P9-BZC-998

Visual Basic 6 Developer's HandBook

Visual Basic® 6 Developer's Handbook™

Evangelos Petroutsos

Kevin Hough

SYBEX®

San Francisco • Paris • Düsseldorf •Soest

Associate Publisher: Gary Masters
Contracts and Licensing Manager: Kristine Plachy
Acquisitions & Developmental Editor: Peter Kuhns
Editors: Suzanne Goraj, Lisa Duran, and Shelby Zimmerman
Project Editor: Fiona Gow
Technical Editors: Don Hergert and Rima Regas
Book Designer: Kris Warrenburg
Graphic Illustrator: Andrew Benzie
Electronic Publishing Specialist: Maureen Forys, Happenstance Type-O-Rama
Production Coordinators: Rebecca Rider and Jeremy Crawford
Indexer: Ted Laux
Companion CD: Ginger Warner and Molly Sharp
Cover Designer: Design Site
Cover Illustrator/Photographer: Gregory MacNicol

Screen reproductions produced with Collage Complete.

Collage Complete is a trademark of Inner Media Inc.

SYBEX is a registered trademark of SYBEX Inc.

Developer's Handbook is a trademark of SYBEX Inc.

TRADEMARKS: SYBEX has attempted throughout this book to distinguish proprietary trademarks from descriptive terms by following the capitalization style used by the manufacturer.

The CD Interface music is from GIRA Sound AURIA Music Library ©GIRA Sound 1996.

The author and publisher have made their best efforts to prepare this book, and the content is based upon final release software whenever possible. Portions of the manuscript may be based upon pre-release versions supplied by software manufacturer(s). The author and the publisher make no representation or warranties of any kind with regard to the completeness or accuracy of the contents herein and accept no liability of any kind including but not limited to performance, merchantability, fitness for any particular purpose, or any losses or damages of any kind caused or alleged to be caused directly or indirectly from this book.

First edition copyright ©1999 SYBEX Inc.
Copyright ©1999 SYBEX Inc., 1151 Marina Village Parkway, Alameda, CA 94501. World rights reserved. No part of this publication may be stored in a retrieval system, transmitted, or reproduced in any way, including but not limited to photocopy, photograph, magnetic or other record, without the prior agreement and written permission of the publisher.

Library of Congress Card Number: 98-87588
ISBN: 0-7821-2283-3

Manufactured in the United States of America

10 9 8 7 6 5

Software License Agreement: Terms and Conditions

The media and/or any online materials accompanying this book that are available now or in the future contain programs and/or text files (the "Software") to be used in connection with the book. SYBEX hereby grants to you a license to use the Software, subject to the terms that follow. Your purchase, acceptance, or use of the Software will constitute your acceptance of such terms.

The Software compilation is the property of SYBEX unless otherwise indicated and is protected by copyright to SYBEX or other copyright owner(s) as indicated in the media files (the "Owner(s)"). You are hereby granted a single-user license to use the Software for your personal, noncommercial use only. You may not reproduce, sell, distribute, publish, circulate, or commercially exploit the Software, or any portion thereof, without the written consent of SYBEX and the specific copyright owner(s) of any component software included on this media.

In the event that the Software or components include specific license requirements or end-user agreements, statements of condition, disclaimers, limitations or warranties ("End-User License"), those End-User Licenses supersede the terms and conditions herein as to that particular Software component. Your purchase, acceptance, or use of the Software will constitute your acceptance of such End-User Licenses.

By purchase, use or acceptance of the Software you further agree to comply with all export laws and regulations of the United States as such laws and regulations may exist from time to time.

Software Support

Components of the supplemental Software and any offers associated with them may be supported by the specific Owner(s) of that material but they are not supported by SYBEX. Information regarding any available support may be obtained from the Owner(s) using the information provided in the appropriate read.me files or listed elsewhere on the media.

Should the manufacturer(s) or other Owner(s) cease to offer support or decline to honor any offer, SYBEX bears no responsibility. This notice concerning support for the Software is provided for your information only. SYBEX is not the agent or principal of the Owner(s), and SYBEX is in no way responsible for providing any support for the Software, nor is it liable or responsible for any support provided, or not provided, by the Owner(s).

Warranty

SYBEX warrants the enclosed media to be free of physical defects for a period of ninety (90) days after purchase. The Software is not available from SYBEX in any other form or media than that enclosed herein or posted to *www.sybex.com*. If you discover a defect in the media during this warranty period, you may obtain a replacement of identical format at no charge by sending the defective media, postage prepaid, with proof of purchase to:

SYBEX Inc.
Customer Service Department
1151 Marina Village Parkway
Alameda, CA 94501
(510) 523-8233
Fax: (510) 523-2373
e-mail: info@sybex.com
WEB: HTTP://WWW.SYBEX.COM

After the 90-day period, you can obtain replacement media of identical format by sending us the defective disk, proof of purchase, and a check or money order for $10, payable to SYBEX.

Disclaimer

SYBEX makes no warranty or representation, either expressed or implied, with respect to the Software or its contents, quality, performance, merchantability, or fitness for a particular purpose. In no event will SYBEX, its distributors, or dealers be liable to you or any other party for direct, indirect, special, incidental, consequential, or other damages arising out of the use of or inability to use the Software or its contents even if advised of the possibility of such damage. In the event that the Software includes an online update feature, SYBEX further disclaims any obligation to provide this feature for any specific duration other than the initial posting.

The exclusion of implied warranties is not permitted by some states. Therefore, the above exclusion may not apply to you. This warranty provides you with specific legal rights; there may be other rights that you may have that vary from state to state. The pricing of the book with the Software by SYBEX reflects the allocation of risk and limitations on liability contained in this agreement of Terms and Conditions.

Shareware Distribution

This Software may contain various programs that are distributed as shareware. Copyright laws apply to both shareware and ordinary commercial software, and the copyright Owner(s) retains all rights. If you try a shareware program and continue using it, you are expected to register it. Individual programs differ on details of trial periods, registration, and payment. Please observe the requirements stated in appropriate files.

Copy Protection

The Software in whole or in part may or may not be copy-protected or encrypted. However, in all cases, reselling or redistributing these files without authorization is expressly forbidden except as specifically provided for by the Owner(s) therein.

To the Joy of my Life

—Evangelos

To my wife, Cheryl, for always being there.

—Kevin

ACKNOWLEDGMENTS

One must publish a few books (or spend a few days at a publishing company such as Sybex) to truly appreciate the effort that goes into the process. It's amazing how much teamwork is involved and how many people work to help authors produce a book in which we can all take pride. It makes writing seem so easy.

I would like to thank all the people involved in this project, starting with the Visual Basic team at Microsoft who delivered an awesome programming environment that brought Visual Basic to the corporate world. Who else would have thought of it, and who else could have done it?

At Sybex, I interacted with many people. First, I want to thank Gary Masters, Associate Publisher, for his unique brand of enthusiasm, vision, and encouragement. Working along with Gary, Peter Kuhns, Acquisitions and Developmental Editor, turned a bunch of ideas into a real book. In the fast-paced universe of computer book publishing, Peter takes the time to be on the author's side, and I can't thank him enough.

Next, I want to thank the various editors who worked on this book: Suzanne Goraj, Lisa Duran, and Shelby Zimmerman. I also want to thank Dan Hergert for his excellent technical editing and helpful remarks. Of course, I shouldn't forget to thank Pat Coleman for her involvement in *Visual Basic 5 Developer's Handbook*.

Special thanks to Ben Ezzell for helping us tap into the power of Visual C++, the interesting examples in Chapter 17, and valuable input on optimization issues.

To publishers, deadlines are as real as the day that follows night, yet for authors like us, these concepts are hard to master. Fiona Gow, our Project Editor, who was involved in every phase, was also burdened with keeping track of time for us.

I also want to thank Rebecca Rider and Jeremy Crawford, our Production Coordinators; Maureen Forys, Electronic Publishing Specialist; Ted Laux, Indexer; Andrew Benzie, Graphic Illustrator; and Molly Sharp and Ginger Warner, CD Specialists.

And a great thank you goes to the people who manage the intricacies of the Internet. This wonderful structure enabled us to stay connected at all times and trivialized two continents and an ocean. In addition, it antiquated an author's favorite excuse—the chapter's in the mail.

—Evangelos Petroutsos, October, 1998

A book project of this size requires the participation and involvement of lots of very gifted and dedicated people. I'd like to take this time to say "Thank you," to everyone who took part in the project and helped make it a reality.

To my friends at Sybex: Associate Publisher, Gary Masters; Acquisitions and Developmental Editor, Peter Kuhns; Contracts and Licensing Manager, Kristine Plachy; Project Editor, Fiona Gow; Editors Suzanne Goraj, Lisa Duran, and Shelby Zimmerman; Technical Editors, Dan Hergert and Rima Regas; Production Coordinators, Rebecca Rider and Jeremy Crawford; Electronic Publishing Specialist, Maureen Forys; Indexer, Ted Laux; Graphic CD Specialists, Ginger Warner and Molly Sharp; and the many others too numerous to name, for all their support, enthusiasm, and expertise.

To the Visual Basic 6 team at Microsoft, for providing VB developers with a distinctive and innovative programming language that will transport them into the next century.

And finally, to my family and friends, for putting up with me!

I truly appreciate it!

—*Kevin Hough, 1998*

CONTENTS AT A GLANCE

TABLE OF CONTENTS

25   Outlook 98 Objects   **1365**

Index to Code Listings   **1392**

INTRODUCTION

Visual Basic is the most popular programming language, but you probably already know that. Version 6 has been enhanced considerably, especially in the area of data access. This version includes support for ActiveX Data Objects through an integrated array of graphical database development tools. In addition, there is a built-in reporting tool and a new suite of ActiveX controls especially designed to provide state-of-the-art database connectivity to SQL Server, Oracle, and other relational database systems.

It's no wonder that there are so many books on Visual Basic, yet most books are either introductory or deal with a single aspect of the language, such as ActiveX components, graphics, database programming, and so on. We believe developers who are familiar with previous editions of Visual Basic, and especially Visual Basic 5, need a book that concentrates on the new capabilities of the language and discusses them from an experienced programmer's point of view. The *Visual Basic 6 Developer's Handbook* fulfills this need. It's written by two longtime developers and is addressed to developers. Because we couldn't cover every topic of the language in depth, we decided to compile a collection of advanced topics and discuss them in depth. We believe every developer will find something of interest in this book.

In our experience, developers don't read books cover to cover. We took care to make the chapters as independent of one another as possible, without repeating ourselves. You will find cross-references in the book, but the chapters are organized to be read independently.

We also believe that you can't master a language through reference material alone. That's why we tried to skip much of the information you can find in the Visual Basic documentation. Where this was not possible, or practical, we moved much of the reference material to appendices (which you will find on the CD that comes with the book). The chapters focus on the concepts and on how you can apply them to day-to-day tasks. To master a language, you have to step through real-world applications, so many of our examples are complete applications. They are not as easy to follow as trivial examples that demonstrate a few functions or methods. We tried to design sample applications that combine many of the techniques involved in building actual applications and that you can use as starting points for other projects.

Who Should Read This Book

Most VB programmers develop database and client/server applications, so more than half of the book deals with topics such as client/server programming, SQL, and the Remote and Active Data Objects. We assume that you are familiar with database programming, and we focus on client/server architectures and techniques for creating and accessing databases.

But there's more to programming than querying databases. Visual Basic is an excellent environment for developing components (code components and ActiveX controls). We discuss these topics in depth and give you practical examples to demonstrate the more advanced techniques. As you undoubtedly know, the Web is making waves in corporate programming, and it's changing the way corporations look at the Internet and intranets. If you are a VB programmer and would like to apply your knowledge to the Web, you'll find much of the information you need in this book. We don't discuss trivial topics, such as how to build Web pages or how to use HTML. Instead, we focus on the topic that will enable you to apply your knowledge of Visual Basic to the Web: the Active Server Pages.

In short, this is a book for result-oriented people. If you have some programming experience in Visual Basic and want to build on your knowledge instead of going through trivial material, or if you want to read about practical techniques instead of general discussions, you will find this book useful.

The Structure of the Book

The book is organized in to five parts that each cover a different aspect of the language. The first part of the book is dedicated to databases. The areas of database connectivity and support have seen major enhancements in Visual Basic 6, and our coverage of these enhancements is exhaustive. The first chapter outlines all of the new database features, and the following chapters expound on many of them. We place a great amount of emphasis on the client/server model, which is the dominant form of database programming in the corporate environment. After a chapter that details the client/server arena, data-access methods, and three-tiered architecture, we move into a chapter that talks about the foundation of SQL Server. Our coverage of SQL Server includes information on how to install SQL Server and set up SQL Server 7, as well as a discussion of what's new in SQL Server 7. Because this book deals with advanced topics, we have included a chapter that demonstrates, through a simple VB application, some advanced SQL programming, including functions and joins. There is also a chapter that shows how to set up a new English Query application, complete with a sample VB project to get you up and running. The last chapter of the database section pulls it all together, as we design and build a complete three-tiered architecture application using Visual Basic and SQL Server.

Objects are the recurring theme of this book. We didn't plan it this way, but that's how it turned out. No matter what you do with Visual Basic, you have to learn and master a number of object models. The second part of the book is dedicated to using and building objects. It starts with an overview of programming with objects in Visual Basic. In the subsequent chapters, we show you how to build ActiveX components (DLL and EXE servers) and ActiveX controls. One special category of ActiveX controls are the data-bound controls, which are discussed in a separate chapter. In the last chapter of this part, we discuss in depth how to extend the Visual Basic IDE with add-ins.

Part III of the book discusses advanced topics such as the Windows API and how to manipulate the Registry. Among the topics discussed in the first chapter are the TreeView and ListView controls. These two controls are not new to Visual Basic 6, but they are not easy to program. In the last chapter of Part III, we discuss optimization techniques. We show you a few simple and efficient ways to optimize your VB applications. However, if the optimized application isn't fast enough, you may want to help Visual Basic with an external DLL. You'll also see how to develop DLLs with Visual C++ (you can speed your applications considerably by implementing a small percentage of the application's calculation-intensive code in Visual C++ and packaging it as a DLL).

VBScript, a subset of Visual Basic, designed to be used for programming Web pages, will present new opportunities for VB programmers; you can use VBScript to program Web pages, create dynamic Web pages by programming the elements of DHTML, and write applications on the server that interact with the clients. We devoted three chapters to VBScript in order to help you apply your knowledge to the Web. In Part IV, you'll find a quick introduction to VBScript and information on how to use VBScript to develop Active Server Pages. In the last chapter of Part IV, you'll learn how to develop two new types of projects: DHTML applications (Web pages enhanced with VBScript) and IIS applications (these applications run on the client and interact with the Web server).

The last part of the book is dedicated to Visual Basic for Applications (VBA). Part V begins by providing you with an overview of VBA. This is followed by a chapter on how to use Visual Basic Editor to create and edit forms for Word and Excel. From there, the chapters move into a discussion of Excel 97, Word 97, and Outlook 98 object models. As a VB programmer, you can apply your skills to programming Office applications, as well as a host of other applications that support VBA. Microsoft Office is the most popular suite of applications in the corporate environment, and once you learn the objects exposed by the Office applications, you'll be ready to apply your knowledge to VBA programming as well.

What's on the CD

This book is accompanied by a CD that contains the following:

- The code for all the example projects discussed in the book
- Demo versions of third-party tools for developers
- Appendix A: Chapter 1 API Functions
- Appendix B: Chapter 2 API Functions

You'll find the code for each chapter's projects in that particular chapter folder within the CD's CH_CODE folder. Each code listing is named after the project. For example, the DEMO project in Chapter 13 is stored in the CH_CODE\CH13\DEMO folder. All the files needed to open the project and run it in the Visual Basic IDE are stored in this folder.

We suggest that you use the installation software on the CD to copy all projects to your hard disk, which will duplicate the structure of the CH_CODE folder on your disk. You can run the projects off the CD, but you can't save them on the CD after editing them.

To edit a project, you must copy the project's folder to your hard disk and then open the project. However, the files copied off the CD will still have their Read-Only attribute set. To deselect Read-Only and gain editing access to the projects, follow these steps:

1. Select all project files on your hard disk with the mouse, then right-click the selection.

2. From the shortcut menu, choose Properties to open the Properties dialog box.

3. In the Attributes section, clear the Read-Only box.

NOTE

The FRACTAL and REVERSE projects of Chapter 17 require that the files FRACTAL.DLL and REVERSE.DLL be in the current path (as discussed in the text) or in the `Windows\ System` folder. If you attempt to run these projects without building the DLLs yourself (see Chapter 17 for details), be sure that the two DLL files are copied to the `Windows\System` folder.

We have also chosen to include a few highly useful and relatively new tools for developers. For details, see the "What's on the CD" page facing the CD at the back of the book.

How to Reach Us

Despite our best efforts, a book this size is bound to contain errors. We will spare no effort in correcting any problem you (or we) discover. If you have any problems with the text and/or the applications in this book, you can contact us directly at:

Evangelos Petroutsos: `76470.724@compuserve.com`

Kevin Hough: `khough@houghtech.com`

Although we can't promise a response to every question, we will endeavor to address any problem in the text and or examples and will provide updated versions. We would also like to hear any comments you may have about the book regarding topics you liked or disliked, as well as your feedback on how useful you found the examples. Your comments will help us revise the book in future editions.

PART I

Database Programming

CHAPTER
ONE

What's New with Visual Basic 6 and Databases

- New database support in Visual Basic 6

- Examining ActiveX Data Objects

- Investigating the new Data Environment

- Working with Data-Bound Controls

- Using the newly integrated Visual Database Tools

Since the introduction of version 2, Visual Basic has provided database support. In version 6, Visual Basic has taken database connectivity and support to a new level.

Today, companies of all sizes are creating business solutions that leverage data from the desktop to the enterprise, and the challenge to provide a business advantage through the best use of data types and access types has become an important aspect of those business solutions. In version 6, Visual Basic has once again moved into the forefront of this challenge.

Visual Basic 6 relies on ActiveX Data Objects (ADO) to provide the main database connectivity. This approach is carried through many of the new database innovations. Visual Basic 6 provides new data controls for connecting data to data-bound controls, an integrated Visual Database Tool, and many new and exciting database innovations to help you satisfy your data access requirements.

This chapter provides some insight into many of the new database and data access features included with Visual Basic 6.

New Database Support in Visual Basic 6

Visual Basic 6 provides an interesting array of new and improved database support features. In the sections that follow, we will take a look at them and demonstrate how they fit into the overall Visual Basic 6 database picture.

Table 1.1 outlines the major new features included in Visual Basic. In addition to the features, the table lists the edition of Visual Basic that provides support for the feature:

TABLE 1.1:   New Database Features Included in Visual Basic 6

Feature	Description	Edition
ActiveX Data Objects (ADO)	New data access technology that features a simpler object model, better integration with other Microsoft and non-Microsoft technologies, a common interface for both local and remote data access, remotable and disconnected recordsets, a user-accessible data binding interface, and hierarchical recordsets.	All Editions

Continued on next page

TABLE 1.1 CONTINUED: New Database Features Included in Visual Basic 6

Feature	Description	Edition
ADO Data Control	A new OLE DB–aware data source control that functions much like the intrinsic Data and Remote Data controls, in that it allows you to create a database application with minimum code.	All Editions
Data Environment	An ActiveX designer that provides an interactive, design-time environment for creating ADO objects.	Professional and Enterprise
Data Form Wizard Enhancements	Now gives you the ability to build code-only forms, using ADO code, where controls are not bound to a data control.	Professional and Enterprise
Data Object Wizard	Automates creating middle-tier objects bound to the Data Environment or UserControls.	Professional and Enterprise
DataGrid Control	An OLE DB–aware version of DBGrid that allows you to quickly build an application to view and edit recordsets. The DBGrid also supports the new ADO Data control.	All Editions
DataList and Data-Combo Controls	Controls that are OLE DB versions of the DBList and DBCombo controls. They also support the new ADO Data control.	All Editions
DataRepeater Control	With insertion of a UserControl, creates a custom view of a database, similar to MS Access forms.	Professional and Enterprise
Data Report	A reporting system that allows you to use drag-and-drop data fields to quickly create reports from any recordset, including hierarchical recordsets.	Professional and Enterprise
Data Sources	Now enables you to create your own User controls and classes that are data sources, to which other controls can be bound.	Professional and Enterprise
Data View Window	Provides access to browse all of the databases you are connected to, allowing you to see their tables, views, stored procedures, etc.	Professional and Enterprise
Enhanced Data Binding	Makes it now possible to bind *any* ADO/OLE DB data source to *any* ADO/OLE DB data consumer.	Professional and Enterprise

Continued on next page

TABLE 1.1 CONTINUED: New Database Features Included in Visual Basic 6

Feature	Description	Edition
File System Objects	Offer a streamlined set of routines to traverse the file system and create text files and directories.	All Editions
Hierarchical FlexGrid Control	An updated version of the FlexGrid control that, in addition to supporting all the functionality of the FlexGrid control, can display a hierarchy of ADO Recordsets.	All Editions
OLE DB Support	Includes a new set of COM interfaces that provide applications with uniform access to data stored in diverse information sources, both relational and non-relational.	All Editions
Passing ADO Recordsets	Now enables you to pass ADO Recordsets across processes, and even across machines (using HTTP or DCOM), which provides an efficient means for moving data between tiers in a multi-tier application.	All Editions
SQL Editor	Allows you to add new stored procedures to existing SQL Server and Oracle databases. You can write triggers using the editor, too.	Enterprise Edition
Visual Database Tools Are Integrated	Now allows you to visually create and modify database schemas and queries, create SQL Server and Oracle database tables, drag and drop to create views, and automatically change column data types from within the Visual Basic development environment.	Enterprise Edition
New Data Enhanced Setup Wizard	Incorporates support into the Package and Deployment Wizard (formerly the Setup Wizard) for ADO, OLE DB, RDO, ODBC, and DAO.	All Editions

In the sections that follow, we will take a closer look at the new database features that are included in Visual Basic 6.

ActiveX Data Objects (ADO)

This new data access technology, available in all editions, features a simpler object model, better integration with other Microsoft and non-Microsoft technologies, a common interface for both local and remote data access, remotable and disconnected recordsets, a user-accessible data binding interface, and hierarchical recordsets.

ADO has been designed to be an easy-to-use application-level interface to any OLE DB data provider. Data providers include relational and non-relational databases, e-mail and file systems, text and graphics, and custom business objects, as well as existing ODBC data sources. Virtually all of the data available throughout the enterprise is available using the ADO data access technology.

The general characteristics of ADO are:

- Ability to return multiple result sets from a single query
- Advanced recordset cache management
- Complex cursor types, including batch and server- and client-side cursors
- Ease of use
- Excellent error trapping
- Flexibility—it works with existing database technologies and all OLE DB providers
- High performance
- Programmatic control of cursors
- Reusable, property-changeable objects
- Synchronous, asynchronous, or event-driven query execution

The simple semantics of ADO and universal application mean minimal developer training, rapid application development, and inexpensive maintenance.

Examining the ADO Object Model

A collection of programmable objects that support the Component Object Model (COM) and OLE Automation to leverage the powerful partner technology called OLE DB define the ADO object model. When compared to other data access objects, such as RDO or DAO, the ADO object model has fewer objects and is simpler to use. With ADO, you do not have to wade through a complex object model, as is the case with DAO and RDO. This simpler object model is shown in Figure 1.1.

FIGURE 1.1:

ADO object model

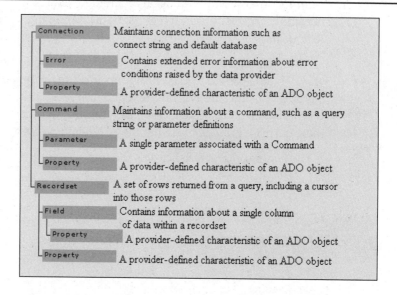

NOTE   See Chapter 4, "The ADO Object," for a complete discussion of this topic.

ADO Data Control

The ADO Data control (shown in Figure 1.2), which is available in all editions of Visual Basic 6, is a new OLE DB–aware data source control that functions much like the original Data and Remote Data controls by allowing you to create a database application with minimum code.

FIGURE 1.2:

ADO Data control

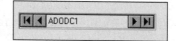

Although you can use the ActiveX Data Objects directly in your applications, the ADO Data control has the advantage of being a graphic control (with Back and Forward buttons) and an easy-to-use interface that allows you to create database applications with a minimum amount of code.

Many of the controls included in Visual Basic 6 can be data-bound, including the CheckBox, ComboBox, Image, Label, ListBox, PictureBox, and TextBox controls. Visual Basic 6 also includes several data-bound ActiveX controls, such as the Data-Grid, DataCombo, DataList and Chart controls. In addition, you can create your own data-bound ActiveX controls, or purchase controls from other vendors.

NOTE   Chapter 6, "Writing Front Ends," provides a more detailed discussion of the ADO Data control, including example projects that have been created with the ADO Data control.

Data Environment

The Enterprise edition of Visual Basic 6 includes the Data Environment designer (shown in Figure 1.3), a graphical designer that provides an interactive, design-time environment for creating programmatic run-time data access. This designer enables you to set property values for Connection and Command objects, write code to respond to ADO events, execute commands, and create aggregates and hierarchies, all at design time. The Data Environment objects can even be dragged onto forms and reports creating data-bound controls.

FIGURE 1.3:

Data Environment designer

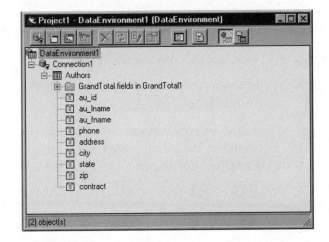

The following tasks can be accomplished easily with the Data Environment:

- Add a Data Environment designer to a Visual Basic project
- Create Connection objects
- Create Command objects based on stored procedures, tables, views, synonyms, and SQL statements
- Create hierarchies of commands based on a grouping of Command objects, or by relating one or more Command objects together
- Write and run code for Connection and Recordset objects
- Drag fields within a Command object from the Data Environment designer onto a Visual Basic form or the Data Report designer

Using a Data Environment with a Visual Basic Application

The Data Environment creates ADO Command and Connection objects for each Command and Connection object defined in the Data Environment designer at run time. In addition, an ADO Recordset object is also created if the Command object is marked as Recordset Returning (on the Advanced tab of the Command Properties dialog box). The ADO Connection and Recordset objects are added as properties and the ADO Command object is added as a method from the Data Environment run-time object.

There are two ways to use a Data Environment in your application at run time:

- As a direct data source for data binding to controls on a form
- To create an instance of the Data Environment in code and execute its Command objects.

The run-time Data Environment contains Commands, Connections, and Recordsets collections. These collections offer another means of programmatically accessing the ADO objects, allowing you to enumerate the various objects.

In the Data Environment, the names of ADO Recordset objects are prefaced with *rs* to distinguish them from their corresponding Command objects. By default, Recordset objects are closed, so when the Recordset object's corresponding

Command method executes, the Recordset object opens. Recordset objects can be opened directly using the ADO Open method.

NOTE   See Chapter 3, "Using SQL Server," for a complete discussion and examples of how to incorporate the Data Environment into your projects.

Data Form Wizard Enhancements

The Data Form Wizard, shown in Figure 1.4, is designed to automatically generate Visual Basic forms that contain individual bound controls and procedures used to manage information derived from database tables and queries. The Data Form Wizard can be used to create either single query forms to manage the data from a single table or simple query, or Master/Detail type forms used to manage more complex, one-to-many data relationships. If you are using a control, you can also create a grid or datasheet type form. The Data Form Wizard is used in conjunction with only the ADO Data control.

FIGURE 1.4:

Data Form Wizard

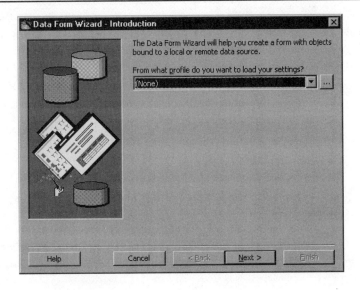

The Data Form Wizard is available as a Visual Basic add-in. Follow these steps to make the Data Form Wizard available:

1. Select Add-In ➢ Add-In Manager to display the Add-In Manager dialog box.

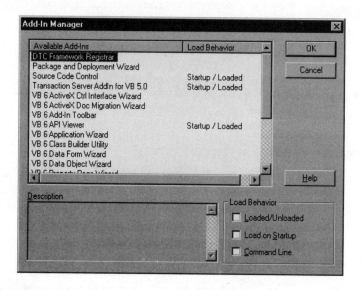

The Add-In Manager dialog box lists all of the add-ins that are currently available.

2. Click the Data Form Wizard on the list to select it.

3. Click the Loaded/Unloaded checkbox in the Load Behavior frame.

4. Click the OK button to add the Data Form Wizard to the list of Add-Ins.

5. Select Add-Ins ➢ Data Form Wizard to open the wizard.

Examining the Data Form Wizard Form Types

The Data Form Wizard provides options (shown in Figure 1.5) to create several different types of forms and also allows you to choose whether your form will be created with an ADO Data control, with ADO code only, or as a class module.

FIGURE 1.5:

Data Form Wizard form-type options

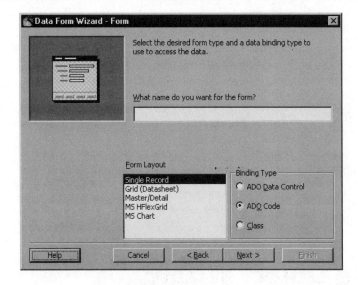

Table 1.2 details the form options available with the Data Form Wizard:

TABLE 1.2: Data Form Wizard Form Types

Form Type	Description
Single Record	Specifies a form that displays one record at a time. This is the default.
Grid (Datasheet)	Specifies a form that displays the selected fields in the Grid (Datasheet) format using the DataGrid control.
Master/Detail	Specifies a form that displays a Master record source and a Detail record source linked together. The Master record source is in single record format and the Detail record source is in a Grid (Datasheet) format. When data in a Master record source row changes, the data in the Detail record source automatically changes based on the link between the two.
MSHFlex Grid	Specifies a form that displays tabular data.
MS Chart	Specifies a form that displays data in a chart format.

In addition to selecting the data form type, you can also select the type of data binding, as outlined in Table 1.3.

TABLE 1.3: Data Binding Types

Binding Type	Description
ADO Data Control	Uses the ADO Data control to access the specified data.
ADO Code	Uses ADO code to access the specified data.
Data Class	Uses data classes to access the specified data.

NOTE   The Data Form Wizard can not only build a complete application for you but can also give you a jump start by creating your forms in a larger application.

Data Object Wizard

The Data Object Wizard (shown in Figure 1.6) is designed to assist you in generating code to create custom data sources and UserControls to display and manipulate data through stored procedures.

FIGURE 1.6:

Data Object Wizard

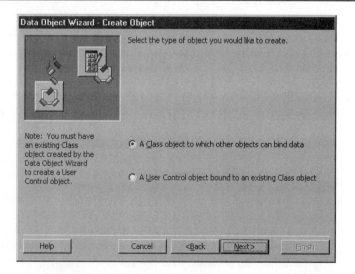

The first step in using the Data Object Wizard is to create a Data Environment. You must first create a Data Environment with commands to retrieve and manipulate data before you can use the Data Object Wizard. The Data Object Wizard uses commands within the Data Environment to retrieve and update your data. The types of commands you can create are:

- A required command, such as the Select Command

- Optional commands, such as the Insert, Update, or Delete commands

Use the Data Object Wizard when you want to perform the following actions:

- Create updatable recordsets from stored procedures.

- Create User controls to display and manipulate data.

- Create User controls that display and allow you to interact with lookup relationships.

- Generate Visual Basic code reflecting relationships between data.

- Assign meaningful text for NULL values.

- Replace cryptic lookup values with meaningful text descriptions.

The Data Object Wizard is a Visual Basic add-in. To make the wizard available, follow the steps in the previous section for adding an add-in to the Visual Basic environment.

DataGrid Control

The DataGrid control (shown in Figure 1.7), available in all Visual Basic editions, is a spreadsheet-like bound control that displays a series of rows and columns representing records and fields from a Recordset object. You can use the DataGrid to create an application that allows the end user to read and write to most databases. The DataGrid control can be quickly configured at design time with little or no code. When you set the DataGrid control's DataSource property at design time, to an existing ADO Data control or Data Environment, the control is automatically filled and its column headers are automatically set from the data source's recordset. You can then edit the grid's columns—delete, rearrange, add headers to, or adjust width of the columns—at design time or run time.

FIGURE 1.7:

DataGrid control

At run time, the DataSource can be programmatically switched to view a different table, or you can modify the query of the current database to return a different set of records.

The following general steps are used to implement a DataGrid control at design time:

1. Select Project ➢ Components to display the Components dialog box.

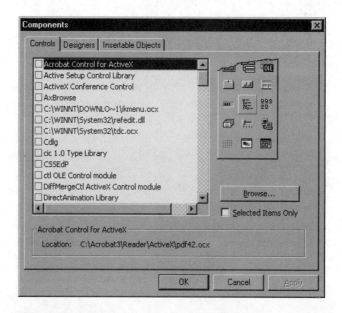

The DataGrid and ADO Data controls are custom controls that must be added to a project through the Components dialog box.

2. Select the Microsoft ADO Data Control 6.0 (OLEDB) and the Microsoft DataGrid 6.0 (OLEDB) from the list of available controls.

3. Click the OK button to add the controls and close the Components dialog box.

4. Place an ADO Data control on a form, and set the ConnectionString property to an OLE DB data source.

5. Type a SQL statement that returns a recordset in the RecordSource field of the ADO Data control, such as:

```
Select * From Authors
```

6. Draw a DataGrid control on a form, and set the DataSource property to the ADO Data control.

7. Right-click the DataGrid control and then click Retrieve Fields.

8. Right-click the DataGrid control and then click Edit.

9. Resize, delete, or add columns to the grid.

10. Right-click the DataGrid control and then click Properties.

11. Using the Property Pages dialog box, set the appropriate properties of the control to configure the grid as you wish it to appear and behave.

NOTE   The DataGrid control is a very powerful, flexible tool; however, this scenario shows only the basics of the control. Chapters 5, "Advanced SQL Examples," and 6, "Writing Front Ends," provide a closer look at the DataGrid control and demonstrate its power and flexibility as it is used in several projects.

DataList and DataCombo Controls

The DataList and DataCombo controls (shown in Figure 1.8) are available in all editions of Visual Basic, and strongly resemble the standard list box and combo box controls provided with Visual Basic 6.

FIGURE 1.8:

DataList and DataCombo controls

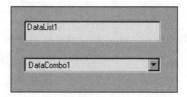

These data-bound controls do provide some important differences that give them great flexibility and usefulness in database applications. The controls can be automatically filled from a database field from the data control to which they are bound. In addition, they can optionally pass a selected field to a second data control, making them ideal for applications that need to "look up" data from another table.

Examining the DataList Control

The DataList control provides the same type of access that is provided by the DBList control, except that it is optimized to work with ADO objects.

The DataList control is a data-bound list box that is automatically populated from a field in an attached data source, and optionally updates a field in a related table of another data source.

The following general steps are required to implement a DataList control in design time:

1. Select Project ➤ Components to display the Components dialog box.

   The DataList control is a custom control that must be added to a project through the Components dialog box, just like the DataGrid control in the previous section.

2. Select the Microsoft ADO Data Control 6.0 (OLEDB) and the Microsoft DataList 6.0 (OLEDB) from the list of available controls.

3. Click the OK button to add the controls and close the Components dialog box.

4. Place an ADO Data control on a form, and set the ConnectionString property to an OLE DB data source.

5. Type a SQL statement that returns a recordset in the RecordSource field of the ADO Data control, such as:

   ```
   Select * From Authors
   ```

6. Draw a DataList control on a form, and set the DataSource property to the ADO Data control.

7. Set the RowSource property to a field from the DataSource. The RowSource property sets a value that specifies the data control from which the DataList control's list is populated.

When the project is run and the form is displayed, the values from the RowSource will be displayed in the DataList.

NOTE   Chapter 6, "Writing Front Ends," provides a detailed look at the DataList control, as well as a sample project.

Discussing the DataCombo Control

The DataCombo control provides the same type of access that is provided by the DBCombo control, except that it is optimized to work with ADO objects.

The DataCombo control is a data-bound combo box that is automatically populated from a field in an attached data source, and optionally updates a field in a related table of another data source.

The main difference between the DataList and the DataCombo controls is that the DataCombo box control provides a text box whose contents may be edited. A DataCombo control also employs two ADO Data controls. One ADO control provides the field whose value is displayed in the edit portion of the DataCombo, and another ADO control provides the list of available values for the DataCombo.

The following general steps are required to implement a DataCombo control in design time:

1. Select Project ➤ Components to display the Components dialog box.

   The DataCombo control is a custom control that must be added to a project through the Components dialog box, just like the DataList control in the previous section.

2. Select the Microsoft ADO Data Control 6.0 (OLEDB) and the Microsoft DataCombo 6.0 (OLEDB) from the list of available controls.

3. Click the OK button to add the controls and close the Components dialog box.

4. Place two ADO Data controls on a form, one for the linked field and one for the values for the field, and set the ConnectionString properties to OLE DB data sources.

5. Type a SQL statement that returns a recordset in the RecordSource field of the ADO Data controls. For example,

```
Select * From Authors
Select City from Cities
```

6. Draw a DataControl control on a form, and set the DataSource property to the ADO Data control and the DataField property to a field in the data source.

7. Set the DataSource property to an ADO Data control and the DataField to the field that will provide the value from the datasource.

8. Set the RowSource property to the other ADO Data control and set the RowMember property to the field in the ADO control that you want to use to provide a list of values.

When the project is run and the form is displayed, the values from the two ADO Data controls will be displayed in the DataCombo control.

NOTE   Chapter 6, "Writing Front Ends," provides a detailed explanation of the Data-Combo control, including a sample project.

DataRepeater Control

A DataRepeater control (shown in Figure 1.9), available in the Professional and Enterprise editions of Visual Basic, has a UserControl inserted into it that is used to create a custom view of a database, similar to a Microsoft Access form. The UserControl can contain TextBox, CheckBox, DataGrid or other controls bound to data fields. The DataRepeater is a very powerful, flexible grid control that can display titles, sections, subheadings, and more.

The DataRepeater control functions as a data-bound container of any User control you create. For example, if you wanted to display records from an Employee table showing an employee's name, address, hire date, and salary level, you could create a UserControl with the proper text boxes and labels.

DataRepeater control

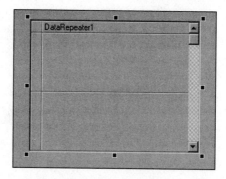

The DataRepeater control's RepeatedControlName property is set to the User-Control after it is compiled into an OCX file. The DataRepeater is then bound to a data source, such as the ADO Data control, which sets up a connection between the UserControl and the Employee database. At run time, the DataRepeater displays several instances of the User control, each in its own row, and each bound to a different record in the database.

At run time, the user can scroll through a recordset using the Home, End, Page Up, Page Down, and right and left arrow keys.

The DataRepeater control could provide the following functionality:

- Create a catalog that includes images of each product.

- Create a bankbook application to track personal finances.

- Create a custom data-bound grid that includes ComboBox or other controls.

NOTE   The DataRepeater is discussed in more detail in Chapter 12, "Building ActiveX Controls."

Data Report

The Microsoft Data Report designer (shown in Figure 1.10) is a versatile data report generator available in the Professional and Enterprise editions of Visual Basic that features the ability to create banded hierarchical reports.

FIGURE 1.10:

Data Report designer

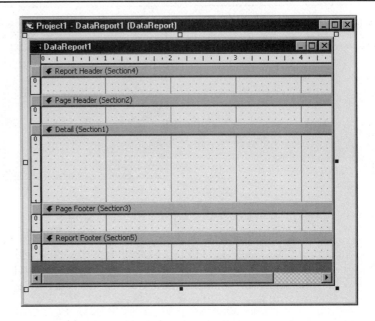

Used in conjunction with a data source, such as the Data Environment designer, the Data Report designer can create reports from several different relational tables. In addition to creating printable reports, you can also export reports to HTML or text files.

Identifying the Data Report Designer Features

The Data Report designer has several features, including:

Asynchronous operation, which allows you to monitor the state of operations and to cancel any that are taking too long by using the Processing-Timeout event. The DataReport object's PrintReport and ExportReport methods are asynchronous operations.

Drag-and-drop functionality for fields, which allows you to drag fields from the Microsoft Data Environment designer to the Data Report designer. Visual Basic automatically creates a text box control on the data report and sets the DataMember and DataField properties of the dropped field. A Command object can also be dragged from the Data Environment designer to the Data Report designer, creating a text box control on the data report for each field in the Command Object. The DataMember and DataField property for each text box will be set to the appropriate values.

Export templates, which allows for the creation of a collection of file templates to be used with the ExportReport method. This is useful for exporting reports in a variety of formats, each tailored to the report type.

File export, which exports the data report information using the ExportReport method. HTML and text are formats included for export.

Print preview, which provides for the preview of the report using the Show method. The data report is then generated and displayed in its own window.

Print reports, which prints a report programmatically by calling the PrintReport method. When the data report is in Preview mode, users can also print by clicking the printer icon on the toolbar.

Toolbox controls, which are a set of controls featured in the Data Report designer; when a Data Report designer is added to a project, its controls are automatically created on a new Toolbox tab named DataReport. Most of these controls are functionally identical to the Visual Basic intrinsic controls. The controls include a Label, Shape, Image, TextBox, and Line control. The sixth control, the Function control, automatically generates one of four kinds of information: Sum, Average, Minimum, or Maximum.

Data Sources

A data source is an object that binds other objects to data from an external source. The foundation for a data source object is a data-aware class module, which is essentially a class module that exposes interfaces to an external source of data. We have already discussed the concepts of data sources and data-bound controls in the discussion of the ADO Data control, and the DataGrid, DataCombo, and DataList controls.

The Professional and Enterprise editions of Visual Basic 6 provide the tools necessary for you to create your own data sources.

Data-aware classes can also be used as the basis for ActiveX components. One common example of a data-aware component is the ADO Data control, which provides a visual interface for binding controls to a database through ADO. Although you could create a data-aware class that does the same thing as the ADO Data control, sharing that class between multiple applications or multiple programmers could prove difficult.

A better approach would be to build on the foundation of the ADO Data control, adding features that your application requires. As with any ActiveX component, this could take any one of several forms: an ActiveX control, an ActiveX DLL, or an ActiveX EXE. No matter how it is created, the custom ActiveX data source can easily be shared by other developers. This would simplify access to data regardless of where that data resides. The data could reside in a local Access database, in SQL Server or another remote database, or even in a private OLE DB data store.

Selecting the Type of Data Source

Visual Basic 6 provides the vehicle for you to create your own custom data sources, as ActiveX controls, ActiveX DLLs, ActiveX EXE, or data-aware classes. With so many choices, it is hard to know what type of data source is appropriate. The following guidelines may help you in this decision:

- Data-aware classes are a good choice when you don't anticipate reusing the data source, such as in a case where you need to keep track of recipes for a party. The data source will only be used once for a very specialized case.

- An ActiveX control is the perfect choice when you need a visual interface for your data source, such as a data control; however, you might also want to combine the display interface as a part of your data source by using a grid, chart, or group of text boxes. ActiveX controls can easily be shared and distributed.

- An ActiveX DLL is a good choice when you need a data source that doesn't require a visual interface and that runs in-process, such as in a case where you need a component to supply today's sold inventory part numbers to a front-end application. This type of component could easily be reused in other applications.

- ActiveX EXEs are an excellent choice for a data source that needs to run out-of-process, such as a middle-tier component that enforces business rules against a database. ActiveX EXEs can also be reused in different applications.

Data View Window

The Data View window (shown in Figure 1.11) presents a view onto one or more database connections, providing access to the entire structure of the database on a particular connection.

FIGURE 1.11:

Data View window

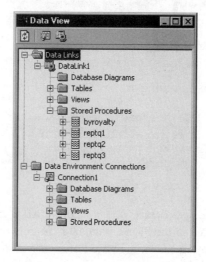

The Data View window, which is available in the Professional and Enterprise editions of Visual Basic 6, provides the means to use the Microsoft Visual Database Tools (Query Designer and Database Designer) to visually manipulate the structure of a database.

> **NOTE** The Data View Window and all of the Visual Database Tools are examined in Chapter 3, "Using SQL Server."

Enhanced Data Binding

In previous versions of Visual Basic, it was only possible to bind controls together on a form. In the Professional and Enterprise editions of Visual Basic 6, it is now possible to bind *any* ADO/OLE DB data source to *any* ADO/OLE DB data consumer. The DataSource property of controls can be set at run time to dynamically bind to data sources. You can create classes that are data sources and consumers, and bind them through the new BindingsCollection object. You can create user controls that are data sources, similar to the ADO Data control and User controls, that are complex-bound, similar to the DataGrid control.

File System Objects

The FSO object model, available in all editions of Visual Basic 6, provides you with the tools and properties to fully interact with the computer's filing system.

Programming in the FSO object model involves three main tasks:

- Use the CreateObject method, or dimension a variable as a FileSystemObject object to create a FileSystemObject object.

- Use the appropriate method on the newly created object.

- Access the object's properties.

The FSO object model is contained in a type library called Scripting, which is located in the file Scrrun.Dll. To gain access to the library, check Microsoft Scripting Runtime in the References dialog box available from the Properties menu. You can then use the Object Browser to view its objects, collections, properties, methods, and events, as well as its constants.

Table 1.4 outlines the objects that are provided in the FSO object model:

TABLE 1.4: FSO Objects

Object	Description
Drive	Allows you to gather information about drives attached to the system, such as the available space and the share name. A "drive" is not necessarily a hard disk. A drive can be a CD-ROM drive, a RAM disk, or any type of drive. Drives are not required to be physically attached to the system; they can also be logically connected through a LAN.
Folder	Allows you to create, delete, or move folders. In addition, you can query the system and return the name, path, and contents.
Files	Allows you to create, delete, or move files. Just as with the Folder object, you can query the system for the file's name, size, type, and much more.
FileSystemObject	The main object of the group. It contains a full complement of methods that allow you to create, delete, gain information about, and generally manipulate drives, folders, and files. Many of the methods associated with this object duplicate those in the other objects.
TextStream	Enables you to read and write text files.

> **NOTE**
>
> Use the Object Browser in Visual Basic (press F2) and look at the Scripting type library for information about the various properties, methods, and events in the FSO object model.

Hierarchical FlexGrid Control

The Hierarchical FlexGrid control (shown in Figure 1.12) is an updated version of the FlexGrid control that is available in all editions of Visual Basic 6.

FIGURE 1.12:

Hierarchical FlexGrid control

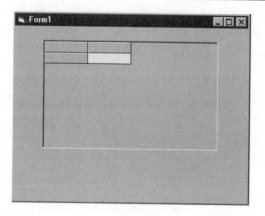

In addition to supporting all the functionality of the FlexGrid control, the Hierarchical FlexGrid control can display a hierarchy of ADO Recordsets. Each Recordset returned is displayed as a separate band within the grid and can be formatted independently.

The Hierarchical FlexGrid control provides advanced features for displaying data in a grid. The control is similar to that of the Microsoft Data Bound grid (DataGrid) control; however, unlike the DataGrid control, the Hierarchical Flex-Grid control does not allow the user to edit data bound to or contained within it. This control allows you to display data to the user while ensuring that the original data remains secure and unchanged.

> **NOTE**
>
> Cell-editing features can be added to the Hierarchical FlexGrid control by combining it with a text box.

While the Hierarchical FlexGrid control is based on the FlexGrid control used in Visual Basic 5, the Hierarchical FlexGrid control is the more flexible of the two. More display options are provided with the Hierarchical FlexGrid control, allowing you to create a custom format that best suits your application's needs.

The following features are provided with the Hierarchical FlexGrid control:

- ActiveX Data Binding when the DataSource and DataMember properties of the control are bound to a specific data provider

- Adaptation to existing Visual Basic code for the DBGrid control

- Additional display options when the Hierarchical FlexGrid is bound to a hierarchy of recordsets

- Binding via the Data Binding Manager in Visual Basic

- Binding directly to grouped and related ADO Recordsets from a Command hierarchy

- Dynamic rearrangement of columns and rows

- Automatic regrouping of data during column adjustment

- Text, a picture, or both allowed in cells

- Flexibility to change cell text in code or at run time

- Automatic data-reading when the Hierarchical FlexGrid is assigned to a data control

- Read-only data binding

- Word-wrapped text within cells

Adding the Hierarchical FlexGrid Control to a Project

The Hierarchical FlexGrid control is a custom control that must be added to your project using the following steps:

1. Select Project ➤ Components to display the Components dialog box (shown in the Data Grid Control section above).

2. Select Microsoft Hierarchical FlexGrid Control 6.0, and click OK. The MSHFlexGrid control is added to the Visual Basic toolbox.

3. Click the MSHFlexGrid control in the Toolbox and draw it on a Visual Basic form.

OLE DB Support

OLE DB is a set of COM interfaces, included in all editions of Visual Basic 6, that provide applications with uniform access to data stored in relational and non-relational sources. These interfaces support the amount of DBMS functionality appropriate to the data source, enabling it to share its data. All the new data-bound controls, the Data Environment, and the Data Report designer are OLE DB–aware.

OLE DB is a new low-level interface that introduces a "universal" data access model. OLE DB is not restricted to ISAM, Jet, or relational data sources, but is capable of dealing with any type of data regardless of its format or storage method. In programming, this versatility means that data can be accessed where it resides. The data can reside in a Microsoft Word document, in a text file, or on a mail server, such as Microsoft Exchange.

OLE DB is accessed through ADO. With Visual Basic, you can even create your own OLE DB Providers.

Passing ADO Recordsets

In all editions of Visual Basic 6, you can pass ADO Recordsets across processes and machines (using HTTP or DCOM), which provides an efficient means for moving data between tiers in a multi-tier application.

The process of passing parameters between two different processes, usually across a network, is referred to as *remoting*. For example, in a three-tiered system, the application makes a call for data on the client machine, passing several parameters as the criteria. On the middle-tier machine, an ActiveX EXE accepts the call, then uses the criteria for retrieving the data.

ADO Recordset objects can be remoted. Armed with this ability, ADO Recordsets are especially suited for use on intranet and Internet client-server applications. For example, imagine creating an HTML or DHTML page that accesses data across the Internet from a Web server application. You can include the Microsoft ActiveX Data Access Recordset 2.0 Library when you create the HTML page, which features only the ADO Recordset object. Since that library doesn't include the Command, Connection, and Parameter objects, your application will have the smallest possible footprint while retaining the functionality of the ADO Recordset features.

SQL Editor

The SQL Editor (shown in Figure 1.13) allows you to create and edit stored procedures and triggers in both SQL Server and Oracle from within the Visual Basic Enterprise edition development environment.

FIGURE 1.13:

SQL Editor

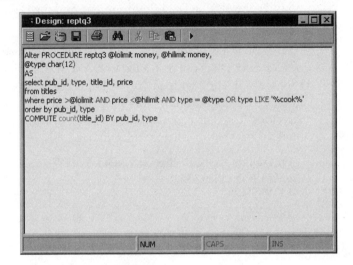

The SQL Editor is part of the Data window. To open the SQL Editor, follow these steps:

1. Select View ➢ Data View Window to open the Data View window.

2. In the Data View window, right-click the Stored Procedures folder or any stored procedure in that folder.

3. Choose Design from the shortcut menu to open the stored procedure in the Stored Procedure Editor.

NOTE   The Data View window and the Stored Procedure Editor are discussed in greater detail in Chapter 3, "Using SQL Server."

Visual Database Tools Are Integrated

With the Enterprise edition of Visual Basic 6, you can visually create and modify database schemas and queries, create SQL Server and Oracle database tables, drag and drop to create views, and automatically change column data types with the integrated Visual Database Tools (shown in Figure 1.14).

FIGURE 1.14:

Database Diagram section of Visual Database Tools

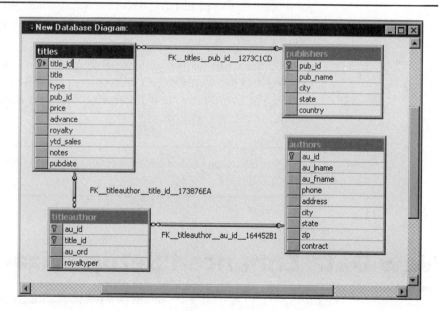

The Visual Database Tools are made up of:

Microsoft Visual Database Tools, which can be accessed from your development environment to help create and manage data-driven applications that rely on live connections to Microsoft SQL Server databases.

NOTE   The specific functionality available in each component depends on the database server you are using.

The Data View component, which provides a visual interface in which you can view live connections to the databases in each project and the objects that are available in each database, organized into folders.

The Query Designer, which enables you to use visual tools to build SQL statements that retrieve data or modify the contents of tables.

The Database Designer, which graphically represents tables and their relationships and enables you to create and modify the database objects that your application relies on. Since all this can be done while you are connected to the underlying database, you can design, query, and populate your databases from within the design environment that you use to build your application.

The Source Code Editor, which enables you to edit stored procedures and triggers and to execute stored procedures and view their results. In addition, if Microsoft Visual C++ Enterprise Edition is installed, you can even debug stored procedures.

NOTE   A complete discussion of Microsoft Visual Database Tools is included in Chapter 3, "Using SQL Server."

New Data-Enhanced Setup Wizard

The Package and Deployment Wizard (shown in Figure 1.15), formerly known as the Setup Wizard, is available in all editions of Visual Basic 6 and incorporates support for ADO, OLE DB, RDO, ODBC, and DAO.

FIGURE 1.15:

Package and Deployment
Wizard

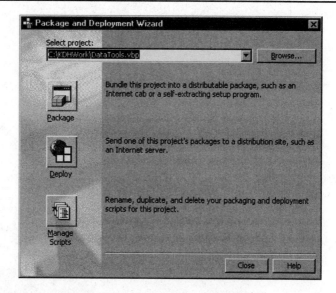

A standard package is a package designed to be installed by a setup.exe program, rather than through the downloading of a .cab file from a Web site. Standard packages are created for Windows-based applications that will be distributed through disks, CDs, or a network share.

If you create an application that employs one of Visual Basic's data access technologies, such as ActiveX Data Objects (ADO), Data Access Objects (DAO), or Remote Data Objects (RDO), two additional steps are performed by the Package and Deployment Wizard during the packaging process:

1. The wizard automatically adds a file called mdac_typ.exe to the list of files to include in your package if your application uses ADO, OLEDB, or ODBC components. Mdac_type.exe is a self-extracting executable that installs all of the components you need for your data access technology.

2. The wizard prompts you to choose the appropriate data access option when your application includes DAO features. You choose the appropriate method—ISAM-based, ODBCDirect, ODBC through Jet, etc.

CHAPTER

TWO

Client/Server Programming

- Understanding the difference between the file-server and the client/server models

- Introducing three-tiered applications

- Deciding to adopt the client/server model

- Looking at the Visual Basic 6 data access options

- Exploring the client/server tools in the Enterprise Edition of Visual Basic 6

Client/server is not a type of computer hardware, nor is it a feature of a software application. Client/server is a computer methodology. In general, the term *client/server computing* means connecting a single-user client machine to a multi-user server machine and sharing the processing load between the two. The client requests services, and the server provides services.

To take full advantage of the client/server relationship, the client should request data, and the server should respond with only the data needed. The client presents the data to the user, and the server processes the data. The client does little processing.

Today, most applications provide some type of data access. More and more developers are adopting the client/server model as the basis for their applications—not because they want to, but because they have to. For the most part, the client/server approach fulfills an important need: The application requires the user interface to connect to an intelligent server database engine, and the client/server provides that connection. A well-designed client application does not have hard-coded Structured Query Language (SQL) statements, and it does not care where or how data is stored or managed, nor does it perform data manipulation. Instead, the client requests raw data at a higher level. The server then processes that data and returns processed records to the client, which then presents them to the user.

The distributed client/server model has both logical and physical partitioning that allows the database tier to be distributed across one or more physical computers to enhance processing speed, increase accessibility, and take advantage of specialized machines.

NOTE   Microsoft SQL Server version 6 introduced the distributed client/server methodology.

As more and more developers use the Microsoft Access database (MDB) to store data, it is important to understand that, even though the MDB supports multiuser access, it is not a true client/server implementation—it is a file server. In the next section, we'll look at these differences in more detail. Then in the rest of the chapter, we'll look at when and why you should adopt the client/server model, the data access options you can choose from, and the Visual Basic 6 client/server tools you can use in developing client/server applications.

File Server versus Distributed Client/Server

In a file-server configuration, no intelligent processing takes place at the server level. All intelligent processing takes place on the individual workstation. When your application needs data, it is the responsibility of the software on the workstation to determine which tables should be read and how to access the network drive. All the data in the database tables must be sent from the server to the workstation, resulting in slower access and increased network traffic.

After the table or file is retrieved, a query can then be run against it to retrieve the needed records. In other words, when a SQL statement is called against an MDB, all the processing takes place on the client side, and only a file request is sent across the network to retrieve the required tables. No logic is executed on the server side, except that needed to provide the tables. Figure 2.1 shows a typical file-server configuration.

FIGURE 2.1:

A typical file-server configuration

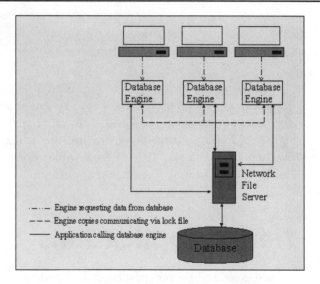

In a distributed client/server environment, the server is responsible for intelligently servicing a client's request for data. The workstation does not request data at a file or table level, but sends a request to the server to execute a query and return specific records. This is a vast improvement over the file-server approach.

For example, if you are looking for a set of address records for the state of Texas, the client sends a SQL statement to the server. The server processes the query and then returns a resultset of Texas addresses only, instead of the entire address file or table. This results in improved access time and reduces network traffic. Figure 2.2 shows a typical client/server configuration.

FIGURE 2.2:

A typical client/server configuration

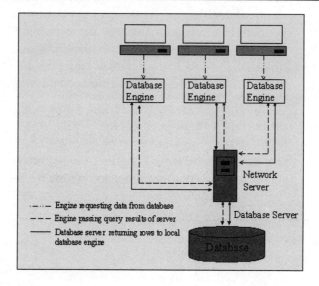

The client/server concept we have been discussing thus far is a two-tiered application—the client and the server. As advanced business methods and technologies are unfolding, however, a new approach is being used in corporate enterprise computing—three-tiered architecture, which we'll look at briefly in the next section. In Chapter 8, "Three-Tiered Applications," we'll look at this topic in depth and present a sample three-tiered application.

Three-Tiered Applications

Three-tiered architecture partitions an application into three logical tiers, or services:

- User services (the front end)
- Business services (the middle)
- Data services (the back end)

Figure 2.3 shows how this works. Using three-tiered architecture, the developer can separate user access, business rules, and data access into separate modules. These tiers do not necessarily correspond to physical locations on the network;

they are conceptual tiers and help the developer to create robust component-based applications. Separate project teams can develop these reusable services, or components, which can be physically located anywhere on the network.

FIGURE 2.3:

The components in a three-tiered application

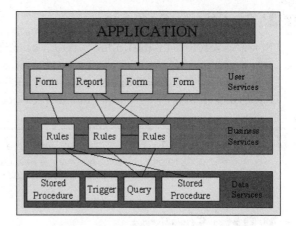

Building the application in tiers also addresses the issue of scalability. The traditional two-tier application can falter as the transaction load increases. With three-tiered applications, the workload is split among the services.

The three-tiered application development method provides many benefits and advantages, including:

Flexibility   Work can be moved from desktop machines to more powerful servers.

Reusability   Many applications can share and reuse code that is written as a component or a service.

Manageability   Large, complex applications can be divided into smaller components.

Maintenance   Maintaining business rules and databases is much easier when they are deployed on central servers rather than on multiple desktop machines.

Tier 1: User Services

User services, commonly referred to as the front end, provide the user interface for presenting information and gathering data. In our case, this service is a Visual

Basic application that provides a graphical interface between the user and the business rules. It is responsible for gathering requirements from the user and presenting data in response to a question or query.

Tier 2: Business Services

Business services are the bridge between user and data services. They respond to requests from the user services for data services. The business services, or middle services, apply defined business rules to the selection of data to narrow the retrieval so that only pertinent data are returned to the user services.

NOTE   A business rule is a condition defined by the application, such as selecting the correct parts to order or printing only the new customers on a customer report.

Tier 3: Data Services

Data services, commonly referred to as the back end, maintain, access, and update data. They also manage and satisfy requests to manipulate data that are initiated by business services. Data services may be supplied by a particular database management system—such as Microsoft SQL Server, Oracle, or Sybase—or by a collection of databases that may reside on multiple platforms. Separating data services allows the data structure and access mechanisms to be maintained, modified, or even re-architected without affecting business or user services.

As you can see, three-tiered applications are ideally suited to the client/server model of separating the client, or first tier, from the server, or third tier. In the next section, we will look at what drives developers to build client/server applications.

Why Adopt the Client/Server Method?

Today, developers are adopting the client/server methodology more than ever before. Why? What drives developers to move to this type of system? We believe they are doing so for three primary reasons:

The need for enterprisewide access to corporate data As technology advances and computers become less expensive, smaller, more powerful, and easier to use, information is becoming more widely distributed across the enterprise. Client/server technology provides flexible links to access and manipulate this data regardless of its location or storage format.

The inadequacy of multiuser file-server applications Client/server applications provide the performance, reliability, and security needed to drive enterprisewide computing into the next century. As database applications grow and become more complex, developers need the assurance that they are on a proven path that can keep pace with ever-increasing demands and plan for the needs of tomorrow.

The downsizing of mainframe and minicomputer database applications Companies are aggressively moving away from text-based applications and file-server applications to provide their users with an easier, friendlier graphical user interface. The power inherent in the client/server model is the basis for this enterprisewide reengineering movement. Reengineering is happening now because it can. Downsizing, however, is more difficult and more expensive, both in capital costs and in resource costs. This makes the move from mainframes to the client/server arena a priority.

Once you decide to move from a file-server to a client/server approach, you'll find that you can use a plethora of Visual Basic data access options, as you will discover in the following sections.

Data Access Options

As we have already discussed, the majority of applications being developed today provide some type of data access. Visual Basic provides a variety of options when it comes to accessing remote client/server databases. In this section, we will explore the following alternatives for client/server data access through the Enterprise Edition of Visual Basic 6:

ActiveX Data Objects (ADO), which eliminates the need to choose DAO and RDO and all the other data access methods and is designed to provide a common bridge between different databases, file systems, and e-mail servers.

ADO Data Control (ADODC), which uses Microsoft ActiveX Data Objects (ADO) to quickly create connections between data-bound controls and data providers.

Data Access Objects (DAO), which communicates with Microsoft Access and other ODBC-compliant data sources through the JET database engine.

Data Control, which binds data-aware controls to Microsoft Access or other ODBC data sources.

ODBCDirect, which allows you to access ODBC data sources through the RDO (Remote Data Objects) with DAO objects, bypassing the JET database engine.

Remote Data Objects (RDO), which provide a framework for using code to create and manipulate components of a remote ODBC database system.

Remote Data Control (RDC), which binds controls to an ODBC remote database.

Open Database Connectivity (ODBC), which is an API call interface to the Open Database Connectivity libraries and drivers to provide data access to Microsoft SQL Server and other databases that provide an ODBC driver.

Visual Basic Library for SQL Server (VBSQL), which is an implementation of the DB_Library API specifically designed to provide access to SQL Server through a Visual Basic application.

Figure 2.4 summarizes these data access models. In the sections that follow, we'll look at each of them in detail.

FIGURE 2.4:

The data access models available in the Enterprise Edition of Visual Basic 6

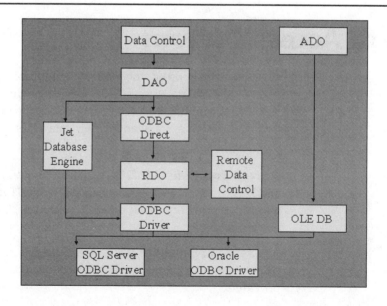

ActiveX Data Objects

Visual Basic 6 supports ActiveX Data Objects (ADO) 2, Microsoft's new, high-level interface to all kinds of data. ActiveX Data Objects is designed to be a cross-language technology for data access that exposes an object model incorporating data connection objects, data command objects, recordset objects, and collections within these objects. The ADO object model provides an easy-to-use set of objects, properties, and methods for creating script that accesses data in databases.

TIP   ADO is available separately from Microsoft and can be downloaded from www.microsoft.com/data/ado. Be sure to also download the ADO help file.

With Visual Basic 6, you can create ADO objects at design time using the updated Data Environment Designer and access a database's entire structure on a connection through the Data View window and Visual Database Tools. Visual Basic also offers new and updated controls specifically designed for working with data. Figure 2.5 shows an ADO connection to a remote data source.

FIGURE 2.5:

An ADO connection to a remote data source

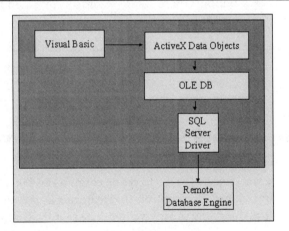

ADO enables you to write a client application to access and manipulate data in a database server through a provider. ADO's primary benefits are ease of use, high speed, low memory overhead, and a small disk footprint.

In ADO, the object hierarchy is de-emphasized. Unlike Data Access Objects (DAO) or Remote Data Objects (RDO), ADO allows you to create objects independently; you no longer have to navigate through a hierarchy to create objects. This allows you to create and track only the objects you need. The ADO model also results in fewer objects, which allows for a smaller working set.

ADO is designed to eventually negate the need for all other interfaces. ADO is not specifically designed for Indexed Sequential Access Method (ISAM) or relational database access, but as an object interface to any data source. ADO is built around a set of core functions that all data sources are expected to implement.

The ADO programming model provides the following features:

- Advanced recordset cache management

- Batch updating

- Different cursor types, including the potential for support of back-end-specific cursors

- Independently created objects

- Support for stored procedures with in/out parameters and return values

- Support for limits on the number of returned rows and other query goals

- Support for multiple recordsets returned from stored procedures or batch statements

NOTE   For a complete discussion of ADO, including code samples, see Chapter 11, "Building ActiveX Controls."

ActiveX Data Objects Data Control

The ADO Data control (ADODC) (shown in Figure 2.6) uses Microsoft ActiveX Data Objects (ADO) to create connections between data-bound controls and data providers. Any controls that feature a DataSource property are data-bound controls, and any source written to the OLE DB specification is a data provider.

Most database access functions can be performed using the ADODC without writing any code. Simply supply a data value for the Connectstring and the recordsource properties and data-bound controls can be bound to the ADODC.

Visual Basic 6 provides several controls that can be data-bound, including the CheckBox, ComboBox, Image, Label, ListBox, PictureBox, and TextBox controls. In addition, it includes several data-bound ActiveX controls, such as the DataGrid,

DataCombo, Chart, and DataList controls. You can also create your own data-bound ActiveX controls in Visual Basic 6.

FIGURE 2.6:

A typical ADODC data access connection

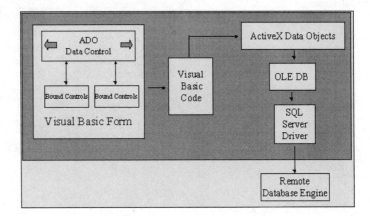

NOTE   You'll find a complete discussion of the ActiveX Data Objects Data Control, including sample code, in Chapter 11, "Building ActiveX Controls."

Data Access Objects

Data Access Objects (DAO) communicate with Microsoft Access and other ODBC-compliant data sources through the JET engine. The DAO model is a collection of object classes that model the structure of a relational database system. They provide properties and methods that allow you to perform all the operations necessary to manage such a system, including the ability to do the following:

- Apply referential integrity

- Create databases

- Define tables, fields, and indexes

- Establish relations between tables

- Navigate and query the database, and so on

Figure 2.7 shows a typical remote data access using DAO and the JET engine.

FIGURE 2.7:

Remote data access using
DAO and the JET engine

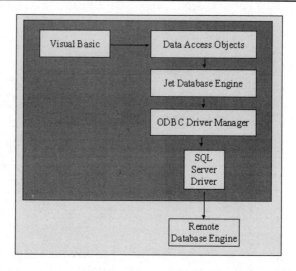

The JET database engine translates these operations on Data Access Objects into physical operations on the database files themselves, handling all the mechanics of interfacing with the different supported databases. This approach simplifies access to the database and insulates you from the underlying mechanics of retrieving and updating data. It affords you great flexibility because the same objects, properties, and methods can be used with a wide variety of supported database formats.

Through DAO and the JET engine, Visual Basic recognizes three categories of databases, and these are summarized in Table 2.1.

TABLE 2.1: Database Categories for DAO and the JET Engine

Category	Description
Visual Basic Databases	Also called native databases, these database files use the same format as Microsoft Access. These databases are created and manipulated directly by the JET engine and provide maximum flexibility and speed.
External Databases	These are Indexed Sequential Access Method (ISAM) databases in several formats, including Btrieve, dBASE III, dBASE IV, Microsoft FoxPro versions 2 and 2.5, and Paradox versions 3.x and 4.
ODBC Databases	These include client/server databases that conform to the ODBC standard, such as Microsoft SQL Server. To create true client/server applications in Visual Basic, you can use ODBCDirect to pass commands directly to the external server for processing.

The DAO programming model provides the following features:

- Advanced resultset management

- An object-oriented programming model that does not require API functions

- A pass-through implementation that allows the JET query processor to be bypassed

- A universal programming model that can access any ODBC database regardless of the ODBC compliance level

- Keyset, static, and forward-only scrolling snapshot cursor implementation

- The ability to fetch and join heterogeneous data from multiple ODBC or ISAM sources

- The ability to create updatable cursors against complex resultsets created as a join product

- Universal error management

Data Control

A data control binds data-aware controls to Microsoft Access or to other ODBC data sources, enabling you to move from record to record and to display and manipulate data from the records in bound controls.

NOTE   A bound control is a control that is assigned to a field in a database.

You can perform most data-access operations with a data control without writing any code. You set the database name and recordsource—a table, a view, or a SQL statement—of the data control at run time or at design time. When a Form that has a data control is opened, the data control is automatically populated with the data from the data control's database and recordsource properties, and the bound controls are loaded with the data from the first record. Figure 2.8 shows the data control and DAO with bound controls.

FIGURE 2.8:

The data control, DAO, and bound controls

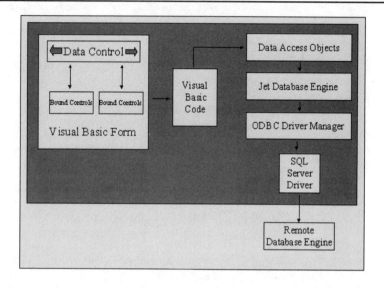

ODBCDirect

ODBCDirect allows you to access ODBC data sources through the RDO with DAO objects, bypassing the Microsoft JET database engine. Originally, DAO was tied to the JET engine, but with DAO 3.5, the DAO object interface was separated from the JET engine, giving developers an alternative—to create ODBCDirect workspaces without the JET engine. When your code opens a DAO Recordset object, the ODBCDirect interface creates an rdoResultSet to retrieve the data. Figure 2.9 shows remote data access using ODBCDirect.

The ODBCDirect programming model is associated with the following advantages:

- It bypasses the JET database engine.

- It reduces resource requirements. Since you don't have to load the Microsoft JET database engine, your application requires fewer resources at the workstation.

- It provides a DAO interface to the RDO libraries.

- Your application can access ODBC data sources directly, making the server responsible for all query processing.

- It provides improved access to server-specific functionality.

FIGURE 2.9:

Remote data access using
ODBCDirect

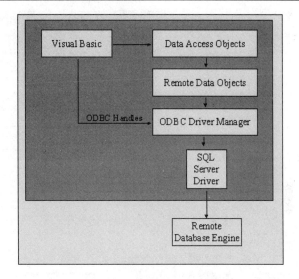

- You can execute a query and perform other operations without waiting for the query to finish. You can then check properties to keep track of the query's execution. This provides greater possibilities for your application in terms of concurrency and optimized performance.

- You can cache recordset changes locally and then submit these changes to the server in a single batch.

- You can handle output parameters and return values from stored procedures.

Remote Data Objects

Remote Data Objects (RDO) and collections provide a framework for using code to create and manipulate components of a remote ODBC database system. Because RDO is a thin object-model layer over the ODBC API, it does not impact data access times.

NOTE   RDO was Visual Basic's flagship interface to relational ODBC data sources until version 6, when ADO took the spotlight.

Figure 2.10 shows a typical remote data access using RDO.

FIGURE 2.10:

Data access with RDO

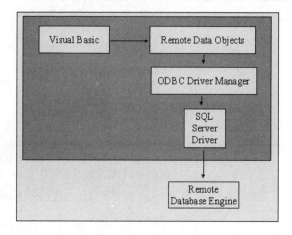

RDO is specifically designed to deal with remote intelligent data sources such as SQL Server and Oracle, as opposed to ISAM databases. Using RDO cuts out the JET layer from the architecture, which can result in significantly higher performance and more flexibility when accessing remote database engines. RDO can execute ordinary table-based queries, but it is especially good at building and executing queries against stored procedures and at handling all types of result-sets. RDO 2 is so adept at providing control over remote data sources that you need not code an ODBC interface, except in unusual cases.

RDO includes a number of objects, properties, and methods specifically designed to work with stored procedures and their arguments, input and output parameters, and return values. RDO will trigger events during and after the completion of an operation, so you no longer have to poll for the status. This allows the developer to leverage the ability of Windows 95 and 98, and Windows NT to run multiple threads of execution. RDO can also handle multiple resultsets generated by a single query.

The following advantages are associated with the RDO programming model:

- It is a universal programming model that can access any 32-bit Level II ODBC data source.

- It can access virtually all Microsoft SQL Server and Oracle remote database engine features.

- It is an object-oriented programming model that does not require the use of APIs.

- Keyset, static, dynamic, and forward-only cursors are implemented on the server side.

- Its operations are fully asynchronous and event-driven.

- It gives you the ability to create stand-alone rdoQuery and rdoConnection objects and to associate queries with connections at design time.

- It supports synchronous, asynchronous, and event-driven connections, queries, and resultset population methods.

- It provides advanced resultset management, including the ability to limit the number of returned rows, to manage multiple resultsets, and to handle input, output, and return value arguments of stored procedures.

- It provides universal error management that exposes not only ODBC error messages but also native errors and messages.

Remote Data Control

The Remote Data Control (RDC) binds controls to an ODBC remote database. The Remote Data Control is similar to the data control, except that it creates and manipulates RDO objects. By using RDO and the Remote Data Control, you can access ODBC data sources through data-aware, or bound, controls without going through the JET engine, resulting in significantly higher performance and greater flexibility when accessing remote data sources. Figure 2.11 shows a typical RDO/Remote Data Control providing access to a remote data source.

FIGURE 2.11:

A typical RDO/RDC data access model

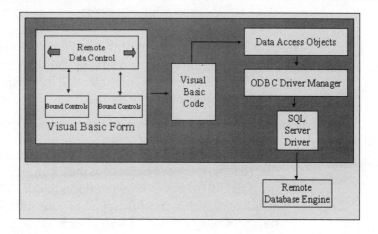

You can perform most remote data access operations using the RDC without writing any code at all. Data-aware controls bound to an RDC automatically display data from one or more columns for the current row or, in some cases, for a set of rows on either side of the current row. Remote Data Controls perform all operations on the current row. The Remote Data Control automatically handles a number of contingencies, adding new rows, editing and updating existing rows, converting and displaying complex data types, and handling some types of errors, including empty resultsets.

Open Database Connectivity

Open Database Connectivity (ODBC) is an API call interface to the Open Database Connectivity libraries and drivers to provide data access to Microsoft SQL Server and other databases that provide an ODBC driver. Figure 2.12 shows a typical ODBC API access to a remote data source.

FIGURE 2.12:

Typical ODBC API access to a remote data source

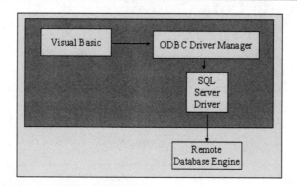

The ODBC API is designed to provide an interface to database front ends that need a fast, small footprint and a relatively stable platform with which to connect to client/server systems. ODBC provides API calls that can expose the application to specific features of the data source.

Generally, there are two approaches to using the ODBC API:

Extending RDO with the ODBC API: Remote Data Objects (RDO) are, for the most part, object interfaces to the ODBC API. Using ODBC handles provided by the object-level interfaces to call ODBC API functions can be an effective way to control aspects of your rdoEnvironment, rdoConnection, rdoQuery, or rdoResultSet objects.

Coding directly to the ODBC API: It is possible to create an application using the ODBC API that does not depend on RDO or other object-style interfaces to allocate handles, open connections, create and manage cursors, or perform complex data retrieval, binding, and update operations. The ODBC API can perform all these functions. Although you might gain some speed in data access, it is far more difficult to code and maintain when compared with using RDO.

The ODBC API programming model provides the following features:

- A native interface to Microsoft SQL Server

- A flexible programming model that can access most database architectures

- Access to virtually all SQL Server features

- Advanced resultset management

- Complete post-call error management

- Fewer API functions than required by VBSQL

- Intelligent handling of stored procedure parameters

- Keyset, dynamic, static, and forward-only cursors

- Support of server-side cursors on Microsoft SQL Server starting with version 6

As the complexity and flexibility of remote data source platforms has evolved, the complexity of using Visual Basic with the ODBC API programming model has also increased. Although it is possible to create applications using the ODBC API from Visual Basic, it no longer affords sufficient benefit over using the Remote Data Object interface or other object-model interfaces.

Visual Basic Library for SQL Server

The Visual Basic Library for SQL Server (VBSQL) is an implementation of the DB-Library API specifically designed to provide access to SQL Server through a Visual Basic application. VBSQL exposes virtually all the DB-Library API functions and is supported as a native interface to SQL Server. Figure 2.13 shows VBSQL accessing the SQL Server.

Use VBSQL when your application needs to connect only to Microsoft SQL Server. You can use VBSQL to open one or more connections, submit queries, create cursors, process resultsets, execute stored procedures, and execute bulk copy operations.

This set of functions invokes equivalent functions in the DB-Library DLL, which is specifically designed to access Microsoft SQL Server.

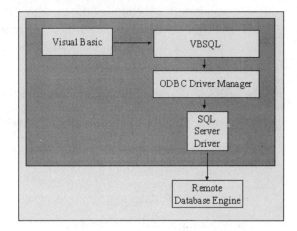

The VBSQL and the OBDC API functions are similar in that they both provide the broadest flexibility and, in some cases, better data access performance than RDO when accessing SQL Server. VBSQL does not support bound controls, so you will have to write all the code to connect, populate, and maintain Form-based controls. VBSQL provides the following features:

- Access to virtually all SQL Server features except two-phase commit

- Access to Microsoft SQL Server

- A native interface to Microsoft SQL Server

- Bulk copy (BCP) interface

- Complete interrupt-driven error and message handlers

- Fully asynchronous operations

- Keyset, dynamic, static, and forward-only scrolling cursors

- 'N' Row buffer resultsets

- Server-side cursor support on SQL Server starting with version 6

- Specific API functions to address all SQL Server features

Client/Server Tools Available in the Enterprise Edition of Visual Basic

The Enterprise Edition of Visual Basic 6 presents a design strategy for building component-based solutions based on the three-tiered services model. This section introduces some of the software tools and utilities that are provided by the Enterprise Edition to assist in building these distributed solutions.

The tools and utilities described here enable developers to connect to a data source, design queries and stored procedures, graphically design and maintain databases, and debug stored procedures.

The following sections briefly introduce and summarize the uses and benefits of each of these tools:

The Data Environment Designer provides an interactive, design-time environment for creating programmatic run-time data access. At design time, you can set property values for Connection and Command objects, write code to respond to ActiveX Data Objects (ADO) events, execute commands, and create aggregates and hierarchies.

Visual Database Tools is a combination of four database design tools (Data View, Database Designer, Query Designer, and Source Code Editor) that work in concert to provide a complete, tightly integrated database development and administration tool for developers.

The T-SQL Debugger is a stored procedure debugger that is fully integrated with the UserConnection Designer and the Data View window to allow you to interactively debug remote stored procedures and queries written in Microsoft SQL Server's Transact SQL dialect, from within the Visual Basic 6 development environment.

Visual SourceSafe is a version control system that enables you to manage individual and team projects.

The Data Environment Designer

As you write client/server applications, you will find that it will become increasingly difficult to stay aware of and maintain your stored procedures and queries.

You will have stored procedures on the Server and Query objects in your VB code, but how do you track all of them?

To solve this problem, the Enterprise version of Visual Basic 6 includes the Data Environment Designer, a graphical designer that provides an interactive, design-time environment for creating programmatic run-time data access. This designer enables you to set property values for Connection and Command objects, write code to respond to ActiveX Data Objects (ADO) events, execute commands, and create aggregates and hierarchies, all at design time. The Data Environment objects can even be dragged onto forms and reports to create data-bound controls.

NOTE   The Data Environment Designer is an improved version of the UserConnection Designer. The UserConnection Designer, used for RDO programming only, is still included in Visual Basic 6.

The following tasks can be accomplished with the Data Environment Designer:

- Add the Data Environment Designer to a Visual Basic project.
- Create Connection objects.
- Create Command objects based on stored procedures, tables, views, synonyms, and SQL statements.
- Create hierarchies of commands based on a grouping of Command objects, or by relating one or more Command objects together.
- Drag fields within a Command object from the Data Environment Designer onto a Visual Basic form or the Data Report Designer.
- Write and run code for Connection and Recordset objects.

This designer provides a simplified method for responding to events raised from connections and queries, as well as for calling stored procedures and client-defined queries at run time.

The Data Environment Designer can be referenced in code at run time or added to a project at design time.

NOTE All of the examples in this chapter rely on a data source called PubsTest. This data source is based on the Pubs sample database that is included with SQL Server. In order to follow along with these examples, you should create a PubsTest data source or substitute PubsTest for a data source that exists on your machine. See the section, Creating an ODBC Data Source, in Chapter 11 if you need help creating the PubsTest data source.

Referencing the Data Environment Designer

Follow these steps to add a reference to a Data Environment:

1. Select Project ➤ References to display the References dialog box.

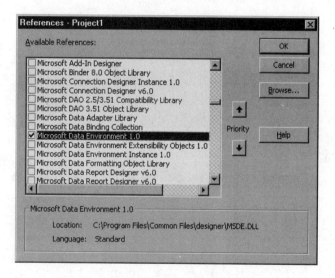

2. Select Data Environment 1.0 from the list of available references.

3. Click OK.

A reference to the Data Environment will be added to your project.

Adding a Data Environment Designer Object to a Visual Basic Project

To add a Data Environment Designer to a Visual Basic project, select Project ≻ Add DataEnvironment. The Data Environment Designer is added to your Visual Basic project, the Data Environment Designer window appears, and a Connection object is added to your Data Environment (shown in Figure 2.14).

FIGURE 2.14:

Data Environment Designer

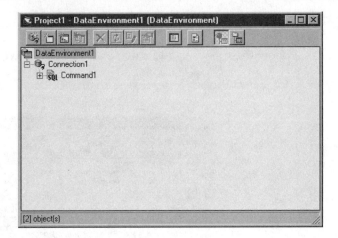

Establishing a Connection in a Data Environment Designer

After a Data Environment Designer has been added to a project, a connection must be established between the Data Environment Designer and a data source. One way to create a connection is to do it manually; add a Command, and then add a table, query, or stored procedure to the Command. Another way to create a connection is to drag a Data Link from the Data View window and drop it onto the Data Environment Designer. This will create a new Connection, create a new Command, and add the object to the Command.

First, let's take a look at the manual process. The Data Link process will be discussed in the Data View window section, later on in this chapter.

Creating the Data Environment Connection

To create a connection to the Data Environment, right-click Connection1 in the Data Environment Designer window, then select Properties from the menu to display the Data Link Properties dialog box.

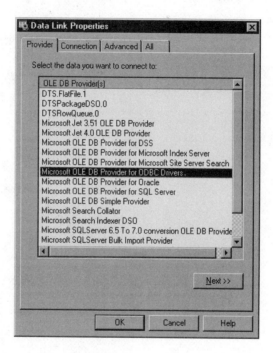

The Data Link Properties dialog box has four tabs that allow you to set and view the connection properties:

- Provider
- Connection
- Advanced
- All

The Provider Tab You use the Provider tab (shown in Figure 2.15) to select the appropriate OLE DB provider for the type of data you want to access. This tab is displayed only if your application allows the OLE DB provider selection to be edited, since not all applications allow you to specify a provider or modify the current selection.

FIGURE 2.15:

The Provider tab

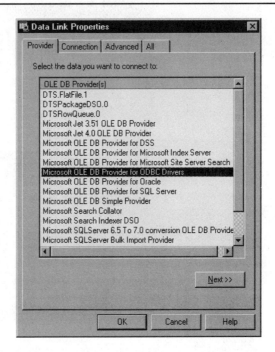

The Microsoft OLE DB provider for ODBC Drivers is selected by default. Accept this provider and click Next to move to the Connection tab.

The Connection Tab The Connection tab (shown in Figure 2.16) is used to specify how to connect to the ODBC data source.

NOTE Regardless of the selected data source type, the Data Environment accesses all data via ADO and OLE DB interfaces.

FIGURE 2.16:

The Connection tab

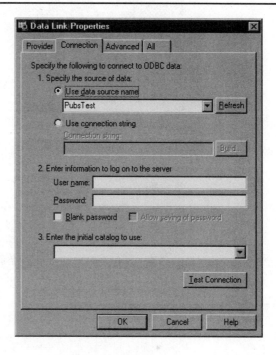

The Connection Tab supplies the following options:

Specify the source of data:

- The **Use data source name** option allows you to select a data source from the drop-down list or to enter the ODBC data source name (DSN) that you want to access. For our test, select the PubsTest data source from the list of available data sources in the drop-down list.

- The **Use connection string** option allows you to enter or build an ODBC connection string, rather than using an existing DSN. This option is very useful if you cannot control the available data sources on your users' machines.

- The **Connection string** field allows you to enter an ODBC connection string.

- The **Build** button opens the ODBC Select Data Source dialog box. Once you select a Data Source, the connection string in that data source will be returned and set into the connection string edit control.

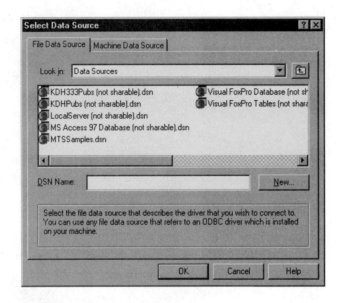

NOTE See Chapter 3, "Using SQL Server," for help with creating an ODBC data source.

If you select a File DSN, the resulting ODBC connection string is DSN-less. The ODBC connection string is persisted in the data link (.udl) file and does not rely on the selected File DSN.

If you select a Machine DSN, the resulting ODBC connection string is DSN-based. The ODBC connection string references the selected Machine DSN. If a user on a different system attempts to access the data link (.udl) file, the user must also have the Machine DSN installed.

Enter information to log on to the server:

NOTE Logon information only needs to be supplied if the database being accessed via the Connection object requires authentication information. You can specify a different set of logon information to be used at design time and run time.

- The **User name** field accepts the User ID to use for authentication when you log on to the data source. Enter a user name if required by your server.

- The **Password** field accepts the password to use for authentication when you log on to the data source. Enter a password if required by your server.

- Checking the **Blank password** option enables the specified provider to return a blank password in the connection string.

- Checking the **Allow saving of password** option allows the password to be saved with the connection string. Whether the password is included in the connection string depends on the functionality of the calling application.

Enter the initial catalog to use:

This field allows you to enter the initial catalog or table to use in the connection. Leave this field blank for our test.

Test Connection:

When you click the **Test Connection** button, Visual Basic attempts a connection to the specified data source. Click the button now. If the connection is established, you will see the Microsoft Data Link dialog box.

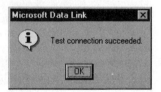

If the connection fails, ensure that the settings are correct and retest the connection.

The Advanced Tab   The Advanced tab (shown in Figure 2.17) supplies network and access options. The Network settings frame provides options to set the impersonation level and the protection level, while the server timeout and access permissions settings are provided by the other frame options.

The **Impersonation level** option sets the level of impersonation that the server is allowed to use when impersonating the client. This property applies only to network connections other than Remote Procedure Call (RPC) connections. These impersonation levels are similar to those provided by RPC. The values of this property correspond directly to the levels of impersonation that can be specified

FIGURE 2.17:

The Advanced tab

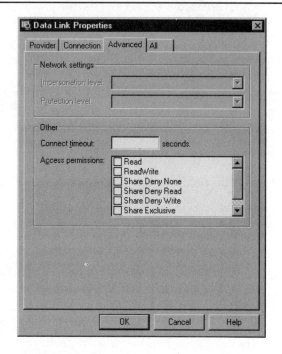

for authenticated RPC connections, but can be applied to connections other than authenticated RPC. Select from the following levels:

- **Anonymous**, where the client is anonymous to the server. With this setting, the server process cannot obtain identification information about the client or impersonate the client.

- **Identify**, where the server can obtain the client's identity. This setting allows the server to impersonate the client for ACL checking, but does not allow access to the system objects as the client.

- **Impersonate**, where the server process can impersonate the client's security context while acting on behalf of the client. With this setting, the information is not obtained on every call, but is obtained when the connection is established.

- **Delegate**, where the process can impersonate the client's security context while acting on behalf of the client. The server process can also make outgoing calls to other servers while acting on behalf of the client.

The **Protection Level** option sets the level of protection of data sent between client and server. This property applies only to network connections other than RPC connections. These protection levels are similar to those provided by RPC. The values of this property correspond directly to the levels of protection that can be specified for authenticated RPC connections, but can be applied to connections other than authenticated RPC. Select from the following levels:

- **None**, which performs no authentication of data sent to the server.

- **Connect**, which authenticates only when the client establishes the connection with the server.

- **Call**, where the source of the data is authenticated at the beginning of each request from the client to the server.

- **Pkt**, which authenticates that all data received is from the client.

- **Pkt Integrity**, which authenticates that all data received is from the client and that it has not been changed in transit.

- **Pkt Privacy**, which authenticates that all data received is from the client and that it has not been changed in transit, and encrypts the data.

The **Other** frame options provide settings for the server timeout and access permissions. (For our test, the settings on this tab are not used.)

The **Connect Timeout** field allows you to specify the amount of time (in seconds) that the OLE DB provider waits for initialization to complete. An error is returned and the connection is not created if initialization times out.

The **Access Permissions** options specify the access permissions. You may select one or more of the following permissions.

- **Read**, which sets the database to read-only.

- **ReadWrite**, which allows the application to read and write to the database.

- **Share Deny None**, which states that neither read nor write access can be denied to others.

- **Share Deny Read**, which prevents others from opening in read mode.

- **Share Deny Write,** which prevents others from opening in write mode.

- **Share Exclusive**, which prevents others from opening in read/write mode

- **Write**, which sets the access to write-only.

The All Tab   The All tab (shown in Figure 2.18) can be used to view and edit all of the OLE DB initialization properties that are available for your OLE DB provider. Properties may vary, depending on the OLE DB provider that you are using.

FIGURE 2.18:

The All tab

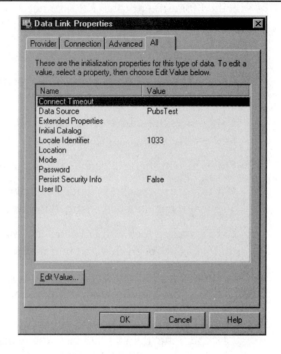

The **Edit Value** button allows you to edit the values for the properties you have set in the dialog box.

All of the settings are now complete and we should have a connection to the PubsTest data source. In the next section, we will create two Commands in the Data Environment that make a connection to the authors table and one that connects to the byRoyalty stored procedure in the Pubs database.

Data Environment Commands

Data Environment Command objects define specific detailed information about what data is retrieved from a database connection. Command objects can be based on either a Database object (such as a table, view, stored procedure, or synonym) or an SQL query.

Creating a Data Environment Command

Follow steps one through seven to create a Command object based on the authors table in the Pubs database:

1. Click Add Command in the Data Environment Designer toolbar.

or

Right-click a Connection object, or your Data Environment designer, and choose Add Command from the shortcut menu to add a command to the connection. Once a Command object is added, the Data Environment's outline view shows the new Command object.

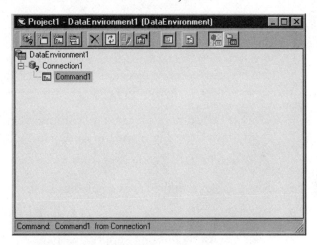

2. Right-click the Command1 object and select Properties from the menu to display the Command1 Properties dialog box.

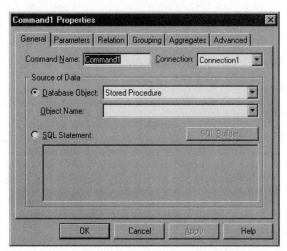

This dialog box allows you to set the options for the command. The available tabs are:

- General
- Parameters
- Relation
- Grouping
- Aggregates
- Advanced

NOTE   The General, Parameters, and Advanced tabs are used for setting properties of the Command and Parameter objects, while the Relation, Grouping, and Aggregates tabs are used for setting properties that are specific to command hierarchies.

3. Change the Command Name to **Authors**. This will rename the command from the default Command1 to Authors.

4. Accept the value of Connection1.

5. Select Table from the list of available Database objects.

6. Select dbo.authors from the list of available tables.

7. Click the Apply button to apply the changes.

The General Tab   The General tab (shown in Figure 2.19) holds the required properties for the command.

- The **Command Name** field is the name of the Command object referencing an individual Command object within a Data Environment object. The default name is Command plus a unique number.

- The **Connection** field sets the object to which the Command object is related. You can view a list of all Connection objects in the current Data Environment object through the combo box.

- The **Source of Data** frame contains the control group that specifies the type of data that is retrieved for the Command object.

FIGURE 2.19:

The General tab

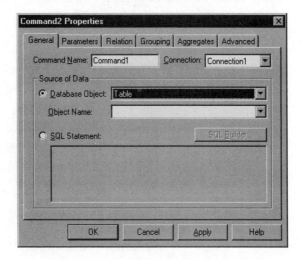

- The **Database Object** combo box specifies the database item on which the Command object is based. The options are Stored Procedure, Table, View, or Synonym.

- The **Object Name** combo box provides a list of all database items of the specified Database object.

- The **SQL Statement** field holds the SQL command that the Command object uses for its data source. Pressing the SQL Builder button opens the Data View window, where you can interactively build a SQL Statement.

NOTE   Only the General tab parameters require setting for our sample. The rest of the tabs are discussed only for information.

The Parameters Tab   The Parameters tab (shown in Figure 2.20) is used to add to a Command object's Parameters collection.

The **Parameters** list box contains all of the Parameter objects that are associated with the Command object. Select a parameter and edit its properties, as appropriate.

FIGURE 2.20:

The Parameters tab

FIGURE 2.20:

The Parameters tab

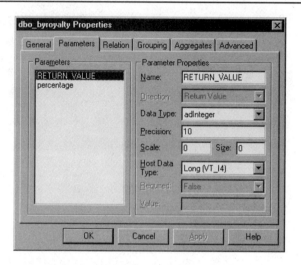

The **Parameter Properties** frame contains the control group with which you can change the property values of the selected Parameter object. This is disabled when no Parameter object is selected. The following properties are available based on the object:

- **Name**, which is the name of the Parameter object. You should change this to a more meaningful and unique name.

- **Direction**, which specifies whether the parameter is an input or output parameter, or both, or if the parameter is the return value from the procedure. Select a value from the combo box: Input, Output, Input and Output, Return Value, or Unknown.

- **Data Type**, which specifies the data type to which a Data Environment Parameter object is converted.

- **Precision**, which sets the maximum number of digits, or precision, of the Data Environment Parameter object.

- **Scale**, which is the maximum number of digits to the right of the decimal point of a Data Environment Parameter object.

- **Size**, which is the maximum size, in bytes, of the Parameter object.

- **Host Data Type**, which is the data type that is used when the Parameter object is referenced by the host application. Changing the host data type affects the data type used in building the typelib information for the host.

- **Required**, which, when selected, indicates that a parameter value is required when executing the Command object.

- **Value**, which is a value for the Parameter object. The Data Environment uses this value for design-time data binding, and run-time Command object execution.

The Relation Tab   The Relation tab (shown in Figure 2.21) specifies the properties for a relation hierarchy.

FIGURE 2.21:

The Relation tab

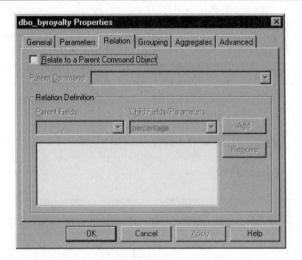

The **Relate to a Parent Command Object** option, if selected, states that the current Command object is the child in a relation hierarchy, and all controls on the tab are enabled. If not selected, the Command object is not the child in a relation hierarchy, and all controls on the tab are disabled.

The **Parent Command** drop-down list contains the Command object that is the parent to the child Command object. This can be any Command object that is associated with the same Connection object.

The **Relation Definition** frame contains the control group that defines the Field and Parameter objects that specify the relationship between two Command objects.

The **Parent Fields** drop-down list contains the Field objects of the parent Command object. When added, these show on the left side of the relate expression in the Relation Definition list.

The **Child Fields/Parameters** drop-down list contains the Parameter or Field objects of the child Command object. The Child Fields/Parameters, when added, are used on the right of the relate expression in the Relation Definition list. If the child Command object has input parameters, these parameters are listed first; if these parameters are required, they must be related to fields in the parent object.

The **Add** button is used to create a new relation definition based on the contents of the Parent Field and Child Field/Parameters lists. The new relation shows in the Relation Definition list (for example, CustomerID TO CustomerID).

The **Remove** button removes a relation from the Relation Definition list.

NOTE   There is no undo mechanism for the Remove action. Therefore, if the wrong relation is removed, it must be added again using the Add feature.

The Grouping Tab   The Grouping tab (shown in Figure 2.22) is used to specify the properties for a grouping hierarchy. You can also use this tab to create, modify, and delete the grouping of a Command object.

FIGURE 2.22:

The Grouping tab

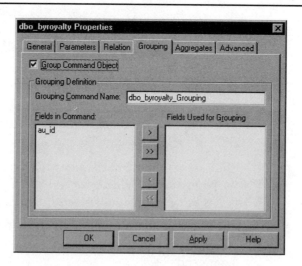

The **Group Command Object** option, if selected, states that the Command object is grouped, and that all controls on the tab are enabled. If not selected, the Command object is not grouped, and all controls on the tab are disabled.

The **Grouping Definition** frame contains the properties for the grouping hierarchy. If Group Command Object is not selected, the contents of this frame are disabled.

The **Grouping Command Name** field sets the name of the grouping Command object that is created when a Command object is grouped. This Command object contains the grouped data, while the current Command object contains the detail data. You should change the default name to a more meaningful name.

The **Fields in Command** list box lists all Field objects that exist in the source Command object.

The **Fields Used for Grouping** list box contains the Field objects by which the Command object is grouped.

The **Arrow** buttons can be used to move fields from one list bow to the other.

- > moves the selected Field object from the Fields in Command list to the Fields Used for Grouping list. This is disabled if no items are listed in the Fields in Command list.

- >> moves all Field objects from the Fields in Command list to the Fields Used for Grouping list. This is disabled if no items are listed in the Fields in Command list.

- < moves the selected Field object from the Fields Used for Grouping list to the Fields in Command list. This is disabled if no items are listed in the Fields Used for Grouping list.

- << moves all Field objects from the Fields Used for Grouping list to the Fields in Command list. This is disabled if no items are listed in the Fields Used for Grouping list.

The Aggregates Tab   The Aggregates tab (shown in Figure 2.23) defines the aggregates associated with a relation or group-based hierarchy.

The **Aggregates** list box lists the aggregates defined for the Command object.

- The **Add** button inserts additional aggregates into the Aggregates box.

- The **Remove** button deletes the selected aggregate from the Aggregates box. This button is disabled if no aggregate is selected.

FIGURE 2.23:

The Aggregates tab

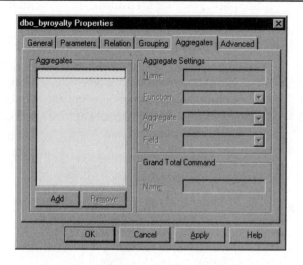

The **Aggregate Settings** frame contains the control group used to change the aggregate properties of the selected aggregate. This is disabled when no aggregate is selected.

- The **Name** field is the name of the Field object that will be added to the Command object. At run time, this field will contain the calculated aggregate value.

- The **Function** drop-down list contains the aggregate function to perform on a Field object. Table 2.2 details the aggregates that are available; you can use one of the following operations for each aggregate that you create.

TABLE 2.2: Function Aggregates

Operation	Description
Any	Returns the default operation of the selected field.
Average	Obtains the average of the values in a particular field.
Count	Returns the count of the number of records in the selection.
Maximum	Returns the highest value in a selected field.
Minimum	Returns the smallest value in a selected field.
Standard Deviation	Returns the standard deviation of the selection.
Sum	Returns the sum of all the values in the selected field.

- The **Aggregate On** drop-down list specifies what the aggregate is based upon: Grand Total, Grouping, or Child Command. The contents of this list will vary, depending on the definition of the Command object. Grand Total is listed only if the current Command object is a top-level object. Grouping is only available if the Command object is grouped. Child Command objects are listed only if the current Command object is a parent.

- The **Field** drop-down list presents the fields that are available for you to create an aggregate. The fields listed are dependent upon the Aggregate On selection.

The **Grand Total Command** frame contains the control group used if the Grand Total constraint is selected in Aggregate On.

The **Name** field allows you to specify a name for the Grand Total Command.

The Advanced Tab   The Advanced tab (shown in Figure 2.24) allows you to specify RecordSet Management and other information relating to the current Command object.

FIGURE 2.24:

The Advanced tab

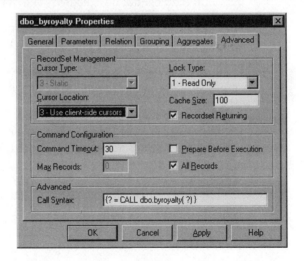

The **RecordSet Management** frame contains the control group pertaining to the management of the Recordset objects.

- The **Cursor Type** drop-down list specifies the type of cursor to use for the Command object: Forward Only, Keyset, Dynamic, or Static. The default is Forward Only.

- The **Cursor Location** drop-down list specifies the location of the cursor library for the Command object.

- The **Lock Type** drop-down list specifies the type of lock that the provider uses to open a Command object: Read Only, Pessimistic, Optimistic, or Batch Optimistic. The default is Read Only.

- The **Cache Size** setting specifies the cache size to use for the Command object. The default is 10 records.

- The **Recordset Returning** option specifies whether the Recordset object returns information. Two Command objects must be created, one with Recordset Returning selected and the other with it not selected, if you want to return both a recordset and an output parameter.

The **Command Configuration** frame contains the control group that specifies timeout and record configuration information.

- The **Command Timeout** option sets the number of seconds to timeout when the Command cannot be executed. The default is 30 seconds.

- The **Max Records** option sets the maximum number of records that can return from a data source. The default is 0, which means infinite.

- The **Prepare Before Execution** option specifies whether the command is prepared on the first invocation. Valid values are True or False. The default is False.

- The **All Records** option specifies whether all records are returned upon execution of the Command object. If selected, Max Records is set to 0 and the edit control is disabled.

The **Call Syntax** field sets the call syntax that ADO uses to call the stored procedure. This can be edited to adjust the number of parameters and presence of the return value.

Using the Data Environment in Your Code

Now that we have added a Data Environment to the project and created a Command object, let's access it in code. The code in Code 2.1 opens a connection, reads the records and prints them to the Debug window, and closes the connection.

Code 2.1	Establishing a Data Environment

```
Private Sub Form_Load()
    Dim DE As New Customers
    'Open the DataEnvironment
    DE.rsauthors.Open

    'Get the first record
    DE.rsauthors.MoveFirst

    'Loop through the records
    Do While DE.rsauthors.EOF = False
        Debug.Print DE.rsauthors(1).Value & ", " _
            & DE.rsauthors(2).Value
        DE.rsauthors.MoveNext
    Loop

    'Close the DataEnvironment connection
    DE.rsauthors.Close
End Sub
```

As you can see, the Data Environment is designed to be the repository for all of your stored procedures and queries.

Visual Database Tools

Visual Database Tools comprises four components included in Visual Basic 6 that you can use to help create and manage data-driven applications that rely on live connections to databases.

Visual Database Tools is tightly coupled with the Data Environment that we discussed in the previous section. The Query Designer enables you to use visual tools to build SQL statements that retrieve data or modify the contents of tables. The interface of the Visual Database Tools is similar to that of Microsoft Access. The Database Designer graphically represents tables and their relationships and lets you create and modify the database objects on which your application relies. All this can be done while you are connected to the underlying database. You can design, query, and populate your databases from within the design environment that you use to build your application. With Microsoft Visual Database Tools, you can:

- Add, update, and delete data stored in database tables.

- Create and modify Microsoft SQL Server 6.5 databases using database diagrams.

- Connect to and explore any ODBC-compliant database.

- Design, execute, and save complex queries.

- Design objects—such as tables, triggers, and stored procedures—in Microsoft SQL Server and Oracle databases.

- Drag database objects onto a design surface, such as an HTML template form, and drop to bind controls to those objects.

Microsoft Visual Database Tools is made up of four components:

Data View provides a graphical environment for creating, viewing, and editing the database objects that reside on a remote database server. Data View is your starting point for managing your database objects, such as database diagrams, tables, triggers, views, and stored procedures.

The Database Designer is used to create, edit, or delete database objects for Microsoft SQL Server 6.5 databases while you're directly connected to the database in which those objects are stored.

The Query Designer is used to create SQL statements to query or update databases. It automatically creates joins and graphically shows table relationships.

The Source Code Editor for Stored Procedures and Triggers is used to create, edit, and debug stored procedures and triggers.

This combination of database design tools provides a complete, tightly integrated database-development and administration tool for developers.

Data View

The Data View component, shown in Figure 2.25, provides a visual interface to live connections to the databases in each project and to objects available in each database, organized into folders. These folders hold the objects that are created with the tools available in Visual Database Tools, or that are created at the server level.

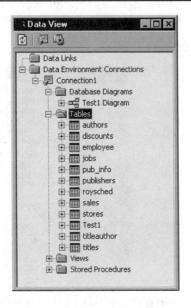

FIGURE 2.25:

The Visual Data Tools Data View

The following folders are available in the Data View window:

Database Diagrams, which is a graphical representation of any portion of a database schema. A database diagram can be either a whole or a partial picture of the structure of a database; it includes objects for tables, the columns they contain, and the relationships among them.

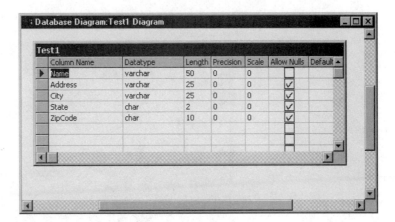

Tables, which can be viewed as a set of rows and columns, similar to the rows and columns of a spreadsheet. In a relational database, the rows are called *records,* and the columns are called *fields.*

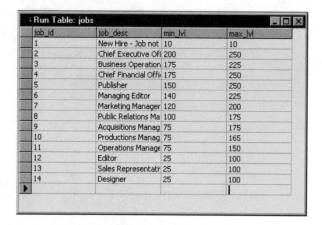

Stored Procedures, a precompiled collection of Transact-SQL statements and optional control-of-flow statements that are stored under a name and processed as a unit. Stored procedures are kept within a database, can be executed with one call from an application, and allow user-declared variables, conditional execution, and other powerful programming features. The stored procedures that SQL Server supplies are called *system stored procedures.*

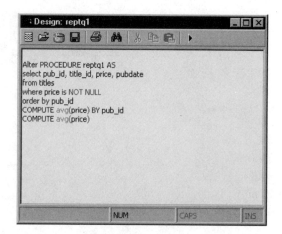

Triggers, which is a special type of stored procedure that is activated when data in a specified table is modified. Triggers are often created to enforce referential integrity or consistency among logically related data in different tables.

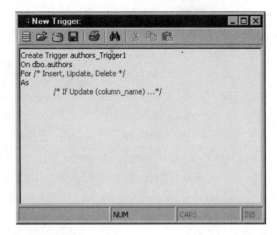

Views, which is another way of looking at data from one or more tables in the database. A view is usually created as a subset of columns from one or more tables. The tables from which views are derived are called *base tables*. A view looks almost exactly like any other database table, and you can display it and manipulate it almost as you can any table.

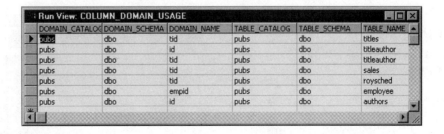

Double-clicking a table, a view, or a stored procedure in Data View opens the object in a window. The data source permitting, you can edit and delete rows or add new rows. Give it a try. Double-click the Employee table in Data View, and the table will open as shown in Figure 2.26.

au_id	au_lname	au_fname	phone	address	city
172-32-1176	White	Johnson	408 496-7223	10932 Bigge Rd.	Menlo Park
213-46-8915	Green	Marjorie	415 986-7020	309 63rd St. #411	Oakland
238-95-7766	Carson	Cheryl	415 548-7723	589 Darwin Ln.	Berkeley
267-41-2394	O'Leary	Michael	408 286-2428	22 Cleveland Av. #	San Jose
274-80-9391	Straight	Dean	415 834-2919	5420 College Av.	Oakland
341-22-1782	Smith	Meander	913 843-0462	10 Mississippi Dr.	Lawrence
409-56-7008	Bennet	Abraham	415 658-9932	6223 Bateman St.	Berkeley
427-17-2319	Dull	Ann	415 836-7128	3410 Blonde St.	Palo Alto
472-27-2349	Gringlesby	Burt	707 938-6445	PO Box 792	Covelo
486-29-1786	Locksley	Charlene	415 585-4620	18 Broadway Av.	San Francisco
527-72-3246	Greene	Morningstar	615 297-2723	22 Graybar House l	Nashville
648-92-1872	Blotchet-Halls	Reginald	503 745-6402	55 Hillsdale Bl.	Corvallis
672-71-3249	Yokomoto	Akiko	415 935-4228	3 Silver Ct.	Walnut Creek
712-45-1867	del Castillo	Innes	615 996-8275	2286 Cram Pl. #86	Ann Arbor
722-51-5454	DeFrance	Michel	219 547-9982	3 Balding Pl.	Gary
724-08-9931	Stringer	Dirk	415 843-2991	5420 Telegraph Av	Oakland
724-80-9391	MacFeather	Stearns	415 354-7128	44 Upland Hts.	Oakland
756-30-7391	Karsen	Livia	415 534-9219	5720 McAuley St.	Oakland
807-91-6654	Panteley	Sylvia	301 946-8853	1956 Arlington Pl.	Rockville
846-92-7186	Hunter	Sheryl	415 836-7128	3410 Blonde St.	Palo Alto
893-72-1158	McBadden	Heather	707 448-4982	301 Putnam	Vacaville
899-46-2035	Ringer	Anne	801 826-0752	67 Seventh Av.	Salt Lake City
998-72-3567	Ringer	Albert	801 826-0752	67 Seventh Av.	Salt Lake City

The Database Designer

You use the Database Designer, shown in Figure 2.27, to create, edit, or delete
database objects for Microsoft SQL Server 6.5 databases while you're directly connected to the database in which those objects are stored.

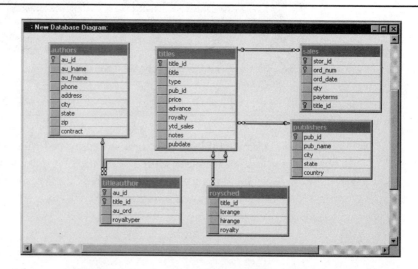

The Database Designer provides a graphical environment in which you can do the following:

- Create and modify the structure of Microsoft SQL Server databases.
- Create, modify, or delete database objects such as tables, relationships, indexes, and constraints.
- Experiment with the design of your Microsoft SQL Server database without affecting the database until you choose to save your new design.

You interact with the server database using database diagrams, which graphically represent tables, the columns they contain, and the relationships among them.

Creating and Managing Database Diagrams   You can use database diagrams to do the following:

- Alter the structure of your database.
- Create new objects and relationships.
- Experiment with database changes without modifying the underlying database.
- Manipulate database objects without writing Transact-SQL code.
- Provide different views of complex databases.
- Perform complex operations to alter the physical structure of your database.

To create a database diagram, follow these steps:

1. Right-click the Database Diagram folder in the Data View window.
2. Select New Database Diagram from the menu.
3. Drag a table from Data View and drop it in the database diagram.

Managing a Database with the Database Designer

In this section, you will use the Database Designer to create, edit, and delete a test database.

Creating the VB6Database Project   Follow these steps to create the TestVB6 database with the Database Designer:

1. Start a new Visual Basic 6 Standard project.
2. Remove Form1 from the project.
3. Save the project under the name VB6Database.vbp.

NOTE
You'll find the VB6Database project in the Ch2Code folder of the CD that comes with this book.

Adding a Data Link to the Project   Follow these steps to add a Data Link to the project:

1. Select View ➤ Data View Window to open the Data View window.

2. Click the Data Link icon in the Data View window to display the Data Link Properties dialog box.

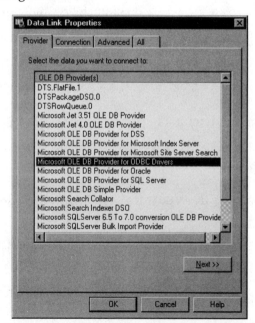

This is the dialog box where you will make a connection to the data source.

NOTE
As are the other examples in this chapter, this example is based on the PubsTest data source.

3. Select the Microsoft OLE DB Provider for ODBC Drivers from the list of available providers.

4. Click Next to move to the Connection tab.

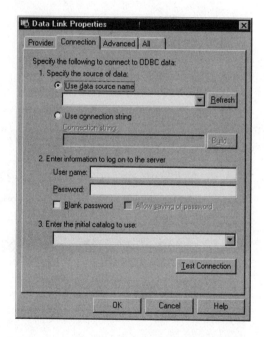

5. Select PubsTest from the list of available data source names.

6. Click the Test Connection button to test the new data link. You should see the Microsoft Data Link message box informing you that the test connection succeeded.

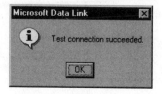

7. Click the OK button to add the Data Link to the Data View window.

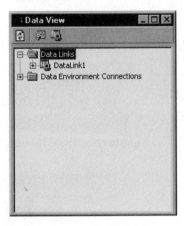

You should now have a connection to the PubsTest data source.

Creating the VBTest Database   Now that you have added a Data Link, it's time to create the TestVB6 database. Follow these steps to open the Database Designer and create the database:

1. Double-click DataLink1 to expose the folders.

2. Right-click the Database Diagram folder and select New Database Diagram from the menu to open a new database diagram screen.

3. Right-click inside the database diagram screen to display the menu. This menu allows you to create a new table, add a text annotation to the diagram, work with links, zoom in or out, and more.

4. Select New Table from the menu to display the Choose Name dialog box.

5. Name the table Test1 and click OK. A new blank table named Test1 will be created and added to the database diagram.

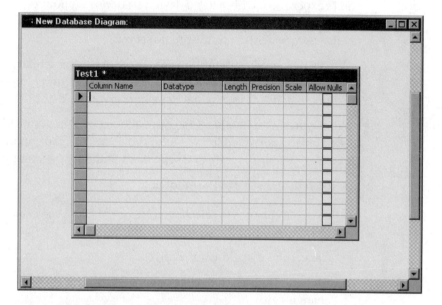

6. Right-click the table to display the menu. This menu provides the options available to you as you manipulate tables in the Database Designer.

7. Enter the column names and other attributes into the Test1 table, as shown in Table 2.3.

TABLE 2.3: Test1 Attributes

Column Name	DataType	Length	Allow Nulls
Name	varchar	50	No
Address	varchar	25	Yes
City	varchar	25	Yes
State	char	2	Yes
ZipCode	char	10	Yes

This will create the table in the database diagram; however, the table is not saved into the database. Saving changes to the database will be discussed in the next section.

Saving Changes   When you create or modify a database object through a database diagram, the modifications you make are not saved in the database until you save the object or the database diagram. This is advantageous because it enables you to experiment with what-if design scenarios without permanently affecting the existing design or data. The tables represented in your diagrams are merely references to tables that reside on the server.

A table that appears in multiple database diagrams actually exists only in the server database itself. When you modify a table in a diagram, your modifications are immediately applied to that table in every other diagram in which it appears.

When you save a database diagram, all the tables in your diagram and their related objects are saved in the server database. You can choose to select only certain tables in your diagram and save them without affecting the others.

You can then do one of the following:

- Save the changes to selected tables or the Database Diagram and have the changes modify the server database.

- Cancel and discard your changes.

- Save the Transact-SQL code generated by your changes to the diagram in a change script.

You control the timing, type, and extent of the changes to your database by choosing how changes to the database diagram affect the server database.

Saving the Test1 Table   Close the database diagram screen and choose Yes in the Save Dialog to save the Test1 table to the Pubs database. Now that the table is saved, you can add rows to it, delete rows, edit the table structure, and delete the table.

The Query Designer

You can use the Query Designer, shown in Figure 2.28, to create SQL statements to query or update databases. It automatically creates joins and graphically shows table relationships. It is similar to the Query tab in Microsoft Access. With the Query Designer you can do the following:

- Drag tables from the Data View into the query and use graphical controls to manipulate the query definition.

- Use a criteria grid to specify search criteria, sort order, and output columns.

- Use a SQL pane to type SQL statements or let the Query Designer generate the SQL statements for your queries.

- Browse and edit live views of data in your database tables.

NOTE   You can copy and paste the SQL statements that the Query Designer creates into your Visual Basic application. This can be especially helpful if your query has a lot of complex joins.

FIGURE 2.28:

The Query Designer

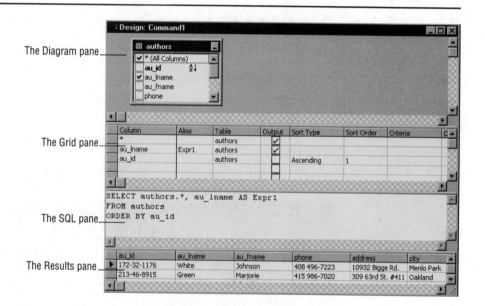

If you are familiar with SQL, you can also do the following:

- Enter SQL statements directly or edit the SQL statements created by the Query Designer.

- Create back-end-specific SQL statements to take advantage of the features of a particular database.

- Execute Microsoft SQL Server stored procedures.

NOTE

You can also copy SQL statements that you code in your Visual Basic applications into the Query Designer and execute them. This is a great way to check your SQL syntax.

Accessing the Query Designer The Query Designer can be accessed through a Data Environment. Follow these steps to access the Query Designer:

1. Add a Data Environment to the VB6Database project and connect it to the PubsTest data source.

NOTE

See the section "Adding a Data Environment Designer Object to a Visual Basic Project," presented earlier in this chapter, if you need help adding a Data Environment.

2. Click the Command icon to add a command to the Data Environment. It is named Command1 by default.

3. Right-click the new Command1 command and select Properties from the menu.

4. Select SQL Statement from the Source of Data frame.

5. Click the SQL Builder button to display the Query Designer.

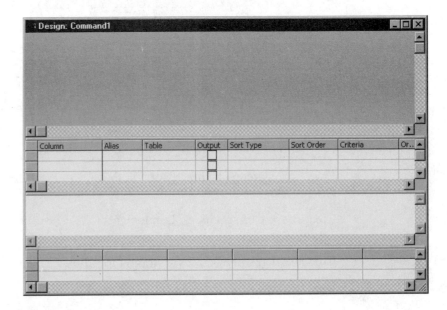

NOTE

After the Source of Data has been set to SQL Statement for the command, you can access the Query Designer by right-clicking the command and choosing Design from the menu.

Query Designer Layout   The Query Designer consists of four panes (as shown in Figure 2.28). Table 2.4 lists and describes each pane.

TABLE 2.4: The Query Designer Panes

Pane	Description
The Diagram pane	Displays the input sources (tables or views) that you are querying. Each input source appears in its own window, showing the available data columns as well as icons that indicate how each column is used in the query. Joins are indicated by lines between the input source windows. Double-click the join lines to get additional information on the join.
The Grid pane	Contains a spreadsheet-like grid in which you specify query options, such as which data columns to display, how the results should be sorted, and which rows to select.
The SQL pane	Displays the SQL statement for the current query. You can edit the SQL statement, or you can enter your own SQL statement. If you edit the SQL statement, the diagram pane is updated to reflect the changes after you run the query.
The Results pane	Shows a grid with the results of the most recently executed query. You can edit the values, add rows, and delete rows from this grid.

NOTE

You can show and hide individual panes by selecting View ➢ Show Panes and then selecting the individual panes from the menu.

Using Different Panes to Create Queries   You can create a query by working in some or all of the panes. You can specify a column to display by choosing it in the Diagram pane and entering it into the Grid pane.

The Diagram, Grid, and SQL panes are synchronized, so when you make a change in one pane, the Query Designer updates the other panes to reflect the change. This allows the Query Designer to represent your query by displaying graphics in the Diagram and Grid panes and displaying text in the SQL pane.

Running the Query   If you are creating a Select query, the results are displayed in the Results pane. The Query Designer enables you to begin viewing rows immediately by running the query in small batches.

The Query Designer dims the contents of the Results pane if the current query changes to indicate that it no longer reflects the current query.

Creating Queries in the SQL Pane   In addition to creating queries in the Diagram and Grid panes, you can enter SQL statements directly into the SQL pane. When you move to another pane, the Query Designer parses the SQL statement and synchronizes the other panes to reflect the new statement. This is a great way to check the syntax of SQL statements in your Visual Basic application. You can copy from Visual Basic, paste into the SQL pane, and run the query. The Query Designer displays any errors that occur.

If you create a SQL statement that cannot be represented in the Diagram and Grid panes, the Query Designer dims those panes to indicate that they no longer reflect the state of the current query.

As you can see, the Query Designer can be a useful tool, helping you create, test, and debug SQL statements.

Querying the Authors Table   Now, let's put it all together and create a query that selects all of the rows from the Authors table and sorts the results by the author's last name. Follow these steps to create a query using the Command1 command from the previous section:

1.   If the Data View window is not open, open it now by clicking the Data View icon. You should have the Query Designer open and the Data View window open.

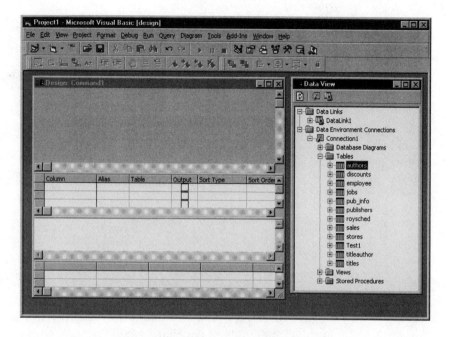

2. Expand the Tables folder, drag the Authors table from Connection1, and drop it on the Diagram Pane of the Query Designer. This adds the table to the designer, but no columns are selected for output.

3. Click the * All Columns box to select all columns for the query.

4. Click on the au_lname column in the Diagram Pane to select it. The au_lname column is already selected for output when you clicked the All Columns box, but it needs to be added again so that we can sort by it.

5. Select Ascending from the Sort Type column in the Grid Pane to set the ORDER BY clause. Notice the SQL statement in the SQL Pane? As you select columns and query options, the Query Designer is building the SQL statement for you.

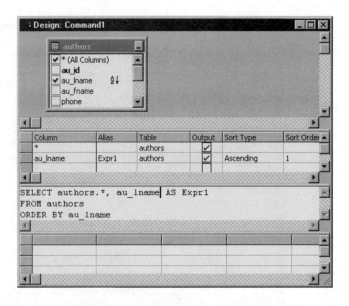

6. Select Query ➢ Run to execute the query and display the results in the Results Pane, as shown in Figure 2.29.

FIGURE 2.29:

Query results

The Source Code Editor

You can use the Source Code Editor, shown in Figure 2.30, to do the following:

- Create stored procedures and triggers.
- Edit stored procedures and triggers.
- Delete stored procedures and triggers.
- Debug stored procedures.

NOTE   To debug stored procedures, you must have Visual C++ Enterprise Edition installed.

FIGURE 2.30:

The Source Code Editor

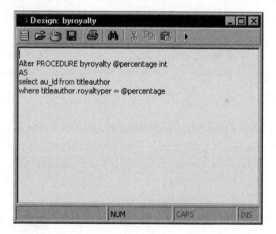

Editing Stored Procedures and Triggers   You can open a procedure stored in your Microsoft SQL Server or Oracle database to view or edit its text. Stored procedures are written in SQL. Follow these steps to open and edit a stored procedure or trigger:

1. In Data View, expand the Stored Procedures folder.

2. Right-click the name of the stored procedure that you want to open.

3. Double-click the stored procedure and it will open the built-in text editor that you can use to edit the SQL statements.

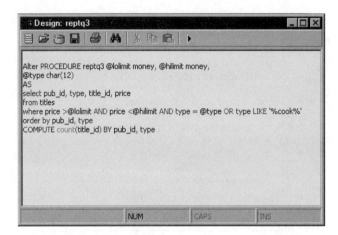

4. Choose File ➤ Save to save the stored procedure or trigger.

NOTE

Stored procedures must have unique names in the database. If the name beside CREATE PROCEDURE in the procedure text is already assigned to another database object, the Server Error(s) dialog box prompts you to choose another name for the stored procedure.

Running Stored Procedures and Triggers   If you are using Microsoft SQL Server, in addition to creating queries, you can execute stored procedures. This feature enables you to take advantage of precompiled queries and system procedures. The project workspace displays a list of stored procedures available in the current database.

To see a list of available stored procedures in Data View, expand the name of your project, expand the name of the data connection you are querying, and then display the Stored Procedures node.

You can execute a stored procedure in the SQL pane of the Query Designer. Follow these steps to execute a stored procedure in the SQL pane:

1. Enter the stored procedure command in the SQL pane using this syntax:

    ```
    EXECUTE procedure_name [parameter [, parameter ] …]
    ```

NOTE

To execute stored procedures in other databases or stored procedures belonging to other owners, you can qualify the name of the stored procedure.

2. Select the Run option to execute the stored procedure.

Any returned rows appear in the Results pane, where you can copy them individually or as a column. However, the Results pane does not display the return value explicitly.

Microsoft Visual SourceSafe

Microsoft Visual SourceSafe (VSS) (shown in Figure 2.31) is a version-control application included with the Enterprise version of Visual Basic that allows you to control and track your projects. VSS provides an easy-to-use way to coordinate your team's efforts and to bring project-oriented version control to all your application or Web site development projects. You get the safety of knowing your files are secure, organized, and efficiently archived in retrievable project-oriented versions, and you get more time for you and your team to develop the best applications and Web sites.

FIGURE 2.31:

Visual SourceSafe Explorer

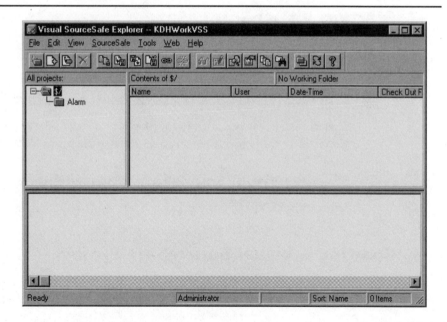

VSS helps you manage your projects, and makes team coordination easy and intuitive, regardless of the file type (text, graphics, binary, sound, or video), by saving files of all types to a database. When you need to share files between two or more projects, you can share them quickly and efficiently. When you add a file to VSS, the file is backed up on the database and made available to other people. Any changes that have been made to the file are saved, so you can recover an old version at any time. Members of your team can see the latest version of any file, make changes, and save a new version in the database.

When a file (or set of files) is ready to deliver to another person, group, Web site, or location, VSS makes it easy to share and secure different versions of the selected set of files.

VSS can be accessed from within many development environments, including Microsoft Access, Visual Basic, Visual C++, Visual FoxPro, and other development tools. If VSS is integrated into your development environment, you do not need to run VSS separately to realize the advantages of source code control.

In the next sections, we will take a closer look at Visual SourceSafe as we work with the Alarm sample application that comes with Visual Basic 6.

Starting Visual SourceSafe

Visual SourceSafe can be started several different ways. You can access it from the Start menu, or you can access it from within Visual Basic.

Starting Visual SourceSafe from the Start Menu

To start Visual SourceSafe from the Start menu, select Start ➤ Programs ➤ Microsoft Visual Basic ➤ Microsoft Visual SourceSafe ➤ Microsoft Visual SourceSafe 6.0.

Starting Visual SourceSafe from within Visual Basic

From within a Visual Basic project, select Tools ➤ SourceSafe ➤ Run SourceSafe.

Creating a Visual SourceSafe Project

In VSS, you create projects that hold your files. A project is a group of related documents or a collection of files. VSS allows you to easily store and organize your projects, in any hierarchy you like.

For this example, we will use the Alarm project that is installed with Visual Basic. You will find the Alarm project in the Samples folder in the Visual Basic directory; for your convenience, it is also included on the CD that comes with this book, in the Ch2Code/Alarm directory.

Creating the Alarm Project in VSS

The first step in using source control is to create a Visual SourceSafe project. Follow these steps to create the Alarm Project:

NOTE
If you want to use the Alarm project from the book's CD, you must copy the Alarm directory to your hard disk and remove the read-only attribute from the files.

---

1. Select Start ➤ Programs ➤ Microsoft Visual Basic ➤ Microsoft Visual SourceSafe ➤ Microsoft Visual SourceSafe 6.0 to open SourceSafe.

2. In the SourceSafe Explorer (shown in Figure 2.31), select File ➤ Create Project to display the Create Project dialog box.

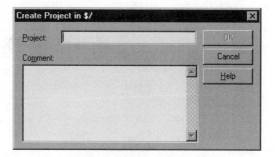

3. Enter "Alarm" as the project name and "Initial Load" as the Comment and click OK to create the Alarm project.

The project is now created; the next step is to add the Alarm.vbp files.

Adding Files to a VSS Project

After your project is created, you can add files or folders to the VSS database. Follow these steps to add files to the Alarm project:

1. Select the Alarm project by clicking it.

2. Select File ➤ Add Files to display the Add File dialog box.

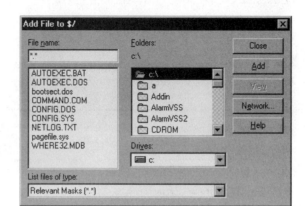

3. Navigate to the Alarm.vbp project and select the files. You can select multiple files by holding down the Shift key.

4. Click the Add button to display the Comment dialog box

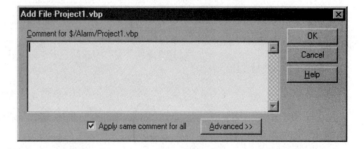

5. Enter "Initial project" in the Comment field and click OK to add the files.

6. Click the Close button to close the Add Files dialog box.

The files have been added to the VSS Alarm Project.

NOTE   You can add files or folders by following the above-described steps, or by dragging files or folders from the Windows Explorer and dropping them on the VSS Explorer.

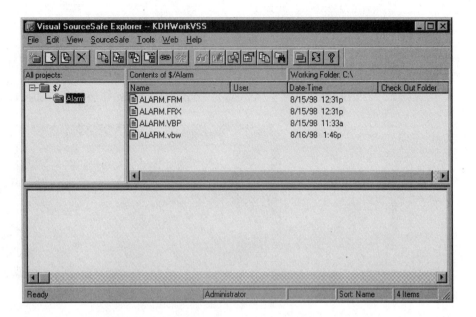

Introducing Working Folders

VSS is used for storing and managing files. When you want to edit or compile files, these actions are performed against a set of files that resides in your working folder. A working folder can be an existing folder or a new folder that VSS creates for you. Your current working folder path is displayed above the list view in the VSS Explorer.

A working folder is set per user, per project, or per machine. If you work on two projects, such as $/Alarm and $/Database, then you would have two different working folders, one for each project. If someone else works on the same two projects, then they would have their own working folders for each project. Multiple developers can work on files from the same project, but the files reside in different folders.

When you set a working folder for a project, you can set it for the entire project, including all subprojects under that project. You can, however, explicitly set a working folder for any subproject.

Setting the Working Folder

You must specify a working folder to perform any action that copies a file out of VSS, including the Check Out, Check In, Undo Check Out, Get Latest Version, and Merge commands. Follow these steps to set a working folder for our Alarm project:

1. Select the Alarm project by clicking it in the VSS Explorer.

2. Select File ➤ Set Working Folder to display the Set Working Folder dialog box.

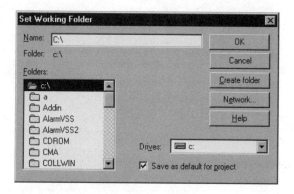

3. Enter c:\AlarmVSS as the folder and click the Create Folder button to create the folder.

4. Click the OK button to close the Set Working Folder dialog box. The VSS Explorer will now display the AlarmVSS folder as the working folder, as shown in Figure 2.32.

FIGURE 2.32:

Working folder displayed

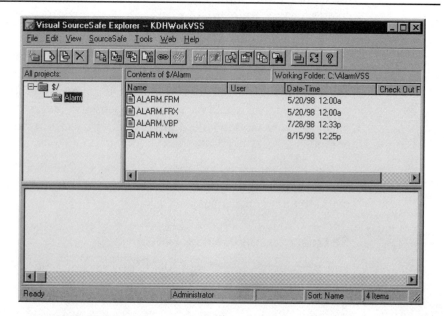

After the working folder is created, it is set as the current working folder, but it does not have any files in it. The files still reside only in the VSS project. In the next section, we will perform the Get Latest Version procedure to get the latest version of the files so that we can access them in Visual Basic.

Getting the Latest Version of Files

Now that we have created the Alarm project in VSS and set the working folder, it is time to add the latest version of the files to the folder. Follow these steps to get the latest version of the Alarm.vbp files:

1. From the VSS Explorer menu, select SourceSafe ➢ Get Latest Version to display the Get Alarm.FRM dialog box.

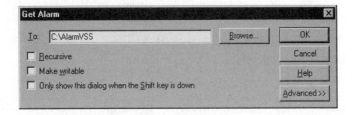

The Get Alarm dialog box asks you to confirm the Get File action. You can set options here for retrieving files recursively, making files writable, and displaying the dialog box.

Recursive: This option gets a project, all the files in the project, and all of its subprojects. Each file in a subproject is copied into its own working folder, which can be a folder anywhere on your computer or an accessible remote computer. To override the working folder settings, and create a file structure that mirrors the VSS project structure, use the Build Tree option.

Make Writable: This option sets the read/write flag so the file is writable. This is not the default behavior. The default is to get a read-only copy of the files. You can change the read status from within Visual Basic with the Check In and Check Out actions that are discussed later in this chapter.

Only Show This Dialog when the Shift Key Is Down: This option, if checked, tells VSS to skip this confirmation dialog box and immediately get the latest version of the files in the current project. If you want to confirm every file, leave this option unchecked.

TIP

If you check the Only Show This Dialog… option, the Get Latest Version operation will go much faster. You can always adjust the files from within Visual Basic, if needed.

2. Click OK to get the latest version of the files. The files will be copied, as read-only, to the Alarm project on your hard drive.

In the next section, armed with a copy of the latest files in our project, we will open a Visual Basic project and work with the files.

Opening a Visual SourceSafe Project in Visual Basic

After you have created a VSS Project, added files to it, created a folder to store a copy of those files, and copied the latest version of the files, it is time to open a Visual Basic project and work with the files. Follow these steps to open a Visual Basic project that is under VSS control:

1. Start Visual Basic normally.

2. Open the Alarm project that you created in the earlier section.

3. Enter a valid Username, Password, and Database in the Visual SourceSafe Login dialog box.

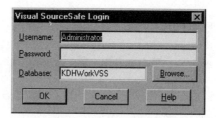

NOTE

In most installations, if you are the VSS Administrator and have a UserID set as "Administrator," you will not see this dialog box.

The project will open and the files will be displayed in the Project window as usual, except that they will be marked as read-only. You can look at the files, but changes are not permitted. As demonstrated in the next section, files that are under VSS control must be checked out before they can be edited.

Checking Out Files

To make changes to a file, you must first check it out of the VSS database. When you Check Out a file, VSS places a writable copy in your working folder. A file that you have checked out cannot be checked out by anyone else unless your installation of VSS has been set up to allow multiple checkouts. This is the main premise of source control. It allows you, or anyone on your team, to make changes to a project or file and then to check those changes in to VSS. This process assures that all changes made to a project or file will be made to the most current copy of those files.

Since a file can only be checked out by one person at a time, VSS marks all files that are checked out with the username of the person who has them checked out. You can see to whom an item is checked out in the User column of the file pane in the VSS Explorer, as shown in Figure 2.33.

FIGURE 2.33:

VSS Explorer with files checked out

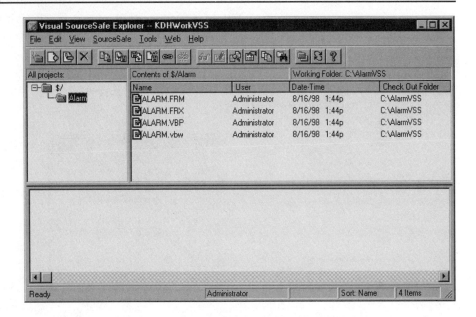

You can check out one file, multiple files, or all files in a project, depending on what items you have selected when you perform the check-out operation.

Follow these steps to check out the files on the Alarm.vbp project:

1. Select Tools ➤ SourceSafe ➤ Check Out to display the Check Out Files from SourceSafe dialog box.

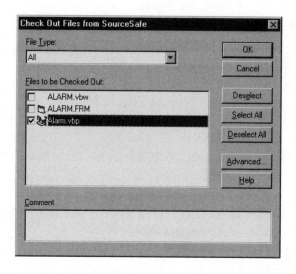

2. Click Select All to select all files.

3. Click OK to check out the selected files.

The files that have been checked out will display a red check next to them in the Project window.

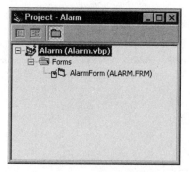

Once a file has been checked out, you are free to edit it as usual.

NOTE   Alternately, you can right-click a file and select Check Out from the menu to check out a project or individual files.

Saving Changes to Files and Projects

Saving changes to a project and its files that are under VSS control is different than saving non-VSS controlled files. If you check out an entire project, you can save it as you would any other project, but if you check out individual files, they must be saved at the file level. For example, let's say that you checked out only the Alarm.FRM file form in the Alarm project. If you make changes to the alarm form and attempt to save the project, you will get a Path/File access error because the project is still read-only. You must save the individual file.

Checking In Projects and Files

As mentioned earlier, when you check out files and make changes to them, you are making changes to the files in your Working Directory. To apply those changes to the VSS project, the files must be checked in. Follow these steps to check in files from within a Visual Basic Project:

1. Select Tools ➤ SourceSafe ➤ Check In to display the Check In Files To SourceSafe dialog box.

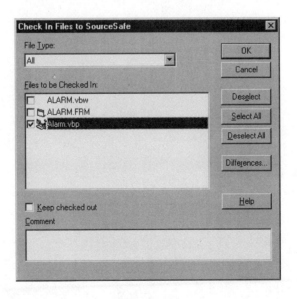

2. Select the files that you want to check in or click Select All to select all of the files.

3. Click OK to check in the files to SourceSafe. This will check in the changes and your copy of the files will once again be read-only.

NOTE   If you want to check in changes and keep the files checked out to perform some additional editing, click the Keep Checked Out checkbox.

After the files have been checked in, another developer can check out the new version and view your changes.

As you can see from this section, Visual SourceSafe can provide version control for all of your projects. In addition to the features outlined in this chapter, Visual SourceSafe provides many additional features, such as maintaining a history of changes, rolling back or undoing changes, and printing reports to provide a record of all SourceSafe activities. This is a portion of what Visual SourceSafe can provide, but there is so much more. VSS has extensive online help that can demonstrate the rest of Visual SourceSafe's potential for you.

CHAPTER
THREE

3

Using SQL Server

- What's new in SQL Server 7

- Installing SQL Server 7

- Using the tools in SQL Server 7

- Creating Database objects in SQL Server 7

- Creating and executing stored procedures and triggers

Most applications being developed today provide some type of data access. With its built-in data replication, powerful management tools, Internet integration, and open system architecture, Microsoft SQL Server 7 is a scalable, high-performance database management system designed specifically for distributed client/server computing.

As businesses streamline processes, decentralize decision making, and depend increasingly on technology to bring users and information together, distributed client/server computing becomes the bridge between data and informed business decisions.

SQL Server 7 includes an array of new and improved features to make it a robust, scalable server capable of solving the needs of many enterprises. It is a defining release for Microsoft's database products, built on the solid foundation established by SQL Server version 6.5.

SQL Server 7 provides a powerful database platform and necessary tools to enable businesses to implement important business applications. It affords an excellent programming platform for developers, by automating standard operations to ease the workload on database administrators and supplying sophisticated tools for more complex operations.

One of the most important areas of innovation in SQL Server 7 is its ability to provide Universal Data Access, a platform for developing multi-tier enterprise applications that require access to diverse relational and non-relational data. This is a collection of software components using a common set of system-level interfaces called OLE DB.

SQL Server 7, designed with the Internet and intranet in mind, provides access to the World Wide Web through many tools and wizards and can offer companies the best features for deploying and maintaining powerful, easy-to-manage, commerce-enabled Web sites, for either business-to-business or business-to-consumer transactions.

In addition, SQL Server is strategically built to handle the most demanding Data Warehouse and Data Mart implementations.

SQL Server 7 is also designed to address mobile-computing requirements by providing scalability from laptop computers to Symmetrical Multiprocessing (SMP) servers, enabling the same application to be deployed on the widest range of options available. It even has a desktop edition that runs on Windows 95, Windows 98, and Windows NT Workstation and is the key for allowing users to take their data and applications on the road with them.

What's New in SQL Server 7

Whether you are new to SQL Server or have been using it all along, it is important to take a look at some of the new and improved features that affect Visual Basic developers.

SQL Server 7 represents a significant new release of Microsoft SQL Server that includes a completely new look and feel. With this version, SQL Server has been redesigned to provide important new server architecture and graphical administration features, while maintaining ANSI and SQL Server 6.x compatibility. The new features can be grouped into five categories:

- Architecture enhancements

- Server enhancements

- Graphical administration improvements and new features

- Development enhancements

- New SQL Server wizards

These new features and enhancements will be explored in the following sections.

Architecture Enhancements

The development, deployment, maintenance, and management of your database applications have been simplified in Microsoft SQL Server version 7 with its redesigned architecture. SQL Server 7 supports applications that span a broad range of platforms, from personal systems, such as desktop and notebook computers, to high-end Symmetric Multiprocessing (SMP) servers with 8 to 16 processors, several gigabytes of memory, and a terabyte or more of disk storage.

Replacing Logical Disk Devices

Databases were created on logical devices in previous versions of SQL Server. In SQL Server 7, databases reside on operating-system files. Files are created to store the data and the log transactions. A database and all of its files can be created with a single CREATE DATABASE statement or with the use of SQL Server Enterprise Manager. A database can be configured so that the associated files expand automatically, eliminating the need for administrators to issue an additional ALTER statement.

Database files can automatically grow from their originally specified size. When you define a file, you can specify a growth increment. Each time the file fills, it increases its size by the growth increment. Each file can also have a maximum size specified. If a maximum size is not specified, the file can continue to grow until it has used all available space on the disk. This feature is especially useful when SQL Server is used as a database embedded in an application where the user does not have ready access to a system administrator. The user can let the files grow automatically to lessen the administrative burden of monitoring the amount of free space in the database and manually allocating space.

When a database is created, files can be set to automatically expand when it fills up. Files can be configured with a maximum size so that they do not fill up all of the available disk space. If a maximum size is not specified, the file will grow until all space is used.

Database files can be used by only one database. When a database is dropped, its files are deleted.

Dynamic Locking

Full row-level locking is now the default in SQL Server 7 for both data rows and index entries. The lock manager has been optimized to complete lock requests faster and with less internal synchronization. Many Online Transaction Processing (OLTP) applications can experience increased concurrency, especially when applications append rows to tables and indexes.

Improved Query Processing for Complex Queries

Support for large databases and complex queries has been engineered into the query processor. This type of support is especially beneficial to complex queries found in decision support, data warehouse, and OLAP applications. New execution strategies have also been added to the query processor to provide improved performance of complex queries.

The query processor in SQL Server 7 now employs hash join, merge join, and aggregation techniques that can scale to larger databases than the ones supported by the nested-loop join technique, the only join technique supported by SQL

Server 7. SQL Server 7 uses index intersection and union techniques on multiple indexes to filter data before it retrieves rows from the database. All indexes on a table are maintained concurrently and constraint evaluations are part of the query processor's execution plan. These two factors speed up and simplify the process of updating multiple rows of a table.

SQL Server 7 supports parallel execution of a single query across multiple processors, allowing SQL Server to perform a query in parallel by using several operating system threads. If a query requires a lot of CPU time to examine a large number of rows of data, the query could benefit if parts of the execution plan were run in parallel. SQL Server 7 automatically determines if a query will benefit from parallelism and, if so, generates a parallel execution plan. If multiple processors are available when the query begins executing, the work is divided across the processors. Parallel query execution is enabled by default.

Increased Capacities

SQL Server 7 has increased table and column capacities. A table can be defined with up to 1024 columns (increased from 250 columns in SQL Server 6.5), and a single query can now reference up to 32 tables. These increases significantly expand power and flexibility by allowing you to store more data in a single table and create more complete and robust queries against your data.

Distributed Query and Update Capabilities

SQL Server 7 now provides SQL Server to SQL Server data sources and OLE DB data sources, allowing for the creation of distributed queries that access data stored in multiple data sources on either the same or different computers. These distributed queries take advantage of OLE DB, the emerging standard for data access of relational and non-relational data sources.

Distributed queries provide SQL Server users with access to data stored in:

- File systems
- Heterogeneous databases
- Multiple servers running SQL Server
- Network sources

Previous versions of SQL Server relied on the Universal Server approach of exporting data into the database. A major concern with this type of approach was that the exported data would immediately be out of date, requiring you to re-export the data or constantly export any data that had changed.

The new approach used in SQL Server 7, known as Universal Access, provides distributed queries using OLE DB technology and allows you to keep data stored where it currently resides and still access all of the data in one query.

New Page and Row Formats Improve Performance and Data Management

New formats are provided to allow the server to easily scale from low-end to high-end systems, while providing improved performance and manageability. These new formats pave the way for additional capabilities in future releases, such as embedded tables, multiple types of rows on a single data page, and databases that can be electronically mailed. New disk formats for pages, rows, extents, data files, and log files are included. The new page and row formats support row-level locking, are extensible for future requirements, and improve performance when large blocks of data are accessed, because each I/O operation retrieves more data. The new page and row formats include:

- 8K page, 64K extent
- Filegroups to improve data placement and provide flexibility for maintenance
- Improved data placement to reduce storage requirements
- Mixed extents (multiple tables within one extent to save space)
- Support for native operating-system files

All database pages are now 8K in size, increased from 2K. The maximum number of bytes in a row is now 8060 bytes, and the limit on character and binary data types is 8000 bytes, increased from 255 bytes. Tables can now have 1024 columns, a significant increase over the 250 columns supported previously.

Enhanced Data Type Support

One of the main roles of SQL Server in an enterprise environment is to provide data storage and retrieval. This data must be stored in database columns that store a certain type of data. To this end, SQL Server 7 provides enhanced data type support to allow you more flexibility in how your data is stored.

One of the most troublesome restrictions of previous SQL Server databases was that the maximum length of the char, varchar, and varbinary data types was only 255 bytes and required long strings to be stored in Text or Image formats. Although this storage could be accomplished, it made it difficult to view the stored data. However, SQL Server 7 has solved this problem by increasing the maximum size for char, varchar, and varbinary data types to 8000 bytes. The enhanced Transact-SQL string functions also support these very long char and varchar values. The use of text and image data types can now be reserved for very large data values. The SUBSTRING function can be used to process text and image columns. The handling of nulls and empty strings has been improved.

A new unique identifier data type is provided for storing a globally unique identifier (GUID).

Providing Support for Windows 95 or Later Operating Systems

Windows NT is no longer the only platform that supports SQL Server. Now, SQL Server 7 can be installed and fully supported by Windows 95/98. Common source code for all platforms, from Windows 95/98 to clustered systems, resolves compatibility issues. Mobile clients are fully supported with merge replication and conflict resolution.

SQL Server 7 for Windows 95/98 is perfect for embedded applications because it provides a full-featured database engine and core components and enables lightweight, full-function, and low-cost applications.

> **NOTE** SQL Server 7 for Windows 95/98 is full-featured, except for a few limitations imposed by the operating system. For example, SMP, asynchronous I/O, and integrated security are not supported on Windows 95/98.

Supporting Unicode

Multi-language support comes to SQL Server in the form of Unicode data type support. In the past, if you needed to support multiple languages in your database, you were required to convert characters and install multiple code pages.

Using Unicode data types, which store character data using two bytes for each character instead of just one byte, a column can store any character that is defined by the Unicode Standard. This includes all of the characters that are defined in the various character sets.

NOTE   Although Unicode data types require twice as much storage space as non-Unicode data types, the requirement is offset by eliminating the need to convert extended characters between code pages.

In SQL Server, the new data types that support Unicode are ntext, nchar, and nvarchar. They are exactly the same as text, char, and varchar, except a wider range of characters is supported and the storage space used is increased.

Indexing Operations

Indexing operations have been enhanced in several areas, including the use of index intersection and index union to implement multiple indexes in a single query. Shared row indicators are used to join two indexes on the same table. Earlier versions of SQL Server employed no more than one index per table in a query.

Storing and Retrieving Text and Image Data

In SQL Server 7, the storage of text and image data has been redesigned by utilizing text and image values more efficiently to allow for the storage of more than one text or image value on a single data page. Parallel retrieval of text and image data is employed to optimize the retrieval of large objects.

Enhancing the Transaction Log

In previous versions of SQL Server, the transaction log was a system table (syslogs) that used ordinary data pages. These pages competed with other data pages for space in the memory cache as they were allocated and de-allocated.

The transaction log in SQL Server 7, significantly different from those in previous versions and no longer represented as a system table, consists of one or more log files. Each log file contains a contiguous set of log records. The new log design enables larger I/Os to the log than were previously possible.

tempdb Database

Tempdb system database is a global resource; it holds the temporary tables and stored procedures for all users connected to the system and fills any other temporary storage needs. Tempdb system database is re-created every time SQL Server is started, so the system always starts with a clean copy of the database.

In SQL Server 7, tempdb system database expands automatically as needed. For example, a query may be executed that needs a lot of space in tempdb. Rather than failing with an out-of-space error, tempdb automatically grows to the size needed to support the temporary tables. In such an instance, tempdb expands automatically and is reinitialized to the configured size by SQL Server the next time the server is started.

Server Enhancements

The redesign of the SQL Server 7 server architecture results in new and improved server functionality. Changes have been made to the server configuration options and server utilities, such as backup, restore, DBCC, and bulk copy. Microsoft SQL Server version 7 provides for parallel query execution, more powerful security, and improved stored procedure performance. In addition, several advancements have been made to SQL Server replication.

SQL Server Enterprise Manager

SQL Server Enterprise Manager (shown in Figure 3.1) is based on a new, common-server management environment called Microsoft Management Console (MMC). This shared framework provides a consistent user interface for Microsoft server applications.

SQL Server Enterprise Manager provides an easy-to-use graphical environment to perform almost all server and database actions. Using SQL Server Enterprise Manager, you can examine and configure your SQL Server 7 system by setting server properties, database properties, remote server properties, and security properties. You can create and alter tables, views, stored procedures, rules, defaults, and user-defined data types, as well as manage alerts and operators, view error logs, create Web Assistant jobs, create and manage full-text indexes, and import and export data.

FIGURE 3.1:

SQL Server Enterprise
Manager

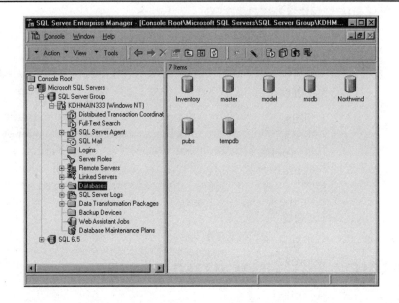

A major advancement in Enterprise Manager is the ability it provides Visual Basic developers to create and view Database Diagrams, allowing you to graphically view the structure of a database and alter that structure without having to create SQL statements and use temporary tables to hold the data.

Configuration Options

SQL Server 7 streamlines and simplifies many server configuration options by increasing allocated resources, when necessary, without over-committing them, and decreasing resources when they are no longer needed. This streamline effect is achieved because, by default, the server dynamically adjusts its memory and lock resource use. In earlier versions of SQL Server, this process required manual adjustment of these settings.

Adding Memory Management

On-demand memory has been provided in SQL Server 7, enabling the memory manager to cooperate with the operating system.

By default, the server's memory and lock resource use are dynamically adjusted. This enables databases to increase their allocated resources when necessary, without committing them, and to decrease resources when they are no longer needed. These actions required manual intervention in earlier versions of SQL Server.

Improved Utilities for Very Large Database (VLDB) Support

Utilities have been improved to provide for Very Large Database (VLDB) support in the areas of backup and restores, support for Microsoft Tape format backup, major performance improvements for the Database Consistency Checker (DBCC), and improved bulk data load performance.

Enhanced Stored Procedures

The stored procedure model has been enhanced in SQL Server 7 to provide improved performance and increased application flexibility by making one copy of the stored procedure available to all users of the stored procedure when it is compiled and placed in the procedure cache. Plans can also be shared SQL statements that are submitted through the ODBC SQLPrepare function and the OLE DB ICommandPrepare interface. Deferred name resolution allows you to create stored procedures referencing objects that don't yet exist, thus providing more flexibility for applications that create and use tables as part of their processing. Stored Procedures are discussed in more detail later in this chapter.

Consistency and Standards Compliance

SQL Server 7 focuses on SQL-92 as the preferred SQL dialect. This focus builds on SQL Server's compliance with the SQL-92 standard. Many of the inconsistencies that existed in earlier versions of SQL Server, including those relating to actual and documented behaviors, have been addressed in SQL Server 7. In addition, several problems that may have been interpreted as features in earlier versions of SQL Server have now been fixed. In these cases, SQL Server 7 has provided options to retain the previous behavior. These options are controlled by the sp_dboption or sp_dbcmptlevel stored procedures.

Trigger Enhancements

SQL Server 7 provides support for multiple triggers of the same type to a single table. This major enhancement allows you to create triggers to enforce different business rules. For example, a single table can now have one delete trigger, multiple insert triggers, and three update triggers. A database option can even be set that allows triggers to call themselves recursively. Triggers are explored in more detail later in this chapter.

Cursor Enhancements

Cursors can now be declared with variables and parameters when they are created with the DECLARE @local_variable statement, and local cursors are supported in SQL Server 7.

Backup and Restore

Backup and restore utilities run much faster, have less impact on server operations, and provide several new features.

Incremental backups capture only those data pages that have changed after the last database backup, thereby often eliminating much of the time the server spends rolling transactions forward. A portion of the database can be restored, or rolled forward, to minimize recovery time in the event of media failure. Restoring a backup is easy because the restore process automatically creates the database and all necessary files.

Database Consistency Checker (DBCC)

The Database Consistency Checker (DBCC) statements have been redesigned to provide substantially improved performance. In addition, bulk copy operations now validate constraints and fire triggers as the data is loaded.

Improved Bulk Data Load Performance

The bulk copy utility (bcp) uses OLE DB to communicate with SQL Server, supports all data types, and is much faster. Index maintenance strategies are improved to make loading data into tables with indexes more efficient.

Support for Microsoft Tape Format Backup

Backup supports the Microsoft Tape Format, allowing SQL Server backups to share the same tape media with other backups, such as those written by the Windows NT Server Backup program.

New SQL Server Security Model

The security architecture provides better integration to Microsoft Windows NT while increasing flexibility. Database permissions can now be assigned directly to Windows NT users, thus eliminating the need to create separate SQL Server users. You can define SQL Server roles to include not only Windows NT users and groups, but also SQL Server users and roles.

A SQL Server user can be a member of multiple SQL Server roles, allowing database administrators to manage SQL Server permissions as Windows NT groups or SQL Server roles, rather than as individual user accounts. Database access and permissions are now managed using Windows NT groups. New fixed server and database roles, such as dbcreator, diskadmin, and sysadmin, provide more flexibility and improved security than the system administrator login.

Replication Enhancements

Replication is built directly into SQL Server 7 and SQL Server Enterprise Manager; it is not a separate add-on. SQL Server 7 replication offers many usability improvements and enhancements, making replication significantly easier to set up, administer, deploy, monitor, and troubleshoot. Wizards are included for most common replication tasks. SQL Server 7 also includes enhancements for Internet replication. Anonymous subscriptions and built-in support for Internet distribution simplify data replication to the Internet.

A COM interface is also included in SQL Server 7 that opens up the store-and-forward replication services, allowing heterogeneous data providers to use the SQL Server 7 replication infrastructure to publish their data.

Adding Full-Text Search

The full-text search facilities in SQL Server 7 provide a complete system where the database developer or administrator can create special full-text-search index columns. These columns provide a means for users to perform full-text searches—not just searches for comparing text, but searches for words or phrases that approximate a search selection.

Upgrading Servers

A fully automated upgrade utility makes easy work of upgrading from SQL Server 6.*x*. The following upgrade options are available:

- Upgrading databases on the same computer using the SQL Server Upgrade Wizard (shown in Figure 3.2). You can upgrade any or all of your databases, transferring all catalog data, objects, and user data.

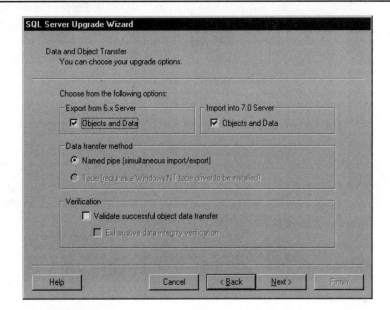

- Upgrading from computer to computer by installing SQL Server 7 on one computer and then connecting to another computer where the existing SQL Server 6.*x* is installed. The upgrade takes place using a Named Pipes connection to transfer data. When the upgrade is complete, SQL Server 7 immediately takes over as the production server.

- Upgrading servers side-by-side takes place on a single computer using a disk-to-disk Named Pipes connection or a tape drive. Upgrades can be done over a direct pipeline with enough disk space. Otherwise, the SQL Server Upgrade Wizard can export the SQL Server 6.*x* catalog data, objects, and databases to a tape backup. When the upgrade is complete, SQL Server 7 immediately takes over as the production server.

Multi-site Management

SQL Server has expanded server administration capabilities to manage multiple servers using one centralized server. SQL Server 7 provides multisite management tools to:

- Create multistep jobs, schedule the job, manage job step flow, and store job success or failure information at a central location.

- Group servers into logical functioning units, such as by departments or business units.

- Perform cross-server transactions, such as creating an application that reviews and transfers product inventory from a remote warehouse to a central warehouse.

Using SQL Server Enterprise Manager, a system administrator can define a multiserver configuration, naming one server as the master server that communicates and distributes jobs, alerts, and event messages to target servers named in the configuration. From a central console running SQL Server Enterprise Manager, the system administrator can manage and monitor server performance and the enterprise's database.

Graphical Administration Improvements and New Features

Microsoft SQL Server 7 has been enhanced to include many new features that make developing and maintaining SQL Server 7 much easier.

Microsoft Management Console

The Microsoft Management Console (MMC) (shown in Figure 3.3) is the new user interface and framework for BackOffice server management. This shared console provides a convenient and consistent environment for SQL Server and other "snap-in" administration tools. The MMC console for SQL Server is SQL Server Enterprise Manager. MMC's point-and-click user interface is similar to Windows Explorer.

FIGURE 3.3:

Microsoft Management
Console

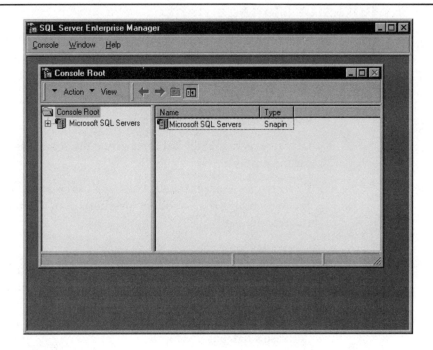

Web Assistant

The SQL Server Web Assistant (shown in Figure 3.4) has been enhanced in SQL
Server 7. In addition to exporting SQL Server data out to an HTML file, it can also
import tabular data from an HTML file and can post to and read from HTTP and
FTP locations.

SQL Server Agent

SQL Server Agent (shown in Figure 3.5) is a Microsoft Windows NT service that
executes jobs, monitors Microsoft SQL Server, fires alerts, and enables you to
automate many administrative tasks. However, you must start the SQL Server
Agent service before your local or multi-server administrative tasks can run
automatically.

FIGURE 3.4:

Web Assistant

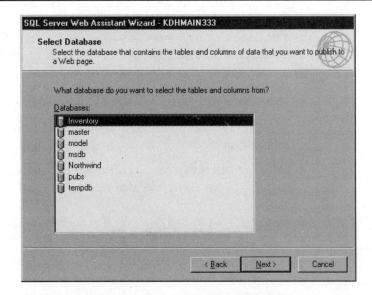

FIGURE 3.5:

SQL Server Agent

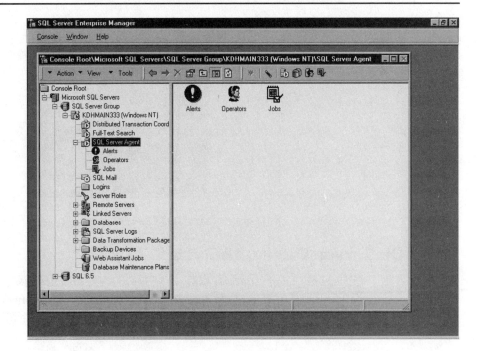

SQL Server Agent monitors events in the Windows NT application event log. When an event occurs, SQL Server Agent compares the event details with the alerts defined for the environment. If a match is found, SQL Server Agent implements the specified alert response. The following actions can be performed with SQL Server Agent:

- Execute a job, which allows SQL Server to perform a predefined server job.

- Perform multiple tasks. SQL Server Agent is not restricted to performing a single task on a single server; the SQL Server Agent can multitask.

- Manage Alerts that can be defined to raise a response when an event occurs with a system or user-defined error or severity level.

SQL Server Service Manager

SQL Server Service Manager (shown in Figure 3.6) is now a taskbar application that enables you to start, stop, and pause the MSSQLServer, MSDTC, MSSearch (only start and stop are applicable), and SQLServerAgent services, and to view their status at any time.

FIGURE 3.6:

SQL Server Service Manager

SQL Server Query Analyzer

SQL Server Query Analyzer (shown in Figure 3.7) provides a graphical way to analyze the plan of a query, execute multiple queries simultaneously, view data, and choose indexes. SQL Server Query Analyzer provides the SHOWPLAN option that is used to report data retrieval methods chosen by the SQL Server optimizer and recommends optimal indexes to improve performance.

SQL Server Query Analyzer

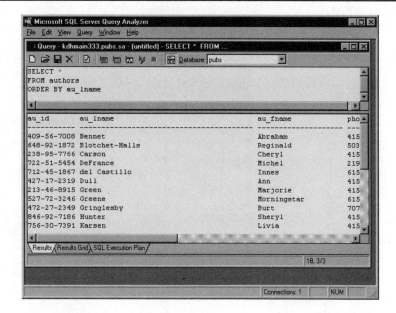

SQL Server Profiler

SQL Server Profiler (shown in Figure 3.8), known as SQL Trace in earlier versions of SQL Server, is a graphical tool that allows you to monitor server events such as:

- Login attempts
- Server connects and disconnects
- Transact-SQL batches
- Deadlocks

Data Transformation Services

Data Transformation Services (DTS) provides the functionality to import, export, and transform data between SQL Server and any OLE DB, ODBC, or text file format. DTS makes it possible to build data warehouses and data marts in SQL Server

FIGURE 3.8:

SQL Server Profiler

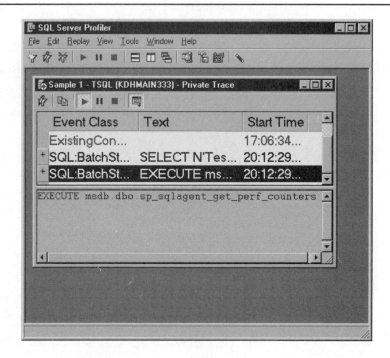

by importing and transforming data from multiple heterogeneous sources interactively or automatically on a regularly scheduled basis (requiring no user intervention). Custom transformation objects can be created that integrate into third-party products. DTS in SQL Server 7 provides the following functionality:

- OLE DB-based interface for defining and executing data transformations

- ActiveScript-based transformations

- Support of high-speed bulk interface for fast loading using OLE DB

- Support for ODBC-based data sources, including Microsoft Access, Microsoft Excel, and flat files

- DTS Export and DTS Import Wizards for quickly moving data and schema into and out of SQL Server

- Scheduled transformations using SQL Server Agent

Index Tuning Wizard

The Index Tuning Wizard (shown in Figure 3.9) allows indexes to be created and implemented without an expert understanding of the structure of the database, hardware platforms and components, or how end-user applications interact with the relational engine.

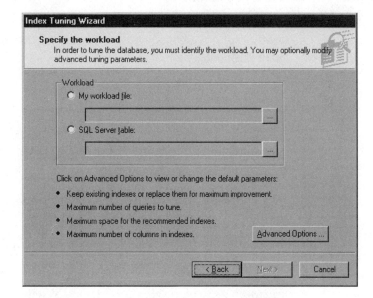

Development Enhancements

Microsoft SQL Server version 7 has additional development flexibility and power and easier application development tools.

It is compatible with SQL Server 6.x applications, provides new and enhanced features for developers, and includes internal enhancements that benefit all applications, such as increased query performance, full row-level locking, and new deadlock avoidance strategies and lock escalation policies that should reduce contention problems. SQL Server 7 now supports OLE DB as a native programming interface. In addition, improvements to the Transact-SQL language and the ODBC programming API are included.

Microsoft English Query

With the Microsoft English Query environment (shown in Figure 3.10), developers and others can turn their relational databases into English Query applications, which give end users the ability to pose questions in English. For example, users can now simply ask, "How many widgets were sold last year in the State of Texas?" instead of forming a query with a SQL statement. The following features are part of the Microsoft English Query application:

- Author improvements, which describe less frequent database design maps to English concepts

- Context-sensitive Help

- Enterprise authoring support, which allows multiple developers to work on the same "model" of the database

- Generation of efficient queries for denormalized databases

- Graphical authoring tool for defining databases to English Query

- Hot swapping of domains (loading a new version of a connection on top of an old version without restarting)

- Information retrieval from SQL Server using English sentences

- Intersentence referencing that provides drill-down into queries

- Microsoft ActiveX object support, which enables embedding of English Query in applications

- Question builder (Knowledge Explorer), which uses English concepts to familiarize users with the database contents

The Microsoft English Query development environment is detailed in Chapter 7.

Improved Transact-SQL

SQL Server 7 offers many new features and enhancements to Transact-SQL, the programming language that developers use to communicate, access, and direct SQL Server. The following enhancements have been made to Transact-SQL:

- Identifiers can now be a maximum of 128 characters, increased from the 30 characters of earlier versions. The left square bracket ([) and right square bracket (]) can be used for delimiting identifiers, in addition to the SQL-92 standard double quotation mark (").

FIGURE 3.10:

Microsoft English Query

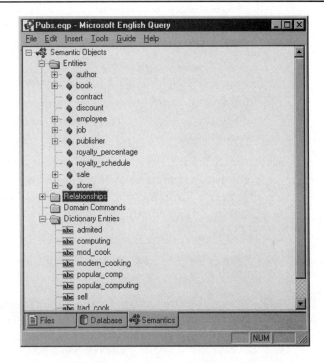

- Developers using SQL Server 7 now have complete flexibility to design and redesign tables.

- Non-nullable columns can be added to a table without having to import data in a separate step.

- Views for the ANSI/ISO schema information tables, as defined in SQL-92, provide a standard way to examine metadata of a SQL Server database.

- Revising database objects is made easier by allowing you to change the definition of a procedure, trigger, or view in place without disturbing permissions or dependencies.

- Deferred name resolution is used in stored procedures, triggers, and statement batches, providing you the power and flexibility to create procedures that reference tables created at run time.

- Multiple triggers of the same type can be added to a single table, allowing a table to have multiple delete, insert, and triggers to enforce business rules and maintain data integrity.

- The maximum length of the char, varchar, binary, and varbinary data types is now 8000 bytes, increased from 255 bytes in SQL Server 6.*x*, and the Transact-SQL string functions also support these very long char and varchar values. You can reserve the use of text and image data types for very large data values.

- The SUBSTRING function can now be used to process text and image columns. The handling of NULLs and empty strings has been improved. SQL Server 7 also includes a new uniqueidentifier data type for storing a Globally Unique Identifier (GUID).

- The SQL Server 7 query processor uses new execution strategies and algorithms (including hash, sort, and merge iterators) to provide improved performance.

SQL Server 7 also includes several new statements that enable you to more easily maintain procedures, triggers, views, and tables:

- ALTER PROCEDURE, which alters a procedure previously created by executing the CREATE PROCEDURE statement, without changing permissions and without affecting any dependent stored procedures or triggers

- ALTER TABLE, which modifies a table definition by adding or removing columns and constraints or by disabling or enabling constraints

- ALTER TRIGGER, which alters the definition of a trigger created previously by the CREATE TRIGGER statement

- ALTER VIEW, which alters a view previously created by executing CREATE VIEW without affecting dependent stored procedures or triggers and without changing permissions

Unicode data types nchar, nvarchar, and ntext have been added, as have a TOP *n* [PERCENT *n*]] extension to the SELECT statement that allows you to select and return a percent of the matching rows of data instead of all the rows.

Also new additions are local cursors, cursor variables, returning cursors as parameters from stored procedures, additional properties for cursors declared through the DECLARE CURSOR statement, and functions and stored procedures for describing cursors.

Programming Interfaces

SQL Server 7 provides a rich set of programming interfaces that allow other applications and development tools to interact with and manipulate it.

ADO

Applications using the ADO API can now use the Microsoft OLE DB Provider for SQL Server instead of using the Microsoft OLE DB Provider for ODBC over the SQL Server ODBC Driver. More SQL Server functionality is exposed by the OLE DB Provider for SQL Server than the Microsoft OLE DB Provider for ODBC, and the number of layers the application must use to communicate with SQL Server is reduced. ADO is discussed in detail in Chapter 4.

OLE DB

SQL Server 7 now provides a native OLE DB Provider for SQL Server that supports the OLE DB 2.0 API. The driver also supports bulk copy operations and the ability to obtain metadata for linked tables used in distributed queries. The OLE DB Provider for SQL Server supports all the new data types and features introduced in SQL Server 7.

SQL Server 7 now provides support for the OLE DB 2.0 in the form of a native OLE DB Provider. This Provider also supports bulk copy operations, the ability to obtain metadata for linked tables used in distributed queries, and all the new data types and features introduced in SQL Server 7.

ODBC

The enhanced SQL Server ODBC Driver now supports the ODBC 3.5 API, as well as the bulk copy functions originally introduced in DB-Library and the ability to obtain metadata for linked tables used in distributed queries. SQL Server ODBC Driver 3.7 supports all the new data types and features introduced in SQL Server 7.

File DSN support makes distributing data sources easier, and the Microsoft Server DSN Configuration Wizard has been created to make creating and managing SQL Server data sources easier. The SQL Server ODBC driver also has other improvements related to connecting to SQL Server 7 servers, such as establishing more efficient connections that are completed in a single roundtrip using default settings.

The SQL Server ODBC 3.5 driver fully supports programs using:

- Active Server Pages (ASP)

- ActiveX Data Objects (ADO)

- Data Access Objects (DAO)

- Internet Database Connector (IDC)

- OLE DB Provider for ODBC

- Remote Data Objects (RDO)

SQL-DMO

SQL Server Enterprise Manager is based on a distributed management framework, SQL-DMO, that allows for centralized administration of all servers running SQL Server in an organization. It also provides COM interfaces for administration activities so that independent software vendors can write custom applications and users can use Visual Basic for Applications or Microsoft JScript to manage their servers. SQL Server 7 extends the capabilities of the framework to include self-managing components, more detailed activity monitoring and filtering, and an event model.

Enhanced Application Support

SQL Server 7 includes features and enhancements specifically designed for certain types of applications. It provides specialized support for the following application types:

- **Administration tools support** is provided by SQL Distributed Management Objects (SQL-DMO) and has been redesigned and expanded to reflect SQL Server 7 features and architecture. SQL Server 7 SQL-DMO objects are very similar to the SQL Server 6.*x* SQL-DMO objects (with some exceptions, such as the replication hierarchy and the Device object).

- **Data warehousing applications** are supported by SQL Data Transformation Services (DTS), which provide a set of COM objects based on OLE DB that let you define and execute complex data conversions between OLE DB data providers.

- **Internet and intranet applications** are supported by the SQL Server Web Assistant, which, in addition to exporting SQL Server data out to an HTML file, can also import tabular data from an HTML file and can post to and read from HTTP and FTP locations. (The SQL Server Web Assistant is demonstrated later in this chapter.)

- **Replication applications** are supported by Replication programming components, including COM objects that you can use to distribute data from third-party data sources. They also include Microsoft ActiveX controls that applications can use to implement distribution and merge functionality without dependency on the SQL Server Agent.

New SQL Server Wizards

SQL Server 7 includes several new wizards to make it easier and quicker to complete many tasks. Table 3.1 lists the wizards that are included in SQL Server 7:

TABLE 3.1: SQL Server 7 Wizards

Wizard	Guides You Through
Create Backup	Backing up a database.
Clustering	Aids in virtual server administration.
Configure Publishing and Distribution	Configuring a publishing and distribution server for replication. Help is included with this wizard.
Create Alert	Creating an alert.
Create Database	Creating a database.
Create Diagram	Creating a database diagram.
Create Index	Creating an index.
Create Job	Creating a job.
Create New Data Service	The installation of an ODBC data source and ODBC driver. Tests the validity of the connection. Help is included with this wizard.

Continued on next page

TABLE 3.1 CONTINUED: SQL Server 7 Wizards

Wizard	Guides You Through
Create SQL Server Login	Granting SQL Server login access to users.
Create Publication	Creating a publication for replication. Help is included with this wizard.
Create Stored Procedures	Creating stored procedures for adding, deleting, and updating rows in a table.
Create Trace	Creating a trace.
Create View	The process of creating a view.
Database Maintenance Plan	Creating a maintenance file that can be run on a regular basis. Works with the sqlmaint utility.
Disable Publishing and Distribution	Disabling a publication and a distribution server for replication. Help is included with this wizard.
DTS Export	Creating DTS packages to export data from a SQL Server database to heterogeneous data sources. Help is included with this wizard.
DTS Import	Creating DTS packages to import heterogeneous data to a SQL Server database. Help is included with this wizard.
Full-Text Indexing	Defining full-text indexing on SQL Server character-based columns. Creates or modifies population schedules that determine when the information stored in the full-text catalog is updated.
Index Tuning	Tuning an index.
Make Master Server	Setting up a master server.
Make Target Server	Setting up a target server and enlisting it into a master server.
Pull Subscription	Enabling a subscription server to pull replicated data from a publication server. Help is included with this wizard.
Push Subscription	Enabling a publication server to push replicated data to a subscription server. Help is included with this wizard.
Register Servers	Registering SQL Servers.

Continued on next page

TABLE 3.1 CONTINUED: SQL Server 7 Wizards

Wizard	Guides You Through
Setup	Installing SQL Server.
Transfer Data	Transferring data to and from SQL Server.
Upgrade	Upgrading SQL Server. The Upgrade Wizard is not supported on the Microsoft Windows 95/98 platform.
Web Assistant	The steps required to create a Web task that creates an HTML page to import data from an HTML page or to run an existing Web task.

Installing SQL Server 7

Microsoft SQL Server provides everything you need to get up and running quickly and easily, including tools to install SQL Server, to bring in all of your existing data, and to take advantage of a number of other technologies. You can:

- Run SQL Server Setup.

- Use the Setup program to add a new installation of SQL Server.

- Upgrade from an earlier version of SQL Server.

- If you are currently using SQL Server version 6.x, you can use the SQL Server Upgrade Wizard to update your databases to SQL Server 7.

- Migrate to SQL Server from other products.

- If your existing data is in products other than SQL Server, you can import it into SQL Server.

- Integrate SQL Server with other tools.

- SQL Server can be used as a stand-alone product, or it can interact with other technologies, access data from other tools, and be used as the core data repository for other applications.

Hardware and Software Requirements for Installing SQL Server

To install the Microsoft SQL Server software or the SQL Server client management tools and libraries, your computer must meet the following minimum requirements.

Item	Requirements
Computer	DEC Alpha AXP and compatible systems or Intel or compatible (Pentium 133 MHz or higher, Pentium PRO, or Pentium II).
Memory (RAM)	32MB (minimum).
Disk drive	CD-ROM drive.
Hard disk space (1)*	190MB (full), 163MB (typical), 74MB (minimum); 73MB (management tools only).
Operating system**	Microsoft Windows NT Server 4.0 or later with SP3 and NT mini-service pack (2), or Windows NT Workstation 4.0 or later with SP3 and NT mini-service pack (2), or Microsoft Windows 95/98, or Windows 95 OSR2.
Network software	Windows NT or Windows 95/98 built-in network software. Additional network software is not required unless you are using Banyan VINES or AppleTalk ADSP. Novell NetWare client support is provided by NWLink. SQL Server can use any of the network adapters supported by Windows NT or Windows 95/98. For information about supported network adapters, see your Windows NT or Windows 95 documentation.

* These figures are the maximum hard disk space required. Setup installs a number of components that can be shared by other applications and may already exist on your computer.

** The Windows NT mini-service pack includes bug fixes for Windows NT with SP3. Setup detects if any of these bug fixes are required and prompts you to install the Windows NT mini-service pack from the SQL Server compact disc.

Installing the Server Software

Follow these steps to install SQL Server 7:

1. Insert the SQL Server 7 CD; it will autostart. Select Install SQL Server 7.0 Prerequisites from the menu, as shown in Figure 3.11.

FIGURE 3.11:

Microsoft SQL Server Setup Main Menu

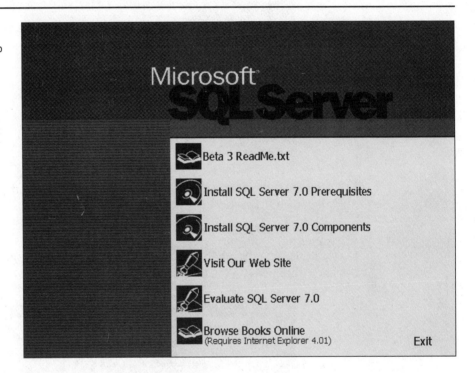

For the Windows 95, Windows NT 4.0 Workstation/Server, and the Windows NT 4.0 operating system, there are prerequisites for installing SQL Server 7. (There are no prerequisites for the Windows 98 or Windows NT 5 operating systems.)

After you select Install SQL Server 7.0 Prerequisites from the menu, the SQL Server 7.0 Prerequisites screen will be displayed.

2. Select your operating system from the list and follow the steps to complete the prerequisites.

NOTE   The prerequisites include the installation of Internet Explorer 4.0 that is required for accessing the online help.

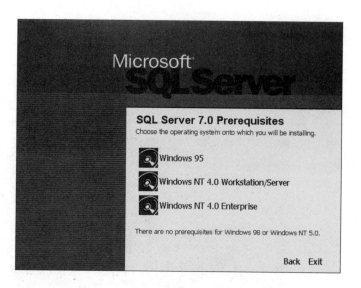

After the prerequisites have been installed, you can continue with the installation of SQL Server 7.

3. Click Install SQL Server from the menu.

4. After reading the Software License Agreement, click Yes to accept the terms and continue with the installation.

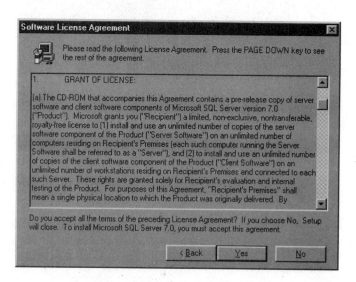

5. Enter your name, company name, and serial number in the User Information screen.

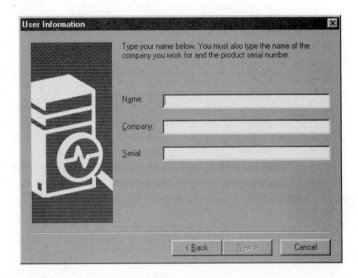

The Setup Type screen will be displayed, allowing you to select the type of installation.

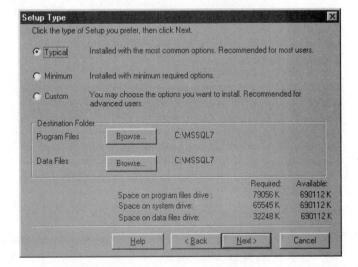

SQL Server 7 provides three types of installations:

1. Typical, which installs all of Microsoft SQL Server using the default installation options that include the SQL Server management tools and SQL Server online documentation. A typical installation does not include full-text search, development tools, or samples. This installation is recommended for most users.

2. Compact, which installs only the minimum configuration necessary to run SQL Server using the default installation options. This is recommended for computers with minimum available disk space. A compact installation does not include any of the SQL Server management tools or SQL Server online documentation.

3. Custom, which installs SQL Server while allowing you to change any or all of the default options. This installation is recommended for expert users. The following options can be specified with Custom installations:

   - Install upgrade tools

   - Install replication support

   - Install full-text search support

   - Install client management tools

   - Install online documentation

   - Install development tools

   - Install samples

   - Set character set

   - Set sort order

   - Set Unicode collation

   - Install network protocols

The following options are given for all three installation types:

- Logon accounts for SQL Server, SQL Server Agent, and Microsoft Distributed Transaction Coordinator (MS DTC).

- The Setup Type screen will be displayed, allowing you to select the type of installation.

- Whether to start SQL Server, SQL Server Agent, and MS DTC automatically each time the computer is restarted.

4. Select the type of installation from the Setup Type screen.

    After you select the Setup Type, the Start Copying Files screen will be
    displayed.

5. Click Next to start copying the SQL Server 7 files to your computer.

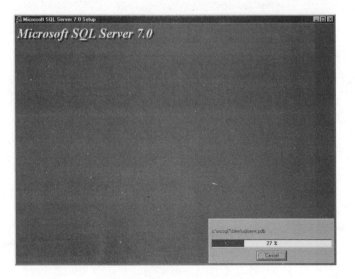

6. Click Finish to restart your computer.

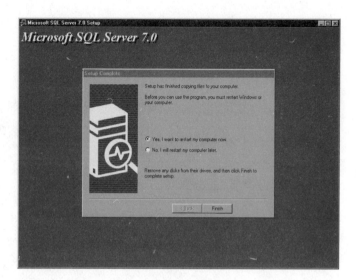

After you reboot, SQL Server is set up, and you can begin using it. Before you do so, however, let's take a look at the tools available in SQL Server 7.

NOTE
If you choose to perform a Custom Installation, there are several other options available, including the ability to automatically convert SQL Server 6.x servers to SQL Server 7, character set selection, and support for network protocols other than TCP/IP.

Tools in SQL Server 7

SQL Server 7 provides a wealth of tools that make it easier to set up, configure, and maintain servers, devices, and databases. Table 3.2 summarizes these tools, and we'll provide details throughout the rest of this section.

TABLE 3.2: The Tools in SQL Server 7

Tool	Description
Microsoft Management Console	The new user interface and framework for BackOffice server management.

Continued on next page

TABLE 3.2 CONTINUED: The Tools in SQL Server 7

Tool	Description
SQL Server Enterprise Manager	A graphical user interface that allows for easy, enterprise-wide configuration and management of SQL Server and SQL Server objects. It allows you to configure servers, manage databases and database objects, schedule events, and configure and manage replication.
SQL Server Books Online	Provides online access to the Microsoft SQL Server documentation set.
SQL Server Client Configuration	Sets the default Net-Library and server connection information on clients, displays the DB-Library version number, and searches for multiple copies of DB-Library and Net-Library in your path.
SQL Server Network Library Configuration	A graphical tool that allows you to load network protocols installed on the server so they are actively listening for client connections, display information about the network libraries currently installed on the server, and configure connection parameters for network protocols.
SQL Performance Monitor	Integrates Windows NT Performance Monitor with SQL Server, providing real-time activity and performance statistics.
SQL Server Profiler	A graphical tool that captures a continuous record of server activity in real-time. SQL Server Profiler monitors events produced through SQL Server; filters events based on user-specified criteria; and directs the trace output to the screen, a file, or a table. SQL Server Profiler allows you to replay previously captured traces.
SQL Server Query Analyzer	A graphical query tool that provides a way to analyze the plan of a query, execute multiple queries simultaneously, view data, and recommend indexes. SQL Server Query Analyzer provides the SHOWPLAN option, which is used to report data retrieval methods chosen by the SQL Server optimizer.
SQL Server Service Manager	A graphical taskbar application that is used for starting, stopping, and pausing SQL Server (MSSQLServer), SQL Server Agent, and the Microsoft Distributed Transaction Coordinator (MSDTC). SQL Enterprise Manager can also be used to start and stop the Microsoft Search (MSSearch) service, which provides full-text indexing and querying capability to SQL Server.
SQL Server Setup	A tool that is used to install and reconfigure the server. You can use the Setup program to change network support options, add a language, rebuild the *master* database, change the character set or sort order, set server options, set security options, or remove SQL Server from your hard drive.

Continued on next page

TABLE 3.2 CONTINUED: The Tools in SQL Server 7

Tool	Description
Version Upgrade Wizard	Used to upgrade SQL Server version 6.x data to SQL Server 7. You can use Version Upgrade Wizard to upgrade databases, replication settings, automated tasks, and most configuration options. The Version Upgrade Wizard is not supported on the Windows 95/98 platform.

Many of these tools were discussed earlier in this chapter in the section "What's New in SQL Server 7."

Creating a Database

Databases are the heart and soul of SQL Server. A relational database management system is made up of related, interacting databases. Each database stores and manages a segment of the business. In this section, we'll focus on using the SQL Enterprise Manager to create a database on SQL Server 7. Table 3.3 lists the major parts of a database on SQL Server 7.

TABLE 3.3: The Major Parts of a SQL Server 7 Database

Part	Description
Database	A repository for data.
Table	A set of rows and columns, similar to the rows and columns of a spreadsheet. In a relational database, the rows are called records, and the columns are called fields.
Key	A field, or fields, in a table that is indexed for fast retrieval.
Index	Specifies the order of records accessed from database tables and whether duplicate records are accepted, providing efficient access to data.
View	A virtual table derived from one or more tables in a database.
Stored Procedure	A precompiled set of instructions written in Transact_SQL.
Trigger	A special kind of stored procedure that is executed automatically when a user attempts to modify data (insert, update, or delete) in the specified table.

Creating the Inventory Database

In the examples that follow, we'll create an inventory database for TeleVision, a fictitious company that distributes TVs and VCRs.

As discussed earlier in this chapter, databases in SQL Server 7 no longer have database devices like the earlier versions of SQL Server did. Instead, databases are created using files.

Understanding Database Files and Filegroups

Databases in Microsoft SQL Server 7 are created using a set of operating system files, instead of database devices like earlier versions of SQL Server.

Examining System Files

All data and objects in the database, such as tables, stored procedures, triggers, and views, are stored within these operating system files. There are three types of database files in SQL Server 7:

- A primary data file is a file that is the starting point of the database. Every database has only one primary data file.

- Secondary data files are optional files used to hold all data and objects that are not on the primary data file. Some databases may not have any secondary data files, while others may have multiple secondary data files.

- Log files hold all of the transaction log information used to recover the database. Every database has at least one log file.

Examining Filegroups

A filegroup is a collection of files. Filegroups allow files to be grouped together for administrative and data allocation/placement purposes. For example, three files (data1.ndf, data2.ndf, and data3.ndf) can be created on three disk drives respectively and then assigned to the filegroup fgroup1. A table can then be created specifically on the filegroup fgroup1. Queries for data from the table will be spread across the three disks, thereby improving performance. Files and filegroups also allow you to easily add new files on new disks. Additionally, if your database exceeds the maximum size for a single Microsoft Windows NT file, you can use secondary data files to allow your database to continue to grow.

Creating the Database

For TeleVision, our fictitious company, we are going to create an inventory database. Follow these steps:

1. To open the Enterprise Manager, choose Start ➤ Programs ➤ SQL Server 7 ➤ SQL Server Enterprise Manager.

2. Click the Database folder in the Console Root to select it.

3. Choose Action ➤ New Database, to display the General Tab of the Database Properties dialog box.

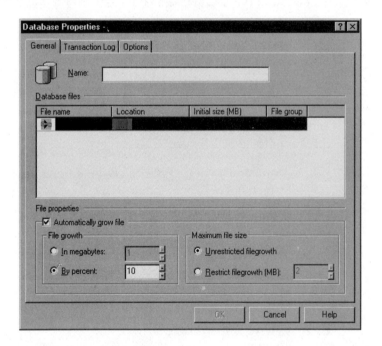

4. In the Name field, enter **Inventory** as the name of the database. The primary database and transaction log files are created using the database name you specified as the prefix, `c:\mssql7\data\Inventory_data.mdf` and `c:\mssql7\data\Inventory_log.ldf`. The initial sizes of the database and transaction log files are the same as the default sizes specified for the *model* database. The primary file contains the system tables for the database. To change the default values provided in the File name, Location, Initial size, and File group (not applicable for the transaction log) columns, click the cell to change and enter the new value. For our example, accept the defaults.

5. Click OK to create the Inventory database and its associated files.

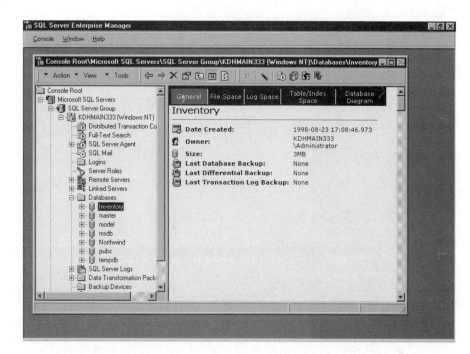

That's all it takes to create a new database in SQL Server 7 using SQL Enterprise Manager. In the next section, we will create and populate two tables for it.

TIP   You can also use the Database Wizard to help you create a database. To invoke the wizard choose Tools ➤ Wizards and select the Create Database Wizard option from the Database section.

Creating a Table in Enterprise Manager

Now that we have created our Inventory database, we are ready to create two tables:

- The OnHand table, which will hold the current inventory for TeleVision

- The Location table, which will define the possible locations where the parts can be stored

Creating the OnHand Table

Follow these steps to create the OnHand table:

1. Click the Inventory folder in the Enterprise Manager.

2. Choose Action ➤ New ➤ Table to open the Choose Name dialog box.

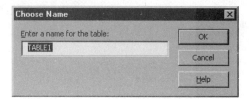

3. Enter **OnHand** as the table name and click OK.

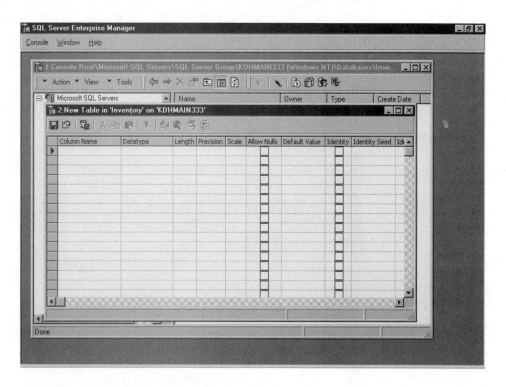

4. Assign the values listed in Table 3.4.

TABLE 3.4: Values for the OnHand Table

Column Name	Data Type	Size	Nulls
PartNumber	char	5	No
QuantityOnHand	int	*	No
ReorderPoint	int	*	No
LocationCode	char	3	No
Comment	char	500	Yes

* You cannot enter a value in the Size column for int type fields. A value of 4 is automatically entered when the table is saved.

5.   Click the Save icon to save the OnHand table.

6.   Close the Manage Tables dialog box.

Now that the OnHand table has been created, we need to populate it with some test data. To do so, we'll use the OnHand.SQL script from the Ch10\OnHand folder on the CD that comes with this book. Follow these steps:

1.   In the Microsoft SQL Enterprise Manager dialog box, choose Tools ➢ SQL Server Query Analyzer to open the Microsoft SQL Server Query Analyzer screen, as shown in Figure 3.12.

FIGURE 3.12:

Microsoft SQL Server Query Analyzer

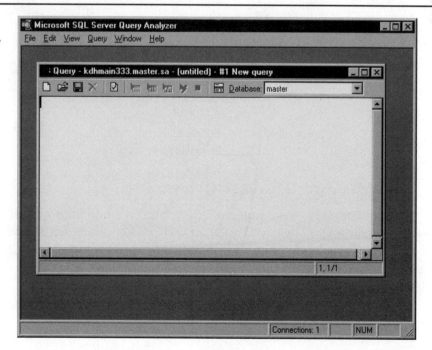

2. Enter a valid Login Name and Password and click OK.

3. Choose File ➤ Open to open the File Open dialog box.

4. Select the OnHand.SQL file from the Ch10 folder on the CD.

5. Choose the Inventory database from the Database list box.

6. Choose Query ➤ Execute Query to run the SQL script. Five records will be added to the OnHand table.

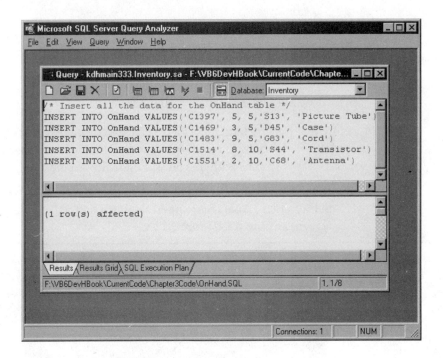

The other table in the Inventory database is the Location table; we will create it using a Database Diagram in the next section.

Using a Database Diagram

One of the new features of SQL Server 7 is the addition of a fully integrated Database Diagram. If you recall from Chapter 2, we discussed Database Diagrams as they related to Visual Basic. Well, the same functionality is built in to SQL Server 7. This added feature opens a new avenue for developers to use in the creation and maintenance of database objects.

Working with Database Objects

Database Diagrams allow you to manage your databases graphically and enable you to create, edit, manage, or delete database objects (tables, table columns, table relationships, constraints, stored procedures, triggers) while you are directly connected to the database in which those objects are stored. Figure 3.13 shows the Database Diagram for the pubs sample database.

In the diagram, you can see the graphical relationship between the objects in the database. You can also define and edit the properties of the database objects, all from within your database diagram.

The tables represented in your diagrams are actually references to tables that reside in the database. Because individual database tables can exist in more than one database diagram, tables that appear in many database diagrams actually exist in only one place, the database itself.

When tables are modified in a database diagram, the modifications are immediately applied to that table in every other diagram in which it appears. Similarly, when you remove a table from a database diagram, it is also removed from the other diagrams. Similarly, if you delete a table in a multi-user environment, the table will be removed from the database diagrams of all other users.

FIGURE 3.13:

Pubs Database Diagram

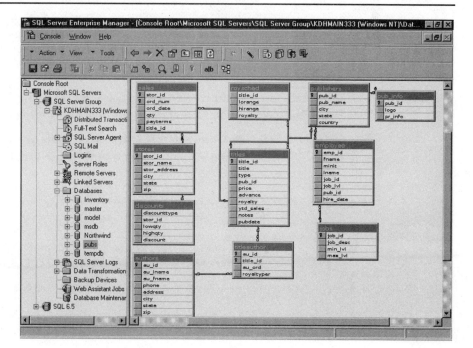

When you save a database diagram, all changes you made to the tables in your diagram and their related objects are saved in the server database. You can choose to select only certain tables in your database diagram and save only those tables, without affecting the other tables in the diagram. This allows you to perform what-if scenarios without actually affecting your database design.

In most databases, if you perform any of the following actions on a database table, the table will be automatically re-created in your database when you save the table or the database diagram. This is the same process that you performed manually in earlier releases of SQL Server; the only difference is that SQL Server does the dirty work now.

- Changes the properties of an existing column

- Appends a column that doesn't allow nulls to the end of an existing table

- Adds a column in the body of an existing table

- Reorders existing columns

- Deletes an existing column

The table must be re-created in the database in order for your database to accept your changes.

When you save a table in which you've performed any of these actions, any triggers, bound defaults, and rules associated with each table are also saved.

Creating a Database Diagram

Database Diagrams can be created in two ways: by using the Create Diagram Wizard or by opening a blank diagram and manually adding tables.

Creating a Database Diagram with the Create Diagram Wizard   Follow these steps to use the Create Diagram Wizard to create a Database Diagram for the pubs database:

1. Choose Start ➤ Programs ➤ Microsoft SQL Server 7 ➤ Enterprise Manager to open the Enterprise Manager.

2. Select the server that holds the pubs sample database and click the plus icon to expand the server objects.

3. Click the plus icon next to the Database Folder to expand the databases.

4. Click the pubs database to select it. This will populate the right panel in the enterprise manager with general information about the database.

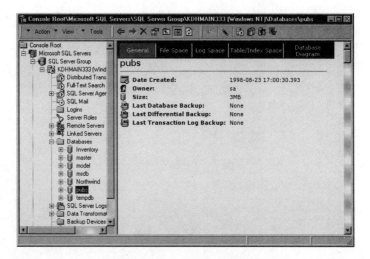

5. Click the Database Diagram link on the title to invoke the Create Diagram Wizard screen.

6. Click Yes to the dialog box asking if you want to create the default diagram and the Create Diagram Wizard Welcome screen will appear.

NOTE

If you click Cancel on the screen, you will have a blank diagram. You can drag tables from the Console Root and drop them onto the blank diagram to manually create a Database Diagram.

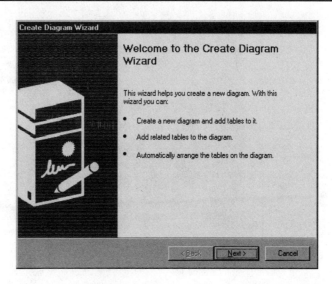

7. Click Next to display the Select Table screen and begin defining the diagram.

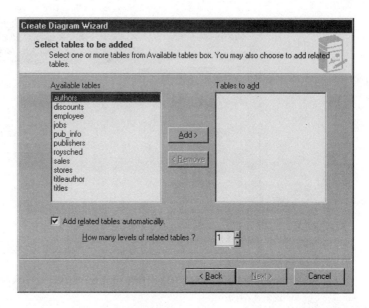

8. Click the Add button for each table to add all of the tables to the diagram.

9. Click Next to display the Select Layout Option screen.

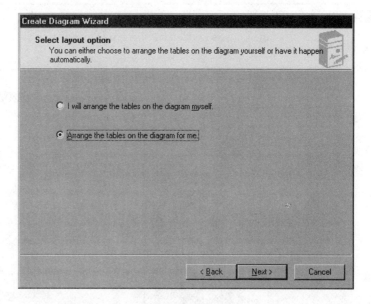

This screen allows you to tell the wizard that you will select the layout of the tables or that you want the wizard to automatically create the layout.

10. Accept the default Arrange the Tables on the Diagram for Me option to have the wizard create the table layout.

11. Click Next to display the Completing the Diagram screen. This screen displays a recap of the tables and the method that will be used to generate the layout.

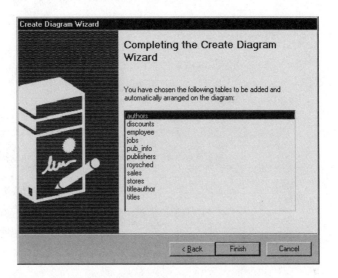

12. Click Finish to create the diagram.

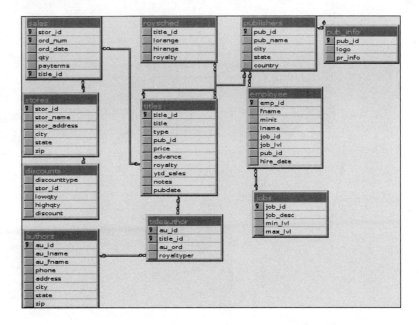

Using a Database Diagram to Create the Location Table

The Location table holds the valid locations for parts to be stored. Follow these steps to create the table using a Database Diagram:

1. In Enterprise Manager, select the Inventory folder.

2. Choose Action ➢ New ➢ Database Diagram to open the Create Diagram Wizard.

3. Click the Cancel button to display the New Diagram screen. Since we want to use a Database Diagram to create a new table, we need to start with a blank diagram.

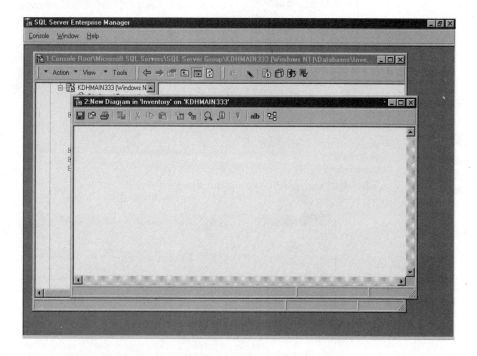

4. Right-click the blank diagram and choose New Table from the menu.

5. Enter **Location** as the table name in the Choose Name dialog box.

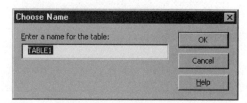

6. Click OK to name the table and display a blank table layout in the diagram.

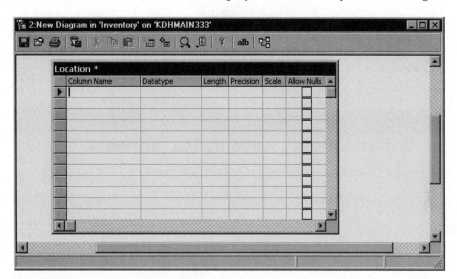

7. Assign the values listed in Table 3.5.

TABLE 3.5: Values for the Location Table

Column Name	Data Type	Size	Nulls
LocationCode	char	3	No
Description	char	100	Yes

8. Right-click the table, and choose Save Selection from the menu to save the Location table.

9. Click the Save icon on the top left menu bar to open the Save As Dialog box.

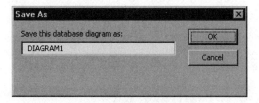

10. Enter **Location** as the name of the Database Dialog and click OK.

The new Database Diagram will be saved. If you want to make any modifications to the Location table, you could use this diagram.

Now that the Location table has been created, we need to populate it with some test data. Do so by running the SQL script Location.SQL from the Ch03 folder on the CD that comes with this book. This script adds five records to the Location table.

NOTE   See the earlier section, "Creating the OnHand Table," for the steps required to run a SQL script.

Understanding Keys in SQL Server 7

There are two types of keys in SQL Server 7:

- Primary

- Foreign

Most tables are designed to have one column or a combination of columns whose values uniquely identify each row of data in the table. This column or combination of columns is the *primary key*.

A primary key ensures that the key value is not null and that duplicate values do not exist in a table. You can create a primary key by defining a Primary Key constraint when the table is created. There can be only one primary key per table. If you define a Primary Key constraint for a table, this constraint automatically creates an index. This index enforces uniqueness in the table and permits quick access to data when you use the primary key in queries.

If you look at the sample data in our OnHand table (Table 3.4), you will see that the PartNumber column is a good candidate for the primary key.

A *foreign key* is a column or a combination of columns whose values match the primary key of another table. A foreign key does not have to be unique. However, foreign key values must be copies of the primary key values; no value in the foreign key except NULL can exist unless the same value exists in the primary key of the referenced table. This sets the basis for referential integrity. There can be an unlimited number of foreign keys per table. A foreign key can be NULL, but if any part of a composite foreign key is NULL, the entire foreign key must be NULL.

Creating a Primary Key

You can create a primary key by defining a Primary Key constraint when you create or alter a table.

Creating keys in SQL Server 7 is an easy task if you employ the help of Database Diagrams. In this section, we will let SQL Server create the default Database Diagram for our Inventory database, then we will use this diagram to create the keys.

Creating a Primary Key for the OnHand and Location Tables

To create a primary key on the PartNumber column of the OnHand table and on the LocationCode column of the Location table that we created earlier, follow these steps:

1. Create the default Database Diagram for the Inventory database.

NOTE   If you need help creating a default Database Diagram, follow the steps outlined earlier in this chapter in the section "Creating a Database Diagram with the Create Diagram Wizard."

---

2. Right-click the PartNumber column in the Onhand table and select Set Primary Key from the menu to set the primary key for the OnHand table.

3. Right-click the LocationCode column in the Location table and select Set Primary Key from the menu to set the primary key for the Location table. The Database Diagram will display a Key image next to the key columns.

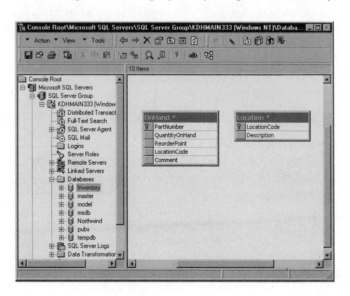

At this point, the diagram reflects the new keys, but the tables have not been saved to the database. You will remember from earlier discussions that changes made to a Database Diagram do not affect the database until you save them.

4. Right-click the diagram and choose Save to display the Save dialog box. This dialog will recap the current changes.

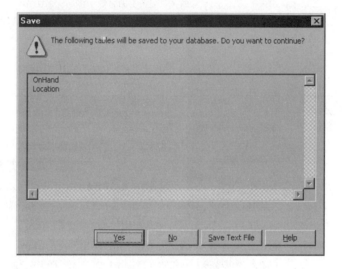

5. Click Save to commit the changes to the database.

The PartNumber column and the LocationCode column are now set as primary keys. In the next section, we will create a foreign key to set up referential integrity on the OnHand and Location tables.

Creating a Foreign Key for the OnHand Table

When a new PartNumber record is added to the OnHand table, we want SQL Server to verify the LocationCode field against the LocationCode field in the Location table. We should not be able to add a PartNumber to a LocationCode that does not exist. We will enforce this rule by adding a foreign LocationCode key to the OnHand table. In SQL Server 7, this can be accomplished by creating a relationship in a Database Diagram.

Follow these steps to create a foreign key for the OnHand table:

1. Open the diagram for the Inventory database by clicking the Inventory folder in the Database folder.

NOTE   If you have not created the Database Diagram and primary keys for the Inventory database, follow the steps described in the sections "Creating a Database Diagram" and "Creating a Primary Key" earlier in this chapter.

2. To create the primary to foreign key relationship, click the LocationCode column in the Location table and drag it to the LocationCode column in the OnHand table. When you release the mouse button, the Create Relationship dialog box will be displayed, as shown in Figure 3.14.

FIGURE 3.14:

Create Relationship
Dialog Box

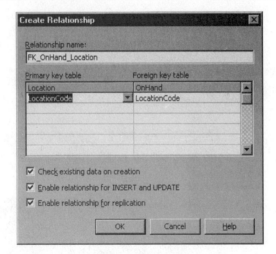

The Create Relationship dialog box enables you to confirm the related columns and to set properties for a new relationship with the following options:

- Relationship name: displays the system-assigned name of the relationship. To rename the relationship, type a new name in the text box.

- Primary key table: shows the name of the Primary key table in the relationship, followed by the columns that make up the primary key. You can select different columns to match the columns shown under Foreign key table.

- Foreign key table: shows the name of the foreign key table in the relationship, followed by the columns that make up the foreign key. You can select different columns to match the columns shown under Primary key table.

- Check existing data on creation: applies the constraint to existing data in the Foreign key table when the relationship is created. An error message will notify you of any data that violates the constraint if this box is selected.

- Enable relationship for INSERT and UPDATE: applies the constraint when data is added to or updated in the Foreign key table using these statements.

- Enable relationship for replication: copies the constraint whenever the Foreign key table is copied to a different database.

- OK: creates the relationship in your database diagram and sets the properties you selected.

- Cancel: erases the relationship line from your database diagram. The relationship is not created.

3. For this example, accept the defaults and click OK to create the relationship.

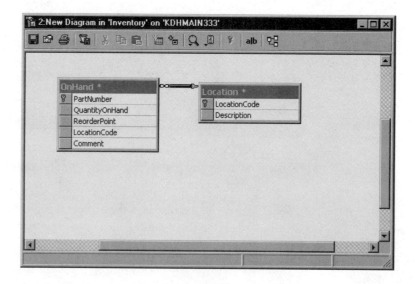

4. Right-click the diagram and choose Save from the menu to save the relationship changes.

NOTE   Remember, if you do not save the diagram, the changes are not saved to the database.

The Foreign key and relationship has now been added and saved, linking the LocationCode field in the OnHand table to the LocationCode field in the Location table. If a new PartNumber record is added to the OnHand table, the Location-Code must already exist in the Location table; however, if it does not already exist, you will get an error message and the record will not be added. Also, you cannot delete a LocationCode from the Location table if a record exists in the OnHand table with the same value in the LocationCode field.

Indexes in SQL Server 7

An *index* is a table structure that SQL Server 7 uses to provide quick access to the rows of a table based on the values of one or more columns. Properly planned indexes provide the most important performance improvement that can be made to your database tables.

SQL Server 7 uses an index in much the same way that you use the index of a book; it searches the index to find a particular value and then follows the pointer to locate the row containing the value.

In SQL Server 7, there are two types of indexes:

- Clustered

- Nonclustered

In a *clustered index*, the physical order of rows is the same as the indexed order of rows. You can create only one clustered index per table. UPDATE and DELETE operations require a large amount of reading, so they are often accelerated by clustered indexes. Typically, if a table has at least one index, that index should be a clustered index; if a table has more than one index, at least one should be clustered.

In a *nonclustered index*, the logical ordering of a table is specified. The physical order of the rows is not the same as their indexed order. You can have multiple nonclustered indexes per table.

To be effective, indexes must be created for the fields that will be used to assess the data. In our TeleVision example, the PartNumber is the index because it is unique in each record. Most of the time, when you need to look up a particular part, you will know the PartNumber. You might think, therefore, that you should index every field. Although that would certainly speed your query searches, it would slow the database because too many indexes would need to be updated.

NOTE   Indexes are not considered part of the logical database design; they can be dropped, added, and changed without affecting the database schema. Experimenting with indexes will not damage the database; it will affect only the performance of a database or an application.

It's good to keep in mind the type of data access and searches that you will require and to plan your indexes accordingly.

SQL Server 7 automatically creates an index for the Primary Key and Unique constraints that you create in your tables. If you want to add more indexes, you will have to create them yourself.

Creating a New Index on the OnHand Table

The OnHand table is currently indexed on the PartNumber field. SQL Server 7 set this index to the primary key field when you created the key. In addition to the PartNumber field, it would be helpful to have an index on the LocationCode field. It would seem logical to allow the users of the database to be able to search for all the parts in a specific location, and an index would speed the searches.

Follow these steps to add an index to the LocationCode field of the OnHand table:

1. Open the Database Diagram for the Location database if it is not already open.

2. Right-click the OnHand table and choose Properties from the menu to display the Properties dialog box (as shown in Figure 3.15).

3. Click the Indexes/Keys tab. The Properties dialog box contains a set of properties for the indexes, primary keys, and unique constraints attached to the tables in your database diagram. Indexes and constraints are not graphically

FIGURE 3.15:

Indexes/Keys Properties
Dialog Box

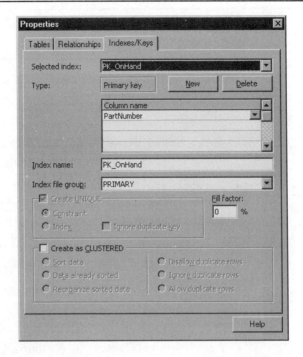

represented in database diagrams. The following options are available from the Properties dialog box:

- Selected Index: Shows the name of the first index for the selected table in your diagram. If more than one table is selected in your diagram, only the name of the first index for the first table is visible. To choose a different index to show properties for, expand the Selected index dropdown list.

- Type: Shows the index/key object type for the selected table: index, primary key, or unique.

- New: Choose this button to create a new index for the selected database table. Enter properties for the index.

- Delete: Choose this button to remove the selected index from the table.

NOTE   To delete a primary key, you must first delete any relationships that the primary key column participates in.

- Column Name: Shows the list of columns in the Index, Primary Key, or Unique constraint. You can add, change, or remove column names in this list.

- Index Name: Shows the name of the selected index. You can rename the index by entering a new name in this box.

- Create UNIQUE: Select this option to create a Unique constraint or index for the selected database table. Select either the Constraint or Index button to specify whether you are creating a constraint or index.

  - Ignore Duplicate Key, which allows you to ensure each value in an indexed column, is unique if you are creating a unique index.

- Fill Factor: Shows the fill factor that specifies how full each index page can be. If a fill factor is not specified, the database's default fill factor is used.

- Create As CLUSTERED: Select this option to create a clustered index for the selected database table.

- Sort Data Options: Identify how the data is ordered in the index as records are added to the index.

  - Sort Data, which is the default, organizes data in ascending order.

  - Data Already Sorted, when selected, accepts the order of existing data.

  - Reorganize Sorted Data reorganizes the data in ascending order. Select this option, for example, when the table becomes fragmented or to rebuild nonclustered indexes.

- Duplicate Row Options: Identify how the index should handle duplicate rows.

  - Disallow Duplicate Rows is the default that prevents the index from being saved if duplicate rows exist. If this option is selected, an error message will appear if duplicate rows exist.

- Ignore Duplicate Rows deletes duplicate rows from the index as it is being created.

- Allow Duplicate Rows creates the index even if duplicate rows exist.

4. Click the New button to create a new index on the OnHand table.

5. Choose LocationCode from the Column Name drop-down list box.

6. Change the Index Name to LocationCode_OnHand in the Index Name field.

7. Click the X at the top of the Properties dialog box to dismiss it. You have now created a new index in the Database Diagram, but guess what? It does not exist in the database. You guessed it! You need to save the diagram to commit the changes to the database.

8. Right-click the diagram and choose Save from the menu to display the Save dialog box.

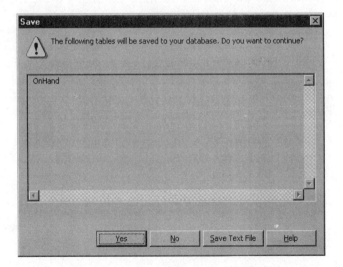

9. Click Save to save the changes to the Inventory database.

NOTE   You can also use the Create Index Wizard to help you create an index. To use the wizard choose Tools ➤ Wizards and select the Create Index Wizard from the Database section.

Understanding Views in SQL Server 7

A *view* is a virtual table that looks like a real table with a set of named columns and rows of data and has contents defined by a query. A view, however, does not exist as a stored set of data values in a database. Instead, the rows and columns of data in a view come from database tables and are produced by the query that defines the view.

Views provide data security by controlling the data that users can see. Views allow users to work with a database in the form they are used to, and they restrict data access without the burden of creating a security layer on top of the database. If, for example, employees must access an Employee Records table, you might create a view that does not include the Salary field.

A view looks and acts exactly like any other database table. You can display, update, and delete data on it just as you can on any other table. Transact-SQL enhances standard SQL so that there are no restrictions on querying through views and there are few restrictions on modifying them.

Creating a View

Let's create a view in our sample Inventory database. Let's say we need to access and manipulate data on the OnHand table, but we do not want the data entry clerks to see or change the QuantityOnHand or the ReorderPoint fields. In addition, we want the clerks to see the description of the LocationCodes from the Location table.

Although we could do all this with a query, we would have to rerun the query every time a clerk wanted to access the data. By creating a view, we can satisfy all our requirements.

Follow these steps to create the sample view:

1. Choose Start ➤ Programs ➤ Microsoft SQL Server 7 Enterprise Manager.

2. Select the server that contains our sample Inventory database from the list of servers.

3. Right-click the Inventory database in the Database Folder.

4. Choose New ➤ SQL Server View from the menu to display the New View screen, as shown in Figure 3.16. This screen is the same as the Query Designer screen discussed in Chapter 2.

FIGURE 3.16:

New View screen

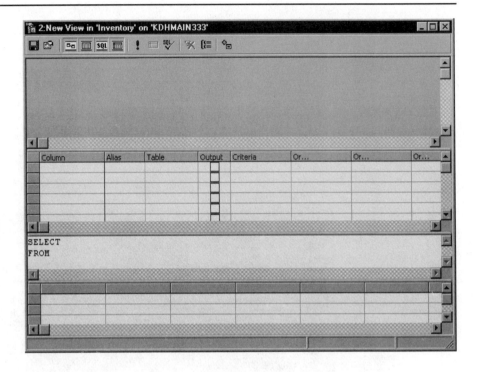

5. Right-click the top Diagram Pane and choose Add Table from the menu to display the Add Table dialog box.

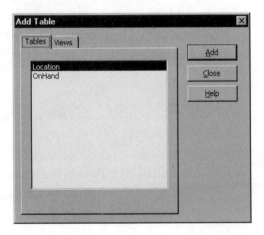

6. Click the Add button to add the OnHand table to the view.

7. Click the Location table to select it.

8. Click the Add button to add it to the view.

9. Close the Add Table dialog box.

10. Click the PartNumber, LocationCode, and Comment columns in the OnHand table to add them to the view.

11. Click the Description column in the Location table to add the Description to the view. Your screen should look like Figure 3.17.

FIGURE 3.17:

View Columns

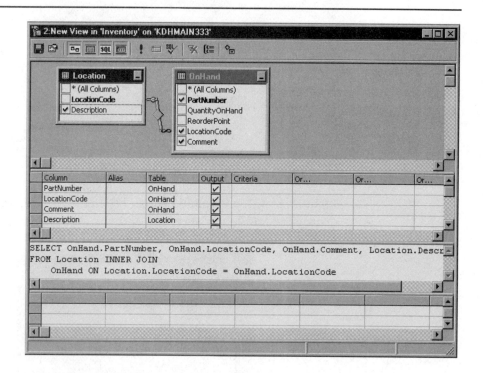

12. Right-click any pane and choose Run from the menu to run the query. The results should look just like we want them to look.

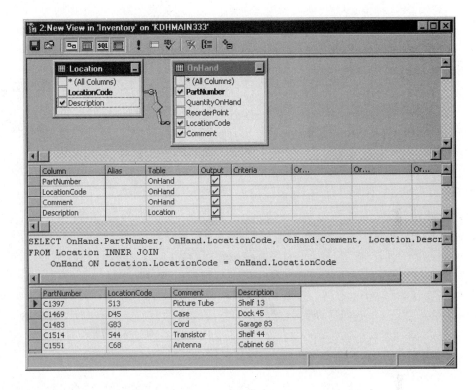

13. Right-click any pane again and select Save from the menu.

14. Enter vwLocate in the Save As dialog box and click OK to save our new view.

Now that the view has been created and saved, let's create a query to look at its contents.

Querying a View

In the previous section, you created the vwLocate view that includes data from the OnHand and Location tables. To create a query that lists the records in the vwLocate view, follow these steps:

1. Choose Start ➤ Programs ➤ Microsoft SQL Server 7 ➤ Enterprise Manager.

2. Select the server that contains our sample Inventory database from the list of servers.

3. Open the Databases folder.

4. Select the Inventory database.

5. Select the SQL Server Views folder to list the available views in the right pane.

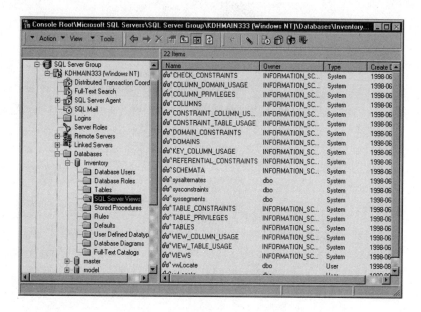

6. Right-click the vxLocate view and choose Open SQL Server View ➤ Return All Rows to display the rows in the view.

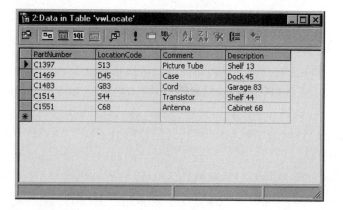

Views are a good vehicle for controlling data security by limiting who can access and manipulate data.

The next section provides an introduction to stored procedures in SQL Server 7.

SQL Server 7 Stored Procedures

Stored procedures are compiled SQL statements that are stored in the database. SQL Server stores the executable stored procedure so that it does not have to be re-created each time the query is executed.

There are two basic types of stored procedures:

- Precompiled
- User-defined

Precompiled stored procedures are special-use stored procedures that are included with SQL Server 7. Here are some examples:

- Catalog-stored procedures provide a uniform catalog interface for accessing database gateways, as well as SQL Server, from the same application

- Extended stored procedures provide a way to dynamically load and execute a function within a dynamic-link library

- System stored procedures make it easy to retrieve information from the administer databases and system tables

User-defined stored procedures are written by the developer in Transact_SQL code. These procedures can be used to perform almost any type of data access and manipulation. Here are some examples:

- Select all records from a Customer table for a mailing list
- Provide a list of all orders placed last month from a Sales table
- List the top five sales areas for the last quarter, show the top salesperson in each area, and give each of them a 5 percent salary increase

Running a Precompiled Stored Procedure

Let's say you want a list of all the columns in the OnHand table and the type of data that can be stored in each column in our test Inventory database. How can you get it? An easy way is to use the sp_columns system stored procedure.

The sp_columns stored procedure returns column information for a single object that can be queried in the current environment. The returned columns belong to a table or a view. The syntax for sp_columns is:

```
sp_columns object_name [, object_owner][, object_qualifier] [, column_name]
```

Table 3.6 explains the parts of the sp_columns stored procedure.

TABLE 3.6: The Parts of the sp_columns Stored Procedure

Part	Description
object_name	Required. Specifies the name of the table or view used to return catalog information.
object_owner	Optional. Specifies the object owner of the table or view used to return catalog information.
object_qualifier	Optional. Specifies the name of the table or view qualifier.
column_name	Optional. Specifies a single column and is used when only one column of catalog information is desired. If column_name is not specified, all columns will be returned.

Follow these steps to execute the sp_columns stored procedure from SQL Enterprise Manager:

1. Choose Start ➢ Programs ➢ Microsoft SQL Server 7 ➢ Query Analyzer to open the Query Analyzer and the Connect to SQL Server dialog box, as shown in Figure 3.18.

FIGURE 3.18:

Query Analyzer

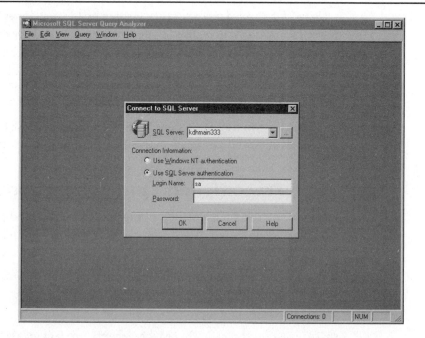

2. Enter a valid User Name and Password and click OK to connect to SQL Server.

3. Select the Inventory database from the list of databases in the Database list box.

4. Enter the following code:

```
sp_columns OnHand
```

5. Click the Execute Query icon or press Ctrl+E to execute the stored procedure. The procedure will run, and the results will be displayed in the Results tab of the Query dialog box:

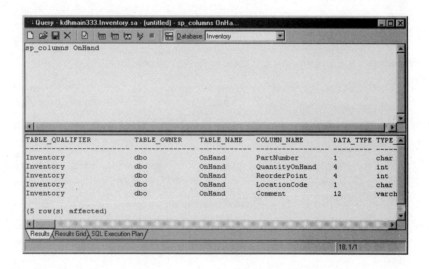

This is just one example of the hundreds of precompiled stored procedures included in SQL Server 7 to help you create, examine, and maintain your servers.

Creating and Executing a User-Defined Stored Procedure

User-defined stored procedures are stored procedures that you write yourself in Transact-SQL. You can write stored procedures to access or create almost every part of your SQL Servers. The general syntax for creating a stored procedure is:

```
CREATE PROCedure [owner.]procedure_name[;number")>
[(parameter1 [,
parameter2]...[parameter255])][{FOR REPLICATION} | {WITH RECOMPILE}
    [{[WITH] | [,]} ENCRYPTION]]AS sql_statements
```

Table 3.7 lists and defines the parts of the stored procedure syntax.

TABLE 3.7: The Parts of the Stored Procedure Syntax

Part	Description
Parameter	Specifies a parameter in the procedure. One or more parameters can optionally be declared in a CREATE PROCEDURE statement. The value of each declared parameter must be supplied by the user when the procedure is executed. A stored procedure can have a maximum of 255 parameters.
Datatype	Specifies the data type of the parameter. All data types except `image` are supported.
default	Specifies a default value for the parameter. If a default is defined, a user can execute the procedure without specifying a value for that parameter.
OUTPUT	Indicates that the parameter is a return parameter. `Text` parameters cannot be used as OUTPUT parameters.
FOR REPLICATION	Is mutually exclusive of the WITH RECOMPILE option. Stored procedures created for replication cannot be executed on the subscribing server.
number	An optional integer used to group procedures of the same name so that they can be dropped together with a single DROP PROCEDURE statement.
procedure_name	The name of the new stored procedure. Procedure names must conform to the rules for identifiers and must be unique within the database and its owner.
RECOMPILE	Indicates that SQL Server does not cache a plan for this procedure and that the procedure is recompiled each time it is executed.
ENCRYPTION	Encrypts the `syscomments` table entry that contains the text of the CREATE PROCEDURE statement.
AS sql_statements	Specifies the actions the procedure is to take. Any number and type of SQL statements can be included in the procedure.

Let's create a user-defined stored procedure that lists the Location codes from the Location table in our test Inventory database.

Creating the procLocationsCode Stored Procedure

Follow these steps to create the stored procedure:

1. Choose Start ➤ Programs ➤ Microsoft SQL Server 7 ➤ SQL Enterprise Manager.

2. Select the server that contains our sample Inventory database from the list of available servers.

3. Expand the `Databases` folder to expose the databases.

4. Select the Inventory database.

5. Right-click the Stored Procedures folder and choose New Stored Procedure from the menu to display the Stored Procedure Properties dialog box.

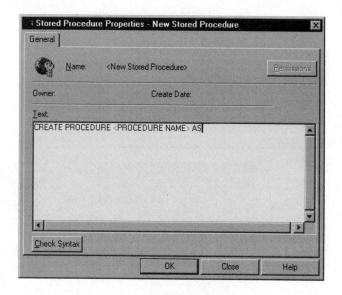

6. Replace the default code with the following code:

```
CREATE PROCEDURE procLocationCodes AS
SELECT LocationCode from Location
```

Table 3.8 explains this code.

TABLE 3.8: The procLocationCodes Stored Procedure Code

Line Number	Code	Explanation
1	Create Procedure procLocationCodes	Names the view procLocationCodes.
2	SELECT LocationCode from Location	Selects the LocationCodes field from the Location table.

7. Click OK to save the stored procedure and close the Stored Procedure Properties dialog box.

Executing the procLocationsCode Stored Procedure

Now that you have created, compiled, and saved the procedure, let's run it and see the results. Follow these steps:

NOTE   If you have just created the procedure, continue here. Otherwise, follow the steps outlined in the previous section "Creating the procLocationsCode Stored Procedure" to create and save the procLocationCodes stored procedure.

1. Choose Start ➤ Programs ➤ Microsoft SQL Server 7 ➤ Query Analyzer to open the Query Analyzer and the Connect to SQL Server dialog box, as shown in Figure 3.19.

FIGURE 3.19:

Query Analyzer and the Connect to SQL Server dialog box

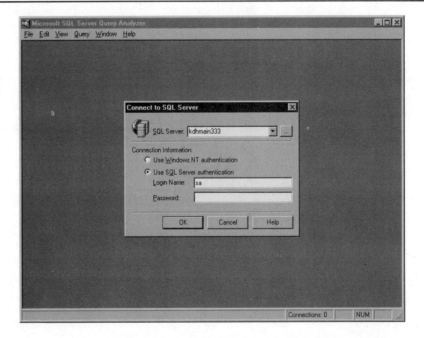

2. Enter a valid User Name and Password and click OK to connect to SQL Server.

3. Select the Inventory database from the list of databases in the Database list box.

4. Enter the following code:

    ```
    procLocationCodes
    ```

5. Click the Run icon or press Ctrl+E to execute the stored procedure.

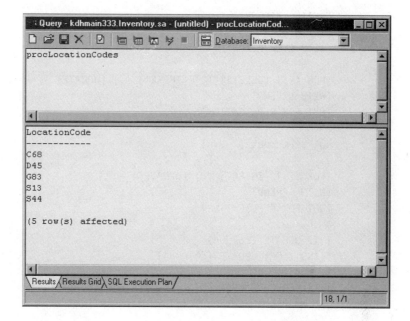

NOTE   You can also use the Create Stored Procedure Wizard to help you create a stored procedure. To invoke the wizard choose Tools ➤ Wizards and select the Create Stored Procedure Wizard option from the Database section.

You can use stored procedures to access and manipulate almost any data that you store in your databases. Stored procedures can be thought of as automatic code runners. A trigger, which is a special kind of stored procedure, also runs code automatically. In the next section, we will take a look at how triggers fit into SQL Server 7 to help you keep your data in sync.

Using Triggers in SQL Server 7

Triggers are special stored procedures that are automatically executed when an Insert, Update, or Delete is performed. A trigger validates data in response to an action statement against a table. A trigger can query other tables, and it can include complex Transact-SQL statements. The trigger and the statement that fires it are treated as a single transaction that can be rolled back from within the trigger. If a severe error is detected, the entire transaction automatically rolls back.

The syntax for a trigger is:

```
CREATE TRIGGER trigger_name
ON table
[WITH ENCRYPTION]
{
{FOR {[,] [DELETE] [,] [INSERT] [,] [UPDATE] }
[WITH APPEND]
[NOT FOR REPLICATION]
AS
sql_statement [ ...n]
}
{FOR {[,] [INSERT] [,] [UPDATE]}
[WITH APPEND]
[NOT FOR REPLICATION]
AS
{ IF UPDATE (column)
[{AND | OR} UPDATE (column)]
[ ...n]
| IF (COLUMNS_UPDATED() {bitwise_operator} updated_bitmask)
{ comparison_operator} column_bitmask [...n]
}
sql_statement [ ...n]}
}
```

Table 3.9 explains the parts of the trigger's syntax.

TABLE 3.9: The Parts of a Trigger's Syntax

Part	Description
trigger_name	Specifies the name of the trigger.
table_name	Specifies the table on which the trigger will be executed.
INSERT, UPDATE, DELETE	Specifies the trigger type and which data modification statements will activate the trigger. Any combination of these (in any order) are allowed in a trigger.
ENCRYPTION	Encrypts the text entries of the CREATE TRIGGER statement.
AS sql_statements	Specifies trigger conditions and actions.

The following SQL statements are not allowed in a trigger:

- All CREATE statements (DATABASE, DEFAULT, INDEX, PROCEDURE, RULE, TABLE, TRIGGER, and VIEW)

- All DISK statements

- All DROP statements

- ALTER TABLE and ALTER DATABASE

- GRANT and REVOKE

- LOAD DATABASE and LOAD TRANSACTION

- RECONFIGURE

- SELECT INTO (triggers cannot create tables)

- TRUNCATE TABLE

- UPDATE STATISTICS

WARNING   If a trigger is defined for an operation (INSERT, UPDATE, or DELETE) that already has a trigger, the existing trigger is replaced without a warning message.

Creating a Trigger

In this section, you will create a trigger on the Location table in our test Inventory database. The trigger, named tgrNewLocation, will print a message notifying the clerks that a new inventory location is available for parts storage.

Follow these steps to create the test tgrNewLocation:

1. Choose Start ➤ Programs ➤ Microsoft SQL Server 7 ➤ Enterprise Manager.

2. Select the server that contains our sample Inventory database from the list of available servers.

3. Expand the Databases folder to expose the databases.

4. Select the Inventory database.

5. Click the Tables folder to display the tables in the details pane.

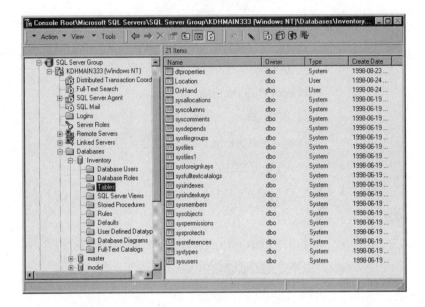

6. Right-click the Location table and choose Tasks ➤ Manage Triggers from the menu to display the Trigger Properties dialog box.

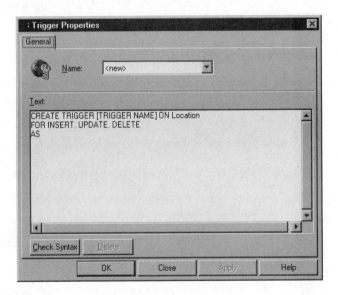

7. Replace the default code with the following code:

```
CREATE TRIGGER tgrNewLocation
ON dbo.Location
FOR INSERT AS
RAISERROR ("A new location code has been added", 0, 1)
```

Table 3.10 explains this code.

TABLE 3.10: The tgrNewLocation Trigger Code

Line Number	Code	Explanation
1	CREATE TRIGGER tgrNewLocation	Names the trigger tgrNewLocation.
2	ON dbo.Location	The name of the table for the trigger.
3	FOR INSERT AS	Defines the trigger as an Insert trigger. The trigger will execute when a new record is added to the Location table.
.4	RAISERROR ("A new location code has been addes",0, 1)	The message that will print when the trigger is executed.

The Trigger Properties dialog box should look like this:

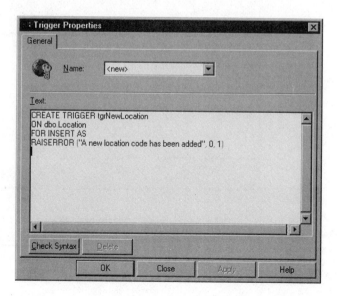

8. Click OK to save the trigger and close the Trigger Properties dialog box.

Executing a Trigger

Now that your trigger has been compiled and saved, let's execute it by adding a new Location record to the Location table. Follow these steps:

1. Choose Start ➤ Programs ➤ Microsoft SQL Server 7 ➤ Query Analyzer to open the Query Analyzer and the Connect to SQL Server dialog box.

2. Enter a valid User Name and Password and click OK to connect to SQL Server.

3. Select the Inventory database from the list of databases in the Database list box.

4. Enter the following code:

   ```
   INSERT INTO Location VALUES ('R48', 'Room 8 on the 4th floor')
   ```

5. Click the Run icon or press Ctrl+E to execute the query.The new record will be inserted into the Location table, and you should see the message "A new location code has been added" in the Results tab of the Query dialog box:

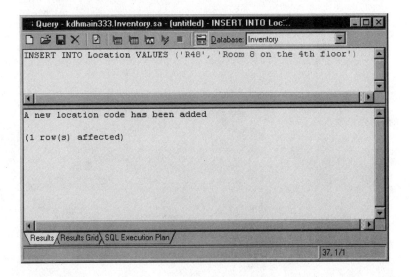

Although this has been a very simple test of a trigger's uses, it serves to demonstrate how easy it is to create and execute your own triggers.

CHAPTER

FOUR

4

The ADO Object

- Creating an ODBC data source

- Exploring the ActiveX Data control

- Using ADO Objects

- Executing stored procedures

- Transaction processing with ActiveX Data Objects

The Data Access Object (DAO) has been the basic mechanism with which we have created and accessed databases since Visual Basic 3, and most VB programmers have learned and mastered this valuable tool. It is, in a sense, the parent of all data access models. The DAO, however, was designed primarily for the Microsoft Access JET engine, and with the advent of the Internet and corporate intranets and the proliferation of SQL Server applications, the time has come to replace the DAO.

The Remote Data Object (RDO) follows a similar paradigm, but is smaller and provides fewer objects. Not that RDO does less than DAO—quite the contrary. The RDO was introduced with Visual Basic 4 to address the needs of client/server developers. It performs better than DAO and provides support for features such as batch cursors and optimistic updates. It is also simpler to use than the DAO because it uses fewer objects. In effect, it's a friendlier interface to the Open Database Connectivity Application Programming Interface (ODBC API).

ActiveX Data Objects (ADO) is the successor to DAO and RDO. ADO 2.0 is most similar to RDO functionally, and there is generally a similar mapping between the two models. ADO "flattens" the object model used by DAO and RDO, meaning that it contains fewer objects and more properties, methods, and events. Much of the functionality contained in the DAO and RDO models was consolidated into single objects, making for a much simpler object model; therefore, you might initially have difficulty finding the appropriate ADO object, collection, property, method, or event. However, although ADO objects, unlike DAO and RDO, are hierarchical, they are also creatable outside the scope of the hierarchy.

ADO currently doesn't support all of DAO's functionality. ADO mostly includes RDO-style functionality to interact with OLE DB data sources, plus remoting and DHTML technology.

In this chapter, we will look at how to connect ADO to a Visual Basic application with a stand-alone connection and with the aid of the ADO Data control, so that your applications can take advantage of all the speed, flexibility, and reliability of SQL Server, Oracle, and any other ODBC database.

Introducing the ADO Object Model

The ADO object model, shown in Figure 4.1 and first discussed in Chapter 1, defines a collection of programmable objects that support the Component Object Model (COM) and OLE Automation to leverage the powerful partner technology called OLE DB.

FIGURE 4.1:

The ADO object model

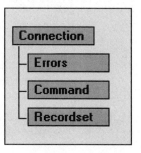

The ADO object model, when compared to other data access objects such as DAO or RDO, is flatter and simpler to use.

The objects in the ADO object model are outlined in Table 4.1.

TABLE 4.1: The ADO Objects

Object	Description
Command object	Maintains information about a command, such as a query string or parameter definitions. A command string can be executed on a Connection object of a query string as part of opening a Recordset object, without defining a Command object. The Command object is useful when you want to define query parameters or execute a stored procedure that returns output parameters. A number of properties are supported by the Command object to describe the type and purpose of the query, and to help ADO optimize the operation.
Connection object	Maintains connection information, such as cursor type, connect string, query time-out, connection time-out, and default database. A Connection is a non-persistent object that represents a connection to a remote database.
Error object	Contains extended error information about error conditions raised by the data provider. The Errors collection can contain more than one Error object at a time because a single statement can generate two or more errors. You can use a For Each statement to loop through the errors in the error collection.
Field object	Contains information about a single column of data within a recordset. The Recordset object uses the Fields collection to contain all of its Field objects. This Field information includes data type, precision, and numeric scale. All of the metadata properties (Name, Type, DefinedSize, Precision, and NumericScale) are available before opening the Field object's recordset. Setting them at that time is useful for dynamically constructing forms.

Continued on next page

TABLE 4.1 CONTINUED: The ADO Objects

Object	Description
Parameter object	A single parameter associated with a command. The Command object uses the Parameters collection to contain all of its Parameter objects. ADO Parameter objects can be created automatically by sending queries to the database. This collection can also be built programmatically to improve performance at run time.
Property object	A provider-defined characteristic of ADO objects. ADO objects have two types of properties, built-in and dynamic. Built-in properties are those properties implemented in ADO and available to any new ADO object. Dynamic properties are defined by the underlying data provider and appear in the Properties collection for the appropriate ADO object. This is one of the greatest features of ADO, in that it lets the ADO service provider present special interfaces.
Recordset object	A set of rows returned from a query, including a cursor into those rows. You can open a Recordset object without explicitly opening a Connection object. However, if you create a Connection object first, multiple Recordset objects can be opened on the same connection.

Creating an ODBC Data Source

You connect ADO to a Visual Basic application through an ODBC data source. ODBC is Microsoft's standard data access interface that relies on specific drivers to access any relational database. It is the layer that sits between the database management system and whatever access mechanism you are using. ODBC's function is to interface DAO and RDO with the actual database.

All the Database Management System (DBMS)-dependent code is placed in a driver, usually supplied by the database's manufacturer, and developers can access the database through a simple, object-based interface.

The sample code and projects in this chapter are based on the Pubs sample database that ships with SQL Server 7.

NOTE   This section shows you how to create a new data source using ODBC 3.5. If you are using a different version, your steps will vary.

Before you can connect ADO to your Visual Basic application, you must create a data source. If you do not already have one, follow these steps to create a data source for the Pubs database using the ODBC Data Source Administrator:

1. Choose Start ➤ Settings ➤ Control Panel to open the Control Panel.

2. Double-click the ODBC32 icon to open the ODBC Data Source Administrator dialog box:

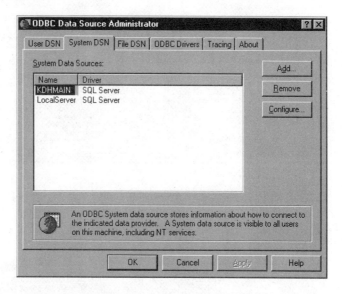

3. Select the System DSN tab, and then click the Add button to open the Create New Data Source dialog box:

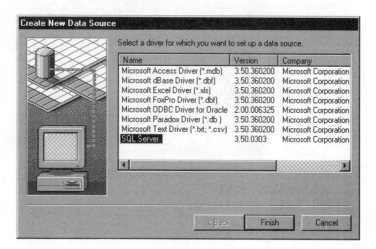

4. Select SQL Server, and then click Finish to open the Create a New Data Source to SQL Server dialog box:

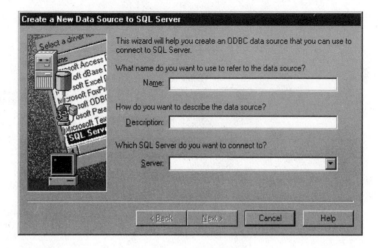

5. In the Name box, enter **Pubs,** and in the Description box, enter **Pubs Test.** From the Server drop-down list box, select the server where the Pubs database is located, and click Next to open the next screen:

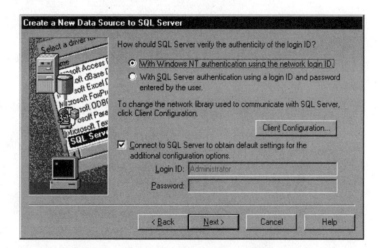

This screen gathers login and connection information. The *How should SQL Server verify the authenticity of the login ID?* section tells the data source how to verify the login ID and password.

6. If you want to use your NT login, select the *With Windows NT authentication using the network login ID* option. If you want to enter a login ID and password for the server, select the *With SQL Server authentication using a login ID and password entered by the user* option.

Clicking the Client Configuration button launches the SQL Client Configuration utility. If you specified a new name in the Server box on the first screen of the ODBC Data Source Administrator, you may need to create an Advanced entry in the SQL Client Configuration utility. To do so, select the Advanced tab. The name you specify for the Advanced entry must match the name in the Server box on the first screen of the ODBC Data Source Administrator.

7. Check the *Connect to SQL Server to obtain default settings for the additional configuration options* checkbox to tell the SQL Server driver to obtain initial settings from the SQL Server for the options on the following screens of the Wizard. The SQL Server driver connects to the SQL Server named in the Server box on the first screen. If you do not select this option, the driver uses standard defaults as the initial settings for the options on the following screens.

8. Enter a login ID and password. This only applies to the connection made to determine the server default settings; it does not apply to subsequent connections made using the data source after it has been created.

9. Click the Next button to open the next screen, in which you select a database and set options for stored procedures, quoted identifiers, and nulls:

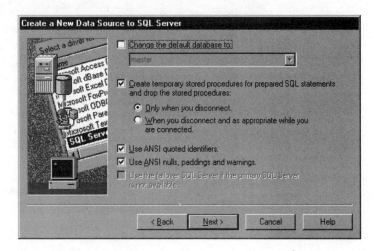

10. Click the *Change the default database to* checkbox and select Pubs from the list of available databases.

11. Check the *Create temporary stored procedures for prepared SQL statements and drop the stored procedures* checkbox. This tells the SQL Server driver to create temporary stored procedures to support the SQLPrepare ODBC function.

12. Check the *Only when you disconnect* checkbox to specify that SQL Server should drop temporary stored procedures created for SQLPrepare when the SQLDisconnect ODBC function is called. This allows the driver to reuse stored procedures and not delete them while the application is running.

13. For our test, accept the default settings *Use ANSI quoted identifiers* and *Use ANSI nulls, paddings, and warnings.* These options specify that QUOTED_IDENTIFIERS be set to On when the SQL Server ODBC driver connects and that the ANSI_NULLS, ANSI_WARNINGS, and ANSI_PADDINGS be set to On when the SQL Server driver connects.

14. Click the Next button to continue and display the screen that allows you to choose a language, define character-set translation, and display regional settings:

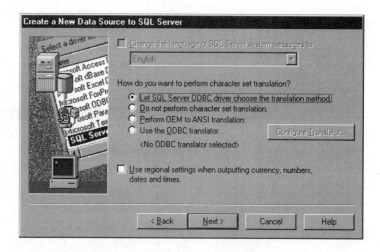

15. If your server is set up with multiple languages, select the language from the drop-down list box.

16. Accept the default choice *Let SQL Server ODBC driver choose the translation method.* This tells the SQL Server driver to automatically configure itself for any needed character-set translations when a connection is made.

17. Leave the *Use regional settings when outputting currency, numbers, dates, and times* checkbox unchecked. Select this option for applications that only display data, not for applications that process data. This specifies that the driver use the regional settings of the client computer for formatting currency, numbers, dates, and times in character output strings.

18. Click the Next button to display the screen that allows you to save query and statistical information to log files:

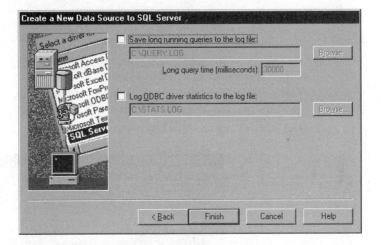

19. The *Save long running queries to the log file* checkbox notifies the driver to log any query that takes longer than the Long Query Time value. We will not run any long queries for our samples, so accept the unchecked default for this checkbox.

20. The *Log ODBC driver statistics to the log file* checkbox specifies that statistics be logged. Accept the unchecked default.

21. Click the Finish button to display the ODBC summary screen, which recaps your choices and gives you an opportunity to test the new data source connection.

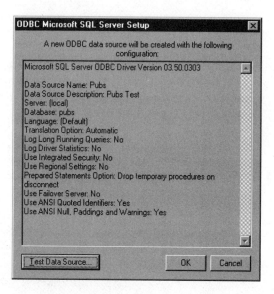

22. Click the Test Data Source button to test the connection. SQL Server will attempt to connect to the database using the options you set. You will see the SQL Server ODBC Data Source Test screen:

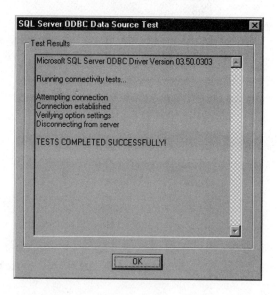

If all went as planned, you will see the message "Tests Completed Successfully."

23. Click OK to close the SQL Server ODBC Data Source Test screen.

24. Click OK to close the Microsoft SQL Server Setup screen. You will see the ODBC Data Source Administrator dialog box.

25. Click OK to close the ODBC Data Source Administrator dialog box and save the new Pubs data source.

Whew! Now that the steps for creating a data source have been completed, let's take a look at the Remote Data Control.

The ADO Data Control

We first discussed the ADO Data control (ADODC) in Chapter 1. The ADO Data control binds data-aware controls to an ODBC remote database. You can perform most remote data access operations using the ADODC without writing any code at all. Data-aware controls bound to an ADODC control automatically display data from one or more columns for the current row. The ADODC automatically handles a number of contingencies, including the following:

- Managing empty recordsets
- Adding new rows
- Editing and updating existing rows
- Converting and displaying complex data types
- Handling some types of errors

Adding the ADO Data Control Component to Your Project

To use the ADODC in an application, you must first add the Microsoft ADO Data Control component to your project. Follow these steps:

1. Choose Project ➤ Components to open the Components dialog box.

2. Choose the Microsoft ADO Data Control 6.0 component from the list of available components.

3. Click the OK button to close the dialog box and add the ADODC to your project.

Now that you have a test data source and the ADODC added to your Toolbox, let's look at the process used for making the actual connection.

Connecting the ADODC

At this point, you have a Visual Basic project, a data source, and an ADODC, but they are not connected to one another. The ADODC provides a ConnectionString property that can be set at design time or at run time to connect the ADODC to a data source.

To set the ConnectionString at design time you can use the Property Pages of the ADO Data control.

You could use the following ConnectionString string for an ADODC for the Pubs data source:

```
Provider=MSDASQL.1;Persist Security Info=False;Data Source=Pubs
```

This string uses SQL Server as the provider and Pubs as the data source. Notice that the parameters are separated by a semicolon. Table 4.2 details the arguments of the ConnectionString property of the ADODC.

TABLE 4.2:   The ADODC ConnectionString

Argument	Description
Provider=	The name of a provider to use for the connection
Data Source=	The name of a data source for the connection
User ID=	A valid user name to use when opening the connection
Password=	A valid password to use when opening the connection
File Name=	The name of a provider-specific file containing preset connection information
Remote Provider=	The name of a provider to use when opening a client-side connection
Remote Server=	The path name of the server to use when opening a client-side connection

After the ConnectionString property is set and you open the Connection object, the contents of the property may be altered by the provider.

The ConnectionString property automatically inherits the value used for the *ConnectionString* argument of the Open method, so you can override the current ConnectionString property during the Open method call.

You cannot pass both the *Provider* and *File Name* arguments because the *File Name* argument causes ADO to load the associated provider.

The ConnectionString property is read-only when the connection is open and read/write when the connection is closed.

In addition to the ConnectionString property, you also must supply a SQL string to populate the ADODC. This can be any valid SQL string, such as:

```
SELECT * FROM authors
```

As do all tools and components, the ADODC has its pros and cons. The ADODC is a great tool if you need to display data from different tables, because you do not have to know the data type. It is also a good choice for conversion programs in which you need to convert data from one table to another, since it is designed to display and update data as it is stored in a database. However, if you need to manipulate the data, perform calculations, or base decisions on the data, the ADODC might not be the best choice. And, building a complete application with the ADODC and bound controls would not be a good idea, as you would likely find yourself fighting with the ADODC instead of taking advantage of its strong points.

Remember, the ADODC is a great tool; however, it is not an application.

NOTE   Chapter 5 includes a complete project built around the ADODC, and Chapter 6 includes projects that employ the ADODC and several bound controls.

Using ADO Objects

As we have discussed earlier, ActiveX Data Objects (ADO) enables you to write a client application to access and manipulate data in a data source through a provider. ADO's primary benefits are:

- Ease of use

- High speed

- Low memory overhead

- A small disk footprint

Adding a Reference to ActiveX Data Objects

To use the ActiveX Data Objects in an application, you must first add a reference to the ADO object library in the References dialog box. Follow these steps:

1. Choose Project ➤ Project Properties to open the References dialog box.

2. Check the Microsoft ActiveX Data Objects 2.0 Library checkbox.

You can now open the Object Browser to look at the objects exposed by the ADO and their members.

The ADO consists of objects and collections that form a framework for manipulating components of a remote ODBC database system. The relationships among objects and collections represent the logical structure of the database system.

Accessing a database through the ADO object model is a straightforward process. First, you create a connection. Once you establish a connection and open the database (which is usually a data source), you can execute SQL statements and stored procedures against the database and process the results of your query. With the Recordset object's methods and properties, you can access the qualified records, edit them (if the type of the Recordset permits editing), and save them back to the database. In the following section, we will discuss these steps and the objects involved in greater detail.

Establishing a Connection

An ADO connection object, shown in Figure 4.2, represents an open connection to a data source.

To establish a connection to a data source with ADO, declare a Connection variable with the following code:

```
Dim cnn As New ADODB.Connection
```

After you have established the connection, you must open the connection. The following code sample can be used to open an ADO connection:

```
'Open ADO connection
strCnn = "DSN=PubsTest;UID=sa;PWD=pwd;"
Set cnn1 = New ADODB.Connection
cnn1.Open strCnn
```

Alternately, you can perform the entire connection opening in one step, as demonstrated in the following code:

```
cnn1.Open "Authors", UserID, Password, Options
```

FIGURE 4.2:

ADO connection object

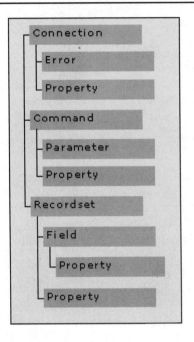

After a connection has been established, you are ready to query a database by executing SQL statements. This process is discussed in the next section.

Executing SQL Statements

After a connection has been established, you can execute SQL statements on the open data source. ADO is a flexible and powerful vehicle for executing SQL statements to read, update, select, and delete records from a data source.

Using ADO, there are two basic ways to execute queries:

- The Execute method of the Command object
- The Execute method of the Connection object

Executing Queries with the Command Object

The Execute Method of the Command object executes the query, SQL statement, or stored procedure specified in the CommandText property. The syntax of this type of Execute statement is as follows:

```
Set recordset = command.Execute( RecordsAffected, Parameters, Options )
```

Table 4.3 defines the parts of the Command Execute statement.

TABLE 4.3: Parts of the Command Execute Statement

Part	Meaning
RecordsAffected	An optional parameter that returns the number of records that were affected by the Execute statement.
Parameters	An optional parameter that contains a Variant array of parameter values passed with a SQL statement.
Options	An optional Long value that indicates how the provider should evaluate the CommandText property of the Command object.

The possible values for the CommandText parameter are listed in Table 4.4

TABLE 4.4: Possible CommandText Values

Value	Description
adCmdText	Informs the provider to evaluate CommandText as a textual definition of a command, such as a SQL statement.
adCmdTable	Informs the provider to evaluate CommandText as a table name.
adCmdStoredProc	Informs the provider to evaluate CommandText as a stored procedure.
adCmdUnknown	Informs the provider that the type of command in CommandText is not known.

The example shown in Code 4.1 employs the Execute method of a Command object to execute a SQL statement.

Code 4.1   **Execute Method of a Command Object**

```
Cnn1.ActiveConnection = ConnectionString
Cnn1.CommandText = "SELECT * FROM Authors"
Cnn1.Execute
```

NOTE

The Execute Method of the Command Object is used in the ADO Stored Procedure project later in this chapter.

Executing Queries with the Connection Object

The Execute Method of the Connection object executes the specified query, SQL statement, stored procedure, or provider-specific text. This method actually employs two types of executions: one for a non-row returning command string, and one for a row returning command string.

Non-Row Returning Command Strings   The syntax for the Execute statement with a Connection object for a non-row returning command string is as follows:

```
connection.Execute CommandText, RecordsAffected, Options
```

Table 4.5 defines the parts of the Connection Execute statement.

TABLE 4.5: Parts of the Connection Execute Statement

Part	Description
CommandText	A required string expression containing the SQL statement, table name, stored procedure, or provider-specific text to execute
RecordsAffected	An optional Long variable to which the provider returns the number of records that the operation affected
Options	An optional value that indicates how the provider should evaluate the Command-Text argument. The possible values for the Options are detailed in Table 4.6

Table 4.6 details the possible values for the Options parameter of the Connection Object Execute method.

TABLE 4.6: Values for the Options Parameter

Value	Description
adCmdText	Informs the provider to evaluate *CommandText* as a textual definition of a command such as a SQL Statement.
adCmdTable	Informs the provider to evaluate *CommandText* as a table name.
adCmdStoredProc	Informs the provider to evaluate *CommandText* as a stored procedure.
adCmdUnknown	Informs the provider that the type of command in the *CommandText* argument is not known.

The Execute method of a Connection object is used to execute a SQL statement in the following example, as shown in Code 4.2.

Code 4.2   Execute Method of a Connection Object

```
Ssql = "SELECT * FROM Authors"
cnn1.Execute ssql, slRecordsAffected
```

NOTE   The Execute Method of the Connection object is used in the New and Update sections of the ADO Project later in this chapter.

Row Returning Command Strings   The Open method of the Recordset object opens a recordset from the specified query, SQL statement, stored procedure, or provider-specific text. The syntax for the Open statement is as follows:

```
recordset.Open Source, ActiveConnection, CursorType, LockType, Options
```

The parts of the Open statement syntax are outlined in Table 4.7.

TABLE 4.7: Parts of the Open Statement

Part	Description
Source	A required Variant that evaluates to a table name or a SQL statement.
ActiveConnection	An optional Variant that evaluates to a string containing a definition for a connection.
CursorType	An optional value that defines a type of cursor for the recordset. Cursor types are examined later in this chapter.
LockType	An optional LockTypeEnum value that determines what type of locking the provider should use when opening the recordset. Lock types are discussed later in this chapter.
Options	An optional CommandTypeEnum value that indicates how the Source argument should be evaluated by the provider.

Code 4.3 presents an example of opening a recordset with ADO:

Code 4.3	**Opening a Recordset**

```
rstAuthors.Open ssql, strCnn, adOpenKeyset, adLockOptimistic, adCmdText
```

NOTE   The Open Method of the Connection Object is used in the RefreshResultset subroutine of the ADO Project later in this chapter.

Identifying ADO Cursor Types

The information in a recordset is returned in a cursor. A cursor is ADO's representation of a set of records from a table, view, or stored procedure. When you use the Open method to return the results of a query, SQL statement, or stored procedure in a Recordset object, ADO sees these rows of data as a cursor.

ADO uses the CursorType property to specify the type of cursor that should be used when opening the Recordset object. Table 4.8 lists the CursorTypeEnum values available in ADO.

TABLE 4.8: Cursor Types Available in ADO

Value	Description
adOpenForwardOnly	A forward-only cursor is the default cursor in ADO and is identical to a static cursor, except that you can only scroll forward through records. Performance is improved with this type of cursor when you need to make only a single pass through a recordset.
adOpenKeyset	A keyset cursor is similar to a dynamic cursor, except for the fact that you cannot see records that other users add. Data changes by other users are still visible.
adOpenDynamic	With a dynamic cursor, additions, changes, and deletions by other users are visible and all types of movement through the recordset are allowed, except for bookmarks if the provider doesn't support them.
adOpenStatic	A static cursor provides a static copy of a set of records that you can use to find data or generate reports. Additions, changes, or deletions performed by other users are not visible.

Examining ADO's Locking Mechanisms

The LockType property in ADO indicates the type of locks placed on records during editing. You should set the LockType property before opening a recordset to specify what type of locking the provider should use when opening it. You can also read the LockType property to determine the type of locking in use on an open Recordset object. The LockType property is read/write when the recordset is closed and read-only when it is open.

Providers may not support all lock types. If a provider cannot support the requested LockType setting, it will substitute another type of locking. The values for the LockType property are detailed in Table 4.9.

TABLE 4.9: LockType Property Values

Value	Description
adLockReadOnly	The default LockType. With this LockType, the data is read-only.
adLockPessimistic	Provides for pessimistic record by record locking. With this option, the provider does what is necessary to ensure successful editing of the records. This is usually achieved by locking records at the data source immediately upon editing.
adLockOptimistic	Sets optimistic record by record locking. Records are locked by the provider only when you call the Update method.
adLockBatchOptimistic	Provides optimistic batch updates. This option locks records for batch update mode, as opposed to immediate update mode.

Manipulating the Recordset Object

The results of a query performed with ADO Recordset object methods are returned in a Recordset object that consists of rows (records) and columns (fields).

To navigate among the rows of the recordset, you can use the Move navigation methods (MoveFirst, MoveLast, MoveNext, and MovePrevious), bookmarks, and the AbsolutePosition property, which determines the absolute row number of a Recordset object's current row. Forward-only Recordset objects can be scanned forward only (using the methods MoveNext and MoveLast).

The number of rows in the Recordset object can be determined by the Row-Count property. Unlike the rowcount property in RDO and DAO, you do not have to access all of the records for the RowCount property to provide the number of records.

You can use the following code to make the first record the current record in a Recordset:

```
'Move to the first record
cnn1.MoveFirst
```

To process the current record, you need to access its fields. To do so, use the ADO Fields collection, which contains one Field object for each column. The total number of fields in the query is given by the property Recordset.Fields.Count. To access each field, use the Fields collection with an index value or the name of the field you want to access. To access all the fields of the Recordset, set up a loop such as the following:

```
For i = 0 To rstRecordset.Fields.Count - 1
    Debug.Print rstRecordset.Fields(i)
Next
```

TIP   Use the Object Browser to find a list of the ADO column object's properties.

In the next section, we will create a sample project that uses the PubsTest data source and ADO to access and manipulate the Authors table of the Pubs sample database.

The AdoObject Project

The AdoObject project (shown in Figure 4.3) uses ADO to access and manipulate the records in the Authors table. The project consists of one Form with the fields from the Authors table, a scrollbar that can be used to navigate among the records, and three Command buttons:

- Clicking the New button adds new records.
- Clicking the Update button updates record changes.
- Clicking the Delete button deletes records.

NOTE   You will find the AdoObject project in the **Ch4\AdoObject** folder on the CD that comes with this book.

FIGURE 4.3:

The AdoObject project

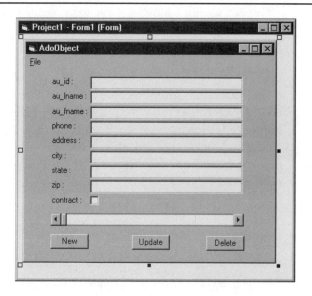

NOTE   The major reason that a Recordset is not updatable with ODBC is that the table does not have a unique nonnull index. When you build your tables, be sure to define a nonnull unique index field.

To load the first record and refresh the recordset after updates, the Refresh-Resultset subroutine is called, as shown in Code 4.4.

Code 4.4   Refreshing the Resultset

```
Public Sub RefreshResultset()
    On Error Resume Next

    'Declare variables
    Dim ssql As String
    Dim strCnn As String
    Dim strID As String
    Dim i

    'Open a connection
    Set cnn1 = New ADODB.Connection
    strCnn = "driver={SQL Server};server=kdhmain333;" & _
```

```
                "uid=sa;pwd=;database=pubs"
          cnn1.Open strCnn

      'Use client cursor to enable AbsolutePosition property
      rstAuthors.CursorLocation = adUseClient

      'Build the SQL statement
      ssql = "SELECT * FROM Authors ORDER BY au_id"

      'Open a recordset
      Set rstAuthors = New ADODB.Recordset
      rstAuthors.CursorType = adOpenKeyset
      rstAuthors.LockType = adLockOptimistic
      rstAuthors.Open ssql, cnn1, , , adCmdText

      'Check for End of File
      If rstAuthors.EOF = True Then
          MsgBox "No records found"
          Exit Sub
      Else
          'No errors
          'Clear all except ID
          For i = 0 To 7
              txtFields(i) = ""
          Next
          chkFields(8) = 1

          'Fill results
          For i = 0 To 7
              txtFields(i) = rstAuthors.Fields(i)
          Next
          If rstAuthors.Fields(8) = True Then
              chkFields(8).Value = 1
          Else
              chkFields(8).Value = 0
          End If

      End If

      dataChanged = False

  End Sub
```

As you can see in this code, several things happen. First, an ADO connection is created, then a client-side cursor is selected to allow for the use of the Absolute-Position property. In the next step, the SQL statement is defined, and the recordset is opened with the Connection object method. Notice the use of the adOpenKeyset type of cursor. This assures that, if the recordset is supported, it will be updatable. The fields are loaded with the value from the ADO Fields property. The fields on the Form are actually a control array of text boxes indexed from 1 to 7. This matches the ADO Fields index, except for the checkbox control for the contract field which is set after the text fields. Finally, the *dataChanged* variable that holds whether a change has been made is reset to False.

The ScrollBar control allows you to move from record to record, as demonstrated in Code 4.5.

Code 4.5   **Moving from Record to Record with the ScrollBar Control**

```
Private Sub HScroll1_Change()
    Dim i
    If dataChanged Then
    Dim reply
        reply = MsgBox("Save changes?", vbYesNo)
        If reply = vbYes Then
            Call UpdateRecord
        End If
    End If
    dataChanged = False
    Call adoMove(HScroll1.Value)
End Sub
```

First, the dataChanged flag is checked. If it is True, a message box is displayed asking if you want to save your changes. If you reply by clicking Yes, the record is saved, and the new record is displayed.

Records are updated in the UpdateRecord subroutine. This subroutine is called from the ScrollBar click event if you move to a new record without saving your changes or if you click the Update button. An interesting aspect of the Update code is how it deals with fields that contain quote marks, such as in O'Leary. If you attempt to execute the update method on a field with a single quote in it, SQL Server will return an error. You cannot have unclosed quotes in a SQL string. To get around this problem, the function CheckForQuote is called with the value from the fields. If an embedded quote is found, a second quote is added to the value: O'Leary becomes O''Leary. SQL Server will then store "O'Leary" as the value for the string. Later in this chapter, you will see how parameter queries deal with this problem.

Let's take a closer look at the process of updating a record. The code required to perform an update to the Authors table is explored in Code 4.6.

Code 4.6   Updating a Record

```
Public Sub UpdateRecord()
    On Error Resume Next

    'Declare variables
    Dim ssql As String
    Dim strCnn As String
    Dim cmdChange As ADODB.Command
    Dim errLoop As ADODB.Error
    Dim slRecordsAffected As Long
    Dim er As Object

    'Clear extraneous errors from the Errors collection
    cnn1.Errors.Clear

    'Build the SQL statement
    'The Function CheckForQuotes checks for a single
    'quote in the field and replaces it with two quotes
    ssql = "UPDATE Authors SET " _
    & "au_lname = '" & CheckForQuote(txtFields(1)) & " '," _
    & "au_fname = '" & CheckForQuote(txtFields(2)) & " '," _
    & "phone = '" & CheckForQuote(txtFields(3)) & "'," _
    & "address = '" & CheckForQuote(txtFields(4)) & "'," _
    & "city = '" & CheckForQuote(txtFields(5)) & "'," _
    & "state = '" & CheckForQuote(txtFields(6)) & "'," _
    & "Zip = '" & CheckForQuote(txtFields(7)) & "'," _
    & "contract = " & chkFields(8).Value & "" _
    & "WHERE au_id = '" & txtFields(0) & "' "

    'Use the Connection object's execute method to
    'execute SQL statement to update the record
    'return the number of records affected into the
    'variable slRecordsAffected
```

```
cnn1.Execute ssql, slRecordsAffected

'Check for errors
If cnn1.Errors.Count > 0 Then
    For Each errLoop In cnn1.Errors
        Debug.Print "Error # : " & errLoop.Number & vbCr & _
        errLoop.Description
    Next errLoop
End If

'Requery to get the latest file
rstAuthors.Requery

'Reset the dataChanged flag
dataChanged = False

End Sub
```

This code clears the ADODB Error object and builds the SQL statement incorporating the CheckForQuote function. The record is updated by calling the Execute method, and if there are no errors, the recordset is refreshed and the Form is filled in with the newly updated record.

As mentioned earlier, the CheckForQuotes function is used to add a second quote to data items that have a single quote. The procedure for accomplishing this is demonstrated in Code 4.7.

Code 4.7   **Checking for Embedded Quotes**

```
Public Function CheckForQuote(str As String)
    Dim slPos1
    slPos1 = InStr(1, str, "'")
    If slPos1 > 0 Then
        CheckForQuote = Mid(str, 1, slPos1) & "'" & _
        Mid(str, slPos1 + 1, Len(str) - slPos1)
    Else
        CheckForQuote = str
    End If
End Function
```

In this code sample, a value is passed in, such as O'Leary. If a quote character is located in the string, a second quote is added, changing O'Leary to O''Leary. This is what SQL Server expects to see, and it will treat it as a text string.

Let's start the AdoObject project and give it a try.

Testing the AdoObject Project

Press F5 to start the AdoObject, as shown in Figure 4.4, and follow these steps to test the project:

1. Click the right arrow on the scrollbar to move to the next record.

2. Click the left arrow on the scrollbar to move to the previous record.

3. Change the state field to TX, and click the right arrow on the scrollbar. Notice that a message box is displayed asking you if the change should be saved. Choose Yes to save the changes.

4. Change the Zip field to 77444, and click the Update button. This will save the changes.

5. Enter new values in the fields, and click the New button to add a new record.

6. Click the Delete button to delete the current record. You will be prompted to confirm your delete request.

Now that you have a good working knowledge of ADO, let's take a look at the ADO and stored procedures.

FIGURE 4.4:

Running the AdoObject project

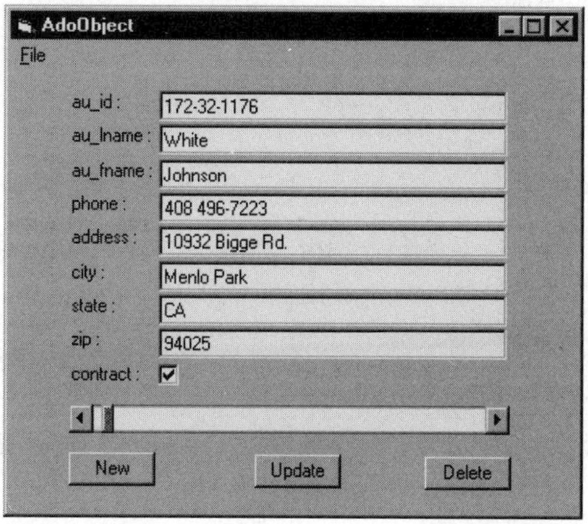

Executing Stored Procedures

The SQL statements executed most frequently on a database should be attached to the database itself as stored procedures. Stored procedures execute faster than SQL statements submitted at run time, and you can make them quite flexible by means of arguments. Essentially, they are small, powerful programs. That is why they are called stored procedures rather than stored SQL statements.

Executing a stored procedure is very similar to executing a query, except the stored procedure exists in the database as an object even after execution is finished. A stored procedure can also be used to hide the complex SQL statements from the application.

To execute a stored procedure with ADO, you use the Command object. When executing stored procedure in a Command object, the adCmdStoredProc value must be specified in the CommandType property. This will cause the corresponding SQL statement for the underlying provider to be generated. With the ODBC provider, the ODBC escape sequences for procedure calls, {[?=]call procedure-name[([parameter][,[parameter]]...)]}, are generated and the SQL Server ODBC driver is optimized to take advantage of these sequences.

Code 4.8 demonstrates this process by calling the sp_who stored procedure.

Code 4.8   **Calling the sp_who Stored Procedure**

```
Dim Cmd As New ADODB.Command
Dim rs As New ADODB.Recordset
Cmd.ActiveConnection = "DSN=pubs;uid=sa"
Cmd.CommandText = "sp_who"
Cmd.CommandType = adCmdStoredProc
Set rs = Cmd.Execute()
Debug.Print rs(0); rs(1); rs(2)
rs.Close
```

This is a simple stored procedure that does not accept any arguments. Stored procedures are usually called with parameters, whose values are supplied by the application. In the next section, we will examine the CreateParameter method used by ADO to create and store parameter values.

Examining the CreateParameter Method

If a stored procedure expects parameters, they must be supplied by using the CreateParameter method in ADO.

The CreateParameter Method in ADO applies to the Command object and creates a new Parameter object with the specified properties. The CreateParameter syntax is as follows:

```
Set parameter = command.CreateParameter (Name, Type, Direction, Size, _
Value)
```

Table 4.10 details the parts of the CreateParameter method.

TABLE 4.10: Parts of the CreateParameter Method Syntax

Part	Description
Name	An optional string that represents the name of the Parameter object.
Type	An optional Long value that specifies the data type of the Parameter object.
Direction	An optional Long value that specifies the type of Parameter object.
Size	An optional Long value specifying the maximum length for the parameter value in characters or bytes.
Value, varValue	An optional Variant value specifying the value for the Parameter object.

You can use the following code to create a parameter with the CreateParameter method for the byRoyalty stored procedure:

```
Set prmByRoyalty = cmdByRoyalty.CreateParameter("percentage", _
adInteger, adParamInput)
```

Notice that this code names the parameter, states the type of value, and states that it is an input type of parameter.

The CreateParameter method does not automatically append the Parameter object to the Parameters collection of a Command object, so you can set additional properties, whose values ADO will validate when you append the Parameter object to the collection. To append the parameter to the Parameter Object, you must use the Append Method, as discussed in the next section.

Appending a Parameter

You use the ADO Append Method to append an object to a collection. In the case of a parameter for a stored procedure, you are appending the parameter to the Parameters object.

The syntax for the Append method is:

```
collection.Append object
```

Collection is the name of the collection. Object is an object variable representing the object to be appended. In the previous example, you could use the following code to append the percentage parameter to the parameters collection:

```
cmdByRoyalty.Parameters.Append prmByRoyalty
```

This code names the collection and appends the prmByRoyalty parameter to it.

In the next section, we will look at the AdoStoredProcedure project and see the byRoyalty stored procedure in action.

The AdoStoredProcedure Project

The AdoStoredProcedure project (shown in Figure 4.5) calls and displays the results of the byRoyalty stored procedure that is included with the Pubs sample database. The project consists of one Form with an MSFlexGrid control and a Command button. The Command button displays an input box that you can use to supply the Percentage parameter required by the stored procedure and then runs the byRoyalty stored procedure.

NOTE   You will find the AdoStoredProcedure project in the `Ch4\AdoStoredProcedure` folder on the CD that comes with this book.

Examining the BYROYALTY Stored Procedure

The byRoyalty stored procedure, shown in Code 4.9, displays the author ID numbers for all authors that have their Royaltyper field equal to the value you enter in the input box.

FIGURE 4.5:

The AdoStoredProcedure
project

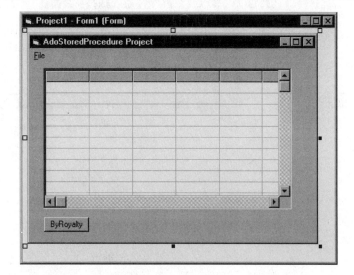

| Code 4.9 | **The byRoyalty Stored Procedure** |

```
CREATE PROCEDURE byroyalty @percentage int
AS
select au_id from titleauthor
where titleauthor.royaltyper = @percentage
```

As you can see, this is a simple stored procedure. The SQL statement selects all au_id fields from the Titleauthor table where the Royaltyper field is equal to the percentage parameter.

The AdoStoredProcedure Project Code

The code in the AdoStoredProcedure project is straightforward. An ADO connection is made, the byRoyalty stored procedure is called, and the results are displayed in the MSFlexGrid.

In the next section, we will call the byRoyalty stored procedure and fill the grid with the results.

Calling the Stored Procedure and Filling the Grid

The byRoyalty button's code on the Form creates the SQL statement and displays an InputBox for you to enter a test percent. ADO objects are then created with the results of the stored procedure, as shown in Code 4.10.

Code 4.10	Calling the byRoyalty Stored Procedure

```
Private Sub cmdRunSP_Click()

    On Error GoTo DisplayDataError

    Dim cnn1 As ADODB.Connection
    Dim cmdByRoyalty As ADODB.Command
    Dim prmByRoyalty As ADODB.Parameter
    Dim rstByRoyalty As ADODB.Recordset
    Dim rstAuthors As ADODB.Recordset
    Dim intRoyalty As Integer
    Dim strAuthorID As String
    Dim strCnn As String
    Dim cl As rdoColumn
    Dim MaxLen As Integer
    Dim Rows As Variant
    Dim i, j, slRow

    'Setup the Grid
    Grid.Cols = 2
    Grid.Row = 0

    'Setup the au_id column
    Grid.Col = 0
    Grid = "au_id"
    Grid.ColWidth(0) = 1100

    'Setup the name column
    Grid.Col = 1
    Grid = "Full Name"
    Grid.ColWidth(1) = 2500

    'Open the ADO connection
    Set cnn1 = New ADODB.Connection
    strCnn = "driver={SQL Server};server=kdhmain333;" & _
```

```
        "uid=sa;pwd=;database=pubs"
        cnn1.Open strCnn
        cnn1.CursorLocation = adUseClient
'Open a command object with one parameter
Set cmdByRoyalty = New ADODB.Command
cmdByRoyalty.CommandText = "byroyalty"
cmdByRoyalty.CommandType = adCmdStoredProc

'Get parameter value and append parameter
intRoyalty = Trim(InputBox("Enter royalty:"))
Set prmByRoyalty = _
    cmdByRoyalty.CreateParameter("percentage", _
    adInteger, adParamInput)
    cmdByRoyalty.Parameters.Append prmByRoyalty
prmByRoyalty.Value = intRoyalty

'Create recordset by executing the command
Set cmdByRoyalty.ActiveConnection = cnn1
Set rstByRoyalty = cmdByRoyalty.Execute

'Open the Authors table to get author names
Set rstAuthors = New ADODB.Recordset
rstAuthors.Open "authors", cnn1, , , adCmdTable

'Set the number of Grid rows
Grid.Rows = rstByRoyalty.RecordCount + 1

'Loop through the records and add to the grid
Do While Not rstByRoyalty.EOF
    slRow = slRow + 1
    strAuthorID = rstByRoyalty!au_id
    Debug.Print "    " & rstByRoyalty!au_id & ", ";
    rstAuthors.Filter = "au_id = '" & strAuthorID & "'"

    'Populate the Grid
    With Grid
        .Row = slRow
        .Col = 0 'au_id
        .Text = "" & rstByRoyalty.Fields(0)
        .Col = 1 'name
        .Text = "" & rstAuthors.Fields(2) _
        & " " & rstAuthors.Fields(1)
```

```
        End With
        rstByRoyalty.MoveNext
    Loop
    'Clean up
    rstByRoyalty.Close
    rstAuthors.Close
    cnn1.Close

    Exit Sub

DisplayDataError:
    MsgBox "Could not display data: " & Err.Description
    Exit Sub

End Sub
```

The previous code uses a Command object to create the BYROYALTY and Authors recordsets based on the percentage parameter that the user enters. After the recordsets are created, the records are displayed on the MSFlexGrid. The code that displays the records on the grid is fairly straightforward. First, it scans the recordset's rows one at a time. For each row, it displays the column values for the au_id from the rstByRoyalty recordset and then, using the Filter method, displays the authors' names from the rstAuthors recordset in consecutive rows on the grid.

Now, with everything in place, let's test the AdoStoredProcedure project.

Testing the AdoStoredProcedure Project

Press F5 to start the project, as shown in Figure 4.6, and follow these steps to test the project:

1. Click the byRoyalty button to start the BYROYALTY stored procedure code.

2. Enter the value **40** in the input box, and click the OK button. The BYROYALTY stored procedure will display all author ID numbers that match the criteria.

Up to this point, we have looked at applications and samples that process one query or action at a time. In the next section, we will discuss how ADO uses transactions that enable you to run two or more action queries, and to cancel or roll back a query if an error occurs.

FIGURE 4.6:

Running the AdoStored-
Procedure project

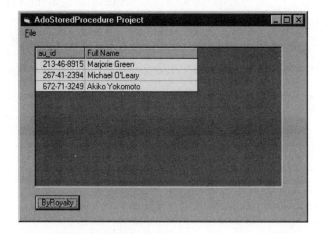

Using Transactions with ADO

So far in this chapter, we have discussed actions that affect only one record or table in one database. However, it is very probable that, at some time, you will need to update multiple records in multiple tables, and for this task, you use transactions.

A *transaction* is a recoverable set of changes that you make to a recordset. You use transactions when you want to verify changes before they are committed to the database. If you decide the changes are correct, you can commit them, but if you find that something went wrong, you can undo the changes. This is called *transaction processing*.

For example, an Inventory application supports the creation of new purchase orders. The process involves adding data to two separate tables:

- The Header table stores the header data, such as the purchase order number, company name, and purchase order date.

- The Detail table holds the detail records for each part that is ordered.

In the update process, you first add a record to the Header table, and then add the detail records to the Detail table for each part that you want to order. This all works well until something happens in one of the updates.

For example, let's say that the update to the Header record works as expected, but an error occurs while adding one of the Detail records. Now you have a problem. The Header record is already in the database, but the Detail record is not. You could simply rerun the operation to add the Detail record, but that would also again add the Header record. This looks like a job for transaction processing.

When you first open a database and no transactions are pending, the transaction state is *auto-commit*. This means that all changes to the database happen immediately and cannot be reversed. When this action is not desirable, you can use transactions to control the timing of your changes.

Visual Basic includes three statements that control transaction processing within a Connection Object:

- BeginTrans
- CommitTrans
- RollbackTrans

When you use transactions, they apply to all open databases, even databases that are opened after the transaction begins. The CommitTrans and RollbackTrans statements affect all pending transactions, regardless of the database.

Beginning a Transaction

The BeginTrans statement marks the beginning of a transaction and takes the next sequence of operations out of auto-commit mode. Once you begin a transaction, you must commit the transactions with the CommitTrans statement or roll them back with the RollbackTrans statement before you close the database or end the program. If you attempt to close a database that has uncommitted transactions, an error will occur. All uncommitted transactions are automatically rolled back when your program ends.

Committing Changes

The CommitTrans statement saves all recordset changes made since the transaction was opened with the BeginTrans statement. The CommitTrans statement saves all changes, ends the transaction, and returns the database state to auto-commit.

Undoing Changes

Calling the RollbackTrans statement reverses all the changes in the current transaction, ends the transaction, and returns the state to auto-commit.

A Transaction Example

The following example, shown in Code 4.11, demonstrates the process of using transactions to update two tables. If an error occurs in either operation, the transaction is reversed with the RollbackTrans statement. It is assumed that a connection called cnn1 is active to a data source.

Code 4.11	Creating a Transaction

```
On Error Resume Next
Dim cnn1 As ADODB.Connection
Dim rstTitles As ADODB.Recordset
Dim strCnn As String
Dim strTitle As String
Dim strMessage As String
Dim errLoop As ADODB.Error
Dim ssql As String

' Open connection.
strCnn = "Provider=sqloledb;" & _
"Data Source=srv;Initial Catalog=pubs;User Id=sa;Password=; "
Set cnn1 = New ADODB.Connection
cnn1.Open strCnn

'Clear extraneous errors from the Errors collection
cnn1.Errors.Clear

'Begin the transaction
cnn1.BeginTrans

'Build the SQL statement
ssql = "INSERT INTO Header VALUES " _
    & "(145, 'Acme Inc.', '11/01/1997')"

'Use the Connection object's execute method to
'execute SQL statement to update the record
'return the number of records affected into the
```

```
'variable slRecordsAffected
cnn1.Execute ssql, slRecordsAffected

'Check for errors
If cnn1.Errors.Count > 0 Then
    'Notify the user of the error
    MsgBox " An error has occurred in the Header update"
    For Each errLoop In cnn1.Errors
        MsgBox "Error # : " & errLoop.Number & vbCr & _
        errLoop.Description
    Next
    'Roll back the transaction
    rdoConn.RollbackTrans
    Exit Sub
End If

'If no errors, create the detail record
'Build the SQL statement
ssql = "INSERT INTO Detail VALUES " _
    & "(150, 'Case', 'CA1397')"

'Use the Connection object's execute method to
'execute SQL statement to update the record
'return the number of records affected into the
'variable slRecordsAffected
cnn1.Execute ssql, slRecordsAffected

'Check for errors
If cnn1.Errors.Count > 0 Then
    'Notify the user of the error
    MsgBox " An error has occurred in the Detail update"
    For Each errLoop In cnn1.Errors
        MsgBox "Error # : " & errLoop.Number & vbCr & _
        errLoop.Description
    Next
    'Roll back the transaction
    rdoConn.RollbackTrans
    Exit Sub
End If

'No errors, so commit the records
rdoConn.CommitTrans
```

This code is a good example of transaction processing. After the adoErrors are cleared out, the SQL statement is built to add the Header record and is executed with the Execute Method. Next, we check for errors. If an error is found, we undo the transaction with the RollbackTrans statement. If no errors are found, we build the SQL statement for the Detail record and execute it. Again, we check for errors. If we find some, we must undo the transactions with the RollbackTrans statement. If all goes as planned, we commit the new records with the CommitTrans statement.

Think of transaction processing as a safety net that can save you from making incorrect changes to your database.

CHAPTER
FIVE

Advanced SQL Examples

■ Reviewing SQL basics

■ Using the SQLControl project

■ Using SQL statements

■ Creating JOINs

■ Using SQL's built-in functions

■ Changing data with SQL

5

Structured Query Language (SQL) enables you to communicate with a relational database to define, query, modify, and control the data. With SQL syntax, you can construct a statement that extracts records according to the criteria you specify.

SQL has quickly become the standard relational database language. It is a declarative fourth-generation language that requires you to tell the database management system what you want as opposed to how you want it. SQL is important to the Visual Basic developer because it is the primary means of communication between Visual Basic and the SQL Server Database Engine.

SQL is a published American National Standards Institute (ANSI) standard. Most of the examples in this chapter are geared toward Microsoft's SQL Server 7; however, SQL as a language is not database specific. Therefore, the code we use here will work with almost all database engines that support ANSI-standard SQL.

The SQL language is used in client-server, file-server, and stand-alone environments. Since it is a set-oriented language, it delivers data as a set of records; how the records are used is up to the application. For example, to access all the addresses in Texas from your Customer table, you would request the following:

```
SELECT * FROM Customer WHERE State = 'TX'
```

This request returns only the records in Texas and not the entire Customer table. This set could then be listed, reported, or altered as needed by your application.

SQL programming is extremely flexible and powerful and allows you to do a lot more than construct queries that retrieve data. You can also use SQL to do the following:

- Create, administer, and maintain databases
- Create and maintain tables
- Insert new data
- Update and delete existing data

In this chapter, we'll take a look at SQL from the Visual Basic developer's point of view.

A Refresher Course in SQL

Although this chapter deals with advanced SQL, we thought it would be helpful to take a brief look at some SQL basics. The SQL language is vast and contains hundreds of statements; however, most of them stem from the following few basic statements:

SELECT identifies which tables and columns in the data source are to be used.

ORDER BY applies a sort order to the recordset.

INSERT adds new records to a recordset.

DELETE deletes records from a recordset.

UPDATE modifies the fields of a record.

WHERE applies a filter that narrows the selection and is used in almost all SQL statements.

These statements are versatile, and you can use them to access and manipulate data in a database, or you can expand and combine them to create a flexible and powerful SQL data manipulation tool. First, let's review these statements in their basic form. Later in the chapter, we will unlock their power to create, access, and maintain SQL Server data.

NOTE   Most of the examples in this chapter refer to the Pubs database, which is created when you install SQL Server 7. To run the examples in this chapter, you must have access to the Pubs database. If it is not installed on your server or if it has been altered, you can run the Instpubs.sql script in the Install subdirectory of SQL Server once it is installed. Although these examples and the SQLControl project demonstrated later in this chapter were created with SQL Server 7, they will also work just fine with SQL Server 6.5.

Coding a SQL SELECT Statement

The most frequently used SQL statement, the SELECT statement, is extremely versatile, and you can use it to retrieve data, compute totals, and create new tables. To use the SELECT statement, you must know what you want to select and where it is located. The syntax for a general SELECT statement is:

```
SELECT [ALL] select list FROM table name WHERE clause ORDER BY sort list
```

NOTE

By convention, SQL keywords are coded in uppercase; however, this is not required. SQL statements are not case-sensitive. In this book we place keywords in uppercase for clarity and to distinguish them from regular code.

Table 5.1 lists the parts of the SELECT statement.

TABLE 5.1: The Parts of the SELECT Statement

Part	Description
ALL	Retrieves all rows in the results. ALL is the default.
select_list	Specifies the columns to select. The select_list can be an asterisk (*), representing all columns in the table; a list of column names, specified in the order in which you want to see them; a column name and column heading that will replace the default column heading; an expression; the IDENTITYCOL keyword instead of the name of a column that has the IDENTITY property; a local variable assignment; or a local or global variable.
FROM	Indicates the specific table(s) and view(s) for the SELECT statement.
WHERE clause	Specifies the restricting conditions for the rows returned in the resultset. There is no limit to the number of conditions that can be included in a SQL statement.
ORDER BY	Sorts the results by columns.

Sample SELECT Statement   To obtain a list of all the first and last names of the authors in the Authors table from the Pubs database sorted by last name, use the following SELECT statement:

```
SELECT au_fname, au_lname FROM authors ORDER BY au_lname
```

NOTE

If you want data presented in a specific order when returned in a query, you use the ORDER BY keyword. The ORDER BY keyword determines how SQL Server collates and presents data in response to database queries. It also determines how certain queries are resolved, such as those involving WHERE and DISTINCT.

Coding a SQL INSERT Statement

You use the SQL INSERT statement to add a new row of data to a recordset. Its general syntax is:

```
INSERT INTO table name VALUES
```

Table 5.2 lists the parts of the INSERT statement:

TABLE 5.2: The Parts of the INSERT Statement

Part	Description
table name	The name of the table in which to insert data.
VALUES	The values to insert into each column in the table.

Sample INSERT Statement   To insert a new row in the Authors table in the Pubs database, use the following statement:

```
INSERT INTO authors VALUES
('555-67-8910','Martin','Robert', '408 555-9657', '15415 Main St.', _
'Bay Shore', 'TX', '77003', 1)
```

Notice that the test strings are enclosed in single quotes and the numeric values are not. This is a SQL rule. All text strings and date fields must be enclosed in single quotes.

Coding a SQL DELETE Statement

You use the SQL DELETE statement to remove rows from a recordset. Use DELETE alone to delete all rows, or use DELETE with a WHERE clause to limit the rows deleted. The general syntax of the DELETE statement is:

```
DELETE [FROM] table name [WHERE clause]
```

Table 5.3 lists the parts of the DELETE statement.

TABLE 5.3: The Parts of the DELETE Statement

Part	Description
table name	The name of the table from which to delete row(s).
WHERE	Conditions to limit the row(s) to delete.

Sample DELETE Statement   To use the DELETE statement to delete the test row that was added in the previous section, use the following code:

```
DELETE FROM authors WHERE au_id = '555-67-8910'
```

Coding a SQL UPDATE Statement

You use the SQL UPDATE statement to change data in existing rows, either by adding new data or by modifying existing data. The general syntax is:

```
UPDATE table name SET column name = new value WHERE clause
```

Table 5.4 lists the parts of the UPDATE statement.

TABLE 5.4: The Parts of the UPDATE Statement

Part	Description
table name	The name of the table to be used in the UPDATE statement.
column name	The name of the column in which the data will be changed.
WHERE	An optional WHERE clause used to limit the rows updated.

Sample UPDATE Statement   To update the phone number of an author in the Authors table from the Pubs database, use the following code:

```
UPDATE authors SET phone = '418 496-7223'
WHERE au_id = '172-32-1176'
```

Understanding SQL Server 7 Data Types

Data types specify the data characteristics of columns, stored-procedure parameters, and local variables. It is important to know the data type of the data you are working with so that you can properly code the SQL statements.

Data types in SQL Server come in two varieties:

- System-supplied
- User-defined

Data types are categorized by the type of data stored within the data type. For example, in a column is the data:

- in the form of text that is to be displayed?
- numbers that are to be added?
- dates that are to be set?

SQL Server assigns a data type to every column in every database. In addition to system-supplied data types, SQL Server allows user-defined data types, which are based on the system data types. Table 5.5 lists the data types supplied for SQL Server 7.

TABLE 5.5: The SQL Server 7 Data Types

Data type	Description
BINARY	Holds as many as 8,000 bytes of fixed-length binary data.
BIT	Holds either 1 or 0. Integer values other than 1 or 0 are accepted but are always interpreted as 1.
CHAR	Holds a character string of fixed-string length up to 8,000 characters. A good data type choice when data in columns will be consistently close to the same size.
DATETIME	Stores date and time in 8 bytes of two 4-byte integers: 4 bytes for the number of days before or after the base date of January 1, 1900, and 4 bytes for the number of milliseconds after midnight. If no value is entered, the default is January 1, 1900.
DECIMAL	Stores numbers as 96-bit (12-byte) unsigned integers scaled by a variable power of 10.
FLOAT	Stores a 4-byte floating point number.
IMAGE	A variable-length data type that can hold as many as 2^{31}, or 1 (2,147,483,647) bytes of binary data.
INT	A data type that holds whole numbers from -2^{31} (-2,147,483,648) through $2^{31} - 1$ (2,147,483,647). Storage size is 4 bytes.
MONEY	Stores monetary values from -922,337,203,685,477.5808 through +922,337,203,685,477.5807, with accuracy to a ten-thousandth of a monetary unit.
NCHAR	Fixed-length Unicode data with a maximum length of 4,000 characters.
NVARCHAR	Variable-length Unicode data with a maximum length of 4,000 characters. sysname is a system-supplied user-defined data type that is a synonym for nvarchar(128) and is used to reference database object names.

Continued on next page

TABLE 5.5 CONTINUED: The SQL Server 7 Data Types

Data type	Description
NTEXT	Variable-length Unicode data with a maximum length of 2^30 - 1 (1,073,741,823) characters.
NUMERIC	Stores numbers as 96-bit (12-byte) unsigned integers scaled by a variable power of 10.
REAL	Stores a floating-point column that has 7-digit precision.
SMALLDATETIME	Stores a date and time data type that is less precise than datetime.
SMALLINT	Holds whole numbers from -2^{15} (-32,768) through 2^{15} - 1 (32,767). Storage size is 2 bytes.
SMALLMONEY	Stores monetary values from - 214,748.3648 through +214,748.3647, with accuracy to a ten-thousandth of a monetary unit.
TEXT	A variable-length data type that can hold as many as 2^{31} - 1 (2,147,483,647) characters.
TIMESTAMP	Is automatically updated every time a row containing a `timestamp` column is inserted or updated. Values in `timestamp` columns are not `datetime` data, but `binary`(8) `varbinary`(8) data, indicating the sequence of SQL Server activity on the row.
TINYINT	Holds whole numbers from 0 through 255. Storage size is 1 byte.
VARBINARY	A variable-length `binary` data type that holds a maximum of 8,000 bytes of variable-length binary data.
VARCHAR	Holds a maximum of 8,000 characters. A good data type choice when you expect null values or a wide variation in the length of the stored data.

Using Character Strings and Quotes

Character strings and dates (*char, varchar,* and *datetime* data types) must be enclosed in single quote marks when you search for them, as in the following:

```
SELECT * FROM authors WHERE au_fname = 'Cheryl'
```

You must use two consecutive single quote marks to specify a single apostrophe within a character entry, as in the following:

```
SELECT * FROM authors WHERE au_lname = 'O''Leary'
```

Arithmetic Operators

Operators are symbols used to perform mathematical computations or comparisons on numeric columns. You can compare columns with like data types without any data conversion. Table 5.6 lists the arithmetic operators used in SQL statements:

TABLE 5.6: Arithmetic Operators

Symbol	Operation
+	Addition
/	Division
*	Multiplication
%	Modula
-	Subtraction

You can use arithmetic operators that perform addition, division, multiplication, and subtraction on any column with a numeric data type (DECIMAL, FLOAT, INT, MONEY, NUMERIC, SMALLINT, SMALLMONEY, or TINYINT). You cannot use the modula operator with money data types.

> **NOTE**   A *modula* is the remainder after the division of two integers. For example, 5 % 2 = 1 because 5 divided by 2 equals 2 with a remainder of 1.

Operator Precedence

Operator precedence becomes an issue when multiplying values. It determines the order of computations or comparisons. Operator precedence is based on the following levels:

- Primary grouping: ( )
- Bitwise: ~
- Multiplication: * / %
- Additive: + −

- Bitwise: ^

- Bitwise: &

- Bitwise: |

- NOT

- AND

- OR

The precedence order is from left to right when all operators in a given expression are at the same level. You can change the order of precedence by using parentheses, in which case the most deeply nested expression is evaluated first. Often, the order in which an expression is evaluated can make a difference in the result.

Comparison Operators in SQL Statements

Comparison operators contrast the difference between two expressions and can only be used between variables and columns of similar data types. Table 5.7 lists the valid comparison operators.

TABLE 5.7: The Valid Comparison Operators

Symbol	Meaning
=	Equal to
>	Greater than
<	Less than
>=	Greater than or equal to
<=	Less than or equal to
<>	Not equal

Keywords Used in a WHERE Clause

The SQL language contains many keywords that can be used in a WHERE clause to limit the records selected. Table 5.8 lists them.

TABLE 5.8: Keywords That Can Be Used in a WHERE Clause

Keyword	Use
ANY	Tests for any values.
ALL	Tests for all values.
AND	Tests for multiple conditions.
OR	Tests for one of two conditions.
BETWEEN	Tests for values between two values.
EXISTS	Tests for values that exist.
NOT EXISTS	Tests for values that do not exist.
NOT BETWEEN	Tests for values not between two values.
IN	Tests for values in a range of values.
NOT IN	Tests for values not in a range of values.
LIKE	Tests for values that are like a value.
NOT LIKE	Tests for values that are not like a value.
IS NULL	Tests for null values.
IS NOT NULL	Tests for values that are not null.

Using Wildcards and the LIKE Keyword

You use the LIKE keyword to select rows containing fields that match a specified portion of a character string. LIKE can be used with CHAR, VARCHAR, DATE-TIME, SMALLDATETIME, and TEXT data types. The LIKE keyword takes one of four wildcard characters, as shown in Table 5.9.

TABLE 5.9: SQL Wildcards

Wildcard	Meaning
-	Any single character.
%	Any string of zero or more characters.
[]	Any single character within a specified range ([a-c]) or in a set ([abc]).
[^]	Any single character not in a specified range ([^a-c]) or in a set ([^abc]).

The wildcard and character string must be enclosed in single quotes when it is part of a SQL statement. Here are some examples:

- LIKE '_heryl' searches for six-letter words ending in the letters *heryl,* such as Cheryl and Sheryl.

- LIKE 'St%' searches for values that begin with *St,* such as Start, Started, and Stop.

- LIKE '%ob%' searches for all words that contain *ob,* such as Robert and Robbery.

- LIKE '[CS]eryl' searches for Cheryl or Sheryl.

- LIKE 'C[^o]' searches for words that start with the letter *C* and do not have the letter *o* in the second position, such as Carpet.

Well, that's a brief review, and now it's time to explore the real power of the SQL language. In the next section, we will take a look at the SQLControl project. The remainder of this chapter is devoted to some really hard-core SQL.

The SQLControl Project

We'll use the SQLControl project, shown in Figure 5.1, as a reference point for the main SQL examples in this chapter. It can also serve as a tool with which you can construct and run SQL statements.

NOTE   You'll find the SQLControl project in the Ch5\sqlcontrol folder on the CD that comes with this book.

The SQLControl project has a Windows Explorer–style tree on the left side that has four main branches:

Statements, which are the SQL example SELECT statements

Functions, which hold the sample aggregate, date, mathematical, niladic, string, system, and text and image functions

JOINs, which create queries by joining two or more tables on common columns

Actions, such as SELECT, DELETE, and UPDATE

FIGURE 5.1:

The SQLControl application

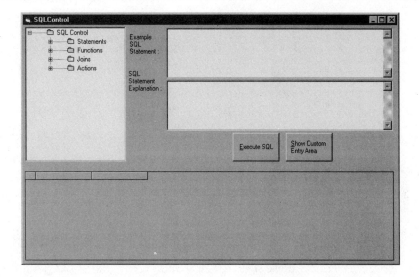

The right side of the SQLControl Form has two text boxes:

- The Example SQL Statement text box displays the example SQL statement for the selected statement.

- The SQL Statement Explanation text box pulls double duty: It provides a description of the current SQL example statement, and it serves as a place for you to enter a SQL statement to be executed.

Below the SQL text box are two Command Buttons:

Execute SQL allows you to execute the current SQL statement.

Show Custom Entry Area allows you to toggle between displaying the current SQL statement and an empty text box in which you can construct a custom SQL statement of your own.

Rounding out the Form is the Results Grid at the bottom. This grid displays the results of the current SQL statement—either the text statement or a custom SQL statement that you enter.

Loading the SQLControl Project

The SQLControl project relies on a SQL Server database. Follow these steps to create and populate the SQLControl database:

1. Choose Start ➤ Programs ➤ Microsoft SQL Server 7 ➤ SQL Enterprise Manager to open the SQL Enterprise Manager.

2. Select the server you want to hold the SQLControl database.

3. Choose Tools ➤ SQL Query Tool to display the Query Tool screen.

4. Choose File ➤ Open and select the `instsqlc.sql` file from the `Ch5Code` subdirectory on the book's CD. This SQL code will create and populate the SQLControl database.

5. Choose Query ➤ Execute or press Ctrl+E to execute the `instsqlc` code.

6. After this code executes, the database is created and populated.

NOTE   See Chapter 3 if you need a refresher in using the SQL Enterprise Manager.

Taking the SQLControl Project for a Test Drive

Follow these steps to select and execute the SELECT statement example:

1. Press F5 to start the project. You should see the SQLControl Form, as shown in Figure 5.1.

2. Click the plus (+) sign next to the STATEMENTS folder.

3. Click the Execute SQL Command Button to populate the text boxes and the Syntax Grid with the SQL statement syntax. The Results Grid will display the results of the example SQL statement, as shown in Figure 5.2.

FIGURE 5.2:

The SQLControl application displaying results

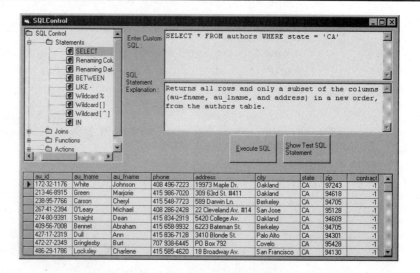

Testing a Custom SQL Statement

As mentioned earlier, the SQLControl Form has a dual role: It presents information about the sample SQL statements in this chapter, and it allows you to enter and execute custom SQL statements. Follow these steps to enter and execute a custom SQL statement:

1. If the SQLControl project is not already running, press F5 to start it. You should see the SQLControl Form, as shown in Figure 5.1 earlier in this chapter.

2. Click the Show Custom Entry Area Command Button.

3. Enter the following SQL statement into the Custom SQL Area:

   ```
   SELECT * FROM authors WHERE state = 'CA'
   ```

4. Click the Execute SQL Command Button or press Alt+E to execute the statement. The Results Grid will display the results (a list of authors residing in California), as shown in Figure 5.3.

FIGURE 5.3:

The results of a custom SQL statement

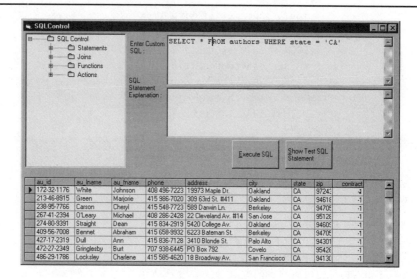

NOTE   The SQLControl application is not designed to execute custom Action queries.

This example demonstrates the ease of use, versatility, and power of the SQL-Control project. The examples in the rest of this chapter are stored in the project. In the next section, we will take a look at some advanced SQL statements that deal with retrieving, presenting, and editing data with queries.

Using SQL Statements

In this section, we will take a look at some advanced SQL statements. For the purposes of this chapter, SQL statements will be considered statements that retrieve, present, and edit data.

Coding the SELECT Statement

In the earlier section "A Refresher Course in SQL," you saw a general SELECT statement. The full syntax of the SELECT statement is:

```
SELECT [ ALL | DISTINCT ]
[ TOP n [PERCENT] [ WITH TIES] ] <select_list>
[ INTO new_table ]
[ FROM <table_sources> ]
[ WHERE <search_conditions> ]
[ [ GROUP BY [ALL] group_by_expression [,…n]]
[HAVING <search_conditions> ]
[ WITH { CUBE | ROLLUP } ]
]
[ ORDER BY { column_name [ ASC | DESC ] } [,…n] ]
[ COMPUTE
{ { AVG | COUNT | MAX | MIN | SUM } (expression) } [,…n]
[ BY expression [,…n]
]
[ FOR BROWSE ]
[ OPTION (<query_hints>) ]
<select_list> :: =
{ [ { <table_or_view> | table_alias }.]*
| { column_name | expression | IDENTITYCOL | ROWGUIDCOL }
[ [AS] column_alias ]
| new_column_name = IDENTITY(data_type, seed, increment)
| GROUPING (column_name)
| { table_name | table_alias}.RANK
| column_alias = expression
```

```
| expression column_name
} [,...n]
<table_sources> :: =
{ <table_or_view>
| (select_statement) [AS] table_alias [ (column_alias [,...m]) ]
| <table_or_view> CROSS JOIN <table_or_view>
| <table_or_view>
{ { INNER
| { FULL | LEFT | RIGHT }
[ OUTER ] [ <join_hints> ] [ JOIN ]
} <table_or_view> ON <join_condition>
}
| <rowset_function>
}
[,...n]
<table_or_view> :: =
{ table_name [ [AS] table_alias ] [ WITH (<table_hints> [...n]) ]
| view_name [ [AS] table_alias ]
}
<table_hints> ::=
{ INDEX(index_name | index_id [,...n])
| FASTFIRSTROW
| HOLDLOCK
| NOLOCK
| PAGLOCK
| READCOMMITTED
| READPAST
| READUNCOMMITTED
| REPEATABLEREAD
| ROWLOCK
| SERIALIZABLE
| TABLOCK
| TABLOCKX
| UPDLOCK
}
<join_hints> ::=
{ HASH | LOOP | MERGE }
<query_hints> :: =
{ { HASH | ORDER } GROUP
| { CONCAT | HASH | MERGE } UNION
| FAST number_rows
| FORCE ORDER
| MAXDOP number
```

```
| ROBUST PLAN
}
<join_condition> :: =
{ table_name | table_alias | view_name }.column_name
<logical_operator>
{ table_name | table_alias | view_name }.column_name
<logical_operator>:: =
{ = | > | < | >= | <= | <> | != | !< | !> }
<rowset_function> :: =
{ CONTAINSTABLE [ [ AS] table_alias]
( table, { column | *}, '<contains_search_condition>'
)
| FREETEXTTABLE [ [ AS] table_alias]
( table, {column | * }, 'freetext_string'
)
| OPENQUERY (linked_server, 'query')
| OPENROWSET
( 'provider_name',
{
'datasource';'user_id';'password'
| 'provider_string'
},
{
[catalog.][schema.]object_name
| 'query'
}
)
<search_conditions> ::=
{ [ NOT ] <predicate> [ { AND | OR } [ NOT ] <predicate> ]
| CONTAINS
( {column | * }, '<contains_search_condition>'
)
| FREETEXT
(
{column | * }, 'freetext_string'
)
| fulltext_table.fulltext_key_column = fulltext_table.[KEY]
} [,...n]
<predicate> ::=
{
expression { = | <> | != | > | >= | !> | < | <= | !< } expression
| string_expression [NOT] LIKE string_expression
[ESCAPE 'escape_character']
```

```
| expression [NOT] BETWEEN expression AND expression
| expression IS [NOT] NULL
| expression [NOT] IN (subquery | expression [,...n])
| expression { = | <> | != | > | >= | !> | < | <= | !< }
{ALL | SOME | ANY} (subquery)
| EXISTS (subquery)
}
```

Whew! It can be a little overwhelming, but we'll cut it down to size in the following examples.

You must use the clauses in a SELECT statement in the order shown. For example, if you want to list the columns to select, you must do so before you set the sort order with the ORDER BY clause.

You can order a resultset either by the column name as:

```
SELECT * FROM authors ORDER BY au_lname
```

or as:

```
SELECT * FROM Authors ORDER BY 2
```

Both statements return a resultset of the Authors table ordered by the authors' last names. Give this a try in the SQLControl application.

SELECT Statement Examples

The following examples show various options used with the SELECT statement against the Pubs database.

SELECT: All Rows, Subset of Columns   This example returns all rows and only a subset of the columns (au_fname, au_lname, and address) from the Authors table:

```
SELECT au_fname, au_lname, address FROM authors
```

Results - Statements - SELECT

au_fname	au_lname	address
Johnson	White	19973 Maple Dr.
Marjorie	Green	309 63rd St. #411
Cheryl	Carson	589 Darwin Ln.
Michael	O'Leary	22 Cleveland Av. #1
Dean	Straight	5420 College Av.
Meander	Smith	10 Mississippi Dr.
Abraham	Bennet	6223 Bateman St.
Ann	Dull	3410 Blonde St.
Burt	Gringlesby	PO Box 792

SELECT: Renaming Columns   The name given to a column when it is returned in a query is used as the default column heading. Sometimes, as developers, we tend to be cryptic in our naming of objects. If a column holds someone's first name, we might name that column fname. This makes perfect sense to us, but to the user it is just a bunch of letters. As you code SQL statements, you can change the column names to be more user-friendly. You do so by renaming a column's display. For example, the following code renames the authors' first name column from au_fname to Author's First Name and renames the authors' last name column from au_lname to Author's Last Name in the Authors table.

```
SELECT 'Author''s First Name' = au_fname, 'Author''s Last Name' = _
au_lname from authors
```

Author's First Name	Author's Last Name
Johnson	White
Marjorie	Green
Cheryl	Carson
Michael	O'Leary
Dean	Straight
Meander	Smith
Abraham	Bennet
Ann	Dull
Burt	Gringlesby

NOTE   Notice the use of double apostrophes in the code. If you want to use an apostrophe in a character entry in a SQL statement, you must use two single apostrophes.

SELECT: Renaming Data   In addition to renaming column headings, you can rename data in a resultset. The following code uses the CASE statement to rename the types from the Titles table.

```
SELECT Section = CASE type WHEN 'mod_cook' THEN 'Modern Cooking'
WHEN 'trad_cook' THEN 'Traditional Cooking'
END, title = title FROM titles WHERE type LIKE '%cook'
```

Section	title
Modern Cooking	Silicon Valley Gastronomic Treats
Modern Cooking	The Gourmet Microwave
Traditional Cooking	Onions, Leeks, and Garlic: Cooking Secrets of the Mediterranean
Traditional Cooking	Fifty Years in Buckingham Palace Kitchens
Traditional Cooking	Sushi, Anyone?

In this example, whenever a record is encountered with a type equal to 'mod_cook', the type is returned as Modern Cooking, and the type 'trad_cook' is returned as Traditional Cooking. These values will make more sense to users and will certainly look better on a printed report.

SELECT: BETWEEN   You use the keyword BETWEEN to select values between two values. The following example returns the sales from January 1, 1993 and December 31, 1993 from the Sales table:

```
SELECT qty, ord_date FROM sales WHERE ord_date BETWEEN '01/01/93' AND
'12/31/93' ORDER BY ord_date [tech changes]
```

qty	ord_date
35	2/21/93
25	3/11/93
30	5/22/93
50	5/24/93
20	5/29/93
25	5/29/93
15	5/29/93
25	5/29/93
15	10/28/93

When using BETWEEN, the values returned are greater than or equal to the first value, and less than or equal to the second value. In our example, you will get records with an ord_date greater than or equal to "01/01/93" and less than or equal to "12/31/93."

Querying with Wildcards and the LIKE Clause

Wildcards can be very useful in writing SQL queries. If you need to query on a group of records that have one or more characters in common, you can make your coding life easier by incorporating wildcards. Let's take a look at some examples using wildcards with the LIKE clause.

SELECT: LIKE_   You use the LIKE keyword to select rows containing fields that match a specified portion of a character string. The LIKE wildcard "_" replaces any single character in a query. If you want to select all authors with the first name of Cheryl or Sheryl, you can use the LIKE keyword combined with the "_" wildcard as in the following:

```
Select * from authors WHERE au_fname LIKE '_heryl'
```

au_id	au_lname	au_fname	phone	address	city	state	zip	contract
238-95-7766	Carson	Cheryl	415 548-772	589 Darwin Ln.	Berkeley	CA	94705	-1
846-92-7186	Hunter	Sheryl	415 836-712	3410 Blonde St.	Palo Alto	CA	94301	-1

This query returns two records—one for Cheryl and one for Sheryl.

SELECT: Wildcard %   You use the % wildcard to select any string of zero or more characters. Let's say that you want to find a certain employee in the Pubs database, but you can't remember the employee's name. You believe that it starts with either an *A* or an *M* and that the employee was hired in 1993. You could use the following SQL statement to query the Employee table to narrow your search:

```
SELECT * FROM employee WHERE (fname LIKE 'A%' or fname LIKE 'M%') AND
hire_date BETWEEN '01/01/93' AND '12/31/93' ORDER BY lname
```

Results - Statements - Wildcard %

emp_id	fname	minit	lname	job_id	job_lvl	pub_id	hire_date
ARD36773F	Anabela	R	Domingues	8	100	0877	1/27/93
MMS49649F	Mary	M	Saveley	8	175	0736	6/29/93

This query returns only those employees hired in 1993 with a first name that starts with an *A* or an *M*. As you can see, it is easy to combine SQL keywords and clauses to create powerful queries.

SELECT: Wildcard [ ]   You can use the wildcard [ ] with the LIKE clause to search for a range of values—for example, you want to find an author who lives in the 415 area code, but you can remember only that the phone number begins with a 5 or an 8. If you want a range, you use [5-8]; simply add a dash between the low and high values. You can retrieve a list of employees with that pattern in their phone numbers with the following SQL statement:

```
SELECT * FROM authors WHERE phone LIKE '415 [58%]'
```

Results - Statements - Wildcard [ ]

au_id	au_lname	au_fname	phone	address	city	state	zip	contract
238-95-7766	Carson	Cheryl	415 548-7723	589 Darwin Ln.	Berkeley	CA	94705	-1
274-80-9391	Straight	Dean	415 834-2919	5420 College Av.	Oakland	CA	94609	-1
427-17-2319	Dull	Ann	415 836-7128	3410 Blonde St.	Palo Alto	CA	94301	-1
486-29-1786	Locksley	Charlene	415 585-4620	18 Broadway Av.	San Francisco	CA	94130	-1
724-08-9931	Stringer	Dirk	415 843-2991	5420 Telegraph Av.	Oakland	CA	94609	0
756-30-7391	Karsen	Livia	415 534-9219	5720 McAuley St.	Oakland	CA	94609	-1
846-92-7186	Hunter	Sheryl	415 836-7128	3410 Blonde St.	Palo Alto	CA	94301	-1

This query returns records that have 415 in the beginning of the phone field and that have either a 5 or an 8 as the next number.

SELECT: Wildcard [^]   You can use the wildcard [^] with the LIKE clause to search for any single character not specified within a range of values. For example, you would like to find all authors who live in California in the 90000 zip code area, but do not live in the Bay Area. The Bay Area has a 4 in the second space of the zip code. You can query for all zips that start with a 9 and that do not have a 4 in the second space with the following SQL code:

```
SELECT * FROM authors WHERE zip LIKE '9[^4]%'
```

au_id	au_lname	au_fname	phone	address	city	state	zip	contract
172-32-1176	White	Johnson	408 496-7223	19973 Maple Dr.	Oakland	CA	97243	-1
267-41-2394	O'Leary	Michael	408 286-2428	22 Cleveland Av. #14	San Jose	CA	95128	-1
472-27-2349	Gringlesby	Burt	707 938-6445	PO Box 792	Covelo	CA	95428	-1
648-92-1872	Blotchet-Halls	Reginald	503 745-6402	55 Hillsdale Bl.	Corvallis	OR	97330	-1
893-72-1158	McBadden	Heather	707 448-4982	301 Putnam	Vacaville	CA	95688	0

This query will return only those authors from the Authors table who have a zip code that starts with a 9 and that do not have a 4 in the next space.

SELECT: IN   You use the IN keyword to select values that match a list of values. For example, if you want to list authors from the Authors table who live in Berkeley, Nashville, or Oakland, you can use the following statement:

```
SELECT * FROM authors WHERE city = 'Berkeley' OR city = 'Nashville' OR
city = 'Oakland'
```

au_id	au_lname	au_fname	phone	address	city	state	zip	contract
172-32-1176	White	Johnson	408 496-7223	19973 Maple Dr.	Oakland	CA	97243	-1
213-46-8915	Green	Marjorie	415 986-7020	309 63rd St. #411	Oakland	CA	94618	-1
238-95-7766	Carson	Cheryl	415 548-7723	589 Darwin Ln.	Berkeley	CA	94705	-1
274-80-9391	Straight	Dean	415 834-2919	5420 College Av.	Oakland	CA	94609	-1
409-56-7008	Bennet	Abraham	415 658-9932	6223 Bateman St.	Berkeley	CA	94705	-1
527-72-3246	Greene	Morningstar	615 297-2723	22 Graybar House Rd.	Nashville	TN	37215	0
724-08-9931	Stringer	Dirk	415 843-2991	5420 Telegraph Av.	Oakland	CA	94609	0
724-80-9391	MacFeather	Stearns	415 354-7128	44 Upland Hts.	Oakland	CA	94612	-1
756-30-7391	Karsen	Livia	415 534-9219	5720 McAuley St.	Oakland	CA	94609	-1

Or you could use the IN keyword and rewrite the SQL statement as follows:

```
SELECT * FROM authors WHERE city IN ('Berkeley', 'Nashville', 'Oakland')
```

This query returns authors from the Authors table who live in Berkeley, Nashville, or Oakland. The IN keyword is useful if you have a long list. You can save yourself a lot of typing.

The SQL statements we have been looking at thus far have involved only one table. If you need to query data from more than one table, you use the JOIN keyword. In the next section, we will explore the world of SQL JOINS.

Querying Multiple Tables with JOIN

In relational databases, the main theory is that no redundant data should be stored in the database. Simply stated, you would not store the name, address, phone number, and like data for an author in the Titles table. Instead, you would create an identification field in the Authors table and use it in other tables. Then, if you need the author's name from the Titles table, you would join the tables on the identification fields.

In a good database design, referred to as *normalized*, each table stores one type of data—a person, a place, a location, an event, or a thing. JOINs are used to present or select data from multiple tables.

Table 5.10 shows the types of ANSI JOINs that are permitted.

TABLE 5.10: ANSI JOINS

JOIN Type	Description
CROSS JOIN	The cross-product of two tables. Returns the same rows as if no WHERE clause were specified.
INNER	Specifies that all inner rows be returned. Discards unmatched rows.
LEFT OUTER	Specifies that all left outer rows be returned, that all rows from the left table that did not meet the condition specified be included in the resultset, and that output columns from the other table be set to NULL.
RIGHT OUTER	Specifies that all rows from the right table that did not meet the condition specified be included in the resultset and that output columns that correspond to the other table be set to NULL.
FULL OUTER	Specifies that if a row from either table does not match the selection criteria, the row is included in the resultset and its output columns that correspond to the other table be set to NULL.

If you are trying to select columns in different tables with the same name, you must use an alias. An *alias* is a value that uniquely identifies each table. If you are not selecting columns from different tables, you can still use an alias.

In the next sections, we will take a look at each type of JOIN.

NOTE In our examples, NULL fields will display blank; they will not show the word NULL.

Creating a CROSS JOIN

A CROSS JOIN is the cross-product of two tables and returns the same rows as if no WHERE clause were specified.

This example returns the cross-product of the Authors and Publishers tables. A list of all possible combinations of au_lname rows and all pub_name rows are returned. This is a JOIN in its simplest form.

```
SELECT au_lname, pub_name FROM authors CROSS JOIN publishers
```

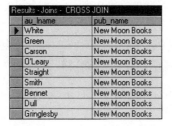

Creating an INNER JOIN

An INNER JOIN specifies that all inner rows be returned, discarding unmatched rows. For example, if you want to query for the titles written by authors Ringer and Green, you INNER JOIN the Authors table with the Titles table.

The Titles table stores the titles, but does not have the authors' names. The Authors table has the authors' names, but does not have the titles. This results in all rows being selected from the Authors table and only rows that match the au_id being selected from the Titles table.

You perform an INNER JOIN on the Authors and Titles tables with the au_id field, as in the following:

```
SELECT authors.au_lname, authors.au_fname, titles.title FROM authors
INNER JOIN titleauthor ON authors.au_id = titleauthor.au_id INNER JOIN
titles ON titleauthor.title_id = titles.title_id WHERE au_lname IN
('Ringer', 'Green') ORDER BY title
```

au_lname	au_fname	title
Ringer	Anne	Is Anger the Enemy?
Ringer	Albert	Is Anger the Enemy?
Ringer	Albert	Life Without Fear
Green	Marjorie	The Busy Executive's Database Guide
Ringer	Anne	The Gourmet Microwave
Green	Marjorie	You Can Combat Computer Stress!

The resulting query returns the first and last names from the Authors table and the titles each has written from the Titles table and then sorts the results by the title.

In the JOINS discussed so far, only matching rows are included in the results. These JOINS eliminate the information in rows that do not match the JOIN criteria.

When you want to retain and display the unmatched rows, you can use an OUTER JOIN. An OUTER JOIN displays all rows from the main table regardless of whether matching data exists in the other table. In the next section, we will explore the ANSI OUTER JOINS.

Creating a LEFT OUTER JOIN

A LEFT OUTER JOIN specifies that all left outer rows be returned, that all rows from the left table that did not meet the condition specified be included in the resultset, and that output columns from the other table be set to NULL.

The following SQL statement selects the order number from the Sales table, the store name from the Stores table, and the title and type from the Titles table. A LEFT OUTER JOIN is performed from the Sales table to the Stores table, returning all rows from the Sales table and setting the store name to NULL if there is not a matching record in the Stores table.

There is also a LEFT OUTER JOIN from the Sales table to the Titles table, returning all rows from the Sales table and setting the values from the Titles table to NULL for any rows that do not match on the title_id. We add a WHERE clause to select only the business and popular_comp type books.

```
SELECT sales.ord_num, stores.stor_name, titles.title, titles.type FROM
sales LEFT OUTER JOIN titles ON sales.title_id = titles.title_id LEFT
OUTER JOIN stores ON sales.stor_id = stores.stor_id WHERE titles.type
IN ('popular_comp', 'business'))
```

Results - Joins - LEFT OUTER JOIN

ord_num	stor_name	title	type
▶ 6871	Eric the Read Books	The Busy Executive's Database Guide	business
423LL930	Bookbeat	The Busy Executive's Database Guide	business
P723	Bookbeat	Cooking with Computers: Surreptitious Balance Sheets	business
X999	Fricative Bookshop	You Can Combat Computer Stress!	business
QQ2299	Fricative Bookshop	Straight Talk About Computers	business
QA879.1	Bookbeat	But Is It User Friendly?	popular_comp
A2976	Barnum's	Secrets of Silicon Valley	popular_comp

NOTE   An easy way to create and test a JOIN is to use the Visual Database Tools for Visual Basic. See Chapter 2 for a discussion of this tool.

The resulting query returns all rows from the Sales table and all rows from the Stores and Titles tables.

NOTE No fields are set to NULL. This means that the LEFT OUTER JOIN found a match for the JOIN fields of sales.title_id to titles.title_id for the first LEFT OUTER JOIN and also found a match for the second LEFT OUTER JOIN from the sales.stor_id to stores.stor_id.

Earlier versions of SQL Server LEFT OUTER JOINS (=*) are supported, as in the following example:

```
SELECT authors.au_lname, titleauthor.title_id
FROM authors, titleauthor
WHERE titleauthor.au_id =* authors.au_id
```

Creating a RIGHT OUTER JOIN

A RIGHT OUTER JOIN specifies that all rows from the right table that did not meet the condition specified are included in the resultset and that output columns that correspond to the other table be set to NULL. A RIGHT OUTER JOIN is useful when you want to see all the data from a given table and match it against the data from a related table.

The following example selects all the publishers from the Publishers table with a pub_id greater than 1300 and, with a RIGHT OUTER JOIN, selects all the titles from the Titles table whether a title exists for the publisher or not. If a publisher does not have a title, the query returns NULL.

```
SELECT publishers.pub_id, titles.title, titles.title_id, publishers.state
FROM titles RIGHT OUTER JOIN publishers ON publishers.pub_id = titles.pub_id
WHERE (publishers.pub_id > '1300')
ORDER BY publishers.pub_id
```

pub_id	title	title_id	state
1389	The Busy Executive's Database Guide	BU1032	CA
1389	Cooking with Computers: Surreptitious Balance Sheets	BU1111	CA
1389	Straight Talk About Computers	BU7832	CA
1389	But Is It User Friendly?	PC1035	CA
1389	Secrets of Silicon Valley	PC8888	CA
1389	Net Etiquette	PC9999	CA
1622			IL
1756			TX
9901			

The resulting query returns all publishers from the Publishers table with a pub_id greater than 1300 and all titles, whether data exists or not, from the Titles table.

Earlier versions of SQL Server RIGHT OUTER JOINS (*=) are supported, as in the following example:

```
Select authors.au_lname, titleauthor.title_id
FROM authors, titleauthor
WHERE authors.au_id *= titleauthor.au_id
```

NOTE   Support for the (*=) JOIN symbols may be dropped in future versions of SQL, so we suggest that you use the ANSI-STYLE JOINS instead. You cannot use both OUTER JOIN operators and ANSI-SQL joined tables in the same query.

Creating a FULL OUTER JOIN

A FULL OUTER JOIN specifies that if a row from either table does not match the selection criteria, the row will be included in the resultset and its output columns that correspond to the other table will be set to NULL.

This example returns the book title and its corresponding publisher in the Titles table for publishers that are not in California or Washington, D.C. It also returns any publishers who have not published books listed in the Titles table and any book titles from a publisher other than the one listed in the Publishers table. The output is sorted by title_id with the ORDER BY clause.

```
SELECT titles.title, publishers.pub_name, publishers.state
FROM publishers FULL OUTER JOIN titles ON titles.pub_id
= publishers.pub_id
WHERE (publishers.state <> 'Ca' AND publishers.state <> 'DC') ORDER BY
titles.title_id
```

Results - Joins - FULL OUTER JOIN		
title	pub_name	state
	Five Lakes Publishing	IL
	Ramona Publishers	TX
	Scootney Books	NY
You Can Combat Computer Stress!	New Moon Books	MA
Is Anger the Enemy?	New Moon Books	MA
Life Without Fear	New Moon Books	MA
Prolonged Data Deprivation: Four Case Studies	New Moon Books	MA
Emotional Security: A New Algorithm	New Moon Books	MA

The resulting query selects all the publishers and all the titles, even if a publisher has not published a book or a book title does not have a publisher.

JOINS make it possible for you to select and view data from multiple tables with ease. Built-in functions are another time-saving feature of the SQL language, whether you want to calculate values, manipulate dates, or perform complex mathematical operations. Functions are a great extension to SQL. In the next section, we will take a look at the role of built-in function extensions.

Using SQL's Built-In Functions

Functions return special information in the form of queries. Functions perform various operations and can be used in a SELECT list, a WHERE clause, or anywhere an expression is allowed. SQL has three types of built-in functions:

Aggregate functions, which operate on a collection of values but return a single, summarizing value.

Rowset functions, which can be used like table references in a SQL statement.

Scalar functions, which operate on a single value and then return a single value.

In the following sections, we will take a closer look at some of the built-in functions.

Returning Summary Values with Aggregate Functions

Aggregate functions return summary values, such as averages, sums, and counts, from all non-null values in a column. They return a single value for each set of rows to which the function applies. You can have multiple function calls in the same query, and each summary value will be in its own column.

You can use aggregate functions with a SELECT clause such as GROUP BY and with a WHERE clause. With a GROUP BY clause, you receive a summary value for each group.

The syntax for aggregate functions is:

```
aggregate_ function ([ALL | DISTINCT] expression)
```

Table 5.11 lists the parts of the aggregate function syntax, and Table 5.12 lists the aggregate functions.

TABLE 5.11: The Parts of the Aggregate Function Syntax

Part	Description
aggregate_function	Specifies an aggregate function as listed in Table 5.12.
ALL	Default. Applies the aggregate function to all values.
DISTINCT	Eliminates duplicate column values before the function is calculated. DISTINCT cannot be used with COUNT(*) and has no meaning in MIN and MAX functions.
expression	The column name or any combination of columns, a constant, or a function.

TABLE 5.12: Aggregate Functions

Aggregate Function	Description
AVG	Calculates the average of all the values or only the DISTINCT values in the expression. AVG can be used with numeric columns only, and null values are ignored.
COUNT	Adds the number of nonnull values in the expression or only the DISTINCT number of unique nonnull values. COUNT can be used with both numeric and character columns, and null values are ignored.
COUNT(*)	Adds the number of rows. No parameters or the DISTINCT keyword can be used, and COUNT(*) includes rows with null values.
MAX	Returns the maximum value in numeric, character, or datetime columns, ignoring any null values. MAX finds the highest value in the collating sequence for character columns. DISTINCT is available, but it is not meaningful with MAX.
MIN	Returns the minimum value in a numeric, character, or datetime column, ignoring any null values. MAX finds the highest value in the collating sequence for character columns. DISTINCT is available, but it is not meaningful with MIN.
SUM	Returns the sum of all the values or only the DISTINCT values in the expression. SUM can only be used with numeric columns and null values are ignored.

In the next sections, we will take a look at some example queries that use the aggregate functions. These examples, like the ones in the previous sections, are available in the SQLControl application under the Functions tree node.

AVG and SUM with GROUP BY Clause The following example calculates the total sales as the SUM of the qty column and the average sales as the AVG of the qty column from the Sales table. The column SUM(qty) is changed to Total Sales, and the column AVG(qty) is changed to Average Sales to be more user-friendly. In addition, the values are grouped and sorted by the stor_id column.

```
SELECT 'Total Sales' = SUM(qty), 'Average Sales' = AVG(qty), stor_id
FROM sales
GROUP BY stor_id ORDER BY 'Total Sales'
```

Results - Functions - AVG and SUM with GROUP BY Clause

Total Sales	Average Sales	stor_id
8	4	6380
60	20	7896
80	20	8042
90	22	7067
125	62	7066
130	21	7131

The query results in three columns—the SUM(qty) column, which is renamed Total Sales, the AVG(qty) column, which is renamed Average Sales, and the stor_id column.

COUNT(*) This example simply returns the number of rows in the Publishers table.

```
SELECT COUNT(*) FROM publishers
```

Results - Functions - COUNT(*)

Column1
8

The result, 8, is the number of publishers in the Publishers table. Null values, if present, are counted.

The remainder of the aggregate functions work the same way. You specify the function name and include the column in parentheses.

In the next sections we will look at scalar functions, beginning with the CONVERT function, which is used to convert one data type to another.

Converting Data Types with the CONVERT Function

The CONVERT function converts an *expression* of one data type to another data type. You can also use it to obtain a variety of special date formats.

SQL Server automatically handles certain data type conversions. You do not need to use the CONVERT functions for the following expressions:

- `char` and `char expressions` of different lengths
- `datetime`
- `smallint`
- `int`

It is never wrong, however, to use the CONVERT function, even when you are comparing two expressions of exactly the same data type.

Here are some general rules to keep in mind when converting data types:

- SQL Server automatically supplies a length of 30 if you do not specify a length for the data type to which the expression is to be converted.

- SQL Server rejects all values it cannot recognize as dates when converting to `datetime` or `smalldatetime`.

- Converting to `bit` changes any nonzero value to 1.

- Integers are assumed to be monetary units when converting to `money` or `smallmoney`.

- Expressions of data types `char` or `varchar` that are being converted to an integer data type must consist only of digits and an optional plus or minus sign. Leading blanks are ignored.

- Expressions of data types `char` or `varchar` that are being converted to `money` can also include an optional decimal point and dollar sign ($).

- Expressions of data types `char` or `varchar` that are being converted to `float` or `real` can also include optional exponential notation (e or E, followed by an optional plus or minus sign and then a number).

- Values that are too long for their new data type are truncated, and SQL Server displays an asterisk (*).

- When converting between data types with a different number of decimal points, the value is truncated.

- You can explicitly convert `text` columns to `char` or `varchar` columns, and you can explicitly convert `image` columns to `binary` or `varbinary` columns, but you are limited to 8,000 characters as the maximum length of the `character` and `binary` data types. If you attempt a conversion that is not possible, SQL Server displays an error message.

The syntax for the CONVERT function is:

```
CONVERT (data type[(length)], expression [, style])
```

The parts of the CONVERT function syntax are listed in Table 5.13.

TABLE 5.13: The Parts of the CONVERT Function Syntax

Part	Description
data type	Any system data type (for example, `char(10)`, `varbinary`, `int` into which the expression is to be converted. User-defined data types cannot be used.
length	An optional parameter with `char`, `varchar`, `binary`, and `varbinary` data types. The maximum allowable length is 8,000.
expression	A column name, a constant, a function, a variable, a subquery, any combination of column names, constants, and functions connected by an operator(s) or a subquery.
style	The style of date representation you want when converting `datetime` or `small-datetime` data to character data.

The following examples demonstrate how to convert data types using the built-in CONVERT function.

CONVERT: Character Data with Select   If you want to perform a string comparison with the LIKE keyword and wildcards, the data type must be of a character type. The following example converts the qty column in the Sales table to `char` so it can be used with LIKE.

```
SELECT stor_id, ord_num, qty FROM sales WHERE CONVERT(char(5), qty) _
LIKE '%25%'
```

Results - Functions - Character Data with Select		
stor_id	ord_num	qty
7131	N914014	25
7131	P3087a	25
7131	P3087a	25
8042	P723	25

This query returns only those records from the Sales table that have 25 in the qty column.

CONVERT: Different Size   When expressions are converted to a data type of a different size, values too long for the new data type are truncated, and SQL Server displays an asterisk (*). In this example, the CONVERT function converts the ytd_sales column in the Sales table to a four-place character string.

```
SELECT title, CONVERT(char(4), ytd_sales) FROM titles
WHERE type like '%cook'
```

title	Column2
Silicon Valley Gastronomic Treats	2032
The Gourmet Microwave	×
Onions, Leeks, and Garlic: Cooking Secrets of the Mediterranean	375
Fifty Years in Buckingham Palace Kitchens	×
Sushi, Anyone?	4095

The results of this query show how SQL Server displays an asterisk (*) for fields that are too long for the converted data type.

In the next section we will look at the date functions in SQL.

Manipulating Datetime Values with Date Functions

Date functions manipulate datetime values by adding to and subtracting from dates and by separating dates into parts. The syntax for the Date functions is:

```
date_function (parameters)
```

You can use the Date functions in the SELECT list or in the WHERE clause of a query. Use the `datetime` data type only for dates after January 1, 1753. When entering datetime values, always enclose them in quotation marks. Store as character data for earlier dates. Table 5.14 lists the parts of the Date function syntax, and Table 5.15 lists the built-in Date functions.

TABLE 5.14: The Parts of the Date Function Syntax

Part	Description
date_function	Specifies the date function as listed in Table 5.15.
parameters	DATEADD, DATEDIFF, DATENAME, and DATEPART

TABLE 5.15: The Built-In Date Functions

Date Function	Description
DATEADD(datepart, number, date)	Produces a date by adding an interval to a specified date resulting in a datetime value equal to the date plus the number of date parts.
DATEDIFF(datepart, date1, date2)	Returns the number of datepart "boundaries" crossed between two specified dates.
DATENAME(datepart, date)	Returns a character string representing the specified date part (datepart) of the specified date (date).
DATEPART(datepart, date)	Returns an integer representing the specified date part (datepart) of the specified date (date).
GETDATE()	Returns the current system date and time in the SQL Server standard internal format for datetime values. GETDATE does not take any parameters.

Table 5.16 provides a list of the valid date parts, abbreviations, and values for the datepart parameter used with the DATEADD, DATEDIFF, DATENAME, and DATEPART functions.

TABLE 5.16: The Datepart Parameters

Date Part	Abbreviation	Values
hour	hh	0–23
minute	mi	0–59
second	ss	0–59
millisecond	ms	0–999
day of year	dy	1–366
day	dd	1–31
week	wk	1–53
weekday	dw	1–7 (Sun.-Sat.)
month	mm	1–12
quarter	qq	1–4
year	yy	1753–9999

NOTE If the year is given with two digits, <50 is the next century, and >=50 is this century. So 25 is 2025, and 50 is 1950.

The datepart weekday, or dw, returns the text of the day of the week (Sunday, Monday, and so on) when used with datename. It returns a corresponding number (Sunday = 1, Saturday = 7) when used with datepart.

Smalldatetime is accurate only to the minute. When a smalldatetime value is used with either datename or datepart, seconds and milliseconds are always 0.

DATEADD and DATEPART   The following example adds one month to the pubdate in the Publishers table with the DATEADD date function and selects only those records with a pubdate greater than 1991. In addition, it sets the new date column heading to Pub Date + 1 Month.

```
SELECT pubdate, 'Pub Date + 1 Month' = dateadd(month, 1, pubdate) FROM
titles WHERE (datepart(year, pubdate) <> 1991)
```

Results - Functions - DATEADD and DATEPART	
pubdate	Pub Date + 1 Month
10/27/97 4:02:08 PM	11/27/97 4:02:08 PM
6/12/94	7/12/94
10/27/97 4:02:08 PM	11/27/97 4:02:08 PM

This query returns two columns: one with the publication date and another with one month added to the publication date for all publication dates not in 1991.

All the Date functions work in the same general way as this example; you state the desired function and provide the parameters.

In the next section, we will explore the mathematical functions provided in SQL.

Performing Mathematical Operations with the Built-In Mathematical Functions

Mathematical functions perform operations on mathematical data. These functions are not keywords. The syntax for mathematical functions is:

```
function_name(parameters)
```

Table 5.17 lists the parts of the mathematical functions syntax, and Table 5.18 lists the built-in mathematical functions.

TABLE 5.17: The Parts of the Mathematical Functions Syntax

Part	Description
function_name	Specifies a mathematical function as listed in Table 5.18.
parameters	The parameters are either numeric_expr, an expression of the decimal, float, int, money, numeric, real, smallint, smallmoney, or tinyint data type or float_expr expressions of the float data type.

TABLE 5.18: The Built-In Mathematical Functions

Function	Parameters	Result
ABS	(numeric_expr)	Absolute value of the numeric expression.
ACOS	(float_expr)	Angle (in radians) whose cosine is the specified approximate numeric (float) expression.
ASIN	(float_expr)	Angle (in radians) whose sine is the specified approximate numeric (float) expression.
ATAN	(float_expr)	Angle (in radians) whose tangent is the specified approximate numeric (float) expression.
ATN2	(float_expr1, float_expr2)	Angle (in radians) whose tangent is (float_expr1/float_expr2) between two approximate numeric (float) expressions.
CEILING	(numeric_expr)	Smallest integer greater than or equal to the numeric expression.
COS	(float_expr)	Trigonometric cosine of the specified angle (in radians) in an approximate numeric (float) expression.
COT	(float_expr)	Trigonometric cotangent of the specified angle (in radians) in an approximate numeric (float) expression.
DEGREES	(numeric_expr)	Degrees converted from radians of the numeric expression.
EXP	(float_expr)	Exponential value of the specified approximate numeric (float) expression.
FLOOR	(numeric_expr)	Largest integer less than or equal to the specified numeric expression.

Continued on next page

TABLE 5.18 CONTINUED: The Built-In Mathematical Functions

Function	Parameters	Result
LOG	`(float_expr)`	Natural logarithm of the specified approximate numeric (`float`) expression.
LOG10	`(float_expr)`	Base-10 logarithm of the specified approximate numeric (`float`) expression.
PI	`( )`	Constant value of 3.141592653589793.
POWER	`(numeric_expr, y)`	Value of numeric expression to the power of y, where y is a numeric data type (`decimal`, `float`, `int`, `money`, `numeric`, `real`, `smallint`, `smallmoney`, or `tinyint`).
RADIANS	`(numeric_expr)`	Radians converted from degrees of the numeric expression.
RAND	`([seed])`	Random approximate numeric (`float`) value between 0 and 1, optionally specifying an integer expression (`tinyint`, `smallint`, or `int`) as the seed.
ROUND	`(numeric_expr, length)`	Numeric expression rounded off to the `length` (or precision) specified as an integer expression (`tinyint`, `smallint`, or `int`).
SIGN	`(numeric_expr)`	Returns the positive (+1), zero (0), or negative (-1) sign of the numeric expression.
SIN	`(float_expr)`	Trigonometric sine of the specified angle (measured in radians) in an approximate numeric (`float`) expression.
SQUARE	`(float_expr)`	Returns the square of the given expression.
SQRT	`(float_expr)`	Square root of the specified approximate numeric (`float`) expression.
TAN	`(float_expr)`	Trigonometric tangent of the specified angle (measured in radians) in an approximate numeric (`float`) expression.

ROUND   This example rounds the number 123.456 to two decimal places.

```
SELECT 'Rounded' = ROUND(123.456, 2)
```

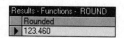

The result of this operation is a column named Rounded with the value 123.460.

SQRT   You can calculate the square root of a number with the SQRT mathematical function. The following example returns the square root of 49:

```
SELECT 'Square Root' = SQRT(49)
```

This query returns one column, Square Root, with a value of 7.

The rest of the mathematical functions perform the same operations as these examples; they specify the mathematical function name and the required parameter(s). In the next section, we will examine the built-in string functions.

Performing Operations with String Functions

String functions perform operations on character strings, binary data, and expressions, and you can use them anywhere an expression is allowed. Most string functions can be used only on char and varchar data types and on data types that implicitly convert to char or varchar.

Concatenation can be used on binary and varbinary columns as well as on char and varchar columns.

String functions can be nested. When you use constants with a string function, enclose them in single quotation marks. The syntax for string functions is:

```
function_name(parameters)
```

Table 5.19 lists the parts of the string function syntax, and Table 5.20 lists the built-in string functions.

TABLE 5.19: The Parts of the String Function Syntax

Part	Description
function_name	The name of a string function as listed in Table 5.20.
parameters	Parameters of char_expr, which are alphanumeric expressions of character data; integer_expt, which is a positive whole number; or float_expr, which is an approximate numeric data type with a decimal point.

TABLE 5.20: The Built-In String Functions

Function	Parameters	Result
+	(expression expression)	Concatenates two character strings, binary strings, column names, or a combination.
ASCII	(char_expr)	Indicates the ASCII code value of the left-most character of an expression.
CHAR	(integer_expr)	Converts a character from an ASCII code that is a value in the range 0 through 255; otherwise, NULL is returned.
CHARINDEX	('pattern', expression)	Returns the starting position of the specified **pattern** in a **char_expr**. The second parameter is an **expression,** usually a column name, in which SQL Server searches for the **pattern.**
DIFFERENCE	(char_expr1, char_expr2)	Shows the difference between the values of two character expressions as returned by the SOUNDEX function. The DIFFERENCE function compares two strings and evaluates the similarity between them, returning a value from 0 through 4, with a 4 signifying the best match indicating that the SOUNDEX values of **char_expr1** and **char_expr2** are identical.
LEFT	character_expression, integer_expression	Returns the number of characters from the left of the specified character string.
LEN	(string_expression)	Returns the number of characters, rather than the number of bytes, of the given string expression, excluding trailing blanks.
LOWER	(char_expr)	Converts uppercase character data to lowercase.
LTRIM	(char_expr)	Removes leading blanks.
NCHAR	(integer_expression)	Returns the Unicode character with the given integer code, as defined by the Unicode standard.
PATINDEX	('%pattern%', expression)	Returns the starting position of the first occurrence of **pattern** in the specified expression or returns zeros if the pattern is not found. You can use wildcard characters in **pattern**, as long as the wildcard character % precedes and follows **pattern** (except when searching for first or last characters).

Continued on next page

TABLE 5.20 CONTINUED: The Built-In String Functions

Function	Parameters	Result
QUOTENAME	(`'character_string'`[, `'quote_character'`])	Returns a Unicode string with the delimiters added to make the input string a valid Microsoft SQL Server delimited identifier.
REPLICATE	(`char_expr, integer_expr`)	Repeats a character expression a specified number of times.
REVERSE	(`char_expr`)	Returns the reverse of `char_expr` in a constant, variable, or column.
RIGHT	(`char_expr, integer_expr`)	Part of a character string starting `integer_expr` characters from the right. If `integer_expr` is negative, a null string is returned.
RTRIM	(`char_expr`)	Removes trailing blanks.
SOUNDEX	(`char_expr`)	Returns a four-digit (SOUNDEX) code to evaluate the similarity of two strings. The SOUNDEX function converts an alpha string to a four-digit code to find similar-sounding words or names.
SPACE	(`integer_expr`)	Returns a string of repeated spaces equal to `integer_expr`. If `integer_expr` is negative, a null string is returned.
STR	(`float_expr` [, `length`[, `decimal`]])	Converts character data from numeric data for a `length` of the total length, including decimal point, sign, digits, and spaces.
STUFF	(`char_expr1, start, length, char_expr2`)	Deletes `length` characters from `char_expr1` at `start` and then inserts `char_expr2` into `char_expr1` at `start`. If the `start` position or the `length` is negative, a null string is returned.
SUBSTRING	(`expression, start, length`)	Returns part of a character or binary string. The first parameter can be a character or binary string, a column name, or an expression that includes a column name. The third parameter specifies the number of characters in the substring.
UNICODE	(`'ncharacter_expression'`)	Returns the integer value, as defined by the Unicode standard, for the first character of the input expression.
UPPER	(`char_expr`)	Converts lowercase character data to uppercase.

String Concatenation   String concatenation is the act of combining two or more string values to make one value. The following example creates one column named Author's Full Name & Address and concatenates the au_fname, au_lname, address, city, state, and zip columns from the Authors table for authors who do not live in California and sorts the list by the author's city:

```
SELECT 'Author''s Full Name & Address' = (au_fname + au_lname + ', ' +
address + ' ' + city + ', ' + state + ' ' + zip) FROM authors WHERE
state <> 'CA' ORDER BY city
```

Results - Functions - String Concatenation
Author's Full Name & Address
Innesdel Castillo, 2286 Cram Pl. #86 Ann Arbor, MI 48105
ReginaldBlotchet-Halls, 55 Hillsdale Bl. Corvallis, OR 97330
MichelDeFrance, 3 Balding Pl. Gary, IN 46403
MeanderSmith, 10 Mississippi Dr. Lawrence, KS 66044
MorningstarGreene, 22 Graybar House Rd. Nashville, TN 37215
SylviaPanteley, 1956 Arlington Pl. Rockville, MD 20853
AnneRinger, 67 Seventh Av. Salt Lake City, UT 84152
AlbertRinger, 67 Seventh Av. Salt Lake City, UT 84152

The result of this query is one column made up of the values from the author's first name, last name, address, city, state, and zip columns from the Authors table.

CHARINDEX   This example uses the CHARINDEX string function to locate the position of the string "cook" from the Type column in the Titles table.

```
SELECT CHARINDEX('cook', type), type FROM titles
```

Results - Functions - CHARINDEX	
Column1	type
0	business
0	business
0	business
0	business
5	mod_cook
5	mod_cook
0	UNDECIDED
0	popular_comp
0	popular_comp

The result is a value representing the location of "cook" in the Type column. A zero is returned if the string is not found.

As you can see, string functions can be a big help in performing all types of operations on character data. In the next section, we take a look at the system functions provided in the SQL language.

Retrieving Special Server or Database Information with System Functions

The syntax for calling system functions is:

```
function_name(parameters)
```

Table 5.21 lists the parts of the system function syntax, and Table 5.22 lists the built-in system functions.

TABLE 5.21: The Parts of the System Function Syntax

Part	Description
function_name	Specifies a function name as listed in Table 5.22.
parameters	The required table name, value, or object.

TABLE 5.22: The Built-In System Functions

System Function	Parameters	Result
@@ERROR	NONE	Returns the error number for the last Transact-SQL statement executed.
@@IDENTITY	NONE	Returns the last-inserted identity value.
@@ROWCOUNT	NONE	Returns the number of rows affected by the last statement.
APP_NAME	()	Returns the program name for the current session if one has been set by the program.
CASE	input_expression WHEN when_expression THEN result_expression [,...n] [ELSE else_result_expression] END	Evaluates a list of conditions and returns one of multiple possible result expressions.
COALESCE	(expression1, expression2, ... expressionN)	Returns the first non-null expression.
COL_LENGTH	('table_name','column_name')	The length of a column.
COL_NAME	(table_id,column_id)	The column's name in the specified table.

Continued on next page

TABLE 5.22 CONTINUED: The Built-In System Functions

System Function	Parameters	Result
CURRENT_TIMESTAMP	NONE	A system function, equivalent to Get-Date(), that returns the current date and time.
CURRENT_USER	NONE	A system function, equivalent to USER_NAME(), that returns the current user.
DATALENGTH	('expression')	The actual length of an **expression** of any data type.
DB_ID	(['database_name'])	The database identification number.
DB_NAME	([database_id])	The database name.
FORMATMESSAGE	(msg_number, param_value[,..n])	Constructs a message from an existing message in sysmessages.
GETANSINULL	(['database_name'])	The default nullability for the database. This function returns 1 when the nullability is the ANSI NULL default.
HOST_ID	( )	The identification number of the workstation.
HOST_NAME	( )	The workstation name.
IDENT_INCR	('table_or_view')	The value that is added to the increment value when a new record is added to the table.
IDENT_SEED	('table_or_view')	The starting number for an identity column.
ISDATE	(expression)	Checks a variable or column with **varchar** data type for valid date format. The function returns 1 when the variable or column contains a valid date; otherwise, it returns 0.
ISNULL	(expression, value)	Replaces NULL entries with the specified value.
ISNUMERIC	(expression)	Returns 1 when the input expression evaluates to a valid integer, floating point number, money or decimal type. Returns 0 otherwise.

Continued on next page

TABLE 5.22 CONTINUED: The Built-In System Functions

System Function	Parameters	Result
NEWID	()	Creates a unique value of type uniqueidentifier.
NULLIF	(expression1, expression2)	The resulting expression is NULL when **expression1** is equivalent to **expression2**.
PARSENAME	('object_name', object_piece)	Returns the specified part of an object name. Parts of an object that can be retrieved are the object name, owner name, database name, and server name.
PERMISSIONS	([objectid [, 'column']])	Returns a value containing a bitmap that indicates the statement, object, or column permissions for the current user.
SESSION_USER	NONE	A niladic function that allows a system-supplied value for the current session's username to be inserted into a table when no default value is specified.
STATS_DATE	(table_id, index_id)	The date that the statistics for the specified index (**index_id**) were last updated.
USER_ID	(['user_name'])	The user's database identification number.
USER_NAME	([user_id])	The user's database username.

HOST_NAME

This system function returns the name of the current workstation. This is an easy way to determine which workstation is currently accessing your application. For example, with this information you can tailor an application to specific user groups—Customer Service, a Help Desk, or clerks. The following example returns the workstation name in a column called Workstation:

```
SELECT 'Workstation' = host_name()
```

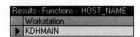

DATALENGTH   This system function returns the length of the data in a column. You supply the column name. This can be a great help if you need to verify whether a text value will fit into a report or print in a given location. You can use the DATALENGTH system function and then loop through the values to make sure they will all fit. The following example returns the length of the data for the address column in the Authors table.

```
SELECT 'Data Length' = DATALENGTH(address), address FROM authors
```

Data Length	address
15	19973 Maple Dr.
17	309 63rd St. #411
14	589 Darwin Ln.
20	22 Cleveland Av. #14
16	5420 College Av.
18	10 Mississippi Dr.
16	6223 Bateman St.
15	3410 Blonde St.
10	PO Box 792

The Data Length column is returned with the length of the data for each author's address and the address.

System functions can be a great help in managing a database, its objects, and the data stored in it. In the next section, which will be our last one on built-in functions in the SQL language, we will discuss the Text and Image functions.

Using Text and Image Functions

The Text and Image functions return commonly needed information about text and image data only. Text and image data are stored in binary format. The syntax for the Text and Image functions is:

```
function_name(parameters)
```

Table 5.23 lists the parts of the Text and Image functions syntax, and Table 5.24 lists the Text and Image functions.

TABLE 5.23: The Parts of the Text and Image Functions Syntax

Part	Description
function_name	The name of the function as listed in Table 5.24.
parameters	A column name or a text pointer.

TABLE 5.24: Text and Image Functions

Function	Parameters	Result
PATINDEX	('%pattern%', expression)	Returns the starting position of the first occurrence of a pattern in a specified expression, or zeros if the pattern is not found, on all valid text and character data types.
TEXTPTR	(column_name)	The text-pointer value in `varbinary` format. The text pointer is checked to ensure that it points to the first text page.
TEXTVALID	('table_name.column_name', text_ ptr)	Checks whether a given text pointer is valid. Returns 1 if the pointer is valid and 0 if the pointer is invalid.

TEXTVALID   This function verifies whether a given text pointer is valid. In this example, we verify the text pointer of the pr_info column, which describes the logo in the pub_info table. A 1 signifies a valid text pointer:

```
SELECT pub_id, 'Valid Text Data = 1'= TEXTVALID('pub_info.pr_info',
   textptr(pr_info)) FROM pub_info
```

pub_id	Valid Text Data = 1
0736	1
0877	1
1389	1
1622	1
1756	1
9901	1
9952	1
9999	1

Results - Functions - TEXTVALID

The previous query returns a 1 in the Valid Text Data = 1 column if the text pointer is valid for the pr_info column.

So far, we have looked at SQL statements and queries that select and return data from databases. In the next section, we will explore action statements in SQL.

Changing Data with SQL

SQL provides INSERT, DELETE, and UPDATE statements for your use to maintain the data in your databases. In this section, you will see how you can use these statements.

Adding Rows with the INSERT Statement

The following are ways to add rows by using the INSERT statement:

- Inserting an empty string (' ') into a varchar or text column inserts a single space.

- Inserting a null value into a text or an image column does not create a valid text pointer and does not create a 2Kb page.

- SQL Server fails and displays an error message if an INSERT statement violates a constraint, a default, or a rule or if the wrong data type is used.

- Trailing spaces are removed from data inserted into varchar columns, except in strings that contain only spaces. These strings are truncated to a single space.

The syntax for the INSERT statement is:

```
INSERT [INTO] {<table_sources>}
{
{
[(column_list)] VALUES
(
{
DEFAULT
| constant_expression
}[,...n]
)
| select_statement
| execute_statement
}
| DEFAULT VALUES
}
<table_sources> :: =
{ <table_or_view>
| (select_statement) [AS] table_alias [ (column_alias [,...m]) ]
| <table_or_view> CROSS JOIN <table_or_view>
{ { INNER
| { FULL
| LEFT
| RIGHT
} [OUTER] [<join_hints>] JOIN
} <table_or_view> ON <join_condition>
```

```
}
| <rowset_function>
}[, …n]
<table_or_view> ::=
{ table_name [ [AS] table_alias ] [ WITH (<table_hints> [ ...m]) ]
| view_name [ [AS] table_alias ]
}
<table_hints> ::=
{ INDEX(index_name | index_id)
| HOLDLOCK
| PAGLOCK
| READCOMMITTED
| REPEATABLEREAD
| ROWLOCK
| SERIALIZABLE
| TABLOCK
| TABLOCKX
}
<join_hints> ::=
{
HASH
| LOOP
| MERGE
}
<rowset_function> :: =
{ OPENQUERY (linked_server, 'query')
| OPENROWSET
( 'provider_name',
{
'datasource';'user_id';'password'
| 'provider_string'
},
{
[catalog.][schema.]object_name
| 'query'
}
)
}
```

As you can see, the INSERT statement's syntax can be very complex. Table 5.25 lists the main parts of the INSERT statement syntax.

TABLE 5.25: The Main Parts of the INSERT Statement Syntax

Part	Description
INTO	An optional keyword.
table_name | view_name	Specifies the name of the table or view used in the INSERT statement.
column_list	Lists one or more columns to which data is to be added.
DEFAULT VALUES	Inserts the default values for all columns.
values_list	The list of values to be added to the columns.
select_statement	A standard SELECT statement used to retrieve the values to be inserted from an existing table.

All Columns This example inserts values into all columns of the Jobs table.

```
INSERT INTO jobs
VALUES('Developer', 75, 175)
SELECT * FROM jobs WHERE job_desc = 'Developer'
```

This query adds one row to the Jobs table. A value is not supplied for the job_id column. This is an Identity column, and SQL Server generates this value. The SELECT statement is used at the end to select the new row and to see if it was added properly. INSERT statements by themselves do not return any rows of data; the rows are simply added to the database.

Specify Columns If you want to insert a row into the Jobs table but you do not know the formal name of the position, you can still insert the row because the job_description field has a default value. When the table was created, the owner created a default value of "'New Position - title not formalized yet'" for the job_desc column. The following example creates a new row in the Jobs table but does not supply a value for the job_desc. In this case, you must tell the server which columns you intend to supply data for.

```
INSERT INTO jobs (min_lvl, max_lvl)
VALUES (55, 95)
SELECT * FROM jobs WHERE job_desc LIKE 'New Position%'
```

This query inserts a new row in the Jobs table, accepting the default value for the job_desc field, and then selects the new row.

As you can see, the INSERT statement is flexible and allows you to dynamically add rows of data. In the next section, we will explore deleting rows of data with the DELETE statement.

Deleting Rows with the DELETE Statement

You use the DELETE statement to remove rows from a recordset. You can use DELETE alone to delete all rows, or you can use it with a WHERE clause to limit the rows deleted. The DELETE statement removes rows one at a time and places each row deletion in the log. The DELETE statement reclaims the space occupied by the data and its associated indexes.

Here are the rules associated with the DELETE statement:

- DELETE can affect only one base table at a time, so you cannot use DELETE with a view that has a FROM clause naming more than one table.

- If you omit a WHERE clause, all rows in the table are removed. The table itself, along with its indexes and constraints, remains in the database.

- You can use the IDENTITYCOL keyword in place of a `column_name` that has the IDENTITY property.

- Cursor operations affect only the single row on which the cursor is positioned.

The syntax of the DELETE statement is:

```
DELETE
[ FROM {table_name | view_name}]
{FROM <table_sources>}
[ WHERE
{ <search_conditions>
| { [ CURRENT OF
{
{ [ GLOBAL ] cursor_name }
| cursor_variable_name
}
```

```
]
}
]
[OPTION (<query_hints> [, ...n])]
<table_sources> :: =
{ <table_or_view>
| (select_statement) [AS] table_alias [ (column_alias [,...m]) ]
| <table_or_view> CROSS JOIN <table_or_view>
| <table_or_view>
{ { INNER
| { FULL
| LEFT
| RIGHT
} [ OUTER ] [ <join_hints> ] [ JOIN ]
} <table_or_view> ON <join_condition>
}
| <rowset_function>
}
[, ...n]
<table_or_view> :: =
{ table_name [ [AS] table_alias ] [ WITH (<table_hints> [...n]) ]
| view_name [ [AS] table_alias ]
}
<table_hints> ::=
{ INDEX(index_name | index_id)
| HOLDLOCK
| PAGLOCK
| READCOMMITTED
| REPEATABLEREAD
| ROWLOCK
| SERIALIZABLE
| TABLOCK
| TABLOCKX
}
<join_hints> ::=
{ HASH | LOOP | MERGE }
<query_hints> :: =
{ { HASH | ORDER } GROUP
| { CONCAT | HASH | MERGE } UNION
| FAST number_rows
| FORCE ORDER
| ROBUST PLAN
```

```
}
<join_condition> :: =
{ table_name | table_alias | view_name }.column_name
<logical_operator>
{ table_name | table_alias | view_name }.column_name
<logical_operator>:: =
{ = | > | < | >= | <= | <> | != | !< | !> }
<rowset_function> :: =
{ OPENQUERY (linked_server, 'query')
| OPENROWSET
( 'provider_name',
{
'datasource';'user_id';'password'
| 'provider_string'
},
{
[catalog.][schema.]object_name
| 'query'
}
)
```

Once again, as you can see, the DELETE statement can be a little overwhelming, but keep in mind that a basic DELETE statement is fairly straightforward. Table 5.26 lists the main parts of the DELETE statement syntax.

TABLE 5.26: The Main Parts of the DELETE Statement Syntax

Part	Description
table_name	view_name	Specifies the table or view used in the DELETE statement.
WHERE clause	WHERE {search_conditions	CURRENT OF cursor_name} is used to perform a searched delete (using search_conditions) or a positioned delete (using CURRENT OF cursor_name).

All Rows   This example deletes all rows from the Jobs table.

```
DELETE jobs
```

NOTE   This DELETE query is not provided as a sample in the SQLControl application. If you use the DELETE statement without a WHERE clause, all rows are deleted from the table.

Selected Rows   If you want to delete selected records from a table, you add a WHERE clause to the DELETE statement. This example deletes the job added in the previous section.

```
DELETE FROM jobs WHERE job_desc = 'Developer'
SELECT * from jobs
```

Results - Actions - DELETE, Selected Rows			
job_id	job_desc	min_lvl	max_lvl
1	New Hire - Job not specified	10	10
2	Chief Executive Officer	200	250
3	Business Operations Manager	175	225
4	Chief Financial Officier	175	250
5	Publisher	150	250
6	Managing Editor	140	225
7	Marketing Manager	120	200
8	Public Relations Manager	100	175
9	Acquisitions Manager	75	175

All rows in the Jobs table with the `job_desc` of Developer are deleted with this query.

Altering Data with the UPDATE Statement

You use the SQL UPDATE statement to change data in existing rows, either by adding new data or by modifying existing data. Here are some rules to keep in mind for the UPDATE statement:

- All trailing spaces are removed from data inserted into `varchar` columns, except in strings that contain only spaces, and they are truncated to a single space.

- An update does not take place and an error message is returned if a column being updated violates a constraint or a rule or if the wrong data type is used.

- Modifying a *text* column with UPDATE initializes it, assigns a valid text pointer to it, and allocates at least one 2K data page (even if updating the column with NULL).

- Updating a `varchar` or `text` column to a column with an empty string (' ') in it inserts a single space. All `char` columns are right-padded to the defined length.

The syntax for the UPDATE statement is:

```
UPDATE {<table_or_view>}
SET
```

```
{column_name = {expression | DEFAULT}
| @variable = expression} [,…n]
[FROM
{
<table_or_view>
| (select_statement) [AS] table_alias [ (column_alias [,…m]) ]
| <table_or_view> CROSS JOIN <table_or_view>
| INNER [<join_hints>] JOIN
<table_or_view> ON <join_condition>
| <rowset_function>
}[, …n]
]
[WHERE
<search_conditions>
| CURRENT OF
{ { [GLOBAL] cursor_name } | cursor_variable_name} }
]
[OPTION (<query_hints>, [,...n] )]
<table_or_view> :: =
{ table_name [ [AS] table_alias ] [ WITH (<table_hints> [...m]) ]
| view_name [ [AS] table_alias ]
}
<table_hints> ::=
{ INDEX(index_name | index_id)
| FASTFIRSTROW
| HOLDLOCK
| PAGLOCK
| READCOMMITTED
| REPEATABLEREAD
| ROWLOCK
| SERIALIZABLE
| TABLOCK
| TABLOCKX
}
<join_hints> ::=
{ HASH | LOOP | MERGE }
<query_hints> :: =
{ { HASH | ORDER } GROUP
| { CONCAT | HASH | MERGE } UNION
| FAST number_rows
| FORCE ORDER
```

```
| ROBUST PLAN
}
<join_condition> :: =
{ table_name | table_alias | view_name }.column_name
<logical_operator>
{ table_name | table_alias | view_name }.column_name
<logical_operator>:: =
{ = | > | < | >= | <= | <> | != | !< | !> }
<rowset_function> :: =
{ OPENQUERY (linked_server, 'query')
| OPENROWSET
( 'provider_name',
{
'datasource';'user_id';'password'
| 'provider_string'
},
{
[catalog.][schema.]object_name
| 'query'
}
)
}
<search_conditions> ::=
{ [ NOT ] <predicate> [ { AND | OR } [ NOT ] <predicate> ]
} [, ...n]
<predicate> ::=
{
expression { = | <> | != | > | >= | !> | < | <= | !< } expression
| string_expression [NOT] LIKE string_expression
[ESCAPE 'escape_character']
| expression [NOT] BETWEEN expression AND expression
| expression IS [NOT] NULL
| expression [NOT] IN (subquery | expression [,...n])
| expression { = | <> | != | > | >= | !> | < | <= | !< }
{ALL | SOME | ANY} (subquery)
| EXISTS (subquery)
}
```

The UPDATE statement, like the other action statements, provides a lot of
power and flexibility. Table 5.28 lists the main parts of the UPDATE statement
syntax.

TABLE 5.28: The Main Parts of the UPDATE Statement Syntax

Part	Description
table_name | view_name	Specifies the name of the table or view used in the UPDATE statement.
SET	A required keyword used to introduce the list of column or variable clauses to be updated. When more than one column name and value pair are listed, separate the names with commas.
column_list =	Specifies a column from the table (table_name) or view (view_name).
WHERE clause	Any valid WHERE clause to limit or define the rows to be updated.

WHERE Clause   You can use a WHERE clause in an UPDATE statement to limit the rows that are updated. The following example increases the price for all books in the business section:

```
UPDATE titles SET price = price * 1.1 WHERE (type = 'business')
SELECT * FROM titles WHERE type = 'business'
```

Results - Actions - UPDATE, WHERE Clause

title_id	title	type	pub_id	price	advance	royalty	ytd_sales	notes
BU1032	The Busy Executive'	business	1389	21.989	5000	10	4095	An overview
BU1111	Cooking with Compu	business	1389	13.145	5000	10	3876	Helpful hints
BU2075	You Can Combat Cor	business	0736	3.289	10125	24	18722	The latest me
BU7832	Straight Talk About [	business	1389	21.989	5000	10	4095	Annotated ar

This will increase the price for all business titles by 10%.

Multiple Columns   You can change the data in multiple columns with the same UPDATE statement. The following example updates an author's complete address consisting of the address, city, state, and zip columns:

```
UPDATE authors SET address = '19973 Maple Dr.', city = 'Oakland',
state = 'CA', zip = '97243' WHERE au_id = '172-32-1176'
SELECT * FROM authors
```

Results - Actions - UPDATE, Multiple Columns

au_id	au_lname	au_fname	phone	address	city	state	zip
172-32-1176	White	Johnson	408 496-7223	19973 Maple Dr.	Oakland	CA	97243
213-46-8915	Green	Marjorie	415 986-7020	309 63rd St. #411	Oakland	CA	94618
238-95-7766	Carson	Cheryl	415 548-7723	589 Darwin Ln.	Berkeley	CA	94705
267-41-2394	O'Leary	Michael	408 286-2428	22 Cleveland Av. #1	San Jose	CA	95128
274-80-9391	Straight	Dean	415 834-2919	5420 College Av.	Oakland	CA	94609
341-22-1782	Smith	Meander	913 843-0462	10 Mississippi Dr.	Lawrence	KS	66044
409-56-7008	Bennet	Abraham	415 658-9932	6223 Bateman St.	Berkeley	CA	94705
427-17-2319	Dull	Ann	415 836-7128	3410 Blonde St.	Palo Alto	CA	94301

CHAPTER

SIX

6

Writing Front Ends

- Selecting a front-end style

- Using data-bound controls

- Incorporating dialog boxes into front-end interfaces

- Accessing menu options with a toolbar

- Developing a front-end application

An application's user interface, or *front end*, is the user's window to the program and is critical to every project. It doesn't matter how technologically advanced, how fast, or how complete an application is if people won't use it. The user must be able to interact comfortably with your application via its interface.

Designing and building a good front end is a difficult task, for it must provide all the information that your application needs to function properly and still be appealing, intuitive, and functional for users.

The tools, controls, and functionality provided in Visual Basic 6 offer the developer a vast array of front-end design solutions to facilitate the task.

While designing an application and considering the interface, you need to answer several key questions:

- Which style should you use?

- How many Forms will you need?

- Which commands will your menus include?

- Will you use toolbars to duplicate and supplement menu functions?

- Will you provide dialog boxes to interact with the user?

Most commercial-quality applications for Microsoft Windows share a familiar and consistent user interface. This improves the usability of the application because the user is not forced to relearn common operations. For example, a user who regularly prints documents from Microsoft Word intuitively looks for a Print option on the File menu when confronted with the task of printing in an unfamiliar application.

Microsoft's user interface services provide a graphical means of displaying information and receiving user input. These services also enable you to interact with the Windows Desktop (shell).

The basic feature of the user interface is *windowing*. Graphical applications use windows, dialog boxes, and property sheets to display information and receive user input. Windows, dialog boxes, and property sheets contain menus to expose commands to users and controls to perform input and output. The common dialog box library contains a set of dialog boxes for performing common tasks. Using the common dialog boxes enables users to take care of common tasks in a consistent manner in applications that use dialog boxes.

Users interact with your Visual Basic application through graphical features. They should be able to control the application by choosing menu commands and, optionally, by clicking icons on a toolbar. They receive information from resources such as bitmaps, carets, cursors, and icons.

In this chapter, we will explore the tools that Visual Basic 6 offers and look at some of the design issues and solutions facing you as you develop Visual Basic front-end solutions.

The Developer's and the User's Viewpoints

Designing and building the front end to any application is difficult. The visual nature of Windows makes the job even more difficult.

The front end to a Visual Basic application must pull double duty: It must provide you, the developer, with all the information you need for the inner workings of the application, the business rules, and the database, and it must be visually appealing, functional, and intuitive to your users.

From the developer's point of view, an application's front end must provide:

- Complete access to all data

- The user's answers to business rule issues

From the user's point of view, an application's front end must provide:

- Complete access to all Forms and data

- Access to information in an intuitive, stress-free environment

- A familiar environment

- Complete error trapping

Selecting a Front-End Style

In today's Windows/Visual Basic application environment, there are three main application styles:

Single Document Interface (SDI), as shown in Figure 6.1, has one main Form and allows the user to open one document at a time. Both Notepad and WordPad are SDI applications.

Notepad is an example of an SDI.

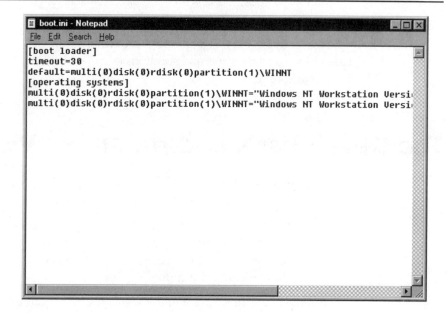

Multiple Document Interface (MDI), as shown in Figure 6.2, maintains multiple Forms within a single container Form. Applications such as Microsoft Excel and Microsoft Word for Windows are multiple document interface applications.

Microsoft Word is an example of an MDI.

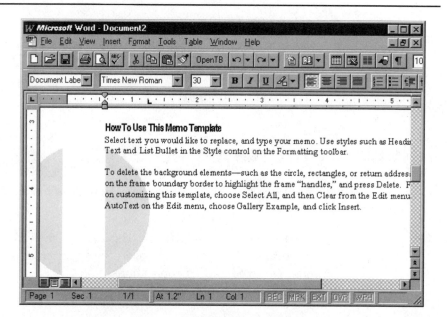

Explorer Interface, as shown in Figure 6.3, is a single window containing two *panes,* or regions, usually consisting of a tree or hierarchical view on the left and a display area on the right, as in the Windows Explorer or Windows RegEdit applications. This type of interface lends itself to navigating or browsing large numbers of documents, pictures, or other files.

FIGURE 6.3:

Windows Explorer is an example of an Explorer Interface.

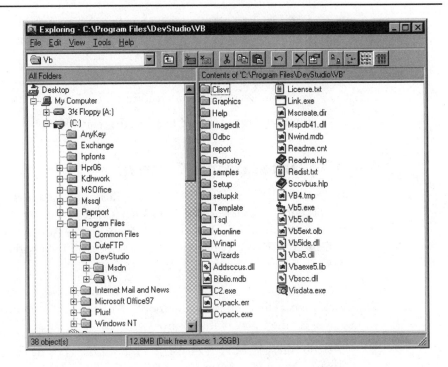

Visual Basic provides many controls and tools that you can use to create functional and user-friendly front ends. In the next section, we will look at some of the data-aware bound controls available in the Enterprise Edition of Visual Basic.

Data-Bound Controls

Data-bound controls, which we have discussed throughout this book, are controls that can be bound to a data source. Visual Basic provides a data-bound control for almost every purpose. The common element is the bound data source. In the

Enterprise Edition of Visual Basic, it is the ActiveX Data control (ADODC). In this section, we'll look at the following data-bound controls:

DataCombo is a data-bound combo box with a drop-down list box that is automatically populated from a field in an attached ADODC control. It optionally updates a field in a related table of another ADODC control.

DataList is a data-bound list box that is automatically populated from a field in an attached ADODC control. It optionally updates a field in a related table of another ADODC control.

DataGrid is a spreadsheet-like bound control that displays a series of rows and columns representing records and fields from a Recordset object.

TextBox is the standard text box that can be bound to an ADODC control.

Using the DataCombo Control

The DataCombo control is automatically filled with data from a field in the Recordset object of an ADODC control to which it is attached. You must populate the standard ComboBox control manually by using the AddItem method. In addition, the DataCombo control has the ability to update a field within a related Recordset object that may reside in a different data control.

The DataCombo control also supports an automated search mode that can quickly locate items in the list without additional code. Figure 6.4 shows the sources for the DataCombo control.

As you can see from Figure 6.4, the DataCombo box has two separate data sources. The first source provides the field value from the current record, and the second provides the data for the drop-down list.

FIGURE 6.4:

The sources for the bound DataCombo control

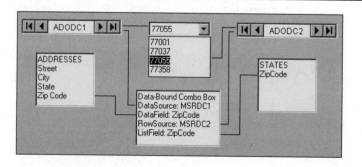

The DataCombo control is commonly used to provide lookup values in another table. For example, if you want the user to enter a valid state or zip code, you can provide a list of selections in a DataCombo box. This simplifies data entry and reduces the possibility of a data-entry error.

Table 6.1 lists the properties used to fill and manage the DataCombo or DataList controls and to bind the selected data to a data control.

T A B L E   6 . 1 :   The Properties of the DataCombo and DataList Controls

Property	Description
BoundColumn	The name of a field in the Recordset object specified by the RowSource to be passed back to the DataField once the user makes a selection.
BoundText	The text value of the BoundColumn field. Once a selection is made, this value is passed back to update the Recordset object specified by the DataSource and DataField properties.
DataField	The name of the field that is updated in the Recordset object specified by the DataSource property.
DataSource	The name of the data control or ADODC that is updated once the user makes a selection.
ListField	The name of a field in the Recordset specified by the RowSource used to fill the drop-down list.
MatchEntry	Defines how the list is searched as the user types characters at run time.
RowSource	The name of the data control or ADODC used as a source of items for the list portion of the control.
SelectedItem	The bookmark of the selected item in the Recordset specified by the RowSource property.
Text	The text value of the selected item in the list.
VisibleCount	The number of items visible in the list (fully or partially).
VisibleItems	An array of bookmarks with a maximum number of items equal to the Visible-Count property.

Adding the DataCombo and the DataList Controls to a Project

Follow these steps to add the DataCombo and DataList controls to a project:

1.   Start a new Visual Basic project.

2. Choose Project ➤ Components to open the Components dialog box.

3. Select Microsoft DataList Controls 6 from the list of available controls.

The DataCombo and DataList controls are added to your Toolbox, as shown in Figure 6.5.

FIGURE 6.5:

The DataCombo and DataList controls added to the Toolbox

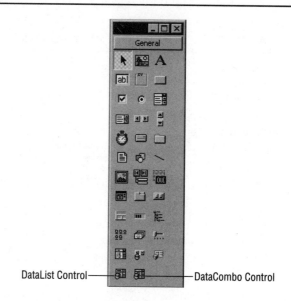

DataList Control —————— DataCombo Control

In the next section, with the DataCombo control added to your toolbar, we will create a sample project using the DataCombo control.

The DataCombo Project

The DataCombo project (shown in Figure 6.6) demonstrates how to use a Data-Combo control as a table lookup. The sample project includes two ADODCs linked to the Pubs database and a DataCombo control that displays the current author's city; it also provides a list of valid cities from the Authors table.

NOTE   You'll find the DataCombo project in the **Ch6/DataCombo** folder on the CD that comes with this book.

The DataCombo project

Creating the DataCombo Project

To create the DataCombo project, start by adding the following to Form1:

- Two ActiveX Data Controls. One will display the current record from the Authors table, and the other will provide the query for the lookup portion of the DataCombo control.

- One DataCombo control.

NOTE   See Chapter 4 for information about adding an ActiveX Data Control to a Form.

Connecting the ActiveX Data Controls

Now you need to set the properties for the ActiveX Data control (named ADODC1). Table 6.2 lists the properties and their values and describes them. Table 6.3 shows the settings for ADODC2.

TABLE 6.2:   The Values for the ActiveX Data Control (ADODC1) Property Settings

Property	Value	Description
ConnectionString	DSN=PubsTest	Sets the server connection string
RecordSource	SELECT * FROM authors	Provides the records for the display portion of the DataCombo control

TABLE 6.3: The Values for the ActiveX Data Control (ADODC2) Property Settings

Property	Value	Description
ConnectionString	DSN=PubsTest	Sets the server connection string
RecordSource	SELECT au_fname FROM authors ORDER BY au_fname	Provides the records for the display portion of the DataCombo control
Visible	False	Makes ADODC2 invisible at run time

NOTE   Substitute your DSN in place of PubsTest or add a PubsTest DSN entry for the Pubs database and supply a valid UID and PWD for your server.

Now that we've set up the ActiveX Data controls, it is time to connect the Data-Combo control.

Connecting the DataCombo Control

The DataCombo control will be connected to both of the ActiveX Data controls; one provides the author's first name from the current record, and the other provides the list of valid authors from the Authors table. Set the DataCombo properties according to Table 6.4.

TABLE 6.4: The DataCombo Property Settings

Property	Value	Description
DataSource	ADODC1	Sets the data source of the display portion to the Authors table through the ActiveX Data control ADODC1
DataField	au_fname	Connects the author's first name from the current record
RowSource	ADODC2	Sets the list portion to the names from the Authors table through the ActiveX Data control ADODC2
ListField	au_fname	Provides the source for the drop-down list portion of the DataCombo control

Testing the DataCombo Project

Press F5 to run the project. You will see the Form with the DataCombo control and the ADODC as shown in Figure 6.6, earlier in this chapter. Click the drop-down arrow on the DataCombo control to see the list of available authors from the Authors table. Change records with the ADODC to display the current author's first name in the DataCombo control.

WARNING   If you change the name by selecting a different name from the drop-down list and then change records, the author's name will be changed in the Authors table.

As you can see from the DataCombo project, the DataCombo control is a great tool to help users select values from a list. If you have an application that needs to present a more visible list to the users, however, you can use the DataList control.

Using the DataList Control

The DataList control is automatically filled with data from a field in the Recordset object of an ADODC control to which it is attached. You must populate the standard ListBox control manually by using the AddItem method. In addition, the DataList control has the ability to update a field within a related Recordset object that may reside in a different data control.

The DataList control also supports an automated search mode that can quickly locate items in the list without additional code. Figure 6.7 shows how the DataList control is bound to a ADODC.

FIGURE 6.7:

The bound DataList control

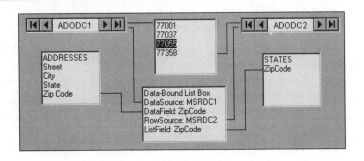

As you can see from Figure 6.7, the DataList control has two separate data sources just as the DataCombo control does. The first provides the field from the current record, and the second provides the data for the list portion.

The DataList control is used, as is the DataCombo box control, to provide a list of data-entry selections for the user. The main difference in the DataCombo control and the DataList control is the way the data is presented to the user. In a Data-Combo control, the data is presented in a drop-down list; in the DataList control, the data is presented in a stationary list.

Table 6.1, earlier in this chapter, lists the properties you use to fill and manage the list and to bind the DataCombo or DataList box controls to a data control or to an ADODC.

The DataList Project

The DataList project (shown in Figure 6.8) demonstrates a DataList control populated with the names from the Authors table.

FIGURE 6.8:

The DataList project

Creating the DataList Project

To create the DataList project, first add the following to Form1:

- Two ActiveX Data controls. One displays the current record from the Authors table, and the other provides the query for the lookup portion of the DataCombo control.

- One DataCombo control.

NOTE   See Chapter 4 for information about adding an ActiveX Data control to a Form.

Connecting the ActiveX Data Controls

Now set the properties for ADODC1. Table 6.5 lists and describes the settings for ADODC1, and Table 6.6 lists and describes the settings for ADODC2.

TABLE 6.5: The ADODC1 Property Settings

Property	Value	Description
ConnectionString	DSN=PubsTest	Sets the server connection string
RecordSource	SELECT * FROM authors	Provides the records for the display portion of the DataCombo control

TABLE 6.6: The ADODC2 Property Settings

Property	Value	Description
ConnectionString	DSN=PubsTest	Sets the server connection string
RecordSource	SELECT au_fname FROM authors ORDER BY au_fname	Provides the records for the display portion of the DataCombo control
Visible	False	Makes ADODC2 invisible at run time

NOTE   Substitute your DSN in place of TestPubs or add a TestPubs DSN entry for the Pubs database and supply a valid UID and PWD for your server.

Now that we've set up the ActiveX Data controls, it is time to connect the DataList control.

Connecting the DataList Control

The DataList control will be connected to both ActiveX Data controls. One provides the author's first name from the current record, and the other provides the list of valid authors from the Authors table. Set the DataList properties according to Table 6.7.

TABLE 6.7: The DataList Property Settings

Property	Value	Description
DataSource	ADODC1	Sets the data source of the display portion to the Authors table through the ActiveX Data control ADODC1
DataField	au_fname	Connects the author's first name from the current record
RowSource	ADODC2	Sets the list portion to the names from the Authors table through the ActiveX Data control ADODC2
ListField	au_fname	Provides the source for the drop-down list portion of the DataCombo control

Testing the DataList Project

Press F5 to run the project. The DataList control will be populated with the names from the Authors table, and the current record will be highlighted.

Navigate through the records with the ADODC, and the DataList control will follow. As with the DataCombo control, if you select a different name in the DataList control and change records, the author's name will be changed to the new value.

The DataCombo and DataList controls display the current record. In the next section, we will explore the DataGrid control, which is capable of displaying multiple records simultaneously.

NOTE The ADODC control that is visible on the Form is bound to the Authors table. As you navigate from row to row, the list box positions itself to the author's first name. The movement will appear to be random, but you are actually seeing the first name from the current author's record.

Using the DataGrid Control

The DataGrid control is a spreadsheet-like bound control that displays a series of rows and columns representing records and fields from a Recordset object. The Results pane in Visual Data Tools, discussed in Chapter 2, "Client/Server Programming," has the same look and feel as the DataGrid control. Also, if you have ever used Microsoft Access or Microsoft Query, you are familiar with the look and feel of the DataGrid control.

The DataGrid control provides a lot of "ready-made" functionality that allows you to browse and edit complete database tables or query results. When you set the DataGrid control's DataSource property to a data control or ADODC, the DataGrid control is automatically filled, and its column headers are automatically set from the data control's recordset.

The DataGrid control provides in-cell editing and allows you to insert or delete entire database records. In addition, the DataGrid control provides a number of properties that can be set at design time or at run time to control the look and feel of the control.

The DataGrid control depends on two major objects:

- The Recordset object of the data control

- The Columns collection of the DataGrid itself

Figure 6.9 shows how the DataGrid is bound to an ADODC.

FIGURE 6.9:

The DataGrid control bound to an ActiveX Data control

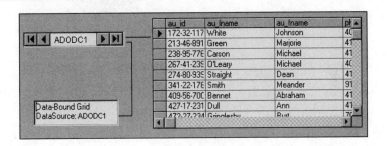

The DataGrid control is a collection of Column objects corresponding to fields in a database and rows corresponding to records in the database.

You can specify the current cell in code, or the user can change it at run time by using the mouse or the arrow keys. When you change the current cell, the underlying data control's recordset is automatically repositioned to the record containing the selected cell.

You can edit cells interactively, by typing in the cell, or programmatically, by changing the Value property of the currently selected Column object. The only property that is used to fill and bind the DataGrid control or the ADODC is the DataSource property. This property contains the name of the ADODC that provides database access for the DataGrid.

The DataGrid control is not added to a new Visual Basic project by default. The next section shows you how to do this.

Adding the DataGrid Control to a Project

Follow these steps to add the DataGrid control to a project:

1. Start a new Visual Basic project.

2. Choose Project ➤ Components to display the Components dialog box.

3. Select Microsoft DataGrid Control 6.0 from the list of available controls.

The DataGrid control will be added to your Toolbox, as shown in Figure 6.10.

FIGURE 6.10:

The Toolbox with the DataGrid control added

DataGrid control

In the next section, with the DataGrid control added to your Toolbox, we will create a sample project.

The DataGrid Project

The DataGrid project (shown in Figure 6.11) demonstrates how a DataGrid control is linked to the Publishers table through a connection to an ActiveX Data control. This sample project includes one ADODC and a DataGrid control.

NOTE You'll find the DataGrid project in the Ch13/DataGrid folder on the CD that comes with this book.

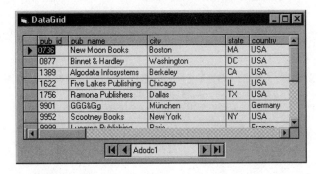

Follow these steps to create the DataGrid project:

1. Add one ADODC to Form1. This will be used to connect to the Publishers table in the Pubs database on your server.

2. Add one DataGrid control. This will display the records from the ADODC.

3. Now connect the ActiveX Data Control by setting the ADODC properties according to Table 6.8.

TABLE 6.8: The ADODC1 Property Settings

Property	Value	Description
ConnectionString	DSN=PubsTest	Sets the server connection string
RecordSource	publishers	Selects the records from the publishers table as the source of the ADODC control

4. Set the DataSource property of the DataGrid control to ADODC1 to connect the DataGrid control to the ActiveX Data control.

Substitute your DSN in place of PubsTest or add a PubsTest DSN entry for the Pubs database, and supply a valid UID and PWD for your server. That's all there is to the setup. Now let's test the project.

Testing the DataGrid Project

Press F5 to start the project. The Form will load, and the DataGrid will display the records from the Publishers table. Notice that the headings are created automatically.

This is truly a drop-in database front end. In the next section, in order to round out our discussion on the bound controls commonly used in database front-end applications, we will look at using a standard TextBox control bound to an ADODC.

Using the Text Box as a Bound Control

You can use a standard TextBox control as a bound control by setting the DataSource property to a data control or ADODC and by setting the DataField property to a valid field in the data source. With these two properties set, the text box will take on the characteristics of a bound control and provide access to a database field. Figure 6.12 shows a text box bound to an ADODC.

FIGURE 6.12:

A bound TextBox control

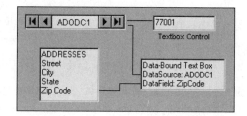

You can change the DataField or DataSource properties of the TextBox control at design time or at run time to change the source of the text box. All the standard properties apply to a bound text box.

NOTE   We'll look at bound TextBox controls in the FrontEnd project later in this chapter.

Bound controls provide an easy, powerful way to begin the process of building a front end. In the next section, we will look at how to use dialog boxes to enhance the functionality of front-end interfaces.

Incorporating Dialog Boxes into Front-End Interfaces

Visual Basic provides a standard suite of predefined dialog boxes in the Common-Dialog control. This control provides dialog boxes for operations such as opening and saving files, setting print options, and selecting colors and fonts. It also has the ability to display Help by running the Windows Help engine.

The CommonDialog control provides an interface between Visual Basic and the routines in the Microsoft Windows dynamic-link library `Commdlg.dll`. To create a dialog box using this control, `Commdlg.dll` must be in your Microsoft Windows `\System` directory.

TIP

You cannot tell the dialog box where to display; however, with a little ingenuity, you can overcome this limitation. Create a separate Form with a CommonDialog control on it. Whenever you need to display a common dialog box, show this new Form at the desired location to position your dialog box where you want it.

You use the CommonDialog control in your application by adding it to a Form and setting its properties. The dialog box displayed by the control is determined by the methods of the control. At run time, a dialog box is displayed or the Help engine is executed when the appropriate method is invoked. Table 6.9 lists the dialog boxes provided as part of the CommonDialog control.

TABLE 6.9: Predefined Dialog Boxes in Visual Basic

Dialog Box	Description
Color	Allows the user to select a color from a palette or to create and select a custom color
Font	Displays a dialog box in which the user can set the font characteristics
PrinterSetup	Displays a dialog box in which the user can select a printer and set printer options
Help	Invokes Windows Help
Open	Displays the standard File Open dialog box to allow the user to specify a drive, directory, file name extension, and file name
Save	Displays the standard File Save As dialog box to allow the user to specify a drive, directory, file name extension, and file name

If your application incorporates predefined dialog boxes where appropriate, it will take on the characteristics of a standard Windows application and, as such, be more likely to be accepted by your users. Another popular feature in front-end applications is the toolbar.

Accessing Menu Options with a Toolbar

Typically, a toolbar contains buttons that correspond to items in an application's menu, thus providing a graphical interface for the user to access an application's most frequently used functions and commands. Users of Windows applications have become accustomed to having toolbars available to them.

NOTE   We look at toolbars in detail in Chapter 16, "The Built In Visual Basic Developer's ActiveX Controls."

With all the tools that Visual Basic provides, it is possible to design and build a commercial-quality Windows standard front end for your database applications. In the next section, we will look at putting the components from this chapter into practice as we create a sample Single Document Interface database front-end application.

The Front-End Project

The easiest and most common type of front-end interface to build is designed around a single Form, commonly referred to as an SDI application. An SDI application consists of one or more single Forms that allow the user to perform one task or to work with a single document. WordPad, Notepad, and Paint are SDI applications.

The sample FrontEnd project (shown in Figure 6.13) provides an interface to the Publishers and Titles tables in the Pubs database.

The FrontEnd Project consists of two Forms:

- The Main Form
- The About Form

The Main Form is a Master/Detail-type Form that shows records from the Publishers table on the top and a DataGrid on the bottom with all the titles for the current publisher. The About Form is used to describe the application and show the current version.

FIGURE 6.13:

The FrontEnd project

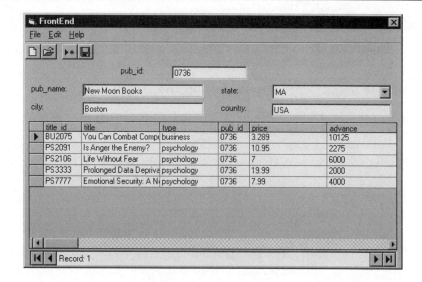

A standard menu and a toolbar allow users to access the most common menu items. Also, whenever possible, we have incorporated Windows standard dialog boxes. In this application, the user will be able to do the following:

- Add records to the Authors table

- Display the predefined dialog boxes, including the Windows Help file

- Edit records for both the Publishers table and the Titles table

- Select the author's state from a DataCombo box

TIP

If you want to be able to delete records from the Publishers table, or Master table, you can write a cascading delete trigger to delete all the associated titles from the Titles table. See Chapter 3, "Using SQL Server," for a discussion of triggers.

Connecting to the Pubs Database

The FrontEnd project connects to the database in three places:

- The adoPrimary

- The adoSecondary

- The adoState ActiveX Data Controls

The adoPrimary is the recordsource connected to the Authors table in the Pubs database and is the main recordsource for the project. The adoSecondary is the recordsource for the associated records from the Titles table. The records are kept in sync in the MoveComplete event of the adoPrimary ActiveX Data control.

Code 6.1 **Repositioning the Detail DataGrid**

```
Private Sub adoPrimary_MoveComplete(ByVal adReason _
    As ADODB.EventReasonEnum, ByVal pError _
    As ADODB.Error, adStatus As ADODB.EventStatusEnum, _
    ByVal pRecordset As ADODB.Recordset)

    Screen.MousePointer = vbDefault
    On Error Resume Next
    adoSecondary.ConnectionString = "DSN=PubsTest"
    'This will synch the grid
    'with the Master recordset
    adoSecondary.RecordSource = _
    "select [title_id],[title],[type],[pub_id]," _
    & "[price],[advance],[royalty],[ytd_sales]," _
    & "[notes],[pubdate] from [titles] " _
    & "where [pub_id]='" & _
    adoPrimary.Recordset![pub_id] & "'"
    adoSecondary.Refresh

    'This will display the current record
    'position for dynasets and snapshots
    adoPrimary.Caption = "Record: " & _
    (adoPrimary.Recordset.AbsolutePosition)
End Sub
```

This code queries the Titles table in the Pubs database for all records where the pub_id field matches in the Publishers and Titles tables. The data source of the ADODC for the DataGrid is set to the results.

The third connection is for the DataCombo box used to provide a list of states. The recordsource for this ADODC is the state field in the Publishers table.

NOTE See Chapter 3, "Using SQL Server," for a complete discussion of how to connect to an ODBC data source.

After the ADODCs are connected, it's time to add the fields to the Main Form.

Adding the Fields for the Main Form

The Main Form in the FrontEnd project includes all the fields from the Publishers table in the Pubs database, with the exception of the state field, which is a Data-Combo box.

Setting Up the State DataCombo Box Control

The state DataCombo box supplies a list of valid state abbreviations that can be used in our sample application. For this application, the user can select a state from the list but cannot enter a state that is not already in use. This is accomplished by setting the Style property to 2, dbcDropDownList. Table 6.10 lists the styles available for the DataCombo box.

TABLE 6.10: Available Styles for the DataCombo Box Control

Style	Value	Meaning
dbcDropdownCombo	0	Default. Drop-Down Combo. Includes a drop-down list and a text box. The user can select from the list or type in the text box.
dbcSimpleCombo	1	Simple Combo. Includes a text box and a list, which doesn't drop down. The user can select from the list or type in the text box. By default, a Simple Combo box is sized so that none of the list is displayed. Increase the Height property to display more of the list.
dbcDropdownList	2	Drop-Down List. Allows selection only from the drop-down list.

The DataCombo box list portion is bound to the adoState ADODC by setting the RowSource property to adoState and by setting the ListField property to State. The state that is displayed from the Authors table is set by setting the DataSource property to adoPrimary, the DataField property to state, and the BoundColumn property to state.

By using two ADODCs, it is possible to display a list of states and to display the current records state from the Publishers table.

TIP   You could add a new State table to the Pubs database that lists the abbreviations of all the states.

Using the Toolbar

The toolbar in our sample project provides easy access to the most frequently used actions. The code for the toolbar calls the matching menu code. This process is used so that you do not have code repeated in two places.

Code 6.2	Responding to Toolbar Clicks

```
Private Sub Toolbar1_ButtonClick(ByVal Button _
    As MSComctlLib.Button)
    On Error GoTo ErrorRoutineErr

    Select Case Button.Key
        Case "OpenFile"
            Call mnuOpenFile_Click
        Case "NewFile"
            Call mnuNewFile_Click
        Case "NewRecord"
            Call mnuNew_Click
        Case "SaveRecord"
            Call mnuSave_Click
    End Select
ErrorRoutineResume:
    Exit Sub
ErrorRoutineErr:
    MsgBox "Project1.frmauthors.Toolbar1_ButtonClick" _
    & Err & Error
    Resume Next
End Sub
```

Notice that error trapping is included. Since this code calls a second subroutine, it will be helpful to know in which subroutine an error occurred. The error routine displays a message box with the subroutines name and the error message.

Accessing Common Dialog Boxes

Another feature of our FrontEnd application is the use of Windows standard common dialog boxes. Code 6.3, taken from the mnuOpenFile subroutine, accesses the dialog boxes.

Code 6.3	**Displaying the Common Dialog Boxes**

```
Private Sub mnuOpenFile_Click()
    On Error GoTo ErrorRoutineErr
    With CommonDialog1
        .DialogTitle = "Open File"
        .CancelError = True
        .ShowOpen
    End With
ErrorRoutineResume:
    Exit Sub
ErrorRoutineErr:
    If Err = 32755 Then
        'user chose cancel
        'put cancel code here
        Resume Next
    End If
    If glDebugMode = "True" Then
        MsgBox "Project1.frmauthors.mnuOpenFile_Click" _
            & Err & Error
    Else
        Call frmError.DisplayErrorForm _
        ("Project1.frmauthors.mnuOpenFile_Click", Err, Error)
    End If
End Sub
```

The only differences between calling an Open dialog box and a Save dialog box are the title and the ShowOpen command.

Notice the following line:

```
CancelError = False
```

If the user chooses the Cancel button on a dialog box, Visual Basic can raise error number 32755. If CancelError is set to True, the error will be raised, and you can write code to intercept and respond to the fact that Cancel was selected. If you do not need to know if the dialog option was canceled, set the CancelError property to False.

Now that we have looked at the major parts of the FrontEnd project, let's take it for a test drive.

Testing the Front-End Project

Follow these steps to test the FrontEnd project:

1. Press F5 to start the application. You should see the application as shown in Figure 6.13, earlier in this chapter.

2. Click the OpenFile toolbar button to display the Open File dialog box.

NOTE   The New File, Open File, and Print Setup options display the appropriate common dialog boxes, but these dialog boxes are just for demonstration purposes. No action is taken in this sample program.

---

3. Click the arrow on the state DataCombo box to display a list of valid zip codes from the Authors table.

4. Select a new state to close the DataCombo box list portion and display the new state.

5. Click the Save icon or choose Edit ➤ Save to save the record with the new state.

6. Choose Help ➤ About to display the About screen. This is just a shell, but it gives you a start to building a complete About box.

7. To see the Windows Help file, choose Help ➤ Windows Help.

CHAPTER

SEVEN

7

Using the Microsoft English Query Engine

- ■ Examining the English Query development Environment

- ■ Creating an English Query application

- ■ Testing an English Query application

- ■ Accessing English Query from Visual Basic

Soon after the first database application was created, users commonly asked, "Why can't we just ask a question in English? Why do we have to use a foreign language to communicate with our data?"

Of course, what they were referring to was the fact that a simple question, such as, "How many Widgets were sold last month?" could not be asked in that particular way. Instead, it had to be asked in a different way, such as "SELECT COUNT(Widgets) FROM ItemsSold WHERE Month = 12"; a way considered by most users to be decidedly not "user friendly." Luckily, however, that's all changed now. Microsoft listened to its users and responded with the Microsoft English Query application.

The Microsoft English Query gives the database developer a vehicle to create an interface that allows users to communicate with databases in English.

Defining a Microsoft English Query Application

An *English Query application* is an application based on a relational database that gives end users the ability to pose queries in English, rather than in a computer language, such as SQL.

The Microsoft English Query development environment provides developers with a vehicle to transform relational databases into English Query applications that can understand and respond to English Queries. These English Query applications give users the ability to present questions or requests in English, as opposed to Transact-SQL or some other programming language. Figure 7.1 provides an overview of this process.

An English Query application is created with the English Query domain editor, as shown in Figure 7.2. With this editor, information about the tables, fields, relationships, and data is used to process English questions posed by the users of the database.

Examining the English Query Development Environment

The Microsoft English Query environment includes two components:

- The domain editor (as shown in Figure 7.2)
- The engine

FIGURE 7.1:

English Query overview

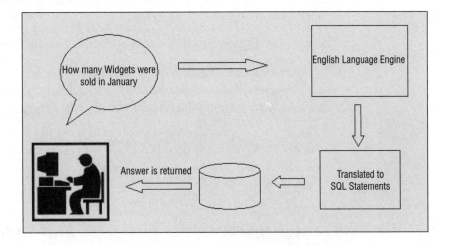

FIGURE 7.2:

The English Query domain editor

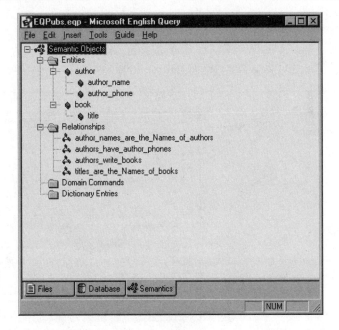

With the domain editor, you define information about the tables, columns, relationships, and data used to process English questions posed by the users of the database. The domain editor is used to create a `*.eqp` file, or project, and to create and test the corresponding connection file (**eqc**). The connection file can then be compiled into an application (**eqd**) file.

There are two types of information used by the domain editor to create a project:

1. The structure or schema of your database is needed, including table names, field names, keys, and relationships. Most of this information is read from the database system tables automatically when the project is first created.

2. The developer provides the definition of semantic objects using the domain editor. These semantic objects include entities and relationships. Entities are usually represented by tables and sometimes by fields. Relationships express how those entities are associated with one another.

Understanding Domains, Entities, and Relationships

An English Query application is made up of a domain, entities, and relationships.

English Query Domains

An English Query domain, shown in Figure 7.3, is a collection of information about the database and semantic objects in a Microsoft English Query application.

FIGURE 7.3:

An English Query domain

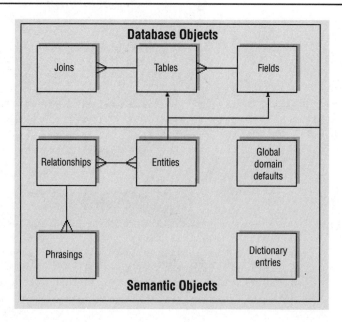

Initially, English Query knows about English and how to generate SQL statements, but it does not know anything about a new database. In particular, it does not know how to connect its knowledge of English with specific elements of the database. The developer and English Query need to know which table contains inventory, which table contains suppliers, which field contains the names of the inventory parts, how the inventory and suppliers are related, and numerous other details about how inventory is stored in the database. Collectively, this information is known as the domain.

English Query Entities

An entity (as shown in Figure 7.4) is an object referred to by a noun, such as a person, place, thing, or idea. For example, people, cities, products, and shipments are all entities. In English Query applications, important entities are typically represented by tables and are known as major entities.

FIGURE 7.4:

English Query entities

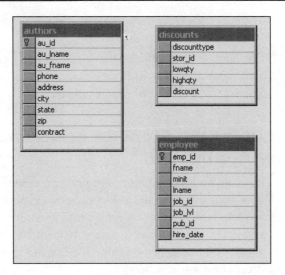

Part Numbers and Suppliers are important entities associated with the Inventory and Suppliers tables, respectively. Entities are sometimes represented by database columns, referred to as minor entities. For example, in a Suppliers table, there may be a Warehouse field. The corresponding Warehouse entity is important for answering questions about branches, but it is not associated with its own table. The least important entities are known as traits and are associated with columns as well. For example, the volume of a shipping carton, the sex of an employee, and the color of a part are all traits.

English Query Relationships

Relationships (as shown in Figure 7.5) represent the third part of the English Query puzzle. A relationship is an association between entities that describes what those entities have to do with one another.

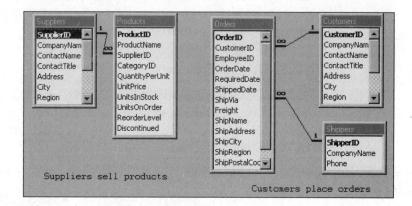

In English, relationships can be described as concise statements: authors write books or authors have phone numbers. Relationships have one or more phrasings that express a relationship in English.

Examining the Steps to Create an English Language Query Application

To create an English Query application, you must start with a well-defined database. Your database should include primary and foreign keys for the tables, so that English Query can create sound joins. After you have established a base database, the steps required to create, test, and build your English Query application can all be accomplished within the English Query development environment. These steps are as follows:

1. Extract the database structure.

2. Create the entities.

3. Create the relationships.

4. Test the questions.

5. Build the application.

In the next section, we will create an English Query application based on the Pubs sample database that is included with SQL Server 7.

Creating the EQPubs English Query Application

In this section, we will create an English Query application based on the Pubs sample database, concentrating on authors and books. For this, we are primarily interested in the Authors and Titles tables. This test application will be able to answer English questions and list information, such as:

- List all authors.
- Who are the authors?
- Which books did Marjorie write?
- How many books did Marjorie write?
- Did Michael O'Leary write a book?

This is just a sample of the kinds of questions and requests that may be presented with Microsoft English Query, so let's get started!

Starting Microsoft English Query

Microsoft English Query is included on the SQL Server 7 CD, but it is not installed as part of the SQL Server 7 installation. Instead, it is a separate application that you must install yourself. If you have not installed Microsoft English Query, follow the steps outlined in the sidebar. With the English Query installed, select Start ➤ Programs ➤ Microsoft English Query ➤ Microsoft English Query to start the English Query, as shown in Figure 7.6.

Installing Microsoft English Query

As we have already mentioned, Microsoft English Query is included on the SQL Server 7 CD, but it is not installed as part of the SQL Server 7 installation. Follow these steps to install it:

1. Insert the SQL Server 7 CD into the CD-ROM reader and it will autostart.
2. Select Install SQL Server Components from the opening menu.
3. Select English Query from the next menu.
4. Select Install English Query to begin the installation process.
5. Follow the online prompts to select the target installation location and install the English Query program.

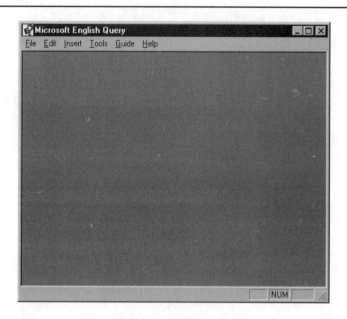

Extracting the Database Structure

The first step in creating an English Query application is to extract the database structure. The structure of the Pubs sample database is shown in Figure 7.7.

The shaded area of Figure 7.7 represents the area of concentration for our sample application.

The structure of the selected database can be extracted by following these steps:

1. Select Start ➤ Programs ➤ Microsoft English Query ➤ Microsoft English Query to start the English Query.

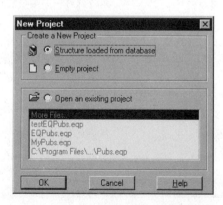

The structure of the Pubs database

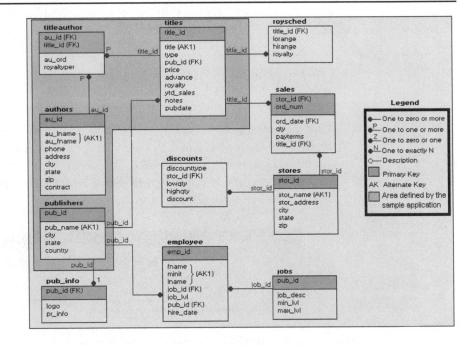

2. Select the Structure Loaded from Database option from the New Project dia-
    log box and click OK. This will display the Select Data Source dialog box,
    where you must tell English Query where the database is located.

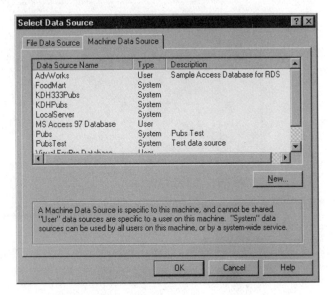

3. Select a data source for the Pubs sample database. If you do not have a data source, click the New button and create one.

NOTE

If you need help creating a new data source, see the section "Creating an ODBC Data Source" in Chapter 4.

---

4. After the data source has been selected, the structure will be extracted. At the end of this process, you may see a dialog box informing you that the Discounts table needs a key added to it. However, you can disregard this message since our example does not deal with the Discounts table. If you do see this message, click OK to continue.

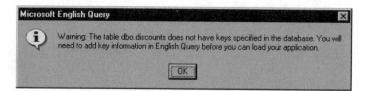

The structure of the Pubs database has been extracted and the English Query screen will be displayed, as shown in Figure 7.8.

FIGURE 7.8:

The English Query screen with the Pubs data structure

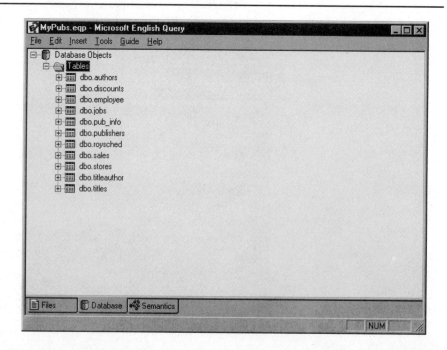

In the next section, we will remove the tables that are not required for our application.

Removing the Unnecessary Tables

Since our application only relies on the Titleauthors, Authors, Jobs, Publishers, and Titles tables, we can delete the others from our domain. Follow these steps to delete the tables:

1. Click the plus icon next to the Tables folder to display the tables in the application.

2. Click the dbo.discounts table to select it.

3. To delete the selected table, either select Edit ➤ Delete from the menu or right-click the table and select Delete from the menu.

4. Click OK to the Confirm Deletion message box.

5. Repeat Steps 3 and 4 for the following tables:

   - dbo.employee
   - dbo.pub_info
   - dbo.roysched
   - dbo.sales
   - dbo.stores

6. This is a good time to save the application. Select Edit ➤ Save Project and save the project as EQPubs.

That completes the extraction of the database structure. In the next section, we will begin creating the semantic objects for our application.

Defining the Semantic Objects

The Pubs database provides several opportunities for creating semantic objects to answer questions about the data. In our application, we will be concerned with only a fraction of the possibilities. Figure 7.9 presents a view of some of the semantic objects that are available. The shaded area represents our application's possible objects.

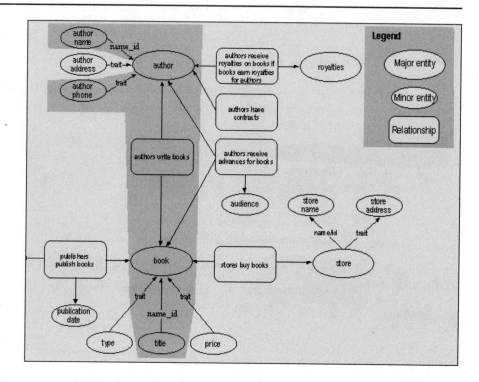

Creating the Book and Titles Entities and Relationships

In our sample English Query application, the users should be able to present general questions or requests about books and titles, such as:

- List the titles.

- How many books are there?

- What are the books?

In the next sections, we will create the entities and relationships necessary to answer these types of questions and requests.

Creating the Book Entity

The Book entity is used to help answer questions or provide information about the titles in the Pubs database, such as "How many books are there?", "List the titles," or "List all of the books." The Book entity is represented by the Titles table.

Follow these steps to create the Book entity:

1. Select Insert ➤ Entity to display the New Entity properties dialog box.

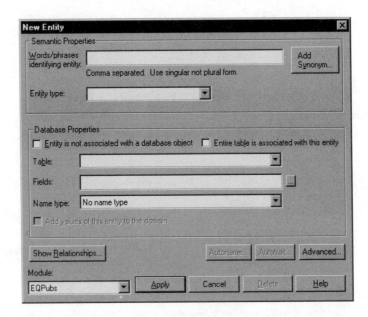

2. Enter the name of this entity, **book**, followed by a comma into the Words/Phrases Identifying Entity field. This will define the entity.

3. Enter some synonyms for book, such as **publication**, **tome**, **work**, **volume**, and **edition**. This will allow you to refer to a book by these names.

4. Select None for the Entity Type.

5. Select Titles from the Table box. This entry specifies that the entity is represented by the rows in the table, not by individual fields. For example, you want to allow a request, such as "Count the books." Associating the Book entity with the entire Titles table, rather than just the Title field, ensures that the count is correct. Since all fields in the Titles table are used in the count to uniquely identify the book, if two books happen to have the same title, they will be counted individually.

6. Enter **title** and **pubdate** in the Fields field. The Fields entry holds the column names from the table that you want displayed whenever a question is asked about this entity. These columns are entered so that the titles and publication dates display whenever questions or requests are presented about books, such as "List the books."

7. If you click the ellipsis box to the right of the Fields field, the Fields dialog box will be displayed. This dialog box lists all of the columns available in the table that you selected in Step 5.

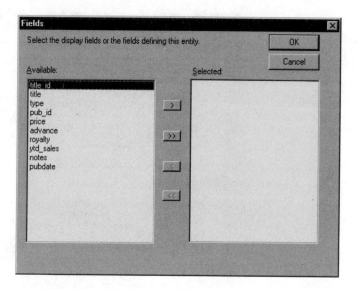

8. Click the Apply button on the New Entity properties dialog box to add this entity to the domain.

Creating the Title Entity

The Title entity is a minor entity. The Title entity is defined to answer specific questions about the books in the Pubs database, such as "What book starts with the word *Computers*?" The Title entity is represented by the Title field in the Titles table. Follow these steps to add the Title entity:

1. Select Insert ➤ Entity to display the New Entity properties dialog box.

2. Enter the name of this entity, **title**, followed by a comma into the Words/Phrases Identifying Entity field. This will define the entity.

3. Enter some synonyms for title, such as **book name** and **designation**. This will allow you to refer to a title by these names.

4. Select None for the Entity Type.

5. Select Titles from the Table box.

6. Enter **title** into the Fields field.

7. Select Proper Name from the Kind of Name list.

8. Click the Add Values of This Entity to the Domain checkbox. Checking this option ensures that the English Query Dictionary can answer questions about particular books and titles.

9. Click the Apply button to add the Title entity to the domain.

Creating the "Titles Are Names of Books" Relationship

Relationships describe what the entities have to do with one another. In the English Query application, you use the Insert Relationship command to define a new relationship in a project.

Defining relationships and their phrasings is necessary because there are many ways to describe an association between objects in English.

You specify phrasings for a relationship as a means to talk about a relationship in English. Table 7.1 lists the types of phrasings that are available in English Query.

TABLE 7.1: Types of Relationship Phrases

Option	Description
Name/ID Phrasing	A relationship in which an entity has a name or ID. For example, parts are the name of inventory parts, or titles are the names of books.
Trait Phrasing	A relationship in which an entity is a trait, or attribute, of another entity. For example, car_colors are the colors of cars.
Preposition Phrasing	A relationship between two entities in which one is the subject and one is the accompanying object of a preposition. For example, a city is in a state. *City* is the subject, *in* is the preposition, and *state* is the object.
Adjective Phrasing	A relationship in which an entity is described by an adjective. For example, desk is brown. (Desk is an entity, and brown may be defined in the project or contained in a field in the database)
Subset Phrasing	An English description of a relationship in which one entity or word is a subset of another entity. For example, some automobiles are trucks. (Trucks are a subset of automobiles.)
Verb Phrasing	Something an entity does: For example, customers buy, or salespeople sell products to customers.

In our sample application, titles are the names of books. This relationship between books and titles must be defined before the English Query can answer questions about titles. Follow these steps to create the relationship:

1. Select Insert ➤ Relationship to display the New Relationship dialog box.

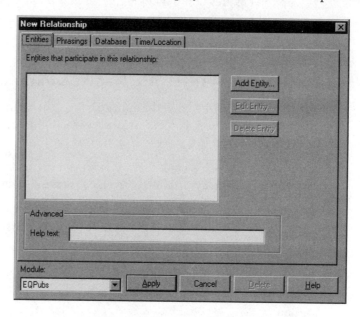

2. Click Add Entity to display the Select Entities dialog box.

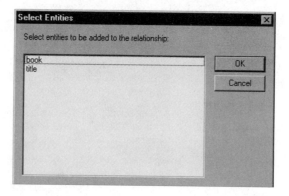

3. Select the Book entity and click OK.

4. On the New Relationship dialog box, click the Add Entity button again to return to the Select Entities dialog box. Select Title from the list of available entities.

5. Click OK to add the Title entity.

6. Click the Phrasings tab to enter a phrase for this relationship. Choose the phrasing that most closely reflects how your users would ask their questions.

7. For the titles or names of books relationships, select the Name/ID Phrasing option and click OK to display the Name/ID Phrasing dialog box.

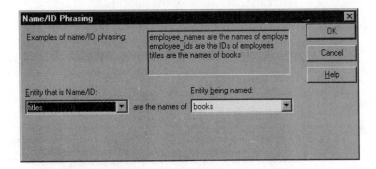

8. Select Titles from the Entity That is Name/ID list.

9. Select Books from the Entity Being Named list.

10. Click OK to add the relationship.

11. Click the Database tab to define database options for this relationship.

12. You can specify database options for a relationship when you want to calculate or identify the table that contains all the links to the tables represented by entities, or if you want to specify a condition for when the relationship is true. For our example, we want to use the default join. Click the Calculate Default Join Table and click OK to have English Query calculate the join for us.

13. Click the Apply button to add this relationship to the domain.

Now that the entities and relationships have been created for the books and titles, in the next section, we will create the entities and relationships for the authors.

Creating the Author Entities and Relationships

In this section, we will create a major entity, the Author, and its trait entries of Author_Name and Author_Phone. In addition, we will define a relationship between these entities to allow the users to ask the following questions:

- What are the names of the authors?

- Who are the authors?

- What is Marjorie Green's phone number?

- How many books did Cheryl Carson write?

Creating the Author Entity

The Author entity, represented by the entire Authors table, is a major entity in our application that is defined to answer general questions and provide information about the authors in the Pubs database, such as "How many authors are there?" or "List the authors." Follow these steps to define the Author entity:

1. Select Insert ➤ Entity to display the New Entity properties dialog box.

2. Enter the name of this entity, **author**, followed by a comma into the Words/Phrases Identifying Entity field. This will define the entity.

3. Enter some synonyms for author, such as **writer, novelist, playwright, poet, artist, reporter**. This will allow you to refer to an author by these names.

4. Select Person for the Entity Type.

5. Select Authors from the Table box.

6. Click the checkbox labeled Entire Table Associated with This Entity to instruct English Query that each row in the Authors table uniquely identifies an author. For example, you want to allow a request, such as "Count the authors." Associating the Author entity with the entire Authors table, rather

than just the Author Name fields, ensures that the count is correct. Because all fields are used in the count to uniquely identify the author, two authors who happen to have the same name are counted individually.

7. Enter **au_fname**, **au_lname**, and **phone** into the Fields field. This instructs English Query to display the values from these columns when author information is requested.

8. Click the Apply button to add the Title entity to the domain.

This completes the settings that are required for the Author entity. In the next section, we will use the Autoname option in English Query to create the Author_Name entity and relationship.

Creating the Author_Name Entity and Relationship

In this section, we will create an Author_Name entity that will allow users of the application to ask questions or request information about specific authors or about the relationship between author names and authors, such as "What do you know about Charlene Locksley?" or "Tell me about Marjorie Green."

Creating an Author_Name entity and its relationship with an author tells English Query that proper nouns (which have initial capitals) correspond to values stored in the Authors table.

Using Autoname to Create the Author_Name Entity and Relationship

Autoname is an option in English Query that allows you to quickly specify the name type and fields used in a Name entity. This option is available for table entities that do not already have a name (a relationship defined as a name phrasing is such that the name entity has a name type other than Unique ID).

Follow these steps to use the Autoname option to create the Author_Name entity and relationship:

1. On the Microsoft English Query screen shown in Figure 7.8, click the Semantics tab at the bottom of the screen. Then double-click the Author entity to display the Entity properties dialog box.

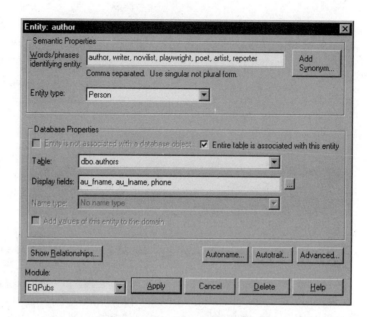

2. Click the Autoname button on the bottom of the dialog box to display the Autoname dialog box.

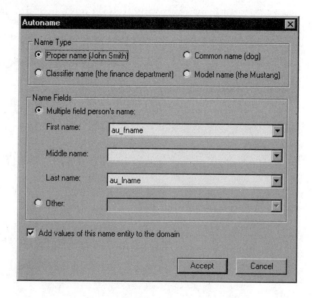

3. Click the Accept button to accept the defaults for the First Name and the Last Name values. The Autoname dialog box will disappear.

4. Click the Apply button on the Entity properties dialog box to save the changes to the domain.

To view the objects created by the Autoname option, click the plus icon next to the Author entity and double-click the Author_Name entity to display the Entity dialog box. This dialog box shows the values of the Author_Name entity that was created by the Autoname option.

To view the new relationship, click the plus icon next to the Relationship folder and double-click the "Author_Names_Are_the_Names_of_Authors" relationship to display the Relationship dialog box.

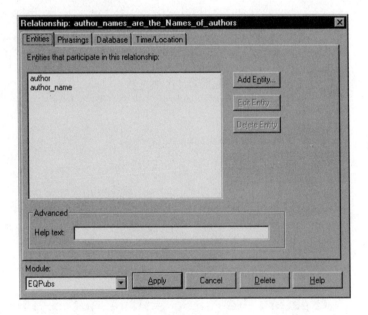

In the next section, we will create a minor entity and relationship of authors and their phone numbers.

Creating the Author_Phone Entity and Relationship

In order for English Query to be capable of presenting general questions or requests, such as "List the authors' phone numbers," and specific questions or requests, such as "What is Dean Straight's phone number?", an Author_Phone entity and a relationship between authors and their phone numbers must be created.

Creating the Author_Phone Entity

The Author_Phone entity, when used in conjunction with a relationship, allows English Query to answer questions or requests about an author's phone number, such as "List the authors and their phone numbers." Along with the relationship between author_name and author, the Author_Phone entity and its relationship with author also answers questions about specific authors, such as "What is Michel DeFrance's phone number?" Follow these steps to create the Author_Phone entity:

1. Select Insert ➤ Entity to display the New Entity properties dialog box.

2. Enter the name of this entity, **author_phone**, followed by a comma, into the Words/Phrases Identifying Entity field. This will define the entity.

3. Enter some synonyms for author phone, such as **phone number** and **telephone number**. This will allow you to refer to an author's phone number by these names.

4. Select None for the Entity Type.

5. Select Authors from the Table box.

6. Enter **au_fname**, **au_lname**, and **phone** into the Fields field. This instructs English Query that you want to see the authors' names as well as their phone numbers, because seeing just phone numbers does not do much good.

7. Click the Apply button to add the Author_Phone entity to the domain.

Creating the Authors_Have_Author_Phones Relationship

To finish this section, we need a relationship that tells English Query that authors have phone numbers. Follow these steps to create the relationship in English Query:

1. Select Insert ➤ Relationship to display the New Relationship dialog box.

2. Click Add Entity to display the Select Entities dialog box.

3. Select Author from the Select Entities box, and click OK.

4. Click Add Entity to display the Select Entities dialog box.

5. Select the Author_Phone entity from the Select Entities box, and click OK.

6. Click the Phrasings tab, and click Add to display the Select Phrasing dialog box.

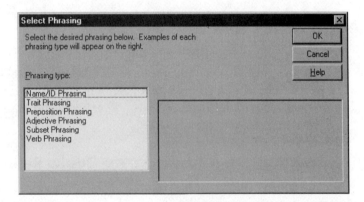

7. Double-click Trait Phrasing to display the Trait Phrasing dialog box.

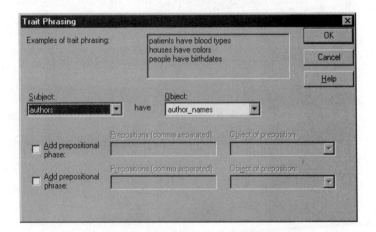

8. Select Authors from the Subject box.

9. Select Author_Phones from the Object box.

10. Click OK to close the Trait Phrasing dialog box

11. Click Apply to add the relationship to the domain.

In the next section, we will create the final relationships to allow the users to ask questions about authors and books.

Relating Authors and Books

In order to establish the relationship between authors and books, two distinct relationships that involve authors and books must first be created: that authors write books, and that books are by authors. These relationships will allow users to pose specific questions, such as "What books did Marjorie Green write?" or "Did Anne Ringer write a book?"

Creating the Authors_Write_Books Relationship

The Authors_Write_Books relationship requires a verb phrase. When creating these relationships, phrase them with active verbs, such as in "authors write books," rather than with passive verbs, as in "books are written by authors." When relationships are specified with active verbs, users can ask questions in either an active or a passive voice, because English Query adds the passive voice automatically. Follow these steps to create the Authors_Write_Books relationship:

1. Select Insert ➤ Relationship to display the New Relationship dialog box.

2. Click Add Entity to display the Select Entities dialog box.

3. Double-click the Authors entity to add it to the relationship.

4. Click Add Entity to display the Select Entities dialog box again.

5. Double-click the Book entity to add it to the relationship.

6. Click the Phrasings tab, and click Add to display the Select Phrasing dialog box.

7. Double-click Verb Phrasing to open the Verb Phrasing dialog box.

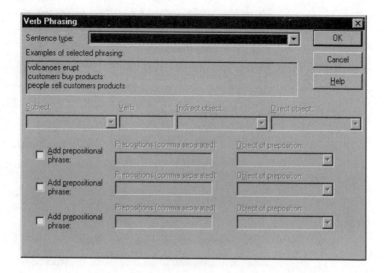

8. Select the sentence type of Subject Verb Object from the Sentence Type list box.

9. Select Authors from the Subject list box.

10. Enter **write** into the Verb list box.

11. Select Books from the Direct Object list box.

12. Click OK to add the phrase.

Creating the Books_Are_by_Authors Relationship

The Books_Are_by_Authors relationship requires a preposition phrase. Preposition phrasing defines a relationship between two entities in which one is the subject and one is the accompanying object of the preposition. For example, in the phrase "books are by authors," books is the subject, by is the preposition, and authors is the object. Follow these steps to create the relationship:

1. Click Add on the Phrasing tab to display the Select Phrasing dialog box.

2. Double-click Preposition Phrasing to open the Preposition Phrasing dialog box.

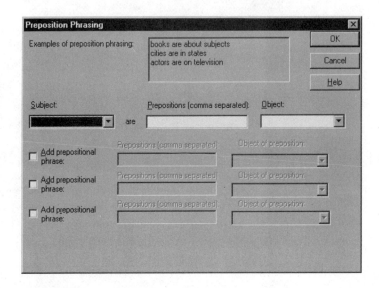

3. Select Books from the Subject list box.

4. Enter **by** into the Preposition field.

5. Select Authors from the Object list box.

6. Click OK to close the Preposition Phrasing dialog box.

7. Click Apply to add the relationships to the domain.

Whew! That was a lot of work, but the results are worth it. In the next section, we will test the English Query application with the built-in testing system.

Testing the English Query Application

The first step in testing our new English Query application is to make sure the application has been saved. Select File ➤ Save Project to save the project.

Your English Query application should look like the one in Figure 7.10.

To test the application, select Tools ➤ Test Application to open the Test Application form, as shown in Figure 7.11.

FIGURE 7.10:

Completed English Query
application

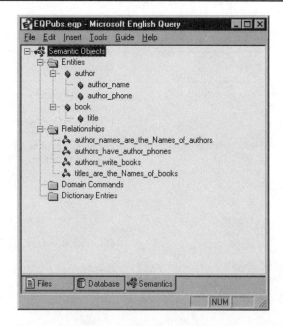

FIGURE 7.11:

Test Application form

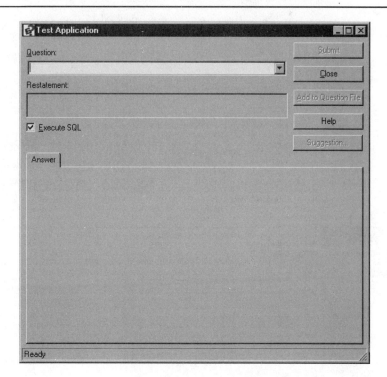

The parts of the Test Application are listed in Table 7.2.

TABLE 7.2: Parts of the Test Application

Part	Description
Question box	Provides an area for you to enter a question. Questions are kept in the list box and can be recalled during the current session. These questions are deleted when you close English Query.
Restatement box	English Query provides an English interpretation of the end user's question or request when you click the Submit button.
Execute SQL checkbox	If checked, the SQL Statement is executed and the results are displayed in the Results tab.
Answer tab	An area that displays the results of the question.
Analysis tab	Provides a list of phrasings that were used to answer a question.
GoTo button (Analysis tab)	If a phrase is selected in the Analysis tab, clicking this button displays corresponding dialog box.
Submit button	Submits the current question or statement in the Question box.
Close button	Closes the Test Application form.
Add to Question File button	Adds the current question or statement to the Question file. This file is used in a front-end interface to English Query, such as Visual Basic.
Help button	Displays the English Query help file for the Test Application.
Suggestion button	Opens the Entity Confirmation dialog box where you can attempt to determine the reason you did not get the desired results.

To test the English Query, enter some questions and statements into the Question box and click the Submit button. Be sure that you check the Execute SQL checkbox so the results are displayed in the Answer tab. Go ahead and give it a try! You can enter the following questions, then make up and enter a few of your own.

> **NOTE** As you enter your questions and statements, click the Add to Question File. This will provide a history of the questions when accessing English Query from a Visual Basic application, later in this chapter.

- Who are the authors?

- How many books did Michael O'Leary write?

- What is Marjorie Green's phone number?

- Did Sheryl Hunter write a book?

- Who wrote the book entitled, "Sushi, Anyone?"? (Notice that the title has been enclosed in quotation marks. When a title consists of more than one word, it must be enclosed in quotation marks.)

- List the authors.

- What is Dean's last name?

- List the authors' telephone numbers.

- How many authors are there?

This is just a small sample of the types of questions that can be asked and the sorts of entities and relationships that can be created. Although implementing an English Query application takes considerable planning and hard work, the results are truly amazing. In the next section, we will access English Query from a Visual Basic 6 application.

Accessing English Query from Visual Basic

To fully enjoy the benefits of English Query, it should be accessed from an environment that your users are familiar with. Visual Basic is a great choice because it can exploit all of the features of an English Query application. In the next sections, we will create a Visual Basic application that will enable you to connect to the English Query application that we built earlier in this chapter and to present your questions. It's time to roll up your sleeves and dig in!

Creating the VB EnglishQuery Project

The Visual Basic EnglishQuery project (EQVB), shown in Figure 7.12, consists of a main form where the user can submit a question and see the results. After the question has been submitted, the application displays a restatement of the question that is used by the English Query engine and interpreted into a SQL statement. In addition, the SQL statement that is passed to SQL Server is available for inspection.

NOTE   The English Query project can be found in the **ch7code\EQVB** folder that comes with this book.

FIGURE 7.12:

English Query project

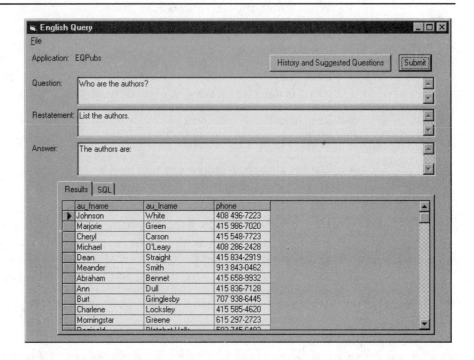

The application includes three support forms:

- An opening form that allows the user to select the location of the English Query files

- A history form where the user can select a question from a list of suggested questions or select a question from a history of previously selected questions

- A clarification form where the user can clarify ambiguous words

NOTE   The source for suggested questions is the History file that we created when we tested the English Query application, earlier in this chapter.

Examining the EQVB Project Code

The code used in the EQVB project demonstrates the major points in creating a Visual Basic interface to an English Query application. To access an English

Query application, you must add a reference to the English Query 2 library in the References dialog box. Adding this reference provides your project access to the properties, methods, and events of the English Query engine. A complete list of these is available in the Object Browser.

Submitting a Question to the English Query Engine

The main action of the EQVB project is to submit a question to the English Query engine. This is accomplished in four major steps:

1. Send the request to the engine for interpretation into an the actual SQL statement.

2. Have the engine restate the question.

3. Execute the SQL statement.

4. Display the results for the user.

These steps are detailed in the following sections.

Retrieving the SQL Statement

In an English Query application, the user is able to present questions and requests in English. It is up to the English Query application to interpret these questions and requests into SQL statements. The code in Code 7.1, taken from the Submit Command button, shows how this can be accomplished.

Code 7.1   **Retrieving the SQL Statement**

```
Private Sub cmdSubmit_Click()
    Dim iNumAnswers As Integer
    Dim strRestatement As String

    'Select Question
    txtQuestion.SelStart = 0
    txtQuestion.SelLength = Len(txtQuestion.Text)
    glCurrentQuestion = txtQuestion.Text
    glrCurrentSQL = ""
    frmHistory.lstHistory.AddItem (glCurrentQuestion)
    frmQuery.txtNextAnswer.Visible = False

    'Send it to Engine
```

```
Screen.MousePointer = MouseHourGlass
iNumAnswers = SubmitQuery(glObjNLSession, glCurrentQuestion, _
    glResponseType, strRestatement, glAnswer, glError, glSQL)
Screen.MousePointer = MouseNormal

If iNumAnswers < 0 Then
    MsgBox strError, vbOKOnly, "Error"
    Exit Sub
End If

glNumDisplays = iNumAnswers
glLastDisplay = 0
If iNumAnswers > 1 Then
    frmQuery.txtNextAnswer.Visible = True
End If

txtRestatement.Text = strRestatement
Select Case glResponseType(0)
    Case iAnswerParse
        txtAnswer.Text = glAnswer(0)
    Case iSQLParse
        glrCurrentSQL = glSQL(0)
        Screen.MousePointer = MouseHourGlass
        Call ExecuteQuery(glSQL(0), 1, 0)
        txtAnswer.Text = glAnswer(0)
        Screen.MousePointer = MouseNormal
        txtSQL = glrCurrentSQL
    Case iSQLYesNo
        glrCurrentSQL = glSQL(0)
        Screen.MousePointer = MouseHourGlass
        txtAnswer.Text = glAnswer(0)
        Call ExecuteQuery(glSQL(0), 1, 1)
        Screen.MousePointer = MouseNormal
    Case Else
        MsgBox "Unknown Reply from SubmitQuery", _
            vbOKOnly, "Error"
        Exit Sub
End Select
End Sub
```

The first part of the code selects the question and adds it to the History List box. Next, the question text is sent to the English Query engine where it is parsed, restated, and returned as a SQL Statement. Then, after this SQL Statement is returned, the parts of the return are dealt with, such as by determining if multiple answers exist and by displaying the Restatement.

The next major part of the subroutine determines the type of SQL statement or answer that is returned. There are three possibilities for the form of the answer:

1. Rows that can be displayed on a grid

2. A True or False answer

3. An error

The type of answer is determined and dealt with in a Select Case statement and, unless there is an error, the ExecuteQuery Function is called.

Executing the SQL Statement and Displaying the Results

After the user's question has been interpreted by the English Query engine and returned as a SQL Statement, it is time to execute the statement by sending it to SQL Server. This is the end result of all of your hard work, both here in the Visual Basic application and in the design and construction of the English Query application, as shown in Code 7.2.

Code 7.2   **Executing the SQL Statement and Displaying the Results**

```
Sub ExecuteQuery(strQuery As String, fDisplayToUser As Integer, _
    fYesNo As Interger

    Dim objResultSet As rdoResultset
    Dim objrdoQuery As rdoQuery
    Dim iNumRDOColumns As Integer, iGridColumns As Integer
    Dim i As Integer

    If (glObjrdocn Is Nothing) Then
        Exit Sub
    End If

    'Execute silently
```

```
            If fDisplayToUser = 0 Then
                glObjrdocn.Execute strQuery, rdExecDirect
                Exit Sub
            End If

            'Execute and populate grid
            Set objrdoQuery = glObjrdocn.CreateQuery(Name:="", _
                SqlString:=strQuery)
            objrdoQuery.MaxRows = MAXANSWERROWS
            Set objResultSet = objrdoQuery.OpenResultset(Type:=rdOpenStatic, _
        LockType:=rdConcurReadOnly, Options:=rdExecDirect)

            'Display Grid
            Set frmQuery.MSRDC1.ResultSet = objResultSet
            frmQuery.MSRDC1.Refresh

            'If  Yes No Answer
            If fYesNo > 0 Then
                iNumRDOColumns = objResultSet.rdoColumns.Count
                If iNumRDOColumns > 0 Then
                    frmQuery.txtAnswer.Text = "Yes."
                Else
                    frmQuery.txtAnswer.Text = "No."
                End If
                Exit Sub
            End If

            Set objrdoQuery = Nothing
        End Sub
```

The first part of this code determines if the data source exists. If the data source does not exist, the subroutine exits. In the next part of the code, the Execute method is used to execute the SQL statement. After the execution of the SQL statement, a resultset is opened that contains the results of the execution and displays them on the grid on the Query form. If the results are in the form of True/False, then Yes or No is displayed in the txtAnswerText box.

You should take a few moments to look around in the sample project. There is a lot of code there that will give you a good head-start on creating a full-blown Visual Basic front-end interface to an English Query application. In the next section, we will take the EQVB project out for a test drive!

Testing the EQVB Project

Press F5 to start the EQVB application. This sample application is based on the TestPubs data source.

NOTE   If you do not have a TestPubs data source, you should create one or change the name to a data source that you do have for the Pubs sample database. This reference can be found in the InitilizeDB function in the **VBEQLib.bas** file.

Follow these steps to test the EQVB application:

1. The Opening form will be displayed. The default English Query files are taken from the English Query application that we built earlier in this chapter. If you saved the files with another name or in another location, enter the new values here.

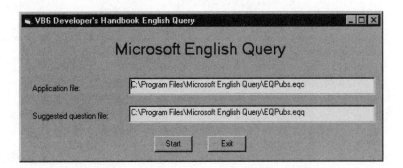

2. Click the Start button to start the application and display the English Query form.

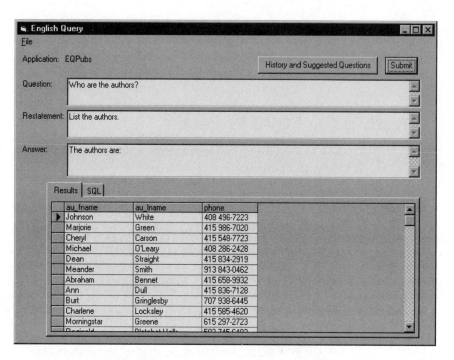

3. Click the History and Suggested Question button to display the History and Suggested Questions form.

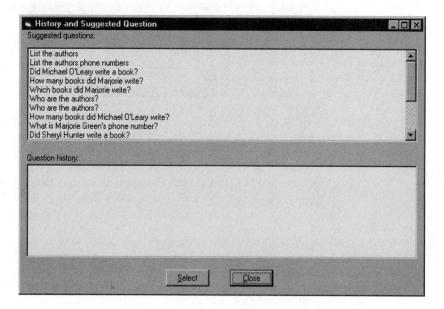

4. Click the "Who are the authors?" question and click the Select button to select this question and close the History form.

5. Click the Submit button to submit the question.

6. The results are displayed in the Results tab, and the restatement and answer text are displayed in the Restatement and Answer areas.

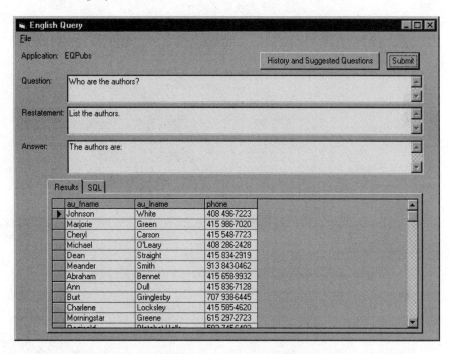

7. Click the SQL Tab to see the SQL Statement that was created by the English Query application and executed on the SQL server.

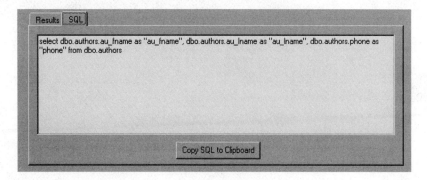

8. The Copy SQL to Clipboard button will copy the SQL statement to the clipboard.

CHAPTER
EIGHT

8

Three-Tiered Applications

- Understanding the Three Tiers

- Developing the Three-Tiered project

In Chapter 3, we discussed some aspects of three-tiered applications. In this chapter, we will build a sample three-tiered application based on the Pubs database and use SQL Server 7.0 as the database engine.

NOTE   Although SQL Server 7.0 is used in this chapter, the examples will work just as well with SQL Server 6.5.

Three-tiered architecture partitions an application into three logical tiers, or services:

- User services (the front end)
- Business services (the middle)
- Data services (the back end)

By using three-tiered architecture, you can develop applications that separate user access, business rules, and data access into separate modules.

Understanding the Three Tiers

In our sample application, tier one, or user services, consists of one Form (shown in Figure 8.1) with the fields from the Authors table that will allow the user to do the following:

- Add new records to the Authors table
- Delete current records from the Authors table
- Find records based on an author's ID number that is actually a Social Security number
- Update records and change the current values

The user interface for tier one incorporates components that we discussed in many previous chapters, including:

- Menus
- Toolbars

- Status bars

- Advanced ActiveX controls

FIGURE 8.1:

The tier one Form

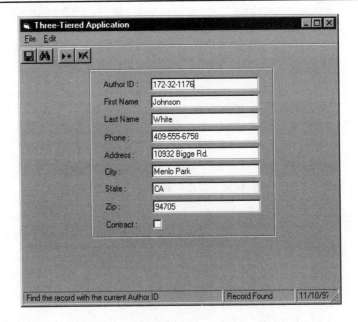

Tier two, business services, is a separate application compiled into a DLL. There is no interface for tier two because it receives requests from tier one and passes them on to the database through ADO 2 (ActiveX Data Objects 2).

NOTE   See Chapter 4 for a complete discussion of ActiveX Data Objects.

Tier three, data services, consists of the Pubs database, which we use throughout this book. It is the same sample database that comes with SQL Server 7.0 and is created when SQL Server is installed. In order to run the examples in this chapter, you must have access to the database. If the Pubs database is not installed on your server or if it has been altered, install it by running the `Instpubs.sql` script included on the CD that comes with this book.

The Three-Tiered Project

The Three-Tiered project is composed of two applications and the database. The front end, or tier one (as shown in Figure 8.1), provides the user interface for presenting information and gathering data. It gathers requirements from the user and presents data in response to a question or a query. The user can add, delete, update, and search records in the Pubs database.

NOTE You will find the TierOne and TierTwo projects in the **Ch8** folder on the CD that comes with this book.

Processing Toolbar Requests

Our application provides a toolbar (shown in Figure 8.2) with which users can interact with the program. The toolbar has four buttons that perform the following actions:

- Save Record sends a request to the TierTwo application to save changes to the current record.

- Find sends a request to find the record that has the current AuthorID.

- New Record sends a request to add a new record to the database using the current field values.

- Delete Record sends a request to delete the current record.

FIGURE 8.2:

The TierOne toolbar

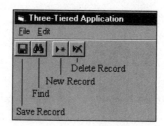

The code used to respond to the users toolbar selection is shown in Code 8.1.

Code 8.1	**The Three-Tiered Application Toolbar**

```
Private Sub Toolbar1_ButtonClick(ByVal Button _
    As ComctlLib.Button)
    On Error GoTo ErrorRoutineErr
    RichTextBox1.Visible = False
    Select Case Button.Key
        Case "Save"
            Call mnuSave_Click
        Case "Find"
            Call mnuFind_Click
        Case "New"
            Call mnuNew_Click
        Case "Delete"
            Call mnuDelete_Click
    End Select
ErrorRoutineResume:
    Exit Sub
ErrorRoutineErr:
    MsgBox "TierOne.Form1.Toolbar1_ButtonClick" _
    & Err & Error
End Sub
```

As you can see, the toolbar simply calls the associated code in the menu to perform the request. This alleviates the need to duplicate the code.

Adding Records

To add a new author's record to the database, you simply click the Add button on the toolbar, as shown in Figure 8.2, or choose Edit ➢ New Record. This will call the mnuNew_click code, as shown in Code 8.2.

NOTE   Remember: Tier one does not actually have any SQL statements or database code. It simply passes requests to tier two.

If all goes well, the record is added to the database, and the status bar is updated to display Record Added, as shown in Code 8.2.

Code 8.2   **Sending a Request to Tier Two to Add a Record**

```
Private Sub mnuNew_Click()
    On Error GoTo ErrorRoutineErr
    'Get the Authors ID
    clsAuthor.AuthorID = txtAuthorID

    'Assign the class values
    Call AssignValues

    'Add the new record
    clsAuthor.Add

ErrorRoutineResume:
    Exit Sub
ErrorRoutineErr:
    MsgBox "TierOne.Form1.mnuNew_Click" & Err & Error
    Resume Next
End Sub
```

NOTE   Notice the use of error-trapping code. Error-trapping code is always important, but here it is essential. You are calling a DLL, and if an error occurs, it is important for you to know where and why.

This code calls the Add subroutine in the TierTwo application, where all the work is performed. Tier one simply gathers requirements from the user and processes requests. It should not know or care how the data is processed.

When a request is processed, one of three things happens:

- The request is processed without any errors.

- A noncritical error occurs (for example, the record is not found).

- A database error occurs.

If the request is successful or if a noncritical error occurs, the TierTwo application raises the Action event in the TierOne application, and the status bar is updated, as demonstrated in Code 8.3.

Code 8.3   **Raising the Action Event in Tier One**

```
Private Sub clsAuthor_Action(ByVal Status As Integer)
    'This event is raised by TierTwo.dll in the event
    'of a non-critical error

    'Define variables
    Dim Msg, Style, Title, Response

    'Clear the status
    StatusBar1.Panels(2).Text = ""

    Select Case Status
        Case 2
            'No record found
            Msg = "No Authors record was located" _
            & "with the AuthorID: " & txtAuthorID
            Title = "No Records Found"
            StatusBar1.Panels(2).Text _
            = "Record Not Found"
        Case 3
            'Record not deleted
            Msg = "No Authors record was located" _
            & "with the AuthorID: " _
            & txtAuthorID _
            & Chr(10) _
            & "No record was deleted"
            Title = "Delete Error"
            StatusBar1.Panels(2).Text _
            = "Record Not Deleted"
        Case 4
            'Record not updated
            Msg = "No Authors record was located" _
            & "with the AuthorID: " & txtAuthorID _
            & Chr(10) _
            & "No record was updated"
            Title = "Update Error"
            StatusBar1.Panels(2).Text _
            = "Record Not Updated"
        Case 100
            'Record Deleted
            StatusBar1.Panels(2).Text _
```

```
            = "Record Deleted"
            Exit Sub
        Case 200
            'Record Found
            StatusBar1.Panels(2).Text _
            = "Record Found"
            Exit Sub
        Case 300
            'record Added
            StatusBar1.Panels(2).Text _
            = "Record Added"
            Exit Sub
        Case 400
            'Record Updated
            StatusBar1.Panels(2).Text _
            = "Record Saved"
            Exit Sub
    End Select

'Display the msgbox
DisplayMsgbox:
    Style = vbOKOnly + vbInformation
    Response = MsgBox(Msg, Style, Title)
End Sub
```

The code in the Action subroutine is passed an integer value from the TierTwo application in response to an action request. If no errors were found, a value of 100, 200, 300, or 400 is passed. The Action code interprets this value and constructs the proper status bar response.

If a record was not found, a value of 2, 3, or 4 is passed back. In this case, in addition to the status bar response, a message box is displayed, notifying the user of the error.

If a database error occurs while the record is being processed, the TierTwo application raises the Errors event in the TierOne application and calls the code in Code 8.4. This code displays a message box, notifying you that an error has occurred, and a RichTextBox control becomes visible between the author fields and the status bar, as shown in Figure 8.3. The rdoErrors, which contains details about remote data access errors, is written to the RichTextBox control, and the status bar displays Processing Error.

FIGURE 8.3:

The Three-Tiered application displaying error messages

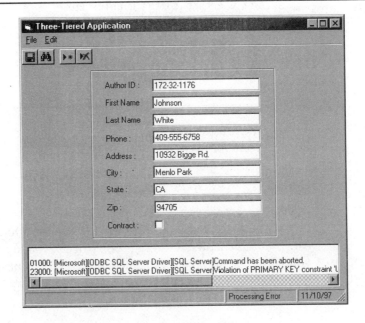

Code 8.4   Raising an Error

```
Private Sub clsAuthor_Errors(ErrMessages As Object)
    'This event is called from the TierTwo.dll
    'if errors are encountered.
    'Errors will be written to the RichTextBox control

    'Define variables
    Dim er As Object

    'Clear the status
    StatusBar1.Panels(2).Text = "Processing Error"

    'Clear the error text
    RichTextBox1.Text = ""

    RichTextBox1.Visible = True
    MsgBox "An error has occurred. Error messages" _
    & " will be displayed in the Errors box."
```

```
      'Write errors to the RichTextBox
      For Each er In ErrMessages
      RichTextBox1.Text = RichTextBox1.Text _
            & Chr(10) & er
      Next
   End Sub
```

This generic error-handling code module is raised, or called, from the TierTwo application in the event of a critical database error.

Deleting Records

Deleting records is easy in our application. With a valid AuthorID present, choose Edit ➤ Delete Record or simply click the Delete button, as shown in Figure 8.2, earlier in this chapter. A message box will ask you to confirm the delete request. If you select Yes, the record is deleted. Select No to cancel the request. When you delete the record, the status bar is updated to display Record Deleted to let you know that the delete was successful.

If an error occurs while the record is being processed, a message box notifies you that an error has occurred, and a RichTextBox control becomes visible between the author fields and the status bar. The rdoErrors is written to the RichTextBox control, and the status bar displays Processing Error.

The TierOne application uses the following code, shown in Code 8.5, to request a delete from the TierTwo application.

Code 8.5   **Sending a Delete Request**

```
Private Sub mnuDelete_Click()
   On Error GoTo ErrorRoutineErr
   'Declare variables
   Dim Msg, Style, Title, Response

   'Get the Authors ID
   clsAuthor.AuthorID = txtAuthorID

   'Confirm the delete request
   Msg = "Delete the current Author's record?"
   Style = vbYesNo + vbQuestion + vbDefaultButton1
```

```
        Title = "Confirm Delete"
        Response = MsgBox(Msg, Style, Title)
        If Response = vbYes Then
            'Delete the record
            clsAuthor.Delete
            Call PopulateTextBoxes
        Else
            'no action
            StatusBar1.Panels(2).Text = "Delete Aborted"
        End If

ErrorRoutineResume:
    Exit Sub
ErrorRoutineErr:
    MsgBox "TierOne.Form1.mnuDelete_Click" & Err & Error
    Resume Next
End Sub
```

This code gets the author's ID from the AuthorID field, which is used to actually locate the record for deletion. Next, a message box is constructed and displayed; it asks you to confirm the delete request. If you select Yes, the request is sent to the DLL; if you select No, the status bar is updated with `Delete Aborted`, and no action is taken.

Finding an Author's Record

Our application also makes easy work of searching for a particular author; you simply enter the author's ID number in the AuthorID field and click the Find icon, as shown in Figure 8.2 earlier in this chapter. The application gets the AuthorID number from the TierTwo application and then sends a request to the application to create a recordset with the AuthorID number.

If the process is completed successfully and the record is found, the fields are filled in with the record, and the status bar is updated to display `Record Found`. As in the other cases, if an error occurs, the text box at the bottom of the screen displays the error messages. The following code, shown in Code 8.6, sends the Find request to the DLL.

Code 8.6 **Sending a Request to Find a Record**

```
Private Sub mnuFind_Click()
    On Error GoTo ErrorRoutineErr
    'AuthorID to find
    clsAuthor.AuthorID = txtAuthorID

    'Lookup
    clsAuthor.Search
    Call PopulateTextBoxes

ErrorRoutineResume:
    Exit Sub
ErrorRoutineErr:
    MsgBox "TierOne.Form1.mnuFind_Click" & Err & Error
    Resume ErrorRoutineResume
End Sub
```

This code is straightforward. First, the AuthorID number is retrieved from the AuthorID text box; then a request is sent to the TierTwo application to perform a search, and, finally, the new records populate the text boxes.

Updating a Current Record

From time to time, you will find it necessary to make changes to current records. Our application supports changes by sending an update request to the TierTwo application. To change a record, you simply locate a current record with the Find method, or add a new record and change one or more fields. Click the Save icon, as shown in Figure 8.2 earlier in this chapter, to send an Update request to the TierTwo application. If the record is successfully changed, the status bar displays Record Updated, notifying you that the change was successful. If an error occurs, the text box at the bottom of the screen displays the error message. The following code, shown in Code 8.7, sends an update request to tier two.

Code 8.7 **Sending an Update Request to Tier Two**

```
Private Sub mnuSave_Click()
    On Error GoTo ErrorRoutineErr
    'Get the Authors ID
```

```
        clsAuthor.AuthorID = txtAuthorID

        'Assign the class values
        Call AssignValues

        'Add the new record
        clsAuthor.Update

ErrorRoutineResume:
        Exit Sub
ErrorRoutineErr:
        MsgBox "TierOne.Form1.mnuSave_Click" & Err & Error
        Resume Next
    End Sub
```

This code looks a lot like the code used to add or delete a record. First, the AuthorID number is retrieved from the AuthorID text box, and then the update request is sent. If the update is successful, the status bar displays Record Updated.

The user interface, or tier one, of a three-tiered application simply gathers requests and passes them to the business services, or second tier. No SQL statements or records are processed. In the next section, we will explore the tier-two application where the records are processed.

The TierTwo Application

In our sample application, the business services, or middle tier, is made up of a class module and is compiled into a dynamic-link library program, or DLL.

The TierTwo application does not have a user interface; in fact, the user really should not even know or care about this application. Its purpose is to receive requests from the front-end application, in our case the TierOne program, to process the requests and to notify the calling application of the status. In our case, this is accomplished with one class module.

Creating Properties, Methods, and Events

We created the class module in our TierTwo application with the help of the Class Builder add-in that comes with Visual Basic 6. The class module we will build consists of properties, methods, and events.

NOTE   For a complete discussion of Visual Basic classes, see Chapter 10.

Defining the Class Properties

The properties in our class are the fields from the Authors table in the Pubs database. Table 8.1 lists and describes them.

TABLE 8.1: The Class Properties

Property	Description
Address	The author's address
AuthorID	The author's Social Security number, which is the key to the table
City	The author's city
Contract	Signifies whether the author is under contract
FirstName	The author's first name
LastName	The author's last name
Phone	The author's phone number
State	The author's state
Zip	The author's zip code

Defining the Class Methods

The methods for our class module are the actions that can be performed from the front end, or the TierOne application. Table 8.2 lists and describes them.

TABLE 8.2: Methods Supported by the TierTwo Application

Method	Description
Add	Adds a new record to the authors table
Delete	Deletes the current record from the Authors table
Search	Locates a record matching the current AuthorID field
Update	Saves changes to the current author's record

Defining the Class Events

The events in our class module are raised and are available in the TierOne application. Table 8.3 lists and describes these events.

TABLE 8.3: Events Raised by the TierTwo Application

Event	Description
Action	Called in response to a method. If the method completes without a critical database error, the Action event is raised.
Errors	Raised if a critical database error occurs.

Accessing the Class Builder Utility

The Class Builder add-in is designed to help you build the class and collection hierarchy for your Visual Basic project. It keeps track of the hierarchy of your classes and collections and generates the framework code for implementing the classes and collections, including the properties, methods, and events.

Follow these steps to open the Class Builder add-in:

1. Choose Add-Ins ➤ Add-Ins Manager to display the Add-In Manager dialog box.

2. Select the VB6 Class Builder Utility from the list of Available Add-Ins and click the Loaded/Unloaded checkbox to load the Class Builder.

3. Click OK to add the Class Builder Utility to the list of add-ins.

4. Choose Add-Ins ➤ VB Class Builder Utility to open the Class Builder dialog box.

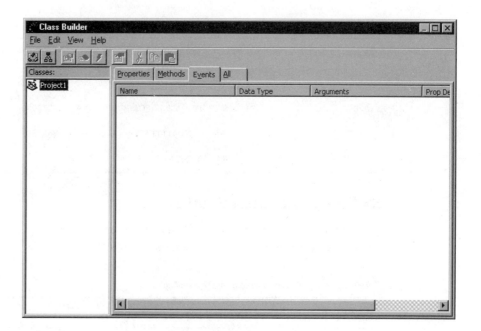

Creating the Class Properties

Now, let's create the properties for our class module with the Class Builder Utility. Follow these steps:

1. Choose File ≻ New ≻ Class to open the Class Module Builder dialog box:

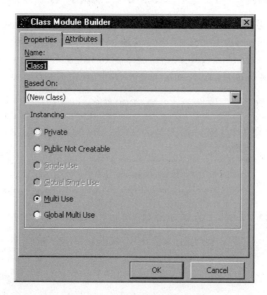

2. In the Name text box, enter **Authors** as the name for the new class.

3. In the Based On text box, accept the default (New Class), and in the Instancing section, select the Multi Use option to create the Class Module for multiuser use. Then click OK.

4. Choose File ➤ New ➤ Property to open the Property Builder dialog box:

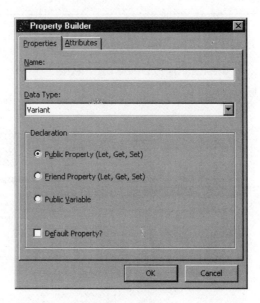

5. In this dialog box, you name the property as well as set the data type and declarations. Add the new properties by typing the name in the Name field according to Table 8.4, and then click OK.

TABLE 8.4: The Property Settings for the Authors Class

Property	Data Type	Declaration
Address	String	Public Property (Let, Get, Set)
AuthorID	String	Public Property (Let, Get, Set)
City	String	Public Property (Let, Get, Set)
Contract	String	Public Property (Let, Get, Set)
FirstName	String	Public Property (Let, Get, Set)
LastName	String	Public Property (Let, Get, Set)

Continued on next page

TABLE 8.4 CONTINUED: The Property Settings for the Authors Class

Property	Data Type	Declaration
Phone	String	Public Property (Let, Get, Set)
State	String	Public Property (Let, Get, Set)
Zip	String	Public Property (Let, Get, Set)

Creating the Methods

Follow these steps to create the methods for the Authors class:

1. Choose File ➤ New ➤ Method to open the Method Builder dialog box:

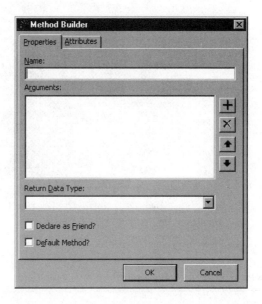

2. You use this dialog box to name the methods. These methods do not need a return value, so leave the Return Data Type text box blank. Create the following methods by typing the name in the Name field and then clicking the OK button:

   Add

   Delete

   Search

   Update

Creating the Events

Follow these steps to create the events for the Authors class:

1. Choose File ➤ New ➤ Event to open the Event Builder dialog box:

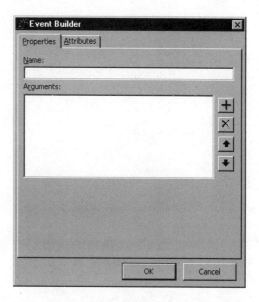

2. Each event will have a name and an argument. Create two events according to Table 8.6. Enter the event's name in the Name text box, enter the argument's name in the Arguments text box, and then click the Plus button.

T A B L E 8.6 : Events for the Authors Class

Event Name	Argument Name	Data Type	By Val
Action	Status	Integer	Yes
Errors	ErrMessages	Object	No

Now that we have created all the properties, events, and methods, select the All tab to see a list of all these items. Choose File ➤ Exit and answer Yes to the confirmation message box to close the Class Builder Utility and update the project.

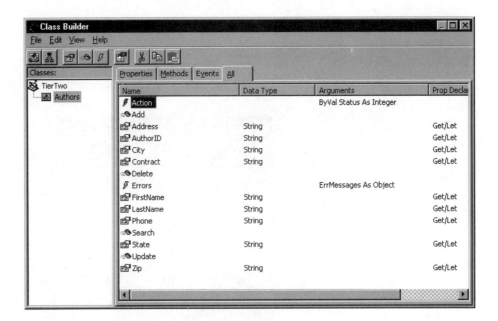

In the next sections, we will discuss the TierTwo application flow and examine some of the code modules.

Writing the Code for Tier Two

As we discussed earlier in this chapter, the business services, or second tier, in a three-tiered application does not include a user interface. It is composed of class modules. In the previous sections, we used the Class Builder Utility to give us a head start on writing the code. In this section, we will examine the major code sections created by the utility.

When we created the properties, events, and methods with the Class Builder Utility, Visual Basic 6 used our entries to generate code for those sections. A Get and Let property was created for each property. Code 8.8 shows the Property Get subroutine for the Address property.

Code 8.8   **The Address Property Get Subroutine**

```
Public Property Get Address() As String
'Used when retrieving value of a property,
'on the right side of an assignment.
```

```
'Syntax: Debug.Print X.Address
    Address = mvarAddress
End Property
```

In addition to the property Get and Let code, the Class Builder Utility generated an empty procedure for the Add, Delete, Save, and Update methods. It is up to you to add code to these procedures. We added the following code, shown in Code 8.9, for the Add method.

Code 8.9	**The Class Builder Utility Add Method Code**

```
Public Sub Add(ByVal Status As Integer)

End Sub
```

As you can see, this is just the beginning of a procedure and has the name and event arguments that you defined.

The last code that the Class Builder Utility adds is for the Action and Errors events that you defined. The code in Code 8.10 has been added to the General Declarations section of the Authors class module.

Code 8.10	**Code Added for Events**

```
'To fire this event, use RaiseEvent
'with the following syntax:
'RaiseEvent Action[(arg1, arg2, ... , argn)]
Public Event Action(ByVal Status As Integer)
'To fire this event, use RaiseEvent
'with the following syntax:
'RaiseEvent rdoe[(arg1, arg2, ... , argn)]
Public Event Errors(ErrMessages As Object)
```

This code defines the events that can be raised for the calling application or, in our example, the TierOne application.

In the next section, we will add code to each of the methods to make them actually perform a function for us.

Coding the Methods

At this point, the methods that we have defined are just empty procedures. We need to add code to each one for it to actually perform a database function.

Adding Code to the Add Method

In our application, the Add method adds a new record to the Authors table in the Pubs database. The following subroutine, shown in Code 8.11, clears the cnn1.Errors object to ensure that we do not get an error message left over from a previous action. Next, an INSERT SQL statement is constructed that inserts a new record in the Authors table based on the value from the text boxes on the TierOne application Form. The values are retrieved by the Property Get procedures in the TierTwo application. After the SQL Statement is constructed, it is executed with the EXECUTE statement.

If an error occurs, the Errors event is raised in the TierOne application. If no errors are encountered, the Action event is raised to notify the user that the record was added.

NOTE   See Code 8.3 earlier in this chapter for an explanation of the Action event, and see Code 8.4 for an explanation of the Errors event.

Code 8.11   **Adding a New Record**

```
Public Sub Add()

    On Error Resume Next
    'Declare variables
    Dim ssql As String
    Dim strCnn As String
    Dim cnn1 As ADODB.Connection
    Dim cmdChange As ADODB.Command
    Dim errLoop As ADODB.Error

    'Open ADO connection
    strCnn = "DSN=PubsTest;UID=sa;PWD=pwd;"
    Set cnn1 = New ADODB.Connection
    cnn1.Open strCnn
```

```
'Clear extraneous errors from the Errors collection
cnn1.Errors.Clear

'Construct SQL statement
ssql = "INSERT INTO Authors(au_id,au_lname," _
    & "au_fname,phone,address,city,state,zip,contract)" _
& "VALUES ('" _
& AuthorID & "','" _
& LastName & "','" _
& FirstName & "','" _
& Phone & "','" _
& Address & "','" _
& City & "','" _
& State & "','" _
& Zip & "'," _
& Contract & ")"

'Use the Connection object's execute method to
'execute SQL statement to add the record
cnn1.Execute ssql

'Check for errors
If cnn1.Errors.Count > 0 Then
    'An error has occurred
    'Pass the rdoErrors to the calling application
    RaiseEvent Errors(cnn1.Errors)
Else
    'No error
    RaiseEvent Action(300)
End If

End Sub
```

Notice the On Error Resume Next statement. We included this because we want the errors to be raised in the Error event of the calling program.

Adding Code to the Delete Method

The Delete method, shown in Code 8.12, deletes a record from the Authors table in the Pubs database. In the Delete subroutine, the cnn1.Errors object is cleared to ensure that we do not get an error message left over from a previous action. Next, a DELETE SQL statement is constructed and executed that attempts to delete the current record from the Authors table based on the value from the AuthorID text box on the TierOne applications form. The value is retrieved with the Property Get AuthorID procedure in the TierTwo application.

If an error occurs during the delete attempt, the Errors event is raised in the TierOne application. In addition to checking for errors, the RowsAffected property of the Execute statement is checked to see if a row was actually deleted. If the RowsAffected value is greater than zero, you know the AuthorID was found and the record was deleted. If not, the Action event is raised with a value of 3. In the Action event in the TierOne application, the return value of 3 is interpreted, and a message notifies the user that the record was not found and was not deleted.

Code 8.12   **Deleting a Record**

```
Public Sub Delete()

    On Error Resume Next
    'Declare variables
    Dim ssql As String
    Dim strCnn As String
    Dim cnn1 As ADODB.Connection
    Dim cmdChange As ADODB.Command
    Dim errLoop As ADODB.Error
    Dim slRecordsAffected As Long

    'Open ADO connection
    strCnn = "DSN=PubsTest;UID=sa;PWD=pwd;"
    Set cnn1 = New ADODB.Connection
    cnn1.Open strCnn

    'Clear extraneous errors from the Errors collection
    cnn1.Errors.Clear

    'Build the SQL statement
    ssql = "DELETE FROM Authors " _
    & "WHERE au_id = '" & AuthorID & "' "

    'Use the Connection object's execute method to
    'execute the SQL statement to delete the record
    'return the number of records affected into the
    'variable slRecordsAffected
```

```
        cnn1.Execute ssql, slRecordsAffected

        'Check for errors
        If cnn1.Errors.Count > 0 Then
            'An error has occurred
            'Pass the rdoErrors to the calling application
            RaiseEvent Errors(cnn1.Errors)
        Else
            If slRecordsAffected > 0 Then
                'No error
                'Clear the values
                AuthorID = ""
                LastName = ""
                FirstName = ""
                Phone = ""
                Address = ""
                City = ""
                State = ""
                Zip = ""
                Contract = ""
                RaiseEvent Action(100)
            Else
                'There were no errors but,
                'no row was deleted
                'The record was not found
                RaiseEvent Action(3)
            End If
        End If
    End Sub
```

Adding Code to the Search Method

The Search method, shown in Code 8.13, locates a record from the Authors table in the Pubs database by searching for the AuthorID. In the Search subroutine, the rdoError object is cleared to ensure that we do not get an error message left over from a previous action. Next, a SELECT SQL statement is constructed, and an rdoResultSet is created with the results of the search of the Authors table based on the value from the Author text boxes on the TierOne application Form. The value is retrieved with the Property Get AuthorID procedures in the TierTwo application.

The EOF, or End of File, property of the recordset is checked to see if a row was actually returned. If the EOF property is True, you know the AuthorID was not found because the recordset is at the end of file; the Action event is passed back with a value of 2, signifying that no record was found. If the recordset is not at EOF, the class properties are filled with the values from the current record in the recordset, and the Action event is raised with a value of 200, signifying that the record was found.

Code 8.13   **Searching for a Record**

```
Public Sub Search()

    On Error Resume Next
    Dim ssql As String
    Dim rstAuthors As ADODB.Recordset
    Dim strCnn As String
    Dim varBookmark As Variant
    Dim strCommand As String
    Dim lngMove As Long

    'Open ADO recordset from Authors table
    strCnn = "DSN=PubsTest;UID=sa;PWD=pwd;"
    Set rstAuthors = New ADODB.Recordset

    'OpenDynamic so changes can be made to data
    rstAuthors.CursorType = adOpenDynamic

    'Build SQL statement
    ssql = "SELECT * FROM Authors " _
    & "WHERE au_id = '" & AuthorID & "' "

    'Open the RecordSet
    rstAuthors.Open ssql, strCnn

    'Check for record found
    If rstAuthors.EOF = True Then
        'Record not found
        LastName = ""
        FirstName = ""
        Phone = ""
        Address = ""
```

```
            City = ""
            State = ""
            Zip = ""
            Contract = ""
            RaiseEvent Action(2)
        Else
            'No errors
            'Clear all except ID
            LastName = ""
            FirstName = ""
            Phone = ""
            Address = ""
            City = ""
            State = ""
            Zip = ""

            'Fill results
            LastName = rstAuthors![au_lname]
            FirstName = rstAuthors![au_fname]
            Phone = rstAuthors![Phone].Value
            Address = rstAuthors![Address]
            City = rstAuthors![City]
            State = rstAuthors![State]
            Zip = rstAuthors![Zip]
            Contract = rstAuthors![Contract]
            RaiseEvent Action(200)
        End If
    End Sub
```

Adding Code to the Update Method

The Update method, shown in Code 8.14, changes a record in the Authors table. In the Update subroutine, the cnn1.Errors object is cleared to ensure that we do not get an error message left over from a previous action. Next, an UPDATE SQL statement is constructed and executed; it attempts to update the current record in the Authors table based on the values from the text boxes on the TierOne application Form.

If an error occurs during the update process, the Errors event is raised in the TierOne application. In addition to checking for errors, the RowsAffected option of the Execute method is checked to see if a row was actually updated. If the RowsAffected value is greater than zero, you know the AuthorID was found and the record was updated. If not, the Action event is raised with a value of 4. In the Action event in the TierOne application, the return value of 4 is interpreted, and a message notifies the user that the record was not found and was not updated.

Code 8.14   **Updating a Record**

```
Public Sub Update()

    On Error Resume Next
    'Declare variables
    Dim ssql As String
    Dim strCnn As String
    Dim cnn1 As ADODB.Connection
    Dim cmdChange As ADODB.Command
    Dim errLoop As ADODB.Error
    Dim slRecordsAffected As Long

    'Open ADO connection
    strCnn = "DSN=PubsTest;UID=sa;PWD=pwd;"
    Set cnn1 = New ADODB.Connection
    cnn1.Open strCnn

    'Clear extraneous errors from the Errors collection
    cnn1.Errors.Clear

    'Build the SQL statement
    ssql = "UPDATE Authors SET " _
    & "au_lname = '" & LastName & " '," _
    & "au_fname = '" & FirstName & " '," _
    & "phone = '" & Phone & "'," _
    & "address = '" & Address & "'," _
    & "city = '" & City & "'," _
    & "state = '" & State & "'," _
    & "Zip = '" & Zip & "'," _
    & "contract = " & Contract & "" _
    & "WHERE au_id = '" & AuthorID & "' "

    'Use the Connection object's execute method to
    'execute SQL statement to update the record
```

```
'return the number of records affected into the
'variable slRecordsAffected
cnn1.Execute ssql, slRecordsAffected

'Check for errors
If cnn1.Errors.Count > 0 Then
    'An error has occurred
    'Pass the rdoErrors to the calling application
    RaiseEvent Errors(cnn1.Errors)
Else
    If slRecordsAffected > 0 Then
        'No errors
        RaiseEvent Action(400)
    Else
        'Record was not found
        RaiseEvent Action(4)
    End If
End If
End Sub
```

The Update code is similar to the Add and Delete code. Now that we have analyzed the program flow and discussed the major code, it's time to test the Three-Tiered application.

Testing the Applications

As we have already discussed, the TierTwo application is a DLL that must be referenced in the TierOne application.

NOTE   For a complete discussion of ActiveX components, see Chapter 10.

Follow these steps to test the applications:

1. Start Visual Basic and open the TierTwo application.

2. Press F5 to run the TierTwo code.

3. Start another instance of Visual Basic, and open the TierOne application.

4. Choose Project ➤ References to open the References dialog box and check the TierTwo reference. This makes the TierTwo class available to the TierOne application.

5. Press F5 to run the TierOne application. The first record is retrieved from the database and displayed on the form:

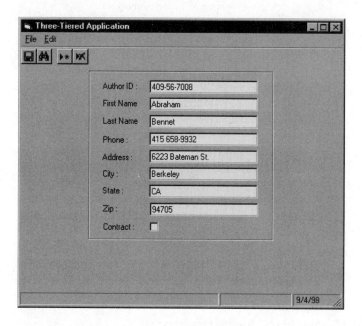

6. In the Author ID field, enter **213-46-8915,** and click the Find button to retrieve the second author's record.

7. Change the Last Name field to Johnston, and click the Save button. The record is saved, and the status bar shows Record Saved.

8. Change the Author ID field to **172-32-5555,** change the data in some of the other fields, and click the New Record button to add this as a new record.

9. With the record 172-32-5555 displayed from step 8, click the Delete Record button to delete this new record.

Now that we have tested the applications, let's look at how to compile the TierTwo application into a DLL.

Creating the TierTwo DLL

In the previous sections, we have been working with the TierTwo application in the Visual Basic design environment. To compile the application into a DLL, follow these steps:

1. Choose File ➢ Make TierTwo.dll to open the Make Project dialog box.

2. Click OK to compile the application and create the `TierTwo.dll` file.

PART II

Object Programming

CHAPTER
NINE

9

Object Programming with Visual Basic

- Understanding objects

- Using components to develop software

- Creating object variables

- Creating controls at run time

- Binding variables

- Using the Object Browser

- Using Collections

As a term, "object-oriented programming" has been around for a quite a while now. At one time, object-oriented versions of popular programming languages, such as C and Pascal, promised to help developers solve many problems, especially with large applications or for projects on which teams of programmers worked. The catch with object-oriented languages and with the object-oriented approach to programming is that developers must learn and master new concepts and get accustomed to a new programming philosophy.

No wonder most developers worked with object-oriented versions of C in a fashion similar to the way they worked with non–objected-oriented languages. The way they worked was determined (to a large extent) by each programmer's education. Object-oriented programming didn't come naturally to those who went to school before the introduction of object-oriented programming or to those who didn't have a degree in computer science. It's a new approach to application development, and, unlike the traditional approach to programming, it's an acquired taste.

So why bother with object-oriented programming? Because you can't go very far without it. Current programming is object oriented, and you must master the object-oriented techniques necessary for developing software with development tools such as Visual Basic. Some of the benefits include the ability to:

- Write code that can be used in multiple applications

- Update objects throughout their life cycle, without breaking the applications that use them

- Coordinate among multiple programmers working on the same project

Much has been written about object-oriented programming, but the bottom line is this: *Object-oriented programming won't simplify your life instantly.* Actually, you'll be hard-pressed to understand topics such as inheritance, encapsulation, and polymorphism and then apply them to your projects. Down the road, however, the object-oriented approach will simplify your life. But not everyone will make the transition.

NOTE   Visual Basic is a unique environment that, over the past seven years, gradually and in subtle ways introduced programmers to the principles of object-oriented programming. Those of you who have worked with Visual Basic since version 1 (it may look arcane now, but it was an extraordinary environment for developing early Windows applications) have been using objects for many years.

The environment of Visual Basic and its approach to programming was carefully crafted so that developers wouldn't have to be aware of features such as encapsulation or polymorphism. Visual Basic literally incorporated the complexity of Windows into a simple language. The average VB developer needn't know that TextBoxes are objects derived from the TextBox class. They are boxes that can be dropped on a Form, and, once there, they carry with them the functionality of a text editor. The same programmer doesn't have to know that objects expose properties and methods and that they communicate with the operating system via events. The Properties window displays all the properties you can set to adjust the appearance of the object, and the methods are like commands that once you had to memorize. The truth is TextBoxes are objects, and they behave like objects on a Form.

So, how do you explain the principles of object-oriented programming? We'll do it gradually, starting with simple topics, such as how to manipulate objects from within your applications. We won't show you how to set properties or how to program with events or deal with other techniques you have mastered already. Instead, we'll focus on the following rather advanced topics:

- How to create object variables

- The early and late binding of variables

- How to create new instances of existing objects

NOTE   This chapter is a compendium of information on manipulating objects, which is a prerequisite for the following chapters. Starting with the next chapter, you'll learn how to build your own objects, how to build your own ActiveX controls, and how to extend the Visual Basic editor with your own add-ins.

The Characteristics of Objects

When you program with Visual Basic, you are actually programming objects. The ActiveX controls you place on a Form are objects, and programming in Visual Basic consists of manipulating their properties and calling their methods. All the action takes place in the events of the objects, which are raised when certain conditions are met. *Objects* are units of code and data, which can be used as black boxes. Developers don't need to know how each object is implemented. All they need to know is:

- Which properties the object exposes

- Which methods the object provides

- Which events the object can raise

Properties and methods constitute the object's interface. This isn't a graphical interface, and it doesn't have visual elements; nevertheless, it's an interface. It stands between you and the object, as you can't access the object's code or data directly.

For example, you can add the functionality of a text editor on your application's user interface by placing a TextBox control on the Form and setting its basic properties through the Properties window (whether the TextBox can display multiple lines of text, the font to use, and so on). In your code, you can program how the TextBox reacts to user actions by providing a subroutine (handler) to the events to which it must react. The properties, methods, and events of the TextBox constitute its interface, and you can bring the functionality of this control to your application, without knowing anything about the code that implements the control. Figure 9.1 shows how this works.

FIGURE 9.1:

Applications communicate with objects through the properties and methods they expose and the events they raise.

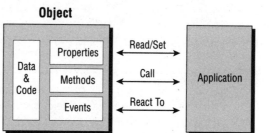

Setting a Property
Text1.ForeColor = RGB(0, 255, 255)

Reading a Property
Comments = Text1.Text

Calling a Method
Text1.SetFocus

Reacting to Events
```
Private Sub Text1_KeyDown(KeyCode, Shift)
If KeyCode = vbKeyF5 Then
    Text1.SelText = Date
End If
End Sub
```

The Change event is raised when the user changes the contents of the control. As a developer, you don't have to monitor the mouse or the keyboard to find out when the text changes. The TextBox control itself will notify your program through an event, and all you have to do is provide the code to react to this event. If you don't provide an event handler for the Change event, the control won't react when the text is changed (it will simply accept the changes, because that is its default reaction to keyboard events).

Finally, the TextBox control provides a few methods that you can call from within your code to manipulate the control. The SetFocus method lets you move the focus to a TextBox control from anywhere in your code and make it the active control. The Refresh method refreshes the control's contents. The TextBox control is in effect an object, which you can manipulate at a high level. You don't have access to its code, and you can neither enhance its operation nor break it. Actually, you can enhance its default operation by programming certain events, but still you don't have to touch its code.

For example, you can capture certain keystrokes and react differently to them. You can think of the TextBox control as an application that exposes a user interface, which consists of properties, methods, and events. Just as users of your application can control it through its user interface, you can only control the objects of your application through the members of the interface they expose.

NOTE　　Restricting access to the code of a control (or any other object) isn't just a strict rule. It serves a practical purpose: It prohibits developers from breaking the control by "enhancing" it. Once users learn what they can do with a TextBox control, they can handle any TextBox, in any application. This consistency in the user interface is a fundamental characteristic of Windows, and objects are designed to enforce this consistency.

Hiding the inner workings of an object is called *encapsulation* or *abstraction*. The object encapsulates (abstracts) complicated operations, such as the breaking of multiple lines, the insertion of new characters, and so on. These are low level details that you don't have to deal with. Instead, you can concentrate on your application, its user interface, and its operation. In this chapter, we are going to discuss the Visual Basic objects at large and the various techniques for working with them. Objects encapsulate complicated operations into a black box, which you can access through its user interface.

Encapsulation is the first buzzword in object-oriented programming; if you had to describe object-oriented programming with a single word, encapsulation would be it. The other terms are not as simple, and we'll explore them in the following chapter.

> **NOTE**
>
> Encapsulation is the ability to wrap code and data in a single unit that can be accessed by a well-defined interface. Developers can carry the functionality of an object to their applications and manipulate it through this interface, but they can't enhance or break the object, because they can't alter the code or make it perform illegal operations.

Encapsulation is often referred to as abstraction because it abstracts complicated operations. If you have used the Data Access Objects, you understand how this abstraction works. Data in a database are stored in a file, with the extension MDB. This file, however, has a complicated structure, and you never access it directly. Instead, you specify the records you're interested in and use the DAO (Data Access Objects) method to retrieve them. Information is presented in the form of rows and columns, which are easy to understand, visualize, and work with. The database file contains the data, index files, pointers, and all kinds of animals that you don't want to deal with. The DAO interface knows how to extract and/or save the desired information to the database.

Component Software Development

The concept of encapsulation leads to another important development in software design methodology: component software. What happens when you're designing applications with Visual Basic? You borrow functionality built into Windows itself and place it on your Forms by dropping controls from the Toolbox onto the Form. Your code is the glue that holds together these "pieces of functionality." And, considering what you can do with a few lines of VB code, the code you provide is really minimal. Most of the functionality of your application is concentrated in the controls.

> **NOTE**
>
> As operating systems and languages evolve, the code behind the applications will become less and less, but today you can't do much better than VB. It's the most compact of all major programming languages in the Windows environment.

Building applications with Visual Basic isn't unlike building a computer with components that you purchase separately. The sure way to build your dream computer is to purchase the components you need and connect them yourself. (Don't try this if you are not a computer whiz, but the best computers we've seen are custom built.) To build your own computer, you must purchase the components you need and put them together. Things may get a bit nasty when time comes to install drivers for SCSII interfaces and huge hard disks, CD-ROM units, or an inexpensive video capture card, but if you know what you're doing, you'll end up with a powerful computer. When a faster processor comes along, you can replace yours with the new processor. Power surge problem? The trip to the local computer store will take you longer than actually replacing the power supply.

The components you put together to build a custom computer encapsulate characteristics, just like the characteristics of programming objects. You don't have to know anything about power supplies, except for the input they require (110 volts, 220 volts, or switching) and the output they provide. All you have to do is make sure that the power supply provides the voltage required by the motherboard. Hard disk? Just find the one with the capacity and performance that suits your needs. They are all designed to fit in a standard bay, and if they don't, use a couple of brackets. These characteristics are the component's properties.

Hardware components have methods too, which are used by the system software. Methods such as GetThisCluster and WriteThatCluster allow the operating system (and the applications) to use the disk. The glue that makes all the components work together is the BIOS and the operating system. Fortunately, both come ready to use, and you don't have to do anything, short of setting a few parameters.

Here we are again. The operating system itself is another object, which encapsulates an incredible amount of functionality. You can adjust certain characteristics of the operating system with the applications provided in the Control Panel or even through the Registry. As a programmer, you know already that you can access the Registry's functions and use them from within your applications, as we discussed in the first part of this book.

When components are designed according to a set of standards that allow them to work in tandem, they can be put together to build a larger system with minimum effort. As far as software development goes, one of the standards that allows components to interact is ActiveX (formerly OLE). Every component you build with Visual Basic supports ActiveX, and you don't have to know much about the ActiveX specifications. A software component designed according to ActiveX will work not only with Visual Basic applications, but also with any programming language, such as Visual C++. It will even work with HTML. You can actually embed ActiveX controls on a Web page by inserting a few lines of code in the page's HTML code and turn static documents into interactive applications.

To summarize, software objects have two characteristics:

1. They encapsulate certain functionality and allow developers to access their functionality through their interface.

2. They interact, which means that they can be placed together on a Form and cooperate.

What this means to you is that you can:

1. Select all the components you need for your application or develop some of them if you can't find off-the-shelf components for your application.

2. Put them together by manipulating them with VB code, using the interface components they provide (properties and methods).

This is how current software is developed, and you've been doing it with Visual Basic for many years.

Before we show you how to create your own objects, we are going to review how built-in objects are manipulated. In the rest of this chapter, we will review a few advanced topics, such as how to create new Forms and objects at run time and how to use type libraries, and then we'll introduce object-oriented programming with the built-in objects. Visual Basic provides a large number of objects, and most of you have been using them in your applications. If you plan to exploit object-oriented programming with Visual Basic, you should take a quick look at the examples in this chapter.

Objects Come from Classes

The controls you see on the Toolbox are actually classes, from which the objects you use on your Forms are derived. The class is a *prototype*, and the object is an *instance* of this prototype. When you place a TextBox control on a Form, Visual Basic creates a new object based on the TextBox class. Because of the way we use ActiveX controls in building an application's user interface, this distinction between classes and objects isn't quite obvious. It will become clear when we build our own classes, and then we'll create new objects based on these classes.

Continued on next page

The classical analogy between classes and objects is that of the cookie cutter and the cookies. All cookies cut with the same cutter are identical (at least as far as their shape and size are concerned). Each TextBox you place on your Form with the TextBox tool of the Toolbox is identical. They all come from the same class, or prototype. Once on the Form, each TextBox can be adjusted, and you can make them all look different. You can change their background and text colors, the font used for rendering the text, and so on. The basic functionality of each TextBox object, however, is the same, and it's determined by the TextBox Class.

Creating Object Variables

To access the functionality of a Class, you must first create an object variable. Objects are Classes (prototypes) that can't be accessed directly. To access the functionality of an object, you must create a special variable that can store a reference to the object. In this section, we'll review the basics of creating object variables to manipulate objects.

Normally, the objects you place on a Form to create the user interface are manipulated from within code through their name (Text1, Command1, and so on). So why create variables to access them? As you will see shortly, on occasion you'll want to be able to access objects through a variable. For example, not all objects can be placed on a Form. If you have done any database programming with Visual Basic, you know that there are two approaches: the simple and limited, no-code approach (through the Data Control), and the serious approach (through the Data Access Objects). To access the objects exposed by the DAO—objects such as Recordsets, fields, and so on—you must create variables that represent these objects, just as you create variables to represent integer values or strings.

Declaring Object Variables

Object variables can be of two types:

- Generic, which can store all types of objects
- Specific, which can store objects of the same type only

Generic object variables are declared as Object type:

```
Dim myObject As Object
```

The *myObject* variable can store any type of object. The type Variant can also store objects, but this type requires more overhead than other types.

Finally, if you need an object variable to store references to controls, use the Control type:

```
Dim myControl As Control
```

The *myControl* object variable can store references to any control, but no other types of objects. If you know the type of object you want to store in an object variable, use this control's name in the declaration, as in the following statements:

```
Dim TBox As TextBox
Dim OKCancel As CommandButton
```

When an object variable is created, it contains nothing. To assign something to the object variable, you must use the Set statement to reference an existing object. The following statement allows you to use the *TBox* variable to access the Text1 TextBox:

```
Set TBox = Text1
```

Both *TBox* and *Text1* reference the same object, the Text1 TextBox (the Text1 object must already exist on the Form). You can change the bold attribute of the control with either of the following statements:

```
TBox.Bold = True
```

or

```
Text1.Bold = True
```

Both statements turn on the bold attribute of the text in the Text1 control.

The Set statement creates a reference to an existing object; it doesn't create a copy of the object. With a regular assignment operation, such as:

```
amount = totalDue
```

a copy of the value of the *totalDue* variable is created, and it's accessed by the name amount. Because the two objects are distinct, changing one of the variables has no effect on the other.

NOTE   When you know the type of object you are going to store in an object variable, you should use a specific type in the Dim statement. This will make your program run faster and also simplify coding. For more details on the effect of object variable declarations, see the section "Early and Late Binding of Variables," later in this chapter.

If you don't need the object variable any longer, release it by setting it to Nothing:

```
Set myControl = Nothing
```

One common use for a Control type variable is to access variables on a different Form. If you need to access the Font property of a control on another Form frequently and if the required statement is:

```
Form3!txtName.Font.Bold
```

you can simplify the code by creating an object variable that points to the control on another Form:

```
Dim TBox As Control
Set TBox = Form3!txtName
TBox.Font.Bold = True
```

You could also create an object variable that references the Font object directly:

```
Dim TBoxFont As Object
Set TBoxFont = Form3!txtName.Font
TBoxFont.Bold = True
```

The New Keyword

The object variables we created in the previous section refer to existing objects. To create a new instance of an existing object, you must use the New keyword, either in the Dim statement or in the Set statement. You can declare that an object variable create a new object with the statement:

```
Dim myObject As New Object
```

and then specify the object with a Set statement:

```
Set myObject = anotherObject
```

Or, you can declare it and then assign a new instance of an object to it:

```
Dim myObject As Object
Set myObject = New anotherObject
```

NOTE   You can use the New keyword either when you declare the object variable (Visual Basic prepares an object for storing a new instance of the object) or when you assign an object instance to the variable with the Set statement.

With the New keyword, you specify that the object variable will not reference an existing instance of the control, but will create a copy of the specified object. As you will see, you can create new instances of just about any object, including Forms, but you can't create new instances of controls. To create new controls at run time, you must use the Load statement, which is described in the section "Creating Controls at Run Time," later in this chapter.

Let's see now how these statements are used and what they can do for your application. In the following sections, we'll discuss a few of Visual Basic's built-in objects and see how and when object variables are used.

The Font Object

Objects represent programming entities, which can be as simple as fonts or as complicated as databases. In object-oriented programming terminology, objects encapsulate, or abstract, the entities they represent. The Font object represents the font used by a Form, by another object, or by the printer. As a programmer, you don't have to know how a font is stored in its file or how the object that uses the font reads this file. If you want the text on a Form to appear in bold, you must set the Bold property of the Font object to True:

```
Font.Bold=True
```

To print in bold on the printer, you can use this statement:

```
Printer.Font.Bold=True
```

To display text in bold on a Form, you can use this statement:

```
Form.Font.Bold=True
```

The Font object encapsulates (or abstracts) the font being used. Since both the Form and the Printer objects use a font, they provide a Font property, and you can change the attributes of the font by manipulating the Font object.

Creating a Font Object Variable

Let's create a Font object variable and make it represent the font of a specific control. You must declare an object variable that represents a font with the Font type. The variable *thisFont*, which is declared with this statement:

```
Dim thisFont As StdFont
```

is a Font object variable. You can use this variable to create a new Font property for a Form. This statement:

```
Set thisFont = Form1.Font
```

makes the *thisFont* variable refer to the Font property of Form1. To change the characteristics of the font being used to render the text on the Form1 Form, you can use statements that manipulate the variable *thisFont*, such as the following:

```
thisFont.Name = "Comic Sans MS"
thisFont.Size = 12
thisFont.Bold = True
thisFont.Italic = False
```

Notice the use of the Set statement. When you want to make an object variable refer to an existing object of the same type, you must use the Set statement. The Set statement tells Visual Basic to create an object that refers to the Font property of Form1.

You can also create a new Font object, with the following declaration:

```
Dim thisFont As New StdFont
```

This object variable refers to a new Font object. You can set its properties with statements such as the following:

```
thisFont.Name = "Courier"
thisFont.Size = 10
thisFont.Bold = False
thisFont.Italic = False
```

At this point, you can assign the *thisFont* object variable to the Font property of an existing object. The statement:

```
Form1.Font = thisFont
```

will cause the text on Form1 to be rendered in regular Courier typeface, at 10 points.

The FontObject Project

The FontObject project demonstrates the two distinct methods of using object variables.

NOTE   You'll find the FontObject project in the `Chapter9\FontObject` folder on the CD that comes with this book.

The main Form of the project, shown in Figure 9.2, contains two Label controls. The top label's font is Verdana 14 point, and the second label has the default font (MS Serif) at 10 points. Clicking the Manipulate Font button changes the attributes of the font of the top label by manipulating its Font property.

FIGURE 9.2:

The FontObject project, after clicking the Create Font button, which manipulates the bottom Label's Font property

NOTE   Load the FontObject project to see how object variables can be used to access existing fonts or represent new fonts.

The Manipulate Font button manipulates the font of the first Label control through an object variable. Code 9.1 shows the code behind the Manipulate Font button.

Code 9.1   The Manipulate Font Button

```
Private Sub Command1_Click()
Dim thisFont As StdFont

' Get original font,
' set its attributes
   thisFont.Bold = True
   thisFont.Italic = True
' and size
   thisFont.Size = 1.5 * thisFont.Size
' Clear object variable
   Set thisFont = Nothing

End Sub
```

The last statement in this subroutine releases the object variable when it's no longer needed by setting it to Nothing. The Nothing keyword is not equivalent to setting a string to an empty string, or a numeric variable to zero. It releases the object variable *thisFont* and returns the resources allocated to the object variable when it was created.

TIP   It's solid programming practice to release any object variable when it's no longer needed.

This subroutine starts by assigning the Font property of the Label1 control to the object variable *thisFont*. It then manipulates the font of the Label control by setting the attributes of the *thisFont* variable. As each statement is executed, the appearance of the font on the Label control changes. You don't need a statement that will assign the new settings of the thisFont property to the Font object of the Label control, because the variable *thisFont* and the property Label1.Font refer to the same object. If you want, you can single step through the code (by pressing F8) to see the effect of each statement on the appearance of the text on the control.

The Create Font button (see Code 9.2) modifies the font of the lower label. It starts by creating a new Font object, initializes it to the value of the Font property of the first label, changes a few attributes, and then assigns the new Font object to the Font property of the second Label control.

Code 9.2   **The Create Font Button**

```
Private Sub Command2_Click()
Dim thisFont As New StdFont

' Use Name and Size properties of the original font
' The Bold and Italic attributes are not inherited
    thisFont.Name = Label1.FontName
    thisFont.Size = 1.5 * Label1.FontSize
    thisFont.Underline = True
    Set Label2.Font = thisFont
    Set thisFont = Nothing

End Sub
```

The object variable *thisFont* is created with the New keyword, when the variable is declared, and it doesn't refer to an existing object. Therefore, it can't affect the appearance of the text on the Label control, unless you specifically assign this object variable to the Font property of the Label control. If you single-step this application and click the Create Font button, nothing will change on the Form until the second to last statement is reached. This statement assigns the characteristics of the object variable to the label's Font property.

Again, you assign the *thisFont* object variable to the Font property of the Label control with the Set statement. Every time you assign an object to another, you must use the Set statement. Simple assignment statements such as the following don't work with objects:

```
Label2.Font = thisFont
```

Simple Tricks with Default Properties

If you attempt to assign the *thisFont* object variable to the Font property of the Label2 control without the Set statement, the text on the label won't change, and you won't get an error message either. What's going on?

The Font object, like all other objects, has a default property, which is the Name property. The statements:

```
Label2.Font.Name = "Courier"
```

and

```
Label2.Font = "Courier"
```

are equivalent. So, the statement:

```
Label2.Font = thisFont
```

is the same as the following one:

```
Label2.Font.Name = thisFont
```

If *thisFont* were a string variable, Visual Basic would set the font's name to another typeface. Because *thisFont* doesn't contain a string, the last statement assigns the default font name (which is MS Sans Serif) to the Font property of the Label control.

The Screen and Printer Objects

Two useful built-in objects are the Screen and Printer objects, which represent the monitor and the current printer. You can use these objects to find out the properties of the monitor (its resolution, the fonts it can display, and so on) and of the printer. The Screen object has a Fonts property, which returns the names of the fonts that can be displayed on the screen (they are not necessarily the same as the fonts that can be used on the Printer object, which also supports the same property). If you had to display the names of the fonts in a ListBox control, you'd use a loop like this one:

```
For i = 0 To Screen.FontCount - 1
    List1.AddItem Screen.Fonts(i)
Next i
```

The Printer object is quite similar and supports many of the same properties and methods. The Screen and Printer objects demonstrate what we call encapsulation, or abstraction. As a developer, you don't have to know how the Printer and Screen objects really work. All you care about is that both objects support the Font property. The implementation details are hidden from the developer, who's free to focus on their application and not on the specifics of the various display adapters or printer models.

This is what abstraction is all about: the ability to tell an object to do something or the ability to change a characteristic of an object without having to know how each specific object carries out its operation. The ScreenPrinterObjects project, discussed later in this chapter, demonstrates how you can simplify your code by exploiting the methods that are common to these two objects.

Forms Are Classes

Forms are Classes that can be created with the Dim statement, and you can control them from within your code. Visual Basic provides four methods for manipulating Forms:

Load loads a new Form in memory, but doesn't show it.

Show displays a Form that has already been loaded or loads and then displays a new Form.

Unload hides a loaded Form and unloads it from memory.

Hide hides a Form, but doesn't unload it from memory.

These methods work on Forms that have already been designed and that exist in the current project. It is also possible to create new Forms at run time and display them as part of the application's user interface with the statement:

```
Dim myForm As Form
```

This statement creates a new Form object variable, which you can use in your code to reference an existing Form or to create a new Form. For example, you can set the *myForm* variable to an existing Form:

```
Set myForm = Form1
```

or to a new instance of the Form1 object:

```
Set myForm = New Form1
```

Form1 is an existing Form, but *myForm* is a new instance of Form1 and can be loaded and displayed with the statement:

```
myForm.Show
```

The Forms Project

If you need one or more special Forms in your application, you can design a prototype and then use it in your application. This prototype can have its own properties and methods and can even raise custom events.

The Forms project is a simple example of a special Form that displays a gradient on its background.

NOTE   You'll find the Forms project in the **Chapter9\Forms** folder on the CD that comes with this book.

We will design a Form with a custom method, the BackGradient method, which accepts a single argument, the direction of the gradient. The gradient's direction can be horizontal or vertical.

You can call it as follows:

```
myForm.BackGradient(gradient)
```

The value of gradient can be:

- 0 (no gradient)

- 1 (horizontal gradient)

- 2 (vertical gradient)

To design a Form with the BackGradient method, start a new project and add a new Form to it. Name the new Form GradForm, and enter the code in Code 9.3 in the Form's Code window.

Code 9.3   **Drawing Gradients**

```
Enum Gradients
    None = 0
    Horizontal = 1
    Vertical = 2
End Enum


Public Sub BackGradient(GradientDirection As Integer)

    If GradientDirection = None Then
        Me.BackColor = RGB(128, 128, 128)
        mGradient = None
        Exit Sub
    End If
    If GradientDirection = Horizontal Then
        For i = 0 To Me.ScaleWidth - 1
            GrComponent = Int(i * 255 / Me.ScaleWidth)
            RGBColor = RGB(GrComponent, GrComponent, GrComponent)
            Me.Line (i, 0)-(i, Me.ScaleHeight - 1), RGBColor
            GrComponent = GrComponent + Me.ScaleWidth / 255
        Next
        mGradient = Horizontal
    End If

    If GradientDirection = Vertical Then
        For i = 0 To Me.ScaleHeight - 1
            GrComponent = i * 255 / Me.ScaleHeight
            RGBColor = RGB(GrComponent, GrComponent, GrComponent)
            Me.Line (0, i)-(Me.ScaleWidth - 1, i), RGBColor
            GrComponent = GrComponent + GradForm.ScaleHeight / 255
        Next
        mGradient = Vertical
    End If

End Sub
```

The Enum type at the beginning of the code allows us to refer to the gradient's direction with a descriptive name (for instance, None, Horizontal, or Vertical) instead of with a number. The BackGradient() subroutine is declared as public, which makes it a method of the Form. (In other words, other procedures outside the Form can call the BackGradient subroutine). To create a new instance of this Form from within another Form's code, you must first create an object variable such as the following:

```
Dim myForm As GradForm
Set myForm = New GradForm
```

After you create the *myForm* instance of the GradForm Class, you can display it with the statement:

```
myForm.Show
```

You can then access its BackGradient method as follows:

```
myForm.BackGradient 1
```

To use the GradForm, create a new Form, the MainForm, and make it the project's Startup object. The MainForm for the Forms project is shown in Figure 9.3. This Form contains a TextBox control and three buttons, which show one instance of the GradForm each. Each time you click one of these buttons, the gradient on the corresponding Form changes (from horizontal to vertical and back).

FIGURE 9.3:

The Forms project

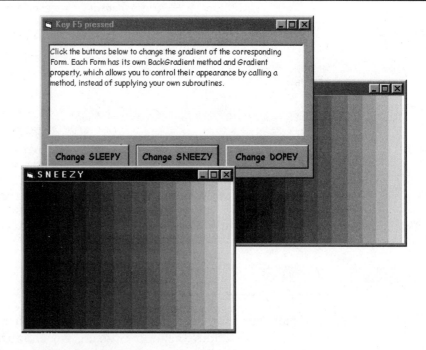

The instances of the GradForm are created with object variables, which are declared in the Main form as follows:

```
Dim Sleepy As GradForm
Dim Sneezy As GradForm
Dim Dopey As GradForm
```

Any part of the application can access these variables. When the main Form is loaded, it executes Code 9.4.

Code 9.4   Loading the Custom Forms

```
Private Sub Form_Load()

Set Sleepy = New GradForm
Load Sleepy
With Sleepy
    .Top = 2000: .Left = 4000
    .Caption = "S L E E P Y"
End With
Set Sneezy = New GradForm
Load Sneezy
With Sneezy
    .Top = 3000: .Left = 7000
    .Caption = "S N E E Z Y"
End With
Set Dopey = New GradForm
Load Dopey
With Dopey
    .Top = 3000: .Left = 2000
    .Caption = "D O P E Y"
End With
End Sub
```

Code 9.5 creates three new instances of the GradForm object and places them on the monitor at different locations. The code behind each button changes the gradient's direction on the corresponding Form and shows it, just in case it was covered by another Form.

Code 9.5   The Change Sleepy Button

```
Private Sub bttnSleepy_Click()
    Sleepy.BackGradient (Sleepy.Gradient Mod 2) + 1
    Sleepy.Show
End Sub
```

Forms with Events

In addition to custom methods, Form Classes can raise custom events. Let's say you want to capture certain keystrokes and react to each one differently. To add a new event to the Form, you declare the event's name at the beginning of the code and then use the RaiseEvent statement to raise the custom event from within the new Form:

```
Event SpecialKey(KeyCode As Integer, Shift As Integer)

Private Sub Form_KeyUp(KeyCode As Integer, Shift As Integer)
    If KeyCode >= vbKeyF1 Or KeyCode <= vbKeyF16 Then
        RaiseEvent SpecialKey(KeyCode, Shift)
    End If
End Sub
```

The SpecialKey event is raised from within the Form's KeyUp event, which examines the code of the key pressed. If it corresponds to a function key, it raises the SpecialKey event and lets the main Form of the application handle the keypress.

Custom events introduce a slight complexity to the project. To declare a Form that raises events, you use the WithEvents keyword in the Dim statement, as follows:

```
Dim WithEvents myForm As GradForm
```

The keyword WithEvents tells Visual Basic to raise the events that occur on the object so that you can handle them from within your code. If you omit this keyword, Visual Basic will create a new Form based on the GradForm Class, but it will not report the events to the object variable that represents the new Form. Now you can create a new instance of the GradForm Form with the statements:

```
Set myForm = New GradForm
myForm.Show
```

To process the special keystrokes, you provide an event handler for the Special-Key event of the custom Form. Follow these steps:

1. Open the Objects drop-down list in the main Form's Code window, and select the Sleepy object.

2. In the Events drop-down list, you will see the name of the custom event, SpecialKey. Select it and enter the following code in the event's handler:

   ```
   Private Sub Sleepy_SpecialKey(KeyCode As Integer, Shift As Integer)
       Me.Caption = "Key F" & Chr(KeyCode - 63) & " pressed"
   End Sub
   ```

3. Now run the project, display the Sleepy Form by clicking the Change Sleepy button, and press a function key.

The main Form's caption displays the key that was pressed on the Sleepy Form. This arrangement allows you to handle certain events of the GradForm's instances from within the main Form's code. The GradForm object will handle other keystrokes or mouse events, and the main Form will never know.

Events Belong to Classes, Not to Objects

If you open the Code window of the GradForm Form, you will see that it doesn't have a SpecialKey event, and you can't program this event for the GradForm Form itself. The Special-Key event can be raised by the instances of the GradForm you created in your code. This is a strange behavior, but there's a simple explanation.

The GradForm was created when you added it to the project by choosing Project ➤ Add Form. At that point, the Form didn't have the SpecialKey event, so its name doesn't appear in the Events drop-down list of the Form's Code window.

Creating Controls at Run Time

You have seen how to create object variables that represent existing, or new objects, such as Forms and fonts. You might expect that it's possible to use the New keyword to create controls at run time, similar to the way that you create Forms. This is not the case, however. If you declare an object variable as:

```
Dim myButton As CommandButton
```

you can then set it to reference an existing command button, but you can't create a new instance of the CommandButton Class. The statement:

```
Set myButton = New Command1
```

will cause a run-time error. You can still use a statement like the following one:

```
Set myButton = Command1
```

that creates a reference to the Command1 button on the Form. If you change the Caption property of the myButton object, you are in effect changing the Caption of the Command1 object.

To create new instances of controls and manipulate them from within your code, you use control arrays. Declaring a Control object variable with the New keyword isn't going to do the trick. Creating new instances of ActiveX controls at run time is the topic of the next section.

Control Arrays to the Rescue

To create multiple instances of new controls at run time, you use a control array. Did you notice that each time you are about to paste a control you have previously copied from a Form, Visual Basic asks whether you want to create a control array? Every time you place multiple instances of the same control on a Form, you have the option of creating an array of controls. All the elements of the array share the same name, and they are distinguished from one another with the help of the Index property.

If you have three command buttons on a Form, you can create the array Three-Buttons. The first Command button is the ThreeButtons(0), the second one is the ThreeButtons(1), and the last one is the ThreeButtons(2). The Index property of the first element in the array need not be zero. You can start indexing the array at any value.

> **NOTE**
>
> The simplest way to create a control array at design time is to copy an existing control and paste it on the same Form. The first time, Visual Basic asks whether you want to create a control array. After that, every time you paste the same control or create a new one with the same name, it is appended to the existing control array. At run time, you must use the Load method, which is explained next.

You use control arrays when two or more controls have similar code that can be simplified with the use of the Index property. If you have the array ThreeButtons with the three elements, you need not provide three different handlers for each Command button's Click event. All the elements of the control array share common event handlers. The Click event handler for an array of controls is:

```
Private Sub ThreeButtons_Click(Index As Integer)
End Sub
```

In your code, you can distinguish the various controls based on their index. When the first Command button is clicked, the Index argument has the value 0, and so on. For example, here is an event handler that changes the caption of the button that was clicked:

```
Private Sub ThreeButtons_Click(Index As Integer)
    ThreeButtons(Index).Caption = "I was clicked!"
End Sub
```

Let's return now to the topic of creating new controls at run time. First, you must create the control you want to repeat and assign the value zero to its Index property. It's also customary to make this control invisible. To create another instance of this control, use the Load method, with a new index value. Assuming that you have created an invisible Command button on the Form with Name = CButton and Index = 0, the following statement will create three instances of this control and display them on the Form:

```
For i = 1 to 3
    Load CButton(i)
    CButton(i).Visible = True
Next
```

When a new control is created at run time, it is initially invisible. That's why you must also set its Visible property.

The CtrlLoad Project

The CtrlLoad project demonstrates how to create new controls using index arrays by creating a Form that can accept a variable number of data points.

NOTE   You will find the CtrlLoad project in the **Chapter9\CtrlLoad** folder on the CD that comes with this book.

When you first run the application, you will see the Form shown in Figure 9.4. Click the New Data Set button, and you'll be prompted to enter the number of data points in the new set. Enter a small number, such as 10, and the Form will be stretched vertically and filled with as many TextBox controls as needed for the entry of the data values. If you specify six data values, the Form of the CtrlLoad application will look like the one in Figure 9.5.

FIGURE 9.4:

The initial state of the CtrlLoad application's main Form

FIGURE 9.5:

The CtrlLoad Form after adding six TextBox controls at run time

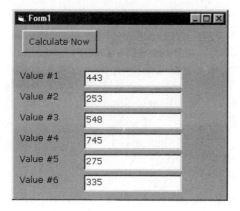

To implement the Form of the CtrlLoad project, start a new project and place the following items on the Form:

- A Command button

- A Label

- A TextBox control

Because the Label and TextBox controls should be invisible when the application starts, set their Visible property to False. At run time, we want to be able to add new instances of these controls on the Form by creating new elements in the control array. The two controls placed on the Form are the first elements in the control array, and you must set their Index property to zero. At run time, you'll be able to add new elements to the array with the Load command and a new index value.

Clicking the New Data Set button executes the code in Code 9.6.

Code 9.6   **Adding Controls on a Form at Run Time**

```
Private Sub Command1_Click()
Dim sum As Double, avg As Double

    If Command1.Caption = "New Data Set" Then
    dataCount = InputBox("How many data values?")
    If Not IsNumeric(Count) Then
        MsgBox "please enter a valid numeric value"
```

```
            Exit Sub
        End If
        For i = 1 To dataCount
            Load Label1(i)
            Load Text1(i)
            Label1(i).Top = Label1(i - 1).Top + 1.25 * Label1(i).Height
            Text1(i).Top = Text1(i - 1).Top + 1.25 * Text1(i).Height
            Label1(i).Visible = True
            Label1(i).Caption = "Value #" & i
            Text1(i).Visible = True
        Next
        Me.Height = Text1(dataCount).Top + 2.5 * Text1(dataCount).Height
        Command1.Caption = "Calculate Now"
    Else
        For i = 1 To dataCount
            If IsNumeric(Text1(i).Text) Then
                sum = sum + Text1(i).Text
            End If
        Next
        avg = sum / dataCount
        MsgBox "The average is " & avg
        For i = 1 To dataCount
            Unload Text1(i)
            Unload Label1(i)
        Next
        Me.Height = 2000
        Command1.Caption = "New Data Set"
    End If

End Sub
```

This code first prompts the user for the number of data points in the data set and then creates that many instances of the Label1 and Text1 controls. It positions each new instance on the Form with respect to the previous instance (the placement of the elements Label1(0) and Text1(0) determines the appearance of the Form). In addition to creating and placing the necessary controls for entering data on the Form, the Command button changes its Caption to Calculate Now. Clicking the Calculate Now button calculates the average of the values entered and removes the controls from the Form with the Unload statement.

> **NOTE**   When new elements are added to a control array, their Visible property is False, and you must manipulate this property from within your code to make them visible. In the CtrlLoad project, the new elements will be invisible anyway, because the initial elements of the array are invisible, but you should always set the Visible property of new control instances to True from within your code.

Manipulating Controls at Run Time

Visual Basic provides a few objects and statements for the manipulation of controls at run time. Let's start with the Control object. We mentioned that, although you can't create new controls at run time by declaring object variables, these variables are frequently used in programming controls. The Control type represents any control on a Form, and you can create variables of Control type with statements such as the following:

```
Dim aControl As Control
```

and then assign instances of other controls to the *aControl* variables with the Set statement:

```
Set aControl = Text1
```

and perhaps later in the code:

```
Set aControl = Command1
```

You can use the *aControl* object to manipulate the properties of the Command1 control. For example, you can change the Command button's Caption property with a statement such as:

```
aControl.Caption = "Click me!"
```

You may be wondering, Why use object variables to manipulate controls and the control names? In some situations, you don't have direct access to a control. Instead, you can access only a variable that represents the control. For example, in programming drag-and-drop operations, you don't have access to the control being dropped. As you will see in the next section, the DragDrop event subroutine passes a reference to the control that was dropped on another control, and not to the control itself. To program the DragDrop event, you must know how to handle object variables that represent controls.

Control Types

Sometimes, you need to know the type of control an object variable represents from within your code. An object variable can store references to any type of control, which is helpful should you need to determine the type of control being referenced within your code. To find out the type of the control referenced by an object variable, use the TypeOf statement, as in the following:

```
If TypeOf aControl Is TextBox Then
```

The keyword TypeOf is followed by the name of the object variable whose type you are seeking, followed by the keyword Is, which is followed by the name of a control's Class. TypeOf is not a function that returns the type of the variable; instead it compares the type of the control to a specific control type and returns a True/False value, which can be used in an If structure, like the one shown here. The TypeOf statement is used frequently in programming drag-and-drop operations to find out the type of the control that was dropped on another control. The following project provides a simple example.

The DragDrop Project

The DragDrop project demonstrates the use of the TypeOf...Is statement with drag-and-drop operations.

> **NOTE**
> You'll find the DragDrop project in the **Chapter9\DragDrop** folder on the CD that comes with this book.

The Form shown in Figure 9.6 contains a TextBox, a Label, and a PictureBox control. The contents of the first two controls can be dragged, so you must set their DragMode property to True. The PictureBox control can't be dragged, but other objects can be dropped on it. All controls can react to the drop of another control, which means you must provide a DragDrop handler for each control.

First, we must decide what happens when a control is dropped on another one. When the TextBox and Label control are dropped on each other, the source's text (Text or Caption property) is copied to the target control. When either control is dropped on the PictureBox control, it is assumed that the text is the path name of an image file, which must be displayed on the control. If the text doesn't correspond to an image file or if, for any reason, the image can't be displayed, an error message is displayed on the PictureBox control, as shown in Figure 9.7.

FIGURE 9.6:

The DragDrop project demonstrates the use of the TypeOf...Is statement in drag-and-drop operations.

FIGURE 9.7:

When the string dropped onto the PictureBox control isn't a valid image file name, an error message is displayed.

Let's start with the DragDrop events of the TextBox and Label controls (see Code 9.7), which are simpler.

Code 9.7	The DragDrop Events of the TextBox and Label Controls

```
Private Sub Text1_DragDrop(Source As Control, X As Single, Y As Single)
    If TypeOf Source Is Label Then
        Text1.Text = Label1.Caption
```

```
        End If
    End Sub

    Private Sub Label1_DragDrop(Source As Control, X As Single, Y As
    Single)
        If TypeOf Source Is TextBox Then
            Label1.Caption = Source.Text
        End If
    End Sub
```

The Source argument represents the control being dropped, and we can use it to access any of the properties of this control. However, we must first examine the type of the control, to avoid calling a property name not supported by the Source control.

The DragDrop event handler of the PictureBox control is quite similar, but instead of copying the Text or Caption property, it attempts to display the specified file. See Code 9.8.

Code 9.8   **Handling the DragDrop Event with Object Variables**

```
    Private Sub Picture1_DragDrop(Source As Control, X As Single, Y As Single)
    Dim imgName
        If TypeOf Source Is TextBox Then
            imgName = Source.Text
        Else
            imgName = Source.Caption
        End If
    On Error GoTo NOIMAGE
        Picture1.Picture = LoadPicture(imgName)
        Exit Sub

    NOIMAGE:
        Picture1.Cls
        Picture1.Font.Bold = True
        Picture1.Print imgName
        Picture1.Font.Bold = False
        Picture1.Print "Can't display file"
    End Sub
```

In addition to the event handlers shown here, the DragDrop project contains the DragOver handler for the various controls, which change the pointer's shape to indicate whether the current control can accept the control being dragged.

The Controls Collection

It is also possible to access from within your code all the controls on a Form through the Controls collection. Each element of the Controls Collection is a control. We'll discuss collections in detail in the section "Collections" later in this chapter, but we'll discuss here how you can use the Controls object to access the controls on the current Form.

The Controls object need not be initialized. It's built in to Visual Basic, and you can access it directly. The Count property of the Controls collection returns the number of controls it contains. To scan its elements, you can set up a For...Next loop such as the following one:

```
For i = 0 To Controls.Count - 1
    { process element Controls(i) }
Next
```

There is, however, a better structure for scanning the elements of a Collection, namely the For Each statement, whose syntax is:

```
For Each iControl In Controls
{ process element iControl }
Next
```

The *iControl* object variable is declared as Control type. At each iteration of the loop, the *iControl* variable is automatically assigned the next control in the Collection. If this control has a Caption property, you can access it with the expression iControl.Caption.

Since all controls have a Name property, you can safely use the expression iControl.Name. Not all properties, however, apply to all controls, and you should use the TypeOf statement to find out whether the current control supports a property. For example, you can change the Text property of all TextBox controls or the Caption property of all Label controls with a loop such as the following:

```
For Each iControl In Controls
    If TypeOf iControl Is TextBox Then
        iControl.Text = "Text Changed"
    Else If TypeOf iControl Is Label Then
        iControl.Caption = "Caption Changed"
    End If
Next
```

The Controls Project

The Controls project demonstrates how to use the Controls Collection and object variables to manipulate the controls on a Form from within your code.

NOTE   You'll find the Controls project in the **Chapter9\Controls** folder on the CD that comes with this book.

The main Form of the application, shown in Figure 9.8, contains two TextBox controls and a Label control, whose colors change when the Command button is clicked.

FIGURE 9.8:

The Controls application demonstrates the use of the Controls Collection.

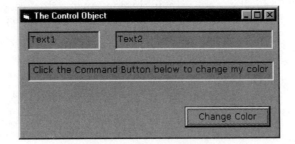

The code behind the Command button (Change Color) scans each element of the Controls Collection and examines its type (see Code 9.9). If it's a TextBox control, it sets the control's background color to yellow. The other elements in the Controls Collection are not processed.

Code 9.9   **The Change Color Button**

```
Private Sub Command1_Click()
Dim iControl As Control

For Each iControl In Controls
    If (TypeOf iControl Is TextBox) Or (TypeOf iControl Is Label) Then
        iControl.BackColor = RGB(200, 200, 0)
        iControl.ForeColor = RGB(0, 0, 200)
    End If
Next
End Sub
```

An alternative approach is to use a For...Next loop to scan all the elements of the Collection:

```
For i = 0 To Controls.Count
    Set iControl = Controls(i)
    iControl.BackColor = RGB(200, 200, 0)
    iControl.ForeColor = RGB(0, 0, 200)
Next
```

Early and Late Binding of Variables

In this section, we are going to discuss an important topic in programming with object variables: their binding. As you do with regular variables, you should declare object variables before they are used. The more Visual Basic knows about a variable's type, the more efficiently it will handle it. If you don't declare the variable, Visual Basic automatically creates a Variant, which is good for storing all types of data values, even objects. Because of their flexibility, Variants can't be processed as quickly. Visual Basic must convert them to the proper type before using them.

The same is true for object variables. For example, if Visual Basic knows in advance that a specific object variable will be used to store a reference to a Font object, it will allocate a structure where information about a Font object can be stored and recalled efficiently. If it doesn't know the type of the object variable, it must set up a structure that can accommodate any type of object and adjust the structure according to the object assigned to the variable at run time. In addition, it must execute quite a number of lines of code at run time, which is when an object is assigned to the object variable. For example, it can't request the value of the Text property unless it makes sure that the control represented by the variable is a TextBox control (or any other control that exposes a Text property). This additional code must execute each time your code attempts to access a member of a generic object variable; this certainly can't help your code run smoothly.

So far, we have seen two ways to declare object variables:

- As objects

- As a specific object type

When the type of the variable is known at design time, Visual Basic will not only protect you from mistakes (such as using nonexistent property names), it will also display the properties and methods that apply to the specific object variable—if you have the Auto List Members feature turned on. Most of the mistakes in your code will be caught by the editor itself as you enter the code or by the compiler before you execute the program. This is called *early binding*. The compiler knows the type of variable and will not compile lines that reference nonexistent properties or methods.

For example, if you declare an object variable as:

```
Dim myBox As TextBox
```

and then attempt to set its Caption property with a statement such as the following:

```
myBox.Caption = "This is a special box"
```

you will get an error message when you compile the application. This error simply can't go undetected. A statement that assigns a value to the *myBox* variable's Text property will compile just fine.

When you declare an object variable as Object, it can be assigned any type of object. This is called *late binding*, because the compiler can't bind members to this variable. In addition, the editor cannot validate the property names you are using. If you declare an object variable with the following statement:

```
Dim thisFontObject As Object
```

it can store any object. You can even store different objects in the same object variable at run time. When you declare a variable without a specific type, it's created the first time it's referenced, which is when you assign an object instance to it. That is also when the exact type of the variable becomes known.

To create an instance of the *thisFont* object variable, you should use a statement such as:

```
Set thisFontObject = Label2.Font
```

If you go back to the FontObject project and change the declaration of the *thisFont* object variable to:

```
Dim thisFont As Object
```

the rest of the code will work just as well. However, the revised application is slower. When the Visual Basic compiler runs into a statement such as:

```
thisFont.Name = Label1.FontName
```

it must generate additional statements, which find out whether the object supports the Name property. These statements must be executed at run time, and if the object doesn't support the Name property, a run-time error message is generated. Had the object variable been declared with a specific type, these statements would never be introduced. Any attempt to refer to a nonexistent property name, such as thisFont.TypeFace, would be caught at compile time.

The main advantage of declaring variables with a specific type is that Visual Basic knows at design (or compile) time whether the object represented by the variable supports a property or a method you call in your code and generates optimal executable code. If the object's type isn't known in advance, Visual Basic generates a lot of overhead code, which is executed at run time, making the program slower. In other words, it generates code to contact the object to find out whether it supports a specific property or method. Only when Visual Basic is sure that the object supports this member does it call the member. You can avoid this overhead by declaring object variables with a specific type.

And this brings us to the second advantage of declaring variables with exact types: You can write applications that run better because many potential errors can be caught at design or compile time. These two methods of declaring variables are known as early binding (object variables of exact type) and late binding (generic object variables). When an object variable's type is known at compile time, the compiler produces shorter, faster executing code. Of course, a few object variable declarations won't make your code crawl, but when you're trying to squeeze every drop of performance out of your code, it's good to know all the tricks.

To get a feel for the difference that early and late binding can make in your code, let's revise the FontObject application. Let's repeat the code of the Manipulate Font button 10,000 times with a loop and measure the elapsed time (see Code 9.10).

Code 9.10   **The Revised FontObject Project**

```
Private Sub Command1_Click()
Dim thisFont As StdFont

StartTime = Timer
For i = 1 To 10000
' Get original font,
    Set thisFont = Label1.Font
' set its attributes
    thisFont.Bold = True
    thisFont.Italic = True
' and size
    thisFont.Size = 1.001 * thisFont.Size
' Clear object variable
    Set thisFont = Nothing
Next
```

```
Debug.Print "10,000 repetition took : " & _
Format(Timer - StartTime, "#.00") & " seconds"
End Sub
```

On a Pentium 75, the elapsed time was 5.77 seconds. Now change the declaration of the *thisFont* object variable to:

```
Dim thisFont As Object
```

and run it again. With late binding, the 10,000 iterations take 7.91 seconds. Granted, not many applications create and release object variables 10,000 times at run time, but this difference would increase with more complicated objects, such as Database objects.

Notice that we changed the line

```
thisFont.Size = 1.5 * Label1.FontSize
```

to

```
thisFont.Size = 1.0 * thisFont.Size
```

The factor 1.5 would result in an overflow after a small number of iterations.

The effect of early binding on speed can be even more dramatic if the object variable has properties that are also objects. Here's an example. An add-in is an extension to the Visual Basic integrated development environment (IDE) that manipulates the various objects of the IDE, such as the controls and code of a Form. The Collection VBProjects, which we'll look at in Chapter 13, can have multiple components (Forms, Modules, and so on). A Form may contain multiple controls, which are accessed through the Controls Collection.

As you will see in Chapter 13, expressions such as:

```
thisForm.VBControls.Item(i).Properties("Index")
```

are common in developing add-ins. This expression represents a control on a specific Form (the variable *i* goes from 1 to the total number of controls on the Form). If Visual Basic doesn't know the exact type of the object variable *thisForm*, it generates code that will find out whether the object represented by the object variable supports the VBControls property. VBControls, in turn, is a collection. If Visual Basic doesn't know it, it will generate additional code to find out whether the *VBControls* object variable supports the Item property.

The expression up to the last dot represents a control. If Visual Basic doesn't have this information at compile time, it generates even more lines to make sure that the object represented by the expression *thisForm.VBControls.Item(i)* has a

Properties property. And only if it does, will it attempt to read the value of the Index property. As you can see, expressions involving object variables can get quite messy, and the more Visual Basic knows about these variables, the better it can handle them—both at design time and at run time.

Dynamic Object Variables

Previously, we mentioned the significant advantages of early binding:

- Code is shorter.

- Code executes faster.

- There are fewer run-time errors.

The run-time errors we are talking about are actually program errors and can't be corrected at run time, as opposed to user errors or unusual conditions, which can be corrected at run time. For example, if your code detects an error with the printer or an invalid data item, it can prompt the user to check the printer connection or re-enter some data. If your code calls a property that a specific object doesn't support, there's nothing to be done about it. A statement that calls a nonexistent property, such as the following:

```
thisFont.Typeface
```

will produce a run-time error that must be caught at design (or compile) time; error trapping isn't going to help you at all. Distributing a program that contains this statement is simply going to embarrass you. Yet, you can avoid this type of error easily by declaring the *thisFont* object variable with an exact type.

This doesn't mean that generic object variables are useless. Because they can be assigned all types of objects at run time, these variables are *dynamic*. You must simply make sure that you don't attempt to access any nonexistent properties or methods.

The ScreenPrinterObjects Project

Let's look at an example of what you can do with late-bound variables. The ScreenPrinterObjects project demonstrates a common programming technique and shows the solution to a problem you may have already faced.

NOTE   You'll find the ScreenPrinterObjects project in the `Chapter9\ScreenPrinter` folder on the CD that comes with this book.

Most commercial applications generate output for the screen and the printer. You are already familiar with the methods that produce shapes and text on a Form or a PictureBox control. The same methods apply to the Printer object. The problem is how to redirect the program's output to the screen or the printer. Should you use statements such as the following:

```
If PrinterOutput Then
        Printer.Line (X, Y) - (X + 100, Y + 100)
Else
        Form1.Line (X, Y) - (X + 100, Y + 100)
End If
```

or is there a more elegant method?

There is indeed a more elegant method, and it uses an object variable to draw on. If the object variable represents a Form object, the output is sent to the screen. If it represents the Printer object, the output is sent to the current printer.

The ScreenPrinterObjects project draws a few simple shapes, as you see in Figure 9.9. The project's main Form contains two option buttons (with their Style property set to Graphical so that they look like buttons) that you can select to specify the output. You can then click the Draw Now button to produce the output.

FIGURE 9.9:

The output of the Screen-PrinterObject project can be redirected to the screen or the printer, depending on the status of the Option buttons.

The program starts by declaring an object variable, *OutputObject*, which is set to the Form1 object or the Printer object, depending on the status of the Option buttons:

```
Dim OutputObject As Object

If Option1 Then
```

```
        Set OutputObject = Form1
    Else
        Set OutputObject = Printer
    End If
```

You can then call the graphics methods, which are common to both objects, to produce the desired output. The sample shapes in Figure 9.9 were produced with the following lines:

```
OutputObject.DrawWidth = 2
OutputObject.ForeColor = RGB(255, 0, 0)
OutputObject.Circle (2000, 2000), 800
OutputObject.DrawWidth = 1
OutputObject.Line (1000, 1000)-(3000, 3000), , B
OutputObject.ForeColor = RGB(0, 0, 255)
OutputObject.CurrentX = 1500
OutputObject.CurrentY = 2400
OutputObject.Print "Graphics methods"
```

Error-Trapping Considerations

The program also contains an error trap, intended for systems without a printer. If you attempt to direct the output to the printer and there's any problem with your printer, the program won't crash.

We were careful not to include any lines that call properties or methods that don't apply to both objects. What if you wanted to change the background color of the Form before printing on it? The statement:

```
OutputObject.BackColor = RGB(230, 230, 0)
```

will work while the *OutputObject* variable refers to the Form1 object, but it will produce a run-time error when the object it refers to is the Printer object. To make sure that the code won't fail, regardless of the current output object, use an If structure, such as the following:

```
If TypeOf OutputObject Is Form Then
    OutputObject.BackColor = RGB(230, 230, 0)
End If
```

Late-bound object variables may have disadvantages over early-bound ones, but if you need to manipulate the object variables dynamically from within your code, you must declare them as late bound (without an exact type).

Using the Object Browser

Where do all these objects come from, and how do you know, at any point, which objects are available and the properties and methods they provide? Each object, whether it's built into Visual Basic or you build it, has a type library. A *type library* is a catalog of the object's properties, methods, and events, which you can consult at any time. Each object, including your custom ActiveX controls and ActiveX components (in EXE or DLL format) has a type library, which can be displayed in the Object Browser. Fortunately, you don't have to take any special action in order to display your component's members. The Object Browser will pick up their definitions from the executable file (you must provide their descriptions, however). You will find more information on this in the following two chapters.

The type libraries of the available objects are displayed in the Object Browser, which is shown in Figure 9.10. We'll demonstrate how to use the Object Browser by building a simple application that manipulates a few of the objects exposed by the Database object. As you will see, you don't have to know every object and every property of these objects in order to use them. A basic understanding of databases and their structure is all you need to program them with the help of the Object Browser.

FIGURE 9.10:

The Object Browser for a simple VB project

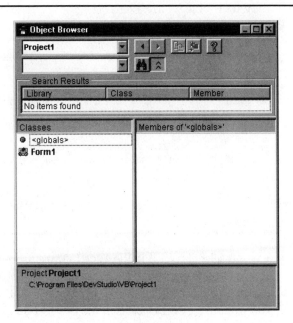

The Object Browser isn't a substitute for the help files or other reference material, but even experienced programmers can't possibly remember the structure of complicated objects such as the Database object. The Object Browser simplifies the task of programming database applications with the Database object, and you will use much of the information in this chapter as you work through the examples Part III.

The Purpose and Structure of the Object Browser

Every class available within Visual Basic or within other applications that expose objects is described in the Object Browser. The Object Browser is an application that gets these descriptions from the corresponding EXE or DLL files and displays them in an easy-to-visualize and navigate fashion. Objects can be as simple as a Form or as complex as an application such as Microsoft Excel or Microsoft Word. Let's explore the Object Browser by starting with a simple project.

Start a new project and click the Object Browser button, or choose View ➤ Object Browser (or simply press F2) to open the Object Browser. At the top of the Object Browser window you see two drop-down boxes. The first contains the available object libraries, from which you can select one. The second contains previous search arguments, which you can activate for new searches. For a new project (a project to which no special objects have been added), the Object Libraries shown in Table 9.1 are available.

TABLE 9.1: The Default Type Libraries

Library	Description
Project1	This is the current project's name. It contains the current project's classes.
Stdole	These are the type libraries of the standard OLE classes, such as the StdFont class.
VB	This is the Visual Basic type library. It contains the type libraries for the ActiveX controls that appear in the Visual Basic Toolbox.
VBA	This is the VBA type library.
VBRUN	This is the Visual Basic run-time library. It contains the classes that are available at run time only.

If you select Project1 in the Type Library drop-down box, you will see the only Class in the project, which is the main Form, Form1 (you know already that, unlike controls, Forms are Classes). In the Classes pane, along with the name of the Form, you will see the entry *globals*. If the project had global variables, their names would appear in the Members pane.

Select the Class Form1, and in the Classes pane you will see all the members of the Form1 class: the properties, methods, and events that the Form1 Form recognizes, as well as any event handlers or procedures you've written. Even the code you entered in the project becomes a member of the Form1 Class, because you can access the Form1 object through the functions and event handlers it provides.

TIP

The Object Browser displays in a compact format all the functionality in a project, whether it was brought into the project by Visual Basic (through its built-in objects) or by the developer (through custom components and controls).

Add a couple of controls on the Form and a couple of event handlers. You can place a couple of Command buttons on it and enter a simple MsgBox function in their Click event. If you open the Object Browser again, you will see that the names of the controls are displayed as properties of the Form1 Class in the Members pane. The event handlers of the Click event for the two Command buttons are also listed in this pane as methods of the Form1 Class. Something wrong here? Click is an event name for the Command1 and Command2 controls. The subroutines Command1_Click() and Command2_Click(), however, are methods, as they can be called from any other subroutine in this Form. Unless they are declared as Private, they can also be accessed by procedures contained in other Forms of the project. So, they are, in effect, members of the Form. If you click the name of the subroutine Command1_Click(), you will see in the description pane that this subroutine is a member of the Class Project1.Form1.

Using the Data Access Object

In this section, we are going to discuss an advanced topic, the Data Access Object. If you are not familiar with database programming, this section should be of particular interest.

Calling All Database Programmers...

Even if you are experienced with programming the Data Access Object, don't skip this section. Our goal is not to explain the Data Access Object, but to show how to use the Object Browser to find out the members of various objects and use them.

If you have any open projects in the Visual Basic editor, close them and start a new Standard EXE project. To use the Data Access Object, you must first add a reference to it, as this Class isn't added by default to every project. Follow these steps:

1. Choose Project ➤ References to open the Reference dialog box (see Figure 9.11), which displays a list of all the available objects you can add to your projects:

FIGURE 9.11:

The References dialog box

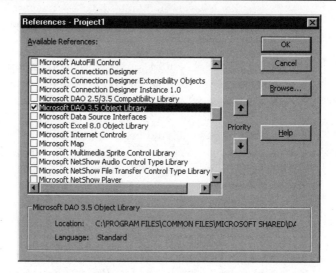

In this dialog box, you see the names of all available Classes on your system. Some were installed with Windows itself; others, by programming languages or applications. (In the next chapter, you will learn how to add your own Classes.) The components referenced in the project are checked.

2. Scroll down the list, locate the entry Microsoft DAO 3.5 Object Library, and check the box in front of its name. Then click OK to close the References dialog box. You have just added a reference to the Data Access Object to your project.

3. Open the Object Browser window again and open the Type Library drop-down list. This time you will see a new object, DAO.

4. Select DAO and take a look at the Classes it exposes in the Classes pane.

In the next section, we'll show you how to use these Classes.

Using the DAO Object

The DAO object has many classes, one of them being the Database class. The Database class represents a database: a structure for storing information in Forms of tables. To work with a database, you must first select a table or a set of records, which are stored in a structure called Recordset.

NOTE A Recordset is a collection of records, such as the invoices issued to customers in California or the best-selling products.

If you scroll down the Classes list in the Object Browser, you will see the Recordset entry. Select the Recordset entry, and you'll see the description of a Recordset at the bottom of the window: "A representation of the records in a base table or the records that result from a query" (the last few words are missing, but we had to complete the sentence anyway).

In the Members pane, you will now see the members of the Recordset class. The BOF property, for example, becomes True when the first record is reached, and the EOF property becomes True when the last record is reached. You use the methods FindFirst, FindLast, FindNext, and FindPrevious to locate records in a Recordset according to criteria you specify.

To access the members of a Database object, you must first open a database and assign it to an object variable. The function for opening a database does not appear anywhere in the Object Browser, because it's not a member of the Database object. A Database object variable doesn't exist before you actually open the database and assign it to the variable. Therefore, the method for opening the database can't be a member of the Database object. OpenDatabase is a method of the DAO object; however, you don't need to prefix it with the name of the DAO object.

To open a database and assign it to an object variable, you first declare the variable as follows:

```
Dim DB As Database
```

and then open a database and set the DB variable to the database:

```
Set DB = OpenDatabase("C:\PROGRAM FILES\DEVSTUDIO\VB\NWIND.MDB")
```

NOTE We assume that the NWIND database is in the default VB folder. If you installed VB in another folder, change the path in the last statement accordingly.

The OpenDatabase() function accepts other optional arguments, and its complete syntax is:

```
OpenDatabase(Name, [Options,] [Read-Only,] [Connect])
```

The arguments in square brackets are optional. The Options argument can be True or False, indicating whether the database will be opened exclusively or will be shared. The Read-Only argument is another True/False argument, indicating whether the database can be written to or is read-only. The last argument sets connection parameters, such as the user name and password.

Selecting Records in Recordsets

The next step is to create a Recordset with the records we want to work with. Let's say we want to explore the Customers table, which contains the names of all customers in the NWIND database. Locate the Recordset Class of the DAO object, and in the Members pane locate the OpenRecordset method. The description of this method is "Creates a New Recordset Object," as shown in Figure 9.12.

The syntax of the method is:

```
OpenRecordset(Name As String, [Type], [Options], [LockEdit]) As Recordset
```

FIGURE 9.12:

Locating the OpenRecordset
method of the Recordset Class

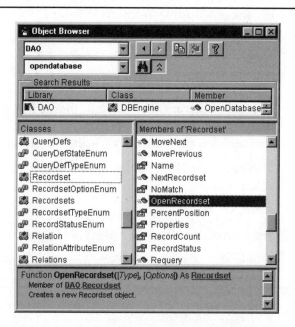

The *Name* entry is the name of the table we want to open or an SQL statement that retrieves the desired records from the database. For the purposes of our example, we'll use the name of the Customers table. You could also specify a SQL statement, such as the following, to retrieve selected customers only:

```
SELECT * FROM Customers WHERE Country = 'Germany'
```

The Type argument specifies the type of Recordset we want to create. You should know the various types of Recordsets you can create, but if you need to be reminded of the constants that describe them, locate the Class RecordsetTypeEnum and select it. In the Members pane, you will see all possible values for the Type argument:

dbOpenDynamic opens a dynamic Recordset (similar to an ODBC dynamic cursor).

dbOpenDynaset opens a Dynaset-type Recordset.

dbOpenForwardOnly opens a forward-only Recordset (it's faster than a Dynaset, but you can only issue the MoveNext and MoveLast methods against this Recordset).

dbOpenSnapshot opens a Snapshot Recordset, which you can use to read from but not write back to the database.

dbOpenTable opens a Table Recordset (an actual table in the database).

If you want to find out the constants that can be assigned to an argument, locate a Class whose name ends with *Enum* in the Classes pane (the name should resemble the name of the argument), and then look up its values in the Members pane. The last argument determines the type of locking for the Recordset, which we will not use in this example. If you want to find out the possible values of this argument, select the LockTypeEnum Class in the Class pane, and you'll see its values in the Members pane.

To create a Recordset with the names of all customers, you declare a Recordset object variable and then assign a newly created Recordset to it:

```
Dim RS As Recordset
Set RS = DB.OpenRecordset("Customers", dbOpenSnapshot)
```

The Recordset type is dbSnapShot, because this type gives the fastest possible access. We don't want to change the Customers table; we only want to read its records.

Exploring the Recordset's Structure

So far we've created a Recordset with the rows of the Customers table. What can we do with this Recordset? In this example, we want to find out the structure of each field, as well as the values of selected fields. If you select the Recordset class in the Classes pane and look at the members of the class, you will see that it has a property called Fields, as shown in Figure 9.12, earlier in this chapter. The icon in front of the Fields member is similar to the icon for properties with a little dot above it. This means that Fields is a Collection.

This make sense, because the Recordset contains multiple records. To access the first field, use the expression RS.Fields(i), where i goes from 0 to the number of fields (columns) in the Recordset minus one. The number of fields in the Recordset is given by the property Fields.Count. Don't remember the name of the property? Select the Fields Class in the Classes pane, as usual, and look it up in the Members pane.

The following loop scans all the fields in the Recordset and displays their names in a ListBox:

```
maxFields = RS.Fields.Count
For i = 0 To maxFields - 1
    List1.AddItem RS.Fields(i).Name
Next
```

Now we'll turn our attention to the rows of the Recordset. Each row is a record, with data about a different customer. The first piece of information we need is the number of rows in the Recordset. Again, select the Recordset class in the Classes pane, and search in the Members pane for a property named RecordCount. Its description is "Returns the number of records accessed in a Recordset." This is the property we need, but there is a detail you should be aware of here. The Object Browser won't be of much help here. The RecordCount property won't return the number of records in the Recordset because it hasn't seen more than the first record. You must first go to the last record in the Recordset with the MoveLast method, and then call the RecordCount property to find out the actual number of records in the Recordset.

The Recordset's rows can't be accessed through a Collection, similar to the Fields Collection. Instead, you must use the MoveNext method to move to the next record. The loop for scanning the rows of the RS Recordset is:

```
Do
    {process fields of current row}
RS.MoveNext
Loop While Not RS.EOF
```

To process the fields of the current row, you must know the names of the fields. We're interested in the fields ContactName and CompanyName. Their values can be accessed with the Value property of the Fields Collection of the RS object. The following code displays the values of the fields ContactName and Company name:

```
Do
    List2.AddItem RS.Fields("ContactName").Value & ",   " _
        & RS.Fields("CompanyName").Value
    RS.MoveNext
Loop While Not RS.EOF
```

Now, let's summarize what we have done so far and then build an application.

1. We opened a database and assigned it to a Database object variable (the DB variable).

2. Then, we called the DB object variable's OpenRecordset method to create a Recordset with the rows of the Customers table. This Recordset was assigned to the RS object variable.

3. Finally, with two loops we extracted the columns (field names) and rows (field values) of the Recordset.

Now we can put it all together and build a small application.

The ObjectLibrary Project

The ObjectLibrary project does the following:

- Opens a database and selects a table—the Customers table

- Displays the names of the fields in the upper ListBox control

- Displays all the values of two fields in the Recordset in the lower ListBox control

The application's main Form is shown in Figure 9.13.

NOTE   You'll find the ObjectLibrary project in the `Chapter9\ObjectLibrary` folder on the CD that comes with this book.

FIGURE 9.13:

The ObjectLibrary project's Form

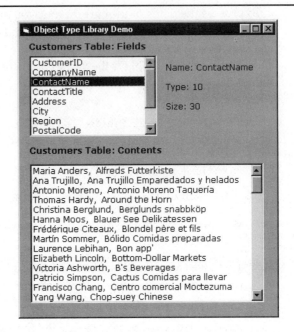

The code starts by declaring two object variables:

```
Private DB As Database
Private RS As Recordset
```

When the Form is loaded, the program opens the NWIND database and assigns it to the DB object variable. The statement that opens the NWIND database is:

```
Set DB = OpenDatabase("c:\Program files\Microsoft Visual
Studio\VB98\nwind.mdb")
```

> **NOTE**
>
> NWIND is a sample database that comes with Visual Basic 6, and we'll be using it a lot in this book's examples. The database's path used in the code segments is the default one. If you installed it in a different folder, you must adjust the code accordingly.

After this statement is executed, the *DB* variable refers to the NWIND database. The following line creates the Recordset with the rows of the Customers table:

```
Set RS = DB.OpenRecordset("Customers", dbOpenSnapshot)
```

After the two object variables are created, the code proceeds with the two loops we presented earlier to populate the lists:

```
List1.Clear
List2.Clear
maxFields = RS.Fields.Count
For i = 0 To maxFields - 1
    List1.AddItem RS.Fields(i).Name
Next

Do
    List2.AddItem RS.Fields("ContactName").Value & ",  " & _
        RS.Fields("CompanyName").Value
    RS.MoveNext
Loop While Not RS.EOF
```

Another event handler in the ObjectLibrary project is the Click event handler of the List1 control, which holds the names of the fields. When you click a field name in the upper list, its characteristics are displayed in three Label controls next to the field names list, as shown in Figure 9.13, earlier in this chapter.

Collections

Arrays are convenient for storing related data, but accessing individual array elements can be a problem. To insert an element at a specific location in an array you may have to move down all the elements that follow it (that could mean copying a large number of elements). Likewise, if you delete an element, the elements that follow must be moved up. And because an array can't be sorted automatically, keeping its elements in some order requires a lot of work. In the past, programmers had to resort to creative programming techniques to manipulate array data to overcome its limitations.

Consider this simple example: Suppose you have a two-dimensional array in which you store city names and temperatures. You want to find out the temperature in Atlanta. Ideally, arrays would be accessed by their contents. So in this instance, you should be able to look up the temperature in Atlanta with a statement such as the following:

```
Temperatures("Atlanta")
```

However, if you haven't or couldn't use the city names to index your array, you would have to either know the index that corresponds to Atlanta or scan each element in the array until you find Atlanta. Clearly, this could be a very cumbersome and time-consuming task.

But Visual Basic provides an alternative—collections. A collection is a very common and very useful structure in working with Visual Basic objects. It is a simple structure that works like an array, storing related items. Collections are objects and, as such, have properties and methods. The advantage of a collection over an array is that the collection lets you access its items via a key. If the city name is the key in the Temperatures() array, you can recall the temperature in Atlanta instantly by providing the key:

```
MsgBox "The temperature in Atlanta is " & Temperatures.Item("Atlanta")
```

Item is a method of the collection that returns a collection item based on its key or index. If you know the index of Atlanta's entry in the collection, you can use a statement such as the following:

```
MsgBox "The temperature in Atlanta is " & Temperatures.Item(6)
```

NOTE   If you are going to access a collection's item with its index, there's no advantage in using collections over arrays.

To use a collection, you must first declare a Collection variable, as follows:

```
Dim Temperatures As New Collection
```

The New keyword tells Visual Basic to set up a new collection and name it Temperatures. Temperatures is not an array. You do not have to specify its size (there are no parentheses after the collection's name), and you can't assign new elements with an assignment operator. Temperatures is an object, and you must use its members to access it.

The Members of a Collection

Collection objects provide three methods and one property:

> **Add Method** adds items to the collection.
>
> **Item Method** returns an item by index or by key.
>
> **Remove Method** deletes an item from the collection by index or by key.
>
> **Count Property** returns the number of items in the collection.

The Add (item, key, before, after) Method

To add a new item to a collection, use the Add method and assign its value to the *item* argument and its key to the *key* argument. To place the new item in a specific location in the array, specify one of the arguments *before* or *after* (but not both). To insert the new item before a specific element whose key (or index) you will specify, use the *before* argument. To place the new item after an item, specify this item's key or index with the *after* argument.

For example, to add the temperature for the city of San Francisco to the Temperatures collection, use the following statement:

```
Temperatures.Add 78, "San Francisco"
```

The number 78 is the value to be stored (temperature), and the string "San Francisco" is the new item's key. To insert this temperature immediately after the temperature of Santa Barbara, use the following statement:

```
Temperatures.Add 78, "San Francisco", , "Santa Barbara"
```

The extra comma denotes the lack of the *before* argument. The Add method supports named arguments, so the previous statement could also be written as follows:

```
Temperatures.Add 78, "San Francisco", after:= "Santa Barbara"
```

Collections aren't sorted; neither do they have a method to automatically sort their items. To maintain an ordered collection of objects, use the *before* and *after* arguments. In most practical situations, however, you don't care about sorting a collection's items. You sort arrays to simplify access of their elements; you don't have to do anything special to access the elements of collections.

The Remove (index) Method

The Remove method removes an item from a collection based on its key or index. By passing the argument to the Remove method, the argument can be either the position of the item you want to delete or the item's key. To remove the city of Atlanta from your collection of temperatures, use the following statement:

```
Temperatures.Remove "Atlanta"
```

Or, if you know the city's order in the collection, specify the index in place of the key:

```
Temperatures.Remove 6
```

The Item (index) Method

The Item method returns the value of an item in the collection, based on its key or index. As with the Remove method, the Index argument can be either the item's position in the collection or its key. To recall the temperature in Atlanta, use one of the following statements:

```
T1 = Temperatures.Item("Atlanta")
T1 = Temperatures.Item(3)
```

The Item method is the default method for a collection object, so you can omit it when you access an item in a collection. The previous example could also be written as:

```
T1 = Temperatures("Atlanta")
```

> **TIP**
>
> Collections maintain their indices automatically as elements are added and deleted. The index of a given element, therefore, changes during the course of a program, and you shouldn't save an item's index value and expect to use it to retrieve the same element later in your program. Use keys for this purpose.

The Count Property

The Count property returns the number of items in the collection. To find out how many cities have been entered so far in the Temperatures collection, use the following statement:

```
Temperatures.Count
```

You can also use the Count property to scan all the elements of the collection with a For...Next loop such as:

```
For city = 1 To Temperatures.Count
{process elements}
Next city
```

Actually, there is a better way to scan the elements of a Collection, which is explained next.

Processing a Collection's Items

To scan all the items in a collection, Visual Basic provides the For Each...Next structure. Its syntax is:

```
For Each member in Temperatures
```

```
    {process member}
Next
```

The *member* variable is the loop counter, but you don't have to initialize it or declare its type. The For…Each statement scans all the items in the collection automatically. At each iteration, the *member* variable assumes the current item's value.

You can also set up a For…Next loop to scan all the items in a collection:

```
For idx = 0 to Temperatures.Count-1
    {process current item}
Next
```

At each iteration of this loop, you can retrieve the value of the current item with the expression Temperatures(idx).

Using Collections

Let's implement a collection for storing the city names and temperatures. Start a new project, and add the following declaration in the Form:

```
Dim Temperatures As New Collection
```

This statement creates a new collection and names it Temperatures. Now enter the following code in the Form's Load event:

```
Private Sub Form_Load()

    Temperatures.Add 76, "Atlanta"
    Temperatures.Add 85, "Los Angeles"
    Temperatures.Add 97, "Las Vegas"
    Temperatures.Add 66, "Seattle"

End Sub
```

You can add as many lines as you wish, read the data from a disk file, or prompt the user to enter city names and temperatures at run time. New items can be added to the collection at any time.

Next, create a Command button, set its Caption property to Show City Temperature, and enter the following code in its Click subroutine:

```
Private Sub Command1_Click()
On Error GoTo NoItem
```

```
city = InputBox("What City?")
temp = Temperatures.Item(city)
MsgBox temp
Exit Sub

NoItem:
MsgBox "This city was not found in our catalog"

End Sub
```

This subroutine prompts users to enter the name of the city's temperature they want to learn. The program then recalls the value of the collection's item, where the key is the city name supplied by the user. If the supplied key doesn't exist, a run-time error is generated, which is why we use the On Error statement. If the user enters a nonexistent city name, a run-time error is generated; Visual Basic intercepts it and executes the statements following the label NoItem. If the key exists in the array, then the temperature of the corresponding city is displayed in a message box.

Finally, add another command button to the Form, set its caption to Show Average Temperature, and enter the following code behind its Click event:

```
Private Sub Command2_Click()
   For Each city In Temperatures
     total = total + city
     Debug.Print city
   Next
   avgTemperature = total / Temperatures.Count
   MsgBox avgTemperature
End Sub
```

The Print statement displays each element in the Immediate window. The name of the loop variable is *city*, and its value is the temperature of the current item, not the city name. (The counter of the For Each loop in the previous example could be named *iCity*, *temp*, or *foo*.)

NOTE The key values in a collection object are not stored as array elements in the collection. They are only used for accessing the items of the collection, just as array indices are used for accessing an array's elements.

CHAPTER

TEN

10

Building ActiveX Components

- Understanding modules and class modules

- Working with the Crypto class

- Working with the Stats class

- Encapsulating database operations

- Building out-of-process servers

- Dealing with synchronous and asynchronous processing

In the last chapter, we discussed how to use the built-in Visual Basic objects and introduced the concepts you need in order to create your own custom objects. This chapter discusses in depth how to build custom ActiveX components and use them within your applications or distribute them to other developers.

An ActiveX component can be any of the following:

- A code component
- An ActiveX control
- An ActiveX document

Code components are server applications that expose their functionality through an interface consisting of properties, methods, and events. The difference between ActiveX controls and code components is that ActiveX controls have a visible interface and are integrated into the Visual Basic IDE. Code components are classes that can be accessed through properly declared object variables with the CreateObject() function.

ActiveX documents are applications that can be hosted in containers such as Internet Explorer and the Office Binder. At this time, there aren't many ActiveX documents on the Internet (at least, we haven't seen any), and it seems it will be a while before they catch up. Developing ActiveX documents for Office Binder is even more questionable. In this book, we won't cover ActiveX documents, which are really simple compared with ActiveX code components and ActiveX controls.

We'll start our exploration of ActiveX components with the so-called code components. Code components provide a functionality similar to that of ActiveX controls, but they aren't as integrated with the development environment (for example, you can't drop a code component on a Form as you can a control), and they don't have a visible interface. Instead, they must be accessed in the same way that built-in objects are accessed, as we discussed in the last chapter, with the help of object variables.

ActiveX components are implemented as classes. They are prototypes that you use to create objects. We'll start our discussion of ActiveX code components with a short presentation of classes, class modules, and the two types of code components.

Modules and Class Modules

Classes are implemented in Visual Basic as class modules. Modules have existed in Visual Basic since the earliest versions. They store variable declarations and code (functions and subroutines) that are available to all other components of an application. For example, if the function ConvertTemperature(degrees As Double) or the function Encrypt(Text As String, Key As String) will be called from several places in your code and from within multiple Forms, implement the function in a module.

Procedures stored in a module can be called from any part of an application. You can think of these procedures as methods of the module, only you don't have to prefix a procedure with the name of the module when you call it. You can also think of the public variables you store in a module as properties of the module. Therefore, a module is not unlike a class, and classes are implemented as special types of modules, called *class modules*.

TIP   Why bother with classes when a module can provide the functionality you need in your application? If you need only a few procedures and global variables for a single project, you're probably better off dumping them in a module. If you plan to use the same procedures in multiple projects, however, you should build a class module.

Let's say you've implemented several functions in a module, tested them with Project A, and are satisfied with them. Later, you build Project B, which uses the same module. You realize that the functions in the module need some tweaking, so you introduce a few additional public variables. Now, although the module works well with Project B, you've inadvertently broken Project A. Even if you're disciplined enough not to touch the module, what if you belong to a group working on a common project? Allowing many programmers to access the same module from within their projects is an accident waiting to happen. One of them will inevitably tweak the code and break some of the existing projects.

If you believe in reusable software, classes are your best friends. To implement a class, you must first design its members so that they address the needs of multiple projects. For example, if your project needs a function that converts degrees Celsius to Fahrenheit, a class should contain a function that converts temperatures from any system to any other system. In the place of the function ConvertTemperature(degrees As Double), implement the function ConvertTemperature(degrees As Double, fromUnits As Integer, toUnits As Integer), which allows the developer to specify the temperature to be converted, as well as the units. You then test the function (which is a method of the class), and finally you cast it in concrete by building a DLL.

Other developers can add a reference to this class in their projects, use the method ConvertTemperature(), and use any other method of the class, but they will never see the code and won't be able to change it. Should conditions necessitate changes in the ConvertTemperature() function (unusual conditions, such as the introduction of a new temperature unit), you can carefully revise the class so that it won't break any code that already works.

Classes exhibit the two most important benefits of object-oriented programming:

Abstraction: The users of the class that exposes the ConvertTemperature method need not know anything about the intricacies of temperature conversion (well, you get the point). In the last chapter, you saw how classes abstract the complexity of objects such as a Database. In this chapter, you'll learn how to hide the complexity of custom operations and give developers simple ways to access them.

Reusability: A class is a real reusable component, at the binary level. As you will see, classes are reusable components on another level too. You can implement new classes that use the features of existing classes, without having to recode them. This is called *polymorphism*, which will be discussed later.

Implementing In-Process and Out-of-Process Servers

A class module is a server—an application that provides its services to the client application. When you create an object variable to access the properties and methods of a class, you are actually invoking an executable file (DLL or EXE) that runs in the background and waits to be contacted. Every time you set or read a property value or call a method, this executable is activated, it performs some action, and, optionally, returns some result to your application.

You can implement servers as ActiveX DLL or ActiveX EXE components. The difference between the two is how the server is executed. An ActiveX DLL is an *in-process server*. The DLL is loaded in the same address space as the executable that calls the server, and it runs on the same thread as the client. At any given moment, however, either the client application or the DLL is running. The benefit of DLLs is that they are faster, because, in effect, they become part of the application that uses them.

An *out-of-process server* runs as a separate process. When a client application creates an object provided by an EXE server for the first time, the server starts running as a separate process. If another client application creates the same object, this object is provided by the running EXE server. In other words, a single EXE server can service multiple clients. Out-of-process servers seem to be more efficient in terms of resource allocation, but exchanging information between servers is a slow process. Therefore, in terms of execution speed, in-process servers are faster.

> **NOTE** The communication between two processes is complicated and is known as *marshaling*.

What we have here is a client/server model. Your application is the client, which makes requests. The ActiveX Component is the server, which services the request. It's hard to think of ActiveX DLLs as servers, since they run in the same process as the client, but this is what they are. ActiveX EXE servers are separate processes, which can also service multiple clients. But more on this in the second half of the chapter.

This distinction between server types has ramifications in testing the components. You can easily test an ActiveX DLL by adding a test project to the ActiveX DLL project. Since both the server component and the test application run in the same process (the current instance of Visual Basic), you don't need two different executables. To test an ActiveX EXE component, however, you need two distinct processes—one instance of Visual Basic with the server and another with the test project. You can't have both the test application and the EXE server running in the Visual Basic environment.

The first few projects in this chapter are in-process servers (ActiveX DLL projects). In the second half of the book, you will see how to design and test out-of-process servers. Out-of-process servers are more difficult to implement because they should be designed so that they can provide their services to multiple clients.

Adding Methods to Class Modules

Adding a method to a class is as simple as declaring a Public function or subroutine. Any procedure that can appear in your code can become a method of a class if you enter it in a class module and declare it as Public. Let's add a really simple method to the class, one that returns its name. We'll call this method Class-Name and implement it as a function:

```
Public Function GetClassName() As String
    GetClassName = "why should you care?"
End Function
```

The class module now contains a method, GetClassName, which always returns the string "why should you care?" Of course, you could implement Get-ClassName as a property (and call it ClassName), whose value is set by the class, and the application can read it (we'll discuss class properties shortly).

Should It Be a Method or a Property?

You can implement some members both as methods and properties, and it isn't always easy to figure out which is best. Fortunately, it's not extremely important either.

You should try to follow the paradigm of the built-in, or third-party, controls. For example, if the class were an ActiveX control, a member you would like to see in the Properties window should be implemented as a property (the opposite isn't necessarily true). Methods should correspond to actions, and properties are attributes.

The naming scheme is also important. A name such as GetClassName suggests a method, and a name such as ClassName suggests a property.

Class modules can also contain private procedures. These procedures can be called from within the class's code, but other applications that use the class can't call them. If you want to track how many times a method is called during the course of an application, you can include a function such as the following:

```
Private Function CallCounter() As Integer
Static Popularity As Integer
    Popularity = Popularity +  1
    CallCounter  = Popularity
End Function
```

This function can be called from within the class's code, but any application that uses this class can't see the CallCounter() function. Because CallCounter() is private, it's not a method of the class. It's a regular function in the class's code.

Declaring Friend Members

In addition to private and public members, classes have a third type of scope modifier, which is called Friend. A Friend member is public for the entire project, and all the classes in the project can access it. In a Standard EXE application, all other modules and Forms can access public variables. In a standard EXE application, however, this is the broadest scope a variable can have.

With ActiveX components, whose public members can also be accessed from other applications, there has to be another type that makes members accessible from anywhere in the project, but not from outside.

NOTE   Only procedures (functions or subroutines) and properties can be declared as Friend. Variables are either private or public. This means that the classes of an ActiveX component can communicate by calling Friend methods and Friend properties.

Adding Properties to Class Modules

Implementing properties for classes requires some extra programming. You can still create properties by declaring public variables. Any variable you declare as public is accessible from outside the class, and other applications can set and read it. If you add the following declaration to the current class module:

```
Public IntProperty As Integer
```

you can access this property from an application and read its value, or you can assign a new value to it, with statements such as the following:

```
Count = Class1.IntProperty
Class1.IntProperty = 999
```

But what if the user attempts to assign an invalid value? A statement such as the following would result in a run-time error:

```
Class1.IntProperty = 99000
```

Implementing properties as public variables can lead to erratic behavior. The application that uses the class is responsible for trapping all possible errors, because your class never has an opportunity to validate the value assigned to the variable-property. Visual Basic provides special procedures for accessing class variables through code: the Property Let and Property Get procedures.

The proper method for implementing a property in your class is to add the following procedures:

```
Private m_IntProperty
Public Property Let IntProperty(newValue As Integer)
    m_IntProperty = newValue
End Property

Public Property Get IntProperty() As Integer
    IntProperty = m_IntProperty
End Property
```

The private variable *m_IntProperty* is local copy of the property's value. Every time an application sets this property's value, the Property Let procedure is automatically invoked, and the value specified is passed as an argument. In other words, the line:

```
IntProperty = 100
```

invokes the following procedure in your class:

```
Property Let IntProperty(100)
```

Assignments to property values trigger a special event, which causes a Property Let procedure (the one with the same name as the property) to execute. The new value is stored in the *m_IntProperty* variable. Likewise, when an application requests the value of the IntProperty property, the value of the local variable *m_IntProperty* is passed to it. In the Property Let procedure, you can insert all the validation code you see fit. For example, here's how you would implement an EMail property (which presumably stores electronic mail addresses):

```
Private m_EMail
Public Property Let EMail(newValue As String)
    If Instr(Email, "@") > 0 Then
        m_EMail = newValue
    End If
End Property

Public Property Get EMail() As String
    EMail = m_EMail
End Property
```

If the application specifies an invalid e-mail address, the class rejects the changes. The amount of validation code depends on the nature of the property, and you can insert as little or as much validation code as you want in the Property Let procedure.

You can also raise errors from within your Property Let procedure, which can be trapped by the application's code. For example, you could implement the EMail property as follows:

```
Public Property Let EMail(newValue As String)
    If Instr(newValue, "@") = 0 Then
        Err.Raise 1999, "Invalid value", _
        "Please supply an address in the form name@server.com"
    Else
        m_EMail = newValue
End Property
```

The error is passed back to the application, and it will either generate a run-time error or be trapped by the application's code.

TIP

The value 1999 was used in this example for reasons of convenience only—it will work, but it's not the suggested method for raising errors. Please read the section "Raising Errors from within a Class" later in this chapter to learn more about raising errors before you implement classes that raise trappable errors.

You might think about displaying a message with the MsgBox() function. This isn't such a good idea, for two reasons.

1. The message box may not be displayed on the user's monitor. If the class resides on a server and is used remotely by an application on a network (or the Internet), the message box will be displayed on the server, not on the client computer. Since the user of the application never sees the message box, he or she will never get a chance to click the OK button. As a result, the application will freeze.

2. Because the error message is produced by the class and not the application's code, in most cases you can't really offer the user more than a short, generic message such as "Please enter a valid value." This action must take place in the application's code, and the best way to react to errors in classes is to raise errors to the calling application.

It is possible, however, to display message boxes from within a class; you can even display an entire Form or a dialog box and request user input. Just remember that the class's visible user interface may become invisible, if the class is executed remotely.

Providing Property Set Procedures

The Property Let procedure is invoked every time the application assigns a new value to a property of a simple data type (Integer, String, and so on). As we saw in Chapter 9, some properties may themselves be objects. If a property is an object, such as Font, the application can't set it with a simple assignment statement like the following:

```
Class1.Font = newFont
```

or

```
Class1.Font = Text1.Font
```

You assign values to object variables with the Set statement:

```
Set Class1.Font = Text1.Font
```

For properties that are set in the code, you must provide a Property Set procedure in place of the Property Let procedure. The Property Set procedure is simply a variation of the Property Let procedure and doesn't require any special coding. For example, here's a Property Set procedure that sets the Font property:

```
Private m_Font As Font
Public Property Set Font (newFont As Font)
    If newFont.Size > 36 Then newFont.Size = 36
    Set m_Font = newFont
End Property
```

This code segment makes sure that the font's size isn't unreasonable. Object properties are read with the Property Get procedure, as usual.

> **NOTE**
>
> Of course, there's very little use for setting a Font property in a class because it doesn't have a visible user interface, but you will be setting Font properties in the next chapter, in which we will discuss ActiveX controls.

You've now seen the basics of building classes. In essence, classes are applications without a visible user interface. They do, however, have an interface, which is made up of the properties, methods, and events they provide (which are collectively called *members*). Actually, you haven't seen how to raise events yet, but we'll discuss this topic in the section "Asynchronous Methods and Properties," later in this chapter. As you recall from the previous chapter, events are raised with the RaiseEvent method. But it's about time to put together the information presented so far to build an actual ActiveX component.

Developing the Crypto Class

In this section, we will develop a class that encrypts text based on a password. Any application that must encrypt text can add a reference to this class and call its Encrypt method. With a class such as Crypto, you'll never have to provide your own encryption procedures, and all your applications can use a consistent encryption method. The same method will also decrypt previously encrypted messages.

The cryptography engine used by the Crypto class is fairly simple, yet it will prevent most occasional intruders. If you need a truly safe encryption, you must tweak the code, and we'll give you a few ideas about how to do this at the end of this section. To simplify the code and focus on the mechanics of implementing a class, we'll implement a simple cryptography engine. (Actually, it's not that simple. Many commercial products use similar methods.)

All encryption techniques are based on the XOR operator, which has the following unique property: If you XOR a character with another character, you'll get an encrypted version of the original character. If you XOR this character with the same key character once again, you will get the original one. For example, if you XOR the value 132 with the value 45, you'll get 169. If you XOR the new value, 169, with 45, you will get the number you started with, 132. This unique feature of the XOR operator is used extensively with drawing methods. You can place a shape over a bitmap and then remove it, using the XOR drawing mode.

To encrypt a string, we'll XOR its first character with the first character of the password, the second character of the string with the second character of the password, and so on, until we run out of characters in the password (see Code 10.1). Then, we must start with the first character of the password again. Figure 10.1 shows which characters will be XORed with each other in encrypting the message "Attack before dawn" with the password TORA.

FIGURE 10.1:

Encrypting by XORing strings with a key

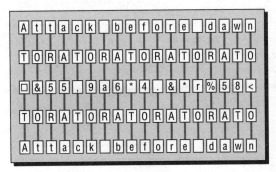
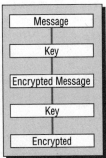

Code 10.1   Encrypting the Message

```
Message = "Attack before dawn"
Key = "TORA"
For i = 1 To Len(Message)
    textChar = Mid(Message, i, 1)
    keyChar = Mid(Key, (i Mod Len(Key)) + 1)
    encryptedChar = Asc(textChar) Xor Asc(keyChar)
    EncryptedMessage = EncryptedMessage & Chr(encryptedChar)
Next
Debug.Print EncryptedMessage
```

The encrypted message is:

```
&55,9a6*4.&*r%58<
```

(The first character is unprintable and, therefore, left blank in the text.) If you run the previous lines using the encrypted text as a message, you'll get back the original string.

TIP

To test the previous lines, place them in the Click event of a Command button. If you want to test them in the Immediate window, be sure that the entire For…Next loop is entered on a single line, using the colon (:) to separate successive statements.

This code segment is the core of the encryption engine we are going to implement in our Crypto class. Before you start coding the class, however, you must design its interface: its properties and methods. In other words, you must decide how other applications will access the functionality of the class. The Crypto class provides three properties and a method, as shown in Table 10.1.

TABLE 10.1: The Crypto Class Members

Member	What It Is
Text	The text to be encrypted
Key	The encryption key (password)
EncryptedText	The encrypted text
Encrypt	The method that performs the encryption by XORing the Text and Key properties

Building the Crypto Class

To build a new class, start an ActiveX DLL project. Visual Basic will add a folder named Class Modules, with a class module in it. Change the name of the Class Module to CryptoClass, and change the project name to Crypto. Then save the components of the project in a new folder.

The Crypto Project on the CD

The components of the Crypto project on the CD are named `Crypto.vbp` and `Test-Project.cls`. The file `Crypt.vbp` contains the class, and the file `TestProject.vbp` contains the test project. To open both the class and the test project and test them at once in the IDE, open the file `Crypto.vbg`.

The first time you open this project from the CD (as well as all other projects in this chapter), you will get the following error message:

```
Unable to set the version compatible component
```

This only means that Visual Basic can't find the Crypto class on your computer, because it hasn't been registered yet. Ignore the warning, click the OK button to open the project, and then run the test project. The Crypto class will be created and registered automatically.

The class's Encrypt method doesn't accept any arguments. It acts on the values of the properties Text and Key and stores the result of the encryption in the Encrypted-Text property. First, add the declarations of the private variables that hold the values of the properties in the class module:

```
Private mvarText As String
Private mvarKey As String
Private mvarEncryptedText As String
```

The next step is to write the Property Let and Property Get procedures for each property (see Code 10.2). Notice that the EncryptedText property is read-only. It doesn't make sense to set the encrypted text from outside the class, so we omit the Property Let procedure for the EncryptedText property. Later, you'll see how you can raise an error message when the application attempts to set the value of a read-only property.

Code 10.2	**The Property Procedures for the Class's Properties**

```
Public Property Get EncryptedText() As String
    EncryptedText = mvarEncryptedText
End Property

Public Property Let Key(ByVal vData As String)
    mvarKey = vData
End Property

Public Property Get Key() As String
    Key = mvarKey
End Property

Public Property Let Text(ByVal vData As String)
    mvarText = vData
End Property

Public Property Get Text() As String
    Text = mvarText
End Property
```

The Property Let procedures don't validate the property values at their assignment. The validation will take place when the Encrypt method is called. Code 10.3 shows the implementation of the Encrypt() function in its simplest form.

Code 10.3	**The Encrypt() Function**

```
Public Function Encrypt() As Integer
Dim textChar As String * 1
Dim keyChar As String * 1
Dim encryptedChar As Integer

    mvarEncryptedText = ""
    For i = 1 To Len(mvarText)
        textChar = Mid(mvarText, i, 1)
        keyChar = Mid(mvarKey, (i Mod Len(mvarKey)) + 1)
        encryptedChar = Asc(textChar) Xor Asc(keyChar)
        mvarEncryptedText = mvarEncryptedText & Chr(encryptedChar)
    Next
    Encrypt = 1
End Function
```

You declare the Encrypt() function as public, and it automatically becomes a method of the class. When it's called, it encrypts the value of the *mvarText* local variable with the key stored in the *mvarKey* local variable and assigns the result to another local variable, *mvarEncryptedText*. The application must then read the EncryptedText property's value to retrieve the encrypted text.

Raising Errors from within a Class

The simple code we presented here doesn't protect the developer from possible errors. What if the key or the text hasn't been specified? The Encrypt method must first make sure that the Text and Key properties have valid values, before it attempts to encrypt the text. If it detects an abnormal condition, it must notify the developer by raising an error. The class shouldn't display error messages or prompt the user to enter the missing data. The Crypto class doesn't have a visible interface, and it should notify the client application by raising an error.

Although it is possible for the class to display message boxes, request user input with the InputBox() function, and even to display Forms and dialog boxes, we generally avoid giving a class a visible user interface, because the class may be running on a remote computer. In that case, any dialog boxes will appear on the server computer and not on the client. Besides, the responsibility for the client application's user interface lies with the developer, not with the class itself. The same class can be used by multiple applications, and each one may handle the same error differently. You must, therefore, offer the means for the developers to detect from within their code any unusual conditions and react to them as they see fit. The best way to detect unusual conditions from within your class and yet leave the responsibility for handling them to the developer is via trappable errors.

To raise an error from within your code, you can call the Raise method of the Err object. The Raise method causes a run-time error and its syntax is:

```
Err.Raise number, source, description, helpfile, helpcontext
```

The number parameter is a Long Integer that identifies the nature of the error. The range 0 to 512 is reserved by Visual Basic; you should never use error numbers in this range. You can use any other error number, but it's recommended that you use small integers and add the vbErrorObject constant to them. If your class can detect eight types of errors, you can assign them the values 1 through 8 and add the constant vbErrorObject. To find out the original error number, the application can subtract the same constant from the Err.Number value. The remaining arguments are optional. The *source* argument is a string that identifies the component that raised the error (for example, Crypto.CryptoClass). Should another control use the same error numbers, you can find out which control generated the error by examining the Err object's Source property. If you omit the source parameter, the programmatic ID of the current Visual Basic project is used. The next argument, *description*, is another string that describes the error. If this is unspecified, Visual Basic examines the value of the Number property. If that Number property corresponds to an existing run-time error, Visual Basic displays this error's description. If no Visual Basic error corresponds to the specified number, the string "Application-defined or object-defined error" is displayed as the error's description.

The last two arguments let you specify additional help. The *helpfile* argument is the path to a Microsoft Windows Help file with information about this error. If this is unspecified, Visual Basic uses the fully-qualified drive, path, and file name of the Visual Basic Help file. The context ID of a topic within *helpfile* that provides help for the specific error is *helpcontext*.

The Encrypt method may discover two error conditions:

- Unspecified text

- Unspecified encryption key

Let's use the numbers 100 and 101 for these two errors and the descriptions "Can't encrypt null text" and "Encryption key not specified." Code 10.4 shows the complete code of the Encrypt() function, which validates the data before acting on them.

Code 10.4   The Complete Encrypt() Function

```
Public Function Encrypt() As Integer
Dim textChar As String * 1
Dim keyChar As String * 1
Dim encryptedChar As Integer

    If mvarText = "" Then
        Err.Raise vbObjectError + 100, _
            "Crypto.CryptoClass", "Can't encrypt null text"
        Encrypt = 0
        Exit Function
```

```
        End If
        If mvarKey = "" Then
            Err.Raise vbObjectError + 101, _
                "Crypto.CryptoClass", "Encryption key not specified"
            Encrypt = 0
            Exit Function
        End If

        mvarEncryptedText = ""
        For i = 1 To Len(mvarText)
            textChar = Mid(mvarText, i, 1)
            keyChar = Mid(mvarKey, (i Mod Len(mvarKey)) + 1)
            encryptedChar = Asc(textChar) Xor Asc(keyChar)
            mvarEncryptedText = mvarEncryptedText & Chr(encryptedChar)
        Next
        Encrypt = 1
    End Function
```

After you enter the complete code, you are ready to test the class. Save all the components of the project (the class module and the test project), and then choose File ➤ Make Crypto.dll. If you saved the class with a different file name, this file name with the extension DLL will appear in the File menu. Select this command and create the DLL in the same folder where you saved the project.

Handling Errors at Design Time

When you are testing a class module with an application that resides in the same project group, errors raised by the class are not passed to the host application. The Encrypt method, for example, raises two errors. If you are testing the class with the test project in the same project group, the program will stop at the line that raises the error, in the class's code.

If you run the test project separately, the code won't break in the class module (developers don't have access to the class's code anyway). Instead, the class will raise an error, which your application will trap. To change this behavior, choose Tools ➤ Options to open the Options dialog box.

Continued on next page

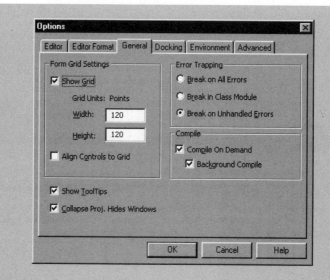

In the Error Trapping section, check the Break on Unhandled Errors option. This causes the class to pass the error to the host application, where it's supposed to be handled by an error-trapping routine. The code will break only if an error is received by a procedure that calls a method or a property of the class and doesn't have its own error handler.

Creating Object Variables

In the last chapter, you saw how to access Classes through object variables. You also saw two ways to declare object variables:

1.   Declare an object variable with the New keyword:

     ```
     Private objectVar As New objectType
     ```

2.   Declare an object variable and then set it to the object you want to access:

     ```
     Private objectVar As objectType
     Set objectVar = New objectType
     ```

Both methods require that Visual Basic knows the objectType. You can expect that Visual Basic knows about Forms, controls, and other types of built-in objects. But how about your custom objects? Visual Basic doesn't know anything about the objects you create; you must tell it that a specific project must access an object by adding a reference to this object to your project. For example, if you want to add the Crypto class to a project, choose Project ➢ References to open the References dialog box:

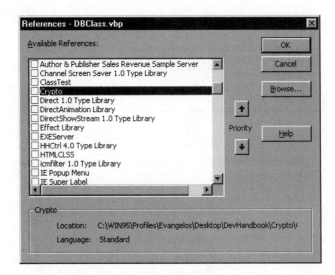

Locate the object you want to reference from within your code, check its box, and click OK.

If you open the Object Browser dialog box after adding a new reference to your project, you will see the Type Library of the recently added object. Select it in the Type Library box to see the classes it exposes in the Classes pane. The Crypto project exposes a single class, the Crypto class. Click the name of the class to see its members.

Unless you add a reference to a specific object to your project, you won't be able to declare variables of this type. You can also declare object variables with the CreateObject function, which requires that you supply the application and class name. First, declare an object variable, and then assign an instance of the class to it:

```
Private cryptoObject As Object
Set cryptoObject = CreateObject("Crypto.CryptoClass")
```

You usually place the Set statement in the Form_Load event or in the procedure that needs to access the class. You can change the declaration of the object variable cryptoObject in the test application with the CreateObject method, as shown here. The rest of the code remains the same.

Testing the Crypto Class

To test the Crypto class, you create a new project, add a reference to this class to the new project, and then create an object variable that represents the Crypto class, as discussed in the previous section. Through this object variable, you can access the class's properties and methods. The test project we'll use for the Crypto class is the TestPrj.vbp project (see Code 10.5). The test project's main Form is shown in Figure 10.2.

NOTE   You'll find the TestPrj.vbp project in the **Chapter10\Crypto** folder on the CD that comes with this book.

FIGURE 10.2:

The main Form of the test project for the Crypto class

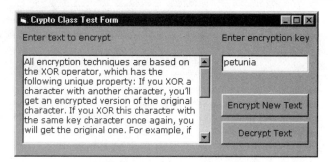

This Form contains two TextBox controls, a multiline one in which the text to be encrypted appears, and a smaller one in which the key is displayed. The Encrypt New Text button encrypts the text in the multiline TextBox with the specified key. The result is stored in a private variable, and clicking the Decrypt Text button decrypts it.

NOTE   The encrypted text isn't displayed in the TextBox, because it's possible for an encrypted character to have the ASCII value zero. This character signifies the end of the text in the TextBox and would truncate the encrypted text in the TextBox control. The test project maintains a Form-wide, private variable, the *secretText* variable, in which the most recently encrypted text is stored. The Decrypt Text button uses this variable's value to decrypt the text.

Code 10.5   **The TestPrj.vbp Project**

```
Private CryptoObj As New CryptoClass
Private secretText As String

Private Sub Command1_Click()
On Error GoTo EncryptionError

    CryptoObj.Key = Text2.Text
    CryptoObj.Text = Text1.Text
    Call CryptoObj.Encypt
    secretText = CryptoObj.EncryptedText
    MsgBox Len(CryptoObj.Text) & " characters encrypted successfully."
    Text1.Text = ""
    Exit Sub

EncryptionError:
    MsgBox Err.Description
End Sub

Private Sub Command2_Click()
On Error GoTo DecryptionError

    CryptoObj.Key = Text2.Text
    CryptoObj.Text = secretText
    Call CryptoObj.Encypt
    Text1.Text = CryptoObj.EncryptedText
    Exit Sub

DecryptionError:
    Debug.Print Err.Number
    MsgBox Err.Description
End Sub
```

You declare the *CryptoObj* variable with the New keyword, so you don't have to set it in the code. The object variable is created not at the moment it's declared, but the first time it's referenced in the code. Notice that the *CryptoObj* object variable is declared in the Form so that both event handlers can access it (see the declarations at the beginning of Code 10.5). Because it was declared with the New keyword and we don't have to set this variable in the code, it doesn't make any difference which event handler will instantiate the variable. The user can click either button for the first time. (It doesn't make much sense to decrypt a string that hasn't been encrypted yet. However, you can try clicking both buttons for the first time and see that this doesn't make any difference to the creation of the object variable.)

The Encrypt method is also used to decrypt a previously encrypted string. Of course, it's going to yield meaningful results only if the application supplies to correct key (the exact same key that was used to encrypt the text). Code 10.6 is the code behind the Decrypt Text command button:

Code 10.6   **The Decrypt Text Button**

```
Private Sub Command2_Click()
On Error GoTo DecryptionError

    CryptoObj.Key = Text2.Text
    CryptoObj.Text = secretText
    Call CryptoObj.Encpyt
    Text1.Text = CryptoObj.EncryptedText
    Exit Sub

DecryptionError:
    MsgBox Err.Description
End Sub
```

As explained earlier, the encrypted text is stored in the *secretText* variable, which is declared at the Form level. The host application will probably retrieve the value of the Encrypted text property and store it to a binary file, from where it can be read later.

Developing More Robust Encryption Schemes

The encryption engine we implemented for the CryptoClass class isn't terribly secure. The problem with this scheme is that it uses a fixed-length key. If the original text contains a (not so unusual) pattern of asterisks, dashes, or other special characters, the length of the key will become evident. If you encrypt the string:

```
******************************
```

with the key abcd, you'll get the following encrypted string:

```
HINKHINKHINKHINKHINKHINKHINKH
```

One can easily spot a pattern in the encrypted text. This pattern reveals the length of the key. In addition, if you XOR the encrypted text with a pattern consisting of special symbols, you'll come up with the encryption key. Let's pretend that we don't know what the original string is, but that we do know that it's made up of a long run of identical characters. If you XOR the encrypted text with several patterns (runs of dashes, spaces, asterisks, and so on), you will eventually discover the encryption key. There are actually applications you reply upon on a daily basis that employ such vulnerable encryption schemes.

One simple trick to make this encryption scheme more secure is to blend the key with the text as you move along. When you run out of characters in the key, you wrap the key and start with its first character again. But you can replace it with a new key, based on the text characters you've encrypted already. For example, instead of using the first character of the key for a second time, you can XOR its first character with the first character of the text and use the result of the operation as the first character of the key. This process is reversible, because when you run out of characters in the encryption key, the first few characters of the original text will be available.

You can also use really convoluted operations between the key and the string to totally eliminate patterns. The new encryption scheme isn't unbeatable, but it will serve the needs of a typical programmer (which is to secure some files on a local area network).

TIP

If you plan to transmit sensitive information over the Internet, look into more advanced encryption schemes, which are readily available.

Setting Project Properties

At this point we'll take a break to discuss the Project Properties dialog box. Most of the entries in this dialog box are obvious, but some aren't. Also, some seemingly obvious options may have ramifications you must be aware of. You can skip this section if you want and come back to it when you need this information. In the Project Properties dialog box, shown in Figure 10.3, you select a project type and set various options for the project.

FIGURE 10.3:

The Project Properties
dialog box

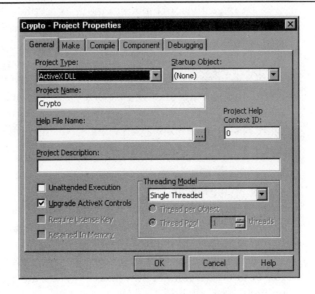

The General Tab

As you can see in Figure 10.3, the General tab of the Project Properties dialog box is selected by default. This dialog box contains the options described in the following sections.

Project Type   This drop-down list box contains the types of projects, as they appear in the File Open dialog box. The following project types are available:

- Standard EXE

- ActiveX DLL

- ActiveX EXE

- ActiveX control

Changing the project type at will isn't always feasible or simple, but many times it is. Switching between ActiveX DLL and ActiveX EXE projects is possible and fairly easy. Let's say you want to build an ActiveX DLL. To simplify the testing and debugging process, you can start a Standard EXE project and add a class module to the project. When the class is working in the context of the current project, you can remove the project's Forms and change the type of the project from Standard EXE to ActiveX DLL. You should also set the StartUp object to None. If you want to execute certain statements when the component is loaded for the first time, place them in its Initialize event.

Startup Object   You use this drop-down list box to specify what will happen when the project is run. You can't execute ActiveX control projects; you must place the ActiveX control on a Form of a Standard EXE project, which is then executed. For Standard EXE projects, the Startup object can be a Form or the subroutine Main. The Main subroutine must reside in a standard module of the project, and it must display the first visible Form of the application. Code components can't start by displaying Forms. The StartUp object of an ActiveX EXE or DLL component must be None or the subroutine Main. If you change the type of a project during its design, you must also change the Startup object.

You can set a different Startup object for each project in a project group. To specify the Startup project, right-click the project's name in the Project window and select Set As Startup.

If the StartUp object is an ActiveX code component or ActiveX control, Visual Basic will present the Debugging tab of the Project Properties dialog box when you attempt to run the component. The Debugging tab offers the following options:

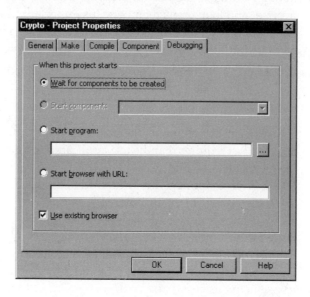

Wait for components to be created   This option will create the new component and register it, so that another instance of VB can use it. If you want to test the component with a test project in a different instance of Visual Basic (this is the case with ActiveX EXE components), select this option.

Start component   This option will start the component. If you're developing ActiveX controls, which can't exist on their own window, Visual Basic will create a small HTML file with the control and will open the page with Internet Explorer. You'll find more information on using ActiveX controls on Web pages in Chapter 18, "Web Development Basics."

Start program This option allows you to select an executable file that exists on the disk already and uses the new component. Select this option to test the control with another project.

Start browser with URL The last option allows you to specify the URL of a Web file, which presumably contains the custom ActiveX control and test the custom control on a Web page.

To test a new class, or control, you must specify that the test project is the StartUp Object, so that Visual Basic will run the test project and display the test Form with the custom component. To do so, right-click the name of the test project in the Project Explorer window and from the shortcut menu select "Set as Start Up."

Project Name This property is the component's name in the Object Browser. In other words, this is how developers will locate your component in the Object Browser and look up its members. It's important to set a proper project name in this field. If you don't, you'll have to differentiate among various Project1 components on your disk. If the component's name is MyComponent and it exposes a class called MyClass, the code can create an object variable to reference the class with the following statement:

```
Set Object1 = CreateObject("MyComponent.MyClass")
```

As you can see, changing the project's name (or the class's name for that matter) after the fact requires that the test application's code be revised too. Use descriptive project names, and avoid generic names such as Test, Example, Server, and so on. ActiveX components are registered to the system; they aren't just files that live in a folder.

Help File Name, Project Help Context ID You use these two fields to specify the help file for the project and the ID. Although we won't discuss help files in this book, any component you plan to release (especially ActiveX controls) must have a help file.

Project Description This is the project's description and appears in the Object Browser when a user selects your component.

Upgrade ActiveX Controls Check this option if you want Visual Basic to automatically upgrade ActiveX controls to their newer versions when the user upgrades one or more of the controls in the project.

Require License Key   This field enables you to protect your components with a license key. When you develop and distribute an ActiveX control, some developers will use it in their applications. The users of these applications should be able to use your control at run time, but you may not want to allow them to use your control in designing new projects. This would be equivalent to distributing your control for free. To protect your software, you can use license keys. If a developer attempts to use your control in the design of an application and doesn't have a license key, Visual Basic won't permit the installation of the control. If you are protecting your components with license keys, check this option.

Unattended Execution   The options in this section apply to multithreaded servers, and we discuss them in the second half of this chapter.

The Make Tab

Now click the Make tab. As you can see, this tab contains mostly developer's information, such as version numbers and conditional compilation arguments.

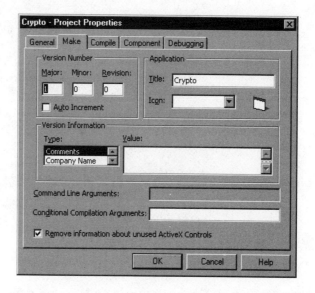

Version Number   Here you can set the version of your component, or you can check the Auto Increment box (which increments the component's version number each time you build a new EXE or DLL file. You should set the version number manually before releasing the component. Releasing a new control with version number 16 isn't the best idea.

Application Here you can specify the name of the application and select an icon for its executable file.

Version Information Enter comments, copyright notices, trademark notes, and other types of information in this section.

Command Line Arguments Enter any command line arguments for Standard EXE projects here.

Conditional Compilation Arguments In this field, you can enter the values of the conditional compilation arguments.

The Compile Tab

Now, click the Compile tab:

This tab lets you specify the various compilation options.

Compile to P-Code, Compile to Native Code These two options let you select how the Visual Basic compiler will optimize the executable file. With older versions of Visual Basic, you could only produce p-Code, but now there's a real compiler. Go for native code and optimize for fast code, right? Not so simple.

Native code isn't necessarily faster than p-Code (it's not slower either). A typical application spends most of its time waiting for user input and performs tasks that take much less than a second. In general, native code runs considerably faster than native code and should be preferred, unless the size of the executable matters. The topic of p-code versus native code and how to optimize VB applications is discussed in detail in Chapter 17, "Optimizing VB Applications."

Advanced Optimizations   Click the Advanced Optimizations button to open the Advanced Optimizations dialog box, in which you can set a number of options (listed to follow) that will marginally improve the speed of the executable. You can turn off some or all of these checks by checking the appropriate checkbox.

> **WARNING**   Enabling these optimizations may prevent the correct execution of your program. You must understand what each option does and be sure that your application doesn't require any of the options you turn off.

Assume No Aliasing: This option tells the compiler that your program does not use aliasing. Aliasing is a technique that lets your code refer to the same variable (memory location) by more than one name. We don't use this technique in this book, so you can safely turn on this option.

Remove Array Bound Checks: By default, Visual Basic checks an array's bounds every time your code accesses the array to determine if the index is within the range of the array. If the index is not within array bounds, a run-time error is generated (which can be trapped from within the code). Select this option to turn off the array bound checking and speed up applications that use arrays. However, the code that will ensure that the array's bounds are not exceeded may cost more in execution time. If an array bound is exceeded, the results will be unexpected.

Remove Integer Overflow Checks: By default, Visual Basic checks every calculation for integer-style data types—Byte, Integer, and Long—to ensure that the value is within the range of the data type. If the magnitude of the value being put into the data type is incorrect, a run-time error is generated. Select this option to turn off the error checking and speed up integer calculations. If data type capacities are overflowed, you will get incorrect results.

Remove Floating Point Error Checks: By default, Visual Basic checks every calculation of a Floating Point data type—Single and Double—to be sure that the value is within range for that data type and that there are no divide-by-zero or invalid operations. If the magnitude of the value being put into the data type is incorrect, an error occurs. Select this option to turn off the error checking and speed up floating-point calculations. If data type capacities are overflowed, no error handling occurs, and you may get incorrect result.

Allow Unrounded Floating Point Operations: When this option is selected, the compiler uses floating-point registers more efficiently, avoids storing and loading large volumes of data to and from memory, and does floating-point comparisons more efficiently.

Remove Safe Pentium FDIV Checks: Checking this option removes the safety checking so that the code for floating-point division is faster. You may, however, get slightly incorrect results on Pentium processors with the FDIV bug.

As you can see, disabling these checks will marginally improve the speed of the code, but it may cause the application to crash.

The Component Tab

Now, select the Component tab.

This tab contains a few options for ActiveX servers and lets you specify the version compatibility, a handy method to ensure that each time you update a component, all projects that used the previous version will be updated as well.

Start Mode In this section, you can specify whether an ActiveX EXE server will start as a standalone application or as an ActiveX server. This option applies to ActiveX EXE components only, and the default is ActiveX Component (it will start when an application contacts the server).

Remote Server   When this option is selected, Visual Basic creates a file with a VBR file name extension and the same file name as the DLL file. This VBR file contains information needed by the Windows Registry to run an ActiveX Server on a remote computer.

Version Compatibility   The options in this section allow you to set the level of version compatibility: how newer versions of ActiveX components and controls will affect existing projects.:

> **No Compatibility**: Compatibility is not enforced.
>
> **Project Compatibility**: If you select this option, the Location dialog box is activated, and you can use it to search for the DLL (or EXE) file with which this project is to be compatible. If this option is not selected, the Location dialog box is not available. If you design an ActiveX control or a code component to be used with a specific project, select this option, and select the name of the project in the last field. By default, this option is selected for all ActiveX projects; so every time you change the control or component's code, the project is also updated.
>
> **Binary Compatibility**: Select this option to maintain compatibility among projects that have been compiled using your component. If this option is selected and you attempt to change the name of a member, Visual Basic will warn you that you're about to break the compatibility mode (any project that calls the member by its previous name will no longer work). You can either break the compatibility, return to the project and undo the changes, or use some other trick to remedy the conditions that are causing compatibility problems.

Classes with Collections

The Crypto class is as simple as it gets. Our next project, the RunningStats class, demonstrates a class that calculates running statistics. It calculates the basic statistics (average and standard deviation) of a data run. The main feature of this class is that it calculates the so-called running statistics; it doesn't require that all the data be supplied at once. As each new data value becomes available, the statistics are updated, and the host application can retrieve their values at any time. The Stats project is a Standard EXE project that has a Form and a class module. Figure 10.4 shows the Stats project at design time.

FIGURE 10.4:

The Stats project at
design time

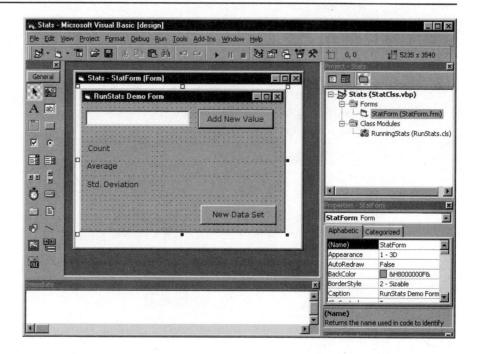

NOTE   You'll find the Stats projects in the **Chapter10\Stats** folder on the CD that comes
with this book.

The benefit of this approach is that you can implement and test the class with a
single project. Since the class module was added to the project, it became immediately part of the project, and you don't have to add a reference to the RunningStats
class through the References dialog box. Yet, the class can be made available for
use by other projects too. To do so, however, you must:

1.   Change the project type from Standard EXE to ActiveX DLL.

2.   Set Instancing Property to MultiUse.

The Instancing property of a class module is discussed in the following section.
Let's return to the Stats project. Table 10.2 lists and describes the members of the
RunningStats class.

TABLE 10.2: The Members of the RunningStats Class

Member	What It Is
NewValue	New data value to be appended to the current data set. Each time a new data value is added to the current data set, all statistics are recalculated.
RunningCount	The number of data values in the data set
RunningAverage	The current average of the data set
RunningDeviation	The current standard deviation of the data set
NewDataSet	This method resets the data set

The average is calculated as the sum of all values in the run, divided by their count. Therefore, we need a private variable that holds the running sum, which is the *m_Sum* variable. At any point, the average can be calculated as:

```
m_Sum / m_var_RunningCount
```

The local variable, *m_var_RunningCount*, stores the RunningCount property.

The standard deviation is calculated according to a standard formula. It's the square root of the difference between the sum of squares, minus the square of the average, multiplied by the number of data values, and divided by the square of the count of the data points. It's implemented with a fairly long line, as you'll see in Code 10.7, but if you aren't interested in statistics, you can ignore the calculations. The deviation is an important attribute of the data set that describes the dispersion of the values around their mean value.

Code 10.7   **The RunningStats Class**

```
Option Explicit
Private m_var_RunningCount As Long
Private m_var_RunningAverage As Double
Private m_var_RunningDeviation As Double
Private m_Sum As Double
Private m_SumSquares As Double

Public Property Get RunningAverage() As Double
    RunningAverage = m_var_RunningAverage
End Property

Public Property Get RunningCount() As Long
```

```
        RunningCount = m_var_RunningCount
End Property

Public Property Get RunningDeviation() As Double
        RunningDeviation = m_var_RunningDeviation
End Property

Public Property Let NewValue(vNewValue As Double)
    m_var_RunningCount = m_var_RunningCount + 1
    m_Sum = m_Sum + vNewValue
    m_var_RunningAverage = m_Sum / m_var_RunningCount
    m_SumSquares = m_SumSquares + vNewValue ^ 2
    If m_var_RunningCount > 1 Then m_var_RunningDeviation = _
        Sqr(m_SumSquares - m_var_RunningCount * _
        m_var_RunningAverage ^ 2) / (m_var_RunningCount * _
        (m_var_RunningCount - 1))
End Property

Public Sub NewDataSet()
    m_var_RunningAverage = 0
    m_var_RunningCount = 0
    m_var_RunningDeviation = 0
    m_Sum = 0
    m_SumSquares = 0
End Sub
```

The Form's code is simple too. First, we create an object variable that references the RunningStats object:

```
Private StatObj As New RunningStats
```

and then we use it from within the AddNew Value button's code to add a new value to the data set and retrieve the updated statistics:

```
Private Sub Command1_Click()
    If IsNumeric(Text1.Text) Then
        StatObj.NewValue = Text1.Text
        Text1.Text = ""
        lblCnt.Caption = StatObj.RunningCount
        lblAvg.Caption = StatObj.RunningAverage
        lblDev.Caption = StatObj.RunningDeviation
    End If
End Sub
```

This class is useful in maintaining running statistics of large data sets, especially if they can be updated from many places in an application. However, it doesn't keep track of the data values. It is possible to build a class that maintains a list of data values (which need not be numeric, by the way) and report them to the application. We'll look at this in the next section.

Array Properties

The Stats class can report the running statistics at any time, but not the data supplied to the class. If the calling application doesn't store them in an array or another structure, the data values will be lost. Of course, the purpose of the Stats class is to avoid keeping track of the data points. As each new data point becomes available, the running statistics are updated, and the value is discarded. Keeping track of the data points in a statistics application requires some careful design, as each run may contain many thousands of data points.

Let's assume that you will use the Stats class to calculate the statistics of a small data run and that it's feasible to maintain an array with the values passed to the class. Storing the data values isn't a problem; a simple array structure will do. But how about retrieving the data values? To access the data values, you need a property such as DataValue, which must accept an index value as an argument: the order of the desired data value in the DataValue array. The Stats1 class demonstrates how to implement array properties.

The Stats1 project is similar to the Stats project, but it implements an additional property, Datapoints. The data values are stored in a Collection, which is declared at the beginning of the code as follows:

```
Private Datapoints As New Collection
```

It would probably be more efficient to use an array of Doubles to store the data values, but the additional code for redimensioning the array when the data values exceed its declared size wasn't worth it for this example. We assume that the class is used with a small number of data values and only for demonstration purposes. Storing an enormous collection of data values in a class isn't a good idea, but in situations where the potential number of data values is limited by the nature of the application, this approach will work nicely.

In the NewValue property's Let procedure, you must add the following line, which appends a new item to the Collection:

```
Datapoints.Add vNewValue
```

In the NewDataSet method, which resets the running statistics for a preparation for a new data run, you must remove all the elements of the Collection:

```
For cItem = Datapoints.Count To 1 Step -1
    Datapoints.Remove cItem
Next
```

The Property Get procedure that implements the array property is shown next:

```
Public Property Get DataValue(Index As Long)
    DataValue = Datapoints(Index)
End Property
```

To test the Stats1 server, you can add a button for displaying all the data values passed to the server so far in the Immediate window. Here's the code for this button:

```
Dim i As Long
For i = 1 To StatObj.RunningCount
    Debug.Print StatObj.DataValue(i)
Next
```

Open the Stats1 project to see the full implementation of the class and the test application.

The Class's Instancing Property

As you have noticed, classes have two properties:

- Name

- Instancing

The Instancing property determines whether applications can use the class and how. Its possible settings are described below.

Private   Only components in the same applications can access Private objects. If you are developing a class that's not needed by other projects or if you don't want to make a class available to other developers, set its Instancing property to Private.

SingleUse   This setting applies to ActiveX EXE code components only, which we will discuss in the second half of this chapter. An ActiveX EXE server is an executable file (an application) that can service one or more clients. If the server's Instancing property is SingleUse, a new instance of the server is started for every client that calls the class's objects. This setting is an inefficient method for creating and using objects, and it's usually avoided. If you need a new instance of the server for each client, you might as well implement the server as an ActiveX DLL.

> **TIP**
>
> For more information on the two types of servers, see the section "Building Out-of-Process Servers" later in this chapter.

MutliUse   This setting is the opposite of Private and can be used only with code components. It allows a single instance of the server to provide as many objects as required by the client applications. Every new ActiveX EXE or ActiveX DLL project you start has its Instancing property set to MultiUse by default.

GlobalSingleUse   This setting creates a global object with SingleUse characteristics. If you are going to implement a global object, make it SingleUse so that all clients that call it can be serviced by a single instance of the server. It's also available with ActiveX EXE and ActiveX DLL components.

GlobalMultiUse   This setting is available with ActiveX EXE and ActiveX DLL projects and should be used rarely. The objects exposed by the GlobalMultiUse component are available to the entire system and can be accessed by any application, as if they were system components. Visual Basic provides its systemwide objects, which are called global objects. The Screen and Printer objects, for example, are global objects because you need not add a reference to them in the applications that use them. If you think you have an object that's important for the rest of the system (and not just the application that needs it) to know about, set its Instancing property to GlobalMultiUse.

PublicNotCreatable   The objects of a class with this setting can be accessed by other applications, but can't be created. Now, what good is this? The objects of a PublicNotCreatable class must first be created by another component in the same object and must be accessed through this component's objects. For example, let's say you have a class that implements database operations. One of the objects exposed by the class represents the database. Another class in the project represents a table of the database. If you allow the developer to access the second object directly, there's a chance they may attempt to open a table without first opening the database. If you make the class that exposes the Database object public, but the class that exposes the Table object PrivateNotCreatable, you can then create a reference to the object that represents the table as soon as the database is opened. The developer can access the Table object directly, but only after it has been created.

NOTE
For an example of PrivateNotCreatable and MultiUse classes, see the DBClass project in the following section.

Registering a Code Component

Classes are registered automatically on the system on which they are designed. When you create the DLL or EXE file that implements the class, Visual Basic registers it as well. But what if you want to make the class available to other developers who are working on different systems? If the component is an EXE server, you can distribute the EXE file. Once it is run on the target computer, the class is registered automatically. No messages or Forms are displayed. You simply execute the server, and it registers itself.

If the file you want to distribute is a DLL server, it must be registered with the REGSVR32 utility, which comes with Visual Basic (it's in the `Tools/RegUtils` folder on the Visual Basic CD). REGSVR32 is a program that allows you to register and unregister in-process servers. Being able to unregister out-of-process servers is just as important. For example, removing the DLL files that implement the code components from the hard disk isn't enough. You must also unregister the components from the Registry, which you can do with the REGSVR32 utility.

To register a DLL, follow these steps:

1. Copy the file to your Windows System folder or to any other folder in the path.

2. Open a Command Prompt window (a DOS window), switch to the folder where the DLL resides, and issue the following command (`filename.dll` is the file that implements the server):

   `REGSVR32 filename.dll`

You can use several options with the REGSVR utility. The /u option uninstalls a previously registered DLL. To unistall the file `filename.dll`, use the following command:

`REGSVR32 /u MyServer.dll`

When a new DLL is registered, the REGSVR utility reports the results of the operation in a message box. To suppress this message box, use the /s (silent) option.

NOTE   Using REGSVR32 is the simplest way to distribute DLL servers. All you have to do is write a small application that copies the DLL file to a folder and then run the REGSVR32 utility on the target computer to register it. If the ActiveX component is part of a project, the Package and Deployment Wizard will include the component in the installation application, and the server will be installed automatically.

Encapsulating Database Operations

The classes we developed so far are fairly straightforward. The essence of a class is to encapsulate fairly complicated data and operations and allow the developer to perform complex tasks with a few statements. In this section, we are going to develop a class that encapsulates database operations. But this is what the DAO does, isn't it? The DAO abstracts many of the low-level details of manipulating databases, but to use its objects, you need a solid understanding of Recordsets, SQL statements, and so on. By abstracting certain operations on a database, you can provide simple tools to other programmers, who can build applications using your classes instead of the DAO itself.

Let's say you have a number of programmers in a corporate environment writing code to display customer names or invoices for their applications. Visual Basic provides the data-bound Grid control, which can be easily connected to a database. But this requires that programmers know how to access a database with the Data Access Objects.

Suppose, however, that you offer programmers a simple class that retrieves customer names and provides them through the following methods:

- GetFirstCustomer
- GetLastCustomer
- GetNextCustomer
- GetPreviousCustomer

The programmer using your class need not know anything about Recordsets (not even that these methods are actually implemented directly on the Recordset). All they have to know is how to set up a small program that scans the customer names (which are already sorted somehow) to display them on a Grid and add them to a ListBox control or to any other control. The fields of the current record are accessed as properties of this class as well. The developer types the name of the object that represents this class and then a period, and the available field names appear in the Auto List Members box.

This class simplifies the task of developing database applications by allowing programmers to access databases without getting into the complexities of DAO. Debugging is also simplified because your class is tested separately, before other applications use it.

The Classes of the DBClass Project

The DBClass project (you'll find it in the DBClass folder on the CD under this chapter's folder) contains four classes. The project is based on the NWIND sample database that comes with Visual Basic, and it implements three classes for retrieving customers, invoices, and invoice details with simple methods, designed specifically for the type of records retrieved by each class. The class that retrieves customer records, for instance, provides the methods GetFirstCustomer, GetNextCustomer, GetPreviousCustomer, and GetLastCustomer.

The current record's fields are properties of the class. The developer using this class need not know how customer records are stored in the database or anything about accessing databases with the Data Access Objects (DAO). In the sections that follow, we'll look at the members of each class.

DefinitionsClass

This class opens the NWIND database and makes it available to the other classes and exposes the following members:

DatabaseName, which must be set to the database's path and a single method

SetDatabase, which opens the specified database. The user need specify only the path of the database, not its name.

CustomersClass

This class exposes the properties and methods for accessing the Customers table in the database and exposes the following members:

> **OpenCustomers**   This method retrieves the customer data. The records are stored in a recordset in the class and can be accessed with the following methods:

> - **GetFirstCustomer, GetLastCustomer, GetNextCustomer, GetPrevious-Customer**: These four methods allow the programmer to move to another record, similar to the MoveFirst, MoveLast, MoveNext, and MovePrevious methods of the Recordset objects. Contrary to the equivalent methods of the Recordset object, the methods of the Customers-Class don't require that the developer know anything about the EOF and BOF properties and their role in scanning the records. These methods return a True/False value, which indicates that the desired record exists (if True) or the records have been exhausted (if False).

> - **CustomerID, CompanyName, ContactName, ContactTitle**: These properties return the values of the fields by the same name in the current record. These properties are read-only to protect the developer from overwriting the data. You can also make them settable if you want to allow the developer to change the data.

InvoicesClass

This class has the same structure as the CustomersClass and exposes the following members:

> **OpenInvoices (CustID)**   This method retrieves the invoices issued to a specific customer, whose ID is passed to the method as an argument. The records are stored in a recordset in the class and can be accessed with the following methods:

> - **GetFirstInvoice, GetLastInvoice, GetNextInvoice, GetPrevious-Invoice**: These are the InvoiceClass's navigational methods.

> - **InvoiceID, CompanyName, OrderDate, ShippedDate, SubTotal**: These properties return the values of the fields by the same name in the current record. They are all read-only.

DetailsClass

This class has the same structure as the two previous ones and exposes the following members:

OpenDetails (InvID): This method retrieves the lines of a specific invoice, whose ID is passed to the method as an argument.

GetFirstLine, GetLastLine, GetNextLine, GetPreviousLine: These are the DetailsClass's navigational methods.

ProductID, ProductName, ProductPrice, Quantity, Units, Discount, ExtendedPrice: These properties return the values of the fields by the same name in the current record. They are all read-only.

As you can see, the classes for accessing customer names, invoices, and invoice lines have the same structure:

- A method that opens a recordset with the appropriate records
- Four navigational methods
- A number of properties that return field values

Their implementation is also quite similar, so we need not present all three of them in detail. Before we look at the implementation of these classes, however, let's see how the developer can use them from within a client application.

Using the DBClass Objects

Figures 10.5 and 10.6 show a few typical examples of using the DBClass objects. The grid in Figure 10.5 contains the list of customers, and each time the user clicks a customer name, the invoices issued to the specific customer are displayed on another grid. The two Forms in this figure are among the test Forms used in the DBClass project.

Figure 10.6 is a similar application, which displays the invoices for a specific customer. When you select an invoice with the mouse, the corresponding lines are displayed in the smaller grid. These are also among the test Forms of the DBClass project.

FIGURE 10.5:

Displaying customers
and invoices with the
CustomersClass and
InvoicesClass objects
of DBClass

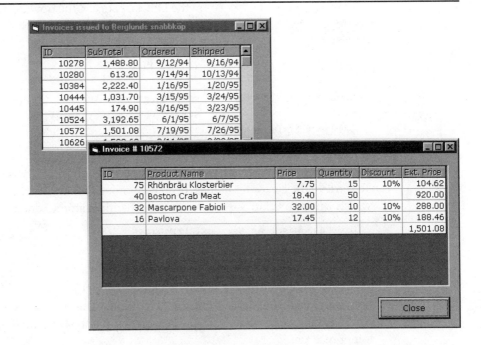

FIGURE 10.6:

Displaying invoices and their
details with the InvoicesClass
and DetailsClass objects of
DBClass

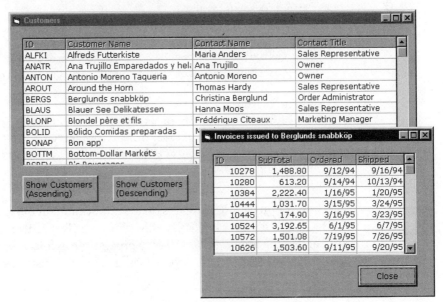

To use the classes exposed by the DBClass server, the developer must first create an object variable to reference the DataBase class and then open the database:

```
Dim DBObject As New DefinitionsClass

DBObject.DatabaseName = "c:\program files\microsoft visual _
                         studio\vb98\nwind.mdb"
DBObject.SetDatabase
```

(Change the value of the DatabaseName property to the path of the NWIND database on your system.) The *DBObject* variable lets you access the database. To retrieve the customer names, declare another object variable, *CustObject*, which will be used to reference a recordset with customer data:

```
Dim CustObject As New CustomersClass

CustObject.OpenCustomers
```

The customer names are stored in a tabular structure, which can be scanned with the CustomersClass navigational methods. The current record's fields can be read with the same object's properties. Here's a loop structure that scans the customer records:

```
Dim CustObject As New CustomersClass
CustObject.OpenCustomers
If CustObject.GetFirstCustomer Then
    {process first record using the properties:
        CustObject.CustomerID, CustObject.CompanyName,
        CustObject.ContactName & CustObject.ContactTitle }

    While CustObject.GetNextCustomer
        {process first record using the properties:
            CustObject.CustomerID, CustObject.CompanyName,
            CustObject.ContactName & CustObject.ContactTitle }
    Wend
End If
```

The type of processing depends on the application. In the test application for the DBClass, we'll simply display the fields on a Grid control. In your code, you could access the InvoicesClass class to process the invoices issued to each customer, calculate statistics for products issued to each customer, and so on.

TIP
If you think you could do this with SQL statements, remember that this class is meant to isolate developers from complicated database operations. It's meant to be used by developers who aren't familiar with the DAO object. For instance, you could provide this class along with your application to allow your customers to write simple customer reports, without having complete access to the database itself.

The loops for scanning the invoices issued to a specific customer or for scanning the lines of an invoice are quite similar. The basic difference is that the customers recordset is opened without an argument. To open the invoices recordset, you must call the OpenInvoices method, passing the customer's ID as an argument:

```
InvObjectClass.OpenInvoices(customerID)
```

The customerID argument is read from the customers recordset (it's the CustomerID property of the CustObject object). Similarly, the OpenDetails method of the Details object requires the invoice's ID as an argument:

```
DetObject.OpenDetails (InvID)
```

In this case, *InvID* is a Long variable that holds the ID of the desired invoice (which will be the InvoiceID property of the InvObject object).

Implementing DBClass

Since all three classes have similar structures, the code is also similar. Therefore, we'll look only at the implementation of the CustomersClass class in detail. First, we declare a recordset where the customer data are stored:

```
Private CustomersRS As Recordset
```

The CustomersRS recordset is private within the class and applications can't access it directly; they must call the methods exposed by the class. This recordset is populated in the OpenCustomers method's code, shown in Code 10.8. This method must be called by the client application to populate the recordset with customer data.

Code 10.8   **The OpenCustomers Method**

```
Public Sub OpenCustomers()
Dim SQLString As String

    SQLString = "SELECT CustomerID, CompanyName, ContactName, _
```

```
                    ContactTitle FROM CUSTOMERS"
            Set CustomersRS = DB.OpenRecordset(SQLString)

    End Sub
```

The code of the other two classes uses more complicated SQL statements, but the principle is the same: Build a SQL statement, use it to open a recordset on the DB database, and then assign it to the CustomersRS object variable.

The Class's navigational methods use the equivalent navigational methods of the recordset to move the record pointer in the recordset. The implementation of the Get-FirstCustomer and GetNextCustomer methods is shown in Code 10.9 and Code 10.10.

Code 10.9   The GetFirstCustomer Method

```
Public Function GetFirstCustomer() As Integer
Dim SQLString As String
On Error GoTo FirstCustomerError

    If CustomersRS.RecordCount > 0 Then
        CustomersRS.MoveFirst
        SetFields
        GetFirstCustomer = 1
    Else
        GetFirstCustomer = 0
    End If
    Exit Function

FirstCustomerError:
    Err.Raise vbError + 1027, "Customers", _
        "Error in reading first customer's data"
    End Function
```

Code 10.10   The GetNextCustomer Method

```
Public Function GetNextCustomer() As Integer
On Error GoTo NextCustomerError

    CustomersRS.MoveNext
    If Not CustomersRS.EOF Then
        SetFields
```

```
        GetNextCustomer = 1
    Else
        GetNextCustomer = 0
    End If
    Exit Function

NextCustomerError:
    Err.Raise vbError + 1027, "Customers", _
        "Error in reading next customer's data"
End Function
```

Notice how these navigational methods handle the EOF property to detect whether the end of the recordset has been reached. The developer need not be concerned with these details. All he or she has to do is examine the value returned by the method and, if it's True, access the fields of the current record.

Each time the pointer is moved to the another record, the SetFields subroutine is called (see Code 10.11). This subroutine extracts the values of the current record's fields and assigns them to private variables, which are later used to implement the class's properties.

Code 10.11   **The SetFields Subroutine**

```
Private Sub SetFields()
On Error GoTo 0
    mvarCustomerID = CustomersRS.Fields("CustomerID")
    mvarCompanyName = CustomersRS.Fields("CompanyName")
    mvarContactName = CustomersRS.Fields("ContactName")
    mvarContactTitle = CustomersRS.Fields("ContactTitle")
End Sub
```

Finally, here's the implementation of a few of the class's properties:

```
Public Property Get CompanyName() As String
    CompanyName = mvarCompanyName
End Property

Public Property Get CustomerID() As String
    CustomerID = mvarCustomerID
End Property
```

The properties are read only, and there are no equivalent Property Let procedures.

Using the members of the DBClass is certainly simpler than using the Data Access Object. Besides isolating developers from the complexity of the DAO, the DBClass offers developers a solid foundation for accessing the database. Should you decide to port the database to the SQL Server, all you have to do is rewrite the class's code; the application programmer may not even notice the difference. However, the test application contains quite a lot of code for placing the record fields on the grid, sizing the grids' columns, and so on.

NOTE   In the following chapter, we'll come back to this project and implement it as an ActiveX control. When the Forms of the DBClass application are converted to ActiveX controls, the developer simply places them on a Form and calls a method to display the data. The appearance of the control is handled internally, and the application's code is reduced to a few method calls.

Building Out-of-Process Servers

In this section, we are going to explore out-of-process servers, which are implemented as ActiveX EXE code components. We'll start by building a simple server that performs complicated calculations, and we'll explain the process step by step because out-of-process servers aren't simple to test (they require that you keep two instances of VB running at the same time and switch back and forth). We will add features to the simple EXE server, and by the end of the chapter you will know how to build an asynchronous server that notifies the client when an operation (such as a method or a property call) has completed. In the meantime, the application can go about its business instead of freezing the client window.

The SERVER1 Project

Start a new ActiveX EXE project. When the class module appears in the Project window, rename the project to SERVER1, and change the name of the class module from Class1 to EXESRV1. Let's start by implementing a method that performs a few simple calculations, but repeats them many times. We simply need a method that takes a few seconds to complete (this method simulates a complicated process that takes a long time to complete). Enter the following code in the class module's Code window:

```
Public Function CalculateLong(Iterations As Long) As Double
Dim i As Long
    Randomize(Time)
    For i = 1 To Iterations
        a = a + Cos(32.33)
        b = b + Sin(0.3233)
    Next
    CalculateLong = a / b
End Function
```

The number of iterations is passed to the method as an argument. The result is a double value that depends on the number of iterations. Any math functions will do; you can even use the Rnd() function to generate a different result every time. We use an argument to specify the number of iterations so that you can adjust the loop's duration according to your computer's speed.

Let's implement another method, the CalculateShort method, which returns almost instantly:

```
Public Function CalculateShort(Iterations As Long) As Double
Dim i As Long
Dim a As Double, b As Double

    For i = 1 To Iterations
        a = a + i
    Next
    CalculateShort = a

End Function
```

Our sample server contains two methods. You can add more methods or properties, but these two are adequate for our purposes. Now, let's build a client application to test our server. As you may have guessed, we'll examine the behavior of the two methods and discuss ways to execute them asynchronously so that the CalculateLong method won't hold the execution of the client application until it completes its execution.

The EXETest Client Application

The test application (shown in Figure 10.7) has two Command buttons, one for each of the server's methods and a Label, at the top left section of the Form where the time is displayed and it's updated every second (to see how the server application affects the execution of the client). The PictureBox on the right reacts to the Click event, by drawing a gradient. This is another CPU intensive operation that will help us observe how the client and server applications share the CPU time (which one executes and when, as well as how to steal cycles from the server application to execute the client application.

To build the test application shown in Figure 10.7, follow these steps (the test project is called EXETest, and you can find it in the EXESERVER1 folder):

1. Start another instance of VB, and create a new Standard EXE project. Place the controls you see on the Form of Figure 10.7, plus a Timer control, which we'll use to update the time on the Label control every second.

2. In order to call the server's methods, we must create an object variable that references the SERVER1 class. First add to the project a reference to the server. Choose Project ➤ References to open the References dialog box, and search for the entry SERVER1. There is no such component in the list of available references. Don't bother browsing for the EXE component, as we have neither saved the ActiveX EXE project nor created the SERVER1.EXE component. The EXE component isn't available because it doesn't exist yet.

FIGURE 10.7:

The EXETest client application's Form at design time

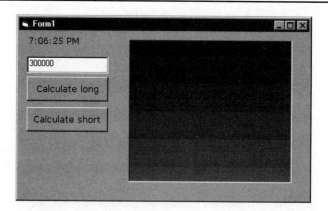

3. Switch to the instance of VB with the SERVER1 project, and press F5 to run it. You will see the Debugging tab of the Project Properties dialog box, which prompts you to select what Visual Basic should do with the project. Check the option Wait for Components to Be Created and click OK. Visual Basic will start the execution of the server application and wait for the client application to contact it.

4. Now, switch back to the test project, and open the References dialog box again. This time, you will see the name of the SERVER1 component in the list.

5. Check the checkbox in front of SERVER1, and click the OK button. Now that you've added a reference to the SERVER1 server to your application.

6. Open the client application's Code window, and enter the following lines:

```
Dim CObject1 As New EXESRV1
Dim CObject2 As New EXESRV1
```

If you have the Auto List Members feature on, as soon as you type the word **New**, you will see the list of object types available to the project. Select the EXESRV1 entry in this list.

7. Enter the following lines in the Command button's Click event:

```
Private Sub Command1_Click()
    MsgBox CObject1.CalculateLong(300000)
End Sub
```

8. Now, enter the following lines in the second Command button:

```
Private Sub Command2_Click()
    MsgBox CObject2.CalculateShort(30000)
End Sub
```

9. Run the application to get a feel for how fast the server responds.

The 300,000 iterations cause a delay of several seconds on a Pentium 166 system. If you start the client application by pressing F8 (to single-step through the code), you will be switched to the EXE Server project when the line that calls the CalculateLong() method is reached. Single-step through a few commands, and then press F5 to continue the program's execution. When the calculations complete, you will be taken back to the instance of VB with the test project. This is an interesting approach. It allows you to single-step through the code of the server and see how the server interacts with the client.

While the server is busy calculating, the client application is frozen. The time display isn't updated, and you can't press any button on the Form or draw the gradient on the PictureBox control. This doesn't happen because the Calculate-Long method doesn't yield control to the processor. Insert the following line in the CalculateLong method's main loop:

```
If (i Mod 100) = 0 Then DoEvents
```

This statement breaks the execution of the loop and gives Windows a chance to attend to other application needs (process keystrokes, refresh windows, and so on). Start the server, and run the client; you won't notice any difference in its behavior.

This leads us to the question: If a server takes too long to respond to a method call, couldn't we let the server go about its business without freezing the client application and notify us with an event when the result is available? Imagine calling a method that downloads an image from a server on the Internet. Would we have to wait for the transmission to complete before allowing the user of the client to press another button on the Form or even move the Form? And what if the user decides not to wait for the download to complete? At the very least, the user should be able to press a Cancel button. (In the next chapter, you will see how to design ActiveX controls that start a download process with the AsyncRead method and receive notification about the file's arrival with the AsyncReadComplete event.) This is indeed possible, but it's a bit involved.

We'll explain the process in detail so that you'll be able to apply the technique in more complicated situations. The server we are building in this section, however, is not what you call a "textbook" example. Many useful servers perform complicated calculations or access databases, format the results (for instance, in HTML format), and notify the clients asynchronously when the data is available.

At this point, you can create an executable of the test project (EXETEST.EXE) and run it outside the Visual Basic environment. You can also start multiple instances of the same application. All running instances of the EXETEST.EXE application are serviced by a single instance of the server—the one running in the Visual Basic IDE. If you switch to Visual Basic and stop the execution of the server application while the client application is running, you'll be warned that another application is accessing an object in the server application. If you stop the server application anyway, the next time you click a button on the test application form, you'll get an automation error, because the server application that supplies the methods is not running.

Synchronous versus Asynchronous Processing

When an application makes a procedure call (which can be a function call, a subroutine call, or a call to a method exposed by an object), it's blocked until the call returns. In other words, no matter how long the procedure takes to complete its task, the code can't proceed past the line that made the call; it just has to wait. This is how computers work. They execute one statement at a time, and you can safely assume that all previous statements have been executed. Consequently, the results of the previous lines are assumed to be known and available when a new line is executed.

NOTE
Parallel computers, which rely on a large number of processors working in parallel, follow a different programming paradigm that allows program lines to be executed out of order. But writing code for parallel computers is an entirely different story.

The same is true when an application calls a method of an ActiveX component. While the method executes, the application has to wait. This type of processing is called *synchronous* because the two processes are synchronized. The advantage of synchronous processing is that the developer need not take any special action to synchronize the application with the server. If the method called must perform time-consuming math calculations, the application must wait. In some situations, however, the application doesn't require the results immediately. For example, in a printing operation the application has no reason to wait for the completed printout. The user should be able to initiate a printing operation and then move about their business. And from your experience with Windows, you know that printing doesn't freeze the application.

Under Windows, it is possible for a method to return control to the calling application immediately, without any results. In the mean time, the component continues its calculations and notifies the client application that the result is available. This type of processing is called *asynchronous*, because the two programs need not be synchronized. The client and server applications work independently of each other, and when the task is complete, the component notifies the client that the result is available. It is possible to implement an asynchronous server, but to do so, we must solve two problems:

- How to return immediately from a method call and defer the execution of the code

- How to notify the client that the results are available when the calculations are complete

Asynchronous Methods and Properties

For the client application to continue its operation, the CalculateLong method must return immediately. And for this to happen and yet carry out its calculations, the server must queue the request and process it in its own good time. We'll now revise the EXESRV1 class so that it queues requests instead of processing them immediately. When it's done with its calculations, the server must trigger an event that will let the client know that the results are available (or that some action has taken place). The revised project is called EXESRV2.

NOTE

You'll find the EXESRV2 project in the **Chapter5\EXESERVER\EXESERVER2** folder on the CD that comes with this book. If you don't want to repeat all the instructions listed here, open the server project in one instance of Visual Basic, and open the test application (the client) in another instance of Visual Basic. Start the server, and then start the client.

To queue the calls to the methods, we need the services of a Timer control—some external event that will remind the server to poll the queue and process the next method. When clients make requests, the server queues them in a Collection (it's the simplest structure for the purpose in terms of coding, but you can use an array if you prefer and if you don't mind writing the code to keep track of the array's size at any moment). Then, from within a Timer's event, the server examines the queue. If there are queued calls to methods, it processes the oldest one and removes it from the queue. In the next Timer event, it repeats the same process, until all suspended calls have been removed from the queue.

The SERVER2 Project

This sounds simple in principle, but how do you add a Timer to a class module? We must add a Form to the project, place a Timer control on the Form, and reference it from within our code. The Form will never be displayed or receive any events, so it doesn't violate the requirement that EXE servers shouldn't have a visible user interface. Let's assume you have declared the *Tmr* object variable, which receives the Timer's Timer event. Let's also assume that you have declared a new Collection, the Queue Collection with the following statement:

```
Private Queue As New Collection
```

The client application will no longer call the CalculateLong method. Instead, it will call the StartCalculations method, which will queue the call:

```
Public Function StartCalculations(Iterations As Long) As Double
    Queue.Add Iterations
End Function
```

Since the CalculateLong method requires a single argument, we store it in the Collection. Normally, you would create an object (or a custom data type) with all the arguments required by the method and append this object to the Collection.

In the *Tmr* object's Timer event (see Code 10.12), we must call the Calculate-Long function (which now is private to the class) and pass it the value of the argument stored in the Queue Collection. At the same time, we must remove this value from the queue.

Code 10.12　　　**The Timer Event**

```
Private Sub Tmr_Timer()
Dim results As Double
Dim CalcIterations As Long
    If Queue.Count = 0 Then
        Exit Sub
    End If
    CalcIterations = Queue.Item(Queue.Count)
    Queue.Remove Queue.Count
    results = CalculateLong(CalcIterations)
    RaiseEvent Done(results)
End Sub
```

If no requests are pending, the code exits. Or, it extracts the argument value stored in the Queue Collection's current item, passes it to the CalculateLong() function, and then returns the result of the function through the Done event to the client application. The Done event is another member of the class. So far, our project is simple and does nothing out of the ordinary.

Incorporating the functionality of the Timer control, which resides on another Form, is a bit more complicated. Follow these steps:

1. Choose Project ➤ Add Form to add a Form to the project.

2. Now, place a Timer control on the Form, set its Enabled property to True, and set its Interval value to 1000 (1 second). At this point, the IDE should look like the one shown in Figure 10.8. Next, you must add the code to load the Form when the server is initialized and create an instance of the Timer control. You must create two object variables that represent the Form and the Timer objects.

FIGURE 10.8:

The EXESRV2 project after the addition of a Form with a Timer control on it

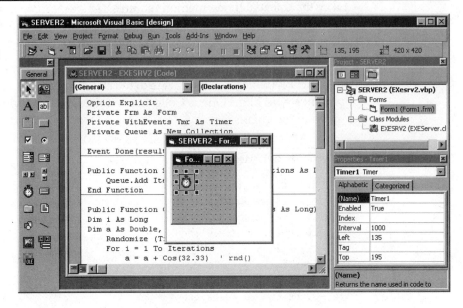

3. Place the following lines in the class's declarations section:

    ```
    Private Frm As Form
    Private WithEvents Tmr As Timer
    ```

    Notice the WithEvents keyword in the *Tmr* variable's declaration. Without it, your code would have access to the Timer control, but wouldn't be able to receive any events.

4. While editing the declarations, add the following event declaration:

    ```
    Event Done(result As Double)
    ```

5. In the class's Initialize event, enter the following lines:

    ```
    Private Sub Class_Initialize()
        Set Frm = New Form1
        Load Frm
        Set Tmr = Frm.Timer1
    End Sub
    ```

    The first two lines create an instance of the Form and load it (the Load method loads the Form into memory, but doesn't display it). Once the Form is loaded, you can create an object variable to access the Timer control on it. The *Tmr* object will receive the Timer event of the Timer control, and the Tmr_Timer event handler we discussed earlier will be activated every second.

You must also release any object variables when the server is terminated. When the last client application releases all references to the server's objects, the *Frm* and *Tmr* object variables will be released automatically (see the listing in Code 10.13).

NOTE   It's a good practice to release any unneeded resources to the system. Not all programs end in an orderly manner.

Code 10.13   **The Class's Terminate Event**

```
Private Sub Class_Terminate()
    Set Tmr = Nothing
    Unload Frm
    Set Frm = Nothing
End Sub
```

The last step is to revise slightly the CalculateLong procedure. It is no longer a method of the server; it's a private function, with a declaration as follows:

```
Public Function CalculateLong(Iterations As Long) As Double
Dim i As Long
Dim a As Double, b As Double
    Randomize (Time)
    For i = 1 To Iterations
        a = a + Cos(32.33)
        b = b + Sin(0.3233)
    Next
    CalculateLong = a + b
End Function
```

Switch to the client application to test the new server. Open the References dialog box before you run the application. You should see that the component SERVER1 has been replaced with the component SERVER2. If not, add a reference to the component SERVER2 manually. Change all instances of the class EXESRV1 to EXESRV2 in the client's code.

TIP

Every time you start a new instance of Visual Basic to build a test project, make sure that the ActiveX EXE project is running. If the server application isn't running, its name will not show in the Components dialog box, and you won't be able to add a reference to the server to the test project.

When VB Can't Find the Server Application

When you add a new component to the server project and then attempt to start the client application, you will see the message:

```
Connection to type library or object library to remote process has
been lost. Press OK for dialog to remove reference.
```

Click the OK button to open the References dialog box, which lists the reference to the SERVER1 object as:

```
MISSING:Server1
```

Clear the checkmark in this box to remove the reference from the list, and then locate the SERVER1 entry and select it. Your project is up-to-date. However, it is important to understand what happened.

The server is running in another instance of Visual Basic and is available only if this instance of Visual Basic is in run mode. Had you created an EXE file, the client application would start the server automatically, by simply requesting one of its objects.

To use the new server, we must further revise the client application. For one thing, it must call the StartCalculations method instead of the CalculateLong method, and we must provide a handler for the Done event. Change the declarations of the objects CObject1 and CObject2 to:

```
Private WithEvents CObject1 As EXESRV2
Private WithEvents CObject2 As EXESRV2
```

The new objects can raise events, and in order for the client application to receive these events, the variables must be recognized with the WithEvents keyword. You can't use the New keyword with the WithEvents keyword. The two object variables must be instantiated explicitly. Enter the following lines in the Form's Load event:

```
Private Sub Form_Load()
    Set CObject1 = New EXESRV2
    Set CObject2 = New EXESRV2
End Sub
```

You must also change the first button's code to call the StartCalculations method instead of the CalculateLong method:

```
Private Sub Command1_Click()
    CObject1.StartCalculations Text1.Text
End Sub
```

The test client application (EXETest) in the EXEServer/EXEServer2 folder on the CD is identical to the test application of the EXESRVR1 project, except for a TextBox control, where you can specify how many times the CalculateLong() function will repeat the calculations. This will help you observe the behavior of the server application with asynchronous notifications, regardless of the speed of your CPU. The value Text1.Text passed as an argument to the StartCalculations method is the number of iterations; you should supply a valid numeric value, because this argument is not validated.

Asynchronous Notification

Finally, you must add the two event handlers for the Done events of the *CObject1* variable. Because we declared these object variables with the WithEvents keyword, they appear in the Object drop-down list of the Code window. Select CObject1 in this list, and the editor creates the definition of the Done event and places the pointer in it. Enter the following lines:

```
Private Sub CObject1_Done(result As Double)
    MsgBox result
End Sub
```

The Calculate Short button calls the CalculateShort method (this method is very fast, and there is no reason to queue calls to this method). Now run the application to see how the new server behaves. Press the Calculate Long button to start the calculations. If your computer is really fast, change the argument to the StartCalculations method. Be sure this method takes a while to complete.

While the calculations take place, the window isn't frozen. The time is updated every second, and you can click the PictureBox to draw another gradient.

NOTE While the gradient is being drawn, the time isn't updated, but that's because the client's code is tight. It has nothing to do with the server.

If you click the Calculate Long button twice in succession, you will see the message box with the results twice, as soon as each deferred invocation of the method completes its execution. If you click the Calculate Long button and then click the Calculate Short button, you will see first the result of the lengthy method and then the result of the short method. That's expected; results arrive in the order in which they were queued by the server.

This leads to another question: What if we have 10 clients, each connecting to the server to request a different method? For example, suppose nine clients need a quick result from the CalculateShort method, and the tenth client calls the CalculateLong method. Delaying the client that requested the services of the lengthy method for a second (perhaps less than that) wouldn't make any difference to the speed perceived by the users of the client application. They would have to wait for the lengthy calculations to complete anyway and only then see the results. It could, however, frustrate the users of the client applications that call the CalculateShort method because they (usually) know whether they've requested a lengthy or a trivial calculation.

One approach to this problem is to prioritize the queued requests: Examine the contents of the queue and execute the ones that take the least time. But in a more practical situation, you aren't going to have methods that take either a fraction of a second or several seconds. Prioritizing the events is rather inflexible, because once a method starts its execution, it must complete it before another one can start.

Let's do another experiment. Stop the test application, and then stop the EXE server application. If you stop them in reverse order, the server instance issues a warning to the effect that another application is accessing the server. Even if the code in the server's method isn't executing, the object variables *CObject1* and *CObject2* in the test application are still alive. Had you set it to Nothing, you would be able to stop the server before the application.

Switch to the server application, and insert a call to the DoEvents statement, right in the loop that performs the calculations, as shown in Code 10.14.

Code 10.14   The Revised CalculateLong Function

```
Public Function CalculateLong(Iterations As Long) As Double
Dim i As Long
Dim a As Double, b As Double
    Randomize (Time)
    For i = 1 To Iterations
        a = a + Cos(32.33)   ' rnd()
        b = b + Sin(0.3233)  ' rnd()
' Remove this line and requests will be serialized
        If (i Mod 100) = 0 Then DoEvents
    Next
    CalculateLong = a + b
End Function
```

The If line is actually commented out in the EXESERVER2 application on the CD. We don't want to call the DoEvents statement frequently, because it can really slow the process. Depending on the nature of the calculations, you can call it more or less frequently. Run the server, switch to the client application, and test it again. Click the Calculate Long button, and then click the Calculate Short button. The client application will first receive the results from the CalculateShort method first and then receive the results from the CalculateLong calculations.

You now have a server application that works nicely and balances short and lengthy methods. Why didn't we implement a method like StartCalculations that would queue calls to the CalculateShort method? Queuing a method that takes less than a second to complete actually makes it slower (the Timer event itself, which would trigger the execution of the function that implements the method, is triggered every second). A method such as CalculateShort takes so little time that we can let it interrupt the CalculateLong function, but not the other way around. Notice that we didn't even insert a DoEvents statement in its code.

Testing the Executables

Now, stop both projects, and save the components of the EXE Server application. Choose File ➤ Make EXESRV2.EXE to build an executable file, which any client application can then use. This action generates the EXE file that implements the server and registers it on the system. Notice that the ActiveX EXE file's name is, by default, the name of the project, and not the name of the Class module. You can start the RegEdit application to see the ClassID of the newly created server. Close the VB instance with the server application, as we no longer need it.

Switch to the instance of VB with the client application. We are going to make an executable file and test it outside Visual Basic's environment. You will not only test the application in "real conditions," you will also be able to run multiple instances of the client and see how they are serviced by a single server.

Run the project one last time in Visual Basic's environment to make sure it works (if it doesn't, be sure you have added a reference to the newly created EXE server and not to an old instance of it). Now, follow these steps:

1. Choose File ➤ Make EXETest.exe to create an executable file.

2. Save the executable file in the same folder as the EXESRV2 project.

3. Close the Visual Basic window, and run the EXETest program by double-clicking its icon.

4. Start two or more instances of the client application, and monitor the behavior of the client application under all conditions.

You can start as many instances of the client application as you wish, but one copy of the server is running. To verify this, press Ctrl+Alt+Enter to open the Close Program dialog box, shown in Figure 10.9. Notice the three instances of the EXETest application and the single instance of the EXESRV2 server.

FIGURE 10.9:

No matter how many clients are running, they are all serviced by a single EXE server.

To simplify the testing of the executables, we added a TextBox control on the test Form, in which you can enter the argument of the method StartCalculations (the number of iterations for the lengthy calculations). Enter the number of desired iterations, and then click the Calculate Long button, as shown in Figure 10.10. You can also click this button several times, using different arguments, before the first result becomes available.

FIGURE 10.10:

The EXETest application lets you specify how many times the calculations will be repeated.

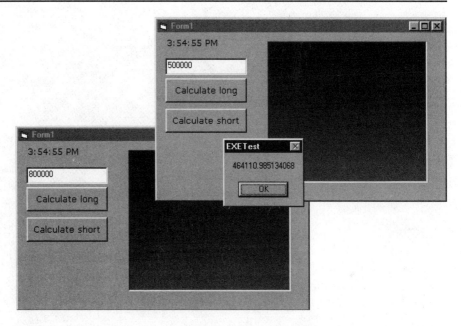

CHAPTER
ELEVEN

Building ActiveX Controls

- Exploring the UserControl object

- The ActiveX Control Interface Wizard

- Designing Property Pages

- Interconnected controls

- Internet-Enabled controls

One of the major features of Visual Basic is the development of ActiveX (formerly OLE) controls. In the past, developing custom ActiveX controls was a task for seasoned C++ programmers. Not only did you have to use a difficult language to develop ActiveX controls, but the process of developing them was complicated, too. Visual Basic, starting with version 5, has simplified one of the most difficult programming tasks. Developing ActiveX controls with Visual Basic is strikingly similar to developing standard applications. Microsoft has done a marvelous job of hiding much of the complexity of ActiveX development, and the included ActiveX Control Interface Wizard takes care of the trivial parts of the code and generates a working skeleton, to which you can add the code that implements the unique functions of the control.

Developing ActiveX controls is also similar to developing classes. ActiveX controls are basically classes with a visible user interface. Implementing the interface of the control (its properties, methods, and events) is similar to writing code for a class. The design of the visible interface is similar to the design of the interface of a standard VB application.

As you will see, there are a few basic concepts unique to ActiveX controls that you must master. We'll start this chapter with a general discussion of the process of ActiveX control development, and we'll explain how the development of ActiveX controls differs from developing standard applications. Then, we'll go through the steps of developing an ActiveX control with the ActiveX Control Interface Wizard and examine the code generated, which is the foundation of any ActiveX control. We'll spot the shortcomings of this computer-made control and see how they can be solved. By then, you will be able to use the Wizard as your starting point and then tweak the code manually to get the functionality you want from the control. Finally, we'll present in detail a few practical ActiveX controls, that you can use, as they are, in your projects.

The Types of Custom ActiveX Controls

The techniques for authoring ActiveX controls are the same, no matter what type of a control you're building. However, there are three types of ActiveX controls you can design, which are discussed in the following sections. Which type of control you are going to build depends on what you want to do and how much of the functionality that you want to include in your control is already available in existing controls. So, before you start designing, consider which of the following types suits your needs.

User-Drawn Controls

This is the kind of control you author from scratch. You are responsible for designing the control's interface, and you are in control of its appearance and visible interface. The code for drawing the control's interface is placed in the Paint event, which is invoked every time the control must be redrawn. You can also call the Paint event handler from within your code to redraw the control in reaction to certain user actions or property changes.

User-drawn controls are more difficult to implement, because you have to code every bit of functionality you need, from the control's programmatic interface to its appearance. They are also the most flexible ones, though, because you don't have to put up with the limitations of other controls.

Enhancing Existing Controls

The simplest type of custom ActiveX control that you can develop is one that is based on an existing control and enhances its operation. (You can enhance any control, no matter how it was developed; it doesn't have to be a VB control.) You can keep most or all of the original control's functionality and then add custom members. One of the built-in controls programmers frequently enhance from within their code is the ComboBox control. When the Style property of the ComboBox is set to 0 (DropDown Combo) or 1 (Simple Combo), the user is allowed to enter a new field value in the edit box of the control, but the new entry isn't appended to the list of available choices. To allow users to add new items to the ComboBox, you must capture the Enter key from within your code and, when the user types Enter, add the entry in the Edit box to the list of options. Actually, you need some more code, as some users may use the Enter key to make a selection, in which case you must avoid adding multiple instances of the same option.

With previous versions of Visual Basic, programmers had to add code to enhance the operation of the ComboBox control on their Forms. Now, you can implement a new control that enhances the ComboBox control—call it SuperCombo or something else—and use this one in your projects instead of the standard ComboBox control.

Building with Constituent Controls

If most of the functionality you want to include in your custom control exists already, you can design a new control that includes other controls. The controls that are part of your custom control are called *constituent* controls. Although you can't alter the appearance of a constituent control, you can choose which of its members to expose. Most of the custom controls you will be authoring will make use of some constituent controls, because much of the functionality required by a typical control is already available in the form of existing controls.

Most controls are user-drawn and use constituent controls as well. In this chapter, you will see examples of this mixed approach, as well as controls based on constituent controls.

NOTE   When designing custom controls with constituent controls, you must make sure you have the appropriate license to distribute these controls. The controls that come with Visual Basic 6 can be distributed free of charge, but you should mention in the About box the original control on which they are based. Most of the third-party controls are also royalty free, but before you decide to distribute your control, you must read the product's documentation or contact the control's manufacturer. By the way, you're free to use the sample controls discussed in this book. You can enhance them, include more error-trapping code, tweak their visible interface, and incorporate them in your projects.

The UserControl Object

An ActiveX control is similar to a class in that it provides properties and methods and fires events. If you can add properties, methods, and events to a class, you can also add these members to a custom ActiveX control. Methods are nothing more than public procedures (subroutines or functions); properties are added with public Property Let and Get procedures, and events are raised with the RaiseEvent statement. Unlike classes, however, controls have a visible interface. An ActiveX control isn't accessed through an object variable, but is placed on a Form and can be edited through the Properties window. The visible interface of an ActiveX control is drawn on an object called *UserControl*, which is very similar to the Form object. As you will see, the UserControl object supports nearly all of the properties and methods of the Form object. If you are designing a user-drawn control, all the drawing must take place on the UserControl object (and usually from within the Paint event). If you are designing a custom control based on constituent controls, they must all be placed on the UserControl object as well. So, designing the visible interface of a custom control is a lot like designing a new Form.

As you might guess, there are some fundamental differences between User-Control and Form objects. A UserControl object can only exist on a Form. You can't display an ActiveX control in its own window on the desktop and you can't run an ActiveX control. You must place it on a Form and then run the project to which the Form belongs.

Actually, ActiveX controls must be placed on containers, which are not necessarily Forms. ActiveX controls can be placed on HTML pages, which can be viewed in Internet Explorer's window. In this chapter we are going to limit our discussion to using ActiveX controls with Visual Basic 6 applications, and we'll focus on Forms as containers. In Part IV of this book, you'll find information on how to use ActiveX controls on the Internet (how to use them on Web pages and download them on a client computer as needed).

Design-Time and Run-Time Behavior

You design Forms in the Visual Basic IDE, and then you test them by running a test application right in the IDE, similar to developing and testing standard VB applications. The process of designing a Form is Design ➤ Run ➤ Stop ➤ Design.

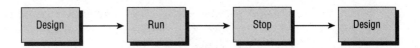

You repeat this process as many times as required to get your application working. During this process, you can add new ActiveX controls on your Form and incorporate them into your design. When ActiveX controls are added to a Form, they have two distinct modes of operation.

- Design-time behavior
- Run-time behavior

For instance, the Timer control won't issue any Timer events in design mode, even if it is enabled and its Interval property has been set. It will start firing Timer events as soon as it's placed in run mode. A simpler example is the Scrollbar control. In design mode, you can't move its button to adjust the control's value. To change the position of the Scrollbar control, you must set the Value property accordingly. If you attempt to move the bar's button with the mouse, you'll end up moving the entire control on the Form. At run time, you can change the Scrollbar's value with the mouse.

Your custom ActiveX controls must support both modes of operations. In addition to these two modes, ActiveX controls have their own design mode. When you design an ActiveX control, you can't test it by pressing F5. To test an ActiveX control, you must follow these steps:

1. Create a new project.

2. Add the ActiveX control on a Form.

3. Test the control's behavior, in the context of the host application, both at design and run time.

As you will see, testing your custom control at design time is an important part of the process. Even when the test project is in design mode, the control's code is running. That's why you can change the control's properties while you're designing the Form. As you change the BackColor property in the Properties window, the background color of the control will change in response.

To make any changes to the control's code, you must stop the test application and switch back to the ActiveX control project. Visual Basic simplifies the design of custom ActiveX controls by allowing the developer to add a test project to the ActiveX control project and switch between the two. The process is quite similar to the process of designing ActiveX DLLs: You open the ActiveX control to make changes to the code, close the project, and then switch to the test project. Because the two projects live together in the IDE, switching from designing and testing the control doesn't require that you close a project to open another one.

We will explain the three modes of operation of an ActiveX control when we build the sample projects later in this chapter. But you must keep this unique characteristic of ActiveX controls in mind as you design and test them. The control's design mode is quite easy to distinguish. When you work with the UserControl object, the control is in design mode. When testing it, the control is running. In your code, you may have to distinguish between the design-time and run-time modes of the project that the control belongs to and react differently in each mode. For example, there are design-time– and run-time–only properties, and your code must know, at any given time, which ones can be set and which ones can't.

Designing a Simple Control

To create a custom ActiveX control, you draw its user interface by placing as many constituent controls as you need on the UserControl object. Then, you implement properties with the Property Let and Property Get procedures, implement methods as public procedures (functions and subroutines), and raise events with the

RaiseEvent method. As with classes, you usually store the properties in local variables and declare the events at the beginning of the code.

If the custom control contains constituent controls, you can expose many of their properties by mapping them to the equivalent properties of the UserControl object. This is best done with the ActiveX Control Interface Wizard, which we'll discuss briefly in the next section. For example, if your custom control accepts text and you provide a TextBox constituent control where users can enter the text, you can map the custom control's Text property (or SecretText or whatever you want to call this property) to the Text property of the TextBox control. Every time you set the Text property of the custom control, Visual Basic will delegate the changes to the TextBox constituent control. Similarly, you can map the custom control's Change event to the TextBox control's Change event, so that each time the text in the TextBox control is changed, the custom control will fire a Change event. All this without writing a single line of code (the wizard will generate the appropriate code for you).

To start the design of an ActiveX control, you must create a new ActiveX Control project. A new ActiveX control project has a folder named UserControls, which contains a UserControl object. (Compare this to a new Standard EXE project that has a folder named Forms, which contains a Form object.)

Your first step is to add a new project—the test project we discussed earlier—and create a project group. This is to simplify testing the control. Without the test project, you'd have to close the ActiveX control project, open a test project to test the control, switch back to the control project to make changes, and then keep repeating the process. To simplify the process of developing custom components, Visual Basic allows you to create project groups and switch from one project to the other with a mouse click.

To add the test project, follow these steps:

1. Choose File ➢ Add Project and in the Project Type dialog box select Standard EXE. A new folder, which contains an empty Form, is added to the Project window.

2. Rename the components of the project.

TIP   Do Step 2 as early in the process as you can, to avoid scattering custom controls with names like Project1 all over your hard disk.

In this book, we will use a separate folder for each project and name the test project of each control TestProject.

Control and Project Names

The name of the custom ActiveX control is quite important, because this is the name developers will see in the Components dialog box when they add your control to their projects.

WARNING   If you don't change the default names before you start coding, you run the risk of creating (and registering) controls with totally meaningless names like Project1. Even worse, you could end up with a multitude of Project1 controls on your computer. While it is possible to have multiple controls with the same name, as long as they are implemented by different OCX files, this is a bad practice.

To rename the components of an ActiveX Control project, follow these steps:

1. In the new ActiveX control project, change the name of the UserControl object to MyControl, and change the project's name to DemoControl.

2. Change the name of the test project to TestProject, and change the name of its Form to TestForm. Save all the components of the project to a new folder.

3. Open the File menu, and you will see the command:

    ```
    Make DemoControl.ocx
    ```

TIP   By default, the name of the OCX file in which the control's code is stored is named after the project. Instead of changing the name of the OCX file, we suggest that you change the name of the project. You should also change it early in the process, to make sure you won't create any controls with names like Project1 or MyControl.

---

4. Select the Make DemoControl.ocx command. You'll be prompted to select the folder where the OCX file will be stored with a File Save dialog box. Select the folder where the project is stored, and store the OCX there. The DemoControl.ocx will be created and registered automatically.

5. Close the control's designer window and open the test project.

In the Toolbox, you will see the generic icon of a custom control. This is your new ActiveX control. If you move the pointer over the icon, its name will appear in a ToolTip box. The new control is named after the UserControl object, MyControl, and not after the OCX file.

You have actually designed your first ActiveX control by doing nothing! The control doesn't do anything on the Form, but it has been integrated into the environment of Visual Basic and can be added to any project through the Components dialog box. You can actually open the Components dialog box at this point and see the entry that corresponds to your new ActiveX control. As you can see in Figure 11.1, the name of the control is DemoControl. If you find this confusing, name the OCX file after the UserControl object when you create it, so that the control has the same name in the Toolbox and the Components dialog box.

FIGURE 11.1:

Once a custom ActiveX control has been registered, its name will appear automatically in the Components dialog box.

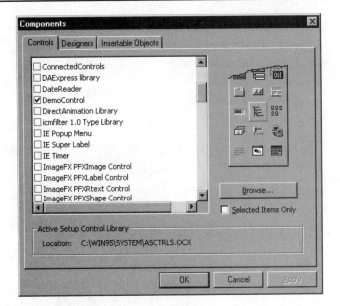

The Test Project's Properties

If you run the test project at this point, you will see the Project Properties window shown in Figure 11.2. The project's StartUp object is the UserControl object, but an ActiveX control can't be executed on its own. Visual Basic needs to know what to do with the project. The first option, Wait for Components to be Created, will create the new control(s) and register it, so that another instance of VB can use it. The option Start Component will attempt to start the component. Since an ActiveX control can't exist in its own window,

Continued on next page

Visual Basic will create a small HTML file with the control and open the page with Internet Explorer. You'll find more information about using ActiveX controls on Web pages in Chapter 18. The option Start Program allows you to select an executable file that exists on the disk already and uses the custom control. Select this option to test the control with another project. The last option, Start Browser with URL, allows you to specify the URL of a Web file, which presumably contains the control, and test the custom control on a Web page.

Which of the options on the Debugging tab should you select? At this point, and for most of the ActiveX controls you will be developing in the future, none of these options is the most appropriate. To test your custom controls, you must specify that the test project is the StartUp object, so that Visual Basic will run the test project and display the test Form with the control. To do this, right-click the name of the test project in the Project Explorer window, and from the shortcut menu select Set as Start Up. When you run the project, the test Form will appear and you won't see the Properties dialog box shown in Figure 11.2 again.

FIGURE 11.2:

If you attempt to run an ActiveX control project without specifying that the test project is the StartUp object, you'll see the Debugging tab of the Project Properties dialog box.

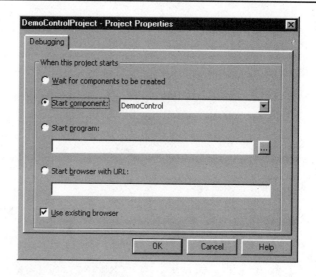

How does the system know about your custom control? As with ActiveX components, every time you create a new component by choosing File ➤ Make, the component is automatically registered in the system and is assigned a ClassID. You can find out the control's ClassID by searching the Registry (run the program RegEdit from the Start menu) for the entry DemoControl. The question now is how will the control be registered to another system so that it can be used by developers? The answer is with the help of a proper setup program. To create a setup program for your custom control, run the Package and Deployment Wizard that comes with VB6 to create an installation and setup program that will install and register the control to the target computer. If the ActiveX control is part of an application, the application's setup program will also install the control along with the application.

TIP   You can also register the OCX file of a new control with the REGSVR32 utility, as explained in Chapter 19, "Active Server Pages." Just replace the name of the class's DLL file with the name of the control's OCX file.

The Package and Deployment Wizard is not described in this chapter, but it is a straightforward application. It locates all the components of the application for which you want to prepare an installation program. Then it creates an executable file that copies all the necessary files on the host computer and registers the control. In Chapter 18, you'll see how you can use the Package and Deployment Wizard to create CAB files that can be downloaded over the Web and install ActiveX controls on the host computer.

The Extender and Ambient Objects

So far, we haven't added any members to the MyControl custom control. Yet, if you place the control on a Form and select it, you will see quite a few properties in the Properties window (see Figure 11.3). Where did they come from? If you examine these properties carefully, you will realize that they are not determined by the control itself. The Width and Height properties, as well as the Top and Left properties, are determined by the developer, when the control is placed on a Form.

Your control can't specify its location on the Form, and the control can't set its own Index property. If the developer decides to build an array of controls, they will determine the Index property. The same is true for the TabIndex property. Your control doesn't know how many controls exist on the Form, and it can't set its own TabIndex property. This property is assigned a value automatically by Visual Basic when the control is placed on the Form; the developer can change it manually.

The properties you see in the Properties window of a minimal control like the one we just designed are provided by the container. The *container* is the Form on which the control is placed. In Visual Basic or Visual C++, the container of the control is a Form. If you are going to use this control on a Web page, the container is Internet Explorer or whatever browser is used to view the page.

FIGURE 11.3:

Each custom control displays
a number of properties that
you don't have to code. These
properties are provided by
the Extender object.

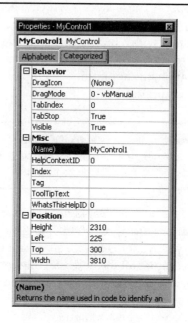

The container object's properties can be accessed from within the control's code, through the Extender object, which represents the container. However, because not all containers are identical and you can't be sure that every container supports the same properties, you must always use error-trapping code when accessing the Extender object.

When you develop the control's code, you don't know the control's Name property. Even though its default name will be something like MyControl1 or MyControl2, the developer can change the control name to anything they please. To find out the Name of your control at run time from within your code, use the expression Extender.Name. You can also find out the location of your control on the Form with the properties Extender.Top and Extender.Left.

The DragMode property is also an Extender object property. You don't have to provide any code to your control to drag it around. Visual Basic will provide this functionality as long as the developer has set the DragMode property to Automatic (1). You can't prohibit dragging your control from within its code, but you can check the value of the Extender.DragMode property to find out whether the control can be dragged.

The Extender object lets you access the properties of your control that are provided by the container, but you can only read the settings of these properties. You can access another group of properties from within your code; these are the properties of the container on which the control is sited. For example, we always try to make the default font of a control the same as the font of the container control. The properties of the container are accessed through an object property named Ambient. To find out the Font and BackColor properties of the container, use the expressions Ambient.Font and Ambient.BackColor. Figure 11.4 shows how this works.

FIGURE 11.4:

The Ambient and Extender objects give you access to the properties of the container and the custom control's properties maintained by the container.

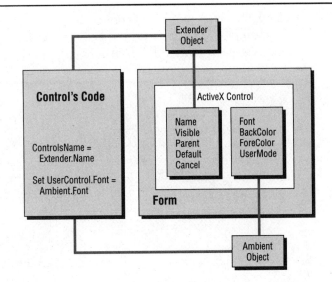

If your control manipulates color palettes, you may want to find out the container's Palette. To do this, use the Ambient.Palette property. This property is set by the developer at design time for the Form, and it applies to all controls on the Form (which means that you can't use a different palette for your custom control).

The most important property of the Ambient object is the UserMode property, which returns True if the project that contains the control is in run mode. Notice that once placed on a container, your custom control is always in run mode. You frequently will want to determine whether the project is in design mode or run mode, and the UserMode property of the Ambient object lets you find out the project's status. We use this property to distinguish between run-time and design-time properties or to assign a different appearance to the control at design time and run time.

As you will see in the examples that follow, when we want to make a property settable at design time only, we use an If statement such as the following:

```
If Ambient.UserMode = False Then Err.Raise 382
```

This statement raises the trappable error 382 if the developer attempts to set the property at run time. Likewise, to make a property settable at design time only, we use the following statement:

```
If Ambient.UserMode Then Err.Raise 393
```

You will see how the ActiveX Control Interface Wizard manipulates run-time and design-time properties in the section "The Custom Properties" later in this chapter.

With the basics of ActiveX control design out of the way, we can now look at a few examples of actual, working ActiveX controls. We'll start with the ActiveX Control Interface Wizard, which automates the process of ActiveX control design.

Opening This Chapter's Sample Apps

When you open the sample applications in this chapter, you'll get a warning to the effect that Visual Basic can't locate a compatible component. This simply means that the ActiveX control used in the project isn't registered on your computer. Here's what to do:

1. Continue loading the project, and then open it.

2. Delete the PictureBox control. (When Visual Basic can't find the OCX file for a control on a Form, it replaces the instance of this control with a PictureBox control.)

3. Select the Custom control on the Toolbox, and draw an instance of this control on the test Form.

Let's say you open the DemoControl project. On the test Form, you will see a PictureBox control named DemoControl1 instead of the DemoControl ActiveX control. Delete the PictureBox control, select the custom ActiveX control on the Toolbox (it's the new icon of a grid with a pen), and then draw an instance of the custom ActiveX control in the place of the PictureBox control. Now you're ready to test the DemoControl project.

The ActiveX Control Interface Wizard

The ActiveX Control Interface Wizard sets up a custom control's interface. Using the Wizard, you can specify the control's properties, methods, and events, and the Wizard will generate the skeleton of the control's code. Of course, the Wizard can only generate the trivial code; the actual code that will make the control do something special is your responsibility. Even so, the Wizard generates a lot of code, freeing you from trivial tasks, such as mapping properties of the control to properties of the UserControl object or mapping them to properties of the constituent controls. If your control has a Font property that you want to map to the Font property of a Label control on the custom control (or the Font property of the UserControl object itself), you can count on the Wizard to produce all the required code. It will also generate the necessary code for design-time– and run-time–only properties, or read-only and write-only properties. These are trivial, error-prone tasks that are best left to a Wizard. However, if you want to implement a custom property that requires special code, you must provide the code yourself. The Wizard will generate the necessary declarations, but you must insert some real code in the Property Let and Property Get procedures.

Let's start by implementing a very simple control. Follow these steps:

1. Place two Label controls and a TextBox control on the UserControl object of the DemoControl project.

2. Assign the strings TransparentLabel and OpaqueLabel to the two labels and set them to a large, bold font (we used 28 pts, Comic Sans MS). The names of the two Label controls are lblTransparent and lblOpaque respectively. The TextBox control's name is Text1.

3. Make the UserControl object large enough to contain its constituent controls, as shown in Figure 11.5.

FIGURE 11.5:

Designing the DemoControl project

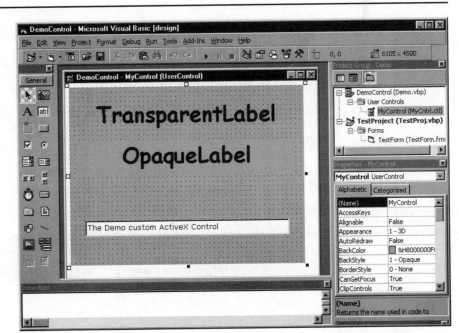

NOTE

You will find the Demo ActiveX control project on the CD, in the Demo folder under this chapter's folder. When you open the project for the first time, you'll get an error message that a component used by the project couldn't be found. Follow the instructions outlined in the sidebar "Opening This Chapter's Sample Apps," earlier in this chapter.

4. Choose Add-Ins ➤ ActiveX Control Interface Wizard to generate the control's code.

TIP

If this Wizard doesn't appear in your Add-Ins menu, select Add-In Manager to install the ActiveX Control Interface Wizard. When you run the Wizard for the first time, you will see a welcome screen. You can disable this by checking the box "Do Not Show This Window in the Future" at the bottom of the window.

5. Click Next to see the first window of the Wizard, the Select Interface Members window, shown in Figure 11.6. In this window, you can select the members of the UserControl object and the constituent controls that you want to become part of your control's user interface. The UserControl's background color will probably become your control's BackColor property.

FIGURE 11.6:

The Select Interface Members window of the Wizard

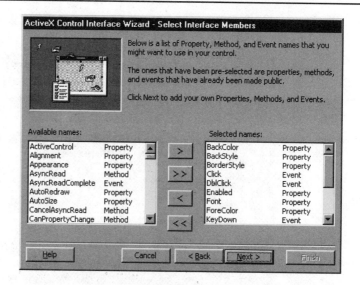

The Available Names list contains the names of members provided by most built-in controls. It's likely that you will need many of these members, so the Wizard displays them all. It also suggests a few members in the Selected Names list. These are the common members of a typical ActiveX control, such as its background and foreground colors, the mouse and keyboard events, and so on. We are going to keep the suggested members and add one more property, the Picture property.

6. Select the Picture member in the Available Names list and click the single right-arrow button to add it to the list of selected members.

7. Click Next to see the Create Custom Interface Members window. In this window, you can specify the custom members of the control.

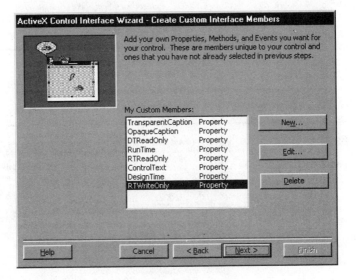

8. To add a new member, click New and you will see a dialog box where you can enter the new member's name and its type (whether it's a property, an event, or a method). Methods are implemented either as public subroutines or as public functions (if they return a value), and you must check the appropriate option button in the New Member dialog box.

9. Add the custom members from Table 11.1 to the DemoControl control (they are all properties).

TABLE 11.1: The DemoControl Control's Custom Members

Member	What It Is
TransparentCaption	The transparent Label's caption
OpaqueCaption	The opaque Label's caption
ControlText	The TextBox control's text
DesignTime	A string property available at design time only
DTReadOnly	A read-only string property available at design time only
RunTime	A string property available at run time only
RTReadOnly	A read-only string property available at run time only
RTWriteOnly	A write-only string property available at run time only

10. Click the Next button again to see the Set Mapping window of the Wizard, shown in Figure 11.7.

FIGURE 11.7:

The Set Mapping window of the Wizard

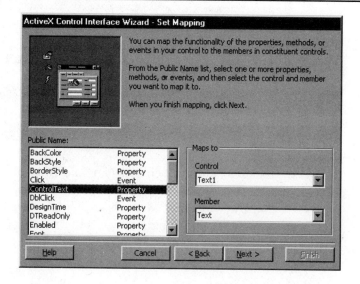

In this window, you can map the control's properties to the equivalent properties of the UserControl object or to the properties of the constituent controls. You can also map properties like BackColor, ForeColor, Font, and Picture, as well as the events, to the UserControl object. Map the custom properties to the equivalent properties of the constituent controls. For example, you would map the OpaqueCaption property to the Caption property of the lblOpaque control, and you would map the TransparentCaption property to the Caption property of the lblTransparent control.

11. Select all the members of the control on the Public Name list except the custom members (use the Shift and/or Control key to select multiple items in the list with the mouse). With the members selected in the Public Name list, expand the Control drop-down list in the Maps To section and select User-Control, as shown in Figure 11.7. The selected members will be mapped to the members of the UserControl object with the same name. You must manually map the remaining members to the appropriate members of the constituent controls.

12. Now select one member at a time from the Public Name list and map it to a property of one of the constituent controls according to Table 11.2.

TABLE 11.2: The Constituent Controls of the DemoControl Project

Property Name	Constituent Control	Property
ControlText	Text1	Text
OpaqueCaption	lblOpaque	Caption
TransparentCaption	lblTransparent	Caption

You can't map the remaining properties to any existing properties. The Wizard will generate the declaration of the properties, but it will not add any lines of code in them.

13. Now click the Next button to see the Set Attributes window.

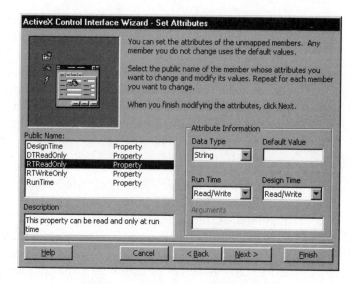

In this window you can set the attributes of the properties, arguments, return types of methods (if they are implemented as functions), and arguments of the event procedures.

You can't set the attributes of multiple properties here, so you must select the members one at a time in the Public Name list and set their attributes according to Table 11.3.

TABLE 11.3: The Attributes of the DemoControl Project's Properties

Property Name	Data Type	Default Value	Run Time	Design Time
DesignTime	String	"Design Time"	Not Available	Read/Write
DTReadOnly	String	"Design Time, Read Only"	Not Available	Read Only
RunTime	String	"Run Time"	Read/Write	Not Available
RTReadOnly	String	"Run Time, Read Only"	Read Only	Not Available
RTWriteOnly	String	"Run Time, Write Only"	Write Only	Not Available

NOTE

Notice that you can't have write-only properties at design time. It wouldn't make much sense to be able to set a property at design time but not be able to read its value.

After setting the properties of the five variables shown in the previous table, click Next again to see the last window of the Wizard, which prompts you to click Finish to generate the code. Click the Finish button and, after the Wizard generates the control's code according to your prompts in the various windows we examined in this section, it will display a text window with simple instructions as to how to proceed. Close this window and open the ActiveX designer's code window.

The Wizard's Code

Let's examine the code generated by the Wizard. Even if you develop your custom ActiveX controls manually from scratch, they will have the same structure. In examining the code generated by the Wizard, we will also discuss the structure of a typical ActiveX control.

Code 11.1 shows the beginning of the code, which contains necessary declarations.

Code 11.1   **Declarations and Constants**

```
'Default Property Values:
Const m_def_DTWriteOnly = ""
Const m_def_DesignTime = ""
Const m_def_DTReadOnly = ""
Const m_def_RunTime = ""
Const m_def_RTReadOnly = ""
'Property Variables:
Dim m_DTWriteOnly As String
Dim m_DesignTime As String
Dim m_DTReadOnly As String
Dim m_RunTime As String
Dim m_RTReadOnly As String
'Event Declarations:
Event Click() 'MappingInfo=UserControl,UserControl,-1,Click
Event DblClick() 'MappingInfo=UserControl,UserControl,-1,DblClick
Event KeyDown(KeyCode As Integer, Shift As Integer) _
      'MappingInfo=UserControl,UserControl,-1,KeyDown
Event KeyPress(KeyAscii As Integer) _
      'MappingInfo=UserControl,UserControl,-1,KeyPress
Event KeyUp(KeyCode As Integer, Shift As Integer) _
      'MappingInfo=UserControl,UserControl,-1,KeyUp
Event MouseDown(Button As Integer, Shift As Integer, X As Single, _
Y As Single) _
      'MappingInfo=UserControl,UserControl,-1,MouseDown
```

```
Event MouseMove(Button As Integer, Shift As Integer, X As Single, _
    Y As Single) _
        'MappingInfo=UserControl,UserControl,-1,MouseMove
Event MouseUp(Button As Integer, Shift As Integer, X As Single, _
Y As Single) _
        'MappingInfo=UserControl,UserControl,-1,MouseUp
```

These declarations are outside any procedure, so that all procedures can access them. The constants are the default values for the various custom properties, and the property variables are private variables that store the values of the custom properties.

NOTE   The naming scheme used by the Wizard makes the code easy to read.

After the variable declarations come the event declarations. All the events raised by the control must be declared, even though they are mapped to the equivalent events of the UserControl object.

Next are the Property procedures for the various properties of the control. The BackColor property, for instance, is implemented with the procedures in Code 11.2.

Code 11.2   **The BackColor Property**

```
Public Property Get BackStyle() As Integer
    BackStyle = UserControl.BackStyle
End Property

Public Property Let BackStyle(ByVal New_BackStyle As Integer)
    UserControl.BackStyle() = New_BackStyle
    PropertyChanged "BackStyle"
End Property
```

As you can see, mapping a property is quite simple. The new setting of the property is assigned to the equivalent property of the UserControl object, in the Property Let procedure. When the value of a mapped property is read, the Property Get procedure returns the value of the same property of the UserControl property. Mapped properties are not stored in local variables. Moreover, the name of a mapped property need not be the same as the name of the property to which it maps. The Property procedures for the OpaqueCaption property, which is mapped to the Caption property of the opaque Label control, are:

```
Public Property Get OpaqueCaption() As String
    OpaqueCaption = lblOpaque.Caption
End Property

Public Property Let OpaqueCaption(ByVal New_OpaqueCaption As String)
    lblOpaque.Caption() = New_OpaqueCaption
    PropertyChanged "OpaqueCaption"
End Property
```

Some properties, like the Font property, are set with the Property Set procedure. These properties have special values (they represent objects), which can't be set with the assignment operator. Code 11.3 lists the property procedures for the Font property.

Code 11.3　　　**The Font Property Procedures**

```
Public Property Get Font() As Font
    Set Font = UserControl.Font
End Property

Public Property Set Font(ByVal New_Font As Font)
    Set UserControl.Font = New_Font
    PropertyChanged "Font"
End Property
```

Raising Events

The custom control's events are raised from within the equivalent events of the UserControl object. Code 11.4 shows the Click and DoubleClick events of the User-Control object.

Code 11.4　　　**The Click and DoubleClick Events of the UserControl Object**

```
Private Sub UserControl_Click()
    RaiseEvent Click
End Sub

Private Sub UserControl_DblClick()
    RaiseEvent DblClick
End Sub
```

By default, the host application does not see the events of the UserControl object. You can insert your own code in these events and handle user actions from within the control's code. To pass these events to the host application, you must call the RaiseEvent method, as shown in these Code examples. If the events pass arguments, you must pass them to the host application as well. Code 11.5 presents the event handler for the MouseMove event of the UserControl object.

Code 11.5   **The Event Handler for the MouseMove Event of the UserControl Object**

```
Private Sub UserControl_MouseMove(Button As Integer, _
            Shift As Integer, X As Single, Y As Single)
    RaiseEvent MouseMove(Button, Shift, X, Y)
End Sub
```

In processing events from within your custom control, you have three options.

- Process them locally and never let the host application see them (simply don't call the RaiseEvent method).

- Process them locally and then pass them to the host application with the RaiseEvent method. In this case, any local processing must take place before passing the event to the host application.

- Ignore an event altogether, as you do with most events in programming VB applications anyway.

The Custom Properties

Now we can look at the Property procedures for the custom properties, which are available in design time or run time only and are read- or write-only. The procedures in Code 11.6 will implement the DesignTime-only property.

Code 11.6   **The DesignTime Only Property**

```
Public Property Get DesignTime() As Variant
    If Ambient.UserMode Then Err.Raise 393
    DesignTime = m_DesignTime
End Property

Public Property Let DesignTime(ByVal New_DesignTime As Variant)
    If Ambient.UserMode Then Err.Raise 393
    m_DesignTime = New_DesignTime
```

```
      PropertyChanged "DesignTime"
  End Property
```

The procedures of properties that are available at design time only examine the value of the Ambient.UserMode property to determine whether the control is in run mode. If so, they raise error 393:

```
Get not supported at run time
```

If the property is available at run time only, then the corresponding Property procedures raise error 382, if the developer attempts to set these properties at design time. Code 11.7 lists the procedures that implement the RunTime property:

Code 11.7   **The RunTime Property**

```
Public Property Let RunTime(ByVal New_RunTime As String)
    If Ambient.UserMode = False Then Err.Raise 382
    m_RunTime = New_RunTime
    PropertyChanged "RunTime"
End Property

Public Property Get RTReadOnly() As String
    RTReadOnly = m_RTReadOnly
End Property
```

Run-time properties don't even appear in the Properties window and therefore can't be set at design time. To exclude a property from the Properties window, you must change its attributes, as explained in the section "Displaying Properties in the Properties Window" later in this chapter. Alternatively, you can omit the Property Let procedure altogether.

Key Events in the Control's Life Cycle

Before we examine the behavior of the minimal control generated by the Wizard, we must discuss the key events in the life cycle of the control. This is another important aspect of the custom control authoring process, and you must be aware of these events while developing custom controls. The events that mark the life cycle of a control are described next. If you want to experiment with the order of these events, start a new ActiveX control object, add a test project, and then follow these steps:

1. Set the control's BackColor property to red, so that you can distinguish it from the Form when you place it there. The control doesn't contain any constituent controls, although you can add some.

2. Locate the following events and place Print statements as shown here:

```
Private Sub UserControl_Initialize()
    Debug.Print "INITIALIZE"
End Sub


Private Sub UserControl_InitProperties()
    Debug.Print "INITPROPERTIES"
End Sub


Private Sub UserControl_ReadProperties(PropBag As PropertyBag)
    Debug.Print "READPROPERTIES"
End Sub


Private Sub UserControl_Terminate()
    Debug.Print "TERMINATE"
End Sub


Private Sub UserControl_WriteProperties(PropBag As PropertyBag)
    Debug.Print "WRITEPROPERTIES"
End Sub
```

3. Now switch to the test project, and add an instance of the new control on the test Form. Read the messages printed in the Immediate window.

4. Run the application by pressing F5 and read the new messages displayed in the Immediate window.

Let's take a look at when the various events are fired and how they are used.

When the Control Is Sited on a Form

When you site an instance of an ActiveX control on a Form, the following events, in the order listed, are triggered:

Initialize: A new instance of the control is created and initialized. This event is the first one received by your control and is fired every time the control is placed on the Form, as well as every time the project is placed in run mode. Place your control's initialization code here.

InitProperties: The InitProperties event follows the Initialize event, when the control is placed on the Form. This event isn't fired when the project starts running. In this event, we place the code for initializing the control's private variables.

When the Project Switches to Run Mode

When the test project switches from design mode to run-time mode (that is, when you press the F5 key), the following events, in the order listed, are triggered:

WriteProperties: The control fires this event to give you a chance to save the values of its properties. As you will see, the design instance of the control will be terminated before a new run-time instance is created. In between, the values of the properties must be stored somewhere, so that the run-time instance of the control can read them. The property values are stored in an object called PropertyBag (which will be discussed shortly). The property values are stored for another good reason. During the execution of the application, properties can change value, usually through code or user actions. When the project returns to design mode, the changes are discarded and the control's properties take on the values they had before the application was switched to run mode.

Terminate: The current (design-time) instance of the control is terminated.

ReadProperties: This event tells your code that it's time to read the values of its properties from the PropertyBag object, where they were stored from within the WriteProperties event. You'll see shortly how the property values are read from the PropertyBag object.

When the Project Switches Back to Design Mode

When the test project switches from run-time mode to design-time mode (that is, when you choose Run ➤ End), the following events, in the order listed, are triggered:

Initialize: When the project's execution is terminated, the run-time instance of the control is terminated, too. A new design instance of the control is created, which is initialized again.

ReadProperties: This event tells your code that it must read the values of the properties from the PropertyBag object. These are the values stored before the previous design-time instance of the control was terminated. In effect, the design-time instance of the control must have the same property values as it did before it was placed in run time. Any changes made to the property values at run time are discarded.

The Wizard generated the listing in Code 11.8 and 11.9 for these key events. If you created the project to follow these events, you should now open the Demo project again.

- The Initialize event contains no code. Normally you use this event to initialize module level variables and properties of the constituent controls. However, you should not access the Extender and Ambient objects from within this event, because the control hasn't been sited on the Form yet. When the Initialize event is triggered, the control knows nothing about its environment yet.

- The InitProperties event initializes the private variables that hold the property values. This is done by assigning the constants declared at the beginning of the code to the private variables, which are also declared at the beginning of the code.

Code 11.8   **The InitProperties Event's Handler for the DemoControl**

```
Private Sub UserControl_InitProperties()
    Set Font = Ambient.Font
    m_DTReadOnly = m_def_DTReadOnly
    m_RunTime = m_def_RunTime
    m_RTReadOnly = m_def_RTReadOnly
    m_DTWriteOnly = m_def_DTWriteOnly
    m_DesignTime = m_def_DesignTime
    m_DesignTime = m_def_DesignTime
    m_RTWriteOnly = m_def_RTWriteOnly
End Sub
```

- The Terminate event is also empty. If your control creates any object variables in the Initialize event, this is the place to release them and return the allocated resources to the system.

- The WriteProperties event handler stores the property values to the Property-Bag object. Every property, including the properties of the UserControl object and its constituent controls, must be written to the PropertyBag object.

- The ReadProperties event handler reads the property values from the PropertyBag and assigns them to the corresponding properties.

The PropertyBag Object

PropertyBag is a complicated object that is used to store all types of property values. Some properties are as simple as numbers, others are strings, and some of them can be objects (such as the Font property). Fortunately, all the complexity of the PropertyBag is hidden from you. To access it, you need two methods:

- The WriteProperty method, which stores a property value

- The ReadProperty method, which reads a property value

The syntax of the WriteProperty method is:

```
UserControl.WriteProperty(PropertyName, Value[, DefaultValue])
```

The *PropertyName* entry is the name of the property you want to save, and *Value* is the property's value (usually the local variable that holds the property value). Although the last argument is optional, you should always supply a default value for every property you save to the PropertyBag object, because the properties with the default values are not saved. This makes the PropertyBag object smaller and faster to access. If you don't supply a default value, Visual Basic 6 will be wasting time saving default values that are (or should be) known to your program.

The syntax of the ReadProperty method is:

```
PropertyValue = UserControl.ReadProperty(PropertyName[, DefaultValue])
```

The *PropertyName* argument is the name of the property whose value you are reading, and *DefaultValue* is the value to be returned if no value has been stored in the PropertyBag object. If you specified a default value in the WriteProperty method, you must supply this default value to the ReadProperty method as well; otherwise the method won't know what value to return.

Now that we have looked at how property values are stored to and read from the PropertyBag object, we can look at the code generated by the Wizard for the WriteProperties and ReadProperties events:

Code 11.9   The WriteProperties and ReadProperties Events

```
Private Sub UserControl_WriteProperties(PropBag As PropertyBag)
    Call PropBag.WriteProperty("BackColor", UserControl.BackColor, _
        &H8000000F)
    Call PropBag.WriteProperty("Font", Font, Ambient.Font)
    Call PropBag.WriteProperty("TransparentCaption", _
        lblTransparent.Caption, "TransparentLabel")
    Call PropBag.WriteProperty("OpaqueCaption", lblOpaque.Caption, _
        "OpaqueLabel")
    Call PropBag.WriteProperty("DTReadOnly", m_DTReadOnly, _
        m_def_DTReadOnly)
End Sub
```

```
Private Sub UserControl_ReadProperties(PropBag As PropertyBag)
    UserControl.BackColor = PropBag.ReadProperty("BackColor", &H8000000F)
    Set Font = PropBag.ReadProperty("Font", Ambient.Font)
    lblTransparent.Caption = _
        PropBag.ReadProperty("TransparentCaption", _
        "TransparentLabel")
    lblOpaque.Caption = PropBag.ReadProperty("OpaqueCaption", _
        "OpaqueLabel")
    m_DTReadOnly = PropBag.ReadProperty("DTReadOnly", m_def_DTReadOnly)
End Sub
```

We only show selected lines in the two subroutines. The actual code contains many more lines, which are quite similar to the ones shown here.

This is the code produced by the Wizard. Our control doesn't do much yet, because we have not added any code; it contains only the code generated by the Wizard, which is too trivial for a meaningful operation. Now we can examine the behavior of the control from a developer's point of view. Then we are going to add the nontrivial code to our control.

A good segment of the code of an ActiveX control is similar to the code of a class. Unlike classes, however, ActiveX controls have a visible interface and behave differently at design time and run time. Once you understand the implications of these differences, you'll start building ActiveX controls with the same ease as you build VB applications.

NOTE   All Property procedures call the PropertyChanged method, passing the name of the property that changed value as argument. The PropertyChanged method notifies Visual Basic that a property value has changed and that it must be saved. The same method is also used to update the setting of a property in the Properties window when another property is changed from within the control's code. You should always call the PropertyChanged method from within any Property Let or Property Set procedure.

Design-Time Behavior of the Demo Control

Once your custom control is placed on a Form, it's actually in run mode. The code you've entered is executed. When the BackColor property of the control is changed via the Properties window, the Property Let Background() procedure is actually called to change the control's background color. The test project, however, is still in design mode. This means that none of the run-time properties that we added to the control will be available.

To test the code, you must take off your control author's hat and put on your VB programmer's hat. While testing the control, you have no access to the control's code, just like a developer using your control. To make any changes, you must switch back to the control project and assume your control author attributes again.

Displaying Properties in the Properties Window

Close all the windows of the ActiveX control project, switch to the test project, and place an instance of the DemoControl custom control on the test Form.

TIP

If the icon of the custom control isn't enabled on the Toolbox, you haven't closed all the ActiveX control project windows.

Select the DemoControl control on the Form and look at the Properties window. If you have developed your own Demo project so far, you will see the run-time properties in the Properties window. Clearly, this isn't the desired behavior. If you have opened the Demo project on the CD, you'll notice that although the RunTime property has a Property Let procedure, it's not displayed in the Properties widow. Actually, none of the run-time properties appear in the Properties window. Why is that? In order to specify whether a property appears in the Properties window, you must follow these steps:

1. Switch back to the control project, open the Code window, and choose Tools ➤ Procedure Attributes.

2. In the Procedure Attributes dialog box, click the Advanced button, and you will see the full window, shown in Figure 11.8.

3. Expand the Name drop-down list and select the RunTime property.

In the Attributes section, the Don't Show in Property Browser option is checked (this option is cleared by default; it is checked in the Demo project). This is how you control which properties are not displayed in the Properties window. The Hide This Member option has a similar effect. It prevents the property from showing up in the Properties window, but it also prevents the member from showing up in the control's type library. This feature allows you to implement "undocumented" features

FIGURE 11.8:

In the Procedure Attributes
dialog box, you specify a
number of attributes for the
control's custom properties.

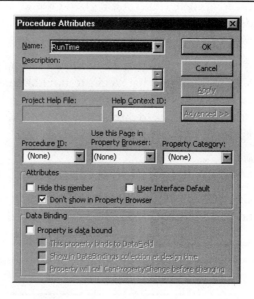

FIGURE 11.8:

In the Procedure Attributes
dialog box, you specify a
number of attributes for the
control's custom properties.

in your controls. The average developer will never know that a member exists, because it doesn't appear in the Object Browser. However, you can write applications that access this member through code.

The User Interface Default option lets you specify that the selected member is the default property of the control. If you make the OpaqueCaption property the default for the custom control, the developer can access this property either as DemoControl1.OpaqueCaption or simply DemoControl1.

Enumerated Properties

You may have noticed a small flaw in the (automated) design of the custom control. Properties with a small number of valid settings normally display a list with the possible settings in the Properties window. This didn't happen with the Back-Style property. The BackStyle property is declared as Integer in the code, and you can enter any integer value in the BackStyle field of the Properties window. If you attempt to enter an invalid value, such as 9, the following message will appear:

```
Invalid property value
```

This message doesn't convey much information to the developer. You must declare a property such as BackStyle as an Enumerated type so that the developer won't be able to set it to an invalid value.

To do this, open the Demo control's Code window and enter the following lines in the declarations section:

```
Enum BackgroundStyles
    Transparent
    Opaque
End Enum
```

An Enumerated type maps strings to integers. The first string, Transparent, corresponds to the value 0. The second string corresponds to the value 1, and so on. Now locate the property procedures of the BackStyle property, and change the type Integer to BackgroundStyles. The revised procedures are as follows:

```
Public Property Get BackStyle() As BackgroundStyles
    BackStyle = UserControl.BackStyle
End Property

Public Property Let BackStyle(ByVal New_BackStyle As BackgroundStyles)
    UserControl.BackStyle() = New_BackStyle
    PropertyChanged "BackStyle"
End Property
```

If you switch back to the test Form, select the Demo control on the Form, and try to set its BackStyle property. You will see a drop-down list in its field in the Properties window. If you expand this field, you will see the values "0 - Transparent" and "1 - Opaque." Developers simply can't set them to an invalid value. Not only that, but if you enter the control's BackStyle property name in the editor's window, as soon as you type the equal sign you will see the Auto List Members list with the valid settings of this property (provided you have turned on the Auto List Members feature of the editor).

Enumerated properties display their members automatically in the Auto List Members list.

Transparency Issues

The lblOpaque constituent control is transparent, which means that the text is displayed on the UserControl object. Change the background color of the control to see how the two Label controls are displayed. You can't change the second Label's background color.

Now change the BackStyle property of the Demo control to 0 (transparent). The top label's caption will be displayed directly on the Form. Constituent controls are made transparent with respect to the control to which they belong. To make them completely transparent, you must also set the UserControl object's BackStyle property to 0 (transparent). Place a Picture on the test Form and you will see the bitmap through the letters of the transparent Label's caption.

Caption and Text Properties

As you design Forms with the Demo control, you will notice another shortcoming: The text properties (ControlText, OpaqueCaption, and TransparentCaption) are not updated on the control as you enter their new values. With the built-in controls, the Text and Caption properties behave differently. The control is updated as you enter its new value in the corresponding field box in the Properties window. To make a text property behave like the standard Text and Caption properties, you must assign the Caption Procedure ID (or Text Procedure ID) to the property. To do so, follow these steps:

1. In the Procedure Attributes dialog box, select the ControlText property in the Name drop-down list, and click the Advanced button.

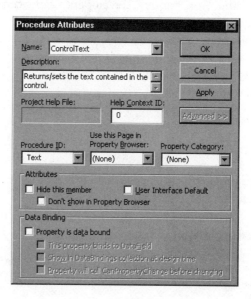

2. In the Procedure ID list, select the entry Text.

    The control's ControlText property will be handled in a way similar to the Text property of the TextBox control. As the developer changes the setting of the property in the Properties list, the control is updated automatically.

3. Select the OpaqueCaption property and set its Procedure ID to Caption. The OpaqueCaption property will behave like a Label's Caption property.

4. Return to the test Form and experiment with the new attributes of the text and caption properties by changing their settings in the Properties window.

If you have more than one text or caption property on the control, you won't be able to assign the same Procedure ID to more than one of them. Each procedure ID can be assigned to a single property. If you assign the same Procedure ID to a second property, the first property's Procedure ID is reset to None.

The last drop-down list on the Procedure Attributes dialog box, the Property Category list, contains the various categories of properties, as displayed in the Properties window when you select the Categorized tab in this window. To specify the category to which a property belongs, follow these steps:

1. Select the property's name in the Name list.

2. Select the category in the Property Category list.

3. Supply a short description for each member of the Demo control in this dialog box. The description will appear in the Properties window when the property is selected, as well as in the Object Browser.

The Run-Time Behavior of the Demo Control

Now, let's test the control in run time. Press F5 to start the test project, and you will see the window shown in Figure 11.9. The top label is transparent and allows the control's background to show through. Since the control's background is also transparent, the Form on which the control is sited shows through. For this figure, we assigned an image to the Form's Picture property. If your control isn't transparent, set its BackStyle property to 0 (transparent).

FIGURE 11.9:

The Transparent control lets
the underlying image show
through, even between the
Label's characters.

Raising Events from Constituent Controls

To test the Click event, enter the following code on the test Form (stop the application and double-click the Form to open its Code window):

```
Private Sub Form_Click()
    MsgBox "Form clicked"
End Sub

Private Sub MyControl1_Click()
    MsgBox "ActiveX Control clicked"
End Sub
```

These two messages let you know which object you clicked. When you click the Form, the Form Clicked message is displayed. That was expected. To see the "ActiveX Control Clicked message, though, you must click the UserControl's object, outside any of the constituent controls. The constituent controls receive the Click event, but they don't pass it to the control. To receive a Click event when the Label control is clicked, you must raise the Click event from within this control's Click event. Stop the project, switch to the Code window of the control project, and enter the following code in the lblOpaque and lblTransparent controls' Click events:

```
Private Sub lblOpaque_Click()
    RaiseEvent Click
End Sub
```

```
Private Sub lblTransparent_Click()
    RaiseEvent Click
End Sub
```

Now run the application again and click the Form, the Demo control, and the constituent controls. The messages tell you which control was clicked.

NOTE   If you click the transparent label, but outside the text, you will receive the Click event from the Form. If you click the transparent label's text, you will receive the Click event from the Demo control. The TextBox constituent control doesn't raise the Click event.

Unique Properties of the UserControl Object

The UserControl object supports nearly all the properties of the Form object (after all, they have the same role in different environments), but you may have noticed a few new property names in the Properties window. The properties unique to the UserControl object are described next.

Alignable

When this property is set to True, Visual Basic automatically adds the Align property in the control's Properties window. This lets the user specify whether the control will be aligned along one of the edges of the Form on which the control is contained. If you need to know the alignment of the control on its Form, you can access the Align property of the Extender object.

ControlContainer

If this property is set to True, the developer can place other controls on top of your custom control. Custom controls that contain constituent controls aren't commonly used as containers, although it's possible. When a control acts as a container, any control placed on top of it belongs to the control. In other words, you can't slide the controls with the mouse outside the container control's boundaries, and when you copy the container control, the contained controls are copied with it. This also means that when you delete the container control, all other controls sited on it are also deleted.

You can access the controls contained on your custom control from within its code with the ContainedControls collection. For example, you can align the contained controls automatically or you can assign common attributes to them. Accessing the ContainedControl collection from within your code is a slow, late-bound process (for more information on late-bound controls and how VB handles them see Chapter 9, "Object Programming with Visual Basic"). The contained controls aren't known before run time and accessing them requires substantial overhead, including serious error-trapping code.

DefaultCancel

When this property is set to True, Visual Basic automatically adds the Default and Cancel properties in the control's Properties window. These two properties are False by default, and the developer can set one of them to True to indicate that the control will function as the default (it will respond to the Enter key) or as the cancel control (it will respond to the Escape key). The Default and Cancel properties are provided by the Extender object, and you can access them from within your code with the expressions Extender.Default and Extender.Cancel.

EditAtDesignTime

Usually, you can edit controls through the Properties window at design time, and you can manipulate their properties through code at run time. You can edit some controls visually at design time. These controls assume a run-time behavior at design time, simplifying the task of editing the control's appearance. To make a control editable with visual tools at design time, set its EditAtDesignTime property to True. This adds the Edit command to the control's shortcut menu. When you select the Edit command, the control's interface behaves as it would at run time.

Let's say you have a control with a Scrollbar control on it. As you know by now, you can't move the Scollbar's button at design time. If you attempt to move the button with the mouse, you'll end up moving the entire control. You can only change the setting of the Scrollbar through the appropriate property in the Properties window.

If you use the Scrollbar control to adjust another attribute of the control, such as its color, "guessing" its value isn't the most convenient way to adjust the control's appearance. Figure 11.10 shows the Color Designer control, which lets the user specify a color by adjusting its red, green, and blue components. This control is similar to the Color common dialog box, but it can be placed directly on a Form, unlike the Color common dialog box, which is displayed in its own window. In addition, you can adjust the color with the mouse at design time, right on the Form to which it belongs. The Color Designer control also demonstrates how to extract the three color components of a given color.

NOTE   The ColorDesigner project can be found in this chapter's folder on the CD.

FIGURE 11.10:

The Edit command of the ColorDesigner control's short-cut menu lets the developer adjust the color by sliding the scrollbars with the mouse at design time.

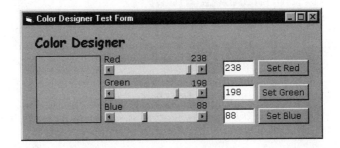

Open the project's test Form and adjust the control's color at design time by scrolling the three scrollbars. We won't present the control's code here, because it's quite straightforward, with the exception, perhaps, of the code that extracts the three basic color components from a long color value. If the variable *Selected-Color* holds a long value representing a color, the following lines extract the red, green, and blue color components:

```
m_RedComponent = SelectedColor And &HFF
m_GreenComponent = (SelectedColor / 256) And &HFF
m_BlueComponent = (SelectedColor / (256 ^ 2)) And &HFF
```

If you experiment with this application, you should notice that as you change the color on the control by sliding the scrollbars, the values of the properties Red-Component, GreenComponent, and BlueComponent in the Properties window change as well, to follow the values you specify visually.

EventsFrozen

This interesting event is available at run time only and lets your code know whether the Form is receiving events. At certain times, the Form can't receive events from the control. For example, if the Form displays a message box, it won't be able to receive any events. If your control must raise one or more events that can't be missed, the code must first read the value of this property. If the EventsFrozen property is True, the event won't be processed (so you shouldn't raise it). Queue the event (store it in a private variable, or store multiple events in an array) and keep checking the EventsFrozen property periodically (possibly with the help of a Timer control). When the EventsFrozen property becomes False again, you can safely raise the queued events. This property is used in special cases, and typical ActiveX controls don't raise events that can be missed.

InvisibleAtRunTime

Some controls remain invisible at run time but can communicate with the application via their interface members. One example is the Timer control. This is always invisible, yet it triggers Timer events as specified by the Interval property. Another invisible control is one that provides methods for calculating math expressions. Such a control need not be visible at run time; as long as you can call its methods and properties to carry out the calculations, users need not see a control with which they can't interact anyway.

Public

Something we haven't mentioned so far is that ActiveX controls can be private within executables or other ActiveX controls. To expose an ActiveX control for use by other applications, set its Public property to True (this is the default value). If you want to use a custom control in an application, yet not make it available to the users of your application as a separate component, set its Public property to False.

ToolboxBitmap

This bitmap appears in the Toolbox when the developer adds your custom control to an application. Assign a bitmap file (BMP) to this property with the icon of the control. The bitmap's dimensions must be 16 × 15 pixels. We designed a Toolbox icon (DBIcon.BMP) for the DBControl project, which we discuss later in this chapter.

> **NOTE**   You'll find the `DBIcon.BMP` file in the `Chapter11/DBControls` folder on the CD that comes with this book.

Designing and Using Property Pages

A control with many properties usually has Property Pages in which users can visually manipulate the control at design time. Related properties are grouped as tabs on the same Property Page, and the user can either change the settings on the Property Page and apply the new settings on the selected control(s) on the Form or cancel the editing operation. To display a Property Page, you usually select Properties from the control's shortcut menu. It is also possible to display an ellipsis (a button with three dots) next to a property's box in the Properties window, which invokes the Property Pages for the selected control(s).

To see the Property Pages in action, start a new project and place a MSFlexGrid, MSChart, or ActiveMovie control on it. The MSChart control's Property Pages have a total of eight tabs, with which you can set just about any of the MSChart control's properties (type, data colors, axis, labels, and so on). Many of the properties that you can set through the MSChart control's Property Pages don't even appear in the Properties window. Without the Property Pages, you'd need quite a lot of code to determine not only the appearance but the function of the control.

Figure 11.11 shows the Property Pages for the MSFlexGrid control. All the properties for setting the general appearance of the grid's cells are collected on the General tab. The other tabs contain related properties. As you change the control's settings, you can click the Apply button from time to time to see their effect on the MSFlex-Grid control, which you can see behind the Property Pages in this figure.

FIGURE 11.11:

The Property Pages for the MSFlexGrid control contains five tabs with related properties.

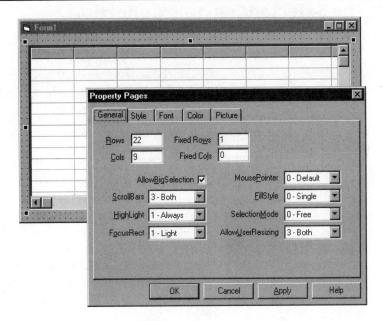

The design of a Property Page is straightforward; there's even a Wizard for designing Property Pages. We'll design a Property Page with multiple tabs shortly, but first let's look at the process.

- A Property Page can contain one or more tabs. Each tab contains a group of related properties. When the user selects a new tab, the settings of the controls on the new tab must be set according to the current settings of the properties of the selected control.

- The user can change the selection on the Form while the Property Page is open. The SelectionChanged event reports this, and you must update the current tab's settings from within the SelectionChanged event's code.

- The user can also click the Apply button to see the effects of the settings on the current tab. Your code doesn't have access to the Apply button. In other words, you can't insert your own code in the Apply button's Click event. Instead, you must insert the code for updating the selected control(s) on the Form from within the ApplyChanges event, which is triggered when the user clicks the Apply button.

The SelectedControls Collection

The selected controls on the Form are accessed by the collection SelectedControls. The number of selected controls is given by the property SelectedControls.Count, and each control in the collection can be accessed as SelectedControls(0), SelectedControls(1), and so on. To read the Caption property of the first selected control on the Form, use a statement such as the following:

```
CaptionText = SelectedControls(0).Caption
```

To set this property from within the code of a Property Page, use a statement such as the following:

```
SelectedControls(0).Caption = "I'm selected"
```

Because the user may have selected multiple instances of the control on the Form, use a loop such as the following:

```
For selControl = 0 To SelectedControls.Count
    SelectedControls(selControl).Caption = txtCaption.Text
Next
```

In this code segment, txtCaption is the name of the TextBox control on the Property Page where the user enters the new setting of the Caption property. If you want to manipulate multiple selections, you must also check all the selected controls to find out if they have a common property setting. If each has a different setting, you disable certain properties on the Property Page or you display a string such as "multiple values." In general, it's not uncommon to act on the first selected control and ignore the remaining ones. Actually, this is what the Property Page Wizard does, by acting on the control SelectedControls(0) only.

Designing Property Pages

In this section, we are going to design a Property Page for the DemoControl. To get started, follow these steps:

1. Switch to the ActiveX control project.

2. Choose Project ➤ Add Property Page.

3. In the Add Property Page dialog box, select the VB Property Page Wizard icon.

Before we go through the windows of this Wizard, let's take a look at the Property Page we are about to design. Figure 11.12 shows the DesignTime tab of the DemoControl and Figure 11.13 shows the Captions tab.

FIGURE 11.12:

The DesignTime tab of the DemoControl Property Page

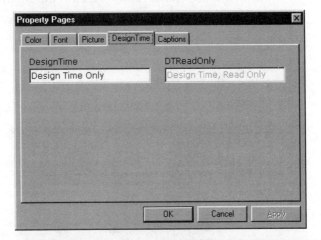

FIGURE 11.13:

The Captions tab of the DemoControl Property Page

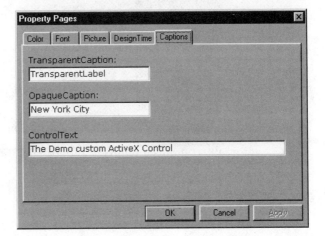

The Property Pages of this control contain three more tabs, which are standard tabs that you have seen many times:

- The Color tab lets you specify the control's background color.

- The Font tab lets you specify the control's Font.

- The Picture tab lets you specify the picture to be displayed on the UserControl object's background.

The Wizard automatically creates these tabs; you don't have to supply a single line of code.

When you add one or more Property Pages to an ActiveX control project, a new folder (the Property Pages folder) is added to the Project window. The Property Pages folder contains the custom tabs of the control's Property Pages.

The simplest way to design a Property Page is with the help of the Wizard. Follow these steps:

1. In the Add Property Page dialog box, select VB Property Page Wizard to open the Wizard's first window, a welcome page.

2. Click Next to open the Select the Property Pages window:

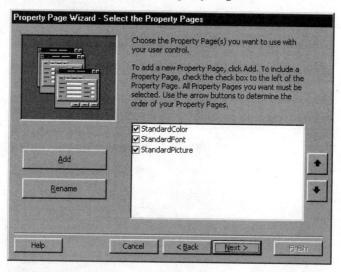

It initially contains the three standard tabs shown in Figure 11.14:

- StandardColor

- StandardFont

- StandardPicture

FIGURE 11.14:

The three standard tabs of a Property Page

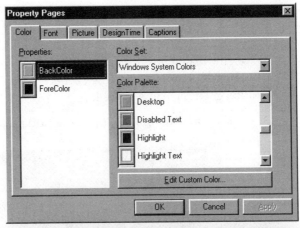

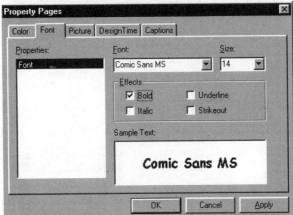

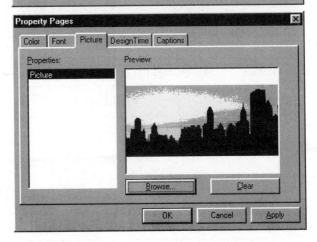

If the control contains a Color, a Font, or a Picture property, the corresponding standard tab is checked automatically. To omit a standard property page from your control's Property Pages, clear the checkbox in front of the corresponding entry. The last two tabs (DesignTime and Caption) will not appear on the dialog box initially. You must add them with the Add button. Click the Add button to open the Property Page Name dialog box in which you can enter the name of the tab.

3. Click the Next button to open the Add Properties window:

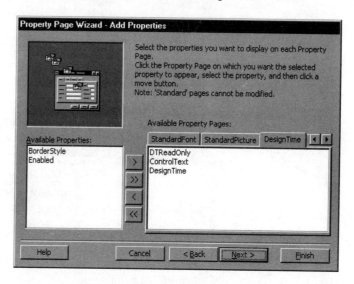

In this window, you can select a tab in the Available Property Pages section and add the properties that will appear on them. Add the following tabs shown in Table 11.4 to the Property Pages and assign the properties shown in the second column of the table to the corresponding tab.

TABLE 11.4: The Properties for the Tabs of the DemoControl's Property Pages

Tab	Property
StandardColor	BackColor, ForeColor
StandardFont	Font
StandardPicture	Picture
DesignTime	DTReadOnly, DesignTime
Captions	TransparentCaption, OpaqueCaption, ControlText

After you specify the properties and their tabs, click Next to open the last window of the Wizard. Click the Finish button to generate the Property Page and the corresponding code. The Wizard will produce some really primitive pages, which you must edit a little. Figures 11.12 and 11.13 show the two custom tabs produced by the Wizard—after a little editing. As you can see, the tabs don't have the OK, Cancel, and Apply buttons that appear in the Property Page. Visual Basic itself manages these buttons.

The Wizard produced Code 11.10 for the DesignTime tab.

Code 11.10   The DesignTime Tab

```
Private Sub txtDesignTime_Change()
    Changed = True
End Sub

Private Sub txtDTReadOnly_Change()
    Changed = True
End Sub

Private Sub PropertyPage_ApplyChanges()
    SelectedControls(0).DesignTime = txtDesignTime.Text
End Sub

Private Sub PropertyPage_SelectionChanged()
    txtDesignTime.Text = SelectedControls(0).DesignTime
    txtDTReadOnly.Text = SelectedControls(0).DTReadOnly
End Sub
```

The Change event of the two TextBox controls sets the Changed property, which is used to enable the Apply button in the Property Page. If no settings have changed, the Apply button is disabled. Clicking the Apply button triggers the ApplyChanges event, which applies the new value of the DesignTime property to the selected control. Finally, when the user selects a new instance of the DemoControl on the Form, the SelectionChanged event is triggered. This event's handler reads the settings of the DesignTime and DTReadOnly properties on the selected control and updates the TextBox controls on the DesignTime tab.

NOTE   The TextBox for entering the value of the DTReadOnly property is locked so that the user can't edit its contents. The property is read-only, so it's displayed on the tab but can't be changed. That's why the corresponding line is missing from the Apply-Changes event handler.

The Captions tab contains three TextBox controls, with which the user can change the settings of the ControlText, OpaqueCaption, and TransparentCaption properties. The code is quite similar, and we need not repeat it here. If you open the Demo project on the CD (in the Demo folder), you will see the complete listing of each tab in the Property Pages. You will also see that the standard tabs don't appear in the Property Pages folder. Visual Basic maintains these tabs, and you cannot access their code. If you don't like their appearance, you can replace them with custom tabs that you must design yourself.

Now that we've explored the techniques for building ActiveX controls and designing Property Pages, it's time to look at some examples that are more complicated and more practical. We'll start with a control that implements a lens-over-image effect. The LensEffect control can display any bitmap and magnify a small section of it, as if you were examining the image with a magnifying lens. You can move the lens around with the mouse, or you can program it to slide around.

The next example, OnLine, demonstrates how to download property values over the Internet and display them on a custom control. The OnLine control shows you how to use the UserControl object's methods and events for downloading data over the Internet asynchronously.

In the last section of this chapter, we'll build an interconnected control that can perform quite complicated tasks with only a few lines of code. We will also present three ActiveX controls that implement the functionality of the DBClass classes (see Chapter 10), but they are far easier to use in an application.

The ImageLens Control

The ImageLens control is an example of the most common type of ActiveX control: a user-drawn control that uses constituent controls. The control we are going to build in this section implements a lens-over-image effect. The UserControl object accepts a bitmap, as shown in Figure 11.15. A small rectangular area of the image is enlarged. This is the area of the image under a magnifying lens. You can move the lens around with the mouse, or you can program it to slide around.

The implementation of the control is quite simple in principle: The rectangular lens is a borderless PictureBox control that displays a small area of the bitmap under it, magnified. The lens's dimensions are 64 × 64 pixels, and it displays an

FIGURE 11.15:

The ImageLens control displaying an image and a magnifying glass over a small area of the bitmap

area of the bitmap with dimensions of 16 × 16 pixels. This area of the bitmap is centered around the center of the lens. The magnification is performed by the PaintPicture method, which copies (and stretches) the 16 × 16 pixel bitmap to the PictureBox control that implements the lens.

> **NOTE**   You'll find the ImageLens project in the ImageLens folder on the CD that comes with this book.

The test Form of the project, shown in Figure 11.15, contains an instance of the ImageLens control and two Command buttons. The first Command button, Load Image, loads an image from the local disk and displays it on the control. Later in this chapter you'll see how you can download an image from a Web server and display it on the control. The second Command button, Scroll Lens, slides the lens around and bounces on the edges of the control. If you click the Scroll Lens button, its Caption becomes Pause, and you must click it again to stop the sliding of the lens. You can then slide the lens around with the mouse.

A More Realistic Lens Control

A more realistic lens control would implement a round lens and would magnify the underlying bitmap unevenly. The magnification at the center should be stronger, and the magnification around the lens's circumference should be smaller.

This operation, however, requires a lot of math and trigonometric operations, and the result would be a slow-moving lens. Our goal is to demonstrate how to build a control with constituent controls and not to explain the math involved (losing our readers in the process).

Those of you who are mathematically inclined and would enjoy experimenting with math and graphics can find a description of the transformations involved in the document at the following site:

http://www.neutralzone.org/home/faqsys/docs/lens.txt

The lens effect is implemented with a single line of code that copies a rectangular area of the bitmap on the UserControl onto the PictureBox control that implements the lens:

```
Picture1.PaintPicture UserControl.Picture, 0, 0, _
Picture1.ScaleWidth, Picture1.ScaleHeight, _
m_LensX + Picture1.ScaleWidth / 4, m_LensY + Picture1.ScaleHeight / 4, _
Picture1.ScaleWidth / 2, Picture1.ScaleHeight / 2, &HCC0020
```

The variables *m_LensX* and *m_LensY* are the coordinates of the lens's upper-left corner. The coordinates of the upper-left corner of the rectangular area of the bitmap to be copied are:

```
(m_LensX + Picture1.ScaleWidth / 4,  m_LensY + Picture1.ScaleHeight / 4)
```

The dimensions of this rectangle are one-half the dimensions of the lens (Picture1 control); so the magnification is 400%.

The actual implementation of the control is straightforward, but the required code is quite lengthy. Let's start with the members of the control's interface. The ImageLens control exposes the members in Table 11.5.

TABLE 11.5: The Members of the ImageLens Control

Member	Description
WidthInPixels, HeightInPixels	The dimensions of the image on the control's background. The control isn't auto-resized, so the image may be smaller or larger than the available display area.
LensX, LensY	The coordinates of the lens's upper-left corner in pixels.
LensWidth, LensHeight	The lens's dimensions.
MoveTo(X, Y)	Method that moves the lens to the specified coordinates.

If you open the project, you'll see that it was designed with the ActiveX Control Interface Wizard. Most of the control's properties are mapped to the UserControl object. Next, we'll describe the custom members.

When you set the coordinates of the lens's upper-left corner, the code must make sure that the specified values are valid (in other words, it won't allow the developer to move the lens outside the control's visible area). Let's start with the Let and Get procedures for the LensX Property (see Code 11.11).

Code 11.11   The Property Let and Get Procedures for the LensX Property

```
Public Property Get LensX() As Integer
    LensX = m_LensX
End Property

Public Property Let LensX(ByVal New_LensX As Integer)
    If ((New_LensX < (UserControl.ScaleWidth - Picture1.ScaleWidth)) _
        And (New_LensX > 0)) Then
            m_LensX = New_LensX
            UserControl_Paint
            PropertyChanged "LensX"
    End If
End Property
```

The Property procedures for the LensY property are similar (see Code 11.12). The WidthInPixels and HeightInPixels properties are mapped to the control's ScaleWidth and ScaleHeight properties, which aren't available directly to the developer. The code relies on the PicturePaint method, which assumes that the source and destination bitmaps are measured in pixels. Moreover, we made these properties read-only by omitting the Property Let procedures.

Code 11.12   **The Property Procedures for the LensY Property**

```
Public Property Get WidthInPixels() As Integer
    WidthInPixels = Int(UserControl.ScaleWidth)
End Property

Public Property Get HeightInPixels() As Integer
    HeightInPixels = Int(UserControl.ScaleHeight)
End Property
```

As expected, the code for drawing a user-drawn control resides in the User-Control's Paint event as shown in Code 11.13.

Code 11.13   **The UserControl's Paint Event**

```
Private Sub UserControl_Paint()
    Picture1.Move m_LensX, m_LensY
    On Error Resume Next
    Picture1.PaintPicture UserControl.Picture, 0, 0, _
        Picture1.ScaleWidth, Picture1.ScaleHeight, _
        m_LensX + Picture1.ScaleWidth / 4, _
        m_LensY + Picture1.ScaleHeight / 4, _
        Picture1.ScaleWidth / 2, Picture1.ScaleHeight / 2, &HCC0020
End Sub
```

The Paint event contains a single line that copies part of the original bitmap to the Picture1 control and magnifies it in the process, as we explained earlier.

Moving the Lens

The most interesting code in this project is in the mouse events of the UserControl. This code captures the movement of the mouse and slides the Picture1 control in the direction of the mouse movement. All three mouse events use the following variables, which are declared on the UserControl object, outside any event:

```
' Program local variables
Private MovingLens As Boolean
Private XStart As Integer
Private YStart As Integer
```

When you press the left mouse button while the pointer is over the Picture1 control, the *MovingLens* variable is set to True in the MouseDown event to indicate that the control can be moved. This variable is examined in the MouseMove event and reset to False in the MouseUp event. Likewise, the variables *XStart* and *YStart* are set to the coordinates of the point where the mouse button was pressed initially. These variables are used in the MouseMove event as well. When the mouse is clicked, the code in Code 11.14 is executed.

Code 11.14   The Event Handler of the MouseDown Event of the Picture1 Control

```
Private Sub Picture1_MouseDown(Button As Integer, Shift As Integer, _
        X As Single, Y As Single)
    If Button = vbLeftButton Then
        XStart = X
        YStart = Y
        MovingLens = True
    End If
End Sub
```

In the MouseMove event of the Picture1 control, we monitor the movement of the mouse and displace the Picture1 control by the difference between the current coordinates of the mouse and the coordinates XStart and YStart where the mouse was pressed initially. The code contains more lines that make sure the lens is not moved outside the visible area of the control. The MouseMove event handler of the Picture1 control is shown in Code 11.15.

Code 11.15   The MouseMove Event

```
Private Sub Picture1_MouseMove(Button As Integer, Shift As Integer, _
        X As Single, Y As Single)
    If Button = vbLeftButton And MovingLens Then
        If Picture1.Left + (X - XStart) > 0 And _
                (Picture1.Left + (X - XStart)) < _
                (UserControl.ScaleWidth - Picture1.ScaleWidth) Then
            m_LensX = Picture1.Left + (X - XStart)
        End If
        If Picture1.Top + (Y - YStart) > 0 And _
                (Picture1.Top + (Y - YStart)) < _
                (UserControl.ScaleHeight - Picture1.ScaleHeight) Then
            m_LensY = Picture1.Top + (Y - YStart)
```

```
                End If
                UserControl_Paint
            End If
        End Sub
```

After the Picture1 control is moved to its new location, the Paint event is called to redraw the control. Finally, in the MouseUp event (shown in Code 11.16), we reset the MovingLens variable to False.

Code 11.16   **The MouseUp Event**

```
Private Sub Picture1_MouseUp(Button As Integer, Shift As Integer, _
        X As Single, Y As Single)
    If Button = vbLeftButton And MovingLens Then
        MovingLens = False
    End If
End Sub
```

The rest of the code is rather trivial; it was created with the ActiveX Interface Wizard. Open the project in the Visual Basic IDE to examine its code and see the implementation of the Picture property. You can ignore the PictureFromURL property for now. In the next section, you'll see how you can download a property value from a Web server.

Internet-Enabled Controls

With the domination of the Internet and the merging of the desktop and the Web—demonstrated by the Active Desktop, the latest release of Internet Explorer, and the Windows operating system—ActiveX controls should be able to connect to the Internet and download information from HTTP servers. No matter how much information you provide along with your control, there will always be more, up-to-date information on a server. An interesting, nearly necessary feature you may want to add to your controls is the ability to connect to HTTP servers and download information on request.

The ActiveX controls you design with Visual Basic support asynchronous downloading of property values. To download a file from a URL, you can use the AsyncRead method, whose syntax is:

```
UserControl_AsyncRead Target, AsyncType [, PropertyName]
```

The Target argument is a string specifying the location of the data, and it can be a URL to a remote HTTP server or the path to a file on a local or network disk. A URL would look something like this:

```
http://www.servername.com/Updates/Latest.txt
```

And a path to a local file would look something like this:

```
file://m:\Software\Updates\Latest.txt.
```

You specify the type of the file to be downloaded with the AsyncType argument, which can be any one of the constants in Table 11.6.

TABLE 11.6: The Possible Settings of the AsyncType Argument of the AsyncRead Method

Constant	Description
vbAsyncTypeFile	The data is provided in a file that Visual Basic can open later.
vbAsyncTypeByteArray	The data is provided as a byte array. The application must handle the elements of the array.
vbAsyncTypePicture	The data is provided in a Picture object.

The last, optional argument is the name of the property to be downloaded. This name is simply an identifier, which you can use later to retrieve the value of the property downloaded or to cancel the downloading of the data. This property is also used to distinguish among multiple properties that are downloaded simultaneously. The PropertyName argument can be any arbitrary name, since its only function is to act as an identifier for this particular data request. The value in PropertyName is used to identify the particular asynchronous read to cancel in the CancelAsyncRead method. It is also used to identify the particular asynchronous read that has completed in the AsyncReadComplete event.

Once the data is requested with the AsyncRead method, control is relinquished to the application, which can continue with other tasks. The download may take a while, so the AsyncRead method performs an asynchronous operation. When the download is complete, the AsyncReadComplete event is raised. The code for handling the downloaded data goes into the AsyncReadComplete event handler.

The AsyncReadComplete event's definition is:

```
Sub UserControl_AsyncReadComplete(PropertyValue As AsyncProperty)
```

The PropertyValue argument is an object that has the properties shown in Table 11.7.

TABLE 11.7: The Properties of the AsyncProperty Object

Property Name	Description
Value	A variant containing the results of the asynchronous download.
PropertyName	The property name, as specified with the last argument in the AsyncRead method.
AsyncType	An integer specifying the type of data in the Value property. It takes the same values as the AsyncType argument of the AsyncRead method, described earlier.

The AsyncReadComplete event will be raised even if an error occurred during the transmission. If the download didn't complete successfully, a run-time error will occur when you access the Value property of the AsyncProperty object.

<table>
<tr><td>

TIP

</td><td>

Always include an On Error statement in the AsyncReadComplete event handler to trap download errors.

</td></tr>
</table>

It is possible to cancel the asynchronous download by calling the CancelAsync-Read method. Its syntax is:

```
UserControl.CancelAsyncRead PropertyName
```

PropertyName is the name of the property being downloaded (the last argument of the AsyncRead method). If PropertyName is not supplied (because no such property was specified in the AsyncRead method), the last AsyncRead method invocation that did not give a PropertyName will be canceled.

The OnLine Project

The asynchronous downloading of property values over the Internet is demonstrated in the OnLine project shown in Figure 11.16. The OnLine control has two panes: the left one is a ListBox control and the right one is a TextBox control. The control connects to a user-specified URL and downloads a list of topics that are displayed in the left pane. When the user clicks a topic, the control connects to the same URL and downloads a text file that is displayed in the pane on the right (the TextBox control).

FIGURE 11.16:

The OnLine control downloads and displays text files over the Internet from an HTTP server.

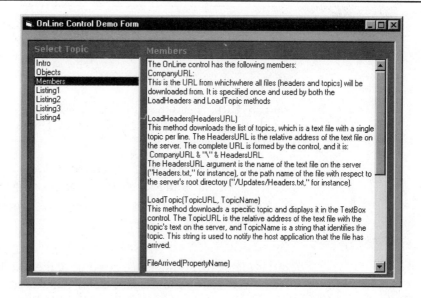

Start a new ActiveX control project and design a UserControl object like the one shown in Figure 11.16. Place a narrow ListBox control on the left and a TextBox control on the right. Since the developer must have the option to resize the control at will, in the Resize event (see Code 11.17) we must resize the two controls according to the control's dimensions.

Code 11.17   The Resize Event

```
Private Sub UserControl_Resize()
    If UserControl.Height < 3000 Then UserControl.Height = 3000
    List1.Height = UserControl.Height - (4 * Label1.Top + Label1.Height)
    If UserControl.Width < 6000 Then UserControl.Width = 6000
    Text1.Height = List1.Height
    Text1.Width = UserControl.Width - Text1.Left - 2 * List1.Left
End Sub
```

This code doesn't resize the two constituent controls proportionally. It simply adjusts the width of the TextBox control. It also enforces a minimum size for the control.

WARNING   Don't make a control such as this one too small; it would be practically useless. Enforce a minimum size from within the control's Resize event.

The OnLine control has the following members:

CompanyURL: This is the URL from which all files (headers and topics) will be downloaded. It is specified once and used by both the LoadHeaders and LoadTopic methods

LoadHeaders(HeadersURL): This method downloads the list of topics, which is a text file with a single topic per line. The HeadersURL is the relative address of the text file on the server. The complete URL is formed by the control, and it is:

```
CompanyURL & "\" & HeadersURL
```

The HeadersURL argument is the name of the text file on the server (`Headers.txt`, for instance) or the path name of the file with respect to the server's root directory (`/Updates/Headers.txt`, for instance).

LoadTopic(TopicURL, TopicName): This method downloads a specific topic and displays it in the TextBox control. The *TopicURL* argument is the relative address of the text file with the topic's text on the server, and *TopicName* is a string that identifies the topic. This string is used to notify the host application that the file has arrived.

FileArrived(TopicName): This event is triggered from within the AsyncReadComplete event and notifies the host application that a download has completed.

OnLineError(ErrorNumber, ErrorDescription): This event is also triggered from within the AsyncReadComplete event and notifies the application that an error has occurred.

TopicClick(TopicName): This event is raised when a topic in the Topics list is selected by the user. The OnLine control starts downloading the selected topic automatically and also notifies the host application that a new topic was selected.

Header: This property returns the selected header (if any) in the left pane.

TopicText: This property returns the text displayed in the right pane.

Using the OnLine Control

Before examining the actual code of the control, let's see how it's used in the test project. The test project consists of a single Form that contains an instance of the OnLine control only.

When the Form is loaded, it assigns the URL of the server on which all the files reside to the CompanyURL property. It then calls the LoadHeaders method to load the list of topics and display them in the left pane.

```
Private Sub Form_Load()
    OnLine1.CompanyURL = "http://127.0.0.1"
    OnLine1.LoadHeaders ("headers.txt")
End Sub
```

The test project need not do anything more. The rest is up to the OnLine control. After the headers are downloaded and displayed, every time the user clicks a topic, the corresponding text file is displayed in the right pane. The test project uses the URL 127.0.0.1, which is the IP address of the local address.

To test this project successfully, you must set up a Web server on your computer and copy all the text files from the OnLine folder on the CD to the Web server's root folder or to a subfolder underneath. You can create a new virtual folder named Online and change the CompanyURL property to the following:

```
http://127.0.0.1/online
```

Under this project folder on the CD, you will find the WEBSrvr folder, which contains a few files you must place in your server's root folder to experiment with the OnLine and DLImage projects. If you don't want to set up your own server, you can copy the files to your own folder on your ISP's computer and change the Company-URL accordingly. The simplest approach is to set up your own Web server, since we are going to use it with other projects in Part IV of this book.

TIP   If you are not familiar with the Personal Web Server, see Chapter 18 for details.

The test project displays the error message (should an error occur) from within the OnLineError event:

```
Private Sub OnLine1_OnLineError(Number As Integer, Description As String)
        MsgBox "ERROR! Data not downloaded." & vbCrLf & _
            Description

End Sub
```

Finally, it prints messages to the Immediate window for demonstration purposes:

```
Private Sub online1_FileArrived(Name As String)
    Debug.Print Name & " arrived"
End Sub

Private Sub online1_TopicClick(topic As String)
    Debug.Print topic & " requested"
End Sub
```

The FileArrived event is triggered every time a new file is downloaded. This applies to both the headers file and the topics file.

The OnLine Control's Code

We used the ActiveX Interface Wizard to add the standard properties of the control. In this section, we'll focus on the procedures that download the headers and the topics. The names of the files with the headers are passed to the method LoadHeaders (shown in Code 11.18) as argument.

Code 11.18   **The LoadHeaders() Method**

```
Public Sub LoadHeaders(HeadersURL As String)
Dim HURL As String
On Error GoTo HeadersError

    HURL = m_CompanyURL & "/" & HeadersURL
    AsyncRead HURL, vbAsyncTypeFile, "Headers"
    Exit Sub

HeadersError:
    RaiseEvent OnLineError(1, "Could not download list of topics.")

End Sub
```

Notice that the complete URL for the headers file is formed by concatenating the company URL and the name of the file. The local variable *m_CompanyURL* stores the CompanyURL property. Before calling the LoadHeaders method from the host application, you must set this property.

The LoadTopic method, shown in Code 11.19, is similar. It accepts two arguments:

- The relative path of the topic file (TopicURL)

- A topic name (*topic*)

Code 11.19   **The LoadTopic Method**

```
Private Sub LoadTopic(TopicURL As String, topic As String)
Dim TURL As String
On Error GoTo TopicURL

    TURL = m_CompanyURL & "/" & TopicURL
    If List1.ListIndex >= 0 Then
        AsyncRead TURL, vbAsyncTypeFile, topic
    End If
    Exit Sub


TopicURL:
    RaiseEvent OnLineError(2, _
            "Could not download topic " & topic)
End Sub
```

The interesting action takes place in the AsyncReadComplete event of the User-Control object, shown in Code 11.20.

Code 11.20   **The AsyncReadComplete Event**

```
Private Sub UserControl_AsyncReadComplete(AsyncProp As AsyncProperty)
Dim FileName As String

On Error GoTo DLoadError
    If AsyncProp.PropertyName = "Headers" Then
        FileName = AsyncProp.Value
        LoadTopicsList (FileName)
        RaiseEvent FileArrived("Headers")
    Else
        For i = 0 To List1.ListCount - 1
            If AsyncProp.PropertyName = List1.List(i) Then
                    FileName = AsyncProp.Value
                    Label2.Caption = AsyncProp.PropertyName
                    LoadTopicText FileName
                    RaiseEvent FileArrived(AsyncProp.PropertyName)
                    Exit For
            End If
        Next
    End If
    Exit Sub
```

```
DLoadError:
    RaiseEvent OnLineError(5, _
                "Error in Downloading topic " & List1.List(i))

End Sub
```

This event is triggered no matter which file has completed downloading, so the code must first figure out if it's the headers file or a topic file. If the property's name is Headers, the code opens the file just downloaded and displays its lines in the ListBox control. When the AsyncRead method downloads a file, the AsyncProp object's Value property is the name of the file where the topic's text was stored on the disk. It has nothing to do with the actual file name on the server. It's a unique file name created by the system in the Temporary Internet Files folder. The Load-TopicsList() subroutine (shown in Code 11.21) uses the name of the file to display the headers in the ListBox.

Code 11.21   **The LoadTopicsList Subroutine**

```
Sub LoadTopicsList(FileName As String)
Dim FNum As Integer
Dim topic As String

    FNum = FreeFile
    List1.Clear
On Error GoTo LoadTopicsError
    Open FileName For Input As FNum
    While Not EOF(FNum)
        Input #FNum, topic
        List1.AddItem topic
    Wend
    Exit Sub

LoadTopicsError:
    RaiseEvent OnLineError(6, "Couldn't load topics")

End Sub
```

This is straightforward VB code that opens a text file and appends its lines to the List1 ListBox control.

Back to the AsyncReadComplete event. If the downloaded file isn't the Headers file, the code scans each topic in the left pane to see which topic name matches the property name of the downloaded file. Once a match is found, the code calls the LoadTopicText() subroutine, which opens the text file and displays it in the right pane.

WARNING   Notice the error-trapping code in all subroutines. When downloading information from the Internet, any number of things can go wrong. The HTTP server may be down, files may be rearranged on the server, transmission errors can occur, and so on. These errors must be trapped and dealt with in a resolute manner.

The OnLine ActiveX control doesn't raise errors; instead, it raises events that notify the application about abnormal conditions. The download of a property value takes place asynchronously, and the host application may be executing any procedure when the error occurs. In other words, you wouldn't know where to place the error-trapping code in the host application. The OnLineError event can be programmed to handle all the errors detected by the control. The number reported by the first argument of the OnLineError event is not an actual error number; you can't retrieve it with the expression Err.Number. It's just a number that differentiates the various error conditions during the download of a topic file. That's why you don't have to add the constant *vbObjectError* to the error number of the OnLineError event.

You might want to add to this project a feature that keeps track of the property being downloaded and prevents the host application from initiating another download of the same property while it's being downloaded. Our code will give a generic error message:

```
Could not download headers
```

or

```
Could not download topic
```

The AsyncRead method can be called to download a file while another one is being downloaded, but it can't download the same file twice simultaneously.

Downloading Image Properties

The AsyncRead method can also download picture properties. You can download pictures as binary files and display them with the LoadPicture method. In addition,

Visual Basic can create a device context and store the downloaded bitmap there. The OnLineImages project (in the OnLineImage folder on the CD) is a variation of the OnLine control, which downloads images. The headers are image names, and each time a new image name is selected in the left pane, it is downloaded and displayed in the right pane, as shown in Figure 11.17.

FIGURE 11.17:

The OnLineImages control downloads images from an HTTP server and displays them.

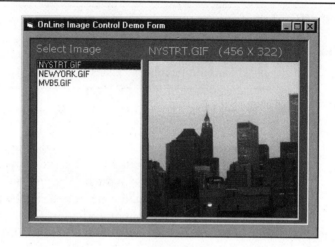

The OnLineImage project is quite similar to the OnLine project, except that it uses the vbAsyncTypePicture constant in the AsyncRead method. Also, the pane in which the selected image is displayed is a PictureBox control. To build this project, copy the components of the projects to a new folder and rename them accordingly.

The data downloaded are stored in a bitmap structure, which can be manipulated like the Image property of the PictureBox control or the Form object. The DownLoadImage method requests the download of an image and is implemented as follows:

```
Private Sub DownLoadImage(TopicURL As String, imageName As String)
On Error GoTo TopicURL

    AsyncRead TopicURL, vbAsyncTypePicture, imageName
    Exit Sub

TopicURL:
    RaiseEvent OnLineError(1025, "Could not download image " & imageName)
End Sub
```

imageName is the image's name on the server. When the download of an image completes, the code shown in Code 11.22 is executed from within the AsyncRead-Complete event:

Code 11.22 **The AsyncReadComplete Event's Handler**

```
Private Sub UserControl_AsyncReadComplete(AsyncProp As AsyncProperty)
Dim FileName As String
Dim i As Integer

On Error GoTo DLoadError
    If AsyncProp.PropertyName = "Images" Then
        FileName = AsyncProp.Value
        LoadTopicsList (FileName)
        RaiseEvent FileArrived("Headers")
    Else
        For i = 0 To List1.ListCount - 1
            If AsyncProp.PropertyName = List1.List(i) Then
                Set Bitmap = AsyncProp.Value
                Label2.Caption = AsyncProp.PropertyName
                ShowImage Bitmap
                Label2.Caption = Label2.Caption & "   (" & _
                Int(ScaleX(Bitmap.Width, vbHimetric, vbPixels)) & _
                    " X " & Int(ScaleY(Bitmap.Height, _
                    vbHimetric, vbPixels)) & ")"
                RaiseEvent FileArrived(AsyncProp.PropertyName)
                Exit For
            End If
        Next
    End If
    Exit Sub
DLoadError:
    RaiseEvent OnLineError(1028, "Error in Downloading file " _
            & AsyncProp.PropertyName)
End Sub
```

The ShowImage() subroutine, which displays the image on the PictureBox control (and is shown in Code 11.23), accepts as argument a bitmap structure. This bitmap structure is created by the AsyncRead method, which stores the downloaded image there. The image is displayed progressively, one line at a time, starting from the top of the image. The code uses the PaintPicture method of the PictureBox control to copy an increasingly wider stripe of the downloaded image.

Code 11.23   **The ShowImage Subroutine**

```
Private Sub ShowImage(Image As StdPicture)
Dim irow
On Error GoTo DisplayError

    For irow = 1 To Picture1.ScaleHeight - 1
        Picture1.PaintPicture Image, 0, 0, _
        Picture1.ScaleWidth, irow, 0, 0, Picture1.ScaleWidth, irow
    Next
    ScrollImage = False
    OldXStart = 0
    OldYStart = 0
    If ScaleX(Image.Height, vbHimetric, vbPixels) > Picture1.ScaleHeight_
        Or ScaleY(Image.Width, vbHimetric, vbPixels) > Picture1.ScaleWidth_
        Then
            ScrollImage = True
    End If
    Exit Sub

DisplayError:
    RaiseEvent OnLineError(1030, "Couldn't display image")

End Sub
```

An interesting feature of this control is that if the image's dimensions exceed the dimensions of the PictureBox control, the user can scroll the image around with the mouse. *ScrollImage* is a Boolean variable that indicates whether the image can be scrolled. If the image fits in the PictureBox control, the *ScrollImage* variable is set to False to prohibit the movement of the image in the control.

Moving the Image

The code for moving the image around in the PictureBox control is located in the three mouse events of the PictureBox control. You can also use this code as your starting point to implement a control that can display large images and allow the user to scroll them with the mouse and bring any portion of the image into view (see Figure 11.18). One shortcoming of the PictureBox control is that it doesn't provide scrollbars that would allow the user to select any part of the image.

FIGURE 11.18:

As the user drags the image around in the control's right pane, the pointer assumes a cross-arrow shape.

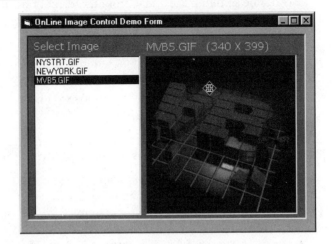

The scrolling starts in the MouseDown event of the PictureBox control, shown in Code 11.24.

Code 11.24	The MouseDown Event of the PictureBox Control

```
Private Sub Picture1_MouseDown(Button As Integer, Shift As Integer, _
    X As Single, Y As Single)
    If Button = vbLeftButton And ScrollImage Then
        Screen.MousePointer = 5
        ScrollNow = True
        XStart = X - OldXStart
        YStart = Y - OldYStart
    End If
End Sub
```

The MouseDown event stores the coordinates of the location at which the mouse was clicked for the first time in the variables *XStart* and *YStart*. The variables *OldXStart* and *OldYStart* are the coordinates of the location at which the mouse was released the last time. It is necessary to subtract these values so that the image won't jump back to its initial position as the user releases the mouse, moves it to another location, and starts sliding the image again.

To see the effect that these two variables have on the movement of the image, comment them out temporarily. The image will jump back to its initial position every time the user starts dragging it. The correct behavior of the program is to continue scrolling the image from its current position. We also change the pointer's shape to a cross-arrow to indicate that the image can be scrolled in all four directions.

In the MouseMove event (shown in Code 11.25), we copy the appropriate portion of the Bitmap image (the downloaded image) to the PictureBox control. We also check the coordinates of the mouse to make sure that the image won't be scrolled beyond its boundaries.

Code 11.25   The MouseMove Event of the PictureBox Control

```
Private Sub Picture1_MouseMove(Button As Integer, Shift As Integer, _
        X As Single, Y As Single)
Dim X1 As Integer, Y1 As Integer

    If Button = vbLeftButton And ScrollNow Then
        X1 = XStart - X
        Y1 = YStart - Y
        If X1 < 0 Then X1 = 0: XStart = X
        If Y1 < 0 Then Y1 = 0: YStart = Y
        If X1 > ScaleX(Bitmap.Width, vbHimetric, vbPixels) - _
            Picture1.ScaleWidth Then _
             X1 = ScaleX(Bitmap.Width, vbHimetric, vbPixels) - _
            Picture1.ScaleWidth
        If Y1 > ScaleY(Bitmap.Height, vbHimetric, vbPixels) - _
            Picture1.ScaleHeight Then _
             Y1 = ScaleY(Bitmap.Height, vbHimetric, vbPixels) - _
            Picture1.ScaleHeight
            Picture1.PaintPicture Bitmap, 0, 0, _
            Picture1.ScaleWidth, Picture1.ScaleHeight, _
            X1, Y1, Picture1.ScaleWidth, Picture1.ScaleHeight
    End If

End Sub
```

Finally, in the MouseUp event we reset the *ScrollNow* variable to False, set the pointer back to its normal shape, and set the variables *OldXStart* and *OldYStart* so that they can be used again by the MouseDown event if the user continues scrolling the image. These actions are implemented in the MouseUp event handler, shown in Code 11.26.

Code 11.26	The MouseUp Event of the PictureBox Control

```
Private Sub Picture1_MouseUp(Button As Integer, Shift As Integer, _
        X As Single, Y As Single)
    Screen.MousePointer = vbDefault
    ScrollNow = False
    OldXStart = (X - XStart)
    OldYStart = (Y - YStart)
End Sub
```

The three mouse events track the movement of the mouse and respond by sliding the image around in the PictureBox (if the image is larger than its container). The code is similar to the code we used in the LensFX control.

Interconnected Controls

In some situations, one control isn't enough. Some interfaces use multiple, interconnected controls. Visual Basic's file system controls are typical. To build a custom file selection Form, you must place all three controls (DriveListBox, DirectoryListBox, and FileListBox) on the Form. These controls are not connected by default, but they are designed so that you can connect them with a few statements. These controls have been replaced for the most part by the Common Dialogs controls, but let's look at a simple example. Figure 11.19 shows a typical Form that combines these three File System controls.

FIGURE 11.19:

A typical Form that combines
the three File System controls

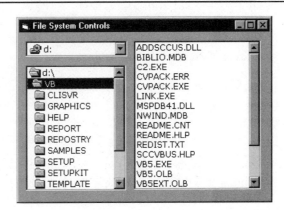

The controls on this Form are connected with the following simple statements:

```
Private Sub Dir1_Change()
    File1.Path = Dir1.Path
End Sub

Private Sub Drive1_Change()
    Dir1.Path = Drive1.Drive
End Sub
```

When the user selects a new drive in the DriveListBox control, the Directory-ListBox control is updated to display the current folder in the new drive. When the user selects a new folder in the DirectoryListBox control, the FileListBox control is updated to display the files in the selected folder. Put these three controls together on a UserControl object along with a few lines of code and you have an ActiveX control for navigating the local disk(s). The FileOpen common dialog box offers much more flexibility, but some situations call for custom dialog boxes. The point we want to make here is that the File System controls are designed to work with one another on a Form; all you have to do is add the code that connects them. All the functionality you need is built into the controls themselves.

> **NOTE**
>
> The File System Controls are not officially labeled interconnected, and you won't find the term *interconnected controls* in Microsoft's documentation (at least, we haven't run into it yet). We're using it here to describe a group of controls that can be tied to one another with a few simple statements. Once connected, they practically work on their own, and they are adequate for building an elaborate user interface.

In this section, we are going to convert the DBClass class we developed in Chapter 10 into a group of ActiveX controls that will not only retrieve records from the NWIND database, but will also display them in Grid controls. Figure 11.20 shows the three interconnected controls:

- CustomersControl

- InvoicesControl

- DetailsControl

The statements between them connect them. What you don't see in Figure 11.20 are the events that contain these lines. As you have probably guessed, these events indicate that a new selection was made in the corresponding control.

NOTE   The three interconnected controls were developed in a common project, which you will find in the DBControls folder on the CD.

FIGURE 11.20:

The three interconnected controls and the statements that connect them

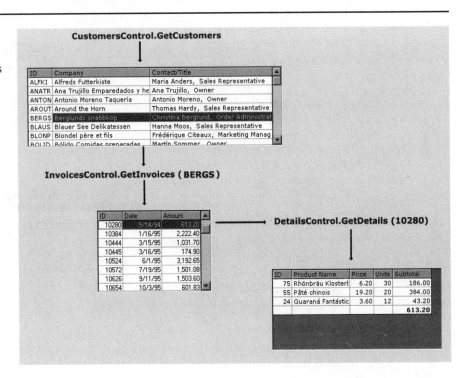

Let's start with the test project to see how the interconnected controls interact on a Form. Figure 11.21 contains the three controls.

On the top is the CustomersControl control, which displays the customer names. When the Form is first loaded, the following code is executed:

```
Private Sub Form_Load()
    Me.Show
    DoEvents
    Me.Caption = "Opening NWIND database..."
    Me.MousePointer = vbHourglass
    CustomersControl.SetDatabase "c:\program files\Micosoft Visual _
        Studio\vb98"
```

FIGURE 11.21:

The CustTest test project for the DBControls ActiveX controls

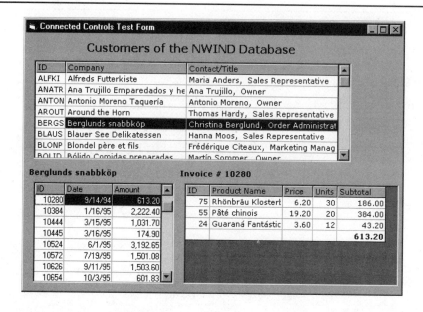

```
        Me.Caption = "Loading Customers Table..."
        CustomersControl.GetCustomers
        Me.MousePointer = vbDefault
        Me.Caption = "Connected Controls Test Form"
    End Sub
```

As you can see, most of this code deals with the shape of the pointer and setting the Form's Caption to reflect the current operation. The two lines of interest here are:

```
CustomersControl.SetDatabase "c:\program files\Micosoft Visual _
    Studio\vb98"
```

```
CustomersControl.GetCustomers
```

The first line opens the NWIND database; it calls the CustomersControl's Set-Database method with the path of the database. The name of the database isn't specified, because all three interconnected controls operate on the same database (which is the NWIND sample database). Well, this may raise some eyebrows, but wait. The interconnected controls might apply to a single database, but they are quite flexible. As you will soon see, they can be used in many projects that manipulate this database.

NOTE
Not all ActiveX controls you will develop will be distributed in the millions. If you work as part of a programming team for a corporation, you will save yourself and your team many hours of work by providing a few controls that address common programming tasks. How many report or invoice-entry screens are designed in a corporation? Every programmer who needs to display customers or invoices could use your controls.

The second line populates the CustomersControl by calling the control's Get-Customers method. This method doesn't have to specify any arguments; the control knows how to populate the Grid.

To display the invoices issued to a customer, the user must click a customer's name. The CustomersControl issues the CustomerSelected event every time the user clicks a customer's name. When the CustomerSelected event is fired, the code in Code 11.27 is executed.

Code 11.27   The Event Handler of the CustomersControl

```
Private Sub CustomersControl_CustomerSelected(customerID As String)
    Me.MousePointer = vbHourglass
    InvoicesControl.ClearGrid
    DetailsControl.ClearGrid
    Label2.Caption = ""
    InvoicesControl.GetInvoices (customerID)
    Label1.Caption = CustomersControl.CompanyName
    Me.MousePointer = vbDefault
End Sub
```

Again, most of this code sets up the appearance of the Form. It changes the shape of the pointer while the invoices are read from the database, it displays the name of the selected customer in a Label on top of the second of the InvoicesControl, and so on. Only one line of code is needed to connect the CustomersControl to the InvoicesControl:

```
InvoicesControl.GetInvoices (customerID)
```

This line calls the InvoicesControl's GetInvoices method, which retrieves the invoices issued to a single customer. The selected customer's ID is passed as an argument and used by the GetInvoices method, which not only retrieves the records, but displays them on the Grid as well. It also calculates the total and displays it after the last invoice.

You've probably guessed what happens when the user clicks an invoice. The program calls another method that displays the lines of the invoice in the DetailsControl. The InvoiceSelected event's handler is shown in Code 11.28.

Code 11.28	The InvoiceSelected Event Handler of the InvoicesControl

```
Private Sub InvoicesControl_InvoiceSelected(InvoiceID As Long)
    Me.MousePointer = vbHourglass
    DetailsControl.ClearGrid
    Label2.Caption = "Invoice # " & InvoiceID
    DetailsControl.GetDetails (InvoiceID)
    Me.MousePointer = vbDefault
End Sub
```

The InvoiceSelected event reports to the host application the ID of the selected invoice, which is later used by the GetDetails method of the DetailsControl to retrieve and display the lines of the selected invoice. Again, a single line of code connects the InvoicesControl to the DetailsControl.

Almost all the work is done by the interconnected controls. All you have to do is detect certain events that let you know that the user has made a new selection and call the method that updates another control. The developer can use the three interconnected controls to set up an elaborate report screen in no time. With some additional effort, you can allow editing of the records. This example isn't suited for editing operations, because invoices shouldn't be edited after the fact; you must void an invoice and issue another one. But all the work will take place in the control, and developers don't need to add a single line of code (short of setting a property that allows a control's contents to be edited).

You may think that the interconnected controls are good enough for a single operation, namely displaying the Form shown in Figure 11.22. Why not package the entire Form as an ActiveX control? Because the interconnected controls can be used in other projects, too, on their own. The InvoicesControl has a GetInvoices-ByDate method that retrieves the invoices issued on a single date. Figure 11.23 shows a second test Form for the same controls. It's called DateTest. This test project uses a date as its starting point and doesn't use the CustomersControl at all.

NOTE	You'll find the DateTest Form in the DBControls folder on the CD that comes with this book. To display this Form, set it as the project's Startup object.

FIGURE 11.22:

The second test Form for the interconnected controls retrieves invoices by date.

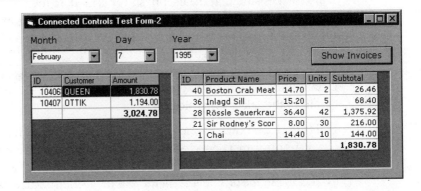

The DateTest Form contains three ComboBox controls, in which the user can specify a date. You could probably use a more elaborate Calendar control in their place, but we're avoiding using controls that may not exist on every system. The Form's Load event handler sets up the ComboBox control and the appearance of the Form. The following line relates to the interconnected controls:

```
InvoicesControl.SetDatabase "c:\program files\Micosoft Visual _
            Studio\vb98"
```

This line opens the NWIND database. Clicking the Command Button executes the following lines:

```
Private Sub Command1_Click()
Dim thisDate As String
    InvoicesControl.ClearGrid
    DetailsControl.ClearGrid
    Me.MousePointer = vbHourglass
    thisDate = MonthBox.Text & "/" & DayBox.Text & "/" & YearBox.Text
    If IsDate(thisDate) Then
        InvoicesControl.GetInvoicesByDate (thisDate)
    Else
        MsgBox "Invalid date selected"
    End If
    Me.MousePointer = vbDefault
End Sub
```

The code clears the two controls and then populates the InvoicesControl with this line:

```
InvoicesControl.GetInvoicesByDate (thisDate)
```

It also makes sure that the user hasn't specified an invalid date with the IsDate() function. The GetInvoicesByDate method accepts an argument, which is a date. It retrieves the invoices issued on the specific date and populates the control. When an invoice is selected in the InvoicesControl, the InvoiceSelected event is triggered. This event's code is the same as that in the CustTest project. It calls the GetDetails method of the DetailsControl to populate the second control with the details of the selected invoice.

Figure 11.23 shows a simplified diagram of how the InvoicesControl and DetailsControl are connected. To populate the InvoicesControl, we call the GetInvoicesByDate method of the Invoices control. When the user selects an invoice by clicking it, the GetDetails method of the DetailsControl is called, which populates the Details control with the lines of the selected invoice.

FIGURE 11.23:

These statements connect the InvoicesControl and Details-Control ActiveX controls when viewing invoices by date.

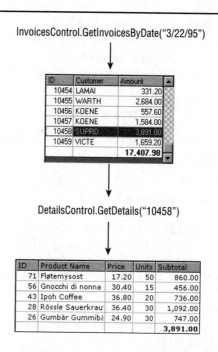

InvoicesControl.GetInvoicesByDate("3/22/95")

ID	Customer	Amount
10454	LAMAI	331.20
10455	WARTH	2,684.00
10456	KOENE	557.60
10457	KOENE	1,584.00
10458	SUPRD	3,891.00
10459	VICTE	1,659.20
		17,407.98

DetailsControl.GetDetails("10458")

ID	Product Name	Price	Units	Subtotal
71	Fløtemysost	17.20	50	860.00
56	Gnocchi di nonna	30.40	15	456.00
43	Ipoh Coffee	36.80	20	736.00
28	Rössle Sauerkrau	36.40	30	1,092.00
26	Gumbär Gummibä	24.90	30	747.00
				3,891.00

As you can see, the three interconnected controls do all the work for retrieving and displaying customer data, invoices, and invoice details. The developer simply drops them on the Form, enters a few lines of code to connect them, and the controls do their work.

TIP   Although these controls operate on a single database, you can use them in many projects. This will reduce development time in a team environment, and it will also ensure a consistent user interface among multiple applications.

Coding the DBControls Project

Now we can look at the code of the DBControls project. The first peculiarity of this project is that it implements three controls in a single project. The project has three UserControl objects in its User Controls folder, and the OCX file it produces will have three controls in it. When you add the ConnectedControls ActiveX control to a project, you will see three new icons in the Toolbox. Although the appearance of the three icons is the same, each has a different name. The icon names are displayed in a ToolTip box when the pointer rests over them, as shown in Figure 11.24.

FIGURE 11.24:

The ConnectedControl component will place three different controls in your Toolbox.

NOTE   You should design a different icon for each control, but it's difficult to create icons that are similar yet different enough to convey information about the controls they represent.

The DBControls project is fairly lengthy, so we are going to concentrate on the core of the code. For this project, we didn't use the ActiveX Interface Wizard. Sometimes it's faster to start typing than to go through the steps of the Wizard to define a few methods. And as you will see, these three controls have the same structure and few properties.

To implement the DBControls custom controls, start a new ActiveX project, and add two more UserControl objects to the project. Name the three UserControl objects as follows:

CustomersControl: which displays customer data

InvoicesControl: which displays invoices

DetailsControl: which displays an invoice's lines

In addition to the three UserControl objects, the DBControls project has a Module. Add a new Module, name it DatabaseModule, and enter the following declaration in it:

```
Public DB As Database
```

The *DB* variable is set to the NWIND database when it's opened with the OpenDatabase method.

Let's examine the structure of the CustomersControl. The control uses a single variable and raises an event. Their declarations are:

```
Event CustomerSelected(CustomerID As String)
Dim CustomersRS As Recordset
```

The CustomersRS argument is a Recordset in which the selected records will be stored. The records are selected with a SQL statement in the GetCustomers method (shown in Code 11.29).

Code 11.29   The GetCustomers Method

```
Public Sub GetCustomers()
Dim SQLString As String
Dim row As Integer
    SQLString = "SELECT CustomerID, CompanyName, ContactName, _
        ContactTitle FROM CUSTOMERS"
    Set CustomersRS = DB.OpenRecordset(SQLString, dbOpenSnapshot)
    CustomersRS.MoveLast
    Customers.Rows = CustomersRS.RecordCount + 1
    CustomersRS.MoveFirst
    row = 1
    While Not CustomersRS.EOF
        Customers.TextMatrix(row, 0) = CustomersRS.Fields("CustomerID")
        Customers.TextMatrix(row, 1) = _
            CustomersRS.Fields("CompanyName")
        Customers.TextMatrix(row, 2) = _
            CustomersRS.Fields("ContactName")& _
            ",  " & CustomersRS.Fields("ContactTitle")
        row = row + 1
        CustomersRS.MoveNext
    Wend
End Sub
```

This code builds the CustomersRS Recordset and then places each record in a new row of the Customers MSFlexGrid control. You could replace the MSFlexGrid control with a data-bound Grid control, which would simplify the code considerably, but we want to show how to populate non–data-bound controls with records. In addition, the MSFlexGrid control offers additional features, such as the display of totals after the last row of data, automatic calculations based on the values of the fields, flexibility to color rows and columns and set fonts, and so on. The other two interconnected controls of the DBControls project are also based on the MSFlexGrid control.

The CustomersControl provides a few properties, too, which are the values of the fields of the selected row. These properties are implemented with the Property Get procedures in Code 11.30 (they are read-only properties and don't have matching Property Let procedures).

Code 11.30   **Field Values As Properties**

```
Public Property Get CustomerID() As String
On Error GoTo CustIDError
    CustomerID = Customers.TextMatrix(Customers.RowSel, 0)
    Exit Property
CustIDError:
    CustomerID = ""
End Property

Public Property Get CompanyName() As String
On Error GoTo CompanyError
    CompanyName = Customers.TextMatrix(Customers.RowSel, 1)
    Exit Property
CompanyError:
    CompanyName = ""
End Property

Public Property Get ContactName() As String
On Error GoTo ContactError
    ContactName = Left(Customers.TextMatrix(Customers.RowSel, 2), _
        InStr(Customers.TextMatrix(Customers.RowSel, 2), ","))
    Exit Property
ContactError:
    ContactName = ""
End Property
```

The values of the fields are read from the Grid control, not from the Recordset itself. There is no simple way to go from the selected row of the Grid control to the corresponding Recordset row.

The CustomerSelected event is raised when the user clicks a row of the Grid control. The code highlights the selected row (in blue) and then retrieves the CustomerID field of the selected row. If this key field is not empty, the RaiseEvent is raised to notify the host application that a new selection was made. The implementation of the Customers control's Click event can be seen in Code 11.31.

Code 11.31   The Click Event of the Customers Control

```
Private Sub Customers_Click()
Dim custID As String * 5
    Customers.Col = 0: Customers.ColSel = 2
    custID = Customers.TextMatrix(Customers.RowSel, 0)
    If custID <> "" Then
        RaiseEvent CustomerSelected(custID)
    End If
End Sub
```

Similarly, the InvoicesControl has a GetInvoices method, which accepts as an argument a customer's ID and retrieves the invoices issued to that customer. The subroutine that implements the GetInvoices method (shown in Code 11.32) builds the appropriate SQL statement and then uses it with the OpenRecordset method on the *DB* object variable to retrieve the invoices.

Code 11.32   The GetInvoices Method

```
Public Sub GetInvoices(custID As String)
Dim SQLString As String
Dim row As Integer
Dim totAmount As Currency

On Error GoTo InvoicesError

    SQLString = "SELECT DISTINCTROW [Order Subtotals].Subtotal AS _
        SaleAmount, Orders.OrderID,"
    SQLString = SQLString & " Customers.CompanyName, Orders.ShippedDate, _
        Orders.OrderDate"
    SQLString = SQLString & " FROM Customers INNER JOIN (Orders INNER _
        JOIN [Order Subtotals] ON Orders.OrderID = [Order _
        Subtotals].OrderID)"
    SQLString = SQLString & " ON Customers.CustomerID = Orders.CustomerID"
```

```
    SQLString = SQLString & " WHERE Orders.CustomerID=" _
        & Chr(34) & custID & Chr(34)
    Set InvoicesRS = DB.OpenRecordset(SQLString, dbOpenSnapshot)
    InvoicesRS.MoveLast
    Invoices.Rows = 1
    Invoices.Rows = InvoicesRS.RecordCount + 2
    InvoicesRS.MoveFirst
    row = 1
    totAmount = 0
    While Not InvoicesRS.EOF
        If Not IsNull(InvoicesRS.Fields("OrderID")) Then _
            Invoices.TextMatrix(row, 0) = InvoicesRS.Fields("OrderID")
        If Not IsNull(InvoicesRS.Fields("OrderDate")) Then _
            Invoices.TextMatrix(row, 1) = InvoicesRS.Fields("OrderDate")
        If Not IsNull(InvoicesRS.Fields("SaleAmount")) Then _
            Invoices.TextMatrix(row, 2) = _
            Format(InvoicesRS.Fields("SaleAmount"), "#,###.00")
        totAmount = totAmount + InvoicesRS.Fields("SaleAmount")
        row = row + 1
        InvoicesRS.MoveNext
    Wend
    Invoices.TextMatrix(Invoices.Rows - 1, 2) = _
        Format(totAmount, "#,###.00")
    Invoices.row = Invoices.Rows - 1: Invoices.Col = 2
    Invoices.CellFontBold = True
    Exit Sub

InvoicesError:
    If Err.Number = 3021 Then
        Exit Sub
    Else
        Err.Raise Error.Number, "GetInvoices", Err.Description
    End If
End Sub
```

In addition to the GetInvoices method, the control provides another method, GetInvoicesByDate, which accepts a date as an argument and returns the invoices issued on that date (regardless of customer). The GetInvoicesByDate method is identical to the GetInvoices method, except for the SQL statement. Here are the lines that build the SQL statement that retrieves invoices by date:

```
SQLString = "SELECT DISTINCTROW [Order Subtotals].Subtotal AS SaleAmount, _
        Orders.OrderID, Customers.CustomerID,"
```

```
SQLString = SQLString & " Customers.CompanyName, Orders.ShippedDate, _
        Orders.OrderDate"
SQLString = SQLString & " FROM Customers INNER JOIN (Orders INNER JOIN _
        [Order Subtotals] ON Orders.OrderID = [Order Subtotals].OrderID)"
SQLString = SQLString & " ON Customers.CustomerID = Orders.CustomerID"
SQLString = SQLString & " WHERE Orders.OrderDate=#" & invDate & "#"
```

In the previous lines, invDate is the date passed to the method as an argument. Although the two subroutines fill the grid's rows, they keep track of the sum of the invoice totals, which they display after the last row.

Similar to the CustomersControls, the InvoicesControl provides a number of properties that return the values of the fields in the selected row. We need not repeat these Property Procedures here; you can open the project and examine the code. The event that signals the selection of an invoice on the InvoicesGrid is called InvoiceSelected and is raised from within the Click event of the Invoices control (shown in Code 11.33).

Code 11.33   **The Click Event of the Invoices Control**

```
Private Sub Invoices_Click()
Dim InvID As Long
    Invoices.Col = 0: Invoices.ColSel = 2
    If Invoices.TextMatrix(Invoices.RowSel, 0) <> "" Then
        InvID = Invoices.TextMatrix(Invoices.RowSel, 0)
        RaiseEvent InvoiceSelected(InvID)
    End If
End Sub
```

This code is quite similar to the code of the Click event of the Customers control.

The third of the interconnected controls, DetailsControl, is implemented along the same lines. It uses a SQL statement (that incorporates the invoice's ID) that retrieves and then displays the lines of the specified invoice. It also provides a number of properties that return the values of the fields on the selected row on the grid, but it doesn't raise any event to signify the selection of an invoice line.

TIP   If you design similar controls frequently, you might want to consider developing a code generator. The controls contain similar statements (only the names of the fields change), which makes them ideal targets for a code generator.

It's been a lengthy project, but we hope to have demonstrated a useful technique for designing ActiveX controls that encapsulate complicated operations. You can incorporate the three interconnected ActiveX controls in many projects that use the NWIND database. If you are working as a programmer in a corporate environment, you know very well how much code is duplicated in designing Forms to display customers, invoices, and invoice lines. With some additional effort, you can adjust these controls to allow editing of their contents as well.

Another benefit of this approach is that the developer doesn't need to know how to build SQL statements or how to manipulate Recordsets. The most important aspect of the three controls is that you can change their implementation without worrying about breaking the application's code. As long as the new implementation provides the same interface members, the applications that use it will work. For example, you could redesign these controls around the Remote Data Object to access the NWIND database on a remote server, or even over the Internet.

CHAPTER
TWELVE

Building Data-Bound ActiveX Controls

- Data Binding properties

- Building data-bound controls

- Building data sources

- The DataRepeater control

Another interesting category of ActiveX controls is those that are bound to data sources. Visual Basic's built-in controls support a few properties that allow the developer to bind them to a Data control (or the ADO Data control) and access a specific field in the database. It is actually possible to design simple database applications with the data-bound controls and a Data control without any code (or very few lines of code). Creating custom data-bound controls is quite simple, but the basic data-bound controls you need to build typical applications already come with the language. To create a useful custom data-bound control, you must add functionality that's not available with the standard data-bound controls. In the examples in this chapter, you will see how to build data-bound controls and how to add extra functionality to accommodate the needs of your application.

Besides simple data-bound controls, which can be connected to a field through a data source, you can also build data sources. A data source is a control like the Data control, or the ADO Data control, which is used to connect simple data-bound controls to the fields of a recordset. Again, the data controls that come with Visual Basic are adequate for accessing most databases you may run into, but you can build your own data controls to perform operations that are specific to your applications.

In the last section of this chapter, you will learn how to use a peculiar, yet quite useful, control: the DataRepeater control. The DataRepeater control's peculiarity is that it can be used with custom data-bound controls only. This control acts like a container and can be populated with many instances of the same control. You can use it to build, with very little programming effort, complex data-bound controls that behave like the DataGrid control.

Basic Data Binding Properties

Data-bound controls come in two distinct flavors: those that are bound to fields and those that act as data sources for other controls. The UserControl object provides two properties that determine the behavior of a data-bound control:

> **DataBindingBehavior:**   This property determines whether the custom control will be data-bound or not. Its possible values are listed in Table 12.1.

TABLE 12.1: The Values of the DataBindingBehavior Property

Property Value	Description
vbNone	The control is not data-bound.
vbSimpleBound	The control is a simple data-bound control, like the TextBox control.
vbComplexBound	The control is a complex data-bound control, like the DataGrid control.

DataSourceBehavior: This property determines whether the custom control will be a data source for data-bound controls on the same Form. Its possible values are shown in Table 12.2.

TABLE 12.2: The Values of the DataSourceBehavior Property

Property Name	Description
vbNone	The control is not a data source.
vbDataSource	The control is a data source.

Designing custom controls to act as data sources is fairly complicated. Visual Basic can't automate this process; you must implement all the methods and properties of the control yourself. You'll see an example of a custom data source control in the section "Building Data Sources" later in this chapter. First, we are going to discuss the process of building data-bound controls and look at a couple of examples.

Building Data-Bound Controls

Let's start with the process of building a simple data-bound control. Any control that exposes a property that can be bound to a field can become data-bound. In other words, any control that can display text, numbers, dates, or any other information that can be bound to a field can be easily converted to data-bound. Of course, there must be a data source control (like the Data control) on the same Form, which will connect the data-bound control to the database. Visual Basic will automatically add the DataSource and DataField properties to the custom control, and the developer will be able to bind the control to a specific field of the data source by setting these two properties without writing a single line of code. At run time, Visual Basic will update the control's data property according to the field's value in the current record. If the user changes the data value of the control, the new value will be written to the database when the data source is repositioned to another record (unless the recordset's type prevents updating the database).

To make an ordinary custom control data-bound, you must first create a custom property that will hold the data-bound value. This property is usually mapped to a constituent control's property, like a TextBox control's Text property. Open the Procedure Attributes dialog box, select the property you want to bind to a data source, and then click the Advanced button to see all the attributes of the selected property, as shown in Figure 12.1. The Procedure Attributes dialog box of Figure 12.1 corresponds to the ControlText property of the Demo control we developed in the previous chapter.

FIGURE 12.1:

The Procedure Attributes dialog box of the Demo control's ControlText property

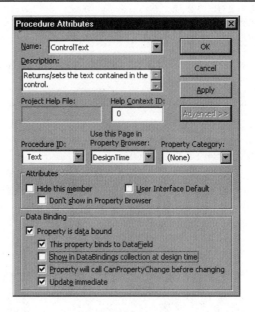

On the Procedure Attributes dialog box, check the option Property Is Data-Bound. As soon as this option is checked, a number of options in the lower section of the dialog box will be enabled:

> **This Property Binds to DataField**   This option tells Visual Basic that the property will be mapped to a field in the current record (the current record is determined by the Data control). If this checkbox is cleared, the control isn't data-bound.

Show in DataBindings Collection at Design Time   If you check this option, the selected property will be added to the DataBindings collection and the developer will be allowed to edit the data binding property at design time. A typical data-bound control provides a single property that's bound to a field through the DataField property. Some controls can expose multiple data-bound properties, but only one of them can be assigned to the DataField property. The other data-bound properties must be set to other fields through the DataBindings property of the control at design time.

Property Will Call CanPropertyChange Before Changing   Check this option if you want the control to call the method CanPropertyChange before it attempts to change the value of the field. The method CanPropertyChange must be implemented in the UserControl object, and it returns a True/False value. This method gives your control a chance to prevent the update of the data-bound field. Use this property to perform data validation from within your control. The developer can also program the control's Validate event to prevent the update of the data-bound field. Notice that you don't have to raise a Validate event from within your control; this event will be raised automatically by the container.

Update Immediate   Check this option if you want the custom control to update field values in the database as soon as their values are changed (provided that the type of recordset allows the update of the database).

The design of a data-bound control is straightforward and you don't have to add any code on your own. Simply select the property that will be bound to a record field, set a few attributes through the Procedure Attributes dialog box, and Visual Basic will do the rest. Let's look at a simple example.

VB6 at Work: The Data-Bound Demo Control

In this section, we are going to convert the Demo control we developed in the previous chapter to a data-bound control. The new control is called DBDemo, and you will find it in this chapter's folder on the CD. All you have to do in order to add data binding capabilities to the Demo control is to make the CaptionText property of the Demo control data-bound. Open the Demo project we developed in the previous chapter, "Building ActiveX Controls," and follow these steps:

1.   Select the UserControl object and set its DataBindingBehavior property to vbBoundSimple.

2. Open the UserControl object's Code window and from the Tools menu select Procedure Attributes.

3. In the Procedure Attributes dialog box, select the ControlText property, click the Advanced button to see all the attributes, and check the box Property Is Data-Bound.

4. The four options at the bottom of the dialog box (discussed in the last section) will be enabled. Check them all. You don't have to check all options pertaining to data binding for every data-bound control, but do so for this example.

5. Click OK to close the Procedure Attributes dialog box.

You have just added data binding capabilities to your new custom control. You didn't do much, but Visual Basic has all the information it needs in order to bind the ControlText property of the Demo control to a database field through a data source control. To test the new data-bound control, switch to the project's test Form and select the custom control (or place a new instance of it on a test Form, if you haven't opened the DBDemo project). Visual Basic has added the following properties to the Properties window: DataSource, DataField, DataBindings, DataMember, and DataFormat. These properties can't be set unless there's a data source control on the Form.

To test the new control, add a Data control on the test form and then set its DataBaseName property to the NWIND database and its RecordSource property to the Customers table. Also set the RecordsetType property to 0 (Table). You can use the ADO Data control as well, if you wish. In the examples in the coming sections, you are going to see how the ADO Data control is used in conjunction with a custom, data-bound control.

Next, select the custom control and set its DataSource property to Data1 (the name of the Data control) and its DataField property to CompanyName. The ControlText property will display the company name in the current record. As you reposition yourself in the recordset with the Data control, the control's ControlText property will change value.

Adjust the captions on the control to reflect the new function of the control. Set the OpaqueCaption property to Customers and the TransparentCaption property to NWIND Database, as shown in Figure 12.2.

FIGURE 12.2:

Binding the ControlCaption property of the Demo control to a database field

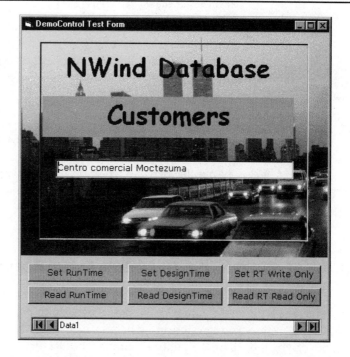

Updating the Database

Press F5 to run the project. As you navigate through the Customers table, the current company's name is displayed on the custom control. If you change a company name, however, the changes won't be posted to the database. Change a company name, move to the next record and then back to the previous record. You'll see that the changes you made are lost. If you examine the settings of the Data1 control again, you'll see that there's nothing that would normally prevent the updating of the field. So, what's keeping our custom control from writing its new value to the database?

Visual Basic doesn't request the value of the data-bound control before it moves to the next record, and that's why it doesn't update the database. It thinks that the ControlText property hasn't changed. Considering that we never call the control's PropertyChanged method when the ControlText property changes value, it's not an unreasonable assumption. If you insert the following line in the Text1 control's Change event, Visual Basic will write the new value of the control to the database, overwriting the existing value:

```
Private Sub Text1_Change()
    If CanPropertyChange("ControlText") Then
```

```
        PropertyChanged "ControlText"
    End If
End Sub
```

As you recall, we require that our control call the method CanPropertyChange before attempting to change a field value (this is a setting we specified in the Procedure Attributes dialog box).

NOTE　　Currently, the CanPropertyChange method returns always True, so you need not call it at all. The statement that enables the data-bound control to update the database is the one that calls the PropertyChanged method. This method tells the control that a data-bound property has changed value, and it must save the new value to the database.

VB6 at Work: The DateBox Data-Bound Control

It's rather unlikely that you'll ever develop simple data-bound controls that merely display a field's value; Visual Basic comes with built-in data-bound controls for all the values you can store in a database. A custom data-bound control should do something more than the built-in controls. The DateBox control is such an example. The DateBox control can display dates in long format. If the field's value is 03/19/1998, the DateBox control will display it as "Thursday, March 19, 1998." Figure 12.3 shows the DateBox control displaying an invoice date. Of course, you can use the DataFormat property of a data-bound control for the same purpose, but we've added a little more functionality to this control. If you click the Set button on the control, the TextBox where the dates appear is replaced by three ComboBoxes that allow the user to set a new date (see Figure 12.4). To commit the changes, the user must click the OK button. This action restores the original long format for dates of the TextBox control.

FIGURE 12.3:

Using the DateBox control to display dates in long format

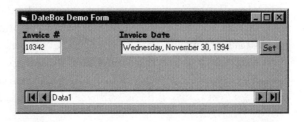

FIGURE 12.4:

Using the DateBox control
to set dates

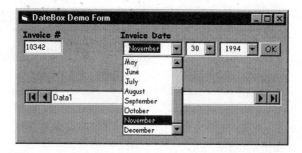

As you can see, the DateBox control operates in two distinct modes. When displaying dates, it uses the long format. To change a date, click the Set button. This action will hide the TextBox and display three ComboBox controls, where you can select a day, a month, and a year. After setting a new date value, click the OK button to return to the display mode. While the control is in selection mode, any changes you make are not committed to the database. Only after the OK button is clicked will the changes affect the database. If you move to another record, the old record's date will remain unchanged and the new record's date will be displayed on the three ComboBox controls.

The DateBox control demonstrates the design of custom data-bound controls with added functionality. Let's start with the design of the control's visible interface. Figure 12.5 shows the DateBox control at design time. The three ComboBox controls at the bottom are hidden, and the control's height is slightly larger than the height of the TextBox control. When the Set button is clicked, the ComboBoxes become visible and the TextBox control becomes invisible. When the OK button is clicked, the ComboBox controls are hidden again and the TextBox becomes visible. Arranging the controls on the UserControl object is the first item to consider. Here's the UserControl object's Resize event:

```
Private Sub UserControl_Resize()
    UserControl.Width = Text1.Width + Command1.Width + 60
    Text1.Left = 15
    Command1.Left = Text1.Left + Text1.Width + 30
    UserControl.Height = Text1.Height + 30
End Sub
```

The numeric values are twips; this code will work on monitors with 15 twips per pixel. To make the code work with different resolutions, replace these values with Screen.TwipsPerPixelX. The value 60, for example, should be 4 * Screen.TwipsPerPixelX.

FIGURE 12.5:

The DateBox custom control at design time

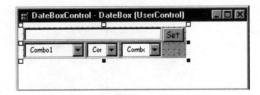

When the control is initialized, the ComboBoxes are populated with the following statements:

Code 12.1   **Populating the ComboBox Controls**

```
Private Sub UserControl_Initialize()
    For i = 1 To 12
        Combo1.AddItem MonthName(i)
    Next
    Combo1.ListIndex = Month(Date)
    For i = 1 To 31
        Combo2.AddItem i
    Next
    For i = 1990 To 2010
        Combo3.AddItem i
    Next
    Combo1.Visible = False
    Combo2.Visible = False
    Combo3.Visible = False
End Sub
```

Consider for a moment what happens when the data source is repositioned to another record. The current value of the TextBox control should be saved to the database and a new value must be displayed on the control. The new date value (the one read from the database) must be assigned to the Text property of the control. Instead of assigning the new value directly to the Text property of the TextBox control, we first format it with the FormatDateTime() function. At the same time, we must save this value to a private variable, *DDate* (you'll see shortly how this variable is used). These actions must take place from within the Text property's Let procedure.

Code 12.2	**Displaying a New Date**

```
Public Property Let Text(ByVal New_Text As String)
    Text1.Text = FormatDateTime(New_Text, vbLongDate)
    DDate = New_Text
    Combo1.ListIndex = Month(DDate) - 1
    Combo2.ListIndex = Day(DDate) - 1
    Combo3.ListIndex = Year(DDate) - 1990
    PropertyChanged "Text"
End Property
```

If the user clicks the Set button, the three ComboBoxes must replace the TextBox on the control's surface. Their values must also be set to the date displayed in the TextBox control. Because Visual Basic doesn't recognize long date formats as dates, we'll use the *DDate* variable. If the button is clicked again (when its Caption is OK), we must extract the date from the three ComboBoxes, make sure it's a valid date, and display it in long format on the TextBox control. The new date must be assigned to the *DDate* private variable, in case the user decides to change it again. The three ComboBoxes must be replaced by the TextBox control, and, finally, we must call the PropertyChanged method for the Text property. This will ensure that the new value will be saved to the database. The Command button's Click event is shown next:

Code 12.3	**Reading a New Date**

```
Private Sub Command1_Click()
    If Command1.Caption = "Set" Then
        Text1.Visible = False
        Combo1.Top = Text1.Top
        Combo2.Top = Text1.Top
        Combo3.Top = Text1.Top
        Combo1.ListIndex = Month(DDate) - 1
        Combo2.ListIndex = Day(DDate) - 1
        Combo3.ListIndex = Year(DDate) - 1990
        Combo1.Visible = True
        Combo2.Visible = True
        Combo3.Visible = True
        Command1.Caption = "OK"
    Else
        newDate = Combo1.ListIndex + 1 & "/" & _
                Combo2.Text & "/" & Combo3.Text
        If Not IsDate(newDate) Then
```

```
            MsgBox "Invalid Date specified"
        Else
            Combo1.Visible = False
            Combo2.Visible = False
            Combo3.Visible = False
            Text1.Text = FormatDateTime(newDate, vbLongDate)
            Text1.Visible = True
            Command1.Caption = "Set"
            DDate = newDate
            PropertyChanged "Text"
        End If
    End If
End Sub
```

We subtract one from the month and date value, because the indexing of the ComboBox control's items starts at zero. Likewise, the third ComboBox control displays the years 1990 through 2010 only, so we must subtract the value 1990 from its actual value to retrieve the index of the selected item.

The rest of the code is quite trivial—it was actually generated by the ActiveX Control Interface Wizard. Open the DateBox project in Visual Basic's IDE and examine the code. Notice that as the Data control is repositioned in its recordset, no special event is raised. It simply reads or sets the value of the data-bound property (the Text property). In so doing, it invokes the Property Let and Property Get procedures. Use these two procedures to insert all the code you want to execute after a new value is retrieved from the database, or before a modified date value is written to the database. You can also raise custom events from within the Property Let procedure to signal that the field has changed value before committing the changes to the database.

Programming the DateBox Control

Let's take a look at the DateBox control's test Form. To test the DateBox control, place an instance of the new control on the test Form, along with a TextBox and a Data control. The Data control is connected to the Orders table of the NWIND database (the property DatabaseName must be set to the path of the NWIND database on your system and the property RecordSource to the Orders table). The other two controls on the test Form are bound to the Data1 control; they display the fields OrderID (the TextBox control) and OrderDate (the DateBox control).

The project's test Form doesn't contain a single line of code. All the action takes place through the data binding properties of the two controls. Run the test project and exercise the custom data-bound control. The TextBox constituent control on the custom control has its Locked property set to True, and you can't change the date while it's displayed in long format. You must click the Set button, set the new date with the help of the ComboBox controls, and then click the OK button to commit the changes to the database. You can also switch to the month/day/year view by clicking the Set button. The dates will be displayed in this format as you reposition yourself in the table.

The DateBox control is a simple data-bound control, which demonstrates the type of functionality you can bring to your custom ActiveX controls without any database programming. If you examine the UserControl object's code, you'll see that there's not a single line of code that accesses the database. By setting a few properties in the Procedure Attributes dialog box, you've told Visual Basic to bind one of the constituent controls to a record's field through a Data control. Each time the Data control is repositioned to another record, Visual Basic calls the Property Get procedure to read the value of the control (and save it to the database) and then it calls the Property Let procedure to assign the new field's value to the Text property. We simply programmed these two procedures to manipulate the appearance of the field's value on the control. You can add as much code as necessary to these two procedures to perform all types of actions on the values furnished by the Data control. For example, you can build data-bound controls with complex validation logic for your applications by incorporating the validation code into the control itself.

Building Data Sources

The tools for creating data-bound controls are adequate for simple controls, but if you want to create complex data-bound controls, such as lists or grids populated with data from different tables, the simple data binding techniques provided by Visual Basic are not adequate. Your custom ActiveX controls have access to all of Visual Basic's capabilities, including its data access mechanisms, and you can build data-bound controls from scratch. In addition, you can build custom ActiveX controls that act as data sources for other controls.

Although Visual Basic comes with data controls for all major databases, you may wish to design data controls with special features. These features are usually determined by the application, so the sample Data Source control in this section can't be used as-is in other applications. However, it demonstrates how to design data controls and how to add extra features.

As you can guess, designing data controls is substantially different from designing custom data-bound controls. To begin with, a custom data control doesn't have many properties that specify its appearance, and it doesn't recognize common events like keyboard events. Instead, it must fire an event when it's repositioned in the recordset, or when it's about to write the changes to the database. Likewise, it must expose methods to move the current record pointer in the recordset (methods like MoveFirst, MoveNext and so on), as well as properties that let the developer examine whether the beginning or the end of the recordset has been reached (properties like EOF and BOF). You should also include properties that let the developer determine how the control should react when it lands on an invalid record (the BOFAction and EOFAction properties of the built-in Data control). In general, you must supply the core of the control's code, because it can't be generated by the wizard.

The basic characteristic of a data source is that it must maintain a recordset. Among the first members you must implement are the Property Set and Property Get procedures for the Recordset property. Notice that this property can't be set directly. The developer should be able to specify the recordset through the properties ConnectionString and RecordSource. In other words, the developer should be able to specify the information that will be retrieved by means of record selection criteria. You must provide the code to create the actual recordset based on the settings of these two properties. We'll demonstrate the design of a data source with the DBControl project.

VB6 at Work: The DBControl Project

In this section, we are going to build an ActiveX control that acts as a data source. Sure, there are few popular databases that can't be accessed by the ADO Data control, but what if you want a peculiar data source? For example, the function of the DateBox control, converting dates to long format, can be easily moved to the data source. The DBControl is nearly identical to the ADO Data control, but it can filter its recordset. The two ComboBox controls on the DBControl let you select a field and set the filter criteria for the current recordset. The DBControl at the bottom of the Form shown in Figure 12.6 has read the Customers table of the NWIND database. At any point, the user can filter the recordset and view contacts from a specific country, or company owners only. Every time the filter is set, the first record matching the criteria is displayed. The navigational buttons move through the subset of recordset that meets the filter criteria, not the entire recordset. The filter can also be reset, in which case the entire recordset becomes active again.

FIGURE 12.6:

The DBControl is a custom data source that lets the user filter its recordset.

WARNING   The data sources you build with Visual Basic are based on the ActiveX Data Objects 2.0 Library. When you start a custom data source control, be sure to add a reference to the ADO 2.0 Library to the project.

The test Form of the DBControl project doesn't contain any code. All the action takes place through the DBControl data control, which lets the user view, filter, and update the records.

To implement a data source, you must first decide which custom members it will expose, as usual. Table 12.3 lists the basic, most essential members of a data source. You can add many more members, but these are the ones you can't do without.

TABLE 12.3: The Members of the DBControl Data Source

Member	Description
ConnectionString	This property allows the designer to specify the database to which the data source will be connected.
RecordSource	This property must be specified after the ConnectionString property has been assigned a value. The RecordSource property is the name of a table in the database specified with the ConnectionString property, a stored procedure, or a SQL statement that acts on the records of the same database.
MoveFirst, MoveLast, MovePrevious, MoveNext	These are the common navigational methods of a data source. The same actions can be invoked by clicking the buttons of the control itself.
Recordset	This property identifies the recordset that is "seen" by the data source.
Repositioned	This event is fired every time the control is repositioned in the recordset.

First, you must design the control's visible interface. In most cases, a control that acts as a data source has a visible interface, which resembles a scrollbar. At the two ends there are buttons, which take the user to the first, previous, next, and last record, respectively. The visible interface consists of a long PictureBox control (or Label control) with two Command buttons at each of its two ends. The Command buttons must be programmed to react to the Click event by moving to another record in the recordset. The same actions should also be performed with navigational methods.

The control can have any appearance; it doesn't have to resemble the existing Data controls. The DBControl example looks like the Data control, with the exception of the controls in the second row. The appearance of your custom data sources is your responsibility.

In addition to the basic navigational buttons, the DBControl provides a few more controls that let the user filter the original recordset. When the recordset is created, the ComboBox control on the lower-left corner is populated with the names of the fields in the recordset. You can select a field and set some criteria for the selected field in the TextBox control on the right. Then, you can click the Set Filter button to apply the filter to the original recordset. Obviously, we must provide the code to populate the ComboBox control and the code to filter the recordset.

The criteria must be in the form of a SQL statement. You can use the usual relational operators (=, >, LIKE, and so on) and literals. If you select the ContactTitle field in the ComboBox control and enter the string **LIKE 'ACCOUNT*'** in the TextBox control, the control's code will generate the following string:

```
ContactTitle LIKE 'ACCOUNT*'
```

This string will be passed to the recordset's Filter method. If you want to combine multiple fields, you must enter their names, along with some criteria, in the TextBox control. To retrieve the owners in Germany, for example, select the field Contact-Title and enter the following string in the TextBox control:

```
LIKE 'OWNER' AND COUNTRY='Germany'
```

Obviously, there's plenty of room for improvement here, but the version of the DBControl on the CD is meant to demonstrate the basics of building data sources with Visual Basic.

Let's start by examining the basic members of the control, which are the ConnectionString and RecordSource properties. These properties are string values, which can be set in the Properties window, and they are saved in private variables. Here are the Property procedures for these properties.

Code 12.4   The ConnectionString Property Procedures

```
Public Property Get ConnectionString() As String
    ConnectionString = m_ConnectionString
End Property

Public Property Let ConnectionString(ByVal New_ConnectionString As
String)
    m_ConnectionString = New_ConnectionString
End Property
```

Code 12.5   The RecordSource Property Procedures

```
Public Property Get RecordSource() As String
    RecordSource = m_RecordSource
End Property

Public Property Let RecordSource(ByVal New_RecordSource As String)
    m_RecordSource = New_RecordSource
End Property
```

The ConnectionString property can be a data source name (DSN), which must already exist on the computer. If you have created a DSN for the NWIND database with the name NWINDDB, you can assign the following string to the ConnectionString property:

```
DSN=NWINDDB
```

The RecordSource property must be assigned the name of a table, stored procedure, or SQL statement. Even if the value of the RecordSource property is the name of a table, you must still enter its name in the corresponding field of the Properties window. With Visual Basic, you can't create an enumerated type with the names of the tables in the database at run time so that you can display them in a drop-down list on the Properties window. To make the control simpler to use, you should probably design a property page, where you can populate a ComboBox control with the names of the tables and let the user select one with the mouse.

Once the control has all the information it needs to connect to a database, you must create the recordset. This must take place in the control's GetDataMember event, which is fired when the control is instantiated, right after the Initialize event. The GetDataMember event's code is shown in the following listing. The code uses two variables declared at the Declarations section of the UserControl object's code with the following statements:

```
Private cn As ADODB.Connection
Private WithEvents rs As ADODB.RecordSet
```

cn is a Connection object. Once the connection to the database has been established with the Open method, the *rs* Recordset object is created. The *rs* variable is used by the rest of the code to access the records of the recordset. Here's the complete listing of the GetDataMember event handler. Notice that most of the code deals with possible errors.

Code 12.6 **The DBControl's GetDataMember Event**

```
Private Sub UserControl_GetDataMember(DataMember As String, _
        Data As Object)
Dim conn As String

On Error GoTo GetDataMemberError
    If rs Is Nothing Or cn Is Nothing Then
        ' make sure various properties have been set
        If Trim$(m_ConnectionString) = "" Then
            MsgBox "No ConnectionString Specified!", _
                    vbInformation, Ambient.DisplayName
            Exit Sub
        End If
        If Trim$(m_RecordSource) = "" Then
            MsgBox "No RecordSource Specified!", _
                vbInformation, Ambient.DisplayName
            Exit Sub
        End If
        If Trim$(m_ConnectionString) <> "" Then
            ' Create a Connection object and establish
            ' a connection.
            Set cn = New ADODB.Connection
            cn.ConnectionString = m_ConnectionString
            cn.Open

            ' Create a RecordSet object.
            Set rs = New ADODB.RecordSet
            rs.Open m_RecordSource, cn, adOpenKeyset, _
                    adLockPessimistic
```

```
            rs.MoveLast
            rs.MoveFirst
        Else
            Set cn = Nothing
            Set rs = Nothing
        End If
    End If
    Set Data = rs
    Combo1.AddItem "Select a field"
    For i = 0 To rs.Fields.Count - 1
        Combo1.AddItem rs.Fields(i).Name
    Next
    Combo1.ListIndex = 0
    Exit Sub

GetDataMemberError:
    MsgBox "Error: " & CStr(Err.Number) & vbCrLf & vbCrLf & _
            Err.Description, vbOKOnly, Ambient.DisplayName
    Exit Sub
End Sub
```

Once the recordset has been created, you can write the code for the UserControl object's constituent controls. Here is the code behind the navigational buttons and the equivalent navigational methods:

Code 12.7   The Code of the DBControl's Navigational Buttons

```
Private Sub bttnFirst_Click()
    rs.MoveFirst
    RaiseEvent Repositioned
End Sub

Private Sub bttnLast_Click()
    rs.MoveLast
    RaiseEvent Repositioned
End Sub

Private Sub bttnNext_Click()
    rs.MoveNext
    If rs.EOF Then rs.MoveLast
    RaiseEvent Repositioned
End Sub
```

```
Private Sub bttnPrev_Click()
    rs.MovePrevious
    If rs.BOF Then rs.MoveFirst
    RaiseEvent Repositioned
End Sub
```

Code 12.8   **The DBControl's Navigational Methods**

```
Public Sub MoveFirst()
    bttnFirst_Click
End Sub

Public Sub MoveLast()
    bttnLast_Click
End Sub

Public Sub MoveNext()
    bttnNext_Click
End Sub

Public Sub MovePrevious()
    bttnPrev_Click
End Sub
```

The code shown here doesn't handle the EOF and BOF conditions in a robust manner. When the control hits the end of the recordset, the code simply displays the last record. You should provide properties that let the developer decide what should happen when the control lands on an invalid record and take into consideration these properties in your code.

Here's a possible implementation of the Next button that takes into consideration the value of the EOFAction property. The EOFAction property can have one of the following values: EOFAddNew, EOFMoveLast, and EOFStay.

```
Private Sub bttnNext_Click()
    If rs.EOF Then
        Select Case m_EOFAction
            Case EOFAddNew        ' (EOFAction = Add New)
                rs.AddNew
            Case EOFMoveLast      ' (EOFAction = Move Last)
                rs.MoveLast
```

```
            Case EOFStay          ' (EOFAction = EOF)
                    Exit Sub
            Case Else
                    Exit Sub
        End Select
    Else
        rs.MoveNext
    End If
End Sub
```

As with all custom controls, you must provide the code to store and retrieve the property values in a PropertyBag object. Here are the UserControl object's Write-Properties and ReadProperties procedures:

Code 12.9   **Saving and Recalling the DBControl's Property Values**

```
Private Sub UserControl_WriteProperties(PropBag As PropertyBag)
    'Write property values to storage
    Call PropBag.WriteProperty("RecordSource", _
        m_RecordSource, m_def_RecordSource)
    Call PropBag.WriteProperty("ConnectionString", _
        m_ConnectionString, m_def_ConnectionString)
End Sub

Private Sub UserControl_ReadProperties(PropBag As PropertyBag)
    'Load property values from storage
    m_RecordSource = PropBag.ReadProperty("RecordSource", _
        m_def_RecordSource)
    m_ConnectionString = PropBag.ReadProperty("ConnectionString", _
        m_def_ConnectionString)
End Sub
```

Filtering the Recordset

The interesting part of the application is the code behind the Set Filter button on the DBControl control. When this button is clicked, the code builds a string with the criteria and passes it as argument to the recordset's Filter method. The matching records form a new recordset, which can be accessed through the *rs* object variable. The control is repositioned to the first record of the new recordset and the host application sees a new set of records. Here's the code of the Set Filter button.

Code 12.10	Filtering the Recordset

```
Private Sub Command1_Click()
    On Error GoTo FilterError
    If Command1.Caption = "Set Filter" Then
        If Combo1.ListIndex = 0 Or _
                Text1.Text = "" Then Exit Sub
        rs.Filter = Combo1.Text & " " & Text1.Text
        If rs Is Nothing Then
            rs.Filter = ""
            rs.MoveLast
            rs.MoveFirst
        Else
            On Error Resume Next
            rs.MoveFirst
            If Err.Number <> 0 Then
                MsgBox "No records match the filter specification"
                Combo1.ListIndex = 0
                Text1.Text = ""
                On Error GoTo FilterError
            End If
        End If
    Else
        Combo1.ListIndex = 0
        Text1.Text = ""
        rs.Filter = ""
        rs.MoveFirst
    End If
    Exit Sub

FilterError:
    MsgBox Err.Description
    rs.Filter = ""
    rs.MoveFirst
End Sub
```

The DBControl data source's test Form doesn't require any code. It simply displays certain field values as the user repositions the control in the recordset. You can program the control using the unique event it raises, the Reposition event. We have included some interesting code that accesses the control's Recordset property. As you recall, the control's code creates a Recordset object from within the

GetDataMember event (and stores it in the *rs* variable). This variable represents the control's recordset and is exposed with the following Property Get procedure:

```
Public Property Get RecordSet() As ADODB.RecordSet
    Set RecordSet = rs
End Property
```

The *rs* variable is maintained for you by Visual Basic. The Recordset property, which is an object, provides a large number of properties and methods, which are exposed by the ADO Recordset object. For example, the number of columns in the recordset is given by the expression MyDataControl1.Recordset.Fields.Count. The following loop displays all the fields of the current record on the Immediate Window (place the following code segment in the control's Repositioned event to experiment with it):

Code 12.11   Accessing the Current Record's Fields

```
Private Sub MyDataControl1_Repositioned()
    Debug.Print "REPOSITION EVENT"
    For i = 0 To MyDataControl1.Recordset.Fields.Count - 1
        Debug.Print MyDataControl1.Recordset.Fields(i)
    Next
End Sub
```

You can also call the Recordset object's methods to add new records (Add method), delete the current record (Delete method), perform batch updates (UpdateBatch method), and so on. Open the DBControl project in the Visual Basic IDE and explore the members of the custom control's Recordset object. You'll realize that Visual Basic does a lot of work behind the scenes, as it maintains a very complicated object (the Recordset property) for you. All you had to do was create a Recordset object with the Open method and store it to an ADODB.Recordset object variable.

The DataRepeater Control

The DataRepeater control is a unique control in the sense that it doesn't do anything on its own. It's a container for custom data-bound controls, and it can host multiple instances of the same custom control. It's a handy tool for creating complex data-bound controls, with a functionality similar to that of the DataGrid and

DataList controls. Figure 12.7 shows a DataRepeater control with multiple instances of a custom data-bound control that displays a product's name and its price. If the DataRepeater control contains many custom controls, or the custom controls are too wide for the control, the appropriate scroll bars are attached automatically (you can control the appearance of the scroll bars with the ScrollBars property).

FIGURE 12.7:

The DataRepeater control acts as a container for multiple custom data bound controls.

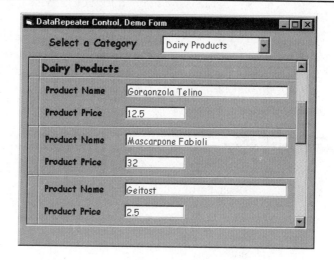

The DataRepeater control saves computer resources by displaying only a single user control—the active control—at a time. The other controls displayed are simple images that do not maintain individual connections to the data source, as would happen if several user controls were contained on a Form.

The DataRepeater control on the Form of Figure 12.7 contains as many instances of a custom data-bound control as needed to display the products of a specific category in the Products table of the NWIND database. Each time you select a new category in the ComboBox control at the top of the Form, the DataRepeater control is populated with a new recordset, with a separate custom control for each record.

To use the DataRepeater control, you must first create a custom data-bound control as described earlier in the chapter. Then you must compile the project and create the control's OCX file. Even if you include a test project in the same project group, you will not be able to use the custom control with the DataRepeater control, unless the control's OCX file exists already.

The ProdDisplay Control

To use the DataRepeater control in a project, you must first create a custom data-bound control. The ProdDisplay control shown in Figure 12.7 is a very simple data-bound control that displays a product's name and price. Let's start by describing the process of designing the ProdDisplay control.

Start a new ActiveX Control project and place two Label and two TextBox controls on the UserControl object. Their names are lblProdName, lblProdPrice, txtProdName, and txtProdPrice, respectively. Then start the ActiveX Control Interface Wizard to design the control. In the Select Interface Members of the wizard, exclude the mouse and keyboard events from the list of Selected Names. If you want to add a Click event to this control, you must call the Raise method from within the Click event of each constituent control. Implementing keyboard events (like KeyPress) is fairly complicated, because you must report not only the key that was pressed, but the constituent control that has the focus as well.

In the next window of the wizard, Create Custom Interface Members, add the ProductName and ProductPrice custom properties. In the Set Mapping window, map all the standard members to the UserControl object and the two custom properties to the Text property of the corresponding TextBox control. Map the Product-Name property to the txtProdName.Text member and the ProductPrice property to the txtProdPrice.Text member. Then click Finish to design the control. As far as the ProdDisplay control's code is concerned, we need not add a single line of code.

To make the control data-bound, and expose multiple bindings, you must set some attributes in the Procedure Attributes dialog box. Open the Tools menu and select Procedure Attributes. In the Name box of the Procedure Attributes dialog box, select the ProductName property and click the Advanced button. In the Data Binding section of the window, check the option Property Is Data-Bound. When the remaining options are enabled, check the option This Option Binds to DataField. The ProductName property is the default property of the custom control, which will be mapped to the field specified by the DataField property in the Properties window.

Then select the ProductPrice property in the Name box and check the option Property Is Data-Bound. Also check the option Show in DataBindings Collection at Design Time. A data-bound control can only be bound to a single field through the DataField property, but it can expose many data-bound properties, which must be set to other fields through the DataBindings dialog box. If you add more custom data-bound properties to the control, set the same procedure attributes as with the DataPrice property.

You can test the ProdDisplay control by adding a new Form to the project's test project. In the following section, we are going to use the custom control with the DataRepeater control.

Using the DataRepeater Control

After the custom control has been created, you must add an instance of the Data-Repeater control on the test Form. Add a new project as usual, name it TestProject, and rename its Form to TestForm. To add the DataRepeater control to the test project's Toolbox, add the Microsoft DataRepeater Control 6.0 component. Finally, place an instance of the DataRepeater control on the test Form.

The most important design time property of the DataRepeater control is the RepeatedControlName property, which must be set to the name of the custom control that will be repeated on the DataRepeater control. If you expand the Repeated-ControlName drop-down list in the Properties window, you will see the names of all custom controls installed on your system, as shown in Figure 12.8. Select the Products.ProdDisplay control in this list.

TIP

If the Products.ProdDisplay control doesn't appear in the RepeatedControlName list, you probably haven't compiled the custom control project. Select the Prod-Display object in the Project Explorer window and from the File menu select Make Products.ocx.

FIGURE 12.8:

The RepeatedControlName list in the Properties window displays the names of all custom controls installed on your system.

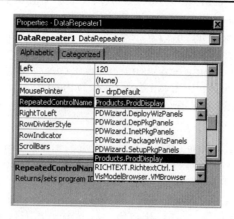

So far, you've told Visual Basic to repeat a ProdDisplay control on the Data-Repeater control. Each instance of the repeated custom control will display a single record, and there will be as many custom controls on the DataRepeater control as there are records in the recordset. Where simple controls display a single field, the custom control can display multiple fields. Next, you must tell it where the records will come from.

Add an ADO Data control on the Form (the DataRepeater is a new control and it doesn't work with the DAO or RDO Data controls) and connect it to a data provider. For this project, I've chosen the NWINDDB data source.

The Products test project uses two ADO Data controls. The first one is used to populate the DataCombo control with all entries in the Categories table. The second ADO Data control is used to populate the DataRepeater control. The second ADO Data control's DataSource property is a SQL statement that changes every time the user selects a new category in the DataCombo1 control.

To design the test Form shown in Figure 12.7, follow these steps:

1. Place an instance of the DataRepeater control on the Form and set its RepeatedControlName to Products.ProdDisplay.

2. Place a DataCombo control and two ADO Data controls on the Form. The two Data controls need not be visible at run time, so set their Visible property to False. If the icons for the ADO data-bound controls don't appear in the Toolbox, add the following components through the Components dialog box: Microsoft ADO Data Control 6.0 (OLEDB) and Microsoft Data List Controls 6.0 (OLEDB).

Populating the DataCombo Control   Let's start by setting the properties needed to populate the DataCombo control.

1. Right-click the first ADO Data control (ADODC1) and from the shortcut menu select ADODC Properties.

2. In the Properties dialog box that will appear, select the General tab and check the option Use ODBC Data Source. From the list below this option, select the NWINDDB data source (or whatever name you have used for the data source that corresponds to the NWIND database).

3. Select the RecordSource tab and set the control's RecordSource property to the Categories table of the NWIND database.

4. Set the properties that will populate the DataCombo control. Start by setting the control's Style property to 2 (dbcDropDownList) to make sure that the user can only select an existing category and not enter a new one.

5.   Set the DataCombo control's data binding properties. Because the control will select all the categories in the table rather than a single record's value, you don't have to set the DataSource and DataField properties. Instead, you must set the control's RowSource property to the ADODC1 (the name of the ADO Data control), its ListField property to the name of the field that will populate the control (CategoryName), and its BoundColumn property to CategoryID. Although the user will select a category by name, the program must be able to retrieve the corresponding records from the Products table by their ID (which is a numeric value). The BoundColumn property of the DataCombo control will be used as part of a SQL statement that causes the second ADO Data control to retrieve the products of the selected category.

Table 12.4 summarizes the settings of the DataCombo1 control.

TABLE 12.4:   The Settings of the DataCombo1 Control

Property	Setting
RowSource	ADODC1
ListField	CategoryName
BoundColumn	CategoryID

Populating the DataRepeater Control   Now you must set the properties of the second ADO Data control (ADODC2) so that it connects to a recordset with the products of the selected category. Open the control's Property pages and set the following attributes:

1.   In the General tab, select the option Use ODBC Data Source Name and set the data source to NWINDDB (or whatever name you have used for the data source that corresponds to the NWIND database).

2.   In the RecordSource tab, specify the SQL statement that will retrieve the products of a specific category. In the Command Type drop-down list, select adCmdText. In the Command Text box, enter the following SQL statement:

```
SELECT ProductName, UnitPrice FROM Products _
    WHERE Products.CategoryID=1
```

(We used the value 1 so that the category with ID=1 is displayed initially.) You will see shortly how the ADODC2 control's RecordSource property is changed from within the application's code.

3.   Click OK to close the ADO Data control's Property Pages.

If you run the project now, the DataCombo1 control will be populated with the names of the product categories. The ADODC2 control is connected to the recordset with the products of the first category (Beverages), but nothing will be displayed on the DataRepeater control. To connect the repeated controls on the DataRepeater control to the ADODC2 control, follow the steps outlined in the next section.

Populating the DataRepeater Control   Since the DataRepeater control will be populated with the recordset of the ADODC2 control, set its DataSource property to ADODC2. Notice that the DataRepeater control doesn't expose a DataField property.

To display the selected product names and prices on the custom controls of the DataRepeater control, right-click the DataRepeater control and from the shortcut menu select Properties. On the control's Property Pages select the RepeaterBindings tab and set the appropriate pairs of PropertyName and DataField. In the Property-Name list you will see the names of the custom control's properties, and in the DataField list you will see the names of the fields in the control's data source. For each pair you specify, click the Add button.

1. Select ProductName in the PropertyName list and ProductName in the DataField list. (The two names happen to be identical, but this is a coincidence. You don't have to name your custom control's properties according to the names of the fields they display.) Then click the Add button, and the property name and field value will be added to the RepeaterBindings list.

2. Select ProductPrice in the PropertyName list and UnitPrice in the DataField list. Then click the Add button to add the new pair to the RepeaterBindings list.

These settings will populate the DataRepeater control with the recordset of the ADODC2 control. Each record will appear in a separate instance of the ProdDisplay control, and all these instances will be tiled vertically in the DataRepeater control.

We want our application to display a different recordset every time a new category is selected in the DataCombo control. This is accomplished with the SQL statement

```
SELECT ProductName, UnitPrice, UnitsInStock " & _
       "FROM Products WHERE CategoryID= " & _
       DataCombo1.BoundText
```

which must be assigned to the ADODC2 control's RecordSource property. This action must take place from within the DataCombo control's Change event, which is fired every time a new item is selected. You shouldn't use the control's Click event, because this event is triggered before and after the selection. To update the records on the DataRepeater control, you must also refresh the ADO Data control. Here's all the code that's required for this application.

Code 12.13	**Updating the ADO Data Control**

```
Private Sub DataCombo1_Change()
    Adodc2.RecordSource = _
            "SELECT ProductName, UnitPrice, UnitsInStock " & _
            "FROM Products WHERE CategoryID= " & _
            DataCombo1.BoundText
    Adodc2.Refresh
    DataRepeater1.Caption = DataCombo1.Tex
End Sub
```

The Products test project's Form contains additional code that demonstrates the basic properties and events of the DataRepeater control, which are discussed in the following section.

The DataRepeater Control's Members

The basic operations you perform on the DataRepeater control at run time are the detection of a selection (when the user selects another record on the control) and the properties of the selected record. There are many more properties that apply to the appearance of the control, as well as events that are fired when the data are changed. In this section, we are going to discuss briefly the members you'll use most often in programming the DataRepeater control.

The RepeatedControl Property   To access the properties of the selected instance of the repeated control, use the RepeatedControl property. The Prod-Display control, for example, exposes the ProdName and ProdPrice properties, and you can access the values of these two properties for the selected record with the expressions

```
DataRepeater1.RepeatedControl.ProdName
```

and

```
DataRepeater1.RepeatedControl.ProdPrice
```

Not all of the repeated control's properties need be displayed on the control. You can implement additional properties, bind them to other fields, and still access their values through the RepeatedControl property. For example, you can implement a ProdStock and a ProdDiscontinued property without adding any new constituent controls to display them. You will still be able to use them from within your code with the DataRepeater1.RepeatedControl.ProdStock and DataRepeater1.Repeated-Control.ProdDiscontinued properties.

The ActiveRowChanged Event and ActiveRow Property   When the user selects another record on the DataRepeater control, the ActiveRowChanged event is fired. This event doesn't report any parameters to the application, but you can access the selected record's fields through the RepeatedControl property. The order of the selected row on the DataRepeater control is given by the Current-Record property. This is not the record's position in the table or the recordset; it's just a sequence number. The total number of rows on the control is given by the RecordCount property. Finally, the selected row's ordinal number on the control is given by the property ActiveRow. You can also set this property to select a new row from within your code. Notice that when the ActiveRow property changes value, the ActiveRowChanged event is fired.

In the Product project's code, we have inserted the following lines to display the number of products in the selected category. The code is placed in the Data-Combo1 control's Change event:

```
Debug.Print "Selected Category: " & _
            DataRepeater1.Caption & _
            " contains :" & _
            DataRepeater1.RecordCount & " records"
```

The RepeaterBindings Collection   Finally, you can access the PropertyName and DataField values (which you set in the DataRepeater's property pages on the RepeaterBindings tab) through your code with the RepeaterBindings collection. Each bound field corresponds to a member of the RepeaterBindings collection and is represented by a RepeaterBinding object. To scan all the members of the Repeater-Bindings collection, declare a RepeaterBinding variable and then set up a For Each …Next loop. The RepeaterBinding object exposes the DataField and Property-Name properties. You can read their values, or set new bindings at run time. The following code segment displays the data fields and the properties bound to these fields:

```
Dim rb As RepeaterBinding
For Each rb In DataRepeater1.RepeaterBindings
    Debug.Print rb.DataField & " >> " & rb.PropertyName
Next
```

If you use these statements with the Products project, the following messages will be displayed in the Immediate window:

```
ProductName >> ProductName
UnitPrice >> ProductPrice
```

You will find this code segment in the control's Click event, but it's commented out.

CHAPTER

THIRTEEN

Extending the IDE
with Add-Ins

- Understanding add-ins

- Exploring the VBIDE class

- Building an add-in

- Programming the Demo add-in project

- Manipulating the IDE menu

- Detecting IDE events

One major strength of Visual Basic is its environment. In Visual Basic's integrated development environment (IDE), you can develop, test, and debug all types of projects, from Standard EXE projects to ActiveX controls and ActiveX documents. And as you know by now, the IDE is extended and enhanced with each new version of Visual Basic.

You can also enhance the IDE by incorporating new commands and even new menus with the help of add-ins. *Add-ins* are components that must be installed on the developer's system, and when developers need the functionality of a specific add-in, they add it to the IDE.

One of the project types you can create with Visual Basic is the Add-In project, which is an application you can hook into the environment to enhance the IDE itself. Using add-ins, you can extend the functionality of the Visual Basic IDE and streamline the design process. Add-ins can be as simple as programs that ensure that all TextBox controls on a Form are aligned or that all data-entry controls use the same font name and size. They can also be complete applications that design Forms and generate code automatically (the so-called Wizards), manipulate databases (such as the Visual Data Manager), and so on.

The proper term for adding an add-in to the environment is *connecting*. When the add-in is no longer needed, it must be *disconnected*. You connect an add-in to the IDE with the help of the Add-In Manager. The process is similar to adding references or components to a project. Here are the steps:

1. Choose Add-Ins ➤ Add-In Manager to open the Add-In Manager dialog box:

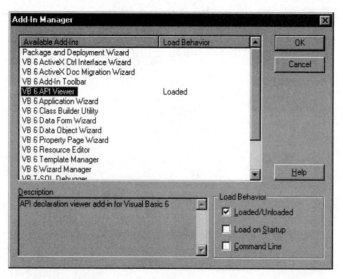

2. To load an add-in, double-click its name.

The add-in's name is added to the Add-Ins menu, and you can activate it from there. Alternatively, you can select the name of the add-in with the mouse and then check the box Loaded/Unloaded. When this box is checked, the selected add-in is loaded; when it's cleared, the selected add-in is unloaded. You can also specify that an add-in connects each time you start Visual Basic by checking the button Load on Startup. If you are using API functions frequently in your applications, load the API Viewer add-in on startup.

Add-ins are part of the project, and each time you open a project to which you have connected an add-in, the add-in is loaded automatically. Add-ins, however, are not part of the executable project. Add-ins are tools for simplifying the development process and are not needed at run time.

Manipulating Visual Basic's IDE is complicated. Even using it isn't always simple. For example, you have to know the difference between in-process and out-of-process servers. You can test in-process servers in the same instance of Visual Basic, but you must test out-of-process servers in a second instance of Visual Basic. In the last chapter, you saw that the behavior of an ActiveX control depends on whether the test project is running in design mode or in run-time mode. However, the ActiveX control is running in both modes. As you can see, the environment of Visual Basic consists of many interacting components, and when manipulating one of them, you must consider the state of other components.

The same is true for an add-in. While a project is in design mode, the add-in's code is running in the background. Testing add-ins isn't as simple as running the project. You need two instances of Visual Basic running at once—one with the add-in, and another with a project with which you'll be testing the add-in.

> **NOTE**   Add-ins are not project components. They are used by the IDE and only in design mode. The project contains no references to the add-ins you have connected to the IDE. Moreover, if you connect the add-ins while a project is open and then open another project or start a new one, the add-ins will remain connected.

Who Needs Add-Ins?

Most of you have managed without building custom add-ins, and chances are that you don't have any compelling reasons to do so now. The add-in market is also small. You can design really useful add-ins to simplify the development process, but marketing them isn't easy. You're better off selling custom ActiveX controls. The add-ins you're using come with Visual Basic itself, and, as you know by now, they are life-savers. Imagine how many lines of code you would have to enter manually to create a simple control that delegates the members of its constituent controls. The ActiveX Control Interface Wizard is basically an application, capable of affecting the IDE itself. You provide the specifications for the interface of a new ActiveX control, and the wizard creates the skeleton of the control (it generates the trivial part of the code and creates the placeholders, where you'll enter your own code).

Another example of a useful add-in is the Visual Data Manager, which is a totally separate application that can be called from within the Add-In menu. The Visual Data Manager allows you to design and manipulate databases while the Visual Basic window is open. You can move back and forth to look up field names and their definitions, perhaps to add a new index to a table according to your application's needs, and so on.

As far as the integration between the Visual Basic IDE and the add-in is concerned, there is none (short of being able to start the add-in from within the IDE). As a proof, you can end Visual Basic, and the Visual Data Manager will remain active. As you probably guessed, this is the simplest type of add-in you can develop; it's an application that can be started from within the IDE. You may claim it's simpler to develop something like the Visual Data Manager as a separate application, which users can start by double-clicking its icon. You're probably right. Personally, I can't think of many add-ins like the Visual Data Manager, although here's an idea for a useful add-in that functions independent of Visual Basic.

Most of us resort to the online help files to get information about constants, especially the ones we need to set up a common dialog box such as the File Open dialog box. You can design a Form that lets the user set all the available options visually and displays the common dialog box that corresponds to these settings. When the developer gets the desired dialog box, the program generates the statements that produce the dialog box and copies them to the clipboard, from where you can paste them anywhere in your code. Turning a VB Form into an add-in isn't difficult, as you'll see, and you can turn many helper applications that you use at design time into add-ins.

The VB 6 Data Form Wizard is an excellent example of the functionality of an add-in. This wizard walks you through a series of dialog boxes where you specify the type of Form you want to create, the fields that will appear on the Form, their organization on the Form, and other optional information. It then creates the corresponding Form, including its visual interface and the supporting code. With a few mouse clicks, you can create elaborate data-entry or report Forms for your applications. Figure 13.1 shows a data-entry Form with the familiar editing buttons.

FIGURE 13.1:

A simple data-entry Form
designed with the Data
Form add-in

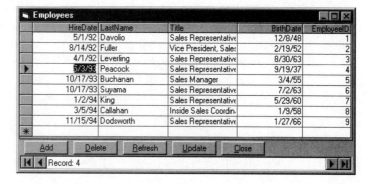

Here's a short segment of the code generated by the add-in:

```
Private Sub cmdDelete_Click()
  With datPrimaryRS.Recordset
    .Delete
    .MoveNext
    If .EOF Then .MoveLast
  End With
End Sub

Private Sub cmdRefresh_Click()
  'This is only needed for multi user apps
  datPrimaryRS.Refresh
End Sub
```

This code doesn't depend on the application. It's generic and performs basic operations in a data-entry application that uses the Data control. If you want additional validation tests or more specific error messages, you can tweak the code generated by the Wizard. The data-entry Form is automatically added to your project, and you can test and edit it as usual.

Designing Forms automatically (in other words, placing the appropriate controls on a Form, aligning them, and assigning initial values to them), as well as generating code for these controls, is one of the most useful things you can do with an add-in, and you will see an example of how this is done in the section "Developing a Form Generator," later in this chapter. But first, we must explore the structure of the objects you will use when designing add-ins.

The VBIDE Class

To allow developers to enhance the development environment, Visual Basic provides the VBIDE class, which represents its own environment. VBIDE stands for Visual Basic integrated development environment, and it exposes all the objects needed to access the integrated environment's components (the various windows, menus, project components, the controls on a Form and the corresponding code, and so on). Every object you work with while designing an application can be accessed and manipulated through the properties and methods of the VBIDE class.

To see the objects exposed by the VBIDE class, follow these steps:

1. Start a new project, and then add a reference to the Microsoft Visual Basic 6.0 Extensibility class through the References dialog box.

2. Start the Object Browser.

3. Select the VBIDE Type Library, and you'll see its classes and their members, as shown in Figure 13.2.

FIGURE 13.2:

The ContainedVBControls class of the VBIDE object and its members

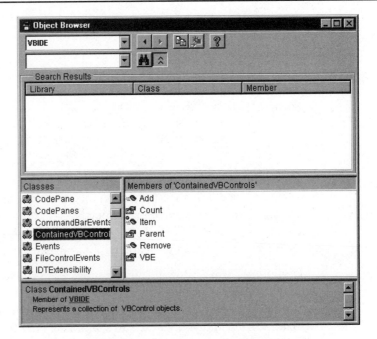

Figure 13.2 shows the members of the ContainedVBControls class, which represents a collection of VB controls that may reside on a Form or on a container control (for example, a Frame control). Its Add member is a method that allows you to add a control to this collection. Writing the code to manipulate the controls on a Form is rather easy, considering all the help provided by the Object Browser. However, you can't enter a few lines of code in the Immediate window or in a Command Button's Click event to test the objects of the VBIDE class. You must first generate an add-in project. The process is similar to developing an ActiveX EXE server. You must first create it and then test it from within another instance of Visual Basic.

At this point, we should probably describe how you create an add-in, integrate it into the Visual Basic IDE, and then make it do something. Creating an add-in requires a few steps that are quite unique. Instead of getting into the details of building your "first add-in" and then examining the objects exposed by the IDE (which you need in order to program the add-in), we will start with an introduction to this object model. This discussion will help you understand what your add-ins can do. It will also help you understand the structure of the objects that allow you to access the IDE's components and its functionality and give you ideas for useful add-ins, which will streamline your development efforts. Then, we'll put these objects together to build many examples that manipulate the environment (add new commands to Visual Basic's menus, manipulate Forms and controls, react to events such as the deletion of a control on a Form, and so on). Some of these examples are lengthy, but you can use many of them as starting points for your add-in projects.

As we mentioned already in several chapters so far, the Object Browser can practically replace the documentation, as long as you are familiar with the structure of an object model. If you are familiar with the concepts of relational databases, you can use the Object Browser to locate the objects of the DAO class you need and then locate their members. The same is true for the objects exposed by the VBIDE, but first you need to get acquainted with the VBIDE object model.

NOTE   In the following sections, you will see code segments demonstrating the most important aspects of the VBIDE object model. Unfortunately, you won't be able to test them immediately. The process of creating an add-in and integrating it in a Visual Basic project (which is the only way to test it) is rather involved. VBIDE is a complicated object, and, instead of presenting long lists of step-by-step procedures to carry out on your own, we will explain the basic principles of programming Visual Basic's environment through the members of the VBIDE object. Then, we are going to look at a number of useful examples. So, bear with us, and you will soon learn about building add-ins and incorporating them into your favorite development environment.

Using the Demo Add-In Project

All the examples we'll discuss in the first part of this chapter will be used later in the Demo add-in. If you want to use these examples and modify them as you go along, follow these steps:

1. Open the Demo project.

NOTE   You'll find the Demo project in the Chapter13/Demo folder on the CD that comes with this book.

---

2. Press F5 to run the project.

The add-in can now be used from within another instance of Visual Basic (but not from within the same instance of VB that's used to develop it).

3. Start another instance of VB6, and create a new Standard EXE project.

4. Choose Add-Ins ➢ Add-In Manager to open the Add-In Manager dialog box.

5. Double-click the Demo Add-in and close the Add-in Manager dialog box.

The Demo add-in has been added to the second instance of VB6, and you can activate it by clicking its name in the Add-Ins menu.

If you want to edit the add-in's code, to experiment with additional objects or properties, disconnect the add-in and then switch to the add-in project and interrupt it. At this point, you can edit the code or enter statements in the Immediate window. When you are done, resume execution by pressing F5 again, switch to the second instance of VB6, and connect the add-in again.

In general, testing and troubleshooting add-ins can be confusing. Use DEBUG .PRINT statements in the add-in's code instead of displaying message boxes, and be sure that the add-in is disconnected from the test project before you stop the add-in project. When the add-in is compiled to an EXE or a DLL file, you no longer need to run the add-in in a separate instance of Visual Basic, and these problems won't be an issue. But for this to happen, you must first make sure the add-in works.

If things get really messy, you can always shut down both instances of Visual Basic and start them again. In nearly all cases, when we had to restart add-in projects, it wasn't Visual Basic's fault. There was always a good explanation for why things went wrong—adding a new command to the wrong menu or leaving behind dead add-in commands on the Add-Ins menu. Knowing what caused the problem was, however, little consolation. When you are working with add-ins, you will make mistakes as usual, but because they affect the very environment in which you work, they will seem more catastrophic than the effects of mistakes you make in developing ActiveX components or regular VB applications.

Some Add-In Tips

As you're working with add-ins, here are some things to keep in mind:

- If you interrupt the execution of the add-in while it's connected, its name remains in the Add-Ins menu, but the add-in isn't connected. If you connect it again, its name will appear twice in the Add-Ins menu. Only the last instance of its name in the menu can be activated. The other one hangs there, but it won't react to the Click event. It will be removed when you shut down this instance of Visual Basic and start a new one.

- The add-in won't react in the test project's environment if the add-in project isn't running. Watch for this when you're troubleshooting and testing your add-ins.

- If you display message boxes from within your add-in or prompt the user for input with the InputBox function, the corresponding dialog boxes won't show up in the test project. Instead, you will get a warning that the other application isn't reacting. You must switch to the other instance of VB6 (the add-in project) to see the message box or input box and close it.

VBInstance: The Environment Variable

To understand the objects exposed by the VBIDE class and their members, consider for a moment what an add-in should be able to do:

- It must expose the objects needed to manipulate the Visual Basic environment.

- It should provide objects that represent the various windows (such as the Code window, the Properties window, and the Toolbox), the components of a project, and so on.

All these objects are properties of the root object, which represents the environment itself (just like every item in a database is accessed via an object variable that represents the open database).

The root component of every add-in is the *VBInstance* object variable, which represents the current instance of Visual Basic. All the components of the VBIDE object are accessed through the *VBInstance* variable (which is declared as VBIDE.VBE type). The name *VBInstance* isn't mandatory, but we have yet to see an add-in that doesn't use it. The *VBInstance* object variable is set by the add-in's code and only when the add-in is attached to a project. In the examples in the following sections, we'll use the *VBInstance* variable to access all the classes and members exposed by the VBIDE object, but we won't show you yet how this variable is created. It's the one variable that must exist in every add-in, and, for now, take it for granted.

The Window Object and the Windows Collection

The most obvious components of the Visual Basic IDE are its windows. The VBIDE class exposes the Windows collection that represents the various windows (the Code window, the Properties window, the Toolbox, and so on) and the Window object, which exposes methods to manipulate these windows (change their location, make visible a specific line in the Code window, and so on). All these windows are members of the Windows collection, which is made up of Window objects. If you've opened the Object Browser window for the VBIDE class, scroll down to the last two classes:

Window, a class that represents a window in the environment

Windows, a collection of Window objects

If you look at the members of these two classes, you'll see that the Window object has a number of properties. The Caption, Width, Height, Top, and Left properties need not be explained any further. These properties let you rearrange the various windows of the IDE on the screen. The SetFocus method lets you move the focus to a specific window. One of the most useful properties of the Window object is the Type property, which returns the window's type. The declaration of this property in the Object Browser's description section is:

```
Property Type As vbext_WindowType
```

All constants of the VBIDE object begin with the prefix *vbext*. Scroll up the Classes list to locate the entry vbext_WindowType, and select it. It's an enumerated type with the following values:

vbext_wt_Browser	vbext_wt_CodeWindow	vbext_wt_ColorPalette
vbext_wt_Designer	vbext_wt_Find	vbext_wt_FindReplace
vbext_wt_Immediate	vbext_wt_LinkedWindowFrame	vbext_wt_Locals

vbext_wt_MainWindow   vbext_wt_Preview   vbext_wt_ProjectWindow

vbext_wt_
PropertyWindow   vbext_wt_Toolbox   vbext_wt_ToolWindow

vbext_wt_Watch

The constant names are self-explanatory. The vbext_wt_Designer signifies that the window is a designer (a Form's or UserControl's design window). In this type of window, you can add new instances of controls. As you can see, you indeed have access to all the windows the user can open in the IDE, and you can figure out the type of each window by examining its Type property.

If you look at the members of the Windows class, you will see that it contains two of the standard members of a collection:

- Count

- Item

The Window object is special in the sense that you can't create new Window objects and add them to the Windows collection with the Add method; nor can you remove existing windows with the Remove method. This is why the Add and Remove methods aren't exposed. (Sure, you can close certain windows, but you can't remove them from Visual Basic's environment.)

To access the windows in the current instance of the Visual Basic IDE, you must set up a loop such as the following:

```
Dim iWindow As VBIDE.Window
For Each iWindow In VBInstance.Windows
    If Not iWindow.Visible Then iWindow.Visible = True
Next
```

Alternatively, you can use a For...Next loop such as the following:

```
For iWindow =1 To VBInstance.Windows.Count
    If Not Windows.Item(iWindow).Visible Then _
       Windows.Item(iWindow).Visible = True
Next
```

Notice here that the Item property is the default member of a collection, so you can omit it. In other words, the element Windows.Item(iWindow) can also be accessed as Windows(iWindow). In this book, we'll use the explicit notation. You can also examine the type of a window by comparing its Type property with the constants listed earlier.

So, can you access an application's code through the Code window? You can indeed access an application's code, but not through the Windows collection (see the CodeModule object, later in this chapter).

The current, active window in the IDE can be read by the MainWindow property of the VBE object. To find out the type of the active window, use an IF statement such as the following one:

```
Dim currentWin As Window
Set currentWin = VBE.MainWindow
If currentWin.Type = vbext_wt_Designer Then ...
```

This IF statement ensures that the current window is a designer window, which means you can place controls on it.

The AddIn Object and AddIns Collection

The AddIn object represents an add-in in the development environment. The add-ins can be accessed through the AddIns collection, which has the same members as the Windows collection (basically you can add new add-ins and disconnect add-ins already connected to the IDE).

We won't discuss this object any further in this book. It's a rather advanced topic and not really needed in developing typical add-ins. You can use it from within an add-in's code during initialization to find out whether another, related add-in has already been connected. To access the add-ins already connected to an application (in other words, the add-ins whose names appear in the Add-Ins menu), use a loop similar to the one we presented for the Windows collection and then examine its Connect property.

The VBProject Object and VBProjects Collection

VBProject is one of the top-level objects of the VBIDE class, and it represents a Visual Basic project. If the current instance of the Visual Basic IDE contains a project group, the VBProjects collection can access each project in the group. To scan the VBProjects collection, use a loop such as this:

```
Dim iProject As VBProject
For Each iProject In VBInstance.VBProjects
    Debug.Print iProject.Name
Next
```

The VBProject object has a number of properties, including:

- **Name**, which is the project's name

- **Type**, which returns the type of the project

- **IsDirty**, which returns a Boolean value that indicates whether a project was edited after the last time it was saved

- **VBComponent**, which represents a project's component, such as a Form, a module, and so on

As you have guessed, the components of a project can be accessed through the VBComponents collection. The VBComponent object is one of the most commonly used objects in programming the IDE, and we'll examine it in detail.

If you look at the members of the VBProjects collection in the Object Browser, you will see that this collection has an Add member. Using the Add member, you can add a new project to the current project group. Creating an entire project in code is quite a task, so the common way to add a new project to a project group is with the AddFromFile method, which adds a project already stored on disk to the current project group. The VBProjects collection contains a number of properties that are not standard collection members. The StartProject property, for instance, returns (or sets) the project that will start executing when the F5 key is pressed. Finally, the VBProjects collection recognizes four events, which are shown in Table 13.1.

TABLE 13.1: The Events of the VBProjects Collection

Event	What It Does
ItemActivated	Notifies the add-in that a project was activated.
ItemAdded	Notifies the add-in that a project was added.
ItemRemoved	Notifies the add-in that a project was removed.
ItemRenamed	Notifies the add-in that a project was renamed.

All these events pass a VBProject object as an argument. This is the project that was activated, added, or deleted. When a project is renamed, the ItemRenamed event passes two arguments: the project being renamed and the old name of the project (they are both string values).

Finally, the FileName property of the Projects collection specifies the full path name of the project's VBG file on the disk. To save the project to another folder, use the SaveAs method. If the project hasn't been saved yet, the FileName property is a blank string. In this case, you must either create a new file name (you will most likely base the file name on the project's name) or activate the Save As command in the File menu to prompt the user for a location and file name for the project. (Yes, you can access the menu commands too and activate them from within your code.)

The active project in a project group is returned by the ActiveVBProject property of the *VBInstance* object variable. The name of the active project is given by the property VBInstance.ActiveVBProject.Name and is the name specified in the Project window. If the user hasn't changed it, it's something like Project1, Project2, and so on.

NOTE   There is no object that represents a project group. A project group is represented by a project object, which is saved to a file with a different extension (VBG instead of VBP).

The VBComponent Object and VBComponents Collection

The VBProject object represents a single project, but each project has a number of components (Forms, classes, Property Pages, and so on). To access the components of a VBProject object, you use the VBComponents collection. Each member of the VBComponents collection is a VBComponent object, whose members you can look up in the Object Browser. The members of the VBComponents collection are similar to the members of the VBProjects collection. This shouldn't surprise you, because a project group has multiple components (projects) just as a project can have multiple components. That's why the two collections have similar members and even support the same events. The VBComponents collection supports two more events, which are shown at the bottom of Table 13.2 (the events unique to the VBComponents collection are the last two in the table).

T A B L E 1 3 . 2 : The Events of the VBComponents Collection

Event	What It Does
ItemActivated	Notifies the add-in that a project component was activated.
ItemAdded	Notifies the add-in that a project component was added.
ItemRemoved	Notifies the add-in that a project component was removed.
ItemRenamed	Notifies the add-in that a project component was renamed.
ItemReloaded	Notifies the add-in that a project component was reloaded from disk.
ItemSelected	Notifies the add-in that a project component was selected (became the active component).

The VBComponents collection also supports the StartupObject property, which returns the startup component of the current project. The Startup component is usually a Form, but it could be the Main subroutine or even None. The programmer can specify the startup component of each project in the Project Properties dialog box (choose Project ➤ Project Properties). From within the add-in's code, you can set the value of the StartupObject property to the name of a startup component (which is usually a Form).

You can examine all the components of the active project with a loop such as the following:

```
Dim thisProject As VBProject
Dim pComponents As Integer
Dim i As Integer

    Set thisProject = VBInstance.ActiveVBProject
    pComponents = thisProject.VBComponents.Count
    For i = 1 To pComponents
        MsgBox "VB Component " & _
            thisProject.VBComponents.Item(i).Name
    ' The component type is given by the property
    Debug.Print thisProject.VBComponents.Item(i).Type
    ' and its name by the property
    Debug.Print thisProject.VBComponents.Item(i).Name
    ' is the startup object the current component?
    If thisProject.VBComponents.StartUpObject.Name = _
        thisProject.VBComponents.Item(i).Name Then _
            Debug.Print "STARTUP OBJECT " & _
            thisProject.VBComponents.Item(i).Name
    Next
```

The object variable *thisProject* is declared as VBProject type and is assigned the current project in the current instance of VB. The number of components in the active project is given by the property VBComponents.Count. The Type property of the VBComponent object can have one of the following values:

Constant Name	Value	Constant Name	Value
vbext_ct_ActiveXDesigner	11	vbext_ct_ClassModule	2
vbext_ct_DocObject	9	vbext_ct_MSForm	3
vbext_ct_PropPage	7	vbext_ct_RelatedDocument	10
vbext_ct_ResFile	4	vbext_ct_StdModule	1
vbext_ct_UserControl	8	vbext_ct_VBForm	5
vbext_ct_VBMDIForm	6		

As usual, the names of the constants are self-explanatory, and they reflect the types of components you can add to a project through the Project menu. Visual Basic can handle all these components (for example, return the controls on a Form, as you will see shortly, or the code for an event handler), with the exception of the Resource File component. Resource Files are created with the Resource Editor, outside Visual Basic, and you can't access their contents from within your add-in.

The expressions that represent the components of a project (or any objects under the root object, for that matter) can be lengthy. To shorten these expressions in your code, you can declare object variables, such as the *thisComponent* variable, which will hold a reference to a project component:

```
Dim thisComponent As VBComponent
```

You can then assign a project component to this variable by using the following statement:

```
ThisComponent = thisProject.VBComponents.Item(i)
```

You can also use the name of the *thisComponent* variable in place of the object expression that represents a component.

The SelectedVBComponent Object

As you recall, the current project is given by the property VBInstance.Active-VBProject. You can also access the currently selected component in the active project, only the property you must use this time doesn't have the word *active* in its name. It's the *SelectedVBComponent* of the *VBInstance* object variable. The following statement prints the name of the active project and the name of the selected component in the active project:

```
Debug.Print "The selected project is " & _
    VBInstance.ActiveVBProject.Name & vbCrLf & _
    "The selected component is " & VBInstance.SelectedVBComponent.Name
```

Let's look at a code segment that puts together the properties discussed in this and the last section to print the names of all the components in a project and the name of the selected component. The code uses a loop to scan all the projects in the Project window of the IDE (there is no property that represents a project group) and a nested loop to scan all the components of the current project. Here's the listing:

```
Dim thisProject As VBProject
Dim nProjects As Integer, nComponents As Integer
Dim i As Integer, j As Integer
Dim projectName As String
```

```
nProjects = VBInstance.VBProjects.Count
For i = 1 To nProjects
    Set thisProject = VBInstance.VBProjects.Item(i)
    projectName = VBInstance.VBProjects.Item(i).Name
    nComponents = thisProject.VBComponents.Count
    For j = 1 To nComponents
        Debug.Print "PROJECT " & projectName & vbCrLf & _
                    "Component #" & j & "  " & _
                    thisProject.VBComponents.Item(j).Name
    Next
Next
Debug.Print "The selected project is " & _
            VBInstance.ActiveVBProject.Name & vbCrLf & _
            "The selected component is " & _
            VBInstance.SelectedVBComponent.Name
```

If you have programmed with objects before, you can certainly understand how the VBIDE objects are used to scan the components of a project group (the outer loop) and the components of each project (the inner loop). Here's the structure of a test project, whose components will be listed in the Immediate window. Figure 13.3 shows the Project window of the test project with the components listed in Table 13.3 and the names of the components as printed in the Immediate window by the add-in's code.

FIGURE 13.3:

A test project with all the types of components you can add to a VB project

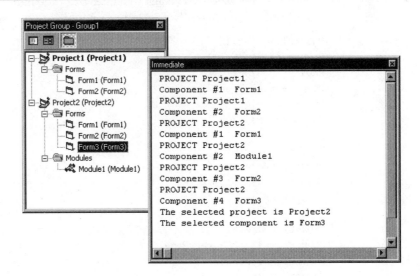

TABLE 13.3: The Components of the Test Project

PROJECT1	
Forms	Form1, Form2
Modules	Module1
Class Modules	Class1, Class2
User Controls	UserControl1
Property Pages	PropertyPage1

PROJECT2	
Forms	Form1, Form2, Form3
Modules	Module1, Module2
Class Modules	Class1, Class2, Class3
Designers	UserConnection1

The code segment we just presented prints the following lines in the Immediate window. Notice that some of the components in the second project are out of order. The order in which the components are printed reflects the order in which they were added to the project. The last two lines print the name of the active project and the name of the currently selected component in this project.

```
PROJECT Project1
Component #1  Form1
PROJECT Project1
Component #2  Form2
PROJECT Project1
Component #3  Module1
PROJECT Project1
Component #4  Class1
PROJECT Project1
Component #5  Class2
PROJECT Project1
Component #6  UserControl1
PROJECT Project1
Component #7  PropertyPage1
PROJECT Project2
Component #1  Form1
PROJECT Project2
```

```
Component #2  Form2
PROJECT Project2
Component #3  Form3
PROJECT Project2
Component #4  Module1
PROJECT Project2
Component #5  Class1
PROJECT Project2
Component #6  Module2
PROJECT Project2
Component #7  Class2
PROJECT Project2
Component #8  Class3
PROJECT Project2
Component #9  UserConnection1

The selected project is Project2
The selected component is Module2
```

The VBControls and ContainedVBControls Collections

OK, we've worked our way from the Visual Basic environment down to the project components. If we can access the controls on each Form (or UserControl object) and the code behind each component, we'll be ready to develop wizards such as the ones that come with Visual Basic. To access the controls on a Form, you use the VBControls collection (made up of VBControl objects) or the ContainedVBControls collection (also made up of VBControl objects). To access the code, you use the CodeModule object, which is described in the next section.

The VBControl object represents a VB control (built-in or custom). To access all the controls on a Form, use the VBControls collection, which contains a VBControl object for each control on the current component (Form or UserControl object). As expected, this collection exposes the standard collection members (Add, Remove, Count, and Item) and recognizes the three events shown in Table 13.4.

TABLE 13.4: The Events of the VBControls Collection

Event	What It Does
ItemAdded	Notifies the add-in that a new control was added to the current component.
ItemRemoved	Notifies the add-in that a control was removed from the current component.
ItemRenamed	Notifies the add-in that a control on the current component was renamed.

If the object variable *thisForm* represents a Form in the current project, the following loop will scan all the controls on the Form with the help of the VBControls collection and print their names:

```
For iControl = 1 To thisForm.VBControls.Count
    Debug.Print _
        thisForm.VBControls.Item(iControl).Properties("Name")
Next
```

The VBControls collection contains all the controls on a Form. But as you know, not all controls may be sited directly on the Form. Some controls may reside on other controls, called *containers*. A typical container control is the Frame control, which is commonly used to group Option buttons. If you want to know not only all the names of the controls that live on the Form, but the control they belong to, you must use the ContainedVBControls collection. The ContainedVBControls collection is made up of VBControl objects too, but it contains only the controls on a container. If the object variable *thisForm* represents a Form, the following loop will print the names of the controls on the Form:

```
For iControl = 1 To thisForm.ContainedVBControls.Count
    Set thisControl = _
        thisForm.ContainedVBControls.Item(iControl)
    Debug.Print thisControl.Properties("Name")
Next
```

If the Form contains the Frame1 control, which in turn contains a few Command Buttons, this loop prints the name of the Frame1 control, but not the names of the controls on the Frame control. Just like the members of the VBComponents collection, the controls are printed in the order in which they were placed on the container. The object variable *thisControl* must be declared with type VBControl.

In programming the Visual Basic environment, we commonly need to access controls, grouped according to the control to which they belong. The code for scanning the controls on a Form and then the controls contained on each control, to any level, isn't complicated, but it is recursive. Let's revise the previous code so that it examines each control on the Form for a contained control. The previous code segment remains as is, but after printing the name of the current control, we'll call a subroutine, the ShowContainedControls() subroutine, that scans for contained controls. This subroutine must accept as an argument a *VBControl* object variable, which represents the current control. Here is the main loop's code:

```
For iControl = 1 To thisForm.ContainedVBControls.Count
    Set thisControl = thisForm.ContainedVBControls.Item(iControl)
```

```
        Debug.Print thisControl.Properties("Name")
        ShowContainedControls thisControl
    Next
```

The ShowContainedControls() subroutine accepts as an argument the control whose name was just printed and scans it for contained controls. In its simplest form, it is:

```
Sub ShowContainedControls(thisControl As VBControl)
Dim iControl As Integer

    If thisControl.ContainedVBControls.Count = 0 Then Exit Sub
    For iControl = 1 To thisControl.ContainedVBControls.Count
        Debug.Print thisControl.ContainedVBControls.Item _
            (iControl).Properties("Name")
    Next
End Sub
```

This subroutine prints the names of the controls contained on the control *this-Control*, but not any controls contained by its individual controls. Now, that's a bit unusual, but because it is possible to nest contained controls at more than two levels, we should call another subroutine, from within this loop, to display the names of any controls that are possibly contained within the current control. This subroutine exists already. It's the ShowContainedControls() subroutine, which must be called recursively. Here's the code of the subroutine that will scan contained controls in any level:

```
Sub ShowContainedControls(thisControl As VBControl)
Dim iControl As Integer
Dim newControl As VBControl

    If thisControl.ContainedVBControls.Count = 0 Then Exit Sub
    For iControl = 1 To thisControl.ContainedVBControls.Count
        Debug.Print thisControl.ContainedVBControls.Item _
            (iControl).Properties("Name")
        Set newControl = _
            thisControl.ContainedVBControls.Item(iControl)
        ShowContainedControls newControl
    Next
End Sub
```

This code is quite simple, as long as you are familiar with recursive procedures. The ShowContainedControls() subroutine calls itself to carry out an identical task. Each time, however, it is called with a different argument (the *newControl* object variable). The actual code in the Demo project contains a few additional lines, to indent the contained controls under the name of the control that contains them. Here, we've skipped these lines to make the code of the subroutine easier to read.

Figure 13.4 shows a Form with several container controls and containers within containers. The names of the controls are the default ones, so they are identical to their captions (some controls have the same caption, which means they are members of a control array). We are going to see how the controls on this Form can be accessed with the VBControls and ContainedVBControls collections.

FIGURE 13.4:

A Form with controls contained within other controls in three levels

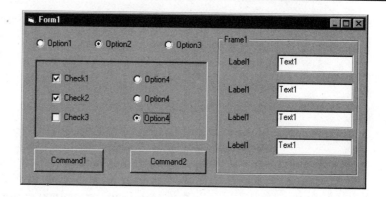

Let's look at the list of control names that the two code segments will print in the Immediate window. The code segment that uses the VBControls collection will print all the controls of the Form, regardless of whether they are sited directly on the Form or on another control:

```
Frame1(1)
Text1(1)
Text1(2)
Text1(3)
Text1(4)
Label1(1)
Label1(2)
Label1(3)
Label1(4)
Option4(0)
Option4(2)
Option4(1)
Picture1
Check1
Check3
Check2
```

```
Option3
Option2
Option1
Command2
Command1
```

The code segment that uses the ContainedVBControls collection (and calls the ShowContainedControls()) subroutine will display all the controls too, but contained controls will be listed under their container's name (they are indented in the following listing). If you omit the call to the ShowContainedControls() subroutine, the second code segment prints only the names of the controls sited directly on the Form.

The button All ContainedControls of the Demo add-in would also print the names of controls sited on other controls that are contained already, and it would indent them properly as shown here. Besides the grouping of the controls according to their container, they are not otherwise ordered within the group to which they belong.

```
Frame1(1)
     Text1(1)
     Text1(2)
     Text1(3)
     Text1(4)
     Label1(1)
     Label1(2)
     Label1(3)
     Label1(4)
Picture1
     Option4(0)
     Check1
     Option4(2)
     Option4(1)
     Check3
     Check2
Option3
Option2
Option1
Command2
Command1
```

The CodeModule Object

And we've come to the last component of a project you can access through the VBIDE object: the project's code. As you know, the project's code is scattered in the various events of the controls and procedures. Each component's code is separate from any other component's code, so you must access each code module in the component to which it belongs. In the context of this discussion, a code module is the smallest self-sufficient piece of code in the Code window. It could be a variable declaration, an event handler, a general procedure, or a Property procedure.

To access the code modules in the current project, use the CodeModule object of the VBIDE. CodeModule is also a property of the VBComponent object and represents the code behind the component. The CodeModule object exposes many properties and methods for accessing the code's modules (declarations, events, methods, and so on). First, it exposes the Members collection, which is made up of CodeModule objects that represent the code module contained in the current component's Code window. All variable declarations, event handlers, property procedures, and general procedures (functions and subroutines) of a component can be accessed through the CodeModule object. Because CodeModule is not a collection, the individual modules must be accessed via the Members property, and not via the Item property.

This may confuse you at first, but CodeModule is an object, not a collection. To access the individual code modules, you must use the CodeModule's Members property, which is a collection.

Let's say you have created a variable that represents the current project:

```
Set thisProject = VBInstance.ActiveVBProject
```

The first component of the current project is:

```
thisProject.VBComponents.Item(1)
```

To access the controls of this component, you have to make sure that it is a Form component and then use the ContainedVBControls or VBControls collection, as discussed in the last section. To access the code behind the module, you use the CodeModule property:

```
thisProject.VBComponents.Item(1).CodeModule
```

This expression represents the code of the module—the entire code on a Form or a class module, for example. To access each of the components, you use the Members property, which is a collection of CodeModule objects. According to the documentation, Members is not a collection. But it looks and behaves like a collection, so we are going to use the term *collection* to describe it. The number of code modules in the first component of the project is given by the property

```
thisProject.VBComponents.Item(1).CodeModule.Members.Count
```

Before we proceed with any examples, let's take a look at the basic properties and methods of the Members collection of the CodeModule object. Each object of this collection is a CodeModule object, so its members are listed under the CodeModule class. The basic properties of the CodeModule object are listed in Table 13.5, and the basic methods are listed in Table 13.6.

TABLE 13.5: The Basic Properties of the CodeModule Object

Property	Description
CountOfDeclarationLines	The number of lines of code in the declarations section in a code module.
CountOfLines	The number of lines of code in a code module.
Lines(startLine, count)	This property acts like a method and returns the specified block of lines (returns count lines starting at *startLine*).
ProcBodyLine(procedureName, procedureType)	Returns the first line of the specified procedure.
ProcCountLines(procedureName, procedureType)	Returns the number of lines in the specified procedure.
ProcStartLine(procedureName, procedureType)	Returns the line in which the specified procedure begins.
ProcOfLine(Line, procedureType)	Returns the name of the procedure that contains the specified line.

TABLE 13.6: The Basic Methods of the CodeModule Object

Method	What It Does
DeleteLines(startLine, count)	Deletes count lines in the code module, starting at *startLine*.
InsertLine(lineNumber, codeLine)	Inserts one or more code lines at the location specified by the *numberLine* argument.
ReplaceLine(lineNumber, codeLine)	Replaces the specified line of code with the line(s) *codeLine*.
Find()	Searches a specified module for a specific string. See the method's description in the Object Browser for an explanation of its arguments.
CreateEventProc(eventName, objectName)	Creates the specified event procedure for the specified object.

Using the members of the CodeModule, you can access the code of a project, edit it, and even create new procedures from within your add-in. We will create a complete add-in that places controls on a Form and code in the Form's code module. The examples here are simple, and they are meant to clarify a few points about using the CodeModule object. You will see more practical examples in the section "Developing a Form Generator," later in this chapter.

Let's start with the basic loop structure that examines each member of the code module of a component.

```
' Set up an array with member type names
Dim MemberType(5) As String
MemberType(vbext_mt_Event) = "EVENT    "
MemberType(vbext_mt_Method) = "METHOD   "
MemberType(vbext_mt_Const) = "CONSTANT"
MemberType(vbext_mt_Property) = "PROPERTY"
MemberType(vbext_mt_Variable) = "VARIABLE"
''''''''''''''''''''''''''''''''''''''''''''
Set thisProject = VBInstance.ActiveVBProject
pComponents = thisProject.VBComponents.Count
For i = 1 To pComponents
    Debug.Print "VB Component " & thisProject.VBComponents.Item(i).Name
    pMembers = _
thisProject.VBComponents.Item(i).CodeModule.Members.Count
    For j = 1 To pMembers
        Set thisCodeModule = _
thisProject.VBComponents.Item(i).CodeModule
        Debug.Print MemberType(thisCodeModule.Members.Item(j).Type) & _
            "  " & thisProject.VBComponents.Item(i).CodeModule. _
            Members.Item(j).Name
    Next
Next
```

The first line after the assignment sets the object variable *thisProject* to the active project. The code then sets up a loop (the outer loop) that scans each component in the project and prints the name of each component and the number of code lines in the component's code module. Then, for each project component, the program calculates the number of code members and sets up a nested loop, which prints each code component's type and name. Notice the lines at the beginning of the code segment that set up an array with the names of the CodeModule's Type property values. The Type property is an enumerated variable and can have one of the values in Table 13.7.

TABLE 13.7: The Possible Types of a CodeModule Object

Value	What It Is
vbext_mt_Const	Constant declaration
vbext_mt_Variable	Variable declaration
vbext_mt_Event	Event declaration
vbext_mt_Method	Method declaration
vbext_mt_Property	Property declaration(Let, Get, or Set property procedure)

The number of code components in a project component is given by the following expression:

```
thisProject.VBComponents.Item(i).CodeModule.Members.Count
```

This is the number of items in the Members collection. To access each code component, you must access a specific item of the collection and read its Type property. The full expression is:

```
thisProject.VBComponents.Item(i).CodeModule.Members.Item(j).Type
```

Object expressions can get really long. Surprisingly, these long expressions are easier to write—especially if you have the Auto List Members option turned on—than they are to read. To keep code lines shorter, you can create intermediate object variables. For the specific example, we can use the *thisCodeModule* object variable, which is of CodeModule type and is set with the following statement:

```
Set thisCodeModule = thisProject.VBComponents.Item(i).CodeModule
```

You can then access individual code components with an expression such as the following:

```
thisModule.Members.Item(i)
```

This object represents a CodeModule, and not the module's code (the actual text). To access the code, you must use one of the properties listed in Table 13.5 or one of the methods listed in Table 13.6 to edit the module's lines. In the following sections, you will see examples that scan the procedures and declarations of a code module, and you will see examples of how to edit a project's code.

Now that we have looked at the major objects of the VBIDE class, we are ready to look at a few examples. First, we'll examine the structure of an add-in. Next, we'll go through the steps that are unique in building and testing add-ins, and then we'll work through a few practical add-ins.

Building an Add-In

Building an add-in isn't much different from building regular VB applications. Basically, an Add-In project type creates the skeleton of an add-in, which you can flesh out with your own code. Unlike VB projects, however, add-ins have special requirements, and you must understand them in order to develop your own add-ins that can be smoothly integrated into the Visual Basic environment.

As we mentioned at the beginning of this chapter, add-ins are displayed in the Add-Ins menu. To add an add-in to this menu, you choose Add-Ins ➤ Add-In Manager to open the Add-In Manager dialog box. You then select the name of the add-in. Something similar happens with ActiveX controls: The user selects the desired control in the Components dialog box. The difference is that ActiveX controls don't require any special code to hook to the Toolbox; neither do you have to provide any code to be executed every time the user clicks the control's icon.

With add-ins, you must supply the code to append the add-in's name to the Add-Ins menu yourself, and you must supply the code to react to the click of the add-in's name (after all, it's a menu command). These extra steps require some lines of code, which may even throw you off if you haven't developed add-ins in the past. Since the structure of an add-in is always the same, we'll start by examining the default Add-In project type. We'll build a simple add-in that connects and disconnects itself to the IDE and displays a Form when selected in the Add-Ins menu.

The Add-In Project Type

Start a New project, and in the New Project window, select AddIn. Visual Basic will add two folders in the Project window:

> **Forms,** which contains the Forms that will be displayed by the add-in (if any). By default, the Forms folder contains one Form, the frmAddin Form.

> **Designers,** which contains an ActiveX Designer, named Connect.

These are the basic components of an add-in. The Connect ActiveX Designer contains the code that connects and disconnects the add-in. If you have developed add-ins with Visual Basic 5, the Connect ActiveX Designer replaces the Connect Class Module. The code of the Connect Class Module is now generated by the Connect ActiveX Designer.

You can change the default names. In this book, we'll use the default names created by the project template.

The Connect ActiveX Designer

The Connect ActiveX Designer is the most important part of an add-in, and most of you will not be familiar with it. The minimum code produced by the Designer should do the following:

- Initialize the add-in

- Disconnect it from the IDE

- React when the user clicks the name of the add-in in the Add-Ins menu

The third procedure isn't really required, but it's disconcerting for users to click a menu command and receive no feedback.

First, you must double-click the Connect Designer to see the dialog box of Figure 13.5. Here, you specify the add-in's name and its description. Replace the generic name My Addin with a more meaningful name early in the design process. In the Advanced tab you can specify a name for the DLL that implements the add-in (if you don't the DLL will be named after the project's name) and additional keys to be written to the Registry when the add-in is installed. You can read the values of the keys when the add-in is loaded to initialize it. Then close the Connect AddIn-Designer window and change the name of the project from MyAddIn to something else.

At this point, you can look at the code produced by the Designer. Select the Connect Designer and click the Code icon on the Project Explorer window. The first few lines contain declarations:

Code 13.1   **Basic Declarations**

```
Option Explicit

Public FormDisplayed           As Boolean
Public VBInstance              As VBIDE.VBE
Dim mcbMenuCommandBar          As Office.CommandBarControl
Dim mfrmAddIn                  As New frmAddIn
Public WithEvents MenuHandler  As CommandBarEvents
```

FormDisplayed is a True/False variable that indicates whether the add-in's Form is displayed or not. VBInstance is an object variable that represents the Visual Basic

FIGURE 13.5:

The Connect ActiveX
Designer

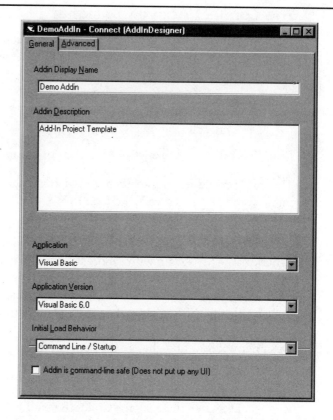

IDE. Later in the code we'll use this variable to access the active project (VBInstance-.ActiveVBProject), the components of the active project (VBInstance.ActiveVB-Project.VBComponents), and so on. The *mcbMenuCommandBar* is another object variable that represents a command in the IDE's Command Bar. This variable will be used to add the add-in's name to the Add-Ins menu. (We will discuss later how to manipulate the menus of the IDE and how to intercept menu commands.)

The *mfrmAddIn* variable represents the add-in's Form (many add-ins don't have a visible user interface). Finally, the *MenuHandler* object variable will be used to program the Click event of the command in the Add-Ins menu that corresponds to the add-in.

Then comes the code required to initialize and install the add-in. We will examine the basic procedures of an add-in in an order different from that in which they appear in the code window.

NOTE

The code produced by the Connect Designer contains all the methods required to connect and disconnect the add-in. The AddinInstance_OnConnection() procedure, for example, is a method. To you, the VB programmer, it looks like an event, but it's a method of the AddinInstance object. Visual Basic doesn't generate an OnConnection event; it simply calls the OnConnection method of the AddinInstance object.

Connecting the Add-In

The OnConnection method of the AddinInstance object is called when Visual Basic installs the add-in, and it contains the code needed to initialize and install the add-in.

Code 13.2   The Default Implementation of the OnConnection Method

```
Private Sub AddinInstance_OnConnection(ByVal Application As Object, _
        ByVal ConnectMode As AddInDesignerObjects.ext_ConnectMode, _
        ByVal AddInInst As Object, custom() As Variant)
On Error GoTo error_handler

    'save the vb instance
    Set VBInstance = Application

    'this is a good place to set a breakpoint and
    'test various addin objects, properties and methods
    Debug.Print VBInstance.FullName

    If ConnectMode = ext_cm_External Then
        'Used by the wizard toolbar to start this wizard
        Me.Show
    Else
        Set mcbMenuCommandBar = AddToAddInCommandBar("My AddIn")
        'sink the event
        Set Me.MenuHandler = _
            VBInstance.Events.CommandBarEvents(mcbMenuCommandBar)
    End If

    If ConnectMode = ext_cm_AfterStartup Then
        If GetSetting(App.Title, "Settings", _
                "DisplayOnConnect", "0") = "1" Then
            'set this to display the form on connect
            Me.Show
```

```
        End If
      End If

      Exit Sub

   error_handler:

      MsgBox Err.Description

   End Sub
```

Visual Basic passes a reference to the current instance of the IDE to this event with the argument *Application*. This reference is saved in the *VBInstance* public variable so that all other parts of the code can use it. The second argument, *ConnectMode*, determines how the add-in was connected. Table 13.8 shows its values.

TABLE 13.8: The Values of the ConnectMode Argument of the OnConnection Method

Value	Description
vbext_cm_AfterStartup	The add-in was started with the project.
vbext_cm_Startup	The add-in was started before any project was opened.
vbext_cm_External	The add-in was started by another program.

The third argument is another object variable that represents the add-in itself. The last argument, custom(), is an array that contains user-defined data.

The code examines the value of the *ConnectMode* argument to figure out how the add-in was started. If it was started by another add-in, it displays the Form. If not, it adds the name of the add-in (you must replace the string "My AddIn" with your add-in's name) to the Add-Ins menu with the AddToAddInCommandBar() function. This is not a built-in function. You can find it later in the code, but you need not change it either. Even if the add-in contains no visible interface, you must place its name in the Add-Ins menu so that users know that the add-in has been installed.

Handling the Add-Ins Menu Events

The AddToAddInCommandBar() function returns an object that represents a menu command. A reference to this object is stored in the *mcbMenuCommandBar* public variable, which is used later in the code to monitor the Click event of the add-in's name. The following line:

```
Set Me.MenuHandler = _
VBInstance.Events.CommandBarEvents(mcbMenuCommandBar)
```

prepares the *MenuHandler* object to detect the events of the *mcbMenuCommandBar* object (it reports the Click event only). If you open the Objects list in the Code window, you will see the name of the MenuHandler object. Select it, and then open the Events list, which contains a single event, Click. The code for this event handler is shown next:

Code 13.3   **The Click Event**

```
Private Sub MenuHandler_Click(ByVal CommandBarControl As Object, _
      handled As Boolean, CancelDefault As Boolean)
    Me.Show
End Sub
```

The Click event displays the add-in's Form. If your add-in has no visible interface, you could use this event to display a message box or an About box with information about the add-in. This is how an add-in's name is added to the Add-Ins menu and how the add-in handles the Click event, which is triggered every time the user selects it. You'll be using the same code for nearly every add-in you build. (We'll discuss the CommandBarControl object in detail later in this chapter.)

The first argument of the event represents the menu command or Command Button that was clicked. The second argument is a Boolean variable, indicating whether the event has been handled already by another add-in. Even if it was handled, your add-in will be notified about the event. If the event has been handled by another add-in, the CancelDefault argument is True, which indicates that your handler's code won't be executed. If you want to handle an event from within your add-in and prohibit other add-ins from handling the same event, set the CancelDefault argument to True.

Disconnecting the Add-In

When the user disconnects the add-in, the AddinInstance_OnDisconnection method is called. This method (which also looks like an event to you) accepts two arguments:

- The RemoveMode, which determines how the add-in was disconnected

- The custom() array, which holds the same custom data with the last argument of the OnConnection method

Table 13.9 lists and describes the values of the RemoveMode argument.

TABLE 13.9: The Values of the RemoveMode Argument of the OnDisconnection Method

Value	Description
vbext_dm_HostShuDown	The add-in was closed by the host application.
vbext_dm_UserClosed	The add-in was closed by the user, through the Add-Ins dialog box.

The code of the OnDisconnection method deletes the mcbMenuCommandBar menu command (which in effect removes the add-in's name from the Add-Ins menu) and then unloads the Form. If your add-in doesn't display a Form, you need to keep only the line that removes the add-in's name from the Add-Ins menu.

Code 13.4   The OnDisconnection Method

```
Private Sub AddinInstance_OnDisconnection(ByVal RemoveMode _
            As AddInDesignerObjects.ext_DisconnectMode, _
            custom() As Variant)
    On Error Resume Next
    'delete the command bar entry
    mcbMenuCommandBar.Delete
    'shut down the Add-In
    If FormDisplayed Then
        SaveSetting App.Title, "Settings", "DisplayOnConnect", "1"
        FormDisplayed = False
    Else
        SaveSetting App.Title, "Settings", "DisplayOnConnect", "0"
    End If
    Unload mfrmAddIn
    Set mfrmAddIn = Nothing
End Sub
```

The OnStartupComplete method is called as soon as the add-in has been successfully connected. It examines the value of the DisplayOnConnect parameter to determine whether it should display the add-in automatically. Although the Add-In template project displays the Form by default, most add-ins don't start automatically.

Code 13.5	The OnStartupComplete Method

```
Private Sub IDTExtensibility_OnStartupComplete(custom() As Variant)
    If GetSetting(App.Title, "Settings", _
            "DisplayOnConnect", "0") = "1" Then
        'set this to display the form on connect
        Me.Show
    End If
End Sub
```

This is the general structure of an add-in. The code that does something is usually placed in the buttons of a Form, although some add-ins don't display any Forms. Later in this chapter, you will see an add-in that detects when the user deletes or renames controls on a Form. The Code Remover add-in prompts the user each time they remove a control as to whether it should remove the control's event handlers. The code for this add-in is contained in the class module.

In the next section, we are going to build a working add-in that demonstrates many of the topics discussed so far in this chapter. You can use this add-in as the starting point for many add-ins and experiment with the objects of the VBIDE object model. We are going to build more advanced, and practical, add-ins later in the chapter.

Testing an Add-In

Testing an add-in is similar to testing an out-of-process ActiveX component. You can compile an add-in into an EXE or a DLL file just as you can compile an ActiveX component into either of those file types. When you create the executable file, the add-in is added to the Registry and is available to the system. To register the component to another system, you must either run the executable (if it's an EXE file) or use the REGSVR32 utility to register it manually or from within a batch file (if it's a DLL file).

To test and debug the add-in, you must first connect it. Follow these steps:

1. Run the add-in project, and then start another instance of Visual Basic.

2. Choose Add-Ins ➢ Add-In Manager to open the Add-In Manager dialog box.

3. Select the add-in you want.

If you haven't changed the default component names for the new add-in, its name will be My Add-In. Once the add-in is added to the list of connected add-ins in the Add-Ins menu, you can activate it by clicking its name. When an error occurs in the add-in's code, Visual Basic will switch you immediately to the add-in's instance of VB6, at the line of the error. You can change the code, press F5 to resume execution, and then switch to the add-in. (In most cases, Visual Basic will take you back to the test project automatically.)

The usual debugging aids apply to add-in projects as well. You can set breakpoints in the add-in project's Code window and single-step the add-in to see what each statement does. While the add-in project is in Break mode, you can issue commands in the Immediate window and examine the structure of the various objects of the VBIDE object model and their properties and methods. Because you can't declare variables in the Immediate window and because the objects of the VBIDE are usually manipulated through object variables, declare all the variables that you may need later in the Immediate window as public in the add-in's code.

Developing add-ins isn't a complicated process, but the object model that allows you to access the IDE is complex, and the expressions can get quite lengthy. If you want to develop custom add-ins, spend some time experimenting with the examples in this chapter to get the hang of the process, and soon you'll be able to apply your VB knowledge to building add-ins.

TIP   Although we usually turn off the Auto List Members feature of the editor, we find this feature handy when working with add-ins.

The Demo Add-In Project

In this section, we are going to put together all the examples we discussed in the first half of the chapter (where we introduced the basic objects of the VBIDE class) and build an add-in. You can use the add-in to experiment with these objects and explore additional objects and their properties and methods. When first connected, and each time it's connected thereafter, the Demo add-in displays the Form shown in Figure 13.6. The buttons on this Form perform many of the operations we've discussed in this chapter. In the previous sections, we focused on the basic lines that carry out each task. Now you are going to see the complete implementation of these examples, including the declarations of the variables and error-trapping code (as needed).

NOTE   You'll find the Demo Add-In project in the Chapter13/Demo folder on the CD that comes with this book.

FIGURE 13.6:

The Demo add-in's Form

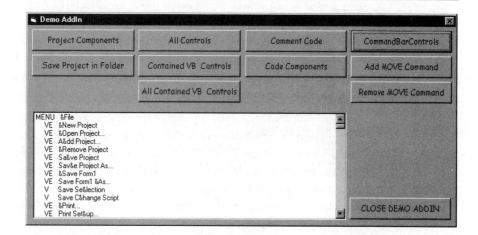

Here is what each button on this Form does:

Project Components displays the open project's components.

Save Project in Folder saves these components to a new folder.

All Controls displays all the controls on the components of the project.

ContainedVBControls displays only the controls sited directly on the currently active (selected) Form.

All ContainedVBControls displays the names of all controls on the project's Forms, grouped according to their container.

Comment Code inserts comment lines in the project's procedures.

Code Components displays all methods and event handlers in the project, along with each procedure's starting line and length (in number of lines).

CommandBar Controls prints the IDE's menu structure (with all its submenus).

Add MOVE Command adds a MOVE custom command to the File menu.

Remove MOVE Command removes the MOVE custom command from the File menu.

In the following sections, we'll discuss the code behind each of these Command Buttons in detail.

Implementing the Demo Add-In

Start a new Add-in project and open the Connect ActiveX Designer by double-clicking its icon in the Project Explorer window. Set its Display Name to Demo and close the Designer's window. Then set the project's name to DemoAddIn. If you open the File menu now, you'll see that the default name for the DLL that implements the add-in is DemoAddIn. The necessary initialization and termination code will be generated by the Designer and there's no need to modify the code of the Connect component.

Then open the frmAddIn Form and delete the OK and Cancel buttons that are placed there by Visual Basic. Make sure you delete their code too. Then place on it the controls you see in Figure 13.6. The large box at the bottom of the Form is a ListBox control. The CLOSE DEMO ADDIN corresponds to the OK button and it closes the add-in's Form. Insert the following lines in its Click event handler:

```
Private Sub bttnOK_Click()
    Connect.Hide
End Sub
```

In the following few sections we are going to develop the code behind each button on the Form. You can already test the add-in by loading it into another project and displaying its main Form. Start a new Standard EXE project, open the Add-Ins menu, and select Add-In Manager. In the Add-In Manager window that will pop up, select the entry Demo and check the option Loaded/Unloaded in the lower-right corner of the window. The add-in will be loaded to the current project. Then close the Add-In Manager window to return to the test project.

Open the Add-In menu again and you'll see the name of the Demo Add-In. Select it and the add-in's main Form will appear. The buttons don't do anything yet, but the add-in was hooked into the environment and you didn't have to supply a single line of code yet. Of course, the name of the add-in will appear in the Add-In Manager window only while the add-in project is running in another instance of Visual Basic. To register the add-in to your system permanently and use it with your projects without having to run it, create the DemoAddIn.dll component with the Make DemoAddIn.dll command of the File menu. This action will register the add-in with your system and you'll be able to add it to any project. Every time you change the add-in's code, you must create a new DLL. While you're designing and testing an add-in, it's simpler to run the add-in and the test project in two separate instances of Visual Basic. After the add-in has been fully debugged, you can create a DLL file and register the add-in to your system.

To follow the examples of the next few sections, start two instances of Visual Basic: one with the add-in and another one with the test project. Just remember to switch the instance of Visual Basic with the add-in to run-mode before using it from within the other instance of Visual Basic with the test project. To change the add-in's code, stop the project, edit it, and then start it again. In the following section, we are going to discuss the implementation of each button on the Demo add-in's Form.

Listing a Project's Components

The Project Components button demonstrates the VBComponents collection, which returns information about all components in a project. You have already seen the core of this add-in in the section "The VBComponent Object and the VBComponents Collection," earlier in this chapter. The Click event handler of this button prints the names of the projects in the Project window, and under each project's name it prints the names of all its components (Forms, class modules, and so on). The last section of the code displays the name of the active project and the name of the selected component in the active project.

Code 13.6	**The Project Components Button**

```
Private Sub bttnComponents_Click()
Dim thisProject As VBProject
Dim nProjects As Integer, nComponents As Integer
Dim i As Integer, j As Integer
Dim projectName As String
Dim msg As String

    nProjects = VBInstance.VBProjects.Count
    List1.Clear
    For i = 1 To nProjects
        Set thisProject = VBInstance.VBProjects.Item(i)
        projectName = VBInstance.VBProjects.Item(i).Name
        nComponents = thisProject.VBComponents.Count
        List1.AddItem "PROJECT " & projectName
        For j = 1 To nComponents
```

```
                    List1.AddItem Space(15) & "Component #" & j _
                        & "  " & thisProject.VBComponents.Item(j).Name
            Next
        Next

    On Error GoTo NoSelectedComponent
        msg = "The selected project is   " & _
                VBInstance.ActiveVBProject.Name & vbCrLf
        msg = msg & "The selected component is " & _
                VBInstance.SelectedVBComponent.Name
        MsgBox msg
        Exit Sub

    NoSelectedComponent:
        MsgBox "No component is selected"

    End Sub
```

The subroutine extracts the number of projects in the project group (property Count of the VBProjects collection) and then sets up a loop that scans the components of each project. This loop starts by setting the object variable *thisProject* to the current project, to shorten the expressions required to access each component. In the rest of the code, the expression VBInstance.VBProjects.Item(i) or VBInstance.VBProjects(i) is replaced by the variable *thisProject*. (You can also shorten the expression that represents the current component by introducing a new object variable, *thisComponent.* You must declare it as VBComponent.)

Each project has a number of components that can be accessed through the VBComponents collection. The code sets up a nested loop that scans the components of the current project. The number of components is given by the property Count of the VBComponents collection. The names of each project's components are printed in the ListBox control, following the name of the project they belong to, as shown in Figure 13.7.

Through the VBComponents collection, you can manipulate the components of the project. You can add a new component to the project with the Add and AddFile methods (the AddFile method adds a component that exists on the disk). The Remove method removes a component from the project. Finally, you can specify the project's startup object by assigning its name to the VBComponents collection's StartUpObject property.

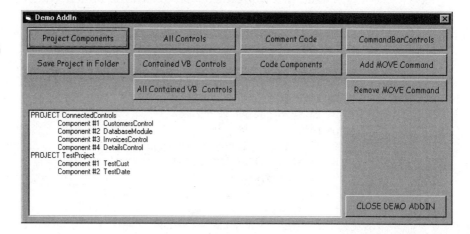

FIGURE 13.7:

The Project Components button of the Demo add-in displays the names of the projects in the current project group, followed by the names of the components in each project.

Once you know how to access each project component, you can also manipulate them through the properties and methods of the VBComponent object. Each member of the collection is a VBComponent object, and you can access an individual component either with the Item property of the collection or with an index value. The Properties property returns the value of any of the properties listed in the Properties window when this component is selected. You can also save the component in a disk file with the SaveAs method or force the IDE to reload it with the Reload method.

NOTE   For the syntax of the methods mentioned in this section, consult the Object Browser.

Listing a Project's Controls

The All Controls, ContainedVBControls, and All ContainedVBControls buttons demonstrate three methods to access the controls on all (or selected) Forms in the current project. (We discussed all three methods in the section "The VBControls and ContainedVBControls Collections," earlier in this chapter.) The VBControls collection returns all the controls on a Form and on any container controls on the Form (if any), and the ContainedVBControls collection returns only the controls sited directly on the Form. If some of these controls contain other controls, the contained controls must be accessed by the ContainedVBControls of the container control. The All ContainedVBControls button demonstrates a recursive routine for scanning each container's contained controls, to any depth.

Let's start with the code of the All Controls button, which is simpler than the others.

Code 13.7　　　**The All Controls Button**

```
Private Sub bttnControls_Click()
Dim thisComponent As VBComponent
Dim thisProject As VBProject
Dim thisForm As VBForm
Dim iProject As Integer, iComponent As Integer, iControl As Integer
Dim thisControl As VBControl
Dim allControls As VBControls

List1.Clear
' the outer loop scans each component of the project
For iProject = 1 To VBInstance.VBProjects.Count
    Set thisProject = VBInstance.VBProjects.Item(iProject)
' the following loop scans each component of the current project
    For iComponent = 1 To thisProject.VBComponents.Count
' and examines its type
        If thisProject.VBComponents.Item(iComponent).Type = _
            vbext_ct_VBForm Or _
            thisProject.VBComponents.Item(iComponent).Type = _
            vbext_ct_UserControl Then
        Set thisForm = _
            thisProject.VBComponents.Item(iComponent).Designer
' the following loop scans each control on the current Form
            For iControl = 1 To thisForm.VBControls.Count
                Set thisControl = thisForm.VBControls.Item(iControl)
' if the control belongs to a control array, its index value
' must be listed along with the control's name
                If thisControl.Properties("Index") >= 0 Then
                    List1.AddItem thisControl.Properties("Name") _
                    & "(" & thisControl.Properties("Index") & ")"
                Else
                    List1.AddItem thisControl.Properties("Name")
                End If
            Next
        End If
    Next
Next
End Sub
```

This code sets up a loop that scans all the projects and a nested loop that scans all the components of the current project. For each component, it examines its Type property, and if the component's type is Form (constant vbext_ct_Form) or User-Control (constant vbext_ct_UserControl), it prints all the components (controls) on the Form. This takes place from within another nested loop, which scans the elements of the VBControls collection and prints the value of the Name property of each control. The program examines the control's Index property, and if the control belongs to a control array, it displays the index value as well. Figure 13.8 shows the output generated by the All Controls button. The project used to create Figure 13.8 is called TestProj and you will find it in the same folder as the Demo-AddIn project.

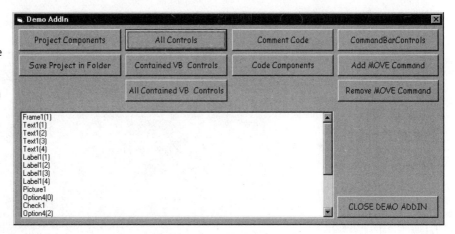

FIGURE 13.8:

The All Controls button of the Demo add-in displays the names of the controls on all Forms in the current project, as well as controls placed on container controls.

Listing Contained Controls

The ContainedVBControls button uses the ContainedVBControls collection to access the controls on the application's Forms. The output generated by the ContainedVBControls button is shown in Figure 13.9. This list contains only the controls that are directly sited on the Form, and not the controls they contain. The Form with the controls that produced the output in Figure 13.9 is shown in Figure 13.10.

The code behind the ContainedVBControls button is similar to the code of the All Controls button. It uses the same three loops to scan projects, components, and controls. However, instead of using the VBControls collection, it uses the ContainedVBControls collection.

FIGURE 13.9:

The ContainedVBControls button of the Demo add-in displays the names of the controls on all Forms in the current project.

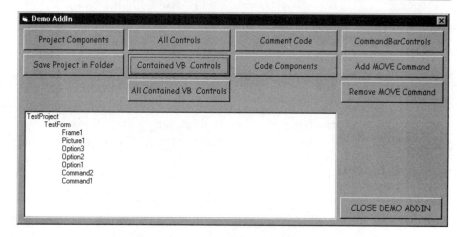

FIGURE 13.10:

The test Form used to produce the list of controls in Figure 13.9

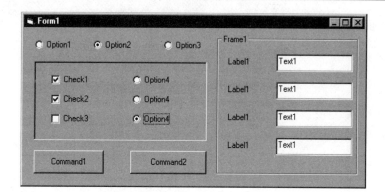

Code 13.8   The ContainedVBControls Button

```
Private Sub bttnContainedControls_Click()
Dim thisComponent As VBComponent
Dim thisProject As VBProject
Dim thisForm As VBForm
Dim iProject As Integer, iComponent As Integer, iControl As Integer

List1.Clear
For iProject = 1 To VBInstance.VBProjects.Count
    Set thisProject = VBInstance.VBProjects.Item(iProject)
```

```
        List1.AddItem thisProject.Name
' the following loop scans each component of the current project
    For iComponent = 1 To thisProject.VBComponents.Count
        Set thisComponent = thisProject.VBComponents.Item(iComponent)
        List1.AddItem Space(10) & thisComponent.Name
' and examines its type.
' If the control belongs to a control array, its index value
' must be listed along with the control's name
        If thisComponent.Type = vbext_ct_VBForm Or _
                thisComponent.Type = vbext_ct_UserControl Then
            Set thisForm = thisComponent.Designer
            For iControl = 1 To thisForm.ContainedVBControls.Count
                List1.AddItem Space(20) & _
                    thisForm.ContainedVBControls.Item _
                    (iControl).Properties("Name")
            Next
        End If
    Next
Next
End Sub
```

The list of all controls, shown in Figure 13.8, doesn't have a particular structure. They are not listed in any order. The list of contained controls, shown in Figure 13.9, has a better structure, but it doesn't contain all the controls on the Form. Ideally, we would like a list of all controls on the Form and the controls they may contain, to any depth, as shown in Figure 13.11. The arrays of the Label and TextBox controls sited on the Frame1(1) container control are listed under the name of the control that contains them, appropriately indented. The list in Figure 13.11 was generated with the All ContainedVBControls button.

The code behind the All ContainedVBControls is interesting. Basically, it uses the same structure to access the components of the project's Forms. After printing the name of each control on the current Form, it calls the ShowContainedControls() subroutine, passing to it as an argument an object variable representing the current control. The ShowContainedControls() subroutine displays the contained controls. This subroutine, in turn, calls itself recursively for each control it prints in the list. Let's start with the code behind the All ContainedVBControls button, and then we'll examine the implementation of the ShowContainedControls() subroutine.

FIGURE 13.11:

The All ContainedVBControls button of the Demo add-in displays the names of the controls and their contained controls on all Forms in the current project.

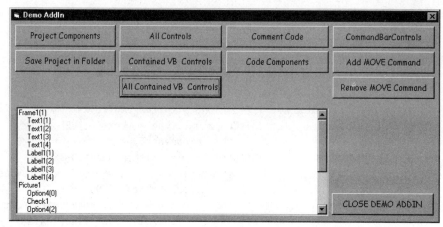

Code 13.9   The All ContainedVBControls Button

```
Private Sub bttnAllContainedControls_Click()
Dim thisComponent As VBComponent
Dim thisProject As VBProject
Dim thisForm As VBForm
Dim iProject As Integer, iComponent As Integer, iControl As Integer
Dim thisControl As VBControl

List1.Clear
For iProject = 1 To VBInstance.VBProjects.Count
    Set thisProject = VBInstance.VBProjects.Item(iProject)
    For iComponent = 1 To thisProject.VBComponents.Count
        If thisProject.VBComponents.Item(iComponent).Type = _
                vbext_ct_VBForm Then
            Set thisForm = _
                thisProject.VBComponents.Item(iComponent).Designer
            For iControl = 1 To thisForm.ContainedVBControls.Count
                Set thisControl = _
                    thisForm.ContainedVBControls.Item(iControl)
                If thisControl.Properties("Index") >= 0 Then
                    List1.AddItem thisControl.Properties("Name") _
                        & "(" & thisControl.Properties("Index") & ")"
                Else
```

```
                        List1.AddItem thisControl.Properties("Name")
                    End If
                    ShowContainedControls thisControl
                Next
            End If
        Next
    Next
    End Sub
```

The ShowContainedControls() subroutine uses the ContainedVBControls collection of the control passed as an argument to display the names of the controls contained on this control. If the current control is a container for additional controls, it calls itself again to print any controls sited on it. (It's quite unlikely that a Form contains multiple levels of container controls, but the code will work anyway.)

Code 13.10   The ShowContainedControls() Subroutine

```
Sub ShowContainedControls(thisControl As VBControl)
Dim iControl As Integer
Dim newControl As VBControl
Static indentLevel As Integer
Dim indentSpace As String

If thisControl.ContainedVBControls.Count = 0 Then Exit Sub
indentLevel = indentLevel + 5
indentSpace = Space(indentLevel)
For iControl = 1 To thisControl.ContainedVBControls.Count
    Set newControl = thisControl.ContainedVBControls.Item(iControl)
    If newControl.Properties("Index") >= 0 Then
        List1.AddItem indentSpace & newControl.Properties("Name") _
            & "(" & newControl.Properties("Index") & ")"
    Else
        List1.AddItem indentSpace & newControl.Properties("Name")
    End If
    ShowContainedControls newControl
Next
indentLevel = indentLevel - 5
End Sub
```

Most of this code deals with formatting the list (indenting the contained controls under their container). Here, however, is the core of this subroutine:

```
If thisControl.ContainedVBControls.Count = 0 Then Exit Sub
For iControl = 1 To thisControl.ContainedVBControls.Count
    Set newControl = thisControl.ContainedVBControls.Item(iControl)
    {DISPLAY CONTROL'S NAME}
    ShowContainedControls newControl
Next
```

First, the program checks the number of contained controls on the current control. If there are no contained controls, the subroutine exits. If there are contained controls, the code scans each element of the ContainedVBControls collection, displays its name on the list, and then calls itself, again passing the current control as an argument (in case this one is also a container control).

NOTE   The ContainedVBControls collection is used in the event handler of the Contained-VBControls button and in the event handler of the All ContainedVBControls button. In the first case, it's a property of the VBForm class (thisForm.ContainedVBControls), and it contains all the controls on the Form. In the second case, it's a property of the VBControl class (thisControl.ContainedVBControls), and it contains all the controls sited on the control represented by the *thisControl* object variable.

Examining and Setting Control Properties

Through the VBControls and ContainedVBControls collection, you can access the properties of the controls on the Forms and set them. We have used the expression newControl.Properties("Index") in our code to access the Index property of the current control. To set the BackColor property of the same control, you would use a statement such as the following:

```
thisForm.ContainedVBControls.Item(i).Properties("BackColor") = _
    RGB(255, 0, 0)
```

To change a property on multiple selected controls, use a statement such as the following:

```
thisForm.SelectedVBControls.Item(i).Properties("BackColor") = _
    RGB(255, 0, 0)
```

(this statement should appear in a loop that uses the variable i as counter).

The Properties property lets you manipulate a control in any way you like. Use it to access the Left and Top properties to align it with other controls, to access the Width and Height properties to resize it, and so on.

The examples in this section demonstrate how to access all the controls on a Form or on a container control. Using the same structure, you can read or set any of the properties of the controls and manipulate them from within your add-in. For example, you can write an add-in that makes sure that all contained controls have the same background color or font as the control that contains them. To access the properties of the container control (or Form, which is usually the case), use the ContainerControl property. The following expression:

```
thisForm.SelectedVBControls.Item(i).ContainerControl
```

returns a VBControl object that represents the container control. Use this object to find the properties of the control that contains the control with which you are working.

All properties that appear in the Properties window when a specific control is selected can be accessed through the Properties property of the VBControl object. Just make sure that the selected control supports the property you want to read (or set) before attempting to access it. Read the control's type first (ClassName property) and then access a property. If you can't be sure that the selected control is a text control, use an If statement such as the following:

```
Set thisControl = thisForm.SelectedVBControls.Item(1)
If thisControl.ClassName = "TextBox" Then
    thisControl.Property("Text") = "I'm a Textbox"
ElseIf thisControl.ClassName = "Label" Then
        thisControl.Property("Caption") = "I'm a Label"
End If
```

The VBControl object doesn't have a Type property, as do most objects. It has a ControlType property, which returns one of the values shown in Table 13.10.

TABLE 13.10: The Values of the VBControl Object's ControlType Property

Value	What It Does
vbext_ct_Container	Returns True if it's a container control.
vbext_ct_Light	Returns True if it's a light-weight control.
cvext_ct_Standard	Returns True if it's a standard control.

The VBControl object's InSelection property returns True if the specific control belongs to the current selection; however, you can't change the selection by setting this property. You can also change the control's order (layer) by assigning a value to the ZOrder property.

You'll see more examples of how to manipulate the properties of the controls on a Form and how to place new instances of controls on a Form from within an add-in in the section "Developing a Form Generator," later in this chapter. Actually, you already have all the information you need to develop an application generator that will create a Form from scratch and place the required code in the event handlers.

Listing a Project's Code Components

The Code Components button on the Demo add-in's Form prints the code components of a component, through the Members collection of the CodeModule object. The list generated by the Code Components button for a typical project (it's the TabOrder add-in demo that comes with Visual Basic) is shown in Figure 13.12. Notice that variable and constant declarations are also code components and that you can access them individually.

FIGURE 13.12:

The Code Components button of the Demo add-in prints the names of all procedures in a project's code, along with their location and size.

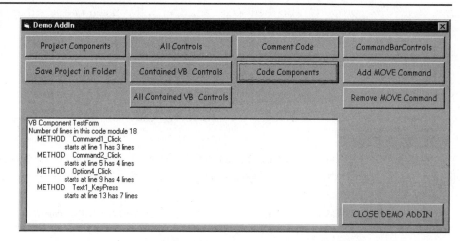

Use the CodeModule object of the VBComponent object to access the code of a component. The CodeModule object exposes several properties and methods that you can use to manipulate the component's code, as discussed in the section "The CodeModule Object," earlier in this chapter. Now we are going to see how to read the code and edit it. In the section "Developing a Form Generator," you will see how to create code modules entirely from within your add-in's code.

As usual, we set up a loop that scans each component in the active project and a nested loop that scans each member of the current component's CodeModule collection. The structure of the two loops is shown next:

```
Set thisProject = VBInstance.ActiveVBProject
pComponents = thisProject.VBComponents.Count
For i = 1 To pComponents
    pMembers = thisProject.VBComponents(i).CodeModule.Members.Count
    For j = 1 To pMembers
        Set thisCodeModule = thisProject.VBComponents(i).CodeModule
        {process current CodeModule object}
    Next
Next
```

> **NOTE** We use a slightly different notation to access the elements of the collection in this segment (we omit the Item property and apply the index directly to the collection's name). The only reason for doing this is to avoid long lines of code that break on the printed page.

Each element in the Members collection represents a declaration line, an event handler, a general procedure, or a Property procedure. The methods that extract the member's starting line and its length require that you know the member's type, which is returned by the Type property. If the member's type is an event or a method, you must call the ProcBodyLine property (which returns the location of the first line) as follows:

```
thisCodeModule.ProcBodyLine(thisProject.VBComponents.Item(i) _
        .CodeModule.Members.Item(j).Name, vbext_pk_Proc)
```

> **WARNING** The syntax of the ProcBodyLine property requires that you specify the member's name and its type. Things get a bit complicated when you want to access Property procedures. The Type property of the Members collection returns the constant vbext_mt_Property. Yet, in the ProcByLine method you must specify one of the constants *vbext_pk_Get*, *vbext_pk_Let*, or *vbext_pk_Set*. If you look at the code, you'll see that we try to extract all three types of Property procedures. If one or more are missing (the Set Property procedure is usually missing), the code uses an error handler to skip the corresponding lines.

The rest of the code is straightforward. First, it sets up an array with the names of the member types:

```
' Set up an array with member type names
Dim MemberType(5) As String
MemberType(vbext_mt_Event) = "EVENT    "
MemberType(vbext_mt_Method) = "METHOD   "
MemberType(vbext_mt_Const) = "CONSTANT"
MemberType(vbext_mt_Property) = "PROPERTY"
MemberType(vbext_mt_Variable) = "VARIABLE"
```

The elements of this array are then used to display the type of the member (EVENT, METHOD, and so on), along with its name:

```
MemberType(thisCodeModule.Members.Item(j).Type) & "  " & _
thisProject.VBComponents.Item(i).CodeModule.Members.Item(j).Name
```

Finally, we call the ProcBodyLine and ProcCountLines methods to extract the member's starting line and length (in number of lines) and display them on the ListBox control. Take a closer look at the lines that handle Property procedures. The code tries to read all three types of Property procedures (Get, Let, and Set), but if one of them is missing, a run-time error is generated. Notice also the long If statement that skips the code if the current component's type isn't one of the following:

- Class Module
- Property Page
- Standard Module
- UserControl
- Form
- MDI Form
- Document Object

Basically, this statement skips the resource files that Visual Basic can't handle.

Code 13.11   The Code Components Button

```
Private Sub bttnCodeComponents_Click()
Dim thisProject As VBProject
Dim thisCodeModule As CodeModule
Dim pComponents As Integer
Dim pMembers As Integer
```

```
Dim i As Integer, j As Integer
Dim line1 As Integer, line2 As Integer
Dim compType As Integer
' Set up an array with member type names
Dim MemberType(5) As String
MemberType(vbext_mt_Event) = "EVENT    "
MemberType(vbext_mt_Method) = "METHOD   "
MemberType(vbext_mt_Const) = "CONSTANT"
MemberType(vbext_mt_Property) = "PROPERTY"
MemberType(vbext_mt_Variable) = "VARIABLE"
''''''''''''''''''''''''''''''''''''''''''''''''
    Set thisProject = VBInstance.ActiveVBProject
    pComponents = thisProject.VBComponents.Count
    List1.Clear
    For i = 1 To pComponents
        List1.AddItem "VB Component " & _
                thisProject.VBComponents.Item(i).Name
        compType = thisProject.VBComponents.Item(i).Type
        If Not (compType = vbext_ct_ClassModule Or _
            compType = vbext_ct_PropPage Or compType = _
            vbext_ct_StdModule Or compType = vbext_ct_UserControl _
            Or compType = vbext_ct_VBForm Or compType = _
            vbext_ct_VBMDIForm Or compType = vbext_ct_DocObject) Then
            GoTo NextLoop
        End If
        pMembers = thisProject.VBComponents.Item(i).CodeModule. _
                Members.Count
        List1.AddItem "Number of lines in this code module " & _
            thisProject.VBComponents.Item(i).CodeModule.CountOfLines
        For j = 1 To pMembers
            Set thisCodeModule = thisProject.VBComponents. _
                    Item(i).CodeModule
            List1.AddItem Space(5) & _
                    MemberType(thisCodeModule.Members.Item(j).Type) & _
                    "  " & thisProject.VBComponents.Item(i). _
                    CodeModule.Members.Item(j).Name
            line1 = 0: line2 = 0
            If thisCodeModule.Members.Item(j).Type = _
                vbext_mt_Event Or thisCodeModule.Members. _
                Item(j).Type = vbext_mt_Method Then
                line1 = thisCodeModule.ProcBodyLine _
                    (thisCodeModule.Members.Item(j).Name, vbext_pk_Proc)
                line2 = thisCodeModule.ProcCountLines _
                    (thisCodeModule.Members.Item(j).Name, vbext_pk_Proc)
```

```
                    If line1 <> 0 And line2 <> 0 Then
                        List1.AddItem Space(20) & "starts at line " _
                            & line1 & " has " & line2 & " lines"
                    End If
            ElseIf thisCodeModule.Members.Item(j).Type = _
                    vbext_mt_Property Then
                On Error GoTo PropertySET
                line1 = 0: line2 = 0
                line1 = thisCodeModule.ProcBodyLine _
                    (thisCodeModule.Members.Item(j).Name, vbext_pk_Get)
                line2 = thisCodeModule.ProcCountLines _
                    (thisCodeModule.Members.Item(j).Name, vbext_pk_Get)
                If line1 <> 0 And line2 <> 0 Then
                    List1.AddItem Space(20) & _
                        "GET Procedure starts at line " & line1 & _
                        " has " & line2 & " lines"
                End If
PropertySET:
On Error GoTo PropertyLET
                line1 = 0: line2 = 0
                line1 = thisCodeModule.ProcBodyLine _
                    (thisCodeModule.Members.Item(j).Name, vbext_pk_Set)
                line2 = thisCodeModule.ProcCountLines _
                    (thisCodeModule.Members.Item(j).Name, vbext_pk_Set)
                If line1 <> 0 And line2 <> 0 Then
                    List1.AddItem Space(20) & _
                        "SET Procedure starts at line " & line1 & _
                        " has " & line2 & " lines"
                End If
PropertyLET:
On Error GoTo EndProp
                line1 = 0: line2 = 0
                line1 = thisCodeModule.ProcBodyLine _
                    (thisCodeModule.Members.Item(j).Name, vbext_pk_Let)
                line2 = thisCodeModule.ProcCountLines _
                    (thisCodeModule.Members.Item(j).Name, vbext_pk_Let)
                If line1 <> 0 And line2 <> 0 Then
                    List1.AddItem Space(20) & _
                        "LET Procedure starts at line " & line1 & _
                        " has " & line2 & " lines"
                End If
EndProp:
            End If
```

```
NextLoop:
            Next
        List1.AddItem " "
    Next
End Sub
```

If you look at the first few lines displayed by the Code Components button for a typical project, you will see that they are the declarations of the module's variables and constants. If the module contains API function declarations, they are listed as METHODS. Figure 13.13 shows the first few lines of the output generated by the Code Components button for the TabOrder project (you will find it in the Samples\CompTool\Addins\TabOrder folder on the VB6 CD). PostMessage is not a method of the project; it's an API function whose declaration (and not its implementation) appears in a module.

FIGURE 13.13:

The first four METHODS in this project are API function declarations, incorrectly classified by Visual Basic as methods.

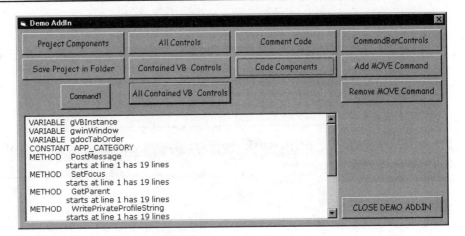

The entry

```
METHOD PostMessage
        Starts at line 1 has 19 lines
```

corresponds to the following declaration in the code:

```
Private Declare Sub PostMessage Lib "user32" Alias "PostMessageA"_
    (ByVal hwnd&, ByVal msg&, ByVal wp&, ByVal lp&)
```

This declaration doesn't start at line 1, and it certainly doesn't have 19 lines. The problem is that Visual Basic (incorrectly) thinks that this is a method, but in reality it's a declaration. Actually, it's a Sub declaration, but nevertheless a declaration. (It contains the keyword Declare and doesn't have a matching End Sub.)

And how about the incorrect line numbers? When the code extracts the first line and length of this method (because this is the component type returned by the Type method), it reads the first line and the length of the entire declarations section. This is a small bug you must live with. You can actually bypass it by reading the number of declaration lines with the CountOfDeclarationLines property and then classifying as a declaration all the methods that start at line 1 and have CountOfDeclarationLines lines of code.

Editing a Module's Code

In addition to reading the code of a module, you can edit it. In fact, this is how you can build a code generator, which is the core of a Wizard application. The Comment Code button is a simple example that inserts a copyright notice after the name of each method and event handler. The button's code uses the Insert Lines method of the CodeModule object, which inserts a string (that may contain multiple lines separated by a carriage return/line feed combination) at a specified location in the Code window. The code is a bit more complicated than that, as it first makes sure the copyright notice isn't already there. Figure 13.14 shows the Code window of a test project before and after the insertion of the copyright notice.

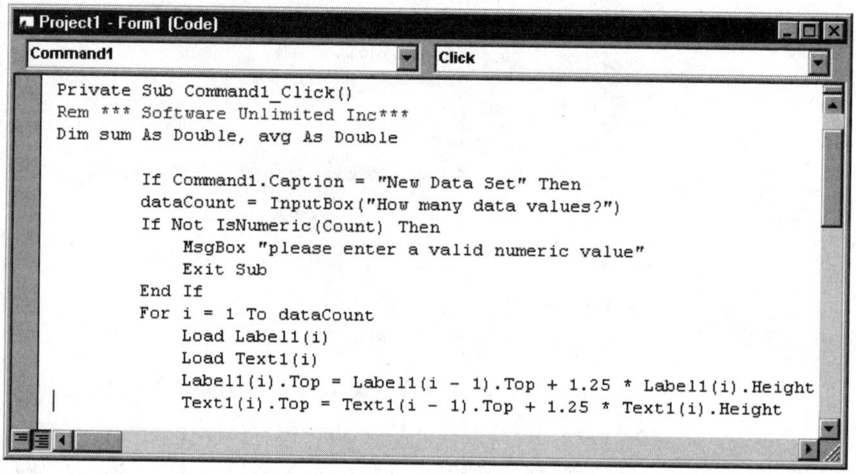

FIGURE 13.14:

The Comment Code button inserts a copyright notice after each procedure's definition line.

```
Project1 - Form1 (Code)

Command1                              Click

    Private Sub Command1_Click()
    Rem *** Software Unlimited Inc***
    Dim sum As Double, avg As Double

            If Command1.Caption = "New Data Set" Then
            dataCount = InputBox("How many data values?")
            If Not IsNumeric(Count) Then
                MsgBox "please enter a valid numeric value"
                Exit Sub
            End If
            For i = 1 To dataCount
                Load Label1(i)
                Load Text1(i)
                Label1(i).Top = Label1(i - 1).Top + 1.25 * Label1(i).Height
                Text1(i).Top = Text1(i - 1).Top + 1.25 * Text1(i).Height
```

The code finds the location of the first line of a code component and reads the first line of code in the module with the Lines method of the CodeModule object.

It then compares it to the copyright message, and if they don't match, the copyright notice is inserted in the code. This step is necessary to avoid filling the code module with copyright notices if the user clicks this button more than once. The rest of the code, which has the same structure as the code of the Code Components button, is shown next.

Code 13.12	**The Comment Code Button**

```
Private Sub bttnCommentCode_Click()
Dim thisProject As VBProject
Dim thisCodeModule As CodeModule
Dim pComponents As Integer
Dim pMembers As Integer
Dim i As Integer, j As Integer
Dim line1 As Integer, line2 As Integer
Dim cpRightLine As String
Const cpRightNotice = "REM *** Software Unlimited Inc***"

    Set thisProject = VBInstance.ActiveVBProject
    pComponents = thisProject.VBComponents.Count
    For i = 1 To pComponents
        pMembers = thisProject.VBComponents.Item(i). _
                CodeModule.Members.Count
        For j = 1 To pMembers
            Set thisCodeModule = thisProject.VBComponents. _
                    Item(i).CodeModule
            If thisCodeModule.Members.Item(j).Type = vbext_mt_Event Or _
                thisCodeModule.Members.Item(j).Type = vbext_mt_Method Then
                line1 = thisCodeModule.ProcBodyLine( _
                        thisProject.VBComponents.Item(i).CodeModule. _
                        Members.Item(j).Name, vbext_pk_Proc)
                line2 = thisCodeModule.ProcCountLines( _
                        thisProject.VBComponents.Item(i).CodeModule. _
                        Members.Item(j).Name, vbext_pk_Proc)
                cpRightLine = thisCodeModule.Lines(line1 + 1, 1)
                If StrComp(Trim(cpRightLine), Trim(cpRightNotice), _
                        vbTextCompare) Then
                    thisCodeModule.InsertLines line1 + 1, cpRightNotice
                End If
            End If
        Next
    Next
End Sub
```

In the next section, you will see an add-in that first creates a Form with user-specified controls on it and then inserts the code for selected event handlers. If you spend a good deal of time developing applications with similar interfaces and/or code, you should consider building an add-in or a Wizard that generates the Forms for you, instead of copying Forms and modifying their existing controls and code.

Developing a Form Generator

In this section, we are going to show you how to develop an application generator as an add-in. It's not just a code generator, but a real application generator that can produce applications with multiple Forms and the code behind them. A complete application generator should have the format of a Wizard and guide the user through a sequence of windows that collect the required information and then build the application.

In this section, we are going to examine the code of the application generator. We'll look at how to create Forms and add controls on them from within the add-in's code and at how to add code to the events. Most of the information we'll present here isn't new to you. We'll use the objects discussed already, and you'll see that building an application generator is a straightforward process, although it requires a lot of typing. From within your code, you must set every property of the controls you place on the Form, including the position and size properties.

First, you must decide what type of application you want the add-in to create. Obviously, you can't write a code generator that can produce all types of applications. Application generators are best suited for data-entry and report screens and for other programs that are used in multiple projects, with small variations—data-entry screens for tables in a database, reports based on different recordsets, and so on. It won't pay to write an application generator for a program that will be used in a single project. If you examine the Wizards that come with Visual Basic, you'll get a good feel for the type of programs that you can streamline with the help of an application generator.

Another good use for an application generator is building Class Modules, such as the ones we looked at in Chapter 10 or the interconnected ActiveX controls we looked at in Chapter 11. The classes we designed in Chapter 10 to access the customers and invoices of the NWIND database had an identical structure and differed only in the names of the properties in which the various fields are stored. If you plan to use the approach shown in those two chapters with other databases, you can save yourself a lot of time and trivial coding by building an add-in to automatically generate these applications.

Adding Controls on a Form

One of the basic operations a Form generator must perform is the placement of new controls on a Form, and we haven't discussed yet how to do it. To add a control on a Form, you use the Add method of the ContainedVBControls collection. The syntax of the Add method is:

```
ContainedVBControls.Add(ProgID As String, [RelativeVBControl As_
    VBControl], [Before As Boolean])
```

ProgID is the programmatic ID of the control you want to add ("Label" for a Label control, "TextBox" for a TextBox control, and so on). The following arguments are optional and are usually omitted in similar applications. The *RelativeVBControl* argument is the name of another control on the same Form, relative to which the new control will be inserted. If you specify this argument and omit the last one, the new control is placed after the specified control. If the last argument, Before, is True, the new control is placed before the specified control. These two arguments are useful in inserting controls in control arrays.

The Add method returns a VBControl object, which represents the newly added control. You can use this object to manipulate the control from within the code. To place a Label control on the current Form and set some properties, use statements such as the following:

```
Set thisControl = thisForm.ContainedVBControls.Add("Label")
thisControl.Properties("AutoSize") = True
thisControl.Properties("Caption") = "VB6 Developer's Handbook"
thisControl.Properties("Top") = currentTop + _
    1.5 * thisControl.Properties("Height")
thisControl.Properties("Left") = 1000
Set thisControl = Nothing
```

You declare the *thisControl* object variable as VBControl, and it's created as soon as you set it with the Add method of the VBControls or ContainedVBControls collection. You can then set any of the properties of the Label control through the Properties property. After you are done, release the object variable by setting it to Nothing.

Sizing Controls

You can rarely set the width of a TextBox or a Label control in twips or other absolute units. The control's size usually depends on its contents. The simplest way to size text controls (such as TextBoxes, Labels, and ListBoxes) is to create a Label control with its AutoSize property set to True. (In Code 13.13 in the next section, this Label control is called *templateLabel*.) Then assign the text control's Text or Caption property to this auxiliary control and make the text control's Width property equal to the Label's Width property.

Because the Label is placed on the same Form as the other text controls, by default it will have the same font as the other controls, and their sizes will match perfectly. As a result, you won't have to deal with font sizes and use the TextWidth property to set the widths of the controls (a rather complicated process).

Prompting the User for Data

The first thing a Form generator will do is prompt the user for the data needed to design the Form. When you invoke the Form Generator add-in by choosing Add-Ins ➤ Form Generator, it starts by displaying the Form shown in Figure 13.15, where the user can specify the fields to be displayed on the Form. The Form produced by the Form Generator add-in for the data shown in Figure 13.15 is shown in Figure 13.16.

FIGURE 13.15:

The Form Specification Data dialog box of the Form Generator add-in

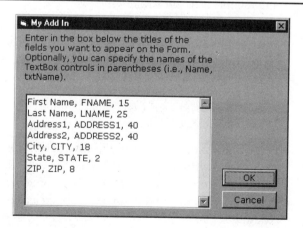

The user must first enter the data needed to build the data-entry Form. Each line in the multiline TextBox corresponds to a separate field, and the fields are placed on the Form in the same order as they appear in the Form Specification Data window. Each line must contain the field's title (which becomes the Caption of the Label control in front of it). Optionally, you can specify two more arguments, which are separated by a comma:

- The name of the field
- The field's length in number of characters

The minimum requirement for a field is its title (UserID or Address, for instance). By default, the name of the TextBox is the field's title, prefixed by the string "fld." If you specify only the field's title, the TextBox in which the field is entered will be named fldUserID or fldAddress. If you want to use another name, append it to the field's title, using a comma to separate the two entities (for instance, "UserID, UIDfield").

Finally, you can specify a length for the field, with a line such as the following:

```
UserID, UIDfield, 12
```

You can't omit the field name and specify a length in its place. The specification "UserID, 12" will attempt to create a TextBox control named 12, and you'll end up receiving an error message.

> **NOTE** This add-in doesn't contain any error-trapping code. Our goal is to demonstrate the basics of building a Wizard-style add-in, and we didn't include any code to deal with common user errors. You can add the required logic for trapping all types of errors and inform the user with your own error messages.

Placing the Controls on the Form

When the user clicks the OK button, the code starts by cleaning all the controls and the code on the Form. The user has presumably selected a new Form in the project or wants to use the specific Form to create a data-entry window. The lines of the TextBox control are then saved in a collection (the Entries collection), where it's easier to read them later in the code.

The code adds one Label control and one TextBox control for each field. The Label's Caption is set to the field's title, and the TextBox control is initially empty.

The Label controls are automatically resized to the dimensions of their captions, and their right edges are aligned. The TextBox controls are left-aligned and sized indirectly, through the templateLabel control. The templateLabel's Caption is set to the string:

```
String(length, "M")
```

in which *length* is the field's length (20 characters if not specified). The Label is resized automatically around its caption, and this length is assigned to the Length property of the corresponding TextBox control. Figure 13.16 shows the Form that corresponds to the specifications shown in Figure 13.15.

FIGURE 13.16:

This Form was generated by the Form Generator add-in, based on the specifications of the dialog box shown in Figure 13.15.

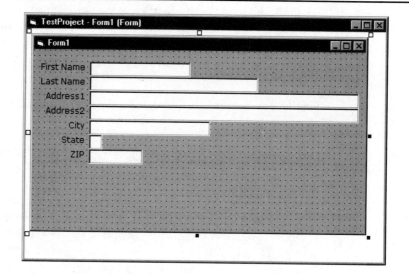

Code 13.13   **Placing the Controls on the Form**

```
' Create and place new controls on the Form
    currentTop = 300
    For i = 1 To Entries.Count
        ' Set up a template Label control
        ' to calculate each TextBox's width
        Set templateLabel = thisForm.ContainedVBControls.Add("Label")
        templateLabel.Properties("AutoSize") = True
        templateLabel.Properties("Top") = 0
''''''''''''''''''''''''''''''''''''''''''''''''''''''''''''''''''''

        Set thisControl = thisForm.ContainedVBControls.Add("Label")
```

```
thisControl.Properties("Name") = "lbl" & _
        MakeControlName(Entries.Item(i))
thisControl.Properties("AutoSize") = True
thisControl.Properties("Caption") = _
        MakeFieldTitle(Entries.Item(i))
If Len(thisControl.Properties("Caption")) > _
        longestLabel Then longestLabel = _
        Len(thisControl.Properties("Caption"))
thisControl.Properties("Top") = currentTop + 1.5 * _
        thisControl.Properties("Height")
thisControl.Properties("Left") = 1000
cHeight = thisControl.Properties("Height")
cTop = thisControl.Properties("Top")
Set thisControl = Nothing

Set thisControl = thisForm.ContainedVBControls.Add("TextBox")
thisControl.Properties("Name") = "txt" & _
        MakeControlName(Entries.Item(i))
thisControl.Properties("Text") = ""
thisControl.Properties("Height") = cHeight
templateLabel.Properties("Caption") = _
        String(GetFieldLength(Entries.Item(i)), "M")
thisControl.Properties("Width") = _
        Val(templateLabel.Properties("Width"))
thisControl.Properties("Top") = cTop
thisControl.Properties("Left") = 2000
currentTop = cTop

Next
```

Each control is placed on the Form as soon as the Add statement of the corresponding VBControl object is set. Initially, the control has the default size and is placed at the same location on the Form, as if you had double-clicked its icon in the Toolbox. The code then uses the object variable returned by the Add method (which represents the new control) to manipulate the properties of the control in order to size and align it on the Form. Although the controls are placed on the Form, we can't align them to their final positions because we need to know the longest caption. The lengthiest caption is stored in the variable *longestLabel*, which is used by another loop that aligns the right edges of the Label controls and the left edges of the TextBox controls.

| Code 13.14 | **Aligning the Controls on the Form** |

```
' Now arrange controls on the Form according to their lengths
controlRight = 500 + longestLabel * 10 * Screen.TwipsPerPixelX
For i = 1 To thisForm.ContainedVBControls.Count
    If thisForm.ContainedVBControls.Item(i).ClassName = _
            "Label" Then
        thisForm.ContainedVBControls.Item(i).Properties("Left") = _
            controlRight - thisForm.ContainedVBControls._
            Item(i).Properties("Width")
    Else
        thisForm.ContainedVBControls.Item(i).Properties("Left") = _
            controlRight + 100
    End If
Next
```

You can edit this code segment to align the controls in any way you see fit for the application. If you want to resize the Form, use the Properties property of the Form variable itself (*thisForm*).

Adding Code to the Form

An application generator should not only place the controls on a Form, but program them as well. If the add-in we are developing in this section were an actual data-entry window connected to a database, we would have to add the code to validate the field values, store them to the database, and then read the next record (just like the Data Form Wizard). Our example is certainly less ambitious, but the same logic applies to other situations too. The idea is to create a long string with the required code and insert it in the Form's CodeModule object.

The Form Generator add-in uses the CodeModule's AddFromString method to add code in the Form's Code window. The application's code is generated on the fly, although you could read it from a file, use constants, and in general use any VB technique with which you're more familiar. In this example, we'll insert a simple handler for the LostFocus event, which will turn the field's value to uppercase. You must place the following lines of code in the loop that places the controls on the Form, just before the Next statement:

```
txtCode = "Private Sub " & _
            thisControl.Properties("Name") & "_LostFocus()"
txtCode = txtCode & vbCrLf & "    " & _
```

```
            thisControl.Properties("Name") & ".Text = _
            UCase(" & thisControl.Properties("Name") & ")"
    txtCode = txtCode & vbCrLf & "End Sub"
    VBInstance.SelectedVBComponent.CodeModule.AddFromString txtCode
```

Executing these lines for a control named fldCity inserts the following text in the
Form's code:

```
Private Sub fldCity_LostFocus()
    fldCity.Text = UCase(fldCity)
End Sub
```

You can create long strings for all the events of the current control, as well as general procedures, variable and constant declarations, and so on. Even though it's
simple in principle, getting the code (along with line breaks and proper indention)
to a string variable can be tricky. If the code you want to insert is complicated, first
test it with a Standard EXE project, and then embed it in the add-in, making sure
you replace the references to control names with the appropriate expressions.

TIP   Remember, the expression Chr(34) inserts a double quote in the text.

The last few lines in the OK button's code generate a message, asking if the user
wants to run the project. These lines are commented out in the actual project on
the CD, and they are meant to demonstrate how you can invoke the IDE's commands from within your add-in's code.

```
Dim reply As Integer
reply = MsgBox("Do you want to run the application now?", vbYesNo)
If reply = vbYes Then
    VBInstance.CommandBars(1).Controls("Run"). _
        Controls("Start").Execute
End If
```

To execute a menu command, call the Execute method of the object variable that
represents the specific command. As you will see in the next section, the first-level
menu options can be accessed through the CommandBars(1).Controls collection.
Each element in this collection is another collection that contains the commands in
the specific submenu.

You can extend this example by adding more Forms to prompt the user for
more data. Organize the data you need in order to build an add-in, place related
data on the same Form, add navigational buttons to take the user from one Form
to the other, and you have built a wizard.

The VB Wizard-Building Wizard

Actually, Visual Basic provides a wizard for building wizards! It's the VB Wizard Manager add-in, and it will create much of the standard code for your add-in. For example, it will generate the code for the navigation buttons that take the user to the previous or next screen, the procedures for connecting and disconnecting the add-in, and much more.

The VB Wizard Manager produces a lot of code, but the information in this chapter will help you work your way through it and build the proper Wizard for your applications.

Manipulating the IDE Menu

So far, you've read about the objects that represent projects (their components, the controls and the code of the components, and so on). In the last part of this chapter, we are going to discuss a few objects that represent the environment itself. These objects allow you to intercept many user actions from within an add-in and react to them. You'll learn how to add new commands to the menu bar, detect events during the design of an application, and so on.

The VBIDE class provides a collection that gives your add-ins access to the commands of the Visual Basic menus. You can find out the state of individual menu commands, add new commands to the menu structure, and even invoke menu commands from within your add-in. This collection is the CommandBars collection, which is made up of Control objects. The CommandBars collection represents the menus, toolbars, and command bars of the environment. They are all objects of the same type to Visual Basic, because they invoke the same commands. The first element of this collection represents the Visual Basic window's main menu, which is the only one we are going to examine in this chapter. The techniques for accessing the other command bars are identical; only the indices will differ.

To access the main menu of the Visual Basic window, you can use one of the following expressions:

```
VBInstance.CommandBars.Item(1)
VBInstance.CommandBars(1)
```

Both expressions return an object of type Office.CommandBarControl. This is a type like all others, but it has a rather odd name. This object was originally designed to allow Visual Basic to control the menus of Office applications. The Count property of this collection returns the number of commands on the Visual Basic menu bar (the first-level commands)—File, Edit, Project, and so on. Each one of these commands leads to a submenu.

The Controls Collection

To access a command's submenu, you use another collection, the Controls collection. Each element in this collection represents an entire submenu. The expression

```
VBInstance.CommandBars(1).Controls(1)
```

represents the entire File menu. Unlike other collections, the elements of the Controls collection can be indexed by name. The File submenu can also be accessed as

```
VBInstance.CommandBars(1).Controls("File")
```

And now we need yet another collection to access the elements of a submenu. A collection for accessing the members of a menu exists already, and it's the Controls collection. To access the third command in the File menu, you can use the expression

```
VBInstance.CommandBars(1).Controls("File").Controls(3)
```

Or, if you know the name of the command, you can use the following equivalent expression:

```
VBInstance.CommandBars(1).Controls("File").Controls("Add Project")
```

This expression represents a menu command or a button on the toolbar. You can find out the name of the command by reading the Caption property, and you can find out its state by reading the Enabled property. In short, the properties of a menu option are also properties of the Controls collection.

The Controls collection is not listed in the Object Browser, and its members won't be listed in the Auto List Member window. Because it represents a menu command, however, it has a few members. Its most important properties are Caption and Enabled (there may be more that we haven't discovered yet). The Execute method invokes the command, as if it were clicked with the mouse. To invoke the Paste command of the Edit menu, use the following statement:

```
VBInstance.CommandBars(1).Controls("Edit").Controls("Paste").Execute
```

and to execute the third command of the File menu, use the following statement:

```
VBInstance.CommandBars(1).Controls("File").Controls(3).Execute
```

Besides reading the commands of Visual Basic's menus, you can also add and remove methods with the Add and Delete methods of the Office.CommandBar-Control control. The Add method's syntax is

```
CommandBars(i).Control(j).Add([Type], [Id], [Parameter], _
            [Before], [Temporary])
```

Notice that all arguments are optional. The Add method returns a Command-BarsControl object, which represents the newly added command. The Type argument determines the type of command and can have one of the following values:

- msoBarTypeMenuBar

- msoBarTypeNormal

- msoBarTypePopUp

The Id argument is a long value, which you can use to refer to the new command. The Before argument is the position of the command, after which the new one will be inserted. The Add method returns an Office.CommandBarControl type object, which represents the newly added command. You can use this variable to access the properties of the command (set its Caption, for instance). To remove a command from a menu, you first create an object variable that represents the command, and then you issue the Delete method of the object variable.

Adding and Removing Menu Commands

The next example demonstrates how you can add new commands to the Visual Basic IDE menu. Later, you will see how to add the code to carry out a task when the new command is clicked. The Demo add-in has two Command buttons, the Add MOVE Command and the Remove MOVE Command, which add and remove a "Move Project" command in the File menu. This command copies all the components of a project to a new folder.

NOTE   Saving the project to another folder with the Save As command doesn't move the files there; only the project (VBP) file will be saved in the new folder. The VBP file will reference the project's files in their original folder. To move an entire project to another folder, you must manually save each component to this folder.

We'll look at the implementation of the Move Project command later in this chapter. In this section, we'll look at the code for adding and removing commands to the various menus of the Visual Basic IDE.

Let's start by looking at the code behind the Add MOVE Command button. The event handler, shown below, scans the commands in the File menu to make sure that the Move Project command isn't already there (in which case, it doesn't add it again). If the command isn't found in the File menu, it adds the Move Project command with the Add method of the Controls collection.

Code 13.15   **The Add MOVE Command Button**

```
Private Sub bttnAddMOVE_Click()
Dim MoveCommand As Office.CommandBarControl
Dim i As Integer

    For i = 1 To VBInstance.CommandBars.Item(1). _
               Controls("File").Controls.Count
        If VBInstance.CommandBars.Item(1).Controls("File"). _
                  Controls(i).Caption = "Move Project" Then
            Exit Sub
        End If
    Next
    Set MoveCommand = VBInstance.CommandBars.Item(1). _
             Controls("File").Controls.Add(1, , , 3)
    MoveCommand.Caption = "Move Project"
End Sub
```

A few explanations are necessary here. The expression VBInstance.Command-Bars.Item(1) represents the main menu bar. Each command in this menu is accessed through the Controls collection. The File menu is the first one, so the object VBInstance.CommandBars.Item(1).Controls("File") represents the File menu. To access the commands of this menu, you must use the Controls collection of this object. You can also declare an object variable, *fileMenu* for instance, and set it to the File submenu with the following statement:

```
Set fileMenu = VBInstance.CommandBars.Item(1).Controls("File")
```

You can then replace the entire expression VBInstance.CommandBars.Item(1).-Controls("File") with the name of the *fileMenu* object variable.

To add a new command to a menu, use the Add method. The last argument of this method is the position of the new command in the menu. Our Move Project command is added right after the New Project and Add Project commands on the File menu. Click the Add MOVE Command Button in the Demo project, and then open the File menu (it should look like the one shown in Figure 13.17).

To remove the command, we must create an object variable that references the Move Project command and then call this variable's Delete method.

FIGURE 13.17:

The File menu after the addition of the Move Project command

Code 13.16 **The Remove MOVE Command Button**

```
Private Sub bttnRemoveMOVE_Click()
Dim MoveCommand As Office.CommandBarControl

    Set MoveCommand = VBInstance.CommandBars.Item(1). _
            Controls("File").Controls(3)
    If MoveCommand.Caption = "Move Project" Then MoveCommand.Delete
End Sub
```

This code removes the third item in the File menu, but not before it examines its Caption (in case the command has already been removed).

NOTE The code shown here isn't quite robust. Another add-in might have added a command before the Move Project command. In this case, the Move Project command won't be at the same position in the File menu, as when we added it there. You should use a loop identical to the one in the event handler of the Add MOVE Command Button, which will actually locate the Move Project command at any location in the File menu and then remove it.

The add-in's code protects you from adding the same command twice, but it doesn't remove the command from the File menu when the add-in is disconnected. The place to insert the code for adding and removing a menu command is not in a Command Button on the add-in's Form, but in the OnConnection and OnDisconnection methods (you'll see shortly how this is done). So, as long as you are experimenting with the Demo add-in, don't forget to remove the Move Project command by clicking the Remove MOVE Command Button.

Handling Menu Events

You've seen how to add and remove commands in the Visual Basic IDE menu bar, but what good is it if you can't detect the Click event for the new command and handle it from within your add-in? In this section, we'll set up an object that receives the Click event of the new command. This object will be added to the Objects list in the Code window, and you'll be able to program its Click event handler.

You already know how to add an event handler for the Click event of a menu command; the Add-In template contains an event handler for the Click event of the add-in's entry in the Add-Ins menu. In your code, you may have to create event handlers for your own custom commands, and here are the steps:

1. In the OnConnection method of the add-in, declare an object variable of Office.CommandBarControl type (it represents a menu command) with the following statement:

   ```
   Dim NewCommand As Office.CommandBarControl
   ```

2. Declare another object variable of type CommandBarEvents, which will be used to access the events of the custom command. You must declare this variable in the Class Module's declarations section, as:

   ```
   Public WithEvents NewCommandHandler As CommandBarEvents
   ```

TIP   Notice the keyword WithEvents; without it, the object variable won't fire any events, and you won't be able to program it.

---

3. Create a new command with the Add method of the CommandBars.Control collection, as explained earlier:

   ```
   Set MoveCommand = _
           VBInstance.CommandBars.Item(1).Controls _
           ("File").Controls.Add(1, , , 3)
   NewCommand.Caption = "New Command"
   ```

This code segment inserts a new command in the third place of the File menu. The command's caption is New Command.

Now you are ready to create the object variable that will detect the events of the new command (the one represented by the *NewCommand* variable) with the following statement:

```
Set Me.NewCommandHandler = _
        VBInst.Events.CommandBarEvents(NewCommand)
```

4. Open the Connect Designer's Code window and select NewCommandHandler in the Objects drop-down list. In the Events drop-down list, the Click event will be selected automatically. Enter the code that implements the new command in this event handler.

5. When the add-in is disconnected, you must remove the custom command from the File menu. Declare the *NewCommand* object variable in the OnDisconnection method of the add-in with a statement such as the following:

```
Dim NewCommand As Office.CommandBarControl
```

6. Add the following code, which actually disconnects the custom command:

```
Set NewCommand = _VBInstance.CommandBars.Item(1).Controls _
                ("File").Controls(3)
NewCommand.Delete
```

The process is straightforward, and you can duplicate it for as many new commands as you wish. Notice that the *NewCommand* object variable isn't public. It's declared in the methods that add the command to and remove it from the IDE's menu. Also notice that a menu command can't be accessed directly; you must first create an object variable that references the command and then call the variable's Delete method.

In the section "The Project Mover Add-In," we are going to build an add-in that adds a custom command to the File menu, which moves an entire project to a new folder. But first, we are going to look at a couple of simpler examples that manipulate menu commands through the CommandBarControl object.

Listing the IDE Menu Commands

The CommandBarControls button of the Demo add-in displays the names of the commands in each of the IDE's submenus, as shown in Figure 13.18.

FIGURE 13.18:

The CommandBarControls button displays the name and status of all the first level submenus of the Visual Basic IDE.

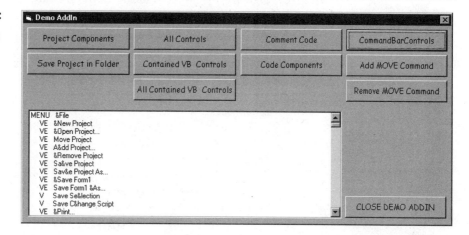

Each submenu is a member of the CommandBars collection of the current instance of the IDE. The first element of the CommandBars collection is another collection that represents the commands in the main menu. The first-level menu commands (File, Edit, and so on) are accessed with the elements of the collection VBInstance.-CommandBars.Item(1).Controls. The File menu is the element VBInstance.Command-Bars.Item(1).Controls.Item(1) or VBInstance.CommandBars(1).Controls(1), if you prefer this latter notation.

To access the commands of the File menu, the code assigns this menu to the variable *currentMenu* and then the File menu's commands through the *current-Menu* variable's Controls collection. The code scans each element of the main menu and all its commands. It displays each command's caption, along with the designators V and E, which stand for Visible and Enabled. If the command is enabled and/or visible, the corresponding digit appears in front of its name.

Code 13.17   The CommandBarControls Button

```
Private Sub bttnCmdBarControls_Click()
Dim mcbMenuCommandBar As Office.CommandBarControl
Dim cmenus As Integer
Dim i As Integer, j As Integer, k As Integer
Dim currentMenu As CommandBarControl
Dim currentSubMenu As CommandBarControl
Dim menuProp As String
    List1.Clear
```

```
' The first element in the CommandBars Collection corresponds
' to the File menu
    cmenus = VBInstance.CommandBars.Item(1).Controls.Count
    For i = 1 To cmenus
        Set currentMenu = VBInstance.CommandBars.Item(1).Controls(i)
        List1.AddItem "MENU    " & currentMenu.Caption
        For j = 1 To currentMenu.Controls.Count
            menuProp = ""
            If currentMenu.Controls(j).Visible Then _
                    menuProp = "V" Else menuProp = "  "
            If currentMenu.Controls(j).Enabled Then _
                    menuProp = menuProp & "E" Else _
                    menuProp = menuProp & "  "
            List1.AddItem "     " & menuProp & "   " & _
                    currentMenu.Controls(j).Caption
            Set currentSubMenu = currentMenu.Controls(j)
            If currentSubMenu.Type = 10 Then
                For k = 1 To currentSubMenu.Controls.Count
                    If currentSubMenu.Controls(k).Visible Then _
                            menuProp = "V" Else menuProp = "  "
                    If currentSubMenu.Controls(k).Enabled Then _
                            menuProp = menuProp & "E" Else _
                            menuProp = menuProp & "  "
                    List1.AddItem "        " & menuProp & _
                        "    " & currentSubMenu.Controls(k).Caption
                Next
            End If
        Next
    Next
End Sub
```

As you know, some menu commands lead to submenus. Most of the commands in the Format menu, for example, lead to submenus, which won't be printed by the previous subroutine. Accessing second-level submenus is a bit trickier (in all honesty it's quite simple, but undocumented). To access a first-level command menu, we used the expression VBInstance.CommandBars.Item(1).Controls(i) (*i* goes from 1 to the number of menus on the menu bar). This menu is assigned to the *currentMenu* object variable, and each command in this menu can be accessed through the *currentMenu* variable's Controls collection. If *currentMenu* represents the Format menu, the following expression:

```
currentMenu.Controls(2)
```

represents the command Make Same Size. This command is a submenu whose elements can be accessed by another Controls collection.

The three commands of the Make Same Size submenu are Width, Height, and Both. The command Width can be accessed with the expression currentMenu.-Controls(2).Controls(1). This looks confusing, and we need to simplify it.

You can create a new object variable to reference the Make Same Size submenu, as follows:

```
Set currentSubMenu = currentMenu.Controls(2)
```

You can then access the commands of the Make Same Size submenu with the following expression:

```
currentSubMenu.Controls(k)
```

in which k goes from 1 (for the Width command) to 3 (for the Both command).

To display the second-level submenus, you need another nested loop that scans each command's submenu.

```
For k = 1 To currentSubMenu.Controls.Count
    If currentSubMenu.Controls(k).Visible Then
        menuProp = "V"
    Else
        menuProp = "  "
            End If
    If currentSubMenu.Controls(k).Enabled Then
        menuProp = menuProp & "E"
    Else
        menuProp = menuProp & "  "
    End If
    List1.AddItem "           " & menuProp & "    " & _
            currentSubMenu.Controls(k).Caption
Next
```

If you insert this loop in the code, you will get an error message for all commands that don't lead to submenus. One would expect the expression current-SubMenu.Controls.Count to be zero for these commands. But this isn't the case. Attempting to access the Count property of an object variable that represents a submenu generates a run-time error. To avoid this error message (without inserting unneeded error handlers), you must examine the value of the current command's Type property.

TIP

A menu command's Type property is normally 1, unless it leads to a submenu, in which case it's 10. These values don't correspond to any constants, and you won't find them in the Object Browser (at least, we couldn't locate the settings of a menu command's Type property in any of the obvious places). Code 13.17 figures out whether a command leads to a submenu, in which case it executes the inner loop.

This trick will work unless there are third-level submenus. The Visual Basic IDE doesn't have nested submenus, but if you create an add-in that implements submenus with commands that lead to other submenus (rather unlikely), you should write a recursive routine that scans each command's submenus. See the section "Listing a Project's Controls," earlier in this chapter, for the description of a similar recursive routine.

The Project Mover Add-In

In this section, we'll put together much of the information presented earlier in this chapter to build an add-in that installs a new command on the File menu and detects the Click event on this command. The command's name is Move Project, and every time the user clicks this command, the current project's components are copied to a new, user-specified folder. The project is called Project Mover.

NOTE

You'll find the Project Mover project in the Chapter13/ProjectMover folder on the CD that comes with this book.

A VB project consists of several to many components that may reside in a number of folders on the hard disk. The Visual Basic project file (VBP) contains a list of the components, including the files' path names. These path names are usually relative to the folder of the project file. When you save the current project with the Save Project or Save Project As command, only the project file is saved. You must save its components separately.

TIP

A simple way to save all the components of a project is to start a new project. Visual Basic will ask whether you want to save the components that have changed since the last save. Click the Yes button, and in the New Project dialog box, click Cancel to return to your project.

It would be useful to have a command that saves the entire project to a new folder, especially if you add existing files to the project. Such a command isn't available on the File menu, so an add-in that implements this operation could be useful to many developers. We'll build a simple add-in that saves all the components in the current project to a user-specified folder. The original files, no matter where they reside initially, will be copied to the new folder. The original files won't be removed from their folders. It's a good practice, however, to maintain a single version of each project, so you might consider adding the code to delete the original files after they have been copied to their destination folder.

WARNING   The examples in this book are meant to demonstrate the topics discussed, so you should test the Project Mover add-in exhaustively before you implement this change in the code.

To build the add-in from scratch, start a new Add-In project and then follow these steps:

1. Remove the frmAddin Form from the project, add a new, blank Form, and name it frmSelect (we'll design this Form later).

2. Remove the code that shows and hides the frmAddin Form from the OnConnection and OnDisconnection methods of the add-in.

3. Declare the *MoveCommandHandler* object variable in the Designer's declarations section, with the following line:

   ```
   Public WithEvents MoveCommandHandler As CommandBarEvents
   ```

4. In the Designer's Code window add the following declarations:

   ```
   Public VBInstance As VBIDE.VBE
   Dim mcbMenuCommandBar As Office.CommandBarControl
   Public WithEvents MenuHandler As CommandBarEvents
   ```

The code that hooks the new command to the File menu and prepares the MoveCommandHandler to intercept the Click event is located in the OnConnection method's subroutine, which is shown next.

Code 13.18   The OnConnection Method of the Add-In

```
Private Sub AddinInstance_OnConnection(ByVal Application As _
    Object, ByVal ConnectMode As AddInDesignerObjects. _
```

```
            ext_ConnectMode, ByVal AddInInst As Object, _
            custom() As Variant)
Dim MoveCommand As Office.CommandBarControl

On Error GoTo error_handler

'save the vb instance
Set VBInstance = Application
Set mcbMenuCommandBar = AddToAddInCommandBar("Move Project")
'sink the event
Set Me.MenuHandler = _
        VBInstance.Events.CommandBarEvents(mcbMenuCommandBar)

Dim i As Integer
For i = 1 To VBInstance.CommandBars.Item _
            (1).Controls("File").Controls.Count
    If VBInstance.CommandBars.Item(1).Controls("File"). _
            Controls(i).Caption = "Move Project" Then
        Exit Sub
    End If
Next
Set MoveCommand = VBInstance.CommandBars.Item(1). _
            Controls("File").Controls.Add(1, , , 3)
MoveCommand.Caption = "Move Project"
Set Me.MoveCommandHandler = _
            VBInstance.Events.CommandBarEvents(MoveCommand)
Exit Sub

error_handler:
    MsgBox Err.Description
End Sub
```

This code is identical to the outline we presented in the last section, except for the loop that scans the commands of the File menu. This loop makes sure that the File menu doesn't contain a Move Project command already. If it does, the code exits and doesn't add it again.

The implementation of the OnDisconnection subroutine is very similar to the one supplied by the template. It doesn't contain the lines that hide the Form and it contains a few additional lines for removing the Move Project command from the File menu.

Code 13.19   The OnDisconnection Method

```
Private Sub AddinInstance_OnDisconnection(ByVal _
    RemoveMode As AddInDesignerObjects.ext_DisconnectMode, _
    custom() As Variant)
Dim MoveCommand As Office.CommandBarControl

    On Error Resume Next
    Set MoveCommand = VBInstance.CommandBars. _
        Item(1).Controls("File").Controls(3)
    MoveCommand.Delete

    'delete the command bar entry
    mcbMenuCommandBar.Delete

    'shut down the Add-In
    SaveSetting App.Title, "Settings", "DisplayOnConnect", "0"

End Sub
```

Coding the Project Mover Add-In

We have implemented all the code for adding a new custom command to the existing menu structure of the Visual Basic IDE. Now, we must provide the code that makes the command do something. This is straight VB code that manipulates the objects of the VBIDE class. The code in this section demonstrates how to access the components of a VB project, find out their type and the names of the files in which they are stored, and save them in a different folder.

The first issue we must deal with is how to allow the user to select the destination folder to which the project will be moved. We must display a dialog box from within our code that will allow the user to select a drive and a folder on the selected drive. This dialog box is shown in Figure 13.19. Add a new Form to the project, and place on it the controls you see in Figure 13.19. The FileListBox control is not really needed; neither can you act on the names of the existing files, but they are displayed to help you locate the desired folder. (Be sure it doesn't contain another project with file names that conflict with the file names of the current application, for example.)

FIGURE 13.19:

The Select Target Folder dialog box allows the user of the Project Mover add-in to select the project's destination folder.

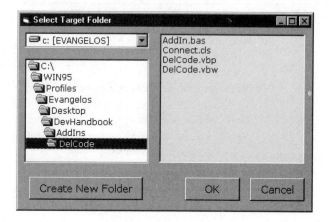

The code behind the controls of the frmSelect Form is trivial, with one exception. The name of the selected folder is a property of the Form so that the add-in can read it (the add-in can't set this property, although it wouldn't be a bad idea to let the add-in select an initial folder).

Code 13.20   **The FrmSelect Form**

```
Private Sub Dir1_Change()
    File1.Path = Dir1.Path
End Sub

Private Sub Drive1_Change()
    Dir1.Path = Drive1.Drive
End Sub
```

When you click the OK button, the code hides the Form and assigns the name of the selected path to the private variable *m_newFolderName*, which stores the value of the NewFolderName Form's property. This is a read-only property, implemented with the following Property Get procedure:

```
Property Get newFolderName() As String
    newFolderName = m_newFolderName
End Property
```

Once the user selects the destination folder, the program can extract its path by reading the frmSelect Form's newFolderName property. In the following section, we are going to look at the code that moves the components of the current project to a new folder.

Saving a Project's Components

Before we look at the code that actually saves the project's components, we must discuss a special requirement of this add-in. If a component has been saved already, we must use the same file name. If not, we must either create a new name, based on the name of the component, or prompt the user for a file name. Since the Project Mover add-in is meant to move projects with components in various folders, we opted for the first approach. If the component UserControl1 hasn't been saved already, we'll use the name UserControl1.ctl for its file name.

When creating file names based on the component name, we must also supply an extension. The extension is based on the component's type, which is returned by the component's Type property. The Type property is an integer, and we use it to build an array of possible extensions, as shown here:

```
' SET UP FILE TYPE EXTENSIONS
extNames(vbext_ct_ClassModule) = ".cls"
extNames(vbext_ct_PropPage) = ".pag"
extNames(vbext_ct_StdModule) = ".cls"
extNames(vbext_ct_ClassModule) = ".bas"
extNames(vbext_ct_ResFile) = ".res"
extNames(vbext_ct_UserControl) = ".ctl"
extNames(vbext_ct_VBForm) = ".frm"
extNames(vbext_ct_VBMDIForm) = ".mdi"
extNames(vbext_ct_DocObject) = ".doc"
```

These extensions are then used to create the default file names, with two statements such as the following:

```
ext = extNames(thisProject.VBComponents(j).Type)
PName = thisProject.VBComponents(j).FileNames(k)
```

in which j is the index of the current component. The property thisProject.VBComponents(j).Type returns one of the constants we used to build the array. Some components are stored in multiple files (like FRM and FRX). The index k determines which of these files is being saved.

The add-in's core code uses two loops (a structure you're accustomed to by now). The outer loop scans the projects in the current project group, and the inner loop scans the components of each project and saves them to a new folder. The code of the Move command handler is almost identical to the code of the Save Project in Folder button of the Demo add-in, and it's shown next.

Code 13.21   **The Move Project Command**

```
Private Sub MoveCommandHandler_Click(ByVal CommandBarControl As _
        Object, handled As Boolean, CancelDefault As Boolean)
Dim thisProject As VBProject
Dim i As Integer, j As Integer, k As Integer
Dim fileCount As Integer
Dim projectCount As Integer, componentCount As Integer
Dim newFolderName As String
Dim SepPos As Integer
Dim PName As String
Dim ext As String
Dim extNames(12) As String

' SET UP FILE TYPE EXTENSIONS
extNames(vbext_ct_ClassModule) = ".cls"
extNames(vbext_ct_PropPage) = ".pag"
extNames(vbext_ct_StdModule) = ".cls"
extNames(vbext_ct_ClassModule) = ".bas"
extNames(vbext_ct_ResFile) = ".res"
extNames(vbext_ct_UserControl) = ".ctl"
extNames(vbext_ct_VBForm) = ".frm"
extNames(vbext_ct_VBMDIForm) = ".mdi"
extNames(vbext_ct_DocObject) = ".doc"
extNames(vbext_ct_ActiveXDesigner) = ".dsr"
''''''''''''''''''''''''''''''''''''''''''''''''''''''''''
    frmSelect.Show vbModal
    newFolderName = frmSelect.newFolderName
    If newFolderName = "" Then
        Beep
        Exit Sub
    End If
' THE SAVE FEATURE
    projectCount = VBInstance.VBProjects.Count
    For i = 1 To projectCount
        Set thisProject = VBInstance.VBProjects(i)
        componentCount = thisProject.VBComponents.Count
        For j = 1 To componentCount
            fileCount = thisProject.VBComponents(j).fileCount
            For k = 1 To fileCount
                ext = extNames(thisProject.VBComponents(j).Type)
                PName = thisProject.VBComponents(j).FileNames(k)
                If Len(PName) > 0 Then
```

```
                    SepPos = InStr(PName, "\")
                    While SepPos > 0
                        PName = Mid(PName, SepPos + 1)
                        SepPos = InStr(PName, "\")
                    Wend
                Else
                    PName = thisProject.VBComponents(j).Name & ext
                End If
                If Dir(newFolderName & "\" & PName) <> "" Then _
                        Kill newFolderName & "\" & PName
                thisProject.SaveAs newFolderName & "\" & PName
                Debug.Print "Saving " & newFolderName & "\" & PName
            Next
        Next
    Next

End Sub
```

This code examines the file name under which the project (VBInstance.VB-
Projects.Item(i).FileName) or the component (thisProject.VBComponents.Item(j).-
FileNames(1)) is saved. If the project or the component hasn't been saved yet, this
property returns a blank string. In this case, the program creates a new file name,
based on the component's name, using an extension based on the component's type.

If the component has been saved already, the FileName property returns the
full path name of the file, and the code parses it (with the While...Wend loop) to
extract the file name. Whether the file name exists or is generated by the code,
the component is saved with the Save method of the VBProjects collection or the
VBComponents collection. If the file exists already in the destination folder, the
add-in overwrites it. We don't ask the user about overwriting the files because
this Move Project command is used just once for a project, and it usually saves
the project's components to a new folder.

Detecting IDE Events

Like Visual Basic applications, add-ins can't do much without events. The most
useful add-ins are those that detect user actions and react to them. In programming the IDE, events are triggered each time the user selects a menu command or
adds or removes components to a project and each time controls are added,
deleted, or renamed.

You know already how to detect and program the Click event of any menu command. The VBIDE object model provides more events, which you can access through the Events class. The Events class exposes six members that detect the events shown in Table 13.11.

TABLE 13.11: The Elements of the Events Class

Element	What It Does
CommandBarEvents	Detects the Command Bar's events
FileControlsEvents	Detects when the user adds/removes file components
ReferencesEvents	Detects when the user adds/removes references to the current project
VBControlsEvents	Detects when the user adds/removes/renames controls on the Form
SelectedVBControlsEvents	Detects when the user changes the current selection on the Form
VBComponentsEvents	Detects when the users selects/reloads/activates/adds/deletes a component

Detecting and programming all the categories of events provided by the IDE is similar, and we'll focus on the VBControlsEvents and SelectedVBControls events. These events are generated constantly in the design process, and you can use them to write add-ins that work in tandem with the user to streamline the design process. We'll limit our discussion to these two categories of events, because they are the most commonly used. The same techniques apply to all other categories of events. To find out the names of the supported events and the arguments passed, consult the Object Browser.

During the design of a Form, the events shown in Table 13.12 are triggered to notify the add-in about user actions related to the design of the user interface.

TABLE 13.12: The Events of the VBControlsEvents Object

Event	Is Triggered
ItemAdded	When a new control is placed on the Form
ItemRemoved	When a control is deleted
ItemRenamed	When a control is renamed

These events are members of the VBControls collection. The first two events are also members of the SelectedVBControls collection. Since you can't rename multiple controls at once, the ItemRenamed event isn't triggered for the SelectedVBControls collection. As with the CommandBar's events, you must first create an object variable that you will use to program these events. This variable must be of VBControlsEvents type. The declaration

```
Private WithEvents ctrlHandler As VBControlsEvents
```

must appear in the declarations section of the class module or Form. Later in the code, you must tell Visual Basic which events to look for. The *ctrlHandler* variable is set with a line such as the following:

```
Set ctrlHandler = _
        VBInstance.Events.VBControlsEvents(thisProject, thisForm)
```

The first argument tells Visual Basic to detect the events on the Form referenced by the *thisForm* variable, of a specific project, referenced by the object variable *this-Project*. If the project *thisProject* has other Forms, their control-related events won't be detected by the *ctrlHandler* variable. To detect these events on every Form of the project, set the second argument of the VBControlsEvents property to Nothing. To detect all events on all Forms, set both arguments to Nothing. If you set the *ctrl-Handler* variable with the following line:

```
Set ctrlHandler = _
        VBInstance.Events.VBControlsEvents(thisProject, thisForm)
```

it will detect all the control-related events in the project. In terms of coding, though, this isn't as convenient as you may think. You must provide the code to detect on which Form the event originated and react accordingly. It's easier to start by deciding which events and on which Forms you want to monitor and then create object variables for these Forms.

ctrlHandler is an object variable that recognizes events, so its name will appear in the Objects list of the Code window, and the events it recognizes will appear in the Events list of the same window. To program a handler for any of the supported events, select the ctrlHandler object in the Objects list, and select the name of the event in the Events list, as shown in Figure 13.20. Unlike controls themselves, the IDE provides only a few control-related events.

You can program the *ctrlHandler* object's events as usual. You can access the entire VBIDE object model from within the event's code and perform all the actions you deem appropriate. In the following section, you will see how you can program the events generated by the IDE every time the user deletes a control on a Form, to remove any event handlers left behind. The same add-in detects the events triggered when controls are renamed too so that you can modify the code automatically.

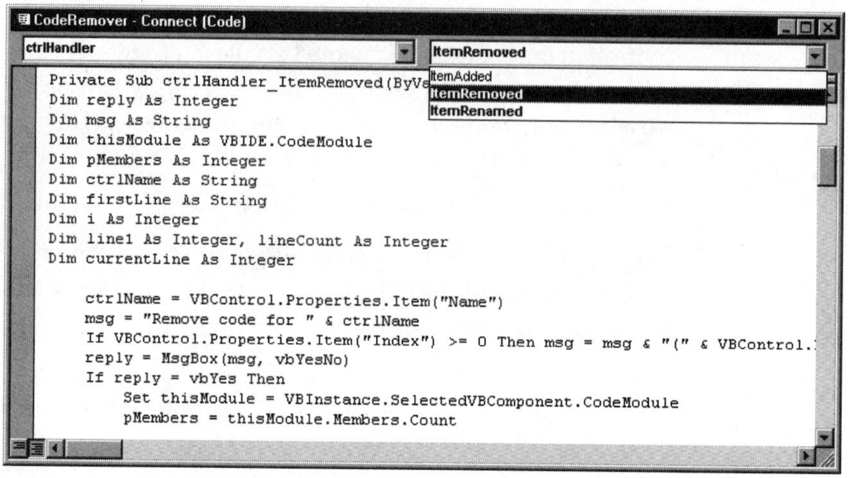

FIGURE 13.20:

The events recognized by object variables declared as VBControlsEvents

```
■ CodeRemover - Connect (Code)                                    _ □ ×

ctrlHandler                      ▼   ItemRemoved                    ▼

    Private Sub ctrlHandler_ItemRemoved(ByVa ItemAdded
    Dim reply As Integer                      ItemRemoved
    Dim msg As String                         ItemRenamed
    Dim thisModule As VBIDE.CodeModule
    Dim pMembers As Integer
    Dim ctrlName As String
    Dim firstLine As String
    Dim i As Integer
    Dim line1 As Integer, lineCount As Integer
    Dim currentLine As Integer

        ctrlName = VBControl.Properties.Item("Name")
        msg = "Remove code for " & ctrlName
        If VBControl.Properties.Item("Index") >= 0 Then msg = msg & "(" & VBControl.
        reply = MsgBox(msg, vbYesNo)
        If reply = vbYes Then
            Set thisModule = VBInstance.SelectedVBComponent.CodeModule
            pMembers = thisModule.Members.Count
```

The Code Remover Add-In

The last example in this chapter demonstrates an add-in that detects events during the design cycle of a Form and handles them silently. This add-in doesn't have a visible interface, and it doesn't install any command in the IDE's menu. When connected, it installs an event handler that detects when the user deletes controls on the Form and prompts the user to delete the corresponding code.

Normally, when a control is deleted during the design of an application, the IDE doesn't remove the event handlers already entered in the Code window because the user might need these procedures for another control. They are simply listed under the General category in the Objects list of the Code window. If you plan to permanently remove a control from your Form, however, you should also remove the associated code. The Code Remover add-in automates the deletion of unneeded code.

This add-in doesn't display any Forms when invoked. Actually, the Code Remover command in the Add-Ins menu does nothing; it simply indicates that the add-in has been installed. The add-in is automatically invoked every time the user deletes or renames a control on the Form and asks the user whether he or she wants to remove the associated code.

To implement the add-in, start a new AddIn project, remove the frmAddIn Form, and then remove the code that shows and hides the Form from within the

Connect Designer's code. The *ctrlHandler* object variable is declared in the OnConnection method with the following line:

```
Set ctrlHandler = VBInstance.Events.VBControlsEvents _
                    (thisProject, thisForm)
```

All the action takes place from within the ctrlHandler's ItemRemoved and ItemRenamed events.

Code 13.22   **The Connect Designer's Code**

```
Public VBInstance As vbide.VBE
Private mcbMenuCommandBar As Office.CommandBarControl
' Detects the RemoveItem/RenameItem events
Private WithEvents ctrlHandler As VBControlsEvents


'-------------------------------------------------------
'this method adds the Add-In to VB
'-------------------------------------------------------
Private Sub IDTExtensibility_OnConnection(ByVal VBInst As Object, _
        ByVal ConnectMode As vbext_ConnectMode, _
        ByVal AddInInst As vbide.AddIn, custom() As Variant)

    On Error GoTo error_handler

    'save the vb instance
    Set VBInstance = VBInst

    'this is a good place to set a breakpoint and
    'test various addin objects, properties and methods
    Debug.Print VBInst.FullName

    Set mcbMenuCommandBar = AddToAddInCommandBar("Code Remover")

' Set up the MenuHandler object variable to detect the
' Edit > Paste ' command selection
    Dim thisProject As VBProject
    Dim thisForm As VBForm

    Set thisProject = VBInstance.ActiveVBProject
    Set ctrlHandler = VBInstance.Events.VBControlsEvents( _
        thisProject, thisForm)
```

```
        Exit Sub

error_handler:

    MsgBox Err.Description

End Sub

'--------------------------------------------------------
'this method removes the Add-In from VB
'--------------------------------------------------------
Private Sub IDTExtensibility_OnDisconnection(ByVal RemoveMode _
        As vbext_DisconnectMode, custom() As Variant)

    On Error Resume Next
    'delete the command bar entry
    mcbMenuCommandBar.Delete
    'shut down the Add-In
    SaveSetting App.Title, "Settings", "DisplayOnConnect", "0"

End Sub

Private Sub IDTExtensibility_OnStartupComplete(custom() As Variant)
    '
End Sub

Private Sub IDTExtensibility_OnAddInsUpdate(custom() As Variant)
    '
End Sub

Function AddToAddInCommandBar(sCaption As String) As _
        Office.CommandBarControl
    Dim cbMenuCommandBar As Office.CommandBarControl   'command bar
object
    Dim cbMenu As Object

    On Error GoTo AddToAddInCommandBarErr

    'see if we can find the Add-Ins menu
    Set cbMenu = VBInstance.CommandBars("Add-Ins")
    If cbMenu Is Nothing Then
        'not available so we fail
```

```
        Exit Function
    End If
Set cbMenuCommandBar = cbMenu.Controls.Add(1)

    'add it to the command bar
'set the caption
    cbMenuCommandBar.Caption = sCaption

    Set AddToAddInCommandBar = cbMenuCommandBar

    Exit Function

AddToAddInCommandBarErr:

End Function
```

After these procedures, you can insert the code that reacts to the ItemRemoved and ItemRenamed events. In the Code Remover add-in, we have implemented the ItemRemoved event only.

Code 13.23   The ItemRemoved Event Handler

```
Private Sub ctrlHandler_ItemRemoved(ByVal VBControl As vbide.VBControl)
Dim reply As Integer
Dim msg As String
Dim thisModule As vbide.CodeModule
Dim pMembers As Integer
Dim ctrlName As String
Dim firstLine As String
Dim i As Integer
Dim line1 As Integer, lineCount As Integer
Dim currentLine As Integer

    ctrlName = VBControl.Properties.Item("Name")
    msg = "Remove code for " & ctrlName
    If VBControl.Properties.Item("Index") >= 0 Then msg = msg & "(" & _
        VBControl.Properties.Item("Index") & ")"
    reply = MsgBox(msg, vbYesNo)
    If reply = vbYes Then
        Set thisModule = VBInstance.SelectedVBComponent.CodeModule
        pMembers = thisModule.Members.Count
        For i = pMembers To 1 Step -1
```

```
        If thisModule.Members.Item(i).Type = vbext_mt_Method Then
            line1 = _
                thisModule.ProcBodyLine(_
                thisModule.Members.Item(i).Name, vbext_pk_Proc)
            firstLine = thisModule.Lines(line1, 1)
            If InStr(firstLine, "Sub " & ctrlName & "_") Then
                currentLine = line1
                lineCount = 1
                While Trim(thisModule.Lines(currentLine, 1)) <>_
                    "End Sub"
                    currentLine = currentLine + 1
                    lineCount = lineCount + 1
                Wend
                thisModule.DeleteLines line1, lineCount
                Debug.Print "deleted " & line1 & ", " & lineCount & _
                    " in " & firstLine
            End If
        End If
    Next
End If

End Sub
```

The ItemRemoved event's handler asks the user whether the event handlers of the deleted control should be removed. If so, the program scans all the items of the CodeModule collection, looking for event handlers. If one is found, it sees if the deleted control's name is in the first line, along with the word *Sub* and followed by an underscore (these characteristics uniquely characterize the definition of an event handler). If the current item is an event procedure of the deleted control, the code removes all lines up to the line End Sub.

TIP   Why didn't we use the ProcCountLines property of the CodeModule method to find out the number of lines in the module and then delete them with the Delete-Lines method? The ProcCountLines property doesn't count empty lines at the beginning of the module, and some special action is required to fix this behavior. The approach here is the simplest, and it will work even if this behavior of the ProcCountLines property is changed in the future. Because it goes through all the lines in the code, however, it's not the most efficient implementation, at least for projects with very long code listings.

The code for changing the program listing when a control is renamed isn't included in the listing. To implement it, you must locate all the instances of the string "Sub oldCtrlName_" (where OldCtrlName is the control's name) and change it to "Sub newCtrlName_" (where newCtrlName is the control's new name). This action will make the event handlers for the original control match the new name of the control.

In addition, you must search the entire code for references to the old control name. If the control Command1 is renamed to OKButton, all instances of the string "Command1." must be changed to "OKButton."

TIP   The period ensures that we change only instances of the control that were renamed, and not another control whose name partially matches the control's old name (like OKButton2, for instance).

In the CodeRemover project on the CD you will find the outline of the ctrlHandler_ItemRenamed procedure, which shows how to use its arguments. The outline of this procedure is

```
Private Sub ctrlHandler_ItemRenamed(ByVal VBControl As _
            vbide.VBControl, ByVal OldName As String, _
            ByVal OldIndex As Long)
Dim reply As Boolean
Dim msg As String

    If VBControl.Properties("Index") >= 0 And _
            OldIndex = -1 Then Exit Sub
    msg = "Revise code for " & OldName
    If OldIndex >= 0 Then msg = msg & "(" & OldIndex & ")"
    reply = MsgBox(msg, vbYesNo)
    If reply = vbYes Then
        ' INSERT CODE TO RENAME ALL INSTANCES OF RENAMED CONTROL
    End If

End Sub
```

With the discussion of the IDE events, this chapter comes to an end. You have seen nearly all the objects of the IDTExtensibility model and many examples that will help you experiment with this object model. We designed these examples so that you can use them as starting points for many new add-ins. We skipped a few objects that aren't quite as useful or are not used commonly in add-in design, but you will find all the information you need about them in the Object Browser.

PART III

Extending Visual Basic

CHAPTER

FOURTEEN

14

Visual Basic and the Windows API

- Understanding API fundamentals

- Using handles in Windows

- Manipulating applications

- Analyzing an application's menu structure

- Programming with the bitmaps and graphics API

- Using the system API functions

In Visual Basic, text boxes already know how to hold and display text, list boxes and combo boxes already know how to present data, command buttons know how to process a click, and windows know how to open and close. When your application needs capabilities that go beyond the core language and these controls, you can make API calls. By calling API procedures in DLLs, or dynamic-link libraries, you can access the thousands of procedures in the WIN32 API system, as well as routines written in other languages.

As their name suggests, DLLs are libraries of procedures that applications can link to and use at run time rather than link to statically at compile time. DLLs are not compiled into the application's executable; thus, DLLs can be updated independently of the application, and many applications can share a single DLL. Microsoft Windows itself is composed of DLLs, and other applications call the procedures within these libraries to display windows and graphics, manage system resources, manipulate the Windows Registry, and do many other tasks. These procedures are sometimes referred to as the Windows API.

Visual Basic is designed to be extended by having access to the API. VB provides a balance by hiding many of the complexities of Windows programming while still providing access to the Windows environment. More than 1000 API calls are available and can be classified in four areas:

Application manipulation   APIs open and close applications, access menu commands, and move and resize windows.

Graphics   APIs create bitmaps and capture screen images.

System information   APIs determine the current drive, available and total memory, current user, and the computer's operating system.

Registry interaction   APIs interact with the Windows Registry beyond the built-in Visual Basic Registry functions of GetSettings and SetSettings to create and query keys and to delete keys, subkeys, and values. (We discuss the Registry API functions in Chapter 15.)

The Win32 API allows Visual Basic to exploit the power of the 32-bit Windows family of operating systems. The functions, structures, messages, macros, and interfaces form a consistent and uniform API for Microsoft Windows 95, Windows 98, and Windows NT operating systems. With a simple API call, you can accomplish tasks that seem overwhelming or even impossible. This chapter introduces the fundamentals of Windows APIs, shows how to access APIs from Visual Basic, and looks at how to declare and reference function arguments. The example projects in this chapter will show you, the developer, how to unleash and harness the power of the Win32 API functions so that your VB projects are able to do the following:

- Find and control a window

- Manipulate other applications

- Find, access, and execute a menu option in another application

API Fundamentals

To use the Windows API functions, you need to understand the functional categories shown in Table 14.1.

TABLE 14.1: API Functional Categories

Category	Description
Windows Management (User32)	Creates and manages a user interface for applications
Graphics Device Interface (GDI32)	Generates graphical output for Windows devices
System Services (Kernel32)	Provides access to the operating system and computer resources
Multimedia	Accesses audio and video services
Remote Procedure Calls (RPC)	Carries out distributed computing

Windows Management

Windows Management (User32) provides the basic functions required to build and manage the display of your program output and to capture user input. The Windows Management layer determines how your application responds to mouse and keyboard input, retrieves and processes messages sent to your application windows, and supports all the clipboard functions. The Windows Management API functions include:

- ShowWindow, which sets the specified window's visibility

- IsWindowVisible, which retrieves the visibility state of the specified window

Graphics Device Interface

The Graphics Device Interface (GDI32) provides the functionality for your application to support all the devices installed on your computer, including the monitor and the printer. The GDI provides the ability to define drawing objects, such as pens, brushes, and fonts and also provides the ability to draw lines, circles, and bitmap functions. The GDI functions include:

- BitBlt, which performs a bit-block transfer of the color data corresponding to a rectangle of pixels from the specified source device context into a destination device context

- CreateCompatibleBitmap, which creates a bitmap that is compatible with the device that is associated with the specified device context

System Services

System Services (Kernel32) provide functions to access the resources of the computer provided by the operating system. These include functions for memory, the file system, and resources running on your system. System Services provide information about the hardware, including the mouse and the keyboard. System Service functions include:

- GetDiskFreeSpace, which retrieves information about the specified disk, including the amount of free space on the disk

- GetVersion, which returns the current version number of Windows and information about the operating system platform

Multimedia Functions

Multimedia functions allow you to add wave audio, AVI video, joystick support, multimedia timers, and MIDI music to your applications. The MCI Command String and Command Message Interface provides support for playing various types of media files. The multimedia functions include:

- mciSendCommand, which sends a command message to the specified MCI device.

- MessageBeep, which plays a waveform sound. The waveform sound for each sound type is identified by an entry in the sounds section of the Registry.

Remote Procedure Calls

Remote Procedure Calls (RPC) give applications the ability to carry out distributed computing, allowing applications to tap the resources and power of computers on a network. You use RPC to create distributed applications consisting of a client that presents information to the user and a server that stores, retrieves, and manipulates data and performs computing tasks for the client. Remote file servers, remote printer servers, and shared databases are examples of distributed applications. The RPC API functions include:

- RpcServerRegisterAuthInfo, which is a server side API that turns on security for the various server interfaces that are registered. It sets up the server, the principal name, the authentication service to use, and any key retrieval function in the RPC_SERVER object.

- RpcMgmtInqServerPrincName, which is used by the server application to inquire about the server's principal name corresponding to the supplied binding handle and the authentication service.

Accessing the Win32 API from Visual Basic

Using a DLL procedure in Visual Basic consists of two steps: declaring it, and then calling it as many times as it is needed. You must tell Visual Basic the DLL or API function you want to use and then supply the arguments it requires.

Declaring API Functions and DLLs

To declare a DLL procedure, you add a Declare statement to the Declarations section of the Code window. If the procedure returns a value, write the Declare statement as a function:

```
Declare Function publicname Lib "libname" [Alias "alias"] [([[ByVal] _
variable [As type] [,[ByVal] variable [As type]]...])] As Type
```

If a procedure does not return a value, write the Declare statement as a subroutine:

```
Declare Sub publicname Lib "libname" [Alias "alias"] [([[ByVal] _
variable [As type] [,[ByVal] variable [As type]]...])]
```

Later in this chapter, we will use the function FindWindow. It is declared as follows:

```
Declare Function FindWindow Lib "user32" Alias "FindWindowA" _
    (ByVal lpClassName As String, ByVal lpWindowName _
    As String) As Long
```

NOTE   The underscore character at the end of code lines is used to break long code into multiple lines.

The FindWindow function in this declaration finds the handle of a window. We will also demonstrate how to use this function later in this chapter.

When you declare DLL procedures in standard modules, they are public by default, and you can call them from anywhere in your application. When you declare DLL procedures in any other type of module, they are private to that module, and you must identify them as such by preceding the declaration with the Private keyword.

NOTE   Procedure names are case-sensitive in 32-bit versions of Visual Basic. In versions before VB5, procedure names were not case-sensitive.

Specifying the Library

The Lib clause in the Declare statement tells Visual Basic where to find the DLL file that contains the procedure. When you reference one of the core Windows libraries (User32, Kernel32, or GDI32), as we did in the FindWindow example, you don't need to include the file name extension. If you do not specify a path for *libname*, Visual Basic searches for the file in the following order:

1. In the directory containing the calling EXE file

2. In the current directory

3. In the Windows system directory (often, but not necessarily \Windows\ System)

4. In the Windows directory (not necessarily \Windows)

5. In the *Path* environment variable

Table 14.2 lists the common operating environment library files.

TABLE 14.2: Common Operating Environment Library Files

Dynamic Link Library	Description
Advapi32.dll	Advanced API services library supporting numerous APIs, including many security and Registry calls
Comdlg32.dll	Common dialog API library
Gdi32.dll	Graphics Device Interface API library
Kernel32.dll	Core Windows 32-bit base API support
Lz32.dll	32-bit compression routines
Mpr.dll	Multiple Provider Router library
Netapi32.dll	32-bit Network API library
Shell32.dll	32-bit Shell API library
User32.dll	Library for user interface routines
Version.dll	Version library
Winmm.dll	Windows multimedia library
Winspool.drv	Print spooler interface that contains the print spooler API calls

Using the API Viewer Application

You can use the API Viewer application (shown in Figure 14.1) to browse through the declarations, constants, and types included in any text file or Microsoft Jet database. When you find the procedure you want, you can copy the code to the clipboard and paste it into your Visual Basic application.

To use the Viewer Application, follow these steps:

1. Choose Add-Ins ➤ API Viewer. If you don't see the API Viewer option, select Add-In Manager and check VB API Viewer to add the API Viewer Application to the list of available Add-Ins.

2. Choose File ➤ Load Text File or File ➤ Load Database File.

FIGURE 14.1:

The API Viewer application

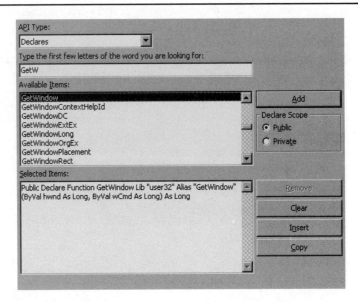

NOTE   For your convenience, Microsoft includes a Win32API file with Visual Basic 6. It is in the WinAPI subdirectory where you installed Visual Basic.

3. Select the function you want from the Available Items list box. The selected function(s) are displayed in the Selected Items list box.

4. Click the Copy button to copy the functions to the clipboard.

5. Paste the functions from the clipboard into your application's Code window.

Passing Arguments

Most DLL routines, including those in the Windows API, are documented using notation from the C programming language. This is only natural, as most DLLs are written in C or C++.

To translate the syntax of a typical API routine into a Visual Basic Declare statement, you have to understand something about how both C and Visual Basic pass arguments. The usual way for C to pass numeric arguments is by *value*—a copy of the value of the argument is passed to the routine.

Sometimes C arguments are pointers, and these arguments are said to be passed by *reference*—the called routine modifies the argument and returns it. C strings and arrays are always passed by reference.

Visual Basic usually passes all its arguments by reference (the default if not specified otherwise). To pass arguments to a C routine that expects its arguments to be passed by value, you use the ByVal keyword with the argument in the Declaration statement.

Visual Basic strings do not use the same format as C strings. In Visual Basic, the ByVal keyword is overloaded to mean "pass a C string" when it is used with a string argument in a Declare statement.

Table 14.3 shows the C argument types and their equivalent declarations in Visual Basic.

TABLE 14.3:   C and Visual Basic Data Types

C Declaration	Visual Basic Data Type	Argument Type
Char	String	ByVal
Handle	Long	ByVal
Integer	Integer	byVal
Integer Pointer (LPINT)	Integer	ByRef
Long	Long	ByVal
Long Integer Pointer	Long	ByRef
Void Pointer	Any	ByRef

NOTE   You will never pass a Visual Basic string or array to a DLL routine unless the DLL was written specifically for use with Visual Basic. Visual Basic strings and arrays are represented in memory by descriptors (not pointers), which are useless to DLL routines that were not written with Visual Basic in mind.

Passing Arguments by Value

When arguments are passed by value, only a copy of a variable is passed. If the procedure changes the value, the change affects only the copy and not the variable itself. Use the ByVal keyword to indicate an argument passed by value.

For example, if you create the following subroutine:

```
Public Sub customSub(ByVal addTo As Integer)
    addTo = addTo + 10
    Debug.Print addTo
End Sub
```

and call customSub() with the following code:

```
x = 5
Call customSub (x)
Debug.Print x
```

the Debug.Print command displays 15 in customSub(), but the value reverts to 5 when it returns to the calling subroutine. The value changes only within the customSub() subroutine.

Passing Arguments by Reference

Passing arguments by reference gives the procedure access to the actual variable contents in its memory address location. As a result, the variable's value can be permanently changed by the procedure to which it is passed. Passing by reference is the default in Visual Basic.

For example, if you create the following subroutine:

```
Public Sub customSub(addTo As Integer)
    addTo = addTo + 10
    Debug.Print addTo
End Sub
```

and call customSub() with the following code:

```
x = 5
Call customSub (x)
Debug.Print x
```

the Debug.Print command displays 15 in customSub(), and the value of x is 15 when it returns to the calling subroutine. The changes to x are global since it was passed by reference.

Handles in Windows

One way or another, Windows API functions can access windows, program instances, bitmaps, files, icons, menus, and all types of objects in Visual Basic.

Windows identifies each object with a 32-bit integer known as a *handle*. This handle is generally referred to as the *Windows hwnd*, a unique Long Integer data type.

Every window in Windows has a handle, which enables you to find a specific window among all the windows currently running in memory. Once you obtain the handle, it is easy to minimize and maximize a window, move a window, and change a window's size.

As the mouse moves over windows on the Desktop, you can use the API function WindowFromPoint to get the handle to the window currently under the mouse. To take this one step further, you can also store the window's handle and use it later in your program. To do so, you implement the same type of process that Visual Basic DragDrop uses.

Clicking the mouse button on a Visual Basic Form triggers the MouseDown event. This sets the Form as a starting point. Releasing the mouse button triggers the MouseUp event. You can then pass the mouse coordinates to the WindowFromPoint API function and obtain the window's handle. Now that you have the handle, you can use the API function GetWindowRect to determine the size and position of the window. The coordinates of the window are returned from GetWindowRect in WindowRect.Left, WindowRect.Right, WindowRect.Top, and WindowRect.Bottom. Code 14.1 shows how these API functions work.

WARNING   When you use API functions in Visual Basic, there is no built-in safety net. If you pass incorrect arguments to a function, unexpected things can happen. You can even cause a General Protection Fault that can crash the system. Therefore, it is good programming practice to use procedure-level error trapping, as we have done in Code 14.1.

Code 14.1   **Sample API Functions**

```
Private Sub Form_MouseUp(Button%, Shift%, x As Single, _
    y As Single)

On Error GoTo ErrorRoutineErr

Dim strCaption$
Dim ptLocation As POINT
Dim i
```

```
        'Convert the current mouse position to screen coordinates
        ptLocation.x = CLng(x)
        ptLocation.y = CLng(y)
        ClientToScreen Me.hwnd, ptLocation

        'Use WindowFromPoint to find out what window we are
        'pointing to
        hwndCurrentWindow = WindowFromPoint(ptLocation.x, _
            ptLocation.y)

        'Create a buffer to hold the caption, and call
        'GetWindowText to retrieve it
        strCaption = Space(1000)
        Caption = Left(strCaption, _
        GetWindowText(hwndCurrentWindow, strCaption, _
        Len(strCaption)))

        'Clear our module-level variable and restore
        'the mouse pointer hwndCurrentWindow = False
        MousePointer = vbNormal

        'Get the rectangle describing the window
        GetWindowRect hwndCurrentWindow, WindowRect

        'coordinates of the window are returned in
        '(WindowRect.Left),(WindowRect.Right)
        '(WindowRect.Top),(WindowRect.Bottom)

ErrorRoutineResume:
    Exit Sub
ErrorRoutineErr:
    MsgBox "FindWindow - frmMain, MouseMove" _
        & Err & " " & Error
    Resume Next
End Sub
```

NOTE   We'll expand on this code later in this chapter in the FindWindow project.

With WindowFromPoint, you can get the handle for any window and then use GetWindowRect to capture the style, size, and position of the window. The projects and examples that follow will give you plenty of ideas and opportunities for integrating (and controlling!) other applications from your Visual Basic application. If you combine the features from the example projects, you can build an even more robust project.

Providing an API Foundation

The Windows API examples in this chapter are designed to provide a foundation from which you can build your own API libraries. Windows includes an API to perform almost any function or task, but they all work the same basic way: declare the function, pass the expected parameters, and perform the actions or manipulate the results. Keep this in mind as you work through the sample applications that follow. Then later, when you work with APIs that are not demonstrated here, you can use these samples to take some of the mystery out of programming the Windows API.

The FindWindow Project

Armed with the window's handle, manipulating the window is easy for VB. We will use the FindWindow application (shown in Figure 14.2) to find and manipulate a window.

NOTE   You will find the FindWindow project in the **Chapter1\FindWindow** folder on the CD that comes with this book.

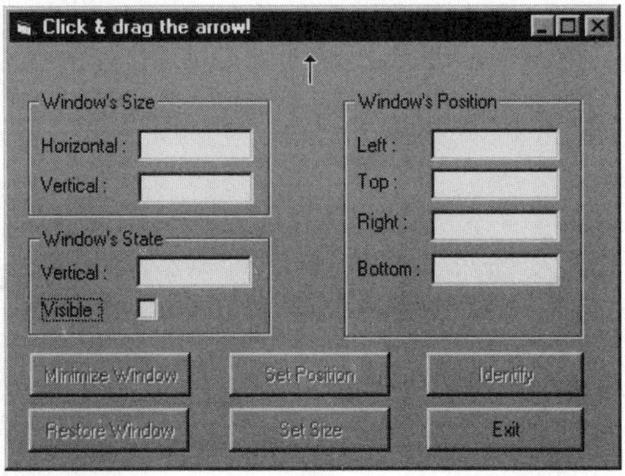

FIGURE 14.2:

The FindWindow application

The FindWindow program gets the handle from a window and allows you to minimize, maximize, move, resize, and flash the title bar of the selected window with API functions. The project consists of three Forms and six Command Buttons on the main Form. These buttons are as follows:

- The Minimize Window button minimizes the selected window by passing SW_MINIMIZE to the ShowWindow function.

- The Restore Window button restores a minimized window to its original size by passing SW_SHOWNOACTIVATE to the ShowWindow function.

- The Set Position button displays the Set Position Form (shown in Figure 14.3). This Form allows you to pass new coordinate positions to the SetWindowPos function and move the window.

- The Set Size button displays the Set Size Form (shown in Figure 14.4). From this Form, you can set new size values and call the SetWindowPos function to resize the window.

- The Identify button calls the FlashWindow API function and causes the window's title bar to change colors.

- The Exit button terminates the program.

FIGURE 14.3:

The SetPosition Form

FIGURE 14.4:

The SetSize Form

The FindWindow Project API Functions

The FindWindow project calls the API functions listed in Table 14.4 to find and manipulate a window.

NOTE   You'll find a complete description of the API functions in Appendix A, which is on the CD that comes with this book.

TABLE 14.4: The FindWindow API Functions

API Function	Description
ClientToScreen	Converts the client coordinates of a given point or rectangle on the display to screen coordinates.
DrawIcon	Draws an icon in the client area of the window.
FlashWindow	Flashes the specified window once.
GetWindowRect	Retrieves the dimensions of the rectangle of the specified window. The dimensions are given in screen coordinates that are relative to the upper-left corner of the screen.
GetWindowText	Copies the text of the specified window's title bar (if it has one) into a buffer. If the specified window is a control, the text of the control is copied.
IsIconic	Determines whether the specified window is minimized (iconic).
IsWindowEnabled	Determines whether the specified window is enabled.
IsWindowVisible	Retrieves the visibility state of the specified window.
IsZoomed	Determines whether a window is maximized.
LoadCursor	Loads the specified cursor.
SetWindowPos	Changes the size, position, and Zorder of a child, pop-up, or top-level window.
ShowWindow	Sets the specified window's visibility.
WindowFromPoint	Retrieves the handle of the window that contains the specified point.

The FindWindow Code in Action

Now that you've seen the API functions needed to convert the mouse pointer's coordinates to find a window's handle, minimize and restore a window's state, move and resize a window, and flash the title bar of a window, let's take a look at the code needed to put the functions into action.

Code 14.2 contains all the declarations, types, and constants required for the API functions in the FindWindow project.

Code 14.2   **Declarations, Types, and Constants for FindWindow**

```
'API Declarations, Types, and Constants
Public Type RECT
    Left As Long
    Top As Long
    Right As Long
    Bottom As Long
End Type

Public Type POINT
    x As Long
    y As Long
End Type

'SetWindowPos() hwndInsertAfter values
Public Const HWND_TOP = 0
Public Const HWND_BOTTOM = 1
Public Const HWND_TOPMOST = -1
Public Const HWND_NOTOPMOST = -2

'SetWindowPos Flags
Public Const SWP_NOSIZE = &H1
Public Const SWP_NOMOVE = &H2
Public Const SWP_NOZORDER = &H4
Public Const SWP_NOREDRAW = &H8
Public Const SWP_NOACTIVATE = &H10
Public Const SWP_FRAMECHANGED = &H20
Public Const SWP_SHOWWINDOW = &H40
Public Const SWP_HIDEWINDOW = &H80
Public Const SWP_NOCOPYBITS = &H100
Public Const SWP_NOOWNERZORDER = &H200
Public Const SWP_DRAWFRAME = SWP_FRAMECHANGED
Public Const SWP_NOREPOSITION = SWP_NOOWNERZORDER

'ShowWindow() Commands
Public Const SW_HIDE = 0
Public Const SW_SHOWNORMAL = 1
Public Const SW_NORMAL = 1
Public Const SW_SHOWMINIMIZED = 2
```

```
Public Const SW_SHOWMAXIMIZED = 3
Public Const SW_MAXIMIZE = 3
Public Const SW_SHOWNOACTIVATE = 4
Public Const SW_SHOW = 5
Public Const SW_MINIMIZE = 6
Public Const SW_SHOWMINNOACTIVE = 7
Public Const SW_SHOWNA = 8
Public Const SW_RESTORE = 9
Public Const SW_SHOWDEFAULT = 10
Public Const SW_MAX = 10


Declare Sub ClientToScreen Lib "user32" (ByVal hwnd _
    As Long, lpPoint As POINT)
Declare Function GetWindowText& Lib "user32" Alias _
    "GetWindowTextA" (ByVal hwnd&, ByVal lpString$, ByVal cb&)
Declare Function GetWindowRect Lib "user32" (ByVal _
    hwnd As Long, lpRect As RECT) As Boolean
Declare Function WindowFromPoint Lib "user32" (ByVal _
    ptY As Long, ByVal ptX As Long) As Long
Declare Function LoadCursor Lib "user32" Alias "LoadCursorA" _
    (ByVal hInstance&, ByVal lpCursor&) As Long
Declare Function DrawIcon Lib "user32" (ByVal hdc As Long, _
    ByVal x As Long, ByVal y As Long, ByVal hIcon As _
    Long) As Long
Declare Function ShowWindow Lib "user32" (ByVal hwnd As _
    Long, ByVal nCmdShow As Long) As Long
Declare Function IsWindowVisible Lib "user32" (ByVal hwnd _
    As Long) As Long
Declare Function IsWindowEnabled Lib "user32" (ByVal hwnd _
    As Long) As Long
Declare Function IsZoomed Lib "user32" (ByVal hwnd As _
    Long) As Long
Declare Function IsIconic Lib "user32" (ByVal hwnd _
    As Long) As Long
Declare Function SetWindowPos Lib "user32" (ByVal hwnd _
    As Long, ByVal _
    hWndInsertAfter As Long, ByVal x As Long, ByVal _
    y As Long, _
    ByVal cx As Long, ByVal cy As Long, ByVal wFlags _
    As Long) As Long
Declare Function FlashWindow Lib "user32" (ByVal hwnd _
    As Long, ByVal bInvert As Long) As Long
```

```
'Define the icon
Global Const IDC_UPARROW = 32516&

' Holds the handle to the captured window
Public hwndCurrentWindow As Long
```

Drawing the Icon   The Form_Load subroutine shown in Code 14.3 sets up the Form and draws a copy of vbUpArrow on the Form using the function DrawIcon. Table 14.5 lists the built-in cursor styles available in Visual Basic. To substitute one of these styles, change the IDC_UPARROW argument in the LoadCursor function.

Code 14.3   **The Form_Load Subroutine**

```
Private Sub Form_Load()
    'Size the form and put instructions in the caption
    With frmMain
        .Caption = "Click & drag the arrow!"
    End With

    'Change the ScaleMode to pixels and turn on AutoRedraw
    ScaleMode = vbPixels
    AutoRedraw = True

    'Draw vbUpArrow into the form's persistent bitmap
    DrawIcon hdc, 170, 0, LoadCursor(0, IDC_UPARROW)

End Sub
```

TABLE 14.5: Cursor Values

Value	Description
IDC_APPSTARTING	Standard arrow and small hourglass
IDC_ARROW	Standard arrow
IDC_CROSS	Crosshair
IDC_IBEAM	Text I-beam
IDC_ICON	Obsolete for applications marked version 4 or later

Continued on next page

TABLE 14.5 CONTINUED: Cursor Values

Value	Description
IDC_NO	Slashed circle
IDC_SIZE	Obsolete for applications marked version 4 or later. Use IDC_SIZEALL.
IDC_SIZEALL	Four-pointed arrow
IDC_SIZENESW	Double-pointed arrow pointing northeast and southwest
IDC_SIZENS	Double-pointed arrow pointing north and south
IDC_SIZENWSE	Double-pointed arrow pointing northwest and southeast
IDC_SIZEWE	Double-pointed arrow pointing west and east.
IDC_UPARROW	Vertical arrow
IDC_WAIT	Hourglass

Tracking the Mouse Position   The MouseMove subroutine tracks the movement of the mouse pointer and converts the location to screen coordinates with the ClientToScreen function. With the WindowFromPoint function, we retrieve the handle to the window. Finally, we pass the handle to the GetWindowText function to set the caption of the main Form to the caption of the window under the mouse pointer.

Code 14.4   The MouseMove Subroutine

```
Private Sub Form_MouseMove(Button As Integer, Shift As Integer, _
    x As Single, y As Single)
    Dim strCaption$
    Dim ptLocation As POINT
    Dim i
    Dim hwndTemp As Long

    'Convert the current mouse position to screen coordinates
    ptLocation.x = CLng(x)
    ptLocation.y = CLng(y)
    ClientToScreen Me.hwnd, ptLocation

    'Use WindowFromPoint to find out what window we are
    'pointing to
    hwndTemp = WindowFromPoint(ptLocation.x, ptLocation.y)
```

```
            'If a window has been captured, then put its caption
            'in our caption
            If hwndTemp Then

                'Create a buffer to hold the caption,
                'and call GetWindowText to retrieve it
                strCaption = Space(1000)
                Caption = Left(strCaption, _
                GetWindowText(hwndTemp, strCaption, Len(strCaption)))
            End If
        End Sub
```

Getting the Handle and Filling the Main Form   The MouseUp subroutine gets the position of the mouse pointer when you release the mouse button and converts the location to screen coordinates with the ClientToScreen function. As in the MouseMove subroutine, we use the WindowFromPoint function to retrieve the handle to the window. Finally, we pass the handle to the GetWindowText function to set the caption of the Main Form to the caption of the window under the mouse pointer, and then we fill in the text boxes with the window's size, position, and state.

Code 14.5	The MouseUp Subroutine

```
Private Sub Form_MouseUp(Button%, Shift%, x As Single, _
    y As Single)

    On Error GoTo ErrorRoutineErr

    Dim strCaption$ ' Buffer used to hold the caption
    Dim ptLocation As POINT ' The location of the window
    Dim i

    'Convert the current mouse position to screen coordinates
    ptLocation.x = CLng(x)
    ptLocation.y = CLng(y)
    ClientToScreen Me.hwnd, ptLocation

    'Use WindowFromPoint to find out what window we are
    'pointing to
    hwndCurrentWindow = WindowFromPoint(ptLocation.x, _
        ptLocation.y)
```

```
        'If a window has been captured, then put its caption
        'in our caption
        If hwndCurrentWindow Then

                'Create a buffer to hold the caption, and call
                'GetWindowText to retrieve it
                strCaption = Space(1000)
                Caption = Left(strCaption, _
                GetWindowText(hwndCurrentWindow, strCaption, _
                Len(strCaption)))

                'If this window does not a caption,
                'it is not a main window, exit out
                If Len(Caption) = 0 Then
                    Exit Sub
                End If

                'Fill the form with the current windows attributes
                Call GetWindowAttributes

                'If we found a window, enable the action buttons
                For i = 0 To 4
                    cmdWindowAction(i).Enabled = True
                Next

        End If
        'Restore the mouse pointer
        MousePointer = vbNormal
ErrorRoutineResume:
        Exit Sub
ErrorRoutineErr:
        MsgBox "frmMain, MouseUp " & Err & " " & Error
        Resume Next
End Sub
```

Managing the Window   The cmdWindowAction button is a control array that minimizes and restores the window with the ShowWindow function, flashing the window's title bar with the FlashWindow function and displaying the NewSize and NewPosition Forms as shown in Code 14.6. Table 14.6 lists the possible values for the ShowWindow function.

Code 14.6	The cmdWindowAction Button

```
Private Sub cmdWindowAction_Click(Index As Integer)
    On Error GoTo ErrorRoutineErr
    Dim rc
    Select Case Index
        Case 0  'minimize window
            rc = ShowWindow(hwndCurrentWindow, SW_MINIMIZE)
        Case 1  'show window
            rc = ShowWindow(hwndCurrentWindow, SW_SHOWNOACTIVATE)
        Case 2  'set new size
            frmNewSize.Show 1
        Case 3  'set new position
            frmNewPosition.Show 1
        Case 4  'identify the window, make the title flash
            rc = FlashWindow(hwndCurrentWindow, -1)
        Case 5  'exit
            End
    End Select
ErrorRoutineResume:
    Exit Sub
ErrorRoutineErr:
    MsgBox "frmMain, cmdWindowAction " & Err & " " & Error
    Resume Next
End Sub
```

TABLE 14.6: The ShowWindow Visibility Values

Value	Description
SW_HIDE	Hides the window and activates another window.
SW_MAXIMIZE	Maximizes the specified window.
SW_MINIMIZE	Minimizes the specified window and activates the next top-level window in the Zorder.
SW_RESTORE	Activates and displays the window. If the window is minimized or maximized, Windows restores it to its original size and position. An application should specify this flag when restoring a minimized window.

Continued on next page

TABLE 14.6 CONTINUED: The ShowWindow Visibility Values

Value	Description
SW_SHOW	Activates the window and displays it in its current size and position.
SW_SHOWDEFAULT	Sets the show state based on the SW_ flag specified in the STARTUPINFO structure passed to the CreateProcess function by the program that started the application.
SW_SHOWMAXIMIZED	Activates the window and displays it as a maximized window.
SW_SHOWMINIMIZED	Activates the window and displays it as a minimized window.
SW_SHOWMINNOACTIVE	Displays the window as a minimized window. The active window remains active.
SW_SHOWNA	Displays the window in its current state. The active window remains active.
SW_SHOWNOACTIVATE	Displays a window in its most recent size and position. The active window remains active.
SW_SHOWNORMAL	Activates and displays a window. If the window is minimized or maximized, Windows restores it to its original size and position. An application should specify this flag when displaying the window for the first time.

Moving the Window To move the window, enter the new Top and Left positions into the text boxes on the NewPosition Form (shown in Figure 14.5 with the Main FindWindow Form) and click the Set button.

FIGURE 14.5:

The NewPosition and Main FindWindow Forms

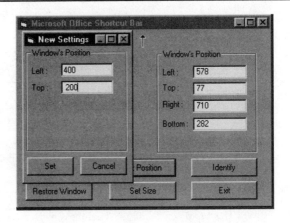

The Set button calls the SetWindowPos function and moves the window to its new location. You must identify the window to precede the positioned window in the Zorder as shown in Code 14.7. This parameter must be a window handle or one of the values in Table 14.7.

Code 14.7   **Moving a Window with the SetWindowsPos API**

```
Private Sub cmdWindowAction_Click(Index As Integer)
    On Error GoTo ErrorRoutineErr
    Dim rc As Long
    Select Case Index
        Case 0  'OK
            rc = SetWindowPos(hwndCurrentWindow, _
                HWND_TOP, txtLeft, txtTop, _
                frmMain.lblHorizontal, frmMain.lblVertical, _
                SWP_NOSIZE)
        Case 1  'cancel
            'cancel the changes and unload the form
            Unload Me
    End Select
ErrorRoutineResume:
    Exit Sub
ErrorRoutineErr:
    MsgBox "frmNewPosition, cmdWindowAction " _
        & Err & " " & Error
    Resume Next
End Sub
```

TABLE 14.7: The SetWindowsPos Values

Value	Description
HWND_BOTTOM	Places the window at the bottom of the Zorder. If the hWnd parameter identifies a topmost window, the window loses its topmost status and is placed at the bottom of all other windows.
HWND_NOTOPMOST	Places the window above all nontopmost windows (that is, behind all topmost windows). This flag has no effect if the window is already a nontopmost window.
HWND_TOP	Places the window at the top of the Zorder.
HWND_TOPMOST	Places the window above all nontopmost windows. The window maintains its topmost position even when it is deactivated.

Resizing the Window   To resize the window, enter the new Horizontal and Vertical dimensions in the text boxes on the NewSize Form (shown in Figure 14.6 with the Main FindWindow Form), and click the Set button. The Set button calls the SetWindowPos function and resizes the window.

FIGURE 14.6:

The NewSize and Main FindWindow Forms

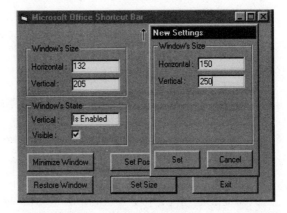

| Code 14.8 | **Setting the Window's Size with the SetWindowsPos API Function** |

```
Private Sub cmdWindowAction_Click(Index As Integer)
    On Error GoTo ErrorRoutineErr
    Dim rc As Long
    Select Case Index
        Case 0  'OK
            rc = SetWindowPos(hwndCurrentWindow, HWND_TOP _
                , frmMain.lblLeft, frmMain.lblTop, _
                txtHorizontal, txtVertical, SWP_NOMOVE)
        Case 1  'cancel
            'Cancel the changes and unload the form
            Unload Me
    End Select
ErrorRoutineResume:
    Exit Sub
ErrorRoutineErr:
    MsgBox "frmNewSize, cmdWindowAction " & Err & " " & Error
    Resume Next
End Sub
```

Taking FindWindow for a Test Run

Now that everything is set up, let's test the FindWindow application and move some windows around. Press F5 to start the program and follow these steps:

1. Move the mouse pointer over the Main Form and press and hold the mouse button.

2. With the mouse button still pressed, move the pointer over a window. Notice that the caption of the Main Form changes to display the title of the window.

3. Release the mouse button, and the Form displays the window's statistics (see Figure 14.7).

4. Now you can experiment with the features of the program.

As you can see from the code samples, finding a window's handle is not difficult. Once you have the handle to a window, it is easy to manipulate it with the API functions. In the next section, we'll explore some of the API functions needed to manipulate an application.

FIGURE 14.7:

The FindWindow application at work

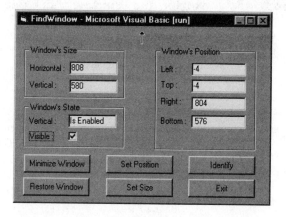

Manipulating Applications

Visual Basic is designed to give you, the developer, lots of control over your application as you are designing and running it, but VB does not give you much control over other applications that may be running concurrently. At times, you need to be able to do the following:

- Start another application from within your VB program.

- Terminate the application and know when that application has ended.

- Start another application and deny access to your VB program until the user closes the new application.

- Terminate any application from within your program.

You can take care of all these tasks with the help of Windows API calls. Here are a few API functions that you can call from within VB to launch a new application:

- OpenProcess opens a handle to an existing process. You can use this function after the Visual Basic Shell function, or you can incorporate the Shell function into the call.

- CreateProcess creates a new process.

- PostMessage terminates a running application after you obtain the handle.

The AppShell Project

We will use the AppShell project (shown in Figure 14.8) to demonstrate the application manipulation API functions.

NOTE   You'll find the AppShell project in the `Chapter1\AppShell` folder on the CD that comes with this book.

AppShell loads a ListBox control with the name and Windows handle of all the processes currently running in memory. These processes include Windows level processes and applications such as Notepad and Calculator. The project has four Command Buttons:

Shell and Continue   Clicking this button displays a File Open dialog box in which you can choose an application (EXE) file to launch. Your VB program monitors the new application and notifies you, through a message box, when it is closed. You remain in control of the VB program.

Process and Wait   This button differs from the Shell and Continue button in that you do not maintain control over the VB program while the new process is active. Clicking this button "freezes" the VB program. Your VB program will notify you through a message box and will again gain control when the new application is terminated.

Terminate App   Clicking this button terminates the application you selected from the ListBox.

WARNING   Terminate App is a powerful command. You can terminate any process, even Windows itself. Since this example program does not employ a lot of error trapping, use caution and only terminate applications such as Calculator or Notepad.

Refresh List Box   Clicking this button refreshes the ListBox control. You can click this button if you launch an application from the Start menu.

FIGURE 14.8:

The AppShell project

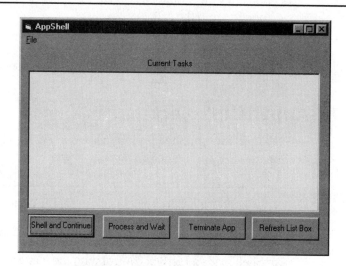

Launching a New Application

To launch a new application from within VB, you can use the OpenProcess API function with the Visual Basic Shell function. The OpenProcess function allows you to control how the application is run. It returns the handle to the newly opened process or application and is declared as follows:

```
Declare Function OpenProcess Lib "kernel32" _
    (ByVal dwDesiredAccess As Long, ByVal bInheritHandle _
    As Long, ByVal dwProcessID As Long) As Long
```

When you have the process handle to the new process, you can use the GetExit-CodeProcess function to determine whether the process is still running in memory. Code 14.9 uses the OpenProcess function to start the Notepad application.

Code 14.9   **The OpenProcess API Function**

```
Private Sub Command1_Click()
    On Error GoTo ErrorRoutineErr

    Dim hProcess As Long
    Dim RetVal As Long
    Dim slAppToRun As String

    slAppToRun = "c:\Windows\Notepad.exe"

    'The next line launches Notepad,
    hProcess = OpenProcess(PROCESS_QUERY_INFORMATION, 1, _
    Shell(slAppToRun, vbNormalFocus))

ErrorRoutineResume:
    Exit Sub
ErrorRoutineErr:
    MsgBox "AppShell.Form1.Command1_Click" & Err & Error
    Resume Next
End Sub
```

The GetExitCodeProcess function returns a value of STILL_ACTIVE if the opened process or application is still running. You can code a subroutine to check this value periodically to determine the state of the new process.

Launching a New Application and Waiting

You can use the CreateProcess API function to load and run any application or process you want. Unlike the OpenProcess function, which uses the Shell function to start the application, CreateProcess actually starts the application before it creates a Windows process. When you use this function, you have complete control over how the launched application is run. After you call the CreateProcess function, you can call the WaitForSingleObject function and force the system to wait until a specified process has finished to continue. You declare the CreateProcess function as follows:

```
Declare Function CreateProcessA Lib "kernel32" _
    (ByVal lpApplicationName As Long, ByVal lpCommandLine As _
```

```
String, ByVal lpProcessAttributes As Long, ByVal _
lpThreadAttributes As Long, ByVal bInheritHandles As _
Long, ByVal dwCreationFlags As Long, ByVal _
lpEnvironment As Long, ByVal _
lpCurrentDirectory As Long, lpStartupInfo As STARTUPINFO, _
lpProcessInformation As PROCESS_INFORMATION) As Long
```

For the WaitForSingleObject function, you pass the handle of the process you want to wait for and the length of time to pause, in milliseconds. You can set the time-out value to INFINITE and cause the system to wait until the user stops the process.

After the user stops the process, the final step is to close the open handle for the just-launched process. This removes all references to the new process. Code 14.10 uses the CreateProcess function to start the Notepad application.

Code 14.10	**The CreateProcess API Function**

```
Private Sub Command1_Click()
    On Error GoTo ErrorRoutineErr

    Dim NameOfProc As PROCESS_INFORMATION
    Dim NameStart As STARTUPINFO
    Dim rc As Long
    Dim slAppToRun As String

    slAppToRun = "c:\Windows\Notepad.exe"

    NameStart.cb = Len(NameStart)
    rc = CreateProcessA(0&, slAppToRun, 0&, 0&, 1&, _
        NORMAL_PRIORITY_CLASS, _
        0&, 0&, NameStart, NameOfProc)

ErrorRoutineResume:
    Exit Sub
ErrorRoutineErr:
    MsgBox "AppShell.Form1.Command1_Click" & Err & Error
    Resume Next
End Sub
```

Terminating an Application

To terminate an application, you use the FindWindow function to retrieve the handle. After you have the handle, it is a good idea to check and be sure that you are not getting ready to close your Visual Basic program. To do this, use the GetWindow function, and compare the handle with your program and with the application you want to terminate. If they are the same, you're getting ready to terminate your Visual Basic program. After this check, use the PostMessage function to actually terminate the application. You declare the PostMessage function as follows:

```
Declare Function PostMessage Lib "user32" Alias _
    "PostMessageA" (ByVal hwnd As Long, ByVal wMsg _
    As Long, ByVal wParam _
    As Long, ByVal lParam As Long) As Long
```

Code 14.11 shows how you can use the PostMessage function to terminate an application whose handle is passed in as TargetHwnd. The FindWindow function ensures that you do not close the current window.

Code 14.11   **The EndTask Subroutine**

```
Function EndTask(TargetHwnd As Long) As Long

    Dim rc As Integer
    Dim ReturnVal As Integer
    If TargetHwnd = Form1.hwnd Or GetWindow(TargetHwnd, _
        GW_OWNER) = Form1.hwnd Then
        End
    End If
    If IsWindow(TargetHwnd) = False Then
        GoTo EndTaskFail
    End If
    If (GetWindowLong(TargetHwnd, GWL_STYLE) _
        And WS_DISABLED) Then
        GoTo EndTaskSucceed
    End If

    If IsWindow(TargetHwnd) Then
        If Not (GetWindowLong(TargetHwnd, GWL_STYLE) _
        And WS_DISABLED) Then
        rc = PostMessage(TargetHwnd, WS_CANCELMODE, 0, 0&)
        rc = PostMessage(TargetHwnd, WM_CLOSE, 0, 0&)
         DoEvents
        End If
    End If
    GoTo EndTaskSucceed
```

```
EndTaskFail:
    ReturnVal = False
    GoTo EndTaskEndSub
EndTaskSucceed:
    ReturnVal = True
EndTaskEndSub:
    EndTask = ReturnVal
End Function
```

The AppShell Project API Functions

The AppShell project calls the API functions listed in Table 14.8 to give Visual Basic a boost in manipulating applications.

NOTE   You'll find a complete description of these API functions in Appendix A, which is on the CD that comes with this book.

TABLE 14.8: The AppShell API Functions

API Function	Description
CloseHandle	Closes an open object handle.
CreateProcess	Creates a new process and its primary thread. The new process executes the specified executable file.
GetExitCodeProcess	Retrieves the termination status of the specified process.
GetParent	Retrieves the handle of the specified child window's parent window.
GetWindow	Retrieves the handle of a window that has the specified relationship (Zorder order or owner) to the specified window.
GetWindowLong	Retrieves information about the specified window. The function also retrieves the 32-bit (long) value at the specified offset into the extra window memory of a window.
GetWindowText	Copies the text of the specified window's title bar (if it has one) into a buffer. If the specified window is a control, the text of the control is copied.
GetWindowTextLength	Retrieves the length, in characters, of the specified window's title bar text (if the window has a title bar). If the specified window is a control, the function retrieves the length of the text within the control.

Continued on next page

TABLE 14.8 CONTINUED: The AppShell API Functions

API Function	Description
IsWindow	Determines whether the specified window handle identifies an existing window.
OpenProcess	Returns a handle of an existing process object.
PostMessage	Posts a message in the message queue associated with the thread that created the specified window and then returns without waiting for the thread to process the message. Messages in a message queue are retrieved by calls to the GetMessage or PeekMessage function.
WaitForSingleObject	Returns when the specified object is in the signaled state or when the time-out interval elapses.

The AppShell Code in Action

The AppShell project uses the API functions in Table 14.8 to help you develop Visual Basic applications that can do the following:

- Launch a new application

- Launch a new application and wait until it is terminated

- Terminate a running application

Code 14.12 highlights the interaction of the VB application and the API functions.

Code 14.12   Declarations, Types, and Constants in the AppShell Project

```
Public Const GW_HWNDFIRST = 0
Public Const GW_HWNDLAST = 1
Public Const GW_HWNDNEXT = 2
Public Const GW_HWNDPREV = 3

Public Const GW_CHILD = 5
Public Const GW_MAX = 5

Global Const NORMAL_PRIORITY_CLASS = &H20&
Global Const INFINITE = -1&

Public Const STILL_ACTIVE = &H103
Public Const PROCESS_QUERY_INFORMATION = &H400
```

```
Public Const GW_OWNER = 4
Public Const GWL_STYLE = -16
Public Const WS_DISABLED = &H8000000
Public Const WS_CANCELMODE = &H1F
Public Const WM_CLOSE = &H10

Public glCurrentHwnd

Type STARTUPINFO
    cb As Long
    lpReserved As String
    lpDesktop As String
    lpTitle As String
    dwX As Long
    dwY As Long
    dwXSize As Long
    dwYSize As Long
    dwXCountChars As Long
    dwYCountChars As Long
    dwFillAttribute As Long
    dwFlags As Long
    wShowWindow As Integer
    cbReserved2 As Integer
    lpReserved2 As Long
    hStdInput As Long
    hStdOutput As Long
    hStdError As Long
End Type

Type PROCESS_INFORMATION
    hProcess As Long
    hThread As Long
    dwProcessID As Long
    dwThreadID As Long
End Type

Declare Function OpenProcess Lib "kernel32" _
    (ByVal dwDesiredAccess As Long, ByVal bInheritHandle _
    As Long, ByVal dwProcessID As Long) As Long
Declare Function GetExitCodeProcess Lib "kernel32" _
    (ByVal hProcess As Long, lpExitCode As Long) As Long
Declare Sub Sleep Lib "kernel32" (ByVal dwMilliseconds As Long)
```

```
Declare Function CloseHandle Lib "kernel32" (hObject As Long) _
    As Boolean
Declare Function WaitForSingleObject Lib "kernel32" (ByVal _
    hHandle As Long, ByVal dwMilliseconds As Long) As Long
Declare Function CreateProcessA Lib "kernel32" _
    (ByVal lpApplicationName As Long, ByVal lpCommandLine As _
    String, ByVal lpProcessAttributes As Long, ByVal _
    lpThreadAttributes As Long, ByVal bInheritHandles As _
    Long, ByVal dwCreationFlags As Long, ByVal _
    lpEnvironment As Long, ByVal _
    lpCurrentDirectory As Long, lpStartupInfo As STARTUPINFO, _
    lpProcessInformation As PROCESS_INFORMATION) As Long
Declare Function IsWindow Lib "user32" (ByVal hwnd As Long) _
    As Long
Declare Function GetWindow Lib "user32" (ByVal hwnd As Long _
    , ByVal wCmd As Long) As Long
Declare Function PostMessage Lib "user32" Alias _
    "PostMessageA" (ByVal hwnd As Long, ByVal wMsg _
    As Long, ByVal wParam _
    As Long, ByVal lParam As Long) As Long
Declare Function GetWindowLong Lib "user32" Alias _
    "GetWindowLongA" (ByVal hwnd As Long, _
    ByVal nIndex As Long) As Long

Declare Function FindWindow Lib "user32" Alias "FindWindowA" _
    (ByVal lpClassName As String, ByVal lpWindowName _
    As String) As Long

Declare Function GetParent Lib "user32" (ByVal hwnd _
As Long) As Long
Declare Function GetWindowTextLength Lib "user32" Alias _
    "GetWindowTextLengthA" (ByVal hwnd As Long) As Long
Declare Function GetWindowText Lib "user32" Alias _
    "GetWindowTextA" (ByVal hwnd As Long, ByVal lpString _
    As String, ByVal cch As Long) As Long
```

Finding All the Windows and Their Handles   The LoadTaskList subroutine
(see Code 14.13) loops through all the windows in memory and uses GetParent,
GetWindowTextLength, and GetWindowText to write the Task Name and handle to
the list box. This includes all Windows-level processes and applications. Table 14.9
lists the values for the GetWindow function.

Code 14.13   The LoadTaskList Subroutine

```vb
Sub LoadTaskList()
    Dim CurrWnd As Long
    Dim Length As Long
    Dim TaskName As String
    Dim Parent As Long

    List1.Clear
    CurrWnd = GetWindow(Form1.hwnd, GW_HWNDFIRST)

    While CurrWnd <> 0
        Parent = GetParent(CurrWnd)
        Length = GetWindowTextLength(CurrWnd)
        TaskName = Space$(Length + 1)
        Length = GetWindowText(CurrWnd, TaskName, Length + 1)
        TaskName = Left$(TaskName, Len(TaskName) - 1)
        If Length > 0 Then
            If TaskName <> Me.Caption Then
                List1.AddItem TaskName & Chr(9) & Chr(9) & _
                    CurrWnd
            End If
        End If
        CurrWnd = GetWindow(CurrWnd, GW_HWNDNEXT)
        DoEvents
    Wend
End Sub
```

TABLE 14.9: The Values for the GetWindow Function

Value	Description
GW_CHILD	The retrieved handle identifies the child window at the top of the Zorder.
GW_HWNDFIRST	The retrieved handle identifies the window of the same type that is highest in the Zorder.
GW_HWNDLAST	The retrieved handle identifies the window of the same type that is lowest in the Zorder.
GW_HWNDNEXT	The retrieved handle identifies the window below the specified window in the Zorder.

Continued on next page

TABLE 14.9 CONTINUED: The Values for the GetWindow Function

Value	Description
GW_HWNDPREV	The retrieved handle identifies the window above the specified window in the Zorder.
GW_HWNDPREV	The retrieved handle identifies the window above the specified window in the Zorder.
GW_OWNER	The retrieved handle identifies the specified window's owner window, if any.

Opening an Application and Continuing   The ShellAndContinue subroutine uses the OpenProcess API and the Visual Basic Shell functions to launch the selected application (see Code 14.14). After it is open, the program monitors the state with GetExitCodeProcess. As soon as the value of GetExitCodeProcess is not equal to STILL_ACTIVE, you are notified through a message box. Table 14.10 lists the access values for the OpenProcess function.

Code 14.14   The ShellAndContinue Subroutine

```
Sub ShellAndContinue(ByVal AppToRun As String)
    Dim hProcess As Long
    Dim RetVal As Long
    Dim Msg, Style, Title, Response

    'The next line launches AppToRun,
    'captures process ID
    hProcess = OpenProcess(PROCESS_QUERY_INFORMATION, 1, _
    Shell(AppToRun, vbNormalFocus))
    Do
        'Get the status of the process
        GetExitCodeProcess hProcess, RetVal

        DoEvents
    'Loop while the process is active
    Loop While RetVal = STILL_ACTIVE

    'Define message
    Msg = AppToRun & " Terminated by user"
    'Define buttons
    Style = vbOKOnly + vbInformation
    'Define title
```

```
        Title = "Termination Notice"
        'Display message
        Response = MsgBox(Msg, Style, Title)

    End Sub
```

TABLE 14.10: The OpenProcess Access Values

Access	Description
PROCESS_ALL_ACCESS	Specifies all possible access flags for the process object
PROCESS_CREATE_PROCESS	Used internally
PROCESS_CREATE_THREAD	Enables using the process handle in the CreateRemoteThread function to create a thread in the process
PROCESS_DUP_HANDLE	Enables using the process handle as either the source or target process in the DuplicateHandle function to duplicate a handle
PROCESS_QUERY_INFORMATION	Enables using the process handle in the GetExitCodeProcess and GetPriorityClass functions to read information from the process object
PROCESS_SET_INFORMATION	Enables using the process handle in the SetPriorityClass function to set the priority class of the process
PROCESS_TERMINATE	Enables using the process handle in the TerminateProcess function to terminate the process
PROCESS_VM_OPERATION	Enables using the process handle in the VirtualProtectEx and WriteProcessMemory functions to modify the virtual memory of the process
PROCESS_VM_READ	Enables using the process handle in the ReadProcessMemory function to read from the virtual memory of the process
PROCESS_VM_WRITE	Enables using the process handle in the WriteProcessMemory function to write to the virtual memory of the process
SYNCHRONIZE	Windows NT only: Enables using the process handle in any of the wait functions to wait for the process to terminate

Opening an Application and Waiting until the User Terminates It

The ShellAndWait subroutine uses the API function CreateProcess to launch the application passed in the AppToRun parameter. This process also uses the function WaitForSingleObject to "freeze" the VB program until the new process is terminated; it then uses the CloseHandle function to close the handle to the process and free the VB project.

Code 14.15   **The ShellAndWait Subroutine**

```
Public Sub ShellAndWait(AppToRun)
    Dim NameOfProc As PROCESS_INFORMATION
    Dim NameStart As STARTUPINFO
    Dim rc As Long

    NameStart.cb = Len(NameStart)
    rc = CreateProcessA(0&, AppToRun, 0&, 0&, 1&, _
        NORMAL_PRIORITY_CLASS, _
        0&, 0&, NameStart, NameOfProc)
    rc = WaitForSingleObject(NameOfProc.hProcess, INFINITE)
    rc = CloseHandle(NameOfProc.hProcess)
End Sub
```

Terminating an Application   The EndTask subroutine first checks with the IsWindow function to make sure you do not close the AppShell program. Next, the GetWindowLong function finds the state of the window you want to close. If it is disabled, you don't close it. If the selected window is not the current window and it is not disabled, use the PostMessage API to cancel and close the handle to the window.

Code 14.16   **The EndTask Subroutine**

```
Function EndTask(TargetHwnd As Long) As Long
    Dim rc As Integer
    Dim ReturnVal As Integer
    If TargetHwnd = Form1.hwnd Or GetWindow(TargetHwnd, _
            GW_OWNER) = Form1.hwnd Then
        End
    End If
    If IsWindow(TargetHwnd) = False Then
        GoTo EndTaskFail
    End If
    If (GetWindowLong(TargetHwnd, GWL_STYLE) And _
WS_DISABLED) Then
        GoTo EndTaskSucceed
    End If

    If IsWindow(TargetHwnd) Then
        If Not (GetWindowLong(TargetHwnd, GWL_STYLE) And
```

```
        WS_DISABLED) Then
            rc = PostMessage(TargetHwnd, WS_CANCELMODE, 0, 0&)
            rc = PostMessage(TargetHwnd, WM_CLOSE, 0, 0&)
             DoEvents
            End If
        End If
        GoTo EndTaskSucceed

EndTaskFail:
    ReturnVal = False
    GoTo EndTaskEndSub
EndTaskSucceed:
    ReturnVal = True
EndTaskEndSub:
    EndTask = ReturnVal
End Function
```

As you can see, APIs are handy for helping VB open applications, create processes, find all the currently running processes, and even terminate processes. Now with everything in place, let's take the AppShell program through its paces.

Give AppShell a Try

Press F5 to start the AppShell application (shown in Figure 14.8, earlier in this chapter), and then follow these steps:

1. Click the Shell and Continue button to open a standard Open dialog box in which you can select an application.

2. Select an EXE file to run. You will notice that you still have control of the AppShell program.

3. Now, close the new application. A message box notifies you that the application has terminated.

4. Click the Process and Wait button, and choose an application. Notice that this time you do not retain control of the AppShell program.

5. Close the new application and control is returned to the AppShell program.

6. Clicking the Terminate App button terminates the application selected in the list box. Be careful with this one; it terminates any application that you select. Test it on an application such as Notepad.

7. Click the Refresh List Box button to refresh the list box with the name and handle of all open processes (see Figure 14.9).

FIGURE 14.9:

The AppShell application at work

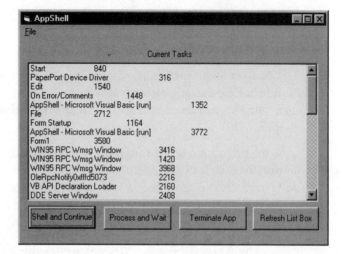

Being able to control applications from within your Visual Basic program is really a plus. It's important to be able to start, monitor, and terminate applications running concurrently with your applications. Just as important to the VB developer is having a way to spy on an application's menu structure and having the power to activate a menu option automatically. The next section examines the API function and procedures necessary to pull this off.

Analyzing an Application's Menu Structure

Most applications we write and encounter have some sort of menu structure. A menu can be a simple one-level structure that includes File and Exit options, or it can be complex, as is the menu structure for Visual Basic 6. With the aid of API functions, you can analyze an application's menu structure and trigger a menu option in another application.

You can use the FindWindow function to get the handle to an application if you already know its name. Once you have the handle, the function GetMenuItemCount returns the number of top-level menu entries. Top-level items are the menu options visible at the top of an application. In Visual Basic, for example, the top-level menus include File, Edit, View, Project, and Format. After you have the top-level menu items, use the function GetMenuItemInfo to retrieve information about the menu, and then use GetSubMenu to obtain information about the pop-up menus.

After you analyze all the top-level and submenus, it is easy to call the Send-Message function and trigger one of the menu options.

The AnalyzeMenu Project

The AnalyzeMenu project, shown in Figure 14.10, reads the menu structure of Notepad, Calculator, WordPad, and Paint. You can easily adjust it to analyze the menu structure of any application by using the techniques we discuss in this chapter.

As the program reads through the menu structure, it creates a new List Box control for each top-level menu item. Using the List Box's AddItem method, it adds the menu items to the list box. Each menu item and its sub items end up in their own list box. An OptionButton is provided for each of the four sample applications. Two Command Buttons and two Text Box controls are included:

> **The Analyze button**   When you click this button, it loops through the application's menu structure and creates and loads a List Box control with the options for each top-level menu. Each top-level menu and its sub- and pop-up menus are placed in a separate list box with the caption of the menu option. The handle to the menu is also provided for all top- and sub-level menu options.

> **The Send button**   Clicking this button triggers the selected menu option with the SendMessage API function.

> **The Menu Handle text box**   Here, the handle of the menu is inserted when you click a menu. Optionally, you can enter the handle of the menu you want to activate.

> **The Number text box**   Here, the menu number is inserted as you click the menu options. Optionally, you enter the number of the menu item to be triggered. Menu items start with zero and advance until you encounter another menu option with a handle.

NOTE   You'll find the AnalyzeMenu project in the **Chapter1\AnalyzeMenu** folder on the CD that comes with this book.

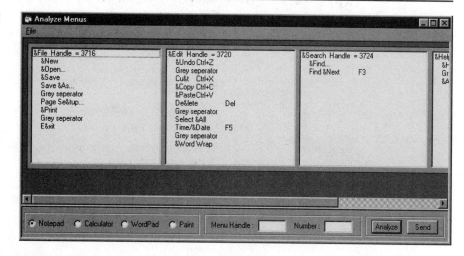

FIGURE 14.10:

The AnalyzeMenu project analyzing Notepad

The AnalyzeMenus Project API Functions

The AnalyzeMenus project calls the API functions listed in Table 14.11 to give Visual Basic the power to analyze and access other applications' menus.

NOTE   You'll find a complete description of these API functions in Appendix A, which is on the CD that comes with this book.

TABLE 14.11: The API Functions in the AnalyzeMenus Project

API Function	Description
FindWindow	Retrieves the handle to the top-level window whose class name and window name match the specified strings. This function does not search child windows.
GetMenu	Retrieves the handle of the menu assigned to the given window.
GetMenuItemCount	Determines the number of items in the specified menu.
GetMenuItemID	Retrieves the menu item identifier of a menu item located at the specified position in a menu.

Continued on next page

TABLE 14.11 CONTINUED: The API Functions in the AnalyzeMenus Project

API Function	Description
GetMenuState	Retrieves the menu flags associated with the specified menu item. If the menu item opens a submenu, this function also returns the number of items in the submenu.
GetMenuString	Copies the text string of the specified menu item into the specified buffer.
GetSubMenu	Retrieves the handle of the drop-down menu or submenu activated by the specified menu item.
SendMessage	Sends the specified message to a window or windows. The function calls the window procedure for the specified window and does not return until the window procedure has processed the message.

The AnalyzeMenus Code in Action

Using the API functions in Table 14.11, the code in the AnalyzeMenus project (see Code 14.17) demonstrates how Visual Basic, with the help of API calls, can spy on the menu structure of other applications and activate menu options.

Code 14.17   **Declarations, Types, and Constants in the AnalyzeMenus Project**

```
'Public Constants
Global hwndHold As Long
Global glSpaces As String
Global Const WM_COMMAND = &H111
Global glApplicationName As String    'hold the window to analyze
Public Const MF_BYPOSITION = &H400&
Public Const MF_BYCOMMAND = &H0&


'API Declarations
Declare Function FindWindow Lib "user32" Alias _
    "FindWindowA" (ByVal lpClassName As String, ByVal _
    lpWindowName As String) As Long
Declare Function GetMenu Lib "user32" (ByVal hwnd _
    As Long) As Long
Declare Function GetSubMenu Lib "user32" (ByVal hMenu _
    As Long, ByVal nPos As Long) As Long
```

```
Declare Function GetMenuItemCount Lib "user32" (ByVal _
    hMenu As Long) As Long
Declare Function GetMenuItemID Lib "user32" (ByVal _
    hMenu As Long, ByVal nPos As Long) As Long
Declare Function GetMenuString Lib "user32" Alias _
    "GetMenuStringA" (ByVal hMenu As Long, ByVal wIDItem _
    As Long, ByVal lpString As String, ByVal nMaxCount _
    As Long, ByVal wFlag As Long) As Long
Declare Function GetMenuState Lib "user32" (ByVal hMenu _
    As Long, ByVal wID As Long, ByVal wFlags As Long) As Long
Declare Function SendMessage Lib "user32" Alias _
    "SendMessageA" (ByVal hwnd As Long, ByVal wMsg As _
    Long, ByVal wParam As Long, lParam As Any) As Long
```

Analyzing the Top-Level Menu Structure   The AnalyzeTopLevelMenus subroutine shown in Code 14.18 loops through the menu structure of the main window and writes the menu text and handle to an array. Figure 14.11 shows the top-level menus for Visual Basic, which include File, Edit, View, and Project. You use the GetMenuItemCount function to get the number of top-level menus for this window. Then, you call the GetSubMenu function to get the handle for the menus. The AnalyzeMenu subroutine uses this handle to determine when to start a new menu. Each time a top-level menu is found, the size of the main Form is increased, and a List Box control is added. This list box holds the menu structure that is found later in the AnalyzeMenu subroutine. Additionally, the value of the menu's handle is stored in the Tag property of the List Box. This handle is used later in the Click Event of the lstMenu list box to populate the txtHandle field.

FIGURE 14.11:

Top-level Visual Basic menus

Code 14.18   The AnalyzeTopLevelMenus Subroutine

```
Public Sub AnalyzeTopLevelMenus(ByVal menuhnd)

    Dim slMenuCounter As Integer
    Dim slNumberOfMenus As Integer

    Dim slMenu As Integer
    Dim slMenuID As Long
    Dim slPopupMenu As Integer

    Dim slMenuInfo As Integer
    Dim slMenuFlags As Integer

    Dim menustring(128) As Byte
    Dim menustring2 As String * 128
    Dim context&

    'This routine can analyze up to 32 popup sub-menus
    Dim trackpopups&(32)

    Dim slXcnt As Integer

    'Find out how many entries are in the menu.
    slNumberOfMenus = GetMenuItemCount(menuhnd)

    'set the number of top level menus
    ReDim aryTopLevel(Str$(slNumberOfMenus))

    'Find out how many entries are in the menu.
    slNumberOfMenus = GetMenuItemCount(menuhnd)

    For slMenu = 0 To slNumberOfMenus - 1
        'Get the ID for this menu
        'It's a command ID, -1 for a popup, 0 for a separator
        slMenuID = GetMenuItemID(menuhnd, slMenu)
        Select Case slMenuID
            Case 0  'It's a separator

            Case -1 'It's a popup menu
                slMenuInfo = GetMenuString(menuhnd, slMenu, _
                    menustring2, 127, MF_BYPOSITION)
```

```
        slMenuFlags = GetMenuState(menuhnd, slMenu, _
            MF_BYPOSITION)
        Debug.Print glSpaces & Left$ _
        (menustring2, slMenuInfo) _
        & " Handle = " & GetSubMenu(menuhnd, slMenu)
        'store the handle to this menu in the array
        aryTopLevel(slMenu) = _
        (GetSubMenu(menuhnd, slMenu))

        'add a list box for each menu and
        'increase the size of the form
        If slMenu > 0 Then
            Load Form1.lstMenu(slMenu)
            Form1.Width = Form1.Width + 3450
            Form1.lstMenu(slMenu).Left = Form1.lstMenu _
                (slMenu - 1).Left + Form1.lstMenu _
                (slMenu - 1).Width + 100
            Form1.lstMenu(slMenu).Visible = True
        End If
        'Store the handle for the menu in the Tag property
        'to use in the Click Event of the listbox to populate
        'the txtHandle and txtNumber fields.
        Form1.lstMenu(slMenu).Tag = GetSubMenu(menuhnd, slMenu)
    End Select
    Next slMenu

End Sub
```

Analyzing the Menu Structure The AnalyzeMenus subroutine uses the Get-MenuItemCount function to return the number of menu items. The GetMenuItemID function tells us if the menu is a separator or a pop-up menu. Figure 14.12 shows the top-level menu of Notepad with the File submenu exposed. New, Open, Save, and Save As are pop-up menus, and the gray line below Save As is a separator.

The AnalyzeMenus subroutine (see Code 14.19) loops through the items in a menu and adds each item with the GetMenuString function; it then uses the Get-SubMenu function to add the handle to a list box. Each top-level menu is added to a separate List Box control. The items are indented to mimic the look of the menu. This subroutine is a good example of API calls and Visual Basic loops. Figure 14.10, earlier in this chapter, shows the menus of Notepad analyzed.

FIGURE 14.12:

The top-level Notepad menus

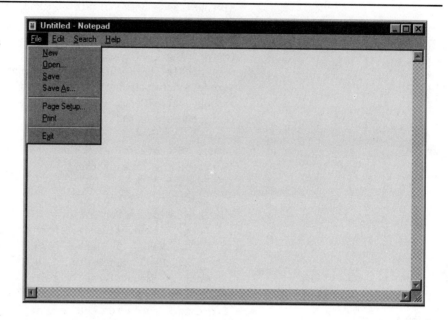

Code 14.19   The AnalyzeMenus Subroutine

```
Public Sub AnalyzeMenus(ByVal menuhnd)

    Dim slMenuCounter As Integer
    Dim slNumberOfMenus As Integer

    Dim slMenu As Integer
    Dim slMenuID As Long
    Dim slPopupMenu

    Dim slMenuInfo As Integer
    Dim slMenuFlags As Integer

    Dim menustring(128) As Byte
    Dim menustring2 As String * 128

    'This routine can analyze up to 32 popup sub-menus
    Dim trackpopups&(32)
```

```
Dim slXcnt As Integer

slPopupMenu = 0

'Find out how many entries are in the menu.
slNumberOfMenus = GetMenuItemCount(menuhnd)

For slMenu = 0 To slNumberOfMenus - 1
    'Get the ID for this menu
    'It's a command ID, -1 for a popup, 0 for a separator
    slMenuID = GetMenuItemID(menuhnd, slMenu)
    Select Case slMenuID
        Case 0  'It's a separator
            Form1.lstMenu(lstNum).AddItem glSpaces & _
                "Grey separator"
        Case -1 'It's a popup menu
            'Save it in the list of popups
            trackpopups&(slPopupMenu) = slMenu
            slPopupMenu = slPopupMenu + 1

            slMenuInfo = GetMenuString(menuhnd, slMenu, _
                menustring2, 127, MF_BYPOSITION)

            'Set the listbox according to the top level menu
            For slMenuCounter = 0 To UBound(aryTopLevel)
                If aryTopLevel(slMenuCounter) = (GetSubMenu _
                    (menuhnd, slMenu)) Then
                    lstNum = slMenuCounter
                    'reset the indention
                    glSpaces = ""
                End If
            Next

            slMenuFlags = GetMenuState(menuhnd, slMenu, _
                MF_BYPOSITION)
            Form1.lstMenu(lstNum).AddItem glSpaces _
            & Left$(menustring2, slMenuInfo) _
            & "  Handle  = " & GetSubMenu(menuhnd, slMenu)

            'At least one popup was found
            If slPopupMenu > 0 Then
                For slXcnt = 0 To slPopupMenu - 1
```

```
                        slMenuID = trackpopups&(slXcnt)
                        glSpaces = glSpaces & "    "
                        AnalyzeMenus GetSubMenu(menuhnd, _
                            slMenuID)
                    Next slXcnt
                    slPopupMenu = 0
                    glSpaces = "    "
                End If

            Case Else 'A regular entry
                slMenuInfo = GetMenuString(menuhnd, slMenuID, _
                    menustring2, 127, MF_BYCOMMAND)
                Form1.lstMenu(lstNum).AddItem glSpaces & _
                    Left$(menustring2, slMenuInfo)
                slMenuFlags = GetMenuState(menuhnd, slMenuID, _
                    MF_BYCOMMAND)
        End Select
    Next slMenu
    glSpaces = ""

End Sub
```

Activating a Menu Option   The subroutine cmdSend uses the handle and menu number from the main Form and calls the API function SendMessage to activate a menu option (see Code 14.20).

Code 14.20   **The cmdSend Subroutine**

```
Private Sub cmdSend_Click()
    Dim hwnd As Long
    Dim hMainMenu As Integer
    Dim hMenu As Integer
    Dim slMenuID As Long
    Dim rc
    Dim X As Long

    slMenuID = GetMenuItemID(txtHandle, txtNumber)

    rc = SendMessage(hwndHold, WM_COMMAND, slMenuID, 0&)

End Sub
```

The ability to activate a menu option from other applications adds a new dimension to the power and flexibility of Visual Basic. As you can see, you can program VB to do the following:

- Open a help file from another application

- Print a report

- Open a file

- Change properties such as font, color, and format

- Access any menu option

Testing the AnalyzeMenu Program

The AnalyzeMenu program is designed to analyze the menu structure of Notepad, Calculator, WordPad, or Paint. You could easily adapt it to analyze the menu structure of any application. For this test, we will analyze the menus of Notepad. Follow these easy steps:

1. Start and minimize the Notepad application.

2. Press F5 to start the AnalyzeMenu program.

3. Select the Notepad button.

4. Click the Analyze button. The top part of the Form will be filled with five list boxes, similar to what you see in Figure 14.10, earlier in this chapter. Each list box contains a top-level menu option and all the submenus and pop-up menus under it.

5. In the MenuHandle text box, enter the handle number for the &Help menu.

6. Enter the number zero into the Number text box. This tells the program that you want to trigger the first option, &Help Topics (remember that menu numbers start with zero).

7. Click the Send button to display the Notepad help file.

Menus are an integral part of Windows applications. By employing the API functions and procedures we looked at in this section, you can program Visual Basic to unlock the power of menus in other applications.

NOTE   If you use the AnalyzeMenu application to activate a menu option that displays a Dialog Box, such as Help About or a Print Setup, keep in mind that the Dialog Box will be displayed behind the AnalyzeMenu application. To access the dialog box, use Alt+Tab to make the dialog box active.

The Bitmaps and Graphics API Functions

In visual programming environments such as Visual Basic and Windows, bitmaps and graphics are important. Graphics and bitmaps are used in almost every part of a Visual Basic application—from the menu to the forms that make up the user interface. Visual Basic does not provide a lot of support for graphics; fortunately, API functions can fill the void. The Win32 API includes a vast array of API functions that can be employed in Visual Basic to do the following:

- Create bitmaps
- Copy bitmaps
- Flood a container with color
- Add bitmaps to menus

And the list goes on and on. One common thread is a bitmap.

Understanding Bitmaps

A bitmap is an object in Windows that holds an image. The two types of bitmaps are:

- Device-dependent bitmaps (DDB)
- Device-independent bitmaps (DIB)

Device-Dependent Bitmaps

All bitmaps in Windows are device-dependent unless otherwise noted. DDBs are described in a single structure, the BITMAP structure. The BITMAP structure defines the type, width, height, color, format, and bit values of a bitmap. Table 14.12 lists and describes the members of a BITMAP structure.

TABLE 14.12: The Members of a BITMAP Structure

Member	Description
bmType	Specifies the bitmap type. This member must be zero.
BmWidth	Specifies the width, in pixels, of the bitmap. The width must be greater than zero.
BmHeight	Specifies the height, in pixels, of the bitmap. The height must be greater than zero.
BmWidthBytes	Specifies the number of bytes in each scan line.
BmPlanes	Specifies the count of color planes.
BmBitsPixel	Specifies the number of bits required to indicate the color of a pixel.
BmBits	Points to the location of the bit values for the bitmap.

Copying and displaying a DDB is much faster than copying and displaying a DIB. All Windows needs to do to move a DDB is to copy memory. You can use the function BitBlt to do this. The key to using DDBs is compatibility. The easiest way to determine if a bitmap is compatible with a device is to use the CreateCompatibleBitmap function. On the other hand, you can use device-independent bitmaps to copy or display bitmaps across devices.

Device-Independent Bitmaps

A device-independent bitmap is a color bitmap in a format that eliminates the problems that occur in transferring DDBs to devices that have a different bitmap format. DIBs provide bitmap information that any display or printer driver can translate. The main purpose of DIBs is to allow bitmaps to be moved from one device to another.

Transferring bitmaps from one device to another was not possible in Microsoft Windows prior to version 3. Now, with DIBs, every device can display a bitmap to the extent of its color resolution. An application can store and display a bitmap regardless of the output device.

A bitmap file consists of a BITMAPFILEHEADER structure and the DIB itself. Table 14.13 lists the members of this structure.

TABLE 14.13: The Members of the BITMAPFILEHEADER Structure

Field	Description
bfType	WORD that defines the type of file. It must be BM.
BfSize	A DWORD that specifies the size of the file in bytes.
bfReserved1, bfReserved2	WORDs that must be set to zero.
BfOffBits	A DWORD that specifies the offset from the beginning of the BITMAPFILEHEADER structure to the start of the actual bits.

The BITMAPINFOHEADER structure follows immediately after the BITMAP-FILEHEADER structure. Table 14.14 lists and describes the members of the BITMAPINFOHEADER structure. The header is made up of two parts: the header and the color table. They are combined in the BITMAPINFO structure, which is what all DIB APIs expect.

TABLE 14.14: The Members of the BITMAPINFOHEADER Structure

Field	Description
BiSize	Should be set to the size of (BITMAPINFOHEADER). This field defines the size of the header (minus the color table).
biWidth, biHeight	Define the width and the height of the bitmap in pixels.
BiPlanes	Should always be 1.
BiBitCount	Defines the color resolution (in bits per pixel) of the DIB. Only four values are valid for this field: 1, 4, 8, and 24.
BiCompression	Specifies the type of compression. Can be one of three values: BI_RGB, BI_RLE4, or BI_RLE8.
BiSizeImage	Should contain the size of the bitmap proper in bytes.
biXPelsPerMeter biYPelsPerMeter	Define application-specified values for the desirable dimensions of the bitmap.
BiClrUsed	Provides a way for getting smaller color tables. When this field is set to 0, the number of colors on the biBitCount field should be set to one of the following values: 1 indicates 2 colors, 4 indicates 16, 8 indicates 256, and 24 indicates no color table.
BiClrImportant	Specifies that the first x colors of the color table are important to the DIB.

The color table follows the header information. The number of entries in the color table matches the number of colors supported by the DIB except for a 24-bit color bitmap that does not have a color table. Table 14.15 shows the structure of a color table for a 16-color DIB.

TABLE 14.15: Color Structure

Field	Description
bmiHeader	BITMAPINFOHEADER information
BmiColors(15)	Colors

The ScreenCapture Project

The ScreenCapture project (shown in Figure 14.13) demonstrates how to use some of the most popular bitmap API functions.

FIGURE 14.13:

The ScreenCapture project

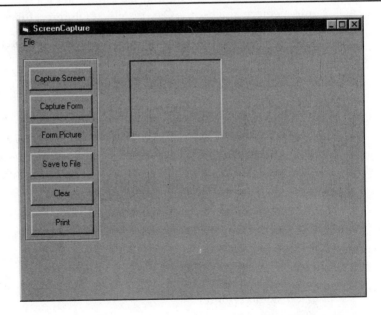

You can use a bitmap to do the following:

- Capture an image
- Store an image in memory
- Display an image at a different location or on a different device

To store an image temporarily, you can call the CreateCompatibleDC function to create a device context that is compatible with the current window device context. After you create the compatible device context, you can create a bitmap with the appropriate dimensions by calling the CreateCompatibleBitmap function. You can then call SelectObject to select it into the newly created device context.

After the compatible device context is created and the bitmap is selected into it, you can use the BitBlt function to capture an image. The BitBlt function performs a bit block transfer. It copies data from a source bitmap into a destination bitmap of the same size. The BitBlt function receives handles that identify two device contexts and copies the bitmap data from a bitmap selected into the source device context into a bitmap selected into the target device context. The target device context is a compatible device context; so when BitBlt completes the transfer, the image is copied into memory. You use the OleCreatePictureIndirect function to redisplay the image.

The ScreenCapture project has six Command Buttons:

Capture Screen   Clicking this button captures the screen and places an image of it in a picture box.

Capture Form   Clicking this button captures the Form and places an image of it in a picture box.

Create Form Picture   Clicking this button, after you capture an image, sets the Picture property of form2 to the captured image. This is an example of how to copy a bitmap into memory and then use it on a Form.

Save to File   Clicking this button opens a standard File Save dialog box, in which you can set the file name and location and save the picture to a file.

Clear   Clicking this button clears the contents of the PictureBox control.

Print   Clicking this button prints the contents of the picture box on the default printer.

NOTE   You'll find the ScreenCapture project in the `Chapter14\ScreenCapture` folder on the CD that comes with this book.

The ScreenCapture API Functions

The ScreenCapture project calls on the API functions listed in Table 14.16 to help Visual Basic perform bitmap functions.

TABLE 14.16: The ScreenCapture API Functions

Function	Description
BitBlt	Performs a bit-block transfer of the color data corresponding to a rectangle of pixels from the specified source device context into a destination device context.
CreateCompatibleBitmap	Creates a bitmap compatible with the device that is associated with the specified device context.
CreateCompatibleDC	Creates a memory device context that is compatible with the specified device.
CreatePalette	Creates a logical color palette.
GetDesktopWindow	Returns the handle of the Windows Desktop window. The Desktop window covers the entire screen. The Desktop window is the area on top of which all icons and other windows are painted.
GetDeviceCaps	Retrieves device-specific information about a specified device.
GetForegroundWindow	Returns the handle of the foreground window (the current window). The system assigns a slightly higher priority to the thread that creates the foreground window than it does to other threads.
GetSystemPaletteEntries	Retrieves a range of palette entries from the system palette that is associated with the specified device context.
GetDC	Retrieves a handle of a display device context for the client area of the specified window. The display device context can be used in subsequent GDI functions to draw in the client area of the window.

Continued on next page

TABLE 14.16 CONTINUED: The ScreenCapture API Functions

Function	Description
GetWindowDC	Retrieves the device context for the entire window, including the title bar, menus, and scroll bars. A window device context permits painting anywhere in a window, because the origin of the device context is the upper-left corner of the window instead of the client area. The GetWindowDC function assigns default attributes to the window device context each time it retrieves the device context. Previous attributes are lost.
OleCreatePictureIndirect	Creates a new picture object initialized according to a PICTDESC structure.
RealizePalette	Maps palette entries from the current logical palette to the system palette.
ReleaseDC	Releases a device context, freeing it for use by other applications. It frees only common and window device contexts and has no effect on class or private device contexts.
SelectObject	Selects an object into the specified device context. The new object replaces the previous object of the same type.
SelectPalette	Selects the specified logical palette into a device context.

The ScreenCapture Code in Action

Let's put these functions to work with VB to see how a bitmap can be used to capture a screen and part of a Form and how it can be used as the Picture property of a Form (see Code 14.21).

Code 14.21   **Declarations, Types, and Constants in the ScreenCapture Project**

```
Global Const INVERSE = 6
Const SOLID = 0
Const DOT = 2

Global HoldX As Single
Global HoldY As Single
Global StartX As Single
Global StartY As Single
Global SavedDrawStyle
Global SavedMode
```

```
Option Base 0

Private Type PALETTEENTRY
peRed As Byte
peGreen As Byte
peBlue As Byte
peFlags As Byte
End Type

Private Type LOGPALETTE
palVersion As Integer
palNumEntries As Integer
palPalEntry(255) As PALETTEENTRY ' Enough for 256 colors
End Type

Private Type GUID
Data1 As Long
Data2 As Integer
Data3 As Integer
Data4(7) As Byte
End Type


Private Const RASTERCAPS As Long = 38
Private Const RC_PALETTE As Long = &H100
Private Const SIZEPALETTE As Long = 104

Private Type RECT
    Left As Long
    Top As Long
    Right As Long
    Bottom As Long
End Type

Private Type PicBmp
    Size As Long
    Type As Long
    hBmp As Long
    hPal As Long
    Reserved As Long
End Type
```

```
Private Declare Function BitBlt Lib "GDI32" ( _
    ByVal hDCDest As Long, ByVal XDest As Long, _
    ByVal YDest As Long, ByVal nWidth As Long, _
    ByVal nHeight As Long, ByVal hDCSrc As Long, _
    ByVal XSrc As Long, ByVal YSrc As Long, ByVal dwRop As Long) _
    As Long
Private Declare Function CreateCompatibleBitmap Lib _
    "GDI32" (ByVal hDC As Long, ByVal nWidth As Long, _
    ByVal nHeight As Long) As Long
Private Declare Function CreateCompatibleDC Lib "GDI32" ( _
    ByVal hDC As Long) As Long
Private Declare Function CreatePalette Lib "GDI32" ( _
    lpLogPalette As LOGPALETTE) As Long
Private Declare Function DeleteDC Lib "GDI32" ( _
    ByVal hDC As Long) As Long
Private Declare Function GetDesktopWindow Lib "USER32" () As Long
Private Declare Function GetDeviceCaps Lib "GDI32" ( _
    ByVal hDC As Long, ByVal iCapabilitiy As Long) As Long
Private Declare Function GetForegroundWindow Lib "USER32" () _
    As Long
Private Declare Function GetSystemPaletteEntries Lib _
    "GDI32" (ByVal hDC As Long, ByVal wStartIndex As Long, _
    ByVal wNumEntries As Long, lpPaletteEntries _
    As PALETTEENTRY) As Long
Private Declare Function GetWindowDC Lib "USER32" ( _
    ByVal hWnd As Long) As Long
Private Declare Function GetDC Lib "USER32" ( _
    ByVal hWnd As Long) As Long
Private Declare Function GetWindowRect Lib "USER32" ( _
    ByVal hWnd As Long, lpRect As RECT) As Long
Private Declare Function OleCreatePictureIndirect _
    Lib "olepro32.dll" (PicDesc As PicBmp, RefIID As GUID, _
    ByVal fPictureOwnsHandle As Long, IPic As IPicture) As Long
Private Declare Function RealizePalette Lib "GDI32" ( _
    ByVal hDC As Long) As Long
Private Declare Function ReleaseDC Lib "USER32" ( _
    ByVal hWnd As Long, ByVal hDC As Long) As Long
Private Declare Function SelectObject Lib "GDI32" ( _
    ByVal hDC As Long, ByVal hObject As Long) As Long
Private Declare Function SelectPalette Lib "GDI32" ( _
    ByVal hDC As Long, ByVal hPalette As Long, _
    ByVal bForceBackground As Long) As Long
```

Capturing the Screen   The CaptureScreen function (shown in Code 14.22) uses the GetDesktopWindow API function to retrieve a handle to the Desktop. After the handle is retrieved, the VB function CaptureWindow is called to copy the bitmap into memory. The screen resolution is passed as well as the handle.

Code 14.22	The CaptureScreen Function

```
Public Function CaptureScreen() As Picture
    On Error GoTo ErrorRoutineErr

    Dim hWndScreen As Long

    'Get a handle to the desktop window
    hWndScreen = GetDesktopWindow()

    'Call CaptureWindow to capture the entire desktop,
    'give the handle and return the resulting Picture object
    Set CaptureScreen = CaptureWindow(hWndScreen, _
    0, 0, _
    Screen.Width \ Screen.TwipsPerPixelX, _
    Screen.Height \ Screen.TwipsPerPixelY)

ErrorRoutineResume:
    Exit Function
ErrorRoutineErr:
    MsgBox "Project1.Module1.CaptureScreen" & Err & Error
    Resume Next
End Function
```

Capturing the Form   The CaptureForm function (shown in Code 14.23) is similar to the CaptureScreen function except that it uses the Visual Basic Handle property hWnd to retrieve the handle to Form1. After the handle is retrieved, the VB function CaptureWindow is called to copy the bitmap into memory. The screen resolution is passed as well as the handle.

Code 14.23	The CaptureForm Function

```
Public Function CaptureForm(frmSrc As Form) As Picture
    On Error GoTo ErrorRoutineErr

    'Call CaptureWindow to capture the entire form
    'given it's window
```

```
          'handle and then return the resulting Picture object
          Set CaptureForm = CaptureWindow(frmSrc.hWnd, 0, 0, _
          frmSrc.ScaleX(frmSrc.Width, vbTwips, vbPixels), _
          frmSrc.ScaleY(frmSrc.Height, vbTwips, vbPixels))

     ErrorRoutineResume:
          Exit Function
     ErrorRoutineErr:
          MsgBox "Project1.Module1.CaptureForm" & Err & Error
          Resume Next
     End Function
```

Processing the CaptureWindow Actions   A lot of work is performed in
this function (see Code 14.24). First, the API function GetWindowDC gets the
device context for the screen or window. Next, CreateCompatibleDC creates a
memory device context for the copy process, and then a bitmap is created with
the CreateCompatibleBitmap function and placed into memory with the Select-
Object function.

The next task is to get the screen properties. To accomplish this, we use the
GetDeviceCaps function to find the raster capabilities and the palette size. If the
screen has a palette, we need to copy it and select it into memory. We get the
palette with the GetSystemPaletteEntries API function, create a copy of it with
CreatePalette, and, finally, select it into memory with SelectPalette.

Now that we are finished with the preliminaries, we can use BitBlt to copy the
image into the memory device context. If the screen has a palette, get it back
with the SelectPalette function. With the bitmap and palette copied into memory,
we can clean up a bit. We use the functions DeleteDC and ReleaseDC to release
the device context resources back to the system. The last task is to call the function CreateBitmapPicture and create the picture object with the API function
OleCreatePictureIndirect.

Code 14.24	**The CaptureWindow Function**

```
Public Function CaptureWindow(ByVal hWndSrc As Long, _
     ByVal LeftSrc As Long, _
     ByVal TopSrc As Long, ByVal WidthSrc As Long, _
     ByVal HeightSrc As Long) As Picture

     On Error GoTo ErrorRoutineErr

     Dim hDCMemory As Long
```

```
Dim hBmp As Long
Dim hBmpPrev As Long
Dim rc As Long
Dim hDCSrc As Long
Dim hPal As Long
Dim hPalPrev As Long
Dim RasterCapsScrn As Long
Dim HasPaletteScrn As Long
Dim PaletteSizeScrn As Long

Dim LogPal As LOGPALETTE

'Get device context for the window
hDCSrc = GetWindowDC(hWndSrc)

'Create a memory device context for the copy process
hDCMemory = CreateCompatibleDC(hDCSrc)
'Create a bitmap and place it in the memory DC
hBmp = CreateCompatibleBitmap(hDCSrc, WidthSrc, HeightSrc)
hBmpPrev = SelectObject(hDCMemory, hBmp)

'Get screen properties
'Raster capabilities
RasterCapsScrn = GetDeviceCaps(hDCSrc, RASTERCAPS)
'Palette support
HasPaletteScrn = RasterCapsScrn And RC_PALETTE
'Size of palette
PaletteSizeScrn = GetDeviceCaps(hDCSrc, SIZEPALETTE)

'If the screen has a palette, make a copy
If HasPaletteScrn And (PaletteSizeScrn = 256) Then
    'Create a copy of the system palette
    LogPal.palVersion = &H300
    LogPal.palNumEntries = 256
    rc = GetSystemPaletteEntries(hDCSrc, 0, 256, _
    LogPal.palPalEntry(0))
    hPal = CreatePalette(LogPal)
    'Select the new palette into the memory
    'DC and realize it
    hPalPrev = SelectPalette(hDCMemory, hPal, 0)
    rc = RealizePalette(hDCMemory)
End If

'Copy the image into the memory DC
```

```
    rc = BitBlt(hDCMemory, 0, 0, WidthSrc, HeightSrc, _
    hDCSrc, LeftSrc, TopSrc, vbSrcCopy)

    'Remove the new copy of the  on-screen image
    hBmp = SelectObject(hDCMemory, hBmpPrev)

    'If the screen has a palette get back the palette that was
    'selected in previously
    If HasPaletteScrn And (PaletteSizeScrn = 256) Then
    hPal = SelectPalette(hDCMemory, hPalPrev, 0)
    End If

    'Release the device context resources back to the system
    rc = DeleteDC(hDCMemory)
    rc = ReleaseDC(hWndSrc, hDCSrc)

    'Call CreateBitmapPicture to create a picture
    'object from the bitmap and palette handles.
    'Then return the resulting picture object.
    Set CaptureWindow = CreateBitmapPicture(hBmp, hPal)

ErrorRoutineResume:
    Exit Function
ErrorRoutineErr:
    MsgBox "Project1.Module1.CaptureWindow" & Err & Error
    Resume Next
End Function
```

Constructing a New Picture Object   The CreateBitmapPicture function (shown in Code 14.25) takes the handles of the bitmap and palettes that were placed into memory in the CaptureWindow function, adds the GUID structure and Pic parts, and with the OleCreatePictureIndirect API, creates a bitmap picture that can be placed in our PictureBox control on Form1.

Code 14.25   The CreateBitmapPicture Function

```
Public Function CreateBitmapPicture(ByVal hBmp As Long, _
    ByVal hPal As Long) As Picture

    On Error GoTo ErrorRoutineErr

    Dim r As Long
        Dim Pic As PicBmp
```

```
        'IPicture requires a reference to "Standard OLE Types"
        Dim IPic As IPicture
        Dim IID_IDispatch As GUID

        'Fill in with IDispatch Interface ID
        With IID_IDispatch
            .Data1 = &H20400
            .Data4(0) = &HC0
            .Data4(7) = &H46
        End With

        'Fill Pic with necessary parts
        With Pic
            'Length of structure
            .Size = Len(Pic)
            'Type of Picture (bitmap)
            .Type = vbPicTypeBitmap
            'Handle to bitmap
            .hBmp = hBmp
            'Handle to palette (may be null)
            .hPal = hPal
        End With

        'Create Picture object
        r = OleCreatePictureIndirect(Pic, IID_IDispatch, 1, IPic)

        'Return the new Picture object
        Set CreateBitmapPicture = IPic

ErrorRoutineResume:
    Exit Function
ErrorRoutineErr:
    MsgBox "Project1.Module1.CreateBitmapPicture" & Err & Error
    Resume Next
End Function
```

As you can see, creating a bitmap in memory involves several steps. Without the help of the Win32API, Visual Basic would never be able to pull it off. Now, it's time to take the ScreenCapture project for a test run.

Testing the ScreenCapture Program

You can use the ScreenCapture project to capture a screen or a form with the aid of API calls and then use the bitmap as the Picture property of a Form. You can create a permanent copy of the bitmap by copying it to a file, and you can print the bitmap to the default printer. To test ScreenCapture, follow these steps:

1. Start the ScreenCapture project from within Visual Basic.

2. Click the Capture Screen button to capture the Desktop to the PictureBox control. Figure 14.14 shows the ScreenCapture project with the Desktop captured.

3. Click the Clear button to clear the picture box.

4. Click the Capture Form button to capture the ScreenCapture Form to the picture box.

5. If you want to save the bitmap to a file, click the Save to File button to open a standard Save As dialog box, in which you can select a path and file name and save the file.

6. Click the Print button to print the contents of the picture box on the default printer.

You can create bitmaps from almost any source, and this project demonstrates only the tip of the iceberg. By combining the techniques in the other sections of this chapter, you can really make APIs and bitmaps work for you to create some unique projects.

FIGURE 14.14:

The Desktop captured

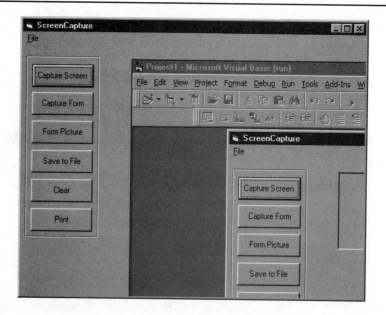

The System API Functions

Visual Basic can tell you a lot about a computer's environment, but as developers we really need even more information. For example, when you get a support call, it's important to know the makeup of the user's system. Many times the problem is simply that the machine running the program does not meet the minimum hardware requirements.

If a computer is running an application that uses a few API functions, developers can have access to information about the following:

- Memory statistics

- Total and free disk space

- Number of colors

- Operating system

- Processor type

You can use the GlobalMemoryStatus API function to investigate the system and report the amount of memory. The GetFreediskSpace API returns, among others, the total disk space and the total free disk space. If your application needs to know the number of colors supported, call the GetDeviceCaps function.

You can use the GetVersionEx function to find out the major version, the minor version (such as NT version 4), the build number, and the service pack level for Windows NT. This last bit of information is especially important for NT users. Most applications written today require at least Service Pack 2 for NT.

Another must in today's programming environment is knowing the type of processor currently running. You can find this information with the GetSystem-Info API function. And if the user is signed on to a network, you can retrieve the user's name with the GetUserName function.

The Statistics Project

We will use the Statistics project (shown in Figure 14.15) to demonstrate some of the API functions you can use to get information about a computer's environment. When the application starts, it makes several API calls to catalog the current environment.

NOTE You'll find the Statistics project in the **Chapter14\Statistics** folder on the CD that comes with this book.

FIGURE 14.15:

The Statistics project

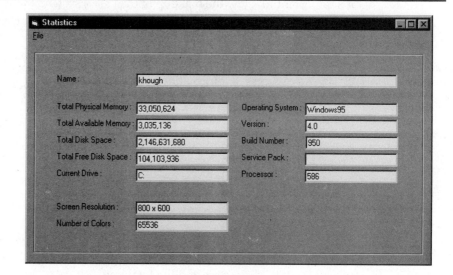

The Statistics Project API Functions

Table 14.17 lists and describes the API functions in the Statistics project.

TABLE 14.17: The Statistics API Functions

Function	Description
GetDeviceCaps	Retrieves device-specific information about a specified device.
GetDiskFreeSpace	Retrieves information about the specified disk, including the amount of free space on the disk.
GlobalMemoryStatus	Retrieves information about current available memory. The function returns information about both physical and virtual memory. This function super-sedes the GetFreeSpace function.
GetUserName	Retrieves the user name of the current thread. This is the name of the user currently logged on to the system.
GetVersionEx	Obtains extended information about the version of the operating system that is currently running.
GetSystemInfo	Returns information about the current system.

The Statistics Project Code in Action

The system statistic API functions listed in Table 14.17 can really give you a head start when it comes to troubleshooting application problems. Let's take a look at Code 14.26 to examine the functions in some code.

Code 14.26	Declarations, Types, and Constants Used in the Statistics Project

```
Global SectorsPerCluster As Long
Global BytesPerSector As Long
Global NumberOfFreeClustors As Long
Global TotalNumberOfClustors As Long
Global BytesFree As Long
Global BytesTotal As Long
Global PercentFree As Long

Public Const VER_Processor_WIN32_NT& = 2
Public Const VER_Processor_WIN32_WINDOWS& = 1

Public Const PROCESSOR_INTEL_386 = 386
Public Const PROCESSOR_INTEL_486 = 486
Public Const PROCESSOR_INTEL_PENTIUM = 586
Public Const PROCESSOR_MIPS_R4000 = 4000
Public Const PROCESSOR_ALPHA_21064 = 21064

Type MEMORYSTATUS
    dwLength As Long
    dwMemoryLoad As Long
    dwTotalPhys As Long
    dwAvailPhys As Long
    dwTotalPageFile As Long
    dwAvailPageFile As Long
    dwTotalVirtual As Long
    dwAvailVirtual As Long
End Type

Public Type SYSTEM_INFO
        dwOemID As Long
        dwPageSize As Long
        lpMinimumApplicationAddress As Long
        lpMaximumApplicationAddress As Long
```

```
            dwActiveProcessorMask As Long
            dwNumberOfProcessors As Long
            dwProcessorType As Long
            dwAllocationGranularity As Long
            wProcessorLevel As Integer
            wProcessorRevision As Integer
End Type

Public Type OSVersionInfo
            dwOSVersionInfoSize As Long
            dwMajorVersion As Long
            dwMinorVersion As Long
            dwBuildNumber As Long
            dwProcessorId As Long
            szCSDVersion As String * 128
End Type


' Holder for version information. Set on form load
Global myVer As OSVersionInfo
Declare Function GetDeviceCaps Lib "gdi32" (ByVal _
    hdc As Long, ByVal nIndex As Long) As Long
Declare Function GetDiskFreeSpace Lib "kernel32" Alias _
    "GetDiskFreeSpaceA" (ByVal lpRootPathName As String, _
    lpSectorsPerCluster As Long, lpBytesPerSector As Long, _
    lpNumberOfFreeClusters As Long, lpTtoalNumberOfClusters _
    As Long) As Long
Declare Sub GlobalMemoryStatus Lib "kernel32" _
    (lpBuffer As MEMORYSTATUS)
Declare Function GetUserName Lib "advapi32.dll" Alias _
    "GetUserNameA" (ByVal lpBuffer _
    As String, nSize As Long) As Long
Declare Function GetVersionEx Lib "kernel32" Alias _
    "GetVersionExA" (lpVersionInformation As OSVersionInfo) _
    As Long
Declare Sub GetSystemInfo Lib "kernel32" _
    (lpSystemInfo As SYSTEM_INFO)
```

Getting the User's Name   A call to GetUserName returns the network logon name of the person currently logged on (see Code 14.27). You can use this name to send mail, verify access levels, mark records for history, and—well you get the idea.

Code 14.27	**The UserName Subroutine**

```
Public Sub UserName()
    On Error GoTo ErrorRoutineErr

    Dim st As String
    Dim slCnt As Long
    Dim slDL As Long
    Dim slPos As Single
    Dim slUserName As String

    'Get the users name
    slCnt = 199
    st = String(200, 0)
    slDL = GetUserName(st, slCnt)
    slUserName = Left(st, slCnt) & slCnt
    slPos = InStr(1, slUserName, Chr(0))
    If slPos > 0 Then
        txtUserName = Left(slUserName, slPos - 1)
    End If

ErrorRoutineResume:
    Exit Sub
ErrorRoutineErr:
    MsgBox "Stats.Form1.UserName" & Err & Error
End Sub
```

Getting System Information   The APIs in this section retrieve a lot of valuable system information. The GlobalMemoryStatus function retrieves and reports on the system's memory position—the total available memory and the total memory (see Code 14.28). After that, a call to GetDeviceCaps gets the number of colors supported. The function GetFreeDiskSpace gets the total disk space and the total free disk space.

Code 14.28	**The SystemInformation Subroutine**

```
Public Sub SystemInformation()

    On Error GoTo ErrorRoutineErr

    Dim ms As MEMORYSTATUS
    Dim slDriveType
```

```
        Dim slDL As Long
        Dim slDrive
        Dim slPosition As Integer
        Dim slFreeBytes As Long
        Dim slTotalBytes As Long

        ms.dwLength = Len(ms)
        GlobalMemoryStatus ms

        'Get memory
        txtTotalPhysicalMemory = Format(ms.dwTotalPhys, "0,000")
        txtTotalAvailableMemory = Format(ms.dwAvailPhys, "0,00")

        'Screen resolution and colors
        txtScreenResolution = Screen.Width \ Screen.TwipsPerPixelX _
            & " x " & Screen.Height \ Screen.TwipsPerPixelY
        txtColors = DeviceColors((hdc))

        'Current drive
        slDrive = Left(App.Path, 2)
        slPosition = InStr(slDrive, " ")
        If slPosition > 0 Then
            slDrive = Left$(slDrive, slPosition - 1)
        End If
        If Right$(slDrive, 1) <> "\" Then slDrive = slDrive & "\"
        txtCurrentDrive = Left(slDrive, 2)

        'Total free disk space
        slDL = GetDiskFreeSpace(slDrive, SectorsPerCluster, _
            BytesPerSector, NumberOfFreeClustors, _
            TotalNumberOfClustors)
            slTotalBytes = TotalNumberOfClustors * _
            SectorsPerCluster * BytesPerSector
            txtTotalDiskSpace = Format(slTotalBytes, "#,0")
            slFreeBytes = NumberOfFreeClustors * _
            SectorsPerCluster * BytesPerSector
            txtTotalFreeDiskSpace = Format(slFreeBytes, "#,0")

ErrorRoutineResume:
    Exit Sub
ErrorRoutineErr:
    MsgBox "Stats.Form1.SystemInformation" & Err & Error
End Sub
```

Getting Version Information The GetVersionEx function finds out the type of operating system and also gets the major version, the minor version (such as NT version 4), the build number, and the service pack level for Windows NT. Among other information, GetSystemInfo can tell us the type of processor on which our application is currently running. See both of these functions in Code 14.29.

Code 14.29 **The VersionInformation Subroutine**

```
Public Sub VersionInformation()
    On Error GoTo ErrorRoutineErr
    Dim flagnum&
    Dim dl&, s$

    Dim vernum&, verword%
    Dim mySys As SYSTEM_INFO

    ' Get the windows flags and version numbers
    myVer.dwOSVersionInfoSize = 148
    dl& = GetVersionEx&(myVer)

    'Get the processor
    If myVer.dwProcessorId = VER_Processor_WIN32_WINDOWS Then
        txtOperatingSystem = "Windows95 "
    ElseIf myVer.dwProcessorId = VER_Processor_WIN32_NT Then
        txtOperatingSystem = "Windows NT "
    End If

    'Get the version, build, and service pack
    txtVersion = myVer.dwMajorVersion & "." _
        & myVer.dwMinorVersion
    txtBuildNumber = (myVer.dwBuildNumber And &HFFFF&)
    txtServicePack = LPSTRToVBString(myVer.szCSDVersion)

    GetSystemInfo mySys

    Select Case mySys.dwProcessorType
        Case PROCESSOR_INTEL_386
                txtProcessor = "386"
        Case PROCESSOR_INTEL_486
                txtProcessor = "486"
        Case PROCESSOR_INTEL_PENTIUM
```

```
              txtProcessor = "586"
        Case Else
              txtProcessor = "586"
    End Select
ErrorRoutineResume:
    Exit Sub
ErrorRoutineErr:
    MsgBox "Stats.Form1.VersionInformation" & Err & Error
End Sub
```

Testing the Statistics Program

Testing the Statistics program is simple. Since all the major calls are in the Form Load procedure, all you have to do is start it up. As you can see in Figure 14.16, the Form is filled with information about the current environment.

FIGURE 14.16:

The Statistics project in action

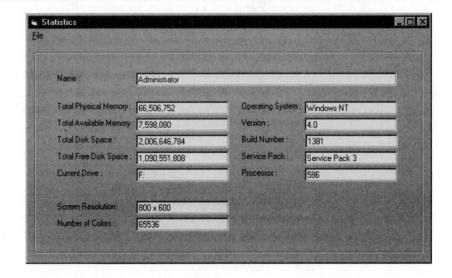

CHAPTER

FIFTEEN

Visual Basic and the Registry

- ■ Understanding the Windows Registry

- ■ Interacting with the Registry from Visual Basic

- ■ Controlling the registration of shareware

You can use the Registry to do the following:

- Store the location, size, and configuration of your Visual Basic Forms so that your users see the application the way they want.

- Store the column widths for grids and set them for each user.

- Store the application's color schemes.

- Keep a list of recently used files or reports. Almost all Windows applications do this.

NOTE   Notice the list of files at the bottom of the File menu in Visual Basic 6? This list of recently used files is stored in the Registry.

As your users' needs or requirements change, you may find it necessary to change or even delete Registry keys. You can take care of all these tasks in VB. In this chapter, we'll show you how to create, open, list, and maintain the Registry from your VB programs and how to take advantage of the Registry when creating time-limited shareware applications.

Understanding the Windows Registry

Applications use the Windows Registry to store configuration data. It replaces the large number of INI files that Windows 3.*x* used, and it is also used heavily by OLE (object linking and embedding). The Registry consists of a hierarchical structure (shown in Figure 15.1) that is divided into six subkeys.

You can access the Registry using the Windows application, RegEdit. Here are the steps:

1. Choose Start ➢ Run.

2. In the Open text box, type **RegEdit** and press Enter to open the Registry Editor, as shown in Figure 15.2.

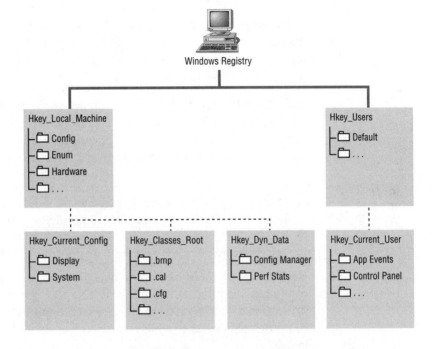

FIGURE 15.1:

The Windows Registry structure

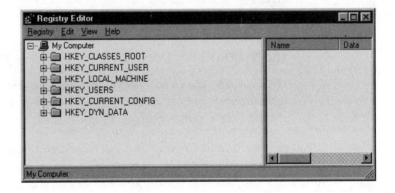

FIGURE 15.2:

The Registry Editor

> **NOTE**   RegEdit is a great tool to use when testing your applications. As you develop a VB program that writes or deletes keys to the Registry, you can use RegEdit to ensure that everything works as you expect.

The six Registry keys are predefined and hold data as follows:

HKEY_CLASSES_ROOT contains the data that associates file types (by file name extension) with the applications that support them. It also contains information about file associations and data associated with COM (communications) objects.

HKEY_CURRENT_USER contains the settings that describe the user profile for the person currently logged on to the local computer. A user profile contains information that defines the appearance and behavior of the individual user's desktop, network connections, and other environment settings.

NOTE HKEY_CURRENT_USER is the main key for VB developers. By convention, you add your Registry keys, subkeys, and values to HKEY_CURRENT-USER\Software\Vb and VBA Program Settings.

HKEY_LOCAL_MACHINE contains the configuration data for the local computer. The information in this database is used by applications, device drivers, and Windows NT to determine configuration data for the local computer, regardless of which user is logged on and which software is in use.

HKEY_USERS contains profiles for all users who can log on to the machine. If only one person is logged on, this key contains only the Default subkey.

HKEY_CURRENT_CONFIG contains font and printer information.

HKEY_DYN_DATA stores dynamic Registry data. The Windows 95 Registry supports both static data (which is stored on disk in the Registry) and dynamic data (which changes frequently, such as performance statistics).

You can create, delete, open, close, query, and enumerate Registry keys in Visual Basic. A Registry key must be created before it can be used. The RegCreateKeyEx function creates a new key if the key does not exist or simply opens the key if it does exist. Once the key is open, you can use the RegSetValueEx function to set or create its value, if necessary. If you only want to find out whether a value already exists, you use the function RegQueryValueEx. When a key is no longer used, you can delete it with the function RegDeleteKey.

WARNING   Changes to the Registry are final once the Registry file is closed. Changing some Registry settings can have drastic and unwanted effects, so exercise caution when working with the Registry. It is a good idea to make a backup of the Registry before you make any changes. To do so, in the Registry Editor, choose Registry ➤ Export Registry File.

The Registry plays an important role in Visual Basic application development by providing a central location for storing and retrieving important information. If you are developing an application with which the user opens and uses files, including a recent file list is a good idea. If your application provides reports for the user, keeping a list of the top five reports that each user requests would be helpful. The Registry is a great place to store each user's preferences for Form sizes and locations, as well as spreadsheets and grids. Users are grateful when an application remembers the way they formatted columns in a spreadsheet or a grid. You can easily store and retrieve all this and more in the Registry.

We'll start our exploration of how Visual Basic and the Registry interact by looking at the Registry project.

The Registry Project

The Registry project (shown in Figure 15.3) demonstrates the API functions necessary to interact with the Registry from within Visual Basic. You can use this project as a stand-alone Registry editor or incorporate the code into your application and use it as a starting point for your own Registry functions.

NOTE   You'll find the Registry project in the **Chapter15\Registry** folder on the CD that comes with this book.

The Registry project does the following:

- Retrieves a list of values associated with a key
- Creates a value
- Changes a value

FIGURE 15.3:

The Registry project

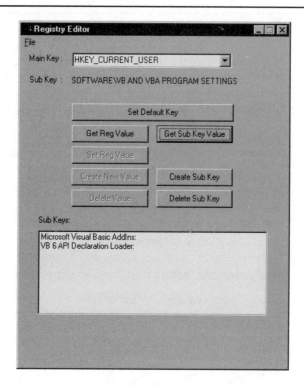

- Deletes a value

- Lists subkeys within keys

- Creates a new subkey

- Deletes a subkey

The Registry project consists of a module that holds the API-specific information and one Form. The Form has a ComboBox control that lists the six predefined keys and the following eight Command Buttons:

Set Default Key allows you to set the current working key location.

Get Reg Value fills a list box with the values associated with the current key and subkey(s). First, the key is opened with the RegOpenKey function, and then RegEnumValue enumerates the values for the specified open Registry key.

Set Reg Value uses the function RegCreateKeyEx (if the key exists, RegCreateKeyEx opens it) to open the key, and then the RegSetValueEx changes the value.

Create New Value creates a new value for the specified key by calling the function RegSetValueEx.

Delete Value uses the function RegCreateKeyEx to open the key and then uses RegDeleteValue to delete the value from the key.

Get Sub Key Value fills the list box with the subkeys defined for the selected key/subkey combination. It uses the function RegOpenKey to open the key, and then the RegEnumKey function enumerates the values for the specified open Registry key. This button is similar to the Get Reg Value button except that it enumerates the keys instead of the values in the keys.

Create Sub Key creates a new subkey with the function RegCreateKeyEx.

Delete Sub Key opens the key with the RegCreateKeyEx function and then deletes the selected subkey by calling the RegDeleteKey API function.

The Registry Project API Functions

Table 15.1 lists and describes the API functions used in the Registry project.

TIP

You'll find a complete description of these functions in Appendix B, which is on the CD that comes with this book.

TABLE 15.1: The API Functions in the Registry Project

API Description	Function
RegCloseKey	Releases the handle of the specified key.
RegCreateKeyEx	Creates the specified key. If the key already exists in the Registry, the function opens it.
RegDeleteKey	Deletes a key and all its subkeys.
RegDeleteValue	Removes a named value from the specified Registry key.
RegEnumKeyEx	Enumerates subkeys of the specified open Registry key. The function retrieves information about one subkey each time it is called.

Continued on next page

TABLE 15.1 CONTINUED: The API Functions in the Registry Project

API Description	Function
RegEnumValue	Enumerates the values for the specified open Registry key. The function copies one indexed value name and data block for the key each time it is called.
RegOpenKeyEx	Opens the specified key.
RegQueryValueEx	Retrieves the type and data for a specified value name associated with an open Registry key.
RegSetValueEx	Stores data in the value field of an open Registry key. It can also set additional value and type information for the specified key.

The Registry Code in Action

Now let's look at the code in the Registry project. To conserve space, we aren't including the declarations, types, and constants required for the Registry API functions here, but they are in this chapter's folder on the CD.

Choose a New Key

Before you can retrieve a key's value, query a key, create or change a value, or delete a Registry key, it must be open. Code 15.1 demonstrates how to choose a new subkey and Code 15.2 demonstrates how to make a key and subkey available by opening it. First, an InputBox is displayed so that a new subkey can be entered, then the code attempts to open the subkey with the function RegOpenKeyEx. If the subkey is opened successfully, it becomes the new subkey, and then the function RegCloseKey closes the key.

TIP

You can also double-click an existing subkey in the list box to open it and make it the current subkey.

NOTE

Notice the On Error statements. As mentioned in Chapter 14, when you use API functions in Visual Basic, there is no safety net. It is important for your applications to trap unforeseen errors.

Code 15.1	The cmdDefaultKey_Click Subroutine

```
Private Sub cmdDefaultKey_Click()
    On Error GoTo ErrorRoutineErr:

    Dim NewKey As String
    Dim phkResult As Long

    'Get Registry SubKey from user
    NewKey = InputBox("Enter SubKey Desired:", , SubKey)

    'Exit if user chose Cancel or entered an empty string
    If NewKey = "" Then
        Exit Sub
    Else
        'Get the new SubKey
        Call SetNewKey(NewKey)
    End If

    Exit Sub

ErrorRoutineErr::
  MsgBox "ERROR #" & Str$(Err) & " : " & Error & Chr(13) _
        & "Please exit and try again."
End Sub
```

Opening a Key

The SetNewKey subroutine demonstrates the process you follow to make a key and subkey available by opening it with the function RegOpenKeyEx. If the subkey is opened successfully, it becomes the new subkey, and then the function RegCloseKey closes the key. The value of the key to open is passed either from the List1 DoubleClick or the cmdDefaulyKey functions.

Code 15.2	SetNewKey

```
Public Function SetNewKey(NewKey As String)
    lblSubKey = NewKey

    'See if the new Registry SubKey given exists
```

```
        If RegOpenKeyEx(hKey, NewKey, 0, 1, phkResult) <> _
            ERROR_SUCCESS Then
            MsgBox "A Valid SubKey is needed to continue." & _
            Chr(13) & "Changes Cancelled."
            Exit Function
        End If

        'Close given SubKey
        RegCloseKey phkResult

        'Set the new default SubKey
        SubKey = NewKey

        'Get the Values for the new SubKey
        Call cmdKeyValue_Click

        Exit Function

ErrorRoutineErr::
    MsgBox "ERROR #" & Str$(Err) & " : " & Error & Chr(13) _
          & "Please exit and try again."
End Function
```

Creating a New Subkey Value

The SetRegValue subroutine (shown in Code 15.3) creates a new value under a subkey. First, RegCreateKeyEx opens the key and the subkey. The RegSetValueEx function then sets the value of the subkey. You can think of this value as a heading. For example, if you want to store a list of recent files used in an application, the value could be "Applications Recent File List." The data for the value could be the list of files.

Code 15.3   **The SetRegValue Function**

```
Function SetRegValue(hKey As Long, lpszSubKey As String, _
                     ByVal sSetValue As String, _
                     ByVal sValue As String) As Boolean

    On Error GoTo ErrorRoutineErr
```

```
    Dim phkResult As Long
    Dim lResult As Long
    Dim SA As SECURITY_ATTRIBUTES

    'Note: This function will create the key or
    'value if it doesn't exist.
    'Open or Create the key
    RegCreateKeyEx hKey, lpszSubKey, 0, "", _
        REG_OPTION_NON_VOLATILE, _
        KEY_ALL_ACCESS, SA, phkResult, Create

    lResult = RegSetValueEx(phkResult, sSetValue, 0, _
        REG_SZ, sValue, _
        CLng(Len(sValue) + 1))

    'Close the key
    RegCloseKey phkResult

    'Return SetRegValue Result
    SetRegValue = (lResult = ERROR_SUCCESS)
    Exit Function

ErrorRoutineErr:
  MsgBox "ERROR #" & Str$(Err) & " : " & Error & Chr(13) _
        & "Please exit and try again."
  SetRegValue = False

End Function
```

Deleting a Subkey's Value

As an application progresses, you may need to delete a subkey's value. Remember, you can think of a value as a heading. If an area of the program is complete and will not be used again, you can delete a subkey's value, freeing the space to be used by another part of the application or by another application. The subroutine cmdDeleteValue (shown in Code 15.4) uses the function RegCreateKeyEx to open the subkey and then deletes the data value with the RegDeleteValue API function. After the value is deleted, the LoadList1 function is called to refresh the list box.

Code 15.4   **The cmdDeleteValue_Click Subroutine**

```
Private Sub cmdDeleteValue_Click()

    Dim Reply As String
    Dim phkResult As Long
    Dim SA As SECURITY_ATTRIBUTES

    If List1.ListIndex = -1 Then
        MsgBox "Please select a Value to delete"
        Exit Sub
    End If
    RegCreateKeyEx Registry.hKey, Registry.SubKey, _
        0, "", REG_OPTION_NON_VOLATILE, _
    KEY_ALL_ACCESS, SA, phkResult, Registry.Create

    'Delete SubKey value specified
    If RegDeleteValue(phkResult, GetValueStr(List1.Text)) _
        = ERROR_SUCCESS Then

        'Refresh the list
        Call LoadList1("Regular")
        lblResult = "Value Deleted"
    Else
        lblResult = "Cannot Delete Value"
    End If

    'Close the current SubKey
    RegCloseKey phkResult
End Sub
```

Creating a New Key

All information in the Registry is stored under a key. Since it is a good idea to keep data separated by application or type of application, you need to create keys to hold subkeys and values. You can think of keys as sections. The function CreateRegKey (shown in Code 15.5) is called from cmdCreateKey_Click, and the RegCreateKeyEx function creates the new keys. The RegCloseKey function then closes the open key.

Code 15.5	The CreateRegKey Function

```
Function CreateRegKey(NewSubKey As String) As Boolean

    On Error GoTo ErrorRoutineErr

    Dim phkResult As Long
    Dim lResult As Long
    Dim SA As SECURITY_ATTRIBUTES

    'Create key if it does not exist
    CreateRegKey = (RegCreateKeyEx(hKey, SubKey & NewSubKey, _
    0, "", REG_OPTION_NON_VOLATILE, _
        KEY_ALL_ACCESS, SA, phkResult, Create) = ERROR_SUCCESS)

    'Close the key
    RegCloseKey phkResult
    Exit Function

ErrorRoutineErr:
    MsgBox "ERROR #" & Str$(Err) & " : " & Error & Chr(13) _
        & "Please exit and try again."
    CreateRegKey = False

End Function
```

Querying a Key's Value

A key's value stores the actual data, such as the list of most recently used files, Form dimensions, or the column widths of a spreadsheet. Double-clicking a value in the list box calls the GetRegValue function (shown in Code 15.6) to return the data value associated with the value of the subkey. The RegOpenKeyEx function opens the key, RegQueryValueEx gets the data value from the value, and RegCloseKey closes the key.

Code 15.6	The GetRegValue Function

```
Function GetRegValue(hKey As Long, lpszSubKey As String, _
    szKey As String, szDefault As String) As Variant

    On Error GoTo ErrorRoutineErr
```

```
Dim phkResult As Long
Dim lResult As Long
Dim szBuffer As String
Dim lBuffSize As Long

'Create Buffer
szBuffer = Space(255)
lBuffSize = Len(szBuffer)

'Open the key
RegOpenKeyEx hKey, lpszSubKey, 0, 1, phkResult

'Query the value
lResult = RegQueryValueEx(phkResult, szKey, 0, _
    0, szBuffer, lBuffSize)

'Close the key
RegCloseKey phkResult

'Return obtained value
If lResult = ERROR_SUCCESS Then
    GetRegValue = Left(szBuffer, lBuffSize - 1)
Else
    GetRegValue = szDefault
End If
Exit Function

ErrorRoutineErr:
    MsgBox "ERROR #" & Str$(Err) & " : " & Error & Chr(13) _
        & "Please exit and try again."
    GetRegValue = ""

End Function
```

Deleting a Key

In the course of your Registry programming, some keys will lose their usefulness. You can delete a key when the information it stores is no longer needed. The subroutine cmdDeleteKey_Click (shown in Code 15.7) uses the RegCreateKeyEx API function to open the selected subkey, and then the RegDeleteKey function deletes it. Remember, a key must be open before you can manipulate it.

Code 15.7	The cmdDeleteKey_Click Subroutine

```
Private Sub cmdDeleteKey_Click()
    'Open current SubKey

    Dim Reply As String
    Dim phkResult As Long
    Dim SA As SECURITY_ATTRIBUTES

    If List1.ListIndex = -1 Then
        MsgBox "Please select a SubKey to delete"
        Exit Sub
    End If
    RegCreateKeyEx Registry.hKey, Registry.SubKey, 0, _
        "", REG_OPTION_NON_VOLATILE, _
        KEY_ALL_ACCESS, SA, phkResult, Registry.Create

    'Delete SubKey specified
    If RegDeleteKey(phkResult, GetValueStr(List1.Text)) _
        = ERROR_SUCCESS Then
        Call LoadList1("Key")
        lblResult = "SubKey Deleted"

    Else
        'Close the current SubKey
        RegCloseKey phkResult
        lblResult = "Cannot Delete SubKey"
    End If
End Sub
```

In this section, we've looked at API functions that perform actions on the Registry—opening a key, deleting a key, and reading a key's value. In the next section, we'll explore the process involved in enumerating, or inspecting, a key's structure. This will include listing the subkeys, the values, and the data in the values.

Enumerating Keys and Loading the List Box

Code 15.8 is a procedure for enumerating a key's structure. You can use this procedure when it becomes necessary to look through a key's structure to find a certain value. Clicking the Get Sub Key Value and the Get Reg Value buttons calls the subroutine LoadList1. In the top part of the code, we use the RegCreateKeyEx function to open the subkey, and then we use the RegEnumKeyEx function inside a While loop to enumerate the subkeys and load them into the list box.

In the bottom part of the code, we load the list box with the values under the selected subkey. The RegOpenKeyEx function opens the key, and then RegEnumValue is used within a While loop to enumerate the values. The RegCloseKey function is called to close the open keys.

Code 15.8 **The LoadList1 Subroutine**

```
Public Sub LoadList1(Action As String)
    On Error GoTo ErrorRoutineErr

    Dim lResult As Long
    Dim Index As Long
    Dim dwReserved As Long
    Dim szBuffer As String
    Dim lBuffSize As Long
    Dim szBuffer2 As String
    Dim lBuffSize2 As Long
    Dim phkResult As Long
    Dim SA As SECURITY_ATTRIBUTES
    Dim lType As Long
    Dim FT As FILETIME

    'Initialize local variables
    Index = 0
    dwReserved = 0
    List1.Clear
    lblResult = ""

    'get keys
    If Action = "Key" Then
    'Add the SubKeys to the list box
        'Open the key
        lResult = RegCreateKeyEx(Registry.hKey, _
            Registry.SubKey, 0, "", REG_OPTION_NON_VOLATILE, _
            KEY_ALL_ACCESS, SA, phkResult, Registry.Create)

        'Loop for each subkey found
        While lResult = ERROR_SUCCESS
```

```
            'Set buffer space
            szBuffer = Space(255)
            lBuffSize = Len(szBuffer)
            szBuffer2 = Space(255)
            lBuffSize2 = Len(szBuffer2)

            'Get next key
            lResult = RegEnumKeyEx(phkResult, Index, _
                szBuffer, lBuffSize, dwReserved, _
                szBuffer2, lBuffSize2, FT)

            'If found a new key, add it to the list
            If lResult = ERROR_SUCCESS Then
                List1.AddItem Left(szBuffer, lBuffSize) & ": "
            End If
            Index = Index + 1
        Wend

    Else ' Enumerate Values

        'Open the key
        lResult = RegOpenKeyEx(Registry.hKey, _
            Registry.SubKey, 0, 1, phkResult)

        'Loop for each value found
        While lResult = ERROR_SUCCESS

            'Set buffer space
            szBuffer = Space(255)
            lBuffSize = Len(szBuffer)
            szBuffer2 = Space(255)
            lBuffSize2 = Len(szBuffer2)

            'Get next value
            lResult = RegEnumValue(phkResult, Index, szBuffer, _
                lBuffSize, dwReserved, lType, _
                szBuffer2, lBuffSize2)

            'If a new value is found, add it to the list
            If lResult = ERROR_SUCCESS Then

                List1.AddItem Left(szBuffer, lBuffSize) & _
```

```
            ": " & GetType(lType)


            '_____
            'As an option, you could use the next line of
            'code to return the value and the data in the value
            '_____

            'List1.AddItem Left(szBuffer, lBuffSize) & ":" _
            '      & GetType(lType) _
            '      & ":" & Left(szBuffer2, lBuffSize2 - 1)


        End If
        Index = Index + 1
        Wend


        End If


    'Close the key
    RegCloseKey phkResult

    'Return true if enumerated all values
    LoadValueList = (lResult = ERROR_NO_MORE_ITEMS)
    Exit Sub

ErrorRoutineErr:
    MsgBox "ERROR #" & Str$(Err) & " : " & Error & Chr(13) _
        & "Please exit and try again."
    LoadValueList = False
End Sub
```

The Registry Project in Action

The code listings in the previous sections highlight the main parts of the Registry project. You can use this code as a basis for building a library of routines that access the Registry from your applications. The Registry project shows how you can use the API functions in a Visual Basic program to store and retrieve data.

Now let's take a look at what happens when you run the program. Press F5 to start the application. Your screen should look like Figure 15.3, shown earlier in this chapter. The default key is HKEY_CURRENT_USER, and the default subkey is SOFTWARE\VB AND VBA PROGRAM SETTINGS.

WARNING   When you set a subkey value, do not add a backslash (\) to the end. If you do, you must remove it to add a new subkey.

The following seven steps demonstrate the major functionality of the Registry project.

1. Click the Get Sub Key Value button. The list box fills with the subkeys that are defined, and the Create Sub Key and Delete Sub Key buttons are enabled.

2. Click the Set Default Key button to set a new subkey. You can enter a value from the list box. For this example, add \API Viewer\File List to the end of the default setting of SOFTWARE\VB AND VBA PROGRAM SETTINGS that is currently displayed in the Input Box.

3. Click the Get Reg Value button to fill the list box with the values associated with a subkey.

4. Double-click a value in the list box to see the value data set for that value.

5. Click the Set Reg Value button to set or change a value data.

6. Click the Create New Value button to create a new value and set the data for the value.

WARNING   Be careful in the next step when deleting a value. Remember that there is no safety net. When you delete a key, a subkey, or a value, it's deleted!

---

7. Click the Delete Value button to delete a value and its data.

As you can see, combining API functions with Visual Basic makes it easy to add, change, and delete Registry keys, subkeys, and values.

Shareware and the Registry

OK, it's time to put the Registry to work! Put on your shareware author's hat, and let's see how you can use the Registry to control the registration of a shareware application. We can use the Registry to hold information about our application. We can store the application name as a subkey, and we can store the number of times the application is launched along with the registration number.

What Is Shareware?

Shareware is a marketing method; it is not a type of software. Shareware is try-it-before-you-buy-it software—an economical way to see if an application meets your needs. In recent years, it has become acceptable for authors to put time-out code in shareware applications.

Many shareware authors allow their applications to be used for a designated period, such as one month, or for a specified number of times before requiring that the user register it. When this trial period expires, the program stops working.

The RegShareware Project

We'll create a shareware application that allows the user to launch it three times during the trial period. During this period, the user can look at the About screen to check the number of remaining launches or to register the software. When the trial period expires, we'll display a message box that allows the user to register the application by entering a registration number. The registration number can be any string, as long as the last character is a five. You can devise a sophisticated registration algorithm, but for now let's keep it simple. For testing purposes, we'll include a Remove Registration button that deletes our entire subkey.

NOTE   You'll find the RegShareware project in the `Chapter15\RegShare` folder on the CD that comes with this book.

The RegShareware project will put the API functions to practical use. In the course of this project, we will do the following:

- Create a key and subkey

- Create a value and add data to the value

- Delete a key

Our project has three Forms (shown in Figure 15.4): a Splash screen, a main Form, and an About screen. The Splash screen, which is displayed first, uses the API function RegOpenKeyEx to try to open our shareware registration key. Since we are launching the application for the first time, we will need to create the Registry entries. We will use the existing HKEY_CURRENT_USER key and the subkey SOFTWARE\VB AND VBA PROGRAM SETTINGS. Under these keys, we will create the following subkeys:

DevHand5Shareware holds the name of our application and has one subkey: Settings.

Settings holds the values of the registration number and the number of times the application is used.

Registration Number holds the actual number the user registers with.

Times holds the number of times the application is launched. We subtract one from this value every time the application is launched. When this value reaches zero, the user is denied access to the application unless he or she enters a valid registration number.

FIGURE 15.4:

The three Forms that make up the RegShareware project

Splash Form

Main Form

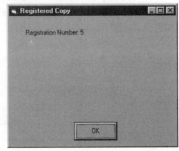

About Form

Figure 15.5 shows the Windows Registry after the application creates the subkeys and values.

FIGURE 15.5:

RegEdit after registration

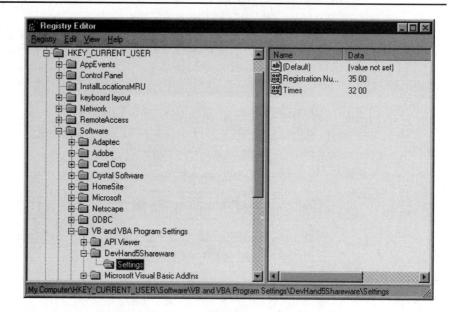

The user can register at any time during the trial period by clicking the Register button on the About screen and entering a valid registration number. Any string that ends in a five is a valid registration number.

Creating the RegShareware Project

To create the RegShareware project, start a new project, and add a Splash Form and a regular Form using the Add Form option. Change the name of form2 to frmAbout. The Splash Form gives the user something to look at while we verify the status of the software, and frmAbout registers the program during the trial period.

NOTE The RegShareware project uses the API functions in Table 15.1, shown earlier in this chapter. See Appendix B on the CD for a complete description of these functions. To conserve space, we didn't include the type, constant, and declare statements here, but they are in this chapter's folder on the CD.

Loading the Splash Form   The Splash Form, shown in Figure 15.4, earlier in this chapter, is the first Form the user sees, and we use it to check the Registry for a valid serial number. The code for the Splash Screen is shown in Code 15.9. If we don't find a valid serial number, this is an unregistered copy of the software, and we must, therefore, check the status of the trial period. The code in the Form_Load subroutine performs the following actions to verify and prepare the shareware environment:

- The first time this code is run, it attempts to create the key, subkeys, and values needed to hold the shareware registration data. The structures SOFTWARE\VB and VBA PROGRAM SETTINGS\DevHand5Shareware will hold our Registry location.

- Once the subkeys and values are created, we track the number of times the program is launched.

- After the program is launched three times, the user must register to continue to use the program.

NOTE   As you look at Code 15.9, pay particular attention to the comments to see how the trial period is used.

Code 15.9   **The RegShareware Splash Screen**

```
Private Sub Form_Load()

    Dim phkResult As Long
    Dim slValue As String
    Dim slData As String
    Dim slTimesRemaining As String
    Dim Msg, Style, Title, Response, MyString
    Dim slRegNumber As String
    Dim rc
    Dim slRegistered

    lblVersion.Caption = "Version " & App.Major & "." _
        & App.Minor & "." & App.Revision
    lblProductName.Caption = App.Title
    'Registry key we want to use
    hKey = HKEY_CURRENT_USER
```

```vb
'Set Registry SubKey
SubKey = "SOFTWARE\VB AND VBA PROGRAM SETTINGS\" _
    & "DevHand5Shareware\Settings"
slValue = "Times"
slData = 3

If RegOpenKeyEx(hKey, SubKey, 0, 1, phkResult) = _
    ERROR_SUCCESS Then

    'Check to see if there is a registration number
    glRegNumber = _
    GetRegValue(hKey, SubKey, "Registration Number", _
        "Not Found")
    If Len(glRegNumber) > 0 Then

        'It's a registered copy, exit
        lblWarning = "Registered Copy"
        glRegistered = True
        Timer1.Enabled = True
        Exit Sub
    End If

    'The key exists so this is not the first time the
    'program has been run
    'Check to see how many runs are left
    slTimesRemaining = _
    GetRegValue(hKey, SubKey, "Times", "Not Found")
    If Val(slTimesRemaining - 1) = 0 Then

        'No time left
        Msg = "Evaluation period has expired." & Chr(13) & _
        "Would you like to register now?."
        Style = vbYesNo + vbCritical + vbDefaultButton1
        Title = "Register Software"
        Response = MsgBox(Msg, Style, Title)
        If Response = vbYes Then

            'Let the user register
            slRegNumber = InputBox("Enter your " & _
            "Registration Number.")

            'Add an algorithm to validate the reg
            'number, here it only has to end in a 5
```

```
                    If Right(slRegNumber, 1) = "5" Then

                        'Put the reg number in the registry
                        If Not SetRegValue(hKey, SubKey, _
                            "Registration Number", slRegNumber) Then
                            MsgBox "Unable to set Value."
                        Else
                            frmAbout.Caption = "Registered Copy"
                            frmAbout.Command1.Visible = False
                            'Set the global registration number
                            glRegNumber = slRegNumber
                        End If
                    Else
                        'Not a validate reg number
                        MsgBox "Registration Number is not valid."
                        End
                    End If
                Else
                    'User does not want to register
                    End
                End If
            Else
                'There is time left so deduct one
                rc = SetRegValue(hKey, SubKey, _
                    slValue, slTimesRemaining - 1)

                lblWarning = "Number of Times remaining = " _
                & slTimesRemaining - 1
                frmAbout.Label1 = "Number of Times" & _
                " remaining = " & slTimesRemaining - 1
            End If
            Timer1.Enabled = True
        Else
            'The key does not exist, this is the first time
            'the program has been run, create the new key
            If CreateRegKey(SubKey) Then

                'If subkey is created, create the value and data
                'For the times counter
                rc = SetRegValue(hKey, SubKey, _
                    slValue, slData)
                rc = ""
                rc = SetRegValue(hKey, SubKey, _
```

```
                    "Registration Number", "")
            Timer1.Enabled = True
            lblWarning = "Number of Times remaining = " _
            & slData
            frmAbout.Label1 = "Number of Times" & _
            " remaining = " & slData
        Else
            MsgBox "Unable to Create Key."
        End If
        Exit Sub
    End If
End Sub
```

Registering the Software   One part of the process that might be overlooked (because it is the end result of all your hard work) is the About box (shown in Figure 15.4, earlier in this chapter). If the user chooses Help ➤ About, the About box is displayed. This Form shows the registration status of the software.

If the software is registered, the About box displays the registration number, and the title is changed to "Registered Copy." If the software is not registered, a Registration button is provided to allow the user to enter a registration number.

Loading the About Form   The subroutine Form_Load (shown in Code 15.10) loads the Form and sets the caption. If the program is registered, the user has entered a valid registration number, and the caption is set to "Registered Copy"; otherwise the caption shows the title.

Code 15.10   **The Form_Load Subroutine**

```
Private Sub Form_Load()
    If glRegistered Then
        'It's a registered copy, set up fields
        Me.Caption = "Registered Copy"
        Label1 = "Registration Number: " & glRegNumber
        Command1.Visible = False
    Else
        'Not registered
        Me.Caption = "About " & App.Title

    End If
End Sub
```

Entering a Registration Number   The subroutine Command1_Click is called from the About box to allow the user to register the software. An Input box is displayed for the user to enter a registration number. If the number matches a set value (in our case, the number must end in a 5), the program is registered by adding the registration number to our Registry key with the API function SetReg-Value, and the user is notified.

Code 15.11	Adding the Registration Value

```
Private Sub Command1_Click()
    Dim slRegNumber

    'Let the user register
    slRegNumber = InputBox("Enter your " & _
    "Registration Number.")

    'Add an algorithm to validate the registration
    'Number, here it only has to end in a 5
    If Right(slRegNumber, 1) = "5" Then

        'Put the reg number in the registry
        If Not Module1.SetRegValue(hKey, SubKey, _
            "Registration Number", slRegNumber) Then
            MsgBox "Unable to set Value."
        Else
            glRegistered = True
            glRegNumber = slRegNumber
            Me.Caption = "Registered Copy"
            Command1.Visible = False
            MsgBox "Registration succeeded."
            'Unload Me
        End If
    Else
        'Not a validate reg number
        MsgBox "Registration Number is not valid."
        End
    End If

End Sub
```

Deleting the Test Key

You can click the Remove Registration button on the main Form (shown in Figure 15.4, earlier in this chapter) to delete the Registry key. The cmdRemove_Click subroutine (shown in Code 15.12) uses the API function RegCreateKeyEx to open the key and then deletes it with RegDeleteKey.

NOTE   This is not part of a normal shareware registration program. We've provided it so that you can delete the key and retest the process.

Code 15.12   **The cmdRemove_Click Subroutine**

```
Private Sub cmdRemove_Click()

    Dim Reply As String
    Dim phkResult As Long
    Dim SA As SECURITY_ATTRIBUTES
    Dim slSubKey As String

    'Open current SubKey
    slSubKey = "SOFTWARE\VB AND VBA PROGRAM SETTINGS\DevHand6Shareware"
    RegCreateKeyEx hKey, slSubKey, 0, _
        "", REG_OPTION_NON_VOLATILE, _
        KEY_ALL_ACCESS, SA, phkResult, 0

    'Delete Settings SubKey
    If RegDeleteKey(phkResult, "Settings") _
        = ERROR_SUCCESS Then
    Else
        'Close the current SubKey
        RegCloseKey phkResult
        MsgBox "Cannot Delete SubKey"
        Exit Sub
    End If

    'Open current SubKey
    slSubKey = "SOFTWARE\VB AND VBA PROGRAM SETTINGS"
    RegCreateKeyEx hKey, slSubKey, 0, _
        "", REG_OPTION_NON_VOLATILE, _
        KEY_ALL_ACCESS, SA, phkResult, 0
```

```
        'Delete SubKey DevHand6Shareware
        If RegDeleteKey(phkResult, "DevHand6Shareware") _
            = ERROR_SUCCESS Then
            MsgBox "Registration removed."
            glRegistered = False
            glRegNumber = ""
            Command1.Enabled = False
        Else
            'Close the current SubKey
            RegCloseKey phkResult
            MsgBox "Cannot Delete SubKey"
        End If
    End Sub
```

Many shareware authors use the process we just described to control the trial period for their applications. Creating and administrating time-limited shareware can be a daunting task, but with the help of a few API functions, we can cut the task down to size.

Testing the RegShareware Application

Let's take our RegShareware application through its paces:

1. Press F5 to start the program. The Splash screen (shown in Figure 15.4, earlier in this chapter) is displayed. Notice the "Number of times remaining = 3" label. This tells the user that the application can be launched three times without being registered. After a couple of seconds, Form1(also shown in Figure 15.4) appears. The Remove Registration button is disabled. After the software is registered, this button is enabled.

2. Choose Help ➤ About Screen to open the About Form (shown in Figure 15.4, earlier in this chapter). Notice that the caption reads "About RegShareware" and that the label reads "Number of times remaining = 3." This reminds the user to register the software.

3. Click the Register button and enter a value that ends in a 5 in the Input box to register the software.

With a little time and effort, you could add a lot of functionality to this program and use it as a starting point for many other applications that require Registry manipulation.

CHAPTER

SIXTEEN

16

The Built-In Visual Basic Developer's ActiveX Controls

- The ImageList control

- The Toolbar control

- The StatusBar control

- The TabStrip control

- The Slider control

- The ProgressBar control

- The TreeView control

- The ListView control

- The CoolBar control

In this chapter, we will explore the Microsoft Windows Common Controls. This suite of nine ActiveX controls comes with Visual Basic and should be part of every serious developer's arsenal:

The ImageList control contains a collection of ListImage objects, each of which can be referred to by its index or key. The ImageList control is not designed to be used alone, but as a central repository to supply other controls with images.

The Toolbar control contains a collection of Button objects that you use to create a toolbar that is associated with an application.

The StatusBar control provides a window, usually at the bottom of a Parent Form, through which an application can display various kinds of status data. The status bar has become a standard feature of all Microsoft Office programs. It can be divided into a maximum of 16 Panel objects that are contained in a Panels collection.

The TabStrip control is similar to the dividers in a notebook or the labels on a group of file folders. By using a TabStrip control, you can define multiple pages for the same area of a window or a dialog box in your application.

The Slider control is a window that contains a slider and optional tickmarks. You can move the slider by dragging it, by clicking the mouse to either side of it, or by using the keyboard.

The ProgressBar control shows the progress of a lengthy operation by filling a rectangle with chunks from left to right.

The TreeView control displays a hierarchical list of Node objects, each of which consists of a label and an optional bitmap. A TreeView typically displays the headings in a document, the entries in an index, the files and directories on a disk, or any other kind of information that might usefully be displayed as a hierarchy. The left side of Windows Explorer and the Windows Registry are examples of the TreeView control.

The ListView control displays items using one of four views. You can arrange items into columns with or without column headings, as well as display accompanying icons and text. The right side of Windows Explorer and the Windows Registry are examples of the ListView control.

The CoolBar control allows for the creation of user-configurable toolbars similar to those found in Microsoft Internet Explorer. The CoolBar control is a container control, able to host child controls. It consists of a collection of one or more resizable regions known as bands. Each band can host a single child control.

Adding the Windows Common Controls to Your Project

The Windows Common Controls are available as a Visual Basic custom control. You'll find them, except for the CoolBar control, in the file MSCOMCTL.ocx. To add the controls to your VB project, follow these steps:

1. Choose Project ➤ Components to open the Components dialog box.

2. Check the Microsoft Windows Common Controls 6.0 checkbox, and then click OK.

The controls are now added to your Toolbox.

To add the CoolBar Control to your VB project, substitute the Microsoft Windows Common Controls 3-6.0 in step 2, as shown above.

In the following sections, we will look at these controls in detail and create sample projects that will demonstrate how they fit together into an application.

The ImageList Control

An ImageList control contains a collection of images that can be used by other Windows Common Controls—specifically the TabStrip, Toolbar, TreeView, and ListView controls.

You can save valuable development time using the ImageList control as a single image repository instead of writing code that loads bitmaps and icon files at run time. With the ImageList control, you can store and refer to images from one central location with the Key value or Index property.

The control uses bitmap (.bmp), cursor (.cur), icon (.ico), JPEG (.jpg), or GIF (.gif) files in a collection of ListImage objects. To use the ImageList control with the Windows Common Controls, you must first associate the ImageList control with the other control and then assign either the Key or the Index property to one of the Windows Common Controls. You can do so at design time or at run time. All the Windows Common Controls, except the ListView control, have an Image-List property that can be set with the name of the ImageList control you are using. The ListView control uses the Icon and SmallIcon properties to associate the ImageList control.

The ImageList control also features the Overlay, ExtractIcon, and Draw methods with which you can create composite images, create icons from bitmaps stored in the control, and draw images on objects with an hDC property.

Adding Images to the ImageList Control at Design Time

To add ListImage objects at design time, you use the ImageList control's Property Pages. Follow these steps:

1. Right-click the ImageList control and click Properties.

2. In the Property Pages, select the Images tab:

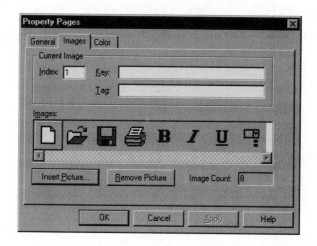

3. Click the Insert Picture button to open the Select Picture dialog box.

4. Locate either bitmap (.bmp), cursor (.cur), icon (.ico), JPEG (.jpg), or GIF (.gif) files, and click Open. You can select multiple files to open.

5. Assign a unique Key to each image by typing a string in the Key box.

NOTE   Optionally, you can assign a Tag to each image by typing a string in the Tag box. Tags do not have to be unique.

---

6. Repeat steps 3 through 5 until the control is populated with the desired images.

Adding Images to the ImageList Control at Run Time

To add an image to the ImageList control at run time, use the Add method for the ListImages collection with the LoadPicture function. Code 16.1 loads an ImageList with a single open bitmap image:

Code 16.1   **The ListImage Add Method**

```
Private Sub Form_Load()
    ImageList1.ListImages.Add , "open",
LoadPicture("d:\chapter3code\toolbar\open.ico")
End Sub
```

As this code shows, just before the Form is loaded, the open bitmap is added to the ImageList control. Also notice that the Key open is used. You can refer to ListImages by their numeric index, or you can use the Key value that you assign.

Using the ImageList Control with Other Controls

The ListImage object's Picture property returns a Picture object, which can be assigned to another control's Picture property. This property can be set to the Picture property for a control that is not part of the Windows Common Controls. The following have a Picture property:

- CommandButton control
- OptionButton control
- Image control
- PictureBox control
- CheckBox control
- Form object
- Panel object (StatusBar control)
- CoolBar control

NOTE   It is a good idea to populate the ImageList control with images before you associate it with another control. Once you associate an ImageList with a control and assign any image to a property of the control, the ImageList control will not allow you to remove images.

The ImageList control is demonstrated in the following sections as we explore the other controls that make up the Windows Common Controls.

The Toolbar Control

A Toolbar control (shown in Figure 16.1) contains a collection of Button objects that correspond to items in an application's menu, providing a visual interface for the user. Although the toolbar usually does not include a button for each menu option, it provides access to the most frequently used actions or commands. The Toolbar control can also hold other controls, such as a Label, ComboBox, or TextBox control.

FIGURE 16.1:

The Toolbar control

A ToolBar can either be shown in 3-D or in a Flat style, like the toolbars in the Microsoft Office programs, as defined by the Style Property shown in Table 16.1.

TABLE 16.1: ToolBar Style Property

Constant	Value	Description
tbrStandard	0 (Default)	Standard toolbar.
tbrTransparent	1	The buttons and toolbar are transparent, button text appears under button bitmaps, and hot tracking is turned on.
tbrRight	2	Similar to tbrTransparent style, except that the button text appears to the right of the image, if any.

You use the Toolbar control to easily create toolbars by adding Button objects to a Buttons collection. Each Button object can have text and/or images, supplied by an ImageList control. You set the image with the Image property, and you set the text with the Caption property for each Button object in the collection. At design time, you use the Toolbar Property Pages to add and remove buttons. At run time, you use the Add and Remove methods to add or remove buttons from the Button object.

Adding Other Controls to a Toolbar

To add other controls to the Toolbar control at design time, simply draw them on the Toolbar. The drawback to this approach is that the controls you draw on the toolbar will not be wrappable; that is, they will not move to the next line with the rest of the Button objects if the Form is resized. If this is a concern, you can create a Button object with a PlaceHolder style and position the desired control over the button in the Resize event. Table 16.2 lists the Button Style properties.

TABLE 16.2: The Properties for the Button Style

Constant	Value	Use
tbrDefault	0	(Default) Button. The button is a regular push button.
tbrCheck	1	Check. The button is a check button, which can be checked or unchecked.
tbrButtonGroup	2	ButtonGroup. The button remains pressed until another button in the group is pressed. Only one button in the group can be pressed at any time.
tbrSeparator	3	Separator. The button functions as a separator with a fixed width of 8 pixels.
tbrPlaceHolder	4	Placeholder. The button is like a separator in appearance and functionality, but has a settable width.
tbrDropDown	5	The button displays a menu when it is clicked.

Double-clicking a toolbar at run time opens the Customize Toolbar dialog box (shown in Figure 16.2), with which the user can hide, display, or rearrange toolbar buttons. You can enable or disable the dialog box by setting the AllowCustomize property. You can invoke the dialog box at run time by calling the Customize method.

NOTE To preserve the state of a Toolbar control, the SaveToolbar method writes to the Windows Registry. You can restore a Toolbar control to a previous state using the RestoreToolbar method to read the information previously saved in the Registry.

FIGURE 16.2:

The Customize Toolbar dialog box

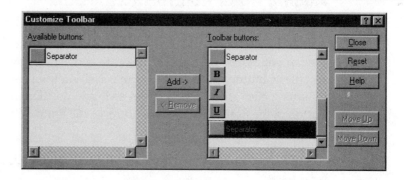

Associating Images to a Toolbar Control

The Button object of a Toolbar control can display only one image for each button. At run time, the Toolbar first determines how the button should be drawn (normal, disabled, or "hot"). After this determination, the image from the appropriate image list (ImageList, DisabledImageList, or HotImageList) is displayed on the button using the sole Image property as the Key. It is important that name usage in the ImageLists is consistent so that the Toolbar control pulls the correct image. For example, if a particular button is making use of all three image types, each of the three images must be defined in their respective image lists to have either the same Index or the same Key.

Adding Buttons to the Toolbar Control at Design Time

To add Button objects to the Toolbar control at design time, use the Toolbar control's Property Pages (shown in Figure 16.3). Follow these steps:

1. Right-click the Toolbar control and click Properties to open the Property Pages.

2. In the General tab, select ImageList from the ImageList box.

3. Select the Buttons tab, as shown in Figure 16.3.

4. Click the Insert Button button to insert a new Button object.

5. Set the Caption, Key, Style, Tag, ToolTipText, Image, Description, and Value as needed.

6. Repeat steps 4 and 5 until you have added all the desired Button objects.

FIGURE 16.3:

The Toolbar Property Pages

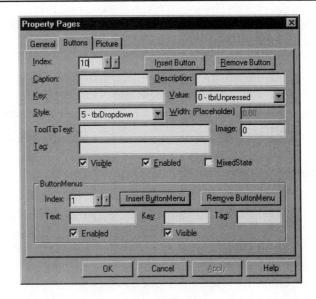

Adding Buttons to the Toolbar Control at Run Time

Use the Add method to add Button objects to the Toolbar control at run time. Code 16.2 adds a Separator Style Button object and a Regular Style Button object.

Code 16.2	Another Way to Add ListImages

```
Private Sub Command3_Click()


    On Error Resume Next

    'Remove the separator the second time through
    Toolbar1.Buttons.Remove (10)
    'Add an image to the ImageList control
    ImageList1.ListImages.Add , "Cut", _
        LoadPicture("d:\Chapter3Code\toolbar\Cut.ico")

    'Add a separator button to the Toolbar control
    Toolbar1.Buttons.Add (10)
    Toolbar1.Buttons(10).Style = tbrSeparator

    'Add a button to the Toolbar control
```

```
        Toolbar1.Buttons.Add 11, "Cut", , , "Cut"
        Toolbar1.Buttons(11).ToolTipText = "Cut"
   End Sub
```

How you use a Toolbar control depends on the type of application you are writing. An application that employs the SDI (Single Document Interface) approach interacts with the Toolbar control differently from an application based on the MDI (Multiple Document Interface).

The SDIToolbar Project

Creating a toolbar for a single Form is easy and can be done entirely at design time. The SDIToolbar project (shown in Figure 16.4) has one Form that contains a Toolbar control and an ImageList control to hold the images used on the toolbar. The Toolbar control has a TextBox and a ComboBox. The Style frame holds the values of the Style property. The six command buttons on the Form demonstrate some of the toolbar's functionality, and a TextBox holds some text to manipulate. Here is a list of the command buttons and what they do:

Disable, Enable disables and enables the first toolbar icon.

Add Button adds an image to the ImageList control and then adds two buttons to the Toolbar control.

Remove Button removes the buttons added with the Add Button command button.

Customize displays the Customize Form (shown in Figure 16.2, earlier in this chapter), which allows the user to customize the look of the toolbar.

Save Toolbar saves the current toolbar configuration to the Registry.

Restore Toolbar restores the saved toolbar configuration to the Registry.

FIGURE 16.4:

The SDIToolBar project

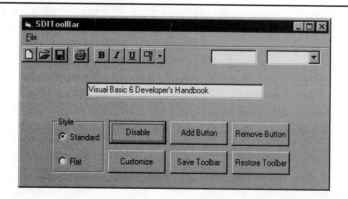

NOTE   You'll find the SDIToolBar project in the `Chapter16\SDIToolbar` folder on the CD that comes with this book.

Creating the SDIToolBar Project

Toolbar controls, after they are set up, rely on code to do almost all their work. Thus, in this section we're including all the code modules so that we can discuss toolbar functionality in depth. Follow these steps to get this project rolling:

1. Start a new Visual Basic project. Form1 is created by default.

2. To Form1, add a Toolbar control, an ImageList control, a TextBox control, and six command buttons.

3. Draw a TextBox control and a ComboBox control on the Toolbar control.

4. Right-click the ImageList control, and click Properties to open the Property Pages.

5. Select the 16 × 16 option button to choose the small image size. Standard Windows 95 and Windows NT toolbar buttons are 16 × 16 pixels.

6. Select the Images tab, and then click the Insert Picture button.

TIP   If you use icons as images and draw them with a transparent background, the Toolbar control automatically adjusts the image to reflect the disabled state of a Button object. You'll find some of the more popular icons already drawn for you if you look in the `Chapter16Code/Toolbar` folder on the CD that comes with this book.

7. From the `Chapter16Code/Toolbar` folder on the CD that comes with this book, select the New, Open, Save, Print, Bold, Italic, and Underline icons. Your ImageList should look like the one in Figure 16.5.

Now that the ImageList is set, let's add the buttons to the Toolbar control.

8. Right-click the toolbar and select Properties to open the Property Pages.

9. On the General tab, select ImageList1 from the ImageList drop-down list box.

10. Select the Buttons tab, as shown in Figure 16.3, earlier in this chapter. Click the Insert Button button nine times to insert nine empty buttons.

FIGURE 16.5:

The ImageList Property
Pages with images

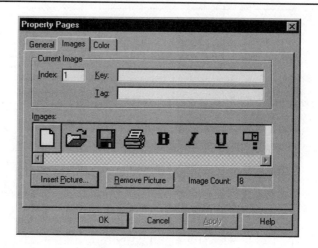

11. Set the Caption, Key, ToolTip, and Image properties as shown in Table 16.3.

TABLE 16.3: The Toolbar Control Properties

Index	Key	Style	ToolTipText	Image
1	New	0-tbrDefault	New	1
2	Open	0-tbrDefault	Open	2
3	Save	0-tbrDefault	Save	3
4		3-tbrSeparator		
5	Print	0-tbrDefault	Print	4
6		3-tbrSeparator		
7	Bold	2-ButtonGroup	Bold	5
8	Italic	2-ButtonGroup	Italic	6
9	Underline	2-ButtonGroup	Underline	7
10	DropDown	5-tbrDropDown	Drop Down	8

12. Set the ButtonMenus options for buttons 1 and 2, according to the settings in Table 16.4.

TABLE 16.4: ButtonMenus Settings

Index	Text
1	Option 1
2	Option 2

Setting the ToolBar's Style

The ToolBar control has a Style property that can be set to control the look of the toolbar. The Style frame contains two Option Buttons that you can use to test the different styles available. The code shown in Code 16.3 adjusts the style setting based on the value of the Option Buttons index.

Code 16.3   **Adjusting the ToolBar's Style**

```
Private Sub Option1_Click(Index As Integer)
    'Set the toolbar style
    Select Case Index
        Case 0 'Standard look
            Toolbar1.Style = tbrStandard
        Case 1 'Flat look like Office applications
            Toolbar1.Style = tbrFlat
    End Select
End Sub
```

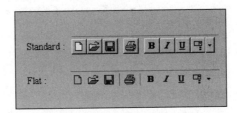

Changing the Form's BackColor

The combo box has been drawn directly on top of the Toolbar control. The code in Code 16.4 is used to change the backcolor of the Form so that it corresponds to the value in the Combo1 combo box on the toolbar.

Code 16.4   **Responding to a Change in BackColor Request**

```
Private Sub Combo1_Click()
    Select Case Combo1.Text
        Case "Grey"
            Form1.BackColor = &H8000000F
        Case "Yellow"
            Form1.BackColor = vbYellow
        Case "White"
            Form1.BackColor = vbWhite
        Case "Blue"
            Form1.BackColor = vbBlue
    End Select
End Sub
```

NOTE   The ImageEdit program included with Visual Basic is a good tool to use to create icons. You'll find the ImageEdit application in the `Tool\ImageEdit` folder on the VB6 CD-ROM.

Enabling and Disabling ToolBar Buttons

Enabling and disabling the Open button on the Toolbar control can be performed at run time, as shown in Code 16.5. If the Image associated with the Toolbar button is a transparent icon, the button will be grayed out by default.

Code 16.5   **Changing the Enabled State of the Open Button**

```
Private Sub Command1_Click()
    If Toolbar1.Buttons(1).Enabled = True Then
        Toolbar1.Buttons(1).Enabled = False
        Command1.Caption = "Enable"
    Else
        Toolbar1.Buttons(1).Enabled = True
        Command1.Caption = "Disable"
    End If
End Sub
```

Clicking Command2 displays the Customize Toolbar dialog box, in which the user can customize the look of the toolbar.

NOTE   The Toolbar configuration can be saved with the SaveToolbar method, discussed later in this section.

Displaying the Customize Toolbar Dialog Box

The Command2_Click subroutine, shown in Code 16.6, demonstrates how to display the Customize Toolbar dialog box.

Code 16.6   **Displaying the Customize Toolbar Dialog Box**

```
Private Sub Command2_Click()
    Toolbar1.Customize
End Sub
```

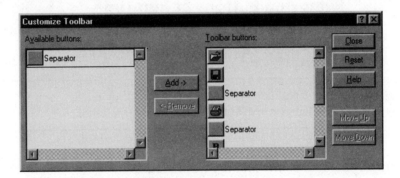

Adding an Image and Buttons at Run Time

The Command3_Click subroutine, shown in Code 16.7, adds an image to the Image-List control and adds two buttons to the Toolbar control. One button is a separator, and the other one is the Cut button with the image added to the ImageList control.

Code 16.7   **The Command3_Click Subroutine**

```
Private Sub Command3_Click()
    On Error Resume Next

    'Remove the separator the second time through
```

```
Toolbar1.Buttons.Remove (11)
'Add an image to the imagelist control
ImageList1.ListImages.Add , "Cut", _
    LoadPicture("d:\Chapter16Code\toolbar\Cut.ico")
'Add a separator button to the toolbar control
Toolbar1.Buttons.Add (11)
Toolbar1.Buttons(11).Style = tbrSeparator

'Add a button to the toolbar control
Toolbar1.Buttons.Add 12, "Cut", , , "Cut"
Toolbar1.Buttons(12).ToolTipText = "Cut"

End Sub
```

NOTE   Change the drive letter in the LoadPicture code to match that of your CD-ROM drive.

Removing Buttons at Run Time

You can use the Remove method to remove Button objects from the Toolbar control. Code 16.8 removes two buttons from the toolbar at run time.

NOTE   You can use the Index, in this case 11, or you can use the Key Cut to access the Button objects of the Toolbar control.

Code 16.8   **The Remove Method**

```
Private Sub Command4_Click()
    On Error Resume Next
    Toolbar1.Buttons.Remove (12)
    Toolbar1.Buttons.Remove (13)
End Sub
```

Saving the Toolbar Configuration to the Registry

After you customize the toolbar to fit your needs, you can save the configuration to the Windows Registry. You save the current toolbar configuration to the Registry with the SaveToolbar method, as shown in Code 16.9. Here are the parameters:

- The Key location in the Registry

- The subkey under the Key

- The name of the toolbar

NOTE   If the Key, subkey, or value you specify doesn't exist in the Registry, it is created.

Code 16.9   **The SaveToolbar Method**

```
Private Sub Command5_Click()
    Toolbar1.SaveToolbar "DHBook", "Toolbar", "UserName"
End Sub
```

Restoring the Toolbar Configuration to the Registry

Visual Basic also provides a way for you to retrieve a saved toolbar. You restore the toolbar configuration to the Registry with the RestoreToolbar method, as shown in Code 16.10. Here are the parameters:

- The Key location in the Registry

- The subkey under the Key

- The name of the toolbar

Code 16.10   **The RestoreToolbar Method**

```
Private Sub Command6_Click()
    On Error Resume Next
    Toolbar1.RestoreToolbar "DHBook", "Toolbar", "UserName"
End Sub

Private Sub mnuExit_Click()
    End
End Sub
```

Responding to the Clicked Button

At the heart of the Toolbar control is its ability to tell you which button the user clicked. In Code 16.11, the Key property is checked to determine which button was clicked, and the code for the action determined by that button is carried out.

Code 16.11   **Responding to a Toolbar Click**

```
Private Sub Toolbar1_ButtonClick(ByVal _
    Button As ComctlLib.Button)
    On Error Resume Next
    Select Case Button.Key
        Case "New"
            MsgBox "New code goes here"
        Case "Open"
            MsgBox "Open code goes here"
        Case "Save"
            MsgBox "Save code goes here"
        Case "Print"
            MsgBox "Print code goes here"
        Case "Bold"
            Text1 = "Bold"
            Text2.SelStart = 0
            Text2.SelLength = Len(Text2.Text)
            Text2.FontBold = True
            Text2.FontItalic = False
            Text2.FontUnderline = False
        Case "Italic"
            Text1 = "Italic"
            Text2.SelStart = 0
            Text2.SelLength = Len(Text2.Text)
            Text2.FontBold = False
            Text2.FontItalic = True
            Text2.FontUnderline = False
        Case "Underline"
            Text1 = "Underline"
            Text2.SelStart = 0
            Text2.SelLength = Len(Text2.Text)
            Text2.FontBold = False
            Text2.FontUnderline = True
            Text2.FontItalic = False
        Case "Cut"
            Text1 = "Cut"
            Text2.SelStart = 0
            Text2.SelLength = Len(Text2.Text)
            Text2.Text - ""
        Case "DropDown"
```

```
          MsgBox "DropDown button"

        End Select
    End Sub
```

The Infamous `readme.txt` File

As a Visual Basic developer, you may sometimes find it difficult to know just where the right places are to add your developer comments or to leave design or application notes for other developers. To make this job a little easier, try adding a Readme file to your projects. Notice the project section named Related Documents in the SDIToolbar project? This is a great place to add your notes and issues and will let other developers know what you are thinking as you design and build an application.

Follow these steps to add a Related Document section to a Visual Basic project:

1. Right-click on the Project window.

2. Select Add ➤ Add File...

3. Check the Add As Related Document check box.

4. Add the file.

5. It will be added under a section named Related Documents.

Testing the SDIToolbar Program

To start the SDIToolBar program, press F5. You'll see the screen shown in Figure 16.4, earlier in this chapter. Clicking a toolbar button displays a message box, and clicking a command button manipulates the toolbar.

Clicking the Disable button disables the Open toolbar button, and the caption of the Disable button changes to Enable. Notice that the look of the toolbar button changes to reflect the disabled state. Here's what happens when you click the other buttons:

- Clicking Command again enables the toolbar button.

- Clicking Add Button adds a new button to the toolbar.

- Clicking Remove Button removes the newly added button.

- Clicking Customize opens the Customize Toolbar dialog box. Select some buttons to remove, and click the Close button. The toolbar changes to reflect the new buttons.

- Clicking Save Toolbar saves the changes to the toolbar in the Windows Registry.

- Clicking Restore Toolbar restores the saved toolbar.

This is a good example of some of the Toolbar control's functionality. The use of the toolbar control in an MDI (Multiple Document Interface) application takes a little more planning.

Using the Toolbar Control in an MDI Application

Using the Toolbar control in an MDI application is different from using it in an SDI application. In an MDI application, you have an MDI Form and usually more than one Child Form. These Forms share the Toolbar control and the code on the MDI Form. If the MDI Form is displayed without any visible Child Forms, you must present the toolbar buttons associated with the MDI Form. When one of the Child Forms is displayed, you need to show that child's toolbar buttons. You can do so by creating the toolbar buttons at run time, depending on the Form displayed, by:

- Calling a routine from the Form_Activate event of the Child Forms to add the proper buttons

- Calling a routine in the Query_Unload event to hide the toolbars

When a button on a Toolbar control is clicked, the code from the toolbar calls the associated menu code in the active Form. This approach keeps track of the active Form and ensures that the proper toolbar buttons are displayed. The MDI-Toolbar project demonstrates this toolbar approach.

The MDIToolbar Project

The MDIToolbar project (shown in Figure 16.6) has one MDI Form with a Toolbar control, an ImageList control, and two Child Forms. The Child Forms do not have Toolbar controls; they share the Toolbar control on the MDI Form.

FIGURE 16.6:

The MDIToolbar project

NOTE   You'll find the MDIToolbar project in the `Chapter16\MDIToolbar` folder on the CD that comes with this book.

Creating the MDIToolbar Project

As with the SDIToolbar project in the previous section, we are including all the code for the MDIToolbar project in this section so that you can see it working together.

Start a new VB project. Form1 is created by default. Now, follow these steps:

1. Add another Standard Form and an MDI Form.

2. Add a Toolbar control and an ImageList control to the MDI Form.

3. Set the MDIChild property of Forms 1 and 2 to True. This will make them Child Forms of the MDI Form.

4. Add a Module to the project to hold the Toolbar collection definitions.

5. To add images to the ImageList control, set the ImageSize to 16 × 16 pixels, and add the icons shown in Table 16.5.

NOTE   For help on how to add images to the ImageList control, see the section "Adding Images to the ImageList Control at Design Time," earlier in this chapter.

TABLE 16.5: The MDIToolbar ImageList Control Settings

Index	Key	File
1	New	New.ico
2	Open	Open.ico
3	Save	Save.ico
4	Print	Print.ico
5	Bold	Bld.ico
6	Italic	Itl.ico
7	Underline	Undrln.ico

NOTE   You'll find the icons in the **Chapter16Code\Toolbar** folder on the CD that comes with this book.

Add the menu structure in Table 16.6 to the MDI Form, add the menu structure in Table 16.7 to Form1, and add the menu structure in Table 16.8 to Form2.

TABLE 16.6: The MDI Form Menu Structure

Caption	Name	Menu Position
&File	mnuFile	Menu
&New	mnuNew	Submenu
&Open	mnuOpen	Submenu
-	Space1	Submenu
E&xit	mnuExit	Submenu

TABLE 16.7: The Form1 Menu Structure

Caption	Name	Menu Position
&File	mnuFile	Menu
&New	mnuNew	Submenu
&Open	mnuOpen	Submenu
-	space1	Submenu
&Save	mnuSave	Submenu
-	space2	Submenu
&Print	mnuPrint	Submenu
-	space3	Submenu
E&xit	mnuExit	Submenu
&View	mnuView	Menu
Form&2	mnuForm2	Submenu

TABLE 16.8: The Form2 Menu Structure

Caption	Name	Menu Position
&File	mnuFile	Menu
&Save	mnuSave	Submenu
&Print	mnuPrint	Submenu
-	space1	Submenu
E&xit	mnuExit	Submenu
Forma&t	mnuFormat	Menu
&Bold	mnuBold	Submenu
&Italic	mnuItalic	Submenu
&Underline	mnuUnderline	Submenu
&View	mnuView	Menu
Form&1	mnuForm1	Submenu

Defining the Buttons for the Main Toolbar

The subroutine ToolbarSetup, as shown in Code 16.12, loads the Keys for the desired buttons into the colToolbarAction collection and loads the ToolTipText, the text that you see when your mouse moves over the toolbar buttons, into the colToolbarTip collection. After this, it calls the CreateToolbar subroutine where the buttons are loaded onto the Toolbar control.

NOTE   Code 16.12 is located in the MDIForm1, General Section. Since this code will be called from Form1 and Form2, be sure to change Private Sub to Public Sub.

Code 16.12   **Setting Up the Button Icons and ToolTipText Values**

```
Public Sub ToolbarSetup()
    On Error GoTo ErrorRoutineErr

    colToolbarAction.Add "New"
    colToolbarAction.Add "Separator"
    colToolbarAction.Add "Open"

    colToolbarTip.Add "New"
    colToolbarTip.Add ""
    colToolbarTip.Add "Open"

    Call MDIForm1.CreateToolbar
ErrorRoutineResume:
    Exit Sub
ErrorRoutineErr:
    MsgBox "MDIForm1.ToolbarSetup " & Err & " " & Error
End Sub
```

Creating the Toolbar Buttons at Run Time

The CreateToolbar subroutine is called from FormLoad of the MDI Form and Form_Activate of Form1 and Form2.

First, the CreateToolbar subroutine, as shown in Code 16.13, clears the buttons from the current toolbar, and then it links the Toolbar control and the ImageList control. Next, a Button object is added to the Toolbar control for each item in the colToolbarAction collection, and the ToolTipText is set. At the end of the routine, the Toolbar and ToolTip collections are set to Nothing to release their resources.

Code 16.13   **The CreateToolbar Subroutine**

```
Public Sub CreateToolbar()
    On Error GoTo ErrorRoutineErr
    Dim slAction As Variant
    Dim slTip As Variant
    Dim slCnt
    Dim btnX As Button

    'Clear the current buttons
    Toolbar1.Buttons.Clear

    'Associate toolbar and imglist
    Toolbar1.ImageList = ImageList1
    'Clear the counter
    slCnt = 0

    'Add button objects to Buttons collection using the
    'add method. After creating each button, set
    'toolTipText properties
    For Each slAction In colToolbarAction
        slCnt = slCnt + 1
        If slAction = "Separator" Then
            Set btnX = Toolbar1.Buttons.Add(, , , tbrSeparator)
        Else
            Set btnX = Toolbar1.Buttons.Add(, slAction, , _
            tbrDefault, slAction)
            btnX.ToolTipText = colToolbarTip(slCnt)
        End If
    Next

ErrorRoutineResume:
    Set colToolbarAction = Nothing
    Set colToolbarTip = Nothing
    Exit Sub
ErrorRoutineErr:
    MsgBox "mdiForm1.CreateToolbar " & Err & " " & Error
End Sub
```

Hiding a Toolbar

The HideToolbar subroutine, as shown in Code 16.14, is called from the Query_ Unload event of Form1 and Form2. It checks the Count property of the Forms collection. If the count equals two, the MDI Form will be the only Form visible when the Query_Unload event completes, so you must call ToolbarSetup to add its buttons, for the main MDI Form, to the Toolbar control.

Code 16.14   **The HideToolbar Subroutine**

```
Public Sub HideToolbar(frm As Form)
    On Error GoTo ErrorRoutineErr

    frm.Visible = False
    'If there are only 2 Forms, show the toolbar for the
    'Main mdi Form, the other Form will be unloaded
    If Forms.Count = 2 Then
        Call ToolbarSetup
    End If

ErrorRoutineResume:
    Exit Sub
ErrorRoutineErr:
    MsgBox "mdiForm1.HideToolbar " & Err & Error
End Sub
```

Loading the Main Form

In the subroutine Form_Load, shown in Code 16.15, we call the ToolbarSetup routine to set up the toolbar for the main MDI Form.

Code 16.15   **The Form_Load Subroutine**

```
Private Sub MDIForm_Load()
    'Setup the MDIToolbar
    Call ToolbarSetup
End Sub
```

Clicking the Toolbar Button

Clicking the Button object on the Toolbar control triggers the Toolbar1_ButtonClick event, as shown in Code 16.16. All the options are prefixed with ActiveForm so that the code in the proper Form is called, and each Form can have different code for the same button. Clicking the buttons on the MDI Form generates an error because there is not an ActiveForm. The On Error Goto ErrorRoutineErr traps this error and processes code for the MDI buttons.

NOTE

For this subroutine to work properly, you must change Private Sub to Public Sub for the menu code in Form1 and Form2. The MDI Form can remain private because it is in the same module as the Toolbar1_Click code.

Code 16.16   **The Toolbar1_ButtonClick Event**

```
Private Sub Toolbar1_ButtonClick(ByVal Button As ComctlLib.Button)
    On Error GoTo ErrorRoutineErr

    Select Case Button.Key
        Case "New"
            ActiveForm.mnuNew_Click
        Case "Open"
            ActiveForm.mnuOpen_Click
        Case "Save"
            ActiveForm.mnuSave_Click
        Case "Print"
            ActiveForm.mnuPrint_Click
        Case "Bold"
            ActiveForm.mnuBold_Click
        Case "Italic"
            ActiveForm.mnuItalic_Click
        Case "Underline"
            ActiveForm.mnuUnderline_Click
    End Select

ErrorRoutineResume:
    Exit Sub
ErrorRoutineErr:
    'If the MDI Form is the only Form open,
    'Then there is no active Form
    If Err = 91 Then
        Select Case Button.Key
            Case "New"
                mnuNew_Click
            Case "Open"
                mnuOpen_Click
        End Select
        Err = 0
```

```
        GoTo ErrorRoutineResume
    End If

    MsgBox "MDIForm1.tbToolbar_ButtonClick" & Err & Error

End Sub
```

Defining the Toolbar Properties for Form1

TheToolbarSetup subroutine loads the Keys for the desired buttons into the colToolbarAction collection and loads the ToolTipText into the colToolbarTip collection. It then calls CreateToolbar in the MDIForm where the buttons are loaded onto the Toolbar control. Code 16.17 is located in Form1.

Code 16.17   **The ToolbarSetup Subroutine**

```
Public Sub ToolbarSetup()
    On Error GoTo ErrorRoutineErr

    colToolbarAction.Add "New"
    colToolbarAction.Add "Open"
    colToolbarAction.Add "Save"
    colToolbarAction.Add "Separator"
    colToolbarAction.Add "Print"

    colToolbarTip.Add "New"
    colToolbarTip.Add "Open"
    colToolbarTip.Add "Save"
    colToolbarTip.Add ""
    colToolbarTip.Add "Print"

    Call MDIForm1.CreateToolbar
ErrorRoutineResume:
    Exit Sub
ErrorRoutineErr:
    MsgBox "MDIForm1.ToolbarSetup " & Err & Error
End Sub
```

Activating the Form

In the Form_Activate module, place the code to set up the toolbar for the Form. That way, whenever the Form becomes active, the proper toolbar buttons will be displayed. Code 16.18 is located in Form1.

Code 16.18   **The Form_Activate Module**

```
Private Sub Form_Activate()
    Call ToolbarSetup
End Sub
```

Unloading Form1

The Form is about to be unloaded, as shown in Code 16.19; check to see if it is the last Form. If it is, set up the buttons for the MDI Form.

Code 16.19   **The Form_QueryUnload Subroutine**

```
Private Sub Form_QueryUnload(Cancel As Integer, _
    UnloadMode As Integer)
    Call MDIForm1.HideToolbar(Me)
End Sub
```

Defining the Toolbar Properties for Form2

The ToolbarSetup subroutine loads the Keys for the desired buttons into the colToolbarAction collection and loads the ToolTipText into the colToolbarTip collection. It then calls CreateToolbar in the MDIForm where the buttons are loaded onto the Toolbar control. Code 16.20 is located in Form2.

Code 16.20   **The ToolbarSetup Subroutine**

```
Public Sub ToolbarSetup()
    On Error GoTo ErrorRoutineErr

    colToolbarAction.Add "Save"
    colToolbarAction.Add "Print"
    colToolbarAction.Add "Separator"
    colToolbarAction.Add "Bold"
    colToolbarAction.Add "Italic"
    colToolbarAction.Add "Underline"

    colToolbarTip.Add "Save"
    colToolbarTip.Add "Print"
    colToolbarTip.Add ""
    colToolbarTip.Add "Bold"
    colToolbarTip.Add "Italic"
    colToolbarTip.Add "Underline"
```

```
        Call MDIForm1.CreateToolbar
ErrorRoutineResume:
        Exit Sub
ErrorRoutineErr:
        MsgBox "MDIForm1.ToolbarSetup " & Err & Error
End Sub
```

Activating the Form

As we did in Form1, place the code to set up the toolbar for the Form. That way, whenever the Form becomes active, as shown in Code 16.21, the proper toolbar buttons will be displayed.

| Code 16.21 | The Form_Activate Subroutine |

```
Public Sub Form_Activate()
        Call ToolbarSetup
End Sub
```

Unloading Form2

The Form is about to be unloaded, as shown in Code 16.22; check to see if it is the last Form. If it is, set up the buttons for the MDI Form.

| Code 16.22 | The Form_QueryUnload Subroutine |

```
Public Sub Form_QueryUnload(Cancel As Integer, _
        UnloadMode As Integer)
        Call MDIForm1.HideToolbar(Me)
End Sub
```

Testing the MDIToolbar Project

To start the MDIToolbar project, press F5. You'll see the MDI Form displayed with a Toolbar control, as shown in Figure 16.6, earlier in this chapter.

NOTE You'll find the MDIToolbar project in the **Chapter16\MDIToolbar** folder on the CD that comes with this book.

To test this project, follow these steps:

1. Choose View ➢ Form1 to open Form1.

Notice that the Toolbar buttons from Form1 are shown on the Toolbar control and that the Menu from Form1 replaces the MDI Forms menu (see Figure 16.7). When Form1 is activated, the code ToolbarSetup in Form1 is run. This passes a collection of buttons to the CreateToolbar subroutine in the MDI Form and tells it to change the Toolbar control's buttons.

FIGURE 16.7:

The MDI Form with Form1

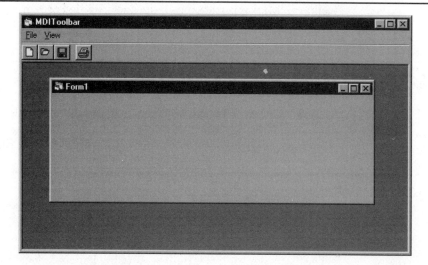

2. Choose View ➤ Form2 to open Form2 with its buttons displayed on the MDI toolbar, as shown in Figure 16.8. The same process that was at work in Step 1 is at work here.

FIGURE 16.8:

The MDI Form with Form2

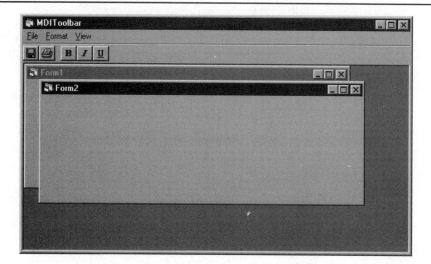

3. With both Form1 and Form2 displayed, activate each Form and notice the toolbar buttons change. If you close both Forms, the toolbar buttons from the MDI Form are displayed. This all happens in the ToolbarSetup and CreateToolbar subroutines.

As you can see from our test, with a little work, the Toolbar control works as well in an MDI application as it does in a single Form application.

The StatusBar Control

A StatusBar control (shown in Figure 16.9) provides a window, usually at the bottom of a parent Form, through which an application can display various kinds of status data. The status bar has become a standard feature of most Windows programs.

FIGURE 16.9:

The StatusBar control

The StatusBar control is built around the Panels collection. It can be divided into a maximum of 16 Panel objects, or sections, that are contained in a Panels collection. At run time, you can dynamically change the text, images, width, and style of any Panel object. You can also add panels and remove panels from the Status-Bar control. At design time, you can create panels and customize their function and style with the StatusBar Property Pages.

A feature of the StatusBar control is its ability to display key states, time, and date by setting the Style property. Table 16.9 lists and describes the values of available styles.

TABLE 16.9: The Values of the StatusBar Control

Style	Value	Description
sbrText	0	Default. Displays text and/or a bitmap image. You set text with the Text property.
sbrCaps	1	Caps Lock key. Displays the letters CAPS in bold when Caps Lock is enabled and dims them when Caps Lock is off.

Continued on next page

TABLE 16.9 CONTINUED: The Values of the StatusBar Control

Style	Value	Description
sbrNumber	2	Number Lock. Displays the letters NUM in bold when Num Lock is enabled and dims them when Num Lock is off.
sbrIns	3	Insert key. Displays the letters INS in bold when the Insert key is enabled and dims them when Insert mode is turned off.
sbrScrl	4	Scroll Lock key. Displays the letters SCRL in bold when Scroll Lock is enabled and dims them when Scroll Lock is off.
sbrTime	5	Time. Displays the current time in the system format.
sbr Date	6	Date. Displays the current date in the system format.
sbrKana	7	Kana. Displays the letters KANA in bold when kana lock is enabled and dims them when kana is turned off. Applies to Japanese systems only.

Use the Bevel, Autosize, and Align properties to control the appearance of the Panel objects.

- Bevel specifies whether the Panel object will have a bevel of inset, raised, or none.

- Autosize determines how a Panel object will be resized when the parent container is resized by the user.

- Align determines where the StatusBar control is placed on the Form.

Adding Panels to the StatusBar Control at Design Time

To add panels to the StatusBar control at design time, you use the StatusBar Property Pages. Follow these steps:

1. Right-click the StatusBar control and click Properties to open the Property Pages.

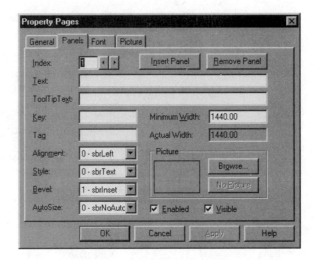

2. Select the Panels tab, and then click the Insert Panel button to insert a Panel object.

3. Set the Text, ToolTipText, Key, Tag, Alignment, Style, Bevel, and AutoSize properties, and add a picture, if desired.

4. Repeat steps 2 and 3 to add all the panels you need.

Adding Panels to the StatusBar Control at Run Time

To add Panel objects at run time, you use the Set statement with the Add method. Declare a *Panel* object variable and then set the object variable to a panel created with the Add method. Code 16.23 adds a panel at run time and adds the application's EXE name and a bitmap image.

Code 16.23   Adding Panels to the Status Bar at Run Time

```
Private Sub Command1_Click()
    'The StatusBar control is named "statusbar1"
    Dim pnlX As Panel
    Set pnlX = StatusBar1.Panels.Add()

    pnlX.Text = App.EXEName
```

```
Set pnlX.Picture = LoadPicture _
(App.Path & "\open.ico")

'Change some text
StatusBar1.Panels(1).Text = "Panel Added"
End Sub
```

The StatusBar Project

The StatusBar project, as shown in Figure 16.10, displays a StatusBar control on a Form and creates a Panel object at run time for each of the panel styles, with the exception of KANA.

FIGURE 16.10:

The StatusBar project

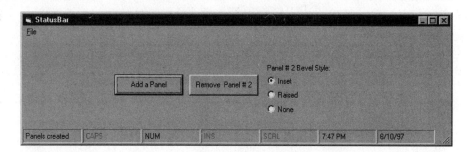

NOTE   You'll find the StatusBar project in the `Chapter16\StatusBar` folder on the CD that comes with this book.

The project contains one Form and a StatusBar control. It also contains two command buttons:

> **Add a Panel,** which adds a Panel object that has text and a bitmap image
>
> **Remove Panel # 2,** which removes the second Panel object

The option buttons cycle the Panel object 2 Bevel property from Inset, Raised, and None.

The StatusBar Project Code

Let's take a look at some of the more interesting code in the StatusBar project.

Adding a Panel at Run Time

The Command1_Click subroutine, shown in Code 16.24, adds a Panel object to the StatusBar control with the Add method, and it adds an icon and sets the Panel Text property.

Code 16.24   **The Command1_Click Subroutine**

```
Private Sub Command1_Click()
    'The StatusBar control is named "StatusBar1"
    Dim pnlX As Panel
    Set pnlX = StatusBar1.Panels.Add()

    pnlX.Text = App.EXEName

    Set pnlX.Picture = LoadPicture(App.Path & "\open.ico")
    'Change some text
    StatusBar1.Panels(1).Text = "Panel Added"
End Sub
```

Removing a Panel Object at Run Time

The Command2_Click subroutine, shown in Code 16.25, removes Panel object number 2 with the Remove method. After the panel is removed, the AutoSize property is set to resize the panels.

Code 16.25   **The Command2_Click Subroutine**

```
Private Sub Command2_Click()

    'Remove panel 2
    StatusBar1.Panels.Remove (2)

    'Change some text
    StatusBar1.Panels(1).Text = "Panel 2 removed"

    'Set the style to AutoSize
    StatusBar1.Panels(1).AutoSize = sbrContents
End Sub
```

The AutoSize property determines the width of the Panel. The values are listed in Table 16.10.

TABLE 16.10: The Values of the AutoSize Property

Constant	Value	Description
sbrNoAutoSize	0	None. This is the default. Autosizing does not occur.
sbrSpring	1	Spring. If there is extra space in the panels as a result of resizing the Form, the panels divide up the extra space. The panels never resize smaller than the amount in the Min-Width property.
sbrContents	2	Content. Panels are resized to fit the contents but never below the MinWidth property setting.

Adding Several Panels at Run Time

When the Form is loaded, as shown in Code 16.26, we add one Panel object and set the Style property to all the styles available, except for KANA.

Code 16.26   The Form_Load Subroutine

```
Private Sub Form_Load()
    Dim pnlX As Panel
    Dim i As Integer
    'Add six Panel objects
    For i = 1 To 6
        'Create a panel and get a reference to it simultaneously
        Set pnlX = StatusBar1.Panels.Add(, "Panel" & i)
        'Set Style property
        pnlX.Style = i
        'Set AutoSize property
        pnlX.AutoSize = sbrContents
    Next i

    Option1(0).Value = True
    StatusBar1.Panels(1).Text = "Panels created"
End Sub
```

Changing the Bevel Property

We change the Bevel style of Panel2 based on the Option Button setting, as shown in Code 16.27.

Code 16.27   **Changing the Bevel Property**

```
Private Sub Option1_Click(Index As Integer)
    Select Case Index
        Case 0
            'Set Panel 2 Bevel = Inset
            StatusBar1.Panels(2).Bevel = sbrInset
            StatusBar1.Panels(1).Text = "Bevel = Inset"
        Case 1
            'Set Panel 2 Bevel = Raised
            StatusBar1.Panels(2).Bevel = sbrRaised
            StatusBar1.Panels(1).Text = "Bevel = Raised"
        Case 2
            'Set Panel 2 Bevel = None
            StatusBar1.Panels(2).Bevel = sbrNoBevel
            StatusBar1.Panels(1).Text = "Bevel = None"
    End Select
End Sub
```

Testing the StatusBar Project

Start the StatusBar program by pressing F5, and then follow these steps:

1. Click the Add a Panel button to add a panel to the end of the StatusBar control. The text in Panel 1 changes to "Panel added." Most StatusBar controls are used to display changes to their programs or environments.

2. Click the Remove Panel # 2 button to remove Panel number 2. The Remove method is used to delete the Panel object from the StatusBar control.

3. Click one of the Option Buttons to change the BevelStyle property of Panel 2.

Status bars have become a fixture in most Windows applications, and this project demonstrates some of the flexibility of the control.

The TabStrip Control

A TabStrip control (shown in Figure 16.11) is similar to the dividers in a notebook or the labels on a group of file folders. By using a TabStrip control, you can define multiple pages for the same area of a window or dialog box in your application.

FIGURE 16.11:

A TabStrip control

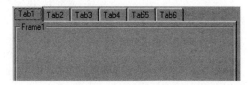

The TabStrip control consists of one or more Tab objects in a Tabs collection. You can add, remove, and/or change the appearance of tabs at design time and at run time. You can also associate an ImageList control with a TabStrip control.

TabStrip Control Properties

The TabStrip control can take on the appearance of notebook tabs (Tabs), push-buttons (Buttons), or flat buttons (FlatButtons) like Microsoft Office style buttons, as determined by the Style property.

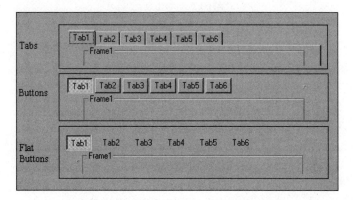

Each page in the TabStrip control consists of a tab and a client area, as shown in Figure 16.12. Visual Basic automatically determines the size and position of the internal area, or ClientArea, of the TabStrip based on the overall size of the control. This area is returned in the Client-coordinate properties of ClientLeft, ClientTop, ClientHeight, and ClientWidth.

FIGURE 16.12:

The TabStrip control's ClientArea

The TabStrip control is not a container. You must use a Frame, a PictureBox, or some other container control to hold the actual pages. After the container controls are created, a technique is required to position them over the TabStrip control's client area. Code 16.28 uses the Move method with the ClientLeft, ClientTop, ClientHeight, and ClientWidth properties to position the containers.

Code 16.28   Positioning the Frames

```
Public Sub ResetFrames()
    Dim i

    For i = 0 To Frame1.Count - 1
    With Frame1(i)
        .Move TabStrip1.ClientLeft + 300, _
        TabStrip1.ClientTop, _
        TabStrip1.ClientWidth - 600, _
        TabStrip1.ClientHeight - 300
    End With
    Next i

End Sub
```

A TabStrip control can contain more than one Tab object; however, you must manage the Tab objects and the associated container controls. You can use the following process to do so:

1. At design time, create as many of the Tab objects as you need.

2. Create a control array of container controls, one for each Tab object.

3. On each container control, draw the controls for that page.

4. At run time, use the SelectedItem property to determine the index of the selected Tab object.

5. Use the Zorder and visible properties to bring the container control to the top and make it visible.

NOTE   If you add a Tab object at run time, you must also create a container control to hold the page controls.

Another feature of the TabStrip control is the MultiRow property. If you set this property to True, a large number of Tab objects will appear in multiple rows, as shown in Figure 16.13. If you set this property to False, the same number of tabs appear in a single row with a pair of scroll buttons at the end, as shown in Figure 16.14.

FIGURE 16.13:

A TabStrip control with multiple rows

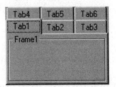

FIGURE 16.14:

A TabStrip control with a single row

Determining the Tabstrip's Appearance

There are several properties that can be combined to control the overall appearance of the TabStrip control:

HotTracking, which determines whether mouse-sensitive highlighting is enabled. Hot tracking is a feature that provides visual feedback when the mouse pointer passes over the control. With HotTracking set to True, the control responds to mouse movement by highlighting the header over which the mouse pointer is positioned.

Placement property, which Sets a value that specifies the placement of tabs—top, bottom, left, or right.

TabStyle property, which determines how remaining rows of tabs in front of a selected tab are repositioned. When the TabStyle is set to tabTabStandard 0 (Default), the remaining tabs remain on the same side of the control. With the TabStyle set to tabTabOpposite, the row of tabs in front of the selected tab are repositioned at the opposite side of the control. This setting does not have an effect on a TabStrip with only one row of tabs.

Associating an ImageList Control with the TabStrip Control

To identify a tab, you can assign an image from the ImageList control to the Tab object. First, associate the ImageList control with the TabStrip control. You can do so at design time or at run time.

To associate an ImageList control with a TabStrip control at design time, follow these steps:

1. Populate the ImageList control with images.

2. Right-click the TabStrip control, and choose Properties to open the TabStrip Property Pages:

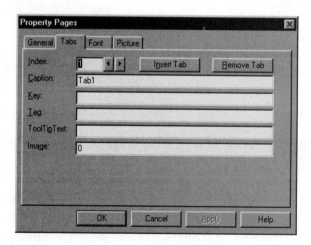

NOTE   You could build the Property Pages dialog box with a TabStrip control.

---

3. Select the General tab, and then select the ImageList control from the Image-List box.

To associate an ImageList control with a TabStrip control at run time, as shown in Code 16.29, set the ImageList property to the ImageList control.

Code 16.29   **Associating the ImageList with TabStrip at Run Time**

```
Private Sub Form_Load()
        TabStrip1.ImageList = ImageList1
End Sub
```

Creating Tabs at Design Time

Follow these steps to create Tab objects at design time:

1. Right-click the TabStrip control, and choose Properties to display the Property Pages.

2. Select the Tabs tab.

3. Click Insert Tab to add a Tab object.

4. Set the Caption, Key, Tag, ToolTipText, and Image properties to customize the Tab object.

Creating Tabs at Run Time

You use the Add method to create a collection of Tab objects at run time, as shown in Code 16.30.

Code 16.30   **Adding Tab Objects at Run Time with the Add Method**

```
Private Sub Form_Load()
    'Use the Add method to create a new Tab object
    TabStrip1.Tabs.Add
    'Count gets the last tab added
    TabStrip1.Tabs(TabStrip1.Tabs.Count).Caption = "Printer"
    TabStrip1.Tabs(TabStrip1.Tabs.Count).Image = "Print"
    TabStrip1.Tabs(TabStrip1.Tabs.Count).Key = "Print"
End Sub
```

The TabStrip Project

The TabStrip project (shown in Figure 16.15) demonstrates a TabStrip control at work. It shows:

- How to add and remove Tab objects at run time
- The procedures necessary to keep all the containers associated with the correct pages
- The use of the MultiRow property
- The use of the Placement property to set the placement of the tabs

FIGURE 16.15:

The TabStrip project

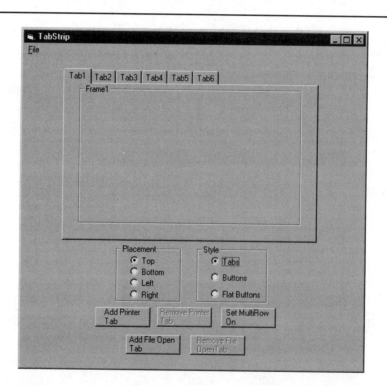

NOTE   You'll find the TabStrip project in the **Chapter16\TabStrip** folder on the CD that comes with this book.

This project consists of a Form with a TabStrip control. Each TabStrip control has a Frame associated with it to hold the page. A Placement Frame that contains options to move the tabs, a Style Frame that provides options to adjust the tab style, and the following five command buttons are included:

Add Printer Tab adds a Tab object at run time. The caption of the Tab contains text and a bitmap image. The image is retrieved from an ImageList control.

Remove Printer Tab removes the Printer Tab object.

Add File Open Tab adds a Tab object at run time. The caption of the tab contains text and a bitmap image. The image is retrieved from an ImageList control.

Remove File Open Tab removes the File Open Tab object.

Set MultiRow On toggles the MultiRow property on and off.

Creating the TabStrip Project

When you use a TabStrip control in your application, keep in mind that the TabStrip control is not a container. You will need some other container control to hold the control for the user. In this case, we will use the Frame control as our container. Let's create the TabStrip project.

1. Start a new project and add one TabStrip control.

2. Create a control array of six Frames, and add five command buttons and an ImageList control.

3. Right-click the ImageList control, and choose Properties to display the Property Pages.

4. From the `Chapter16Code\TabStrip` folder, add an Open icon and a Printer icon to the ImageList control.

NOTE   You'll find a number of common icons you can use in your projects in the `Chapter16\TabStrip` folder on the CD that comes with this book.

---

5. Right-click the TabStrip control, and click Properties to display the Property Pages.

6. Select the General tab, and then select ImageList1 from the ImageList box.

7. Select the Tabs tab, and click the Insert Tab button five times to add five Tab objects. Tab 1 is created by default.

8. Set the Caption property of each Tab object to Tab and the index of the tab. Tab1 should have a Caption property set to Tab1; Tab2 caption is Tab2. Do this for each Tab object.

Moving the Frames to the Client Area

The ResetFrames subroutine, shown in Code 16.31, moves the Frames to the ClientArea of the Tab by looping through the frames and aligning them with the ClientArea of the TabStrip control.

Code 16.31   The Reset Frames Subroutine

```
Public Sub ResetFrames()
    Dim i

    For i = 0 To Frame1.Count - 1
    With Frame1(i)
        .Move TabStrip1.ClientLeft, _
        TabStrip1.ClientTop, _
        TabStrip1.ClientWidth, _
        TabStrip1.ClientHeight
    End With
    Next i

End Sub
```

Adding a Tab at Run Time

The Command1_Click subroutine adds a new Printer Tab object and then sets properties on the new tab, as shown in Code 16.32. After the Tab is created, the frames are reset by calling the ResetFrames subroutine.

Code 16.32   Creating a Printer Tab Object

```
Private Sub Command1_Click()

    'Use the Add method to create a new Tab object
```

```
TabStrip1.Tabs.Add
TabStrip1.Tabs(TabStrip1.Tabs.Count).Caption = "Printer"
TabStrip1.Tabs(TabStrip1.Tabs.Count).Image = "Print"
TabStrip1.Tabs(TabStrip1.Tabs.Count).Key = "Print"

'Reset the frames
Call ResetFrames

Command1.Enabled = False
Command2.Enabled = True
End Sub
```

Deleting a Tab at Run Time

The Command2_Click subroutine deletes the Print Tab object with the Remove Method and calls ResetFrames, as shown in Code 16.33. If the TabStrip control has a large number of Tab objects, you will need to realign them.

Code 16.33   **Deleting a Tab Object**

```
Private Sub Command2_Click()
    'If you delete the current tab,
    'make Frame1(0) visible
    If TabStrip1.SelectedItem.Index = TabStrip1.Tabs.Count Then
        Frame1(0).Visible = True
    End If

    'Remove the printer tab
    TabStrip1.Tabs.Remove ("Print")

    'Set the command buttons
    Command1.Enabled = True
    Command2.Enabled = False

    'Reset the frames
    Call ResetFrames

End Sub
```

Adding a Tab with the Add Method

The Command3_Click subroutine uses the Add method to create a new File Open Tab object, as shown in Code 16.34. The Add Method allows you to combine the add and property settings into one command. The Add method has the following parameters:

Object, which is a TabStrip control.

Index, which is optional and is an integer specifying the position where you want to insert the tab.

Key, which is optional and is a unique string that identifies the tab. Use Key to retrieve a specific tab.

Caption, which is optional and is the string that appears on the tab.

Image, which is optional and is the index of an image in an associated ImageList control.

Code 16.34   **Adding a Tab Object with the Add Method**

```
Private Sub Command3_Click()
    'Use the Add method to create a new Tab object
    'This is the same as in the Command1 Printer add except
    'it is all in one command
    TabStrip1.Tabs.Add TabStrip1.Tabs.Count + 1, _
        "Open", "Open File Tab", "Open"

    'Reset the frames
    Call ResetFrames

    Command3.Enabled = False
    Command4.Enabled = True
End Sub
```

Setting the MultiRow Property

The Command5_Click subroutine toggles the MultiRow property on and off, as shown in Code 16.35. If you set the MultiRow property to True, a large number of Tab objects will appear in multiple rows, as shown in Figure 16.16 earlier in this chapter. If you set this property to False, the same number of tabs appear in a single row with a pair of scroll buttons at the end, as shown in Figure 16.17 earlier in this chapter.

Code 16.35	**Setting the MultiRow Options**

```
Private Sub Command5_Click()
    If TabStrip1.MultiRow = True Then
        TabStrip1.MultiRow = False
        Command5.Caption = "Set MultiRow On"
    Else
        TabStrip1.MultiRow = True
        Command5.Caption = "Set MultiRow Off"
    End If
    Call ResetFrames
End Sub
```

Clicking a Tab

The TabStrip1_Click subroutine, shown in Code 16.36, checks for the current tab, makes the associated frame visible, and puts it at the top of the Zorder. Make all other frames invisible.

Code 16.36	**Maintaining the Correct Frame**

```
Private Sub TabStrip1_Click()
    Dim i

    'Loop through the tabs
    For i = 0 To Frame1.Count - 1
        If TabStrip1.SelectedItem.Index = i + 1 Then
            'Make the current frame visible
            Frame1(i).Visible = True
            Frame1(i).ZOrder 0
        Else
            'All others are invisible
            Frame1(i).Visible = False
        End If
    Next
End Sub
```

The previous code loops through the Frame controls one at a time. When the current frame is located, it is made visible and moved to the top of the stack. All other frames are rendered invisible.

Testing the TabStrip Project

To test the TabStrip project, press F5 to run the project and then follow these steps:

1. Click the six tabs, and notice that the Frame associated with the tab is visible and lined up in the Tab object's ClientArea.

2. Click the options in the Placement frame to move the tabs around on the TabStrip.

3. Select the options in the Style Frame to change the style of the tabs.

4. Test the other features by clicking the Add and Remove buttons.

5. Try this with the MultiRow property on and again with the MultiRow property turned off. If your project must remain in a limited area, setting MultiRow off can save space.

TabStrip controls have become permanent features in most Windows applications as dialog boxes and list containers. In fact, the use of TabStrip controls for dialog boxes will help your programs maintain the Windows standard.

The Slider Control

The Slider control (shown in Figure 16.16) is a window containing a slider and optional tickmarks. You can move the slider by dragging it, clicking the mouse to either side of the slider, or using the arrow keys on the keyboard. As you move the slider, the current value is displayed in a ToolTip either above or below the slider, based on the setting of the TextPosition property.

FIGURE 16.16:

The Slider control

A Slider control consists of a scale defined by the Min and Max properties and a "knob" that can be moved by using the mouse or arrow keys. You can set the Min and Max properties of the Slider control at run time to dynamically change the range of the control.

The appearance of the Slider is controlled by the TickStyle and TickFrequency properties. Set the ticks (shown in Figure 16.17) according to Table 16.11.

FIGURE 16.17:

The Slider control tickmarks

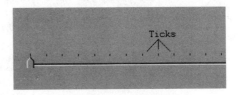

TABLE 16.11: The Properties of the Slider Tick Style

Constant	Value	Description
sldBottomRight	0	Bottom/Right. Tickmarks are positioned along the bottom of the slider if the control is oriented horizontally or along the right side if it is oriented vertically.
sldTopLeft	1	Top/Left. Tickmarks are positioned along the top of the slider if the control is oriented horizontally or along the left side if it is oriented vertically.
sldBoth	2	Both. Tickmarks are positioned on both sides or the top and the bottom of the slider.
sldNoTicks	3	None. No tickmarks appear on the slider.

The TickFrequency property returns or sets the frequency of tickmarks on a Slider control in relation to its range. For example, if the range is 100 and the TickFrequency property is set at 2, there will be one tick for every 2 increments in the range and a total of 50 ticks.

Setting the Min and Max Properties at Design Time

The Min and Max properties determine the minimum and maximum limits of the Slider control. To set these properties at design time, right-click the control and choose Properties to open the Property Pages.

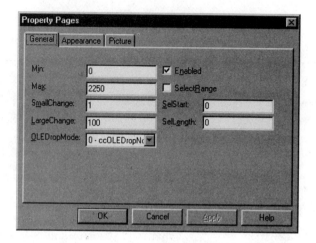

Setting the Min and Max Properties at Run Time

To set the Min and Max properties at run time, you can use Code 16.37.

Code 16.37   **Setting Min and Max Properties**

```
Private Sub Command2_Click()
    Slider1.Min = 100
    Slider1.Max = 1000
End Sub
```

Changing the Position of the Slider Knob

In addition to adjusting the TickStyle, TickFrequency, Min, and Max properties, you can adjust the SmallChange and LargeChange properties to determine how the slider control increments and decrements. The SmallChange property sets the number of ticks the slider will move when you press the Left or Right Arrow keys, and the LargeChange property sets the number of ticks the slider will move when you press the Page Up or Page Down keys or when you click the mouse to the left or the right of the slider.

Selecting Ranges with the Slider

As you have seen, you can use the Slider control to select a value between the Min and Max properties. You can also use the Slider control to select a range of values by setting the SelStart and SelLength properties. When a range of values is selected, the Slider changes its appearance (as shown in Figure 16.18) to notify the user that it is ready to accept a range. If the user presses the Shift key while clicking the Slider control, the MouseDown event occurs. Code in that event sets the SelectRange and SelStart properties. When the user releases the mouse button, the MouseUp event occurs, and in that code the SelLength property is set, from which a range of values can be extracted.

FIGURE 16.18:

The Slider control in
Selected mode

The Slider Project

The Slider project (shown in Figure 16.19) sets the caption of a Label control according to the value of the Slider control. The Slider project has one command button that is used to toggle between selecting a single value and selecting a range of values and two Option Frames that set the Tick Style and the TextPosition properties.

FIGURE 16.19:

The Slider project

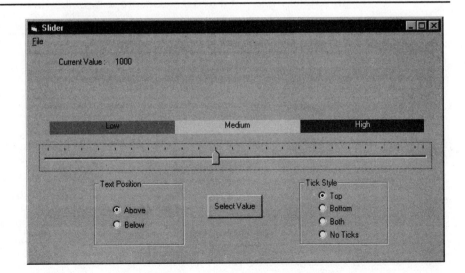

NOTE   You'll find the TabStrip project in the `Chapter16\TabStrip` folder on the CD that comes with this book.

The Slider Project Code

Let's take a look at some of the code in the Slider project that demonstrates how to set the Min and Max values and to select a range of values.

Showing the Slider's Value

The Scroll event is triggered whenever the knob of the Slider is moved. As the knob is moved, we put the value in a label.

```
Private Sub Slider1_Scroll()
    lblValue = Slider1.Value
End Sub
```

Getting the SelStart

When the SelRange property of the Slider control is True and the user presses Shift and clicks the control, the MouseDown event is triggered. In the Mouse-Down subroutine, shown in Code 16.38, we capture the starting point, the Sel-Start property, and put it into the label property of lblMinValue.

Code 16.38   **The MouseDown Subroutine**

```
Private Sub Slider1_MouseDown(Button As Integer, Shift _
    As Integer, x As Single, y As Single)

    If Shift = 1 Then
        Slider1.SelStart = Slider1.Value
        lblMinValue = Slider1.Value
        ' Set previous SelLength (if any) to 0.
        Slider1.SelLength = 0
    End If

End Sub
```

Getting the SelLength

When the user releases the mouse button, the MouseUp event is triggered. In the MouseUp event, shown in Code 16.39, the SelLength and SelStart properties are captured and put into labels.

Code 16.39	The MouseUp Event

```
Private Sub Slider1_MouseUp(Button As Integer, _
    Shift As Integer, x As Single, y As Single)

    If Shift = 1 Then
    ' If user selects backwards from a point,
    ' an error will occur.
    On Error Resume Next
    ' Else set SelLength using SelStart and
    ' current value.
        Slider1.SelLength = _
        Slider1.Value - Slider1.SelStart
    Else
        'If user lifts SHIFT key, set SelLength
        ' to 0 (to deselect the SelRange) and exit.
        Slider1.SelLength = 0
    End If
    lblLengthValue = Slider1.SelLength
    lblMaxValue = Slider1.Value
End Sub
```

Testing the Slider Program

There is only one button to work with in the Slider application, and it toggles the Range property on and off. To test the Slider project, follow these steps:

1. Press F5 to start the project.

2. Click the slider knob and move it to the right. Notice that the Current Value is increased. Move the slider knob to the left, and the value goes down.

3. Click the Select Range button, and the Slider control expands to notify you that it is in the SelectRange mode.

4. Press and hold the Shift key, click the Slider knob and move it to the right about midway, release the mouse button, and then release the Shift key.

Notice that the Min, Max, and Length values are now the labels in the Range frame, as shown in Figure 16.20.

FIGURE 16.20:

The Slider project in SelectRange mode

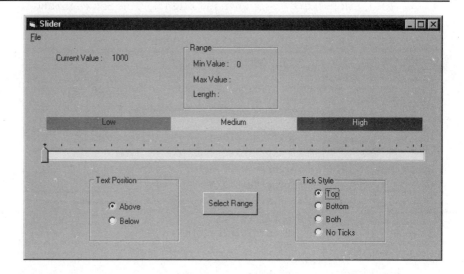

5. Select the options in the Text Position frame and move the slider. Notice that the ToolTips are displayed either above or below the slider knob.

6. Select the options in the Text Position frame to adjust the Ticks.

Well, that's about all there is to the Slider control. Not very difficult, but a great tool with which you can set values and limits in your applications.

The ProgressBar Control

The ProgressBar control (shown in Figure 16.21) shows the progress of a lengthy operation by filling a rectangle from left to right. The ProgressBar can fill in the rectangle with chunks, the default, or with a smoother movement by setting the Scrolling property at run time or design time. A ProgressBar control allows your application to graphically represent the progress of an operation, such as:

•   Copying or transferring a file

•   Sorting a huge database

- Loading a long or complex array or collection with data
- Performing any task that takes more than a few seconds

FIGURE 16.21:

A ProgressBar control

If users have no indication that an operation is taking place, they may assume that the application has stopped responding. Also, when users get feedback, they feel that the operation is taking less time than it actually is. The ProgressBar is a great tool to use for that reason.

The Value property determines how much of the control has been filled, and the Min and Max properties set the minimum and maximum points.

Setting the Value Property and Min and Max Properties to Show Progress

To show the progress of a lengthy operation, the Value property is continually increased until the value in the Max property is met. The number of blocks displayed in the ProgressBar control is a ratio of the Value property to the Min and Max properties. You can use Code 16.40 to display a ProgressBar and show the progress.

Code 16.40   The ProgressBar

```
Private Sub Command1_Click()
    On Error Resume Next
    Dim Progress As Integer

    Dim TestArray(2250) As String
    ProgressBar1.Min = LBound(TestArray)
    ProgressBar1.Max = UBound(TestArray)
    ProgressBar1.Visible = True

    'Set the Progress's Value to Min.
    ProgressBar1.Value = ProgressBar1.Min
```

```
'Loop through the array.
For Progress = LBound(TestArray) To UBound(TestArray)
    'Set initial values for each item in the array.
    'Workarea(Counter) = "Initial value" & Counter
    ProgressBar1.Value = Progress
Next Progress
ProgressBar1.Visible = False
ProgressBar1.Value = ProgressBar1.Min
End Sub
```

The ProgressBar Project

We will use the ProgressBar project (shown in Figure 16.22) to demonstrate the use of the ProgressBar control.

FIGURE 16.22:

The ProgressBar project

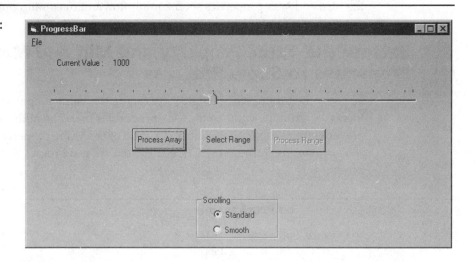

NOTE   You'll find the ProgressBar project in the `Chapter16\ProgressBar` folder on the CD that comes with this book.

This project consists of one Form, a Slider control to set the Max value of the ProgressBar, and a ProgressBar control. (See the previous section, "The Slider Project," for a complete discussion of the Slider control.)

There is also a label to show the value of the Slider control. One command button is provided to start the ProgressBar. The ProgressBar control notifies you of the progress as a counter advances from zero to the value of the Slider control.

The ProgressBar Code

Let's take a look at the code used to actually start the ProgressBar and give users some feedback about the status of an operation.

Moving the ProgressBar

The *Counter* variable is set to the Slider's Value property. The Min property is set to zero, and the Max property is set to the value of the Slider control. The counter starts at the Min value and counts by one until it reaches the Max. As the counter advances, the ProgressBar is set to the value of the counter, as shown in Code 16.41.

Code 16.41   **Setting ProgressBar Values**

```
Private Sub Command1_Click()
    On Error Resume Next

    Dim Counter As Integer

    ProgressBar1.Min = 0
    ProgressBar1.Max = Slider1.Value
    ProgressBar1.Visible = True

    'Set the Progress's Value to Min.
    ProgressBar1.Value = ProgressBar1.Min

    'Loop until Slider1.Value is met
    For Counter = Slider1.Min To Slider1.Value
        ProgressBar1.Value = Counter
    Next Counter

    ProgressBar1.Visible = False
    ProgressBar1.Value = ProgressBar1.Min
End Sub
```

As you can see, the ProgressBar control is not a difficult control to program, and it helps provide the user with feedback that draws attention away from what might be a lengthier-than-usual operation.

Testing the ProgressBar Project

To test the ProgressBar project, follow these steps:

1. Press F5 to start the project.

2. Move the Slider knob to the right.

3. Click the Process Array button.

4. Select the options in the Scrolling Frame to select the type of scrolling, either in chunks or smooth.

The ProgressBar has become a staple in the developer's bag of tools. Almost every application that performs an operation that takes more than a couple of seconds calls on the ProgressBar control to keep users informed of the progress. It does not require a lot of code, and the return is an informed user.

The TreeView and ListView Controls

A TreeView control displays a hierarchical list of Node objects, each of which consists of a label and an optional bitmap. A TreeView typically displays any information that might benefit from a hierarchical arrangement, for example:

*   The headings in a document

*   The entries in an index

*   The files and directories on a disk

The left side of the Windows Explorer (File Manager) and the Windows Registry Editor are examples of the TreeView control.

The ListView control displays items using one of four views:

*   In Icon view, which is the default, each ListItem object is represented by a full-sized icon and a text label.

*   In SmallIcon view, small icons represent the ListItems, and a text label appears to the right of each icon. Each ListItem appears horizontally.

- In List view, small icons represent the ListItems, and a text label appears to the right of the icon. Each ListItem appears vertically and on its own line with information arranged in columns.

- In Report view, each ListItem is displayed with its small icons and text labels. Additional information can be added in columns with optional column headings.

The right side of the Windows Explorer (File Manager) and the Windows Registry Editor are examples of the ListView control.

The TreeView control is often used with the ListView control. The combination allows the end user to look through several hierarchical layers, with the TreeView displaying the larger structure and the ListView displaying the individual sets of records as each Node object is selected, as shown in Figure 16.23.

FIGURE 16.23:

TreeView and ListView controls

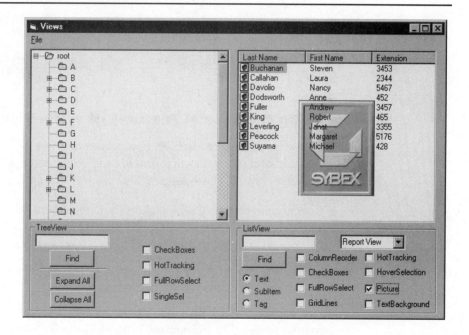

Let's take a look at the individual controls before we examine them together in a project.

The TreeView Control

The TreeView control (shown in Figure 16.24) is designed to display data that is hierarchical in nature, such as lists of names, database records, or a phone list. A tree is composed of cascading branches of "nodes" that can consist of images, set with an ImageList, and text.

FIGURE 16.24:

A TreeView control

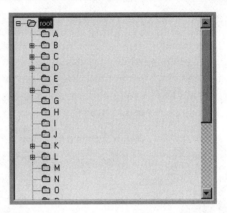

Examining the Special Features of a TreeView Control

In addition to the regular features and properties of a TreeView control, there are several features and properties that provide a special operation and appearance to the TreeView control. These features and properties include:

Checkboxes property, which allows you to add checkboxes to the items in a TreeView list. When this property is set to True, the NodeCheck event will be fired when the user checks a checkbox next to a node.

FullRowSelect property, which instructs the TreeView control to select the entire row when any part of the row is selected.

HotTracking, which provides feedback to the user when the mouse pointer passes over the control. With HotTracking set to True, the control responds to mouse movement by highlighting the header over which the mouse pointer is positioned. HotTracking gives the TreeView control the look and feel of the Internet.

SingleSel property, which instructs the TreeView control to collapse the previously selected item and expand the currently selected item.

NOTE   These features and properties are explored in the List Project shown later in this chapter.

Associating an ImageList Control with the TreeView Control

To identify a Node, you can assign an image from the ImageList control to the TreeView control. First, associate the ImageList control with the TreeView control. You can do so at design time or at run time. Follow these steps:

1. Populate the ImageList control with images.

2. Right-click the TreeView control, and choose Properties to open the TabStrip Property Pages.

3. On the General tab, select the ImageList control from the ImageList box.

To associate an ImageList control with a TreeView control at run time, set the ImageList property to the ImageList control, as shown in Code16.42.

Code 16.42   **Associating an ImageList with a TreeView Control at Run Time**

```
Private Sub Form_Load()
        TreeView1.ImageList = ImageList1
End Sub
```

All about Nodes

As we have already discussed, a tree is composed of cascading branches of "nodes" that can consist of images, set with an ImageList and text. These nodes belong to the Nodes collection. After you create a TreeView control, you can add, remove, rearrange, expand, collapse, and manipulate nodes in code.

Adding Node Objects to the Nodes Collection

To add a node to the tree, you can use the Add method, whose syntax is:

```
object.Add(relative, relationship, key, text, image, selectedimage)
```

The Add method can take the arguments shown in Table 16.12.

TABLE 16.12: The Arguments of the Add Method (Nodes Collection)

Argument	Description
object	Required. An object expression that evaluates to an object in the Applies To list.
relative	Optional. The index number or key of a preexisting Node object. The relationship between the new node and this preexisting node is found in the relationship argument.
relationship	Optional. Specifies the relative placement of the node object, as described in Settings.
key	Optional. A unique string that can be used to retrieve the Node with the Item method.
text	Required. The string that appears in the node.
image	Optional. The index of an image in an associated ImageList control.
selectedimage	Optional. The index of an image in an associated ImageList control that is shown when the node is selected.

Table 16.13 shows the settings for node relationships.

TABLE 16.13: The Node Relationship Settings for the Add Method

Constant	Value	Description
tvwFirst	0	First. The node is placed before all other nodes at the same level of the node named in relative.
tvwLast	1	Last. The node is placed after all other nodes at the same level of the node named in relative. Any node added subsequently may be placed after one added as Last.
tvwNext	2	(Default) Next. The node is placed after the node named in relative.
tvwPrevious	3	Previous. The node is placed before the node named in relative.
tvwChild	4	Child. The node becomes a child node of the node named in relative.

Because the Add method returns a reference to the newly created Node object, it is most convenient to set properties of the new node using this reference. Code 16.43 can be used to add nodes to the Nodes collection at run time.

Code 16.43   Adding Nodes

```
Private Sub Form_Load()

    'Declare the Node object
    Dim nodX As Node

    'Add Root Node object
    Set nodX = TreeView1.Nodes.Add(, 4, , "root", "closed")
    'Add an A, child node
    Set nodX = TreeView1.Nodes.Add(1, tvwChild, , "A", "closed")
    'Set the Enabled property
    nodex.Enabled = True
End Sub
```

This code adds a Root node and an "A" child node under the Root and sets the Enabled property of the child node to True.

Another Way to Add Nodes

You can also add nodes using the Set statement with the Add method. The Set statement sets the object variable to the new node as shown in Code 16.44. After the Set statement is used, other properties can be set.

Code 16.44   Using "Set" and "Add" to Add a Node

```
Private Sub Command5_Click()
    Dim nodex As Node
    Set nodX = TreeView1.Nodes.Add("1 node", tvwChild)
    nodX.Key = "New Node"
    nodX.Tesx = "Added Node"
    nodX.Image = "Closed"
End Sub
```

Node Relationships

Each node can be either a parent or a child, depending on its relationship with other nodes. If a node has child nodes, it can be expanded or collapsed. A tree can have any number of child nodes, but there can be only one Root node. You can use Code 16.45 to expand all the nodes of a TreeView control.

Code 16.45   **Expanding Nodes**

```
Private Sub Command4_Click()
    Dim i As Integer

    For i = 1 To TreeView1.Nodes.Count - 1
        TreeView1.Nodes(i).Expanded = True
    Next
End Sub
```

As you can see, we loop through all the nodes and set the Expand property to True. This causes the nodes to expand as shown in Figure 16.25.

FIGURE 16.25:

A TreeView control with collapsed and expanded nodes

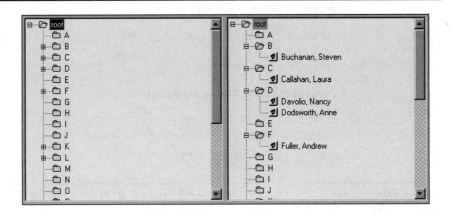

To collapse nodes, you use code that loops through the nodes and sets the Expand property to False, as shown in Code 16.46:

Code 16.46   **Collapsing All Nodes**

```
Private Sub Command2_Click()
    Dim i As Integer

    For i = 1 To TreeView1.Nodes.Count - 1
        TreeView1.Nodes(i).Expanded = False
    Next

End Sub
```

Finding Items in a TreeView Control

The TreeView control does not have a defined Find method, so we're on our own. To find a specific item in a node, you can loop through the nodes and compare the node text to a text string. Code 16.47 shows one way to accomplish this. Here are the steps:

1. Loop through the nodes one by one.

2. When you find the string, use the EnsureVisible method to scroll the tree to the node that has the string you want.

3. Set the Selected property to True to highlight the text.

TIP

When you use this type of find method, which is one in which you compare one text value to another text value, the comparisons are case sensitive. To set the VB application to case insensitive, use the Option Compare Text statement in the General Declaration section. When you add the Option Compare Text statement to the Declarations section of a module, Visual Basic compares the two strings on a case-insensitive basis.

Code 16.47   Finding a String in a TreeView Control

```
Private Sub Command1_Click()
    Dim i As Integer
    For i = 1 To TreeView1.Nodes.Count - 1
        If TreeView1.Nodes(i).Text = Text1.Text Then
            TreeView1.Nodes(i).EnsureVisible
            TreeView1.Nodes(i).Selected = True
            Exit Sub
        End If
    Next
    MsgBox "No match found"
End Sub
```

You can use this procedure to find text in any node on the tree.

Now that you understand the TreeView control and some basic Node fundamentals, let's take a look at the ListView control. We'll then pull it all together in a sample project.

The ListView Control

The ListView control (shown in Figure 16.26) displays data as ListItem objects. Each ListItem object can have an associated icon. The control is best at displaying items of data, such as database records, lists, and indexes.

FIGURE 16.26:

The ListView control

Last Name	First Name	Extension
Buchanan	Steven	3453
Callahan	Laura	2344
Davolio	Nancy	5467
Dodsworth	Anne	452
Fuller	Andrew	3457
King	Robert	465
Leverling	Janet	3355
Peacock	Margaret	5176
Suyama	Michael	428

Examining the Special Features of a ListView Control

In addition to the regular features and properties of a ListView control, there are several features and properties that provide a special operation and appearance to the control. These features and properties include:

AllowColumnReorder property, which determines if the columns of the ListView can be reordered by the user using the mouse.

Checkboxes property, which allows you to add checkboxes to the items in a ListView list. When this property is set to True, the ItemCheck event will be fired when the user checks a checkbox next to an item.

FullRowSelect property, which instructs the ListView control to select the entire row when any part of the row is selected.

GridLines property, which determines if the ListView control, in Report view, displays gridlines.

HotTracking property, which provides feedback to the user when the mouse pointer passes over the control. With HotTracking set to True, the control responds to mouse movement by highlighting the header over which the mouse pointer is positioned. HotTracking gives the ListView control the look and feel of the Internet.

HoverSelection property, which determines if a ListItem object is selected when the mouse pointer hovers over it.

Picture property, which sets a graphic to be displayed in the ListView control. You can load the graphic from the Properties window at design time. At run time, you can also set this property using the LoadPicture function on a bitmap, icon, or metafile. When setting the Picture property at design time, the graphic is saved and loaded with the form. If you create an executable file, the file contains the image. When you load a graphic at run time, the graphic isn't saved with the application. Use the SavePicture statement to save a graphic from a form or picture box into a file.

TextBackground property, which determines if a ListItem object's text background is opaque or transparent. The rectangular field which surrounds the ListItem object's text is the text background. The TextBackground property is used when the ListView control displays a picture (by assigning a picture to the Picture property). When a ListItem object is positioned over the picture and the property is set to transparent, the background picture will be visible behind the text. If the TextBackground property is set to opaque, the picture will not show through the text background.

NOTE   These special features and properties of the ListView control will be explored in the List project, shown later in this chapter.

Views

The ListView control can display data in different views, as listed in Table 16.14. Each view has its advantages and is suited for different data.

TABLE 16.14: Views of the ListView Control

Constant	Value	Description
lvwIcon	0	(Default) Icon. Each ListItem object is represented by a full-sized icon and text.
lvwSmallIcon	1	SmallIcon. Each ListItem is represented by a small icon that appears to the right of the item. The items appear horizontally.

Continued on next page

TABLE 16.14 CONTINUED: Views of the ListView Control

Constant	Value	Description
lvwList	2	List. Each ListItem is represented by a small icon and text that appears to the right of the icon. Each ListItem appears vertically and on its own line with information arranged in columns.
lvwReport	3	Report. Each ListItem is displayed with its small icons and text. The icons, text labels, and information appear in columns, with the left-most column containing the small icon, followed by the text. Additional columns display the text for each of the item's subitems.

Figures 16.27, 16.28, 16.29, and 16.30 show the ListView views.

FIGURE 16.27:

The ListView Icon view

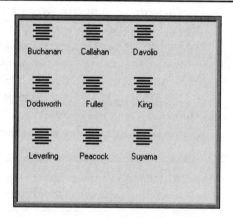

FIGURE 16.28:

The ListView Small Icon view

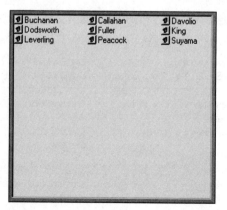

FIGURE 16.29:

The ListView List view

FIGURE 16.30:

The ListView Report Icon view

Associating an ImageList with the ListView Control

The ListView control, unlike other controls, can use two ImageList controls:

- A ListItem object, which consists of a label and an optional image supplied by an ImageList

- The ImageList control, which is associated to the ListView with the Icon, SmallIcon, and ColumnHeader Icon properties

In the List, SmallIcon, and Report views, you can use a small icon as an image for the ListItem object. You can associate the ImageList control at run time or at design time.

ImageList and the List, SmallIcon, and Report Views   To associate an ImageList control with a ListView control in the List, SmallIcon, or Report view at design time, follow these steps:

1.   Populate the ImageList control with images.

2.   Right-click the ListView control, and choose Properties to open the ListView Property Pages:

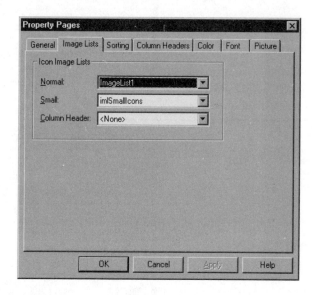

3.   In the Image Lists tab, select the ImageList control from the Small ImageList box.

To associate an ImageList control with a ListView control at run time, as shown in Code 16.48, set the SmallIcons property to the ImageList control.

Code 16.48   **Associating an ImageList at Run Time**

```
Private Sub Form_Load()
    ListView1.SmallIcons = ImageListSmall
End Sub
```

ImageList and the Icon View   When the ListView control is in the Icon view, it uses a different set of images supplied by a second ImageList control. You can set the ImageList control at design time by following the procedure discussed earlier and choose the images from the Normal Icon Image List list box or at run time with the Code 16.49.

Code 16.49   **Associating a Second ImageList at Run Time**

```
Private Sub Form_Load()
    ListView1.Icons = ImageListIcons
End Sub
```

The Report View Has Column Headers

As an added feature, the Report view has the ability to display column headers, as shown in Figure 16.31.

FIGURE 16.31:

The ListView control column headers

Last Name	First Name	Extension
Buchanan	Steven	3453
Callahan	Laura	2344
Davolio	Nancy	5467

The control contains a ColumnHeader object. There is always one column in the ListView control, which is Column 1. This column contains the ListItem objects. The other columns contain subitems. You can add ColumnHeaders with the Add method, as shown in Code 16.50.

Code 16.50   **Adding ColumnHeaders to a ListView Control**

```
Private Sub Command5_Click()
    'Create an object variable for the ColumnHeader object
    Dim clmX As ColumnHeader
    'Add ColumnHeaders. The width of the columns
    'is the width of the control divided by the
    'number of ColumnHeader objects
    Set clmX = ListView1.ColumnHeaders. _
        Add(, , "Last Name", ListView1.Width / 3)
    Set clmX = ListView1.ColumnHeaders. _
        Add(, , "First Name", ListView1.Width / 3)
    Set clmX = ListView1.ColumnHeaders. _
        Add(, , "Extension", ListView1.Width / 3)
End Sub
```

Here, we declare a ColumnHeader object and then use the Add method to add three ColumnHeaders.

SubItems

In all the list views, except the Report view, the ListItem object displays only one label. In the Report view, ListItems can have any number of other text items.

The number of ColumnHeader objects determines the number of subitems each ListItem object in the control can have, and the number of subitems is always one less than the number of ColumnHeader objects. When you delete a ColumnHeader object, all subitems associated with the column are also deleted. Each ListItem object's subitem array shifts to update the indices of the ColumnHeader, causing the remaining column headers' SubItemIndex properties to change. Subitems are arrays of strings representing the ListItem object's data that are displayed in Report view. For example, in Figure 16.30, shown earlier, First Name and Extension are subitems.

A ListItem object can have any number of associated item data strings (subitems), but each ListItem object must have the same number of subitems.

Corresponding column headers are defined for each subitem.

You cannot add elements directly to the subitems array. Use the Add method of the ColumnHeaders collection to add subitems, as shown in Code 16.51.

Code 16.51   **Adding SubItems to a ListView Control**

```
Private Sub Command5_Click()
    Dim itmX As ListItem
    'Use the Add method to add a new ListItem
    'and set an object variable to the new _
    'reference
    'Use the reference to set properties
    Set itmX = ListView1.ListItems.Add(, , "Buchanan")
    intCount = intCount + 1
    itmX.Tag = intCount

    'Set SubItem 1 to FirstName
    itmX.SubItems(1) = "Steven"

    'Set SubItem 2 to Extension
    itmX.SubItems(2) = "3453"

End Sub
```

This code declares a ListItem object and then adds a ListItem object and two subitems.

Finding Items in a ListView Control

Another nice feature of the ListView control is the FindItem method. The FindItem method finds and returns a reference to a ListItem object in a ListView control. Once the item is found, you can use the EnsureVisible method to scroll the found item into view. The syntax for the FindItem method is:

```
object.FindItem (string, value, index, match)
```

The FindItem method syntax has the parts shown in Table 16.15, the values shown in Table 16.16, and the match settings shown in Table 16.17.

TABLE 16.15: The Parts of the FindItem Method

Part	Description
object	Required. An object expression that evaluates to a ListView control.
string	Required. A string expression indicating the ListItem object to be found.
value	Optional. An integer or a constant specifying whether the string will be matched to the ListItem object's Text, Subitems, or Tag property, as described in Settings.
index	Optional. An integer or a string that uniquely identifies a member of an object collection and specifies the location from which to begin the search. The integer is the value of the Index property; the string is the value of the Key property. If no index is specified, the default is 1.
match	Optional. An integer or a constant specifying that a match will occur if the item's Text property is the same as the string, as described in Table 16.16.

TABLE 16.16: The FindItem Settings

Constant	Value	Description
lvwText	0	(Default) Matches the string with a ListItem object's Text property.
lvwSubitem	1	Matches the string with any string in a ListItem object's SubItems property.
lvwTag	2	Matches the string with any ListItem object's Tag property.

TABLE 16.17: The FindItem Match Settings

Constant	Value	Description
lvwWholeWord	0	(Default) An integer or a constant specifying that a match will occur if the item's Text property begins with the whole word being searched. Ignored if the criterion is not text.
lvwPartial	1	An integer or a constant specifying that a match will occur if the item's Text property begins with the string being searched. Ignored if the criterion is not text.

Code 16.52 demonstrates how you can use the FindItem and the EnsureVisible methods to locate an item. Here are the steps:

1. Create a reference to hold the found item.

2. Use the FindItem method to find the requested item.

3. Use the EnsureVisibility method to scroll the ListView control so that the item is in view.

Code 16.52   **Finding an Item in the ListView Control**

```
Private Sub Command5_Click()

    'FindItem method returns a reference to the found item, so
    'you must create an object variable and set the found item
    'to it

    ' FoundItem variable
    Dim itmFound As ListItem

    Set itmFound = ListView1. _
    FindItem("Steven", lvwText, , lvwPartial)

    'Scroll ListView to show found ListItem.
    itmFound.EnsureVisible
    itmFound.Selected = True
    'Return focus to the control to see selection.
    ListView1.SetFocus
    End If
End Sub
```

The List Project

As you can see from the sections on the TreeView and ListView controls, you can use these controls to present all sorts of data to users in ways that make it easy to view, select, and find just the right data when it is needed. The List project (shown in Figure 16.32) uses the TreeView and ListView controls to display the Employee's table from the NWIND sample database.

NOTE   You'll find the List project in the `Chapter16Code\List` folder on the CD that comes with this book. The NWIND sample database comes with Visual Basic and is installed by default in the main Visual Basic directory.

FIGURE 16.32:

The List project

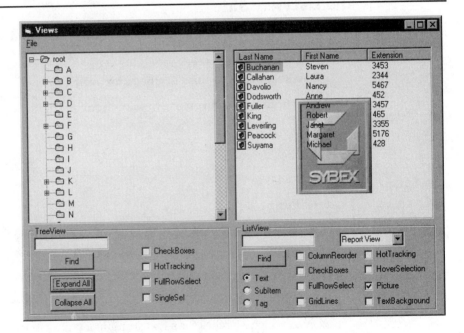

The TreeView Side

The TreeView control is on the left side of the List Form and has a text box in which you can enter a text string. It has three command buttons:

Find searches through the nodes of the TreeView control for a string value. If it is found, it is selected, and the EnsureVisibility method is used to expand the node and scroll it into view.

Expand All expands all nodes in the TreeView control.

Collapse All collapses all nodes in the TreeView control.

Also included are checkboxes to control the special features discussed earlier in this chapter. They are:

- CheckBoxes, which displays or hides the Node's checkboxes

- HotTracking, which turns HotTracking on or off

- FullRowSelect, which controls the row selection

- SingleSel, which determines if a previous selection is hidden

The ListView Side

The ListView control is on the right side of the List Form and has the following controls:

TextBox, which you use to enter a text string to find.

ComboBox, which you use to select from one of the four available views:

- Icon

- SmallIcon

- List

- Report

FindButton, which searches the ListView control for a text string, subitem, or tag as selected by one of three option buttons:

Text, which searches for a text string in the ListItem.

SubItem, which searches for a text string in a subitem.

Tag, which searches for a text string in a tag.

Checkboxes, which control the special features and properties introduced earlier in this chapter. They are:

- ColumnReorder property, which toggles whether the user can reorder the columns

- Checkboxes, which determines if checkboxes are displayed next to the ListItems

- FullRowSelect, which sets if an entire row is selected

- GridLines, which controls the gridline display

- HotTracking, which turns HotTracking on or off

- HoverSelection, which determines if the cursor highlights the selected item

- Picture, which lets you decide whether or not to display a picture in the control

- TextBackground, which toggles the background of the text objects from opaque to transparent

Filling the Controls

The FillList subroutine populates the TreeView and ListView controls with data. A Data control is used to create a recordset of the records from the Employee table in the NWIND sample database. After the records are retrieved, the column headings for the Report view of the ListView are set with the ColumnHeaders property. To ensure a clean start, the controls are cleared with the Clear method and the LineStyle property is set to trwRootLines. Table 16.18 shows the settings for the LineStyle property.

TABLE 16.18:   The Values for the LineStyle Property

Constant	Value	Description
tvwTreeLines	0	(Default) Tree lines. Displays lines between node siblings and their parent node.
tvwRootLines	1	Root lines. In addition to displaying lines between node siblings and their parent node, also displays lines between the root nodes.

Now that everything is set up, we use a For loop to add the data. A loop is set up to add the letters of the alphabet from A to Z in the TreeView control. The Index and Tag properties are set also.

NOTE   We store the index of the current node. This is used later in the program to ensure that the detail names fall under the parent node that is set to the letters A–Z.

Each iteration of the loop checks for any employee records that have the same first letter of the last name as the current node letter. If one is found, it is added to the TreeView node and to the ListView ListItem, as shown in Code 16.53.

Code 16.53	**Filling the List and Tree Views with Records**

```
Public Sub FillLists()

    On Error GoTo ErrorRoutineErr
    Dim nodX As Node
    Dim i As Integer
    Dim intIndex
    Dim gRs As Recordset
    'Create an object variable for the ListItem object
    Dim itmX As ListItem
    Dim intCount As Integer
    'Create an object variable for the ColumnHeader object
    Dim clmX As ColumnHeader

    Data1.RecordSource = _
        "Select * from Employees order by lastname;"
    Data1.Refresh
    Set gRs = Data1.Recordset

    'Add ColumnHeaders. The width of the columns
    'Is the width of the control divided by the
    'Number of ColumnHeader objects
    Set clmX = ListView1.ColumnHeaders. _
        Add(, , "Last Name", ListView1.Width / 3)
    Set clmX = ListView1.ColumnHeaders. _
        Add(, , "First Name", ListView1.Width / 3)
    Set clmX = ListView1.ColumnHeaders. _
        Add(, , "Extension", ListView1.Width / 3)

    'Set BorderStyle property
    ListView1.BorderStyle = ccFixedSingle

    'Clear the views
    TreeView1.Nodes.Clear
    ListView1.ListItems.Clear

    'Set TreeView control properties
    TreeView1.LineStyle = tvwRootLines   ' Linestyle 1
```

```
'Add Node objects.
Set nodX = TreeView1.Nodes.Add(, 4, , "root", "closed")

'Fill top level A-Z of the treeview
For i = 0 To 25
    Set nodX = TreeView1.Nodes.Add _
        (1, tvwChild, , Chr(65 + i), "closed")
    'Set the tag property of the main nodes
    nodX.Tag = "Name"
    'Set index to current node
    intIndex = nodX.Index
    'Add Names
    Do While Not gRs.EOF
            If UCase(Left(gRs!LastName, 1)) = _
            Chr$(65 + i) Then '
            Set nodX = TreeView1.Nodes.Add _
                (intIndex, tvwChild, , gRs!LastName + _
                ", " + gRs!FirstName, "word")

                'Use the Add method to add a new ListItem
                'And set an object variable to the new _
                'Reference
                'Use the reference to set properties
                Set itmX = ListView1.ListItems.Add _
                    (, , CStr(gRs!LastName))
                intCount = intCount + 1
                itmX.Tag = intCount

                'If the FirstName field is not Null,
                'Set SubItem 1 to FirstName
                If Not IsNull(gRs!FirstName) Then
                    itmX.SubItems(1) = CStr(gRs!FirstName)
                End If
                itmX.SmallIcon = "word"
                itmX.Icon = "center"

                'If the Extension field is not Null,
                'Set SubItem 2 to Extension
                If Not IsNull(gRs!Extension) Then
                    itmX.SubItems(2) = gRs!Extension
                End If

                'Move to next record
                gRs.MoveNext
```

```
            Else
                Exit Do
            End If
        Loop
    Next i
    TreeView1.Nodes(1).Expanded = True
    'Set the ListView control to report view
    Combo1.ListIndex = 0
    ListView1.View = lvwReport

ErrorRoutineResume:
    Exit Sub
ErrorRoutineErr:
    If Err = 3021 Then
        Resume Next
    End If
    MsgBox Err & " " & Error
    Resume Next
End Sub
```

Finding a TreeView Record

The Command1_Click subroutine searches one by one through the nodes of the TreeView control, shown in Code 16.54, to find a match with the text entered in theText1 text box. If the text is found, the control is scrolled with the EnsureVisibility method and highlighted with the Selected property. If a match is not found, the user is notified with a message box.

Code 16.54   Performing a Tree Search

```
Private Sub Command1_Click()
    Dim i As Integer
    For i = 1 To TreeView1.Nodes.Count - 1
        If TreeView1.Nodes(i).Text = Text1.Text Then
            TreeView1.Nodes(i).EnsureVisible
            TreeView1.Nodes(i).Selected = True
            Exit Sub
        End If
    Next
    MsgBox "No match found"
End Sub
```

Expanding All the TreeView Nodes

In the Command4_Click subroutine, the Expanded property is set to True as we loop through the nodes of the TreeView control, expanding them as we go, as shown in Code 16.55.

Code 16.55   **Expand All the Nodes**

```
Private Sub Command4_Click()
    Dim i As Integer

    For i = 1 To TreeView1.Nodes.Count - 1
        TreeView1.Nodes(i).Expanded = True
    Next

End Sub
```

Collapsing All the TreeView Nodes

In the Command2 subroutine, the Expanded property is set to False as we loop through the nodes of the TreeView control, collapsing them as we go, as shown in Code 16.56.

Code 16.56   **Collapse All the Nodes**

```
Private Sub Command2_Click()
    Dim i As Integer

    For i = 1 To TreeView1.Nodes.Count - 1
        TreeView1.Nodes(i).Expanded = False
    Next

End Sub
```

Selecting a ListView View

As the Form is loaded, we populate the combo box with the four views of the ListView control. When you select a view from the combo box, the ListView property is set, as shown in Code 16.57.

Code 16.57   **Setting the Four Views**

```
Private Sub Form_Load()
    Data1.Refresh
    'Load the listview combo box
    With Combo1
        .AddItem "Icon View"        '0
        .AddItem "SmallIcon View"   '1
        .AddItem "List View"        '2
        .AddItem "Report View"      '3
        .ListIndex = 3
    End With
    Option1(0).Value = True

    Call FillLists
End Sub

Private Sub Combo1_Click()
    'LvwIcon = 0
    'LvwSmallIcon = 1
    'LvwList = 2
    'LvwReport = 3
    ListView1.View = Combo1.ListIndex
End Sub
```

Finding an Item in the ListView Control

The ListView control provides a handy FindItem method we can use to find a text string in the ListItem, a subitem, or the Tag.

Code 16.58 gets FindOption—either the ListItem, subitem, or Tag—from the option buttons. It calls the FindItem method with the string from the text box, and it calls FindOption from the option buttons. If the find is successful, the EnsureVisibility method is used to scroll to the item, and the selected property is set to True to highlight the item.

Code 16.58   **Finding a List Item**

```
Private Sub Command3_Click()
    Dim slFind As String
    Dim slFindOption As Integer
```

```
If Option1(0).Value = True Then
    slFind = txtListFind
    slFindOption = lvwText
End If
If Option1(1).Value = True Then
    slFind = txtListFind
    slFindOption = lvwSubItem
End If
If Option1(2).Value = True Then
    slFind = txtListFind
    slFindOption = lvwTag
End If

'FindItem method returns a reference to the found item, so
'you must create an object variable and set the found item
'to it
Dim itmFound As ListItem

Set itmFound = ListView1. _
FindItem(slFind, slFindOption, , lvwPartial)

'If no ListItem is found, then inform user and exit. If a
'ListItem is found,
'scroll the control using the EnsureVisible
'method, and select the ListItem
If itmFound Is Nothing Then
    MsgBox "No match found"
    Exit Sub
Else
    'Scroll ListView to show found ListItem
    itmFound.EnsureVisible
    'Select the ListItem
    itmFound.Selected = True
    'Set focus to the control to see selection.
    ListView1.SetFocus
End If
End Sub
```

The List project demonstrates the major functionality of the TreeView and ListView controls. Now, let's run the project and see it in action.

Testing the List Project

To test the List Project, follow these steps:

1. Start the project by pressing F5.

2. Click the Expand All and Collapse All buttons to see the TreeView nodes expand and collapse.

3. Press the Collapse All button to collapse the nodes.

4. Type **King, Robert** in the text box under the TreeView control, and click the Find button. The TreeView control will scroll, expand, and select the node "King, Robert."

5. Check and uncheck the checkboxes to change the appearance and functionality of the controls.

6. Click the different views in the combo box on the ListView side to see the views.

Next, let's test the Find option of the ListView.

1. Select the Report view.

2. Type **Fuller** in the text box, select the Text option button, and click the Find button. The ListView will highlight the Fuller record.

Now, let's test the SubItem find.

1. Click the SubItem option button.

2. Enter **Michael** in the text box, and click the Find button. The ListView highlights the last record. The ListItem, column1, is always selected regardless of the type of find performed.

Finally, let's test the Tag find option. The Tag property is set to the record number in the FillList subroutine.

1. Click the Tag option button.

2. Enter **4** in the text box, and click the Find button. The fourth record will be selected.

As you can see, the List controls are flexible and provide lots of options for the developer and the user. If your application needs to show data from a database, a list, an index, or most any kind of tabular data, the TreeView and ListView controls might be just what the user ordered.

The CoolBar Control

The CoolBar control (shown in Figure 16.33) allows you to create toolbars similar to those found in Microsoft Internet Explorer. The CoolBar control is a container control, able to host child controls. It consists of a collection of one or more resizable regions known as bands. Each band can host a single child control.

FIGURE 16.33:

The CoolBar Control

The CoolBar control is a container control that acts as a host for other controls. The main control that you will use with the CoolBar is a ToolBar control.

Working with Bands

A Band object represents an individual band in the Bands collection of the CoolBar control. A band is a region within a CoolBar control that can contain a single child control (such as a ToolBar or a Text Box), caption, and image. Each Band may be moved and resized independently by the user at run time.

At design time, use the Insert Band and Remove Band buttons on the Bands tab in the Properties Page of the CoolBar control to insert and remove Band objects from the Bands collection. At run time, you can add and remove Band objects by using the Add and Remove methods of the Bands collection.

Adding Controls to a CoolBar Control at Design Time

The method for adding child controls to a CoolBar control is slightly different than that of adding controls to other containers. The control must first be associated with a Band object; there is a limit of one child control per band. Follow these steps to add a control to a CoolBar:

1. With the CoolBar control selected, select a control from the ToolBox and draw it on the CoolBar.

2. Open the Property Page for the CoolBar and select the Bands tab.

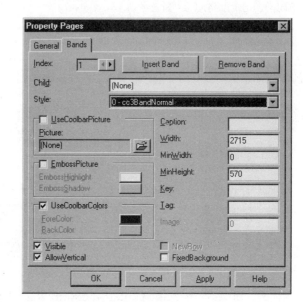

3. Use the Index button to select the index of the Band object on which you want the control to appear.

4. Select the control from the Child list. The child control will then move and resize with the Band object at run time.

NOTE
If you add a control without associating it to a band, it will appear as a floating control over the CoolBar at run time.

Adding Controls to a CoolBar Control at Run Time

Use the Add Method to add Band objects to the CoolBar control at run time. You can also add a control, such as a Text Box or Combo Box, to the Band at run time. The CoolBar control can only host controls that expose a Window handle. Lightweight controls, such as Label, Image, and Shape controls, do not expose a Window handle and cannot be used. Although you can place these controls on the CoolBar, they will not appear at run time and will not be listed in the Child list box on the Property Page.

NOTE
To assign a new child control to a band at run time, use the Set keyword. This will replace the existing control on the Band object.

Code 16.59 can be used to add a new Band object to a CoolBar and associates a Combo Box control to the new band.

Code 16.59	**Adding Bands at Run Time**

```
Private Sub cmdAddBand_Click()
    'Add a new band
    CoolBar1.Bands.Add 4, "History", "History", , True, cboHistory
End Sub
```

NOTE
To associate a Combo Box or other control to a Band object, the control must be drawn on the CoolBar control at design time. You can draw the controls that you will need and set their Visible property to False until they are used.

The CoolBar Project

The CoolBar project (shown in Figure 16.33, shown earlier) demonstrates how to incorporate a CoolBar into a project. The CoolBar project includes a CoolBar control with three bands. Two of the Bands have Toolbar controls as the Child control, and the third Band has a Text Box as the Child control. In addition, there is a command button and a Frame control that are used to demonstrate some of the CoolBars features.

The Add History Band command button is used to add or remove a History Band to the CoolBar. When you first click the button, a new History Band will be added to the CoolBar. The History Band has a Combo control as a Child control. When you click the button, the caption changes to "Remove History Button." Another click of the button will remove the History Band and change the caption back to "Add History Band."

The Button Captions Frame contains two Option Buttons that add and remove captions from the buttons on the main Toolbar.

FIGURE 16.34:

The CoolBar project

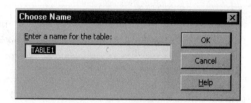

NOTE   You'll find the CoolBar project in the `Chapter16\CoolBar` folder on the CD that comes with this book.

Creating the CoolBar Project

As we have already discussed, a CoolBar control is a container control. To make the CoolBar useful, you must add Child controls to it. The most common Child controls for the CoolBar are Toolbars and Text Boxes. The CoolBar project uses one of each. Let's start with the CoolBar project.

1. Start a new project and add the Microsoft Windows Common Controls 6.0 and the Microsoft Windows Common Controls 3-6.0 components from the list of available Components.

2. To Form1, add a CoolBar control, a command button, a frame, and three ImageList Controls.

NOTE   By default, the CoolBar will be created with three Band objects. This will be the container control for the CoolBar project.

3. Draw a ToolBar control on top of the top Band of the CoolBar control. This will be the Main Toolbar.

4. Draw a Text Box control on top of the left Band on the second line of Bands.

5. Draw a Toolbar control on top of the third band.

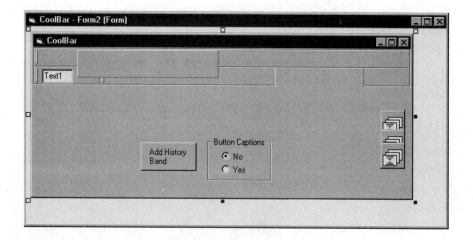

Adding Images to the ImageList Controls

The CoolBar project utilizes three ImageList controls to provide the following images:

> **ImageList1,** which provides the Images for Toolbar1
>
> **ImageList2,** which provides the HotImages for Toolbar1
>
> **ImageList3,** which provides the images for Toolbar2

Add the images from the Chapter16Code/CoolBar/Images folder to ImageList1.

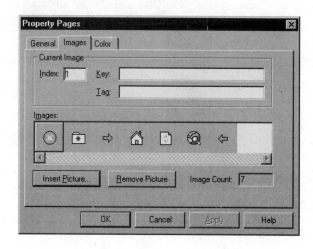

Add the images from the Chapter16Code/CoolBar/HotImages folder to ImageList2.

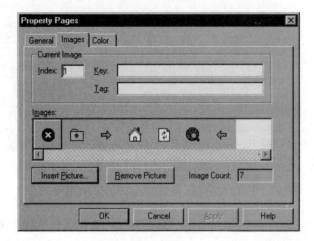

Add the images from the Chapter16Code/CoolBar/LinkImages folder to ImageList3.

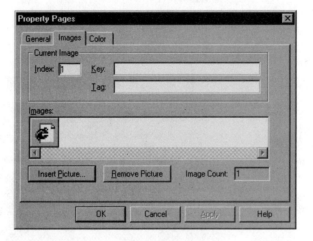

NOTE For detailed help on adding images to an ImageList control, see "The ImageList Control" section at the beginning of this chapter.

Adding Child Controls to the CoolBar Project

The next step in building the CoolBar project is to associate the Toolbars and Text Box controls as CoolBar Child controls.

1. Open the CoolBar property pages and select the Bands tab.

2. Select ToolBar1 from the list of available Child controls. This is the top Toolbar in the CoolBar project.

3. Click the Apply button.

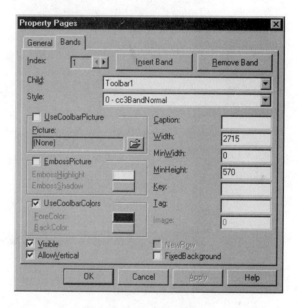

4. Click the Right Arrow by the Index to make Band 2 the current Band. This is the Band that will host the Text Box control.

5. Select Text1 from the list of available Child controls.

6. Set the Caption to "Address."

7. Set the Width to 4500.

8. Click the Apply button.

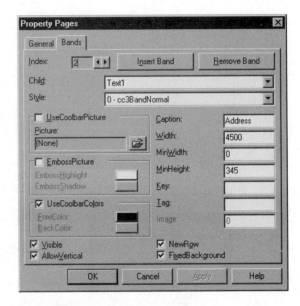

9. Click the Right Arrow by the Index to make Band 3 the current Band. This is the Band that will host the Link Toolbar.

10. Select ToolBar2 from the list of available Child controls.

11. Click the Apply button.

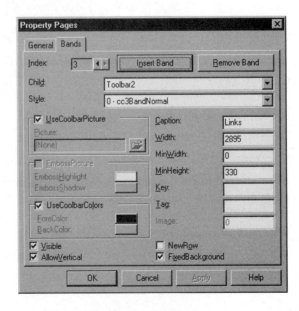

Draw a Combo Box control on the CoolBar. This will be used in the Add History Band command button.

Adding Buttons to the Toolbars

The next step in the process is to add buttons to the two Toolbar controls. Set the properties for Toolbar, as shown in Table 16.19.

TABLE 16.19: Toolbar1 Control Properties

Index	Key	Style	Image	DropDown Text	DropDown Key
1	Back	5-tbrDropDown	7	List Back History	Back
2	Forward	5-tbrDropDown	3	List Forward History	Forward
3		3-tbrSeparator			
4	Stop	0-tbrDefault	1		
5	Refresh	2-ButtonGroup	5		
6	Home	2-ButtonGroup	4		
7		3-tbrSeparator			
8	Search	0-tbrDefault	6		
9	Favorites	5-tbrDropDown	2	List Favorites	Favorites

Set the properties for Toolbar2 as shown in Table 16.20.

TABLE 16.20: Toolbar2 Control Properties

Index	Caption	Key	Style	Image
1	SYBEX	SYBEX	0-tbrDefault	1
2	Microsoft	Microsoft	0-tbrDefault	1

NOTE See The "SDI Toolbar Project section," earlier in this chapter, for a detailed discussion of Toolbars.

Adding a History Band

You can use the Add and Remove methods with the Band collection to add or remove Bands from the CoolBar control at run time. Code 16.60 demonstrates this process.

Code 16.60   **Adding a Band at Run Time**

```
Private Sub cmdAddBand_Click()
    Select Case cmdAddBand.Caption
        Case "Add History Band"
            'Add a new band
            CoolBar1.Bands.Add 4, "History", "History", , _
                True, cboHistory
            cmdAddBand.Caption = "Remove History Band"
            'Remove the History Band
        Case "Remove History Band"
            CoolBar1.Bands.Remove 4
            cmdAddBand.Caption = "Add History Band"
    End Select
End Sub
```

Examining the Add Bands Syntax   The syntax for the Add Bands method is:

```
object.Add ([index As Long], [key As String], [caption As String],
[image As Variant], [newrow As Boolean], [child As Object], [visible As
Boolean])
```

Table 16.21 details the parts of the Add Bands syntax.

TABLE 16.21: Parts of the Add Bands Syntax

Part	Description
object	An object expression that evaluates to the Bands collection of a CoolBar control.
index	Optional. A long integer that uniquely identifies a band within a Bands collection.
key	Optional. A unique string that identifies the Band object. Use this value to retrieve a specific Band object.
caption	Optional. A string containing the caption to be displayed on the band.

Continued on next page

TABLE 16.21 CONTINUED: Parts of the Add Bands Syntax

Part	Description
image	Optional. An integer or unique string specifying the ListImage object to use with object. The integer is the value of the Index property; the string is the value of the Key property.
newrow	Optional. Default = False. A Boolean expression specifying whether the new Band will be displayed in its own row.
child	Optional. An object reference specifying the control that will be a child of the band.
visible	Optional. Default = False. A Boolean expression specifying whether a new band will be visible at run time.

Displaying Button Captions

A popular option for buttons on the CoolBar is to offer captions for the buttons. Captions can be easily added to a Toolbar control by setting the Caption property. In addition to setting this property, you will need to adjust the height of the Toolbar and of the CoolBar Bands. The process of adding and removing button captions is shown in Code 16.61.

Code 16.61   Adding and Removing Button Captions

```
Private Sub Option1_Click(Index As Integer)

    Dim i As Integer

    'Add or remove button captions
    Select Case Index
        Case 0 'No
            Toolbar1.ButtonHeight = 590

            'Loop through the Buttons and
            'remove the captions
            For i = 1 To 9
                Toolbar1.Buttons(i).Caption = ""
            Next

            'Adjust the height of the CoolBar
            CoolBar1.Bands(1).MinHeight = 600
```

```
        Case 1 'Yes
            'Adjust the Toolbar height
            Toolbar1.ButtonHeight = 780

            'Set the Button captions
            Toolbar1.Buttons(1).Caption = "Back"
            Toolbar1.Buttons(2).Caption = "Forward"
            Toolbar1.Buttons(3).Caption = ""
            Toolbar1.Buttons(4).Caption = "Stop"
            Toolbar1.Buttons(5).Caption = "Refresh"
            Toolbar1.Buttons(6).Caption = "Home"
            Toolbar1.Buttons(7).Caption = ""
            Toolbar1.Buttons(8).Caption = "Search"
            Toolbar1.Buttons(9).Caption = "Favorites"


            'Adjust the CoolBar height
            CoolBar1.Bands(1).MinHeight = 790
    End Select
End Sub
```

The first part of the code removes the caption and resets the Toolbar and Cool-Bar Band heights.

The second part of the code sets the height of the Toolbar to 590, adds captions for the buttons, and then adjusts the size of the CoolBar Band object to compensate for the newly added caption.

Responding to Toolbar Buttons as They Are Clicked

When a user clicks a Toolbar button, they must process the code associated with the button. Code 16.62 shows the code necessary to respond to the Toolbar1 buttons.

Code 16.62   Responding to Toolbar Clicks

```
Private Sub Toolbar1_ButtonClick(ByVal Button _
    As ComctlLib.Button)
    On Error Resume Next
    Select Case Button.Key
        Case "Back"
            MsgBox "GoBack code goes here"
```

```
        Case "Forward"
            MsgBox "GoForward code goes here"
        Case "Stop"
            MsgBox "Stop code goes here"
        Case "Refresh"
            MsgBox "Refresh code goes here"
        Case "Home"
            MsgBox "Home code goes here"
        Case "Search"
            MsgBox "Search code goes here"
        Case "Favorites"
            MsgBox "Favorites code goes here"
    End Select
End Sub
```

Testing the CoolBar Project

Now that we have designed, built, and coded the CoolBar project, let's give it a try. Follow these steps to test the CoolBar project:

1. Press F5 to run the project.

2. Move your mouse over the Toolbar buttons and notice that the images change. These images are coming from ImageList2 or the HotImageList.

3. Click one of the buttons and a Message box will be displayed.

4. Click the Add History Band Command button to add a new Band to the CoolBar control.

5. Select the Yes option in the Button Caption Frame to add captions to the buttons on Toolbar1.

   The CoolBar control is the toolbar that is used in Internet Explorer. Adding it to your applications will give them an original Internet look and feel.

CHAPTER

SEVENTEEN

17

Optimizing VB Applications

- Understanding the Visual Basic compiler

- Optimizing Visual Basic code

- Optimizing graphics operations with API functions

- Building DLLs with Visual C++

- Understanding dynamic-link libraries

- Calculating fractals

- Calling DLL functions from Visual Basic

- Manipulating strings with Visual C++

Visual Basic is the most popular language for rapid application development, the simplest language to use, and in most respects as powerful as any other language, such as Visual C++. But Visual Basic also has limitations, some of which are inherent in the interpreted nature of the language and others which are simply part of the functionality supplied by VB. This is not to decry the value of Visual Basic, but simply to point out that in certain areas it is valuable to be able to extend or enhance the functionality of the language.

One of these areas is speed. Visual Basic relies on an interpreter, which generates p-code. P-code stands for pseudocode, a language designed to be machine independent yet easily mapped to processor commands. P-code is translated into executable statements by the Visual Basic run-time module.

> **NOTE**   You'll find detailed information on p-code in the section "What's P-Code?" later in this chapter.

Visual Basic 6 comes with a native code compiler, which can generate optimized code similar to the code produced by the VC++ compiler. It's not quite as efficient as the VC++ compiler yet, but it produces code that runs considerably faster than the equivalent p-code. Whether native code runs marginally or significantly faster than p-code depends on the application.

In this chapter, we are going to discuss the Visual Basic compiler, look at what the native code compiler can do for your applications, and give you a few tips on how to optimize math and string operations. Some applications just can't be made fast enough. You can use all the tricks in the book and still not be happy with their performance. A relatively simple method to speed VB applications is to call API functions instead of Visual Basic's built-in functions. (The API functions are discussed in detail in Chapter 14, "Visual Basic and the Windows API.") In this chapter, we'll demonstrate how to speed up graphics operations, which are inherently slow, using API functions. To stretch this limit, we'll show you how to implement computation-intensive procedures with Visual C++ and package them as DLLs. Although Visual Basic's native code compiler can improve performance over the interpreted code significantly, Visual C++ is even faster. How much faster depends on the type of processing. You'll see examples of both math and string operations in the following sections. But first, let's see how to optimize VB code and how to get the most out of the Visual Basic compiler.

The Visual Basic Compiler

Visual Basic comes with a true compiler that produces machine-specific code that the CPU can execute directly. These executable files are the same as those generated by the Visual C++ compiler or the Delphi compiler.

Up to version 5, Visual Basic couldn't produce native code, only p-code. Even with Visual Basic 6, you're actually running p-code when you run a project in the IDE. Any project will run faster when it's compiled to native code and executed outside the Visual Basic IDE. To understand why native code performs better than p-code, you must first understand the nature of p-code and how Visual Basic uses it.

NOTE　　In short, p-code is what makes the environment of Visual Basic so popular and unique. Without p-code, you wouldn't be able to stop your applications, edit the code, and resume execution.

What's P-Code?

P-code is close to machine language, but it's not quite machine language; in other words, it can't be executed as is. It must be translated into commands for a specific processor. Whether you develop on a Pentium or a PowerPC, the p-code is the same. But before it can be executed on either processor, it must be translated into the target processor's command set. Moreover, this translation must take place while the application is running, which means that p-code will never be as fast as native code.

The text you enter in the Visual Basic editor is translated into p-code as you enter it. Each time you press Enter to move to the next line, the IDE translates the line you are leaving into p-code. All the syntax checking and color coding of the statements takes place after the line is translated into p-code—which explains why the current line isn't colored as you type.

To run p-code, Visual Basic uses a so-called execution engine: a DLL that translates p-code into machine-executable code, or native code. This is how your projects are executed in the Visual Basic IDE. To distribute the application, you can create an executable file that contains the p-code plus the execution engine. The EXE files produced by previous versions of Visual Basic were nothing more than p-code and the run-time DLL. That's why running an executable file outside the IDE wasn't any faster than running the application in the IDE.

NOTE
Visual Basic applications were always slower than other compiled applications. All benchmarks showed that languages such as Visual C++ and Delphi were consistently faster than Visual Basic. The reason is that every line of p-code must be translated into machine-specific instructions before it can be executed. This was the price we had to pay in exchange for an unmatched development environment in which we could edit, run, edit, and resume execution of the application.

The native code compiler, however, is similar to a traditional compiler, such as the one used by Visual C++. It produces processor-specific instructions that can be executed directly, without any additional translation. It's easy to understand why native code executes faster than p-code. You might actually expect a significant improvement over p-code, but Visual Basic's p-code is highly optimized. (It seems that Microsoft couldn't improve it any further, and the introduction of a native code compiler was inevitable.)

Another reason native code outperforms p-code is that the compiler can do global optimizations. P-code is generated on the fly, and it's executed one line at a time. The native code compiler can see the big picture (many lines of source code at once) and produce optimal executable code that takes into consideration the peculiarities and dependencies among multiple lines of code. A native code compiler for Visual Basic was long overdue, and we expect future versions of Visual Basic to produce executables that match the speed of executables generated by Visual C++ or Delphi.

Compiler Options

So, now that we have a native code compiler, which produces faster-running executables, you might think that we could just forget all about p-code. But the native code compiler doesn't come without a price. It produces longer files that take longer to load and, if you are distributing your software on the Internet, also take longer to download. If these restrictions don't apply to you, you can compile your applications to native code, see what difference the compiler makes, and then decide how to distribute them.

NOTE
Programmers who use Visual Basic to implement scientific and graphics algorithms, which benefit the most by the native code compiler, will be more than glad to exchange some disk space for performance.

Applications compiled to native code don't always run faster. Real-world business applications spend most of their time doing disk I/O, screen updates, and other tasks that you can't speed up from within your VB code. For example, when you call an API function, you're no longer in control. When the API function is executing, there's nothing you can do to improve its speed no matter how much you've optimized the rest of the code. In a way, this is a barrier you can't break, regardless of whether you compile to p-code or to native code.

To create the executable file, start Visual Basic (if necessary), and choose File ➤ Make *File.exe* (*File.exe* is the application's name). Before selecting this command, you must set certain compiler parameters in the Project Properties dialog box. Choose Project ➤ Project Properties to open it and then select the Compile tab, as shown in Figure 17.1.

FIGURE 17.1:

The Compile tab of the Project Properties dialog box

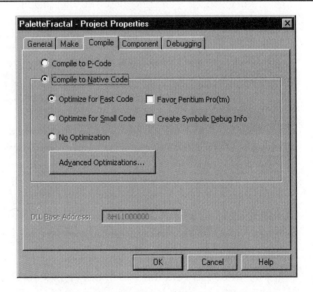

The type of executable that will be created depends on the settings you choose in the Compile tab of this dialog box:

Compile to P-Code compiles a project using p-code. The main benefit of p-code is that it's compact and (in many practical cases) not much slower than purely executable code.

Compile to Native Code compiles a project using native code, which is the machine language the CPU understands and executes.

NOTE

The generated executable created by selecting Compile to Native Code is faster than the equivalent p-code executable by as much as 2000 percent, according to Microsoft. Only applications designed to exploit the compiler will exhibit such behavior; we have witnessed improvements of no more than 100 percent, and in most cases less than that.

In the Fractals/Bench folder in this chapter's folder on the CD, you will find the Fractal application, which generates fractals such as those shown in Figure 17.2. We'll use this application to exercise the VB6 compiler. In the same folder, you will find three executable files: PCODEFractal.exe, VBFractal1.exe, and VBFractal2.exe.

NOTE

For instructions on using these two applications, see the next sidebar, "Having Fun with Fractals."

PCODEFractal.exe is a p-code executable. The other two files are native code executables, with different optimization settings (the VB6 compiler lets you specify various optimization settings, which are discussed in the section "Options for Optimizing Native Code," later in this chapter). The application is calculation intensive and was not designed to demonstrate the superiority of one type of code over the other. However, we expected to see a significant difference between p-code and native code for this type of application. If you run the PCODEFractal.exe and VBFractal2.exe (the fully optimized executable), you'll see that the native code executable is nearly three times faster than the p-code executable. This is not typical for all applications. Most of our applications run approximately 30 percent to 50 percent faster when compiled to native code.

The VBFractal2.exe file is 28KB, and the PCODEFractal.exe file is 20KB. Other applications can generate much larger executables, but p-code executables are consistently smaller than native code executables. However, we don't think the size of the executable is an important consideration, especially for an application such as a fractal generator.

In the Fractals folder on the CD you will find the DLLFractal subfolder, which contains a version of the Fractal application that uses a DLL written in Visual C++; it's considerably faster than the VB version of the application. If you want to use the faster version of the application, make sure that the FRACTAL.DLL file (in the same folder) has been copied to the Windows/System folder. The DLLFractal application uses FRACTAL.DLL and should be able to locate it on your hard disk.

FIGURE 17.2:

A fractal generator compiled in both native code and p-code demonstrates the differences between the two executables.

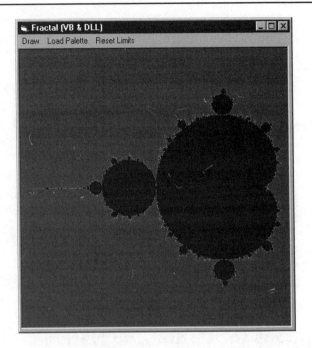

Having Fun with Fractals

The Fractal application displays the Mandelbrot set. The application uses palettes, and it may not work well (that is, it may not display the correct colors) on many true color systems. If your video board is set to display true color (16- or 24-bit color), change the color depth to 8 bits (256 colors). To change the palette, click Load Palette and select one of the palettes in the DIBS folder. If, instead of a colored fractal, the window of the Fractal application is filled with a solid color, select the Reset Limits command in the menu.

After displaying the entire Mandelbrot set by clicking the Draw menu command, you can zoom in to any area of the fractal image by drawing a rectangle with the mouse around the desired area. Click the upper-left corner of the desired area and, while holding the button down, drag the mouse to the lower-right corner of the selection and release the button. Then click the Draw command. If you get lost in the filaments of the Mandelbrot set, click Reset Limits to return to the original limits of the Mandelbrot set.

Continued on next page

You will notice that the Fractal application can't be stopped. To change this behavior, insert a DoEvents statement in the main loop of the program (we explain this later in the chapter). You can also capture keystrokes and end the drawing of the fractal when the Escape key is pressed. We didn't implement these features, because our primary goal is to compare the performance of the native code and p-code executables.

The Load Palette command lets you select the current palette by selecting a DIB file with a range of colors. The DIB files are stored in the DIBS folder in the application's folder. You can open these DIB files with any application that can manipulate palettes, such as BitEdit or PaintShop Pro, and adjust their contents or create new ones. Notice that the palette files contain smooth gradients (ranges of similar colors).

We have included two versions of the Fractal application on the CD. In the **Bench** folder, you will find the VB version of the application—which is slow, but you can easily adjust its code. In the **Palette** folder, you will find a version of the application that uses a DLL developed with Visual C++ and is significantly faster than the VB version of the application. The implementation of the DLL is discussed later in this chapter.

Options for Optimizing Native Code

The native code compiler must balance various and usually conflicting requirements. For example, it can't produce the most compact and most efficient code. The Compile to Native Code section of the Project Properties dialog box contains processor-specific optimizations and a number of advanced options that may or may not apply to your project. You specify the options that produce the type of executable that best matches your application and the target systems:

Optimize for Fast Code maximizes the speed of the executable file by instructing the compiler to favor speed over size. To optimize the code, the compiler can reduce many constructs to functionally similar sequences of machine code. This will inevitably increase the size of the executable file.

Optimize for Small Code minimizes the size of the executable file by instructing the compiler to favor size over speed.

No Optimization compiles without specific optimizations. It balances speed and size.

Favor Pentium Pro optimizes the code to favor the Pentium Pro processor. Use this option for programs meant only for the Pentium Pro. Code generated with this option will run on other Intel processors, but it will not perform as well.

Create Symbolic Debug Info generates symbolic debug information in the executable. An executable file created using this option can be debugged using Visual C++ or debuggers that use the CodeView style of debug information. Setting this option generates a PDB file with the symbol information for your executable. This option is most often used by Visual C++ programmers who also use Visual Basic.

Advanced Optimizations displays the Advanced Optimizations dialog box, which is shown in Figure 17.3. You use the options in this dialog box to turn off certain checks that normally take place and ensure that your application works properly. To increase the speed of the executable file, you can turn on some or all of these options by checking the appropriate checkbox.

WARNING Enabling the options in the Advanced Optimizations dialog box may prevent the correct execution of your program. You must understand what each option does and be sure that your application requires any of the options you turn on.

FIGURE 17.3:

The Advanced Optimizations dialog box

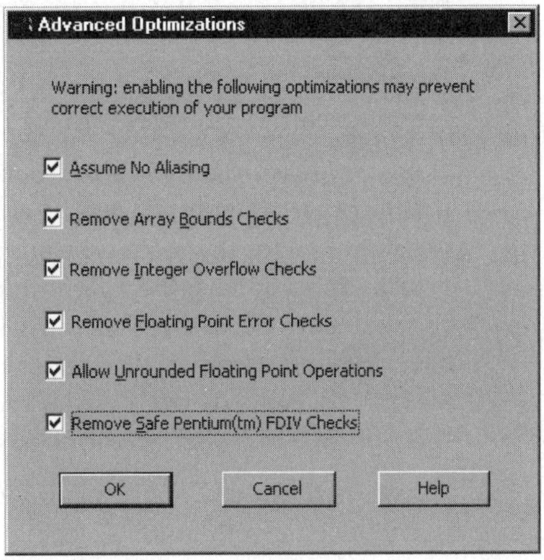

The following options from the Advanced Optimizations dialog box may be checked to ensure that your application works efficiently.

Assume No Aliasing tells the compiler that your program does not use aliasing. Aliasing is a technique that lets your code refer to the same variable (memory location) by more than one name. We don't use this technique (of dubious value, anyway) in this book, so you can safely turn on this option.

Remove Array Bound Checks looks for array bounds and speeds up applications that use arrays when checked. By default, Visual Basic checks an array's bounds every time your code accesses the array to determine if the index is within the range of the array. If the index is not within array bounds, a run-time error is generated (the out-of-bounds error), which can be trapped from within the code. However, the code that will ensure that the array's bounds are not exceeded may cost more in execution time. If an array bound is exceeded, the results will be unexpected. You can turn on this option if the application doesn't use arrays or if you know that your code will not attempt to access nonexisting array elements. For example, a loop that uses the LBound and UBound functions to scan the elements of an array will not cross the array's boundaries.

Remove Integer Overflow Checks looks for errors and speeds up integer calculations when checked. By default, Visual Basic checks every calculation for integer-style data types—Byte, Integer, and Long—to ensure that the value is within the range of the data type. If the magnitude of the value being put into the data type is incorrect, a run-time error is generated. If data-type capacities are overflowed, you will get incorrect results, but no errors. It's really difficult to make sure that calculations with integers do not result in overflows, and it's even trickier to find out where the overflow occurred. You must test your application thoroughly for numeric overflows before you turn on this option.

Remove Floating Point Error Checks examines every calculation of a floating-point data type—Single and Double—to be sure that the value is within range for that data type and that there is no division by zero or invalid operations. If the magnitude of the value being put into the data type is incorrect, an error occurs. Check this option to turn off the error checking and speed up floating-point calculations. If data-type capacities are overflowed, no error occurs, and you may get incorrect results. Avoid this optimization with scientific applications.

Allow Unrounded Floating Point Operations uses floating-point registers more efficiently, avoids storing and loading large volumes of data to and from memory, and does floating-point comparisons more efficiently (floating-point numbers are slightly truncated when moved from registers to memory).

Remove Safe Pentium FDIV Checks removes safety checking so that the code for floating-point division is faster. Checking this option may produce slightly incorrect results on Pentium processors with the FDIV bug. (The new Pentiums, 120MHz or faster, are exempt from the floating-point division flaw.)

This is how you can automatically speed up your application: by producing a native code executable. Unless the EXE is really large (and you plan to distribute it by means other than a CD), generate EXE files optimized for speed. However, a few bad coding techniques can easily offset any benefit introduced by the native code compiler. If your application calculates squares in a loop that's executed many times and you code it as $x \wedge 2$, no advanced optimization option is going to help your application. As you will see shortly, coding this operation as $x * x$ will make a p-code executable run faster than a native code executable that squares a variable with the statement $x \wedge 2$. The trick to writing fast-running applications is to start by optimizing the code itself. In the following sections, we are going to present a few useful optimization techniques. They are quite simple, but efficient. Even if you are an experienced VB programmer, you should take a look at the following pages. You may discover simple optimization tricks you are not familiar with.

Optimizing VB Code

Code optimization depends on the type of application you're writing. In most cases, you'll be optimizing small, tight sections of code that are executed frequently (such as loops or frequently called procedures). Code optimization requires a combination of experience, an eye for detail, and a basic understanding of processors. Seasoned programmers, who have done some assembly-language programming in their days, have an advantage here, but you can pick up a lot along the way.

> **TIP**
>
> Never think your code has been optimized completely, and never underestimate your capabilities. Some expert programmers start with the code produced by the compiler and optimize it. So don't count too much on the machine. Learn its limitations and work around them.

Although there are no hard and fast rules for optimizing code, there are some tricks you can use and some guidelines you can follow. We'll discuss these in the next sections and then look at how these tricks affect the native code and p-code compilers.

There are some simple rules that every BASIC programmer knows. For example, Integer and Long variables are handled faster than Single and Double variables. If your calculations permit it, use Integer instead of Long variables, and use Single instead of Double variables. Another, even more important, optimization trick is to avoid the use of undeclared variables.

Avoid Variants

Variants are convenient when putting together a short program to display the ASCII character set or the ASCII values of the function keys, but avoid variants in your code. They take up much more memory than other data types, and they can't be processed immediately. The compiler must find out their proper type, convert them to this type, and then use them in a calculation. For example, if a variant holds the value 45, the compiler must convert it to a numeric value before using it in a numeric calculation or to a string before using it in a string operation.

Some developers defend variants and explain to you why they are so cool, pointing out that they free the programmer from having to declare variables and use them consistently. They also give you some neat examples—mostly one-liners that could normally be implemented with two or three lines of code. If you're trying to squeeze every drop of performance from your application, avoid variants.

The VBVariables application, shown in Figure 17.4, performs a number of calculations.

> **NOTE**
>
> You'll find the VBVariables application in this chapter's folder on the CD that comes with this book.

FIGURE 17.4:

The VBVariables application demonstrates the inefficiency of variants.

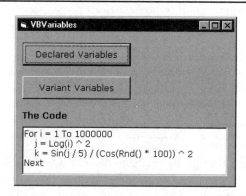

The Declared Variables button performs the calculations using variables declared as Doubles. The Variant Variables button does the same calculations using variants. The time to complete the calculations is displayed on a Label next to each button. The actual calculations are shown in the TextBox control at the bottom of the Form. A few math operations are repeated 1,000,000 times. As you can see, using properly declared variables speeds up the calculations by more than 10 percent (11.78 versus 10.64 seconds on a Pentium 233 system).

The code of the VBVariables application is shown next. The calculations are trivial, but are typical of scientific and engineering applications. You may notice the exceptionally inefficient implementation of some operations; more on this later.

Code 17.1   **The VBVariables Project**

```vb
Private Sub Command1_Click()
    T1 = Timer
    Screen.MousePointer = vbHourglass
    Dim i As Long, j As Double, k As Double
    For i = 1 To 1000000
        j = Log(i) ^ 2
        k = Cos(Rnd() * 100) ^ 2
    Next
    Label1.Caption = Format(Timer - T1, "##.000")
    Screen.MousePointer = vbDefault
End Sub

Private Sub Command2_Click()
    T1 = Timer
    Screen.MousePointer = vbHourglass
    For i = 1 To 1000000
        j = Log(i) ^ 2
        k = Cos(Rnd() * 100) ^ 2
    Next
    Label2.Caption = Format(Timer - T1, "##.000")
    Screen.MousePointer = vbDefault
End Sub
```

Let's compile the VBVariables application and see how the equivalent native code does. Follow these steps:

1. In the Project Properties dialog box, check the Compile to Native Code option and the Optimize for Fast Code option.

2. Click the Advanced Optimizations button to open the Advanced Optimizations dialog box.

3. Check all the options to enable all optimizations.

4. Now choose File ➤ Make VBVariables.exe to generate the executable file.

5. Minimize the Visual Basic window, locate the VBVariables.exe file, and run it.

The equivalent times on the same system are now 8.895 and 9.609 seconds respectively. The native code compiler helped the variants a little, but the calculations with typed variables were executed faster. Notice also that the native code compiler improved execution by almost 20 percent.

Now let's experiment with the optimization options. Go back to the Advanced Optimizations dialog box and clear the option Allow Unrounded Floating Point Operations. The compiler will round the results of each operation, as if they were moved to memory, in between calculations. This will add a few cycles, and we are going to lose some accuracy too (one wonders why this is even an option). The calculations with typed variables will take 9.95 seconds, and those with variants will take 11.334 seconds. Rounding intermediate results has a profound effect on execution time.

TIP

It is possible to use variants by calling the wrong form of certain functions. The functions Mid(), Left(), and so on are different from the string functions Mid$(), Left$(), and so on. The functions without the dollar sign in their names are more flexible (they work on both strings and numbers), but they return variants. If you are working exclusively with strings, use Left$() instead of Left() and Right$() instead of Right().

Simplify the Math

Now we are going to optimize the code in the loop. There isn't much you can do here, except for the ^ operator, which raises a number to a power, even a non-integer number. Raising a number to a non-integer power is accomplished with an algorithm that is more complicated than multiplying a number by itself (which is what the square of a number is). Many programmers will use the proper operator (x ^ 2) to calculate the square of x, because they don't know better or (in most cases) because they are translating a math formula into Visual Basic statements.

Let's revise the code to avoid the ^ operator. Replace the following line

```
j = Log(i) ^ 2
```

with the line

```
j = Log(i) * Log(i)
```

And replace the following line

```
k = Cos(Rnd() * 100) ^ 2
```

with this line:

```
k = Cos(Rnd() * 100)* Cos(Rnd() * 100)
```

Make sure that the advanced optimization options are checked, create a new executable, and run it. The calculations take only 2.22 seconds to complete with typed variables and 4.72 seconds with variants. So, most of the time in the previous runs was spent by the ^ operator. Notice also that, although the calculations with variants improved, they are now much slower than the calculations with typed variables. The reason? With simple math tricks you can improve the performance of your code, but there's nothing you can do about the overhead involved with variants.

You can use the same tricks with cubes and other integer powers. You will still save time if you multiply a number by itself three times, rather than raising it to the cube with the ^ operator.

Another way to optimize code that implements math operations is to save intermediate results. For example, the following statements:

```
Xnew = X * X + X0: Ynew = Y * Y + Y0
{other calculations}
If X * X + Y * Y > 0 Then ...
```

will execute faster if you save the results of the operation X * X to a temporary variable, as shown next:

```
XSquare = X * X : YSquare = Y * Y
Xnew = Xsquare + X0: Ynew = Ysquare + Y0
{other calculations}
If Xsquare + Ysquare > 0 Then ...
```

The improvement will be more impressive if you store more complicated operations, such as X ^ 2.8 or Y ^ -0.3, to temporary variables and reuse them.

Manipulate Strings Efficiently

The single most important trick in speeding up string operations is to remember that Mid() is not only a function. It's also a statement. In the following line, the Mid() function returns the third through the tenth characters of a string:

```
subString = Mid$(originalString,3,10)
```

But in the following line:

```
Mid$(originalString,3,10) = "1234567890"
```

Mid$() is used as a statement to change part of the string.

Let's say you want to reverse a long string. Many VB programmers would start by building a new string and appending to it the characters of the string to be reversed, starting with the last character of the original string and working up to the first, with a loop such as the following:

```
For i = 1 To Len(AString)
    BString = BString & Mid$(AString, Len(AString) - i + 1, 1)
Next
```

In this listing, *AString* is the string to be reversed, and *BString* is the new string. If you run this code with a 30KB string, you'll spend almost a minute looking at the hourglass. It won't be bad with a shorter string, say 5KB, but as the length of the string increases, Visual Basic needs more and more time to handle it. Reversing a 30KB string isn't six times slower than reversing a 5KB string six times. Not even close.

Let's start with setting up a long string, which is a more fundamental problem. We are going to build a string using random characters. In a practical application they could be read from a file or an incoming stream from a Web server. The basic problem is that a string grows as new characters are attached to it. The following code appends random characters to the end of the string *AString*:

```
AString = ""
For i = 1 To 30000
    AString = AString & Chr(Rnd() * 26 + 48)
Next
```

It's simple, but very slow. On a Pentium 233 system, it took 23 seconds. If the string were only 3,000 characters, filling it with random characters would take less than a second. There seems to be something wrong here. The longer the string, the more time it takes Visual Basic to manipulate it. This is a consequence of the way Visual Basic stores strings in memory, but this isn't something you can change.

To speed up the code, we can set up two nested loops, such as the following:

```
AString = ""
For j = 1 To 10
    BString = ""
    For i = 1 To 3000
```

```
        BString = BString & Chr(Rnd() * 26 + 48)
    Next
    AString = AString & BString
Next
```

The inner loop creates a 3,000-character string (variable BString) at a time and appends it to the AString variable. It must build ten of those strings to fill the long string. This structure took only half a second on the same Pentium. By limiting the size of the string variable we use to append individual characters, we brought the total execution time of more than 20 seconds down to less than a second.

TIP   The conclusion is that you shouldn't manipulate very long strings with Visual Basic. Break long strings into shorter ones, manipulate them individually, and when you're done, concatenate the processed strings. Execution times will be reduced tremendously.

The application VBStrings, shown in Figure 17.5, demonstrates the two techniques.

NOTE   You'll find the VBStrings project in this chapter's folder on the CD that comes with this book.

FIGURE 17.5:

The VBStrings application demonstrates efficient string manipulation techniques.

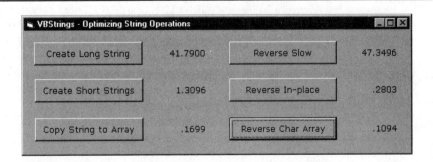

The Create Long String button builds a very long string (30,000 characters) by appending characters to the end of a string variable. The button Create Short Strings builds the same string, using shorter segments, as described here.

Let's process a long string now. The processing is trivial; we'll reverse the order of the characters in the string. Again, here's how many programmers would initially code this operation:

```
For i = 1 To Len(AString)
    BString = BString & Mid(AString, Len(AString) - i + 1, 1)
Next
```

As you might suspect, this is another slow operation. It's implemented with the Reverse Slow button on the VBStrings Form. How long does it take on the same Pentium 233? Nearly 48 seconds! A trivial operation like this. What if we wanted to scramble the characters or do a more intensive operation?

We can improve the string reversal operation by using the Mid statement. To enhance the example, we are going to reverse the string in place—we'll reverse its characters without copying it to another string. If you want to keep the original string too, copy *AString* to *BString* and then reverse *AString* in place. Here's the code for reversing the *AString* variable in place:

```
For i = 1 To Len(AString) / 2
    tmpChar = Mid(AString, Len(AString) - i + 1, 1)
    Mid(AString, Len(AString) - i + 1, 1) = Mid(AString, i, 1)
    Mid(AString, i, 1) = tmpChar
Next
```

This operation is implemented with the Reverse In-Place button in the VBStrings application. The time? Only 0.33 seconds! This can't be considered an optimization trick; it's more like bad initial coding, right? We bet that many programmers would reverse the string with the first method. They would test their program with a 20-character string and think they had a functional application.

Perhaps we can stop here. Reversing a string in less than a second isn't bad. But maybe we can do even better with character arrays. Let's start by copying the characters of the *AString* variable to an array:

```
For i = 1 To Len(AString)
    A(i) = Mid(AString, i, 1)
Next
```

This operation (which is implemented by the Copy String to Array button) took approximately half a second. If we can speed our string manipulation routines by using the character array we just created, the time to copy the string to an array is well spent. Here's the code for reversing the characters in the array:

```
UB = UBound(A)
For i = 1 To UB
```

```
        B(i) = A(UB - i + 1)
    Next
```

The string reversal operation in an array took 0.172 seconds. Indeed, the time to copy the string to an array was well spent, especially if you use the array for more complicated types of processing or multiple string operations.

In this section, we measured times while the project was running in the IDE. If you compile the project to native code and run it, you won't see much improvement. The compiler will help all operations a little, but it will primarily help the string reversal operation with the array. So, if you are doing lots of string processing in your code, consider copying the strings onto character arrays and process the array elements instead. When you're done, you can copy the array's characters back to the string.

Access Properties Indirectly

Another simple but effective optimization technique is to avoid referencing the same property many times. Let's say you have an incoming stream of data that you want to display on a TextBox control. You already know what to do: Create small string variables and append them to the control's Text property.

Another common mistake is to reference a property such as Text1.Text in a loop. Let's say you want to reverse the characters of the text displayed in a TextBox. Even if you use the Mid statement in a loop such as the following, the process is going to be very slow.

```
Dim Astring As String
Astring = " "
With Text1
    For i = 1 To Len(.Text)
        tmpChar = Mid(.Text, Len(.Text) - i + 1, 1)
        Mid(AString, i, 1) = tmpChar
        Astring = Astring + " "
    Next
    .Text = Astring
End With
```

Because a lot of overhead is involved every time you access a control's property, avoid too many references to the same property. Copy the Text property's value to the string *AString,* and process this variable. Then, assign the processed variable to the Text property. Reversing 3,000 characters on a TextBox control took 4.33 seconds using the Text property, while the same operation using a temporary string variable took less than half a second on the same computer. Clearly, you should avoid referencing control properties directly in your code, especially within loops that are executed many times.

Optimize for Worst-Case Scenarios

Many times we write less than optimal code because we don't test our applications with real-world data or under worst-case scenarios. We write code that works well with short text files, and we assume it will behave similarly with any text file. If an operation takes 90 milliseconds, why optimize it? Because, as we have demonstrated, it may deteriorate by a factor of 100 when the string's length is increased by a factor of 20.

In addition, don't trust anyone's code—not that of the compiler, a code generator, your colleagues or boss, your professors, or book authors. No code (except for truly trivial segments) can be proven optimal, so if you are not happy with its speed, optimize it.

Maximize Apparent Speed

No amount of optimization is going to do you much good unless the users of your application *think* it's fast. Conversely, the sloppiest application need not be optimized if users think it's fast. The most important metric of the speed of an application is its so-called *apparent speed*. Apparent speed can't be measured in time units (or any units, for that matter). Apparent speed is how fast the application appears to the user. If your Forms load slowly, any amount of optimization in the code that follows the loading of the Form isn't going to help. For example, which image-processing application do you open more often? The one that loads the fastest, right?

Apparent speed can be improved in two ways:

- By loading Forms faster

- By displaying flash screens and animation while the program is busy for more than a few seconds

Your best bet is to load Forms at startup and keep them in memory. The Load command loads a Form, but doesn't display it. Once the Form is in memory, you can display it instantly with the Show method. The application may take longer to start, but once it's started, Forms can be displayed and hidden instantly (unless they contain large bitmaps).

Another way to increase the apparent speed is to load new Forms and then ask the user to wait for a lengthy operation to complete. While the user takes a few seconds to study the controls on the Form and think about their next move (which parameters to adjust or which button to click), your application calculates the values that will be displayed on the Form or retrieves data from a database.

But how about the initial delay, when the user has to wait for your application's Forms to load? This initial delay is just about the worst thing you can do for the application's apparent speed, but it helps the apparent speed of the rest of the application. When a time-consuming operation takes place, we use the hourglass to indicate that the user should wait. And we've all watched more than our share of hourglasses. Sometimes users go as far as to shake them to see if the sand will move. Well, an hourglass isn't improving the application's apparent speed, and we need something more amusing, something fresher.

An animated cursor or an AVI file with a few small frames isn't going to make the application run faster, but it's not going to slow it down noticeably either. A typical example is the animation that takes place while documents are sent to the Recycle Bin. Another example is the information displayed on the screen while applications are being installed. The flash screens keep the user from getting utterly bored, and they are more fun to watch than an hourglass. The excitement, however, grows thinner over time, and users want more speed. You may have optimized your VB application as best as you can. Perhaps there are no more milliseconds to be squeezed out, and still you (or your users) are not happy with the application. It may be time to help Visual Basic with an external component.

Optimizing Graphics Operations with API Functions

If your application's code has been optimized but you're still not happy with its speed, you should consider alternatives outside Visual Basic. Some of Visual Basic's built-in functions and methods are slow—graphics methods are notoriously so. If your application uses graphics methods extensively, you should consider replacing them with the equivalent API functions.

API (Application Programming Interface) is a vast collection of functions for performing common (and uncommon) programming tasks. The API functions are the foundation of the Windows operating system, and C programmers are using them all the time. Just about every Visual Basic method and function has an equivalent API function. In many cases, Visual Basic methods are masquerading API functions. The PaintPicture method, for example, calls the BitBlt() API function behind the scenes. Shape-drawing functions also do the same. If your application calls the equivalent API functions directly, it will actually run a bit faster than the application that relies on Visual Basic methods for drawing.

There are API functions for tasks that have no equivalent VB methods. There are filling functions, for example, that let you fill an area of a PictureBox control or a Form with a solid color or pattern. If you want to fill a closed, irregular shape (which is usually delimited by the intersections of other shapes like lines and circles), you must use an API function, because Visual Basic lacks an equivalent method.

API functions are part of Visual Basic and you can access their declaration through the API Viewer add-in. Once you have copied the declaration of an API function to your application's code, you can call it as if it were a Visual Basic function. In this section, we are not going to discuss the topic of API functions. We are assuming you have used API functions in your Visual Basic application already. Instead, we'll show you how a few API functions can increase the speed of your graphics applications. As we mentioned already, Visual Basic's graphics methods are inherently slow and the use of graphics API functions can increase speed considerably. If you need more information on calling API functions and passing arguments, see Chapter 14, "Visual Basic and the Windows API."

All graphics methods have equivalent API functions, but you won't gain anything by drawing a few lines or circles with the LineTo() and Ellipse() API functions. There aren't many applications that draw thousands of lines or circles. The slowest graphics operations are those that manipulate pixels, and it's easy for an application to read or examine the values of many thousands of pixels in a loop. Let's take a look at a couple of techniques for speeding bitmap manipulation.

Figure 17.6 shows the CopyPixels application, which moves pixels from one PictureBox control to another. The fastest method to copy the pixels is to call the built-in PaintPicture method, or the BitBlt() API function. However, if you must process the pixels while copying them (or if your application generates the pixel values on the fly instead of reading them off another control), you must copy them one at a time. To copy the pixels using straight VB code, you must set up two nested loops that copy the pixels one column (or row) at a time, as shown next:

```
For i = 0 To Picture1.ScaleWidth - 1
    For j = 0 To Picture1.ScaleHeight - 1
        clrValue = Picture1.Point(i, j)
```

```
            Picture2.PSet (i, j), clrValue
        Next
    Next
```

The straight VB code is extremely slow. Run the CopyPixels application on the CD and click the Copy VB button to see how long it takes to transfer the pixel values from the top to the bottom PictureBox control.

FIGURE 17.6:

The CopyPixels application demonstrates how to manipulate device contexts directly to speed graphics operations.

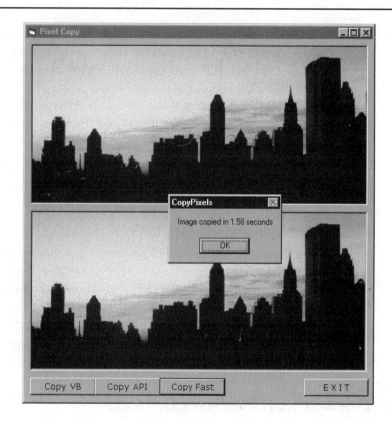

To speed the operation, you must replace the calls to Point and PSet methods with the equivalent GetPixel() and SetPixel() API functions.

The SetPixel() and GetPixel() API Functions

In Chapter 14, "Visual Basic and the Windows API," you learned about the Set-Pixel() and GetPixel() functions, which perform the same operation as the Pset and Point methods but are faster. Let's replace the call to the PSet method in the code with a call to the SetPixel() function and the call to the Point method with a call to the GetPixel() function. The two functions must first be declared with the following statements:

```
Declare Function SetPixel Lib "gdi32" (ByVal hdc As Long, _
        ByVal x As Long, ByVal y As Long, _
        ByVal crColor As Long) As Long
Declare Function GetPixel Lib "gdi32" (ByVal hdc As Long, _
        ByVal x As Long, ByVal y As Long) As Long
```

The argument hdc is the handle to the device context. To read or set a pixel on a PictureBox control or a Form, pass the hdc property of the object. *X* and *y* are the coordinates of the pixel and CrColor is a long value that represents the color of the pixel. The code behind the Copy API button is identical to the code of the Copy VB button, except that it uses the API functions to read and set pixel values. We have also combined the two statements into one:

```
SetPixel hDestDC, i, j, GetPixel(hSourceDC, i, j)
```

where the hSourceDC and hDestDC arguments are declared Long and are assigned the hdc property of the source and destination PictureBoxes outside the loop:

```
hSourceDC = Picture1.hdc
hDestDC = Picture2.hdc
```

Run the application now and time the two operations. On a Pentium 233 computer, the straight VB code takes over 30 seconds to copy the pixel values, while the equivalent code with API functions takes 2.5 seconds on the average. Still, 2.5 seconds is a lot of time for a trivial operation like moving pixels from one control onto another. You can do better than that by drawing directly on the control's device context. The process is a bit involved, but it will speed up the copying process considerably.

Drawing on Device Contexts

To speed up the drawing operations, we are going to draw directly on the bitmap that corresponds to the rectangle of the control on the screen. Visual Basic doesn't draw directly on the PictureBox control. Instead, it updates a special area in the memory, where a copy of the image is stored. Whenever Windows gets a chance, it transfers the contents of this memory area to the screen. Windows gets a chance to update the image on the control when no code is executed, or when the DOEVENTS or the PICTURE1.REFRESH statement is executed. This indirect method of drawing on controls places a significant burden on Visual Basic.

It is possible to access the memory where the copy of the bitmap is stored and update the pixel values there. After the entire bitmap has been modified, we can transfer it to the PictureBox control. The drawback of this method is that, while drawing on the bitmap, the image on the PictureBox control won't be updated. If the processing takes a few seconds only, that's something we can live with. And as you'll see shortly, updating the bitmap in memory is quite fast.

Let's start by reviewing the process. In order to access the bitmap that stores the image of the first PictureBox control, we must create a bitmap structure. This is done with the CreateCompatibleBitmap() API function, which creates a bitmap of specific dimensions and makes it compatible with the bitmap displayed on the control. The variable *hBMP* created with the following statement points to a bitmap that's compatible with the bitmap displayed on the Picture1 control and has the same dimensions as the control (provided that the control's ScaleMode is set to 3 pixels).

```
hBMP = CreateCompatibleBitmap(Picture1.hdc, Picture1.ScaleWidth, _
                        Picture1.ScaleHeight)
```

The hBMP structure can't be accessed directly by Visual Basic either. The pixel manipulation API functions, and specifically the SetPixel() function, can only write a so-called *device context*. To use the SetPixel() function, you must also create a device context with the CreateCompatibleDC() API function:

```
hDestDC = CreateCompatibleDC(Picture1.hdc)
```

The device context is compatible with the PictureBox control and you can use any of the drawing functions to draw on it. However, your drawing won't end up on the PictureBox control unless you connect the *hDestDC* device context and the compatible bitmap *hBMP*. This is taken care of by the SelectObject() API function, which connects the two objects (or "mounts" the bitmap on the device context):

```
SelectObject hDestDC, hBMP
```

The hDestDC argument context is the device context of the PictureBox control. In other words, it's equivalent to the hDC property of the PictureBox control. Where we were drawing on the PictureBox control with the statement

```
SetPixel Picture1.hdc, j, i, RGB(red, green, blue)
```

we can now draw on the device context with the statement

```
SetPixel hDestDC, j, i, RGB(red, green, blue)
```

After the entire device context has been updated, we must transfer it to the PictureBox control with the BitBlt() function. After you have copied all pixels of the first PictureBox control to the device context of the second PictureBox control and the new bitmap exists in the control's device context, you must transfer it to the PictureBox control with the BitBlt() function:

```
BitBlt Picture1.hdc, 1, 1, Picture1.ScaleWidth - 2, _
        Picture1.ScaleHeight - 2, hDestDC, 1, 1, &HCC0020
```

The Copy Fast button uses all the API functions discussed in this section to read the pixels of the top PictureBox control and transfer them to the bottom one. Here's the Copy Fast button's code:

Code 17.2   **The Copy Fast Button's Code**

```
Private Sub Command3_Click()
Dim i As Integer, j As Integer
Dim tStart As Long, tEnd As Long
Dim wWidth As Integer, wHeight As Integer
Dim hBMPSource As Long, hBMPDest As Long
Dim hDestDC As Long, hSourceDC As Long

    Picture2.Cls
    Screen.MousePointer = vbHourglass
' set up source bitmap
    tStart = timeGetTime()
    hBMPSource = CreateCompatibleBitmap(Picture1.hdc, _
            Picture1.ScaleWidth, Picture1.ScaleHeight)
    hSourceDC = CreateCompatibleDC(Picture1.hdc)
    SelectObject hSourceDC, hBMPSource
' set up destination bitmap
    hBMPDest = CreateCompatibleBitmap(Picture2.hdc, _
            Picture2.ScaleWidth, Picture2.ScaleHeight)
    hDestDC = CreateCompatibleDC(Picture2.hdc)
    SelectObject hDestDC, hBMPDest
    ' Copy picture bitmap to source bitmap
    BitBlt hSourceDC, 0, 0, Picture1.ScaleWidth - 1, _
            Picture1.ScaleHeight - 1, Picture1.hdc, 0, 0, &HCC0020
' Copy pixels between bitmaps
    wWidth = Picture1.ScaleWidth
    wHeight = Picture1.ScaleHeight
    For i = 0 To wWidth - 1
        For j = 0 To wHeight - 1
            SetPixel hDestDC, i, j, GetPixel(hSourceDC, i, j)
        Next
    Next
```

```
' transfer the copied pixels to the second PictureBox
    BitBlt Picture2.hdc, 0, 0, Picture1.ScaleWidth - 1, _
           Picture1.ScaleHeight - 1, hDestDC, 0, 0, &HCC0020
' finally, clean up memory
    tEnd = timeGetTime()
    Call DeleteDC(hSourceDC)
    Call DeleteObject(hBMPSource)
    Call DeleteDC(hDestDC)
    Call DeleteObject(hBMPDest)
    Screen.MousePointer = vbDefault
    MsgBox "Image copied in " & (tEnd - tStart) / 1000 & " seconds"
End Sub
```

The Copy Fast button copies the bitmap in 1.4 seconds on the average—a considerable improvement over using the GetPixel() and SetPixel() API functions only, but still not as fast as using the PaintPicture method. As we mentioned already, if you want to process the pixels while copying them, you can't rely on the PaintPicture method, which simply copies the bitmap.

Here's an interesting experiment. If you comment out the line that copies the pixel (the single line that constitutes the body of the inner loop), the operation will complete in 0.25 seconds. Graphics operations are actually quite slow in the Windows environment, and you should use API functions to speed up applications that process or manipulate pixels, such as the Fractal application, which we'll explore later in this chapter.

A final note: If you run the CopyPixels application, you may get strange results. The Copy API button may transfer the pixels faster than the Copy Fast button. If your display is not set for optimal performance, the API functions will not work as advertised. If you have set your computer to display 256 colors, for example, the process of copying the colors will be much slower than if you set it to display true color.

Building DLLs with Visual C++

You may have optimized your VB application as best as you can. Perhaps there are no more milliseconds to be squeezed out, and still you (or your users) are not happy with the application. It may be time to help Visual Basic with an external component. A DLL written in Visual C++ is a prime candidate, and we are going to look at the basics of implementing simple, time-consuming operations in Visual C++ and packaging them as DLLs. By *time-consuming operations*, we mean CPU-intensive calculations, string manipulation, and the like. Accessing a database isn't going to get any faster, no matter what language you use. The JET Engine or the SQL Server, for example, doesn't know what language is contacting it. The same is true for API calls. You simply can't make these operations any faster. However, you can make other operations, especially math operations, significantly faster with the help of an external DLL.

Do You Have to Learn Visual C++?

Are we suggesting that you learn Visual C++ to simply make Visual Basic faster? Yes and no. Visual Basic programmers, for whatever reasons, don't like C. But experienced VB programmers shouldn't have any problem picking up the basics of writing C code. We'll show you the mechanics of converting VB code to C and compiling it as a DLL.

Writing code to perform math operations in C isn't any more complicated than writing VB code. Sure, you must end each line with a semicolon and get used to the notation counter++ (which increases the value of the counter variable) and other syntactical differences, but the actual statements aren't that different from the equivalent VB statements.

In this section, we'll show you how to design a DLL with Visual C++, how to call the DLL's functions from within your VB application, and how to pass parameters (including arrays) back and forth. You don't have to master C to reap some of its benefits. Sometimes you can succeed without trying really hard, but don't make it your banner. To get this far in this book, you've already tried hard.

What Are Dynamic-Link Libraries?

Dynamic-link libraries, or DLLs, are libraries of executable code that another application can call at run time through dynamic linking to provide functions and procedures to perform tasks that are not supplied by the application itself. In your VB application, you must declare the procedure in a DLL and provide the path to the DLL so that your application can connect to it at run time. These DLLs are similar to the ActiveX DLLs discussed in the second part of the book, but they only expose procedures, which are called directly like the API functions. Let's look at this process in more detail.

First, a *library* is a block of code that has been compiled to produce a machine-executable product. A library can consist of a single function or procedure or contain a variety of separate procedures, all of which are externally accessible. These public functions or procedures can be called by other applications to perform specific tasks, to execute calculations and return results, and even to call on the services of other libraries.

A DLL can also contain procedures that are not accessible outside the library but that are used by procedures within the library. These private functions or procedures differ principally in the manner in which they are exposed for external access. We'll discuss both types in detail later in this chapter.

Second, like any Windows application, a DLL can contain resources such as dialogs, bitmaps, and so on that are used by functions within the DLL and that are visible to the user. These resources are not, however, directly accessible to applications using the DLL. (There are exceptions by which resources may be made available externally, but these are not the usual methods for using resources.) The DLLs we'll describe in this chapter don't have a visual interface; we'll leave that task to Visual Basic, and the DLL will take care of CPU-intensive calculations.

Third, unlike a static library that is linked at the time the application is created, a DLL remains independent and separate from the application and is linked only at run time and only if and when specific functions supplied by the DLL are requested. Further, again in contrast to a static library, the machine code supplying the service is not incorporated in the application but remains a part of the dynamic-link library.

You can think of a DLL as a black box that can be asked to perform specific tasks and/or to return specific results, but that does not require the programmer to know anything about what is inside.

Of course, the ignorance permitted for those using a DLL does not apply if you are interested in writing a DLL, which is precisely what this section is about.

Advantages of DLLs

Several advantages are associated with using dynamic-link libraries. Some of them apply to any application written in any language and others apply principally to using DLLs with Visual Basic.

Common Services

The functions supplied by a DLL can be shared by more than one application at different times or even simultaneously by several applications. When separate applications call a DLL, each individual client application receives a separate instantiation of the requested function—at least in the sense that the data used by the function remains separate for each calling application—even though only one copy of the executable code exists.

The Windows Common Dialog Library, which provides such functions as the Save File and Find File dialog boxes, is an example. In addition to sharing a single functionality across all applications, the shared file also ensures that all applications present a common interface when opening or saving files. Thus, when you are using the Common Dialog control to build an Open dialog box, the users of your application will see the familiar Windows File Open dialog box.

Compact Size

While the current trend toward code bloat seems to almost make a mockery of falling memory prices and increasing CPU speeds, using DLLs is still a valid and useful way to reduce the size of executables. When functions supplied by a static library are used in an application, the code for each function is incorporated into the application's code, becoming a part of the EXE program file.

Some years ago, when an application used a library, the entire library was linked into the compiled application, regardless of how much or how many of the services supplied by the library were actually needed by the application. Later, as smart linkers came into use, only those portions of a library that were actually needed and used were linked to become a part of the executable.

But, regardless of how the application is compiled—or even whether it is compiled or interpreted—the functions supplied by the DLL are never incorporated in the application's EXE file. Instead, all functions supplied by the DLL remain in the dynamic-link library and are called as needed. Further, because there is only one copy of the DLL even when the services are shared among many applications, additional savings in space are realized over duplicating the code.

Ease of Revision

A DLL can be revised at any time to incorporate improvements. In this respect, a DLL is similar to an ActiveX component, except that your application doesn't have to access the exposed functions via an object variable.

Likewise, revised DLLs can include additional public functions that were not provided in the original DLL, without affecting applications using the earlier version. Of course, applications that are taking advantage of elements added to a later revision will not be able to function using the earlier version.

TIP

To avoid potential version conflicts and crashes, provide a way to test the DLL version in your application.

Speed of Execution

The primary reason for using a DLL with Visual Basic is the need for speed. For example, a graphics application may require a large number of calculations. By implementing a calculation-intensive process as a DLL written in Delphi or C/C++, you can significantly reduce calculation time. In many areas, however, Visual Basic is just as fast as other languages.

NOTE

If a DLL written in Visual C++ could run circles around your Visual Basic application, you'd be really disappointed, wouldn't you? Visual Basic is not only an excellent development environment, but a fast language too. It just isn't always as fast as Visual C++.

Third-Party Libraries

With a DLL, you can use third-party libraries to supply functions, features, or utilities instead of developing them yourself. Libraries of functions in DLL format were popular, but are being slowly replaced by classes. However, there is still a significant market for DLLs that contain useful procedures, especially if they are implemented in a fast language such as Visual C++.

Disadvantages of DLLs

Although the advantages of using DLLs far outweigh the disadvantages, shortcomings may occur in a few areas.

Loss of Customization and Adaptability

When you are developing every aspect of your application entirely on your own, you are certainly free to adapt every aspect and every element of the application exactly and precisely as you would prefer. By off-loading tasks to DLLs that are not developed in-house, you give up some freedom of design and customization.

Also, DLLs are not as readily adaptable as Visual Basic code, and, when working across languages, trying to debug operations inside a DLL can be a major headache at best and impossible at worst.

Of course, since the ultimate in customization and adaptability would be to design your own operating system, every application consists of some form of compromise. In the case of DLLs, the usual compromise is trading some flexibility for increases in execution speed and savings in development time.

Compatibility Problems

You can encounter compatibility problems between DLLs written in one language and applications written in another. Of course, the same can be said of DLLs and applications that are written in different versions of the same language.

For example, an integer in Visual Basic is not the same as an integer in Visual C/C++. In most cases, such as passing an integer parameter by value, this discrepancy will not be apparent or relevant. In other cases, this difference can be a major problem if you do not take it into consideration. (See the section "When an Int Is Not an Int" later in this chapter.)

The key, of course, is to be sure that you know what the DLL expects and what the calling application can provide. And, obviously, test your application with the DLL to ensure that they are communicating in a compatible fashion. (See the section "Array Dimensions in VB versus VC" for more on this.)

Fractal Calculations

In this section, we'll use the Mandelbrot set in an example, mainly because displaying the set depends on extensive floating-point calculations and is intrinsically slow. Calculating a fractal is a computationally intensive operation, and we chose it to demonstrate how much difference a DLL written in Visual C++ can make.

The Fractal application (written in Visual Basic) calculates an image that is 400 × 400 pixels, a total of 160,000 pixels. Further, since each pixel requires 50 iterations (an approximate average), this gives us a total in the neighborhood of 8 million iterations. However, each iteration requires multiple floating-point operations (FLOPs), bringing us to many million FLOPs to display a single image of the Mandelbrot set.

The Visual Basic version of this operation takes nearly a minute for an image that's 400 × 400 pixels. Therefore, we developed the Fractal.DLL library using Visual C++. The DLL provides one function for performing the calculations (which are the most time-consuming portion of the task) and returning the result (as an altitude) to the Visual Basic program for display. Different altitudes are colored differently.

We'll start by looking at the VB code for calculating and displaying the Mandelbrot set. This application will be the reference point for comparing the speed improvements introduced with the Visual C++ DLL.

You are probably familiar with fractal images, but you may not be familiar with the algorithms used to produce them. Fractal images are generated mathematically. In this chapter, we'll concentrate on the calculations (which aren't complicated, but are repeated millions of times). For more information on what fractals represent, see the `fractal.doc` file on the companion CD.

Fractals and Fractal Dimensions

The term *fractal* was first coined by the mathematician Benoit B. Mandelbrot in 1975 as shorthand for any object—mathematical or physical—that exhibits the characteristics of a fractional dimension. A detailed discussion of the Mandelbrot set and fractals is beyond the scope of this chapter, but if you are interested in exploring fractals and other mathematically intriguing entities, check out the following:

Fractals Everywhere by Michael Barnsley

Fractal Programming in C and *Advanced Fractal Programming in C*, both by Roger Stevens

Computer Graphics: Principles and Practice by Foley, van Dam, Feiner, and Hughes

Graphics Programming in Turbo C by Ben Ezzell

The Fractal Application

Don't worry if you are not familiar with the fractal algorithms. They are straightforward, and you need not understand all the details. Each point of the fractal must be calculated separately. Let's call the Mandelbrot() function, which calculates the color of each point. It accepts as arguments the coordinates of the point and returns the color. The entire image is calculated with two For ... Next loops, which scan the columns of the pixels (the outer loop) and the pixels across each column (the inner loop). Here's the structure of the application that calculates and displays the fractal:

```
nLimit = 100
XStep = (XMax - XOrg) / XSize
YStep = (YMax - YOrg) / YSize
```

```
For i = 0 To XSize
    For j = 0 To YSize
        XPos = XOrg + i * XStep
        YPos = YOrg + j * Ystep
        {calculate nSteps}
        Picture1.PSet (i, j), QBColor(nSteps Mod 16)
    Next
    Picture1.Refresh
Next
```

The variables *XOrg*, *XMax*, *YOrg*, and *YMax* represent the limits of the Mandelbrot set. By changing these values, you can zoom in to any area of the Mandelbrot set.

The calculations are repeated up to 100 times (variable *nLimit*) for each pixel. The current pixel is painted according to the number of iterations. Points lying in the "fractal sea" exhaust all 100 calculations (or as many as you specify with the *nLimit* variable). To simplify the code, the current point is painted with the QBColor() function.

NOTE   The fractals that are produced with the QBColor() function—which supports only 16 colors—will not look as nice as those colored with palettes, but this isn't the issue at hand. At the end of the chapter, we'll show you how to build smoothly colored fractals.

The actual calculations take place in the section marked as {calculate nSteps} in the previous listing. We didn't implement them as a separate function because this function would be called for each point; we preferred to code the calculations inline. The statements that calculate the color of each point are shown in the next listing.

Code 17.3   Calculating the Mandelbrot Set

```
XSize = Picture1.ScaleWidth
YSize = Picture1.ScaleHeight
Picture1.BackColor = QBColor(15)
Picture1.Cls
XStep = (XMax - XOrg) / XSize
YStep = (YMax - YOrg) / YSize
For i = 0 To XSize
    XPos = XOrg + i * XStep
    For j = 0 To YSize
        YPos = YOrg + j * YStep
        XIter = 0#: YIter = 0#
        bDone = False
```

```
            nSteps = 0
            Do
                XSqr = XIter * XIter
                YSqr = YIter * YIter
                XTemp = XSqr - YSqr + XPos
                YIter = 2 * (XIter * YIter) + YPos
                XIter = XTemp
                nSteps = nSteps + 1
                If (XSqr + YSqr) >= 4# Then bDone = True
                If (nSteps >= nLimit) Then bDone = True
            Loop Until bDone = True
            Picture1.PSet (i, j), QBColor(nSteps Mod 16)
        Next
        Picture1.Refresh
    Next
```

Even if you aren't familiar with the math involved, you can easily see that painting each pixel requires a lot of floating-point operations. In the Fractal application, shown in Figure 17.7, choose Draw Direct ➤ Mandelbrot to display the entire Mandelbrot set, or choose Draw Direct ➤ Mandelbrot (Zoom) to display a detail of the Mandelbrot set. These two commands are implemented in Visual Basic.

FIGURE 17.7:

The Fractal project calculates and displays the Mandelbrot set.

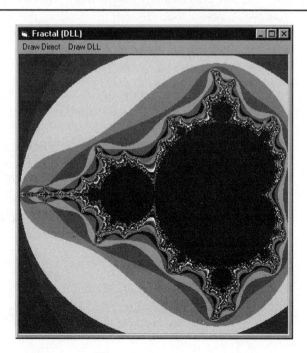

TIP

In our code, we evaluate some squares. As you can see, to calculate the square of a variable, we multiply it by itself. If you didn't know better, you might code these lines with the ^ operator (XIter^2 instead of XIter * XIter). Doing so will make your code much slower! The ^ operator invokes a procedure that raises a number to any power. When it comes to integer powers, though, the ^ operator is slow, and you should never, never use it. This trick won't make a difference in a typical application, but avoiding the ^ operator in a loop that repeats millions of times will make a world of difference in your application's speed!

The rule for breaking the calculations is that the square root of the sum of the squares XIter ^ 2 and YIter ^ 2 be less than 2. This rule is implemented with the line:

```
If (XSqr + YSqr) >= 4# Then bDone = True
```

To avoid calculating a square root for each iteration, for each point, we took the squares of both sides of the inequality. The variables *XSqr* and *YSqr* hold the values of the *XIter* and *YIter* variables squared.

In the Fractal application, shown in Figure 17.7 earlier in this chapter, choosing Draw DLL ➤ Mandelbrot and choosing Draw DLL ➤ Mandelbrot (Zoom) is identical to using the commands on the Draw VB menu, but the Draw DLL menu uses the DLL we are going to develop in the next section, FRACTAL.DLL. We still use the same two nested loops to scan the pixels of the image, but instead of using the VB code shown in Code 17.3 to calculate the color of the current point, we call the DLLMandelbrot() function, which is implemented in Visual C++ and is provided to our application by the FRACTAL.DLL.

Before getting down to the details of constructing a DLL in Visual C++, let's look at what the DLL did for the application. Run the Fractal application (in the Chapter17/Fractal/DLLFractal folder on the CD) from within the Visual Basic IDE. The commands on the Draw VB menu draw the Mandelbrot set with straight VB code, and the first two commands on the Draw DLL menu draw the same views of the Mandelbrot set using a DLL function to perform the calculations. It takes nearly 40 seconds to draw the Mandelbrot set with straight VB code (with the Draw VB ➤ Mandelbrot command) and just 15 seconds to draw the same image with the help of the DLL (with the Draw DLL ➤ Mandelbrot command). The VB/DLL code is nearly three times faster, which is an enormous improvement.

However, this isn't quite fair to VB. The DLL contains native code, optimized by the Visual C++ compiler. If you create a native code executable for the Fractal application and run it, you'll see that the VB compiler will do a great job. Run the FRACTAL.exe file in the DLLFractal folder (or create a new executable), and you'll see that the Mandelbrot set is drawn in approximately 17.3 seconds with VB code and in 13.3 seconds with the VB/DLL code. The VB compiler helped the VB implementation of the program a lot, as expected. The DLL can't be helped by the VB compiler (the compiler doesn't do anything to the DLL; it simply calls one or more of its functions). Even so, the VB/DLL approach is more than 20 percent faster than straight VB. Given that calculating a fractal image is an inherently slow process, it makes sense to help VB with a DLL written in Visual C++. Let's look at the implementation of the function that calculates each pixel's color with Visual C++.

NOTE   Before calling a function supplied by a DLL, you must declare the function's name, the DLL it belongs to, and its argument, just as you do with API functions (see the section "Calling DLL Functions from Visual Basic," later in this chapter). The commands on the Draw DLL menu will not work if the FRACTAL.DLL file isn't copied to the Windows/System folder. Alternatively, you can specify the DLL file's full path name in the declaration line, but this approach depends on the system on which the application is run and should be avoided.

Constructing a DLL in Visual C++

Constructing a DLL using Visual C++ is a relatively simple process, but begins with a choice of either using the standard C/C++ format or basing the DLL on the Microsoft Foundation Classes. In both cases, of course, the Visual C App Wizard can be used to create the project, but your choice of Form has definite ramifications.

In short, Visual C/C++ allows creation of three types of DLL: non-MFC DLLs, a statically-linked MFC-based DLL, or a dynamically-linked MFC-based DLL.

A non-MFC DLL is a DLL that does not use MFC internally. Because the exported functions from the DLL use the standard C interface, the DLL can be called by either MFC or non-MFC applications.

Alternatively, either a statically-linked or dynamically-linked MFC-based DLL can use the MFC classes internally while still using the standard C interface for all exported functions, insuring that the DLL can, again, be called by either MFC or non-MFC applications.

If, however, an MFC-based DLL expects exported functions to be called using MFC classes as arguments (variables), then the DLL could only be called from another MFC-based application. And, rather obviously, since Visual Basic does not recognize the Microsoft Foundation Classes, such a DLL could not be called by a VB application.

To allow a non-MFC application to communicate with a DLL using MFC-class arguments, an intermediate DLL—accepting non-MFC arguments—can convert the calling arguments to MFC classes before calling the MFC-based DLL. An example of this 'translated' approach can be found in the DLL libraries chapter in *Developing Windows Error Messages* by Ben Ezzell. Here, the ErrorMessage.DLL is an MFC-based library and expects MFC-class arguments when exported functions are called.

This MFC-class dependency makes the library's exported functions unreachable from either non-MFC C/C++ or Visual Basic applications. However, a second DLL—ErrorShell.DLL—is also provided in which all exported functions use the standard C interface and standard arguments. The ErrorShell.DLL then 'translates' the supplied arguments into MFC classes before passing the function calls to the ErrorMessage.DLL.

Here, where the intention is to create a DLL for use explicitly with a Visual Basic application (even though we are going to use Visual C/C++), all of the functions supplied for export will use the standard C interface and will use standard data types as arguments. This makes the Fractal.DLL library compatible with Visual Basic applications as well as Visual C/C++ applications, irrespective of whether they use the Microsoft Foundation Classes.

Creating a Dynamic-Link Library

The first step in creating a dynamic-link library requires that you have Visual Studio (Visual C++) installed.

From Visual C++, select the File ➤ New menu option and then select the Projects tab (see Figure 17.8).

FIGURE 17.8:

Creating a new project

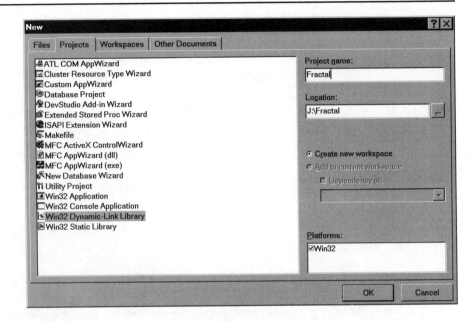

The Projects tab offers a wide choice of different project types. Only two of these—MFC AppWizard (dll) and Win32 Dynamic Link Library—are of interest here.

- **MFC AppWizard (dll)**   This option creates a skeletal application for a dynamic-link library using the Microsoft Foundation Classes. As this book is for Visual Basic programmers, the MFC AppWizard (dll) option is not suggested because (a) most Visual Basic programmers are not familiar with MFC and (b) avoiding dependence on the Microsoft Foundation Classes ensures that all exported functions will use only conventional C-calling parameters.

- **Win32 Dynamic Link Library**   This option creates a skeletal application for a dynamic-link library without depending on the Microsoft Foundation Classes. All exported functions will depend on conventional C-calling parameters, and the finished DLL should be compatible with all applications created using Visual Basic, Visual C, or other compilers.

After selecting the Win32 Dynamic Link Library option, enter a project name—in this case, the name **Example**—which will also be the name of the DLL. Optionally, we can also specify a directory where the project will be created.

Last, click OK to launch the Win32 Dynamic Link Library wizard, which is shown in Figure 17.9.

FIGURE 17.9:

The Win32 Dynamic Link Library wizard

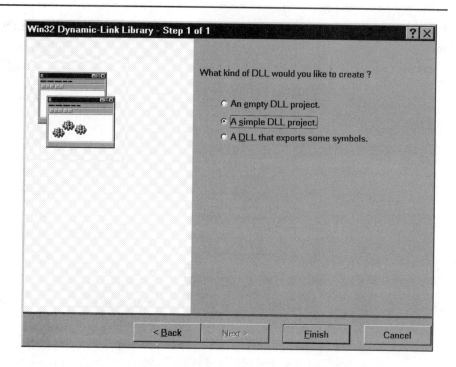

The Win32 Dynamic Link Library wizard offers three choices ranging from an absolute minimal project to a sample DLL illustrating how functions, variables, and classes are exported. The second option, recommended, provides a blank DLLMain function but leaves the bulk of the application for the programmer to create.

The three options offered are:

- **An empty DLL project**   This option creates a DLL project with the specified name but adds no files to the project. Use this when you intend to supply all of the appropriate source files.

- **A simple DLL project (recommended)**   This option creates a .DSP file based on the specified project name and creates a .CPP file with a blank DLLMain function. The project skeleton also includes StdAfx.CPP and StdAfx.H files and sets compiler options to create the precompiled header file.

- **A DLL that exports some symbols**   This option creates the dynamic-link library equivalent of a simple "Hello World" application. The created DLL demonstrates exporting symbols (a function, a variable, and a class).

After selecting the simple DLL project option, the Project Wizard creates four principal source files, listed in Table 17.1.

TABLE 17.1: Major Project Files

File	Function
Example.dsp	The project file contains information at the project level and is used to build a single project or subproject.
Example.cpp	The main DLL source file.
StdAfx.h, StdAfx.cpp	These files are used to build a precompiled header (PCH) file named Example.pch and a precompiled types file named StdAfx.obj.

The Example.CPP file created by the Project Wizard is quite brief and consists of a dummy DllMain function as shown:

```
// Example.cpp : Defines the entry point for the DLL application.
//
#include "stdafx.h"
```

Notice that there is an #INCLUDE statement for the StdAfx.h header but there is none for an Example.h header. If you need a header file for your main source file—which is likely—then you may include it here or place the appropriate #INCLUDE statements in the StdAfx.h header

Last, the supplied Example.CPP source file provides a DllMain function.

```
BOOL APIENTRY DllMain( HANDLE hModule,
                       DWORD  ul_reason_for_call,
                       LPVOID lpReserved
                     )
{
    return TRUE;
}
```

The DllMain function provided by the Project Wizard is essentially the same as the one used in the Fractal.CPP file—the only differences are minor elements of syntax and nomenclature. Functionally, we are not expecting the DllMain procedure to accomplish anything except to provide the default entry point for the library.

Optionally, we could use the entry point to perform initialization or to retrieve setting information from the Registry or any similar tasks. It is, however, better practice to leave it to the calling applications to supply any necessary initialization.

Because DLLs are commonly shared among different applications, leaving this responsibility to the calling application avoids invalid settings created by some other application's initialization—i.e., separate applications may share a single DLL but each supplies its own settings.

Likewise, DLLs should never be expected to store global values for the calling applications.

TIP

As always, rules are made to be broken and there may be occasional circumstances where global values or global initialization for a DLL may be appropriate. These should always, however, be exceptions and not conventional practice.

While the DllMain function has been supplied for you, the rest of the DLL—i.e., the real mechanisms—remains for the programmer to create. We will discuss this next.

The StdAfx.cpp source file is very brief and consists principally of an include statement for the StdAfx.h header:

```
// stdafx.cpp : source file that includes just the standard includes
//    Example.pch will be the pre-compiled header
//    stdafx.obj will contain the pre-compiled type information
#include "stdafx.h"
// TODO: reference any additional headers you need in STDAFX.H
// and not in this file
```

The StdAfx.h header file offers a couple of elements of interest:

```
// stdafx.h : include file for standard system include files,
//  or project specific include files that are used frequently, but
//       are changed infrequently
//
#if
!defined(AFX_STDAFX_H__C45FACC3_2D4A_11D2_BD12_004005360DEC__INCLUDED_)
#define AFX_STDAFX_H__C45FACC3_2D4A_11D2_BD12_004005360DEC__INCLUDED_
```

The preceding #DEFINE statement is a generated UUID (Universally Unique ID) that simply ensures that the header file is ignored if it has already been referenced during compilation. Other than this, the UUID provided has no value and is not a part of the completed DLL.

```
#if _MSC_VER > 1000
#pragma once
```

```
#endif // _MSC_VER > 1000
// Insert your headers here
#define WIN32_LEAN_AND_MEAN    // Exclude rarely-used stuff from _
Windows headers
```

The #DEFINE WIN32_LEAN_AND_MEAN statement is a useful flag because this instructs the compiler to ignore a lot of rarely used elements that are found in the standard Windows headers. If, however, your project does not compile and responds with error messages saying that some API function or functions cannot be found, you might—before panicking—try commenting out the preceding statement.

```
#include <windows.h>
// TODO: reference additional headers your program requires here
```

An #INCLUDE statement is provided for the windows.h header file, and other #INCLUDE references for additional headers can be added here.

In the Fractal.CPP source file—which does not use the optional StdAfx files—two additional #INCLUDE references are used for the Math.h and Fractal.h headers. The first is because the DLL uses math functions and the second, of course, is the header supplying the function definitions for the main source file.

TIP   When system header files are referenced by #INCLUDE statements, the convention is to place the name of the header file in brackets, as #INCLUDE <windows.h> or #INCLUDE <math.h>. Alternatively, when the referenced header is specific to the project, the name of the header file is in quotation marks, as #INCLUDE "fractal.h". This nomenclature serves to identify the location where the headers will be found—i.e., either in the compiler's ..\Include directory or in the project's local directory. If, for any reason, the header files are found in some other location, an explicit path reference may also be used.

```
//{{AFX_INSERT_LOCATION}}
// Microsoft Visual C++ will insert additional declarations _
immediately before the previous line.
#endif // !defined(AFX_STDAFX_H__C45FACC3_2D4A_11D2_BD12_
_004005360DEC__INCLUDED_)
```

Both the StdAfx.cpp and StdAfx.h files are optional. The Project Wizard supplies these for your convenience, but both may be omitted if they are not wanted. As an example, in the Fractal and Reverse DLL projects, the StdAfx files were not used simply because there were no considerations depending on them.

Standard C++ versus the Microsoft Foundation Classes

The simplest form of DLL begins with a .cpp source file, a .h header file and an (optional) .def definition file, contains no derived classes, and does not depend on the Microsoft Foundation Classes or the MFC DLLs for support. The advantage of such a DLL is that it is lean and mean (figuratively speaking) and does not require ensuring that other DLLs are installed before it can be used.

On the other hand, if Visual C's App Wizard is used to create an MFC-based DLL, then you have the advantages of being able to use the MFC classes—including the CString and CFile classes—within the DLL-supported operations and, of course, being able to derive your own custom classes from the MFC library.

But, at the same time, in addition to installing your DLL you will also have to ensure that the appropriate supporting libraries are also installed.

Since the expectation here is that you are programming in Visual Basic and are creating a DLL to provide specialized support, there is probably little point in basing your DLL on the MFC classes.

For one reason, Visual Basic already provides support paralleling virtually all of the MFC classes—particularly the CString and CFile operations—so there is no need to duplicate these services.

And, for another reason, creating a straight C/C++ DLL is just simpler—particularly for anyone who is more accustomed to programming in VB than in VC.

Last, the Project Wizard also offers a cautionary note:

> When created, this DLL does not export any symbols. As a result, it will not produce a .lib file when it is built. If you wish this project to be a project dependency of some other project, you will either need to add code to export some symbols from the DLL so that an export library will be produced, or you can check the "doesn't produce lib" checkbox in the Linker settings page for this project.

Please note, however, that this caution does not apply to exported functions—only to exported symbols. The former are implicitly inherent in any DLL, while the latter are purely optional and rarely—if ever—used.

Still, for exported functions, no export library is required and, even though both the Fractal.DLL and Reverse.DLL projects will create .lib files, these can be freely ignored.

The key to determining which functions—in either library—are available externally (i.e., can be referenced by the calling application) is found in the EXPORT declaration used when the function is defined. This is demonstrated in the next section.

Declaring Functions for Export

One of the first tasks in creating a Dynamic Link Library is to define functions for export. While you may have any number of functions within the library, it is the exported functions that provide the access for other applications to use the DLL.

The .def file, or definitions file, provides a list of exported functions, making them available in the compiled DLL in a format that is accessible to external applications. Although you can compile and link the DLL without including the .def file and without producing any error reports, the resulting library will not have identifiable entry points when the VB application calls it.

The Fractal.DEF file is simple, consisting of a list of exported functions by name only, and can also include an ordinal value for each exported function. The sample definition file is:

```
; Fractal.def : Declares the module parameters for the DLL.

LIBRARY      "Fractal"
DESCRIPTION  'Fractal Windows dynamic-link libraries'
```

A standard .DEF file begins with the Library and Description statements. The Library statement simply defines the name of the DLL library. The Description statement is purely optional and simply offers an opportunity to enter a description of the library's purpose.

Next, following the Exports statement, the names of the library's exported functions are listed; optionally, each function name can be followed by an ordinal value.

```
EXPORTS
    ; Explicit exports can go here
    DLLMandelbrot           @1
    DLLMandelbrotArray      @2
    DLLPaintMandelbrot      @3
```

If you do not explicitly define any ordinal values, default ordinal values are assigned (sequentially) when the DLL is compiled and linked.

The Header File

Unlike the optional .def file, the .h header file is absolutely essential. If you have experience with C/C++ programming, you may think it is redundant to call the .h header *essential*, since all C/C++ files are expected to be accompanied by .h headers. This format of .cpp and .h files as pairs, however, is more custom and convenience than a hard and fast requirement, and, in many cases, there is really no need for an .h header.

For the Fractal.DLL library, the Fractal.H header serves several purposes:

• The .h header contains the names and specifications for the exportable functions (but may also contain declarations for local functions that are not exported).

• Any other C/C++ applications that want to use the Fractal.DLL library will use the .h header (in an #INCLUDE statement) to make the exported functions accessible within the application. (Visual Basic does not use the .h header, but does require parallel function definition statements, which we'll discuss presently.)

• The .h header provides a reference for programmers to see which functions are provided by the library and which parameters and arguments are required or returned.

The first item in the Fractal.H header is a #DEFINE statement, which identifies the Export macro as

```
extern "C" __declspec( dllexport )
```

Wherever the term EXPORT appears in the header file or in the .cpp source file at compile time, this macro is expanded to the full term:

```
#define EXPORT extern "C" __declspec( dllexport )
```

Such macros—and many macros are used in C/C++—are simply a convenient shorthand format for expressing complex terms, tests, or other provisions without having to write them out in full each time. The Export macro identifies the exported functions listed both in the header and in the source file.

Following the macro definition, you define three exported functions (as you will see later when the other two procedures are used):

```
EXPORT int CALLBACK DLLMandelbrot(double, double );
EXPORT int CALLBACK DLLMandelbrotArray(int*, int, int,
                                       double, double,
```

```
                                   double, double );
EXPORT int CALLBACK DLLPaintMandelbrot(HDC*, int, int,
                                   double, double,
                                   double, double );
```

Here, the EXPORT term identifies each of these functions as external functions, as using the C calling format for arguments, and, for the library, as exported functions. The int for each function is the value returned by the function to the calling application, and the Callback macro, which is already defined in Visual C/C++, expands to FAR PASCAL, identifying the handling required to call the function.

Since the Export and Callback macros are essentially fixed elements, you need not be concerned with them. Note, however, that local functions (functions that will not be exported) will not include the Export macro but will still specify a return value (or void if nothing is returned) and will be identified as CALLBACK.

Following the function name, the calling parameters are identified by their types. Optionally, here in the header, the function definitions can also include variable names. For example, the DLLMandelbrot function definition could also be written as:

```
EXPORT int CALLBACK DLLMandelbrot( double dXPos, double dYPos );
```

However, although you must include the variable names in the function entries in the .CPP file, they are optional in the .H header, and you can include them or omit them. The operational point is that only the types are important; the variable names proper, which are internal to the functions themselves, are not needed outside the source file.

TIP   Visual Basic requires that the complete statement appear on a single line and interprets a CR/LF pair (in the source code) as the end of a statement. In contrast, Visual C (and all versions of C) permits statements to extend over several lines in the source code and, instead of line breaks, requires semicolons as statement terminators.

The DLL Entry Point

Every dynamic-link library requires an entry point that, by custom and practice, is always named DllMain, just as the entry point for an executable under Windows is always named WinMain and under DOS is always named Main. Likewise, the parameters accompanying the call to DllMain are also predefined and do not vary.

In short, the entry point function for the DLL, in its simplest form, appears in the .CPP source file as:

```
int WINAPI DllMain(HINSTANCE hInstance, DWORD dwReason,
                   PVOID pvReserved )
{
    return TRUE;
}
```

Within the DllMain procedure, you can make additional provisions if, for example, you have some need or reason to perform some special initialization for the library. In general, however, the DllMain procedure does not need to perform any special tasks other than assuring the system that the DLL has been loaded correctly by returning True.

Once you provide the DllMain procedure, your source file is ready to compile and link and will produce a valid DLL library.

Of course, it will also be a library that doesn't do anything yet, so the next step is to add some functionality by providing at least one exported procedure.

DLL Procedures

A DLL procedure is not particularly different from any C/C++ procedure except, of course, for the EXPORT specification. The procedure definition from the .H header is repeated in the source file, but this time it does not have the terminating semicolon and does have the variable names as well as the variable type identifiers.

```
EXPORT int CALLBACK DLLMandelbrot( double dXPos, double dYPos )
{
```

Within the procedure, define any local variables that will be used. Unlike Visual Basic, in which variables can be used without being defined, C/C++ always requires that you explicitly define variables before you reference them:

```
double  dXIter, dYIter, dXTemp;
int     nSteps, nLimit = 100;
bool    bDone;
```

Once you define the variables, you assign a few initial values. Again, unlike Visual Basic, which has the grace to zero out variables when they are defined (or dimensioned), Visual C/C++ does not automatically clear the memory allocated for a variable. Instead, any allocated variable must have an explicit value assigned even if it is only a matter of explicitly zeroing the variable:

```
dXIter = 0.0;
dYIter = 0.0;
```

```
bDone  = FALSE;
nSteps = 0;
```

Once these local variables are initialized, we're ready to enter a Do…While loop, using the variable *bDone* as our exit condition. We started by assigning a value of False (0) to the *bDone* variable, and the loop is set up to continue until *bDone* has a value of True (1). This means that the loop will not terminate until we explicitly change the value of *bDone* in response to one of two tests.

Before performing any tests, however, we need to carry out an iteration of the Mandelbrot equation for the supplied coordinates:

```
do
{
    dXTemp = dXIter * dXIter - dYIter * dYIter + dXPos;
    dYIter = 2 * ( dXIter * dYIter) + dYPos;
    dXIter = dXTemp;
    nSteps++;
```

The values for *dXTemp*, *dXIter*, and *dYIter* were all initialized as zero, and the *dXTemp* variable is used for temporary storage so that the value in *dXIter* is not updated until the second calculation is complete.

Also, each time these calculations are reiterated, the *nSteps* variable is incremented. The value in *nSteps*, assuming that the calculated distance for this coordinate pair does increase without bounds, will identify the altitude for the point. The following statement

```
nSteps++;
```

increases the value of the *nSteps* variable by one.

NOTE   This notation was introduced not to make the code more compact, but to help the compiler optimize the native code it produces.

The following line

```
result = limit * nSteps++;
```

tells the compiler to produce code to multiply the variables *limit* and *nSteps* and store the result in the variable *result*. After the operation is complete and while the *nSteps* variable is in one of the processor's registers, it increases its value. If the variable *nSteps* is increased in a separate statement (nSteps = nSteps + 1), the value of the variable would have to be read from memory (an operation that can be avoided).

Last, after the current iteration is complete, one test is performed to determine the distance for the resulting values before a second test checks *nSteps* to decide if *nLimit* has been reached. If either condition is satisfied, the variable *bDone* is set to True, and the Do …While loop is allowed to terminate:

```
If ( dXIter * dXIter + dYIter * dYIter ) >= 4.0 )
    bDone = TRUE;
if( nSteps >= nLimit )
    bDone = TRUE;
}
while( ! bDone );
```

The ! operator in C/C++ is the equivalent of the logical Not operator. The Not operator in C/C++ inverts every bit of the following variable. Likewise, the logical And operator in C/C++ is &, and the logical Or operator is |. The And, Or, and Not operators are numeric operators that act on each bit of variable(s). The And operator in *value1* And *value2* will And each bit of the variable *value1* with the corresponding bit of the variable *value2* and return the new value. These operators are also known as bitwise operators because they process one bit at a time and don't treat variables as logical ones (True/False values).

Finally, if *nSteps* is less than *nLimit*, the function returns the *nSteps* value modulo 15 (that is, the remainder after dividing by 15) for use as a color index to indicate the altitude of this point. Or, if *nSteps* equals *nLimit* (or is greater), the value of 15 is returned since this is the color index for white in the default palette that Visual Basic uses:

```
if( nSteps < nLimit )
    return( nSteps % 15 );
else
    return( 15 );
}
```

And this completes the DLLMandelbrot procedure. We'll discuss the process for calling the DLLMandelbrot function in the section "Calling DLL Functions from Visual Basic," later in this chapter.

Using Arrays As Parameters

Let's see if we can improve the speed of the application by reducing the number of calls to the DLLMandelbrot procedure. The DLLMandelbrot procedure is called once for each point. For an image 400 × 400 pixels, it must be called 160,000 times. Let's see if we can save any seconds by calling another function in the DLL that calculates the values of all points and returns an array with the pixel color values.

We are going to develop another procedure, the DLLMandelbrotArray, that will set up an array whose dimensions are the same as the dimensions of the Picture-Box control, on which the fractal is displayed, in pixels. The DLL procedure will fill in all the values of the array's elements and pass it back to the VB application, which will use the values stored in the array to paint each pixel on the PictureBox.

WARNING This approach is just about the worst as far as the apparent speed is concerned, since the user won't see the fractal being drawn as it's calculated. The calculations must complete before any pixels can be drawn. It's not a very good approach, but we'll explore it anyway.

Besides ruining the apparent speed of the application, this approach does not improve the actual speed of the application. We'll discuss it because we want to show you how to use arrays to process large sets of data with a Visual C++ DLL. Some interesting issues arise when you pass arrays back and forth to DLLs, and if you are going to use arrays in your Visual C++ DLLs, you will find this informa-tion useful.

In the second exported function in the Fractal DLL, an array of integers is expected as a parameter. Or, more accurately, instead of an array of integers, a pointer to the first element in the array is expected, along with two arguments giving the size of the array. (A two-dimensional array is assumed here.)

Since this version will calculate values (altitudes) for all the points in the array, the last four parameters are the dXStart/dYStart and dXEnd/dYEnd arguments, which set the boundaries for the region of the Mandelbrot set that we want to explore:

```
EXPORT int CALLBACK DLLMandelbrotArray(int *pA,
                                       int nXSize, int nYSize,
                                       double dXStart, double dYStart,
                                       double dXEnd, double dYEnd)
{
    double    dXStep, dYStep;

    dXStep = ( dXEnd - dXStart ) / nXSize;
    dYStep = ( dYEnd - dYStart ) / nYSize;
    for( int j=0; j<nYSize; j++ )
        for( int i=0; i<nXSize; i++ )
        {
            *pA = DLLMandelbrot(dXStart + i * dXStep,
```

```
                              dYStart + j * dYStep );
             pA++;
          }
       return TRUE;
    }
```

Rather than repeating the code for calculating the point values, the same exported DLLMandelbrot function is also called locally. Even though a function is explicitly exported, nothing prevents us from using it locally as well.

Because we have a pointer to the first element in the array, the inner loop simply increments the address of the pointer to the next element in the array after performing the calculations for one point in the array, instead of passing the entire array as a fixed size. The variable *pA* is a pointer to the array, and it's declared as *pA. When you declare a variable with the asterisk in front of it, like

```
int *pA
```

you create a variable that points to an integer value in memory. In the code, you use the expression *pA to access the integer you're pointing at. If you assign a value directly to the *pA* variable, you cause it to point to a different area in memory. The array is a collection of integers stored in sequential memory locations. When you increase the variable that points to the first element of the array, the compiler knows that it should not add 1 to the current value of the variable *pA*. When you increase a pointer, it should point to the next integer, which is 8 bytes away. The compiler will increase the value of the variable *pA* by 8 so that *pA will point to the next element in the array.

Notice also that the array we pass from the Visual Basic application is two-dimensional, but in the DLLMandelbrotArray() function, we address it as one-dimensional. No matter how many dimensions an array has, its elements are stored in sequential memory locations, one row at a time. Therefore, when we reach the last element of the first row and attempt to access the next element, this will be the first element of the next row. This trick allows you to access any two-dimensional array declared in VB from within a DLL function, without knowing its exact dimensions.

Pointers are at the heart of C programming, yet they are a sore spot for VB programmers. However, you don't really need to master all aspects of pointers (they can get quite nasty, as you can have pointers to pointers and pointers to functions and other beasts) in order to write a few simple DLLs to speed a segment of your VB application. You've seen how to pass numeric variables and arrays from a VB application to a Visual C++ function. Later in this chapter, you'll learn how to pass arrays of characters back and forth, and we don't think you need to learn more about pointers.

Although this procedure is valid, on occasion problems can occur. For more on this, see the section "When an Int Is Not an Int," later in this chapter.

When you choose Draw DLL ➤ Mandelbrot (Array), the program displays the time it takes to calculate the color values of the pixels and the time it takes to display these values. It takes 2.85 seconds to calculate the entire Mandelbrot set and slightly more than 3 seconds to display it. The DLLMandelbrot() function is very fast. By decoupling the calculations from the manipulation of the display, we were able to pinpoint the major source of delay.

If you are using Visual Basic to design applications that do a lot of drawing on the screen, you have already noticed that Visual Basic isn't extremely fast when it comes to drawing operations. It's almost puzzling, but on a fast Pentium it takes longer to display the pixels than to calculate them. Let's see how much more we can improve the Fractal application by moving the painting of the pixels from the VB application to the DLL. Our last attempt is to design a Visual C++ procedure that not only calculates the fractal, but draws it on the screen as well.

Notice that the time it takes to paint the pixels depends on the display settings. Because the code uses the QBColor() function, the code runs fastest on systems set to display 256 colors. The same code is considerably slower on True Color systems. We verified this behavior on three different systems and it's rather unlikely that it will behave differently on your system. We suggest that you test all versions of the Fractal application after setting your display to 256 colors; besides, the application doesn't display more than 256 colors anyway.

Using Direct Paint

The DLLPaintMandelbrot function accepts a pointer to the device context handle for the PictureBox control on the VB Form. Along with the device context, this function is called with the limit values for the region to be explored. With this much information, the DLLPaintMandelbrot function attempts to perform all the calculations and the paint operations by calling the SetPixelV() function.

Code 17.4　　　**Calculating and Painting the Mandelbrot Set**

```
EXPORT int CALLBACK DLLPaintMandelbrot( HDC *pDC,
                                        double dXStart, double dYStart,
                                        double dXEnd,   double dYEnd )
{
    double  dXStep, dYStep;
    int     nIndex, nXSize, nYSize;
```

```
nXSize = nYSize = 1001;
dXStep = ( dXEnd - dXStart ) / nXSize;
dYStep = ( dYEnd - dYStart ) / nYSize;
for( int i=0; i<nXSize; i++ )
{
    for( int j=0; j<nYSize; j++ )
    {
        nIndex = DLLMandelbrot( dXStart + i * dXStep,
                                dYStart + j * dYStep );
        if( nIndex < 15 )
            SetPixelV( *pDC, i, j, PALETTEINDEX( nIndex ) );
    }
}
return TRUE;
}
```

To test the new implementation of the Mandelbrot algorithm, run the Fractal application and choose Draw DLL ➤ Mandelbrot (Paint). When executed from within the IDE, the Mandelbrot set takes 3.75 seconds to complete. The compiled version of the application is marginally faster (3.25 seconds). The VB compiler can't help this procedure significantly, because nearly all the work (both the calculation and the display of the fractal) is done by the DLL.

The two numbers you should compare are the time it takes for Visual Basic to calculate and display the Mandelbrot set, 10.50 seconds, and the time it takes for the Visual C++ DLL to display the same image, which is only 3.25 seconds. The function MandelbrotPaint(), implemented in Visual C++, is nearly three times faster than the equivalent VB code. Our effort to build a DLL in Visual C++ certainly paid off.

Another Approach

Visual C++ isn't much faster than Visual Basic when it comes to drawing operations. This shouldn't surprise you, because both languages call the same API function. Instead of using either the PSet or SetPixelV operations—both of which are inherently slow—you can write the pixel values to the pixel data elements within a bitmap structure to achieve a major improvement in speed. You should modify the Fractal application and incorporate the technique discussed earlier in the section "Drawing on Device Contexts" to make it as fast as it can get.

Calling DLL Functions from Visual Basic

Now that we've created a dynamic-link library and have provided several exported functions, the next step is to call these functions from within a Visual Basic program.

The Fractal application includes the Draw Direct and the Draw DLL menus. The Draw Direct menu contains two items:

- Mandelbrot
- Mandelbrot (Zoom)

Both draw views of the Mandelbrot set on the PictureBox control using only Visual Basic code (the first command draws the entire Mandelbrot set; the second draws a detail of the Mandelbrot set).

The Draw DLL menu contains four items:

- Mandelbrot
- Mandelbrot (Zoom)
- Mandelbrot (Array)
- Mandelbrot (Paint)

The first two commands are equivalent to the commands of the Draw Direct menu, only they use the DLLMandelbrot function. The other two commands call the DLLMandelbrotArray and DLLPaintMandelbrot functions. To compare the times required for internal and external calculations and drawing operations on the Visual Basic side of the application, a timer receives the system clock information before drawing the set and then compares times with the system clock when the drawing operation is complete. The difference, which is the elapsed time, is then reported through a dialog box.

A similar dialog box reports on each of the menu items. Choosing Draw DLL ➢ Mandelbrot (Zoom) displays an enlarged view, as shown in Figure 17.10.

The zoomed region, magnified 100 times, shows features that are similar to the set as a whole. This recursion of similarities can be found along the shores of the fractal sea at almost any location and any magnification.

FIGURE 17.10:

A zoomed view into the
Mandelbrot set

External Function Declarations

Just as the C/C++ DLL has a .H header file with declarations for both local and
exported functions, the Visual Basic program also requires forward declarations
for the DLL-accessible functions. For the VB version, however, a .H header is not
compatible. Instead, the forward declarations for the Fractal.DLL exported functions appear at the top of the code section of the Fractal.frm file as

```
Private Declare Function DLLMandelbrot Lib "Fractal.DLL"
     ( ByVal XPos As Double, ByVal YPos As Double ) As Integer
```

The DLLMandelbrot procedure is declared as a function, meaning that it returns a
value or result. The function name, DLLMandelbrot, is used in the dynamic-link
library for the desired function. The term Lib following the function name indicates
that the function is located in an external library, and the name "Fractal.DLL" identifies the library itself.

In this case, the assumption is that the dynamic-link library (the DLL file) is
located in the \Windows\System directory (or somewhere else in the current path
where it will be found without difficulty). As an alternative, the specification can
also include an explicit path or drive/path for the DLL file.

Following the DLL name is a list of the calling parameters in parentheses. These parameters, of course, have been translated from Visual C/C++ into Visual Basic terminology, as has the return value for the function following the closing parenthesis.

Translating parameter arguments from C/C++ to Visual Basic is an excellent way to generate serious errors that may or may not be caught by the compiler. The DLLMandelbrot function there doesn't appear to present much opportunity for error; two doubles are passed, by value, as arguments, and an integer value is returned. So what can go wrong? In this case, not much. The difference is unimportant since the return value is a color index that is easily contained in either a long or a short int.

NOTE   Do take a look at the sidebar "When an Int Is Not an Int," later in this chapter. The integer expected on return may not be precisely the same as the integer returned by the DLL function.

The next two declarations are not quite as forgiving:

```
Private Declare Function DLLPaintMandelbrot Lib "Fractal.DLL" _
   ( ByRef hDC As Any, _
     ByVal nXSize As Integer, ByVal nYSize As Integer, _
     ByVal dXStart As Double, ByVal dYStart As Double, _
     ByVal dXEnd As Double,   ByVal dYEnd As Double) As Integer
```

In the DLLPaintMandelbrot declaration, the first argument is a handle to a device context, and handles must be passed by reference, not by value. However, since VB doesn't really have a "type" for this, we used the type Any as a catchall.

Two integer values are being passed that are actually short integers (2-byte), but the DLL function is expecting long integers (4-byte). In this case, no conflict occurs because the arguments are passed by value.

In the DLLMandelbrotArray function, however, we find another potential for an error in translation. The declaration for this DLL function—from the Fractal.H header—indicates that the first parameter is expected to be a pointer to an integer:

```
EXPORT int CALLBACK DLLMandelbrotArray( int*, int, int,_
        double, double, double, double );
```

In the Visual Basic code, again there is no exact equivalent type, so the forward declaration again uses the type Any and passes the parameter by reference (ByRef), the VB equivalent of a pointer:

```
Private Declare Function DLLMandelbrotArray Lib "Fractal.DLL" _
```

```
( ByRef A As Any, _
    ByVal nXSize As Integer, ByVal nYSize As Integer, _
    ByVal dXStart As Double, ByVal dYStart As Double, _
    ByVal dXEnd As Double,   ByVal dYEnd As Double) As Integer
```

Okay, a pointer is a pointer, right? There's no problem here, right? Well, yes and no. The declaration is perfectly correct, but the form of the declaration, as we will discuss in a moment, can inadvertently disguise a more serious problem.

Passing Parameters by Value

By default—that is, if not otherwise specified—arguments in VC++ applications are passed by value. Not only is this convenient, but it allows the operating system to mask what could otherwise be conflicts between types. As long as arguments are only exchanged as values, the raw value data is translated into the expected format without conflict if a short integer is passed to a function expecting a long integer.

On the other hand, if a long integer is being translated as a value to a short integer, information can be lost because the short int will contain only the data from the low word of the long value.

In most cases, the worst that you can expect is a loss of data, but the Visual Basic defaults are not the same as the defaults used by 32-bit C/C++ compilers. Get in the habit of specifying the ByVal keyword in front of the arguments you pass to your DLLs (the same is true with nearly all the Windows API function declarations).

Passing Parameters by Reference

Although passing parameters by value is the simple choice and, in many cases, is perfectly appropriate, in a number of circumstances parameters must be passed by reference.

For example, to call the DLLPaintMandelbrot function from the DLL, the handle to the device context must be passed by reference, not by value. Here, the value of the handle is irrelevant; it is simply an identifier that the operating system uses. What's important is that there is only one device context, and, by passing a pointer to the handle to the DLL, the device context is being shared, giving the DLL access to the original device context.

When you call the DLLMandelbrotArray function from your VB application, another parameter must also be passed by reference (although, this time, for a slightly different reason). Here, a pointer is being passed to the first element in an array so that the DLL can fill in the million-plus array elements with individual values (it wouldn't make a lot of sense to copy the million-plus array elements and pass them by value, not to mention that the values stored in the array by the function wouldn't make it back to the VB application).

If the array is passed by value, the DLL function receives a copy of the array, but any values entered in the copy are not returned to the calling function. The copy is strictly local and is lost (discarded from memory) when the called function returns.

Alternatively, you could treat an array as a structure and pass it by reference to the entire array. This, however, requires a fixed array size and, of course, needs identical definitions in both VB and VC (which in turn means that every time you want to change the size of the fractal image, you must change the DLL's code and recompile). Instead, by passing a reference to the first element of the array only, the called function can calculate a value to be written to that address and then offset the address to the next element in the array. In this fashion, a two-dimensional array (or even a one-dimensional array) of any size can be filled because the array size has been passed separately. And, because the array belongs to the calling application (only an address is being passed), the resulting values remain available even after the DLL-supplied function terminates.

Of course, when you're working with arrays, you also need to keep in mind the following:

- Different languages can mean quite different things even when the terms are the same (for more on this, see the "When an Int Is Not an Int" section later in this chapter).

- Visual Basic and C/C++ differ subtly in how arrays are dimensioned (for more on this, see the "Array Dimensions in VB versus VC" section later in this chapter).

As long as you avoid these two conflicts (and there are probably others that are less apparent), passing parameters by reference is a useful way to make it possible for a DLL (or any other remote procedure) to return values more complex than a simple integer or a double.

Problems and Conflicts between Visual Basic and C/C++

When you mix languages—for example, when you use a DLL written in Pascal or C/++ with Visual Basic—some conflicts will not show up in the compile/build operation. And, in some cases, the problems may not show up at all, at least not in a form that can be conveniently identified and debugged. Other problems will make themselves entirely too apparent by causing a compiler crash, and debugging them can be annoying. Here are a couple of these types of conflicts.

When an Int Is Not an Int

Visual Basic defines an integer as a 2-byte or WORD value. In contrast, Visual C/C++ (the current, 32-bit version) defines an integer as a 4-byte value (a DWORD or double WORD). In most cases, this difference does not affect development, even when you use a VC-developed DLL with a VB application. When Visual Basic passes an integer parameter (2 bytes) to a DLL that is expecting an integer argument (4 bytes), the translation is automatic.

Likewise, when the VC DLL returns an integer (4-byte) value, the VB application "sees" a 2-byte integer without a conflict. Of course, if the returned value is greater than 0xFFFF (65535), the data that the Visual Basic program recognizes will not correspond to what the DLL intended to return because the high word value will be lost in translation.

One solution, of course, is for the VB application to always pass INT values as LONG when the DLL is expecting integers and to expect a LONG return when the DLL is returning an integer result. This accommodation, rather obviously, is a shortcoming in Visual Basic, which has simply not fully entered the world of 32-bit operations. When passing arguments by value, this is not a problem, as Visual Basic performs the necessary conversions. When passing arguments by reference, however, you are responsible for providing the proper variable types. In some circumstances, however, no automatic accommodation is possible, and serious results can easily eventuate from such discrepancies in sizes. For example, in the DLL-MandelbrotArray function in the Fractal.DLL library, the first parameter expected is the address of an array of integers, and the second and third parameters are the dimensions of the array, arguments passed as integers (2-byte) and expected as integers (4-byte).

As we mentioned earlier, these second and third parameters are passed and accepted without conflict. The first parameter, however, is passed as an address (ByRef) and does have potential for error—a serious error—if the Visual Basic application declares an array of integers as

```
Private Sub MandelbrotArray_Click()
    Dim A(1000, 1000) As Integer
```

and then passes the address of the array to the DLL's DLLMandelbrotArray function as

```
bResult = DLLMandelbrotArray( A(0, 0), ...
```

Initially, when the DLL is called, there is no obvious problem. However, within the DLL, the array is recognized only as an address of the first element of an array, and the DLL enters values in the array by incrementing the address to reach successive elements of the array. The address pointer is incremented, however, as if the elements in the array were 4 bytes in size.

Two errors result:

- The DLL is only writing results to every second element in the original array supplied by the Visual Basic application.

- Once the original array is exhausted, the DLL will be writing additional information to an area beyond the array.

In most cases, this addressing error will simply result in the VB application crashing *after* the DLL returns, but, in a worst-case scenario, the result could be the corruption of the system (that is, a system crash).

The solution, of course, is simple. When the DLL expects an array of integers, the VB application should declare an array of Long:

```
Private Sub MandelbrotArray_Click()
    Dim A(1000, 1000) As Long
    bResult = DLLMandelbrotArray( A(0, 0), ...
```

The point, however, is not as simple as the solution shown here. Because VB is not fully 32-bit compliant, be very sure when using a DLL that you know what you are passing as arguments and what you are expecting returned. Even though it is called an integer in both cases, an integer is not the same in both languages.

Array Dimensions in VB versus VC

Visual Basic and Visual C/C++ also differ in the way that they dimension arrays.

WARNING   Be aware that passing the wrong array variable or attempting to access nonexisting elements of the array from within the Visual C++ code will frequently lead to crashes.

In Visual Basic, when an array is declared as

```
Dim A(10) As Long
```

the array actually has 11 elements. In this example, VB allocates and numbers elements as A(0), A(1), A(2), A(3), A(4), A(5), A(6), A(7), A(8), A(9) and A(10).

In C/C++, the corresponding declaration would be

```
int A[10];
```

but this array has only 10 elements, allocated and numbered as A[0], A[1], A[2], A[3], A[4], A[5], A[6], A[7], A[8], A[9]. There is no A[10] (eleventh) element.

Therefore, if you tell a DLL function that you have passed a pointer to an array with dimensions of (1000, 1000), the DLL will expect the array to include only 1,000,000 elements when the actual array contains 1,002,001 elements (1001 to the square), a discrepancy of 2,001 elements. The solution, obviously, is to always declare the actual array dimensions (1001, 1001) and not the index limits.

Code 17.5 **Visual C++ Program Listing for Fractal DLL**

Fractal.DEF
```
; Fractal.def : Declares the module parameters for the DLL.
LIBRARY      "Fractal"
DESCRIPTION  'Fractal Windows Dynamic Link Library'
EXPORTS
     ; Explicit exports can go here
     DLLMandelbrot              @1
     DLLMandelbrotArray         @2
     DLLPaintMandelbrot         @3
```

Fractal.H
```
#define EXPORT extern "C" __declspec( dllexport )
EXPORT int CALLBACK DLLMandelbrot( double, double );
EXPORT int CALLBACK DLLMandelbrotArray( int*, int, int, double, _
double, double, double );
EXPORT int CALLBACK DLLPaintMandelbrot( HDC*, int, int, double, _
double, double, double );
```

Fractal.CPP
```
#include <windows.h>
#include <math.h>
#include "fractal.h"

int WINAPI DllMain(HINSTANCE hInstance,
                DWORD dwReason, PVOID pvReserved )
{
```

```
        return TRUE;
}

EXPORT int CALLBACK DLLMandelbrot(double dXPos, double dYPos )
{
    double      dXIter, dYIter, dXTemp;
    int             nSteps, nLimit = 100;
    bool      bDone;

    dXIter = 0.0;
    dYIter = 0.0;
    bDone  = FALSE;
    nSteps = 0;
    do
    {
        dXTemp = dXIter * dXIter-dYIter * dYIter + dXPos;
        dYIter = 2 * ( dXIter * dYIter) + dYPos;
        dXIter = dXTemp;
        nSteps++;
        if( sqrt( dXIter * dXIter + dYIter * dYIter ) >= 2.0 )
            bDone = TRUE;
        if( nSteps >= nLimit )
            bDone = TRUE;
    }
    while( ! bDone );
    if( nSteps < nLimit )
        return( nSteps % 15 );
    else
        return( 15 );
}

EXPORT int CALLBACK DLLMandelbrotArray(int *pA, int nXSize,
                                       int nYSize,
                                       double dXStart, double dYStart,
                                       double dXEnd, double dYEnd )
{
    double      dXStep, dYStep;

    dXStep = ( dXEnd - dXStart ) / nXSize;
    dYStep = ( dYEnd - dYStart ) / nYSize;
    for( int j=0; j<nYSize; j++ )
        for( int i=0; i<nXSize; i++ )
          {
             *pA = DLLMandelbrot( dXStart + i * dXStep,
                                  dYStart + j * dYStep );
```

```
                pA++;
            }
        return TRUE;
    }

    EXPORT int CALLBACK DLLPaintMandelbrot(HDC *pDC,
                                           int nXSize, int nYSize,
                                           double dXStart, double dYStart,
                                           double dXEnd, double dYEnd )
    {
        double     dXStep, dYStep;
        int        nIndex;

        SetMapMode( *pDC, MM_ANISOTROPIC );
        SetWindowExtEx( *pDC, nXSize, nYSize, NULL );
        SetViewportExtEx( *pDC, nXSize, nYSize, NULL );

        RealizePalette( *pDC );

        dXStep = ( dXEnd - dXStart ) / nXSize;
        dYStep = ( dYEnd - dYStart ) / nYSize;
        for( int i=0; i<nXSize; i++ )
        {
            for( int j=0; j<nYSize; j++ )
            {
                nIndex = DLLMandelbrot( dXStart + i * dXStep,
                                        dYStart + j * dYStep );
                if( nIndex < 15 )
                    SetPixelV( *pDC, i, j, PALETTEINDEX( nIndex ) );
            }
        }
        return TRUE;
    }
```

Fractal Images and Palettes

The Fractal application we used in the previous sections to demonstrate how to build DLLs in Visual C++ produces 16-color fractals (not the most exciting images). It's certainly possible to modify the code to produce fractals with many colors and smooth coloring schemes. In the `Fractals\Palette` folder in this chapter's folder on the CD, you will find another project, also named Fractal, that draws smoothly colored fractals. This fractal

Continued on next page

application uses 236 iterations in calculating each pixel's color and is significantly slower than the version of the Fractal application we use in this chapter to demonstrate the Fractal DLL. The new Fractal project, which uses palettes to color the fractal images, is implemented in Visual Basic so that it can be used by those of you who would rather experiment on fractal images without resorting to Visual C++.

If you open this project in the Visual Basic IDE, you will see that the line

```
Picture1.PSet (i, j), QBColor(nSteps Mod 16)
```

is replaced by the line

```
Picture1.PSet (i, j), &H1000000 + nSteps + 10
```

The color expression in the above statement corresponds to an entry in the current palette. Because the first 10 and last 10 colors in a palette are reserved for system use, we skip them and use the remaining 236 colors of the palette. The number of iterations is mapped to a palette color that is used to paint the current pixel.

The fractals shown below were produced by the revised Fractal application and show a few details of the Mandelbrot set. You can experiment by trying different palettes to see which one is best suited for each image.

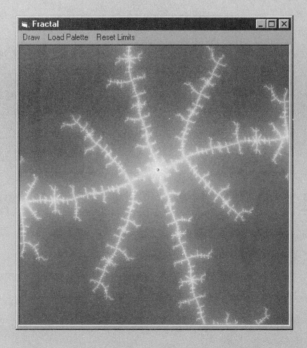

Continued on next page

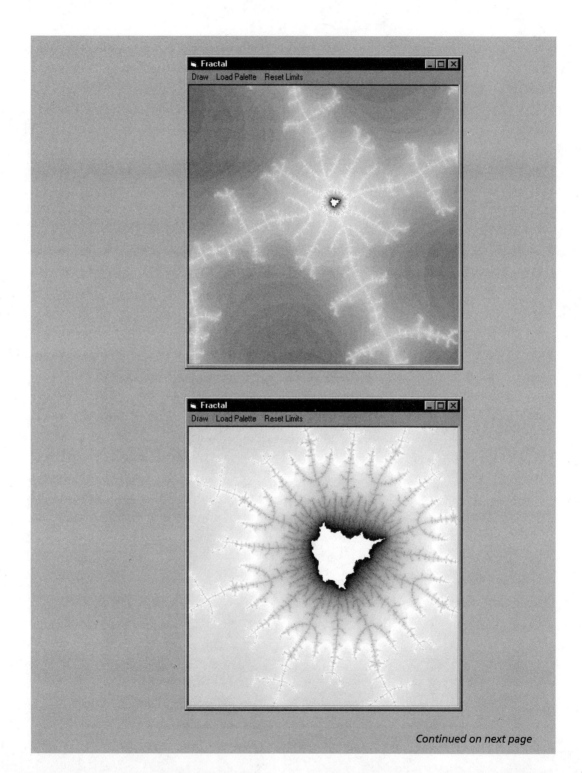

Continued on next page

The `FRACTAL.DLL` file contains yet another function, the MandelbrotMax() function, whose declarations are

```
Private Declare Function MandelbrotMax Lib "fractal.dll" _
(ByVal XPos As Double, ByVal YPos As Double, ByVal MaxIterations _
As Long) As Long
```

This function accepts the same arguments as the DLLMandelbrot() function, plus the maximum number of iterations. The Fractal application in the `Palette` folder uses the MandelbrotMax() function to generate the fractals shown in this sidebar.

Manipulating Strings with Visual C++

C/C++ DLLs can be particularly helpful in sorting or ordering large blocks of data. For example, the ReverseString function in the Reverse.DLL accepts a string that can be a maximum of 100Kb. First, the string is reversed entirely, and then, in a second operation, the individual words are re-reversed (restored). Thus, the following sentence:

```
The quick red fox jumped over the lazy brown dog
```

becomes:

```
dog brown lazy the over jumped fox red quick The
```

Although this example is rather trivial, it is by no means without a practical value, and it does illustrate how to handle character strings in a VC++ DLL. The Visual Basic Instr() function locates instances of a string in a longer string, but it always starts from the beginning of the long string. A function that locates the same instances in the reverse order (starting from the end of the string) would also be useful, but to implement it efficiently, you would have to reverse both strings and then perform a search with the Instr() function.

The Visual Basic routine to reverse the string in place would look something like this:

```
For i = 1 To Len(AString) / 2
    tmpChar = Mid(AString, Len(AString) - i + 1, 1)
    Mid(AString, Len(AString) - i + 1, 1) = Mid(AString, i, 1)
    Mid(AString, i, 1) = tmpChar
Next
```

All this routine does is reverse the original string, character for character:

god nworb yzal eht revo depmuj xof der kciuq ehT

You can reverse a 30Kb string in approximately 0.6 seconds, as you may recall from the section "Manipulate Strings Efficiently" earlier in this chapter.

Alternatively, the ReverseString function in the Reverse.DLL is called in a slightly different fashion. First, the declaration of the function appears as

```
Private Declare Function ReverseString Lib "Reverse.DLL" (ByVal Str As
Any, ByVal StrLen As Integer) As String
```

The string argument is passed by value, not by reference, and here it is passed as a type Any, although actually it makes little difference whether the type is identified as Any or as String.

Next, to call the external function, the local variable *TempStr* receives a copy of the string to be modified. This is important because if you try to pass the property Text1.Text, your application will malfunction with a page fault error.

Also, we supply a size argument, StrLen, that contains the length of the string. This is necessary because, as you will see in a moment, the ReverseString function has no knowledge of the size of the string or even that it is looking at a string:

Code 17.6   **VB Code to Reverse a String**

```
Private Sub Command1_Click()
    Dim T1 As Single
    Dim T2 As Single
    Dim Msg
    Dim TempStr As String

    TempStr = Text1
    StrLen = Len(TempStr)
    T1 = Timer
    Text2 = ReverseString(TempStr, StrLen)
    T2 = Timer - T1
    Msg = Format(T2, "###0.000")
    Debug.Print "Elapsed time = " & Msg & _
                " seconds to reverse string (dll)"
End Sub
```

These provisos aside, the ReverseString function returns the modified text string in a form that can be copied to the Text2 member for display. What is not immediately apparent here is that the TempStr argument itself has also been altered, and the value returned by the ReverseString function is actually a pointer to the TempStr member, which has been used as a buffer for the transfer both to and from the external function.

Most important, using the same 30Kb text file as the sample to be processed, the execution time becomes approximately 0.050 seconds. It is more than 10 times faster while executing a more complex operation (it reverses the order of the words in the string, not just the characters). The ReverseString() function ignores punctuation, but you can easily modify the C code for various types of sequential character manipulation.

The Reverse project, shown in Figure 17.11, demonstrates the ReverseString function implemented in REVERSE.DLL. You'll find the Reverse project in this chapter's folder on the CD that comes with this book.

To test this function, copy a large segment of text from another application and paste it in the TextBox control on the Form. Then click the Reverse button.

FIGURE 17.11:

The Reverse project demonstrates the ReverseString function, which is implemented in REVERSE.DLL.

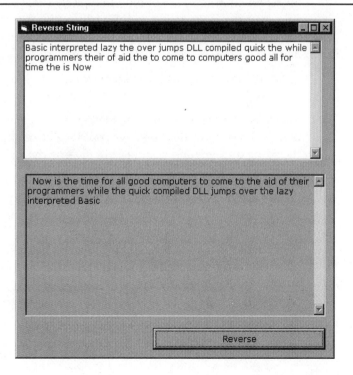

The first time you click the Reverse button, the operation will complete in almost a second. Visual Basic needs the additional time to load the DLL. After the DLL is loaded, the string is reversed in practically no time.

The Magic Black Box

Now, let's look inside the magic black box, the DLL function. C/C++ does not have particularly sophisticated string-handling functions; although, more recently, the MFC CString class has introduced a variety of member functions that parallel the Visual Basic string functions. These CString members, however, are not what we will be using here. Instead, we will rely on much more primitive (and faster) mechanisms.

Neither does C/C++ have a string data type. Instead, strings are simply arrays of characters (char data type in C). In VB, strings are also arrays of characters, but VB's strings are not readily accessible as arrays, whereas C/C++ strings are only accessible as indexed arrays.

The ReverseString function does not actually accept a string argument even though that is what the Visual Basic operation has passed. Instead, the Reverse-String function accepts a pointer to type char that essentially is the address of the first character in the string. In this fashion, the ReverseString function does not begin with a copy of the original string but, instead, has a pointer to the memory address for the string that belongs to the Visual Basic application:

```
EXPORT char* CALLBACK ReverseString( char* pStr, int nStrLen )
{
```

Because the string is not local, the ReverseString function needs to know the length of the string. (Granted, we could scan from the address to find the end of the string by searching for nulls, but passing the length, which VB already knows, is simpler.)

Internally, ReverseString declares two arrays of char, each 100KB in size. Although it's possible to allocate these dynamically, according to the size information provided by nStrLen, this static declaration is simpler for the present example. You might keep this alternative in mind, however, because other types of sort and order operations may well need to use dynamic allocation for buffer space.

```
char strTemp1[102400], strTemp2[102400];
char *pTemp;
int  i, j, k, n;
```

Next, before taking any actions, it is only prudent to clear the two buffers. Unlike Visual Basic, C/C++ does not automatically clear allocated memory, and you must explicitly set the entire range of memory to zeros:

```
//=== clear both buffers
memset( strTemp1, '\0', 102400 );
memset( strTemp2, '\0', 102400 );
```

Next, reverse the entire string. Because the source information is not in a local array and we have only a pointer to the data, we begin by duplicating the pointer. We do this because we will need the original pointer (address) again later:

```
pTemp = pStr;
```

Now that the pTemp pointer points to the same memory location as pStr (the string passed to the function by VB), we can set up a loop that will scan the original array of characters backward and append each character to the end of a new string (strTemp1):

```
// copy remote buffer (incoming) to local buffer in reverse order
for( i=nStrLen-1; i>=0;  )
{
    strTemp1[i-] = *pTemp;
    pTemp++;
}
```

After copying each character, we also increment the pointer pTemp. Notice that the loop counter is not decremented in the For statement. Instead, this operation takes place in the loop. The expression i does the following: First, it uses the current value of the variable *i* to address an element of the character array strTemp, and after the value is copied, the variable is decreased by one. Earlier, we discussed problems that can arise when VB and C/C++ don't correctly understand array types. This problem, however, does not arise here, and we can simply increment the address without concerns.

If, however, we were doing this for other types of arrays—such as an array of structures, for example—we would need to make appropriate provisions for incrementing the address pointer according to the size of the structure.

But, once we have our local array, which is now in reverse order, our next task is to re-reverse the individual words to put them in forward order—that is, to restore *sdrawkcab* to *backwards*. We'll begin with several index variables, initializing three of these as zero:

```
i = j = n = 0;
```

Next, we'll use a Do...While loop to terminate when our index *i* reaches nStrLen:

```
do
{
```

Within the Do...While loop, we execute another While loop to look for a non-alphanumeric character, using the isalnum() function to test each character in the array and incrementing *i* until a space, punctuation, or other nonalphanumeric character is found:

```
while( isalnum( strTemp1[i] ) ) i++;
```

The isalnum() function is only one of the character-test functions supplied by C/C++. C/C++ provides a variety of useful tests, and we could also include punctuation or exclude numbers or whatever our test required.

In this case, however, as soon as we find a nonalphanumeric character, we've reached the end of the word, and we need another loop to re-reverse the characters belonging to the word:

```
for( k=i-1; k>=j; k- )
    strTemp2[n++] = strTemp1[k];
```

We've used i-1 to exclude the space (or punctuation or other characters) at the end of the word. But, of course, we need a separator between words, so we'll insert a space.

```
strTemp2[n++] = ' ';
```

Each time we write a char to the strTemp2 array, we're incrementing the *n* index.

And, last, we increment the *i* index before copying the value to the *j* index. (The expression ++i says that *i* is incremented before anything else happens. If the expression is i++, *i* is incremented last, after it is used in the operation.)

```
j = ++i;
}
while( i < nStrLen );
```

Now, when our original Do...While loop finishes, we have a copy of the original text that is in reverse word order. (We've also dropped all punctuation, but that's not important here.)

However, this reverse-order copy is a local copy, and, once the ReverseString function exits, these local arrays will be lost—freed from memory—which means that their contents will also be lost. Therefore, our last operation is to copy the data from the local array back to the buffer maintained by the Visual Basic application that called ReverseString. And this is also why we've been careful to maintain our original address pointer. Now we need it again:

```
// write changed buffer (local) back to original buffer (remote)
pTemp = pStr;
```

However, since we still aren't done with the original pointer, we assign pTemp to the same initial address again. And then we initiate another loop to copy the indexed element from strTemp2 back to the memory location addressed by pTemp before incrementing pTemp to the next address:

```
for( i=0; i<nStrLen; i++ )
{
    *pTemp = strTemp2[i];
    pTemp++;
}
```

And, finally, we'll return the pStr pointer to the calling application:

```
    return pStr;
}
```

Remember, pStr is the same pointer that the calling application supplied as the address of the local buffer containing the original data. In this last loop, we've copied the local array back to the original string (TempStr) and then returned the address of the original string to the calling application where it is assigned to a new string member (Text2). And, because we're changing the string that was passed as an argument, we have another reason for passing a copy (TempStr) rather than the real original (Text1).

Now that you have seen the code of the ReverseString function, let's review all the operations it performs on a 30Kb string. First, it copies the string to a local array, reverses all characters, then reverses each word in the string, and finally copies the processed array back to another string, which is returned to the VB application. All these operations don't take more than a few dozen milliseconds, which is really impressive. Visual C++ is extremely efficient when it comes to handling characters, and you should consider a Visual C++ DLL for operations that manipulate strings extensively. One thing to keep in mind is that Visual Basic can handle small strings very fast too, but it slows down quickly as the strings grow large.

Code 17.7   **Visual C++ Program Listing for Reverse DLL**

Reverse.DEF

```
; Reverse.def : Declares the module parameters for the DLL.

LIBRARY      "Reverse"
DESCRIPTION  'Reverse Windows dynamic-link libraries'

EXPORTS
    ; Explicit exports can go here
    ReverseString            @1
```

Reverse.H

```
#define EXPORT extern "C" __declspec( dllexport )

EXPORT char* CALLBACK ReverseString( char*, int );
```

Reverse.C

```
#include <windows.h>
#include "reverse.h"

int WINAPI DllMain( HINSTANCE hInstance,
                    DWORD dwReason, PVOID pvReserved )
{
    return TRUE;
}

EXPORT char* CALLBACK ReverseString( char* pStr, int nStrLen )
{
    char strTemp1[102400], strTemp2[102400];
    char *pTemp;
    int  i, j, k, n;

    //=== clear both buffers
    memset( strTemp1, '\0', 102400 );
    memset( strTemp2, '\0', 102400 );

    //=== copy remote buffer (incoming) to local buffer in reverse
order
    pTemp = pStr;
```

```
    for( i=nStrLen-1; i>=0;  )
    {
        strTemp1[i-] = *pTemp;
        pTemp++;
    }

    //=== now re-reverse each word in the strTemp buffer
    i = j = n = 0;
    do
    {
        while( isalnum( strTemp1[i] ) ) i++;
        for( k=i-1; k>=j; k- )
            strTemp2[n++] = strTemp1[k];
        strTemp2[n++] = ' ';
        j = ++i;
    }
    while( i < nStrLen );

    //=== write changed buffer (local) back to original buffer (remote)
    pTemp = pStr;
    for( i=0; i<nStrLen; i++ )
    {
        *pTemp = strTemp2[i];
        pTemp++;
    }
    return pStr;
}
```

PART IV

Programming for the Web

CHAPTER

EIGHTEEN

Web Development Basics

- Understanding the Web client/server model

- Using Forms and controls

- Embedding a script

- Passing parameters to the server

- Using ActiveX controls on the Web

This part of the book discusses how to use Visual Basic on the Web. You can apply your VB knowledge to the Web in many ways. For example, you can create ActiveX controls and deploy them on the Internet. You know how to design ActiveX controls, and you can easily place them on a Web page. You can also turn your VB applications into ActiveX documents and deploy them on the Web as well. Visual Basic comes with the ActiveX Document Migration Wizard that will do the conversion for you. These technologies, however, are not yet mature, and they are not the bread and butter of Web developers and authors.

Only a small percentage of sites are using ActiveX controls, and ActiveX Documents are simply not used on the Web. (Some intranets must make use of ActiveX Documents, but they still can't be considered mainstream technology.) One technology, however, has matured and is used on many Web sites: Active Server Pages (ASP). Corporations are interested in flashy sites, but their primary concern is to get their databases on the Web so that visitors can search their databases and so that they can collect data (orders, whenever possible) from visitors. Corporations aren't interested in putting together a game in Dynamic HTML; they need applications that will allow visitors to interact with their sites. And this is exactly what Active Server Pages are all about.

Using ASP, VB programmers can apply their knowledge in a profitable area of the Web. ASP may not be the most interesting of all the technologies developed by Microsoft to activate the Web, but it is surely the most practical. That's why we'll focus on ASP and show you how to publish databases on the Web and how to design pages that let visitors interact with a Web server.

Another reason for including Active Server Pages in this book is that the Web is another implementation of the client/server architecture that you are so familiar with by now. As far as database programming and client/server architectures are concerned, you are ready to develop Web applications. The language you'll be using is VBScript, a subset of Visual Basic. As you will see, Active Server Pages use the ActiveX Data Objects to contact databases on the server, and they also rely on objects.

We'll cover ASP in detail in the following chapter. In this chapter, we'll deal with the prerequisites:

- How clients and servers interact
- The role of VBScript in building active Web pages
- The role of the server that makes this interaction possible

ASP is a component that runs on the server, and, in order to develop Active Server Pages, you must understand the role of the Web server, as well as how clients interact with the server. If you are familiar with this topic, you can jump to the next chapter. If you have only used the Web as a resource to retrieve information, you need the information in this chapter.

Clients and Servers on the Web

The computers that make up the World Wide Web can be classified in two categories:

- Clients
- Servers

The *clients* (the machines that run a browser such as Internet Explorer) request information. The *servers* (the machines that run a Web server such as the Internet Information Server) provide the requested information. The role of the Web server is to supply the documents requested by the client. This is an easy task, and setting up a Web server is straightforward. Today's Web servers, however, do a lot more than simply supply HTML documents. They process requests made by the clients, handle security, and more. To understand what the Web server does and to understand how to develop applications that interact with the server, let's start by examining what goes on between a client and a server on the Web.

When a client requests a document, it sends a URL (Uniform Resource Locator) to the server. A URL is a unique address for every entity on the Web. Each server has a unique URL, and each document on the server has a unique URL. The Web server looks at the URL to determine the desired response for any given request. A Web server can process requests for:

- Ordinary Web pages (HTML documents)
- Common Gateway Interface (CGI) applications
- Active Server Pages (ASP)

Web pages are HTML documents that the browser renders on the screen as they arrive. These documents live on the server, and the server supplies them whenever a client requests them. CGI applications and scripts are applications that run on the server, and they produce HTML pages on the fly. CGI applications are used mostly on UNIX machines (and most Web servers run on UNIX machines), and they look a lot like C programs. Active Server Pages are simpler. They look a lot like HTML pages, and they contain VBScript code.

The URL is the string displayed in the browser's Address box every time you click a hyperlink (or the string you enter in the Address box to connect to a server). It looks like this:

```
http://www.servername.com/website/home.htm
```

A URL contains the following:

- Protocol (http://)

- Domain name (www.servername.com)

- Path (/website/home.htm) to the desired document

Within the path, rather than specifying a static HTML page as shown here, you can enter the filename of a script to run. In doing so, the server will commence the operation requested, if possible. If the server cannot fulfill the request properly, it will return an error message or the static contents of the file. In any case, the Web server returns the result of some local processing as an HTML document. Not all servers can process all types of requests mentioned here, but Microsoft's Web servers (Internet Information Server and the Personal Web Server) can do so.

A URL that requests an application on the Web server looks like this:

```
http://www.servername.com/website/register.asp?UserName=Evangelos&Email _
=EP@Sybex.com
```

This URL contains the name of an application to run on the server (instead of an HTML document), followed by some parameters. The ASP file needs these parameters. The application on the server will process these values, and the results (for example, a confirmation message indicating that the user has been successfully registered or a report based on a database search) will be sent back to the client.

Sending information to the server is simple. The browser sends a string that looks like the URL of a document. For all the browser knows, it is requesting an HTML document. The server receives the request, sees that the client is contacting an application, and starts the application. At the same time, it passes the string with the parameters to the application. The application on the server processes the parameters, creates an output in HTML format, and submits it to the client. The client sees another HTML document and renders it on the screen.

How about HTML?

To develop Web sites, whether you're interested in working with the server or the client, you must learn HTML, which is a simple document formatting language. As a VB programmer, you can do so in less than a day with a good book.

NOTE   You might want to start with *Mastering HTML*, by Deborah S. Ray and Eric J. Ray, available from Sybex. Some excellent tutorials and reference material are available at the Microsoft Web site (`www.microsoft.com`). If you are going to do any work with HTML, you should also visit Microsoft's workshop site at `www.microsoft.com/workshop/default.asp`, a Web site dedicated to Web authors and developers and loaded with information and authoring tools.

We're including here the shortest introduction to HTML you'll probably ever find. This quick reference will give you the information you need to continue working through this chapter. It's not meant to explain HTML, but to convince you that not knowing HTML shouldn't keep you from getting involved with the Web and starting to develop Web pages immediately.

HTML is a lot like the RTF (Rich Text Format) language. An HTML document consists of text, which is displayed on the client as is, and formatting tags, which determine the appearance of the text in the browser's window. For example, to display a few words in bold, enclose them in a pair of <B> tags:

```
Some words in this sentence appear <B>in bold type</B>
```

The string "in bold type" will be displayed in bold. The <I> tags display text in italic, the <U> tags underline text, and so on. You can use the <FONT> tag to specify font attributes, as in the following example:

```
<FONT FACE = "Verdana" SIZE = 8>
```

Other, more complicated tags rearrange the text on the screen. You can use the table-related tags to create really elaborate tables. And you even insert images on a Web page with text tags. To insert an image at the current location on a page, use the <IMG> tag, whose syntax is:

```
<IMG SRC = "Bunny.bmp" ALT="Bunny Image">
```

When the browser sees the <IMG> tag, it contacts the server, requests the specified image file (the Bunny.bmp image happens to be in the same folder as the current document), and then displays it. While the image is being downloaded, the string "Bunny Image" is displayed in its place on the browser.

The tag that makes the Web tick is the <A> tag, which inserts hyperlinks. A hyperlink is a string, usually rendered in blue, that reacts to the mouse pointer. When the mouse pointer is over a hyperlink, it assumes the shape of a hand pointing up. If you click the mouse button on a hyperlink, the browser reads the destination of the hyperlink, contacts the server, and displays the new page. Here's how you would insert a hyperlink to Microsoft's home page in an HTML document:

```
For more information visit the <A HREF="http://home.microsoft.com"> _
Microsoft Web site</A>
```

The string "Microsoft Web site," which is enclosed in a pair of <A> tags, is displayed as a hyperlink when the document is rendered on the client computer. When the visitor clicks this hyperlink, the browser displays Microsoft's home page.

The most common use of hyperlinks is to take the visitor to another document on the same Web (our Web). The following hyperlinks create a table of contents when displayed:

```
<A HREF="HTMLDoc.htm">HyperText Markup Language</A>
<P>
<A HREF="VBSDoc.htm">Programming with VBScript</A>
<P>
<A HREF="JSDoc.htm">Programming with JavaScript</A>
<P>
```

To complete this speedy introduction to HTML, let's look at the structure of an HTML document. The <HEAD> section of an HTML document contains its title (which appears in the browser's title bar) and the scripts (if any). Next comes the <BODY> section, with the document's contents. If the page contains controls, where the visitor can enter information (such as registration data), they appear in a <FORM> section.

```
<HTML>
<HEAD>
<TITLE>The document's title</TITLE>
<SCRIPT LANGUAGE = VBScript>
Sub Window_OnLoad()
    MsgBox "You are about to enter our brave, active world!"
End Sub
</SCRIPT>
</HEAD>
<BODY>
<H1>The document's header</H1>
```

```
Here comes the document's body.
<P>
It consists of text, but we throw in a few pictures from time to time:
<IMG SRC = "Action1.gif">
<P>
No Web page would be complete without a hyperlink. So, click
<A HREF="http://www.nasa.org">here</A> to view some spectacular space _
images.
Have fun with HTML!
</BODY>
</HTML>
```

This is a (not so) minimal HTML document, and with the exception of tables, you've seen all the tags you need in order to build Web pages. Indeed, the examples in the next chapter aren't much more complicated than that. If you can understand that the <TABLE> tag signifies the beginning of a table, that the <TR> tag signifies the beginning of a new row within a table, and that the <TD> tag signifies the beginning of a new cell in a row, you are ready to build tables, too.

So don't let your ignorance of a simple language like HTML stop you from applying your hard-earned knowledge of Visual Basic on the Web. Of course, you can build complicated documents with HTML, and we don't want to downplay the importance of the language. But let's face it: HTML is not nearly as difficult as Visual Basic, and you can pick it up as you go along.

Activating the Client with VBScript

The Web is by nature a client/server environment. The load is balanced between the server, where the information is stored, and the client, which does the processing. Until recently, processing consisted of rendering a Web page (including its graphics) on the client. With VBScript, you can add small programs to your pages, which are executed on the server. With the introduction of Dynamic HTML (DHTML), scripting languages such as VBScript and JavaScript, and ActiveX controls for the Web, an increasing amount of processing will move from the server to the client.

Web pages are by definition interactive: Each time visitors click a hyperlink, they are taken to another page. But this isn't the type of interaction with which Windows users are familiar. In addition, this type of interaction requires a trip to the server at each step. The Web page can't respond to events, such as the click of a button, because HTML isn't a programming language. It can't display the date or do a simple calculation. The latest trend in Web design is to make pages active.

An *active page* behaves like an application. It has its own user interface, composed of the common Windows elements (Command buttons, text boxes, and all the new ActiveX controls released for the Web), and interacts with the visitor in a manner similar to a Windows application. An active page doesn't require a trip to the server to display the date or do some calculations.

The embedded application is called a *script*. Scripts are simple programs that are embedded into the HTML page as ASCII text. When the page is downloaded, the script is downloaded with it and is executed by the browser on the client computer. The idea behind active pages is to exploit the computing power of the client computer. With straight HTML, the client computer's task is to render the HTML documents on the screen. But most clients out there are powerful PCs, and they could do much more than simply display Web pages. Active pages can exploit the available computing power by passing much of the processing that would otherwise take place on the server to the client.

In the following sections, we are going to look at the differences between Visual Basic and VBScript, at the limitations of VBScript, and at a few features that are unique to VBScript 2. VBScript is a lightweight version of Visual Basic, but before you start developing scripts, you must understand the design philosophy of VBScript. The design environment is also quite different. VBScript doesn't come with an integrated editor. To insert a script on a page, you must edit the HTML file and insert the appropriate code. Once you learn the structure of a script and how it interacts with the rest of the document, you'll be ready to script your Web pages. You'll also be ready to design documents with Dynamic HTML, which relies on VBScript for the manipulation of its elements in real time.

VBScript and Windows 98

VBScript was designed to activate HTML pages, but it's not limited to the Web. Most of you probably remember the batch language that you could use to automate many tasks through BAT files. Windows 98 will be the first version of Windows to support a scripting language, and this language will be VBScript.

If you learn how to use VBScript on the Web, you will soon be ready to program the Windows 98 interface. After activating the Web, Microsoft is about to activate the Desktop, and the tool that does it is based on your favorite language.

VBScript Variables

To begin with, VBScript is a typeless language. All variables are treated as Variants, and VBScript converts them to the proper type before using them. You can declare variables before you use them, but not their type. For example, to declare the *UserName* variable, use the following statement:

```
Dim UserName
```

The language supports the usual data conversion functions, which you must use to call methods that expect their arguments to be of a specific type. You'll never have to convert argument types when calling VBScript procedures, which can only accept Variant arguments. However, if an ActiveX component provides a method that expects a double number as its argument, you must convert the value you pass to the method to a double value with the CDbl() function.

VBScript supports the VarType() function, which returns information about how your data is currently stored in a Variant data type. The VarType() function returns an integer that represents the type of its argument. The TypeName() function returns the actual name of a variable's type. You can also check for a specific data type by using the Is functions:

IsArray()

IsDate()

IsEmpty()

IsError()

IsNull()

IsNumeric()

IsObject()

VBScript variables declared in the procedures are local to these procedures. Variables declared outside procedures are global and are visible from within any procedure on the page. Since VBScript treats all variables as Variants, the only benefit of declaring variables is to write clean code and simplify debugging.

The variables declared in a procedure are local, and they have a limited scope. Only the function (or subroutine) in which they were declared can access them. They have a limited lifetime, too. They exist only for as long as the procedure's code is executed. When the procedure exits, the local variables cease to exist. If the same procedure is called again, a new set of local variables is created and initialized. To make a local variable maintain its value between calls, declare it with the Static keyword. Static variables have a limited scope (they are local to the procedure), but the same lifetime as global variables. In other words, they maintain their values as long as the page with the script is active, but they can be accessed from within a specific procedure only. You can also make a variable global by declaring it with the Dim statement (and no type) outside any procedure.

VBScript Arrays and Dictionaries

VBScript supports arrays too, as well as a structure called *Dictionary*, which is equivalent to the Visual Basic collection. An array is declared with a Dim statement, without a type. The following statements declare two arrays:

```
Dim Days(7)
Dim Months(12)
```

VBScript arrays are zero based, and they may have multiple dimensions. For example, the array Temperatures, which holds the temperatures in various cities, can be declared as:

```
Dim Temperatures(1,99)
```

This array has enough elements to hold 100 city names and their temperatures. Since arrays are not typed, you can store any type of data in an array's elements.

Dictionaries are objects that can store index information, just like Visual Basic collections. The difference between an array and a Dictionary object is that in the array you use an index value to access the array's elements; in a Dictionary object, you use a key.

Back to our Temperature array. To read the temperature in a given city, you must know the city's index to the array and request the corresponding element. If New York's index in the array is 23, the temperature in New York is Temperatures(23,1), and the name of the city is Temperatures(32,0).

If Temperatures were a Dictionary object, you would access the desired temperature by the name of the corresponding city, as in Temperatures("New York"). To use a Dictionary object in your code, you must first create an object variable with the CreateObject() function:

```
Dim Temperatures
Set Temperatures = CreateObject("Scripting.Dictionary")
```

In this case, *Temperatures* is an object variable, not an array. The *Temperatures* variable holds items, which can be any type (numeric or string). Each item is associated with a unique key that is used to retrieve an individual item and is usually an integer or a string, but can be anything.

To populate a *Dictionary* variable, use the Add method, which accepts two arguments: a value and a key. The following statements add cities and temperatures to the Temperatures Dictionary:

```
Temperatures.Add "New York", 82
Temperatures.Add "Atlanta", 79
Temperatures.Add "Houston", 73
```

If you attempt to add a pair with a key that already exists, an error will occur. You can either insert the appropriate error-trapping code or use the Exists method. The Exists method accepts as an argument a key and returns True if the key exists in the Dictionary; otherwise, it returns False. Call the Exists method every time you want to add a new pair to the Dictionary to avoid multiple instances of the same value:

```
If Not Temperatures.Exists("Atlanta") Then
    Temperatures.Add "Atlanta", 79
End If
```

You can also remove items from the Dictionary with the Remove method, which accepts a key as an argument and removes the corresponding pair from the Dictionary. To remove the entry that corresponds to the temperature in Atlanta, use statements such as the following:

```
If Temperatures.Exists("Atlanta") Then
    Temperatures.Remove "Atlanta"
End If
```

You can also clear the entire Dictionary by removing all the pairs with the RemoveAll method, whose syntax is:

```
Temperatures.RemoveAll
```

These are the methods that let you set up Dictionaries and assign data to them. To retrieve a value stored in a Dictionary object, use the name of the *Dictionary* variable and pass the key to it as an argument. The temperature in Houston is:

```
Temperatures("Houston")
```

By default, keys are case-sensitive, and the keys "HOUSTON" or "houston" won't locate the desired item in the Dictionary. To change this behavior, use the CompareMode property, which sets (or returns) the comparison mode for comparing string keys in a Dictionary object. Its syntax is:

```
Temperatures.CompareMode = 0
```

This property's value can be 0 (for binary, or case-sensitive, comparisons) or 1 (for text, or case-insensitive, comparisons).

To access the items and their keys in the Dictionary object, you must use the Items and Keys methods. The Items method returns an array containing all the items in a Dictionary object. Likewise, the Keys method returns an array containing all the keys in a Dictionary object. To access the elements of these two arrays, declare a new variable and then assign the result of the corresponding method to the variable. The following lines demonstrate how to access the keys and their items:

```
Dim DItems, DKeys
{statements to assign values to the collection Temperatures}
DItems = Temperatures.Items
DKeys = Temperatures.Keys
For i = 0 To Temperatures.Count - 1
    Document.write DKeys(i) & " " &  DItems(i) & "<P>"
Next
```

This code segment displays the list of cities and their temperatures in the two columns of a table. The table is created on the fly with Document.write statements, which place strings directly on the current document.

In addition to the Items and Keys methods, which let you examine the items in a Dictionary object, you can use the Item and Key properties to manipulate the Dictionary's items. The Item property sets (or returns) an item for a specified key in a Dictionary object. To change the temperature of a city in the Dictionary object of the example, use a statement such as the following:

```
Dictionary.Item("Houston") = 84
```

You can also change the key of a given item with the Key property, although this isn't common practice. If users are looking up the temperature in Los Angeles using the key "LA," you can change the key of this item with a statement such as the following:

```
Dictionary.Key("Los Angeles") = "LA"
```

Finally, the Count property of the Dictionary object returns the number of items stored in it. To scan all the items in a Dictionary object, set up a For…Next loop that goes from zero to the value of the Count property minus 1.

VBScript Procedures

Like Visual Basic, VBScript supports two kinds of procedures:

- Subroutines
- Functions

Event handlers are implemented as subroutines, and their names are made up of the name of the control and the name of the event they handle, separated by an underscore character.

A subroutine is a block of VBScript statements, enclosed by the Sub and End Sub statements, that perform a specific action but don't return a value. To call a subroutine procedure from within another, type the name of the subroutine along with values for its arguments, separated by a comma. The Call statement is not required, but if you do use it, you must enclose any arguments in parentheses.

Functions are similar to subroutines, but they return a value. Functions consist of a block of VBScript statements enclosed by the Function and End Function statements. If a function doesn't require any argument, its Function statement must include an empty set of parentheses. The return type of a Function procedure is always a Variant data type.

Like Visual Basic, VBScript procedures accept arguments by value or by reference. The default is by reference, which means that the procedure accepts the actual argument (an address in memory where the argument is stored). Any changes to the arguments made by the procedure are permanent. If you want to pass an argument by value so that the procedure can't change its value, use the ByVal keyword.

And also like Visual Basic, event handlers in VBScript are implemented as subroutines. Any element on a Web page that has a name can recognize the usual mouse events. To implement a handler for an event, write a subroutine whose name consists of the element's name, the underscore character, and the name of the event.

VBScript Input/Output Functions

VBScript is limited when it comes to input and output functions. It supports the InputBox and MsgBox functions of Visual Basic, but your best bet is to avoid using them. This is not the way to build a user interface in the Windows environment. In Visual Basic, we use controls on Forms to design elaborate user interfaces. HTML pages can also contain Forms with controls, only VBScript doesn't support as many controls.

NOTE   We are going to discuss VBScript's Forms and controls in the section "Forms and Controls."

VBScript doesn't provide any functions for writing output directly on the screen. You can use VBScript to update the display, but everything must be done within the framework of the current page. All you can do is create HTML code that can affect the current page, but there is no way to access a single pixel outside the client's window.

VBScript has no functions for opening and reading files. The reason is that VBScript is a "safe" language. Web pages that deploy scripts shouldn't be able to access the client system. Otherwise, every page you open with your browser would be a clear and present danger for your computer. To make VBScript safe, its designers had to eliminate many of the features of Visual Basic.

Updating the browser's window is usually done through the server. The visitor supplies information or simply clicks a hyperlink. The browser contacts the server, which supplies another Web page. It's quite simple, and it works very well. With the help of ActiveX controls, you can build elaborate user interfaces, but this requires that your visitors upload the ActiveX controls, which aren't safe.

By and large, visitors are reluctant to download and install new components on their computers from every Web site they visit. Eventually, the most commonly used and most useful ActiveX controls will be distributed with Internet Explorer, and Web developers will be able to use them. This, in turn, will make their pages dependent on Internet Explorer. The techniques we discuss in this book don't rely on specific ActiveX controls, and they apply to all browsers.

Web pages contain special sections called Forms on which you can place controls such as Command buttons, CheckBoxes, and so on. These controls accept user input, and you can program them, just as you can program Visual Basic controls. But there is a major difference between scripts and Visual Basic applications. Visual Basic applications have Forms, and Forms can communicate via Public variables, but Web pages can't communicate.

You will find more information on passing information among the scripts of the various pages that make up a Web site in the next chapter in the section on cookies. In the following section, we are going to discuss how to create Web pages with Forms that can interact with the user.

Forms and Controls

As you know already, HTML pages contain controls that let the user enter information, similar to the usual Windows controls: text boxes, option buttons, and so on. The areas on the HTML page where these controls appear are called Forms, and the controls themselves are called *intrinsic controls*. HTML provides special tags for placing intrinsic controls on a Form.

> **NOTE**
>
> In addition to intrinsic controls, you can place ActiveX controls on your Forms. Because ActiveX controls must be downloaded to the client, and many visitors don't allow the installation of ActiveX controls on their systems, we are not going to discuss them.

Before placing a control on the page, you must create a Form with the <FORM> tag. Its syntax is:

```
<FORM NAME=name ACTION=action METHOD=method>
</FORM>
```

All the controls must appear between these two tags. The NAME attribute (it's optional) is the name of the Form and is used when a page contains multiple Forms. The ACTION attribute is the name of an application on the server that will be called to process the information. The METHOD attribute specifies how the controls' values will be transmitted to the server. All the information needed by the browser to contact an application on the server is contained in the <FORM> tag. But more on this later, in the section "Passing Parameters to the Server."

HTML provides support for the following intrinsic controls. Figure 18.1 shows a Web page with a Form that contains most of HTML's intrinsic controls. You are going to see the HTML code that produced the page of Figure 18.1 in the section "The FORM.htm Web Page," later in this chapter.

The Text Control

The Text control is a box in which visitors can enter a single line of text (such as name, address, and so on). To insert a Text control on a Form, use the following tag:

```
<INPUT TYPE = TEXT NAME = "Publisher" VALUE = "Sybex">
```

The VALUE attribute specifies the initial value. After the visitor changes this entry, VALUE holds the new string. To edit the contents of a Text control, the visitor can use the common editing keys (Home, Del, Insert, and so on), but the text can't be formatted.

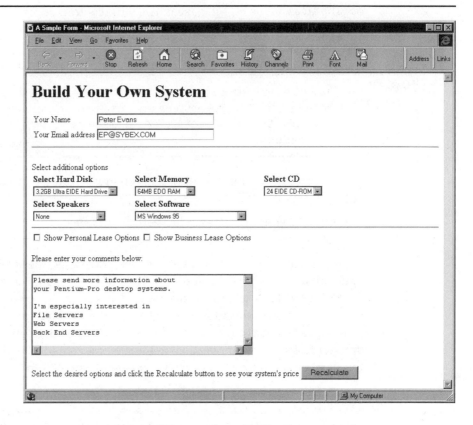

To control the size and contents of the control, use the SIZE and MAXLENGTH attributes. The SIZE attribute specifies the size of the control on the Form, in number of characters, and the MAXLENGTH attribute specifies the maximum number of characters the user can type in the control. A variation of the Text control is the Password control, which is identical but doesn't display the characters as they are typed. Instead, it displays asterisks, and it is used to enter passwords.

The TextArea Control

The TextArea control is similar to the Text control, but it allows the entry of multiple lines of text. All the usual navigation and editing keys work with the TextArea control. To place a TextArea control on a Form, use the <TEXTAREA> tag:

```
<TEXTAREA NAME = "Comments" ROWS = 10 COLS = 30>
The best editor I've ever used!
</TEXTAREA>
```

Because the TextArea control allows you to specify multiple lines of initial text, it's not inserted with the usual <INPUT> tag, but with a pair of <TEXTAREA> tags. The ROWS and COLS attributes specify the dimensions of the control on the page, in number of characters. Notice that the line breaks you insert between the two <TEXTAREA> tags are preserved when the text is displayed on the control. Even if you include HTML tags in the initial text, they will appear on the control.

The CheckBox Control

The CheckBox control is a little square with an optional checkmark, which acts as a toggle. Every time the visitor clicks it, it changes state. It is used to present a list of options, from which the visitor can select one or more. To insert a CheckBox control on a Form, use the <INPUT> tag:

```
<INPUT TYPE = CHECKBOX NAME = "Check1">
```

To initially check a CheckBox control, specify the CHECKED attribute in the corresponding <INPUT> tag. The control's value can be 0 or 1, indicating whether it's checked (1) or cleared (0).

The RadioButton Control

The RadioButton control is round and contains a dot in the center. RadioButton controls are used to present lists of options, similar to CheckBox controls, but only one of them can be selected at a time. Each time a new option is checked by the visitor, the previously selected one is cleared. To insert a RadioButton control on a Form, use the following:

```
<INPUT TYPE = RADIO NAME = "Radio1">
```

Whereas each CheckBox control has a different name, a group of RadioButtons have the same name. This is how the browser knows that a number of RadioButton controls belong to the same group and that only one of them can be checked at a time. To specify the control that will be initially checked in the group, use the CHECKED attribute. The following lines insert a group of four RadioButton controls on a Form:

```
<INPUT TYPE = RADIO NAME = "Level">Beginner <BR>
<INPUT TYPE = RADIO NAME = "Level">Intermediate <BR>
<INPUT TYPE = RADIO NAME = "Level" CHECKED>Advanced<BR>
<INPUT TYPE = RADIO NAME = "Level">Expert <BR>
```

The Multiple Selection Control

The Multiple Selection control is basically a list that can contain a number of options. The visitor can select none, one, or multiple items in the list. The list is delimited with a pair of <SELECT> tags. Each item in the list is inserted with a separate <OPTION> tag. To place a Multiple Selection List on the Form, add the following lines:

```
<SELECT  NAME = "MemoryOptions" SIZE = 3 MULTIPLE = multiple>
<OPTION VALUE=16> 16 Mbytes</OPTION>
<OPTION VALUE=32> 32 Mbytes</OPTION>
<OPTION VALUE=64> 64 Mbytes</OPTION>
<OPTION VALUE=128> 128 Mbytes</OPTION>
<OPTION VALUE=256> 256 Mbytes</OPTION>
</SELECT>
```

The SIZE attribute specifies how many lines will be visible. If you omit it, the list will be reduced to a single line, and the visitor must use the up and down arrow keys to scroll through the available options. If the list contains more lines, a vertical scrollbar is automatically attached to help the visitor locate the desired item. The MULTIPLE attribute specifies that the visitor can select multiple items in the list by clicking on their names while holding down the Shift or Control key. If you omit the MULTIPLE attribute, each time an item is selected, the previously selected one is cleared.

The <OPTION> tag has a VALUE attribute that represents the value of the selected item. If the viewer selects the 64 Mbytes option in the earlier list, the value 64 is transmitted to the server. Finally, to initially select one or more options, specify the SELECTED attribute:

```
<OPTION  SELECTED VALUE=128> 128 Mbytes</OPTION>
```

The Command Button Control

Clicking a Command button triggers certain actions. Without VBScript, Command buttons can trigger only two actions:

- Submit the data entered on the controls to the server

- Reset all control values on the Form to their original values

With VBScript, Command buttons can trigger any actions you can program in your pages.

You can place three types of buttons on a Form:

- Submit

- Reset

- Button

The most important is the Submit button: It transmits the contents of all the controls on the Form to the server. The Reset button resets the values of the other controls on the Form to their initial values. The Reset button doesn't submit any values to the server. Most Forms contain Submit and Reset buttons, which are inserted like this:

```
<INPUT TYPE = SUBMIT VALUE = "Send data">
<INPUT TYPE = RESET VALUE = "Reset Values">
```

The VALUE attribute specifies the string that will appear on the Command button. The Submit button reads the name of the application that must be contacted on the server (the <FORM> tag's ACTION attribute), appends the values of the controls to this URL, and transmits it to the server.

The third, generic type of button has as its type simply Button and functions similar to the other buttons in the Windows interface. Clicking it triggers an event, which you can use to execute some VBScript code. To insert a generic Button control on your Form, use the <INPUT> tag:

```
<INPUT TYPE = BUTTON NAME = "ShowDate">
```

Every time this button is clicked, it triggers the ShowDate_Click event. Obviously, you must place the code that you want to execute every time this button is clicked in this event's handler:

```
Sub ShowDate_Click()
    MsgBox "The date is " & Date()
End Sub
```

TIP   If you're going to validate the data on the client's side, you shouldn't use the Submit button because that would transmit the data to the server as soon as the button is clicked. Instead, you must use the Button control to trigger your data validation routine. After you validate the data, you can submit it with the Submit method.

Here's a typical Command button script that validates the data entered by the visitor and then submits the Form's contents to an ASP application on the server.

The Command button is a generic one and is placed on the Form with the following:

```
<INPUT TYPE = BUTTON NAME = SendData VALUE = "Register Now">
```

Code 18.1   **The Event Handler for the SendData Button's Click Event**

```
<SCRIPT LANGUAGE = VBScript>
Sub SendData_Click()
    If Instr ("e", EMAIL.Value) = 0 Then
        MsgBox "Invalid e-mail address." & chr(13) & _
                "Please enter a string like yourname@yourserver.com"
    Else If RealName.Value = "" Then
        MsgBox "You can't register without a name"
    Else
        RegistrationForm.Submit
End If
End Sub
</SCRIPT>
```

This script is invoked when the SendData button is clicked. First, it checks the contents of the EMail Text control. If the specified address isn't in the form name@server.com, it prompts the user to enter a valid e-mail address. It then checks the value of the RealName Text control. If the user hasn't specified a name, they are prompted accordingly. If both tests fail, the script submits the data on the Form (the Form may contain other controls, too) with the Submit method. The Form's Submit method is equivalent to the Submit button. They both cause the browser to contact the application specified by the ACTION attribute of the <FORM> tag and pass to it the values of the controls as parameters. For the previous example, the browser will submit a string such as the following:

```
http://www.servername.com/Register.asp?EMail=EP@SYBEX.COM&Name=Evangelos+P
```

EMail and *Name* are the names of the parameters, as expected by the Register .asp application on the server. The values shown could be anything. Notice that strings are not enclosed in quotes, and spaces are replaced by plus signs.

Embedding a Script

The script is contained in the event handlers of the various controls, as well as procedures, just like regular Visual Basic applications.

You place scripts in the HTML file's SCRIPT section, which is delimited with a pair of <SCRIPT> tags. Because there is more than one scripting language, you must also specify the script's language in the <SCRIPT> tag. Here's a typical SCRIPT section:

```
<SCRIPT LANGUAGE = VBScript>
    {your scripting code}
</SCRIPT>
```

When the browser hits the <SCRIPT> tag, it calls the VBScript interpreter to compile and execute the following code. The code is usually placed in event handlers, but you can insert procedures that will be called from within event handlers. If some code appears outside any handler, as shown in the next listing, it is executed as soon as the page is downloaded and before the browser renders the document on the screen. The following script displays the current date as soon as the page that contains it is loaded:

```
<SCRIPT LANGUAGE="VBScript">
    MsgBox "The date is " & Date
</SCRIPT>
```

All intrinsic controls have a Name property (or attribute) that can be used to identify them in the script. Since the intrinsic controls are always placed on a Form, their complete name is the name of the Form, followed by a period and then the name of the control. The Button control, placed on a Form called RegisterForm with the following line

```
<INPUT TYPE=BUTTON NAME="DateBttn" VALUE="Show Date">
```

can be accessed from within a script with this expression:

```
AppForm.DateBttn
```

For example, you can change the caption of the DateBttn with a statement such as the following:

```
AppForm.DateBttn.Value = "DATE"
```

All intrinsic controls, with the exception of the Select control, have a *Value* property, too. A button's value is its caption, and a Text control's value is the text displayed on the control. The equivalent property of the Select control is the *SelectedIndex* property, which is the index of the item currently selected. You can manipulate the Value and SelectedIndex properties of the various controls from within your script.

Finally, the most common event in scripting Web pages is the Click event, which is generated when the visitor clicks a control. The Text, TextArea, and

Select controls don't recognize this event. The most common event for these controls is the Change event, which takes place when the text in a Text or TextArea control is changed or when the visitor makes a new selection in the Select control.

This is all the information you need to start scripting your Web pages. VBScript is similar to Visual Basic, and we can look at an example next.

Passing Parameters to the Server

For the client to interact with the server, there must be a way for the browser to send information to the server, along with the name of the requested document. We mentioned already that every time the viewer clicks a hyperlink, the browser sends a URL to the server. The hyperlink is the URL of another document.

To build truly interactive documents, browsers should be able not only to request documents, but to invoke applications on the server and pass to the server data entered by the visitor. Indeed, this is how clients interact with the server. Instead of requesting another HTML document, they request an application, which is executed on the Web. Along with the name of the application, they pass visitor-supplied data. The application reads the data, processes them, and passes the results in the form of another HTML page, which is generated on the fly. Figure 18.2 shows a simple Web page (assuming that categories don't change daily) that displays the categories of the products stored in the NWIND database. When the visitor clicks a category name, the products in the selected category are displayed on a new page, shown in Figure 18.3.

Each category could be a hyperlink, pointing to a different document, but you'd have to build a different HTML document for each category. This wouldn't be too time-consuming if products and prices didn't change frequently. In most cases, however, maintaining a separate document for each product category is more than a Webmaster can handle. If you wanted to display invoices, this approach simply wouldn't work.

Clearly, you should be able to write a program that runs on the server, accepts the category name (or category ID) as an argument, builds a new HTML page with the requested products (as shown in Figure 18.3), and submits it to the client. The HTML page generated by the application on the server exists only while it's being transmitted; it's not saved on the server. The client, on the other hand, has no idea what's happened; it sees another HTML page, which it renders on the screen.

FIGURE 18.2:

A Web page displaying product categories. Each category name is a hyperlink that leads to a page, like the one shown in Figure 18.3.

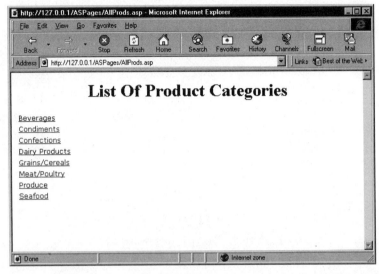

FIGURE 18.3:

The destinations of the hyperlinks on the page in Figure 18.2 display the products of the selected category.

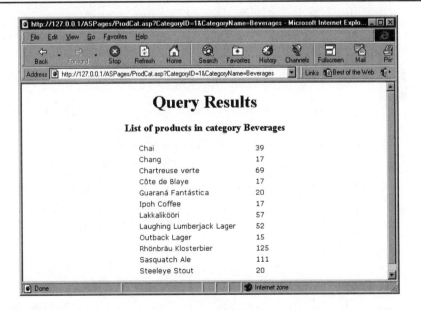

The application that runs on the server is an Active Server Page. The HTML file shown in Figure 18.2 requests the document PRODUCTS.ASP. Along with the name, it passes to the server the value of the parameter CategoryID. The complete URL of the requested document is something like this:

```
http://www.myserver.com/products.asp?CateogryID=32
```

Everything preceding the question mark is the URL of a document. This document is not an HTML page, but the client doesn't care; it will receive an HTML document anyway. The question mark separates the URL of the requested document from the parameters. Parameters have a name and a value, and they are specified as:

```
parametername = parametervalue
```

The *parametername* parameter is the name, and *parametervalue* is the value of the parameter. If you are using a Form to collect information from the visitor, the parameter names are the names of the controls on the Form. Multiple parameters are separated by the ampersand (&) sign, as shown next:

```
http://www.myserver.com?LName=Evans&FName=Peter
```

If a value contains spaces, each space is replaced by the plus sign (+). With a different set of values, the previous URL would be:

```
http://www.myserver.com?LName=von+Kaiser&FName=Richter
```

Many characters have special meaning in HTML and the HTTP protocol, and they can't appear in the parameter string. For example, double quotation marks (") can't appear in the parameter string following the application's URL. Other illegal characters are the forward slash (/) and the ampersand (&). All special characters (that is, every character that's not a letter or a numeric digit) are replaced with the hexadecimal representation of their ASCII value, prefixed with the percent (%) symbol. The ampersand (&) is encoded as %26, and the percent symbol itself is encoded as %25.

The parameters are encoded by the client, but you must be aware of this encoding scheme if you choose to create the URL from within a script. In some cases, you must also be able to decode the parameter string on the server, from within your application, by replacing the hexadecimal codes with the symbols they represent.

How does the client create the parameter string and append it to the URL of the application? When you include a Form in a Web page, you must supply the <FORM> tag. The <FORM> tag requires two parameters (it recognizes more optional parameters):

- ACTION

- METHOD

The ACTION parameter is the name of the application that will process the request. For the purposes of this book, this application is an Active Server Page (a file with the extension ASP). The METHOD parameter indicates the type of form-handling protocol that will be used to pass the parameters to the application, and it can have one of the values GET and POST. The application that receives the information usually dictates the method. Active Server Pages recognize both methods but handle them differently. The simpler method is the GET method, and we are going to use it in our examples.

The browser, therefore, picks up the URL of the application from the <FORM> tag and appends the parameter/value pairs to it. Each pair corresponds to a control on the Form: The control's name is the parameter name, and the control's value is the parameter value. The whole thing is done automatically, and you don't have to provide any client scripts. And when does the browser submit the request to the server? When the Submit button is clicked. The Submit button's role on a Form is to submit the visitor-supplied values to the server.

The FORM.htm Web Page

At this point, we can look at an example of a Web page with a Form that lets the visitor enter information, which is then submitted to the server. The FORM.htm page is shown in Figure 18.4, and it contains many of the controls we discussed in the previous sections.

FIGURE 18.4:

The FORM.htm page lets the visitor submit information to the server.

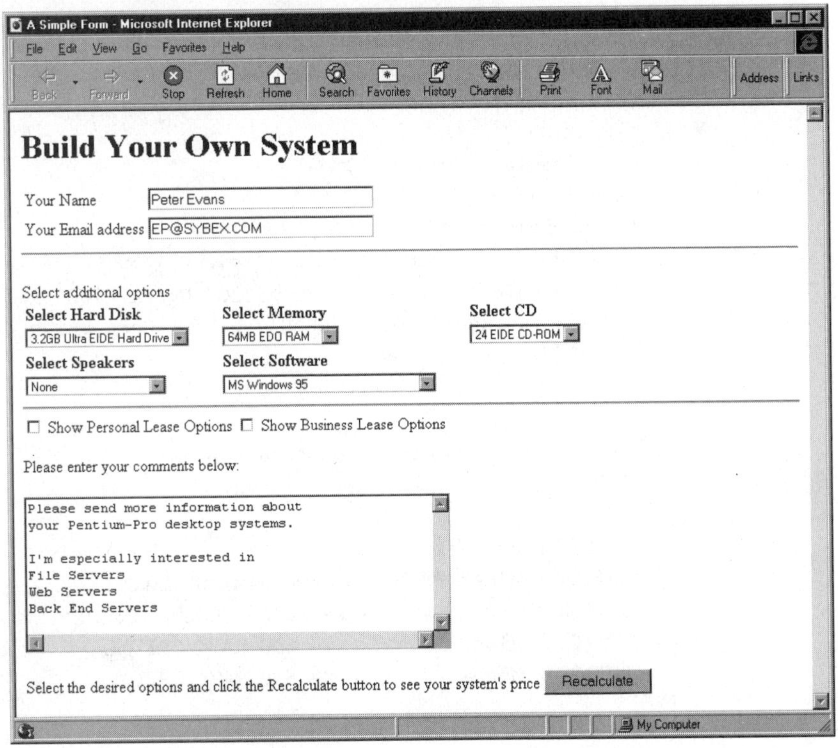

The HTML code of the page is straightforward, and you will be able to understand it even if you don't know HTML. The <TABLE> tag inserts a table at the current location in the HTML document and is used frequently to align controls (which explains why we used it in this document; the table isn't an essential feature of the page, but it wouldn't look nearly as good without it).

Code 18.2 **The FORM.htm Page**

```
<HTML>
<TITLE>A Simple Form</TITLE>
<H1>Build Your Own System</H1>
<FORM name=ORDER method="POST"
action="http://127.0.0.1/aspages/param.asp">
<TABLE>
<TR><TD>Your Name</TD> <TD><INPUT TYPE=TEXT SIZE=30 MAXSIZE=30 _
NAME="Name"></TR>
<TR><TD>Your Email address</TD> <TD><INPUT TYPE=TEXT SIZE=30 _
MAXSIZE=30 NAME="EMail"></TR>
</TABLE>
<HR>
<P>
Select additional options
<TABLE>
<TR><TD><B>Select Hard Disk</B></TD>
<TD></TD>
<TD><B>Select Memory</B></TD>
<TD></TD>
<TD><B>Select CD</B></TD></TR>
<TR><TD><SELECT name="HardDisk" size="1">
<OPTION selected value="3.2G">3.2GB Ultra EIDE Hard Drive </OPTION>
<OPTION  value="4.3G">4.3GB Ultra EIDE Hard Drive </OPTION>
</SELECT>
</TD>
<TD>
      
</TD>
<TD>
<SELECT name="Memory" size="1">
<OPTION  value="32">32 MB EDO RAM</OPTION>
<OPTION selected value="64 MB">64MB EDO RAM</OPTION>
<OPTION  value="128">128 MB EDO RAM</OPTION>
<OPTION  value="256">256 MB EDO RAM</OPTION>
```

```
</SELECT>
</TD>
<TD>
      
</TD>
<TD>
<SELECT name="CD" size="1">
<option   value="">None</option>
<option selected value="CD12">12 EIDE CD-ROM</option>
<option selected value="CD24">24 EIDE CD-ROM</option>
</SELECT>
</TD>
</TR>
<TR>
<TD><B>Select Speakers</B></TD>
<TD></TD>
<TD><B>Select Software</B></TD>
<TD></TD>
</TR>
<TR>
<TD>
<SELECT name="Speaker" size="1">
<option selected value="">None</option>
<option value="S90">Altec ACS90 Speakers</option>
<option value="S290">Altec ACS290 Speakers</option>
</SELECT>
</TD>
<TD></TD>
<TD>
<SELECT name="Software" size="1">
<option selected value="WIN95">MS Windows 95</option>
<option value="WIN98">Microsoft Windows 98</option>
<option value="WINNT">Microsoft Windows NT Workstation 4.0 </option>
</SELECT>
</TD>
</TABLE>
<HR>
<INPUT TYPE=CHECKBOX VALUE=1> Show Personal Lease Options
<INPUT TYPE=CHECKBOX VALUE=2> Show Business Lease Options
<P>
Please enter your comments below:
<P>
<TEXTAREA NAME=Comments ROWS=8 COLS=50>
```

```
Please send more information about
your Pentium-Pro desktop systems.

I'm especially interested in
File Servers
Web Servers
Back End Servers
</TEXTAREA>
<P>
Select the desired options and click the Recalculate button to see _
your system's price
<INPUT TYPE=SUBMIT VALUE="Recalculate">
</FORM>
</HTML>
```

Let's take a look at the parameters passed to the server by the FORM.htm page. For the data shown in Figure 18.4, this is the URL prepared by the browser when the Command button at the bottom of the Form is clicked (notice that the lines of the TextArea control are separated by carriage return characters):

```
http://127.0.0.1/aspages/param.asp?Name=Peter+Evans&EMail=EP@SYBEX.COM&
HardDisk=3.2G&Memory=64+MB&CD=CD24&Speaker=&Software=WIN95&Comments=Ple
ase+send+more+information+about+your+Pentium-Pro+desktop+systems.
I'm+especially+interested+in+
File+Servers
Web+Servers
Back+End+Server
```

This is a lengthy string, but it isn't going to introduce any problems. The Web server will extract the values of the control, and you'll be able to access them through your Active Server Page as if they were variables. We'll discuss this topic in the next chapter.

The URL of the ASP application on the server (http://127.0.0.1/aspages/ param.asp) is mentioned in the <FORM> tag's ACTION attribute. The names and values of the parameters are extracted from the controls on the Form and are encoded for transmission to the Web server. The PARAM.ASP application, which we'll present in the next chapter, displays the values submitted by the client in another HTML document.

You've seen how the client passes information to the server. In the next chapter, you will see how an application running on the server processes this information. Between the client and the application that runs on the server is another program that coordinates them. As you probably know, this program is the Web server. The Web server communicates with the clients by receiving their requests, extracting the parameters they pass to the server, sending back HTML documents, and coordinating multiple clients. Without the Web server, your application would have to keep track of the connections and each client's requests, and, in short, it would be difficult to set up a Web site. The Web server is the most important part of the Web, and it's practically transparent to your applications.

Many Web servers are out there, and most of them run on UNIX machines. Microsoft has released two Web servers:

- Internet Information Server (IIS)
- Personal Web Server (PWS)

IIS is the professional Web server and can handle heavy traffic. The PWS is suitable for designing Web sites, as it runs on both Windows 95/98 and Windows NT. However, it supports Active Server Pages, and we are going to use it in the next chapter to demonstrate how to access ASP applications on the server.

The Personal Web Server

We'll end this chapter with a brief overview of the Personal Web Server. Microsoft's Personal Web Server (PWS) is the simplest way of sharing information with other users on an intranet or with the rest of the world on the Internet. PWS is a desktop Web server that simplifies Web site setup and maintenance and supports advanced features such as Active Server Pages (ASP). You can use it to develop and test Web sites and then move them to the Internet Information Server. The Personal Web Server 4 supports a maximum of 10 connections, so it isn't intended for running real Web sites. The Personal Web Server comes with Visual Studio 6. To make sure you have the most recent version of the PWS (for both Windows 98 and Windows NT), go to the following site:

www.microsoft.com/msdownload/ntoptionpack/beta3

NOTE   You can also order the software on CD.

Installing the software is practically automatic and takes place as you download nearly 40MB of data. A new icon is placed on the Desktop, which starts the Personal Web Manager application, as shown in Figure 18.5.

FIGURE 18.5:

Use the Personal Web Manager to manage your Web server.

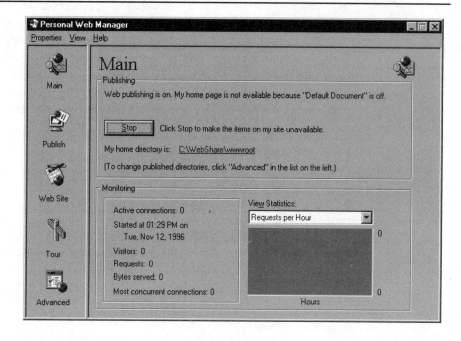

To test the PWS, start Internet Explorer and enter the following URL:

`127.0.0.1`

This is the IP address (Internet Protocol address) of the local computer, and it will connect you to the PWS on your own computer. You should see the home page that comes with the PWS. Any visitor who connects to your computer through the active Internet connection will also see this file. You should modify this document accordingly.

The window in Figure 18.5 contains a narrow frame on the left, where you can select an administrative function. Each time you select a function, the contents of the right frame change. Clicking the Main icon displays the Main frame that you see in Figure 18.5.

In the following section, we are going to examine the Main and the Advanced functions of the Personal Web Manager. You can explore the other functions on your own:

- The Publish icon lets you create simple documents and publish them.

- The Web Site icon lets you structure your Web site (determine the documents you want to share with other users).

- The Tour icon is a guided tour of the product.

IP Addresses

Most computers on the Internet don't have a domain name. If you don't work for a corporation that has its own domain name (for example, `www.sybex.com`), you can run the WINIPCFG program to find out your current IP address (as well as some other information about your connection). Follow these steps:

1. Choose Start ➢ Run to open the Run dialog box.

2. In the Open text box, type **WINIPCFG** and click OK.

You'll see your current IP address in the IP Configuration dialog box. It will be something like `192.210.54.102`.

Any user with an active connection to the Internet can contact you at this address. If you disconnect from your ISP, the next time you connect, your IP address will be different. If you are on a network, any user can contact your site by specifying the IP address or the name of the machine on which the Web server is installed.

The Main Window

You start and stop the Web server in the Main window. To make the Web site available to other users, click the Start button. If the server is running and you want to stop sharing the Web site, click the Stop button. In the same frame, you can see the address of the machine on which the Web server is running and the site's home directory (this is where visitors are connected by default if they specify only the Web server's address). Both strings are hyperlinks, and you can click them to see the site's home page.

In the lower half of the Main window, you can monitor the activity of the Web server. You can see the number of visitors currently connected (Active connections), when the server was last started, the total number of visitors, how many requests they've made, and how many bytes have been sent out by the server. You can also view statistics on the usage of the Web site in the graph—by visitors or requests and on an hourly or daily basis.

The Advanced Window

The Advanced window, shown in Figure 18.6, also contains the most important settings of the site, at least as far as Active Server Pages are concerned. In the upper zone of the window, you can edit the virtual directories. The home directory is your site's home. When users connect to the URL of the server, they are automatically connected to the home directory. If the home directory contains a home page, this page is displayed on the client.

FIGURE 18.6:

The Advanced window of the Personal Web Manager

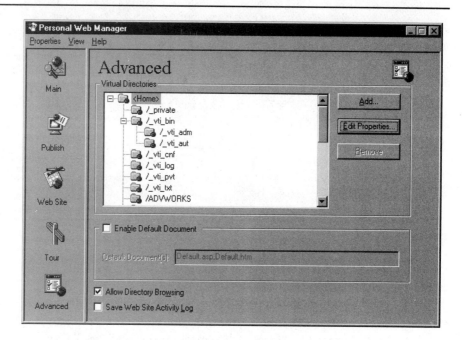

Virtual Directories

To publish from any directory not contained within your home directory, you must create a virtual directory. A virtual directory is a directory that is not physically contained in the home directory, but that appears to clients as though it were. You can choose to store your images in a folder that's not even on the same disk as the Web site. Instead of specifying long path names in your Web pages, you can create a virtual name for this folder—let's say you call it Images—and it will appear to be nested under the home directory. You can then reference any image in your Web page as Images\Planets.bmp, and the server looks for the Planets.bmp file in the physical folder that's mapped to the virtual name Images.

Virtual directories have aliases, which not only simplify coding, but add some security. Visitors don't know where your files are physically located on the server and cannot use that information to modify the actual files. Aliases make it easier for you to move directories in your site too. You can move an entire Web to another folder, map the home directory's virtual name to the new folder, and everything will work as before.

To add a new virtual folder, follow these steps:

1. Click the Add button to open the Add Directory dialog box:

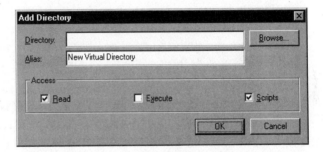

2. In the Directory text box, enter the name of the physical folder or click Browse to locate it.

3. In the Alias box, enter a virtual name.

4. In the Access section, set the permissions for the new virtual directory and then click OK:

    -   Check Read if you want clients to read documents stored in this folder. If a client requests a document in a virtual directory that doesn't have Read permission, the Web server returns an error message. Virtual directories that contain HTML documents should have their Read permission checked. Directories that contain scripts or executable files should not have Read permission.

    -   Check Execute if the folder contains applications that can be executed on the server (ActiveX DLLs, for example).

    -   Check Scripts if the folder contains scripts such as ASP applications.

NOTE   Scripts are text files, and you can easily check to see if they are doing anything to the system. Executable files that can be called from scripts aren't easy to control, so you should not trust other users to place executable files in a folder with Execute permission.

Home Directory and Default Documents

When visitors connect to your site by specifying a URL such as `www.server.com` or an IP address, the Web server connects them to the home directory. The home directory contains a default document. For example, when you connect to the site `www.sybex.com`, the Web server at the specified location displays the default document in the home directory.

A default document is the document, usually in HTML format, that the server presents to site visitors when they have not specified a filename in the URL. Visitors can also specify the name of another document in the URL, in which case the Web server supplies the specified document instead of the default document.

Visitors can also specify a virtual directory, without a document name. If the specified directory has a default document, this document is sent to the client. By placing a default page in every virtual directory, you can assure that visitors find a home page on your site, regardless of how they got there. If no document is specified, they can either be allowed to browse the current directory or see an error message indicating that the requested document was not found.

> **NOTE**   Of course, if visitors know the name of an HTML file, they can request it. This technique is used sometimes to allow trusted visitors to connect to a Web site. If the home directory contains the file `Secret.htm`, only visitors who know the name of the file can connect to the site by specifying the URL `www.server.com/Secret.htm`.

If you want to use default documents on your site, specify their names in the Default Document(s) text box. PWS supports the use of multiple default document names. When a request without a filename arrives, PWS searches for the first default document name in the directory specified in the URL. If it does not find a document with that name, it checks for the second default document name, and so on. In other words, you can have multiple default names and use a different one in each virtual directory. The simplest approach is to use the same filename for all virtual directories. The Personal Web Manager suggests the names `Default.htm` and `Default.asp` (depending on whether a directory contains HTML documents or ASP applications). The most common names are `Default.htm` and `Index.htm`.

Navigating by Using Directory Browsing

If you disable the Default Document(s) box and enable Allow Directory Browsing, visitors can view a list of all files in the directory specified in their URL. PWS automatically formats the file list in HTML format and transmits it to the client. When a visitor clicks the filename, the content of the document is displayed (assuming the visitor has a program compatible with the file format of the document).

When testing Web pages and ASP applications, consider disabling Default Document(s) and enabling Allow Directory Browsing. Each time you create a new document and you want to test it, you won't have to specify its name or rename it to Default.htm or whatever the default document name is. With Allow Directory Browsing enabled, visitors can also navigate the subdirectories of the home directory.

Check the Save Web Site Activity Log if you want to log the activity of the Web server. Every new connection and every request for a document is logged by the server in a text file, which you can open later with a text editor.

Deploying ActiveX Controls on the Web

Your custom ActiveX control can be used not only with desktop applications, but on Web pages as well. The process of deploying ActiveX controls on the Internet, however, is a bit more involved. The ActiveX controls must be downloaded along with the page and installed on the client computer. When a custom ActiveX control is used on a Form of a VB application, the control is included in the setup program, which installs the application and its components on the target computer. After an ActiveX control is installed on the target computer, any application can use it. There's no need to install it again.

Something similar happens with Web pages that contain ActiveX controls. The ActiveX controls used by a page must be downloaded from the Web server and installed on the client computer. Once installed, they can be used by other Web pages or desktop applications. The process, however, is quite different. Web pages are text files, which means they can't contain the control's OCX file. The control must be downloaded and installed separately. Indeed, the Web page contains enough information to allow Internet Explorer to download the control and install it. The installation process is the responsibility of the browser and of your Web page.

The major issue regarding the use of custom ActiveX controls on the Web is security. Would you allow every site you visit to install and use custom ActiveX controls on your system? Most people wouldn't, and that's why Internet Explorer will not, by default, download any ActiveX control it encounters. When Internet Explorer opens a page with a custom ActiveX control, it will issue a warning asking your permission to install the control. If you trust the site, you will allow Internet Explorer to download the control and display the page. There aren't many users who would not allow the installation of a new control from Microsoft's Web site. But not too many sites enjoy the same respect.

To allow ActiveX controls to be downloaded, you must change the default settings of Internet Explorer, too. Open the View menu, select Internet Options, and in the Internet Options dialog box, select the Security tab. Check the Custom button and then click Settings to see the dialog box shown in Figure 18.7. The options "Download unsigned ActiveX controls" and "Initialize and script ActiveX controls not marked as safe" are disabled by default. Check the Prompt button for both. Internet Explorer will issue a warning when it's about to download controls that are not signed (or execute associated scripts) and you can decide whether the controls will be installed on your system or not.

FIGURE 18.7:

Internet Explorer's Security
Settings

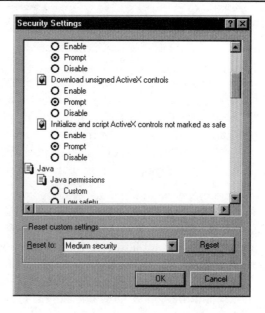

In the following section, we'll describe the process of deploying custom ActiveX controls on the Web. The process is quite simple, thanks to the Package and Deployment Wizard, a tool that comes with VB6 and creates setup programs for your applications. The same tool should also be used to create setup programs for distributing your applications on CDs or other media.

Using the Package and Deployment Wizard

To create the CAB file required for the installation of a custom ActiveX control, start the Package and Deployment Wizard. On the first screen of the wizard, you must select the project for which you want to create the setup files. Click the Browse button to locate the VBP file. Notice that you can't select a group. You must also make sure you don't select the test project (all test projects in this book are named TestProj.vbp). In the following section, you will prepare the CAB file for the ImageLens control.

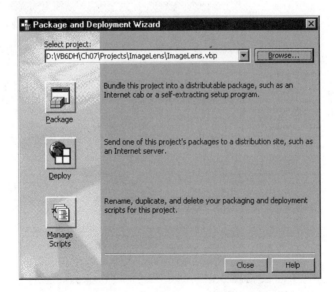

Then you must specify the type of installation files you want to create. Select a packaging script or specify a new one (you'll see later what the script does). You can leave this entry as is (Internet Package). Click Next to move to the next window, the Package Type window.

The Package Type Window   In this window, you specify the type of package you want to create. You have the following options:

Standard Setup Package   This option creates a package that will be installed by a `setup.exe` program. Select it if you plan to create an installation program that will be distributed with a CD or diskettes.

Internet Package   This option creates a CAB-based installation package that will be downloaded from a Web site or posted to a Web server. Select this option to create setup files for deploying your custom ActiveX controls on the Web.

Dependency File   This option creates a file listing information about the run-time components required by your application. Use this option to create a file that will document the installation application. The output produced with this option will not install the component.

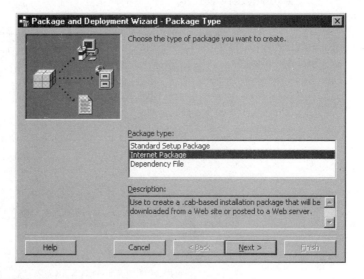

Select the second option, Internet Package, and click Next to move to the Package Folder window.

The Package Folder Window   In this window, you must specify the folder where the installation files (produced by the wizard) will be stored. By default, the wizard will suggest the Package folder under the project's folder. If you have already created a CAB file for your project, you'll be prompted as to whether the existing files must be overwritten. Click Next to see the Included Files window of the wizard.

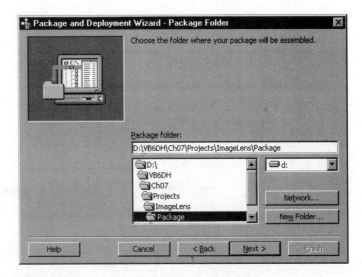

Included Files   In this window, you'll see the support files required by the component. If you plan to install the component on the computers in a local area network and you know that certain files exist on all computers, you can exclude these files from the EXE file or the CAB files by clearing the box in front of their names.

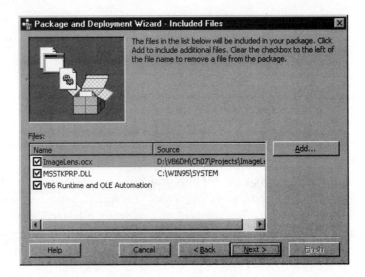

If your application requires additional auxiliary files, like images, font files, registry files, ActiveX controls, resources, and other support files, add them to the package with the Add button. After you have specified the included files, click Next to move to the File Source window of the wizard.

File Source   In this window, you specify the location of the included files (the ones displayed in the previous window). If you plan to distribute the application through the Internet, you may decide to include only the files that are unique to your application. Some support files are common to all applications (like system DLLs or the VB6 RunTime module). These files can be included in your EXE or CAB files, or be downloaded from the Microsoft Web site. In this window, you can specify the source of each file.

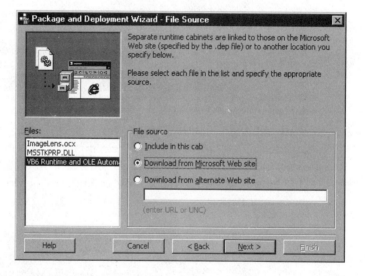

If the Web page with the ActiveX control will be viewed in a corporate environment, you may choose to have some files downloaded from a specific server. Likewise, if your Web server is too busy, you may choose to have some files downloaded from Microsoft's Web site. For the purpose of testing your custom control, include all files in the CAB file. Then click Next to move to the Safety Settings window.

Safety Settings   In this window, you must specify whether your component(s) is Safe for Scripting and/or Safe for Initialization. A custom ActiveX control can be quite harmless on its own, but through the script on the HTML page, it could possibly delete system files. By specifying that your control is safe for scripting, you're basically telling the viewers of your page that the script can't harm their computers. For example, the control doesn't expose any members that could harm the host computer. Whether viewers will believe you and download the control is a different story, of course.

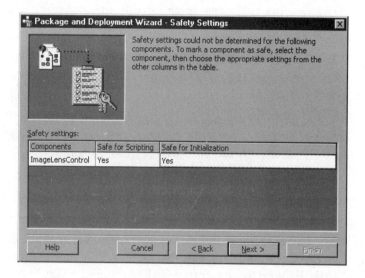

A custom ActiveX control could also harm the target computer during initialization. By marking your control as safe for initialization, you are again telling your viewers that your control isn't going to harm their computers. Click Next. You'll be prompted to click Finish and the wizard will generate the CAB in the Package folder.

The wizard will generate two files, `Alarm.CAB` and `Alarm.HTM`, as well as a new folder called Support. Any additional files you have specified in the Included Files window will also be placed in the Package folder. Since the CAB file you've prepared is meant to be distributed over the Internet, the wizard has created a minimal Web page that shows you how to place an instance of the custom control on a Web page with the `<OBJECT>` tag. Here's the `ImageLens.htm` file listing:

Code 18.3   **The ImageLens.htm File**

```
<HTML>
<HEAD>
<TITLE>ImageLens.CAB</TITLE>
</HEAD>
<BODY>
<!--If any of the controls on this page require licensing, you must
    create a license package file. Run LPK_TOOL.EXE to create the
```

```
required LPK file. LPK_TOOL.EXE can be found on the ActiveX SDK,
http://www.microsoft.com/intdev/sdk/sdk.htm. If you have the Visual
Basic 6.0 CD, it can also be found in the \Tools\LPK_TOOL directory.

The following is an example of the Object tag:
```

```
<OBJECT CLASSID="clsid:5220cb21-c88d-11cf-b347-00aa00a28331">
    <PARAM NAME="LPKPath" VALUE="LPKfilename.LPK">
</OBJECT>
-->

<OBJECT ID="ImageLensControl"
CLASSID="CLSID:36FDB80E-3532-11D2-9049-F3C13EDD060E"
CODEBASE="ImageLens.CAB#version=1,0,0,0">
</OBJECT>
</BODY>
</HTML>
```

This file simply shows you how to use the ImageLens control on a Web page. The CODEBASE tag tells the browser where it can find the ImageLens control's CAB file on the server. The CAB file should reside in the same folder on the server as the Web page (or, you should modify the location of the CAB file in the CODE-BASE attribute).

Double click the ImageLens.htm file in the Package folder to open it with Internet Explorer. You will see that the page contains an instance of the control and nothing else. The control has already been registered with your system, and that's why it's displayed instantly. On another system, the browser would have to download the CAB file from the server and install the control on the target computer before it could display it on the page.

No image will be displayed on the control because the sample page doesn't contain a script, but the lens rectangle will be white and you'll be able to drag it around. To complete the test, open the ImageLens.htm page and implement the following changes:

1. Add a Command button below the control, which will load an image on the control with the following tag:

    ```
    <INPUT TYPE=Button NAME=bttnLoad VALUE="Download Image">
    ```

2. Insert the following script for the button's onClick event:

    ```
    <SCRIPT LANGUAGE=VBscript>
    Sub bttnLoad_onClick()
    ```

```
        ImageLensControl.PictureFromURL = "nysky.gif"
    End Sub
    </SCRIPT>
```

This script loads the NYSKY.GIF image, which resides in the same folder as the HTML document. The script must be inserted inside the HEAD section of the document.

3. You should also change the default dimensions of the ImageLens control by adding the WIDTH and HEIGHT attributes to the <OBJECT> tag. Here's the revised <OBJECT> tag that matches the dimensions of the image:

    ```
    <OBJECT ID="ImageLensControl"
    CLASSID="CLSID:36FDB80E-3532-11D2-9049-F3C13EDD060E"
    CODEBASE="ImageLens.CAB#version=1,0,0,0"
    WIDTH=500 HEIGHT=230>
    </OBJECT>
    ```

Now you can open the `ImageLens.htm` page, click the Download Image button to load the NYSKY.GIF image on the control, and then slide the lens around with the mouse.

Testing the CAB File

Obviously, you can't test the CAB file on the same computer on which the control was developed. The control has already been registered on this system and need not be downloaded ever again. To actually download the control's CAB file and force Internet Explorer to install it again, you must first uninstall the control from your computer (or use another computer on the network, if you have one).

Let's unregister the control and see what will happen. Open a DOS window, switch to the folder with the IMAGELENS.ocx file, and issue the following command:

```
REGSVR32 /u IMAGELENS.ocx
```

This command will remove the control's entry from the Registry. It will not delete the OCX file on your hard disk, but for all intents and purposes, your system knows nothing about the ImageLens control.

If you double-click the `Alarm.htm` file again, Internet Explorer will extract the OCX file (and any required support files) from the CAB file and install the control. As part of the installation process, the control will also be registered. This process will take several seconds, and you'll experience a small delay. While the control is being installed and registered, a small square will appear at the top of

Internet Explorer's window (at the same place where the ImageLens control will be displayed later).

As a last test, you can create a Web page and open it through the Web server. The simplest method is to create a new virtual folder on the Web server and place the necessary files there. Since the wizard has placed the CAB file and the sample HTML file in the Package folder, make this folder a virtual folder on your Web server and call it ImgLens. Then unregister the control again, as explained earlier in this section. Start Internet Explorer and connect to the following URL:

```
127.0.0.1/ImgLens/ImageLens.htm
```

Again, you should experience a delay as the browser downloads the control's CAB file from the Web server and installs the control on your computer. Then the ImageLens control will appear on the Web page and you'll be able to load the image and test the control by sliding the mouse over it.

Alternatively, you can specify your computer's IP address on the Internet instead of the local IP address (12.0.0.1). Run the WINIPCFG utility by selecting Start ➢ Run, and entering WINIPCFG. The utility will report your address on the Internet (something like 194.104.89.203), and you can use this address to connect to your own Web server. You can also give this address to a friend, who can connect to your Web server over the Internet. The ImageLens control will be downloaded and installed on their computer, and the ImageLens.htm page will function on the browser's window.

CHAPTER
NINETEEN

19

Active Server Pages

- Understanding Active Server Pages

- Exploring the objects of Active Server Pages

- Creating an ASP page

- Using ActiveX Data Objects

- Understanding the File Access component

- Accessing Objects on the Web server

In the last chapter, you saw how a Web server sends information to the client in the form of HTML documents and how the client interacts with the server with hyperlinks. You also saw how to design Web pages that collect information from visitors on the client and submit it to the server along with the URL. When the server receives parameter values from a client, it must process them and return the results to the client in HTML format. In this chapter, we are going to discuss how parameters are processed on the server.

The parameters that a client submits can be anything—registration data, search arguments, customization data, anything. Businesses are interested in the information that is stored in databases and that must be retrieved as needed. To retrieve up-to-the-minute information through a Web server, the client must send back more information than simply the name of a hyperlink. For example, the user on the client might request the sales of a specific product in North Carolina or the most active customers in Texas. This information is encoded in a special format and transmitted to the server. As far as the client is concerned, it thinks it's requesting another URL.

Figure 19.1 shows a typical Web page that prompts the user to enter information, which will be used later to extract information from a database on the server. The site shown in Figure 19.1 is Infoseek, a widely used search engine on the Web. The search argument is "VB +books" (this searches for documents about VB that also contain the word *books*).

When the Search button is clicked, the client sends the following URL to the server:

```
http://www.infoseek.com/Titles?qt=VB+%2Bbooks&rf=11&lk=noframes&st=10
```

Titles is the name of an application on the server that will search the database and supply the results. It's not an ASP application, but that doesn't make any difference. The same arguments would be supplied if it were an ASP application, and the same document would be returned to the client.

The parameters follow the question mark. The first parameter is `qt`, and its value is the string "VB+%2Bbooks". The space was replaced with a plus sign, and the plus sign in the original search argument was substituted with %2B (2B is the hexadecimal representation of the plus sign's ASCII value). The parameter `lk=noframes` tells the application on the server to generate an HTML document without frames, and the parameter `st=10` specifies that it should display the second batch of 10 matching titles. The search of Figure 19.1 recalled nearly 50,000 documents, but they can be displayed on the client 10 at a time. Each time you click the

The Infoseek site searches
the Web for documents
that contain user-supplied
keywords.

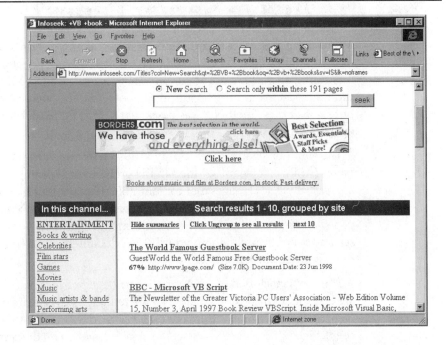

Next 10 hyperlink, the value of st is increased by 10 (and each time you click the Previous 10 hyperlink, the value of the parameter st is decreased by 10). This is all the information that the Titles application on the server needs to display the appropriate page with the results of the search.

The Web server can't decipher the requested URL, but it does have the intelligence to invoke the program whose name appears in the URL string and pass to it the parameters following the program's name. Traditionally, the programs that process client requests in real time on the server are called *scripts*, and most of them were written in Perl.

NOTE   Perl is an acronym formed from Practical Extraction and Report Language and is a scripting language for Unix systems with which you can write powerful data and text manipulation routines. However, compared with Visual Basic and VBScript, Perl is a cryptic language, and it's not a language with which Windows programmers are familiar.

What Are Active Server Pages?

Microsoft introduced several methods for developing scripts on the server—some of them quite simple (such as the Internet Database Connector and the SQL Web Assistant), and others not as simple. There was a confusing time when companies did their best to simplify the development and deployment of server-side scripts, but none of these methods was particularly easy for Visual Basic developers, or even for Web authors.

The situation changed drastically in 1996 with the introduction of Active Server Pages (ASP), an elegant solution to the problem of scripting. Active Server Pages are basically HTML pages that contain VBScript code that is executed on the server. The HTML code is transmitted to the client, as is. As a consequence, every HTML page you have authored can be turned into an Active Server Page. Not that you'll see any benefits in renaming your HTML documents, but you're ready to activate them with the inclusion of scripts.

The scripts included on an Active Server Page produce text and HTML tags that are also sent to the client, where they are rendered on the screen. An Active Server Page can produce any output, but only HTML documents can be rendered on the client. Since VBScript can contact the objects installed on the server, you are not limited to VBScript's native commands. You can contact ActiveX components to carry out complicated data processing, access databases, and so on. Which brings us once again to the ubiquitous objects. We didn't plan this book to revolve around objects, but there simply isn't a way around them! If you're planning to do some serious programming with Visual Basic, you can't go far without them.

Using the Server's Objects

In the last couple of years, we witnessed a dramatic shift from static Web pages to interactive applications that run in the browser's environment. Visual Basic's ActiveX documents are a perfect example. ActiveX documents, however, have not matured, and we have chosen not to discuss them in this book. They can't be considered mainstream technology yet, and many people still doubt their usefulness. (It doesn't take much longer to download a VB application that contacts your site to retrieve all types of information.) Instead, we decided to focus on more mature and far more popular methods of developing interactive Web pages, such as Active Server Pages. In Chapter 20, we'll discuss Visual Basic's built-in tools for developing applications for the Web, but a good understanding of HTML and server-side VBScript is essential. This chapter focuses on the basics of building Web applications, and the topics discussed here are more or less required for the next chapter.

HTML is a great language for displaying information on the client. HTML extensions made Web pages colorful, then interactive. But HTML is a simple language. It wasn't designed to be a programming language, and no matter how many extensions are introduced, HTML will never become a proper programming language.

To design interactive Web pages, we need a programming tool. VBScript could be the missing link, but VBScript (and any other scripting language) is also seriously limited because of security considerations. A scripting language that runs on the client must be safe, and, practically speaking, making a language safe for scripting is like crippling it. So, the answer is to do more on the server. The programming tool is still VBScript. But with the server's ability to create new objects, VBScript can now be extended with objects.

Among the objects you can access from within your Active Server Pages are the objects exposed by applications that support VBA, such as the Microsoft Office applications. Let's say you want to calculate complicated math expressions that the user entered on the client. Excel's Evaluate function is probably the simplest solution. Just pass the expression as entered by the visitor to the Evaluate function, wait for the result, and pass it to the client on a new HTML page.

To access databases, you can write custom objects similar to the ones we developed in Chapter 9. However, the simplest way to access databases through an ASP is via the Database component, which is based on the ActiveX Data Objects (ADO). ADO is a component that's installed along with ASP, and you can call it from within your ASP pages to access databases. The ADO component provides high-performance connectivity to any ODBC-compliant database or OLE DB data source. As such, it can be used from within a Web page's script to directly access remote databases. In other words, you can use the ADO component on the client script (provided that the component is already installed on the client computer) to build a Web front end for accessing corporate data, without developing additional scripts on the server. You will find more information on using the ActiveX Data Objects with Visual Basic in Chapter 4.

Why Use Active Server Pages?

Before we look at the structure of Active Server Pages and the objects they use, let's summarize the benefits of using Active Server Pages versus other, more traditional methods of server scripting. Active Server Pages enable HTML authors and Web developers to mix HTML with inline scripting using any authoring tool they are accustomed to (as long as they can comfortably open and edit the HTML documents). The scripts can reference components running on the server to perform complicated processing on the data submitted by the user.

Open Architecture

Active Server Pages are not limited to a particular scripting language. Currently, they support VBScript and Jscript, but third parties can provide support for other languages such as REXX (the OS/2 batch programming language), Perl, and so on. In addition, multiple scripting languages can be used interchangeably in the same ASP file.

You can create ActiveX components in virtually any language. This includes Visual Basic, which opens up a new field for VB programmers. You can easily apply your knowledge of Visual Basic components to Web development (several chapters on building ActiveX components are in the second part of this book). Even though most scripts in use today are still written in Perl (you see, Microsoft wasn't among the first to see the future of the Web and help it grow), the situation is changing rapidly with the introduction of Active Server Pages and the Internet Information Server. Any language that can produce ActiveX components can also be used in Web development.

Ease of Development

Active Server Pages make it easy for HTML authors to activate their Web pages on the server. You can develop customized pages immediately, without writing complicated CGI programs in unfamiliar languages. You can start developing Active Server Pages by writing an HTML document, using any tools you like, and then add the script section, which provides the functionality that can't be achieved with HTML. You can also include server-side and client-side scripts on the same page, to balance the load between the two computers.

Processing on the Client or on the Server

In principle, any processing that can be carried out on the client shouldn't be moved to the server. Of course, a lot depends on the developer's abilities or on other factors, such as the processing power of the client.

If an action takes a long time to complete on the client, consider bringing this part of the script to the server. This approach will work better with intranets, however, because the time required to contact the Web server on the Internet and download a new page through a modem will more than offset any speed gained in processing the information.

Separation of Content and Logic

Web sites are designed by teams of professionals, including artists, HTML authors, programmers, and so on. One of the challenges in setting up a large Web site is to enable these professionals to work together efficiently. Developing large sites with straight HTML and traditional scripting tools leads frequently to one developer cutting into another developer's work.

The components provided by Active Server Pages allow teams to separate the programming from the design of visual elements. Each developer can focus on his or her part of the process (programming, back-end database management, advertisement rotation, visual design, and so on). This separation of the programming logic from the content allows more flexibility in Web site design, especially when it involves teams.

The last component of Active Server Pages is the scripting language, VBScript, which is the glue that holds these components together. Active Server Pages support multiple scripting languages, but in this book we'll focus on VBScript. Being a Visual Basic programmer, you will be able to apply your knowledge to the Web immediately—especially your knowledge of building and using ActiveX components.

Browser Independence

The output produced by an ASP is straight HTML code, which can be viewed with any browser. All application logic needs to generate dynamic content resides on the server. The server-side script can be as complicated as you can make it. Your visitors, however, don't see this complexity, and they aren't required to have a specific browser. Any browser that can handle the latest version of HTML will do. In the HTML documents you produce, you can include features that are unique to Internet Explorer, but this is up to you. Avoid browser-specific issues, and your ASP pages can be contacted by any browser.

The Objects of Active Server Pages

Active Server Pages follow the component-based development paradigm. All the standard functionality you need to build a Web site comes in the form of objects, which can be classified in two major categories:

- Intrinsic
- Basic

Intrinsic objects provide methods and properties that you need to access details of the incoming requests (such as the parameters of the request), handle cookies, and create the response to send back to the client. Basic objects provide functionality that is commonly used in Web development, such as the ADO component for accessing databases, the file system component for writing to and reading from local files on the server, and more. In the following two sections, we'll discuss these objects and give you examples of how they are used in Web development. It goes without saying that you can build your own objects to address specific requirements.

Intrinsic Objects

ASP includes a number of built-in objects that free the developer from much of the grunt work of writing code to access details such as extracting the parameters submitted along with the URL, storing and retrieving cookies on the client computer, and directing the output to the client.

Request   This object gives you access to the parameters passed to the server by the client, along with the URL. These parameters are usually the values of the controls on the Form, but can be any string constructed on the client by a local script. Through the Request object, you can also recall the values of existing cookies on the client or create new ones.

Response   This object provides the methods you need to build the response, which is another HTML document. The Response object represents the output stream, which is directed by the Web server to the client, as if it were another HTML document.

Application   This object maintains information that's common to all users of an ASP-based application. The Application object provides events that let you set up variables that will be used by all users of the application.

Session   This object maintains information for individual users while they are interacting with the application. A separate Session object is associated with each user, and its basic function is to maintain a state between sessions for that user. You can define variables in the Session object, and they will maintain their value even when the user jumps between pages in the application. The Session object's variables are released when the user terminates the session.

Server   This object allows your server-side script to create instances of ActiveX components that reside on the server. The Server object's CreateObject method is almost identical to the Visual Basic function by the same name, and it lets you incorporate the functionality of ActiveX components into your applications. Similarly, you can create object variables with the Server object and extend your Web pages with capabilities that are way beyond HTML.

Base Objects

To help you create Web applications, the Active Server Pages components of the Web server expose the following objects that provide the functionality that is not necessary (as is the functionality of the built-in objects), but that is commonly used in building applications for the Web.

Database   This object provides connectivity to any ODBC-compliant database or OLE DB data source. It is based on the ActiveX Data Objects and allows Web developers to easily link a database to an active Web page to access and manipulate data.

File Access   This is another useful object that lets you access text files stored on the server. As with client-side scripts, server-side scripts must be safe for the host system. The File Access object is fairly safe, because it allows developers to write and read only text files and only in specific folders on the server.

Content Linking   This object manages a list of URLs so that you can treat the pages in your Web site like the pages in a book. You author the pages, and the Content Linking object automatically generates and maintains tables of contents and navigation links to previous and following Web pages. With the methods and properties exposed by the Content Linking object, you can add, delete, and rearrange pages without editing the individual HTML files.

Browser Capabilities   With this object, ASP files can recognize the capabilities of the requesting browser and dynamically optimize the site's content for specific browser features. If you weren't able to write code that automatically recognizes the type of browser for a session, you'd have to create (and maintain) a series of duplicate pages for each browser, or you'd have to notify users that special features on your site can be viewed only with a specific browser.

Advertisement Rotator   As people realize the potential of the Web as a business medium and more and more sites become commercial, the need to manage ads on a Web increases. Web managers can't afford to manually place ads in their designs. Ads must not only be rotated, but selected according to user preferences. If your Web site has a search engine, it wouldn't make sense to advertise cars to a viewer who's looking for books or advertise magazines to people who are searching for programming tools. To simplify the handling of ads on a Web site, Active Server Pages comes with the Advertisement Rotator object. You can use this object to display ads based on preset criteria every time an ASP file is requested.

In this chapter, we'll cover only a few of the basic components of Active Server Pages. We'll discuss the built-in objects and a few of the basic objects, which will help you leverage your VB knowledge to the Web. We won't get into every ASP-related topic.

Creating an ASP Page

The simplest way to create an ASP page is to change the extension of an existing HTML document, from HTM (or HTML) to ASP. Then place the file in a new folder under your Web server's root folder. For the examples in this chapter, we will use the ASPages folder. All examples will reference ASP pages in the ASPages folder.

> **NOTE** You'll find all the Active Server Pages examples discussed in this chapter in the ASPages folder under this chapter's folder on the CD that comes with this book.

ASP Files and Execute Rights

ASP files are text files by content, but they are also programs. When called, their scripts are compiled on demand, and the executable parts are loaded in the cache. Therefore, they must be placed in a folder with Scripts rights.

Through the Web server's administration utility, create a virtual directory, name it **ASPages**, and map it to the ASPages folder under the Web's root folder. (You can create the ASPages directory anywhere on your hard disk, but it's commonly placed under the root folder.) Then set the folder's Scripts permission. You need not set the Execution rights for the folder, because ASP files are not executable files.

Here's a simple HTML file that displays the time on the client.

Code 19.1	**The** DATETIME.htm **File**

```
<HTML>
<HEAD>
<TITLE>Simple ASP Demo</TITLE>
<SCRIPT LANGUAGE=VBScript>
Document.Write "<FONT SIZE=3 FACE='Verdana'>"
Document.Write "<H1>Welcome to the Active Server Pages</H1>"
Document.Write "The date is <B>" & Date() & "</B> and the time is _
<B>" & Time() & "</B>"
Document.Write "<P>"
</SCRIPT>
</HEAD>
<BODY>
<B>Active Server Pages</B> contain text, HTML code and scripts that _
are executed on the client, just like ordinary HTML documents. The _
DateTime.asp file contains a client-side script, which prints the _
date and the time on the client and then displays the document's body.
<BR>
In addition, server-side scripts contain scripts that are executed _
on the server and produce HTML output. The client never sees the _
server-side script, just the output it produces.
</BODY>
</HTML>
```

The date and time are displayed from within a client-side script, which calls the functions Date() and Time(). This script is executed on the client, and as a consequence the date and time are read from the local computer's clock.

We'll revise this page to display the time on the server. To do so, we'll add statements that are executed on the server. Copy the DATETIME.HTM file to the SRVR-TIME.ASP file and replace the <SCRIPT> tag with the following:

```
<SCRIPT LANGUAGE = VBScript RUNAT = Server>
Response.Write "<FONT SIZE=3 FACE='Verdana'>"
Response.Write "<H1>Welcome to the Active Server Pages</H1>"
Response.Write "The date is <B>" & Date() & "</B> and the time is _
<B>" & Time() & "</B>"
Response.Write "<P>"
</SCRIPT>
```

The Response object is equivalent to the Document object, but the server can't access the Document object, which is available only on the client. Instead, it must use the Response object. The new page will produce the same output, but the date and time displayed will be the date and time on the server. The modifier RUNAT in the <SCRIPT> tag tells the Active Server Pages to execute this script on the server, not on the client.

Server-side scripts can also be enclosed in a pair of <% and %> tags. These tags enclose all the statements that must be executed on the server. Everything between these two tags is considered a server-side script, which is replaced by its output and never seen by the client.

Displaying the HTML Code

To open an ASP file (or ASP application, if you prefer), follow these steps:

1. Connect to your Web server. If you are developing on the machine where the Web server is installed, connect to the URL 127.0.0.1.

2. Open the ASPages folder.

3. Click the name of the ASP file you want to open.

If you double-click the name of an ASP file, you will see the HTML code, but none of the server-side statements will be executed. The browser skips the server-side script tags (<% and %>) because it doesn't know how to render them. These statements must be executed on the server, which happens only if a Web server furnishes the document.

Here's a more useful ASP page along the same lines. This page displays a different greeting depending on the time of the day.

Code 19.2   **An HTML Page with a Greeting**

```
<HTML>
<BODY>
<%
If Time() >=#12:00:00 AM# And Time() < #12:00:00 PM#  Then
  greeting = "Good Morning!"
Else
  greeting = "Good Afternoon!"
```

```
End If
%>
<H1> <% =greeting %> </H1>
<BR>
<H2>and welcome to the Active Server Pages.</H2>
<BR>
More HTML lines follow
</BODY>
</HTML>
```

The statements between the first pair of server-side tags (<% and %>) do not produce any output for the client. They simply assign the proper value to the *greeting* variable. The value of this variable is then sent to the client by the line <% =greeting %>. The rest is straight HTML, which is rendered on the client as usual.

HTML and server-side statements can coexist on the same line too. The last example could have been implemented as follows:

```
<HTML>
<BODY>
<% If Time()  > = #12:00:00 AM# And Time() < #12:00:00 PM#  Then %
<H1>Good Morning!</H1>
<% Else %>
<H1>Good Afternoon!</H1>
<% End If %>
<BR>
<H2>and welcome to the Active Server Pages.</H2>
<BR>
More HTML lines follow
</BODY>
</HTML>
```

Your server-side script can also call procedures you supply in addition to built-in procedures such as the Date() and Time() functions. You can write a function that returns the date formatted in a specific way with the FormatDate() function. To call this function from within your script, enclose its name in the server-side script tags:

```
<% =FormatDate %>
```

The actual definition of the function must appear somewhere in the same file. Since the entire procedure will be executed on the server and since it doesn't contain any HTML code to be sent to the client, you can place it in a pair of <SCRIPT> tags, similar to the client-side scripts, with an added qualifier:

```
<SCRIPT RUNAT=SERVER LANGUAGE=VBScript>
  function  FormatDate ()
  {
      function's statements
  }
</SCRIPT>
```

The procedure will be executed and will return the current date in a format determined by the code.

Included Files

Multiple scripts can use procedures such as the FormatDate() function. To avoid repeating code or to maintain identical code in multiple files, you can include a file with one or more procedure definitions in an ASP file. The included file can also contain HTML code; it doesn't really matter. It is inserted as is in the current ASP file and processed along with the rest of the file.

HTML provides the #INCLUDE directive, which inserts the contents of another text file into an ASP file before processing it. The #INCLUDE statement is called a directive because it's not an executable statement; it merely instructs ASP to perform a simple insertion.

> **NOTE** C programmers will be quite familiar with the term *directive*. Normally, directives are processed by the preprocessor to prepare a file for the compiler.

The syntax of the #INCLUDE directive is:

```
<!-- #INCLUDE VIRTUAL|FILE="filename" -->
```

The comment tags ensure that this line will not be sent to the client by mistake. If the file resides in a virtual folder (or a subfolder under a virtual folder), use the VIRTUAL keyword. If you'd rather specify an absolute path name, use the FILE keyword. Either keyword must be followed by the path name to the file to be included. Included files do not require a special extension, but the extension INC is commonly used.

To include the `DateFunctions.inc` file in the `Support` folder under ASPages, use the following line:

```
<!--#INCLUDE VIRTUAL="/ASPages/Support/DateFunctions.inc"-->
```

If the `DateFunctions.inc` file resides in the same folder as the ASP file in which it will be included, you can use the #INCLUDE directive with the FILE keyword:

```
<!--#INCLUDE FILE="DateFunctions.inc"-->
```

If the included file resides in the `Support` subfolder under the folder of the ASP file, the following line will insert it in the current ASP file:

```
<!--#INCLUDE FILE="Support/DateFunctions.inc"-->
```

Relative paths use the ASP file's folder as the starting point. You can also use the ../ qualifier to specify parent folders:

```
<!--#INCLUDE FILE="../Support/DateFunctions.inc"-->
```

Included Files: Dos and Don'ts

Included files can, in turn, include other files. You must ensure that the #INCLUDE directives don't form a loop. For example, `Document1.asp` includes `file1.inc`, which, in turn, may include `file2.inc`. However, `File2.inc` can't include `file1.inc` (and neither can an included file include itself). ASP detects circular references and aborts the processing with an error message, which will appear in the browser.

Advanced programmers might even attempt to use the script to generate the included file's name. This is an interesting technique with VB applications, but it won't work with Active Server Pages. The #INCLUDE directives are processed before the script is executed, and the name of the included file won't be available the moment it must be inserted.

Finally, an included file must contain scripts in their entirety. In other words, you can't start a script in one included file and end it in another; neither can you include a file in the middle of script. The following script won't work:

```
<%
    {server-side script statements}
    <!--#INCLUDE FILE="DateFunctions.inc"-->
    {more statements}
%>
```

You must break the script into two segments, as follows:

```
<%
    {server-side script statements}
%>
    <!--#INCLUDE FILE="DateFunctions.inc"-->
<%
    {more statements}
%>
```

Mixing Server-Side and Client-Side Scripts

An ASP file can contain both server-side and client-side scripts. If you want to include a script section in your Web page, simply insert the scripting commands between the <SCRIPT> tags in the file. Figure 19.2 shows the output of another ASP file that is a variation of the script that displays the server's date on the client. The ServerTime page displays the time on the client through a client-side script, and it displays the time on the server through a server-side script. If the client and server computers are in different time zones, the difference in the time is an integer number of hours, plus a few seconds that it may take for the HTML code to arrive at the client.

FIGURE 19.2:

The ServerTime.asp script combines client-side and server-side scripts to display the time on the client and the server.

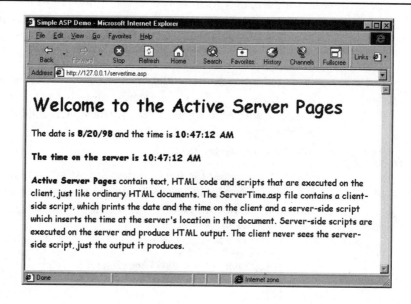

Here is the listing of the ServerTime.asp file. Notice that the client-side script is inserted with the <SCRIPT> tag, as if it were included on a regular HTML page. The server-side script isn't really a script, just a call to the Time() function. You could have inserted as many statements as necessary, as long as they were included in a pair of <% and %> tags.

Code 19.3	The ServerTime.asp Script

```
<HTML>
<HEAD>
<TITLE>Simple ASP Demo</TITLE>
<SCRIPT LANGUAGE=VBScript>
Document.Write "<FONT SIZE=3 FACE='Comic Sans MS'>"
Document.Write "<H1>Welcome to the Active Server Pages</H1>"
Document.Write "The date is <B>" & Date() & "</B> and the time is _
<B>" & Time() & "</B>"
Document.Write "<P>"
</SCRIPT>
</HEAD>
<BODY>
<B>The time on the server is <% =Time() %></B>
<P>
<B>Active Server Pages</B> contain text, HTML code and scripts that _
are executed on the client, just like ordinary HTML documents. The _
ServerTime.asp file contains a client-side script, which prints the _
date and the time on the client and a server-side script which inserts _
the time at the server's location in the document. Server-side scripts _
are executed on the server and produce HTML output. The client never _
sees the server-side script, just the output it produces.
</BODY>
</HTML>
```

After this introduction to the basic structure of ASP files, we can turn our attention to the objects of the Active Server Pages and see how they can help you develop interactive Web pages. In developing ASP applications, we are primarily interested in interacting with the client, rather than writing elaborate HTML code or even client-side scripts.

The emphasis is in writing server-side code that reads data submitted by the client, processes them on the server (in most cases with ActiveX components that reside on the server), and produces Web pages on the fly, which are transmitted back to the client. With any other server, this process requires CGI scripts and, in general, programming in C-like languages. With Active Server Pages and the built-in objects, the tasks that would normally require Perl or C++ programming can be taken care of with VBScript.

In the rest of the chapter, we are going to examine these objects and see how they simplify scripting on the server. At the end of the chapter, we'll look at some of the basic components, especially the Database component, which lets your script access databases on the server.

The Response Object

Use the Response object to send information to the client. ASP files may contain straight HTML code that's sent directly to the client. However, if you want to control the output programmatically from within the script, you must write it to the Response object. The Response object supports the following methods and properties.

Write Method

```
<HTML>
<SCRIPT LANGUAGE=VBScript RUNAT=Server>
  Response.Write "<HTML>"
  Response.Write "<HEAD>"
  Response.Write "<TITLE>Response.Write Demo</TITLE>"
  Response.Write "</HEAD>"
  Response.Write "<H1>"
  Response.Write "Response Object:Write Method"
  Response.Write "</H1>"
  Response.Write "This document was created on the fly by an ASP file _
on the server"
  Response.Write "</HTML>"
</SCRIPT>
</HTML>
```

The outer pair of HTML tags delimits the ASP file (they are not really required), and the pair of HTML tags written to the Response object delimits the HTML file seen by the client. If there's one method used in nearly every ASP file, it is the Response.Write method, and you will see many more examples of it in this chapter.

NOTE	The Write method of the Response object is the primary way to send data to the client. ASP also uses this method behind the scenes. Let's say you want to output the value of a variable, and you mistype the expression, as shown here: Welcome back < % =UserName %>. (The mistake is an extra space between the characters < and %.) When the script that contains this line is processed, the error message that is displayed on the client indicates that the error occurred in the method Response.Write, even though this method is not directly called by the script!

Here's a more practical example of the Response object's Write method. Let's say you are constructing a page with various levels of headings that are determined by the variable *iHead*. This variable is incremented and decreased by an algorithm you provide. If *iHead* is 2, a level 2 heading is inserted, with a statement such as the following:

```
Response.Write "<H" & iHead & ">"
```

When this statement is executed with iHead = 2, the tag <H2> is sent to the client.

Later in this chapter, you will see how to use the File Access object to read from text files on the server. If you want to read the text and send it to the client, you use the Write method to write the incoming text stream to the Response object.

Redirect Method

This method redirects the client to another URL. If you move your site to another URL, write a short ASP application such as the following to redirect the visitor automatically to the new URL.

```
<HTML>
<%
Response.Write "Our site was moved at a new URL."
Response.Write "Your browser will be redirected to the new URL
automatically."
Response.Redirect newURL
%>
</HTML>
```

The *newURL* variable is the Web's new URL.

Clear Method

This method clears the data written to the Response object and is used only when the Buffer property is set to True (when the output is buffered until the entire page has been processed, before it's sent to the client).

> **NOTE**   See the discussion of the Buffer property, later in this section, for more details on using the Clear method.

ContentType Property

This property determines the type of document you will send to the client. The ContentType property applies to the entire page and must be set before you write any information to the output stream with the Write method.

> **NOTE**   You'll find the various content types in the File Types tab of the Windows Explorer's Options dialog box. (In any Explorer window, choose View ➤ Options and select the File Types tab.)

For example, if you want to send source code of an ASP page, set ContentType to text/plain, rather than to text/html, which is the default content type:

```
<% Response.ContentType = "text/plain" %>
```

Cookies Property

Use this property to send cookies to the client. Cookies are special strings that are stored on the local computer, and your ASP application can read them back with the Request method.

In effect, cookies are a way to pass values between the pages of your Web site. The HTTP protocol used on the Web is stateless. Each document is requested by the client and transmitted by the server, and the transaction completes at this point. If the same client requests another document from the same server, neither the client nor the server has any recollection of the previous transaction.

Maintaining variables between different pages is a problem with a stateless protocol, which is solved with the help of cookies. If your Web pages use a consistent, but user-defined, background color, you can store this value to a cookie—let's call it BColor—and then read it before constructing and transmitting a new page. *BColor* is the name of a variable that is stored on the client computer with the Cookies method of the Response object. To read its value, you access the Cookies property of the Request object.

NOTE For more information on using cookies, see the section, "Storing and Recalling Cookies," later in this chapter.

Buffer Property

By default, the Response object sends its output to the client as soon as it can, and it doesn't wait for the entire page to complete. If you want to process the entire page before sending any output to the client, set the Buffer property of the Response object to True. Let's say that as you process the page (with an ActiveX component or by reading data from a database), you discover that you need not send the previous data to the client or that you must redirect the client to another URL. If the Buffer property was set to True, you can cancel the processing and clear the output stream with the Clear method of the Response object. Here's a typical scenario:

```
<%
Reponse.Buffer = True
{script statements}
If SupplierName = UserName Then
    Response.Clear
    Response.Redirect "/Suppliers/AllSuppliers.html"
    Response.End
End If
%>
```

This script builds a page by reading data from a database, until it discovers that the visitor is actually one of the suppliers; then it clears the output created so far, ends the Response object, and redirects the visitor to another page. If your script takes too long to process, however, nothing will appear on the client's monitor, and visitors may think they are not getting a response. Normal HTML pages are not buffered, so you should not buffer your ASP pages by default.

The Request Object

To interact with the visitor, your script should be able to request information that the visitor enters on a Form and read the values of cookies. Reading data back from the client has been a sore point in server scripting. ASP has simplified the process of reading the data submitted by the client by encapsulating all the complexity of the operation into a few properties of the Request object. This single feature of ASP would be adequate to make it a major server-scripting tool.

The Request object has five properties, all of which are collections:

QueryString contains the values passed to the server with the GET method.

Form contains all the Forms on the page.

Cookies contains all cookies that have been written to the client by the Web site.

ServerVariables contains all the HTTP variables, which are determined by the server.

ClientCertificate contains all the client certificates installed on the client.

The QueryString Collection

The collection you'll be using most often in developing ASP applications is the QueryString collection. This property lets you access all the parameters passed along with the URL by the client. If the names of the parameters are known at the time you develop the ASP file, you can request their values by name, with expressions such as the following:

```
reqProdName = Request.QueryString("ProductName")
```

If the names of the parameters are not known when you develop the ASP file, or if you want to process them all serially, you can use a loop such as the following:

```
Set Params = Request.QueryString
    For Each param in Params
    {process parameter param}
Next
```

Figure 19.3 shows a simple HTML page with a Form; the visitor can enter information by selecting options in list boxes.

NOTE   The HTML page is called ServerForm.HTM, and you will find it in this chapter's folder on the CD.

FIGURE 19.3:

A typical Form on an
HTML page

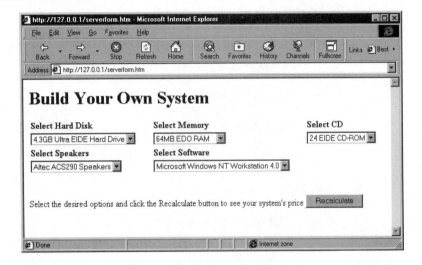

The names of the List Box controls on the ServerForm page are: HardDisk, Memory, CD, Speaker, and Software. The possible values for each setting are listed in the <OPTION> tags of each <SELECT> tag. The options of the Select Memory list box have the values 32, 64, 128, and 256. The Memory query parameter will have one of these values, depending on which option was selected on the Form.

Code 19.4   **The** ServerForm.htm **File**

```
<H1>Build Your Own System</H1>
<FORM name=ORDER method="GET"
action="http://127.0.0.1/aspages/param.asp">
<TABLE>
<TR>
<TD><B>Select Hard Disk</B></TD>
<TD></TD>
<TD><B>Select Memory</B></TD>
<TD></TD>
<TD><B>Select CD</B></TD>
</TR>
<TR>
<TD><SELECT name="HardDisk" size="1">
<OPTION selected value="3.2G">3.2GB Ultra EIDE Hard Drive </OPTION>
<OPTION  value="4.3G">4.3GB Ultra EIDE Hard Drive </OPTION>
```

```
</SELECT>
</TD>
<TD>
      
</TD>
<TD>
<SELECT name="Memory" size="1">
<OPTION  value="32">32 MB EDO RAM</OPTION>
<OPTION selected value="64 MB">64MB EDO RAM</OPTION>
<OPTION  value="128">128 MB EDO RAM</OPTION>
<OPTION  value="256">256 MB EDO RAM</OPTION>
</SELECT>
</TD>
<TD>
      
</TD>
<TD>
<select name="CD" size="1">
<option  value="">None</option>
<option selected value="CD12">12 EIDE CD-ROM</option>
<option selected value="CD24">24 EIDE CD-ROM</option>
</select>
</TD>
</TR>
<TR>
<TD><B>Select Speakers</B></TD>
<TD></TD>
<TD><B>Select Software</B></TD>
<TD></TD>
</TR>
<TR>
<TD>
<select name="Speaker" size="1">
<option selected value="">None</option>
<option value="S90">Altec ACS90 Speakers</option>
<option value="S290">Altec ACS290 Speakers</option>
</select>
</TD>
<TD></TD>
<TD>
<select name="Software" size="1">
```

```
<option selected value="WIN95">MS Windows 95</option>
<option value="WIN98">Microsoft Windows 98</option>
<option value="WINNT">Microsoft Windows NT Workstation 4.0 </option>
</select>
</TD>
</TABLE>
<BR><BR>
Select the desired options and click the Recalculate button to see _
your system's price
<INPUT TYPE=SUBMIT VALUE="Recalculate">
</FORM>
</HTML>
```

The script that processes this Form (Param.asp) doesn't do much (it doesn't actually recalculate the price of the configuration, but once you know the options specified by the visitor, it's relatively easy to calculate the price of the selected configuration). It generates another HTML page on the fly with the names and values of the parameters and sends it back to the client. The server's response is shown in Figure 19.4.

FIGURE 19.4:

The names and values of the query parameters submitted to the server by the Form in Figure 19.3

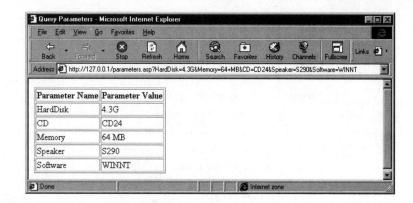

The Parameters.asp script that processed the data on the server uses a For Each loop to scan all the items of the QueryString collection and display their names and values in a new table. Each parameter is stored in the variable *PValue*. The default property of this variable is the name of the parameter. To access the value of the parameters, use Params(PValue).

Code 19.5   **The** Parameters.asp **File**

```
<HTML>
<TITLE>Query Parameters</TITLE>
<%
  Response.Write "<HTML>"
  Response.Write "<BODY>"
  Response.Write "<H2>
  Response.Write "<TABLE BORDER RULES=ALL>"
  Response.Write "<TR><TD><B>Parameter Name</B></TD><TD><B>Parameter _
Value</B></TD></TR>"
  Set Params = Request.QueryString
  For Each PValue in Params
  Response.Write "<TR><TD>" & PValue & "</TD><TD>" & Params(PValue) & _
"</TD></TR>"
  Next
  Response.Write "</TABLE>"
  Response.Write "</HTML>"
%>
</HTML>
```

To access individual parameters, you can use the collection Request.QueryString followed by the name of the parameter whose value you want. The following lines will return the specifications of the memory and the hard disk, as entered by the visitor on the Form in the page ServerForm.htm:

```
MemorySpec = Request.QueryString("Memory")
HDiskSpec = Request.QueryString("HardDisk")
```

TIP

It is possible for multiple controls on a Form to have identical names. In this case, the QueryString collection contains an array of values. For example, if the Form contains three TextBoxes named "Name," you can access them as Request.Query-String("Name")(1), Request.QueryString("Name")(2) and Request.QueryString-("Name")(3).

The Form Collection

This collection is similar to the QueryString collection in that it contains data that the visitor entered on a Form. Whereas the QueryString collection contains all the parameters submitted to the server, regardless of whether they belong to a Form, the Form collection contains the values of the parameters that come from controls. It is possible to build a URL followed by a number of parameters on the fly, from within a client script. These parameters will be reported by the QueryString collection, but not by the Form collection.

NOTE   You will see examples of URLs with parameters constructed by the client in the section "Using the ActiveX Data Objects" later in this chapter.

To access the value of a specific parameter in the Form collection, use a statement such as the following:

```
FullName = Request.Form("LastName") & ", " % Request.Form("FirstName")
```

The ServerVariables Collection

This collection contains a number of standard environment variables, which you can access from within your script. Basically, the ServerVariables collection contains all the information available about the client and the server. Here are some of the most commonly used server variables:

SERVER_NAME   The server's DNS or IP address.

SERVER_PROTOCOL   The name and revision number of the protocol used for the request. It's usually *HTTP/1.0*.

SERVER_PORT   The TCP/IP port number on which the server accepts requests. It's usually *80*.

SERVER_SOFTWARE   The name and version of the HTTP server software on the server machine.

SCRIPT_NAME   The path to the script being executed.

QUERY_STRING   The information that follows the question mark (?) in a URL. The GET method uses this variable, and you can retrieve it with the QueryString collection. This string is encoded according to the following two rules:

- Spaces are converted to plus signs.

- Any character may be represented as a hexadecimal number (representing the character's ASCII value) prefixed with the percent sign. The plus sign is encoded as %2B.

REQUEST_METHOD The HTTP method being used to send client data to the server. The possible values are GET and POST.

CONTENT_TYPE The type of data sent to the server. This variable is always *application/x-www-form-urlencoded*.

CONTENT_LENGTH The length of the string holding the data. This variable is used with the POST method.

REMOTE_HOST The full domain name of the client that made the request.

REMOTE_ADDR The IP (Internet Protocol) address of the requesting client.

The file SrvrParam.asp contains a short script that displays all the server variables, as shown in Figure 19.5.

NOTE   You'll find the SrvrParam.asp file in this chapter's folder on the CD that comes with this book.

Code 19.6   **The** SrvrParam.asp **File**

```
<HTML>
<%
   Response.Write "<HTML>"
   Response.Write "<BODY>"
   Response.Write "<TABLE BORDER RULES=ALL>"
   Response.Write "<TR><TD><B>Parameter Name</B></TD> _
          <TD><B>Parameter Value</B></TD></TR>"
   Set Params = Request.ServerVariables
   For Each Pvalue in Params
   Response.Write "<TR><TD>" & Pvalue & "</TD><TD>" & _
          Params(pValue) & "</TD></TR>"
   Next
   Response.Write "</TABLE>"
   Response.Write "</HTML>"
%>
</HTML>
```

The SrvrParams.asp script displays the names of all server variables and their values on a Web page.

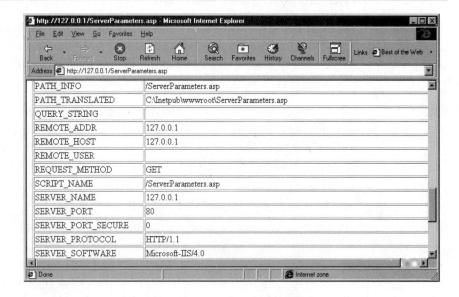

PATH_INFO	/ServerParameters.asp
PATH_TRANSLATED	C:\Inetpub\wwwroot\ServerParameters.asp
QUERY_STRING	
REMOTE_ADDR	127.0.0.1
REMOTE_HOST	127.0.0.1
REMOTE_USER	
REQUEST_METHOD	GET
SCRIPT_NAME	/ServerParameters.asp
SERVER_NAME	127.0.0.1
SERVER_PORT	80
SERVER_PORT_SECURE	0
SERVER_PROTOCOL	HTTP/1.1
SERVER_SOFTWARE	Microsoft-IIS/4.0

The Cookies Collection

This collection is discussed in detail in the "Storing and Recalling Cookies" section, later in this chapter. Cookies are basically variables stored by the server on the client computer and can be accessed by name, similar to parameters.

The ClientCertificates Collection

This collection contains all the certificates installed on the client computer and is needed only when your ASP applications install ActiveX components on the client. This property is supported only by Internet Explorer clients.

The Server Object

The Server object controls the environment in which the server-side scripts are executed. The single most important member of the Server object is its CreateObject method, which can create a new instance of an object from a registered class.

The CreateObject Method

The Server object's CreateObject method is identical to the Visual Basic CreateObject function. It accepts the programmatic ID of the object as an argument and returns an instance of the object. The syntax of the CreateObject method is

```
Server.CreateObject("progID")
```

To access a database through the ADO component, for instance, you first create a Connection object and a Recordset object with the following statements (see the section "Using ActiveX Data Objects," later in this chapter, for more details on accessing databases through ASP):

```
Set ADOConnection = Server.CreateObject("ADODB.Connection")
Set ADORS = Server.CreateObject("ADODB.Recordset")
```

Similarly, you must create object variables to access the other basic components of ASP, such as the File Access component and the Advertisement Rotator component. You can also use the Server's CreateObject method to create object variables for accessing your own custom ActiveX components. For example, you can use the DBClass ActiveX server we created in Chapter 10 to contact Microsoft Access databases. Or you can build an ActiveX component that contacts Excel to evaluate math expressions with the Evaluate method. In short, the CreateObject method lets you extend Active Server Pages by plugging into it almost any component you need.

The MapPath Method

Another commonly used method of the Server object is the MapPath method, which maps virtual folders to actual path names. This method is useful in developing server-side scripts for a very simple reason: All the files you access are stored in virtual folders. You can rearrange the entire folder structure of a Web site and then rename a few virtual folders, and your scripts will never know. In some situations, however, you need to know the actual path to a file, and the MapPath method will return this value.

> **NOTE**   In the last section of this chapter, "The File Access Component," you will find an example of using the MapFolder method.

The Session and Application Objects

The Session object maintains variables that apply to a specific session. Before we examine the members of this object and how it's used in developing an ASP application, let's look at how the ASP component maintains sessions with a stateless protocol.

As we mentioned, HTTP is a stateless protocol. Each time the client requests a new document, a new transaction is initiated. Then how does the ASP know that a new request from a client belongs to an existing session? The answer is that ASP uses cookies.

When the client connects for the first time, the server sends the ASPSESSIONID cookie, which is stored on the client computer. Then, every time the client contacts the server, the ASPSESSIONID cookie is transmitted along with the request's header.

NOTE   The header contains information that both computers use to communicate, but you don't have to know what type of information is transmitted or change the default headers.

ASP processes this cookie and uses it to restore the variable values saved previously in the Session object. The ASPSESSIONID cookie doesn't have an expiration value and expires automatically when the client disconnects. The next time the same client connects, a new cookie is sent, and a new session is created. To maintain information between sessions, you must store a cookie with an expiration date on the client, read it as soon as the client connects to the Web server, and use it as a key to a database with relevant data (such as user preferences, access rights, and so on).

NOTE   Some browsers don't support cookies (a rather rare situation today). These browsers don't support sessions either. Basically the only limitation that ASP imposes on the client (if it can be considered a limitation) is that it support cookies.

The Application object plays a similar role. It maintains a set of variables, not for each session, but for the application. Simple examples are a welcome message that's displayed on each client's window and a visitor counter. To implement a visitor counter with ASP, all you have to do is create an application-wide variable and increment it every time a client hits your home page (which must be an ASP document).

To create a new Session or Application variable, you need only reference it in your code (this is VBScript; you are not required to declare variables). The statement:

```
<% Session("UName") = Request.QueryString("UserName") %>
```

assigns the value of the cookie UserName (which presumably has been set by the client) to the Session variable *UName*. You can also assign function values to the Session variables, as the following statement does:

```
<% Session("Connected") = Now() %>
```

The name of the variable is on the left side of the above expressions. You can use Session variables to build all types of expressions and statements with VBScript. The following statement terminates a client connection if it's been active for more than 12 hours:

```
<% If Hour(Now() - Session("Connected")) > 12 Then
    Session.Abandon
End If
%>
```

The Abandon method terminates the current session.

Application variables are declared and used in the same manner, but since multiple scripts can access Application variables, there is always a chance that more than one script will attempt to change the value of an Application variable. The Application object provides the Lock and Unlock methods, which must be called before and after setting the variable:

```
Application.Lock
Application("VisitorCounter") = Application("VisitorCounter") + 1
Application.Unlock
```

The Session and Application objects support object variables too, created with the CreateObject method of the Server object. The difference is that object variables stored in the Session object can't be accessed by other sessions. If you have many clients accessing the same object (the same component on the server), you will be creating many instances of the same component, which may affect performance. This isn't as simple as it sounds. An object can be accessed by multiple sessions only if it has been designed to support multiple threads of execution.

The Start and End Events

Both the Session and the Application objects support a Start and an End event, which signal when a Session or Application starts and when it ends. The Start events are:

- Session_OnStart
- Application_OnStart

The End events are:

- Session_OnEnd

- Application_OnEnd

These procedures include code you want to run whenever an application or a session starts or ends. If an application and a session start at the same time, the Application_OnStart event is executed first. These events are important in developing ASP applications, but they are not available from within the script. You must enter them in the GLOBAL.asa file, which lives in the root folder of the application (the folder where the first ASP file to be requested by the client is stored). Typically, the GLOBAL.asa file contains the Start and End events of the Session and Application objects, as well as variable definitions.

For example, if you want to implement a variable that stores the number of visitors hitting the site, initialize it in the Application_OnStart event. Enter the following code in the GLOBAL.asa file:

```
<SCRIPT LANGUAGE=VBScript RUNAT=Server>
Sub Application_OnStart
    Application("Visitors") = 0
End Sub
</SCRIPT>
```

This event takes place every time the Web server software starts. Since you don't want to reset this counter every time you stop and restart the server, you can save the value of the variable *Visitors* to a text file on the server's disk, as explained in the sections "The FileSystemObject Object" and "The TextStream Object" later in this chapter. In the Application_OnStart event you read the value of the variable from the text file, and in the Session_OnStart event you increase it by one:

```
<SCRIPT LANGUAGE=VBScript RUNAT=Server>
Sub Session_OnStart
    Application.Lock
    Application("Visitors") = Application("Visitors") + 1
    Application.Unlock
End Sub
</SCRIPT>
```

You must also enter this procedure in the GLOBAL.asa event. This technique works well. The number will not increase each time a visitor hits the home page during the same session, because the Session_OnStart event is only triggered the first time.

Displaying a fancy counter on your pages is a different story. You can simply display this number in a large font on your home page, or you can generate a GIF file on the fly and display it on the home page. The Structured Graphics control that comes with Internet Explorer 4 lets you create elaborate graphics with text commands. This control is probably the easiest method to display a graphic that shows the number of visitors.

If your pages call a specific component frequently during a session, you can declare an object variable in the session's Start event. This variable will be available from within any page during the current session. Here's a simple example that creates an object variable referencing the MyObject component:

```
<SCRIPT LANGUAGE=VBScript RUNAT=Server>
Sub Session_OnStart
    Set Session("MyObj")=Server.CreateObject("MyObject")
End Sub
</SCRIPT>
```

Any page in the current session can use the *MyObj* object variable, and each session's *MyObj* variable is independent of the other sessions' *MyObj* variable.

Storing and Recalling Cookies

You have certainly noticed that some of the sites you've visited (Microsoft's home page is one of them) can be customized according to the visitor's preferences. How is it done? How does the server know each visitor's preferences between sessions? If each user had a fixed IP address, it would be possible (although not practical) for the server to maintain a database with IP addresses and the preferences for each visitor. The IP address of the client computer is given by the ServerVariables collection of the Server object. But most clients have different IP addresses each time they connect, so this approach is out of the question.

If you think about it, you will see that the only way for the server to maintain information about specific clients is to store this information on the client computer itself and recall it each time the client connects to the server. The information is stored on the client computer by the browser, in a special folder, in the form of variables and values. But instead of variables, they are called *cookies*.

NOTE   Cookies is another Unix term, if you were wondering what cookies have to do with your computer. And, no, cookies can't be used as Trojan horses.

Cookies are also used to pass information between pages on the same site. Let's say you're building a Web site for online orders. The site is made up of many pages, and visitors can order items on many pages. How do you keep track of the visitors' orders? Each page can have its own script, and each page can have its own global variables, but their scope is limited to the page on which they were declared. There is no way for two or more pages to share common variables. This is a direct consequence of HTTP being a stateless protocol. Each time a new page arrives at the client, the browser forgets everything about the current page (except for its URL, so that it can jump back to it). Orders made on one page can be stored on the client computer in the form of cookies and can be read by any other page on the same site.

Since cookies are managed by the browser, Web pages can't access your computer's hard disk directly (that's why cookies are safe). Moreover, when a page requests the values of the cookies, the browser supplies only those cookies that were stored by pages on the same site. In other words, cookies left on your computer by Microsoft's Web site can't be read by pages of other sites. The browser supplies to each page only the cookies left by other pages on the same site.

Cookies have expiration dates too. If a cookie is stored without an expiration date, it ceases to exist after the current session. A cookie with an expiration date remains on the client computer until it expires.

To store a cookie to the client computer, use the Cookies property of the Response object. The Cookies property is a collection, and you can create and access individual cookies by name. To create a new cookie, use a statement such as the following:

```
<% Response.Cookies("FavoriteSport")="Hockey" %>
```

If the cookie FavoriteSport exists on the client computer, its value is overwritten. If not, a new cookie is created. This cookie is released as soon as the current session ends.

You can specify the expiration date and time with the Expires property of the cookie, as follows:

```
<% Response.Cookies("FavoriteSport").Expires = _
        "December 31, 1998 12:00:00 GTM" %>
```

Cookies have other properties too:

> **Domain**   If specified, the cookie value is sent only to requests from this domain. This property is used along with the Path property.

Path If specified, the cookie is sent only to requests made from this path on the server, and not to every page on the same site.

HasKeys Specifies whether the cookie contains multiple keys (in which case, it's a dictionary). This property is read-only.

To create cookies with keys, use the same cookie name with multiple attributes, as in the following statements:

```
<%
Response.Cookies("Preferences")("Books") = "Mystery"
Response.Cookies("Preferences")("News") = "Sports"
%>
```

To request the value of a specific cookie from the client, use the Cookies collection of the Request object. The number of cookies in the Cookies collection is given by the Request.Cookies.Count property.

You can write a For...Next loop that scans the collection, or you can write a For Each...Next loop such as the following:

```
<%
For Each cookie In Request.Cookies
    {process current cookie, which is Request.Cookies(cookie)}
Next cookie
%>
```

Normally, the script on the server knows the names of the cookies and can request them by their names:

```
BookType = Request.Cookies("FavoriteSport")
```

If you need to find out the names of the cookies, use the For Each...Next structure. At each iteration, the value of the *cookie* variable is the name of the cookie, and Request.Cookies(cookie) is its value.

If a cookie has keys, you must access them as elements of a collection. Let's assume you've sent a cookie with keys to the client with the following statements:

```
<%
Response.Cookies("Background") = "Planets.bmp"
Response.Cookies("Preferences")("Books") = "Mystery"
Response.Cookies("Preferences")("News") = "Sports"
%>
```

The first cookie determines the visitor's favorite background patterns. The next two values can be used to create a custom home page. The following loop reads all the cookie values, including the key values:

```
<%
For Each cookie In Request.Cookies
    If Request.Cookies(cookie).HasKeys Then
        For Each cookie In Request.Cookies(cookie)
            { Process current cookie. Its value is
              Request.Cookies(cookie)(scookie) }
        Next
    Else
        { Process current cookie. Its value is Request.Cookies(cookie)}
    End If
Next
%>
```

Cookies are used for many purposes other than to exchange information among different pages on the same site. Every site that provides customized start pages uses cookies to store user information. Some Web sites may store information about the topics you search most often and adjust the ads they present to you.

Using ActiveX Data Objects

The most important component of ASP is the Database component, which is nothing other than the ADO. We left this topic for last so that we can use the objects discussed earlier in this chapter to build more elaborate and practical examples. Although you can use other components to access databases on the server, most Web developers use the ADO component.

As you recall from our discussion in Chapter 4, the ADO is the simplest object for accessing databases. Its object model is much simpler than that of DAO (Data Access Objects) or even RDO (Remote Data Objects). Yet, the ADO is the most powerful component and is used on most sites that deploy Active Server Pages. You can also use the DAO component and even develop your own ActiveX components to access databases on the server. This approach will work, but if you are setting up a new Web site, you should seriously consider ADO. It's faster, consumes fewer resources on the server (an important consideration for servers with a heavy load), and will eventually replace the DAO.

Setting Up an ODBC Data Source

To access a database on the server through the Database component, you must first define a System ODBC data source for the database, using the ODBC Data Source Administrator. Follow these steps:

1. Choose Start ➤ Settings ➤ Control Panel.

2. Double-click 32bit ODBC (the ODBC Administrator) to open the ODBC Data Source Administrator dialog box. In your System DSN tab you will probably see different data source names.

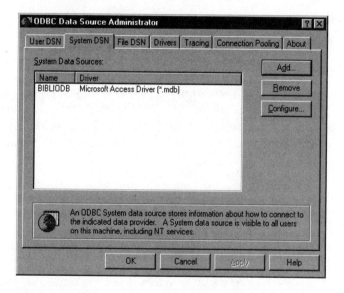

3. Select the System DSN tab to see the installed data sources. For the examples in this chapter, we are going to use the NWIND sample database, so we'll create a data source for the NWIND database.

4. Click the Add button to open the Create New Data Source Wizard. In this window, you will see the names of all ODBC drivers. Select the Microsoft Access driver and click Finish.

5. In the ODBC Microsoft Access 97 Setup dialog box, enter **NWINDDB** in the Data Source Name text box (you'll use this name to access the database). Enter a description in the Description text box, and then click Select to select the NWIND.mdb database in your VB folder.

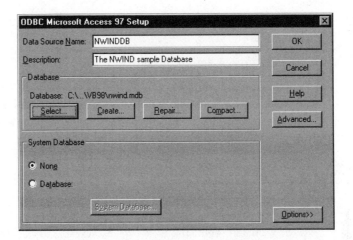

6. Click OK to return to the ODBC Data Source Administrator dialog box. The new data source will now appear in this window.

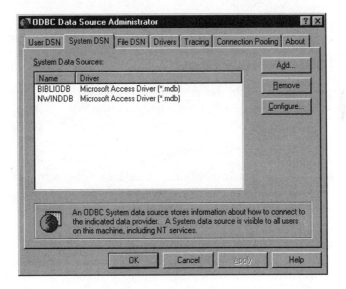

Opening the Database

To access the NWIND database from within an Active Server Page, you must create a Connection object with the Server.CreateObject method, as shown here:

```
Set DBConnection = Server.CreateObject("ADODB.Connection")
```

This variable establishes a connection to the database when you call its Open method, whose syntax is

```
DBConnection.Open "NWINDDB"
```

The first argument following the Open method's name must be the name of the data source that corresponds to the database you want to access. After you access the database to build the HTML page, you must release the Connection object by closing the connection with the Close method:

```
DBConnection.Close
```

TIP   This is the preferred method for accessing Microsoft Access databases. If you use the SQL Server instead, you can set up the *DBConnection* variable in the Application_OnStart event. This way it will be available to all clients that need to access the NWIND database. SQL Server supports multiple threads, and this technique will work. The Microsoft Access ODBC driver does not. Instead, there's a pool of connections, and the first available one is used. That's why you must release each connection object when you no longer need it.

Building a Recordset

After you establish a connection to the database, you can access it with SQL statements. To issue a SQL statement, use the Execute method of the Connection object, and pass the SQL statement as an argument. The syntax of the Execute method is

```
DBConnection.Execute SQLStatement
```

The SQLStatement argument can be a string with the SQL statement or the name of a stored procedure. If the SQL statement returns records (as does the SELECT statement), the Execute method returns a recordset and should be called as follows:

```
Set SelRecords = DBConnection.Execute(SQLStatement)
```

The Execute method accepts two optional arguments:

- The number of records affected by the operation (this parameter is set by the driver)

- Whether the SQL statement is SQL text or the name of a stored procedure

The method's complete syntax is

```
DBConnection.Execute SQLStatement, numRecords, SQLText
```

The SQLText argument can have the value adCmdText or adCmdStoredProc.

A second way to execute a SQL statement against the database is to create a Command object with the statement

```
Set SQLCommand = Server.CreateObject("ADODB.Command")
```

You can then execute SQL statements with the SQLCommand object's Execute method. The Command object exposes several properties that let you specify the statement and how it will be executed.

For example, you can specify the Connection object to which the Command object applies (should you have multiple connections open), specify parameter values for stored procedures, and so on.

NOTE   For a complete discussion of the ADO object, see Chapter 4, "The ADO Object."

Here's how the Command object is typically used:

```
Set DBConnection = Server.CreateObject("ADODB.Connection")
Set SQLCommand = Server.CreateObject("ADODB.Command")
Set ParamItem = Server.CreateObject("ADODB.Parameter")

SQLCommand.ActiveConnection = DBConnection
SQLCommand.CommandText = "ProductsByCategory"
SQLCommand.CommandType = adCmdStoredProc
SQLCommand.ParamItem
SQLCommand.ParamItem.Name = "@ProductCategory"
SQLCommand.ParamItem.Value = 31
SQLCommand.Parameters.Append ParamItem
SQLCommand.Execute
```

These statements set up the SQLCommand Command object to execute a stored procedure with a single parameter, the ProductCategory parameter. The same code can be simplified using a With structure:

```
Set DBConnection = Server.CreateObject("ADODB.Connection")
Set SQLCommand = Server.CreateObject("ADODB.Command")
Set ParamItem = Server.CreateObject("ADODB.Parameter")

With SQLCommand
    .ActiveConnection = DBConnection
    .CommandText = "ProductsByCategory"
    .CommandType = adCmdStoredProc
```

```
With ParamItem
    .Name = "@ProductCategory"
    .ParamItem.Value = 31
    .Parameters.Append ParamItem
EndWith
.Execute
End With
```

Name and Value are properties and they specify the parameter's name and value. The Append method adds the newly defined query to the Command object, and the Execute method executes the query against the database.

Using the Recordset

Most ASP applications that access databases use recordsets to retrieve and display records, rather than edit them remotely. Recordsets have two important properties:

CursorType indicates the type of cursor used with the Recordset object.

LockType indicates the type of lock to be placed on a record during editing.

Cursors are similar to DAO's Recordset types: They determine the degree of navigation and the freshness of the recordset. There are four Cursor types:

ForwardOnly   This cursor is the most efficient and the fastest, but the least flexible. Its contents do not reflect the changes made by other users. It contains an image of the records at the moment they were retrieved from the database. ForwardOnly recordsets can only be scanned forward; they support only the MoveNext method.

KeySet   This cursor is more flexible than the ForwardOnly cursor. It lets you scan forward and backward and use bookmarks, but it doesn't automatically reflect changes made by other users. However, you can synchronize the recordset with the database using the ReSync method. Except for an initial overhead, the KeySet cursor is more efficient than a Dynamic cursor (discussed next), but if you don't want the recordset to be continuously synchronized, you should prefer the KeySet cursor over the Dynamic Cursor type.

Dynamic   This is the most flexible, but the most expensive, Cursor type. It can be scanned forward and backward and reflects changes made to the records by other users. To make sure that the cursor's records are always up-to-date, the driver is constantly checking the records in the database to see if any have changed. Don't use this type of recordset on the Web, because records can change while their previous values are being transmitted.

Static   KeySet and Dynamic cursors do not contain the actual fields of the records. Instead, they contain keys to the records and retrieve them from the database as needed. Static cursors contain the actual records (avoid them with very large recordsets) and provide forward and backward navigation. They do not reflect changes made by other users.

The LockType property determines when pages are locked and can have one of the following values:

- ReadOnly (default)
- Optimistic
- Pessimistic
- Batch Optimistic

To navigate through the recordset, use the MoveNext, MovePrevious, MoveFirst, and MoveLast methods. You can also bookmark certain records so that you can return to them instantly. To display all the records in the recordset, set up a loop like the following:

```
<%
Do While Not SelRecords.EOF
    {process fields}
    SelRecords.MoveNext
Loop
%>
```

To access the fields of the recordset, use the name of the recordset and the name of the field or its order in the recordset. For example, to access the field Product-Name in the current record of the SelRecords recordset, use the expression

```
SelRecords("ProductName")
```

Or, if the ProductName field is the first one (this is determined by the SQL SELECT statement), use the expression

```
SelRecords(1)
```

NOTE   We discuss the ActiveX Data Object in detail in Chapter 4.

The overview we presented in this chapter should be adequate for building interactive ASP Web applications that access databases on the server and display selected records. In the examples that follow, you will see how these objects are used in building Active Server Pages. The following examples are all based on the NWIND sample application, and we are assuming that you have set up a data source for this database.

The Products Application

Products is a Web application consisting of two simple pages. The Categories page displays a list of all the product categories in the NWIND database, as shown in Figure 19.6.

NOTE

You'll find all the scripts of the Products application in the **ProductSales** folder under this chapter's folder on the CD that comes with this book.

The ASP page retrieves the category names and formats them as hyperlinks. When the visitor clicks a category name, the hyperlink takes him or her to another ASP page, the CategoryProducts.asp page, which displays all the products in the selected category, along with their prices and the number of units in stock. The output of the Categories.asp page is shown in Figure 19.7.

FIGURE 19.6:

The Categories.asp page displays the product categories in the NWIND database as hyperlinks.

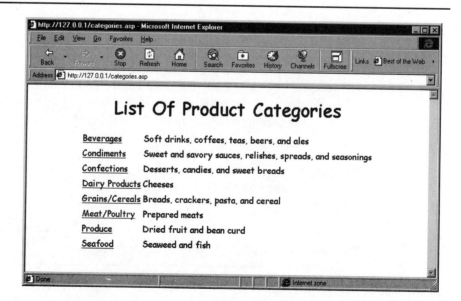

FIGURE 19.7:

The CategoryProducts.asp file displays the products in the category selected in Figure 19.6.

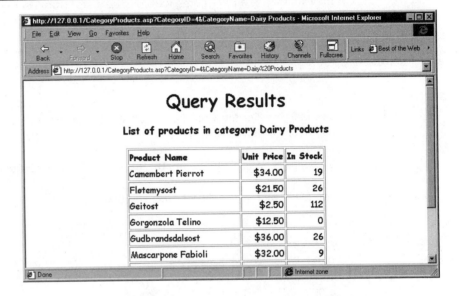

Let's start by looking at the code of the Categories.asp page. There's very little HTML code on this page; it's a server-side script that opens the NWINDDB database, creates a recordset with all the category names, and displays the category names as hyperlinks.

The line that inserts the hyperlinks is the most interesting code in this listing. If you ignore the expression surrounded by the server-side script tags, it's a simple HTML tag for inserting a hyperlink. Because the hyperlink's name and destination are not known at the time of this file's design, we insert them as expressions, which are substituted by the Active Server Pages when the file is processed.

Notice that all hyperlinks call the same URL on the server (the script Category-Product.asp), but each hyperlink passes a different parameter to it. The parameter is the ID of the category, since this is the field stored in the Products table of the NWIND database along with each product. The CategoryProduct page uses this parameter to retrieve the products that correspond to the selected category. In addition, it passes the name of the category as the second parameter. This value is not needed in extracting the requested products from the database, but the script uses it to display the name of the selected category. Had we omitted this parameter, the CategoryProducts.asp page would have to open the Categories table to find out the name of the selected category, display it in the page's header, and then open the Products table to retrieve the product names. By passing the name of the category as a parameter, we save the script from establishing a new connection to the database to read a value that's already known.

Code 19.7   **The** Categories.asp **File**

```
<HTML>
<%
Set DBObj = Server.CreateObject("ADODB.Connection")
DBObj.Open "NWindDB"

SQLQuery = "SELECT CategoryID, CategoryName, Description FROM
Categories"
Set RSCategories = DBObj.Execute(SQLQuery)
%>

<CENTER>
<FONT FACE="Comic Sans MS">
<H1>List Of Product Categories</H1>
<FONT FACE="Comic Sans MS" SIZE=2>
<TABLE>
<% Do While Not RSCategories.EOF %>
  <TR>
  <TD>
    <% CategoryName = RSCategories("CategoryName") %>
    <A HREF="/ASPages/ProdCat.asp?CategoryID= _
          <% =RSCategories("CategoryID") %>&CategoryName= _
          <% =CategoryName %> "> <% = CategoryName %> </A>
  <TD>
    <% =RSCategories("Description") %>
    </FONT>
<%
RSCategories.MoveNext
Loop
DBObj.Close
%>
</HTML>
```

The CategoryProducts.asp file, which processes requests made by the Categories.asp page, is a bit more complicated. First, it must extract the values of the parameters passed by the client. The following statements

```
ReqCategory=Request.QueryString("CategoryID")
ReqName=Request.QueryString("CategoryName")
```

store these values to the variables *ReqCategory* and *ReqName*. The QueryString collection contains these values for you, and you don't have to do anything special to read them. Simply access them by name. The value of *ReqCategory* is then used to build the SQL statement that will retrieve the records from the Products table:

```
SQLQuery = "SELECT ProductName, UnitPrice, UnitsInStock FROM Products _
WHERE CategoryID = " & ReqCategory & " ORDER BY ProductName"
```

This SQL statement returns a recordset with the products in the selected category. The script scans the records, one at a time, and displays each record on a new row of a table. The code that builds the table looks quite complicated because it combines HTML code and script statements. Replace every expression that appears between the <%> tags with a likely value (a product name for the expression <% = RSProducts("ProductName") %> and so on) to see how these lines gradually build the table in Figure 19.8, later in this chapter.

Code 19.8   The `CategoryProducts.asp` **File**

```
<HTML>
<%
ReqCategory=Request.QueryString("CategoryID")
ReqName=Request.QueryString("CategoryName")
Set DBObj = Server.CreateObject("ADODB.Connection")
DBObj.Open "NWindDB"
SQLQuery = "SELECT ProductName, UnitPrice, UnitsInStock FROM
Products WHERE CategoryID = " & ReqCategory & " ORDER BY ProductName"
Set RSProducts = DBObj.Execute(SQLQuery)
%>

<CENTER>
<FONT FACE="Comic Sans MS">
<H1>Query Results</H1>
<H3>List of products in category <% = ReqName %></H3>
<TABLE BORDER=ALL>
<TR>
<TD><B>Product Name</B><TD><B>Unit Price</B><TD ALIGN=RIGHT>
<B>In Stock</B>
<% Do While Not RSProducts.EOF %>
  <TR>
  <TD>
      <% = RSProducts("ProductName") %>
  <TD ALIGN=RIGHT>
      <% = FormatCurrency(RSProducts("UnitPrice")) %>
  <TD ALIGN=RIGHT>
```

```
        <% = RSProducts("UnitsInStock") %>
<%
RSProducts.MoveNext
Loop
%>
</TABLE>
</HTML>
```

This example was fairly simple. Some of the code may look complicated, but try to separate the expressions that will be evaluated on the server from the pure HTML code. You can use symbolic names—*ProdName* and *UnitPrice* in your code—and after you make sure it works, replace these symbolic expressions with the actual server-side script variables.

The ProductSales Application

Our next example is along the same lines, but the script is a bit more complicated. This time we'll start with the list of product categories. When the user selects a category, its products are displayed in the table shown in Figure 19.8. Each category hyperlink calls the ProductSales.asp script, which responds by generating the page shown in Figure 19.8. The code of the ProductSales.asp page is similar to the code of the CategoryProducts page we examined in the previous section, except that the lines that build the output are a bit more complicated.

FIGURE 19.8:

The ProductSales.asp page displays a table with details about the products of a specific category.

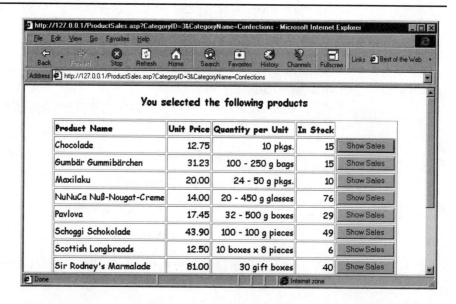

Not only can you see more details about each product, but you can click the Show Sales button to see the total sales for the specific product. From within the Click event of each button, the page requests another URL—the Invoices.asp script—and passes the product's name and ID as a parameter. The Invoices.asp page displays the total sales for the product, as shown in Figure 19.9. You can add more controls to the page in Figure 19.9 to let the user specify a time interval in which the totals will be calculated.

FIGURE 19.9:

The Invoices.asp page retrieves and displays the total sales for a product.

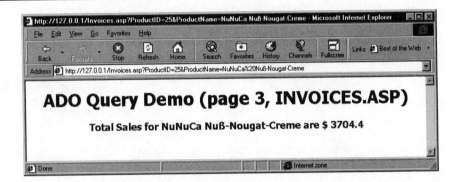

The code behind the ASP pages of this example is quite similar to the code of the Products application, and we are not going to repeat it here. You will find all the files on the CD, and you can examine them. We will only discuss briefly the code that generated the table with the Command Buttons.

Code 19.9   **Constructing the Table**

```
<% Do While Not RSProducts.EOF %>
  <TR>
  <TD>
      <% =RSProducts("ProductName") %>
  </TD>
  <TD ALIGN=right>
      <% RSProducts("Price") %>
  </TD>
  <TD ALIGN=right>
      <% =RSProducts("QuantityPerUnit") %>
  </TD>
  <TD ALIGN=right>
    <% =RSProducts("UnitsInStock") %>
    </FONT></TD>
```

```
<TD ALIGN=center>
  <%
    ProdName=RSProducts("ProductName")
    ProdName=Replace(ProdName, "'", "%27")
    ProdID=RSProducts("ProductID")
    InvParam="Invoices.asp?ProductID=" & ProdID & "&ProductName=" & _
ProdName
    HString="Window.Navigate (" & "'" & InvParam & "')"
  %>
  <INPUT TYPE=SUBMIT VALUE="Show Sales" OnClick=" <% =HString %> " _
>
  </TR>
<%
RSProducts.MoveNext
Loop
%>
```

The syntax of the tag for inserting a command button on an HTML page is

```
<INPUT TYPE=SUBMIT VALUE="caption" ONCLICK="action">
```

The OnClick option lets you specify the action to take place when a button is clicked. Usually, we call a procedure on the same page (a client-side script) to carry out some action. In this example, we call the Navigate method of the Window object. The line is fairly lengthy, but looking at the code it produces when processed might help you understand it. If you open the ProductSales.asp file with Internet Explorer and look at the source code (choose View ➤ Source), you will see the actual HTML code generated by the ASP application. Here are the lines that correspond to the first product:

```
<TR>
  <TD>
      Boston Crab Meat
  </TD>
  <TD ALIGN=right>
      18.40
  </TD>
  <TD ALIGN=right>
      24 - 4 oz tins
  </TD>
  <TD ALIGN=right>
    123
```

```
    </FONT></TD>
  <TD ALIGN=center>
    <INPUT TYPE=SUBMIT VALUE="Show Sales" _
      OnClick="Window.Navigate('Invoices.asp?ProductID= _
          32&ProductName=Boston Crab Meat')"
  </TR>
```

With these two examples, we end our discussion of using the Database component with Web pages. The Database component is based on the ActiveX Data Objects, and you should read Chapter 4 for information on this very flexible and powerful data component.

The File Access Component

The second basic component of the Active Server Pages we are going to discuss is the File Access component, which gives your server-side scripts access to text files on the server. The File Access component consists of two objects:

- FileSystemObject
- TextStream

The FileSystemObject object gives your script access to the server computer's file system, and the TextStream object lets your script open, read from, and write to text files.

The FileSystemObject Object

The FileSystemObject object gives your script access to the server computer's file system. To gain access to the server's file system, you create a FileSystemObject object with the CreateObject method of the Server object, as usual:

```
Set fs = Server.CreateObject("Scripting.FileSystemObject")
```

The CreateTextFile Method

This method creates a text file and returns a TextStream object that can be used to read from or write to the file. The syntax of the CreateTextFile method is

```
fs.CreateTextFile(filename, overwrite, unicode)
```

The *filename* variable is the path of the file to be created and is the only required argument; overwrite is a Boolean value that indicates whether you can overwrite an existing file (if True) or not (if False). If the overwrite argument is omitted, existing files are not overwritten. The last argument, unicode, indicates whether the file is created as a Unicode or as an ASCII file. If omitted, an ASCII file is assumed.

To create a new text file, you first create a FileSystemObject object variable and then call its CreateTextFile method as follows:

```
Set fs = CreateObject("Scripting.FileSystemObject")
Set TStream = fs.CreateTextFile("c:\testfile.txt", True)
```

The *TStream* variable represents a TextStream object, whose methods allow you to write to or read from the specified file.

NOTE   We'll discuss the TextStream object later in this section.

The OpenTextFile Method

In addition to creating a new text file, you can open an existing file with the OpenTextFile method, whose syntax is

```
Set Tstream = fs.OpenTextFile(filename, iomode, create, format)
```

The OpenTextFile method opens the specified file and returns a TextStream object that can be used to read from or write to the file. The *filename* argument is the only required one. The value of the *iomode* argument is one of the following constants:

ForReading: The file is opened for reading.

ForAppending: The file is opened for appending data.

The optional argument *create* is a Boolean value that indicates whether a new file can be created if the specified file name doesn't exist. The last argument, format, is also optional, and if it's True, the file is opened in Unicode mode. If it's False or omitted, the file is opened in ASCII mode.

To open a TextStream object for reading from a text file, use the following statements:

```
Set fs = CreateObject("Scripting.FileSystemObject")
Set TStream = fs.OpenTextFile("c:\testfile.txt", ForReading)
```

The TextStream Object

After you create a TextStream object with one of the FileSystemObject object's methods, you can use it to read from and write to the file.

The Methods of the TextStream Object

The methods of the TextStream object are equivalent to Visual Basic's file I/O functions. They allow you to read lines from and write lines to text files. The following methods apply to a *TextStream* object variable, which represents a file that has already been opened for input and/or output.

Read   This method reads a specified number of characters from a TextStream object. Its syntax is

```
TSream.Read(characters)
```

The *characters* variable is the number of character to be read from the TextStream object.

ReadAll   This method reads an entire TextStream (text file) and returns the resulting string. Its syntax is simply

```
TStream.ReadAll
```

ReadLine   This method reads one line of text at a time (up to, but not including, the newline character) from a TextStream file and returns the resulting string. Its syntax is

```
TStream.ReadLine
```

Skip   This method skips a specified number of characters when reading a TextStream file. Its syntax is

```
TStream.Skip(characters)
```

The *characters* variable is the number of characters to be skipped.

SkipLine   This method skips the next line when reading from a TextStream. Its syntax is

```
TStream.SkipLine
```

The characters of the skipped lines are discarded, up to and including the next newline character.

Write   This method writes a specified string to a TextStream file. Its syntax is

```
TStream.Write(string)
```

The *string* variable is the string (literal or variable) to be written to the file. Strings are written to the file with no intervening spaces or characters between them. Use the WriteLine method to write a newline character or a string that ends with a newline character.

WriteLine   This method writes the specified string, followed by a newline character to the file. Its syntax is

```
TStream.WriteLine(string)
```

The *string* variable is the text you want to write to the file. If you call the WriteLine method without an argument, a newline character is written to the file.

WriteBlankLines   This method writes a specified number of blank lines (newline characters) to the file. Its syntax is

```
TStream.WriteBlankLines(lines)
```

The *lines* variable is the number of blank lines to be inserted in the file.

The Properties of the TextStream Object

The TextStream object provides a number of properties that allow your code to know where the pointer is in the current TextStream.

AtEndOfLine   This is a read-only property that returns True if the file pointer is at the end of a line in the TextStream object and False otherwise. The AtEndOfLine property applies to files that are open for reading. You can use this property to read a line of characters, one at a time, with a loop similar to the following:

```
Do While TSream.AtEndOfLine =False
    newChar = TStream.Read(1)
    {process character}
Loop
```

AtEndOfStream   This is another read-only property that returns True if the file pointer is at the end of the TextStream object. The AtEndOfStream property applies only to TextStream files that are open for reading. You can use this property to read an entire file, one line at a time, with a loop such as the following:

```
Do While TStream.AtEndOfStream = False
    newChar = TStream.ReadLine
    {process line}
Loop
```

Column   This read-only property returns the column number of the current character in a TextStream line. The first character in a line is in column 1. Use this property to read data arranged in columns, without tabs or other delimiters between them.

Line Property   This read-only property returns the current line number in the TextStream. The Line property of the first line in a TextStream object is 1.

Using the TextStream Object

Here's a simple ASP page that demonstrates several of the TextStream object's methods. When this file is requested by the client, it creates a text file on the server computer and writes a few lines in it. Then, it opens the file, reads its lines, and displays them on an HTML page, which is returned to the client computer. As you will see, it uses the Write method of the Response object to send its output to the client.

Code 19.10	Writing to and Reading from Text Files

```
<HTML>
<HEAD>
<TITLE>Working with Text Files</TITLE>
</HEAD>
<CENTER>
<H1>Working with Text Files</H1>
</CENTER>
<%
  Set FileObj = Server.CreateObject("Scripting.FileSystemObject")
  TestFile = Server.MapPath ("/AXPages\textfile.txt")
  Set OutStream= FileObj.CreateTextFile (TestFile, True, False)
  str1 = "This file was created on " & Now()
  OutStream.WriteLine Str1
  OutStream.WriteLine "This is Tip # 1"
  OutStream.WriteBlankLines(1)
  OutStream.WriteLine "This is Tip # 2"
  Set OutStream = Nothing

  Response.Write "The contents of the textfile.txt '" & TestFile &
"':<BR>"
  Response.Write "<HR>"
  Set InStream= FileObj.OpenTextFile (TestFile, 1, False, False)
%>
</BODY>
</HTML>
```

The Server object's CreateObject method creates a FileSystemObject through which the script can access the server's hard disk. It then calls the MapPath method to map a virtual folder to the actual folder name and specify a full path name. The path name of the text file is then passed to the CreateTextFile method to create the *OutStream* object variable. The second argument of the CreateTextFile method specifies that the text file should be overwritten if it already exists. After the desired lines have been written to the file, we set the *TextStream* object variable to Nothing to release it.

In the second half of the script, we create another TextStream object to read the lines of the same file. The file's lines are read with a While…Wend loop, which examines the value of the TextStream object's AtEndOfStream property to find out how many lines to read from the file:

```
While InStream.AtEndOfStream = False
    Line = Instream.ReadLine
    {process Tline text line}
Wend
```

Server-side scripts don't use text files frequently. Information is usually stored in databases, but it's not uncommon to store common variables in text files. We already discussed how you can implement a visitor counter with an Application variable. To make sure that this variable isn't reset every time you restart the Web server, you can store it to a text file. You can also use text files from within your scripts to store debugging information or to log information that's not available through the server's administration logging utilities (such as the duration of each session). In general, short pieces of information that don't justify the use of a database are usually stored in text files on the server.

Contacting Server Applications

Active Server Pages can also contact any server application on the Web server and retrieve all types of information that can't be accessed directly through a Web page. You are probably familiar with Web services that provide e-mail accounts, which let you view and send messages through the browser. With a service like this, you can check your mail no matter where you are; there's no need to connect to your ISP's computer. You can use any computer that has access to the Web, view your messages, and create and send new ones. After you're done, nothing is stored on the computer you used to access your mail. All the information is stored on a secure server and the messages are exchanged in HTML format.

In this section, we are going to build a very basic Web application that allows you to view your messages in Outlook's Inbox folder and reply to any message.

The application is rather simple, but it demonstrates many of the issues of recalling live information from a specialized database application (such as Outlook) and passing information from the client to the application that runs on the server computer. Let's start by looking at the application, and then we'll examine the code behind it.

NOTE   This example assumes some familiarity with the objects exposed by Outlook. These objects, and their properties and methods, are discussed in Chapter 25, "Outlook 98 Objects," in the last part of the book.

The home page of the application is the Messages.asp page, which is shown in Figure 19.10. This Active Server Page opens Outlook's Inbox folder and reads all the messages. Then, it creates a HTML document that contains the basic items for each message (sender, subject, and date sent) and sends it to the client. The messages' subjects are hyperlinks that point to individual messages. As you can guess, these hyperlinks don't point to HTML documents on the server. Instead, they pass to the server the information needed to retrieve the selected message (this information is the EntryID field of the corresponding message).

FIGURE 19.10:

The Messages.asp page

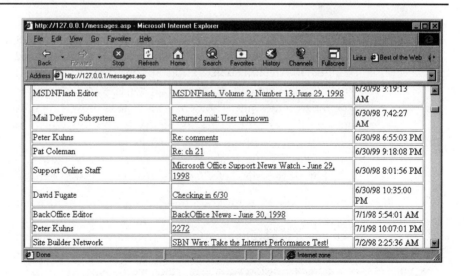

All hyperlinks on the Messages.asp page call the ShowBody.asp page, passing the message's EntryID field as parameter. The script on the server uses the EntryID field to retrieve the selected message and format it as another HTML document, shown in Figure 19.11. The Command Button at the bottom of the page (you can't see it in the figure) allows the user to reply to the message by composing new one. Once you understand how the script handles the Reply operation, you can implement additional operations, such as Delete, Forward, and so on.

FIGURE 19.11:

The ShowBody.asp page

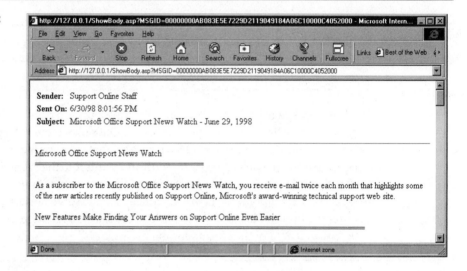

When the user clicks the Reply button, a new ASP script is called on the server, the Reply.asp file. This script displays the message's recipient, which can't be changed; the default subject ("Re:" followed by the original message's subject), which can be changed by the user; and a TEXTAREA control, where the user can type the new message. The Reply.asp page is shown in Figure 19.12. To send the message, the user must click the Send Now button, which submits the information to the server and mails the message via Outlook 98, or the Cancel message, which takes the user back to the previous page. When the message is sent, a confirmation page is displayed and the user is returned to the initial Messages page.

Let's examine the application's code by looking at its pages. The various pages communicate with each other by passing the appropriate information to the server, each time a page calls another one. There are other ways to maintain state among the pages of the application and you should experiment with the application. You could create Session variables, which would also speed up the application. Or you can use cookies on the client and read them with the Request.Cookies method. Outlook 98 is an interesting application to experiment with.

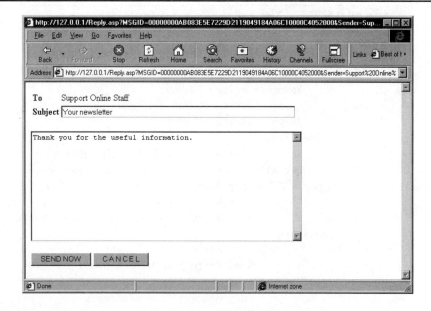

The Messages.asp Page

When the user connects to the application's home page, a server-side script (in the Messages.asp file) contacts Outlook 98 and retrieves all the messages in the Inbox folder. One of the first things to try is to provide the controls that allow the user to select a range of messages (such as a starting and ending date, or a different folder). For example, you can scan the Inbox folder and display all its subfolders as hyperlinks. The user can then select the folder to work with. This process is described in Chapter 25, later in this book.

The Messages.asp script is quite simple. It creates an object variable to access Outlook and then creates a collection of all messages in the Inbox folder. If you have organized your incoming messages into subfolders under the Inbox folder, move a few messages to the Inbox folder to test the application and then back to the folders where they belong (or use another folder instead of the Inbox folder, such as the Deleted Items folder).

Then the script scans each message, retrieves its sender, subject, and date sent fields, and places it in a new line of a table that's built gradually. After the table is complete, it's submitted to the client. Here's the listing of the Messages.asp script.

Code 19.11	**The** Messages.asp **file**

```
<%
Set OLApp = CreateObject("Outlook.Application")
If Error Then
    Response.Write "<HTML>"
    Response.Write "Could not start Outlook"
    Response.Write "</HTML>"
Else
    Set mNameSpace = OLApp.GetNamespace("MAPI")
    Set AllMessages = mNameSpace.GetDefaultFolder(6).Items
    If AllMessages.Count > 0 Then
        Response.Write "<HTML>"
        Response.Write "<H4>The following messages were found in your _
mailbox</H4><P>"
        Response.Write "<TABLE BORDER>"
        Response.Write "<TR><TD><B>Sender</B><TD
WIDTH=400><B>Subject</B><TD WIDTH=150><B>Date</B>"
        For Each message In AllMessages
            Response.Write "<TR>"
            Response.Write "<TD>" & message.SenderName
            HRef="ShowBody.asp?MSGID=" & message.EntryID
            Response.Write "<TD WIDTH=400> <A HREF=" & chr(34) & HRef _
& chr(34) & ">" & message.Subject & "</A>"
            Response.Write "<TD WIDTH=150>" & message.SentOn
            Response.Write "</TR>"
        Next
        Response.Write "</TABLE>"
        Response.Write "</HTML>"
    End If
End If
Set AllMessages=Nothing
Set OLApp=Nothing
%>
```

Notice that the object variables *OLApp* and *AllMessages*, which represent the Outlook application and the messages in the Inbox folder, respectively, are released at the end of the script. If this application is being accessed by many users, there will be a noticeable delay. The *OLApp* and *AllMessages* variables should be initialized in the Session_OnStart event, so that they need not be created every time the user hits the

Messages page. Of course, if new messages arrive after the AllMessages collection has been populated, they will not be added to the collection automatically. You must provide another button that will allow the user to refresh the collection at will.

Notice also how the code builds the destination of the hyperlink. All hyperlinks call the ShowBody.asp script on the server. For each message, a different parameter is passed along with the name of the script, and this parameter is the message's EntryID field. This field uniquely identifies a message and allows the script to retrieve the corresponding message instantly with the GetItemFromID method.

The ShowBody.asp Page

The ShowBody.asp script uses the parameter passed along with its name to retrieve a message with the GetItemFromID method of the MAPI data store. The message is stored in the variable *thisMessage*. Then, the following statements retrieve the basic items of the message:

```
Set thisMessage=mNameSpace.GetItemFromID(MessageID)
MsgBody=Replace(thisMessage.Body, chr(13), "<BR>")
Sender=thisMessage.SenderName
Subject=thisMessage.Subject
```

The line breaks in the message's body won't be preserved when displayed on a HTML page, so we must convert them to <BR> tags. That's what the Replace() function does: it replaces all instances of the Chr(13) character—line feeds—with the <BR> tag.

The Reply button at the bottom of the Form uses the Navigate method to call the Reply.asp script on the server. The script with the button's onClick event handler is inserted with Response.Write statements, but here's the script that will be inserted in the HTML document:

```
Sub bttnReply_onClick()
    DestinationURL= _
        "Reply.asp?MSGID=<msgID>&Sender=<sender>&Subject=<subject>"
    Window.navigate DestinationURL
End Sub
```

where <msgID>, <sender>, and <subject> are the appropriate strings with the message's ID, its sender, and its subject. You'll see shortly how these strings are used by the Reply.asp script.

Here's the complete listing of the ShowBody.asp script.

Code 19.12   **The** ShowBody.asp **File**

```
<%
Set OLApp = CreateObject("Outlook.Application")
If Error Then
    Response.Write "<HTML>"
    Response.Write "Could not start Outlook"
    Response.Write "</HTML>"
Else
    Set mNameSpace = OLApp.GetNamespace("MAPI")
    MessageID=Request.QueryString("MSGID")
    Set thisMessage=mNameSpace.GetItemFromID(MessageID)
    MsgBody=Replace(thisMessage.Body, chr(13), "<BR>")
    Sender=thisMessage.SenderName
    Subject=thisMessage.Subject
    Response.Write "<HTML>"
    Response.Write "<SCRIPT LANGUAGE=VBScript>" & vbCrLf
    Response.Write "Sub bttnReply_onClick()" & vbCrLf
    DestinationURL="Reply.asp?MSGID=" & "" & MessageID & "" & _
"&Sender=" & _
              "" & Sender & "" & "&Subject=" & "" & Subject & ""
    Response.Write "    Window.navigate " & chr(34) & DestinationURL & _
              chr(34) & vbCrLf
    Response.Write "End Sub" & vbCrLf
    Response.Write "</SCRIPT>" & vbCrLf
    Response.Write "<TABLE>"
    Response.Write "<TR><TD><B>Sender:</B><TD>" & _
              thisMessage.SenderName & vbCrLf
    Response.Write "<TR><TD><B>Sent On:</B><TD>" & _
              thisMessage.SentOn  & vbCrLf
    Response.Write "<TR><TD><B>Subject:</B><TD>" & _
              thisMessage.Subject  & vbCrLf
    Response.Write "</TABLE>"
    Response.Write "<P><HR>"
    Response.Write MsgBody
    Response.Write "<HR>"
    Response.Write "<INPUT TYPE=BUTTON NAME=bttnReply VALUE='Reply'>"
    Response.Write "</HTML>"
End If
Set OLApp=Nothing
%>
```

The Reply.asp Page

The Reply.asp page script accepts the basic items of the selected message and prepares a new page, where the user can specify his or her reply. The message's sender automatically becomes the new message's recipient and the message's subject is set to the string "Re:" followed by the original message's subject. The user can edit the subject (it's displayed on a Text control), but can't change the message's recipient, or specify additional recipients. After reading the chapter on Outlook's objects, you will be able to add more features, such as multiple recipients, CC recipients and so on.

You may have noticed that the ShowBody page passes the message's EntryID field, along with the message's original body, subject, and recipient. If you know the message's ID, you can easily retrieve it from the Inbox folder, right? The Reply.asp script doesn't contact Outlook, something that would be costly in terms of performance. All the information we need is already available to the ShowBody.asp page, so why not pass it to the Reply.asp script? The EntryID field isn't required by the Reply page. As you will see, the Reply page will pass this value to the SendReply.asp script, which will send the new message. All this information could be stored in Session variables, or in cookies at the client, instead of being moved from one script to the other. You can experiment with alternate implementations of this Web application.

The complete listing of the Reply.asp script is shown next. Because the Reply.asp script outputs mostly VBScript code to be executed on the client, we didn't use the Response.Write method to create the output. The Reply.asp script contains a short segment of code that's executed on the server, and the rest is straight HTML and VBScript code that's output to the client as is.

Code 19.13 **The** `Reply.asp` **File**

```
<%
MessageID=Request.QueryString("MSGID")
SendTo=Request.QueryString("Sender")
MsgSubject=Request.QueryString("Subject")
DestinationURL=chr(34) & "SendReply.asp?MSGID=" & MessageID &
"&SENDER=" & "'" & SendTo & chr(34)
%>
<HTML>
<SCRIPT LANGUAGE=VBScript>
Sub bttnSend_onClick()
```

```
    MsgBody=MsgForm.MsgBody.Value
    If Trim(MsgBody)="" Then
        reply=MsgBox("Do you want to send a message with a blank _
body?", vbYesNo)
        If reply=vbNo Then
            Window.History.Back
        End If
    End If
    MsgBody=Replace(MsgBody, chr(13), "%0C")
    Window.navigate   <% =DestinationURL %> & "&SUBJECT=" & _
        txtSubject.Value & "&BODY=" & MsgBody
End Sub

Sub bttnCancel_onClick()
    Window.History.Back
End Sub
</SCRIPT>

<TABLE>
<TR><TD><B>To</B><TD><% =SendTo %>
<TR><TD><B>Subject</B><TD><INPUT TYPE=TEXT SIZE=60 NAME=txtSubject _
    VALUE= 'Re:<% =MsgSubject %>' >
</TABLE>

<FORM NAME="MsgForm">
<TEXTAREA ID="MsgBody" COLS=60 ROWS=12>
</TEXTAREA>
<P>
<INPUT TYPE=BUTTON NAME=bttnSend VALUE="SEND NOW">
<INPUT TYPE=BUTTON NAME=bttnCancel VALUE="C A N C E L">
</FORM>
</HTML>
```

The SendReply.asp Page

The last page of the application sends the reply message and displays a confirmation page. The SendReply.asp script is called from within the Reply page's code along with the following parameters: the original message's ID, the original message's sender, and the reply's subject and body. The message's ID is used by the SendReply.asp script to retrieve the original message. The Reply method of the MailItem object creates a new message, which is the reply (the message's sender and recipient are swapped). Then, the script assigns the new subject and body to the reply and sends it with the Send method. Here's the SendReply script's code:

Code 19.14   The `SendReply.asp` **File**

```
<SCRIPT LANGUAGE=VBScript RUNAT=Server>
Set OLApp = CreateObject("Outlook.Application")
If Error Then
    Response.Write "<HTML>"
    Response.Write "Could not start Outlook"
    Response.Write "</HTML>"
Else
    Set mNameSpace = OLApp.GetNamespace("MAPI")
    MessageID=Request.QueryString("MSGID")
    ReplyBody=Request.QueryString("BODY")
    ReplySubject=Request.QueryString("SUBJECT")
    Set thisMessage=mNameSpace.GetItemFromID(MessageID)
    Set newMessage=thisMessage.Reply
    newMessage.Body=ReplyBody
    newMessage.Subject=ReplySubject
    newMessage.Send
    Response.Write "<HTML><H1> Message Sent <H1></HTML>" & vbCrLf
    Response.Write "<SCRIPT LANGUAGE=VBScript>" & vbCrLf
    Response.Write "Sub BackToMessages_onClick" & vbCrLf
    Response.Write "    Window.Navigate " & Chr(34) & _
                    "Messages.asp" & Chr(34) & vbCrLf
    Response.Write "End Sub" & vbCrLf
    Response.Write "</SCRIPT>" & vbCrLf
    Response.Write "<FORM NAME=BttnForm>" & vbCrLf
    Response.Write "<INPUT TYPE=BUTTON NAME=BackToMessages _
                    VALUE='Return to Messages'>" & vbCrLf
    Response.Write "</FORM>" & vbCrLf
  End If
  Set OLApp=Nothing
</SCRIPT>
```

As you have noticed, the Reply.asp script doesn't need the message's ID, but it accepts it as a parameter when it's called and passes it on to the SendReply.asp script. Without the message's ID, creating the reply message from within the last script wouldn't be as simple as calling the Reply method.

You can use this sample application to check your mail through the Web. The code we presented here is the absolute minimum, and you can test it on a single machine. The Personal Web Server must also be running on the machine that receives the mail. In a corporate environment, you must request the user's name and password and log them into Outlook before they can access their individual Inbox folders. Use the Logon method of the NameSpace object to specify the user's profile and password. You must also disable the display of the Login dialog box, as this dialog box will appear on the server computer and the remote user will never see it.

Another problem of the application is that new messages may not be mailed immediately. You should change Outlook's options, so that it sends messages as soon as they appear in the Outbox folder and not at specified intervals.

CHAPTER

TWENTY

Developing Internet Applications

- Dynamic HTML

- The Tabular Data control

- DHTML projects

- IIS projects

- WebClasses

In this chapter, we'll discuss two new types of projects you can develop with Visual Basic 6. They are the DHTML applications and IIS applications. These two project types are new to Visual Basic 6, but they are not new to you. DHTML applications are collections of DHTML pages that form a Web site. Visual Basic is not an HTML editor, so you shouldn't expect that you can use it to develop Web sites, but it can help you with the programmable elements on the pages of your site. In other words, you can design the Web site with a tool like FrontPage and import the Web pages you want to script into VB, add the code, and save them back.

An IIS application is a VB application that runs on the server and services client requests. Where DHTML applications move much of the processing to the client, IIS applications rely on the Web server to do most of the processing. If you've read the previous chapters, you already know that DHTML applications contain client-side scripts and IIS applications contain server-side scripts. Here's the first difference between DHTML and IIS applications: DHTML applications rely on Internet Explorer 4.0, while IIS applications can run in any browser that supports plain HTML. DHTML applications are meant to be used on corporate intranets (provided every workstation on the network is equipped with IE 4).

This chapter starts with an overview of Dynamic HTML: the properties of the various elements of an HTML page, the events these elements trigger, and the methods used to program them. Among the topics we'll discuss is the Tabular Data Control (TDC). The TDC comes with Internet Explorer and allows you to create a table and manipulate the table data on the client computer. For example, you can sort them or display selected rows without additional trips to the server. Internet Explorer supports a number of controls for displaying dynamic content, but they are not discussed in this book. You can read about these controls at Microsoft's Workshop site (`www.microsoft.com/workshop`).

Then we'll discuss the two new types of projects, DHTML applications and IIS applications. DHTML applications are Web sites that contain DHTML pages. Visual Basic comes with a DHTML Designer that streamlines the programming of the elements of a DHTML page, but it's not an HTML editor. You can't rely on the DHTML Designer to build a Web site. IIS applications are far more interesting, as they allow you to build Web applications using Visual Basic. IIS applications are very similar to ASP scripts, but to you, the developer, they look like VB applications.

NOTE   To test the projects in this chapter, you must have Internet Explorer 4.0 (or a more recent version, when it becomes available) and a Web server, like the Internet Information Server or the Personal Web Server. The PWS is an optional component of Visual Studio 6 and you must install it now in order to follow the examples of this chapter. If you're using Windows NT, you must have IIS installed, either on the same machine or on another machine on the network. No matter which Web server you're using, Visual Basic will detect it (as long as it's running) and will set up the appropriate Web sites when you run an IIS application.

Dynamic HTML

HTML was fine for designing static documents, and it was constantly enhanced through its history with new tags that allowed developers to create dynamic content. A drastic departure from the basic HTML model was needed in order to create highly dynamic content that would resemble an application rather than a static document. This departure was the introduction of a scripting language and the ability to script the elements of a page. Dynamic HTML, or DHTML, is nothing more than programmable HTML. The program, or script, which makes the page dynamic, is included in the page and executed on the client.

In Chapter 18, "Web Development Basics," you learned how to script the intrinsic controls of HTML and the objects of the ASP component on the server. In the first half of this chapter, you'll see how you can script the elements of an HTML page and make it behave like an application. You have certainly seen many pages on the World Wide Web that react to user actions (to the movement of the mouse, for instance) by changing their appearance, structure, or contents. Here are a few of the things you can do with DHTML that are practically impossible to do with straight HTML:

- Hide text and/or images in your document and reveal them in response to a user action.

- Animate text and images in your document, apply transitions as the user moves from one page to another, change the z-order of the various elements at run time, and so on.

- Create tables that can be sorted according to any column and display more or fewer lines depending on user-specified criteria, without another trip to the server.

DHTML achieves these effects by modifying the current document and automatically reformatting and redisplaying the document to show changes. It does not fetch another document from the server; instead, it uses the power of the client computer to perform calculations and display the results. Furthermore, DHTML does not require additional support from applications or ActiveX controls to interact with the user. DHTML documents are self-contained. Both content and logic are included in the same file, which is downloaded to the client and activated there.

Programming HTML Elements

To make the elements on a Web page programmable, you must first define the elements you want to program. You do so with the <DIV> tag and the ID attribute. The ID attribute is an identifier (name) you can assign to an existing element. The following tag inserts a hyperlink:

```
<A HREF=www.sybex.com>Sybex</A>
```

If you want to program this element on the page (for example, make it change color as the user moves the pointer over it), name it with the ID attribute of the <A> tag:

```
<A ID=link1 HREF=www.sybex.com>Sybex</A>
```

The hyperlink is now an object; it can recognize events and invoke event handlers similar to Visual Basic's objects. If you provide an event handler for the onmouseover event (which is fired when the mouse pointer enters the area under an element), this handler will be automatically invoked. To italicize the hyperlink's text when the pointer enters it and restore it to normal when the pointer leaves the area of the element, supply the following two event handlers:

```
Sub link1_onmouseover()
    link1.Style.fontStyle = "Italic"
End Sub
Sub link1_onmouseout()
    link1.Style.fontStyle = "Normal"
End Sub
```

Many tags recognize the ID attribute. You can also turn a sequence of characters into an object that can be programmed just as easily, by supplying an ID attribute to the <P> tag that marks the beginning of the text:

```
<P ID=string1>This text can be programmed</P>
```

Notice that you must supply the closing </P> tag, or else all the text to the following <P> tag will be treated as an object. The string "This text can be programmed" in the previous example is an object, and you can access its properties through its ID. For example, you can change the text's color with the statement

```
string1.style.color="red"
```

The examples so far have used the element's `style` property, but there are more attributes you can program. If you assign an ID to the <IMG> tag, as in the following statement, you can program any of the usual attributes of the same tag:

```
<IMG ID=image SRC="sky.gif">
```

The following event handlers enlarge the image when the user moves the mouse on top of it. When the mouse moves outside the image, its size is restored. The image must be placed on the page with the following tag:

```
Name this planet<IMG SRC="mars.gif" ID=image1 WIDTH=50>
```

Here are the event handlers that resize the image in reaction to the movement of the mouse:

```
Sub image1_onmouseover()
    image1.border=3
    image1.width=image1.width*2
End Sub
Sub image1_onmouseout()
    image1.border=0
    image1.width=image1.width/2
End Sub
```

You can also change the image displayed by manipulating the SRC attribute, but this trick will work only on an intranet. By the time the new image is downloaded from an HTTP server, the user will have probably moved the mouse outside the image's area.

The <DIV> and <SPAN> Tags

Sometimes you'll want to program a large chunk of the document (for instance, a paragraph, a table, or a couple of images) as a single object. If the part of the document you want to program isn't a single HTML tag, you can mark part of the document with the <DIV> and <SPAN> tags and turn any part of the document into a single object.

The <DIV> tag groups a series of elements into a larger group. For example, you can group multiple paragraphs and their headings using the <DIV> tag. <SPAN> is used within an element to group a part of it that is too small to capture with regular HTML tags. For example, you can use the <SPAN> tag to group a few words in a paragraph in order to perform actions that affect only that text. Another difference between the two tags is that the <DIV> tag inserts a line break above and below the elements it delimits. <SPAN> does not change the placement of the elements in the document.

The <DIV> and <SPAN> tags were introduced so that developers could apply various styles to sections of the document. Here's a simple example. The following DHTML document uses the <DIV> tag to apply a uniform background color to a section of the document (the publisher's data). The text within the <DIV> tag is split into two different sections with the <SPAN> tag. These two sections of the document in the following example (delimited with the <SPAN> tag) use a different text color.

```
<DIV id="Publisher" style="background:yellow;font-size:14pt">
<B>Sybex</B>
<BR>
<SPAN id="PublisherAddress" style="color:red;font-size:12pt">
1151 Marina Village Parkway</SPAN>
<BR>
<SPAN id="PublisherPhone" style="color:red;font-size:12pt">
1-800-2272346</SPAN>
</DIV>
```

The <DIV> and <SPAN> tags in this document have an ID attribute, which means that they can be programmed from within the page's script. And this is what DHTML documents are all about. They are HTML documents, whose elements can be programmed with VBScript or JavaScript. Of course, for the page to be dynamic, it must recognize events. Your code must be inserted in the handlers for these events. The events are actually recognized by the browser, and the corresponding event handlers are invoked automatically. Before we discuss the DHTML events, let's look at the properties of the elements you can manipulate through your code.

Manipulating Styles

As you have seen in the examples in the previous paragraphs, the appearance of the various elements is manipulated through the style object. Style is a property of every element and is itself an object. It exposes a number of properties, which are explained in the documentation (under the topic Platform SDK ➢ Internet ➢ Intranet ➢ Extranet Services). Table 20.1 lists only the names of these properties, which are self-explanatory.

TABLE 20.1: The Properties of the Style Object

background	backgroundAttachment	backgroundColor
backgroundImage	backgroundPosition	backgroundPositionX
backgroundPositionY	backgroundRepeat	border
borderBottom	borderBottomColor	borderBottomStyle
borderBottomWidth	borderColor	borderLeft
borderLeftColor	borderLeftStyle	borderLeftWidth
borderRight	borderRightColor	borderRightStyle
borderRightWidth	borderStyle	borderTop
borderTopColor	borderTopStyle	borderTopWidth
borderWidth	clear	clip
color	cssText	cursor
display	filter	font
fontFamily	fontSize	fontStyle
fontVariant	fontWeight	height
left	letterSpacing	lineHeight
listStyle	listStyleImage	listStylePosition
listStyleType	margin	marginBottom
marginLeft	marginRight	marginTop
overflow	paddingBottom	paddingLeft
paddingRight	paddingTop	pageBreakAfter
pageBreakBefore	pixelHeight	pixelLeft
pixelTop	pixelWidth	posHeight
position	posLeft	posTop
posWidth	styleFloat	textAlign
textDecoration	textDecorationBlink	textDecorationLineThrough
textDecorationNone	textDecorationOverline	textDecorationUnderline
textIndent	textTransform	top
verticalAlign	visibility	width
zIndex		

DHTML Events

The programming model of DHTML is quite similar to the Visual Basic programming model. The code is located in the various event handlers, which are invoked automatically when a specific event takes place on a specific element. When the user clicks the button named bttnSend, the bttnSend_onclick event handler is invoked. Most events in the Dynamic HTML object model are similar to the equivalent events in Visual Basic, but their names are different. All event names in DHTML are preceded by the word "on" (onclick, onload, and so on) and are always in lower case. Table 20.2 summarizes the events of DHTML.

TABLE 20.2: DHTML Events

Keyboard Events	
onkeydown	Fires when a key is pressed and reports the key that was pressed.
onkeypress	Fires when a user presses a key.
onkeyup	Fires when a user releases a key.
Mouse Events	
onclick	In addition to occurring when a user clicks on an element, this event also fires when the user presses Enter on an element that can receive focus, such as a button.
ondblclick	Fires when the user double-clicks an element.
onmouseout, onmousedown, onmouseup, onmousemove, onmouseover	The onmousedown and onmouseup events fire when the user presses and releases the mouse button, respectively. When moving between elements, the onmouseout event fires first to indicate that the mouse has left the original element. Next, the onmousemove event fires, indicating that the mouse has moved. Finally, onmouseover fires to indicate that the mouse has entered the new element.
Focus and Selection Events	
onfocus	Fires when the user moves to an element capable of receiving input.
onblur	Fires when the user moves out of an element capable of receiving input.
onselectstart, onselect	The onselectstart event fires when a selection is first initiated—for example, when the user clicks a character or object in the document. The onselect event fires when the user completes their selection on the page.
ondragstart	Fires when the user first begins to drag the selection.

Continued on next page

TABLE 20.2 CONTINUED: DHTML Events

Other Events

onchange	Fires when the user tabs off or presses Enter on an element, moving out of it (it's equivalent to the Visual Basic Change event).
onerror	Fires when an error occurs loading an image or other element or when a scripting error occurs.
onready, statechange	The onready event fires when the page has initialized, and the statechange event fires when all the content (including images, sounds, and ActiveX controls) has been loaded.
onload	Fires after the document is loaded and all the elements on the page have been completely downloaded.
onresize	Fires when the browser's window is resized. You need not program this event to resize and/or reposition elements, since HTML resizes the page automatically.
onscroll	Fires when the page is scrolled.
onunload	Fires immediately prior to the document being unloaded (when navigating to another document).

Unique DHTML Events

onabort	Fires when the user aborts the download of a page by pressing the Stop button.
onreset	Fires when the user selects a Reset button on a form.
onsubmit	Fires when the user selects a Submit button on a form.

Changing Text and Tags

Additional useful properties in manipulating the elements of a DHTML document are the InnerText, OuterText, InnerHTML, and OuterHTML properties. Frequently, you'll want to change the text displayed on a page, or its surrounding tags, in reaction to a user event. When you want to replace the text of an element, you use the InnerText and InnerHTML properties. Let's say you have a heading like the following one:

```
<H1 ID=head1>Document Title</H1>
```

The text enclosed by the <H1> tags is a single element. You know already how you can change its appearance with the help of the style property. To change the actual text of the heading, you must use the head1 object's InnerText property:

```
head1.InnerText = "Alternate Title"
```

The value of the InnerText property is the text between the <H1> tags. After the execution of the last statement, the document's heading will become

```
<H1 ID=head1>Alternate Title</H1>
```

If you want to change the enclosing tags as well, use the InnerHTML property instead. The InnerHTML tag is first parsed and then inserted in the document. For example, if you want to change the heading as before, but set it into italics as well, use the statement

```
Head1.InnerHTML="<I>Alternate Title</I>"
```

After the execution of this statement, the document's heading will become

```
<H1 ID=head1><I>Alternate Title</I></H1>
```

Figure 20.1 shows the InnerText document, which demonstrates the use of the InnerText property. When the pointer moves over the heading, the document's heading changes. When the pointer leaves the area under the head1 element, the heading is restored to its original state.

FIGURE 20.1:

The InnerText.htm document demonstrates the use of the InnerText property.

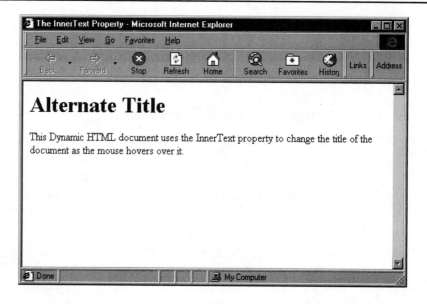

Open the InnerText.htm document with Internet Explorer and see how it reacts to the movement of the mouse. The listing of the InnerText.htm document is shown next:

Code 20.1   **The InnerText.htm Document**

```
<HTML>
<SCRIPT LANGUAGE=VBScript>
Sub h1_onmouseover()
    h1.InnerText="Alternate Title"
End Sub
Sub h1_onmouseout()
    h1.InnerText="Document Title"
End Sub

</SCRIPT>
<H1 ID=h1>Document Title</H1>
This Dynamic HTML document uses the InnerText property to change the _
title of the document as the mouse hovers over it.
```

The InnerHTML.htm document, which is quite similar to the InnerText.htm, demonstrates the use of the InnerHTML property. The document reacts to the movement of the mouse in a similar manner, only this time it changes the text, as well as the color of the head1 element. Here's the listing of the InnerHTML.htm document:

Code 20.2   **The InnerHTML.htm Document**

```
<HTML>
<SCRIPT LANGUAGE=VBScript>
Sub h1_onmouseover()
    h1.InnerHTML="<I><FONT COLOR=red>Document Title</FONT></I>"
End Sub
Sub h1_onmouseout()
    h1.InnerHTML="Document Title"
End Sub

</SCRIPT>
<H1 ID=h1>Document Title</H1>
This Dynamic HTML document uses the InnerHTML property to change the _
appearance of the document as the mouse hovers over it.
```

To change both the text and the surrounding tags of an element, use the properties OuterText and OuterHTML. Both properties replace the text enclosed in the HTML tags for a specific element and the element tags themselves. OuterText replaces the entire element, including the <DIV> tags that delimit the element, with the specified text. OuterHTML replaces the entire element, but the replacement string can include HTML tags. It is actually possible to change the ID of the element by specifying a new <DIV> tag, or any other tag that delimits the element.

Let's say you have inserted the following element in a Web page:

```
<H1 ID=Summary><B>Product Summary<B></H1>
```

To convert this element to plain text from within your code, you must execute the following statement:

```
Summary.outerText = Product Description
```

After the execution of this statement, the string "Product Summary" (in bold) will be replaced by the string "Product Description" (in plain text). The new string will not be an element, and you won't be able to manipulate it from within your code any longer.

To change the text and replace the surrounding elements, use the OuterHTML property:

```
Summary.outerHTML = <H2 ID=Description><I>ProductSummary</I></H2>
```

The original header will be demoted to level 2 and will appear in italics. In addition, you'll be able to further manipulate this element from within your code, which can now be accessed as "Description" (the new ID of the element).

A DHTML List

Let's design a DHTML page to demonstrate that's not as simple as the previous examples. The DHTMLList page, shown in Figure 20.2, is a list of books. The document consists of two frames, the left one being an index. When the pointer hovers over a title, additional information about the specific title is displayed. When the pointer is moved over another title, this first title's information disappears and the second title's data lines are displayed under its name. When a title is clicked, a lengthier description appears in the right pane of the browser.

FIGURE 20.2:

The DHTMLList page

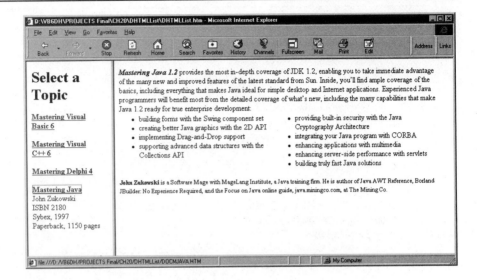

The DHTMLList.htm document's listing, shown below, is quite simple. It sets up two frames and their relative widths.

Code 20.3   **The DHTMLList.htm File**

```
<HTML>
<HEAD>

<META content="text/html; charset=iso-8859-1" http-equiv=Content-Type>
</HEAD>
<FRAMESET COLS=20%,80%>
    <FRAME SRC="Books.HTM" NAME="RIGHT">
    <FRAME NAME="LEFT">
</FRAMESET>
</HTML>
```

The file BOOKS.HTM is a Dynamic HTML document that displays the titles and a few data lines for each title. The document contains all the information, including the book titles and their data. Here's the HTML code for the first two titles (there are similar lines in the BOOKS.HTM file for the other titles).

Code 20.4   **The Body of the BOOKS.htm Document**

```
<H1>Select a Topic</H1>
<SPAN ID=MVB6><B>
<A HREF="DOCMVB6.HTM" TARGET="LEFT">Mastering Visual Basic 6</A>
</B></SPAN>
<SPAN ID=MVB6text>
<BR>
Evangelos Petroutsos
<BR>
ISBN 2272
<BR>Sybex, 1998
<BR>
Paperback, 1285 pages
</SPAN>
<P>
<SPAN ID=MJAVA><B>
<A HREF="DOCMJAVA.HTM" TARGET="LEFT">Mastering Java</A>
</B></SPAN>
<SPAN ID=MJAVAtext display:none>
<BR>
John Zukowski
<BR>
ISBN 2180
<BR>Sybex, 1997
<BR>
Paperback, 1150 pages
</SPAN>
```

The actual file contains more lines. In the interest of conserving space, we show only the lines that correspond to the titles *Mastering VB5* and *Mastering Java*.

Each book's section in the left window consists of two <SPAN> sections. The first section is the book's title (which is also a hyperlink) and the second section contains technical data about the book (its ISBN, author, pages, and so on). The two sections of the first book, for example, are two separate objects called *MVB6* and *MVB6text*. Notice that the <HREF> tag contains the TARGET attribute, which displays the book's description in the right frame.

The interesting part of the document is the script that displays and hides the data lines under each title. The script manipulates the display property of the style element. When this property is "none," the corresponding element is hidden. To display the element, you must set this property to "block." When the page is loaded, the display property of all titles is set to "none." In the onmouseover event handler of each title's <DIV> section you must set the display property to "block," and in the onmouseout event handler set the same property to "none." Here's the script of the DHTMLList.htm page:

Code 20.5   **The Script of the BOOKS.htm Document**

```
<SCRIPT LANGUAGE=VBScript>
Sub window_onLoad()
    MVB6text.style.display="none"
    MVCPPtext.style.display="none"
    MDtext.style.display="none"
    MJAVAtext.style.display="none"
End Sub
Sub MVB6_onmouseover()
    MVB6text.style.display="block"
End Sub
Sub MVB6_onmouseout()
    MVB6text.style.display="none"
End Sub
Sub MJAVA_onmouseover()
    MJAVAtext.style.display="block"
End Sub
Sub MJAVA_onmouseout()
    MJAVAtext.style.display="none"
End Sub
</SCRIPT>
```

Again, we show only the lines for two titles.

As you can see, creating DHTML documents is straightforward and very similar to programming a VB Form. The browser detects the various events and automatically invokes the corresponding event handler (if one exists). The event handlers contain VBScript code that manipulates the properties of the various elements.

DHTML pages can also interact with the Web server, just like normal HTML pages. Because DHTML pages are meant to run on the client computer, a number of new controls were designed to enable DHTML to perform even more complicated tasks. The multimedia controls, which allow Web developers to create rich multimedia content with very little overhead, are typical examples. These controls are not discussed in this book. Instead, we will present the Tabular Data

Control, which allows you to download a data set to the client and manipulate it from within the script at the client computer.

The Tabular Data Control

A very good reason to use DHTML pages is that you can download all the data you need to the client and manipulate the data there, without additional trips to the server. For example, you can use the Tabular Data control (TDC) to reformat a data set at run time. With the Tabular Data control, you can display the data on a table, or other controls on the Form, sorted in any way you like, or filtered according to criteria specified by the user. The Tabular Data control downloads data from the server (they must be stored in a text file). After the data have been downloaded, you can manipulate them on the client computer through the appropriate scripts.

Figure 20.3 shows a data set that is downloaded to the client computer along with the page. The user can sort the data according to the values of any column by clicking the header of the appropriate column.

FIGURE 20.3:

The data shown in the table of this figure are downloaded once to the client.

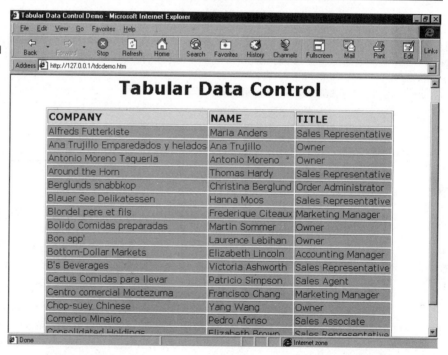

FIGURE 20.4:

The same data shown in Figure 20.3 after they have been sorted according to customer names

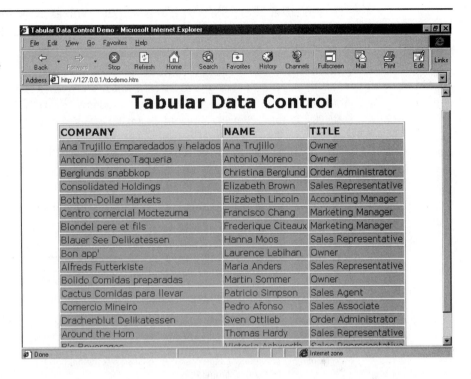

To use the data control on a Web page, you must first insert the appropriate <OBJECT> tag:

```
<OBJECT id=Customers CLASSID="clsid:333C7BC4-460F-11D0-BC04-0080C7055A83">
    <PARAM NAME="DataURL" VALUE="Customers.txt">
    <PARAM NAME="UseHeader" VALUE="True">
</OBJECT>
```

The DataURL property specifies the URL of the file with the data to be downloaded. The value of this property can be an absolute or a relative URL (as in this example). By default, the TDC will not download its data from another domain, other than the one from which the page that contains it was downloaded. You'll see shortly how you can change this behavior.

The DataURL property can also be a file's name, if the page is going to be used on a local area network:

```
<PARAM NAME="DataURL" VALUE="file://\\ServerComputer\Data\Customers.txt">
```

The `Customers.txt` file is a plain ASCII file, with each record on a separate line and successive fields on the same line delimited by commas. The first few lines of the `Customers.txt` file used in the example in this section are shown next:

```
CustomerID, CompanyName, ContactName, ContactTitle
ALFKI, Alfreds Futterkiste, Maria Anders, Sales Representative
ANATR, Ana Trujillo Emparedados y helados, Ana Trujillo, Owner
ANTON, Antonio Moreno Taqueria, Antonio Moreno, Owner
```

The first line contains the titles of the table's columns. The UseHeader property tells the control how to interpret the first line in the data file (as headers, if True, or as a record, if False).

The DTC supports a few more properties, which are shown in Table 20.3.

TABLE 20.3: The Properties of the Tabular Data Control

CharSet	Identifies the character set used by the data file. The default character set is latin1.
DataURL	Specifies the location of the data file as a URL.
EscapeChar	Identifies the character to be used as an escape character in the data file (there is no default escape character).
FieldDelim	Identifies the character that delimits the fields in the data file. The default delimiter is the comma (,).
Language	Specifies the language used to render the data on the client. The default language is "eng-us."
TextQualifier	Specifies the optional character that surrounds a field.
RowDelim	Identifies the character that delimits each row of data. The default delimiter is the newline (NL) character.
UseHeader	Specifies whether the first line of the data file contains header information. The default value is FALSE.

When the browser hits the `<OBJECT>` tag, it places an instance of the Tabular Data control on the Form and downloads the data file specified. Somewhere in the page there must be a table, which will display the rows of the data file. In the `<TABLE>` tag, you must specify the DATASRC attribute with the name of the TDC that will populate the rows of the table. Each column of the table must include a `<DIV>` tag with the DATAFLD attribute, which specifies the name of the column that will appear in the corresponding column. Here's a simple table that displays the first two columns of the Customers.txt file:

```
<TABLE DATASRC=#Customers>
<TR>
<TD><DIV DATAFLD="CustomerID"></DIV></TD>
<TD><DIV DATAFLD="CompanyName"></DIV></TD>
</TR>
</TABLE>
```

The table will be populated by the TDC, but it will be a static table—as if you had prepared an HTML page with the table's data on the server. To change the appearance of the table at the client, you must provide a script that calls the Filter and Sort properties and the Reset method. The Filter and Sort properties specify how the data will be filtered (the selection criteria) or sorted. To apply the changes to the table, you must call the Reset method. The Sort property's value must be the name of the column, prefixed with the symbol "+" (for ascending sort) or "-" (for descending sort). You can sort a table according to multiple field values, by separating their names with a semicolon. If you had a list of names to sort, you could specify the following value for the Sort property:

```
Names.Sort = "+LastName;+FirstName"
```

This specification will sort the rows of the data according to the value of the field LastName. If multiple rows have the same last name, then these rows will be sorted according to the value of the field FirstName.

NOTE   If the data file doesn't contain a header line, you can use the names Column1, Column2, and so on to specify how the rows will be sorted.

The Filter property is another string that specifies selection criteria. Only the rows meeting these criteria will be displayed. Even if the Filter attribute is specified in the <OBJECT> tag, all the rows of the text file will be downloaded, but only some of them will be displayed. To display the rows with a valid CustomerID field, you should specify the following Filter string:

```
Customers.Filter = "CustomerID <> ' '"
```

You can also combine multiple criteria with the AND and OR operators. However, you must use the C-like notation for these operators: & for AND and | for OR. The following filter will display the customers from California and Nevada only:

```
Customers.Filter = "State = 'CA' | State = 'NE'"
```

Setting the Sort of Filter property in your script isn't going to affect the appearance of the table. You must first call the Reset method, to force the changes to take effect.

To undo the sorting and/or filtering of the rows and return to the original data set, set the Sort and Filter properties to an empty string and then call the Reset method again:

```
Customers.Filter = ""
Customers.Sort = ""
Customers.Reset
```

The TDCDemo.htm Page

Although it is possible to specify the settings of the Sort and Filter properties in the <OBJECT> tag, these properties are usually set from within a script, in reaction to user actions. The TDCDemo.htm page contains a table whose contents are downloaded from the same server as the page. The user can click the headers of the three columns to sort the rows of the table according to the values of the selected column.

The Tabular Data Control was inserted with the following <OBJECT> tag on the page:

```
<OBJECT id=Customers CLASSID="clsid:333C7BC4-460F-11D0-BC04-
0080C7055A83">
    <PARAM NAME="DataURL" VALUE="http://127.0.0.1/customers.txt">
    <PARAM NAME="UseHeader" VALUE="True">
</OBJECT>
```

The table was placed on the page with the standard tags. The <TABLE> tags contain the DATASRC attribute and each <TD> contains a DATAFLD attribute. Notice that the table has two sections: the table's header and the table's body. The headers of the columns are enclosed in <DIV> tags, so that they can be programmed.

```
<TABLE BORDER=ALL DATASRC="#Customers">
<THEAD BGCOLOR=yellow>
<TR>
<TD><DIV ID=Col1><B><FONT SIZE=4>COMPANY</FONT></B></DIV>
<TD><DIV ID=Col2><B><FONT SIZE=4>NAME</FONT></B></DIV>
<TD><DIV ID=Col3><B><FONT SIZE=4>TITLE</FONT></B></DIV>
</THEAD>
<TBODY BGCOLOR=cyan>
<TR>
<TD><DIV DATAFLD="CompanyName"></DIV>
```

```
<TD><DIV DATAFLD="ContactName"></DIV>
<TD><DIV DATAFLD="ContactTitle"></DIV>
</TR>
</TBODY>
</TABLE>
```

The script of the TDCDemo.htm page sets the Sort property of the Customers TDC according to the column that was selected by the user. Code 20.6 shows the complete listing of the TDCDemo.htm page.

Code 20.6   **The TDCDemo.htm Document**

```
<HTML>
<HEAD>
<TITLE>Tabular Data Control Demo</TITLE>
<SCRIPT LANGUAGE=VBScript>
Sub Col1_onclick()
    Customers.Sort = "+CompanyName"
    Customers.Reset()
End Sub
Sub Col2_onclick()
    Customers.Sort = "+ContactName"
    Customers.Reset()
End Sub
Sub Col3_onclick()
    Customers.Sort = "+ContactTitle"
    Customers.Reset()
End Sub
</SCRIPT>
</HEAD>

<BODY>
<FONT FACE=Verdana SIZE=3>
<OBJECT id=Customers CLASSID="clsid:333C7BC4-460F-11D0-BC04-
0080C7055A83">
    <PARAM NAME="DataURL" VALUE="http://127.0.0.1/customers.txt">
    <PARAM NAME="UseHeader" VALUE="True">
</OBJECT>
<CENTER>
<H1>Tabular Data Control</H1>
<TABLE BORDER=ALL datasrc="#Customers">
<THEAD BGCOLOR=yellow>
<TR>
```

```
<TD><DIV ID=Col1><B><FONT SIZE=4>COMPANY</FONT></B></DIV>
<TD><DIV ID=Col2><B><FONT SIZE=4>NAME</FONT></B></DIV>
<TD><DIV ID=Col3><B><FONT SIZE=4>TITLE</FONT></B></DIV>
</THEAD>
<TBODY BGCOLOR=cyan>
<TR>
<TD><DIV datafld="CompanyName"></DIV>
<TD><DIV datafld="ContactName"></DIV>
<TD><DIV datafld="ContactTitle"></DIV>
</TR>
</TBODY>
</TABLE>
</BODY>
</HTML>
```

This example concludes our introduction to Dynamic HTML. With a basic understanding of HTML and your knowledge of VB programming, you can easily create DHTML documents—especially with a programmer's editor, such as the one we'll present in the next section. In short, a DHTML document is a Web page, whose elements are identified by name and can be programmed with VBScript (or JavaScript). The various HTML elements have properties that can be manipulated from within the page's script. Finally, a DHTML page recognizes a number of events, which are similar (in many cases identical) to the equivalent Visual Basic events.

In the second half of the chapter, we are going to explore two new types of projects, introduced with Visual Basic 6: DHTML projects and IIS projects. DHTML projects are simple types of projects that can be created with other tools as well. DHTML applications don't interact with the server as much and are not as interesting as IIS applications. IIS applications are basically ASP applications, but they are highly integrated with Visual Basic. Writing them is like writing ASP applications with Visual Basic. We'll outline the process of designing DHTML applications in the next section and then move on to IIS applications.

Building a DHTML Project

A DHTML application is a group of HTML pages that work together, similar to a VB project that consists of multiple Forms. The user interface of a DHTML application is not as rich as the interface of a VB application, as you are limited to the components you can place on an HTML page, but it runs in the browser. A DHTML application does most of its processing on the client computer, although it is possible to make calls to the server. However, you must design the application so that the majority of processing takes place on the client, thus avoiding frequent trips to the client. According to Microsoft, corporations can lower the cost of training and support associated with their applications by presenting commonly used information and applications through the browser. Of course, this is a major shift in corporate programming and it may be a while before this paradigm becomes commonplace.

DHTML applications are designed to work most optimally on intranets. Because intranets are not subject to slow connections, the trips to the Web server do not bring the application to its knees when it's downloading images or large files, and users can safely download and install custom ActiveX controls.

Visual Basic lets you create DHTML pages that act as the user interface of your application, either from scratch or by bringing any existing Web page into Visual Basic and modifying it. In addition, you can write VB code to react to certain events on the client. These events are reported to the server, which reacts by supplying another page.

If your application must interact heavily with the Web server, you should implement it as an IIS application. In this section, we are going to look at the tools of the Visual Basic IDE for developing DHTML pages. In the following section, we'll discuss in greater detail another type of application, the IIS applications. These applications are far more useful and common than DHTML applications.

To demonstrate the basics of developing DHTML applications in the Visual Basic IDE, we are going to build the Books.htm page of the last section, this time using the tools provided by VB. Start a new project, and in the Project Type dialog box select DHTML Application. Visual Basic will add a module (the modDHTML module) and an ActiveX Designer (DHTMLPage1) to the project. Open the ActiveX Designer and you will see the window of Figure 20.5.

The Designer's window consists of two parts:

- The **Treeview pane**, which shows the elements that make up the HTML page and their relationship to the overall object model for the application. When you first begin a project for a DHTML application, the treeview contains three elements: the Document object, the page's Body element, and a paragraph, or <P>, tag.

- The **Detail pane**, which shows the HTML page as it will appear in the browser and is the area you use to draw and manipulate your page's appearance.

FIGURE 20.5:

The DHTMLPage ActiveX
Designer

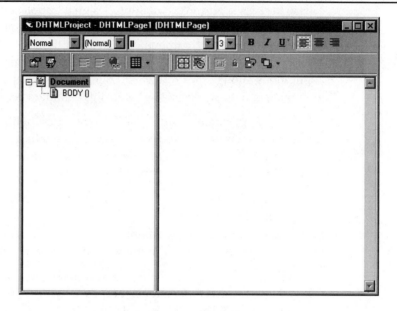

The Treeview pane displays each tag on the HTML page, including all visible elements on the page, such as buttons, text, images, checkboxes, and options boxes, and all the <DIV> and <SPAN> tags. The elements that can be programmed appear in bold. These elements are the ones that have an ID attribute, so that you can reference the element from within your script.

Notice that every time you select an element in either pane on the Designer window, the corresponding item in the other pane is also highlighted. You can also select an element in the Properties dialog box. The corresponding entries in the Details and Treeview pane are highlighted automatically.

To build the Books.htm page, enter the text for the first book title in the Details pane. Then format the title and the following lines accordingly. After the formatting of the text, your Designer's window should look like the one in Figure 20.6.

Our next step is to enclose all the lines following the book title in a pair of <SPAN> tags. Select the text with the mouse and click the button "Wrap Selection in <SPAN>...</SPAN>" on the toolbar. While the text is still selected, switch to the Properties window and set the ID property to MVB6text. Then select the book's title, and set its ID property in the Properties window to MVB6.

So far, you have inserted the elements that correspond to the first title. They both have an ID property, so they can be programmed. Double-click the item

FIGURE 20.6:

The DHTMLPage Designer
after the formatting of
the text

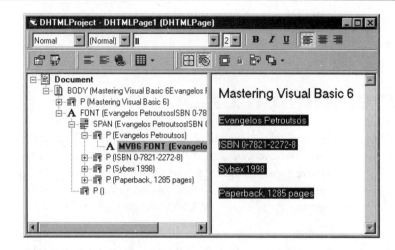

MVB6 in the Treeview pane and you will see the Code window with the MVB6
element's onclick event handler. Select the onmouseover event from the Events
list, as shown in Figure 20.7, and enter the following lines in this event handler:

```
Sub MVB6_onmouseover()
    MVB6text.style.display="block"
End Sub
```

Then select the onmouseout event and enter the following line:

```
Private Sub MVB6_onmouseout()
    MVB6text.Style.display = "none"
End Sub
```

FIGURE 20.7:

Programming the MVB6
element on the page

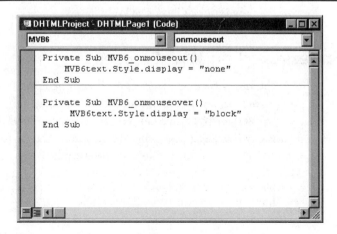

At this point, you can test the application. Press F5 and you will see the DHTML page you designed in Internet Explorer. Move the mouse in and out of the title's area to see how the document reacts to the movement of the mouse.

Developing IIS Applications

Where DHTML applications are groups of HTML pages that move as much of the processing as possible to the client, typical business applications rely on servers where enormous amounts of information are stored. Applications that need to frequently access databases shouldn't be implemented as DHTML applications, because there's very little processing that can take place on the client.

IIS applications are VB applications that use HTML pages for their user interface and Visual Basic code on the server. As you recall, ASP scripts consist of VBScript code that runs on the Web server and produces HTML pages that are downloaded to the client. Because VBScript is a seriously limited subset of Visual Basic, it can't do much processing on its own. The existing version of server-side VBScript has been enhanced with special objects (like the FileSystemObject object) and the Create-Object( ) function, which allows it to contact any ActiveX component on the server, including the Active Data Objects (ADO). You learned in the last chapter how to build ActiveX DLLs to facilitate the processing of client requests on the client. IIS applications do the same, but you can use VB code on the client. As a consequence, you need not build separate ActiveX components; you can use straight VB code to process the client data and prepare HTML pages to download to the client.

Of course, IIS applications are not simply server-side scripts written in Visual Basic. In order to understand how to build IIS applications, you must first understand a new type of Class, the WebClass.

Understanding WebClasses

A WebClass is the basic item of an IIS application. In the last chapter, you learned how to develop ASP scripts that run on the server and communicate with the client. An ASP script on its own can't do much. It can read the values of the parameters passed by the client and generate output in HTML format, which is automatically sent to the client. This is a lot, considering how easy it is to access the parameter values with VBScript, but the processing must take place on the server. And in order to process the data on the server, you'll either use existing servers (like the

ADO library, for example) or build your own components, which the scripts can contact with the CreateObject function.

A WebClass replaces the custom component. You must still write the code using Visual Basic, but you don't have to package it as a DLL and then use it with the script. You can develop the procedures you need in VB and test them in the browser. When an error occurs, you're taken back to the Visual Basic IDE to fix it and then continue (if possible). A WebClass lets you combine VB code with the objects of the ASP component to create HTML files. There's nothing new here. We'll do the same thing we did in Chapter 19, only this time we'll use WebClasses.

Here's another way to look at WebClasses. Web pages contact ASP scripts (or CGI scripts) on the server. When you design IIS applications with Visual Basic, WebClasses are the equivalent of an ASP file. The Web page passes the URL of the WebClass to the server, along with parameter values. The Web server passes the parameter values to the WebClass, which processes the request and sends the appropriate output to the client. Behind the scenes, Visual Basic will create the appropriate ASP file(s) on the server and the Web page will actually see this ASP file. The developer, however, need not deal with the details of creating the Web site, moving the files there, and maintaining the Web site.

Building an IIS Application

Start a new IIS Application project. Figure 20.8 shows the Visual Basic IDE for the IIS Application project. The folder Designer contains a WebClass item; this item's designer appears in the middle of the window. The WebClass item may contain HTML Template WebItems and custom WebItems. So, at the heart of an IIS Application you'll find the WebItems. A WebItem is like a Class; it contains procedures (including event handlers) that a Web page can request.

An HTML Template file is an HTML page that is associated with the application and can be downloaded to the client as is. The HTML template may also contain replacement sections, which the WebClass will replace with specific HTML elements (text, images, tags) before sending the file to the client.

As you'll recall from the last chapter, the server component (the ASP script) can create an HTML page on the fly with the Response.Write method. The HTML template simplifies the task of generating Web pages on the fly. The template contains the structure of the page: its title, some text that's always the same, the background, and so on. The parts of the page that change from client to client and from request to request are inserted by the WebClass, as the page is transmitted to the client.

FIGURE 20.8:

The default components of an IIS application

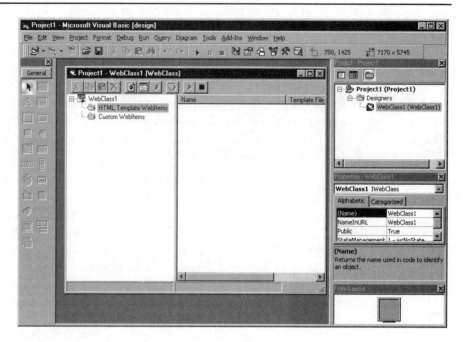

The HTML templates allow you to separate the content from the logic of a Web site. A Web author will create the template, which involves mostly visual design and artistic work. The programmer will supply the script or the parts of the page that must be generated programmatically. This is probably the most compelling reason for creating IIS applications in the Visual Basic environment. You'll see shortly how this is done.

Let's return to the IIS project's Designer window. Click the View Code button on the Project Explorer to see the code inserted automatically by Visual Basic:

```
Option Explicit
Option Compare Text

Private Sub WebClass_Start()

    'Write a reply to the user
    With Response
        .Write "<html>"
        .Write "<body>"
        .Write "<h1><font face=""Arial"">WebClass1's Starting _
Page</font></h1>"
```

```
        .Write "<p>This response was created in the Start event of _
WebClass1.</p>"
        .Write "</body>"
        .Write "</html>"
    End With

    End Sub
```

The Start event of the WebClass is fired when the application starts. This is not a Visual Basic application, however. It's an IIS application and it will start when a client contacts the URL of the WebClass. In the Start event, you can insert the code to create a Web page on the fly. As you can see, the WebClass supports the ASP objects, such as the Response object.

If you run the project now by pressing F5, the Debugging Properties tab of the Project Properties dialog box will appear, as shown in Figure 20.9. Since an IIS project is implemented as a DLL, you must specify what will happen when the application starts. Visual Basic suggests that the project start with the WebClass1 component.

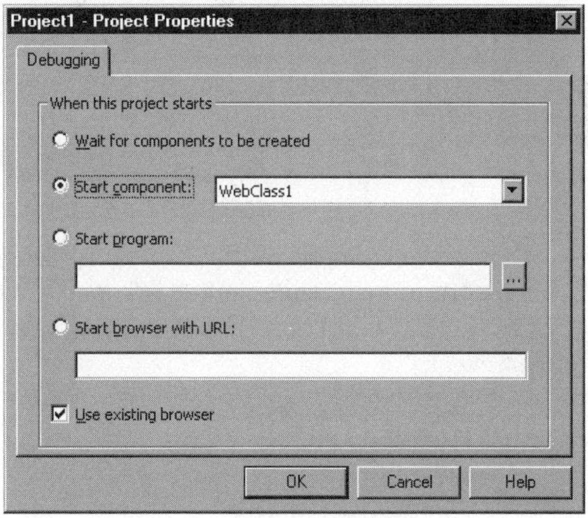

FIGURE 20.9:

The Debugging tab of the Project Properties dialog box

Visual Basic will start Internet Explorer using the URL of the IIS application, which is

```
http://localhost/WebTest1/WebClass1.ASP
```

As you can see, the project was tested with the local Web server (IIS or Personal Web server running on the same computer). If the Web server is installed on another machine on the network, the *localhost* part of the URL will be different. Visual Basic has created an ASP file, the `WebClass1.ASP` file, which invokes the WebClass component of the application.

The ASP file resides in the `WebTest1` virtual folder of the Web server. This virtual folder was created automatically by Visual Basic (normally, you should create this virtual folder yourself and map it to the application's folder). The document that will be displayed on the browser is quite simple (see Figure 20.10).

FIGURE 20.10:

The sample page created by the default IIS application

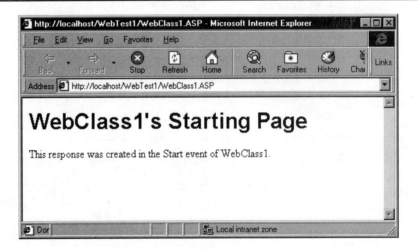

Let's revise the project's code so that it uses an HTML template. We'll create another document, again with the Response.Write method, which will contain a hyperlink that invokes an HTML page. Here's the revised code of the WebClass's Start event:

```
Private Sub WebClass_Start()
    'Write a reply to the user
    With Response
        .Write "<html>"
        .Write "<body>"
        .Write "<h1><font face=""Arial"">WebClass1's Starting _
Page</font></h1>"
        .Write "<p>This response was created in the Start event of _
WebClass1.</p>"
```

```
        .Write "<p>Click <A HREF=""" & URLFor(Template1) & """>here _
</A> to see another document"
        .Write "</body>"
        .Write "</html>"
    End With
End Sub
```

The code is straightforward, except for the code that generates the hyperlink. The URLFor function will insert the URL of the Template1 component. Now, we can create the Template1 HTML template.

Switch to the Designer window and right-click the item WebClass1. From the shortcut menu select Add HTML Template. Visual Basic will display a message box, indicating that the project must first be saved, before an HTML template is added. Save the project's components to a new folder (you can find the project in the IISDemo1 folder on the CD). Invoke the Add HTML Template command again and you'll see the File Open dialog box, where you must select an existing HTML file. (Visual Basic doesn't come with a built-in HTML editor that would allow you to create an HTML file in the same environment.) Click Cancel to close the dialog box, switch to a text editor (use Notepad for a simple HTML file like the one we'll use in this example), and create a new file with the following contents:

```
<HTML>
<FORM NAME=Frm1 ACTION="WebClass1.asp?WCI=webitem1" METHOD=post>
<INPUT TYPE=Input NAME="Text1" VALUE="TEXT1: Enter more text here">
<INPUT TYPE=Input NAME="Text2" VALUE="TEXT2: Enter more text here">
<INPUT TYPE=submit NAME="BttnSend" value="Submit Query">
</FORM>
</HTML>
```

Save this file as HTMLForm.htm in the same folder as the project. Make sure it's saved with the extension ASP, and not with extension TXT. Do not return to the IIS project to add the template yet.

This is a very simple HTML file that contains a Form with two Text controls, where the user can enter data to be passed to the server. The ACTION attribute of the <FORM> tag tells the browser which application it must contact on the server when the Submit button is clicked. The ACTION attribute's value is the name of the script that will process the parameter values and generate the response to the client request. Even though you didn't write an ASP file, Visual Basic created it for you and placed it in the application's folder in the Web server.

Our first task is to create a component to process the client request. This component is a WebItem: a special object that's invoked automatically by the ASP file when the Submit button of the document is clicked. Right-click the WebClass1 entry in the Designer window and select Add Custom WebItem. The new WebItem will be named by default WebItem1. Don't change the name.

If you open the Code window and select WebItem1 in the Objects list, you'll see that the WebItem recognizes three events:

- **ProcessTag** This event takes place when the HTML template is read, and gives the WebItem a chance to modify it before sending the HTML code to the client. Use this event to replace specific sections of the HTML template with HTML code (text and tags). The process of replacing sections of the template file before submitting it to the client is described in the section "Processing Template Tags" later in this chapter.

- **Respond** This event is fired every time the WebItem is contacted by the client.

- **UserEvent** This event is fired every time the client raises a custom event (you'll see shortly how you can fire custom events).

The event we're interested in is the Respond event of the WebItem1. This event will be fired when the HTMLForm.htm page requests the WebItem1 object on the server. The HTML file will pass the values on its two Text controls, which are named Text1 and Text2. The event handler must extract these values, process them, and pass an HTML document back to the client. You know already that the parameter values must be read with the Request.Form property and the output must be generated with the Response.Write method. WebItem1 should respond to the request with the following code:

```
Private Sub WebItem1_Respond()
    Response.Write "WEBITEM1_RESPOND invoked "
    Response.Write "with the following values<P>"
    Response.Write Request.Form("Text1") & "<P>"
    Response.Write Request.Form("Text2") & "<P>"
End Sub
```

So far, we've created the HTML template and the procedure that will process the HTML file's request. The HTML template (the HTMLForm.htm) invokes the WebItem1 object on the server, and as a consequence you cannot add it to the project before the WebItem1 object. If you attempt to add an HTML template that references a non-existing component, a message to that effect will be displayed.

When the hyperlink on the initial page of the application is clicked, the Template1 component of the application will be contacted. The Template1_Respond event will be invoked, and you must provide the code to display the HTML-Form.htm page. Insert the following line in the Template1_Respond event:

```
Private Sub Template1_Respond()
    Template1.WriteTemplate
End Sub
```

The WriteTemplate method sends the HTML file as is to the client.

At this point, your project contains a WebClass, which in turns contains an HTML Template (Template1) and a custom WebItem (WebItem1). Here's the project's code:

Code 20.7   The IISDemo1 Project's Code

```
Option Explicit
Option Compare Text

Private Sub Template1_Respond()
    Template1.WriteTemplate
End Sub

Private Sub WebClass_Start()
    'Write a reply to the user
    With Response
        .Write "<html>"
        .Write "<body>"
        .Write "<h1><font face=""Arial"">WebClass1's Starting _
Page</font></h1>"
        .Write "<p>This response was created in the Start event of _
WebClass1.</p>"
        .Write "<p>Click <A HREF=""" & URLFor(Template1) & """>here _
</A> to see another document"
        .Write "</body>"
        .Write "</html>"
    End With
End Sub

Private Sub WebItem1_Respond()
    Response.Write "WEBITEM1_RESPOND invoked "
    Response.Write "with the following values<P>"
    Response.Write Request.Form("Text1") & "<P>"
    Response.Write Request.Form("Text2") & "<P>"
End Sub
```

IISDemo1 is a simple IIS application that demonstrates the basic functions of WebClasses and WebItems. We are going to look at a more complicated example, but first let's summarize three key items in writing code for a WebClass:

- **URLFor Function**   Use this method to insert the URL of any component. Visual Basic will generate the proper URL and you don't have to worry about absolute or relative URLs and what will happen when the application is moved to another computer or folder.

- **Respond Event**   Every time the client contacts a component, the component's Respond event is triggered automatically. All you have to do is code this event.

- **WriteTemplate Method**   Use this method to send an HTML file to the client as is. You can also process the HTML file, using the ProcessTag event (discusses in the next section).

Connecting Events to WebClasses

Let's return our attention to the <FORM> tag of the HTMLForm.htm file, which is repeated here:

```
<FORM NAME=Frm1 ACTION="WebClass1.asp?WCI=webitem1" METHOD=post>
```

The ACTION attribute is the URL of the server application (or the server-side script in the case of Active Server Pages). The application's name is WebClass1.asp and there's nothing peculiar so far. But the name of the server application is followed by a parameter, the WCI parameter. As you can see, the name of the WebItem that will process the request on the server is passed as a parameter. Obviously, any additional parameters will be appended to this URL by the browser automatically. WCI stands for WebClass Item; this is how you specify the name of a WebItem in the application's WebClass.

By default, when the user selects the hyperlink on the HTMLForm.htm page (the Template1 component in the project) the WebItem1_Respond event is fired. This is the event where we inserted the code to display the values of the parameters passed by the browser to the server in the previous example.

In this example, we inserted all the required attributes manually. It is also possible, and preferable, to let the Designer insert the appropriate tag. To do so, you must first edit the HTMLForm.htm file and remove the ACTION attribute from the <FORM> tag. If you switch to a text editor and change the HTM file outside the Visual Basic environment, when you switch back to Visual Basic's window you must right-click the Template1 entry in the left pane of the Designer's window and select Refresh HTML Template in the shortcut menu. This will force Visual Basic to read the contents of the file and update the contents of the Designer's right pane.

You can also right-click the Template1 entry and select Edit HTML Template from the shortcut menu. Your designated HTML editor will start with the Template1 HTML file. You can specify the HTML editor of your choice through the Advanced tab of the Options dialog box (Tools ➤ Options). Figure 20.11 shows our favorite HTML editor.

FIGURE 20.11:

Use the Advanced tab to specify the HTML editor to be invoked by Visual Basic when you select to edit an HTML Template.

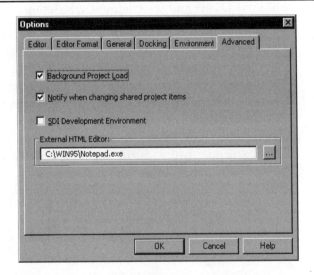

If you save the changes to the HTM file and return to the Visual Basic IDE, you'll be prompted to refresh the HTML template. So, it's safer to edit the template from within the Visual Basic IDE, to make sure that the changes will take effect immediately.

Assuming that you have removed the ACTION attribute from the HTML template, open the WebClass Designer and select the template that contains the hyperlink (or any other tag) you want to connect to WebItem1. In the right pane of the Designer you will see the elements of the Template. Template1 contains a <BODY> and a <FORM> tag. The Form is named Frm1 and there is no action associated with it. To specify an action, right-click the Frm1 item in the right pane of the Designer. In the shortcut menu, select Connect to WebItem; the Connect to WebItem dialog box will appear. This dialog box contains all the components in the project. Click the

WebItem1 entry and click the OK button. When the dialog box is closed, the Action for the Frm1 item in the right pane of the Designer will be set to WebItem1. You have just connected the Form's ACTION attribute to the WebItem1 component.

If you open the HTMLForm.htm file you will see that the Designer has modified its contents. The new <FORM> tag is

```
<FORM NAME=Frm1 ACTION="WebClass1.ASP?WCI=_
            WebItem1&amp;WCU" METHOD=post>
```

To disconnect the attribute from the WebItem, you can right-click the Frm1 item in the right pane of the Designer and select Disconnect from the shortcut menu. The WCU keyword is explained in the following section.

In addition to invoking WebItems on the server, an element on the Web page can also call a custom event of the Template1 WebItem on the server. To do this, select the Template1 entry in the left pane of the Designer and right-click the Frm1 item in the right pane. From the shortcut menu select Connect to Custom Event. An event will be automatically added to the Template1 entry in the right pane of the Designer window. The event's name is by default the same as the Template's element name (Frm1). Change the name of the custom event to Frm1Event. Visual Basic will modify the <FORM> tag in the HTMLForm.htm file automatically. The new <FORM> tag is shown next:

```
<FORM NAME=Frm1 ACTION="WebClass1.ASP?WCI=Template1&amp; _
WCE=Frm1Event&amp;WCU" METHOD=post>
```

The WCE keyword specifies the name of the event to be invoked. The WebItem to which the event will be reported is specified with the WCI keyword.

When the user clicks the Submit button on the Form, the Template1 WebItem's custom event will be fired. Therefore, we must add another event handler to the project, which will process the parameters submitted by the HTML page. This event handler is quite similar to the WebItem1_Respond event handler.

```
Private Sub Template1_FRM1Event()
    Response.Write "TEMPLATE1_FRM1EVENT invoked "
    Response.Write "with the following values<P>"
    Response.Write Request.Form("Text1") & "<P>"
    Response.Write Request.Form("Text2") & "<P>"
End Sub
```

The revised project, in which the HTML page invokes a custom event of the Template1 WebItem, can be found in the EventDemo folder under the IISDemo folder.

There's a third method to contact a procedure on the server, namely to invoke an event of a custom WebItem. First, you must add a custom event to the WebItem. Right-click the entry WebItem1 in the right pane of the Designer and from the shortcut menu select Add Custom Event. Rename the custom event to **WebEvent**. Then edit the HTML template and change the <FORM> tag to

```
<FORM NAME=Frm1 ACTION="WebClass1.ASP?WCI=_
        WebItem1&amp;WCU=WebEvent&amp;" METHOD=post>
```

Then open the Code window and enter the following code in the custom event's handler:

```
Private Sub WebItem1_WebEvent()
    Response.Write "WEBITEM1_WEBEVENT invoked "
    Response.Write "with the following values<P>"
    Response.Write Request.Form("Text1") & "<P>"
    Response.Write Request.Form("Text2") & "<P>"
End Sub
```

This project is identical to the IISDemo project, only it contacts a custom event of the WebItem1 object on the server. The revised project can be found in the UEventDemo folder under the IISDemo folder on the CD.

In the following section, we are going to build an IIS application that demonstrates the separation of the application's content and logic. The sample application will show you how to process HTML templates before they are sent to the client and how to contact other server components (the Active Data Objects, in specific).

Processing Template Tags

It is possible to customize an HTML template by using the special <WC@> tag. This tag marks a section in the template that will be replaced by another string, just prior to sending the response to the client. Each <WC@> tag must be followed by a name and the matching closing tag. Let's say you want to display a greeting with the viewer's name, which is stored in the *VName* variable. This variable may hold a cookie value; the value is set once and used every time the same user connects to the site. The following line, which can be customized for each viewer, will insert a message into the HTML template file:

```
The order for <WC@customer>CustomerName</WC@customer> _
will be processed immediately.
```

If the HTML template contains <WC@> tags, the ProcessTag event of the WebItem is fired, just before the response is sent to the client. The event's declaration is

```
Private Sub WebItem1_ProcessTag(ByVal TagName As String, _
                    TagContents As String, SendTags As Boolean)
```

This event is fired for each <WC@> tag in the template file, and is fired by the WriteTemplate method. The *TagName* argument reports the tag being processed and the *TagContents* argument reports the string between the two tags (the string to be replaced). The last argument is a Boolean value, which you can set to True to omit the entire tag from the output. When the <WC@> of the previous example is processed, the arguments of the ProcessTag event will report the following values:

```
TagName = customer
TagName = Customer Name
```

In the event's handler, you can perform the substitution with a code segment like the following one:

```
Sub WebItem1_ProcessTag(ByVal TagName As String, _
            TagContents As String, SendTags As Boolean)
    Select Case TagName
        Case WC@customer: TagContents = VName
        Case WC@address: TagContents = VAddress
        {more cases}
    End Select
End Sub
```

Normally, the WebClass scans the HTML template sequentially and replaces all <WC@> tags, one at a time. It is possible for the replacement string to contain another <WC@> tag, in which case the template must be scanned again. Since you can't force the ProcessTag event from within your code, you must tell the Web-Class to search again by setting the WebItem's ReScanReplacements property to True. The ReScanReplacements property causes the WebClass to make an additional pass through the replacement tags during the ProcessTag event.

The WCDemo Project

The example in this section is an IIS application that uses the ADO library to retrieve records from the NWIND database and present them to the client. This example will also demonstrate how to separate the site's content from its logic (not in a dramatic way, unfortunately; this could only be demonstrated clearly with a large-scale project, which can't be presented in this book). Let's start by looking at the various pages of the application.

When the user connects to the IIS application's home page, they see a list with the names of the product categories in the NWIND database, as shown in Figure 20.12. The user can select a category in the list and click the Send Data button to see the products in the selected category.

FIGURE 20.12:

The home page of the WCDemo IIS application

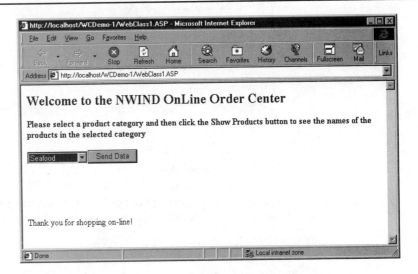

The next window, shown in Figure 20.13, displays the products in the selected category, along with prices and a checkbox for each. To select a product, the user must check the box in front of its name. After the desired products have been selected, the user can click the Order button to submit the order to the server.

The application on the server confirms the order by displaying a page with the IDs of the selected products. The WCDemo application is incomplete, but once the application that processes the order on the server has the IDs of the selected products, it can update the database, issue invoices, and so on.

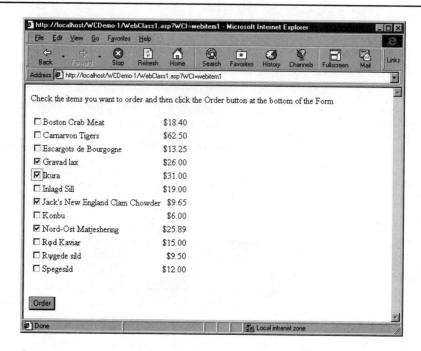

The WCDemo application demonstrates the separation of the application's project from its logic. The initial page of the application doesn't contain the list box with the categories. Instead, it contains a specially marked section, which is replaced with the appropriate <SELECT> tag when the page is downloaded. Here's the listing of the HTML page that displays the product categories:

```
<BODY><H2>Welcome to the NWIND OnLine Order Center</H2>
<B>Please select a product category and then click the Show
Products button to see the names of the products in the selected _
category</B>
<P>
<WC@OPTIONS>
PLS ENTER AN OPTION CONTROL HERE
<BR>
AND A  SUBMIT BUTTON
</WC@OPTIONS>
<P>
<BR><BR><BR><BR>
Thank you for shopping on-line!
</BODY>
</HTML>
```

Notice the section of the document enclosed by the <WC@OPTIONS> and </WC@OPTIONS> tags. This section of the page will not appear on the browser. It's inserted there by the Web author as a reminder to a VB developer. The developer must replace these lines with the appropriate tags.

The WCDemo application consists of an HTML Template WebItem (the CategoriesPage) and two custom WebItems. When the application starts, the WebClass_Start event is fired. From within the Start event's handler we must display the CategoriesPage template:

```
Private Sub WebClass_Start()
    'send a Web page to the user
    CategoriesPage.WriteTemplate
End Sub
```

As the CategoriesPage template is read and downloaded to the client computer, the WebClass must replace the specially marked section with the tags that will produce the list of categories. This action must take place in the Template's ProcessTag event handler. This event is fired before an HTML template is downloaded to the client.

Code 20.8   **The ProcessTag Event Handler**

```
Private Sub CategoriesPage_ProcessTag(ByVal TagName As String, TagContents
As String, SendTags As Boolean)
If TagName = "WC@OPTIONS" Then
    TagContents = "<FORM NAME=Frm1 ACTION=""" &
"WebClass1.asp?WCI=webitem1""" & " METHOD=post>" & vbCrLf
    TagContents = TagContents & "<SELECT NAME=Categories SIZE=1>" & vbCrLf
    TagContents = TagContents & "<OPTION SELECTED VALUE='1'>Beverages _
</OPTION>" & vbCrLf
    TagContents = TagContents & "<OPTION SELECTED VALUE='2'>Condiments _
</OPTION>" & vbCrLf
    TagContents = TagContents & "<OPTION SELECTED VALUE='3'>Confections _
</OPTION>" & vbCrLf
    TagContents = TagContents & "<OPTION SELECTED VALUE='4'>Dairy _
Products</OPTION>" & vbCrLf
    TagContents = TagContents & "<OPTION SELECTED VALUE='5'>Grains/ _
Cereals</OPTION>" & vbCrLf
    TagContents = TagContents & "<OPTION SELECTED VALUE='6'>Meat/Poultry _
</OPTION>" & vbCrLf
    TagContents = TagContents & "<OPTION SELECTED VALUE='7'>Produce _
</OPTION>" & vbCrLf
```

```
    TagContents = TagContents & "<OPTION SELECTED VALUE='8'>Seafood _
</OPTION>" & vbCrLf
    TagContents = TagContents & "</SELECT>"
    TagContents = TagContents & "<INPUT TYPE=Submit VALUE=""" & "Show _
Products" & """>" & vbCrLf
    TagContents = TagContents & "</FORM>"
End If
End Sub
```

The code is straightforward. We don't even read the categories from the database (assuming that the categories don't change frequently). This is how you modify HTML templates on the fly. The TagContents argument contains the text that will replace the section of the HTML file enclosed in the <CW@> tags. The template may contain multiple sections to be replaced, as long as they have different names. The Web author, or designer, can add as much content to the page as they want, as long as they know roughly how much space is needed for the display of the categories. Placing a Form with the appropriate controls on the page is the responsibility of the VB developer.

The Form's ACTION attribute is straightforward. It calls the WebItem1 component of the WCDemo.asp application. Right-click the Custom WebItems entry in the Designer's left pane and select Add Custom WebItem. The new WebItem will be named WebItem1.

WebItem1 will be called when the user clicks the Send Data button. Thus, we must program its Respond event to generate another HTML file on the fly. This time we are going to open the NWIND database and retrieve the selected products directly from the database. The code uses the ADO component to open the NWIND database. The same statement would have been used in a VB application to retrieve the recordset with the desired products. Here's the WebItem1_Respond event handler:

Code 20.9   The WebItem1_Respond Event Handler

```
Private Sub WebItem1_Respond()
Dim selectedCategory As Integer
Dim SQLQuery As String
Dim DBConnection As ADODB.Connection
Dim RSProducts As ADODB.Recordset

    selectedCategory = Request.Form("Categories")
```

```
Set DBConnection = Server.CreateObject("ADODB.Connection")
DBConnection.Open "NWINDDB"
SQLQuery = "SELECT ProductID, ProductName, UnitPrice " & _
           "FROM Products " WHERE CategoryID=" & _
           selectedCategory & " ORDER BY ProductName"
Set RSProducts = DBConnection.Execute(SQLQuery)
Response.Write "Check the items you want to order and _
           then click the Order button at the bottom of the Form"
Response.Write "<FORM NAME=ORDERFORM ACTION=""" & _
           "WebClass1.asp?WCI=webitem2""" & "METHOD=POST>"
Response.Write "<TABLE>"
While Not RSProducts.EOF
    Response.Write "<TR>" & vbCrLf
    Response.Write "<TD><INPUT TYPE=Checkbox NAME=SelProduct _
            VALUE=PROD" & RSProducts.Fields("ProductID") & vbCrLf
    Response.Write "<TD>" & RSProducts.Fields("ProductName") & _
            "<TD ALIGN=right>" & _
            FormatCurrency(RSProducts.Fields("UnitPrice"), 2)
    Response.Write "</TR>"
    RSProducts.MoveNext
Wend
Response.Write "</TABLE>" & vbCrLf
Response.Write "<BR><BR>"
Response.Write "<INPUT TYPE=SUBMIT VALUE=Order>"
Response.Write "</FORM>"
Set RSProducts = Nothing
Set DBConnection = Nothing
End Sub
```

The user will select the desired products by checking the box in front of their names. To avoid keeping the recordset open, we store the product IDs in the page itself. The name of the CheckBoxes are formed by concatenating the string "PROD" and the product's ID. If the product codes were not numeric values, we could have named the CheckBoxes after these IDs. When the Order button on this page is clicked, the names of the selected CheckBoxes will be passed to another component of the server application, which can use them to prepare the order (issue the invoice, update the stock, and so on; these operations are not shown in this example).

As you can see in the <FORM> tag, the parameters will be passed to the WebItem2. The WebItem2_Respond event handler of the WCDemo application creates another page with the names of the selected product codes. We don't process the data passed back to the server at all, but this is all the information you need to process the order.

For example, you can store the selected product codes and names to an array, design pages that allow the user to review the selected items (and possibly drop some of them), add products from multiple categories, and finally place the order.

Maintaining State in WebClasses

Normally, a new instance of the WebClass is created each time a request is made and destroyed after the response has been sent to the browser. However, you can use the StateManagement property of the WebClass to alter this behavior. You can set the StateManagement property to wcRetainInstance to keep the WebClass alive between requests. This enables you to use variables within the WebClass to store information between browser requests.

There are other methods to maintain variable values between requests. All the methods discussed in the last chapter (including cookies) can be used with a WebClass as well. In addition to these methods, you can use the URLData property to manage your site's state. This is a peculiar technique; it doesn't store the information on either the client or the server. It keeps the information alive by moving the information back and forth.

The URLData property appends information to specific URLs that the WebClass sends to the browser. When the browser submits another request using one of these URLs, the information can be passed back to the Web server for further processing. In this way, you can send and retrieve state information without storing it in either location. The very nature of this technique imposes a serious limitation. URLData is restricted in the amount of data it can send. The size limitation varies from browser to browser, but most browsers can handle about 2K of data in the URL.

The URLData property can add information to URLs in the WebClass's responses in two cases:

- when the WebClass calls a WriteTemplate method

- when the WebClass calls the URLFor method

To set state information with URLData, you must assign a value to the URL-Data property in your event procedure. The following statement shows how you can set state data within a custom event called SetID:

```
Private Sub WebItem1_Set()
    URLData = "CustomerID#77788"
    Response.Write "<A HREF=""" & URLFor(WebItem2) & _
                "">Customer Information</A>"
End Sub
```

The CustomerID will be transmitted to the client and the client will return it back to the server when the user clicks the "Customer Information" hyperlink. The information sent to the browser will be returned to the server when the Web-Class processes the URL that contains the data, and you can retrieve the value of the URLData property in order to manipulate and process the state information on the Web server.

For example, the following code shows how you might retrieve state data within the Respond event for WebItem1:

```
Private Sub WebItem1_Respond()
    Response.Write "The customer's name is " & _
                    CustomerNameFromID(Me.URLData))
End Sub
```

Presumably, CustomerNameFromID is a function, which operates on data on the server or accesses a database on the server.

The Structure of an IIS Application

Let's end this chapter by reviewing the structure of an IIS application. Normally, this discussion should appear at the beginning of the chapter, but we found it hard to introduce so many concepts and objects without examples. Now that you have a good idea about what WebClasses and WebItems are, you'll find it much easier to understand the structure of an IIS application.

An IIS application is a Visual Basic application that uses HTML pages to interact with the user. Unlike Visual Basic applications, IIS applications can't be distributed; they must be executed on a Web server. The developer, however, doesn't have to be concerned with the Web server. Visual Basic installs and configures an ASP application and connects it to the WebClass object of the IIS application. These are troublesome operations, which are taken care of for you by Visual Basic.

The IIS application consists of a WebClass, which contains one or more WebItems. When a user connects to the URL of the application, the WebClass object is contacted and its Start event is invoked. In the WebClass_Start event handler, you must supply the code to display the home page. This page can be displayed in two ways:

- **On the fly** Use the Response.Write method to create the HTML page on the fly. The default event handler for this event generated by Visual Basic generates a simple page by writing HTML code to the Response object.

- **With a Template** Use an existing HTML file (or HTML Template WebItem) and send it to the client with the WriteTemplate method. In addition to sending the HTML file as is, you can replace certain segments of the template file the moment it's send to the client. Place the code to replace the <WC@> tags in the ProcessTag event of the WebItem object.

The home page of the application must interact with the server, somehow. Several tags on an HTML page can trigger events in the server application when selected, and these tags must contain a URL. A hyperlink, for example, can invoke the Web-Class and pass parameter values to it.

A WebClass has an Initialize and a Terminate event, which you use to insert the code to initialize (by creating object variables, populating arrays, and so on) or terminate (by cleaning up any object variables) the WebClass. However, it doesn't support a Respond event. In other words, the WebClass cannot respond to client requests directly. You must create WebItem objects under the WebClass and use them as hyperlink destinations. When a custom WebItem is specified as the URL of an event in the HTML file, the WebItem's Respond event is invoked. The Visual Basic code to process the request must be inserted in this event handler.

In addition to default Respond event, you can also define custom events for each WebItem. Custom events can be fired directly from the browser through the URLFor method. To insert the URL of a custom event, use the URLFor method and specify the name of the WebItem, along with the name of the custom event. Here's how you would insert a hyperlink to invoke the ReadCustomer event of the Customers WebItem:

```
Response.Write _
    "<A HREF=""" & URLFor(Customers, "ReadCustomer") & """></A>"
```

In the WebClass's code window, you must supply the Customers_ReadCustomer event handler. The Customers_ReadCustomer event handler is nothing more than a subroutine, which should generate another HTML page on the fly and send it to the client. The event handler can use the Request object to find out the values submitted by the client. The code of the event handler has a similar structure to the VBScript code you would use to handle a client request with a server-side script, but it is not limited to VBScript. It's actually a Visual Basic subroutine.

You can also specify a URL manually, using the WCI and WCU keywords. Use the WCI keyword to specify the WebItem and the WCU keyword to specify the custom event, as shown here:

```
http://www.myserver.com/Project1_Orders.asp?WCI=OrderTotal;WCU=GetOrders
```

As far as the code of the WebClass's events is concerned, it's straight Visual Basic code. You can't use any components with a visible user interface, but you can use any statements that would appear in a standard VB application. You can also access any objects that exist on the server computer, as well as the Active Server Objects, which we discussed in the previous chapter.

IIS Applications versus ASP Applications

By now, you should also have a good feel for the differences between IIS and ASP applications. But you may have a few doubts about the usefulness of IIS applications. What is there that you can do with an IIS application that you can't do with an ASP application? Basically, they do the same thing. They both use the Active Server Pages object model, and if you can write ASP applications, you can write IIS applications.

While to the end user they look the same (they are series of HTML pages), IIS applications are Visual Basic applications. They are developed and tested in the Visual Basic IDE, which simplifies the programming. You have at your disposal the entire repertoire of Visual Basic commands and you can contact code components on the Web server as you would with a straight VB application. Where ASP applications borrow some of Visual Basic's functionality by means of VBScript, IIS applications bring the functionality of Active Server Pages to Visual Basic. The advantage of IIS applications is that they look and feel like regular VB applications, but they can run on the client and interact with the Web server. Of course, they can't take advantage of Visual Basic's rich user interface capabilities, but then again they wouldn't run in every browser.

PART V

Programming Office 97

CHAPTER
TWENTY-ONE

21

An Introduction to VBA

- Programming with objects

- Using the VBA Editor to create macros

- Automating Microsoft Office applications

- Designing and using VBA Forms with Visual Basic

For several years, VBA (Visual Basic for Applications) was the programming language to use with Microsoft Office applications. VBA is a simple programming language that allows programmers (and power users as well) to do the following:

- Extend and automate Office applications
- Integrate Office applications and their data with other applications

The basic idea is really simple: Create a common language and programming environment for a number of applications so that people can customize applications and add capabilities to suit their own environment. As such, VBA had to be simple. You can't use VBA to develop just any type of application you may need or think of. VBA provides only the basic control structures, math and string functions, and variable manipulation capabilities. The real power of VBA comes from the objects of the applications that support it.

With the introduction of VBA 5, Microsoft started licensing the language to manufacturers who wanted to add programmable features to their products—for example, Autodesk's AutoCAD. AutoCAD has been a programmable environment for many years, but its programming language was unique to AutoCAD and couldn't be shared with other applications. Many other manufacturers included scripting languages or other means of automating their software. But the need for a global language that would act as the glue in putting together the pieces of many applications was clear. Finally, Microsoft came up with a version of VBA that meets the needs of other manufacturers, and VBA is on its way to becoming a universal language for automating applications under Windows.

Most companies today use off-the-shelf software and need to customize it. More than half of the corporations in the United States use Microsoft Office products, and many of them use VBA to customize those applications to suit their business needs. This trend will continue and become stronger in the future. There is already a need not to simply customize applications, but to tie them together so that they can communicate. VBA does this too, and as a result, the need for VBA programmers will increase in the next few years.

Today's applications are so powerful and so feature-rich that it no longer makes sense to develop custom applications. Instead, it makes sense to customize existing applications and make them work together. Even the Office 97 applications are adequate for addressing most of the day-to-day computer operations of a typical corporation. With a host of third-party applications supporting VBA, you can easily guess its importance in corporate environments.

In this chapter, we'll introduce you to the parts and pieces of VBA and show you in general how you can use it with Visual Basic. In the following three chapters, we'll get into the specifics, discuss the objects of the major Office applications, and give you some concrete examples of how you can use them from within your own applications.

The examples in this chapter and the following three chapters assume that you have Word and Excel installed on your system. You can automate other applications with VBA, but we are going to focus on the primary Office applications, since most of the VBA code written today applies to them. Because VBA depends on the functionality and the objects exposed by each individual application, you can apply the information in this chapter to other applications.

Programming with Objects

The theme running throughout this book is object programming. We have looked at all types of objects you will run into as a VB programmer, and VBA is no exception. The goal of VBA is to access the functionality of applications and either automate them (with macros—procedures made up of VBA commands) or control them from within other applications. And, as you no doubt know so well by now, applications make their functionality available to other applications via objects. Applications expose objects, which represent their programmable entities. For instance:

- The Visual Basic IDE exposes the CommandBars collection, which represents the toolbars of the Visual Basic IDE.

- The DAO (Data Access Objects) exposes the Database object, which represents an entire database.

- Word exposes the ActiveDocument object, which represents the current document, the Selection object, which represents the current selection, and so on.

- Excel exposes a different set of objects, better suited for the type of data it can handle. Instead of the ActiveDocument object, it exposes the Active-Sheet object, which represents the active worksheet.

All of these objects have properties that are also objects or collections of objects. For instance, the Documents collection contains an item for each open document. Each Document object, in turn, contains a Paragraphs collection, which represents all the paragraphs in the document. You already know that you can access each paragraph of a DOC document, and as you will see, you can also access individual words and characters.

For example, to access the first paragraph of the document DevHandbook.doc, you use an expression such as the following:

```
Documents("DevHandbook.doc").Paragraphs(1)
```

To set the Bold attribute of this paragraph, you must use an even longer expression:

```
Documents("DevHandbook.doc").Paragraphs(1).Font.Bold
```

NOTE   Bold is a property of the Font object, as you may recall from Chapter 9.

Expressions involving objects exposed by Office applications can get quite lengthy, but they are usually simple to build and understand. The object model of each application forms a hierarchy, which represents the structure of the documents each application can handle.

When an application is manipulated from within another, we say that the application is *automated*. You can't really program Word to do something it doesn't know how to or can't do. You must call functions already built into Word to access the objects exposed by Word itself. In essence, you are automating Word. You are telling Word to carry out an action that isn't implemented as a menu command, to carry out an action repeatedly on each paragraph, and so on. VBA is not a complete language. Instead, it relies on the functionality of the applications that support VBA and expose it via an object model.

The same object can also be used from within other applications. You can write Word macros that rely on Excel to retrieve data and then format them as DOC files. You can also borrow the functionality of Office applications from within your Visual Basic applications. You will see later in this chapter how to use Word's spell-checking capabilities to verify the spelling of a document from within a Visual Basic application and how to use Excel capabilities to evaluate a math expression from within your Visual Basic application.

The New VBA Editor

VBA is not a new language; it's been around for several years, although limited to Office applications. And, as you probably know, the simplest way to program in VBA is to record a macro. Every operation you can perform with the keyboard and menu commands in Word or Excel can be recorded as a macro. Macros can be executed (played back) to perform the same operation on different data.

The most common use of macros is to assign formatting commands to keystrokes. Let's say you are using Word to prepare elaborate documents, with many formatting options. If your documents contain code segments, you probably want to format these segments in Courier New, 10 or 11 point, and indent their left edge more than the text. Instead of selecting every code segment in the document and then applying the formatting manually, you can record a macro that contains all the commands you must issue to apply the desired formatting. You can also assign these commands to a keystroke, such as Alt+C. Then, each time you want to format a section as a code segment, all you have to do is select the text and press Alt+C.

In older versions of VBA, macros were the only means of programming, or automating, Office applications. You could edit macros, but there were no debugging tools and no special editor (an editor with an Auto List Members features, for example). With VBA 5, a new editor was introduced that is nearly identical to the IDE editor of Visual Basic 5. As you type the name of an object variable, the editor displays the names of its members in a drop-down list, where you can select the desired member. The new VBA editor is a programmer's editor, and it simplifies the manual coding of macros as much as an editor can. VBA 5 comes with an integrated development and debugging environment, which was sorely missing from previous versions of VBA.

Using the Auto List Members Feature

If you're a seasoned programmer, you may find the Auto List Members feature a real annoyance. But you will find it extremely useful with VBA because Office applications expose their own objects and most VB programmers just aren't familiar with these objects. A reminder won't hurt.

If you want, you can turn off the Quick Tip feature and type the names of the members in lowercase. If the member is supported by the object, the VBA editor will adjust the spelling of the member's name the moment your pointer leaves the line.

For example, you can type the following:

Application.activeprinter

If the Application object supports the property ActivePrinter, the editor automatically changes the name of the property to Application.ActivePrinter when you press Enter (or move the pointer to another line).

Another limitation of previous versions of VBA was the lack of Forms. VBA macros were limited to the user interface of the application. You could add a few dialog boxes, but not elaborate Forms, such as the ones you can design with Visual Basic. VBA 5 has a Form Designer that lets you design Forms, just as you do with Visual Basic, and incorporate them in a macro. As you can see, with a proper editor, debugging tools, and a Form Designer window, VBA is no longer a macro language. It's a fully developed language with which you can write real applications in the environment of Office 97, not just customize applications.

Recording Macros

The example of a paragraph formatting macro is a trivial one, but you will see shortly how to develop more elaborate macros that behave like applications. But let's start with the simplest operation of all—recording a macro.

No matter how elaborate your VBA programs are, macros are indispensable. The Macro Recorder will generate most of the trivial code of your macro. As you will see, VBA is a verbose language, and the more code you can generate automatically, the better—less typing, fewer chances for mistakes, and less testing.

Let's start by looking at the VBA code of a common operation, searching for a string:

1. Start Word and open an existing file, or create a new one and enter some text.

2. Choose Tools ➤ Macro ➤ Record New Macro to open the Record Macro dialog box:

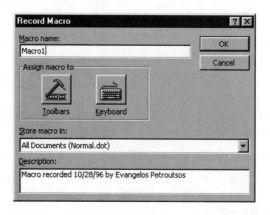

3. In the Macro Name box, enter the name of the new macro. You can click the Toolbars or the Keyboard button to assign the new macro to a keystroke or to the toolbar. (This is a simple test, and you don't need to make the macro permanent. We'll delete it shortly anyway.)

4. The default macro name is Macro1, and if a macro by the same name exists, Word will ask you whether it should overwrite it.

5. Click OK, and you will see a small window on your screen, with two VCR-style buttons: Stop Recording and Pause Recording. Every action you perform on the current document with the keyboard or the mouse from now on will be recorded. To pause the recording of the commands (say you want to look up the Help files), click the Pause Recording button. To end the recording of the macro, click the Stop Recording button.

Now perform the following actions:

1. Press Ctrl+Home to move to the top of the document.

2. Choose Edit ➤ Find to open the Find and Replace dialog box.

3. In the Find What box, enter the string you want to look for (in this example, our text included the word *macro,* and we searched on that string), and click the Find Next button. Word locates and highlights the first instance of the word *macro* in the document. Because we did not check the Match Case box or the Find Whole Words Only box, it locates any instance of the word, regardless of case or whether the word is part of another word.

4. The macro is now recorded. Click the Stop Recording button.

Now let's open the macro to see its code. Follow these steps:

1. Choose Tools ➤ Macro ➤ Macros to open the window where all available macros are displayed.

2. Select the Macro1 entry (or whatever the macro's name is) and then click the Edit button to open the VB Editor window. You will see the listing of the Macro1 macro, as shown in Figure 21.1.

FIGURE 21.1:

In the Visual Basic Editor window, you can edit any macro recorded in a Word session.

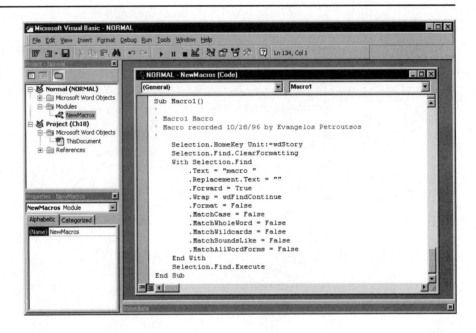

Code 21.1   **The Macro1 Macro**

```
Sub Macro1()
'
' Macro01 Macro
' Macro recorded 10/26/96 by Evangelos Petroutsos
'
    Selection.HomeKey Unit:=wdStory
    Selection.Find.ClearFormatting
    With Selection.Find
        .Text = "macro"
        .Replacement.Text = ""
        .Forward = True
        .Wrap = wdFindContinue
        .Format = False
        .MatchCase = False
        .MatchWholeWord = False
        .MatchWildcards = False
```

```
        .MatchSoundsLike = False
        .MatchAllWordForms = False
    End With
    Selection.Find.Execute
End Sub
```

The first line of code represents the Ctrl+Home keystroke, which took us to the beginning of the document. All the following lines represent the Find operation. Since we are not replacing the word we found, you can omit the following line:

```
.Replacement.Text = ""
```

To find another word, simply replace the string macro with any other string. If you want to perform a more elaborate search, use the macro recorder to capture the appropriate commands. Figure 21.2 shows the Find and Replace dialog box with the arguments of another, more complicated search operation. By specifying the word *replace* and checking the Find All Word Forms box, you're telling Word to find not only the instances of the word *replace*, but the words *replaced* and *replacing* as well. The new macro is identical to the previous one, except for the last option:

```
.MatchAllWordForms = True
```

FIGURE 21.2:

The Find and Replace dialog box for a more complicated search

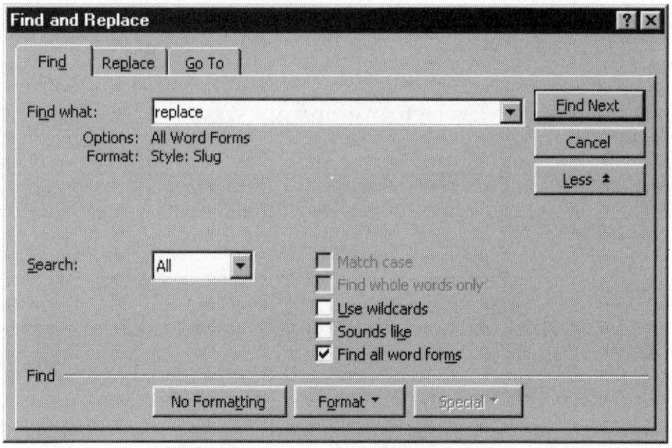

The With Structure

You are probably familiar with the With structure. It's a shorthand notation for referencing objects' properties and methods. Objects can have really long names. The expression Selection.Find represents the Find dialog box, and each option in this dialog box is another property of this object. The expression Selection.Find.Text represents the text to search for.

Instead of repeating the object's name over and over (thus making the code harder to type and read), you can type the names of the properties within a With structure. The object name following the With keyword determines the object to which these properties apply.

Developing a "Real World" Word Macro

Let's look at a more meaningful example of automating Word. When preparing long documents with many figures, such as this chapter, we avoid inserting figures in the text. This would slow down many normal editing operations, not to mention that, in general, the figures are not available at the time of the writing or they must be revised later.

To make sure that we have all the figures we need for a chapter, we like to collect all the figure captions at the end of the chapter or in a separate file and use this file to capture the appropriate figures. When all figure captions, along with their numbers, are listed in the same order as they appear in the text, we can easily check whether we've skipped a figure number. This simple operation is done with the CollectCaptions macro we'll develop in this section.

NOTE   You'll find the CollectCaptions macro in the `Ch21\Wmacro` folder on the CD that comes with this book.

The CollectCaptions macro is based on the one you recorded earlier, only it repeats the search as many times as necessary to extract all the captions from the text. Clearly, we must place the lines generated earlier by the Macro Recorder into a loop structure, which will repeat them as many times as there are captions in the document. The captions copied by the macro will be appended to a string variable, and, when done, we'll paste this variable at the end of the document.

To implement the new macro in the Visual Basic Editor of Word, follow these steps:

1. Start Word, and choose Tools ≻ Macro ≻ Visual Basic Editor to open the VB Editor window for Word, which looks a lot like the Visual Basic window.

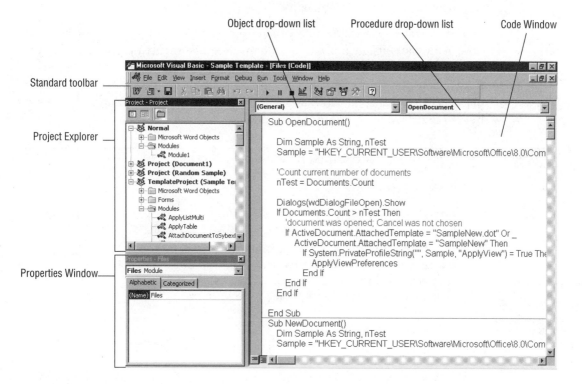

Object drop-down list   Procedure drop-down list   Code Window

Standard toolbar

Project Explorer

Properties Window

NOTE

In the next chapter, we'll explore the components of the Visual Basic Editor interface in detail.

---

2. Open the Code window and create a new subroutine and name it Collect-Captions. In other words, enter the following lines in the Code window:

```
Sub CollectCaptions()
End Sub
```

3. Copy the contents of the Macro1 macro and paste them in the new procedure's body.

The specification `.Wrap = wdFindContinue` tells Word to ask the user whether to continue searching the document from the beginning once it reaches the end. Since we are going to start the Find operation at the first character of the document, we don't need to display this prompt; so remove this line from the code or comment it out as we've done in the listing.

Next, we must decide how many times to loop. Since we don't know in advance how many captions the document contains, we must set up a While…Wend loop that will keep finding the next caption until a search operation ends unsuccessfully. When a Find operation ends unsuccessfully, the Found property of the Find object is False. Our code will examine the value of this property and end the loop by setting the value of the FindMore variable.

Code 21.2   **The CollectCaptions Macro**

```
Sub CollectCaptions()
'
' CollectCaptions Macro
' Macro recorded 10/25/96 by Evangelos Petroutsos
' This macro collects all figure captions in the text
' and appends them to the document.
' Captions are formatted with the Caption style, which is
' used to locate them in the text

Dim CaptionsText As String

' Move to beginning of document
Selection.HomeKey Unit:=wdStory
' Set up the Find & Replace dialog box's parameters
Selection.Find.ClearFormatting
Selection.Find.Style = ActiveDocument.Styles("Caption")
With Selection.Find
    .Text = ""
    .Replacement.Text = ""
    .Forward = True
'    .Wrap = wdFindAsk
    .Format = True
    .MatchCase = False
    .MatchWholeWord = False
    .MatchWildcards = False
    .MatchSoundsLike = False
    .MatchAllWordForms = False
```

```
End With
' Now execute the Find operation
Selection.Find.Execute
CaptionsText = CaptionsText & Selection.Text
If (Not Selection.Find.Found) Or Selection.End Then
    FindMore = False
End If
FindMore = True
' Repeat the Find operation as long as there are more instances
' of the text being searched
While FindMore
    Selection.Find.ClearFormatting
    Selection.Find.Execute
' Stop searching if last find operation was not successful
    CaptionsText = CaptionsText & Selection.Text
    If (Not Selection.Find.Found) Then
        FindMore = False
    End If
Wend
' Insert spaces before the list of captions
CaptionsText = vbCrLf & vbCrLf & vbCrLf & "L I S T   O F   C A P T I O N S"
& vbCrLf & CaptionsText
' Append list of captions to text
Selection.EndKey Unit:=wdStory
Selection.Text = CaptionsText
' Set Normal style, or else it may be formatted in the
' document's last paragraph's style
Selection.Style = "Normal"
End Sub
```

Figure 21.3 shows the CollectCaptions macro being edited in Word's Visual Basic Editor. Notice that the Find object's properties need not be defined at each iteration. We can simply call the Execute method of the Find object. Each time a new caption is located in the text, we copy it and append it to the local variable *CaptionsText*. When the loop ends, we paste the variable *CaptionsText* at the end of the document. We move to the end of the document and paste the string as a Selection object. This highlights the new text so that we can apply the Normal format to it. If you don't reformat the pasted text, it will be formatted according to the format of the last paragraph in the document (which could be another caption, for all we know).

FIGURE 21.3:

The CollectCaptions macro being edited in the VBA Editor

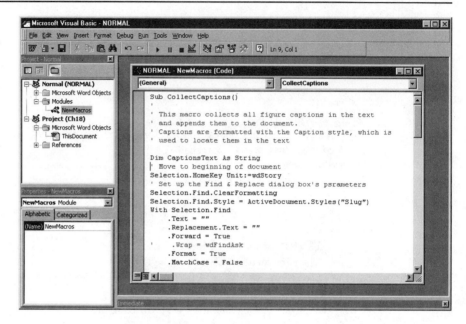

FIGURE 21.3:

The CollectCaptions macro being edited in the VBA Editor

Automating Office Applications

In this section, we'll explore how you can automate Office applications from within your Visual Basic applications. The idea is to exploit the functionality of the various applications without having to rewrite the code. One of the things you can do so well with Word is spell-check your documents, but this feature is useful in the context of other applications. If you want to add spell-checking capabilities to a VB application, you can "borrow" the spell-checking capabilities of Word and incorporate them in your application. You can even hide Word, and users need not know you are contacting Word to do all the work. However, the Word application must be installed on the host system.

To access an Office application from within a VB application, you must first create an object variable that references the desired application, just as you did for the ActiveX components you developed in Chapter 10. You declare this variable as Object, with the following statement (change the name of the variable according to the application you want to access):

```
Dim AppExcel As Object
```

Rich Services and the Operating System

Shouldn't basic services, such as document editing, spell-checking, charting, and so on, be part of the operating system? Right now, they are part of Office applications, and you can't assume that Office applications will be available on every system.

It would work much better if these basic features were part of the operating system, but these features are costly. Someone has to pay for their development, and Microsoft decided that including them with Office applications is the best way to recover the cost.

Eventually, all these services may end up in the operating system, and you will be able to expect that your applications will run on every host system. You can also purchase a spell-checker and install it along with your application. However, Office applications are popular, and you can expect to find them installed on many host systems. Moreover, by developing custom applications based on the Office applications, you may be able to justify the cost of installing Office on a stand-alone system or on a corporate network.

To actually instantiate the AppExcel, you use the CreateObject or the GetObject function. The CreateObject function creates a new instance of an object. To create a new instance of Excel from within your VB application, use this statement:

```
Set AppExcel = CreateObject("Excel.Application")
```

The string Excel.Application is the programmatic ID of the application that supplies the object. This variable references the application itself. The CreateObject function starts a new instance of the application (or ActiveX component), even if an instance of it is already running.

If one or more instances of the application is already running, you can contact this instance of the application instead of creating a new one. The obvious advantage of this technique is that no additional resources are required. To do so, use the GetObject function, whose syntax is:

```
Set objectvariable = GetObject([pathname] [, progID])
```

The pathname argument can be the path to an existing file or to an empty string, or it can be omitted entirely. If you omit it, the *progID* argument is required. If you specify the path to an existing file, the GetObject function will create an object using the information stored in the file (it will start the application associated with this file). If it's a DOC file, for example, it opens the specified file in an existing instance of Word. If Word isn't running at the moment, it will be started, and the specified file will be opened in its main window. Using an empty string for the first argument causes GetObject to act like CreateObject—it creates a new object of the class whose programmatic identifier is *progID*.

To open the file SALES97.XLS with Excel, you can use the statements

```
Dim XLObj As Object
Set XLObj = GetObject("C:\SALES\SALES97.xls")
```

When the second line executes, the file SALES97.xls either opens in a running instance of Excel or starts a new instance of Excel and opens the XLS file in it. When you supply the *pathname* argument (the filename of a document), you need not specify the *progID* argument.

If you omit the name of the file in the GetObject() function, the function returns a handle to the running instance of Excel or an error message if Excel isn't running. If you want to use the running instance of Excel to evaluate a math expression (an operation that doesn't entail any changes in the currently open document), you can contact a running instance of Excel, call its Evaluate method, and then release the object variable, as shown here:

```
Dim XLObj As Object
Set XLObj = GetObject(, "Excel.Application")
If Err.Number <> 0 Then
    ' Excel isn't running, you must start a new instance
    Set XLObj = CreateObject("Excel.Application")
End If
X = XLObj.Evaluate("3*sin(2/log(45.5))"
```

Object Variables and Early Binding

The object variables we created in the previous section are not of a specific type. As we mentioned time and again in the second part of this book, Visual Basic doesn't have enough information about them at design or compile time to check the validity of their members. This means that the variables will be late bound; not only will the application be slower at run time, but any reference to nonexistent members will cause a run-time error. Whenever possible, declare object variables with specific types.

If you enter the following line in the Visual Basic Editor (not the VBA Editor), you would expect to see a variable type that matches the object you want to reference.

```
Dim AppWord As
```

Such a type doesn't appear in the drop-down list. Does this mean you can't use early binding with object variables that reference Office applications and/or their objects? Not at all. You don't see the Word or Excel object in the Auto List Members drop-down box because Visual Basic doesn't know that you want to reference another application from within your program. When the line that sets the object variable is reached during execution, Visual Basic locates the application you are referencing in the Registry and starts it in the background.

To be able to declare the *AppWord* and *AppExcel* variables with an explicit type (and not as Object type), you must first add a reference to the type library of the application you want to reference. To do so, follow these steps:

1. Choose Project ➤ References to open the References dialog box.

2. Check the boxes Microsoft Excel 8.0 Object Library and Microsoft Word 8.0 Object Library, as shown in Figure 21.4.

FIGURE 21.4:

Use the References dialog box to add the object libraries of other applications to your Visual Basic application.

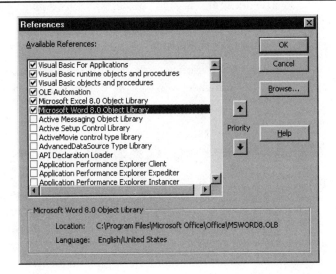

NOTE   See Chapter 22 for much more information on the References dialog box.

3. Now enter the same line in the Form's declaration section and scan the list of available variable types in the Auto List Members drop-down list box (shown in Figure 21.5).

FIGURE 21.5:

Add the object libraries of the applications you want to reference, and their types will appear in the Auto List Members box as you enter VB code.

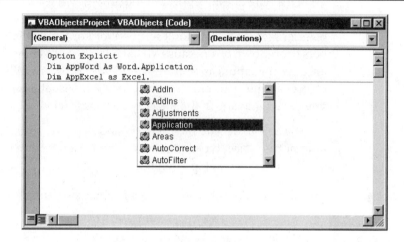

The declarations of the object variables *AppExcel* and *AppWord* should be

```
Dim AppWord As Word.Application
Dim AppExcel As Excel.Application
```

These declarations are all the information Visual Basic needs to early bind the variables and check the validity of their members at design time.

The VBAObjects Application

Now that we have seen how to create object variables that represent the Office applications, let's build an application that demonstrates these techniques. The VBAObjects application lets you start a new instance of Excel or Word, create a new Word document or a new Excel worksheet, and manipulate it from within a Visual Basic application. The application's main Form is shown in Figure 21.6.

NOTE   You'll find the VBAObjects application in the Ch21\VBAObjs folder on the CD that comes with this book.

When you run VBAObjects, all buttons are disabled except for the two buttons that reference Excel and Word. When these buttons are clicked, the program creates a new instance of Excel or Word and enables the remaining buttons on the Form. (We'll discuss the operation of these buttons later in this chapter.)

FIGURE 21.6:

The main Form of the VBAObjects application

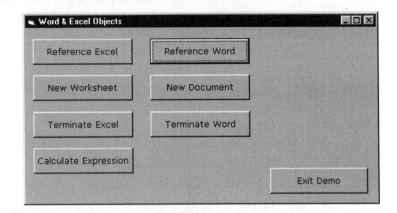

The object variables that represent the two applications are declared outside any procedure:

```
Dim AppWord As Word.Application
Dim AppExcel As Word.Excel
```

Both buttons create a new instance of the application, and they assign it to an object variable, which is used later by the other procedures in the program.

| **Code 21.3** | **The Click Event Handler of the Reference Excel Button** |

```
Private Sub Command1_Click()

    Screen.MousePointer = vbHourglass
    Set AppExcel = CreateObject("Excel.Application")
    Screen.MousePointer = vbDefault
    Command3.Enabled = True
    Command5.Enabled = True
    Command8.Enabled = True

End Sub
```

The code for the Reference Word button is similar, except that it passes the Class Word.Application to the CreateObject method.

We will examine the code behind the other buttons on the VBAObjects Form later, but you can run the application now. Instantiate the *AppExcel* and *AppWord* object variables, and then break the application and check out the members of the two object variables in the Immediate window. (In the examples below, the results displayed in the Immediate window are indented to the right.) You can find the names of the applications that these two variables reference.

```
Print AppExcel.Name
    Microsoft Excel
Print AppWord.Name
    Microsoft Word
```

Or you can ask Excel to evaluate math expressions:

```
Print AppExcel.Evaluate ("log(999.333)")
    2.99971022893117
```

You can use the AppWord object to find out whether a word is spelled correctly:

```
Print AppWord.CheckSpelling("Antroid")
    False
```

Or you can display the names of the fonts installed:

```
For i=1 To AppWord.FontNames.Count: Print AppWord.FontNames(i):Next
    Times New Roman
    Arial
    Courier New
    {more font names}
```

Simply type the name of the object variable followed by a period and then select a member (property or method) from the drop-down list that appears automatically, as shown in Figure 21.7.

You might want to change the declarations of the *AppWord* and *AppExcel* object variables to generic object variables to see how they are going to affect the application at design time and at run time. The Auto List Members feature will be practically useless, and all references to the wrong members will cause run-time errors.

FIGURE 21.7:

Use the Visual Basic Immediate window to check out the members of the *AppWord* and *AppExcel* object variables.

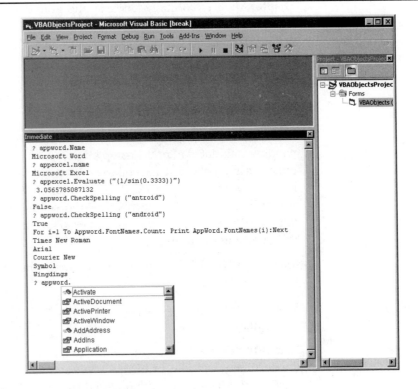

The Application Object

When an application is executed in the background, you can access it via the Application object, which represents the running application and is common to all Office applications. You can think of the Application object as a container for the application's objects. Besides being your back door to the running application, the Application object has a few members of its own. Here are the most important:

ActivePrinter   Returns or sets the name of the active printer.

ActiveWindow   Returns the handle to the application window that has the focus.

Caption   Returns or sets the string that appears on the application window's title bar. You can use this property to find out whether a window contains a specific document.

DisplayAlerts   Normally, Office applications display dialog boxes to confirm certain actions (such as deleting a large amount of data) or irreversible actions (such as closing a document without saving it). If you are running the application in the background and you don't want users to see any dialog boxes other than the ones displayed by your application, set this property to False. When your procedure ends, the DisplayAlerts property is reset to True automatically.

ScreenUpdating   Normally, when a macro is executed, the application's window is updated after the completion of each command. This is usually unnecessary, as these actions take place too quickly and the user can't follow them anyway. In general, it's a good idea to turn off the updating of the screen from within your macros. To do so, set the ScreenUpdating property to False. When you are done, remember to turn it on again; this property isn't reset automatically.

Top, Left   These two properties return or set the position of the application's window.

Width, Height   These two properties return or set the dimensions of the application's window.

UsableWidth, UsableHeight   These properties return the dimensions of the document window within the application's window. Normally, they are the window's total width (or height), minus the space taken by scroll bars, menu bars, and toolbars.

Visible   Hides (if False) or displays (if True) the application's window.

Windows   This property is a collection of Window objects that represent the application's windows.

WindowState   This property returns or sets the state of the application's main window. The window's state can be:

Maximized   xlMaximized or wWindowStateMaximize

Minimized   xlMinimized or wWindowStateMinimize

Normal   xlNormal or wWindowStateNormal

The Application object supports a few methods as well, which are different depending on the application. You can use these methods to tap into the functionality unique to the application. Both Excel's and Word's Application objects provide the OnTime method, which executes a procedure at a specified time. Its syntax is:

```
Application.OnTime when, name, tolerance
```

The argument When is a date and time expression indicating when the procedure will be invoked; Name is the name of the procedure that will be executed, and the Tolerance argument is the delay (in seconds) you are willing to tolerate, with respect to the argument When.

Another common method is the Move method, which repositions the window on the screen and is equivalent to changing the Top and Left properties. The methods that apply to all applications are more or less generic. However, a few methods expose unique functionality that you can access from within your applications. One of them is the CheckSpelling method, which can spell-check a word or an entire document. The CheckSpelling method is a member of the Application object and of the Selection object, which represents the current selection. When used as a method of the Application object, its syntax is:

```
Application.SpellCheck(word, CustomDictionary, IgnoreUpperCase)
```

The Word argument is the word to be spelled, CustomDictionary is the filename of a custom dictionary, and *IgnoreUpperCase* specifies whether words in upper-case will be ignored. The SpellCheck method returns a True/False result, indicating whether the word is spelled correctly. The same method is also available with Excel's Application object.

In the following sections, we are going to look at the basic objects of Word and Excel, and we'll present a few examples. In the following chapters, we are going to look at each application's objects in depth and show you how to automate Office applications with macros or from within your VB applications.

Working with Word VBA Objects

Word provides numerous objects with which you can program any action that can be carried out with menu commands. Under the Application object is the Documents collection, which contains a Document object for each open document. Using an object variable of Document type, you can access any open document (or create and open a new document). The most important object that each document exposes is the Range object, which represents a contiguous section of text.

This section can be words, part of a word, characters, or even the entire document. Using the Range object's methods, you can insert new text, format or delete existing text, and so on.

To address specific units of text, use the following collections:

- Paragraphs, which are made up of Paragraph objects

- Words, which are made up of Word objects

- Characters, which are made up of Character objects

These objects represent a paragraph, word, or character in the object to which they apply. For example, if you access the Paragraphs collection of a specific document, you retrieve all the paragraphs of the document. If you apply the same method to the current selection (represented by the Selection object), you retrieve all the paragraphs in the selected text.

The Documents Collection and the Document Object

The first object under the Word Application object hierarchy is the Document object, which is any document that can be opened with Word or any document that can be displayed in Word's window. All open documents are represented by a Documents collection that is made up of Document objects. Like all other collections, it supports the Count property (the number of open documents), the Add method, which adds a new document, and the Remove method, which closes an existing one. To access an open document, you can use the Item method of the Documents collection, specifying the document's index:

```
Application.Documents.Item(1)
```

or the document's name:

```
Application.Documents.Item("VBHandbook.doc")
```

Since Item is the collection default property, you can omit its name altogether:

```
Application.Documents(1)
```

To open an existing document, use the Documents collection's Open method, whose syntax is:

```
Documents.Open(fileName)
```

The *fileName* argument is the document file's path name.

To create a new document, use the Documents collection's Add method, which accepts two optional arguments:

```
Documents.Add (template, newTemplate)
```

The argument *template* specifies the name of a template file to be used as the basis for the new document. The *newTemplate* argument is a Boolean value. If it's set to True, Word creates a new template file.

Most of the operations you will perform on text apply to the active document, which is represented by the ActiveDocument object. This is the document in the active Word window. You can also make any document active by calling the Activate method of the Document object. To make the document MyNotes.doc active, use the following statement:

```
Documents("MyNotes.doc").Activate
```

After the execution of this statement, the MyNotes.doc document is active, and your code can refer to it through the object ActiveDocument.

Objects That Represent Text

The basic object for accessing text in a Word document is the Range object, which represents a contiguous segment of text. To extract some text from a document, you can use the Document object's Range method, which accepts as arguments the positions of the starting and ending characters in the text. The syntax of the Range method is:

```
Document.Range(start, end)
```

The *start* and *end* arguments are two numeric values. Oddly enough, the first character's position in the document is zero. The statement

```
Range1 = Document.Range (0, 99)
```

extracts the first 100 character of the document represented by the *Document* object variable. These characters are assigned to the *Range1* object variable, which represents a Range object.

In the previous expressions, the *Document* variable must first be set to reference an existing object, with a statement such as the following:

```
Set Document = Documents(1)
```

You can also replace the variable *Document* with the built-in object AppWord.ActiveDocument, which represents the active document (the one you've set with the Activate method).

Words, sentences, and paragraphs are more meaningful units of text than characters. We mentioned these collections earlier in this chapter, and you'll find more information on them in the following chapters. The Word, Sentence, and Paragraph objects are better suited for text manipulation, and you commonly use these objects to access documents. These objects, however, don't support all the properties of the Range object. Therefore, in addition to the Range method, there is a Range property, which returns a Word, Sentence, or Paragraph object as a Range.

For example, the statement

```
Document.Paragraphs(3).Range
```

returns the third paragraph in the document as a Range object. You can then access the Range object's properties to manipulate the third paragraph. The Paragraph object doesn't have a Font property or a Select method. To change the appearance of the third paragraph in the document, you can use a statement such as the following:

```
Document.Paragraphs(3).Font.Bold = True
```

Document is a properly declared Document variable, or you can use the App-Word.ActiveDocument object.

The following statement selects (highlights) the same paragraph:

```
Document.Paragraphs(3).Select
```

Once a paragraph (or any other piece of text) is selected, you can apply all types of processing to it (edit it, move it to another location, format it, and so on).

The two methods of the Range object that you will use most often are:

- InsertAfter, which inserts a string of text after the specified Range

- InsertBefore, which inserts a string of text in front of the specified Range

The following statements insert a title at the beginning of the document and a closing paragraph at the end:

```
AppWord.ActiveDocument.Select
AppWord.ActiveDocument.Range.InsertBefore "This is the document's title"
AppWord.ActiveDocument.Range.InsertAfter "This is the closing paragraph"
```

The Select method of the ActiveDocument object selects the entire text. The selected text is assigned to the Range object. The InsertBefore and InsertAfter methods place some text before and after the Range object.

VBAObjects: Creating a New Document

Now we can examine the code behind the New Document button of the VBAObjects application, which we looked at earlier in this chapter. When this button is clicked, the program does the following:

- Connects to a new instance of Word

- Creates a new document

- Inserts some text and formats it

- Counts the paragraphs, words, and characters in the new document and displays them in a message box

These actions take place from within the Visual Basic application, and Word is running in the background. The user doesn't see Word's window, not even as an icon on the taskbar. Clicking the OK button in the message box opens the Word window and displays the newly created document, as shown in Figure 21.8. At this point you can edit the document or shut down Word.

The code behind the New Document button is straightforward. It uses the object AppWord.Documents(1).Range to manipulate the text (insert new paragraphs and format them). Notice how it changes the alignment of the first text paragraph with the Alignment property of the Paragraph object.

FIGURE 21.8:

This document is created by a Visual Basic application, which manipulates the objects exposed by Word.

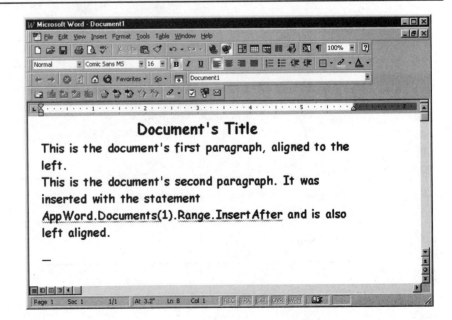

Code 21.4 **The New Document Button**

```
Private Sub Command4_Click()
Dim wDoc As Document
Dim tmpText As String
Dim parCount As Long, wordCount As Long, charCount As Long
Dim msg As String

    If AppWord.Documents.Count = 0 Then
        AppWord.Documents.Add
    End If
    AppWord.Documents(1).Range.InsertAfter "Document's Title" & vbCr
    AppWord.Documents(1).Range.Font.Bold = True
    AppWord.Documents(1).Range.Font.Size = 16
    AppWord.Documents(1).Range.Font.Name = "Comic Sans MS"
    AppWord.Documents(1).Range.InsertAfter "This the document's first _
        paragraph, aligned to the left." & vbCr
    AppWord.Documents(1).Range.InsertAfter "This the document's second _
        paragraph. "
    AppWord.Documents(1).Range.InsertAfter "It was inserted with the _
        statement "
    AppWord.Documents(1).Range.InsertAfter _
        "AppWord.Documents(1).Range.InsertAfter "
    AppWord.Documents(1).Range.InsertAfter "and is also left aligned." _
        & vbCrLf

    parCount = AppWord.Documents(1).Paragraphs.Count
    wordCount = AppWord.Documents(1).Words.Count
    charCount = AppWord.Documents(1).Characters.Count
    msg = "The new document contains " & vbCrLf
    msg = msg & parCount & " paragraphs" & vbCrLf
    msg = msg & wordCount & " words" & vbCrLf
    msg = msg & charCount & " characters"
    MsgBox msg

    AppWord.Documents(1).Paragraphs(1).Alignment = _
        wdAlignParagraphCenter
    AppWord.Visible = True

End Sub
```

The code behind the Terminate Word button is more interesting. To shut down Word, all you really need is the Quit method of the Application object. It would be quite simple if Word were running in the background only. But since we display Word's window, the user can close it before switching back to the VBAObjs application. If we attempt to close an application that has been closed already, we'll end up with a run-time error. To avoid a run-time error, the procedure that terminates Word uses an error handler.

The program closes Word with the Quit method and resumes with the next statement, if an error occurs. The next executable statement attempts to read the name of the application. If the error occurs because this particular instance of Word was already closed, an error will occur again, and the program will simply disable the New Document and Terminate Word buttons. If no error occurs, the two buttons are not disabled and the procedure ends.

Code 21.5   **The Terminate Word Button**

```
Private Sub Command6_Click()

    On Error Resume Next
    AppWord.DisplayAlerts = False
    AppWord.Quit
Dim wRunning As String
    wRunning = AppWord.Application.Name
    If Error Then
        Command4.Enabled = False
        Command6.Enabled = False
    End If
End Sub
```

Spell-Checking Documents

One of the most useful features of Word (and of every Office application) is the ability to spell-check a document. This functionality is also exposed by Word's VBA objects, and you can borrow it for use within your VB applications. This is not only possible, it's quite simple. To call upon Word's spell-checking routines, you need to know about two objects:

- The ProofreadingErrors collection
- The SpellingSuggestions collection

The ProofreadingErrors collection is a property of the Range object, and it contains the misspelled words in the specified Range. If you want Word to spell-check a range of text and populate the ProofreadingErrors collection, call the Range object's SpellingError method. This method returns a result that must be stored in an object variable of type *ProofreadingErrors*:

```
SpellCollection As ProofreadingErrors
Set SpellCollection = DRange.SpellingErrors
```

The second line populates the *SpellCollection* variable with the misspelled words. You can then set up a loop to read the words from the collection.

Besides locating spelling errors, Word can also suggest a list of alternate spellings or words that sound like the misspelled one. To retrieve the list of alternate words, you call the GetSpellingSuggestions methods of the Application object, passing the misspelled word as an argument. Notice that this is a method of the Application object, not the Range object you are spell-checking. The results returned by the GetSpellingSuggestions method must be stored in a similar object variable, declared as SpellingSuggestions type:

```
Public CorrectionsCollection As SpellingSuggestions
Set CorrectionsCollection = AppWord.GetSpellingSuggestions("antroid")
```

The second line retrieves the suggested alternatives for the word *antroid*. To scan the list of suggested words, you set up a loop that retrieves all the elements of the CorrectionsCollection collection. The example in the next section demonstrates the use of both methods from within a Visual Basic application.

The SpellDoc Application

In this section, we are going to look at the SpellDoc application (see Figure 21.9), a VB application that uses Word's methods to spell-check a document.

NOTE   You'll find the SpellDoc application in the **Ch21\Spelldoc** folder on the CD that comes with this book.

The user can enter text in the multiline TextBox control (or paste it from another application) and then spell-check it by clicking the Check Document button.

The Spelldoc application's
main Form

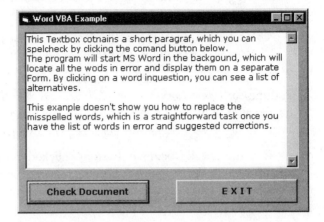

The results, which are the misspelled words, are displayed on a different Form, shown in Figure 21.10. The ListBox control on the left shows all the misspelled words returned by Word. Word can not only locate misspelled words, but suggest alternatives as well. To view the correct words suggested by Word for each misspelled word, click the corresponding entry in the list of misspelled words. The Spelldoc application doesn't replace the misspelled word in the document with the selected alternative, but this is straightforward code that manipulates strings. Once you have the list of misspelled words and the alternatives, you can design any number of interfaces that allow the user to correct the original document with point-and-click operations.

This Form of the Spelldoc
application displays the
misspelled words and
possible alternatives.

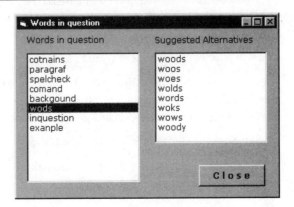

The program uses three public variables, which are declared as follows:

```
Public AppWord As Application
Public CorrectionsCollection As SpellingSuggestions
Public SpellCollection As ProofreadingErrors
```

The *SpellCollection* variable is a collection that contains all the misspelled words, and the *CorrectionsCollection* variable is another collection that contains the suggested alternatives. The *CorrectionsCollection* variable's contents are assigned every time the user clicks another misspelled word.

When the Check Document button is clicked, the program contacts the Word application. First, it attempts to connect to an existing instance of Word, with the GetObject function. If no instance of Word is currently running, it starts a new instance of Word.

Code 21.6   The Check Document Button

```
Set AppWord = GetObject("Word.Application")
    If AppWord Is Nothing Then
        Set AppWord = CreateObject("Word.Application")
        If AppWord Is Nothing Then
            MsgBox "Could not start Word. Application will end"
            End
        End If
    End If
```

After contact with Word is established, the program creates a new document and copies the text there, using the InsertAfter method of the Range object:

```
AppWord.Dcouments.Add
DRange.InsertAfter Text1.Text
```

Now comes the interesting part. The VB code calls the Range object's SpellingErrors method, which returns a collection of Word objects. The result of the SpellingErrors method is assigned to the object variable *SpellCollection*:

```
Set SpellCollection = DRange.SpellingErrors
```

The following lines add the words contained in the *SpellCollection* variable to the left list of the second Form, and then they display the Form.

Code 21.7   **The Check Document Button**

```
Private Sub Command1_Click()
Dim DRange As Range

    Me.Caption = "starting word ..."
On Error Resume Next
    Set AppWord = GetObject("Word.Application")
    If AppWord Is Nothing Then
        Set AppWord = CreateObject("Word.Application")
        If AppWord Is Nothing Then
            MsgBox "Could not start Word. Application will end"
            End
        End If
    End If
On Error GoTo ErrorHandler
    AppWord.Documents.Add
    Me.Caption = "checking words..."
    Set DRange = AppWord.ActiveDocument.Range
    DRange.InsertAfter Text1.Text
    Set SpellCollection = DRange.SpellingErrors
    If SpellCollection.Count > 0 Then
        SuggestionsForm.List1.Clear
        SuggestionsForm.List2.Clear
        For iWord = 1 To SpellCollection.Count
            SuggestionsForm!List1.AddItem SpellCollection.Item(iWord)
        Next
    End If
    Me.Caption = "Word VBA Example"
    SuggestionsForm.Show
    Exit Sub

ErrorHandler:
    MsgBox "The following error occurred during the document's
spelling" & vbCrLf & Err.Description
End Sub
```

On the second Form of the application, all the code is concentrated in the "Words in Question" list's Click event. Every time an entry in this List is clicked, the code calls the AppWord object's GetSpellingSuggestions method, passing the selected word as an argument. Notice that we add 1 to the List's ListIndex property to offset the fact that the indexing of the elements of a collection starts at one, while the indexing of the elements of a ListBox control starts at zero. The GetSpellingSuggestions method returns another collection, with the suggested words, which are placed in the list on the right.

Code 21.8   **The List's Click Event**

```
Private Sub List1_Click()

    Screen.MousePointer = vbHourglass
    Set CorrectionsCollection = _
        AppWord.GetSpellingSuggestions(SpellCollection.Item _
        (List1.ListIndex + 1))
    List2.Clear
    For iSuggWord = 1 To CorrectionsCollection.Count
        List2.AddItem CorrectionsCollection.Item(iSuggWord)
    Next
    Screen.MousePointer = vbDefault

End Sub
```

The SpellDoc application can become the starting point for many VB applications that require spell-checking but that don't need powerful editing features. This situation isn't common, but in some cases you might want to customize spelling. In a mail-aware application, for example, you can spell-check the text and exclude URLs and e-mail addresses. You first scan the words returned by the SpellingErrors method to check which ones contain special characters and omit them.

As you can see, tapping into the power of the Office applications isn't really complicated. Once you familiarize yourself with the objects of these applications, you can access the Office applications by manipulating a few properties and calling the methods of these objects.

Working with Excel VBA Objects

The objects that Excel exposes have different names, but they form an equally sensible and structured hierarchy for accessing data stored in a tabular arrangement. Just as Word's basic unit of information is the text segment (not characters or words), Excel's basic unit of information is a Range. A Range object can contain a single cell or an entire worksheet (and everything in between).

The Application object represents an instance of Excel, and it supports most of the basic properties and methods of Word's Application object. In addition, it supports a few more methods that are unique to Excel. The most important methods of Excel's Application object are:

- Calculate
- OnKey
- Evaluate

The Calculate method recalculates all open worksheets. The OnKey method allows the programmer to specify a procedure to be executed each time the user presses a specific keystroke. The syntax of this method is

```
Application.OnKey(key, procedure)
```

The Key argument represents the keystrokes that will initiate a procedure, and the Procedure argument is the procedure that will be executed each time the specified key combination is pressed. Table 21.1 shows the strings you can use for the Key argument.

TABLE 21.1: The Settings of the OnKey Method's Key Argument

Key	Expression
Arrow Dn	"{DOWN}"
Arrow Left	"{LEFT}"
Arrow Rt	"{RIGHT}"
Arrow Up	"{UP}"
Backspace	"{BACKSPACE}"
Break	"{BREAK}"
Caps Lock	"{CAPSLOCK}"
Delete	"{DELETE}", "{DEL}"
End	"{END}"

Continued on next page

TABLE 21.1 CONTINUED: The Settings of the OnKey Method's Key Argument

Key	Expression
Enter	"{ENTER}", "{~}"
Esc	"{ESCAPE}", "{ESC}"
Home	"{HOME}"
Help	"{HELP}"
Insert	"{INSERT}"
Num Lock	"{NUMLOCK}"
PgDn	"{PGDN}"
PgUp	"{PGUP}"
Scroll Lock	"{SCROLLLOCK}"
Tab	"{TAB}"
F1–F12	"{F1}"–"{F12}"

The Evaluate method evaluates math expressions and returns the result. The statement

```
Application.Evaluate "cos(3/1.091)*log(3.499)"
```

returns a numeric value that is the value of the math expression passed to the Evaluate method as an argument. You can also use variables in your expressions, as long as you store their values in specific cells and use the addresses of these cells in the expression. The statement

```
Application.Evaluate "log(" & Application.Range("A1") & ")"
```

returns the logarithm of the numeric value stored in cell A1. The Range object represents one or more cells, depending on the address you supply. In this example, we addressed a single cell (A1). You will see how you can address and access specific cells in an Excel worksheet in the following two sections.

The Sheets Collection and the Sheet Object

Each workbook in Excel contains one or more worksheets. The Worksheets collection, which is similar to Word's Documents collection, contains a Worksheet object for each worksheet in the current workbook. To add a new worksheet, use the Add method, whose syntax is

```
Application.Worksheets.Add(before, after, count, type)
```

The Before and After arguments let you specify the order of the new worksheet in the workbook. You can specify one of the two arguments, and if you omit both, the new worksheet is inserted before the active worksheet. The Type argument specifies the type of the new worksheet and can have one of the following values:

xlWorksheet (the default value)

xlExcel4MacroSheet (a worksheet with Excel 4 macros)

xlExcel4IntlMacroSheet (a worksheet with Excel 4 international macros)

To access a worksheet, use the collection's Item method, passing the index or the worksheet's name as an argument. The following expressions are equivalent (if the second worksheet is named SalesData.xls):

```
Application.Worksheets.Item(2)
Application.Worksheets.Item("SalesData.xls")
```

Since Item is the collection default property, you can omit its name altogether:

```
Application.Worksheets(2)
```

Excel is an application for manipulating units of information stored in cells, but the basic object for accessing the contents of a worksheet is the Range object, which is a property of the Worksheet object. There are several ways to identify a Range (and we discuss them in detail in Chapter 23), but here's the basic syntax of the Range method:

```
Worksheet.Range(cell1:cell2)
```

Here, *cell1* and *cell2* are the addresses of the two cells that delimit a rectangular area on the worksheet. They are the addresses of the upper-left and lower-right corners of the selection (which is always rectangular; you can't select disjointed cells on a worksheet). Of course, you can address cells in several ways, but we will not discuss them here. In this section, we are going to use the standard Excel notation, which is a number for the row and a letter for the column (for example, C3 or A103).

You can also retrieve a single cell as a Range object, with the Cells method, whose syntax is

```
Worksheet.Cells(row, col)
```

The *row* and *col* arguments are the coordinates of the cell as numbers. Finally, the Rows and Columns methods return an entire row or column by number. The two expressions

```
Worksheet.Rows(3)
Worksheet.Columns("D")
```

return the third row and the fourth column as Range objects.

The Range object is not a collection, but you can access individual cells in a Range object with the Cells method. The Cells method accepts a single argument, which is the index of the cells in the range. The index 1 corresponds to the upper-left cell in the range, the index 2 corresponds to the second cell of the first row, and so on up to the last cell in the first row. The next index corresponds to the first cell of the second row and so on up to the last row. The Text property returns the cell's contents as a string, and the Value property returns the cell's contents as a string (if it's text) or as a numeric value (if it's numeric).

Another way to work with cells is to make a selection and access the properties and methods of the Selection object. To create a Selection object (which represents the cells that are highlighted if you select them with the mouse), use the Range object's Select method:

```
Range("A2:D2").Select
```

This statement creates a new Selection object, which you can access by name. Because a worksheet has only one selection, you don't have to specify any arguments. To change the appearance of the selection, for instance, use the Font property:

```
Selection.Font.Bold = True
Selection.Font.Size = 13
```

Now that we've looked at the basic objects of Excel VBA, we can examine the code behind the New Worksheet button of the VBAObjs application.

VBAObjects: Creating a New Worksheet

The VBAObjs application's New Worksheet button demonstrates how to access a worksheet, populate it with data, and then format the data. The program starts by examining the number of open workbooks. If no workbook is open, the program creates a new one. If a workbook exists, the program assigns it to the *wBook* object variable:

```
Dim wSheet As Worksheet
Dim wBook As Workbook

    If AppExcel.Workbooks.Count = 0 Then
        Debug.Print "Adding a new Workbook"
        Set wBook = AppExcel.Workbooks.Add
    End If
    Set wSheet = AppExcel.Sheets(1)
```

TIP

Before you run the VBAObjs application, be sure that you don't have an instance of Excel with useful data running. Or, add a new worksheet to the workbook, and give it a unique name (unless you don't mind overwriting the data of the open worksheet, of course).

The code then populates the first four cells on the first and second rows. Figure 21.11 shows the worksheet after it has been populated and formatted by the VBAObjs application. To populate the worksheet, the program uses the Cells object, as shown in the following lines:

```
wSheet.Cells(2, 1).Value = "1st QUARTER"
wSheet.Cells(3, 1).Value = 123.45
```

FIGURE 21.11:

The VBAObjs application populated and formatted this worksheet.

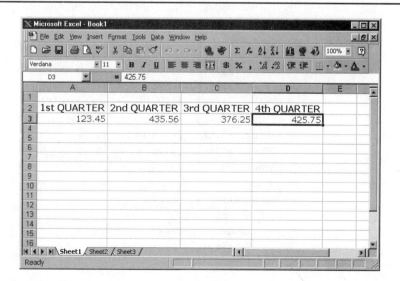

To format a range of cells, the code uses the Select method of the Range object to create a selection and then manipulate the appropriate properties of the Selection object. The following lines format the headings of the worksheet shown in Figure 21.11:

```
Range("A2:D2").Select
With Selection.Font
    .Name = "Verdana"
    .FontStyle = "Bold"
    .Size = 12
End With
```

While the worksheet is being populated and formatted, Excel is running in the background. Users can't see Excel, although they will notice activity (the disk is spinning, and the pointer assumes an hourglass shape for several seconds). After all operations complete, the program displays Excel by setting its Visible property to True.

Code 21.9   **The New Worksheet Button**

```
Private Sub Command3_Click()
Dim wSheet As Worksheet
Dim wBook As Workbook

    If AppExcel.Workbooks.Count = 0 Then
        Debug.Print "Adding a new Workbook"
        Set wBook = AppExcel.Workbooks.Add
    End If
    Set wSheet = AppExcel.Sheets(1)
    wSheet.Cells(2, 1).Value = "1st QUARTER"
    wSheet.Cells(2, 2).Value = "2nd QUARTER"
    wSheet.Cells(2, 3).Value = "3rd QUARTER"
    wSheet.Cells(2, 4).Value = "4th QUARTER"
    wSheet.Cells(3, 1).Value = 123.45
    wSheet.Cells(3, 2).Value = 435.56
    wSheet.Cells(3, 3).Value = 376.25
    wSheet.Cells(3, 4).Value = 425.75

    Range("A2:D2").Select
    With Selection.Font
        .Name = "Verdana"
        .FontStyle = "Bold"
```

```
            .Size = 12
        End With

        Range("A3:D3").Select
        With Selection.Font
            .Name = "Verdana"
            .FontStyle = "Regular"
            .Size = 11
        End With

        Range("A2:D2").Select
        Selection.Columns.AutoFit
        Selection.ColumnWidth = Selection.ColumnWidth * 1.25
        Range("A2:E2").Select
        Selection.HorizontalAlignment = xlCenter

        AppExcel.Visible = True

    End Sub
```

VBAObjects: Using Excel as a Math Parser

In the section "Spell-Checking Documents," you saw how you can steal the spell-checking capabilities of Word. Now, we'll do something similar with Excel. Excel is a great tool for doing math. At the same time, Visual Basic doesn't provide a function or a method for evaluating math expressions. With the little information on VBA programming we have presented so far, you can exploit this capability of Excel and use it as a background server to calculate math expressions.

To calculate a math expression such as

```
1/cos(0.335)*cos(12.45)
```

with Excel, all you have to do is enter the expression in a cell and let Excel calculate the cell. For Excel to recognize that the text you've entered is a formula and treat it accordingly, you must prefix the expression with the equals sign.

That's exactly what the Calculate Expression button does. It contacts Excel, builds a new worksheet (if needed), and then copies a user-assigned math formula to a cell. The formula is prefixed with the equals sign so that Excel will calculate the value of the expression and place it in the same cell. The value of this cell is then read back and displayed from within the VBObjs application (see Figure 21.12).

Code 21.10   **The Calculate Expression Button**

```
Private Sub Command8_Click()
Dim wSheet As Worksheet
Dim wBook As Workbook
Dim expression

    expression = InputBox("Enter math expression to evaluate _
        (i.e., 1/cos(3.45)*log(19.004)")
    If Trim(expression) <> "" Then
        If AppExcel.Workbooks.Count = 0 Then
            Debug.Print "Adding a new Workbook"
            Set wBook = AppExcel.Workbooks.Add
        End If
        Set wSheet = AppExcel.Sheets(1)
        On Error GoTo CalcError
        wSheet.Cells(1, 1).Value = "=" & expression
        wSheet.Calculate
        MsgBox "The value of the expression " & expression & vbCrLf & _
            " is " & wSheet.Cells(1, 1).Value
    End If
    Exit Sub

CalcError:
    MsgBox "Error in evaluating expression"
End Sub
```

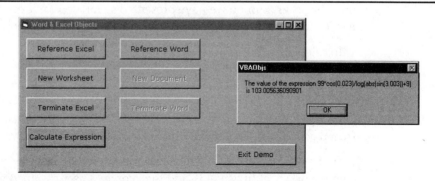

FIGURE 21.12:

Using Excel's Evaluate method to evaluate math expressions

VBA and Form Design

Besides the VB Editor, Office applications come with a Form Designer that is similar to the Form Designer in the Visual Basic IDE. With VBA 5, you can create Forms and display them from within your VBA applications. In the past, VBA programs were limited to the user interface of the Office application. A Word macro that called some of Excel's methods to streamline the transfer of data from Excel to Word and format them in Word could use the user interface of Word or Excel and display a few simple dialog boxes on its own, but not a real Form such as the ones you can build with Visual Basic. Custom Forms were not an option.

The situation has changed, and now you can design Forms similar to Visual Basic Forms, program their events, and display them from within your macros. This significant development was the next step in the evolution of Word and Excel applications to fully programmable environments. In the following sections, we'll describe how to design and use Forms with Excel's Visual Basic Editor and how to import these Forms into Visual Basic applications.

VBA Forms

We'll demonstrate the VBA Form Designer with a simple, but typical, example: the VBAExcel application. The Form shown in Figure 21.13 is displayed from within Excel. It summarizes the data shown on the Excel spreadsheet. You could just as easily process the data in Excel, but in some situations it is best to extract the information from a spreadsheet, process it, and display the results on a different Form.

NOTE   You'll find the VBAExcel application in the `Ch21\VBAExcel` folder on the CD that comes with this book.

The data come from the NWIND database (we've used it many times in the previous chapters of the book), but you won't find the spreadsheet on the CD. To import the data into Excel, follow these steps:

1. Start Access, and open the NWIND database (you will find it in the VB folder).

2. In the Queries tab of the Database window, double-click the Order Details Extended box to display all the invoice details.

3. Select the data on the data grid (shown in Figure 21.13) and copy them.

FIGURE 21.13:

The Order Details Extended
query returns the details of
all invoices in the NWIND
sample database.

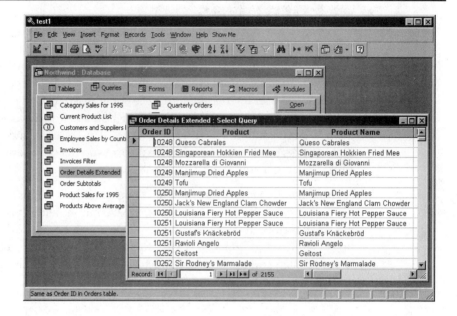

4.   Start Excel.

5.   Paste the data from the clipboard into the first cell.

6.   Select the following columns (by clicking their headings) and remove them
from the grid by choosing Edit ➤ Delete:

- Product

- Unit Price

- Quantity

- Discount

What you now have on the spreadsheet are the details of all invoices recorded
in the NWIND database. Your Excel window should look like the one shown in
Figure 21.14. However, there are no totals for each invoice. The specific query
returns the detail lines. Notice that the same invoice number is repeated on the
spreadsheet as many times as there are lines in the invoice.

Assuming we are not interested in taxes or other charges, we can calculate the
total for each invoice by running down the details and summing the Extended
Prices for all lines with the same OrderID field. All it takes is a macro that loops

FIGURE 21.14:

The invoice details of the grid shown in Figure 21.13 in an Excel spreadsheet

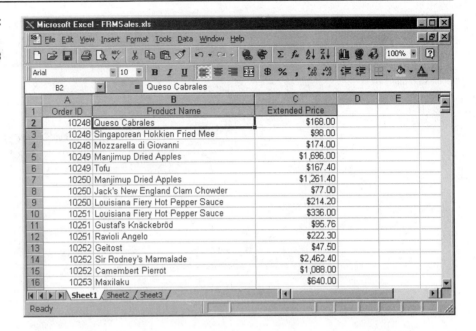

FIGURE 21.14:

The invoice details of the grid shown in Figure 21.13 in an Excel spreadsheet

through the spreadsheet's rows, compares the OrderID cell with the previous one, and adds the Extended Price to the running total. But how about displaying the totals? One approach is to insert a new row after each invoice's line. Another is to place the total in the cell next to each invoice's last Extended Price cell.

To demonstrate the design of Forms, we are going to display the totals for each on a separate Form, as shown in Figure 21.15. This Form looks like an ordinary VB Form, but it was designed with Excel's Visual Basic Editor and displayed in Excel's environment. You don't even need to have Visual Basic installed to design and display this Form. In the next section, we are going to export this Form and use it with a VB application.

You may be wondering, Why deploy a new Form instead of using Excel's subtotaling features? Keep in mind that this is a simple example. The processing of the data may be more complicated, and it may not always be convenient to display the results on the same spreadsheet. This example does not demonstrate the need to deploy custom Forms, but everyone who's programmed Excel in the past will admit that they wished they could pop up a similar Form at one time or another.

FIGURE 21.15:

The totals for the invoices shown in Figure 21.14 displayed in a ListBox control on a VBA Form

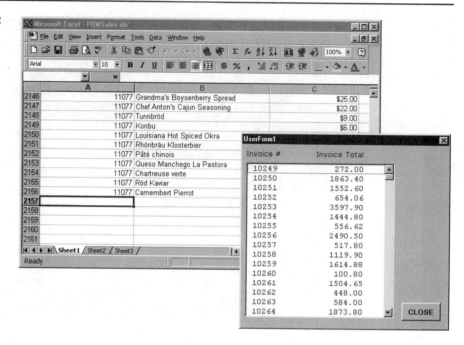

Forms are the next step in Excel's evolution toward a fully programmable environment. Once you understand the structure of a spreadsheet and the objects that expose this structure to other applications, programming Excel will be no different from programming with Visual Basic, including Form design. You can even "dress your application up" with Forms so that users will see very little Excel, and they may even think that the spreadsheet is another data-entry window in your application.

Designing a Form

To design a new VBA Form with Excel, open a new worksheet and choose Tools ➤ Macro ➤ Visual Basic Editor. You will see the window shown in Figure 21.16. To get the Form shown in Figure 21.16, open the VBA Editor and choose Insert ➤ UserForm. This window contains the usual Project, Properties, and Form panes, just like the Visual Basic Editor. The Project pane contains all the components of the Excel project, including the spreadsheets and the modules (recorded macros are stored in the project's main module). If you select the Form, you will see a Toolbox, similar to the one in the Visual Basic editor, except that it doesn't contain as many controls. If you don't see the Toolbox, click the Form to display it. When you are not designing a Form's interface, the Toolbox remains hidden.

FIGURE 21.16:

The Visual Basic Editor's window for a typical Excel project

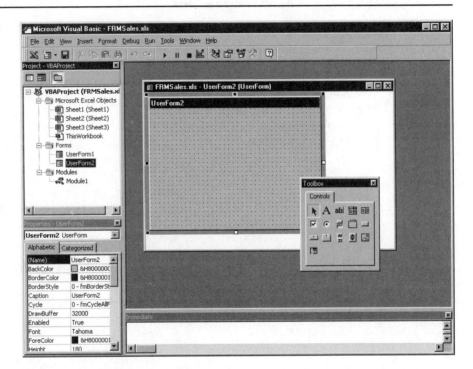

To design the Form shown in Figure 21.15 earlier in this chapter, place the List-Box control on it, add a Command Button to the right side of the control, and place two Label controls on top of the List control. The exact placement of the two labels depends on the size of the tab character between the two columns on the ListBox control, and the initial placement will be approximate.

The data should be loaded when the Form is initialized, which is signaled by the Initialize event. In this event's handler, we must set up a loop to scan all the rows of the spreadsheet and sum the prices while the OrderID field is the same. As each invoice is processed, the new total is added to the list. The OrderID fields are accessed by the expression

```
Range("A" & curRow)
```

in which *curRow* is the row's number, which is increased by one with every iteration. Many of the lines deal with formatting the numbers, and you can ignore them initially.

Code 21.11   The Initialize Event

```
Private Sub UserForm_Initialize()
Dim InvoiceValue As String

curRow = 2
Range("A" & curRow).Select
curInvoice = ActiveCell.Value
curRow = curRow + 1
While curInvoice <> ""
    Range("A" & curRow).Select
    InvoiceNumber = ActiveCell.Value
    If InvoiceNumber = curInvoice Then
        invoicetotal = invoicetotal + Range("C" & curRow).Value
    Else
        InvoiceValue$ = Format$(invoicetotal, "#.00")
        InvoiceValue$ = Space(12 - Len(InvoiceValue$)) & InvoiceValue
        ListBox1.AddItem InvoiceNumber & Chr(9) & Chr(9) &
InvoiceValue$
        invoicetotal = Range("C" & curRow).Value
        curInvoice = InvoiceNumber
    End If
    curRow = curRow + 1
Wend
DoEvents
End Sub
```

The List's Font property is set to a monospaced font to simplify alignment. There are better ways to align multiple columns in a ListBox control, but for this example we want to keep the code's complexity to a minimum.

To display the Form, press F5, or choose Run ➢ Run Sub/User Form. The Form will be loaded, and a couple of seconds later the invoice totals will appear, as shown in Figure 21.15. The Close button simply hides the Form with the following statement:

```
Me.Hide
```

Using VBA Forms with Visual Basic

You can use the Forms and applications that you design with VBA with Visual Basic by making a few adjustments in the code. This means that you can start with VBA and move your designs to Visual Basic, or vice versa. Both the user interface and the code can be reused and shared by people in different environments.

To reuse a VBA Form in a Visual Basic application, first export it by choosing File ➢ Export.

> **NOTE**   VBA Forms are saved automatically with the current project, and you don't have to save them separately. Every time you save the workbook, the Forms (and macros) you designed in the current session are also saved as part of the project.

Choosing File ➢ Export saves the current Form in an FRM file. You can then import this file into a Visual Basic project by choosing Project ➢ Add Form. Save the Form you designed in the last section (you can also find it in the VBAExcel folder on the CD) and then start a new Visual Basic project.

Choose Project ➢ Add Form to add the VBA Form. Visual Basic creates a new folder in the Project window, the Designers folder, and places the VBA Form there. This folder contains Forms designed outside Visual Basic. The UserForm1 Designer is quite similar to a Visual Basic Form, but you can't add to it all the controls you can use with regular Visual Basic Forms. If you click UserForm1, you will see the same Toolbox as you see in the VBA Editor (see Figure 21.17). The Designer should be usable in the environment in which it was created, even after it's been edited with Visual Basic.

If you open the UserForm1 Form's Code window, you will see that it doesn't support all the events recognized by regular Forms. Most of the events are still present, and the code you entered in the VBA Editor is still there.

To complete the application VBExcel, add a new module (the InvModule) and enter the following lines:

```
Public appExcel As Object

Sub Main()
    On Error Resume Next
    Set appExcel = GetObject(App.Path & "\FRMSales.xls", _
        "Excel.Application")
    If appExcel Is Nothing Then
```

```
            Set appExcel = CreateObject("Excel.Application")
            appExcel.Workbooks.Open App.Path & "\FRMSales.xls"
        End If
        VBEXCEL.Show
    End Sub
```

FIGURE 21.17:

To adjust the interface of a Designer, you must use the same Toolbox as the application in which the Designer was created.

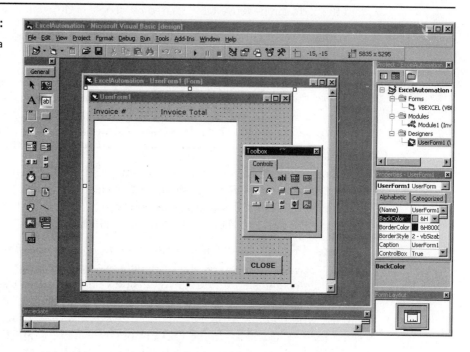

As you can guess, the code of the UserForm1 Form's code isn't going to work as is. When executed from within Excel's VB Editor, it can safely assume it's connected to an instance of Excel. This is no longer the case. The VB application must first establish a connection to an instance of Excel and then show the Form.

The code of the Main subroutine does exactly that. It instantiates the *appExcel* object variable, assigns the FRMSales spreadsheet to it, and then displays the VBExcel Form, shown in Figure 21.18. This Form simply waits for the user to click the Show Invoice Totals button or terminate the application. The project's Startup object is the subroutine Main (open the Project Properties window and select Sub Main in the Startup Object list).

The code of the Show Invoice Totals button's Click event doesn't do much. It simply loads and displays the UserForm1 Form with the statement

```
UserForm1.Show
```

FIGURE 21.18:

The VBExcel application's starting Form. As the program reads the invoice lines, it displays its progress on the Form.

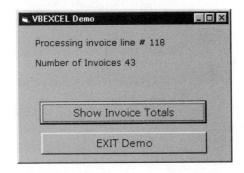

When UserForm1 is loaded, its Initialize event is triggered, and the data are read from Excel. We must adjust the code of the Initialize event. The necessary corrections are quite simple. When this code is executed in Excel's environment, we don't have to tell it which spreadsheet to access. We can call the Range method to access the cells of the active spreadsheet. Now, however, the Range method isn't adequate. We must now tell Visual Basic to contact a server application (appExcel) and request data from the first worksheet ("Sheet1" or any other name you may have used in Excel). All instances of the methods called in the Initialize event handler must now be prefixed with the following string:

```
appExcel.Sheets("Sheet1")
```

To read the value of the active cell, for example, we use the expression

```
appExcel.ActiveCell.Value
```

The revised code of the UserForm1 object's Initialize event handler is shown next.

Code 21.12   **The UserForm1_Initialize Event Handler**

```
Private Sub UserForm_Initialize()
Dim InvoiceValue As String

curRow = 2
appExcel.Sheets("Sheet1").Range("A" & curRow).Select
curInvoice = appExcel.ActiveCell.Value
curRow = curRow + 1
While curInvoice <> ""
    appExcel.Sheets("Sheet1").Range("A" & curRow).Select
    InvoiceNumber = appExcel.ActiveCell.Value
    If InvoiceNumber = curInvoice Then
```

```
          invoicetotal = invoicetotal + _
              appExcel.Sheets("Sheet1").Range("C" & curRow).Value
      Else
          InvoiceValue$ = Format$(invoicetotal, "#.00")
          InvoiceValue$ = Space(12 - Len(InvoiceValue$)) & InvoiceValue
          ListBox1.AddItem InvoiceNumber & Chr(9) & Chr(9) & _
              InvoiceValue$
          invoicetotal = appExcel.Range("C" & curRow).Value
          curInvoice = InvoiceNumber
          InvCounter = InvCounter + 1
      End If
      VBEXCEL.Label1.Caption = "Processing invoice line # " & curRow
      VBEXCEL.Label2.Caption = "Number of Invoices " & InvCounter
      curRow = curRow + 1
      VBEXCEL.Refresh
  Wend
  End Sub
```

If you load the VBExcel application from the CD, be sure that the FRMSales.xls file (the worksheet with the invoice details) has been prepared and resides in the same folder as the application. Moreover, you may have to change the addresses of the cells. In the project's code, we assume that the OrderID values are stored in the first column (A) and the prices in the third column (C). If you paste the data into a different location on the worksheet, adjust the references in the code accordingly. Figure 21.19 shows the Form being used within a VB application.

NOTE The NWIND database contains more than 2,000 invoice lines, and processing them won't be instant, even on a fast machine.

This example concludes our introduction to the basic objects exposed by Excel and Word. You have now seen how you can build VB applications to control other applications that act as OLE servers by manipulating their objects. In the following chapters, you will find a complete discussion of all the objects exposed by Word and Excel and lots of examples.

FIGURE 21.19:

A VBA Form being used from within a Visual Basic application

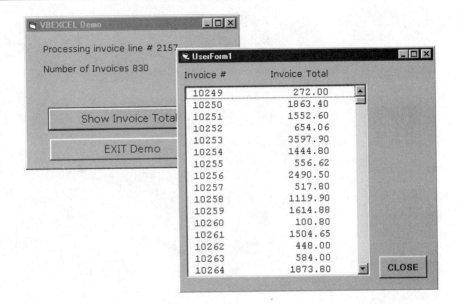

CHAPTER

TWENTY-TWO

Using the Visual Basic Editor with Word and Excel

- Using the Visual Basic Editor

- Choosing options for the Visual Basic Editor

- Recording and creating macros

- Creating Forms

- Finding the VBA objects you need

In this chapter, we'll discuss how to use the Visual Basic Editor to create and edit code and Forms for Word and Excel. If you're familiar with the Visual Basic Integrated Development Environment (IDE), you'll find that many of the features in the Visual Basic Editor are familiar, though some work in somewhat different ways in the Visual Basic Editor than in the Visual Basic IDE.

> **NOTE** You'll find that the Word documentation and help files use the term `userform` instead of `Form`, which is the term we use throughout this book. The terms are synonymous. Excel (which we discuss in the next chapter) uses both of them.

Word and Excel use the same Visual Basic Editor, but always in separate sessions launched from the host application: You run a Visual Basic Editor session for Word from Word, and you run a Visual Basic Editor session for Excel from Excel. If you have the Visual Basic Editor open for Word and choose to display the Visual Basic Editor for Excel, Excel opens its own session of the Visual Basic Editor.

We'll start by discussing the components of the Visual Basic Editor, what they do, and how to use the Visual Basic Editor. We'll then run through how to use the Visual Basic Editor to create code and Forms for Word and Excel. Finally, we'll look at how to find the objects you need in VBA.

> **NOTE** Most of the information in this chapter also applies to using the Visual Basic Editor with PowerPoint, but we won't discuss PowerPoint in this chapter.

Opening the Visual Basic Editor

You can open the Visual Basic Editor for Word and Excel in any of several ways:

- Choose Tools ➤ Macro ➤ Visual Basic Editor.

> **NOTE** If the Visual Basic Editor for the current application is already displayed, Word or Excel switches to it. If a session of the Visual Basic Editor is open for another application, Word or Excel starts its own session of the Visual Basic Editor.

- Press Alt+F11 from within Word or Excel.

- Choose Tools ➤ Macros ➤ Macros (or press Alt+F8) in Word or Excel to display the Macros dialog box. Select the macro you want to edit, and click the Edit button. (Alternatively, you can create a macro by typing a name for it in the Macro Name text box in the Macros dialog box and then clicking the Create button. Word or Excel displays the Visual Basic Editor and creates the macro in it ready for editing.)

To switch back to Word or Excel from the Visual Basic Editor, click the View Microsoft Word button or the View Microsoft Excel button on the Standard toolbar. Alternatively, press Alt+F11.

The Visual Basic Editor Interface

Parts of the Visual Basic Editor will be immediately recognizable to you from the Visual Basic IDE. As you can see in Figure 22.1, the Visual Basic Editor typically displays three windows—the Project Explorer, the Properties window, and the Code window—and a Standard toolbar.

FIGURE 22.1:

The Visual Basic Editor

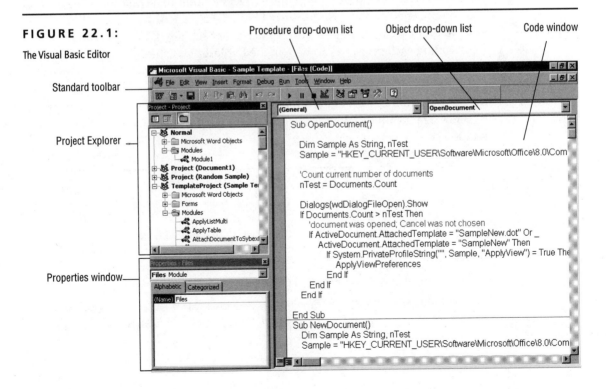

In the previous chapter, we took a quick look at the components of the Visual Basic Editor. Now, we'll look at them in detail and discuss how to use them.

> **NOTE**
>
> If you've spent any time working with macros in earlier versions of Word or Excel, you'll find a number of differences in the Visual Basic Editor that take some getting used to. Whereas Word versions through Word 95 and Excel versions through Excel 95 used a macro-editing window within the host application window, the Visual Basic Editor runs as a separate application window. It has its own Taskbar button so that you can switch to it easily and close it from the Taskbar. (Be warned though, the Visual Basic Editor shares the same memory space as the host application. If you crash the Visual Basic Editor (which may not take down the application itself), it's wise to close and restart the application. Or, if you're using Windows 95, shut down and restart the operating system. If you crash Word or Excel, it will almost invariably take down its session of the Visual Basic Editor as well.)

The Project Explorer

As in the Visual Basic IDE, you use the Project Explorer to navigate among projects and components of projects in the Visual Basic Editor for Word and Excel. The Project Explorer lists all open projects for the current session of the host application, representing each project as an item in the Explorer-style hierarchical list. You can click the boxed plus sign (+) to the left of a project or project component to expand the view to display the contents of the project component. You can click the resulting boxed minus sign (–) to the left of a project or project component to collapse the view again. You can double-click an item to display it or its code in the Code window.

> **NOTE**
>
> Because the Project Explorer provides fast and efficient navigation among the various elements of your VBA projects, it's usually best kept displayed unless you're desperately short of screen space. Given that you'll usually be working with multiple projects in Word and Excel, the Visual Basic Editor can quickly become more cluttered than the Visual Basic IDE normally does. So it makes sense to keep the Project Explorer displayed to ease navigation from one project element to another.

To display the Project Explorer, choose View ➤ Project Explorer, press Ctrl+R, or press the F4 key. To close the Project Explorer, click its Close button.

Similarities between the Visual Basic Editor and the Visual Basic IDE

The first time you display the Visual Basic Editor for Word and Excel, you'll be struck by its similarities to the Visual Basic IDE. Not only does the interface of the Visual Basic Editor have a similar layout to that of the Visual Basic IDE, but many (if not most) of the features in the Visual Basic Editor are the same as or similar to those in the Visual Basic IDE.

For example, most of the code-completion and visual help features from the Visual Basic IDE—such as the Complete Word feature, the List Properties/Methods and List Constants features, and the Quick Info and Parameter Info features—are present in the Visual Basic Editor as well. Likewise, most of the keyboard commands in the Visual Basic Editor are the same as those in the Visual Basic IDE.

For example, you can press the F7 key to view the code for an object, and you can press Shift+F7 to return from viewing the code to viewing the object to which the code belongs. Furthermore, as you'll see later in this chapter, the commands for arranging controls on Forms in the Visual Basic Editor are mostly the same as those in the Visual Basic IDE.

However, you'll also notice a number of differences, such as the following:

- The Visual Basic Editor has no Form Layout window to give you a quick view of the Form you're creating.

- The Visual Basic Editor has no Property Pages.

- The Visual Basic Editor does not have explanatory help text at the bottom of the Properties window as does the Visual Basic IDE.

- The Visual Basic Editor has fewer controls available than the Visual Basic IDE.

- When you drag an object on a Form, the Visual Basic Editor does not display the coordinates at which the outline of the object is currently located as does the Visual Basic IDE.

Projects in the Project Explorer for Word

In this section, we'll discuss the projects that you'll see in the Project Explorer in Word. Figure 22.2 shows the Project Explorer window in the Visual Basic Editor for Word with several projects open.

FIGURE 22.2:

The Project Explorer with several Word projects open

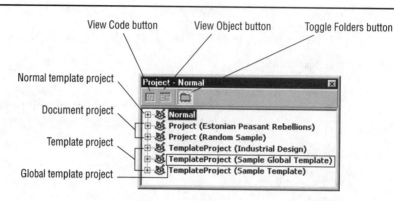

View Code button   View Object button   Toggle Folders button

Normal template project

Document project

Template project

Global template project

The Visual Basic Editor for Word displays the following projects in the Project Explorer:

- The template project for the NORMAL.DOT template (the global template). This project is identified as Normal and appears at the top level of the Project Explorer. This project is always displayed, even when no document is open.

- One template project for each open global template. Each project is identified by the keyword TemplateProject, followed by the name of the global template in parentheses. For example, the project for a global template named NADIR CO. GLOBAL TEMPLATE would appear as TemplateProject (Nadir Co. Global Template) in the Project Explorer. As you can see in Figure 22.2, the Project Explorer does not present a global template differently from a regular template, but you can identify a global template because the project for any global template loaded is always displayed, even when no document is open. You'll also notice that the project for each global template is locked: You cannot edit a global template when it is loaded. (The locking isn't peculiar to global templates, because any template can be locked, but it can be a hint that a template is a global template.)

- One document project for each open document. Each document project is identified by the keyword Project, followed by the name of the document in parentheses. For example, the project for a document named ESTONIAN PEASANT REBELLIONS.DOC would appear as Project (Estonian Peasant Rebellions) in the Project Explorer.

- One template project for each open document template. This project is identified by the keyword TemplateProject, followed by the name of the template in parentheses. For example, the project for a global template named INDUSTRIAL DESIGN.DOT would appear as TemplateProject (Industrial Design) in the Project Explorer.

Running Multiple Word and Visual Basic Editor Sessions

If you run multiple sessions of Word, you can open a session of the Visual Basic Editor for each Word session. Each session of the Visual Basic Editor will show the open projects in the corresponding session of Word. As long as you do not have the same document or template open in two or more sessions, you can make and save changes to the document projects and template projects. However, the Normal template will be controlled by the first Word session and its corresponding Visual Basic Editor session.

If you try to save changes to the Normal template from a second or subsequent Word session, or from its corresponding Visual Basic Editor session, while the first Word session is running, Word will prompt you to save the template under a different name.

If you try to save changes to the Normal template from a second or subsequent Word session or its corresponding Visual Basic Editor session after closing the first Word session, Word will warn you that NORMAL.DOT was being edited by another Word session and that saving these changes as NORMAL.DOT will overwrite any changes made in the other session. You can then choose to overwrite the previous copy of NORMAL.DOT or to save the other session of the template under a different name.

The order in which the document projects and template projects are listed varies from session to session and will change as you open and close documents. The project for the Normal template is always listed first in the Project Explorer.

Components of Word Projects

As in the Visual Basic IDE, you can expand the projects in the Project Explorer to view their contents by clicking the plus (+) sign to the left of the project name. Figure 22.3 shows the expanded view of a typical project.

FIGURE 22.3:

The expanded view of a typical project, showing its component objects

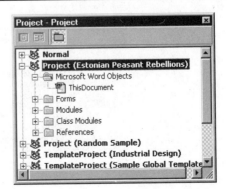

Each Word project can contain the following elements:

Microsoft Word objects   Typically, each document project or template project contains an object named ThisDocument that contains the properties for the document or template. For example, the project for the Normal template contains an object named ThisDocument that contains the properties for the Normal template.

Userforms (for dialog boxes or Forms)   You can save a Form to a separate FRM file.

Modules (that typically contain macros, procedures, and functions)   You can save a module to a separate BAS file.

Class modules   You can save a class module to a separate CLS file.

References   You can add template references to object type libraries, ActiveX controls, or other projects. For example, when you need to use a Form or procedure stored in a different document or template, you can add a reference to that document or template to make it available to the current project. Each document project contains a reference to the template to which it is currently attached.

Projects in the Project Explorer for Excel

In this section, we'll discuss the projects that you'll see in the Project Explorer in Excel. Figure 22.4 shows the Project Explorer for the Visual Basic Editor for Excel with several projects open.

FIGURE 22.4:

The Project Explorer with several Excel projects open

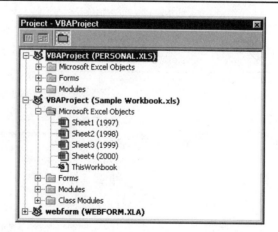

The Visual Basic Editor for Excel displays the following projects in the Project Explorer:

- One project for each add-in file (XLA) you have loaded. This project is identified by the name of the add-in, followed by its file name in parentheses. For example, if you load the Web Form Wizard add-in (webform), its project will appear in the Project Explorer as webform (WEBFORM.XLA). Projects for add-ins are always displayed while the add-ins are loaded, even when no workbook is open.

- The project for the Personal macro workbook, if one exists for this copy of Excel and (for systems with multiple users defined) for this user. This project is identified as VBAProject (PERSONAL.XLS) and is displayed whether the Personal macro workbook is hidden or displayed. This project is always displayed in the Project Explorer, even when no workbook is open.

- One project for each open workbook. Each workbook project is identified by the keyword VBAProject, followed by the name of the document in parentheses. For example, the project for a workbook named NEW MODEL WORKBOOK.XLS would appear as VBAProject (New Model Workbook.xls) in the Project Explorer.

Running Multiple Excel and Visual Basic Editor Sessions

As with Word, you can run multiple sessions of Excel, with a separate session of the Visual Basic Editor for each Excel session. However, Excel is more protective of the PERSONAL.XLS Personal macro workbook than Word is of the NORMAL.DOT Normal template. If you start a new Excel session when an Excel session is already running, Excel displays the File Reservation dialog box shown here to warn you that the Personal macro workbook is being modified. (If you don't have a Personal macro workbook, Excel will not display this message box.)

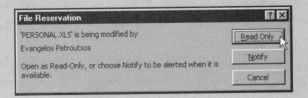

Continued on next page

You then have three choices:

- Click the Read Only button to open PERSONAL.XLS as a read-only file (so that you will not be able to modify it).

- Click the Notify button to open a second (or subsequent) Excel session without PERSONAL.XLS. After you close the first Excel session, the second Excel session will display the File Reservation dialog box shown here to notify you that PERSONAL.XLS is available for editing. Click the Read-Write button to open PERSONAL.XLS for editing.

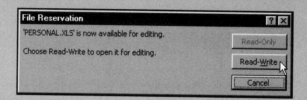

- Click the Cancel button to open a second (or subsequent) Excel session without PERSONAL.XLS.

Now that you can make changes to PERSONAL.XLS from only one Excel session at a time, there's no possibility of two sessions trying to write changes to PERSONAL.XLS. You can safely make changes to any Excel workbook project or template project open in any Visual Basic Editor session.

Components of Excel Projects

Each Excel project can have the following components:

Microsoft Excel Objects   Each workbook project or template project contains an object named ThisWorkbook that contains the properties for the workbook or template. For example, the project for the PERSONAL.XLS macro workbook contains an object named ThisWorkbook that contains the properties for PERSONAL.XLS. Each worksheet appears as an object identified by a default name based on its position in the workbook (Sheet1, Sheet2, and so on) and any name assigned to its tab. For example, in Figure 22.4, earlier in this chapter, Sheet1 is named 1997, and Sheet2 is named 1998.

Forms (for dialog boxes or Forms)   You can save a Form to a separate FRM file.

Modules (for macros, procedures, and functions)   You can save a module to a separate BAS file.

Class modules   You can save a class module to a separate CLS file.

The Code Window

As in the Visual Basic IDE, the Code window in the Visual Basic Editor is where you'll do most of the actual work of creating and editing your macros. The Visual Basic Editor provides a Code window for each open project, for each document section within the project that can contain code, and for each code module and Form in the project. Each Code window is identified by the project name, the name of the module within the project, and the word *Code* in parentheses.

The Visual Basic Editor Code window provides a half-dozen features for helping you create code efficiently and accurately. You'll recognize most of these features if you're familiar with the Visual Basic IDE.

Complete Word completes the word you're typing once you've typed enough letters to distinguish that word from any other. To activate Complete Word, press Ctrl+spacebar or click the Complete Word button on the Edit toolbar.

Quick Info, which is on the Edit toolbar, displays syntax information on the current variable, function, method, statement, or procedure.

List Properties/Methods displays a pop-up list box containing properties and methods for the object you've just typed so that you can quickly complete the expression. List Properties/Methods is switched on by default and will automatically pop up the list box when you type a period within an expression. You can select a property or a method by clicking it with the mouse, by using the page up arrow and the page down arrow, or by typing the name of the property or method until the Visual Basic Editor can identify it. To enter the property or method into the code, you can double-click it or do one of the following:

- Press Tab or the spacebar and continue working on the same line.

- Press the period key (.) and continue working on the same line.

- Press Enter and start a new line.

List Constants displays a pop-up list box containing constants for a property that you've typed so that you can quickly select the constant needed to complete the expression. Again, you can use either the mouse or the keyboard to select the constant, and you can enter the constant by double-clicking it or by pressing Tab (to continue working on the same line) or Enter (to start a new line).

Data Tips displays a screentip containing the value of a variable that the mouse pointer moves over. This feature works only when the Visual Basic Editor is in Break mode.

Margin Indicators lets you quickly set a breakpoint, the next statement, or a bookmark by clicking in the left margin of the Code window.

Apart from these features, the Visual Basic Editor includes standard Office editing features such as Copy and Move, Cut and Paste, and Drag-and-Drop. Drag-and-Drop is particularly useful because you can drag code from one macro or module to another.

The Properties Window

The Visual Basic Editor provides a Properties window that you can use to view the properties of an object such as a project, a Form, or a control. Use the drop-down list at the top of the Properties window to select the item whose properties you want to view. The Alphabetic tab presents an alphabetic list of the properties in the item, and the Categorized tab presents a list of the properties broken down into categories. Figure 22.5 shows the properties for a relatively straightforward Word document.

FIGURE 22.5:

Use the Properties window to view the properties of a project, a Form, or a control.

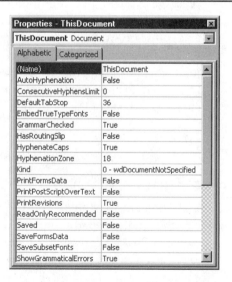

These properties map to document or template information (in Word), or workbook or template information (in Excel), that you're probably familiar with. For example, the Saved property stores information on whether the document or workbook contains unsaved changes. If the document or workbook does not contain unsaved changes, this property will be set to True (because all the information in the document or workbook is saved); if the document or workbook does contain unsaved changes, this property will be set to False.

To display the Properties window, press F4, click the Properties Windows button on the Standard toolbar, or choose View ➤ Properties Window. To change a property, click in the right column and change the value. You'll be able to choose different values depending on the type of property. For a True/False property, you'll be limited to those two choices in the drop-down list; for a text property such as Name, you can enter any valid Visual Basic name.

Other Windows in the Visual Basic Editor

In this section, we'll discuss the other windows that the Visual Basic Editor provides for working with code:

- Object Browser
- Locals
- Watch
- Immediate

Unlike the Project Explorer, the Code window, and the Properties window, these windows are not displayed by default in the Visual Basic Editor; you can display them whenever you find them helpful. Like the Project Explorer, the Code window, and the Properties window, these windows work in a similar way to their equivalents in the Visual Basic IDE.

The Object Browser

The Object Browser in the Visual Basic Editor provides information classes, properties, methods, events, and constants for both built-in objects and custom objects you create. Figure 22.6 shows the components of the Object Browser.

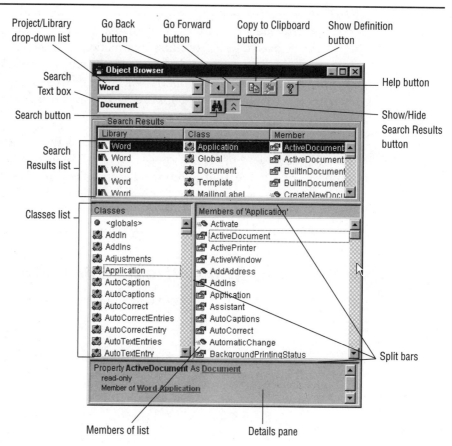

FIGURE 22.6:

The Object Browser provides information on built-in objects and custom objects.

Here's what the elements of the Object Browser do:

- The **Project/Library** drop-down list provides a list of object libraries available to the current project. Use the drop-down list to choose the object libraries you want to view.

- In the **Search Text** box, enter the string you want to search for: Either type it in, or choose a previous string in the current project session from the drop-down list. Then either press Enter or click the Search button to find members containing the search string.

TIP

To make your searches more inclusive, you can use wildcards such as ? (representing any one character) and * (representing any group of characters). You can also choose to search for a whole word only (rather than matching your search string with part of another word) by right-clicking anywhere in the Object Browser (except in the Project/Library drop-down list or in the Search Text box) and choosing Find Whole Word Only from the shortcut menu. The Find Whole Word Only choice will have a checkmark next to it in the shortcut menu when it is active; to deactivate it, choose Find Whole Word Only again on the shortcut menu.

- Click the **Go Back** button to go back one by one through your previous selections in the Classes list and the Members Of list. Click the **Go Forward** button to go forward through your previous selections one by one. The Go Back button will become available when you go to a class or a member in the Object Browser; the Go Forward button will become available only when you have used the Go Back button to return to a previous selection.

- Click the **Copy to Clipboard** button to copy the selected item from the Search Results box, the Classes list, the Members Of list, or the Details pane to the clipboard so that you can paste it into your code.

- Click the **Show Definition** button to display a Code window containing the code for the object selected in the Classes list or the Members Of list. The Show Definition button will be available (undimmed) only for objects that contain code, such as macros and Forms that you've created.

- Click the **Help** button to display any available Help for the currently selected item.

- Click the **Search** button to search for the term entered in the Search Text box. If the Search Results pane is not open, the Object Browser will open it at this point.

- Click the **Show/Hide Search Results** button to toggle the display of the Search Results pane on and off.

- The **Search Results** list in the Search Results pane contains the results of the latest search you've conducted for a term entered in the Search Text box. If you've performed a search, the Object Browser will update the Search Results list when you switch to a different library by using the Project/Library drop-down list.

- The **Classes** list shows the available classes in the library or project specified in the Project/Library drop-down list.

- The **Members Of** list displays the available elements of the class selected in the Classes list. A method, constant, event, property, or procedure that has code written for it appears in boldface. The Members Of list can display the members either grouped into their categories (methods, properties, events, and so on) or ungrouped as an alphabetic list of all the members available. To toggle between grouped and ungrouped, right-click in the Members Of list and choose Group Members from the shortcut menu. When members are grouped, the Visual Basic Editor displays a checkmark next to the menu item.

- The **Details** pane displays the definition of the member selected in the Classes list or in the Members Of list. For example, if you select a macro in the Members Of list, the Details pane displays its name, the name of the module and template, document, or workbook in which it is stored, and any comment lines you inserted at the beginning of the macro. The module name and template name will contain hyperlinks so that you can quickly move to them.

- Drag the three **split bars** to resize the panes of the Object Browser to suit you.

Adding and Removing Object Libraries

You can add and remove object libraries by using the References dialog box (we looked at this dialog box briefly in the previous chapter). By adding object libraries, you can make available additional objects to work with; by removing object libraries that you do not need to view or use, you can reduce the number of object references that VBA needs to resolve when it compiles the code in a project, thus allowing it to run faster.

You can also adjust the priority of references by adjusting the order in which the references appear in the References dialog box. The priority of references matters when you use, in your code, an object whose name appears in more than one reference: VBA checks the order in the References list of the references that contain that object name and uses the first of them.

To add or remove object libraries, follow these steps:

1. Right-click anywhere in the Object Browser window other than in the Search Text box and choose References from the shortcut menu, or choose Tools ➢ References in the Visual Basic Editor, to display the References dialog box (shown here).

Continued on next page

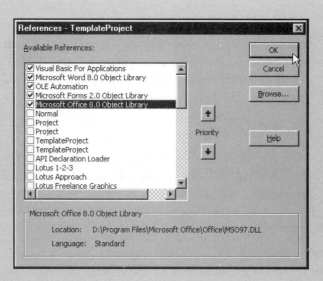

2. In the Available References list box, select the checkboxes for the references you want to have available, and clear the checkboxes for the references you want to remove.

3. Adjust the priority of the references if necessary by selecting a reference and using the up- and down-arrow Priority buttons to move it up or down the list. Usually, you'll want to keep Visual Basic for Applications and the Microsoft Excel 8.0 Object Library at the top of your list when you're working with Excel, and the Microsoft Word 8.0 Object Library when you're working with Word. You can add further reference libraries by clicking the Browse button to display the Add Reference dialog box, selecting the library file, and clicking the Open button.

4. Choose the OK button to close the References dialog box and return to the Object Browser.

The Locals Window

The Locals window provides a quick readout of the value and type of all expressions in the active procedure via a collapsible tree view. The Expression column displays the name of each expression, listed under the name of the procedure in which it appears; the Value column displays the current value of the expression (including Empty if the expression is empty, or Null or Nothing as appropriate); and the Type column displays the data type of the expression, with variants listed as "Variant" along with their assigned data type (for example, "Variant/String" for a variant assigned the string data type).

To display the Locals window, click the Locals Window button on the Debug toolbar or choose View ➤ Locals Window; to remove the Locals window, click its Close button. From the Locals window, you can also click the button marked with an ellipsis (...) to display the Call Stack dialog box.

The Watch Window

In the Watch window you can track the values of variables and expressions as your code executes. To display the Watch window, click the Watch Window button on the Debug toolbar or choose View ➤ Watch Window in the Visual Basic Editor. To hide the Watch window, click its Close button.

The Watch window displays watch expressions you set ahead of time to give you a running display of the value of a variable or an expression. This allows you to pinpoint the location of an unexpected value for a variable or an expression as your code executes. The Watch window lists the names of the watched expressions or variables in the Expression column, their values in the Value column, their type (Integer, Byte, String, Long, and so on) in the Type column, and their context (the module and macro in which they are operating) in the Context column.

> **NOTE** If a variable or an expression in the Watch window has not been initialized, the Watch window will display "<Out of Context>" in the Value column and "Empty" (for a variable other than a Variant) or "Variant/Empty" (for a Variant) in the Type column.

The Visual Basic Editor updates all watch expressions in the Watch window whenever you enter Break mode and whenever you execute a statement in the Immediate window (more on this window in the next section). So if you step through a macro in the Code window, you can watch the value of a variable or an expression as each statement executes. This is a great way to pinpoint the location of an error or an unexpected value and is much easier than moving the mouse over each variable or expression in question, checking each value with the Auto Data Tips feature.

Before you can display a variable in the Watch window, you need to declare it. Otherwise, the Visual Basic Editor will respond with a "Variable not created in this context" error.

Because watch expressions slow execution of your code, the Visual Basic Editor does not save them with the code—you need to place them separately for each editing session. The Visual Basic Editor stores watch expressions during the current editing session, so you can move from procedure to procedure without losing your watch expressions.

To set a watch expression, add it to the list in the Watch window:

1. Select the variable or expression in your code, or position the insertion point in it. (This step is optional, but recommended.)

2. Right-click in the Code window or in the Watch window and choose Add Watch from the shortcut menu, or choose Debug ➢ Add Watch to display the Add Watch dialog box. If you selected a variable or an expression in Step 1, it will appear in the Expression text box.

3. If necessary, change the variable or expression in the Expression text box, or enter a variable or an expression if you didn't select one in Step 1.

4. If necessary, adjust the settings in the Context group box. The Procedure drop-down list will be set to the current macro, and the Module drop-down list will be set to the current module.

5. In the Watch Type group box, adjust the option button setting if necessary:

   • The default setting, Watch Expression, adds the variable or expression in the Expression text box to the list in the Watch window.

   • *Break when value is true* causes VBA to enter Break mode whenever the value of the variable or expression changes to True.

   • *Break when value changes* causes VBA to enter Break mode whenever the value of the watch expression changes. Use this setting either when dealing with a watch expression whose value you do not expect to change but which appears to be changing or when dealing with a watch expression whose every change you need to observe.

TIP The *Break when value is true* option button allows you to run your code without stepping through each statement that does not change the value of the watch expression to True. The *Break when value changes* option button allows you to run your code and stop with each change of the value.

---

6. Click the OK button to add the watch expression to the Watch window.

TIP   You can also drag a variable or an expression from the Code window to the Watch window. This sets a default watch expression in the current context; to set *Break when value is true* or *Break when value changes*, edit the watch expression after dragging it to the Watch window.

To edit a watch expression, right-click the watch expression in the Watch window and choose Edit Watch from the Shortcut menu, or select the expression in the Watch window and choose Debug ➤ Edit Watch. Either action displays the Edit Watch dialog box with the watch expression selected in the Expression box. Change the context or watch type for the watch expression by using the settings in the Context group box and the Watch Type group box, and then click the OK button to apply your changes.

To delete a watch expression, right-click it in the Watch window and choose Delete Watch from the shortcut menu. You can also delete the current watch expression by clicking the Delete button in the Edit Watch dialog box.

Using the Quick Watch Feature

For times when you don't want to create a watch expression for an expression or a variable, you can use the Quick Watch feature, which displays the Quick Watch dialog box showing the context and value of the selected expression.

To use Quick Watch, select the expression or variable in the Code window and then click the Quick Watch button on the Debug toolbar, choose Debug ➤ Quick Watch, or press Shift+F9. (If you're already working in the Quick Watch dialog box, you can click the Add button to add the expression to the Watch window.)

The Immediate Window

The Visual Basic Editor provides an Immediate window that you can use as a virtual scratchpad to enter lines of code that you want to test without entering them in the macro itself or to display information to help you check the values of variables while a macro is executing. In the first case, you enter code in the Immediate window; in the second, you use statements entered in the Code window to display information in the Immediate window, where you can easily view it. You can execute code in the Immediate window *only* when your code is running—for example, when you have a project in Break mode and are stepping through it.

To display the Immediate window, click the Immediate Window button on the Debug toolbar, choose View ➤ Immediate Window, or press Ctrl+G. To hide the Immediate window again, click its Close button.

A number of restrictions apply to the code you can use in the Immediate window:

- You cannot use declarative statements (such as DIM, PRIVATE, PUBLIC, OPTION EXPLICIT, STATIC, or TYPE) or control-flow statements (such as GOTO, SUB, or FUNCTION). These will cause VBA to throw an "Invalid in Immediate Pane" error.

- You cannot use multiline statements (such as block IF statements or block FOR...NEXT statements) because there is no logical connection between statements on different lines in the Immediate window; each line is treated in isolation. You can get around this limitation by entering block If statements on a single line, separating the statements with colons, and using the underscore line-continuation character to break the resulting long lines into two physical lines while keeping them as one logical line.

- You cannot place breakpoints in the Immediate window.

The Immediate window supports most standard Windows key combinations and most of the Visual Basic Editor keystrokes and key combinations (such as F5 to start a procedure or Form running). There are, however, two exceptions:

- Pressing Enter runs the current line of code.

- Pressing Ctrl+Enter inserts a carriage return.

As well as entering statements in the Immediate window for quick testing, you can include in your macros statements to print information to the Immediate window by using the Print method on the Debug object. This provides you with a way of viewing information as a macro runs without having to be in Break mode or having to display a message box or dialog box that stops execution of the macro.

The syntax for the Print method is

```
Debug.Print [outputlist]
```

The outputlist argument, which is optional, specifies the expression or expressions to print. For example, you could print the names and paths of all open documents to the Immediate window by using the following statements in a macro for Word:

```
For Each doc in Documents
    Debug.Print doc.FullName
Next
```

The Visual Basic Editor Toolbars

The Visual Basic Editor for Word and Excel provides four toolbars:

- Standard
- Edit
- Debug
- UserForm

You can display and hide these toolbars by using conventional Office methods: Right-click anywhere in the menu bar or in any displayed toolbar and choose the name of the toolbar from the shortcut menu of toolbars; or choose View ➢ Toolbars and make your selection from the Toolbars submenu.

The following sections discuss each of the toolbars in detail.

Standard Toolbar

The Standard toolbar (see Figure 22.7) provides commands for working with and running macros.

FIGURE 22.7:

Use the buttons on the Standard toolbar for working with macros.

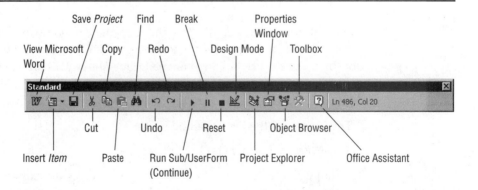

This is what the buttons on the Standard toolbar do:

View Microsoft Word displays Word.

Insert Item inserts the currently selected item—UserForm, Module, Class Module, or Procedure. You can click the drop-down button and select a different item from the drop-down list.

Save Project (*Project* is the name of the current project) saves the current project and all code in it.

Cut, **Copy**, and **Paste** work as usual.

Find displays the Find dialog box for finding and replacing text.

Undo and **Redo** work as usual.

Run Sub/UserForm (Continue) starts the current procedure or Form running. If the current procedure or Form is already running and is stopped in Break mode, clicking the Run Sub/UserForm (Continue) button starts the procedure or Form running again. (If no procedure is current, clicking this button displays the Macros dialog box for you to choose the macro to run.)

Break places the Visual Basic Editor in Break mode, interrupting the execution of any code that is running. (When the Break button is not visible, you can enter Break mode by pressing Ctrl+Break.)

Reset stops the current procedure and clears all its variables.

Design Mode toggles Design mode on and off.

Project Explorer displays the Project Explorer window (if it is not displayed) and activates it.

Properties Window displays the Properties window (if it is not displayed) and activates it.

Object Browser displays the Object Browser (if it is not displayed) and activates it.

Toolbox displays or hides the Toolbox when it is available.

Office Assistant starts the Office Assistant.

Edit Toolbar

The Edit toolbar (see Figure 22.8) provides more commands for running and editing macros.

FIGURE 22.8:

Use the buttons on the Edit toolbar for running and editing macros.

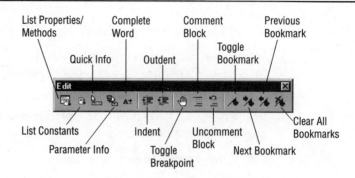

Here's what the buttons on the Edit toolbar do:

List Properties/Methods displays the pop-up List Properties/Methods list box when it is available.

List Constants displays the pop-up List Constants list box when it is available.

Quick Info displays information about the code at which the insertion point is currently located.

Parameter Info displays pop-up information about the parameter at which the insertion point is currently located.

Complete Word completes the word in which the insertion point is currently located.

Indent and **Outdent** indent and un-indent the current line of code or the currently selected lines.

Toggle Breakpoint toggles on and off a breakpoint at the current line.

Comment Block comments out the current line or selected lines by putting an apostrophe at the beginning of the line. The Visual Basic Editor displays comment lines in a different color (by default, green) so that you can readily identify them.

NOTE

When you comment a block, any lines already commented receive a second apostrophe. When you uncomment a block, the Visual Basic Editor removes only the first apostrophe from each line so that any lines commented before the block was commented remain commented. You can remove such commenting by clicking the Uncomment Block button again.

Uncomment Block removes commenting from the current line or selected lines.

Toggle Bookmark adds a bookmark to the current line (if it doesn't already have one) or removes a bookmark if the line already has one.

Next Bookmark moves the insertion point to the next bookmark.

Previous Bookmark moves the insertion point to the previous bookmark.

Clear All Bookmarks removes all bookmarks from the current project.

Debug Toolbar

The Debug toolbar (see Figure 22.9) contains commands for running and debugging your macros. The Debug toolbar shares three buttons—Run Sub/UserForm (Continue), Break, and Reset—with the Standard toolbar; the others are specific to running and debugging macros.

FIGURE 22.9:

The Debug toolbar provides 13 commands for debugging your macros.

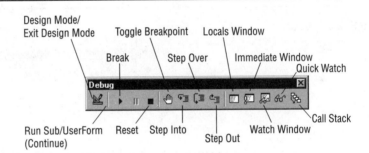

Here's what the buttons on the Debug toolbar do:

Design Mode/Exit Design Mode toggles in and out of Design mode, which you use for creating Forms.

Run Sub/UserForm (Continue), **Break**, and **Reset** work as described in the "Standard Toolbar" section earlier in this chapter.

Toggle Breakpoint toggles on and off a breakpoint at the current line.

Step Into steps into the current procedure in Break mode.

Step Over executes the whole of a procedure or function called from the current procedure (instead of stepping through the called procedure statement by statement). This button becomes available when you enter Break mode.

Step Out runs the rest of the current procedure. This button becomes available when you enter Break mode.

Locals Window displays the Locals window.

Immediate Window displays the Immediate window.

Watch Window displays the Watch window.

Quick Watch displays the Quick Watch dialog box containing the context and value of the selected expression.

Call Stack displays the Call Stack dialog box.

UserForm Toolbar

The UserForm toolbar (see Figure 22.10) contains buttons for working with Forms. This toolbar contains some of the same buttons as the Form Editor toolbar in the Visual Basic IDE.

FIGURE 22.10:

The UserForm toolbar

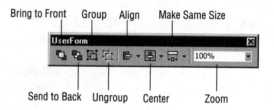

Here's what the buttons on the UserForm toolbar do:

Bring to Front places the selected object, objects, or group of objects in front of the other objects on a form.

Send to Back places the selected object, objects, or group of objects behind the other objects on a form.

Group groups the selected objects.

Ungroup ungroups the selected objects.

Align aligns the selected objects using the alignment last chosen (for example, Align Middles). The Align drop-down list offers the horizontal alignments Lefts, Centers, and Rights; the vertical alignments Tops, Middles, and Bottoms; and To Grid.

Center centers the selected object, objects, or group of objects using the centering last chosen (for example, Center Vertically). The Center drop-down list offers the choices Horizontally and Vertically.

Make Same Size makes the selected objects the same size in the dimension or dimensions last used (for example, Make Width Same Size). The Make Same Size drop-down list offers the choices Width, Height, and Both.

Zoom zooms the controls on the Form.

Choosing Options for the Visual Basic Editor

The Visual Basic Editor provides a number of options to let you customize its look and its actions. You'll find many of these options similar to those in the Visual Basic IDE.

To choose options for the Visual Basic Editor, select Tools ➢ Options to open the Options dialog box and make choices on the four tabs. The following sections describe the options.

Editor Tab Options

The Editor tab of the Options dialog box (see Figure 22.11) includes the following settings:

Auto Syntax Check controls whether the Visual Basic Editor automatically checks your syntax as you type expressions. This is usually helpful because the Visual Basic Editor can instantly point out errors that otherwise would have remained unseen until you tried to run or debug your code. But if your style is to flit from one unfinished line of code to another (and ultimately finish lines at your convenience), you may want to turn off this feature.

Require Variable Declaration governs whether you declare variables explicitly or implicitly. Select this checkbox to have the Visual Basic Editor require you to declare variables explicitly. The Visual Basic Editor will place an Option Explicit statement at the beginning of each module you create when this option is selected.

Auto List Members controls whether the List Properties/Methods and List Constants features automatically suggest properties, methods, and constants as you work in the Code window.

Auto Quick Info controls whether the Quick Info feature automatically displays information as you work in the Code window.

Auto Data Tips controls whether the Visual Basic Editor displays screentips when you move the mouse pointer over a variable.

Auto Indent controls whether the Visual Basic Editor automatically indents subsequent lines of code after you've indented a line.

Tab Width sets the number of spaces in a tab. You can adjust this from 1 to 32 spaces.

Drag-and-Drop Text Editing controls whether the Visual Basic Editor supports drag-and-drop. (Enabling this is usually a good idea.)

Default to Full Module View controls whether the Visual Basic Editor displays all the macros in one module together in one list or displays them one at a time. If you're working with short macros, you may find the list view useful; for most other purposes, the individual view provides a less cluttered and more workable effect. To switch to individual view, clear this checkbox, close the Options dialog box, and then open the module you want to work with by choosing it from the Procedure drop-down list at the top of the Code window. (If you already have the macro displayed in the list view, you'll need to close this window to switch to the individual view.)

Procedure Separator controls whether the Visual Basic Editor displays horizontal lines to separate the macros within a module shown in list view in the Code window. Usually these lines are helpful, providing a quick reference to where one macro ends and the next begins. (If you're using the individual view, this checkbox is not relevant.)

Editor Format Tab Options

The Editor Format tab of the Options dialog box (see Figure 22.12) controls how text in the Visual Basic Editor appears. You can change the default colors for various types of text used in macros by choosing any of them (one at a time) in the Code Colors list box and selecting colors from the Foreground, Background, and Indicator drop-down lists.

FIGURE 22.11:

The Editor tab of the Options dialog box

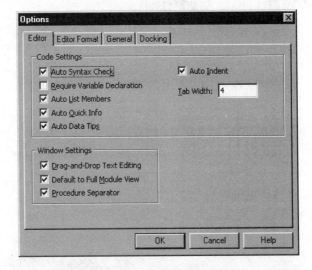

FIGURE 22.12:

The Editor Format tab of the Options dialog box

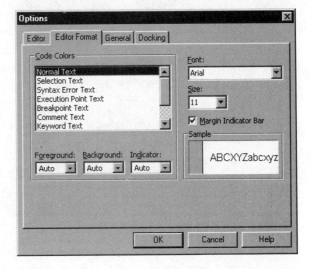

You can change the font and size of all the text in the Code window by using the Font and Size drop-down lists. To increase the size of the Code window a fraction, you can also prevent the display of the margin indicator bar (in which items such as the Next Statement and Breakpoint icons appear) by clearing the Margin Indicator Bar checkbox.

General Tab Options

The General tab of the Options dialog box (see Figure 22.13) contains categories of settings. The Form Grid Settings control how the Visual Basic Editor handles Forms for items such as dialog boxes. Note that unlike the Visual Basic IDE, the Visual Basic Editor uses twips as its measurement unit for the grid.

- Select the Show Grid checkbox if you want the Visual Basic Editor to display the grid pattern of dots on Forms.

- Specify the distance between the lines in the grid pattern by setting the Width and Height text boxes.

- Select the Align Controls to Grid checkbox if you want the Visual Basic Editor to automatically snap the controls to the grid as you place them.

FIGURE 22.13:

The General tab of the Options dialog box

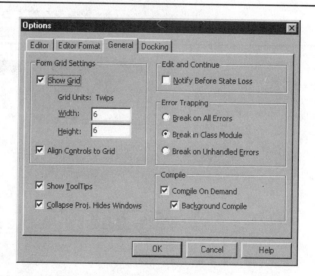

The Notify Before State Loss checkbox controls whether the Visual Basic Editor warns you when you're running a module and you try to take an action that will require VBA to reset the values of all variables in the module.

The Error Trapping group box controls how VBA handles errors that occur when you're running code:

Break on All Errors sets VBA to enter Break mode when it encounters any error, no matter whether an error handler is active or whether the code is in a class module. This option is useful for pinpointing where errors occur; if you have an error-handling mechanism in place, you probably won't want to use this option.

Break in Class Module is the default setting for the Error Trapping group box, and it's the most useful option for general use. When VBA encounters an unhandled error in a class module, it enters Break mode at the offending line of code in the module.

Break on Unhandled Errors is useful when you have constructed an error handler to handle predictable errors in the current module. If there is an error handler, VBA allows the handler to trap the error and does not enter Break mode; but if there is no error handler for the error generated, VBA enters Break mode on the offending line of code. An unhandled error in a class module, however, causes the project to enter Break mode on the line of code that invoked the offending procedure of the class, thus enabling you to identify (and alter) the line that caused the problem.

The Compile group box controls when the Visual Basic Editor compiles the code for a project. Select the Compile On Demand checkbox if you want the code to be compiled only as needed; if you do so, you can also select the Background Compile checkbox to have the Visual Basic Editor use idle CPU time to compile the code while the project is not running.

The Show ToolTips checkbox controls whether the Visual Basic Editor displays ToolTips (a.k.a. screentips) for its toolbar buttons.

The Collapse Proj. Hides Windows checkbox controls whether the Visual Basic Editor hides the Code window and other Project windows that you collapse in the Project Explorer.

Docking Tab Options

The Docking tab of the Options dialog box (see Figure 22.14) controls whether the various windows in the Visual Basic Editor are dockable or not—that is, whether they attach automatically to a side of the window when you move them there. As in the Visual Basic IDE, keeping windows dockable usually makes for a more organized interface, but you may find it useful to make the windows undockable so that you can drag them off the edge of the screen as necessary and generally arrange them however makes most sense to you.

FIGURE 22.14:

The Docking tab of the
Options dialog box

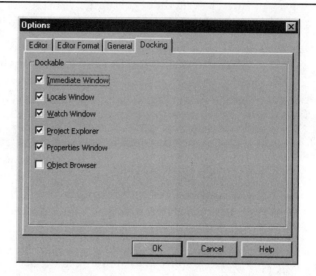

Working with the Visual Basic Editor and the Visual Basic IDE

Both the Visual Basic IDE and the Visual Basic Editor provide an enormous amount of help when you're working in them. In most cases, the best way of creating code that uses VBA and the Office applications is to use all the help that you can get. This means working in the environment most suited to helping you create the code you need.

As discussed earlier in this chapter, the Visual Basic Editor interface provides help and prompting for creating VBA code to work with the host application for the Visual Basic Editor session through features such as Auto Complete and List Properties/Constants. Because these and other features of the Visual Basic Editor are not available when you are working in the Visual Basic IDE and referencing Word or Excel VBA objects, it's usually a good idea to create the prototype for the code in the Visual Basic Editor and then transfer it to the Visual Basic IDE when you're sure it works: When creating a Visual Basic project that manipulates Word, create the Word statements in the Visual Basic Editor in a session started from a Word session. (The Visual Basic Editor provides help on the host application only.

If you reference another application—for example, if you use VBA in Word to create an Excel object—the Word VBA session cannot provide help on Excel VBA.)

When you move code from the Visual Basic Editor to the Visual Basic IDE, you will have to adjust the references in the code from the Visual Basic Editor to correspond with the command structure you've used in the Visual Basic IDE. But doing so is usually much faster than debugging code, statement by statement in the Visual Basic IDE, because you've missed (or mistyped) an argument that the Visual Basic Editor could have supplied (or highlighted) instantly had you been working in it.

Recording a Macro

If you're not intimately familiar with the object model of Excel or Word (which we'll be examining in Chapters 23 and 24), recording a macro is by far the easiest way of creating VBA code that you can then move to the Visual Basic IDE: You simply switch on the macro recorder and record the actions you want the macro to take. When you finish recording, you can switch to the Visual Basic Editor and work with the code representing the actions.

Even if you *are* familiar with the object models of the Office applications, a macro can still be a handy way of quickly assembling the details of the code you need. Either way, you will usually want to adjust the code recorded in a macro before moving it to the Visual Basic IDE.

In Chapter 21, we gave you the short version of how to record a macro. Here's a more detailed look:

1. Start the macro recorder by choosing Tools ➤ Macro ➤ Record New Macro. (In Word, you can double-click the REC indicator on the status bar instead.) Excel or Word displays the Record Macro dialog box. Figure 22.15 shows the Record Macro dialog box for Word; Figure 22.16 shows the Record Macro dialog box for Excel.

2. Enter a name for the new macro in the Macro Name text box. The macro name can be a maximum of 80 characters and can contain both letters and numbers, but it must start with a letter. It cannot contain spaces, punctuation, or special characters (such as ! or *), though underscores are allowed.

FIGURE 22.15:

In the Record Macro dialog box, enter a name for the macro you're about to record, and enter a description in the Description box if necessary. This is the Record Macro dialog box for Word.

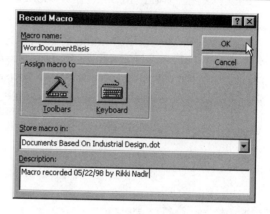

FIGURE 22.16:

The Record Macro dialog box for Excel

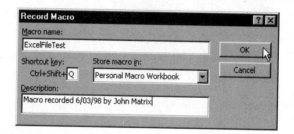

NOTE   Neither Excel nor Word will prevent you from typing a space or a forbidden character in the Macro Name text box. But when you click the OK button, Excel will display a message box telling you the name is not valid and will return you to the Record Macro dialog box to allow you to fix the name. Word will display a message box telling you that the procedure name is invalid and will close the Record Macro dialog box.

3. If you care to, you can enter a description for the macro in the Description box. This description is to help you (and anyone you share the macro with) identify the macro. If you're creating the macro with the intention of cannibalizing it immediately for a Visual Basic project, don't waste time adding a description to it.

4. In Word, if you want to restrict the macro to the current template, choose that template from the Store Macro In drop-down list. If you want the macro to be available no matter which template you're working in, make sure the default setting, All Documents (NORMAL.DOT), appears in the Store Macro In drop-down list box.

In Excel, if you want the macro to be available only to the current workbook, choose This Workbook in the Store Macro In drop-down list. If you want the macro to be available to all workbooks, choose the Personal Macro Workbook option. If you want to store the macro in a new workbook, choose the New Workbook option.

5. Next, you can assign a way to run the macro. Again, if you're creating a scratch macro for immediate reuse, this isn't worth the effort. Otherwise, see the sidebar for how to assign a toolbar button, menu item, or shortcut key.

6. Excel or Word will now be ready to start recording the macro. You'll see the application display the Stop Recording toolbar and add a cassette-tape icon to the mouse pointer to remind you that you're recording. In Word, the REC indicator in the status bar will be darkened (activated) as well.

7. Now record the sequence of actions for the macro:

    -   In Word, you can use the mouse to select items from menus and toolbars and to make choices in dialog boxes, but not to select items within a document window—to select items in a document window, you must use the keyboard.

    -   To perform any actions that you don't want recorded, you can pause the macro recorder at any time by clicking the Pause Recording button on the Stop Recording toolbar. Click the Pause Recording button again to resume recording.

NOTE   When you make choices in a dialog box—for example, the Paragraph dialog box in Word—the macro recorder records the current settings for *all* of the options on that tab of the dialog box when you click OK. So when you make a change to, say, the left indention of a paragraph, Word records all the other settings on the Indents and Spacing tab as well (Alignment, Before and After spacing, and so forth). You'll need to edit the unnecessary commands out of the resulting macro.

8. To stop recording, click the Stop Recording button on the Stop Recording toolbar. The macro recorder will have recorded the VBA commands for the actions you performed. If you chose to assign the macro to a control or a keystroke, the application will have assigned it.

You'll probably need to edit the macro you've recorded, either to adapt it or to tighten it. We'll look at editing macros in the Visual Basic Editor in just a moment, in "Debugging a Macro in the Visual Basic Editor."

Assigning a Way to Run a Macro

You can assign a macro to a toolbar button, to a menu item, or to a shortcut key. The process is a little different depending on whether you're working in Excel or in Word.

In Excel, click in the Shortcut Key text box and press the key that you want to use with Ctrl as a shortcut key. Press the Shift key if you want to add Shift to the key combination. (For example, you can use Ctrl+K and Ctrl+Shift+K to run different macros stored in the same workbook if you so choose.)

In Word, click the Toolbars button or the Keyboard button in the Assign Macro To group box. If you choose Toolbars, Word displays the Customize dialog box with the Commands tab displayed and Macros selected in the Categories list box. Now, follow these steps:

1. Click the macro's name in the Commands list box and drag it to any convenient toolbar or to the menu bar. Word will add a button or menu item for the macro, giving it the macro's full name and context, such as NORMAL.NEWMACROS.MyNewMacro.

2. You can now rename the button or menu item by right-clicking it and entering a suitable (and probably shorter) name in the Name text box on the shortcut menu that appears.

3. To assign an access key to an item, put an ampersand (&) before the character that you want to use as the access key.

4. Click the Close button to close the Customize dialog box.

If you choose Keyboard, Word displays the Customize Keyboard dialog box. Place the insertion point in the Press New Shortcut Key box and then press the key combination you want. A key combination can be any one of the following:

- Alt plus either a regular key not used as a menu access key or a function key

- Ctrl plus a regular key or a function key

- Shift plus a function key

- Ctrl+Alt, Ctrl+Shift, Alt+Shift, or Ctrl+Alt+Shift plus a regular key or function key

Check the Current Keys list box to make sure the key combination you chose isn't already in use (if it is, press Backspace and select another combination), and then click the Assign button. Click the Close button to close the Customize Keyboard dialog box. Excel or Word will now be ready to start recording the macro.

Creating a Macro from Scratch in the Visual Basic Editor

Instead of recording a macro from Excel or Word, you can create the macro from scratch in the Visual Basic Editor. There are a couple of main advantages to doing so:

- First, you can write code that you will not need to tighten or edit down. If you want to use only one setting in, say, the Paragraph dialog box in Word, you will not need to record every other setting on that tab of the dialog box as well.

- Second, you can create code that you would not be able to record using the macro recorder. For example, while working interactively with Excel or Word, you can work only with the active workbook or document: Any workbook or document that you need to work with, you must first make active. By writing VBA code, on the other hand, you can work with workbooks or documents other than the active one. This can greatly help you write efficient macros.

The disadvantage to writing a macro from scratch is that you need to know which objects you want to manipulate—or be prepared to do some research. This is why the macro recorder makes a great tool for getting a macro started.

You can start creating a macro from scratch in any of several ways:

- From Excel or Word, choose Tools ➤ Macro ➤ Macros to open the Macros dialog box. Enter the name for the new macro in the Macro Name text box, add a description in the Description text box if necessary, select the template, document, or workbook to store the macro in, and then click the Create button. Excel or Word opens the Visual Basic Editor and displays the macro in a Code window.

    Excel will store the macro in a new module named Module*n*—Module1, Module2, and so on, where *n* is the number higher than any consecutive number used so far for such a module name. Excel will continue to use this module for further macros you create in the same Excel session. For macros you create in a subsequent Excel session, Excel will create a new module with the next higher consecutive number.

Word will store the macro in a module named NewMacros, creating the module if it does not already exist.

• From the Visual Basic Editor for the appropriate host application, open the module in which to store the macro. Choose Insert ➤ Procedure to open the Add Procedure dialog box (see Figure 22.17). Enter the name for the new procedure in the Name text box. In the Type group box, choose the type of procedure to create: Sub, Function, or Property. (For a macro, choose Sub.) In the Scope group box, select the Public option button or the Private option button to specify public or private scope for the procedure. Click the OK button to close the Add Procedure dialog box. The Visual Basic Editor places the appropriate statements for the macro—for example, Public Sub *MacroName*( ), a blank line, and an End Sub statement—in the module.

FIGURE 22.17:

Name the macro and specify its scope in the Add Procedure dialog box.

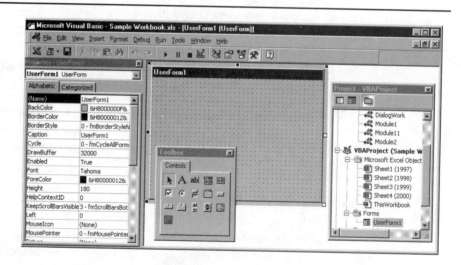

• In the Code window, type **Sub** (or **Private Sub** or **Public Sub**, as appropriate for the scope of the macro you want to create), followed by the name you want the macro to have, and press Enter. The Visual Basic Editor will automatically add parentheses (unless you typed them), a blank paragraph, and an End Sub statement.

You can now create the macro by entering code in the Code window, using the help features that the Visual Basic Editor provides.

Debugging a Macro in the Visual Basic Editor

In this section, we'll touch on the types of errors to expect in VBA and the main ways of debugging a macro in the Visual Basic Editor. Both these topics should be familiar to you from Visual Basic and the Visual Basic IDE, so we won't linger on them. We'll simply point out the few differences between debugging in the Visual Basic Editor and debugging in the Visual Basic IDE.

Types of Errors to Expect

You can confidently expect to see language errors, compile errors, and run-time errors when working with VBA. Whether you see program logic errors as well is up to you.

The Visual Basic Editor's help features help eliminate language errors (also known as *syntax errors*) and some compile errors when entering code. For example, the Visual Basic Editor will alert you to an error such as omitting the Then from an If…Then construction by checking the statement when you move the insertion point to another line in the Code window. Language errors that the Visual Basic Editor doesn't catch as you create them usually show up as compile errors when the Visual Basic Editor compiles the code for a procedure.

Compile errors occur when VBA cannot compile a statement correctly—when it cannot turn a statement that you've entered into viable code. For example, if you tell VBA to use a property for an object that doesn't have that property, you'll cause a compile error. Likewise, if you mistype an argument in a statement, as in the example below (FILEMAME instead of FILENAME), it will usually show up as a compile error.

```
ActiveDocument.SaveAs FileMame:="My File.doc"
```

As well as the errors that the Visual Basic Editor actively helps you avoid, as in the examples above, you can avoid other errors by watching the Visual Basic Editor's behavior closely as you're creating your code. Say you're trying to enter a DOCUMENTS.CLOSE statement and mistype Documents as Docments—easy enough to do. In this case, the Visual Basic Editor will not display the Properties/Methods list because you haven't entered a valid object. Not seeing the list should alert you that something is wrong, unless you've turned off the Auto List Members option.

If you continue anyway and enter the DOCMENTS.CLOSE statement (again, easy enough to do if you're not watching the screen), the Visual Basic Editor will not spot the mistake, and it will show up as a "Run-time error 424: Object required" when you try to run the macro.

In a similar vein, if you specify a property or a method for an object to which that property or method does not apply, VBA will generate a compile error. For example, say you forget the Add method and enter Documents.Create instead. VBA will highlight the offending word and will generate a compile error "Method or data member not found," which tells you there's no Create method for the Documents collection.

Run-time errors occur while code is executing, caused by a statement that makes VBA try to perform an impossible operation. For example, your code might require opening a document that doesn't exist, closing a workbook when no workbook is open, or performing something mathematically impossible such as dividing by zero.

Program logic errors—errors that produce incorrect results, though the code compiles and runs correctly—are entirely up to you. They also tend to be the hardest errors to catch, because you'll have less of an indication as to where things start going wrong—or how many things are going wrong.

Troubleshooting Problems in Procedures

This section contains some suggestions for troubleshooting problems in procedures in the Visual Basic Editor.

First, make the most of Break mode for pinpointing where things go wrong in your code:

- When a macro stops and the Visual Basic Editor displays the Microsoft Visual Basic *Code execution has been interrupted* dialog box, click the Debug button to access and view the problem line in your code straightaway. If your code gets stuck in a loop, press Ctrl+Break to enter Break mode and display this dialog box.

- Alternatively, set breakpoints at lines of code that may be problematic.

- Use Stop statements if you need to keep a breakpoint in your code from one editing session to another. Like the Visual Basic IDE, the Visual Basic Editor doesn't save breakpoints with your code: You have to place them for each editing session. This serves as a handy way to avoid leaving breakpoints in your code unintentionally, but at times you'll want to use a Stop statement instead to halt execution.

- Use the Step Through and Step Out commands to avoid stepping command-by-command through code that you know to be working fine.

- After you fix an error in the code in Break mode, use the Set Next Statement command to continue execution from wherever is most advantageous. Click in the line from which to start and choose Debug ➤ Set Next Statement, or right-click in the line and choose Set Next Statement from the shortcut menu.

Don't let your error handlers hide errors from you:

- Make your error handlers as specific as possible. When you're creating an error handler, use a Debug.Print statement to place the error number in the Immediate window and then copy the number into your handler. Check to make sure that this error number solves the problem: Often, you'll get various errors from the same line of code, depending on the condition of the host application. For example, if the user tries to specify a drive that is not available, VBA responds with an error that is different from the one it displays when a user tries to access a folder that does not exist. Trap each error by number, and take action accordingly, rather than using a blanket error handler that will quash any other error that you encounter.

- If you're using one or more error handlers that prevent you from seeing certain errors in your code, use the Break on All Errors setting in the Options dialog box to cause VBA to enter Break mode from any error without your having to disable your error handler or handlers.

Comment out lines that may be problematic, and rerun the code to see if that makes a difference.

Keep a close eye on the value of variables and expressions:

- When you hit an error, check as many of the variables and expressions as possible, looking for unexpected values.

- Use the Immediate window to test data or expressions or to print information at strategic points in the macro.

- Use the Locals window to track the values of all the declared variables in the current procedure.

- Use the Watch window (and the Quick Watch dialog box when necessary) to watch the value of selected expressions.

- Use the Call Stack dialog box to track which procedures are called.

To watch what is happening as a macro executes, arrange the Visual Basic Editor and the host application windows so that you can see them both. Then step through the questionable part of the macro command by command. Watching the effect of each command as it is executed is a powerful tool in helping to establish what's going wrong. Is a macro failing because the required object is not available (for example, because the relevant document or workbook is not open when the macro expects it to be) or because the wrong object is being manipulated (for example, if you have selected a different range than you intended)?

NOTE Beyond the differences in the menus, necessary for dealing with the different capabilities of the Visual Basic IDE and the Visual Basic Editor, you'll find small inconsistencies that take a little getting used to. For example, the Run menu in the Visual Basic IDE contains a Restart command with the access key R, whereas the Run menu in the Visual Basic Editor contains the Reset command instead, also with the access key R. This Reset command performs the equivalent of the Visual Basic IDE's Run ➤ End command. If you're used to using Alt+R, R to restart a project from Break mode, you'll get a little surprise when you use that key combination in the Visual Basic Editor.

Creating Forms in the Visual Basic Editor

Creating Forms in the Visual Basic Editor is similar to creating Forms in the Visual Basic IDE. In this section, we'll briefly discuss the process of creating Forms in the Visual Basic Editor, touching on some of the differences from the Visual Basic IDE. We'll look at how the controls in the Visual Basic Editor compare with those in the Visual Basic IDE and at how you can customize the Toolbox in the Visual Basic Editor.

To create a new Form in a project, follow these steps:

1. Right-click the project in the Project Explorer and choose Insert ➢ UserForm from the shortcut menu. The Visual Basic Editor creates and displays a new Form of the default size and names it UserForm*n*, where *n* is the next higher unused consecutive number. Figure 22.18 shows a new Form in the Visual Basic Editor. The Visual Basic Editor places this Form in the Forms collection for the project. If the project does not have a Forms collection yet, the Visual Basic Editor creates one and places the Form in it. The Visual Basic Editor also displays the Toolbox.

NOTE   If you don't have the Project Explorer displayed, choose Insert ➢ UserForm, or click the Insert button on the Standard toolbar and choose UserForm from the drop-down list. The Insert button has four manifestations: Insert UserForm, Insert Module, Insert Class Module, and Insert Procedure, depending on the last item created from this button. If the current button is Insert UserForm, you can click the button to create a Form rather than using the drop-down list.

FIGURE 22.18:

Creating a Form in the Visual Basic Editor

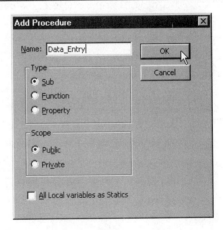

2. Add controls to the Form. Click the Toolbox button for the control you want to create. The mouse pointer changes to a crosshair with the button symbol for the item that you will create. Click once in the Form to place a default-size control; the upper-left corner of the control will be placed where you click. Click and drag in the Form to place and size a custom control. You can

drag in any direction after clicking—the point at which you click does not have to be the upper-left corner of the control.

3. Adjust the controls as necessary:

   • Drag them about with the mouse.

   • Use the Properties window to adjust their properties.

   • Use the commands on the UserForm toolbar and on the Format menu to adjust the placement, grouping, and layering of the controls.

4. Add code to the code sheet for the Form:

   • Display the code sheet for the Form. You can do so in several ways: Press F7; right-click the Form itself or the Form's name or icon in the Project Explorer and choose View Code from the shortcut menu; select the Form's name in the Project Explorer and click the View Code button on the Project Explorer's toolbar; or choose View ➤ Code. To create a procedure associated with a particular control, double-click that control. The Visual Basic Editor will display the code sheet for the Form and will create a private procedure for the default event of that control. For example, if you double-click an option button named optAutomatic, the Visual Basic Editor will create a procedure associated with the Click event for the option button and name it Private Sub optAutomatic_Click. (If a procedure with that name exists already, the Visual Basic Editor will display the procedure.)

   • Enter the code for the procedures as usual.

   • Create an initialization macro if you need to initialize any of the controls in the Form. This macro does not take the name of the Form. It needs to be named UserForm_Initialize:

```
Private Sub UserForm_Initialize()
'Commands for initializing the Form
End Sub
```

5. Adjust the tab order of the controls on the Form as necessary. Choose View ➤ Tab Order to display the Tab Order dialog box. Select one or more controls in the Tab Order list box (Shift+click to select multiple contiguous controls, Ctrl+click to select multiple controls individually) and click Move Up and Move Down to get the controls into the appropriate order. Click the OK button to close the Tab Order dialog box.

6. If necessary, create a macro to display the Form:

- To load a Form, use the Load statement. To unload a Form, use the Unload statement. The Load statement loads the Form into memory so it is available to the program, but does not display the Form. The Unload statement unloads the Form from memory and reclaims any memory associated with that object. If the Form is displayed when you run the Unload statement on it, VBA removes the Form from the screen. The following statement loads the Form named frmOptions:

```
Load frmOptions
```

- To display a Form, use the Show method. You can display a Form by using the Show method without explicitly loading the Form with a Load command first; VBA takes care of the implied Load command for you. To hide a Form, you use the Hide method. The following statement displays the Form named frmOptions:

```
frmOptions.Show
```

NOTE If you run a Hide method without having loaded the dialog box into memory by using the Load statement or the Show method, VBA will load the dialog box but will not display it on-screen.

Controls in the Visual Basic Editor

Although the Visual Basic Editor provides fewer controls for Forms overall than the Visual Basic IDE, it has a number of controls that the Visual Basic IDE does not. Table 22.1 shows how the controls stack up in the Visual Basic IDE and the Visual Basic Editor.

TABLE 22.1: The Visual Basic IDE Controls and the Visual Basic Editor Controls

Visual Basic IDE Control	Visual Basic Editor Control
CheckBox	CheckBox
ComboBox	ComboBox
CommandButton	CommandButton

Continued on next page

TABLE 22.1 CONTINUED: The Visual Basic IDE Controls and the Visual Basic Editor Controls

Visual Basic IDE Control	Visual Basic Editor Control
Data	—
DirListBox	—
DriveListBox	—
FileListBox	—
Frame	Frame
HscrollBar	—
Image	Image
Label	Label
Line	—
ListBox	ListBox
—	MultiPage
OLE	—
OptionButton	OptionButton
PictureBox	—
Shape	—
—	SpinButton
—	TabStrip
TextBox	TextBox
Timer	—
—	ToggleButton
VScrollBar	ScrollBar

As you can see, the Visual Basic Editor does not provide the DriveListBox, DirList-Box, and FileListBox controls for working with drives, directories (folders), and files. Instead, you can use list boxes or combo boxes to display arrays of files. But you'll often find it easier to use built-in dialog boxes in the Visual Basic Editor than list boxes or combo boxes with arrays. For example, you can display a built-in dialog box such as the Open dialog box to allow the user to choose a file—either to open it or simply to select it. Alternatively, you might want to select or open a file by using a Form in the Visual Basic IDE before manipulating it in the Visual Basic Editor.

Neither does the Visual Basic Editor provide a Timer control. You can use the OnTime method of the Application object to run a procedure at a specified time.

The Visual Basic Editor provides only a vertical scrollbar control, named Scroll-Bar, whereas the Visual Basic IDE provides the VScrollBar vertical scroll bar control and HScrollBar horizontal scroll bar control.

The Visual Basic Editor provides the following controls that are not present in the basic set of controls in the Visual Basic IDE:

ToggleButton toggles between an On state and an Off state.

SpinButton increments and decrements numbers. Typically, you use a SpinButton control to adjust the value of another control, in many cases in preset increments or decrements (for example, adjusting the cost of a service in five-cent steps).

TabStrip presents sets of controls. For example, you might use a TabStrip control to move from one record to another, where each record used the same set of controls.

MultiPage presents different sets of controls on pages of a Form, as in dialog boxes such as the Options dialog box in the Visual Basic IDE and the Visual Basic Editor. The pages in MultiPage controls are often described as "tabs." The MultiPage control is similar to the Microsoft Tabbed Dialog control that you can add to the controls in the Visual Basic IDE Toolbox.

There are some minor differences between the Visual Basic Editor and the Visual Basic IDE when it comes to working with controls:

- To denote the access key for a control, in the Visual Basic Editor you set the Accelerator property for the control to the appropriate letter. In the Visual Basic IDE, you place an ampersand before the appropriate letter.

- To copy an object in the Visual Basic Editor, you can hold down Ctrl and drag the object (instead of using a Copy command).

- You can also use Copy and Paste to copy an object. Unlike the Visual Basic IDE, the Visual Basic Editor will not ask if you want to create an array, but will create a copy of the object, resetting its name to the next generic name for that type of object but leaving all relevant properties set as they were.

For example, if you create a CommandButton object named cmdOK, set its properties as you want them and then copy it, the Visual Basic Editor will name the copy CommandButton1 (or CommandButton2 or Command-Button3, as appropriate) but will leave the other properties as they were.

Customizing the Toolbox

In the Visual Basic Editor, as in the Visual Basic IDE, you can customize the Toolbox. You can change the controls on its default page if you wish, or you can add extra pages to it and place on them both existing controls and custom controls of your own creation.

By customizing the Toolbox, you can avoid having to create custom controls from scratch each time you need them. For example, in most dialog boxes, you'll want to have an OK button and a Cancel button. You can create these easily by using CommandButton objects and setting the relevant properties (Name, Height, Width, Accelerator, Default, and so on). Once you've created one CommandButton object with the right properties, you can simply put a copy of it in your Toolbox and reuse it when you need it.

You can also add to the Toolbox complex controls that extend the things you can do with dialog boxes and Forms.

Working with Toolbox Pages

Here's how to work with Toolbox pages. You can add pages, rename them, move them to different positions in the Toolbox or even save them to separate files.

To Add a Page to the Toolbox   Right-click the tab at the top of a page (or the label on the tab) and choose New Page from the shortcut menu. The Visual Basic Editor adds a new page named New Page, to which it will add the Select Objects control. This control appears on every tab in the Toolbox (so that it's always at hand), and you cannot remove it.

To Change the Name of a Page   You'll usually want to change the name of a page after adding it to the Toolbox. Right-click its tab or label, and choose Rename from the shortcut menu to display the Rename dialog box. Enter the name for the page in the Caption text box, enter any control tip text you want to appear in the Control Tip Text text box, and click the OK button to close the dialog box.

To Remove a Page from the Toolbox   Right-click its tab or label, and choose Delete Page from the shortcut menu. The Visual Basic Editor removes the page from the Toolbox without any confirmation, whether the page contains controls or not.

To Save Toolbox Pages As Separate Files   You might want to do this when creating a backup or for distribution purposes. Toolbox pages have a PAG extension. To import a Toolbox page, right-click the tab or label on an existing page in the Toolbox and choose Import Page from the shortcut menu to display the Import Page dialog box. Select the page you want to import and choose the Open button. The Visual Basic Editor adds the new page after the last page currently in the Toolbox and names it New Page. To export a Toolbox page, right-click its tab or label and choose Export Page from the shortcut menu to display the Export Page dialog box. Enter a name for the page (change folders if necessary) and click the Save button to save it.

To Move a Page in the Toolbox   Right-click its tab or label and choose Move from the shortcut menu to display the Page Order dialog box. In the Page Order list box, select the page or pages that you want to move (Shift+click or Ctrl+click to select multiple pages) and use the Move Up and Move Down buttons to rearrange the pages as desired. Click the OK button to close the Page Order dialog box when you've finished.

Working with Toolbox Controls

To customize the pages of the Toolbox, you can add and remove controls, rename controls, and assign pictures to their Toolbox icons.

To Add Controls to the Toolbox   You can add to the Toolbox either custom controls from a displayed Form or additional controls installed on your computer:

- To copy a control from a displayed Form to the Toolbox, drag the control from the Form and drop it where you want it in the Toolbox.

- To add controls to the Toolbox, right-click in the tab to which you want to add controls, and choose Additional Controls from the shortcut menu to display the Additional Controls dialog box (see Figure 22.19). In the Available Controls list box, select the checkboxes for the controls you want to add to the Toolbox, and then click the OK button. (To collapse the list to only the items currently selected, select the Selected Items Only checkbox in the Show group box.)

You can move a control from one page of the Toolbox to another by dragging it from the page it is on, moving the mouse pointer (still dragging) over the tab of the destination page to display that page, then moving the mouse pointer down (again, still dragging) into the body of that page, and dropping the control on it. To copy a control from one page to another, hold down the Ctrl key as you drag the control.

FIGURE 22.19:

In the Additional Controls dialog box, select the checkboxes for the controls you want to add, and then click the OK button.

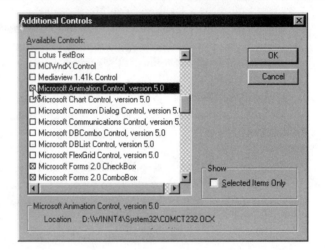

To Rename a Toolbox Control Right-click it in the Toolbox and choose the Customize item from the shortcut menu to display the Customize Control dialog box, shown in Figure 22.20. (The menu item will be identified by the name of the control—for example, if the control is identified as New Label, the menu item will be Customize New Label.)

FIGURE 22.20:

In the Customize Control dialog box, enter the name for the control in the Tool Tip Text text box, and then click the Edit Picture button or the Load Picture button to assign a button to it.

Enter the name for the control in the Tool Tip Text text box; this name will appear as a screentip when the user moves the mouse pointer over the control in the Toolbox. Then, if you wish, assign a different picture to the control's Toolbox icon as described in the next section, or click the OK button to close the Customize Control dialog box.

To Assign a Picture to a Control's Toolbox Icon To edit the picture assigned to the control, right-click the control, choose Customize from the Shortcut menu to display the Customize Control dialog box, and click the Edit Picture button to display the Edit Image dialog box. Here, you can adjust the picture in the Picture edit box, pixel by pixel, by choosing the appropriate color or choosing the Erase tool in the Colors group box and clicking in the square you want to change. Click the Move buttons to move the entire image around the edit box (each direction button is available only if the image does not touch that edge of the edit box); click the Clear button to erase the entire image so that you can start from scratch. Use the Preview group box to see how the picture looks at the resolution at which it will be displayed in the Toolbox. When you finish adjusting the image, click the OK button to return to the Customize Control dialog box, and click the OK button to close that dialog box.

To load an existing picture for a control, right-click the control, choose Customize from the Shortcut menu to display the Customize Control dialog box, and click the Load Picture button in the Customize Control dialog box to display the Load Picture dialog box. Select the picture and click the Open button to load it.

To Remove a Control from the Toolbox Right-click it, and choose Delete from the shortcut menu. The item will be identified by the name of the control— for example, if you right-click a control named Company Name Combo Box, the menu item will be named Delete Company Name Combo Box. If the item is a custom control, this action gets rid of the control, and you will not be able to restore it (unless you have a copy elsewhere). If the item is a Microsoft-supplied control, you can restore it from the Additional Controls dialog box by selecting the checkbox for the appropriate object (for example, Microsoft Forms 2 CommandButton).

You can also remove controls from the Toolbox by deleting the entire page they are on, as we discussed earlier in this chapter.

Finding the VBA Objects You Need

In this section, we'll discuss how to find the VBA objects, methods, and properties you need. You find objects, methods, and properties in the same way in both Excel and Word, though the specifics naturally vary.

In addition to the List Properties/Methods feature and to recording a macro to identify the objects you need to manipulate, you can find objects in two main ways:

- By using the Object Browser
- By using the Help system

Navigating with the Object Browser

The Object Browser in the Visual Basic Editor works in a similar way to the Object Browser in the Visual Basic IDE, which we looked at in Chapter 9. Here's how to find the objects you need by using the Object Browser:

1. Display the Object Browser (see Figure 22.6, earlier in this chapter) by choosing View ➤ Object Browser, by pressing the F2 button, or by clicking the Object Browser button on the Standard toolbar. If the Object Browser is already displayed, make it active by clicking in it or by selecting it from the list at the bottom of the Window menu.

2. In the Project/Library drop-down list, select the name of the project or the library that you want to view. The Object Browser displays the available classes in the Classes list.

3. In the Classes list, select the class you want. For example, if you chose a template in Step 2, select the module you want to work with in the Classes list.

4. If you want to work with a particular member of the class or project, select it in the Members Of list. For example, if you're working with a template project, you might want to choose a specific macro or Form to work with.

5. Once you select the class, member, or project, you can take the following actions:

   - View information about it in the Details pane at the bottom of the Object Browser window.

- View the definition of an object by clicking the Show Definition button. Alternatively, right-click the object in the Members Of list and choose View Definition from the shortcut menu. (The definition of a macro is the code that it contains; the definition of a module is all the code in all the macros that it contains; the definition of a Form is the code in all the macros attached to it.) The Show Definition button will be available (undimmed) only for objects that contain code, such as macros and Forms that you've created.

- Copy the text for the selected class, project, or member to the clipboard by clicking the Copy to Clipboard button or by issuing a standard Copy command (for example, Ctrl+C or Ctrl+Insert).

Using Help to Find the Object You Need

VBA's Help system provides another easy way to access the details of the objects you want. The Help files provide you with a hyperlinked reference to all the objects, methods, and properties in VBA, including graphics that show how the objects are related.

The quickest way to access VBA Help is to activate the Visual Basic Editor and then press the F1 key. (If you've disabled the Office Assistant, you can also choose Help ➤ Microsoft Visual Basic Help.) VBA will respond by displaying the Visual Basic Reference window.

TIP   To get help on a specific object, keyword, and so on referenced in your code, place the insertion point in the appropriate word before pressing the F1 key. VBA will display the Help for that topic.

Click the Help Topics button at the top-left corner of the Visual Basic Reference window to display the Help Topics dialog box. Click the Index tab to display it if it isn't already displayed. In the top text box, type the name of the object about which you want to get information, and then select the appropriate entry in the list box and click the Display button to display the entry.

For example, if you display help on the Word Document object, you'll see a Help window like the one shown in Figure 22.21.

FIGURE 22.21:

Here's what you'll get if you search for help on the Document object.

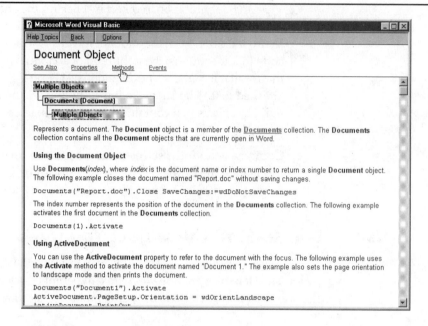

Apart from the regular Help information you'll find in the Help window, you can use the following features to get some additional information:

- Use the graphic at the top of the Help listing to understand the relationship of the current object to the object (or objects) that contains it and to the objects it contains. Click either of these objects to display a list of the relevant objects.

- Click any See Also hyperlink at the top of the window to display a Topics Found dialog box showing associated topics.

- Click the Properties hyperlink at the top of the window to display a Topics Found dialog box listing the help available on the properties of the object. You can then display one of the topics by selecting it in the list box and clicking the Display button or by double-clicking it in the list box.

- Click the Methods hyperlink at the top of the window to display a Topics Found dialog box listing the help available on the methods available for use on the object. Again, you can display one of these topics by selecting it in the list box and clicking the Display button or by double-clicking it in the list box.

- Some objects also have one or more events associated with them. If the object has any events associated with it, you can access them by clicking the Events hyperlink at the top of the window to display a Topics Found dialog box.

Saving Your Work and Closing the Visual Basic Editor

To save your work in the Visual Basic Editor, choose File ➤ Save *projectname* to save the document, template, or workbook and the changes you've made to it. Then choose File ➤ Close and Return to Microsoft Word or File ➤ Close and Return to Microsoft Excel to close the Visual Basic Editor and return to Word or Excel.

NOTE   You can also press Alt+Q to quit the Visual Basic Editor and return to its host application.

CHAPTER
TWENTY-THREE

Excel 97 Objects

- Understanding the Excel object model

- Working with the Excel application

- Working with workbooks and worksheets

- Working with ranges

- Using Find and Replace

- Using Excel's built-in dialog boxes

In this chapter, we'll discuss the objects in Excel 97, the Excel object model that describes how they are arranged, and how to work with them to get things done in VBA.

To manipulate Excel with VBA, you use the VBA objects that Excel exposes. These objects range from the Application object that represents the Excel application to Range objects that can be used to represent ranges of cells. By controlling these objects, you can take actions in Excel.

Because Excel is such a complex application, it exposes many more VBA objects than we can deal with in this chapter. So here we'll discuss the most important Excel objects—those you are most likely to work with first when automating procedures involving Excel. In discussing these objects, we will highlight the most useful properties and methods for each. We will not list or discuss every single property and method for each object. Likewise, for each method we mention, we will present the most useful arguments, not an exhaustive list of every argument that can be used with the method. The goal of this chapter is to give you the information you need to start working effectively with Excel through Visual Basic, not to bore you to tears.

Understanding the Excel Object Model

The Excel object model describes the theoretical architecture underlying Excel. By understanding the Excel object model, you can manipulate the objects in Excel and work effectively with VBA.

The Application object, at the top level of the Excel object model, represents the Excel application. Figure 23.1 shows the objects and collections contained in the Application object. From the Application object, you can access almost any Excel object by manipulating the appropriate object or collection. The plural names with singular names in parentheses indicate collections and the individual objects they contain. For example, the Addins collection is comprised of all Addin objects in the Application object, and the Workbooks collection contains all the open Workbook objects in the Application object.

The most-used objects in the Application object are the Workbooks collection, the Worksheets collection, and the Windows collection. By using these, you can manipulate the workbooks, the worksheets, and the windows that are open. Figure 23.2 shows the collections and objects contained in the Workbooks collection.

FIGURE 23.1:

The Excel Application object. The shaded boxes denote objects and collections; the unshaded boxes denote objects only.

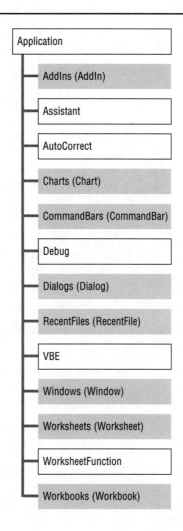

The Worksheets collection gives you access to the worksheets in the active workbook (when you access the Worksheets collection from the Application object) or in the specified workbook (when you access the Worksheets collection from a Workbook object). Figure 23.3 shows the collections and objects contained in the Worksheets collection.

The Windows collection provides access to the windows in the active workbook (when you access the Windows collection from the Application object) or in the specified workbook (when you access the Windows collection from a Workbook object).

FIGURE 23.2:

The collections and objects contained in the Workbooks collection

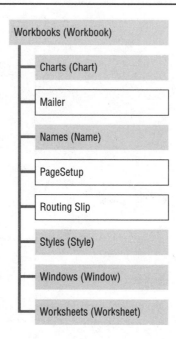

FIGURE 23.3:

The collections and objects contained in the Worksheets collection

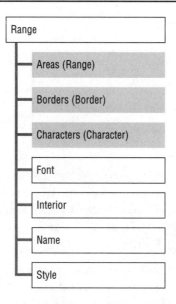

Working with the Excel Application

The Application object represents the Excel application. It contains properties that control application-wide settings, such as options in the Options dialog boxes. For example, the following statement turns off the EditDirectlyInCell property, the equivalent of clearing the Edit Directly in Cell checkbox on the Edit tab of the Options dialog box:

```
Application.EditDirectlyInCell = False
```

The following statement displays a message box containing the Path property of the Excel application:

```
Msgbox Application.Path
```

Accessing the Application Object

You can access the Excel Application object from within the Excel VBA environment. You can also access it using VBA, either from another Office application (for example, from Word) or from Visual Basic.

The Application property returns the Application object. You can apply properties to the Application object to access objects and collections within it. The following statement accesses the Caption property of the first Window object in the Windows collection in the Application object:

```
Application.Windows(1).Caption
```

You can access top-level objects such as ActiveCell, ActiveSheet, and Active-Window through the properties available in the Application object, but it is usually simpler to use the top-level objects without the Application object qualifier. The following statements both return the Address property of the active cell. The first statement uses the ActiveCell property of the Application object, whereas the second statement is more concise and easier to use:

```
Application.ActiveCell.Address
ActiveCell.Address
```

To access the Application object from within another VBA environment or from Visual Basic, use the GetObject function or the CreateObject function. The Get-Object function returns a reference to an existing object, and the CreateObject function creates a new object and returns a reference to it.

The following statements create a new Excel Application object and return a reference to it:

```
Dim vbExcel As Object
Set vbExcel = CreateObject("Excel.Application")
With vbExcel
    'Statements here
End With
```

The following statements return a reference to an existing Excel object:

```
Dim MySpreadsheet As Object
Set MySpreadsheet = GetObject("c:\Corporate\Sales Forecast.xls")
With MySpreadsheet
    'Take actions here
End With
Set MySpreadsheet = Nothing
```

To display an Excel object that you have created or accessed, set its Visible property to True:

```
vbExcel.Visible = True
```

To close the Excel application, use the Quit command:

```
With vbExcel
'Take actions here
.Quit
End With
```

Once you've closed the Excel application or the Excel object, use a Set statement with the Nothing keyword to release the memory:

```
Set vbExcel = Nothing
```

Working with Workbooks

The Workbooks collection represents all open workbooks. You can either work with Workbook objects that you access through the Workbooks collection or with the ActiveWorkbook object, which represents the currently active workbook.

Depending on the type of procedure you are creating, it's usually easy to decide whether to work with one or more Workbook objects in the Workbooks collection or to work with the ActiveWorkbook object. Use the Workbooks collection when you need to specify a workbook by name or when you need to work with a workbook that is not (or may not be) the active workbook. When performing complex procedures for the user, it is sometimes beneficial to work with a workbook other than the active workbook so that the user cannot see what Excel is doing. Use the ActiveWorkbook object when you do not know (or need to know) the name of the workbook you're working with (for example, in a simple macro the user runs on a workbook of their choosing), to find out which workbook is active, or when you want to display a procedure on screen so that the user can see it.

Activating a Workbook

To activate a workbook, use the Activate method. The Activate method makes the specified workbook the active workbook, so you can work with it as the Active-Workbook object.

The following statement makes the open workbook named CANDIDATES.XLS the active workbook:

```
Workbooks("Candidates.xls").Activate
```

NOTE   Running the Activate method on a workbook that is already the active workbook does no harm.

Opening a Workbook

To open a workbook, use the Open method with the appropriate Workbook object. The following statement opens the file named CONTRIBUTION ANALYSIS.XLS in the U:\VPS\FINANCE\ folder:

```
Workbooks.Open "u:\vps\finance\Contribution Analysis.xls"
```

NOTE   If the workbook you want to open is in the current folder, you do not need to specify the path. For example, the previous statement could be simply `Workbooks .Open "Contribution Analysis.xls"`. However, unless you can be sure that the current folder contains the workbook you want to open, it's wise to include the full path in the statement.

The only argument required when opening a workbook in Excel is the File-Name string argument, which can be supplied implicitly, as in the previous example.

Important optional arguments for opening workbooks include the following:

- Use the UpdateLinks argument to specify how to update any links in the workbook. Use the value 0 to specify that no links be updated, 1 to specify that external references be updated but remote references not be updated, 2 to specify that remote references be updated but external references not be updated, or 3 to specify that both external references and remote references be updated. If you omit the UpdateLinks argument and the workbook being opened contains one or more links, the user will be prompted to choose how to update the links. The following statement opens the workbook C:\TEMP\MY_LINKS.XLS and updates all references in it:

  ```
  Workbooks.Open FileName:="c:\temp\My_Links.xls", UpdateLinks:=3
  ```

- To open a workbook in read-only mode, use the optional ReadOnly argument set to True:

  ```
  Workbooks.Open FileName:="c:\temp\My_Links.xls", _
      UpdateLinks:=3, ReadOnly:=True
  ```

- To add the workbook you're opening to the most recently used file list for Excel, use the AddToMRU argument set to True, as shown in the following statement. (The default value of the AddToMRU argument is False; so if you omit this argument, the workbooks you open from VBA will not be added to the most recently used file list.) The following statement opens the workbook C:\TEMP\MY_LINKS.XLS and adds it to the most recently used file list:

  ```
  Workbooks.Open FileName:="c:\temp\MyWork.xls", AddToMRU:=True
  ```

> **NOTE**
>
> When you open a workbook using VBA, Excel does not run any Auto_Open macro associated with the workbook—so you don't need to worry about automatic macros when opening a workbook programmatically.

Closing a Workbook

To close a workbook, use the Close method with the appropriate Workbook object. The following statement closes the active workbook:

```
ActiveWorkbook.Close
```

You can use the Close method without any arguments, but usually in automated procedures you'll want to allow for the workbook containing unsaved changes. To do so, use the optional SaveChanges argument to specify whether to

Opening a Recently Used File

As well as opening any file by name, you can open a recently used file. Excel stores the list of recently used files as RecentFile objects in the RecentFiles collection, which can contain 0 to 9 files, depending on the Recently Used File List setting chosen on the General tab of the Options dialog box.

To open one of the recently used files, access its RecentFile object by its index number in the RecentFiles collection. For example, to access the most recently used file, use the following statement:

```
Application.RecentFiles(1).Open
```

To open all the recently used files, you could use the following code segment:

```
With Application
For i = 1 to .RecentFiles.Count
.RecentFiles(i).Open
Next i
End With
```

save changes to the workbook: A value of True saves the changes to the workbook; a value of False closes the workbook without saving changes. If you omit the SaveChanges argument and the workbook contains unsaved changes, Excel prompts the user with a message box asking whether to save changes. The following statement closes the workbook named COMPETITIVE REPORT.XLS and saves any unsaved changes:

```
Workbooks("Competitive Report.xls").Close SaveChanges:=True
```

You can also use a FileName argument to specify the file name under which the workbook should be saved as it is closed. The following statement closes the workbook named COMPETITIVE REPORT.XLS and saves any unsaved changes under the name UPDATED COMPETITIVE REPORT.XLS:

```
Workbooks("Competitive Report.xls").Close SaveChanges:=True, _
FileName:="Updated Competitive Report.xls"
```

Note that if a file with the name specified by the FileName argument already exists, Excel will prompt the user whether to replace it. If the user selects the No button or the Cancel button in the dialog box, the Close method will fail, causing an error.

NOTE When you close a workbook using VBA, Excel does not run any Auto_Close macro associated with the workbook.

Creating a Workbook

To create a new workbook, use the Add method with the Workbooks collection.

- To create a new workbook based on a template, specify the template by using the Template argument. The following statement creates a new workbook based on the INVOICE.XLT template in the C:\PROGRAM FILES\MICROSOFT OFFICE\TEMPLATES\SPREADSHEET SOLUTIONS\ folder.

  ```
  Workbooks.Add Template:="c:\Program Files\Microsoft Office\ _
  Templates\Spreadsheet Solutions\invoice.xlt"
  ```

- To create a new workbook based on the default template, omit the Template argument:

  ```
  Workbooks.Add
  ```

- To create a new template, start a new workbook using one of the above techniques, and then save it as a template, as discussed in the next section.

Saving a Workbook

To save an existing workbook under its current name and path, use the Save method, which takes no arguments. (If the workbook has never been saved, Excel will save it under its default name, such as BOOK2.XLS.) The following statement saves the active workbook:

```
ActiveWorkbook.Save
```

To save a new workbook for the first time or to save a workbook under a different name, use the SaveAs method with the appropriate Workbook object. Use the FileName argument to specify the file name under which to save the file. Include the path in FileName unless you want to save the workbook in the current folder. If you do not specify FileName, Excel will save the workbook under the current name (for example, BOOK1.XLS for a new, unsaved workbook).

The following statement saves the active workbook as C:\TEMP\OUTPUT.XLS:

```
ActiveWorkbook.SaveAs "c:\temp\Output.xls"
```

Important optional arguments for saving a workbook include the following:

- Use the FileFormat argument to specify the file format in which to save the file. The following list shows the most commonly used file formats:

xlAddIn	Excel add-in
xlCSV	Comma-separated value
xlExcel4	Excel 4 format
xlExcel5	Excel 5 format
xlWorkbookNormal	Excel 97 format
xlTemplate	Excel template

- Use the CreateBackup argument with a value of True to create a backup file of the workbook. Note that the backup of a workbook is created only the second and subsequent times the workbook is saved, not the first time.

- To add the workbook you're saving to the most recently used file list for Excel, use the AddToMRU argument set to True. (The default value of the AddToMRU argument is False, so if you omit this argument, the workbooks you save from VBA will not be added to the most recently used file list.)

The following statement saves the workbook named TORQUE FRAGILITY.XLS under the name TORQUE FRAGILITY TESTS.XLS in Excel 5 format in the current folder:

```
Workbooks("Torque Fragility.xls").SaveAs _
    FileName:="Torque Fragility Tests.xls", FileFormat:=xlExcel5
```

Printing a Workbook

To print a workbook, use the PrintOut method. The following statement prints the current print area of the active workbook:

```
ActiveWorkbook.PrintOut
```

NOTE   You can also use the PrintOut method with other objects, such as a worksheet or a window.

Important optional arguments for the PrintOut method include the following:

- Use the From variant argument to specify the number of the page at which to start printing.

- Use the To variant argument to specify the number of the page at which to stop printing.

- Use the Preview variant argument set to True to display Print Preview of the workbook before printing.

- Use the Copies variant to specify the number of copies of the item to print. If you omit the Copies argument, VBA prints one copy.

The following statement prints three copies of pages 2 through 4 of the active workbook:

```
ActiveWorkbook.PrintOut From:=2, To:=4, Copies:=3
```

Code 23.1   Creating, Saving, and Closing a Workbook

```
Dim vbExcel As Excel.Application
Set vbExcel = CreateObject("Excel.Application")
With vbExcel
    .Workbooks.Add
    With .ActiveWorkbook
        .SaveAs "z:\common\Manufacturing Capacity.xls"
        'Manipulate the contents of the workbook
        .Close SaveChanges:=True
    End With
    .Quit
End With
```

Working with Worksheets

The Sheets collection represents the worksheets within a workbook. You can use the Sheets collection to access worksheets, activate worksheets, add worksheets, delete worksheets, or rename worksheets. You can use the ActiveSheet object to work with the active worksheet, and you can use the SelectedSheets collection in the active window to work with all selected sheets.

To work with worksheets within a workbook, you use the Sheets collection. You can return the Sheets collection by using the Worksheets property:

- Use the Worksheets property with the Application object, with the Active-Workbook object, or without an object to return the Sheets collection for the active workbook. All three of the following statements return the Sheets collection for the active workbook:

```
Set mySheets = Application.Worksheets
Set mySheets = ActiveWorkbook.Worksheets
Set mySheets = Worksheets
```

- Use the Worksheets property with the Workbook object to return the Sheets collection for that workbook. For example, to print a list of the worksheets in the open workbook named EXPANSION PLANS.XLS to the Immediate window, you could use the following statements:

```
For Each wks In Workbooks("Expansion Plans.xls").Worksheets
    Debug.Print wks.Name
Next
```

To select a worksheet, use the Select method. The following statement selects the worksheet named Frame Relay Charges in the active workbook:

```
ActiveWorkbook.Sheets("Frame Relay Charges").Select
```

To add a worksheet to a workbook, use the Add method with the Sheets collection. The following statement adds a worksheet to the workbook named GIGABIT.XLS:

```
Workbooks("Gigabit.xls").Sheets.Add
```

To delete a worksheet from a workbook, use the Delete method. The following statement activates the workbook named 1999 SALARY PROJECTIONS.XLS and deletes the worksheet named Vice-Presidents from it:

```
Workbooks("1999 Salary Projections.xls").Activate
Sheets("Vice-Presidents").Delete
```

You cannot delete all the worksheets in a workbook, because each workbook needs to contain at least one visible sheet at all times. The following statements check to make sure that not all worksheets in the active workbook are selected before deleting the selected sheets. If all the worksheets in the workbook are selected, a message box warns the user of the problem.

```
With ActiveWindow
    If .SelectedSheets.Count < ActiveWorkbook.Sheets.Count Then
```

```
            .SelectedSheets.Delete
    Else
            MsgBox "You cannot delete all the sheets in the workbook.", _
                vbOKOnly + vbCritical, "Deletion Failed"
        End If
    End With
```

To rename a worksheet, change its Name property. The following statement changes the name of the active sheet in the active workbook to Spot Prices:

```
ActiveSheet.Name = "Spot Prices"
```

To move a worksheet within a workbook, use the Move method. The Move method takes either a Before argument or an After argument, specifying the worksheet before which or after which to place the worksheet being moved. The following statement moves the worksheet named Results in the workbook named REMOTE OFFICES.XLS to the position after the worksheet named Projections:

```
Workbooks("Remote Offices.xls").Sheets("Results").Move _
    After:=Sheets("Projections")
```

NOTE   Without a Before argument or an After argument, Excel will create a new default workbook and move the specified sheet to it.

To move a worksheet from one workbook to another, specify the destination workbook in the Before or After argument, as appropriate. The following statement moves the worksheet named Results in the workbook named REMOTE OFFICES.XLS to the position before the worksheet named Vice-Presidents in the workbook named 1999 SALARY PROJECTIONS. Note that the destination workbook will be the active workbook after the worksheet is moved.

```
Workbooks("Remote Offices.xls").Sheets("Results").Move _
    Before:=Workbooks("1999 Salary Projections.xls").Sheets("Vice-Presidents")
```

To copy a worksheet from one workbook to another, use the Copy method with either a Before argument or an After argument, as appropriate.

The following statements provide an example of how you might use Visual Basic to copy a worksheet from a workbook located on a local drive to a workbook located on a network drive.

Code 23.2	Copying a Workbook from One Drive to Another

```
Set vbExcel = CreateObject("Excel.Application")
With vbExcel
    'Open source workbook and destination workbook
    .Workbooks.Open "d:\Finance\Office Current.xls"
    .Workbooks.Open "\\Mercury\Mercury_D\Finance\Company Current.xls"
    'Copy worksheet from one to the other
    .Workbooks("Office Current.xls").Sheets("October Sales").Copy _
        Before:=.Workbooks("Company Current.xls").Sheets(1)
    'Save destination workbook
    .Workbooks("Company Current.xls").Save
    'Close both workbooks
    .Workbooks("Company Current.xls").Close
    .Workbooks("Office Current.xls").Close
    'Close Excel application object
    .Quit
End With
'Release object variable to free memory
Set vbExcel = Nothing
```

Working with Ranges

The Range object can represent any range of cells, from a single cell to a 3-D range of cells. The Range object does not have an associated Ranges collection object—you might say it acts as its own collection when it represents more than one cell.

Specifying a Range

To work with a range, you first specify it. You can specify a range in several ways:

- To specify a simple range (consisting of one contiguous block of cells), use an A1-style reference. The first of the following statements sets the Formula property of cell Z28 on the second worksheet in the active workbook to =SUM(C28:Y28). The second statement sets the Value property of the cells in the range A1:L1 to 1999.

```
ActiveWorkbook.Sheets(2).Range("Z28").Formula = "=SUM(C28:Y28)"
ActiveWorkbook.Sheets(2).Range("A1:L1").Value = 1999
```

- Alternatively, use the Range property with Cell1 and Cell2 arguments to specify the extent of a range. The following statements create a range named newRange that refers to cells A2:E2 on the third worksheet and then apply bold font formatting to the range:

```
Set newRange = Worksheets(3).Range(Worksheets(3).Cells(2, 1), _
Worksheets(3).Cells(2, 5))
newRange.Font.Bold = True
```

- You can also create a range by specifying its row index and column index. The following statement sets the font of cell E4 (the fourth row, the fifth column) on the specified worksheet to Times New Roman:

```
Workbooks("Sales Forecast.xls").Sheets("Western Region") _
.Cells(4, 5).Font.Name = "Times New Roman"
```

- To specify a range by its position offset from another range, use the Offset property with Row and Column arguments. The following statements select the range named Conclusions in the active sheet; create a range named Cost offset from the selection by three rows (down) and no columns, spanning the columns A through F of the rows in question; and enter **Cost** in each cell in the range:

```
Conclusions.Select
Set Cost = Selection.Offset(3, 0).Range("A1:F1")
Cost.Value = "Cost"
```

- To specify a multiple-range area consisting of two or more contiguous blocks of cells, use the Union method with as many Range *n* arguments as necessary. The following statements create a range named EmphasisRange that consists of the ranges Headings, Totals, and Conclusions; apply font formatting to it if it is not already applied:

```
Dim EmphasisRange As Range, Headings As Range
Dim Totals As Range, Conclusions As Range
Set Headings = Range("A1:F1")
Set Totals = Range("A7:F7")
Set Conclusions = Range("A11:F11")
Set EmphasisRange = Union(Headings, Totals, Conclusions)
With EmphasisRange.Font
    If .Name <> "Gill Sans Ultra Bold" Then _
    .Name = "Gill Sans Ultra Bold"
    If .Size <> 24 Then .Size = 24
End With
```

Looping on Row Numbers of Column Numbers

Specifying the row index and column index of a cell is less intuitive than using an A1-style reference, but it enables you to create For… Next loops on row numbers or column numbers. The following statements check the values of the cells in the range named Totals and apply red font color to any cell whose value is 1000 or greater:

```
With Range("Totals")
    For i = 1 to .Columns.Count
        If .Cells(1, i).Value >= 1000 Then _
        .Cells(1, i).Font.ColorIndex = 3
    Next i
End With
```

TIP   Use the Areas property to find out how many areas are in a given selection before trying to take an action that works only with simple selections.

Identifying the Current Range

If you allow users to specify a range in your code, you may need to identify the range they select in order to work with it effectively. Two useful tools for doing so are the CurrentRegion property and the UsedRange property.

Using the CurrentRegion Property

The CurrentRegion property returns the current region of the specified sheet. The current region is the range of contiguous cells around the insertion point, bordered by either empty rows or columns, or the boundaries of the spreadsheet. For example, if a worksheet contains entries in every cell in the range C3:Z28, an entry in cell A1, and an entry in cell Z80, the current region will be C3:Z28 if the active cell is within the C3:Z28 block. If the active cell is cell A1, the current region will be cell A1. If the active cell is cell Z80, the current region will be Z80.

The following statements check that the current region is large enough for a procedure to have enough data to operate. If the current region does not contain at least 10 columns and 5 rows, a message is displayed asking the user to place the active cell in a suitable range.

```
With ActiveCell.CurrentRegion
    If .Rows.Count < 5 Or .Columns.Count < 10 Then
        MsgBox "Please place the active cell in a range of data at
least 10 columns wide by 5 rows deep.", vbOKOnly, "Select Range for
Procedure"
        End
    End If
End With
```

Using the UsedRange Property

The UsedRange property defines the range of cells used on the specified worksheet. The used range is understood to be the range marked by the first (upper-left) and last (lower-right) cells used in the worksheet. For example, if a worksheet contains entries in every cell in the range C3:Z28, an entry in cell A1, and an entry in cell Z80, the used range will be A1:Z80. The following statement returns the used range for the active worksheet:

```
MsgBox ActiveSheet.UsedRange
```

Manipulating a Range

Once you've specified a range, you can manipulate its properties and methods and those of the objects contained within it:

- To select a range, use the Select method. The following statement selects the range named EmphasisRange:

  ```
  EmphasisRange.Select
  ```

- To access a cell within the range, specify it by reference within the range: The top-left cell in a range is Cells(1, 1) for the range, the cell to its right is Cells(1, 2), and so on. The following statement selects the second cell in the second row of the range qRange:

  ```
  qRange.Cells(2,2).Select
  ```

- To apply formatting to the range, manipulate the properties of the appropriate object for the range: Use the Style object to return or change the style of the range, use the Font object to return or change the font of the range, and so on. The following statements create a range named TR referring to cell

K11 (of the active sheet) and truncate the contents of the cell to five characters if the contents are more than five characters long:

```
Set TR = Cells(11, 11)
If TR.Characters.Count > 5 Then
    TR.Value = TR.Characters(1, 5).Text
End If
```

- To copy the contents of a range to the clipboard, use the Copy method. To copy the contents of a range to another range, set the value of the second range to the value of the first. The following statement copies the content of the range named TempRange into the range named PermRange:

```
Range("PermRange").Value = Range("TempRange").Value
```

- To clear the contents of a range, use the ClearContents method. The following statement clears the contents of the range named TempRange:

```
Range("TempRange").ClearContents
```

Working with Name Objects

You can use the Names collection and the Name objects it contains to work with named objects in a workbook. Because named objects let you easily access predefined areas of a workbook without specifying the location by worksheet or by cell, they are useful for automated procedures.

To return the Names collection for a workbook, use the Names property of the workbook. The following statement returns the Names property of the first named object in the workbook:

```
n1 = Names(1).Name
```

To return the range a named object refers to, use the RefersTo property. The following statements display a message box containing a list of the named objects in the active workbook together with their ranges. If the active workbook contains no named objects, the message box displays a message to that effect.

```
Dim Msg As String, msgTitle As String
msgTitle = "Named Objects in " & ActiveWorkbook.Name
If Names.Count = 0 Then
    Msg = "The workbook contains no named objects."
Else
    Msg = "The workbook contains the following named objects: _
        " & vbCr & vbCr
```

```
End If
For j = 1 To Names.Count
    Msg = Msg & Names(j).Name & ": " & Names(j).RefersTo & vbCr
Next j
MsgBox Msg, vbOKOnly + vbInformation, msgTitle
```

To add a named object to the Names collection, use the Add method with a Name argument specifying the name and a RefersTo argument specifying the address. Specify the RefersTo argument using A1-style notation, including dollar signs when the reference should be absolute rather than relative to the active cell. The following statement creates a named object called InterestRates that refers to the range Q33:Q36 on the sheet named 1999 in the active workbook:

```
Names.Add Name:="InterestRates", RefersTo:="1999!$Q$33:$Q$36"
```

To delete a named object, use the Delete method with the appropriate item in the Names collection. The following statement deletes the named object Interest-Rates in the active workbook:

```
Names("InterestRates").Delete
```

Working with Windows

VBA provides two Windows collections: one containing Window objects that represent the windows available in the Application object, and another containing Window objects in a Workbook object. Usually, you'll want to work with the Windows collection for the Application object, though at times it's useful to work with the Windows collection for a Workbook object. Each Window object contains a Panes collection of Pane objects that represent the panes for the window.

These are the actions you're most likely to need to perform with Window objects and the Windows collection:

- Use the window name or index number with the Windows collection to return a Window object. Windows(1) is always the active window. The following statement displays a message box containing the name of each Window object in turn:

  ```
  For i = 1 To Windows.Count
      MsgBox Windows(i).Caption
  Next i
  ```
- Use the WindowState property to return or adjust the window state of the active window. Use the arguments xlMaximized to maximize the window,

xlMinimized to minimize the window, or xlNormal to "restore" the window. The following statements maximize the active window if it is not already maximized:

```
With ActiveWindow
    If .WindowState <> xlMaximized Then .WindowState = xlMaximized
End With
```

- Use the Zoom property to adjust the zoom level in the window. The following statement sets the zoom percentage to 90 percent:

```
ActiveWindow.Zoom = 90
```

- Use the DisplayVerticalScrollBar property and the DisplayHorizontalScroll-Bar property to return or set the display of the scroll bars in the window. The following statements make sure both scroll bars are displayed:

```
With ActiveWindow
    If .DisplayHorizontalScrollBar = False Then _
    .DisplayHorizontalScrollBar = True
    If .DisplayVerticalScrollBar = False Then _
    .DisplayVerticalScrollBar = True
End With
```

- Use the Arrange method with the ArrangeStyle argument to arrange the open document windows in the application window. Use xlArrangeStyleTiled (or omit the argument) to tile the windows. Use xlArrangeStyleCascade to cascade the windows (overlapping, with the title bar of each visible). Use xlArrange-StyleHorizontal to arrange the windows horizontally. Use xlArrangeStyle-Vertical to arrange the windows vertically. The following statement cascades the windows:

```
Windows.Arrange ArrangeStyle:=xlArrangeStyleCascade
```

- Use the Count property of the Windows collection for a Workbook object to make sure the appropriate number of windows (usually only one) are displayed for a workbook you want to work with.

- Use the Split property to split or unsplit a window, and use the FreezePanes property to freeze or unfreeze the panes of a window. Both Split and Freeze-Panes are Boolean properties. The following statements work with the active window to unfreeze the panes if they are frozen and unsplit the window if it is split:

```
With ActiveWindow
    If .FreezePanes = True Then .FreezePanes = False
    If .Split = True Then .Split = False
End With
```

Working with the Active Cell

The ActiveCell property returns the ActiveCell object, which represents the active cell. The ActiveCell object has the same properties and methods as a Range object.

If you do not specify a Window object, Excel returns the active cell in the active window. The following statements both return the active cell in the active window:

```
ActiveCell
ActiveWindow.ActiveCell
```

You can specify a Window object to return the active cell from that window. The following statement displays a message box containing the contents of the active cell in the window 2000 SALARY PROJECTION.XLS:

```
MsgBox Windows("2000 Salary Projections.xls").ActiveCell
```

> **NOTE**
>
> If no worksheet is displayed, the ActiveCell property fails. If a range of cells is selected, the ActiveCell property returns the active cell within the range—not the whole range.

To manipulate the active cell, work with its properties and methods and those of the objects it contains. For example, to return the address of the active cell, use its Address property:

```
ActiveCell.Address
```

The following statements enter the text from a text box named txtMyText in a Visual Basic Form in the active cell:

```
Dim vbExcel As Object
Set vbExcel = CreateObject("Excel.Application")
vbExcel.Workbooks.Add
vbExcel.ActiveCell.Value = txtMyText.Text
```

You can set the active cell by using the Activate method on a cell. For example, to make cell Z80 on the worksheet named Captains of Industry the active cell, enter the value "Moderator" into it, and apply the style named Emphasis; you could use the following statements:

```
With Worksheets("Captains of Industry")
    .Activate
    .Range("Z80").Activate
    With ActiveCell
```

```
        .Value = "Moderator"
        .Style = "Emphasis"
    End With
End With
```

To move the active cell, you can use the Activate method with the Offset property of the ActiveCell object. The Offset property uses two optional variant arguments, RowOffset and ColumnOffset, for specifying the number of rows and columns by which to move the active cell. The following statement moves the active cell down one row:

```
ActiveCell.Offset(1,0).Activate
```

Working with Find and Replace

You can use the Find and Replace methods in your macros and procedures to find or replace specific information in a given range.

Using the Find Method

The Find method in VBA corresponds to the Edit ➢ Find command in the Excel user interface. The Find method has the following syntax:

```
Expression.Find(What, After, LookIn, LookAt, SearchOrder, _
SearchDirection,MatchCase)
```

The Expression argument and the What argument are required:

- *Expression* is an expression that specifies the Range object for the Find operation. The Find operation starts in the upper-left cell in the range unless you specify a different starting location by using the After argument. Find wraps to the beginning of the range after reaching the end, so if you use an After argument, you will sometimes need to stop Find from wrapping by comparing the location of the currently found cell with the location of the first found cell. If Find does not find a match for the specified information, it returns Nothing.

- *What* is a variant argument specifying the data you want to search for.

The following statements use a Set statement to perform a Find operation for the string "Paris". If the string is found, VBA displays a message box showing the address. If it is not found, VBA displays a message box informing the user.

```
Set Found = Cells.Find(What:="Paris")
If Found Is Nothing Then
     MsgBox "The item was not found.", vbOKOnly, "Find Unsuccessful"
Else
     Found.Cells.Font.Bold = True
     MsgBox Found.Cells.Address, vbOKOnly + vbInformation, "Location"
End If
```

Find operations such as this do not move the selection or the active cell. Use the Activate statement to perform a Find operation and move the active cell to the information found, as happens in searches performed through the user interface. The following statement searches for the string "Paris" on the active worksheet and moves the active cell to the first instance of it (if there is one):

```
Cells.Find(What:="Paris").Activate
```

These are the most useful optional arguments for the Find method:

- Use the After variant argument to specify the cell after which to begin the search. This argument must be a single cell rather than multiple cells and must be in the range being searched. The following statement specifies that the search begin after the active cell:

  ```
  Set Found = Cells.Find(What:="Paris", After:=ActiveCell)
  ```

- Use the LookIn variant argument to specify whether to look in formulas (xlFormulas), values (xlValues), or notes (xlNotes). This corresponds to the Look In drop-down list in the Find dialog box in the Excel user interface.

- Use the LookAt variant argument to specify whether to search for a whole cell (xlWhole) or a part of a cell (xlPart) containing the specified item. This corresponds to the Find Entire Cells Only checkbox in the Find dialog box.

- Use the SearchOrder variant argument to specify whether to search by rows (xlByRows) or by columns (xlByColumns). This corresponds to the Search drop-down list in the Find dialog box.

- Use the SearchDirection variant argument to specify whether to search down (xlNext) or up (xlPrevious). The default setting is xlNext.

- Use the MatchCase variant argument set to True to perform a case-sensitive search. The default setting is False.

NOTE   Like the settings in the Find dialog box, which they affect and which affect them, the settings for LookIn, LookAt, SearchOrder, and MatchCase are sticky. So if you set SearchDirection to xlPrevious in one procedure, it will remain set to xlPrevious until you change it. It's a good idea to set each argument explicitly when you use the Find method, to make sure you get the effect you intended.

Finding the Next or Previous Instance

To find the next instance of the item you last searched for, use the FindNext method. Use an After argument if you need to specify the cell after which to start the search. The following statement searches for the next instance of the last item searched for:

```
Set nFound = Cells.FindNext(After:=ActiveCell)
```

To find the previous instance of the item you last searched for, use the Find-Previous method. Use an After argument if you need to specify the cell *before* which to start the search.

Using the Replace Method

The Replace method corresponds to the Edit ➤ Replace command in the Excel user interface. Replace works in a similar way to the Find method and has the following syntax:

```
Expression.Replace(What, Replacement, LookAt, SearchOrder, MatchCase)
```

Here, Expression, What, LookAt, SearchOrder, and MatchCase work in the same way as their counterpart arguments for the Find method; Expression and What are required, and LookAt, SearchOrder, and MatchCase are optional. Replacement is a required string expression specifying the replacement string for the Replace operation; Replacement corresponds to the Replace With text box in the Replace dialog box. As with the Find method, the arguments for Replace operations stick and affect (and are affected by) the settings in the Replace dialog box, so it's best to specify them in each Replace operation.

The Replace method returns True if the specified item is found one or more times in the specified range.

The following statement replaces all instances of the word *prognosis* in the sheet named March in the workbook SALES RESULTS.XLS with the word *forecast*:

```
Workbooks("Sales Results.xls").Sheets("March").Cells.Replace _
What:="prognosis", Replacement:="forecast", LookAt:=xlWhole
```

Looping through an Excel Collection

By looping through a collection, you can check or take action on each item in the collection without having to establish how many items there are. Earlier in the chapter, we looked at how to open all the recently used files by looping through the RecentFiles collection using a For...Next loop. You can also loop through a collection by using a For Each...Next loop.

The For Each...Next loop performs one iteration of the loop for each object in the collection. The following statements use a For Each...Next loop to close any workbook that has never been saved to disk. The statements check the Path property of each of the workbooks in the Workbooks collection. If the Path property of a workbook is an empty string—that is, if it has never been saved to disk—the workbook is closed without saving changes.

```
For Each wBook In Workbooks
    If wBook.Path = "" Then wBook.Close SaveChanges:=False
Next
```

Using Excel's Built-In Dialog Boxes

In this section, we'll discuss how to use Excel's built-in dialog boxes in procedures you create. You can use Excel's built-in dialog boxes to get past the limitations of the standard selection of controls that the Visual Basic Editor provides for Forms. Moreover, you can save time and trouble by using a built-in dialog box, and you can be confident that users of your applications or procedures will recognize the dialog box and know how to use it, particularly if it is a common dialog box (for example, an Open dialog box, a Save dialog box, or a Print dialog box).

Displaying a Built-In Dialog Box

Built-in dialog boxes in Excel are identified by constants starting with *xlDialog*, followed by the name of the dialog box. For instance, the constant for the Open dialog box is xlDialogOpen, the constant for the Print dialog box is xlDialogPrint, and the constant for the Save As dialog box is xlDialogSaveAs. The naming conventions are not entirely consistent. For example, the constant for the Delete dialog box is xlDialogFileDelete rather than xlDialogDelete, because there is also an xlDialogEditDelete dialog box that identifies itself only as Delete.

To identify a dialog box, use its constant with the Dialogs property of the Application object, which returns the Dialogs collection. The following statement refers to the Delete dialog box:

```
Application.Dialogs(xlDialogFileDelete)
```

To display a dialog box, use the Show method. The Show method displays the specified Dialog object and executes the actions the user takes in the dialog box. For example, if you use the Show method to display the xlDialogOpen dialog box and the user chooses a file to open and clicks the Open button, VBA will open the file.

In VBA, Excel treats its multipage dialog boxes as individual dialog boxes, except for the Page Setup dialog box, which has its regular four tabs. For example, you cannot display the same Format Cells dialog box through VBA that you can display when working live in Excel, but you can display the six pages (tabs) of the Format Cells dialog box—Number, Alignment, Font, Border, Patterns, and Protection—individually by using the constants xlDialogFormatNumber, xlDialogAlignment, xlDialogActiveCellFont, xlDialogBorder, xlDialogPatterns, and xlDialogCell-Protection. Similarly, the Excel Options dialog box is divided into its eight component pages.

If you look through the list of built-in dialog boxes for Excel, you'll notice a number of other peculiarities, including multiple copies of a number of dialog boxes. For example, there are four Paste Special dialog boxes, each of which has arguments suitable for a different situation.

WARNING   Don't try to display the xlDialogMacroOptions dialog box. It generates enough of an error to crash Excel.

Setting Options in a Built-In Dialog Box

Most of the built-in Excel dialog boxes have a number of arguments that you can use for retrieving or setting values in the dialog box. To set an option in a built-in dialog box, you use the appropriate argument. For example, the xlDialogSaveAs dialog box has the arguments shown in Table 23.1.

TABLE 23.1:   The Arguments for the xlDialogSaveAs Dialog Box

Argument	Type	Explanation
document_text	Text	The name in the File Name text box
type_num	Numeric	The entry in the Save As Type drop-down list
prot_pwd	Text	The password for opening the file
backup	True/False	Whether the Always Create Backup checkbox in the Save Options dialog box is selected
write_res_pwd	Text	The password for modifying the file
read_only_rec	True/False	Whether the Read-Only Recommended checkbox in the Save Options dialog box is selected

> **TIP**
>
> The names of arguments tend to be cryptic and are almost impossible to guess from the names of the corresponding options in the dialog boxes. To access a list of Excel dialog boxes and the names of the arguments they take, look up the topic "Built-In Dialog Box Argument Lists" in the Index of the VBA Help file for Excel.

You can specify the arguments either explicitly or implicitly. The following statement uses explicit arguments to display the Save As dialog box with the suggested file name of MY TEST FILE.XLS, a file-opening password of **mytest**, a file-modifying password of **testme**, and the backup option selected:

```
Application.Dialogs(xlDialogSaveAs).Show arg1:="My Test File.xls", _
   arg3:="mytest", arg4:=True, arg5:="testme"
```

The following statement uses the arguments implicitly. Note the extra comma to indicate that the second argument is skipped:

```
Application.Dialogs(xlDialogSaveAs).Show "My Test File.xls",, "mytest", _
   True, "testme"
```

Returning the Button the User Chose in a Dialog Box

To find out which button the user clicked in a dialog box, check the return value of the Show method. The OK button or equivalent (the Open button, the Save button, and so on, depending on the dialog box) returns True, whereas the Cancel button or equivalent (the Close button, say) returns False.

For example, you could display the Open dialog box so that the user could open a workbook. By checking the return value of the Open dialog box, you could display a warning (or terminate the procedure) if the user clicked the Cancel button instead of opening a workbook. The following statements prompt the user to terminate the procedure:

```
TryAgain:
Clicked = Application.Dialogs(xlDialogOpen).Show
If Clicked = False Then
    If MsgBox("Do you want to terminate this procedure?", _
    vbYesNo + vbExclamation, "Terminate Procedure?") = vbYes Then
        End
    Else
        GoTo TryAgain
    End If
End If
```

The following procedure, run from Visual Basic, accesses a Word document, brings information from it into Excel, and prompts the user to save the resulting workbook under a different name.

NOTE   To display a built-in Excel dialog box from Visual Basic, add a reference to the Microsoft Excel 8.0 Object Library to the Visual Basic project.

Code 23.3:   **Working with Excel from Visual Basic**

```
'Declare object variables for Excel and Word
Dim vbExcel, As Excel.Application, vbWord As Word.Application
'Return Excel and Word application objects
Set vbExcel = CreateObject("Excel.Application")
Set vbWord = CreateObject("Word.Application")
'Open Word document, select bookmark, copy it
'Close Word document without saving changes; quit Word
```

```
With vbWord
\temp\newinfo.doc"
    .Documents("newinfo.doc").Bookmarks("info").Select
    .Selection.Copy
    .Documents("newinfo.doc").Close SaveChanges:=wdDoNotSaveChanges
    .Quit
End With
'Release Word object variable
Set vbWord = Nothing
'Display Excel, open workbook, add and name sheet
'Display Save As dialog box for user to save workbook under a new name
'Close workbook and quit Excel
With vbExcel
    .Visible = True
    .Workbooks.Open "u:\testing\fiscal\FY99 Master.xls", ReadOnly:=True
    .Sheets.Add Before:=Sheets(1)
    .Sheets(1).Name = "Antwerpen"
    With .Sheets("Antwerpen")
        .Cells(2, 2).Select
        .Paste
    End With
    .Dialogs(xlDialogSaveAs).Show arg1:="u:\testing\fiscal\FY99 Master
(adapted).xls"
    .ActiveWorkbook.Close SaveChanges:=False
    .Quit
End With
'Release Excel object variable
Set vbExcel = Nothing
```

CHAPTER

TWENTY-FOUR

Word 97 Objects

- The Word object model

- Working with documents

- Working with windows and panes

- Working with ranges and the Selection object

- Looping through a collection

- Using Word's built-in dialog boxes

In this chapter, we'll discuss the objects in Word 97, the Word object model that describes how they are arranged, and how to work with them to get things done in VBA.

To manipulate Word with VBA, you use the VBA objects that Word exposes. These objects range from the Application object that represents the Word application, to Document objects that represent individual documents, to collections such as Words and Paragraphs that represent components of documents. By controlling these objects and adjusting their properties, you can take actions in Word.

Like Excel, Word is highly complex and exposes many more VBA objects than we can deal with in this chapter. To get you started manipulating Word with VBA, we'll discuss the most important Word objects—the objects likely to be most useful to you when you are accessing Word from Visual Basic. As in the previous chapter, we'll highlight the most useful properties and methods for each object but will not list or discuss every single property and method for each object. We'll present the most useful arguments for each method discussed here, not a complete list of the arguments for the method.

We'll start by looking at the Word object model and examining the logical structure of the application as VBA sees it.

VBA Takes Over from WordBasic

VBA is new to Word 97, replacing the WordBasic language used in previous versions of Word up to Word 95. In many ways, VBA is the most important new feature in Word 97, because it provides far greater capabilities overall than any other new feature.

If you've used WordBasic in previous versions of Word, there's good news and bad news. The bad news is that VBA works very differently from WordBasic, and you'll have to adjust your thinking to VBA's object-dominated structure. The good news is in two parts: First, if you know Visual Basic, you'll find VBA straightforward; and second, VBA in Word includes full support for WordBasic through the WordBasic property.

In a pinch, you can leverage your knowledge of WordBasic through VBA to get things done. For a few disparate maneuvers, you will find that WordBasic offers functionality that VBA does not or that by using a WordBasic statement through the WordBasic property, you can achieve the same effect more concisely than you can with VBA. In most cases, though, VBA offers equivalent functionality to or greater functionality than WordBasic.

Continued on next page

If you have Word 6 or Word 95 templates containing macros that you need to use with Word 97, you can open the templates and have Word convert the macros to VBA procedures, with some statements using the WordBasic property. VBA's conversion is impressive and mostly successful, though some WordBasic structures are beyond its conversion capabilities; you'll have to fix such structures manually when the converted macros fail. You'll also find less-than-concise renderings that you can improve manually if you have the inclination.

The Word Object Model

In this section, we'll look at the Word object model, which describes the theoretical architecture underlying Word. By understanding the Word object model, you can manipulate the objects from which Word is built and work quickly and effectively with VBA.

Because the Word object model is extremely complex, we will look only at the most important objects in this chapter. But by understanding the structure of Word, and by using the techniques described in Chapter 23, you should be able to easily find the objects you need.

The Application object, at the top level of the Word object model, represents the Word application. Figure 24.1 shows the Application object and the objects it contains. The plural names with singular names in parentheses indicate collections and the individual objects they contain. For example, the Addins collection comprises all Addin objects in the Application object, and the Documents collection contains all the open Document objects in the Application object. The arrows to the right of the AutoCorrect, Documents, Selection, Templates, and Windows objects indicate that these objects and collections contain further objects.

The three most-used objects in the Application object are the Documents collection, the Windows collection, and the Selection object. By using these, you can manipulate the documents that are open, the windows that are open, and the current selection in the active document. Figure 24.2 shows the collections and objects contained in the Documents collection and the Document object.

FIGURE 24.1:

The Application object and the objects it contains. The unshaded boxes denote objects and collections; the shaded boxes denote objects only.

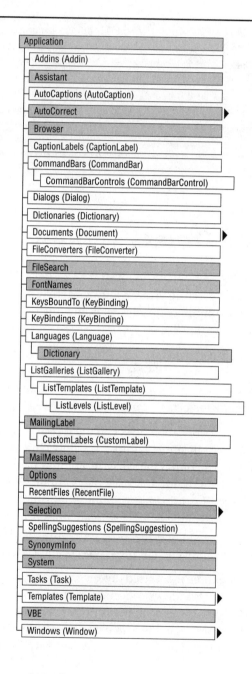

The collections and objects contained in the Documents collection and the Document object

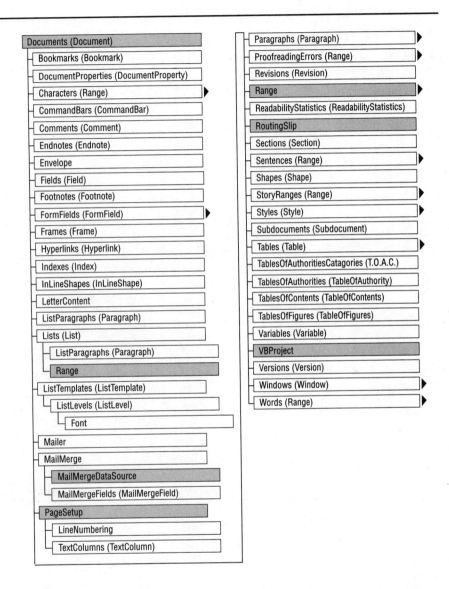

The Selection object enables you to work with the current selection. Figure 24.3 shows the collections and objects contained in the Selection object.

FIGURE 24.3:

The collections and objects contained in the Selection object

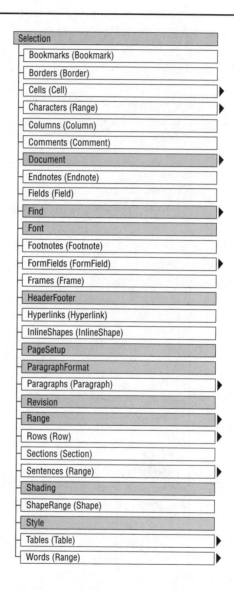

The Windows collection gives you access to the Window objects for all the available windows in the application. Figure 24.4 shows the collections and objects contained in the Windows collection.

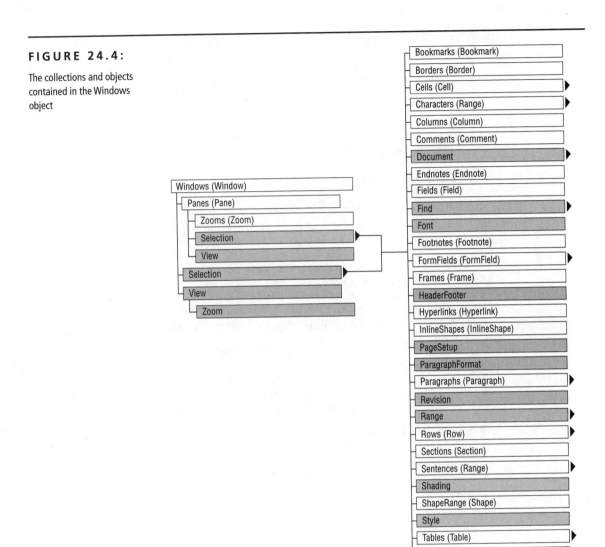

FIGURE 24.4:

The collections and objects contained in the Windows object

Working with the Word Application

As we just mentioned, the Application object represents the Word application. You can use the Application object to control many aspects of Word's behavior, from the size of the application window to global preferences such as whether AutoCorrect features are switched on.

The Application object contains properties and methods that return top-level objects, including:

- An ActiveDocument property to return the active document
- A Documents property to return the Documents collection
- A CommandBars property to return the CommandBars collection

You can access the most-used interface objects without using the Application object qualifier. For example, both the following statements display the name of the active document; the second statement is more concise:

```
MsgBox Application.ActiveDocument.Name
MsgBox ActiveDocument.Name
```

To set application-wide preferences, set the appropriate property of the Application object. For example, to make Word visible or to hide it, set the Visible property to True or False:

```
Application.Visible = False
```

To run Word from another application, use the CreateObject function or the GetObject function, as discussed for Excel in Chapter 23:

```
Set vbWord = CreateObject("Word.Application")
With vbWord
    'Statements here
    .Quit
End With
Set vbWord = Nothing
```

Working with Documents

To work with documents in Word, you can use either the Documents collection or the ActiveDocument object. The Documents collection represents all open documents; the ActiveDocument object represents the currently active document.

Depending on the type of procedure you are creating, it's usually easy to decide whether to work with one or more Document objects in the Documents collection or to work with the ActiveDocument object. Use the Documents collection when you need to specify a document by name or when you need to work with a document that is not (or may not be) the active document. For example, in some procedures you might prefer to work with a document other than the active document so that the user cannot see what is happening. Use the ActiveDocument object when you do not know (or need to know) the name of the document you're working with (for example, in a simple macro that users run on a document of their choosing), to find out which document is active, or when you want to display a procedure on screen so that the user can see it.

> **TIP**   To prevent the user from seeing what is happening, you can also turn off screen updating by setting the ScreenUpdating property of the Application object to False, as discussed in Chapter 21.

Activating a Document

To activate a document, use the Activate method on its Document object. The Activate method makes the specified document the active document, and you can then work with it using the ActiveDocument object. The following statement makes the open document URUGUAY VISIT.DOC the active document:

```
Documents("Uruguay Visit.doc").Activate
```

> **NOTE**   Running the Activate method on a document that is already the active document does no harm.

Opening a Document

To open a document, use the Open method with the appropriate Document object. The following statement opens the document named VP MEMO.DOC in the folder F:\USERS\JSMITH\:

```
Documents.Open "f:\users\jsmith\VP Memo.doc"
```

> **TIP**   Before trying to open a document, be sure that it exists. Alternatively, trap the run-time error 5174 that results when a document does not exist, or trap the run-time error 5273 that results when the path does not exist.

The only argument required when opening a document is the FileName string argument, which can be supplied implicitly, as in the above example. Important optional arguments for opening documents include the following:

- Use the ConfirmConversions variant argument set to True if you want Word to display the Convert File dialog box if the file is in a format other than Word 97.

- Use the ReadOnly variant argument set to True to open the document as read-only.

- Use the AddToRecentFiles variant argument set to True if you want Word to add the file name to the list of recently used files at the foot of the File menu. (The default is not to add the file to the recently used files list.)

- The Revert argument is a variant that specifies what Word should do if the FileName argument matches a file already open. By default, Revert is set to False, so Word activates the open instance of the document (if it is not the active document) and does not open the saved instance. Set Revert to True if you want Word to open the saved instance of the document and discard any changes to the open instance.

- Use the Format variant argument with the appropriate wdOpenFormat constant (see the list below) to specify the file converter with which to open the document:

Constant	Effect
wdOpenFormatAuto	Word chooses a converter automatically. This is the default setting.
wdOpenFormatDocument	Word opens the document as a Word document.
wdOpenFormatRTF	Word opens the document as a Rich Text Format file.
wdOpenFormatTemplate	Word opens the document as a template.
wdOpenFormatText	Word opens the document as a text file.
wdOpenFormatUnicodeText	Word opens the document as a Unicode text file.

- Use the Format variant argument with the appropriate FileConverter object and the OpenFormat property to specify an external file format (one not included in the above list). The following statement opens the Write file TEST.WRI in the current folder:

```
Documents.Open FileName:="Test.wri", _
    Format:=FileConverters("MSWinWrite").OpenFormat
```

Finding FileConverter Objects

Here's how to find out the names of the FileConverter objects you need:

1. In Word, choose Help ➤ About Microsoft Word to display the About Microsoft Word dialog box; or, in the Visual Basic Editor, choose Help ➤ About Microsoft Visual Basic to display the About Microsoft Visual Basic dialog box.

2. Click the System Info button to run the Microsoft System Information application in its own window.

3. In the tree in the left panel, expand the Text Converters object (if it's collapsed) by clicking the boxed plus sign to its left.

4. Select the Registry Settings item under Text Converters. Microsoft System Information will display a list of installed text converters in the panel on the right. The Key column shows the name you need to specify. For example, the import filter for Word 6 is named MSWord6, and the import filter for WordPerfect 6.*x* is WordPerfect6*x*. Specify this name for the FileConverter object.

To close Microsoft System Information, click its Close button or choose File ➤ Exit.

Closing a Document

To close a file, use the Close method with the appropriate Document object. The following statement closes the active document:

```
ActiveDocument.Close
```

Important optional arguments for the Close method include the following:

- SaveChanges is an optional variant you can use to specify how to handle unsaved changes. Use wdDoNotSaveChanges to discard changes, wdPromptToSaveChanges if you want Word to prompt the user to save changes, or wdSaveChanges to save changes without prompting.

- OriginalFormat is an optional variant you can use to specify the save format for the document. Use wdOriginalDocumentFormat if you want Word to use the original document format, wdPromptUser if you want Word to prompt the user to choose a format, or wdWordDocument to use the Word 97 document format.

The following statement closes the document ESTONIAN PEASANT REBELLIONS .DOC and saves any unsaved changes to it:

```
Documents("Estonian Peasant Rebellions.doc").Close _
SaveChanges:=wdSaveChanges
```

The following statement closes all open documents, prompting the user whether to save any document that contains unsaved changes:

- `Documents.Close SaveChanges:=wdPromptToSaveChanges`

Creating a Document

To create a new document, use the Add method with the Documents collection. The following statement creates a new document based on the Normal template:

```
Documents.Add
```

To create a new document based on a template other than the Normal template, use the optional Template argument. Specify the path unless the template is in the default template folder or global template folder. (If you omit Template, Word uses the Normal template.) The following statement creates a new document based on the template INDUSTRIAL DESIGN.DOT stored in the folder U:\COMMON\PROGRAM FILES\MICROSOFT OFFICE\TEMPLATES\:

```
Documents.Add Template:="u:\common\Program Files\Microsoft _
Office\Templates\Industrial Design.dot"
```

To create a template rather than a document, use the NewTemplate variant argument set to True. The following statement creates a new template based on the Normal template:

```
Documents.Add NewTemplate:=True
```

NOTE You can also create a new document by using the SaveAs method (discussed later in this chapter) on an existing document.

Saving a Document

To save a document or a template, use the Save method or the SaveAs method, depending on whether you're saving a previously saved file, saving a file for the first time, or saving a previously saved file under a new name.

Saving a Previously Saved File

To save a previously saved file, use the Save method. The following statement saves the active document:

```
ActiveDocument.Save
```

The following statement saves the open document named STRIFE IN GEORGIA.DOC:

```
Documents("Strife in Georgia.doc").Save
```

The following statement saves all open documents:

```
Documents.Save
```

NOTE If you use the Save method the first time you save a file, Word displays the Save As dialog box for the user to enter a name and choose a drive and folder for the document.

Saving a File for the First Time

To save a file for the first time, use the SaveAs method. Use the FileName optional variant argument to specify the name and path for the document. (FileName is optional in that if you omit the argument, VBA will use the current folder and the default file name of DOC*N*.DOC for a document and DOT*N*.DOT for a template, where *n* is the next higher unused consecutive number.) If a document with the name and location specified in FileName already exists, VBA will overwrite it without warning.

The following statement saves the active document under the name TEST DOCUMENT.DOC in the folder C:\TEMP\:

```
ActiveDocument.Save FileName:="c:\temp\Test Document.doc"
```

Use the FileFormat optional variant argument to specify the format in which to save the document. Word provides eight wdSaveFormat constants for quick reference, as shown in Table 24.1.

TABLE 24.1: The Word wdSaveFormat Constants

Constant	Saves Document As
wdFormatDocument	A Word 97 document
wdFormatDOSText	A DOS text file
wdFormatDOSTextLineBreaks	A DOS text file with layout
wdFormatRTF	A Rich Text Format file
wdFormatTemplate	A Word template
wdFormatText	A text file (plain ASCII)
wdFormatTextLineBreaks	A text file with line breaks
wdFormatUnicodeText	A text file with Unicode characters

The following statement saves the active document as a text file under the name INVESTIGATION.TXT in the current folder:

```
ActiveDocument.SaveAs FileName:="Investigation.txt", _
FileFormat:=wdFormatText
```

Use FileFormat with the appropriate value for the SaveFormat property of the FileConverter object to save a document in a different format. The following statement saves the active document in Word 5.1 for the Macintosh format:

```
ActiveDocument.SaveAs FileFormat:=FileConverters("MSWordMac51").SaveFormat
```

To add the document to the list of recently used files, use the AddToRecentFiles variant argument set to True:

```
Documents(11).Save FileName:="c:\temp\Test Document.doc", _
AddToRecentFiles=True
```

Saving a Document under a Different Name

To save a previously saved document under a different name, use the SaveAs method and specify the FileName argument implicitly or explicitly. The following statement saves the open document named OCTOBER REPORT.DOC under the name NOVEMBER REPORT.DOC in the current folder:

```
Documents("October Report.doc").SaveAs "November Report.doc"
```

Printing a Document

To print a document, use the PrintOut method on the appropriate document object. The following statement prints the open document named GENERATING LEADS.DOC:

```
Documents("Generating Leads.doc").PrintOut
```

The PrintOut method has a number of optional arguments that correspond to options in the Print dialog box and the Print tab of the Options dialog box. Use the Range variant argument to specify the range to print:

- Use wdPrintAllDocument to print the whole document.

- Use wdPrintCurrentPage to print the current page.

- Use wdPrintFromTo with From and To arguments to print a simple range of pages (from one numbered page to another numbered page):

```
Documents("Generating Leads.doc").PrintOut Range:=wdPrintFromTo,
From:=11, To:=22
```

- Use wdPrintRangeOfPages with a Pages argument to print a simple range of pages or a complex range of pages:

```
Documents("Generating Leads.doc").PrintOut
Range:=wdPrintRangeOfPages, Pages:="1, 3, 5, 11-21"
```

- Use wdPrintSelection to print the current selection.

Checking Whether a Document Contains Unsaved Changes

To find out whether a document contains unsaved changes (if it is dirty) or not (if it is clean), check the Saved property of its Document object. This Boolean property reads True if the document contains no unsaved changes and False if the document contains unsaved changes. The following statement checks the active document for unsaved changes and saves it if it contains any:

```
If ActiveDocument.Saved = False Then ActiveDocument.Save
```

NOTE   A newly created document is considered clean until you make changes to it, even if it contains a vast amount of text from the template on which it is based. So a document that has never been saved to disk can be clean or dirty, and you won't necessarily be able to tell from its contents (or lack of them). As soon as the user enters even a space in the document or deletes existing content, it becomes dirty.

Checking Whether a Document Exists

To check whether a document exists, use the Dir function with the file name. The following procedure prompts for a file name to test and displays a message box saying whether the file exists:

```
Sub UsingDir()
    Dim TestName As String, Msg As String
    TestName = InputBox("Enter the name and path of the document:", _
        "Demonstration of Dir Function")
    If Dir(TestName) <> "" Then
        Msg = TestName & " exists."
    Else
        Msg = TestName & " does not exist."
    End If
    MsgBox Msg, vbOKOnly + vbInformation, _
        "Demonstration of Dir Function"
End Sub
```

Deleting a Document

To delete a document (or other file) from VBA, use the Kill statement with the path and file name. The following statement deletes the document C:\TEMP\SCRATCH1.DOC:

```
Kill "c:\temp\Scratch1.doc"
```

WARNING   Two quick caveats: First, *Kill deletes files irrevocably*—it does not send them to the Recycle Bin. Second, Kill will not work if the file in question is open—instead, you'll get a run-time error 75 in Windows 95 ("Path/File access error") and a run-time error 70 in NT ("Permission Denied"). If you need to kill an open file, close it first.

The following statements provide an example of how you can close and delete the active document. If the document has never been saved, there is no need to use the Kill statement—closing it gets rid of it:

```
Dim DocToKill As String, TestDoc
DocToKill = ActiveDocument.FullName
ActiveDocument.Close
TestDoc = Dir(DocToKill)
ActiveDocument.Close SaveChanges:=wdDoNotSaveChanges
If Len(TestDoc) <> 0 Then Kill DocToKill
```

To delete multiple files at the same time, use the wildcards * (for multiple characters) and ? (for single characters). The following statement deletes all the DOC files in the C:\WINDOWS\TEMP\ folder:

```
Kill "c:\windows\temp\*.doc"
```

Getting Document Information

Word keeps a full set of information on each document. Here's how to return the most useful information:

- Use the Path property to return a document's path:

  ```
  MsgBox ActiveDocument.Path
  ```

- Use the Name property to return the file name without the path:

  ```
  MsgBox ActiveDocument.Name
  ```

- Use the FullName property to return a document's full path and name:

  ```
  MsgBox ActiveDocument.FullName
  ```

- Use the Application.PathSeparator property to add to the path the backslash used to separate folders and drive letters:

  ```
  MsgBox ActiveDocument.Path + Application.PathSeparator
  ```

- Use the Count property of the Characters, Words, Sentences, or Paragraphs collection to get a count of the characters, words, sentences, or paragraphs in the document.

You can also retrieve built-in document properties by using the BuiltInDocument-Properties property for a document. Word provides the built-in document properties shown in Table 24.2.

TABLE 24.2: The Built-In Document Properties of Word

Property	Meaning
wdPropertyBytes	The number of bytes the file occupies.
wdPropertyCharacters	The number of characters in the document, not including spaces, paragraph marks, and other "noncharacter" characters.
wdPropertyComments	The contents of the Comments field in the Properties dialog box.
wdPropertyKeywords	The contents of the Keywords field in the Properties dialog box.
wdPropertyLastAuthor	The name of the last user to work on the document.
wdPropertyLines	The number of lines in the document.
wdPropertyPages	The number of pages in the document.
wdPropertyParas	The number of paragraphs with contents in the document; does not include blank paragraphs.
wdPropertyRevision	The number of times the document has been saved.
wdPropertySubject	The subject of the document (as set in the Properties dialog box).
wdPropertyTemplate	The template to which the document is attached.
wdPropertyTimeCreated	The date and time at which the document was first created.
wdPropertyTimeLastPrinted	The date and time at which the document was last printed. This property returns an error if the document has never been printed.
wdPropertyTimeLastSaved	The date and time at which the document was last saved. Returns an error if the document has never been saved.
wdPropertyTitle	The title of the document (as set in the Properties dialog box).
wdPropertyVBATotalEdit	The time spent editing the document.
wdPropertyWords	The number of words in the document.

To use one of these built-in document properties, specify it like this:

```
ActiveDocument.BuiltInDocumentProperties(wdPropertyWords)
```

Changing the Default File Paths

Word maintains a number of default file paths, from the program path to the tutorial path (where tutorial files are located). You'll often want to retrieve these paths to establish where particular types of files should be located on a computer; occasionally, you may want to change the paths in your macros.

Table 24.3 displays the most useful of Word's default file paths. Some of these are accessible on the File Locations tab of the Options dialog box; others are accessible only through the Registry.

TABLE 24.3: Default File Paths in Word

Constant	Specifies the Path To
wdAutoRecoverPath	AutoRecover files
wdCurrentFolderPath	The current folder
wdDocumentsPath	The default location for documents
wdGraphicsFiltersPath	The location of graphics filters (usually the COMMON FILES\MICROSOFT SHARED\GRPHFLT\ folder)
wdProgramPath	The location of the Word EXE files (usually the MICROSOFT OFFICE\OFFICE\ folder)
wdStartupPath	The Startup folder
wdTempFilePath	The folder where Word stores temporary files
wdTextConvertersPath	The folder containing the text converters (usually COMMON FILES\MICROSOFT SHARED\TEXTCONV\)
wdToolsPath	The folder containing Word tools (usually the MICROSOFT OFFICE\OFFICE\ folder)
wdUserOptionsPath	The folder in which user options are stored
wdUserTemplatesPath	The folder containing user (local) templates (usually the PROGRAM FILES\TEMPLATES\ folder)
wdWorkgroupTemplatesPath	The folder containing workgroup (shared) templates

To return a default file path, use the DefaultFilePath property of the Options object with the appropriate argument. The following statement displays a message box containing the program path:

```
MsgBox Options.DefaultFilePath(wdProgramPath)
```

The following statement sets the workgroup templates path:

```
Options.DefaultFilePath(wdWorkgroupTemplatesPath)= "f:\common\Templates"
```

Working with Folders

VBA provides the following commands for working with folders:

- Use the Dir function with \nul to check whether a folder exists. The following statements save a document if the specified folder exists and display a warning message box if the folder does not exist:

  ```
  If Dir("d:\temp\nul") <> "" Then
      ActiveDocument.SaveAs "d:\temp\Sample Document.doc"
  Else
      MsgBox "The folder d:\temp does not exist.", vbOKOnly + _
  vbCritical
  End If
  ```

- Use the ChDir statement to change the current directory or folder on the specified drive. The following statement changes the current folder on drive D to D:\TEMP:

  ```
  ChDir "d:\temp"
  ```

- Use the ChDrive statement to change the current drive. ChDrive uses only the leftmost character of the string you give it. The following statements both change the current drive to D:

  ```
  ChDrive "d"
  ChDrive "d:\temp\testing"
  ```

- Use the CurDir function to return the current folder:

  ```
  MsgBox "The current folder is " & CurDir & ".",, "Current Folder"
  ```

- Use the MkDir statement to create a folder. MkDir takes a path argument specifying the path of the folder to create. The following statement creates the folder C:\WINDOWS\TEMP\TESTING\:

  ```
  MkDir "c:\Windows\Temp\Testing"
  ```

- Use the RmDir function to delete a folder. RmDir takes a path argument specifying the path of the folder to delete. Before using RmDir, you need to remove all the contents of the target folder (for example, by using a Kill statement) and make sure the target folder is not the current folder.

- To delete a folder and its contents, use a Shell statement and the DELTREE command. Shell uses a DOS box.

Working with Windows and Panes

VBA provides two Windows collections: one containing Window objects that represent the windows available in the Application object, and one containing Window objects in a Document object. Usually, you'll want to work with the Windows collection for the Application object, though at times it's useful to work with the Windows collection for a Document object.

Each Window object contains a Panes collection of Pane objects that represent the panes for the window. Each window and pane can have a different Selection object, though only one Selection object can be active at a time.

These are the actions you're most likely to need to perform with Window and Pane objects and their collections:

- Use the window name or index number with the Windows collection to return a Window object. The following statement displays a message box containing the name of each Window object in turn:

```
For i = 1 To Windows.Count
    MsgBox Windows(i).Caption
Next i
```

- Use the WindowState property to return or adjust the window state of the active window. Use the arguments wdWindowStateMaximize to maximize the window, wdWindowStateMinimize to minimize the window, or wdWindowStateNormal to "restore" the window. The following statement maximizes the active window if it is not already maximized:

```
If ActiveWindow.WindowState <> wdWindowStateMaximize Then _
    ActiveWindow.WindowState = wdWindowStateMaximize
```

- Use the View object to adjust the view in the window. For example, for many procedures you will want a document to be in Normal view rather than Outline view, Print Preview, or another unsuitable view. The following statements store the current view, change to Normal view if necessary, and then restore the previous view if necessary:

```
With ActiveWindow
    If .View <> wdNormalView Then
        CurView = .View
        .View = wdNormalView
    End If
    'Take other actions here
```

```
        If CurView <> "" Then .View = CurView
    End With
```

- Use the Zoom property of the View object to adjust the zoom level in the window. The following statement sets the zoom percentage to 125%:

```
ActiveWindow.View.Zoom = 125
```

- Use the Arrange method with the ArrangeStyle argument to arrange the open document windows in the application window. Use wdTiled to tile maximized or "restored" windows, or use wdIcons to arrange minimized window icons:

```
Windows.Arrange ArrangeStyle:=wdTiled
```

- Use the Count property of the Windows collection for a Document object to make sure that only one window is displayed for a document you want to work with. Note that Print Preview uses a second window.

- For many procedures, you'll want to make sure that the insertion point is in the main document before taking action. This enables you to, say, avoid creating a whole document in a header, footnote, or comment pane. To find out which pane the insertion point is in, try using the SplitSpecial property of the View object for the appropriate pane. (We say "try using" because for us, SplitSpecial consistently causes GPFs under both Windows 95 and NT.) Failing that, you can close every pane beyond the first to make sure the main document is active:

```
With ActiveWindow
    Do While .Panes.Count > 1
        .Panes(.Panes.Count).Close
    Loop
End With
```

Inserting Text in a Document

You can insert text in either the active document or a specified Document object.

When working with the active document, you can use the Selection object for working with text:

- To insert text at the position of the insertion point, use the TypeText method of the Selection object:

```
Selection.TypeText "Report for April 1, 1998"
```

NOTE Before inserting text, make sure the current selection is suitable, as discussed in the next section. Usually, you'll want to make sure the selection is wdSelectionIP.

- To insert text before or after the current selection, use the InsertBefore and InsertAfter methods on the Selection object. VBA will extend the selection to include the inserted text. The following statements insert Professor and a space before the current selection and the content of the string expression Course after it:

```
Selection.InsertBefore "Professor"
Selection.InsertAfter Course
```

To insert text in a document other than the active document, identify the document and the position in which to insert the text. The following statement inserts the string Title at the beginning of the document named Weekly Report.doc:

```
Documents("Weekly Report.doc").Characters(1).InsertBefore Title
```

You can insert a paragraph in any of several ways:

- Use the InsertParagraph method to insert a paragraph at the current position of the insertion point:

```
Selection.InsertParagraph
```

- Use the InsertParagraphAfter or InsertParagraphBefore method to insert a paragraph either after or before the selection or range:

```
Selection.InsertParagraphBefore
```

- Use the TypeText method to enter the vbCr constant or the carriage-return character, Chr(13):

```
Selection.TypeText vbCr
Selection.TypeText Chr(13)
```

Working with the Selection Object

The Selection object represents the selection in the Application object, a Window object, or a Pane object. Use the Selection object with the Application object to return the active selection in the active document; use the Selection object with a Window object or a Pane object to return the selection in that pane. Each window in each open document can have a Selection object, but only one Selection object can be active at any time in any Word session: the selection in the active document. The Selection object is analogous to the insertion point or current selection when you are working interactively with Word.

The Selection object can be collapsed to an insertion point, or it can contain one or more characters or document items, up to the entire content of any document story. (Word recognizes eleven *stories*—parts of a document—including the main text, the comments section, text in frames, and the header and footer sections. See "Using Range Properties" later in this chapter for a list of Word stories and their associated constants and values.)

Checking the Type of Selection

To find out what type of selection you currently have, return the Type property of the Selection object:

```
If Selection.Type = wdSelectionIP Then MsgBox "Insertion point"
```

Word differentiates the types of selections shown in Table 24.4.

TABLE 24.4: The Types of Selections in Word

wdSelectionType constant	Value	Meaning
wdNoSelection	0	There is no selection.
wdSelectionIP	1	The selection is a plain insertion point—nothing is selected.
wdSelectionNormal	2	A "normal" selection, such as a selected word or sentence.
wdSelectionFrame	3	A frame is selected.
wdSelectionColumn	4	A column or part of a column (two or more cells in a column, or one cell in each of two or more columns) is selected.
wdSelectionRow	5	A full row in a table is selected.
wdSelectionBlock	6	A block is selected (a vertical part of one or more paragraphs).
wdSelectionInlineShape	7	An inline shape or graphic is selected.
wdSelectionShape	8	A shape object is selected.

Manipulating the Current Selection

To manipulate the current selection, use the properties and methods of the Selection object and the objects and collections it contains. The Text property contains the text of the Selection object:

```
MsgBox Selection.Text
```

You can perform operations such as cut, copy, and paste. The following statement copies the current selection from the active document:

```
Selection.Copy
```

To work with part of the current selection, specify it by using the appropriate object. The following statement sets the font size of the second word in the selection to 48 points:

```
Selection.Words(2).Font.Size = 48
```

To work with the current paragraph (the paragraph in which the insertion point resides, or the paragraph that is selected or partly selected), use the Paragraphs object to specify it:

```
Selection.Paragraphs(1)
```

Extending a Selection

To extend a selection, use the EndOf method for a Range or Selection object. EndOf takes an optional Unit argument (see Table 24.5) and an optional Extend variant argument: wdMove moves the selection or range and is the default setting; wdExtend extends the selection or range.

TABLE 24.5: Unit Arguments

Unit	Meaning
wdCharacter	A character
wdWord	A word (the default setting if you omit Unit)
wdSentence	A sentence
wdLine	A line (can be used only with Selection objects, not with ranges)
wdParagraph	A paragraph
wdSection	A section of a document

Continued on next page

TABLE 24.5 CONTINUED: Unit Arguments

Unit	Meaning
wdStory	The current story
wdCell	A cell in a table
wdColumn	A column in a table
wdRow	A row in a table
wdTable	A whole table

The following statement extends the current selection to the end of the paragraph:

```
Selection.EndOf Unit:=wdParagraph, Extend:=wdExtend
```

The following statement moves the selection (that is, the insertion point) to the end of the paragraph:

```
Selection.EndOf Unit:=wdParagraph, Extend:=wdMove
```

The following statement selects from the current insertion point or selection to the end of the current Word story:

```
Selection.EndOf Unit:=wdStory, Extend:=wdExtend
```

Canceling a Selection

You can cancel (deselect) a selection in any of several ways:

- Collapse the selection to the start of the selection by using the Collapse method:

  ```
  Selection.Collapse wdCollapseStart
  ```

- Reduce the selection to just one point by setting the end of the selection to be equal to the start of the selection:

  ```
  Selection.End = Selection.Start
  ```

- Reduce the selection to one point by setting the start of the selection to be equal to the end of the selection:

  ```
  Selection.Start = Selection.End
  ```

- Collapse the selection and move the insertion point to the end of the selection:

  ```
  Selection.Collapse wdEnd
  ```

Getting Other Information about the Current Selection

VBA can provide full information about the current selection, from its font and size to its borders. To access this information, check the property of the relevant object.

For further information, use the Information property to return information about a selection or range and about what's happening in the Word environment. Table 24.6 lists the available information.

TABLE 24.6: Information Available in the Information Property

wdInformation Constant	Returns this Information
Environment Information	
wdCapsLock	True if Caps Lock is on.
wdNumLock	True if Num Lock is on.
wdOverType	True if Overtype mode is on.
wdRevisionMarking	True if change tracking is on.
wdSelectionMode	The current selection mode: 0 indicates a normal selection; 1 indicates an extended selection (Extend mode is on); and 2 indicates a column selection.
wdZoomPercentage	The current zoom percentage.
Selection and Insertion Point Information	
wdActiveEndAdjustedPage-Number	The number of the page containing the active end of the selection or range. This number reflects any change you make to the starting page number; wdActiveEndPageNumber does not.
wdActiveEndPageNumber	The number of the page containing the active end of the selection or range.
wdActiveEndSectionNumber	The number of the section containing the active end of the selection or range.
wdFirstCharacterColumnNumber	The character position of the first character in the selection or range. If the selection or range is collapsed to an insertion point, this returns the character number immediately to the right of the insertion point. (This "column" is relative to the currently active left margin and does not have to be inside a table. This is the number that appears in the Col readout in the status bar.)

Continued on next page

TABLE 24.6 CONTINUED: Information Available in the Information Property

wdInformation Constant	Returns this Information
Selection and Insertion Point Information	
wdFirstCharacterLineNumber	In Page Layout view and Print Preview, returns the line number of the first character in the selection. In non-layout views (for example, Normal view), this returns −1.
wdFrameIsSelected	True if the selection or range is a whole frame or text box.
wdHeaderFooterType	A value that specifies the type of header or footer containing the selection or range: −1 indicates that the selection or range is not in a header or footer; 0 indicates an even-page header; 1 indicates an odd-page header in a document that has odd and even headers, and the only header in a document that does not have odd and even headers; 2 indicates an even-page footer; 3 indicates an odd-page footer in a document that has odd and even footers, and the only footer in a document that does not have odd and even footers; 4 indicates a first-page header; and 5 indicates a first-page footer.
wdHorizontalPositionRelativeToPage	The horizontal position of the selection or range—the distance from the left edge of the selection or range to the left edge of the page, measured in twips (20 twips = 1 point; 72 points = 1 inch).
wdHorizontalPositionRelative-ToTextBoundary0	The horizontal position of the selection or range—the distance from the left edge of the selection or range to the text boundary enclosing it, measured in twips.
wdInCommentPane	True if the selection or range is in a comment pane.
wdInEndnote	True if the selection or range is in an endnote (this is defined as appearing in the endnote pane in Normal view or in the endnote area in Page Layout view).
wdInFootnote	True if the selection or range is in a footnote (this is defined as appearing in the footnote pane in Normal view or in the footnote area in Page Layout view).
wdInFootnoteEndnotePane	True if the selection or range is in a footnote or endnote.
wdInHeaderFooter	True if the selection or range is in a header or footer (defined as appearing in the header or footer pane in Normal view or in the header or footer area in Page Layout view).
wdInMasterDocument	True if the selection or range is in a master document (a document containing at least one subdocument).

Continued on next page

TABLE 24.6 CONTINUED: Information Available in the Information Property

wdInformation Constant	Returns this Information
Selection and Insertion Point Information	
wdInWordMail	A value that specifies the WordMail location of the selection or range: 0 indicates that the selection or range is not in a Word-Mail message; 1 indicates that it is in a WordMail send note; and 2 indicates that it is in a WordMail read note.
wdNumberOfPagesInDocument	The number of pages in the document in which the selection or range appears.
wdReferenceOfType	A value that specifies where the selection is in relation to a footnote, endnote, or comment reference.
wdVerticalPositionRelative-ToPage	The vertical position of the selection or range—the distance from the top edge of the selection to the top edge of the page, measured in twips.
wdVerticalPositionRelative-ToTextBoundary	The vertical position of the selection or range—the distance from the top edge of the selection to the text boundary enclosing it, measured in twips.
Table Information	
wdWithInTable	True if the selection is in a table.
wdStartOfRangeColumnNumber	The number of the table column containing the beginning of the selection or range.
wdEndOfRangeColumnNumber	The number of the table column containing the end of the selection or range.
wdStartOfRangeRowNumber	The number of the table row containing the beginning of the selection or range.
wdEndOfRangeRowNumber	The number of the table row containing the end of the selection or range.
wdAtEndOfRowMarker	True if the selection or range is at the end-of-row marker in a table (not the end-of-cell marker).
wdMaximumNumberOfColumns	The largest number of table columns in any row in the selection or range.
wdMaximumNumberOfRows	The largest number of table rows in the table in the selection or range.

Creating and Using Ranges

In Word, a *range* is a contiguous area of a document with a defined starting point and ending point. For example, you can define a range that consists of the first paragraph in a specified document. The starting point of the range will be the beginning of the paragraph, and the ending point of the range will be the end of the paragraph. Likewise, you can define a range that consists of the 100th to 200th characters in a document or a range that consists of a specified number of words in a certain paragraph.

You can use ranges with VBA for the same reason you use bookmarks when working interactively with Word: to mark a location in a document that you want to be able to access quickly or manipulate easily. Like a bookmark, a range can contain any amount of text in a document, from a single character to all the contents of the document; a range can even have the same starting point and ending point, which gives it no contents and makes it in effect an invisible mark in the document that you can use to insert text. Once you've created a range, you can refer to it, access its contents or insert new contents in it, or format it, all by using the properties of the range and the methods that apply to it.

In practical terms, the main difference between a range and a bookmark is that the lifetime of a range is limited to the VBA procedure that defines it, whereas a bookmark is saved with the document or template that contains it and can be accessed at any point (whether or not a procedure is running).

Using range objects gives you far more flexibility than working with the current selection. Whereas there can be only one active selection in a given Word session, you can define multiple ranges in each of the documents you have open. Moreover, you can define and manipulate ranges in documents other than the active document, and you can work with ranges without affecting the current selection.

Defining a Named Range

You can create a Range object by using a Set statement in either of two ways:

- Use the Range method on a Document object.

- Use the Range property for an object that supports it.

To use the Range method, use the following syntax, where RangeName is the name you are assigning to the range, and Start and End are optional arguments specifying the starting and ending points of the range:

```
Set RangeName = Document.Range(Start, End)
```

To use the Range property, use the following syntax:

```
Set RangeName = Object.Range
```

The following statement uses the Range property of the Paragraphs collection to define a range named FirstPara that consists of the first paragraph of the active document:

```
Set FirstPara = ActiveDocument.Paragraphs(1).Range
```

The following statements uppercase the first three words of the active document:

```
With ActiveDocument
    Set FirstThree =.Range(Start:=.Words(1).Start, End:=.Words(3).End)
    FirstThree.Case = wdUpperCase
End With
```

The first statement defines the range FirstThree as a range in the active document, from the beginning of the first word to the end of the third word. The second statement changes the case of the FirstThree Range object to uppercase. Because FirstThree is now defined as a Range object for the duration of the procedure that declares it, you can return to FirstThree and manipulate it later in the procedure if you want to.

Working with Unnamed Ranges

You don't have to assign a name to a range to work with it—you can also use the Range object without assigning a name. For example, if you didn't want to revisit the FirstThree range that we defined in the previous example, you could skip the step of naming the range and instead apply the Case method to the Range object, as in the following statement:

```
With ActiveDocument
    .Range(Start:=.Words(1).Start, End:=.Words(3).End).Case = _
wdUpperCase
End With
```

Redefining a Range

To redefine a range, use the SetRange method with the optional Start and End arguments. The following statement redefines the range FirstThree (which was defined as the first three words of the active document) to refer to the first character of the document:

```
FirstThree.SetRange Start:=0, End:=1
```

NOTE   You can also redefine a range by using the Set method again, in essence re-creating the range from scratch.

Using Range Properties

The Range object has a large number of other properties associated with it, from contents properties such as a Words property and a Characters property (as well as a Cells property, a Columns property, and a Rows property for ranges that contain tables) to formatting properties such as a Font property, a Bold property, and an Italic property. For manipulating a range, the most important properties are the Start property, the End property, and the StoryType property:

- Use the Start property to set or return the starting character position of the range.

- Use the End property to set or return the ending character position of the range.

- Use the StoryType property to set or return the type of story (document area) associated with the Range:

wdStoryType Constant	Value	Meaning
wdMainTextStory	1	Main text of the document
wdCommentsStory	4	Comments section
wdEndnotesStory	3	Endnotes section
wdFootnotesStory	2	Footnotes section
wdTextFrameStory	5	Text in frames
wdPrimaryFooterStory	9	Main footer
wdEvenPagesFooterStory	8	Even-page footer
wdFirstPageFooterStory	11	First-page footer
wdPrimaryHeaderStory	7	Main header
wdEvenPagesHeaderStory	6	Even-page header
wdFirstPageHeaderStory	10	First-page header

The following statement compares the story type of the range MyRange to the main text of the document and terminates the macro if it is not the main text of the document:

```
If MyRange.StoryType <> wdMainTextStory Then End
```

Working with a Range

Once you've defined a range, you can specify it by name to quickly work with its contents. The following statements define a range named WorkRange that references the first sentence in the document and then works with it:

```
Set WorkRange = ActiveDocument.Sentences(1)
With WorkRange
    .Font.Name = "Arial"
    .Font.Size = "48"
    .Font.Underline = wdUnderlineSingle
End With
```

Working with Formatting and Styles

By using VBA, you can apply the same three types of formatting to your documents as you can manually: paragraph styles, character styles, and direct formatting.

Applying Paragraph Styles

To apply a paragraph style, use the Style property of either the Paragraphs collection, a Range object, or the Selection object. The following statement applies the Heading 1 style to the current selection:

```
Selection.Style = "Heading 1"
```

You can apply a style to all the paragraphs in a document by specifying the Paragraphs collection. The following statement applies the Body Text style to all the paragraphs in the document A QUESTION OF STYLE.DOC:

```
Documents("A Question of Style.doc").Paragraphs.Style = "Body Text"
```

Applying Character Styles

To apply a character style, identify the target text and use the Style property of a suitable object, such as the Characters collection or the Words collection. The following statement applies the character style Bold Italic to the first word of the second paragraph of the active document:

```
ActiveDocument.Paragraphs(2).Range.Words(1).Style = "Bold Italic"
```

To apply a character style to selected text, use the Style property of the Selection object. The following statement applies the character style Dialog Text to the current selection:

```
Selection.Style = "Dialog Text"
```

NOTE   You cannot apply a character style to a Paragraph object directly—you need to specify a range, some characters, or some words.

Applying Direct Formatting

You can apply direct formatting as well as (or instead of) paragraph styles and character styles. Although direct formatting has a number of disadvantages (for example, carelessly applying other styles to text that has direct formatting can remove formatting attributes from it), you may want to use it from time to time in your macros. Here are two examples.

To apply font formatting, manipulate the Font property of the object in question. The following statement italicizes the first paragraph in the document named ARIZONA SALES.DOC:

```
Documents("Arizona Sales.doc").Paragraphs(1).Range.Font.Italic = True
```

To apply paragraph formatting to a paragraph, use the ParagraphFormat object. The following statement applies Left alignment to the current selection:

```
Selection.ParagraphFormat.Alignment = wdAlignParagraphLeft
```

Working with Find and Replace

Word's Find and Replace features are as powerful tools in procedures as they are for working interactively with Word. You can use Find and Replace operations on either the ActiveDocument object or a Document object.

The Find Object

The Find object, which applies to the Range and Selection objects, has properties and methods that match the options in the Find and Replace dialog box. The easiest way to use the Find object is with the Execute property, specifying the parameters for the Find operation as arguments in the Execute statement. You can also set the parameters beforehand using properties.

Table 24.7 describes the most useful properties for common search operations. You'll see a lot of overlap between these and the arguments for the Execute statement, which we'll look at in a moment; essentially, they cover the same ground, but with different syntax.

TABLE 24.7: Properties for Common Search Operations

Find Property	Meaning
Font	Font formatting you're searching for (on either specified text or an empty string).
Forward	A Boolean argument specifying whether to search forward (True) or backward (False) through the document.
Found	A Boolean property that is True if the search finds a match and False if it does not.
Highlight	A Long argument controlling whether highlighting is included in the formatting for the replacement text (True) or not (False).
MatchAllWordForms	A Boolean property—True or False—corresponding to the Find All Word Forms checkbox.
MatchCase	A Boolean property corresponding to the Match Case checkbox.
MatchSoundsLike	A Boolean property corresponding to the Sounds Like checkbox.
MatchWholeWord	A Boolean property corresponding to the Find Whole Words Only checkbox.
MatchWildcards	A Boolean property corresponding to the Use Wildcards checkbox.
ParagraphFormat	Paragraph formatting you're searching for.
Replacement	Returns a Replacement object containing the criteria for a replace operation.
Style	The style for the search text. Usually, you'll want to use the name of a style in the current template, but you can also use one of the built-in Word constant style names, such as wdStyleHeading1.

Continued on next page

TABLE 24.7 CONTINUED: Properties for Common Search Operations

Find Property	Meaning
Text	The text you're searching for—what you would enter in the Find What box in the Find and Replace dialog box. To search only for formatting, use an empty string ("").
Wrap	A Long property that governs whether a search that starts anywhere other than the beginning of a document (for a forward search) or the end of a document (for a backward search), or a search that takes place in a range, wraps when it reaches the end or beginning of the document or the end or beginning of the selection.

The Replacement Object

The Replacement object specifies the replace criteria in a replacement operation. The Replacement object has the following properties, which correspond to the properties of the Find object (but pertain to the replacement operation instead):

- Font

- Highlight

- ParagraphFormat

- Style

- Text

Using the Execute Method

The easiest way to execute a Find operation is to use the Execute method with the Find object. The syntax for the Execute method is:

```
Find.Execute(FindText, MatchCase, MatchWholeWord, _
MatchWildcards, MatchSoundsLike, MatchAllWordForms, _
Forward, Wrap, Format, ReplaceWith, Replace)
```

The parts of this statement are as follows:

- FindText is an optional variant specifying the text for which to search. Though this argument is optional, you'll almost always want to specify it, even if you specify only an empty string ("") to allow you to search for formatting. (If you do not specify FindText, you run the risk of searching inadvertently for the previous item searched for.) You can search for special characters (such as ^p for a paragraph mark or ^a for an annotation) and for wildcards by using codes. For wildcards to work, set MatchWildcards to True. To search for a symbol, enter a caret and a zero followed by its character code. For example, to search for a smart double closing quote, specify **^0148**, because its character code is 148.

- MatchCase is an optional variant that you can set to True to make the search case-sensitive.

- MatchWholeWord is an optional variant that you can set to True to restrict the search to finding whole words rather than words contained in other words.

- MatchWildcards is an optional variant that you can set to True to use wildcards in the search.

- MatchSoundsLike is an optional variant that you can set to True to have Word find words that sound similar to the Find item specified.

- MatchAllWordForms is an optional variant that you can set to True to have Word find all forms of the Find item specified.

- Forward is an optional variant that you can set to True to have Word search forward (from the beginning of the document toward the end) or False to have Word search backward.

- Wrap is an optional variant that governs whether a search that begins anywhere other than the beginning of a document (for a forward search) or at the end of a document (for a backward search), or a search that takes place in a range, wraps (continues) when it reaches the end or beginning of the document. Word offers the following options for Wrap:

WdFindWrap Constant	Value	Meaning
wdFindAsk	2	Word searches the selection or range from the insertion point to the end or beginning of the document and then displays a message box prompting the user to decide whether to search the rest of the document.

WdFindWrap Constant	Value	Meaning
wdFindContinue	1	Word continues to search after reaching the end or beginning of the search range or the end or beginning of the document.
wdFindStop	0	Word stops the Find operation upon reaching the end or beginning of the search range or the end or beginning of the document.

- Format is an optional variant that you can set to True to have the search operation find formatting as well as (or instead of) any Find text you've specified.

- ReplaceWith is an optional variant specifying the replacement text. You can use an empty string for ReplaceWith to simply remove the FindText text; you can also use special characters for ReplaceWith as you can for the FindText argument. To use a graphic object, copy it to the clipboard and then specify ^c (the contents of the clipboard).

- Replace is an optional variant that controls how many replacements the Find operation makes: one (wdReplaceOne), all (wdReplaceAll), or none (wdReplaceNone).

To clear formatting currently set for the Find object or the Replace object, use the ClearFormatting method. The following statements clear formatting on both the Find and Replacement objects:

```
With ActiveDocument.Content.Find
    .ClearFormatting
    .Replacement.ClearFormatting
End With
```

Find and Replace in Action

The simplest way to use Find and Replace is to specify as many parameters as you need in an Execute statement, leaving out any optional parameters that you don't need to specify. For example, to replace all extra paragraph marks in the active document, you could search for **^p^p** and replace it with **^p** with the following statement:

```
ActiveDocument.Content.Find.Execute FindText:="^p^p" _
ReplaceWith:="^p",Replace:=wdReplaceAll
```

Alternatively, use a With statement to specify the properties for a Find and Replace operation:

```
With ActiveDocument.Content.Find
    .Text = "^p^p"
    .Replacement.Text = "^p"
    .Forward = True
    .Wrap = wdFindContinue
    .Execute Replace:=wdReplaceAll
End With
```

Working with Bookmarks

Word's bookmarks provide a way of identifying and referring to parts of documents quickly and easily. Bookmarks are particularly useful for automating the flow and transfer of information from document to document or from Word to another application. To access bookmarks, use the Bookmarks collection.

NOTE   VBA's ranges provide another way of working with a specified part of a document. The advantage of a bookmark over a range is that you can save a bookmark in a document, whereas a range lasts only while the procedure that defines it is running.

Not only can you create bookmarks of your own, but Word includes a number of hidden, built-in bookmarks that you can use to access information about a document.

Working with User-Defined Bookmarks

In this section, we'll discuss how VBA handles user-defined bookmarks—the ones that you add to a document either manually or by using macros.

Inserting a Bookmark

To insert a bookmark, use the Add method. The Add method takes a required Name string argument that specifies the name of the bookmark. Bookmark names can contain underscores but not spaces, can contain alphanumerics but not symbols, and can be a maximum of 40 characters. You can also use an optional variant Range argument to specify the range for the bookmark to mark. The range can contain text or graphical elements or can be collapsed to a single point.

The following statement adds a bookmark named Meeting_Location to the active document at the current position of the insertion point or the current selection:

```
ActiveDocument.Bookmarks.Add Name:="Meeting_Location"
```

The following statement uses a Range argument to add a bookmark named Request_Number to the first word of the open document named PERSONNEL REQUEST.DOC:

```
Documents("Personnel Request.doc").Bookmarks.Add _
    Name:="Request_Number", _
    Range:=Documents("Personnel Request.doc").Words(1)
```

Finding Out Whether a Bookmark Exists

To find out whether a bookmark exists, use the Exists property for the Bookmark object in the Bookmarks collection. The following statements display a message box stating whether the bookmark Request_Number exists in the document PERSONNEL REQUEST.DOC:

```
With Documents("Personnel Request.doc")
    If .Bookmarks.Exists("Request_Number") = True Then
        MsgBox "The bookmark exists."
    Else
        MsgBox "The bookmark does not exist."
    End If
End With
```

Going to a Bookmark

To move the insertion point to a bookmark, use the Select method for the Bookmark object. The following statement moves the insertion point to the bookmark named MyTemp in the active document:

```
ActiveDocument.Bookmarks("MyTemp").Select
```

Finding Out Where a Bookmark Is Located

To find out where a bookmark is located, use the Start and End properties of its Range object, which return the character position of the start and end of the bookmark's range. The statements below display a message box listing the start and end positions of the bookmark named CEO_Salary:

```
Set CurDoc = Documents("Industry Survey.doc")
BookStart = CurDoc.Bookmarks("CEO_Salary").Range.Start
BookEnd = CurDoc.Bookmarks("CEO_Salary").Range.End
MsgBox "Start position:" + Str(BookStart) & vbCr & "End position:" _
  & Str(BookEnd), vbOKOnly + vbInformation, "Bookmark Information"
NOTE
```

NOTE   If the start and end of the bookmark's range are in the same place—that is, if the bookmark marks a collapsed selection—the start and end positions will be the same.

Returning the Contents of a Bookmark

To return the contents of a bookmark, use the Text property of the Range object of the Bookmark object. The following statement returns the contents of the bookmark CEO_Salary in the active document:

```
MsgBox ActiveDocument.Bookmarks("CEO_Salary").Text
```

To find out whether a bookmark is empty, check to see if its Empty property is True.

Deleting a Bookmark

To delete a bookmark, use the Delete method with the Bookmark object. The following statement deletes the bookmark named Employee_Idea in the document NEW IDEAS.DOC:

```
Documents("New Ideas.doc").Bookmarks("Employee_Idea").Delete
```

To delete all the bookmarks in a document, you could use a For Each…Next statement with the Bookmarks collection. The following macro deletes all bookmarks in the active document:

```
Sub Delete_All_Bookmarks()
    With ActiveDocument
        For Each Mark In .Bookmarks
            .Bookmarks(Mark).Delete
        Next Mark
    End With
End Sub
```

Using Word's Built-In Bookmarks

Word provides a number of built-in bookmarks (see Table 24.8) that it uses in the background to perform standard operations. You can use these bookmarks for your own purposes.

TABLE 24.8: Word's Built-In Bookmarks

Bookmark	Returns
\Sel	The current selection.
\PrevSel1	The location of the most recent edit (Shift+F5 manually).
\PrevSel2	The location of the second most recent edit (Shift+F5 twice manually).
\StartOfSel	The start of the current selection if there is one; otherwise, the location of the insertion point.
\EndOfSel	The end of the current selection if there is one; otherwise, the location of the insertion point.
\Line	The first line of the current selection if there is one; otherwise, the line on which the insertion point resides. If the insertion point is positioned at the end of any line other than the last line in the paragraph, this bookmark includes the whole of the next line. If there's a space after the insertion point at the end of the line, you'll get the current line instead of the next line.
\Char	The first character of the current selection if there is one; otherwise, the character to the right of the insertion point.
\Para	The current paragraph, or the first paragraph if part or all of two or more paragraphs are selected. This bookmark includes the paragraph mark unless the paragraph in question is the last paragraph in the document.
\Section	The current section, or the first section if there is a selection that contains part or all of two or more sections.
\Doc	All the contents of the active document except for the last paragraph mark.
\Page	The current page, or the first page if there is a selection that spans two or more pages. If the page in question is the last page in the document, this bookmark does not include the last paragraph mark.
\StartOfDoc	The beginning of the document.
\EndOfDoc	The end of the document.

Continued on next page

TABLE 24.8 CONTINUED: Word's Built-In Bookmarks

Bookmark	Returns
\Cell	The current cell in a table, or the first cell if there is a selection that spans two or more cells.
\Table	The current table, or the first table if there is a selection that spans part or all of two or more tables.
\HeadingLevel	The current heading and any subordinate headings or text. If the current selection is not a heading, VBA selects the heading that precedes the selection, together with any subordinate headings or text.

> **NOTE**   Before using the PrevSel1 or PrevSel2 bookmark, check that it exists by using a statement such as If ActiveDocument.Bookmarks.Exists("\PrevSel2") = True Then ActiveDocument.Bookmarks("\PrevSel2").Select.

The following statements delete the current paragraph in the active document:

```
ActiveDocument.Bookmarks("\Para").Select
Selection.Delete
```

Looping through a Collection

By looping through a collection, you can quickly perform an action on all the objects in it without testing to see how many objects there are. To loop through a collection, use a For Each…Next statement. The following statements set the ShowAll property (which displays paragraph marks, spaces, tabs, and so on) for each window to False and the WrapToWindow property to True:

```
For Each Win In Windows
    Win.View.ShowAll = False
    Win.View.WrapToWindow = True
Next Win
```

The following procedure shows how you might search the contents of each document for a particular word or phrase and close each document that did not contain it:

```
Sub Close_Documents_without_Specified_Text()
    Dim SearchText As String
```

```
SearchText = InputBox("Enter the text to search for:", _
    "Close Documents without Specified Text")
For Each Doc In Documents
    With Selection.Find
        .Text = SearchText
        .Execute
        If .Found = False Then Documents(Doc).Close
    End With
Next Doc
End Sub
```

Using Word's Built-In Dialog Boxes

In this section, we'll discuss how to use Word's built-in dialog boxes in procedures you create. Using the built-in dialog boxes is an easy way to present the user with choices that Word already offers. Furthermore, you can use built-in dialog boxes to get past the limitations of the standard selection of controls that the Visual Basic Editor provides for Forms. (For example, as we saw in Chapter 23, the Visual Basic Editor does not offer the FileListBox, DirListBox, and DriveList-Box controls that the Visual Basic IDE offers.) Moreover, you can save time and trouble by using a built-in dialog box, and you can be confident that users of your applications or procedures will recognize the dialog box and know how to use it, particularly if it is a common dialog box (such as an Open dialog box, a Save dialog box, or a Print dialog box).

The main disadvantage to using a built-in dialog box is that it may not be 100 percent suitable for what you want it to do: It may not offer all the actions you want, or it may offer the user actions that you do not want them to take. For example, you might require the user to open a file only from a given folder, in which case the Open dialog box would not be suitable, as it lets the user access any folder to which they have file-viewing rights.

You can choose whether to display a built-in dialog box and let the user use it in the normal fashion or to display a built-in dialog box, check the choices the user makes in it, and execute only appropriate choices. Doing the latter enables you to prevent the user from taking inappropriate actions in the dialog box.

Displaying a Built-In Dialog Box

Built-in Word dialog boxes are identified by constants starting with wdDialog, followed by the name of the dialog box. The name is derived from the menu commands required to display the dialog box. For example, the constant for the Open dialog box is wdDialogFileOpen (File ➤ Open); the constant for the Print dialog box is wdDialogFilePrint (File ➤ Print); and the constant for the Font dialog box is wdDialogFormatFont (Format ➤ Font).

NOTE   To display a Word dialog box from Visual Basic, you need to add a reference to the Microsoft Word 8.0 Object Library.

To display a dialog box, you use its constant with the Dialogs collection. There are two methods for displaying a built-in dialog box:

- The Show method displays the specified Dialog object and executes the actions the user takes in the dialog box. For example, if you use the Show method to display the wdDialogFileSaveAs dialog box and the user enters a name for the file in the File Name box and clicks the Save button, VBA will save the file with the given name in the specified folder (and with any options the user chose). The following statement displays the Save As dialog box:

      ```
      Dialogs(wdDialogFileSaveAs).Show
      ```

- The Display method displays the dialog box on-screen but does not execute the actions the user takes in the dialog box. Instead, it allows you to return the settings from the dialog box once the user dismisses it and use them for your own purposes. For example, you could display the Open dialog box to allow the user to select a file. Instead of opening the file, you could then manipulate it in a different way. The statements below use the Display method to display the Open dialog box and then display a message box containing the name of the file selected:

      ```
      Set MyFileOpen = Dialogs(wdDialogFileOpen)
      MyFileOpen.Display
      MsgBox "You chose " & MyFileOpen.Name & "."
      ```

If the dialog box has tabs, the tabs have names built from the name of the dialog box, the word *Tab*, and the name of the tab. So the constant for the Bullets and Numbering dialog box is wdDialogFormatBulletsAndNumbering, and the constant for its Outline Numbered tab is wdDialogFormatBulletsAndNumbering-TabOutlineNumbered. Likewise, the Character Spacing tab of the Font dialog box is wdDialogFormatFontTabCharacterSpacing. To specify the tab to display, you use the DefaultTab property. The following statements display the Font dialog box with the Character Spacing tab foremost:

```
With Dialogs(wdDialogFormatFont)
    .DefaultTab = wdDialogFormatFontTabCharacterSpacing
    .Show
End With
```

To execute the settings in a built-in dialog box displayed with the Display method, use the Execute method. The statements below display the Open dialog box and then execute the user's choices in it. The comment line indicates where you could take actions to ensure the user had chosen a suitable file.

```
Set MyFileOpen = Dialogs(wdDialogFileOpen)
With MyFileOpen
    .Display
    'Check the file chosen by the user; set options as appropriate
    .Execute
End With
```

> **NOTE** You can also use the Execute method on a built-in dialog box you've displayed using the Show method, but typically you won't need to, because the user's actions will make the dialog box execute appropriately.

Setting Options in a Built-In Dialog Box

To set an option in a built-in dialog box, use a Set statement to return a dialog object that refers to the object in the Dialogs collection. For example, to set the contents of the File Name text box in the Save As dialog box, you could use the statements shown below:

```
Set SaveMe = Dialogs(wdDialogFileSaveAs)
SaveMe.Name = "Baroque Castles in Bavaria, Introduction.doc"
```

Alternatively, you can use a With statement to work with the dialog box:

```
With Dialogs(wdDialogFileSaveAs)
.Name = "My Visit to Neuschwanstein"
.Display
End With
```

Most of the built-in Word dialog boxes have a number of arguments that you can use for retrieving or setting values in the dialog box. For example, the Open dialog box has arguments for Name, ConfirmConversions, ReadOnly, LinkToSource, AddToMRU (adding the document to the Most Recently Used document list at the foot of the File menu), PasswordDoc, and more. Some of these are options that you'll see in the Open dialog box itself; others are associated options that you'll find on the various tabs of the Options dialog box.

You can deduce the names of many of the arguments for a built-in dialog box from the names of the options in the dialog box. For example, in the Font dialog box (wdDialogFormatFont), the Font drop-down list is identified by the Font argument, and the Color drop-down list is identified by the Color argument. Other options, however, have different names. For instance, the Size drop-down list in the Font dialog box is identified by the Points argument.

TIP   Look up the topic "Built-in Word dialog boxes, argument list" in the Index of the VBA Help file for Word to get a list of all the built-in Word dialog boxes and the names of the arguments they take.

For example, you could display the Open dialog box showing all the TXT files in the \PUBLIC\COMMON\ folder on the networked drive \\ERASER_D\ by setting the Name argument for the dialog box to *.txt and using the ChangeFileOpen-Directory statement to change the folder displayed in the Open dialog box:

```
ChangeFileOpenDirectory "\\Eraser_D\public\common"
With Dialogs(wdDialogFileOpen)
    .Name = "*.txt"
    .Show
End With
```

TIP   To change the folder in the Open dialog box, use the ChangeFileOpenDirectory method before displaying the dialog box. ChDrive and ChDir will not affect the folder displayed in the Open dialog box. The File-Open-Directory setting is set to a default folder when Word is launched, and it changes when the user manually changes folders in the Open dialog box.

Retrieving Values from a Built-In Dialog Box

When you use the Display method to display a dialog box, you'll need to return information from the dialog box so that you can take action with it. You may also need to return information from a dialog box displayed using the Show method.

To return a value from a built-in dialog box, use a Set statement to identify the dialog box:

```
Set mySaveAs = Dialogs(wdDialogSaveAs)
```

Then display the dialog box to let the user choose settings. If you want to be able to approve the settings before implementing them, use the Display method instead of the Show method so that VBA does not execute the settings when the user dismisses the dialog box. Then check the settings, change any that need changing, and use the Execute method to apply the settings.

For example, you could display the User Info tab of the Options dialog box from Visual Basic and make sure the user had entered text in each of the three text boxes by using the following code. Note that the dialog box uses the Execute method to execute any changes the user made to the information in the dialog box even when the user has not supplied complete information. Without this Execute method, the Display method will not bring in updated information on each loop back to the Redisplay label.

```
Set MyWord = CreateObject("Word.Application")
With MyWord
    .Visible = True
Redisplay:
    With Dialogs(wdDialogToolsOptionsUserInfo)
        .Display
        'Substitute a more effective check for the next line
        If .Name = "" Or .Initials = "" Or .Address = "" Then
            .Execute
            MsgBox "Please complete your information.", vbOKOnly _
            + vbCritical, "Information Inquisition 1.1"
            GoTo Redisplay
        Else
            .Execute
        End If
    End With
    .Quit
End With
Set MyWord = Nothing
```

Getting the Current Values for a Dialog Box

To get the current values for a dialog box, use the Update method. For example, the following statements show how you might display the Find and Replace dialog box, take other actions (indicated by the comment line), and then use the Update method to get the current values for the Find and Replace dialog box:

```
Set MyFind = Dialogs(wdDialogEditReplace)
MyFind.Display
'Take other actions here
MyFind.Update
```

> **NOTE** In most cases, it makes more sense to delay calling the dialog box until it is needed. By doing so, you will get the current values for the dialog box and will not need to use the Update method.

Returning the Button the User Chose in a Dialog Box

To find out which button the user clicked in a dialog box, check the return value of the Show method or the Display method. Table 24.9 shows the return values.

TABLE 24.9: The Return Values of the Show and Display Methods

Return Value	Button Clicked
−2	Close
−1	OK
0	Cancel
1	The first Command Button
2	The second Command Button
>2	Subsequent Command Buttons

For example, you could display the Paragraph dialog box and check which button the user clicked by using the following statements:

```
With Dialogs(wdDialogFormatParagraph)
    ButtonClicked = .Display
```

```
      Select Case ButtonClicked
      Case -1                              'User clicked the OK button
          MsgBox "You clicked the OK button.", vbOKOnly
      Case 0                               'User clicked the Cancel button
          MsgBox "You clicked the Cancel button.", vbOKOnly
      End Select
  End With
```

Specifying a Timeout for a Dialog Box

You can a specify a timeout for a built-in dialog box, instead of having it displayed until the user dismisses it, by using the TimeOut variant argument with the Show method or the Display method. You specify TimeOut as a number of units, each of which is approximately a thousandth of a second (if the system is busy with many other tasks, the units may be longer). So you could display the User Information tab of the Options dialog box for about 15 seconds by using the following statements:

```
With Dialogs(wdDialogToolsOptions)
    .DefaultTab = wdDialogToolsOptionsTabUserInfo
    .Show (15000)
End With
```

NOTE   The TimeOut argument works only for built-in Word dialog boxes; it does not work for custom dialog boxes.

CHAPTER
TWENTY-FIVE

Outlook 98 Objects

- Outlook's folders

- Scanning and creating folders

- The MailItem object

- The ContactItem object

- Creating new messages

- Creating new contacts

Incorporating e-mail capabilities into desktop applications is becoming increasingly popular in modern-day software. To make your applications e-mail aware, you can use the MAPI control or program Outlook's objects. We are going to discuss how to mail-enable your VB applications through Outlook VBA, because Outlook is simple, manages more types of information than just messages, and is a practical tool for carrying out day-to-day operations. Many corporations use Outlook to automate tasks like appointment scheduling, sending routine mail, and so on. We can't examine all the functions of Outlook 98 in this chapter, and many of them are not of interest to the majority of VB programmers. So we'll focus on the objects you need to add mailing capabilities to your VB applications and show you how to access messages and contacts stored in Outlook.

A difference between Outlook and the other Office applications is that where Excel and Word can be both programmed and automated with VBA, Outlook can only be programmed with VBScript. Both VBA and VBScript, however, manipulate the same objects, which we are going to explore in the following sections.

The Outlook 98 Object Model

The root object of the Outlook 98 object model is the Application object, which gives you access to all other objects. Unlike the Word and Excel applications, Outlook 98 doesn't expose a single object, like Document or Worksheet, that gives you access to the units of information it can handle. Outlook 98 contains several objects, such as mail messages, contacts, notes, tasks, and so on, which are organized in folders. In order to work with a particular type of object, you must open the appropriate folder. To work with contacts, you must open the Contacts folder (or a subfolder under the Contacts folder). Likewise, to work with messages you must open the Inbox, Outbox, or Sent Items folder. You won't find information about your contacts in the InBox folder, or pending messages in the Calendar folder.

The basic unit of information in Outlook is a folder. Different folders store drastically different types of information. Mail messages are represented by objects that are totally different from objects that represent appointments or contacts. Under the Application object, there's a collection of MAPIFolder items, the Folders collection. Each MAPIFolder object, in turn, contains a number of Item objects in the Items collection. The Items collection contains the items in a specific folder, and different folders contain different types of items.

To contact Outlook and program its objects, you must first add a reference to the "Microsoft Outlook98 Object Model" library through the References dialog box. Then, you must create an object variable that represents the Application object with statements like the following:

```
Dim OLApp As Outlook.Application
Set OLApp = CreateObject("Outlook.Application")
```

To access Outlook's folders through the *OLApp* object variable, you must create another object variable, of type NameSpace. A NameSpace object can represent any data source, such as a MAPI (Messaging Application Programming Interface) data source. The current release of Outlook supports only MAPI message data sources, but there could be others in the future.

The method GetNameSpace of the Application object returns a NameSpace object variable that references all the folders in Outlook 98. To create such a variable, use a statement such as the following:

```
Set OLFolders = OLApp.GetNameSpace("MAPI")
```

where *OLFolders* must be declared as follows:

```
Dim OLFolders As NameSpace
```

You'll use the following statements in every application that contacts Outlook 98:

```
Dim OLApp As Outlook.Application
Dim OLFolders As NameSpace
    Set OLApp = CreateObject("Outlook.Application")
    Set OLFolders = OLApp.GetNamespace("MAPI")
```

Outlook's Folders

Through the *OLFolders* variable, you can access the various folders of Outlook. The method for accessing a folder is the GetDefaultFolder method, which accepts as argument the name of the folder and returns an object variable. The type of object variable returned by GetDefaultFolder method is MAPIFolder, and it provides properties and methods that give your application access to the items stored in the folder.

The GetDefaultFolder method returns the default folder for each category of items. If you want to access the contacts you have entered in Outlook 98, the

GetDefaultFolder will return the contact items stored in the Contacts folder. Most users organize the various items in subfolders. Figure 25.1 shows a typical organization of Oulook's folders. The contact items in this particular computer are organized in two main folders (Business and Personal) under the Contacts folder. Under each of these folders there are more subfolders. The default folder for the contact items is the Contacts folder; this is the folder returned by the GetDefault-Folder method if it's called with the olFolderContacts argument.

FIGURE 25.1:

Outlook items are usually stored in nested folders.

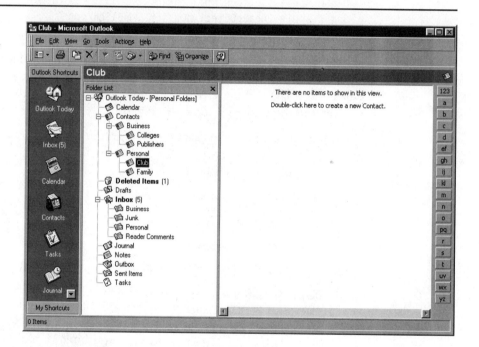

The various default folders maintained by Outlook can be accessed with the following constants:

TABLE 25.1: Outlook's Default Folders

Constant Name	Description
OlFolderContacts	Default folder for ContactItem objects
OlFolderInbox	Default folder for MailItem objects

Continued on next page

TABLE 25.1 CONTINUED: Outlook's Default Folders

Constant Name	Description
OlFolderOutbox	Storage area for items that are completed but not sent
OlFolderSentMail	Storage area for items that have been sent
OlFolderNotes	Default folder for NoteItem objects
OlFolderJournal	Default folder for JournalItem objects
OlFolderDeletedItems	Storage area into which all item objects are moved when they're marked for deletion
OlFolderCalendar	Default folder for AppointmentItem objects
OlFolderTasks	Default folder for TaskItem objects

Each folder contains items of different types, which in turn expose a large number of properties. Discussing all types of items and their members is beyond the scope of this book. ApppointmentItems, JournalItems, and TaskItems are important when building very specific applications, and we'll not discuss them here. Instead, we'll focus on the members of the ContactItem and MailItem objects, which are the most general items of Outlook and can be used to add mail capabilities to your applications.

. The various items you can create and store with Outlook are represented by different object types that are stored in different folders. They are mail messages, appointments, meeting requests, tasks, task requests, contacts, journal entries, posts, mail delivery reports, remote mail items, and notes. Table 25.2 summarizes the various Outlook items.

TABLE 25.2: The Items Stored in the Folders of Outlook 98

Object	Description
AppointmentItem	Represents an appointment in the Calendar folder. An AppointmentItem object can represent either a one-time or a recurring meeting or appointment. An appointment becomes a meeting when the MeetingStatus property is set to *olMeeting* and one or more resources (either personnel, in the form of required or optional attendees, or physical resources, such as a conference room) are designated. These actions result in the creation of a MeetingRequestItem object.

Continued on next page

TABLE 25.2 CONTINUED: The Items Stored in the Folders of Outlook 98

Object	Description
ContactItem	Represents a contact in a Contacts folder. A contact can represent any person and provides a number of properties for storing information about the person (physical and electronic addresses, job title, and so on).
JournalItem	Represents a journal entry in a Journal folder. A journal entry represents a record of all Outlook-moderated transactions for any given period of time.
MailItem	Represents a mail message in a mail folder (including the Sent Items and Deleted Items folders). The MailItem object is the default item object and, to some extent, the basic element of Outlook. The MailItem object exposes many properties for creating new messages (recipient, message text, attachments, and so on) as well as methods for sending messages. In addition to the MailItem object, Outlook also has a parallel PostItem object that has all of the characteristics of the mail message, differing only in that it's posted (written directly to a folder) rather than sent (mailed to a recipient).
MeetingRequestItem	Represents a change to the recipient's Calendar folder, initiated either by another party or as a result of a group action. Unlike other Outlook objects, you cannot create a MeetingRequestItem object or find an existing one in the Items collection. This object is created automatically when you set the MeetingStatus property of an AppointmentItem object to *olMeeting* and send it to one or more users. To return the AppointmentItem object associated with a MeetingRequestItem object and work directly with the AppointmentItem object to respond to the request, use the GetAssociatedAppointment method.
NoteItem	Represents a note (an annotation attached to a document) in a Notes folder.
PostItem	Represents a post in a public folder that other users can browse. This object is similar to the MailItem object, differing only in that it's posted (saved) directly to the target public folder, not sent (mailed) to a recipient. Use the Post method, which is analogous to the Send method for the MailItem object, to save the post to the target public folder instead of mailing it.
RemoteItem	Represents a remote item in the Inbox folder or another mail folder. This object is similar to the MailItem object, but it contains only the Subject, Received, Date, Time, Sender, Size, properties, and the first 256 characters of the body of the message. You use it to give someone who's connecting in remote mode enough information to decide whether or not to download the corresponding mail message.
ReportItem	Represents a mail-delivery report in the Inbox folder or another mail folder. This object is similar to the MailItem object, and it contains a report (usually the nondelivery report) or error message from the mail transport system.

Continued on next page

TABLE 25.2 CONTINUED: The Items Stored in the Folders of Outlook 98

Object	Description
TaskItem	Represents a task (an assigned, delegated, or self-imposed task to be performed within a specified time frame) in a Tasks folder. Like appointments or meetings, tasks can be delegated. Tasks are delegated when you assign them to one or more delegates, using the Assign method.
TaskRequestItem	Represents a change to the recipient's task list, initiated either by another party or as a result of a group assignment. Unlike other Outlook objects, you cannot create a TaskRequestItem object or find an existing one in the Items collection. It's created automatically when you apply the Assign method to a TaskItem object to assign (delegate) the associated task to another user. To return the TaskRequestItem object and work directly with the TaskItem object to respond to the request, use the GetAssociatedTask method.

Each one of these objects provides numerous properties, which are the attributes of the item it represents. A ContactItem object, for example, provides properties for setting just about any attribute of a contact (name, e-mail addresses, job title, even birthday and anniversary). To see the properties of the ContactItem object; open the Object browser, select Outlook in the Class box, and in the Classes list, click the ContactItem entry, as shown in Figure 25.2. The members of the selected Class will appear in the right pane. The properties you'll use most often in your applications are LastName and FirstName, Email1Address, Title and the properties that begin with HomeAddress and BusinessAddress. These are the fields you usually set in the Contact dialog box when you add or edit contacts from within Outlook. If you need additional fields, you can add your own custom properties. The custom properties are accessed by name, but I'm not going to discuss them here. You should see Outlook's help files for more information on adding custom properties.

The MailItem object exposes all the properties you need to create new messages, as well as methods for sending, forwarding, deleting, and replying to messages. The basic properties of the MailItem object are Body (the message's text), HTMLBody (the message's text in HTML format), To (the main recipient of the message), Recipients (a collection with the message's recipients), Subject, and SentOn (the date the message was sent). The Reply method creates a new MailItem object and sets its destination and subject (which is the same as the original message's subject with the "Re:" prefix). All you have to do is specify the reply text and send the message. To create and send a new message, set up a new MailItem object variable and call its Send method.

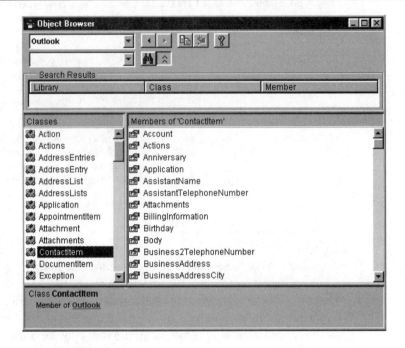

In the following section, we'll briefly present the members of the MailItem and ContactItem objects, which are the two objects we'll use in our examples in the rest of the chapter.

The Members of the MailItem Object

The MailItem object represents messages sent, received, or pending transmission. MailItem objects are contained in the folders Inbox, Outbox, Drafts, Sent Items, and Deleted Items. You can also create new messages and prepare them for transmission. New messages are stored in the Drafts folder, until you call their Send method. Then, they are moved to the Outbox folder, from where they will be transmitted, according to Outlook's settings (in the Delivery tab of the Options dialog box you can specify when messages are actually sent).

Attachments Property

The Attachments property is a collection of all items (files) attached to the current message. To access the individual attachments, create an Attachments collection and then use a For Each…Next loop to scan the attachments. Code 25.1 is a code segment that scans all the attachments in MailItem *thismessage* (an object variable that represents a message):

Code 25.1   **Enumerating the Attachments of a MailItem**

```
Dim thisAttachment As Attachment
Dim MessageAttachments As Attachments

    Set MessageAttachments = thismessage.Attachments
    For Each thisAttachment In MessageAttachments
        {process current attachment}
        {thisAttachment.PathName}
        {thisAttachment.Type}
    Next
```

In the loop's body you can retrieve the path name of the location where the attachment is stored with the property thisAttachment.PathName and the type of the attachment with the property thisAttachment.Type.

Body and HTMLBody Properties

Use these properties of the MailItem object to access a message's text in plain text or HTML format. You can also set these properties to create a new message.

DeleteAfterSubmit Property

Set this Boolean property to True to delete a message you've generated in your code after its submission. Normally, sent messages are stored in the Sent Items folder. Mass-mailing applications, which need not store hundreds of messages in the Sent Items folder, should set the DeleteAfterSubmit property of each new message to True.

Recipients Property

Recipients is a collection of Recipient objects. Each Recipient object in the Recipients collection is a destination for a message. To view the Recipient object's members, open the Object Browser, select Outlook in the Type Library list, and locate the Recipient item in the Classes list.

To add a new recipient to a message, create a MailItem object and call the Recipients collection's Add method, specifying either a valid e-mail address or the name of a contact in the Contacts folder. The address some_address@some_server.com is a valid address. You can also specify contacts from the Contacts folder. If you designate contacts by name, you can specify the contacts' last and first names in any order. If an entry in your Outlook folder is "John, Doe," you can define the corresponding recipient as either "John, Doe" or "Doe, John." For an example on how to use the Recipients collection to specify destinations for messages, see the description of the Resolve method.

Resolve and ResolveAll Methods

When you specify multiple addresses from within your code via the Recipients collection, it's likely that some of them are incorrect or invalid. Outlook can resolve the specified addresses with the Resolve and ResolveAll methods. Resolve is a method of the Recipient object and it resolves a single address. The Resolve method returns True if the address is valid (i.e., if its format is valid, like name@server.com or a name in the Contacts folder). ResolveAll is a method of the Recipients collection and resolves all addresses in the collection. If one or more of the addresses in the Recipients collection can't be resolved, the ResolveAll method returns False.

Code 25.2 creates a new message and adds a few recipients by appending items to the Recipients collection. Some of the recipients are valid, some are not. (You should replace the addresses and names with entries from your Contact folder.)

Code 25.2   **Adding Recipients to a Message**

```
Dim thisMessage As MailItem
Dim person As Recipient

    Set thisMessage = OLApp.CreateItem(olMailItem)
    thisMessage.Recipients.Add "Dave, Fugaro"
    thisMessage.Recipients.Add "pevangelos@usamail.net"
    thisMessage.Recipients.Add "Knoppf, Piere"
    thisMessage.Recipients.Add "Piere, Knoppf"
    thisMessage.Recipients.Add "bad address"
    thisMessage.Recipients.Add "some_address@some_server.com"
    If Not thisMessage.Recipients.ResolveAll Then
        For i = thisMessage.Recipients.Count To 1 Step -1
            Set person = thisMessage.Recipients.Item(i)
            If Not person.Resolve Then
                Debug.Print "Couldnt resolve address: " & _
                        thisMessage.Recipients.Item(i)
```

```
                thisMessage.Recipients.Remove (i)
        Else
                Debug.Print "Resolved address: " & person.Address
        End If
    Next
End If
```

Notice that the recipient Piere Knoppf was added in two different formats. If an entry with first name "Piere" and last name "Knoppf" exists in the Contact folder, both addresses are valid.

The code calls the ResolveAll method to find out whether the list of recipients contains invalid addresses. If one or more addresses can't be resolved, it scans the entire list of recipients and calls the Resolve method for each contact. The ones that can't be resolved are removed from the list. Both valid and invalid addresses are displayed in the Immediate window, with the appropriate prefix.

Reply and ReplyAll Methods

Use these methods to create a reply to an existing message. Outlook will create a new message and set up as many of its fields as possible (list of recipients, the original message's text, and so on). You can set more fields, change the text (by inserting your response), and send the reply to its recipient(s). The Reply method generates a reply message addressed to the sender, and the ReplyAll method generates a reply message addressed to the sender and all recipients of the original message.

SenderName Property

This is a read-only property with the name of the message's sender.

Send Method

Call a MailItem's Send method from within your code to send the corresponding message to its destination. The MailItem object must exist already and all its fields must be set.

Sent Property

This is another read-only property of the MailItem object, which returns True if the message has been sent.

SentOn

This is another read-only property of the MailItem object, which returns the date on which the message was sent.

Subject

This property returns or sets the message's subject.

To

This property returns or sets the message's main recipient.

The Members of the ContactItem Object

The ContactItem object represents the items in the Contacts folder. The ContactItem object supports a large number of properties, which you can view in the Object Browser or on Outlook's Contact window as you're editing or adding new contacts. Most of the properties are self-explanatory. The properties with the E-mail prefix store e-mail addresses. Each contact can have up to three e-mail addresses (Email1Address, Email2Address, and Email3Address). Each contact has a First-Name and LastName field, as well as a Company field. Outlook will automatically generate a number of read-only properties, which can be used to locate contacts or format contacts for printouts. They are as follows:

CompanyAndFullName	CompanyLastFirstNoSpace
CompanyLastFirstSpaceOnly	FullName
FullNameAndCompany	LastFirstAndSuffix
LastFirstNoSpace	LastFirstNoSpaceCompany
LastFirstSpaceOnly	LastFirstSpaceOnlyCompany

The fields with the Business prefix (BusinessAddress, BusinessHomePage, and so on) store information about the contact's workplace and the fields with the Company prefix store information about the contact's business. The ContactItem doesn't provide any special methods, just a few methods for saving and printing a contact's information and other trivial operations.

The EntryID Property

The EntryID property, a long value generated by Outlook that uniquely identifies each item, is a property that's common to all items. Of course, you can't present IDs to the user to select a contact or a message, but you can use them to bookmark items or as keys in a TreeView, or other, control. The user can select items based on more meaningful information, such as name and company, message subject, and so on. Then, you can instantly locate the desired item in the corresponding folder with its ID (you'll learn how the EntryID property is used in the examples of this chapter).

As you can see, none of the fields of the MailItem or ContactItem objects are unique, with the exception of the electronic address. But then again, not all objects have an electronic address (NoteItems don't, for example). The EntryID is a unique identifier used by every object in the Outlook object model (even folders) that you can use in your code as you see fit. In addition, the various items are indexed by this field and can be retrieved instantly.

The Display Method

All objects in Outlook, including the MailItem and ContactItem objects, support a Display method, which opens the item's Form in Outlook. If you're preparing a new message and you want the user to enter a few fields or confirm the various field values, you can call the MailItem's Display method. Likewise, if you want to offer the user a chance to review the fields of a new contact and then save the changes, call the ContactItem's Display method.

The Display method accepts a single optional argument, vbModal, which specifies that the corresponding Outlook Form should not return control to the application that opened it before the user has closed it. If you call the Display method without an argument, then the program control will be returned to the statement following the one that called the Display method, and your code will continue its execution. It's rare that you'll call the Display method without the vbModal argument.

Working with Folders

Let's return to the Outlook folders at the top of the Outlook object model. To access mail and contact items (or any other item supported by Outlook), you must first locate and open the folder to which it belongs.

To work with a specific folder, you must first create an object variable that represents the contents of a specific folder. If all items are stored in the default folder (for example, if all ContactItems are stored in the Contacts folder, and not in subfolders under the Contacts folder), you can easily create this object variable with the GetDefaultFolder method. First, declare a MAPIFolder variable with the statement:

```
Dim contactsFolder As MAPIFolder
```

and then Set this variable to the Contacts folder with the statement:

```
Set contactsFolder = OLFolders.GetDefaultFolder(olFolderContacts)
```

The Contacts folder may contain ContactItems, subfolders, or both. To access the ContactItems in the Contacts folder, use the Items collection. As a collection, the Items object exposes the Count property (the total number of ContactItems) and the Item property, which allows you to retrieve individual items. Each item in this collection is a ContactItem. Had you requested the Inbox default folder, then each item would be a MailItem. The properties exposed by each object type are different, but you'll use the same techniques for accessing individual items in any folder you open.

The number of ContactItems in the Contacts folder is given by the expression contactsFolder.Items.Count. The first one is contactsFolder.Items.Item(1), the second one is contactsFolder.Items.Item(2), and so on. If you print the values of these expressions in the Immediate window, you'll see the names of the contacts (this is the default property). The loop in Code 25.3 will print the names of the contacts stored in the Contacts folder (but not any contacts stored in a subfolder under Contacts):

Code 25.3　　　**Enumerating a Folder's Items**

```
Dim contactsFolder As MAPIFolder
    Set contactsFolder = _
            OLFolders.GetDefaultFolder(olFolderContacts)
    If contactsFolder.Items.Count > 0 Then
        For i = 1 To contactsFolder.Items.Count
            Debug.Print contactsFolder.Item.Items(i)
        Next
    End If
```

You can access the messages in any of the folders that hold MailItems with the same statements (as long as you change the constant *olFolderContacts* to *olFolderInbox* and the names of the variables accordingly). The techniques for accessing folders and subfolders are the same, regardless of the type of information stored in the folder.

If the Contacts folder contains subfolders (and in most cases it does), you can access its subfolders through the Folders collection. The following loop will print the names of the subfolders under the Contacts folder:

```
Dim contactsFolder As MAPIFolder

    Set contactsFolder = _
            OLFolders.GetDefaultFolder(olFolderContacts)
    If contactsFolder.Folders.Count > 0 Then
        For i = 1 To contactsFolder.Folders.Count
            Debug.Print contactsFolder.Folders(i).Name
        Next
    End If
```

For the folder structure shown in Figure 25.1, the above loop will print the following folder names:

```
Business
Personal
```

As you can see, only the first level subfolders under the Contacts folder are returned. Scanning the subfolders recursively to any depth requires some additional programming. You'll see how you can scan a folder recursively in the section "Scanning Folders Recursively."

Adding New Folders

The Folders collection provides an Add method, too, which lets you create new folders from within your code. Code 25.4 will add a folder named "New Contacts," under the Contacts folder:

Code 25.4	Adding a New Folder

```
Dim contactsFolder As MAPIFolder

On Error GoTo FolderAddError
    Set contactsFolder = _
            OLFolders.GetDefaultFolder(olFolderContacts)
    contactsFolder.Folders.Add ("New Contacts")
    MsgBox "New Contacts folder added successfully"
```

```
        Exit Sub

FolderAddError:
        MsgBox "Could not add new folder." & vbCrLf & _
               "OUTLOOK ERROR" & vbCrLf & Err.Description
```

The error-trapping code is an essential part of the code. If for any reason , the Add method fails (this will happen if the New Contacts folder exists already), the program will fail with an error message.

To retrieve the newly added folder, use the following statements:

```
Dim contactsFolder As MAPIFolder
Dim newContactsFolder As MAPIFolder
    Set contactsFolder = OLFolders.Folders.Item _
        ("Personal Folders").Folders.Item("Contacts")
    Debug.Print contactsFolder.Parent.Name & " > " & _
        contactsFolder.Name
    Set newContactsFolder = contactsFolder.Folders.Item _
        ("New Contacts")
        Debug.Print newContactsFolder.Parent.Name & _
        " > " & newContactsFolder.Name
```

If you want to delete a MAPIFolder object, call its Delete method. To delete the New Contacts folder, retrieve it as shown with the previous statements and then call the Folder object's Delete method, with a statement like the following:

```
newContactsFolder.Delete
```

Each time you access a folder, you can enumerate its subfolders with the Get-First, GetLast, GetNext, and GetPrevious methods, or you can delete a subfolder with the Remove method. These are methods of the Folders collection. Notice that the name of the method for deleting a folder is called Delete if you have access to the MAPIFolder object you want to delete, and Remove if you have access to the Folders collection to which the MAPIFolder object to be deleted belongs.

Adding New Items

In addition to adding new folders to the Outlook structure, you can add items to each folder. To add an item, you must first create the appropriate Item object, set its properties, and finally call the Save method. To create a new contact and store it in the New Contacts folder, use the statements in Code 25.5.

Code 25.5	**Adding a New ContactItem**

```
Dim contactsFolder As MAPIFolder
Dim newContactsFolder As MAPIFolder
Dim newContact As ContactItem

    Set contactsFolder = OLFolders.Folders.Item _
        ("Personal Folders").Folders.Item("Contacts")
    Set newContactsFolder = _
            contactsFolder.Folders.Item("New Contacts")
    Set newContact = newContactsFolder.Items.Add
    newContact.LastName = "Clinton"
    newContact.FirstName = "Bill"
    newContact.JobTitle = "President"
    newContact.EmailAddress = "billy@worldleaders.org"
    newContact.Save
```

The Add method creates a new ContactItem object (variable *newContact* in the listing), but doesn't store it in the corresponding folder. The statements that follow the Add method set the basic properties of the contact, and then the Save method is called to actually store the contact to the New Contacts folder.

If you place these statements in a Command button's Click event handler and click the button twice, two identical contacts will be added to the folder. The only property that will be different in these two items is their EntryID property.

Scanning Folders Recursively

Most users organize their items in subfolders to simplify the process of locating the desired items. Scanning a folder recursively (i.e., scanning its subfolders and their subfolders to any depth) is not as simple. This operation calls for a recursive routine. In this section we'll present a procedure that scans the Contacts folder recursively and maps its structure to a TreeView control. Each subfolder under the Contacts folder is a node of the tree; the user can see the contacts in a specific subfolder by clicking its name. Figure 25.3 shows the Form of the Contacts project, which you will find in this chapter's folder on the CD. Click the Populate Tree button to create a tree structure with the subfolders of the Contact folder on the TreeView control. After the TreeView control has been populated with the folder names, you can click a folder to see its contents (the ContactItems stored in the corresponding subfolder).

FIGURE 25.3:

The Contacts project maps the structure of the Contacts folder on a TreeView control.

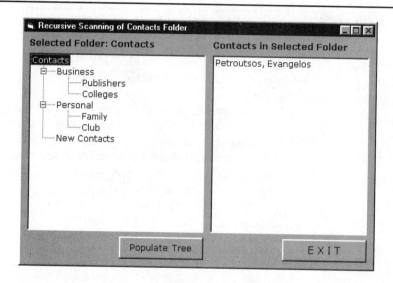

Let's start with the trivial code. First, declare the following object variables, which must be accessed by multiple procedures:

```
Public OLApp As outlook.Application
Public OLObjects As outlook.NameSpace
Public OLContacts As outlook.MAPIFolder
```

Then, in the Form's Load event, enter the statements in Code 25.6 to create a new instance of Outlook and the object variables needed to access the folders of Outlook:

Code 25.6   **Creating an Outlook Object Variable**

```
Private Sub Form_Load()
    Set OLApp = CreateObject("Outlook.Application.8")
    If Err Then
        MsgBox "Could not create Outlook Application object!", _
               vbCritical
        End
    End If
    Set OLObjects = OLApp.GetNamespace("MAPI")
    Set OLContacts = OLObjects.GetDefaultFolder(olFolderContacts)
    If Err Then
        MsgBox "Could not create MAPI Namespace!", vbCritical
    End If
End Sub
```

The *OLApp* variable represents the application. The *OLObjects* variable represents all the folders exposed by Outlook, and *OLContacts* represents the Contacts folder.

Populating the TreeView Control

The core of the Contacts project is the code that populates the TreeView control (the Populate Button's Click event handler). Code 25.7 contains the code that populates the TreeView control:

Code 25.7   Populating the TreeView Control

```
Private Sub Command1_Click()
Dim allFolders As outlook.Folders
Dim Folder As outlook.MAPIFolder
Dim Folders As outlook.Folders
Dim thisFolder As outlook.MAPIFolder
Dim newNode As Node

' Add root node
Set newNode = TreeView1.Nodes.Add(, , OLContacts.EntryID, "Contacts")
newNode.Expanded = True
' Get all Folders under Contacts
Set allFolders = OLContacts.Folders
' Process each Folder under Contacts
For Each Folder In allFolders
    Set newNode = TreeView1.Nodes.Add(OLContacts.EntryID, _
            tvwChild, Folder.Name, Folder.Name)
    Set Folders = Folder.Folders
    For Each thisFolder In Folders
        Set newNode = TreeView1.Nodes.Add(Folder.Name, _
            tvwChild, thisFolder.EntryID, thisFolder.Name)
        newNode.Expanded = True
        ' now scan the current folder's subfolders
        ScanSubFolders thisFolder
    Next
Next
End Sub
```

The TreeView control is populated as follows. First, we add the root node, which is the Contacts folder. This node has no parent node and its key is the Contact's folder EntryID property value:

```
Set newNode = TreeView1.Nodes.Add(, , OlContacts.EntryID, _
            "Contacts")
newNode.Expanded = True
```

As soon as the node is added, it's expanded, so that the user will see the names of the subfolders under it and the plus sign in front of their names (should they contain subfolders). Then we must create the *allFolders* collection, which contains all the subfolders of the Contacts folder:

```
Set allFolders = OlContacts.Folders
```

The following loop scans each item in this collection, then it adds the name of the current folder to the TreeView control. The new node becomes a child node of the Contacts node, and its Key is the EntryID property of its parent node.

Next, we must create another collection, the *SubFolders* collection, with the current folder's subfolders. This collection's items are added to the TreeView control, and then we call the ScanSubFolders() subroutine to scan the subfolders of each item. The code of the ScanSubFolders() subroutine is shown in Code 25.8:

Code 25.8   **The ScanSubFolders() Subroutine**

```
Sub ScanSubFolders(thisFolder As Object)
Dim subFolders As outlook.Folders
Dim subFolder As outlook.MAPIFolder

    Set subFolders = thisFolder.Folders
    If subFolders.Count <> 0 Then
        strFolderKey = thisFolder.EntryID
        For Each subFolder In subFolders
            TreeView1.Nodes.Add thisFolder.EntryID, _
                tvwChild, subFolder.EntryID, subFolder.Name
            ScanSubFolders subFolder
        Next
    End If
End Sub
```

This is a recursive subroutine, which creates a collection with the current folder's subfolders—the *subFolders* collection. Then, it scans each item in the collection, adds its name to the TreeView control, and scans it recursively by calling itself and passing the name of the current folder as an argument. Notice that each MAPIFolder object's key in the TreeView control is its EntryID property. As a result, all nodes have a unique key, which will allow our code to instantly access any folder selected on the control.

Viewing a Folder's Contacts

After populating the TreeView control with the structure of the subfolders under the Contacts folder, you can select a folder in the TreeView control with the mouse to display its contacts on the ListBox control in the right-hand side of the Form. When you click on an item in the TreeView control, the NodeClick event is triggered. This event reports the Node clicked, and you can use the event's argument to retrieve the node's key, which is the ID of the selected folder. Once you know the ID of the selected folder, you can create a reference to this folder (variable *thisFolder*) and use it to scan the contact items in the actual folder. Code 25.9 is the code of the TreeView control's NodeClick event:

Code 25.9   **Listing the Items of the Selected Folder**

```
Private Sub TreeView1_NodeClick(ByVal Node As ComctlLib.Node)
Dim thisFolder As outlook.MAPIFolder
Dim contacts As outlook.Items
Dim Contact As outlook.ContactItem

On Error Resume Next
    List1.Clear
    Label1.Caption = "Selected Folder: " & Node.Text
    Set thisFolder = OLObjects.GetFolderFromID(Node.Key)
    If Err Then
        Exit Sub
    Else
        Set contacts = thisFolder.Items
        For Each Contact In contacts
            List1.AddItem Contact.LastName & ", " & Contact.FirstName
        Next
    End If
End Sub
```

The code displays only the contact's *LastName* and *FirstName* properties, but you can modify the code to display any fields. For example, you can retrieve the contact's e-mail address and send automated messages. Add a TextBox control on the Form where the user can enter some text, and then create and send a message to the selected recipients (you'll see shortly how to create messages and send them from within your application).

Creating and Sending Messages

The process of creating and sending messages is quite similar. First, you must create a MailItem object, set its properties, and then send it to its recipient with the Send method. The code in Code 25.10 creates a new message and sends it. The message's recipient is hardcoded, but you have seen already how to retrieve e-mail addresses from the Contacts folder(s).

The Send method doesn't actually send the message. It places it in the Outbox folder of Outlook so the message will be delivered with the next batch of messages.

Code 25.10   **Creating a New Message**

```
Dim thisMessage As MailItem
Dim strMsg As String

    strMsg = Text1.Text      ' the message's text
    Set thisMessage = OLApp.CreateItem(olMailItem)
    With thisMessage
        .Recipients.Add "billy@worldleaders.org"
        .Subject = "News from Sybex " & Format(Date, vbLongDate)
        .Body = strMsg
        .Send
    End With
```

If the message has a single recipient, you can use the To property instead of the Recipients collection.

The Find Methods

When you request a collection of items (any type of items), you can filter the collection and retrieve only the items you're interested in. To filter the messages, use the Find and FindNext methods of the Items object that contains the items. The syntax of the Find method is:

```
Items.Find(filterstring)
```

where *filterstring* is an expression that specifies the desired criteria. The Find method returns an object, whose type depends on the type of the Items collection. If you apply the Find method to the InBox folder, it will return a MailItem object; if you apply it to the Contacts folder, it will return a ContactItem object. After you have retrieved the first item that meets the criteria, you can retrieve the following ones by calling the FindNext method, without specifying any arguments.

The *filterstring* argument is a string expression that combines field names, logical operators, and values. To retrieve the messages sent by WebBuilder's Network, use the following string:

```
[SenderName] = "WebBuilder's Network"
```

To retrieve all messages sent in October of '97, use the following string:

```
[SentOn] => "10/01/97" And [SentOn] <= "10/31/97"
```

You can combine as many fields as needed with the usual comparison and logical operators. The field names for each item type can be found in the Object browser. Select the desired item (MailItem, ContactItem, and so on) and look up its properties in the Members pane.

The values of the various fields in the *filterstring* argument are commonly specified as variables. To specify a filter string with values entered by the user on various controls on a Form, you must enclose the names of the controls (or variables) in double quotes. In other words, you must build a string with embedded double quotes. To enclose the variables' values in double quotes, use two consecutive double quotes.

Let's say you want to retrieve messages sent by a contact whose name is retrieved from a ComboBox control and whose messages were sent between two dates specified in the DateTo and DateFrom TextBox controls. Here's the code that builds the filter string:

```
ContactName = Combo1.Text
filterString = "[SenderName] = """ & ContactName & """"
filterString = "[SentOn] > """ & _
DateFrom.Text & """ And [SentOn] < """ & DateTo.Text & """"
filterString = filterString & " and [SentOn] > """ & _
    DateFrom.Text & """ And [SentOn] < """ & DateTo.Text & """"
```

If the value of the *ContactName* variable is "Sybex" then the statement:

```
"[SenderName] = """ & ContactName & """"
```

will produce the following string:

```
[SenderName] = "Sybex"
```

The *filterstring* variable is built slowly, according to the values entered by the user on the Form. Then, it is passed to the Find method of a collection of MailItem objects.

To retrieve the messages in the Inbox folder that were sent in October '97, declare a variable of Items type:

```
Dim AllMessages As Items
```

Then assign the collection of all items in the Inbox folder to the *AllMessages* variable:

```
Set OLApp = CreateObject("Outlook.Application")
Set mNameSpace = OLApp.GetNamespace("MAPI")
Set AllMessages = NameSpace.GetDefaultFolder(olFolderInbox).Items
```

Then apply the filter string to the *AllMessages* variable with the following statements:

```
Filterstring = "[SentOn] => "10/01/97" And [SentOn] <= "10/31/97"
Set thismessage = AllMessages.Find(filterString)
```

The variable *thismessage* holds the first MailItem object that meets the specified criteria (if any). If this variable is Nothing, you need not continue. If not, it means that at least one message meets the criteria. You can then iterate through the qualifying messages with a loop like the following one:

```
If thismessage Is Nothing Then
    MsgBox "No messages sent in the specified interval."
Else
    While Not thismessage Is Nothing
        {process the MailItem represented by thismessage}
        Set thismessage = AllMessages.FindNext
    Wend
End If
```

In the loop's body, you can access the message's subject with the expression thismessage.Subject, its sender with the expression thismessage.Sender, and so on.

Retrieving Messages

The last example of this chapter demonstrates some techniques for retrieving mail items. Messages are stored in the InBox and OutBox folders, or subfolders created by the user under these two folders. The Messages example retrieves the messages from the InBox folder only. If you don't have any messages in this folder, move some incoming messages from your custom folders to the InBox folder so you can test the application; then move them back to their original folders when you're done.

FIGURE 25.4:

The Messages project demonstrates how to read Outlook's incoming messages from within your VB applications.

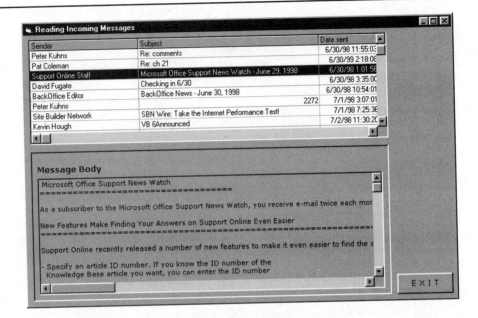

The Messages project is stored in this chapter's folder on the CD, and its Form is shown in Figure 25.4. When the application starts, it populates a Grid control with the headers of the messages. Only the message's sender, subject, and date are displayed, but you can easily expand the grid to display more fields. The Grid control is set up with 999 rows. If you have a lot of messages in your Inbox folder, you should increase this value accordingly (or filter the messages displayed as explained in "The Find Methods" sections earlier in this chapter).

In the Form's Load event we create the AllMessages variable, which is a collection of all MailItem objects in the Inbox folder. The variable is declared with the statement:

```
Dim AllMessages As Items
```

And it's created with the following statements:

```
Set OLApp = CreateObject("Outlook.Application")
Set mNameSpace = OLApp.GetNamespace("MAPI")
Set AllMessages = _
        mNameSpace.GetDefaultFolder(olFolderInbox).Items
```

Then the code scans the elements of the AllMessages collection with a For Each...Next loop and populates the rows of the Grid control.

```
For Each thismessage In AllMessages
        MSFlexGrid1.Row = MSFlexGrid1.Row + 1
        MSFlexGrid1.Col = 0
        MSFlexGrid1.Text = thismessage.SenderName
        MSFlexGrid1.Col = 1
        MSFlexGrid1.Text = thismessage.Subject
        MSFlexGrid1.Col = 2
        MSFlexGrid1.Text = thismessage.SentOn
    Next
```

After the Grid has been populated, you can click a message's header to view its body. The program extracts the number of the row that was clicked and uses it to index the AllMessages collection to retrieve the selected message. The Grid control's Click event handler is shown in Code 25.11:

Code 25.11 **Extracting a Message's Body**

```
Private Sub MSFlexGrid1_Click()
Dim thismessage As MailItem
    currentrow = MSFlexGrid1.Row
    MSFlexGrid1.Col = 0
    MSFlexGrid1.ColSel = 2
    Set thismessage = AllMessages.Item(currentrow)
    txtBody.Text = " " & thismessage.Body
End Sub
```

The actual code contains some error-trapping code and sets up the widths of Grid control's columns. Open the Messages project in the Visual Basic IDE to examine its code. You can modify the code to add more selection criteria or work with different folders (the OutBox folder, a subfolder under the InBox folder, and so on).

The application uses the AllMessages collection to store the messages and accesses them by their index. You could also use a hidden column in the Grid control (one whose width is 0 pixels) and store the EntryID fields of the messages there. This value would then be used from within the Grid control's Click event to retrieve the corresponding message directly from Outlook's Inbox folder, with the GetItemFromID method.

INDEX TO CODE LISTINGS

INDEX

Note to the Reader: Throughout this index **boldface** page numbers indicate primary discussions of a topic. *Italicized* page numbers indicate illustrations.

F

M

O

S

W

SYBEX BOOKS ON THE WEB

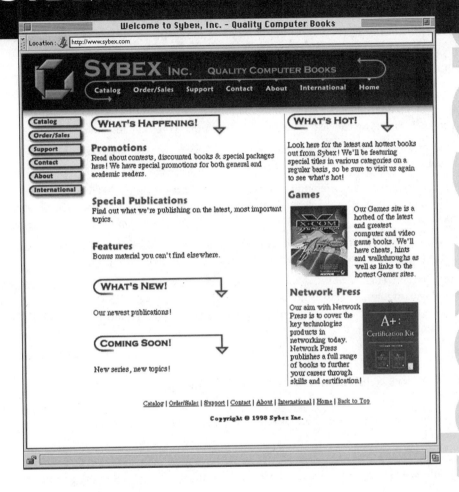

At the dynamic and informative Sybex Web site, you can:

- view our complete online catalog
- preview a book you're interested in
- access special book content
- order books online at special discount prices
- learn about Sybex

www.sybex.com

SYBEX Inc. • 1151 Marina Village Parkway, Alameda, CA 94501 • 510-523-8233

Visual Basic 6 Developer's Handbook Companion CD-ROM

For Windows 95, 98, and NT4 users, this autoplay CD-ROM automatically displays the Sybex interface for access to the different products on the CD. Just insert it in the CD-ROM drive and let the autoplay CD boot the Sybex interface. At this interface, you'll find the following products:

- **Adobe Acrobat Reader 3**   Provides the fastest way to publish any document online. It empowers everyone to create and share documents across platforms while maintaining the documents' original look and feel.

- **Data Widgets 3**   The premier set of database components for developing in Visual Basic, C++, or Internet Explorer just got better. Now you can also print, export, and format your data to paper or HTML.

- **InstallShield Express 2.1**   A completely visual development tool that gives you the fastest route to developing Windows 95/NT-compliant installations for your applications targeting Windows 3.1, Windows 95, and Windows NT.

- **LEADTools 10**   The leading image development toolkit, with controls for almost 300 functions, methods, and properties, with imaging technology in 12 general categories including scanning, color conversion, display, annotation, image processing (more than 50 different filters with region of interest), animation, and compression.

- **RoboHELP HTML 6**   An HTML Help authoring tool that provides rich WYSIWYG editing capabilities with full drag-and-drop support, automated project management, and complete testing features.

- **WinZip 7**   Brings the convenience of Windows to the use of Zip files and other archive and compression formats. The optional wizard interface makes unzipping easier than ever. WinZip features built-in support for popular Internet file formats, including TAR, gzip, Unix compress, UUencode, BinHex, and MIME. ARJ, LZH, and ARC files are supported via external programs. WinZip interfaces to most virus scanners.

- **Complete Code from the book**   All the code from the book's chapters in one easy-to-transfer .exe file.

In addition, two appendices are included in pdf format. You can view these appendices with the included Adobe Acrobat Reader.

- **Appendix A: Chapter 1 API Functions**   Includes the declarations, parameters, and return values for all WIN32 API functions used in Chapter 1. A remarks section is included in some functions to provide additional information.

- **Appendix B: Chapter 2 API Functions**   Lists and explains API functions used in Registry projects in Chapter 2.

Installation and Usage   You must install the CD's software and project code to your hard drive before you will be able to access the project code and appendices. (Most of the third-party tools have their own Setup programs). You can:

- Copy the project code to your hard disk (removing the read-only attribute from the files).

- Set up and run the third-party add-ons by copying them directly from the CD to your hard drive. Be sure to read and comply with each program's license agreement, and see the readme files for other important information.

Where specified in files on the CD, owners retain copyright to their respective contents. Where not otherwise noted, all contents copyright ©1999 Sybex, Inc.